Amharic English - Amharic Dictionary

MW00471169

2nd Edition
Revised & Updated

Editor: Endale Zenawi

© 2007 Simon Wallenberg ISBN 1-84356-015-1
Second Edition

First Edition 1975
University of Addis Ababa & Simon Wallenberg

All rights reserved. Printed in the USA. No part of this book may be used or reproduced in any form or by any means, or stored in a database or retrieval system, without prior written permission of the publisher and the author's estate except in the case of brief quotations embodied in critical articles and reviews.

Published by The Simon Wallenberg Press
wallenberg.press@gmail.com

© Book Block & Cover design Simon Wallenberg Press
Printed in the United Kingdom

Published by The Simon Wallenberg Press

The Addis Ababa University Library System (AAULS), formerly known as Haileselassie I University Library, is the largest academic library in Ethiopia. At this time the AAULS is serving the University community and others with a collection of more than 500,000 catalogued volumes, 632 micro formats, more than 7000 print and electronic serial titles, and other electronic formats.

Amharic - English
English - Amharic
Dictionary

Editor: Endale Zenawi

Simon Wallenberg Press

This Dictionary is dedicated to the memory of Professor Getaneh Assefa

Professor Dateline Assefa passed away suddenly due to a car accident. He was laid to eternal peace on Monday, 7 May 2007 at the St. Trinity Cathedral in Addis Ababa.

He was a distinguished member of the University Staff and highly regarded across the academic world.

Professor Assefa began his primary education at Molale Elementry School and continued his secondary education at Hailmariam Mamo Secondary School in Debre Berhan. He then joined the then Haile Selassie I University in Addis Ababa where he obtained his Bachelor of Science in 1959. He continued further studies at the University of Florida where he obtained his Ph.D. From the University of Minnesota.

Prof Assefa began his academic career at Addis Ababa University as an assistant and rose quickly up the ladder to become full professor in 1985 E.C. In his research undertakings, Getaneh Assefa was a dynamic, innovative and productive scholar.

He was undoubtedly one of the most recognized and esteemed Ethiopian academicians of our time.

He will be missed by students and staff at the University.

Professor Andreas Esheté
President
Addis Ababa University.

Ethiopia

Located in the heart of the Horn of Africa, Ethiopia is the tenth largest African country by land area and the third largest African nation in terms of population. Ethiopia is bordered by Eritrea to the north, Djibouti and Somalia to the east, Kenya to the south and Sudan to the west.

A land of contrasts, the scenery in Ethiopia changes constantly from one region to another, creating a microcosm of an entire continent in a nation the size of France and Spain combined. The scenery changes from hot, dry areas to rolling hills and fertile highlands, to savanna and mountainous regions where it sometimes even snows. The contrasting land is largely due to the volcanic activity that shaped the area some forty million years ago when the Ethiopian land mass was shaken by a massive upheaval. This opened deep faults in the bedrock and its overlying sedimentary layers, through which white-hot basaltic lava slowly spread over a large expanse of the land. Later, erosion produced some of the sharp contrasts that travelers visiting Ethiopia can see today.

Ethiopia's dramatic geographic contours, which were formed over one million years ago, have been hailed by some as probably the most spectacular in the world. The most sensational geographical feature is the East African Rift Valley, which runs from north to south, cleaving the country into three distinct regions: the western highlands, the eastern highlands, and the Rift Valley lowlands.

The central highlands stand at altitudes from 7,800-12,000 feet, rising to Ras Dashen at 15,100 feet, the highest peak in the Simien Mountains. Deep gorges surround the high plateaus, dipping far below sea level. From the highlands of Gojjam Province in Amhara, the Blue Nile River crashes over the Tissisat Falls, where it begins its 1,000 mile journey to join the White Nile in Sudan. The eastern highlands run along the Rift Valley escarpment, sloping steeply to the east and widening and descending into the Danakil Depression at 380 feet below sea level.

History

The history of Ethiopia, known to many as Abyssinia, is rich, ancient, and still in part unknown. Anthropologists believe that East Africa's Great Rift Valley is the site of the origin of humankind. The first recorded account of the region dates back to almost 5,000 years ago during the time of the Egyptian pharaohs, when the ancient Egyptians sent expeditions down the Red Sea in quest of gold, ivory, incense, and slaves.
It is in the Afar region of Ethiopia where scientists discovered the remains of "Lucy" or Dinkenesh, meaning "thou art wonderful," as she is known to the Ethiopians. "Lucy" lived more than three million years ago, and her bones now rest in the Ethiopian National Museum.

The country's rich history is woven with legends of King Solomon and the Queen of Sheba; the Ark of the Covenant that is said to rest in Axum; the great Axumite kingdom and the birth of Christianity; the rise of Islam; and the story of King Lalibela, who is believed to have constructed eleven rock-hewn churches, still standing today and considered the eighth wonder of the world.

Ethiopia is the only African nation that was not colonized by European colonial forces. It was briefly occupied by the Italians between 1936 and 1941.

In recent history, between 1889 and 1913, Emperor Menelik II reigned, fending off the encroachments of European powers. Italy posted the greatest threat, having begun to colonize part of what would become its future colony of Eritrea in the mid 1880s. In 1896, Ethiopia defeated Italy at the Battle of Adwa, which was considered the first victory of an African nation over a European colonial power.

Menelik's successor, Haile Selassie I (who reigned from 1930-1974) was left with the task of dealing with Italy's resurgent expansionism. In the early years of World War II, Ethiopia was liberated from the Italians by the joint forces of the Resistance Movement and the British Army.

After being restored to power, Emperor Selassie attempted to implement reforms and modernize the state. However, increasing internal pressures, including conflict with Eritrea and severe famine, placed strains on Ethiopian society that contributed in large part to the 1974 military rebellion that ended the Haile Selassie regime.

The biggest impact of the coup d'etat was the emergence of Lieutenant Colonel Mengistu Haile Mariam as the head of state, and the re-orientation of the government and national economy from capitalism to Marxism. During the 17 years of the military controlled government, the economy deeply worsened, while civil unrest grew beyond the control of the military.

Growing civil unrest and a unified force of Ethiopian people, led by the Ethiopian Peoples Revolutionary Democratic Front (EPRDF) against their communist dictators finally led to the demise of the Mengistu regime in 1991. Between 1991 and 1995, the transitional government of Ethiopia, a coalition of 27 political and liberation organizations, embarked on its path to transform Ethiopia from a centralized, military-controlled country to a free and democratic federation.

In 1994, a new constitution was written, setting up a bicameral legislature and a judicial system, and guaranteeing equal rights and freedom of expression to all of the Ethiopian citizens. In May 1995, Ethiopia's first free and democratic elections were held in which Meles Zenawi was elected Prime Minister and Negasso Gidada was elected President. Representatives to the Parliament were also elected at that time. Ethiopia's second national multiparty elections took place in May of 2000 and individuals were once again elected to the House of the Federation and to the House of Peoples' Representatives. Prime Minister Meles was re-elected Prime Minister in October 2000, and a new president, Lieutenant Girma Wolde-Giorgis, was elected the following year, in October 2001.

Ethiopia is a mosaic of diverse people who live peacefully, side-by-side speaking a multitude of different tongues, practicing different religions and customs, and celebrating a rich and eclectic history.

Language

Amharic is the official language of Ethiopia, while English, French and Italian are widely spoken, especially in business and academic circles. In fact, there are over 80 different languages with 200 dialects spoken around the country. The many languages can be broken down into four main groups: Semitic, Hametic, Omotic and Nilo-Saharan.

The Semitic languages are related to both Hebrew and Arabic. They are mostly spoke in the Northern and Central parts of the country. The principal Semitic language is Amharic. The Hametic languages are found mainly in the East, West, and South. Of this group, Oromiffa is the predominant language. The Omotic group of languages are spoken in the Southwest and have been given that name in recent years because they are spoken in the general area of the Omo River. Finally, the Nilo-Saharan languages are spoken in a wide area along the Sudan frontier.

Some of the written languages use the Ge'ez alphabet, the language of the of the ancient Axumite kingdom. As a matter of fact, Ge'ez is the only indigenous written language in all of Africa. Today some of the written languages in Ethiopia are using the Latin alphabet.

Ethnicity

There are more than 78 ethnic groups in Ethiopia, with 69% of them found in the Southern Nations, Nationalities and Peoples' State.

Highest population percentages (1994 census): Oromo, 32%; Amhara, 30%; Tigray, 6%; Somali, 6%; Guragie, 4%; Sidama, 3%; Wolaita, 2%; Afar, 2%; Hadiya, 2%; and Gamo, 1%.

Religion

The religions in Ethiopia are predominantly Ethiopian Orthodox (or Monophysite Christianity) and Islam. Other religions that are also practiced include Judaism and Animism. The Animist faith is found mainly in southern regions of Ethiopia. Further south in Somali and surrounding areas, Islam is practiced. Christianity is more common in the northern and central parts of Ethiopia, where Judaism and Islam can be found as well.

Traditions

People usually greet each other by bowing heads. A greeting in Ethiopia can be a long and lively process- the longer the greeting, the closer the friends. Another custom is to kiss the cheek of your friend three times when you greet them.

The coffee ceremony is a sacred tradition in Ethiopia, where the beverage originated and is an integral part of the Ethiopian lifestyle. Performing the ceremony is almost a requirement when you have a visitor at any time of the day. The special coffee ceremony can take up to a few hours. The beans are roasted by hand and then ground in a special way. The coffee is prepared in a special pot and poured into a special cup. Of course, food is prepared with the coffee, practically making a full meal of the affair. In most parts of Ethiopia, the coffee ceremony takes place three times per day-- in the morning, at noon, and in the evening.

Festivals

The Ethiopian Year is full of colorful festivals and both religious and secular holidays.
September 11 New Year
September 27 Maskal Day (Finding of the True Cross)
January 7 Christmas
January 19 Timkat (Epiphany)
February 8 (date varies) Ramadan
March 2 Battle of Adwa
April 17 Id Al Adha (Arefa)
April 25 (date varies) Ethiopian Good Friday
April 27 (date varies) Ethiopian Easter
May 1 Labor Day
May 5 Ethiopian Patriots Victory Day
May 28 National Holiday
July 17 (date varies) Birth of the Prophet Mohammed

Clothing

As diverse as their own backgrounds are the traditional costumes of each region. While European dress is worn in the major urban centers, the traditional shemma is seen frequently on both men and women in the highlands. The shemma is a white cotton dress with a border of bright colors. The pastoral peoples of the lowlands wear mainly leather clothing with bead or shell ornamentation or brightly colored garments. Fine-featured Hararies wear colorful, tight trousers and gauzy veils. Among the Oromos the young girls wear their hair in two buns behind their ears. In addition, their foreheads are encircled with wreaths of silver, leaves or flowers.

Food

Injera, a flat, sourdough pancake made of the indigenous grain called t'ef, is the country staple. The injera is typically served with either meat or vegetable sauces. To eat it, you tear off a bit of injera and use it to pick up pieces of meat or to mop up the sauce.

T'ef is a nutritional miracle food. It contains 2-3 times the iron of wheat or barley. The calcium, potassium and other essential minerals are also many times what would be found in an equal amount of other grains. T'ef has 14% protein, 3% fat and 81% complex carbohydrates.

T'ef is the only grain to have symbiotic yeast. Like grapes, the yeast is on the grain, so no yeast is added in the preparation of injera.

T'ef is milled into flour and made into a batter. The batter is allowed to sit so the yeast can become active. When the batter is ready, it is poured on a large, flat oven and allowed to cook. This process is much harder than it sounds. I t has taken years (literally centuries) of practice for Ethiopians to perfect this injera.

Berbere, the blend of spices that gives Ethiopian food its characteristic taste, can be quite hot. A popular food called wot is a hot spicy pepper sauce, which is eaten with basic ingredients like vegetables, meat and chicken. Kotcho, another popular food, is a pancake made of "ensete" stem and root.

The meat that Ethiopians eat is beef (either cooked, dry or raw).

Mutton is eaten in the high altitudes, while camel and goat are eaten in the lower altitudes. They eat cooked and dried fish in the coastal regions.
A traditional Ethiopian meal involves a gathering of people, who eat together from one large circular plate. The guests will have the choice morsels of meat placed in front of them, which they wait to eat last after filling up on injera and sauce.

You eat with your right hand, and you should wash your hands ahead of time. Typically, a jug of water and a bar of soap are brought to you for that purpose.

Along with the traditional Ethiopian meal, one would normally drink either t'ej, a type of honey wine, or a local beer called t'ella. Ethiopia produces its own wines: Dukam and Gouder are dry reds; Crystal is a dry white; and Axumite is a sweet red.

Calendar

Ethiopia uses the Julian Solar calendar, which is made up of 12 equal months of 30 days each and a thirteenth month consisting of 5 or 6 days, depending on the year.

Ethiopia is endowed with vast agricultural, mineral, and energy resources, which remain virtually untapped. In 1992, following the collapse of the military dictatorship and command economy, Ethiopia has taken a major policy shift towards democracy and economic development.

The Government of the Federal Democratic Republic of Ethiopia has introduced an economic reform plan that emphasizes the use of free market mechanisms and liberalized trade and investment laws to encourage foreign investment and trade, as well as domestic entrepreneurs.

As the result of the reforms, the direct role of the State in economic activity has progressively declined. In particular, tariffs were substantially reduced, quota constraints relaxed, licensing procedures simplified, foreign exchange controls eased, and privatization of public enterprise became widespread. The government has also adopted the strategy of Agricultural Development Led Industrialization (ADLI) as a central plank of its development program. This strategy emphasizes productivity growth in smallholder agriculture and labor-intensive industrialization.

Agriculture

Ethiopia is a predominantly agricultural country with over 80 percent of its population farming on about 15 - 20 percent of the arable land. The agricultural sector accounts for over half of the GDP and 90 percent of export earnings, the most important of which is coffee. Some of the finest and rarest coffees in the world are grown in the highlands of Ethiopia, and Ethiopia is Africa's third largest producer of coffee, after Uganda and the Ivory Coast. In addition, Ethiopia has one of the largest livestock resources in the world.

Given the key role that agriculture plays in the economic development of the country, the Government has placed special focus on agriculture in its development agenda. Agriculture can be a stimulus to improve land utilization and productivity, generate income and be used as a spring-board for growth in the industrial and service sectors.

Industry

The industry and manufacturing sector plays an important role in the economy by supplying consumer goods, generating employment opportunities, absorbing agricultural raw materials and earning foreign exchange through exports. This sector comprises light manufacturing products such as construction materials, metal and chemical products as well as basic consumer goods such as food, beverages, leather, clothing and textiles. Production is concentrated in and around Addis Ababa and mostly caters to the domestic market, although the number of exported goods is steadily growing.

To help the industrial sector grow, the Government is making concerted efforts to dismantle barriers to investment and private sector participation caused by excessive regulation from past regimes.

Mining

The mining sector of the economy has immense potential for

development. A limited scale of gold tantalum and platinum mining is currently being undertaken. Several countries have signed contracts with Ethiopia to conduct gold exploration in certain parts of the country.
The development of Ethiopia's mineral wealth is one of the Government's leading economic objectives. Mining operations are expected to be an important economic catalyst for the Government's export-oriented development strategy. The goal is to get the minerals sector up to 10 percent of GDP within 10 years.

Entertainment

Night Life

In the large cities there is a wide range of entertainment in the evenings. In Addis Ababa, there are several international nightclubs. In Addis Ababa, and in many other towns, the cinema is a popular form of entertainment with films in both English and other languages. Theatrical performances are confined to the main centers, but in every town you will find local bars, surprisingly called Buna bet (coffee house) where the local people will be pleased to make you welcome. Traditional folklore dances will often be held in the main hotels and tourist sites.

Food and Drink

The food and drink of Ethiopia reflect the many different cultures. A typical dish is wot, a hot spicy stew of meat or vegetables, seasoned with a blend of berbere. It is often made with doro (chicken) and normally served with injera, the traditional spongy pancake made from fermented teff flour batter.

In most good restaurants, or in the local Buna bet, or coffee house, you will find delicious dishes that reflect the customs and the ingredients of the region.

In Addis Ababa as in most of the larger cities, visitors will also find a wide range of other restaurants that reflect the influence of other cuisines. All large hotels have international restaurants, but our in the city you can tempt your taste buds in Chinese, Indian, Middle Eastern, Italian, French, Greek and other restaurants.

Ethiopia produces its own wines. Dukam and Gouder are red and quite dry, while Axumite is a sweet white wine. Crystal is our dry white wine. Our famous honey wine or tej is found all over the country, as is tella a local beer and Katikala, distilled liquor.

Crafts of Ethiopia

Ethiopia is rich in traditional crafts and our artisans work with local raw materials, creating artifacts that are both useful as well as being items of great beauty.

Shopping in Ethiopia can be an exciting experience. The bustling markets are the places to try out the age-old skills of bargaining and in some small workshops you can achieve a more reasonable price after a little bit of haggling.

In Addis Ababa the Merkato is the place to head for, but in all towns, markets and roadside stalls will display the crafts made in the locality.

In Harar visitors will find colorful basketwork or silver filigree, while in the crosses of Gonder are famous. Hand-woven carpets come from Debre Brhan, while Jimma is well known for its three-legged stools. All over the country you will find historical artifacts.

In all regions modern skills are being combined with traditional methods to produce modern handicrafts that make splendid souvenirs. Pottery, woodcarving and modern jewelers make wonderful keepsakes of a visit to Ethiopia. Other treasures include hand-carved furniture, wall hangings, and beautiful embroidery and costume dolls.

Our modem designers have now created ranges of fashionable clothes that will enchant you. Women could explore some of the smaller boutiques in Addis Ababa, while both men and women will delight in the excellent leather goods for which Ethiopia is famous.

Sporting activities available for the Tourist

Ethiopia is a country for outdoor orientated people where so many open-air activities can be enjoyed. The opportunities to enjoy the attractions of Ethiopia, while participating in a favorite pastime, make a holiday in Ethiopia even more fun.

Some activities may provide a relaxing interlude in an Ethiopian tour, while others will be an important factor in choosing to come to Ethiopia. So take time out, and explore the opportunities that Ethiopia offers. In any remote area, or when undertaking any form of hazardous activity, we strongly recommend you take a local guide. In National Parks ranger guides accompany trekking parties.

Walking and Trekking

The beautiful landscapes of Ethiopia, and the sometimes wild and dramatic terrain, make Ethiopia perfect hiking country, whether you are looking for a trek across the vast moorlands of the Bale plateau, or the Simien mountain, the dramatic countryside around Lalibella, or the wilderness of the Awash river, camping under the light of a thousand stars. Less strenuous, and more relaxing, are the pleasant local trails that follow the banks of Rift Valley lakes, or resort areas close to Addis Ababa, such as a walk through the vineyards of Ambo.

Mountain Climbing

Much of Ethiopia is rugged mountainous country, and the opportunities to conquer demanding peaks and crags are endless. The Simien Mountains, the Bale Plateau and many other areas provide perfect climbs. Equipment is rarely available locally and should be brought with you.

Caving

In many areas, particularly those with limestone Crags, underground caves and caverns may be discovered. Near Dire Dawa there is evidence of prehistoric habitation. Skilled expeditions will find great opportunities, but local guides are essential.

Fishing

With so many lakes and rivers, excellent fishing is available in most parts of Ethiopia. Brown and rainbow trout abound in the torrents and rivers of the Bale Mountains, while in most of the Rift Valley lakes, Nile Perch, Catfish, Tilapia and Tiger Fish offer great sport. Just ask any local fisherman.

Riding/Pony Trekking

In such a rugged environment, horses and mules play an important part in the transportation of people and goods. So it is not surprising that horse riding can be enjoyed in most parts of Ethiopia. A trek in the Simien Mountains on a sure-footed pony allows visitors to get to areas even 4x4 vehicles find difficult.

Camping

Camping is often the only way to see some of the more beautiful, but remote, areas of Ethiopia. In most areas camping is safe, but local advice should be sought. As little camping gear is available to hire in the country, all the necessary equipment should be brought with you.

Swimming

Opportunities for swimming abound in Ethiopia. Apart from pools at the main hotels, lakes Langano and Shalla are bilharzias-free and resort areas have been set aside for swimming. Especially attractive are pools created by natural springs which can be found in Awash National Park, or at Sodere Filwoha.

Water Sports

Sailing on Lake Tana, or some of the Rift Valley lakes is a popular pastime. Many of the local fishermen will be happy to take out their boat for you. A trip in a dugout canoe, or traditional papyrus boat, is another wonderful experience. Lake Langano is also popular with wind-surfers, and water-skiers. White water rafting is a new adventure that can be experienced on part of the Omo River and the Blue Nile.

Rastafari movement

Rastafari movement, is a religion that accepts Haile Selassie I, the former Emperor of Ethiopia, as God incarnate, whom they call Jah.

The movement emerged in Jamaica among working-class and peasant black people in the early 1930s, arising from an interpretation of Biblical prophecy partly based on Selassie's status as the only African monarch of a fully independent state, and his titles of King of Kings, Lord of Lords, and Conquering Lion of Judah (Revelation 5:5). Other characteristics of Rastafari include the spiritual use of cannabis, and various Afrocentric social and political aspirations,[2] such as the teachings of Jamaican publicist and organiser Marcus Garvey (also often regarded as a prophet), whose political and cultural vision helped inspire a new worldview.

The Rastafari movement has spread throughout much of the world, largely through interest generated by reggae music—most notably, that of Jamaican singer/songwriter Bob Marley. By 2000, there were more than one million Rastafari faithful worldwide. About five to ten percent of Jamaicans identify themselves as Rastafari. Many Rastafari follow an ital diet which essentially means living by the dietary Laws of Leviticus and Deuteronomy in the Old Testament.

Doctrines

Rastafari developed among an oppressed people who felt society had nothing to offer them except more suffering.[2] Rastas may regard themselves as conforming to certain visions of how Africans should live,[2] reclaiming what they see as a culture stolen from them when their ancestors were brought on slave ships to Jamaica, the movement's birthplace.The messages expounded by the Rastafari promote love and respect for all living things and emphasize the paramount importance of human dignity and self-respect. Above all else they speak of freedom from spiritual, psychological as well as physical slavery and oppression. In their attempts to heal the wounds inflicted upon the African race by the civilized nations of the world, Rasta's continually extol the virtue and superiority of African culture and civilization past and present.

The doctrines of Rastafari depart radically from the norms of the conventional modern western mind, a trait of the movement deliberately encouraged by Rastas themselves. Unlike many religious groups that stress compliance with and recognition of the "powers-that-be," Rastafari instead stresses loyalty to their vision of "Zion," and rejection of modern society (called Babylon), which they see as thoroughly corrupt. "Babylon" in this case is considered to be rebelling against "Earth's Rightful Ruler" (JAH) ever since the days of king Nimrod.

This "way of life" is not merely to be assented to intellectually, or "belief" as the term is often used; it is used for the finding and knowledge of one's true identity. To follow and worship JAH Rastafari is to find, spread and "trod" the unique path to which each individual Rasta was rightfully born. The movement is difficult to categorize, because Rastafari is not a centralized organization.[2] Individual Rastafari work out their religion for themselves, resulting in a wide variety of doctrines nevertheless also covered under the general umbrella of Rastafari.

Afrocentrism

Socially, Rastafari has typically been viewed as a response to racist negation of black people as it was experienced, both in the world as a whole (where Selassie was the only black leader recognised in international circles), and in Jamaica, where in the 1930s black people were at the bottom of the social order, while white people and their religion and system of government were at the top. Marcus Garvey's encouragement of black people to take pride in themselves and their African heritage inspired the Rastas to embrace all things African. They teach that they were brainwashed while in captivity to negate all things black and African. They turned the white image of them--as primitive and straight out of the jungle--into a defiant embrace of the African culture they see as having been stolen from them when they were taken from Africa on the slave ships. Africa is associated with Zion. Africa/Zion is the starting place of all human ancestry as well as the original state of mind that can be reached through meditation and the ganja herb.

Living close to and as a part of nature is seen as African. This African approach to "naturality" is seen in the dreadlocks, ganja (marijuana), ital food, and in all aspects of Rasta life. They disdain the modern approach (or, as they see it, non-approach) to life for being unnatural and excessively objective and rejecting subjectivity. Rastas say that scientists try to discover how the world is by looking from the outside in, whereas the Rasta approach is to see life from the inside, looking out. The individual is given tremendous importance in Rastafari, and every Rasta has to figure out the truth for himself or herself.

Another important Afrocentric identification is with the colours red, gold, and green, of the Ethiopian flag as well as, with the addition of black, the colors of "Pan-African Unity" for Marcus Garvey. They are a symbol of the Rastafari movement, and of the loyalty Rastas feel toward Haile Selassie, Ethiopia, and Africa rather than for any other modern state where they happen to live. These colors are frequently seen on clothing and other decorations. Red stands for the blood of martyrs, green stands for the vegetation of Africa, while gold stands for the wealth and prosperity Africa has to offer.

Some Rastafari learn Amharic, which some consider to be the original language, because this is the language of Haile Selassie I, and in order to further their identity as Ethiopian. There are reggae songs written in Amharic. Most Rastas speak either a form of English, or a form of their native languages, that embraces non-standard dialects and has been consciously modified to accord with and display an individual Rasta's world view (e.g. "I-an-I" rather than "we").

Amharic - English Dictionary

Part I

ሀ

ሀሁ — *hahu* n. alphabet, "abc"

ሀብት — *habt* n. wealth

  ምጣኔ— — *məṭṭane*— n. economy

  ሀብታም — *habtam* adj. wealthy, rich

  ሀብታምነት — *habtamənnät* n. wealthiness

  ባለሀብት — *balä habt* adj. rich, wealthy; owner

  የተፈጥሮ ሀብት — *yätäfäṭro habt* n. natural resources

ሀይ ሀይ አለ — *hai hai alä* v.t. conciliated, calmed down conflict, cooled down

  ሀይ ሀይ ባይ — *hai hai bai* n. one who conciliates, calms down conflict, cools down

ሀገር — *hagär* n. country (*also* አገር)

ሁለት — *hulätt* adj. two

ሁሉ — *hullu* adj. all, every, everybody

  ሁለመና — *hullämäna* adv. all over (*the body*)

  ሁሉም — *hullumm* all of them

  — ቦታ — *-bota* adv. everywhere

  ሁልቀን — *hulləqän* adv. daily

  ሁልጊዜ — *also* ሁሌ *hulgize*, *hulle* adv. always, all the time

  ሰው ሁሉ — *säw hullu* everybody, everyone

ሁከት — *hukät* n. disturbance, unrest, trouble, violence

  ሁከተኛ — *hukätäñña* adj. trouble maker, disturber

  አዋኪ — *awwaki* adj. trouble maker, disturber, nuisance

ሃች — *hačč* in እዚያሃች *əzziya hačč* adv. there, over there

  ሀቻምና — *haččamna* adv. the year before

ሃያ — *haya* adj. twenty

  ሃያኛ — *hayañña* adj. twentieth

ሂስ — *his* n. criticism

  ሂስና ግለሂስ — *hisnna gəllähis* criticism and self-criticism

ሃይማኖት — *haimanot* n. religion

  ሃይማኖተኛ — *haimanotäñña* adj. religious

  ሃይማኖታዊ — *haimanotawi* adj. religious

ሄደ — *hedä* v. went

  ሂያጅ — *hiyağ* n. one who goes; riotous liver; profligate; libertine

  ሂደት — *hidät* n. process

ህላዌ — *həllawe* n. existence

  ህልውና — *hələwna* n. existence

ህንድ — *hənd* n. India

  ህንዳዊ — *həndawi* adj. Indian

ህዋእ — *həwa'ə* n. space

ሆሳዕና — *hossa'ana* n. Palm Sunday

ሆመጠጠ — *homäṭṭäṭä* v. was acid, turned sour

  ሆምጣጣ — *homṭaṭa* adj. sour, acid, tart

  ሆምጣጤ / ኮምጣጤ — *homṭaṭṭe*/ *komṭaṭṭe* n. vinegar

ሆነ — *honä* v.i. became, happened

  ሁነኛ — *hunäñña* n. trustworthy person

  ሁኔታ — *huneta* n. condition, situation

  ሆነለት — *honällät* he succeeded, he made it

  ሆን ብሎ — *hon bəlo* adv. intentionally, deliberately

  ሆኖም — *honomm* adv. nevertheless, at any rate

  ለመሆኑ — *lämähonu* by the way

  መሆን — *mähon* inf. to be, become

  ምንም ቢሆን — *mənəmm bihon* whatever happens, by any means

  በዚህም ሆነ በዚያ — *bäzzihəmm honä bäzziya* one way or the other, at any rate

  ቢሆን ቢሆን — *bihon bihon* at least

  ባይሆን — *bayhon* at least

  አኳኋን — *akkuʷahuʷan* n. situation, manner, condition

እንደሆን *əndähon in* የመጣ- *yämaṭṭa* — if he comes, in case he comes

የሆነ ቢሆንም *yähonä bihonəmm* in any event; whatever happens

የሆነ ያልሆነ *yähonä yalhonä* all sorts of things, irrelevent things

የሆነውን ያህል *yähonäwən yahəl* as much as possible

የማይሆን *yämmayhon* adj. inappropriate, impossible

ያልሆነ *yallhonä* adj. inappropriate, improper

ያም ሆነ ይህ *yamm honä yəh* in any case

ይሆናል *yəhonal* it is possible, it is probable

ሆይ *hoy* interj. oh!

ልዑል ሆይ —*lə'ul hoy* Oh! Prince!

ክቡር ሆይ *kəbur hoy* Your Excellency!

ጃንሆይ *ǧanhoy* Your Majesty! His Majesty!

ሆታ *hota* n. cheering, acclaim, shout

ሆቴል *hotel* n. hotel, restaurant

ሆድ *hod* n. stomach, belly abdomen

— ቁርጠት —*qurṭät* n. stomachache, colic

— ድርቀት —*dərqät* n. constipation

ሆደ ሰፊ *hodä säffi* adj. phlegmatic, not susceptible, patient

— ባሻ *hodä bašša* adj. excitable, susceptible, easily hurt

ሆዳም *hodam* adj. greedy, gluttonous, big eater

ሆድቃ *hodəqa* n. guts *(innards)*, entrails

ሆጃ *hoǧǧa* n. title deed *(Harar)*

ለ

ለ *lä* prep. for, to

ለምን *lämən* why?

ለሱ ንገረው *lässu nəgäräw* tell him

ለሀጭ *lähač̣* n. dribble

ለሁጫም *lähuč̣am* adj. dribbling

ለሖቴ *lähote* n. whetstone

ለመለመ *lämällämä* v.i, v.t. became green *(of landscape of vegetation)*; stripped leaves *(from a tree)*

ለምለም *lämläm* adj. green; soft

ለምለም ጆሮ *lämläm ǧoro* n. lobe

ለምለምነት *lämlämnənät* n. greenness, verdure

ለምላሚ *lämlami* adj. green, verdant

ልምላሜ *ləmlame* n. greenness, verdure

ተለመለመ *tälämällämä* v.i. was stripped, for tree, *etc.*

አለመለመ *alämällämä* v.t. became green

አለማለም *allämaläm* n. turning green

ለመሰሰ *lämässäsä* v.t. smoothed *(hair)*; trampled or flattened *(grass, etc.)*

ተለመሰሰ *tälämässäsä* v.i. was smoothed; was trampled or flattened

ለመነ *lämmänä* v.t. asked, beseeched, begged

ለማኝ *lämmañ* adj. beggar

ለማኝነት *lämmaññənnät* n. beggary

ልመና *lәmmäna* n. begging, imploring

ተለመነ *tälämmänä* v.i. was begged

ተለማኝ *tälämmañ* adj. *(person)* entreated

ተለማመነ *tälämammänä* v.i. pleaded with

ተለማማኝ *tälämamañ* adj. pleading; pleader

አለማመነ *allämammänä* v.t. supported a plea, helped in begging

አላመነ *allammänä* v.t. supported a plea, helped in begging

አላማኝ *allamañ* n. helper in begging

አስለመነ *aslämmänä* v.t. caused or allowed to beg

ለመዘገ *lämäzzägä* v. pinched very hard

ተለመዘገ *tälämäzzägä* v.t. was pinched very hard

ለመደ *lämmädä* v.t. became accustomed to, got used to

ለማዳ *lämmada* adj. tame, domestic *(animals)*

ለማዳነት *lämmadannät* n. tameness

ለማጅ *lämaǧ* adj. n. beginner, trainee, learner

ልማድ *lәmad* n. custom, habit

ልማደኛ *lәmadäñña* adj. habitual, customary

ልምድ *lәmd* n. custom, habit

መልመጃ *mälmäǧa* n. exercise, drill

ለማመደ *lämammädä* v. t started to be accustomed, began to learn

ልምምድ *lәmәmmәd* n. experience, training; exercise *(military, sport)*

ተለመደ *tälämmädä* v.i. used, became used

ተለማጅ *tälämmaǧ* adj. habitual or customary

ተለማመደ *tälämammädä* v.i. practiced, trained himself

ተለማማጅ *tälämamaǧ* n. trainee

መለማመጃ *mällämamäǧa* n. means of training

ተላመደ *tälammädä* v.i. got gradually accustomed to

ተላማጅ *tälamaǧ* n. trainee

አለመደ *alämmädä* v.t. trained

አልማጅ *almaǧ* adj. trainer *(animals, persons)*

አለማመደ *alämammadä* v.t. trained or tamed to some extent

አለማመደ *allämammädä* v.t. caused to become aquainted with each other

አላመደ *allamädä* v.t. caused to get used to each other

አስለመደ *aslämmädä* v.t. caused or allowed to become accustomed, taught

አስለማጅ *aslämmaǧ* n. trainer instructor

ለመጠ *lämmäṭä* v.t./v.i. bent; stroke

ለማጣ *lämmaṭṭa* adj. flattering; insincere

ልምጥ *lәmmәṭṭ* adj. curved

ለመጥ አለ *lämmäṭ alä* v.i. bent a little

ልምጥ አለ *lәmmәṭṭ alä* v.i bent forcefully

ተለመጠ *tälämmäṭä* became warped, was bent

ተለማጭ *tälämmač* adj. bendable, flexible

ተለማመጠ *tälämammäṭä* v.t. curried favour, cajoled

ተለማማጭ *tälämamač* n. one who curries favour

አለመጠ *alämmäṭä* v.t. made fun of, mocked

አልማጭ *almač* n. mocker

ለመጠጠ *lämäṭṭäṭä* v.t. burned; stung with whip

ተለመጠጠ *tälämäṭṭäṭä* v.i. was burned; was strung (with whip)

ለማ *lämma* v.i. was developed; blazed up *(fire)*

ለሚ *lämi* adj. developing

ለም *läm* adj. fertile, rich (soil, farmed land)

ለምነት *lämənnät* n. fertility *(land)*; the state of being developed

ልማት *ləmat* n. development

አለማ *alämma* v.t. developed; made fertile

አልሚ *almi* adj.n. developing, developer

—ምግብ *—məgəb* nutritious food

አስለማ *aslämma* v.t. caused to become developed or fertile

ለምቦጭ *lämboč* n. thick lip

ለምቦጫም *lämbočam* adj. thick-lipped

ለምን *see* ምን

ለምድ *lämd* n. sheepskin *(used as cloak for shepherds etc.)*

ለምጽ *lämṣ* n. discoloured skin, *also* ለምጥ

ለምጻም *lämṣam* adj/n. one who has a discoloured skin, *also* ለምጣም

ለሰለሰ *läsälläsä* v. i was or became tender, smooth

ለስላሳ *läslassa* adj. smooth, tender, soft

ለስላሳነት *läslassannät* n. tenderness

ልስላሴ *ləsəllasse* adj. smooth, soft

ልስልስ *ləsləs* adj. smooth, soft

ተለሳለሰ *täläsalläsä* v.i. was tender; became idle

አለሰለሰ *aläsälläsä* v.t. smoothed, made tender, softened

አለሳለስ *alläsaläs* n. smoothness, tenderness

ለሰሰ *lässäsä* v.i. became lukewarm

ለስ አለ *läss alä* v. became a little warm *(for water)*

ለስታ ቅቤ *lästa qəbe* n. fresh butter

ለሰነ *lässänä* v. plastered

ለሳኝ *lässañ* n. plasterer

ልስን *ləssən* adj. plastered

ተለሰነ *tälässänä* v.i. was plastered; kept silent

አላሰነ *allassänä* v.t. helped to plaster

አስለሰነ *aslässänä* v.t. caused to be plastered

ለሸለሸ *läšälläšä* v.t. flattened *(crops, grass* etc.)

ለቀለቀ *läqälläqä* v.t. daubed; smeared

ልቅላቂ *ləqəllaqi* n. dish-water

ልቅልቅ *ləqləq* n. something daubed

ለቅለቅ አደረገ *läqläqq adärrägä* v.t. daubed or rinsed a little

ተለቀለቀ *täläqälläqä* v.i. was smeared, was daubed

ተለቃለቀ *täläqalläqä* v.i. rinsed slightly; smeared each other

መለቃለቂያ *mälläqaläqiya* n. washing water, rinsing water

አለቀለቀ *aläqälläqä* v.t. rinsed

አለቃለቀ *aläqalläqä* v.t. rinsed slightly

አስለቀለቀ *asläqälläqä* v.t. caused to be smeared

ለቀመ *läqqämä* v.t./v.i. picked, picked up; reaped, gathered

ለቀማ *läqäma* n. picking, gathering

ለቃሚ *läqami* adj. picker, gatherer

ልቃሚ *ləqqami* n. leavings or rubbish

ልቅም *ləqqəm* adj. free from impurities (grain etc.); polite

ለቀም አደረገ *läqämm adärrägä* v.t. grabbed

ለቃቀመ *läqaqqämä* v.t. picked, gathered a little here and there; picked out

ለቃቃሚ *läqaqami* n. scavenger

ልቅም አደረገ *ləqqəmm adärrägä* v.t. removed all impurities (*grain etc.*)

ተለቀመ *täläqqämä* v.i. was picked *(e.g. crops)*

አለቀመ *aläqqämä* v.t. grazed, took to pasture *(specially in a dry season)*

አላቀመ *allaqqämä* v.t. helped to pick, helped to gather

አስለቀመ *asläqqämä* v.t. made *(s/o)* pick

*ለቀሰ *see* አለቀሰ

ለቀቀ *läqqäqä* v.t./v.i. let go; released; abandoned; gathered; threaded on to distaff

ልቃቂ *ləqqaqi* n. distaff

ልቃቂት *ləqqaqit* n. distaff

ልቅ *ləqq* n/adj. loose liver; abandoned *(moral)*

ልቅነት *ləqqənnät* n. abandon, loose living

ለቀቅ አደረገ *läqäqq adärrägä*, v.t. relaxed one's hold on s/o

ልቅቅ አደረገ *ləqəqq addärrägä* v.t. let go, set free

ተለቀቀ *täläqqäqä* v.i. was set free, released

ተላቀቀ *tälaqqäqä* v.i. became separated; got free from

አላቀቀ *allaqqäqä* v.t. made free from, caused to be free from

አስለቀቀ *asläqqäqä* v.t. caused to be free from, separated

ለበለበ *läbälläbä* v.t. scorched, burnt slightly, singed

ለብላቢ *läblabi* adj. scorching

ልብልብ *ləbləb* adj. scorched

ተለበለበ *täläbälläbä* vi. burnt, scorched

አለብላቢት *aläblabit* n. nettle

አስለበለበ *asläbälläbä* v.t. caused to be burnt

ለበሰ *läbässä* v.t. dressed, put on clothes, wore

ልባስ *ləbas* n. cloth; covering

ልባሽ *ləbbaš* adj. worn out *(clothes)*

ልብስ *ləbs* clothes, garment

ልብስ *ləbbəs* adj. worn out *(clothes)*

ለባበሰ *läbabbäsä* v.t. put on clothes

ተለባበሰ *täläbabbäsä* v.i. was kept secret, hidden

አለበሰ *aläbbäsä* v.t. dressed *(s/o)*

አልባሽ *albaš* n. dresser, valet

አለባበሰ *aläbabbäsä* v.t. caused to be dressed, covered; kept hidden *(secret)*

አላበሰ *allabbäsä* v.t. helped in dressing

አስለበሰ *asläbbäsä* v.t. made *(s/o)* get dressed

ለበቀ *läbbäqä* v.t./v.i. bended;

ለበቅ *läbäq* n. lath

ለባቃ *läbbaqqa* adj. bent, flexible; cowardly

ልብቅ *ləbbəq* adj. flexible

ተለበቀ *täläbbäqä* v.i. was bent

ተለባቂ *täläbbaqi* adj. flexible

ለበበ *läbbäbä* v.t. put a halter or head-stall on

ልባብ *ləbab* n. halter, head-stall

ተለበበ *täläbbäbä* v.i. was harnessed

አስለበበ *asläbbäbä* v.i. caused to be harnessed

ለበደ — *läbbädä* v.t. covered with leather etc. (e.g. *scabbard*)

ልብዳት — *ləbbədat* n. leather covering etc.

ልብድ — *ləbbəd* adj. covered with leather etc.

ተለበደ — *täläbbädä* v.i. was covered with leather etc.

አስለበደ — *asläbbädä* v.t. caused to be covered with leather, etc.

ለበጠ — *läbbäṭä* v.t. covered with cloth (*e.g. cushions*)

ልብጥ — *ləbbəṭ* adj. covered with cloth

ተለበጠ — *täläbbäṭä* v.i. was covered with cloth

አስለበጠ — *asläbbäṭä* v.t. caused to be covered with cloth

ለብ አለ — *läbb alä* v. became luke-warm

ለብታ — *läbbəta* slight drunkenness

ለብ አለው — *läbb aläw* v.i. was slightly drunk

ለተመ — *lättämä* v.t hit; crashed into

ተለተመ — *tälättämä* v.i. was hit; crashed into

ለካ — *läkka* (particle indicating surprise, remorse, sorrow, discovery etc.)

ለካ — *läkka* v.t. measured

ልክ — *ləkk* n. measurement

ልክ ልኩን ነገረው — *ləkk ləkkun näggäräw* he told him off, scolded him

ለኰሰ — *läkuʷäsä* v.t. set fire to, lit; (*cigarette etc.*)

ለኰፈ — *läkkuʷäfä* v,i. stroked gently, tapped

ለወሰ — *läwässä* v.t. kneaded (*flour for bread*), mixed powder and liquid; crippled (*disease*)

ለዋሳ — *läwwassa* adj. crippled

ተላወሰ — *tälawwäsä* v.i. moved to and fro, started moving

ለወጠ — *läwwäṭä* v.t. changed, exchanged, shifted, altered; cashed (*a check*)

ለውጥ — *läwṭ* n. change; exchange

ልዋጭ — *ləwwač̣* n. things given in return

ልውውጥ — *ləwəwwəṭ* n exchange

ተለወጠ — *täläwwäṭä* vi. was changed, changed

ተለዋጭ — *täläwwač̣* n. substitute

— አባል — *—abal* n. alternate member

ተለዋወጠ — *täläwawwäṭä* v.i. exchanged (*mutually*), interchanged

ተለዋዋጭ — *täläwawač̣* adj. changeable, inconsistent, variable

መለዋወጫ — in የመኪና መለዋወጫ *yämäkina mäläwawäč̣a* n. spare parts (*car*)

መለወጫ — in የዘመን መለወጫ *yäzämän mälläwäč̣a* n. New Year

ለውዝ — *läwz* n. peanut, ground nut

ለዘበ — *lazzäbä* v.i. was tender; was gentle

ለዘብተኛ — *läzzäbtäñña* adj moderate (*pols.*)

ልዝብ — *ləzzəb* adj. gentle, smooth, soft

አለዘበ — *aläzzäbä* v.t. smoothed; rehearsed, (*music, song*)

ለዛ — *läzza* n. charisma (*in speaking*)

—ቢስ — *—bis* adj. unattractive (*in speech etc.*)

— የለሽ — *—yälläš* adj. (*same as above*)

ለየ — *läyyä* v.t. separated divided; distinguished, differentiated; recognized, identified.

ልዩ — *ləyyu* adj. special, different; private; extraordinary

— ልዩ — *—ləyyu* adj. various

—መልእክተኛ —mälə'ktäñña n. envoy extraordinary

—ጸሐፊ —ṣähafi n. private secretary

ልዩነት ləyyunnät n. difference, distinction; division, variation

የዘር— yäzär – n discrimination *(race)*

ለያየ läyayyä v.t. classified; separated; dismantled

ተለየ täläyyä differed, was different; parted from

መለዮ mälläyyc n. badge, insignia; uniform

በተለይ bätäläyy adv. especially, in particular

ተለያየ täläyayyä v.i. differed *(in opinion)*, was different; branched off

የተለያየ yätäläyayyä adj. different, varied

አለያየ alläyayyä v.t. detached, took apart; created enmity among people

ላይ lay prep./adv. on, upon, above

—ላዩን –layun adv. superficially, externally

ላይኛ layəñña adj. upper, top

በ...ላይ bä...lay on, on top of ...e.g በጠረጴዛው ላይ on the table በዚህም ላይ on top of this

አንድላይ andlay adv. together

እዚህ ላይ əzzih lay adv. at this point

ከመጠን በላይ kämäṭän bälay adv. unusually, too much

ከዚህ ላይ käzzih lay at this point

ከዚህ በላይ käzzih bälay adv. moreover, furthermore

ወደላይ wädälay adv. upwards

ለጋ läga adj. fresh, e.g. ለጋ ቅቤ fresh butter

ለጋ lägga v.t. hit *(the ball)*, served *(tennis etc.)*

አላጋ allagga v.t. dashed *(against s/t. boat etc)*

ለገመ läggämä v.i. worked with ill will and badly

ልግመኛ ləgmäñña n. resentful worker

ለገሰ läggäsä v.i. was charitable, was generous

ለጋስ läggas adj. generous

ለጋስነት läggasənnät n. generosity

ልግስና ləggəsənna n. charity, generosity

*ለገጠ •läggäṭä

አላገጠ allaggäṭä vt. made fun of, mocked, derided

ልግጫ ləgč̣a *n.* mocking, mockery, derision

አላጋጭ allagač̣ n. mocker

ለግላጋ läglagga adj. young and well-built; sturdy (of person)

ለጐመ läggu"ämä v.t. fitted with bridle; kept quiet

ልጓም ləgu"am n. bridle

ልጉም ləggum adj. fitted with bridle

ተለጐመ tälägu"ämä v.i. was bridled

አለጐመ aläggu"ämä v.i. criticized others *(while being lazy oneself)*

አልጓሚ algu"ami adj./n hypocritical; sarcastic

አልጉም algum adj. critical; sarcastic

አስለጐመ asläggu"ämä v.t. made *(s/o)* fit a bridle; had *(an animal)* bridled

ለጐደ läggu"ädä v.t. covered, stained with mud

ለጠለጠ läṭälläṭä v.t. compressed oil seed

ልጥልጥ ləṭləṭ n. lump of compressed oil seed

ተለጠለጠ täläṭälläṭä v.i. was compressed, squeezed *(oil seed)*

አለጠለጠ *alăţällăţă* v.i. grew to be in fine physical condition *(i.e. with round strong face)*

ለጠቀ *läţţäqä* v.t. went behind (s/o *i.e. in moving line)*

ለጣቂ *läţţaqi* adj./n. one who follows, goes behind s/o

ለጠጠ *läţţäţä* v.t. expanded stretched *(elastic, spring, arms etc.)*

ልጥጥ *ləţţəţ* adj. stretched, expanded; proud; boastful

ልጣጭ *ləţţač* n. peel, rind

ተለጠጠ *täläţţäţä* v.i. was stretched; was proud, boastful

ተለጣጭ *täläţţač* adj. stretchable, elastic

አስለጠጠ *aslaţţäţä* v.t. had s/t stretched, expanded,

ለጠፈ *läţţäfä* v.t. stuck *(s/t)* on to *(s/t)*, stuck *(s/t)* together; threw against a wall *(to make stick)*; accused falsely

ልጥፋት *ləţţəfat* n. pad *(e.g. wound dressing)* poultice

ልጥፍ *ləţţəf* adj. padded, patched

መለጠፊያ *mäläţţäfiya* n. s/t used for jointing, sticking; glue; jointing piece; sticking plaster

ተለጠፈ *täläţţäfä* v.i. was stuck, joined together; was hidden to eavesdrop, eavesdropped

ተለጣጠፈ *täläţaţţäfä* v. was glued up, stuck together

አስለጠፈ *asläţţäfä* v.t. made (s/o) stick (s/t) together, had (s/t) stuck

ለጥ አለ *läţţ alä* v.i. lay flat; was submissive *(e.g. to a superior power after a battle)*

ለጥ ያለ *läţţ yalä* adj. lying flat; submissive, subdued

—ሜዳ *—meda* n. wide plain

ለፈለፈ *läfälläfä* v. i. talked too much; chattered

ለፍላፊ *läflafi* adj. over-talkative, chatterbox

ልፍለፋ *ləfläfa* n. rambling conversation, prattle

ተለፋለፈ *täläfulläfä* v. chattered together, held idle conversation

ተለፋላፊ *täläfalafi* adj. chattering

አስለፈለፈ *asläfälläfä* v.t. interrogated, made *(s/o)* talk

ለፈፈ *läffäfä* v.t. announced, spread the news, heralded

ለፋፊ *läfäfi* n. public announcer, herald, spreader of tidings

ልፈፋ *ləffäfa* n. public announcement, proclamation

ተለፈፈ *täläffäfä* v.i. was announced, was proclaimed publicly

አስለፈፈ *asläffäfä* v.t. had *(s/t)* announced

ለፋ *läffa* v. worked very hard, toiled

ለፊ *läfi* adj. n. hard worker

ልፊያ *ləffyia* n. romping

ልፋት *ləfat* n. weariness, extreme tiredness

ተላፋ *tälaffa* v.t. horsed around, pretended to fight with each other

ተላፊ *tälafi* adj./n. one who plays around *(physically)*

አለፋ *aläffa* v.t. fatigued, made *(s/o)* tired, tired *(s/o)* out; tanned *(leather, skins)*

አስለፋ *asläffa* v.t. had *(s/t)* tanned *(leather, skins)*

ሉህ *luh* n. legal size paper

ሉል *lul* n. pearl; regal orb; globe

ሉካንዳ *lukanda* n. butcher's shop

ሉጫ *luččа* n. smooth hair

ሊቅ *liq* n. learned, wise,

ሊቀ መንበር *liqä mänbär* n. chairman, president *(of a meeting)*

ሊቅነት *liqənnät* n. learning, scholarliness

ሊትር *litər* n. litre

ሊጋባ *ligaba* n. chief usher, senior official *(for ceremonies etc.)*

ሊጥ *liṭ* n. dough mixture *(for preparing ənǧära)*, dough

ሊጦን *liṭon* n. litany

ላላ *lalla* v.i. was loose, relaxed, was supple *(physically)*; not geminated *(of consonants)*

ልል *ləl* adj. soft, loose, relaxed; easy going, not hard in manner

አላላ *alalla* v.t. made soft, loose, relaxed s/t *(one's grip,hold)*;eased off *(e.g, belt, harness law, restriction)*

ላመ *lamä* v.i. became powdered, fineley ground

ልም *ləm* adj. powdery, finely ground

አላመ *alamä* v.t. ground finely, reduced to powder

አላላም *allalam* n. powdery quality, fineness

አስላመ *aslamä* v.t. had *(s/t)* ground finely

ላመል *lamäl* adv. lightly, slightly, barely, only, *see also* አመል

ላም *lam* n. cow

ላምባ *lambba* n. kerosene, lamp *(oil or paraffin)*

ላምፋ *lamfa* n. husk, *also* ላንፋ

ላሰ *lasä* v.t. licked

ላሽ *laš* n. ring worm, tinea

መላስ *mälas* n. tongue; inf. to lick

ምላስ *məlas* n. tongue

ምላሰኛ *məlasäñña* adj. talkative

ምላሰኛነት *məlasäññənnät* n. talkativeness

ምላሳም *məlasam* adj. talkative

ተላሰ *tälasä* v.i. was licked

አላሰ *alasä* v.t. sweetened *(ṭäǧǧ with honey)* *have* s/o lick s/t *(e.g. from fingers)*

ማላሻ *malaša* n. honey *(used to sweeten ṭäǧǧ)*

አስላሰ *aslasä* v.t. had s/o lick s/t

ላሸ *laššä* v.t. became weak, tender, very soft

አላሸ *alaššä* v.t. made *(s/t)* weak, tender, soft

ላሸቀ *laššäqä* v.i. become churned up *(e.g. mud)*; kneaded forcefully

አላሸቀ *alaššäqä* v.t. churned up, made muddy

ላቀ *laqä* v.t. was superior, excelled

ሊቅ *liq* adj. learned, scholarly

ሊቅነት *liqənnät* n. learning, scholarliness

ላቂያ *laqqiya* n. superiority in ከሁሉም ልቆ *kähullumm ləqo* more than any thing

ይልቅ *yəlq* conj. than *(rather than)*

ከሁሉም— *kähullumm*-above all, more than this, more than that

ከኔ ይልቅ *käne yələq* more than I.

ላቅ አለ *laqq alä* v.i. was slightly better than, excelled *(a little than)*

አላቀ *alaqä* v.t. made *(s/o)* better; preferred

ላቈጠ *läqquʷäṭä* v.i. became churned up, muddy; was kneaded

አላቈጠ *alaqquʷäṭä* v.t. made muddy, churned up; kneaded

ላባ *laba* n. feather

ላባም *labam* adj. feathered, covered with feathers

ላብ *lab* n. sweat, perspiration

ላቦት *labot* n. sweat, perspiration

አላበ *alabä* v.i. made to sweat

ላቦራቱዋር *laboratuʷar* n. laboratory (*Amh. also* ቤተ ሙከራ)

ላቲን *latin* n. Latin

ላት *lat* n. fat (*on sheep's tail only*)

ላታም *latam* adj. fat-tailed (*sheep only*)

ላንቃ *lanqa* n. soft palate

ላከ *lakä* v.t. sent (*message, letter etc.*)

ላኪ *laki* n. sender

መላክት *mälakt* n. message

መላክተኛ *mälaktäñña* n. messenger

መልእክት *mälə'əkt* n. message *also* መልክት

መልእክተኛ *mälə'ktäñña* n. messenger *also* መልክት

ተላከ *tälakä* v.i. was sent

ተላኪ *tälaki* adj. n (*one who*) is sent, messenger

ተላላከ *tälalakä* v.i. acted as a messenger; corresponded

ተላላኪ *tälulaki* n. runner, messenger

ተላላኪነት *tälulakinnät* n. the job of being a messenger

አላላከ *ullalakä* v.t. made enquiries

አስላከ *aslakä* v.t. had (*s/t*) sent

ላከከ *lakkäkä* v.t. put the blame on (*s/o.*); stuck onto

ተላከከ *tälakkäkä* v.i. was stuck to, stuck onto

ላዕላይ *la'lay* adj. upper

—መዋቅር *—mäwaqər* n. superstructure

ላይ *lay* adv. on, above

ላይኛ *layəñña* adj. top, upper

በ+noun+ላይ። e.g. በጠረጴዛው ላይ on the table

በ+ infinitive +ላይ ነው e.g. የምርምሩን ጥናት በመጨረስ ላይ ነው። He is in the process of completing his research

በዚህ ላይ። in addition to this

አንድ ላይ። together

እዚህ ላይ። there, at this point (*also* ከዚህ ላይ)

ከመጠን በላይ unusually, beyond measure, too much

ከዚህም በላይ furthermore, besides, moreover

የበላይነት *yäbälayənnät* n. superiority

ላይዳ *layda* n. winnowing fan (*made of wood*)

ላገ *lagä* v.t. planed (*wood etc. in carpentry*)

ተላገ *tälagä* v.i. was planed

አስላገ *aslagä* v.t. had (*s/t*) planed, made smooth

መላጊያ *mälagiya* plane

ላጠ *laṭä* v.t. peeled (*fruit, etc.*); unsheathed

ልጣጭ *ləṭṭač* n. peel, outer skin

ልጥ *ləṭ* n. bark (*of plant, tree*)

መላጣ *mälaṭa* adj. bald-headed

መላጫ *mälača* n. peeling knife, peeler; shaving instrument

ላላጠ *lalaṭä* v.t. cut shavings from

መላላጫ *mälalača* n. chicken leg, drumstick (*chicken*)

ተላጠ *tälaṭä* v.i. was peeled

ተላጭ *tälač* adj. capable of being peeled

ተላላጠ *tälalaṭä* v.i. was peeled off *(skin)*

አስላጠ *aslaṭä* v.t. had *(s/t)* peeled

ላጨ *laččä* v.t. shaved, shaved off; fooled *(s/o)*

ላጭ *lač̣* adj, n one who shaves

መላጫ *mälač̣a* n. shaving instrument

ምላጭ *məlač̣č̣* n. razor, blade; adj. cunning

ጢም ላጭ *ṭim lač̣* n. barber

ተላጨ *tälaččä* v.i. was shaved, was shaved off

አስላጨ *asläččä* v.t. had *(s/o)* shaved

ላጲስ *lappis* n. eraser

ላፈ *lafä* v.t. burned off, singed; guzzled

ተላፈ *tälafä* v.i. was burned off, singed; was guzzled

ላፒስ *lappis* n. eraser; indelible pencil

ሌሊት *lelit* n. night, night-time

ሌላ *lela* adj. other, extra. additional, another

— ሌላውን —*leluwən* something else

— ጋ —*ga* elsewhere, *also* ሌላ ዘንድ

ከዚህ — *käzzih* — besides this

ከዚያም *käzziamm*— besides, moreover

ሌማት *lemat* n. basket tray *(for serving ənǧära bread)*

ሌባ *leba* n. thief

ሌባሻ *lebaša* n. thief catcher

ሌባ ጣት *leba ṭat* n. index finger

ሌብነት *lebənnät* n. thieving, skill in thieving

ሌጋሲዮን *legasion* n. legation

ሌጣ *leṭa* adj. not pregnant; (single, unmarried

—ሴት *leṭa-set* n. spinster, unmarried woman

ሌጣነት *leṭannät* n. the single state, bachelorhood, spinsterhood

ሌጦ *leṭo* n. hide *(sheep or goat only)*

ለ *lə*, *with imperfect* in order that, so that *with imperfect*+ ነው is about *with imperfect*+ ነበር was about to

ለሙጥ *ləmuṭṭ* adj. plain, undecorated

ለሙጥነት *ləmuṭṭnät* n. plainness

ለምጭ *ləmməč̣č̣* n. lath, thin whippy stick

ለሳን *ləssan* n. tongue; language; organ (pols.

ለሻን, ሊሻን *ləšan*, *lišan*, ኒሻን *nišan* n. decoration. *(medal)*

ለባብ *ləbab* harness

ለቡና *ləbbuna* n. conscience

ለቅሶ *ləqso* n. crying, mourning, lamentation

ለብ *ləbb* n heart; courage, mental acuteness

ለበ ሰፊ *ləbbä säffi* adj. tolerant; long-suffering

— ቅን —*qən* adj. kind-hearted, well-disposed

— ቈራጥ —*qʷärraṭ* adj. courageous; decisive in manner

— ቢስ —*bis* adj. forgetful,

— ተራራ —*tärara* adj. indomitable, unyielding

— ደንዳና —*dändanna* adj. stout-hearted

— ደፋር —*däffar* adj. daring. courageous

ልባም *ləbbum* adj. conscientious, mindful *(of details)*

ልባዊ *ləbbawi* adj. cordial; warm

ልዑል *lə'ul* n. prince

ሉዓላዊ *lu'alawi* adj. raised, *(dais/or platform)*, sovereign

ልዕልት *lə'əlt* n. princess

ልዕልና *lə'lənna* n. princeliness. nobility; greatness ; supremacy

ልደት *lədät* n. birthday; Christmas

ልደታ *lədäta* n. first day of the month *see* ወለደ

ልጅ *ləǧ* n. child; esq. *(general title for aristocracy)*

ልጃገረድ *ləgaǧäräd* n. young girl; virgin

ልጃገረድነት *ləgaǧärädənnät* n. youth *(for girls)*; virginity

ልጅነት *ləǧənnät* n. childhood

የልጅ ልጅ *yäləǧ ləǧ* n. grandchild

ልፕ *see* ላጠ

ልጨኛ *ləččäñña* adj. polite, courteous

ልፋጭ *ləffač̣* n. gristle, sinew; tough, inedible meat

ልፍስፍስ *see* ተልፈሰፈሰ

ሎሌ *lole* n. old retainer

ሎሌነት *lolennät* n. long service *(as a domestic)*

ሎሚ *lomi* n. lime *(fruit)*

ባህረ — *bahrä*—n. grape fruit

ሎሚታ *lomita* n. metal ornament. *(at point of scabbard)*

ሎሚናት *lominat* n. lemonade

ሎተሪ *lotäri* n. lottery

ሎቲ *lotti* n. ear pendant

ሎጋ *loga* n. slim, tall and young

ሎጣዊ *loṭawi* n. homosexual *(male)*, sodomite

ሎፊሳ *lofisa* n. leather saddle cloth

ሐ

ሐሙስ *hamus* n. Thursday

ጸሎተ— *ṣälotä*—n. Maundy Thursday

ሐማል *hammal* n. coolie *(Harar)*

ሐማልነት *hammalənnät* n. coolie work

ሐሜት *hammet* n. backbiting, malicious gossip

ሐሜተኛ *hamatäñña* n. backbiter, gossip *see* አማ

ሐምሌ *hamle* n. tenth Ethiopian month *(July)*

ሐምራዊ *hamrawi* n. purple

ሐሞት *hamot* n. bile

ሐሞተ ቢስ *hamotä bis* adj. lacking initiative; dull

ሐረርጌ *harärge* n. one of the Administrative Regions, Eastern Ethiopia *(Hararge)*

ሐረር *harär* n. the city of Harar

ሐረግ *haräg* n. shoot of a creeping plant; decoration *(in printed book)*

ሐረገ ወይን *harägä wäyn* n. vine shoot

ሐሩር *harur* n. heat-wave; spell of hot weather

ሐራ ጥቃ *haraṭəqa* n. heretic

ሐራጅ *harraǧ* n. auction

ሐር *harr* n. silk

የሐር ትል *yäharr təl* n. silkworm

ሐሰት *hassät* n. lie, falsehood

ሐሰተኛ *hassätäñña* n. liar

ሐሳዌ መሲሕ *hassawe mäsih* n. false prophet

ሐሳብ *see* አሰበ

ሐቅ *haqq* n. truth

ሐቀኛ *haqqäñña* adj. truthful

ሐቀኛነት *haqqäññannät* n. truthfulness

ሐበሻ *habäša* adj/n. Abyssinian; Abyssinia

ሐብል	*habl* n. necklet
ሐብሐብ	*habhab* n. watermelon
ሐተታ	*hatäta* n. investigation (scientific, academic); discursiveness
ሐተተኛ	*hatätäñña* adj. discursive, digressive
አታች	*attač* adj. discursive digressive
ሐች	*hačč* adv. yonder, over there
ሐኪም	*hakim* n. physician, doctor
—ቤት	*—bet* n. hospital
ሕክምና	*həkkəmənna* n. medical profession, medical treatment,
ሐኬት	*haket* n. laziness
ሐካይ	*hakkay* adj. lazy
ሐኬተኛ	*haketäñña* adj. lazy
ሐኬተኛነት	*haketäññannät* n. laziness
ሐዋላ	*hawwala* n. money transfer *(through bank)*
ሐዋርያ	*hawarəya* n. appostle
ሐዋርያነት	*hawarəyannät* n. apostleship
ሐዋርያዊ	*hawarəyawi* adj. apostolic
ሐውልት	*hawəlt* n. statue
ሐዘን	*see* አዘነ
ሐይቅ	*hayq* n. lake
ሐዲስ ኪዳን	*haddis kidan* n. New *Testament*
ሐዲድ	*hadid* n. railway line *(metal)*, track
(የ)ባቡር—	*(yä)babur—*n. railway line, track
ሐጂ	*hağği* n. one who has made the pilgrimage to Mecca *(title)*
ሐፍረት	*hafrät* n. shame
ሐፍረተ ሥጋ	*hafrätä səga* n. sexual organ *(male or female)*, *see* አፈረ
ሑር ወጣ	*hurr wäṭṭa* v.i. was set free
ሑርነት	*hurrənnät* n. freedom *(e.g. as given to slave)*
ሑዳዴ	*hudade* n. lent
ሒሳብ	*hisab* n. calculation; mathematics; account, bill *see* አሰበ
ሔዋን	*hewan* n. Eve
ሕልም	*həlm* n. dream, *see* አለመ
ሕመም	*həmäm* n. sickness, disease
ሕመምተኛ	*həmämtäñña* n. sick person, patient
ሕማም	*həmam* n. pain
ሕማማት	*həmamat* n. Holy Week, *see* አመመ
ሕቅ አለ	*həqq alä* v.i. hiccoughed, hiccupped
ሕቅታ	*həqqəta* n. hiccough, hiccup
ሕንፃ	*hənṣa* n. building *(usually of stone) see* አነጠ *and* አነፀ
ሕዋስ	*həwas* n. sense *e.g. hearing, sight etc.)* cell *(pols)*
ተሕዋስያን	*tähawasəyan* n. small crawling insects *(general term)*
ሕዝብ	*həzb* n. people, population
ሕዝባዊ	*həzbawi* adj. popular, public, social *(of the people)*
ሠራዊት	*—särawit* n. militia
ተራ ሕዝብ	*tära həzb* n. crowd, masses
አሕዛብ	*ahəzab* infidels, gentiles
የሕዝብ ካፒታሊዝም	*yähəzb kappitalism*, people's capitalism
ሕይወት	*həywät* n. life
ሕይወቱን ሳተ	lost consciousness
—አሳለፈ	gave one's life
በሕይወት ኖረ	or ቆየ kept alive
—አለ	be alive
የሕይወት	biography, memoires
ታሪክ	autobiography
— ዋስትና	life insurance
ዘለዓለማዊ ሕይወት	eternal life
ሕያው	*həyaw*-animate; vivid
ሕያውነት	*həyawənnät* n. immortality
ሕግ	*həgg* n. law, rule, regulation; virginity matrimony pl. ሕግጋት *or* ሕገጋት
ሕገ ወጥ	*həggä wäṭṭ* adj. illegal, lawless

ሕጋዊ	*həggawi* adj. lawful, legitimate, legal, juridical
—ወራሽ	—*wäraš* n. legal heir
ሕጋዊነት	*həggawinnät* n. legality
የሕግ መወሰኛ ምክር ቤት	*yähəgg mäwässäña məkər bet* n. parliament
— ሚስት	— *mist* n. legal wife
ሕግ ተላለፈ	*həgg tälaläffä* v.t. broke the law
—አስከባሪ	—*askäbbari* n. public prosecutor
—አወጣ	—*awäṭṭa* v.t. legislated, drew up rules.
—አውጪ	—*awṭi* legislator lawgiver, lawmaker,
— የለሽ	—*yälläš* lawless
ሕገ መንግሥት	*həggä mängəst* constitution
— ወጥ	*wäṭṭ* outlaw, illegal; irregular
የሕግ ረቂቅ	*yähəgg räqiq* draft *(of law)*, bill
ጠቅላይ ዐቃቤ ሕግ	*ṭäqlay aqqabe nəgg* Procurator General
ሕግ ጣሽ	*həgg ṭaš* n. law breaker
ሕፃን	*həṣan* n. child, baby pl. ሕፃናት
ሕፃንነት	*həṣannənnät* n. babyhood, early childhood

መ

መሀል	*mähal* n. centre
—ሠፋሪ	— *säfari* n. vacillator *(pols)* neutral, *(pols.)*
—ከተማ	— *kätäma* n. city-centre
መሀንዲስ	*mähandis* n. engineer, civil engineer, architect
መሀንዲስነት	*mähandisənnät* n. the work of an engineer
መሀከል	*mähakkäl* n. middle, centre
መሀከለኛ	*mähakkäläñña* adj. central, middle, medium
መሃይምን	*mähayyəmn* n. illiterate person: layman
መሃይምነት	*mähayyəmənnät* n. illiteracy; status of layman
መለለ	*mällälä* v. t. became attenuated, grew thin and long
መለሎ	*mälälo* adj. tall and slim; attractively built *(person)*
መላላ	*mälala* adj. tall
ሰላላ—	*sälala*— adj; tall and slim
መለል አለ	*mäläll alä* v.i. grew fairly tall and slim
መለመለ	*mälämmälä* v. t. stripped off leaves; made a selection *(of people)*, recruited; pruned
መልማይ	*mälmay* adj. n. *(one who)* strips; selects; prunes
ምልመላ	*məlmäla* n. the action of stripping; pruning; selecting; recruiting
ምልምል	*məlməl* n. selected person, chosen candidate; young paramour for rich widow; gigolo
ተመለመለ	*tämälämmälä* v. i. was pruned, stripped, was selected, recruited

መለሰ mälläsä v.t. answered; returned; put back; gave back; translated

መላሽ mällaš adj./n. (one) who answers, returns; gives back, etc.

መልስ mäls n. answer; return invitation (esp. after marriage)

መልሶ ማቋቋም mälləso maquʷaquʷam n. rehabilitation

ምላሽ məllaš n. answer; change (from purchase)

ምልስ məlləs adj. pliant, complaisant

ተመለሰ tämälläsä v.i. returned, came back

ተመላሽ tämällaš adj./n. (one) who returns, comes back

ተመላለሰ tämälallässä v.i. went to and fro

ተመላላሽ tämälalaš adj/n. (one) who goes to and fro

አመላለሰ ammälallässä v.t. transported, carried from place to place

አመላላሽ ammälalaš adj/n (one) who transports, carries from (place to place)

ማመላለሻ mammälaläša n. means of transportation

አስመለሰ asmälläsä v.t. had (s/t) brought back; vomited

*መለከተ see አመለከተ / ተመለከተ

መለከት mäläkät n. long, single-note trumpet, ceremonial trumpet

*መለከ see አመለከ

መለኮት mäläkuʷät n. Divinity

መለኮታዊ mäläkuʷätawi adj. Divine

መለኮትነት mäläkuʷätənnät n. Divine power

መለዮ mälläyyo see ለየ

መለጠ mälläṭä v.t. removed all the hair from

መላጣ mälaṭa adj. bald; bare; barren (for land)

መላጣነት mälaṭannät n. baldness

ምልጥ məlṭ adj. skinless, hairless

ተመለጠ tämälläṭä v.i. was made bald; was peeled

ተመላለጠ tämälalläṭä v.i. became, was made completely bald; was completely stripped of skin

አመለጠ amälläṭä v.t. slipped from the hands; escaped (from custody, danger etc.)

አመለጠው amälläṭäw v.t. broke wind

አስመለጠ asmälläṭä v.t. caused (s/o) to escape; caused (s/t) to fall from the hands

መላ mäla n. idea for solving a problem, scheme

—መታ —mätta v.t. predicted, foresaw, made a guess

—ምት —mət n. hypothesis, guess

—ቢስ —bis adj. without hope (person); unsolvable

—ቅጡን አጣ —qəṭun aṭṭa v.i. was thrown into utter confusion, was at a loss

—ተናገረ —tänaggärä v.t. made a helpful suggestion

—የሌለው —yälelläw adj. without hope; unsolvable

መላ mälla adj. whole, entire

መልሕቅ mälhəq n. anchor

መልቲ mälti adj. mischievous, roguish

መልቲነት mältinnät n. roguishness, mischievousness

መልአክ mäl'ak n. angel

መልአከ ሞት mäl'akä mot n. the Angel of Death

መልአከ ዑቃቢ *mäl'akä uqabi* n. guardian angel

መልከኛ *mälkäñña* n. landlord

መልካም *mälkam* adj. good, nice, well

መልክ *mälk* n. face; appearance

መልከ መልካም *mälkä mälkäm* adj. beautiful, handsome

— ቀና *—qänna* adj. attractive, good - looking

— ጥፉ *—ṭəfu* adj. ugly,

መሐለቅ *mähälläq* n. coin

መሐላ *mähalla* n. oath, *see* ማለ

መሐረም(ብ) *mäharäm(b)* n. handkerchief

መምህር *mämhər* n. professor, high-level teacher

መምህርነት *mämhərənnät* n. teaching profession

ምሁር *məhur* n. scholar

ምሁራዊ *məhurawi* adj. scholarly

መሠረተ *mäsärrätä* v.t. established, founded

መሠረት *mäsärät* n. foundation; reason

መሠረታዊ *mäsärätawi* adj. basic, fundamental

መሥራች *mäsrač* n. founder

ተመሠረተ *tämäsärrätä* v.i. was founded, established

አመሠራረት *ammäsärarät* n. manner of establishing

አስመሠረተ *asmäsärrätä* v.t. had *(s/t)* established

መሠሪ *mäsärri* n. malicious, uncharitable, vicious

መሠሪነት *mäsärrinnät* n. maliciousness, uncharitableness

መሥመር *mäsmär* n. line, circuit \ *see also* ሠመረ

መረመረ *märämmärä* v.t. investigated, examined; scrutinised, checked

መርማሪ *märmari* n. investigator

ምርመራ *mərmära* n. investigation

ምርምር *mərmmər* n. investigation; research

ተመረመረ *tämärâmmärä* v.i. was investigated, checked

ተመርማሪ *tämärmari* n. person under investigation

ተመራመረ *tämärammärä* v.t. researched into *(s/t)*, studied *(s/t)* deeply

ተመራማሪ *tämäramari* adj/n. *(one)* who researches, studies; a researcher

አመራመረ *ammärammärä* v.t. tried to get the truth; pursued an investigation

አመራመር *ammäramär* n. method of investigation

አመራማሪ *ammäramari* n. informer's fee *also* የአመራማሪ ገንዘብ

አስመረመረ *asmärämmärä* v.t. had *(s/t)* investigated, checked

መረረ *märrärä* v.i. was bitter, *(to the taste)*

መረረው *märräräw* v.i. was bitter about it

መራሪ *märari* adj. bitter-tasting

መራራ *märara* adj. bitter-tasting

መራራነት *märarannät* n. bitterness

መራር *märrar* adj. bitter *(fig. e.g. sorrow)*

መራርነት *märrarənnät* n. bitterness

ምሬት ምረት *mərret, mərrät* n. bitter taste

ምር *mərr* n. serious-mindedness

የምር *yämərr* adv. seriously

የምሩን ነው *yämərrun näw* he is very serious

ምርር አለ *mərərr älä* v.i. became very bitter; was very sad

ተመረረ *tämärrärä* v.t. was irritated by; was impatient with; was embittered

ተማረረ *tämarrärä* v.i. took to heart; became serious about *(e.g.*

fighting, reciprocal)

አመረረ *amärrärä* v.t. became serious about *(s/t)*; took too much to heart; became offended *(e.g. if it goes too far)*; made up one's mind *(finally, surprisingly)*

አምራሪ *amrari* adj. n. *(one* who takes *(s/t)* too seriously

አማረረ *ammarrärä* v. i. complained, grumbled; caused others to quarrel

አማራሪ *ammarari* adj/n. *(one)* who grumbles

አስመረረ *asmärrärä* v.t. made *(s/o)* embittered

መረቀ *märräqä* v.t. wished *(s/o)* well; blessed, gave benediction to; made an outright gift; inaugurated

ምሩቅ *mərruq* n. graduate; one who completes a course of instruction successfully

መራቂ *märraqi* adj. n. *(one)* who blesses; wishes *(s/o)* well; makes a gift to; inaugurator

ምረቃ *mərräqa* n. graduation

ድህረ — *dəhərä* — n. graduate studies, post graduate studies

ምርቃት *mərrəqat* n. blessing; good wishes; outright gift

ምርቃን *mərrəqan* n. blessing; good wishes; outright gift

ተመረቀ *tämärräqä* v.i. was blessed; was given graduating certificate

ተመራቂ *tämärraqi* adj./n. *(one)* who is blessed: graduate

አስመረቀ *asmärräqä* v.t. had *(s/o)* blessed; treated one's friends *(after buying a new car, suit, etc.)*

መረቅ *märäq* n. broth, bouillon

መረቀዘ *märäqqäzä* v.i. suppurated *(after seeming to be healed)*; turned sour *(of a relationship)*

አመረቀዘ *amäräqqäzä* v.i. suppurated; turned sour. broke out afresh *(wounds, hatred)*

መረባ *märäbba* adj. square*(for measurement - as 'square metre'- arch.)*

መረብ/መርበብ *märäb/märbäb* n. net *(for fishing, tennis etc.)*

— ጣለ *—ṭalä* v.t. netted *(fish)*

— ጣይ *—ṭay* n. fisherman

መረተ *märrätä* v.i. yielded; was cleaned and threshed *(grain)*

ምርት *mərt* n. production; yield, crop

ስልተ ምርት *səltä mərt* mode of productoin

አመረተ *amärrätä* v.t. threshed crop, harvested; produced

አምራች *amrač* n. producer

መረነ *märränä* v.t. tied with a thong *(joined ploughshare to handle)*

ምራን *məran* n. leather thong

መረን *märän* adj/n. loose-living, libertine

መረዋ *märäwwa* n. bell *(large, e.g. of church)*

መረዘ *märräzä* v.t. poisoned; hated strongly

መራዥ *märraž* adj/n. *(one)* who poisons; *(one)* who hates strongly

መርዛኛ *märzäñña* adj. poisonous

መርዛም *märzam* adj. full of poison

መርዝ *märz* n. poison

ተመረዘ *tämärräzä* v.i. was poisoned

ተማረዘ *tämarräẓä* v.i. hated each other *(very strongly)*

አማረዘ *ammarräzä* v.t. caused

(people) to hate each other

አስመረዘ *asmärräzä* v.t. had *(s/o)* poisoned; caused *(s/o)* to be hated

መረጀ *see* አረጀ

መረገ *märrägä* v.t. daubed *(cement)*, plastered

መምረጊያ *mämrägiya* n. tool, method used in plastering, daubing

መራጊ *märagi* adj./n. *(one)* who plasters, daubs

ምርጊት *mərgitt* n. plaster *(usually mud or dung)*

ምርግ *mərg* adj. plastered, daubed with mud *(wall, etc.)*

ተመረገ *tämärrägä* v.i. was plastered, daubed

አማረገ *ammarrägä* v.t. helped *(s/o)* to plaster, daub

አስመረገ *asmärrägä* v.t. had *(s/t)* plastered

መረግድ *märägd* n. emerald

መረጠ *märrätä* v.t. chose, selected, voted for, preferred

መረጣ *märäta* n. choice, election

መራጭ *märač* adj/n. *(one)* who chooses, votes

መራጭነት *märačənnät* n. process of voting, choosing

መምረጫ *mämräča* n. polling booth; place where choice is made

ምራጭ *mərrač* n. second best, what is left over after choice is made

ምርጥ *mərt* adj/n. *(that)* which is chosen; best

ምርጫ *mərča* n. choice; election

ተመረጠ *tämärrätä* v.i. was chosen, selected

ተመራጭ *tämärrač* n. candidate for selection; preference

ተመራጭነት *tämärračənnät* n. candidature

አማረጠ *ammarrätä* v.t. helped in choosing; decided between the best

አማራጭ *ammarač* adj/n. *(one)* who selects the very best; alternative

አስመረጠ *asmärrätä* v.t had *(s/o, s/t)* chosen

መራ *märra* v.t. led; led in singing, chanting; distributed land

መሪ *märi* n. leader

መሪነት *märinnät* n. leadership

መሪጌታ *märigeta* n. choir leader, chant leader *(in church)*

መርህ *märh* n. principle

መምሪያ *in* የመምሪያ ኃላፊ *yämämriya halafi* department head *(in a ministry etc.)*

ምሪት *mərrit* n. the assigning of plots of land, lodging

ተመራ *tämärra* v.i. was led; was assigned *(plot of land)*

ተመሪ *tämäri* adj/n *(one)* who is led; assigned *(plot of land)*

መመሪያ *mämmäriya* n. policy, guideline

ተማራ *tämarra* v.t. led each other *(e.g. two blind people)*

አመራ *amärra* v.t. took one's course, went one's way; headed for; went towards

አመራር *ammärar* n. way of guiding, leading; leadership

አስመራ *asmärra* v.t. had *(s/o)* guided, led

መሬት *märet* n. land, earth, ground, soil

— ነው *—näw* he is patient

ባለመሬት *balä märet* n. landowner

የመሬት —ይዞታ *yämäret yəzota* n. land tenure

— ከበርቴ *—käbbärte* n. landlord

ከመሬት ተነሥቶ *kämäret tänästo* without any reason, provocation

ድንግል መሬት *dəngəl märet* virgin land

መር አለ *märr alä* v.i. jumped, leaped

መርበብ *märbäb* n. net *(for fishing) also* መረብ

— ጣለ *—ṭalä* v.t. cast net

— ጣይ *—ṭay* n. fisherman

መርከብ *märkäb* n. ship, large boat, large vessel

መርከበኛ *märkäbäñña* n. sailor

መርዶ *see* አረዳ

መርፌ *märfe* n. needle *(sewing, hypodermic)*; injection

— ቀዳዳ *—qädada* n. eye of a needle

—ቁልፍ *—qulf* n. safety pin

— ወጋ *—wägga* v.t. gave an injection

መሮ *märo* n. chisel

መሰለ *mässälä* v.t. resembled; pretended to be; made a model of; spoke in parables

መሳይ *mäsay* adj/n. *(one)* who resembles, pretends

ምሳሌ *məssale* n. example; parable

ምስለኔ *məsläne* n. district officer *(in earlier days lowest Govt. rank in Ethiopia)*

ምስል *məsəl* n. statue; model; graven image

ተመሰለ *tämassälä* v.t. took the form, shape of *(s/t)*

ተማሰለ *tämassälä* v.t. was stirred, mixed, homogenised; resembled each other

አማሰለ *ammassälä* v.t. stirred, broth etc; assessed points of similarity

ማማሰያ *mammasäya* n. stirring stick, stirrer

አመሳሰል *ammäsasäl* n. point or resemblance

አስመሰለ *asmässälä* v.t. spoke convincingly; pretended

አስመሳይ *asmässay* adj/n. *(one)* who pretends, speaks convincingly; pretender, impostor

መሰላል *mäsälal* n. ladder

* መሰቃቀለ *see* አመሰቃቀለ

መሰነ *mässänä* v.i. became barren *(for animals)*

መሲና *mäsina* adj./n. fat and sterile *(cow)*

መሰንቆ *mäsänqo* n. *also* ማሲንቆ *masinqo* n. single-string violin *(Ethiopian)*

— መቺ *—mäči* adj./n. *(one)* who plays a *mäsänqo*

መሰከረ *mäsäkkärrä* v.i. testified, acted as witness

መስካሪ *mäskari* adj/n. *(one)* who testifies, acts as witness

መስካሪነት *mäskarinnät* n. act of testifying

ምስክር *məsəkkər* n. witness *(in court)*

ምስክራ *məskära* n. testimony

ተመሰከረ *tämäsäkkärä* v.i. was certified by witnesses

ተመሳከረ *tämäsakkärä* v.t. produced witnesses against each other

አመሳከረ *ammäsakkärä* v.t. made *(both parties)* testify; compared *(two things of the same kind)*

አመሳካሪ *ammäsakari* adj/n. *(one)* who compares; *(one)* who makes *(both parties)* testify

አስመሰከረ *asmäsäkkärä* v.t. had *(s/o)* testify; had *(s/o)* testify by proxy

አስመስካሪ *asmäskari* adj.*(one)* who has *(s/o)* testify on his behalf

መሰከነ *mäsäkkänä* v.i.. became very poor

ምስኪን *məskin* adj. very poor; pathetic

ምስኪንነት *məskinənnät* n. extreme poverty

መሰገ *mässägä* v.t. packed into *(animals into stable)*, put in a fold
ምስግ *məssəg* n. fold
*መሰገነ *see* አመሰገነ
መሰጠ *mässäṭä* v.t. took *(one's)* attention, absorbed *(one's thought, plan etc.)*
መሳጭ *mässač* adj. absorbing
ተመሰጠ *tämässäṭä* v.t. was absorbed *(in thought)*
*መሰጠረ *see* ተመሳጠረ *and* ምስጢር
መሲሕ *masih* n. Messiah
መሲሓዊ *mäsihawi* adj. Messianic
መሳ *mässa* adj. half *(e.g. "the tea was half water")*
— ለመሳ *—lämässa* adj. half and half
መስቀል *see* ሰቀለ
መስቃ *mäsqa* n. unjustified reproach
መስተአምር *mästä'ammər* n. article *(gram.)*
መስተዋድድ *mästäwadəd* n. preposition
መስተጋብር *mästägabər* n. interaction
መስተፃምር *mästäṣamər* n. conjunction *(gram.)*
መስተዋት *mästäwat* n. mirror; glass; window glass
መስቲካ *mästika* n. chewing-gum
መስኖ *mäsno* n. irrigation
መስከረም *mäskäräm* n. first Ethiopian month *(Sept. / Oct.)*
መስክ *mäsk* n. field, meadow *(pasture)*
— አልፋ *—alfa* adj. idle, loafer
መስኮብ *mäskob* n. Russia
መስኮባዊ *mäskobawi* adj. Russian
መስኮብኛ *mäskobəñña* n. *Russian (language)*
መስኮት *mäskot* n. window
መስጊድ *mäsgid* n. mosque
መስፍ *mäsf* n. anvil
መስፍን *mäsfən* n. nobleman *(used as title, equivalent to "Duke")*
መሳፍንት *mäsafənt* n. the nobility
መሶብ *mäsob* n. food-table *(made of basketwork, peculiar to Ethiopia)*
መሶበወርቅ *mäsobäwärq* n. small food-table *(highly decorated)*
መሸ *mäššä* v.i. night fell, became evening, got dark
ምሽት *məššət* n. evening, dusk
አመሸ *amäššä* v.i. spent the evening, was late in the evening
እንዴት አመሸህ *əndət amäššäh* good evening
አምሽቶ መጣ *amšəto maṭṭa* he came late in the evening
አማሸ *ammaššä* v.t. kept *(s/o)* company *(for the evening)*
አማሺ *ammaši* adj/n. one who keeps *(s/o)* company *(for the evening)*
አስመሸ *asmäššä* v.t. made *(s/o)* late *(in the evening)*
መሸተ *mäššätä* v.t. prepared drink for sale *(beer or ṭäg)*
መሸተኛ *mäšätäñña* adj/n. *(one)* who frequents drinking houses
መሸታ *mäšäta* n. a drink in a public house; a drinking spree
መሸታ ቤት *mäšäta bet* n. public house; bar
መሸገ *mäššägä* v.t. built a fortification; manned a barricade
ምሽግ *məššəg* n. barricade, fortification
አስመሸገ *asmäššägä* v.t. had *(a place)* fortified
መቀመቅ *mäqämäq* n. abyss
መቀስ *mäqäs* n. scissors
መቀነት *see* ቀነት

መቃ *mäqa* n. reed
— ብዕር —*b'ər* n. reed pen
መቅሠፍት *see* ቀሠፈ
መቅረዝ *mäqräz* n. candle stick, lampholder
መቅን *mäqn* n. bone marrow
መቅኖ ቢስ *mäqno bis* adj. short-lived; lacking support; having no hope of success; in a desperate situation
መቋሚያ *mäquʷamiya* n. staff *(e.g. priest staff)*, *see* ቆመ
መበለት *mäbällät* n. nun *(in Ethiopia, usually a widow who has vowed the remainder of her life to the Church)*
መባ *mäba* n. holy vow; small offering given to the Church
መባቻ *mäbaća* n. first day of any month
መብረቅ *mäbräq* n. lightning; thunderbolt
መብት *mäbt* n. right *(as in "the rights of the citizen")*
ባለ — *balä* — adj/n. *(one)* who is within his rights
መተረ *mättärä* v.t. chopped *(meat, etc.)*
መታሪ *mätari* adj/n. *(one)* who chops *(meat, etc)*
ምትር *mətər* adj. chopped up
መታተረ *mätattärä* v.t. chopped *(a certain amount of)*
ተመተረ *tämättärä* v.i. was chopped up
አስመተረ *asmättärä* v.t. had *(s/t)* chopped up
መተት *mätät* n. magic, spell
መታ *mätta* v.t. hit, struck; put *(animals)* together for breeding
ምታት *mətat*, *also* ምትሐት *məthat* n. conjuring trick, optical illusion
ራስ ምታት *ras mətat* n. headache
ምት *mət* n. way of hitting; beat

ምች *məčč* n. attack of fever
መታታ *mätatta* v.t. tapped gently
ተመታ *tämätta* v.i. was hit, struck
ተማታ *tämatta* v.t. hit each other; hit, struck; was confused
ተማች *tämač* adj/n. *(one)* who tends to use his fists, violent person, bully
አማታ *ammatta* v.t. made s/o hit s/o; confused *(s/o)* in order to deceive
አማች *ammač* adj/n *(one)* who makes others hit each other; *(one)* who confuses in order to deceive
አምታታ *amtatta* v.t. deceived, beguiled
አምታች *amtač* n. deceiver
አስመታ *asmätta* v.t. had *(s/o)* hit
መትረየስ *mäträyyäs* n. machine gun
መቶ *mäto* adj./n. hundred
መቶኛ *mätoñña adj.* hundredth
መቶ በመቶ fully, wholly; hundred per cent
— አለቃ lieutenant
— ዓመት century
በመቶ *or* ከመቶ percent, percentage
መቶኛ ዓመት centennial, centenary
መቸ *see* ተመቸ
መቼ *mäče* መች *mäč* adv/conj. when
መቼም *mäččem* interj. well of course, after all, any way
መቼ አጣሁት *mäče aṭṭahut* I know it well
— ጠፋኝ — *ṭäffañ* I know it well.
መቼውንም *mäččewənəm* adv. all the time
ከመቼ ጀምሮ *kämäčče ǧämməro* since when?

ከመቼውም kämäččewəmm more than ever before

መነመነ mänämmänä v.i. got thin; became emaciated

ምንምን mənmən adj. thin; emaciated

መንማና mänmanna adj. very thin, emaciated

አመነመነ amänämmänä v.t. made thin

መነቀረ mänäqqärä v.t. gouged out; churned up *(ground)*

መንቃራ mänqarra adj./n. *(one)* who walks clumsily, ungraceful in walking

መነቃቀረ mänäqaqqärä v.t. disarranged, messed up; gouged; churned up completely

መነተፈ mänättäfä *also* ሞነተፈ monättäfä v.t. snatched, grabbed *(for thief)*

መንታፊ mäntafi adj/n. *(one)* who snatches, thief

ተመነተፈ tämänättäfä v.i. was snatched, grabbed, was stolen

መነቸከ mänäččäkä *also* ችክ አለ čəkk alä v.t. importuned, annoyed by asking; would not come clean *(laundry, etc.)*

መንቻካ mänčakka adj/n. *(one)* who is stubborn, importunate

አመነቸከ amänäččäkä v.t. made *(s/t)* too dirty for washing ,cleaning

መነነ männänä v.i. became a hermit; forsook the world

መናኝ männañ n. hermit

ምናና mənnäna n. the action of retiring from the world

ምናኔ mənnane n. the action of retiring from the world

መመነኛ mämännäña n. place of retirement from the world; hermitage

አስመነነ asmännänä n. caused *(s/o)* to become a hermit

መነኰሰ mänäkkʷäsä v.t. became a monk

መነኩሴ mänäkwəse n. monk

መንኳሽ mänkuʷaš n. religious novice *(male or female)*

ምንኩስና mənkʷəsənna n. state of being a monk, monkhood

የምንኩስና ኑሮ yämənkʷəsənna nuro monastic life

አመነኰሰ amänäkkʷäsä v.t. made *(s/o)* a monk

አስመነኰሰ asmänäkkʷäsä v.t. had *(s/o)* made a monk

መነዘረ mänäzzärä v.t. gave change *(money)*, changed *(money)*

መንዛሪ mänzari adj/n. money changer

ምንዝር mənzər adj/n. fornication, adultery; follower *(of a chief)* e.g. አለቃና ምንዝር a leader and his followers

መነዛዘረ mänäzazzärä v.t. changed completely *(i.e. break down total amount into small change)*

ተመነዘረ tämänäzzärä v.i. was changed *(money)*

መመንዘሪያ mämänzäriya n. place where money is changed

አመነዘረ amänäzzärä v.i. committed adultery, fornicated

አስመነዘረ asmänäzzärä v.t. had *(money)* changed

መነገገ mänäggägä. v.t. forced *(s/o's)* mouth wide open

መንጋጋ mängaga n. lower jaw, mandibles

መነጠረ mänäṭṭärä v.t. cleared, uprooted completely *(to clear land for ploughing)*

ምንጣሪ *mənəṭṭari* n. s/t. which is uprooted

ምንጥር *mənṭər* adj. uprooted *(plants, tree stumps etc.)*

ምንጠራ *mənṭära* n. the action of uprooting. clearing *(of land)*

መነጣጠረ *mänäṭaṭṭärä* v.t. uprooted completely, cleared completely *(land)*

ተመነጠረ *tämänäṭṭärä* v.i. was uprooted

አስመነጠረ *asmänäṭṭärä* v.t. had *(s/t)* uprooted, cleared *(e.g. field)*

መነጠቀ *mänäṭṭäqä see also* ነጠቀ *näṭṭäqä* v.t. snatched, grabbed *(took rudely, forcibly)*

መንጠቆ *mänṭäqqo* n. fish-hook

ተመነጠቀ *tämänäṭṭäqä* v.i. was snatched, grabbed *(rudely)*; walked off *(angrily, abruptly)*

መነጥር *mänäṭṭər* n. eyeglasses, spectacles *also* መነፅር

መነጨ *mänäččä* v.i. sprang out *(for water)*; sprang from the mind *(idea, suggestion)*

ምንጭ *mənč* n. spring, source

መነጨረ *mänäččärä* v.t. clawed at

መንጫራ *mänčarra* adj. ungainly, clumsy

መነጨቀ *mänäččäqä* v.t. snatched, grabbed

መንጫቃ *mänčaqqa* adj. irritable, ill-tempered

አመነጫጨቀ *ammänäčaččäqä* v.t denigrated

አመናጨቀ *ammänaččäqä* v.t. denigrated

መነጽር *mänäṣṣər* n. eyeglasses, spectacles

መና *mäna* adj. useless, unsuccessful

— ቀረ *—qärrä* was without hope, was irredeemable

መና *männa (in the Bible, food provided by God for the Israelites)*

መናኛ *mänaňňa* adj. commonplace, of the lowest grade

መናፍቅ *mänafəq* adj/n. heretic, heretical

መንሽ *mänš* n. pitchfork, fork *(farm tool)*

መንበር *mänbär* n. throne

መንታ *mänta* adj/n. twin

— መንገድ *—mängäd* n. fork *(in road)*

መንካ *mänka or* ሙንካ *munka* n. spoon

መንኮራኩር *mänkorakur* n. wheel; rocket

ሰው ሠራሽ *säw särraš* – n space satellite

መንደሪን *mändärin* n. tangerine *(orange)*

መንደር *mändär* n. village

መንደረኛ *mändäräňňa* n. villager, one who lives in a village

መንደርተኛ *mändärtäňňa* adj/n fellow-villager

መንገድ *mängäd* n. road, way; method, system

መንገደኛ *mängädäňňa* n. traveller, passerby

እግረ መንገዴን *əgrä mängäden* on my way

አቋራጭ መንገድ *aquʷarač mängäd* crosscut

የአየር መንገድ *yä'ayyär mängäd* airlines

የእግር መንገድ *yä'əgər mängäd* footpath, path, track

መንጋ *mänga* n. flock *(of sheep, goats, etc.)* swarm *(of locusts, birds etc.)*

— ፈሪ *—färi* n. bunch of cowards

መንጋጋ *mängaga* n. lower jaw mandible *see* መነገገ

መንግሥት *see* ነገሠ

መንጠቆ *see* ነጠቀ

መንጦ *mänṭo or* ሜንጦ *menṭo* n. hook

መንጮረር *mänčorär* n. duct

መንፈሳዊ *mänfäsawi* adj. spiritual, religious; theological

መንፈሳዊነት *mänfäsawinnät* n. spirituality. *see also* ነፈሰ

መንፈቅ *mänfäq* n. period of six months

መንፈቀ ሌሊት *mänfäqä lelit* n. midnight

መኖ *männo* n. fodder, animal food

መከረ *mäkkärä* v.t. advised, counselled

መካሪ *mäkari* adj/n. *(one)* who advises, advisor

ምክር *məkər* n. advice

— ቤት *—bet* n. parliament

የምክር ቤት አባል *yäməkər bet abal* n. member of parliament

መካከረ *mäkakkärä* v.t. gave a certain amount of advice to

ተመከረ *tämäkkärä* v.i. was advised

ተማከረ *tämakkärä* v.i. gathered together *(e.g. to study a problem)*, held a seminar; asked advice from s/o; took counsel together, consulted each other

ተመካከረ *tämäkakkärä* v.t. discussed *(a problem)* together, took counsel, sought advice, consulted

አማከረ *ammakkärä* v.t. asked advice ; gave advice, consulted with s/o

አማካሪ *ammakari* adj/n. *(one)* who asks, gives, advice; counsellor, member of parliament

የሕግ — *yähəgg* – legal advisor

አስመከረ *asmäkkärä* v.t. had *(s/t)* discussed

መከራ *mäkära* n. trouble, distress, hardship, misfortune, tribulation

መከረኛ *mäkäräñña* adj. mischievous, trouble-making; *(one)* who is prone to trouble

መከር *mäkär* n. harvest-time; autumn also መኸር *mähär*

መከተ *mäkkätä* v.t. defended oneself *(from a blow etc.)*

መካች *mäkkač* adj/n. *(one)* who defends himself

መከታ *mäkäta* n. structure of a wall, lath; screen *(against cold air, draughts)*; barricade

ተመከተ *tämäkkätä* n. was defended

መከነ *mäkkänä* v.i. became sterile, barren *(women)*

መካን *mäkkan* adj/ n. *(one)* who is sterile, barren

መካንነት *mäkkänənnät* n. sterility, barrenness

አመከነ *amäkkänä* v.t. made *(s/o)* sterile, barren

መከዳ *mäkkädda* n. pillow, cushion

*መከኘ *see* አመካኘ

መኪና *mäkina* n. machine, mechanical device; motor car

— ነጂ *—näği* n. driver, chauffeur

በመኪና ጻፈ *bämäkina ṣafä* v.t. typed *also* ተየበ

የመኪና መሪ *yämäkina märi* n. steering wheel

የጭነት መኪና *yäčənät mäkina* n. lorry, truck

የጽሕፈት መኪና *yäṣəhəfät mäkina* n. typewriter

መካከል *mäkakkäl* adj. central, middle, medium; n. centre, middle

መካከለኛ *mäkakkäläñña* adj. medium, average

መካከለኛው ምሥራቅ Middle East

መከረጅ *mäkräğ* n. tea kettle

መክሰስ *mäksäs* n. snack; quick meal *(not at set mealtime)*

መኰንን *mäkʷännən* n. officer *(army)*

ዕጩ — *əčču-* n. cadet

መውጅ *mäwǧ* n. sea wave, storm wave

መዐልት *mä'alt* n. daytime

መዐት *mä'at* n. horror; wrath of God; huge number *(for crowd of people)*, calamity

— አውሪ *-awri* n. doom sayer

መዐተኛ *mä'atäñña* adj. shocking, horrifying

መዐዛ *mä'aza* n. fragrance, odour

መዘመዘ *mäzämmäzä* v.t. sucked; drew out *(molten gold, silver)*

ምዝምዝ *məzməz* adj. drawn out *(molten gold, silver)*

ተመዘመዘ *tämäzämmäzä* v.i. was sucked; was drawn out *(gold, silver)*

መዘበረ *mäzäbbärä* v.t. looted, pillaged, exploited

መዝባሪ *mäzbari* adj/n. *(one)* who loots, pillages

ምዝበራ *məzbära* n. looting pillaging; exploitation

ተመዘበረ *tämäzäbbärä* v.i. was looted, pillaged, was exploited

መዘነ *mäzzänä* v.t. weighed, balanced

መዛኝ *mäzzañ* adj/n. *(one)* who weighs; *(one)* who has good judgement

ሚዛን *mizan* n. scale; balance; weight

የሌባ ሚዛን *yäleba mizan* n. false scale

መመዘኛ *mämäzzäña* n. instrument, place for weighing; criterion

ተመዘነ *tämäzzänä* v.i. was weighed

ተመዛዘነ *tämäzazzänä* v.t. was comparable *(with)*, was in equilibrium, balanced one another

ተመዛዛኝ *tämäzazañ* adj/n. *(one)* who is comparable *(with)*, comparable, equivalent, symmetrical

አመዘነ *amäzzänä* v.t. gave weight to; was heavier than, surpassed

አመዛዘነ *ammäzazzänä* v.t. compared; balanced; had good judgement, evaluated; took into account

አመዛዛኝ *ammäzazañ* adj/n. *(one)* who compares; *(one)* who balances; *(one)* who has good judgement; judicious *(person)*

አስመዘነ *asmäzzänä* v.t. had *(s/t)* weighed

መዘዘ *mäzzäzä* v.t. drew out *(e.g. thread from cloth, sword from sheath)*

መዘዝ *mäzäz* n. bad behaviour, fault

መዘዘኛ *mäzäzäñña* adj. troublesome

ተመዘዘ *tämäzzäzä* v.i. was drawn out

ዱላ ተማዘዘ *dulla tämazzäzä* took up cudgels *(to start fighting)*

—አማዘዘ *—ammäzzäzä* v.t. caused *(s/o)* to start fighting *(took up cudgels)*

አስመዘዘ *asmäzzäzä* v.t. had *(s/t)* drawn out

መዘገበ *mäzäggäbä* v.t. registered, kept a record, had on file; enrolled; catalogued

መዝጋቢ *mäzgābi* n. registrar

መዝገበ ቃላት *mäzgäbä qalat* n. dictionary, lexicon

መዝገብ ቤት *mäzgäb bet* n. archives, record office

—ያዘ *—yazä* v.t. kept records

የሒሳብ መዝገብ *yähisab mäzgäb* n. accounts

መዥገር *mäžgär* n. crab lice, tick

መዥገራም *mäžgäram* adj. ticky

መደመደ *mädämmädä* v.t. made level *(by cutting)*

መደበ *mäddäbä* v.t. allotted, shared out, apportioned; put in the kitty *(gambling)*

ምደባ *mәddäba* n. allotment, share; money put in bank or kitty *(gambling)*

መደብ *mäddäb* n. allotment apportion; class *(political)*

የመደብ ትግል *yämäddäb tәgәl* n. class-struggle

የሠራተኛው— *yäsärratäññaw* – the working class

የገዢው— *yägäžәw*– the ruling class

ተመደበ *tämäddäbä* v.i. was allotted; was put aside was stationed, put into position

አስመደበ *asmäddäbä* v.t. had *(s/t, s/o)* allotted, positioned

መደብር *mädäbbәr* n. department store, large shop; warehouse

መደደ *mäddädä* v.i. acted foolishly

መደዳ *mädäda* n. row, series; position in line, *(often irrespective of rank)*

መደዴ *mädäde* n. beginner, novice

መዲና *mädina* n. metropolis

መዳብ *mädab* n. copper

መዳፍ *mädaf* n. palm *(of the hand)*

መድረክ *mädräk* n. threshold; stage, platform, tribune, rostrum; forum

መድን *in* የመድን ድርጅት *yämädәn dәrәǧǧәt* n. insurance company *see also* ዳነ

መድፍ *mädf* n. cannon, artillery

መድፈኛ *mädfäñña* n. artilleryman

መዶሻ *mädoša* n. hammer

መጀመሪያ *see* ጀመረ

መጅ *mäǧ* n. upper millstone, upper griadstone; callus

መገለ *mäggälä* v.t. gave out pus *(for a wound)*

መግላም *mäglam* adj. full of pus

መግል *mägәl* n. pus

አመገለ *amäggälä* v.t. squeezed out pus

መገመገ *mägämmägä* v.t. drank greedily, with relish *(making sucking noise with lips)*

መገበ *mäggäbä* v.t. fed, gave food to

መጋቢ *mäggabi* adj/n. *(one)* who feeds; catering manager ; quartermaster, administrator of a church, monastery

—መንገድ *—mängäd* n. feeder-road

ምግብ *mәgәb* n. food, meal, nourishment, aliment

—ቤት *—bet* n. restaurant, dining—room

የምግብ አዳራሽ *yämәgәb addaraš* n. dining—hall

-ሸቀጣሸቀጥ መደብር *– šäqäṭašäqäṭ mädäbbәr* n. grocery store

—ዝርዝር *—zәrzәr* n. menu

—ዘይት *—zäyәt* n. edible oil

ዋና ምግብ *wanna mәgәb* n. staple food

ተመገበ *tämäggäbä* v.t. ate, was given food

ተመጋቢ *tämäggabi* adj/n. *(one)* who is fed; lodger, *(one)* supported by a household; *(one)* who eats at a hotel, restaurant

አመጋገብ *ammägagäb* n. diet *(general sense)*

አስመገበ *asmäggäbä* v.t. had *(s/o)* fed; made *(s/o)* eat

መጋላ *mägäla* n. market place *(mainly Harar)*

መጋዘን *mägazän* n. store-room, ware house

መጋዝ *mägaz* n. saw *(tool for cut ing wood)*

መጋቢት *mäggabit* n. March

መጋዣ *mägaža* n. pack horse

መግላሊት *mäglalit* n. clay pot lid

መግነጢስ *mägnäṭis* n. magnet *also* ማግኔት

መጠመጠ *mäṭämmäṭä* v.t. sucked *(lemons etc.)*, suckled

መጠቀ *mäṭṭäqä* v.i. soared

ምጥቀት *mǝṭqät* n. the action of soaring

አመጠቀ *amäṭṭäqä* v.t. launched, caused to soar up

መጠነ *mäṭṭänä* v.t. judged accurately *(amount)*, measured out the right amount

መጠነኛ *mäṭänäñña* adj/n average, of medium size, medium sized, moderate, proportionate

መጠን *mäṭän* n. size, amount, measure, proportion, magnitude

—የሌለው *—yällelläw* adj. inordinate, enormous

በተቻለ— *bätäčalä–* as much as possible

ከመጠን በላይ *kämäṭän bälay* too much, unusually, beyond measure

መጣኝ *mäṭṭäñ* adj/n. *(one)* who judges *(amounts)* accurately

ምጣኔ *mǝṭṭane* n. accurate judgement *(of quantity)*

—ሀብት *—hǝbt* economy

ምጥን *mǝṭṭǝn* n. pea, bean powder *(highly spiced)*

ተመጠነ *tämäṭṭänä* v.p. was judged accurately

ተመጣጠነ *tämäṭaṭṭänä* v.i. was equal in quantity, standard; was proportionate, was comparable

ተመጣጣኝ *tämäṭaṭañ* adj/n *(s/t, s/o)* equal in quantity, standard, *(s/t)* correspondingly sufficient

—ምግብ *—mǝgǝb* balanced diet, *also* የተመጣጠነ ምግብ

አመጣጠነ *ammäṭaṭṭänä* v.t. made correspondingly equal *(e.g. wages equal to work)*

መጠወተ *mäṭäwwätä also* መጸወተ *mäṣäwwätä* v.t. gave *(alms to the poor)*

መጥዋች *mäṭwač* adj/n. *(one)* who gives alms

ምጥዋት *mǝṭwat* n. alms

ምጥዋተኛ *mǝṭwatäñña* adj/n. *(one)* who takes alms

ተመጠወተ *tämäṭäwwätä* v.i. was given alms

ተመጥዋች *tämäṭwač* adj/n. *(one)* who is given alms

አስመጠወተ *asmäṭäwwätä* v.t. caused *(s/o)* to receive alms

መጢያ *see* ተጠጋ

መጠጠ *mäṭṭäṭä* v.t. sucked

መጣጭ *mäṭač* adj/n. *(one)* who sucks

መጣጣ *mäṭaṭa* n. vinegar adj. emaciated

ምጣጭ *mǝṭṭač* n. remains of sucked lemon, orange, etc.

ተመጠጠ *tämäṭṭäṭä* v.t. was sucked

አመጠጠ *amäṭṭäṭä* v.i. dried out a little *(e.g. wet clothes)*

አስመጠጠ *asmäṭṭäṭä* v.t. gave *(s/o, s/t)* to suck

ማምጠጫ *mämṭäča* n. blotting paper; wiping up cloth

መጠጥ *see* ጠጣ

መጢቃ *mäṭiqa* adj/n. crossbreed, crossbred *(animals, particularly sheep)*

መጣ *mäṭṭa* v. came

መጤ *mäṭṭe* adj. recent arrival

መጥ in አዲስ መጥ *addis mäṭṭ* newcomer

ምጣት *məṭat* n. Day of Judgement

የመጣው ቢመጣ *yämäṭṭaw bimäṭa* whatever may be

—ይምጣ *—yəmṭa* come what may!

የሚመጣው ሳምንት/ ዓመት next week/ year

አመጣ *amäṭṭa* v.t. brought, brought about

አማጣ *ammaṭṭa* v.t. helped to bring *(s/t)*

አማጭ *ammač* n. go-between *(in marriage negotiations)*

አስመጣ *asmäṭṭa* v.t. had *(s/t, s/o)* brought

አስመጪ *asmačči* adj/n. *(one)* who has *s/o, s/t* brought, importer *(of goods)*

አስመጪና ላኪ *asmäččinna laki* n. import- export businessman

መጥፎ *see* ጠፋ

መጣጢስ *mäṭaṭis* n. sweet potato *also* በጣጢስ

መጨመጨ *mäčämmäčä* v.t. kissed closely

መጸወተ *mäṣäwwätä* v.t. gave alms to the poor *also* መጠወተ

መጽሐፍ *see* ጻፈ

መጸው *mäṣäw* n. season after the summer rains, autumn

መጻጉዕ *mäṣagwu'ə* adj/n. cripple, handicapped, person; stunted

መፍትሔ *mäftəhe* n. solution *(of a problem) see* ፈታ

ሙሀቻ *muhačča* n. storage vessel *(for the liquid dough used in making əngära)*

ሙላ *mula* n. hip-joint

ሙልሙል *mulmul adj.* oblong

ሙሬ *mure or* ሙሪ *muri* n. brush *(for cleaning ground grain)*

ሙርጥ *murṭ* n. penis

ሙሴ *muse* n. head of a self help fraternity (ማኅበር)

ሙሾ *mušo* n. dirge, funeral chant

—አውራጅ *—awrağ* n. funeral chant leader

ሙቀጫ *muqäčča* n. mortar *(for grinding coffee, grain etc.), see* ወቀጠ

ሙዋለጠ *muwälläṭä or* ሟለጠ *mu^{w}alläṭä* v.i. became slippery; was worn smooth

ሙልጥ *mulṭ* adj. slippery; worn smooth

ሙልጭ *mulč* adj. slippery worn smooth; poverty-stricken

ሙዋላጣ *mu^{w}alaṭa* adj. slippery

ሙዋሙዋ *muwammuwa or* ሟሟ *mu^{w}amm^{w}a* v.i. dissolved, melted

ሙዋሚ *muwami* adj/n. *(s/t)* which can be easily dissolved, melted

ሙዋርት *muwart* n. pessimism

ሙዋርተኛ *muwartäñña* adj. pessimistic; *(one)* who is a prophet of doom; ill–wisher

አሟረተ *amu^{w}arrätä* v.t foretold disaster

አሟራች *amu^{w}arač* n. one who predicts disaster

ሙዋሸሸ *muwaššäsä or* ሟሸሸ *mu^{w}aššäsä* v.i. shrank, softened; became shrunken and soft

ሙዋጠጠ muwaṭṭäṭä or ሟጠጠ muʷaṭṭäṭä v.t. ate up everything (*impolite in Ethiopia*); took every thing away

ሙጣጭ muṭṭač̣ n. crumb, scraps cf. ፍርፋሪ

ተሟጠጠ tämʷaṭṭäṭä v.t. was eaten up, was removed completely

ለዛው የተሟጠጠ läzzaw yätämuʷaṭṭäṭä adj. graceless, uncouth

ሙዋጨ muwač̣č̣ä or ሟጨ mʷač̣č̣ä v.t. cleaned one's teeth (*especially with the small stick used in Ethiopia*)

መሙዋጫ mämuwač̣a n. s/t used to clean the teeth

ሙዋጨረ muwač̣č̣ärä or ሟጨረ mʷač̣č̣ärä v.t. scratched (*with the fingernails*); scribbled

ሙጭረት muč̣č̣ərat n. a scratch

ሙጭርጭር muč̣ərč̣ər adj/n. (s/t) which is scratched, scribbled

ሞጫጨረ moč̣ač̣č̣ärä v.t. scratched slightly, scribbled

ተሟጨረ tämuʷač̣č̣ärä v.t. was scratched, was scribbled

ተሞጫጨረ tämoč̣ač̣č̣ärä v.i: was scratched all over; was scribbled all over

አስሟጨረ asmuʷač̣č̣ärä v.t. had s/o scratched by s/t

ሙዚቃ muziqa n. music

—ተጫወተ —täč̣awwätä v.t. played music

ሙዚቀኛ muziqäñña n. musician

ሙዝ muz n. banana

ሙያሌ muyyale n. jigger, chigoe

ሙዳ mudda n. hunk of meat

ሙዳይ muday n. small woven basket (*decorative, for buttons etc.*)

ሙዳየ ምጽዋት mudayä məṣwat n. alms box

ሙጃ muǧǧa n. tall weed grass

ሙጃማ muǧǧamma adj. covered with weed grass

ሙገሳ *see* * ሞገሰ

ሙጢ muṭi adj. talkative

ሙጢአፍ muṭi'af adj. talkative *also* ሙጢያፍ

ሙጥኝ muṭṭəññ n. protection (*e.g. aegis of a stronger person*)

ሙጥኝ አለ muṭəññ alä v.t. sought protection; clung to (*s/o, s/t*)

ሙጫ muč̣č̣a n. gum, resin (*of tree*)

ሚሊዮን milliyon or መልዮን mälyon adj/ n. million

ሚስት mist n. wife

ባልና— balənna—couple

ባልና—ቁልፍ balənna—qulf n. press-stud

ሚኒስትር ministr n. minister

ሚኒስቴር minister n. ministry

ሚዜ mize n. best man

ሚና mina n. role

ሚዳቋ midaqqʷa n. bush duiker

ሚዶ mido n. comb

ሚጥሚጣ miṭmiṭṭa n. chilli (*pepper*)

ማ ? ma *inter. pron.* who?

ማህደር mahədär n. leather book case, folder, *see also* አደረ

ማለ malä v.t. swore (*an oath*)

ማላ malla or መሐላ mähalla n. oath

ማለለ mallälä v.t. implored

ማለደ mallädä v.i. went out (*early in the morning*); was early (*in doing things*); interceded

ማለዳ maläda n. early in the morning

ምልጃ məlǧa n. intercession

ተማለደ *tămallădă* v.i. was approachable *(as a source of help)*

መማለጃ *mămmalağa* n. gift *(to smooth the way for intercession)*

አማለደ *ammallădă* v.t. interceded for s/o

አማላጅ *ammalağ* adj/n. *(one)* who makes intercession; job of being a go-between

አማላጅነት *ammalağənnăt* n. intercession; job of being a go-between

መማለጃ *mămmalăğa* n. gift *(to smooth the way for intercession)*

ማለገ *mallăgă* v.i. became sticky, viscous

ማላጋ *malaga* adj. sticky *(e.g. dough mixture)*, viscous

ማላጋነት *malagannăt* n. stickiness, gluey consistency, viscosity

ማሕሌት *mahəlet* n. ecclesiastical song of praise

ማሕሌተኛ *mahəletăñña* n. one who sings hymns of praise in church, cantor

ማሕሌታይ *mahəletay* n. cantor

ማኅሌተ ገንቦ *mahəletă gămbo* n. priests' song in praise of founder of a feast

ቅኔ ማሕሌት *qəne mahəlet* n. middle section of Ethiopian church i.e. between the Holy of Holies, corresponds to chantry of European church

ማሕፀን *mahəṣăn* n. womb, uterus

ማሚቴ *mammite* n. form of address for small girl

ማሚቶ *mammito* n. echo

የገደል— *yăgădăl*—n. echo

ማሞ *mammo* n. form of address for small boy

ማረ *mară* v.i. forgave, was merciful; cancelled a debt

መሓሪ *măhari* adj. merciful

ምሕረት *məhrăt* n. mercy, forgiveness; compassion

ዓመተ— *amătă*— n. Year of Grace, Anno Domini *(A.D.)*

ያለ — *yală* - adv. ruthlessly

ተማረ *tămară* v.i. was forgiven

ተማማረ *tămamară* v.i. forgave each other

አስማረ *asmară* v.t. had *(s/o)* forgiven

ማረረ *marrără* v.t. gleaned, picked up

ማራሪ *marari* adj/n. gleaner

ማረከ *marrăkă* v.t. took captive; took the attention of

ማራኪ *maraki* adj/n. *(one)* who takes s/o captive; who is attentive, takes the attraction of

ምርኮ *mərko adj/n.* *(one)* who is taken captive, booty

ምርኮኛ *mərkoñña* adj/n *(one)* who is taken captive

ተማረከ *tămarrăkă* v.t. was taken captive

ተማራኪ *tămaraki* adj/n. *(one)* who is taken captive

ማረፊያ *see* ዐረፈ

ማራገቢያ *marragăbiya* n. fan *see also* ረገበ

ማር *mar* n. honey

ማርመላታ *marmălata* n. jam, marmalade

ማርሽ *marš* n. gear *(of car)*

ማርክ *mark* n. grade *(in exam.)*

ማርያም *maryam* n. Mary

ምርኩዝ *see* ተመረኰዘ

ማርዳ *marda* n. glass ring *(used as neck charm)*

ማሰ *masä* v.i. dug a hole

ማሳ *masa* n. tilled land, farm

ማሰሮ *masäro* n. pot, pitcher *(usually of earthenware)*

ማሲንቆ *masinqo or* መሰንቆ *mäsänqo* n. Ethiopian single-stringed violin

ማሳሰቢያ *see* አሰበ

ማሽላ *mašəlla* n. white sorghum

የባሕር— *yäbahər–* n. maize, *also* ባርማሽላ

ማሸንክ *mašənk* adj. spiteful, vicious

ማቀቀ *maqqäqä* v.i. languished *(in prison)*

ማቅ *maq* n. coarse woollen cloth

ማተብ *matäb* n. neck-band *(worn under the shirt, sign of Christianity)*; religion *(Christian)*

ማቲ *mati* n. crowd of small children

ማታ *mata* evening

የማታ— *yämata*—at last, at the end

ማቴማቲክ *matematik* n. mathematics

ማት *mat also* መዓት *mä'at* n. wrath of God; multitude, crowd of people

ማቶት *matot* n. coffee-pot stand

ማኅበር *mahəbär* n. association; self-help group; company *see* አበረ

ማኅበር (ረ) ተኛ *mahəbär(ä)täñña* n. member of a society, association, self-help group;

ማኅበራዊ *mahəbärawi* adj. social; pertaining to society or group;

ኅብረት *həbrät* n. unity; union

ኅብረተሰብ *həbrätä säb* n. society

ማኅተም *mahətäm* n. seal, rubber stamp, *see* አተመ

ማን *man* inter. adj. who

ማንም *manəmm* pron. nobody, not anyone, not anything; anybody, anyone, everyone

ማንኛውም *mannəññawəm* pron. whoever

ማን አለብኝ ባይ *man alläbbəññ bay* n. despot

ማንዘራሽ *manzärraš* n. riffraff, street-boy, person of no family

እነማን *ənnämann* pron. pl. who?

ማንቆርቆርያ *see* አንቆረቆረ

ማንቁርት *manqurt* n. Adam's apple

ማንቁርታም *manqurtam* n. person who has a large Adam's apple

ማንካ *manka also* መንካ፥ማንኪያ n. spoon

ማክሰኞ *see* ማግሰኞ

ማዕረግ *ma'əräg* n. rank, title

ማዕረገ ቢስ *ma'ərägä bis* n. one who acts below his station, in an undignified way

ማዕረገኛ *ma'ərägäñña or* ማረ ገኛ *marägäñña* n. a pretentious person, one who gives himself airs

ማዕቀብ *ma'əqäb* n. sanction

ማዕበል *ma'əbäl* n. storm *(at sea)*

ማዕከል *ma'əkäl* n. centre

ማዕከላዊ *ma'əkälawi* adj. central

—መንግሥት *—mängəst* n. central government

ማዕዘን *ma'əzän* n. corner, angle

ማዕዘነ ዓለም *ma'əzänä aläm* n. cardinal points of the compass

ማዕድ *ma'add* n. the meal-table *also* ማድ *madd*

—ቤት *—bet also* ማድቤት *madbet* n. kitchen

ማዕድን *ma'əddən* n. mine; minerals

ማድቤት *see* ማዕድ

ማየ ዐይኅ *mayä ayh* n. Noah's flood *(lit. water of destruction)*

ማይል mayl n mile (English distance measure)
ማይክሮስኮፕ mavkroskopp n. microscope
ማዲያ see አዲለ
ማድያት madiyat n. blemish
ማድያታም madyatäm n. blemished
ማድጋ madəgga n. large water pot (earthenware)
ማዶ mado adv. opposite; yonder
ባሕር— bahər — n. abroad
ማጀት mağät n. larder
ማጅራት mağərät n. nape of the neck
—መቺ —mäči n. gangster
ማገ magä v.t. drunk
አማገ amagä v.t. sipped loudly, sucked up (to wash down food which is difficult to swallow)
ማማጊያ mamagiya n. a drink to wash down food
ማገረ maggärä v.t. fitted reinforcing beams (in house walls)
ማገር magär n. wall reinforcing beam
ተማገረ tämaggärä v.i. was fitted with reinforcing beams
አማገረ ammaggärä v.t. helped (s/o) to reinforce a wall
አስማገረ asmaggärä v.t. had (a wall) fitted with reinforcing beams
ማገደ maggädä v.t. stoked up, fuelled (e.g a wood burning oven)
ማገዶ magädo n. firewood
ተማገደ tämaggädä v.i. was stoked up, fuelled
ማገጠ maggäṭä v.i. became idle, lax in, lazy in his work
ማጋጣ magaṭa adj. idle, slack, lazy
ማጋጣነት magaṭannät n. idleness
ማጋጭ magač adj. idle, slack, lazy
ማጋጭነት magačənnät n. idleness
አማገጠ amaggäṭä v.t. influenced (s/o) to be lazy, idle, spoiled (a child)
አማጋጭ amagač adj/n. (one) who influences (s/o) to be idle, lazy; (s/t) that spoils (a child)
ማግ mag n. weft (in cloth weaving), woof
ማግሥት magəst n. the morrow, the next day
በማግሥቱ bämagəstu the following morning, the following day
ማግሰኞ magsäñño also ማክሰኞ maksäñño n. Tuesday
ማጥ maṭ n. swampy place, bog
ማጣም maṭam adj. swampy, boggy
ማጭድ mačəd n. sickle see አጨደ
ሜትር metər n. metre
መተረ mättärä v.t. measured (with a metre)
ሜንጦ menṭo n. hook
ሜካኒክ mekanik n. mechanic
ሜዳ meda n. field, grassy plain
የጦር— yaṭor —n. battlefield
ሜዳማ medamma n. level plain, level ground
ሜዳ ፍየል medafəyyäl n. gazelle
ሜዳይ meday n. medal
ሜጀር ጀኔራል meğär ğeneral n. major-general
—ም —m suffix. also, too and
ምሁር məhur n. intellectual, learned, scholar
ምህዋር məhwar n. orbit
ምላጭ see ላጨ

ምስራች *massəračč* n. good tidings, good news

ምሥራቅ *məsraq* n. East

መካከለኛው— *mäkakkäläññaw*— the Middle-East

ምሥራቃዊ *məsraqawi* n. Eastern

ምስጢር *məstir* n. secret; private affairs

ምስጢረኛ *məstiräñña* n. confidant

ምስጢራዊ *məstirawi* adj. confidential, secret

በምስጢር *bäməstir* adv. confidentially

ምራቅ *məraq* n. saliva

ምራቁን የዋጠ *məraqun yäwaṭä* adj. well-experienced *(in life)*; serious - minded

ምራት *mərat* n. daughter-in-law, sister-in -law

ምር *mərr* n. *in* የምር *yämərr* adj. serious e.g. የምሬን ነው I am serious

ምርቅ *mərq* n. beard *(of grain)*.

ምሰሶ *məsässo* n. central-pillar *(of traditional Ethiopian house)*

ምሳ *məsa* n. lunch

ምሳር *məssar* n. axe

ምስ *məss* n. personal preference, thing one likes most *(zar etc.)*

ምስማር *məsmar or* ሚስማር *mismar* n. nail *(carpentry etc.)*

ምስሪት *məssərit* n. lens

ምስጥ *məsṭ* n. termite

ምሽት *məšt see also* ሚስት *mist* n. wife

ምሽት *məššət* n. evening *see* መሸ

ምቀኛ *məqqañña* adj. envious, spiteful

ምቀኝነት *məqqäññənnät* n. envy, spite

ምኑ *mənu* inter adj. pron. which ?

ምናልባት *mənalbat* adv. perhaps

ምናምን *mənamən* pron. something; anything; nothing

ምናምንቴ *mənaməntе* adj. degraded, worthless *(of people)*

ምን! *mən* int. adj. pron. what ?

ምንም *mənəmm* pron. nothing

ምንኛ *mənəñña* conj. phrase however...., whatever

ምን ቆርጦኝ *mən qorṭoññ* I wouldn't dare do such a thing *(except that... this phrase introduces an excuse)*

አለበት *—alläbbät* what does it matter? what is wrong with it ?

—አልባት *-albat also* ምናልባት *mənalbat* adv. perhaps, possibly

ምንድን *mənddən* n. interj. adj. what !

ምንኛ *mənəñña* excl. how.!

ምን ገዶኝ *mən gäddoññ* excl. phr. what do I care

ለምን *lämən* what for ?

ስለምን *səlämən* why?

በምን ጊዜ *bämən gize* when ?

ምንቸት *mənčät* n. clay amphora *(medium sized, for making ṭälla)*

ምንደኛ *məndäñña* n. hired shepherd

ምንዳ *mənda* n. wages *(for hired shepherd)*, wage

ምንጅላት *mənağəllat* n. great-great grand-mother, great- great grandfather

ምንጯር *mənçər* n. lower lip

ምንጣፍ *see* * ነጠፈ

ምኞት *məññot* n. wish, desire, aspiration, ambition, *see* ተመኘ

ምኩራብ *məkurab* n. synagogue

ምዕራብ *mə'ərab* n. west

ምዕራባዊ *mə'rabawi* western

—በስተ ምዕራብ *bästä mə'rab* towards the West

ምዕራፍ *mə'əraf* n. chapter, *see also* ዐረፈ

ምድር *mədər* n. earth, country, land

የምድር ወገብ *yämədər wägäb* n. equator, *also* የምድ ሰቅ

—ዋልታ *walta* n. pole

ምድረ ባዳ *mədrä bäda* n. wilderness, desert

ምድራዊ *mədrawi* adj. earthly, of the earth

ምድጃ *mədəǧǧa* n. oven, fireplace

ምግባር *məgbar* n. virtue

ምጣድ *see* ጣደ

ምጥ *məṭ* n. labour *(pains of childbirth)*

አማጠ *amaṭä* v.t was in labour

ምጥማጥ *see* ሽለምጥማጥ

ምጸት *məṣṣät* n. irony

ምጽአት *məṣ'at also* ምጣት *məṭat* n. the second Advent, Judgement Day, the second coming of Christ *see* መጣ

ሞለለ *mollälä* v. was oval, egg-shaped; was sausage-shaped

ሙልል አለ *muləll alä* v. was slightly oval, egg-shaped

ሞላላ *molala* adj. oval, egg-shaped; sausage-shaped

ሞላላነት *molallannät* n. oval shape; sausage shape

ሞለሞለ *molämmolä* v. was oval, egg- shaped, sausage-shaped

ሙልሙል *mulmul* adj. oval egg-shaped, sausage-shaped

ሞልጓላ *molmʷalla* adj. sausage shaped

ሞለቀቅ *moläqäq* adj. spoiled *(child), also* ሞልቃቃ

ሞለጨ *molläčä* v.t. cropped close *(hair, grass etc)*

ሙላጭ *mulllač* n. last scrap *(soap, etc.)*

ሙልጩን ወጣ *mulučun wäṭṭa* v.t. went broke, was bankrupt

ሙልጭ *mulč* adj. destitute, having lost everything

ሞላጫ *mollačča* n. swindler, dishonest, cheater

ተሞለጨ *tämolläčä* v.t. was robbed completely, was fleeced

አሞለጨ *amolläčä* v.i. slipped *(e.g wet soap from grasp)*

አሟላጭ *amuʷalač* adj. slippery

ሞለፈጠ *moläffäṭä* v.i. laughed inanely, laughed for nothing cf. ገለፈጠ

ሞልፋጣ *molfaṭṭa* adj. given to inane laughter

ተሞላፈጠ *tämolaffäṭä* v.i laughed inanely, pointlessly

ሞላ *molla also* መላ *mälla* v.i. v.t was full, became full; filled out, filled up; was plentiful; overflew; charged *(battery)*; wound *(a watch)*

ሙሉ *mulu* adj. full, whole complete

—ልብስ *—ləbs* n. suit

—ቁጥር *—quṭər* n. even number

—በሙሉ *bämulu* adv. entirely, fully, completely, wholly

በሙሉ/ በሞላ *bämulu/ bämolla* adv. entirely, fully, in full, all over

—ልብ *ləbb* adv. wholeheartedly

ከሞላ ጎደል *kämolla goddäl* by and large, roughly, approximately, more or less

አሞላ *amolla* v.i. was fattened.

ሙላት *mulat* n. extent to which s/t. is filled; overflow; abundance

የውሃ— *yäwəha*—n. flood

መሙያ *mämuya* n. device for, means of filling; noun in apposition

ሞላላ *molalla* v.t poured out *(e.g. from glass to glass)*

ተሞላ *tämolla* v.p. was filled

ተሟላ *tämʷalla* v.i. was successful *(in an enterprise, undertaking, etc.;)* was complete, was done completely

የተሟላ *yätämuʷalla* adj. full, exhaustive, complete, perfect

ያልተሟላ *yaltämuʷalla* adj. incomplete, imperfect, inadequate

አሟላ *ammʷalla* v.t. made up *(a sum of money)* to the required amount; completed, met the need

ማሟያ *mammʷaya* n. means of making up to required amount; complement *(gram.)*

አሞላላ *ammolalla* v.t. filled up *(one vessel, container, from several partially full)*

አስሞላ *asmolla* v.t. has s/o fill

ረሞረ *morämmorä* v.i. was extremely hungry, felt the pangs of extreme hunger

ሞረደ *morrädä* v.t. filed s/t *(i.e. with a metal file)*

ሙረዳ *murräda* n. action of filing

ሞረድ *moräd* n. file *(metal)*

ተሞረደ *tämorrädä* v.i. was filed

አስሞረደ *asmorrädä* v.t. had *(s/t)* filed

ሞራ *mora* n. abdominal fat

ራል *moral* n. morale, morals

ሞርሳ *morsa* n. mandrel, clamp *(It.)*

ሞሸለቀ *mošälläqä* v.t. burned scalded *(e.g. with boiling water)*

ሞሽላቃ *mošlaqqa* adj. n. utterly dishonest, without scruple; persistently and deliberately untruthful

ተሞሸለቀ *tämošälläqä* v.t. was scalded, badly burned; was robbed completely

ሞሸረ *moššärä* v.t. accommodated and entertained newly wed couple

ሙሽሪት *mušərrit* n. bride

ሙሽራ *muššərra* n. bride groom

ተሞሸረ *tämoššärä* v. spent *(one's honeymoon)*

ሞቀ *moqä* v.i. got hot, became warm *(weather)*,

ሞቀኝ *moqäññ* I feel hot

ሞቀው *moqäw* felt warm; got slightly drunk

እሳት ሞቀ *əsat moqä* warmed oneself by the fire

ፀሐይ— *ṣähai*—warmed oneself in the sun

ሙቅ *muq* adj. hot, warm; n. thick broth *(made mainly of flour and butter)*

ሙቀት *muqät* n. heat, temperature, warmth

ሞቃት *moqqat* adj. warm, hot

አሞቀ *amoqä* v.t. warmed *s/t.)*, made s/t warm, heated up, kept warm

ማሞቂያ *mamoqiya* n. heater, device for heating

ተሟሟቀ *tämʷamʷaqä* v.t. gave warmth to each other, reached a climax *(party, ceremony, song etc.)*

የተሟሟቀ *yätämuʷamuʷaqä* adj. animated, full of cheer

አሟሟቀ *ammʷamʷaqä* v.t. caused *(s/t)* to reach its climax: made *(the party)* go, gave life, enlivened up *(a party etc.)*

አሟሟቂ *ammʷamʷaqi* n. one who makes a party lively, gets things going

አስሞቀ *asmoqä* v.t. had *(s/t)* warmed

ሞቀሞቀ *moqämmoqä* v.i. became morbid, infected *(of wound)*; became rotten *(fruit etc.)*

ሙቅሙቅ *muqmuq* adj. swollen, morbid, full of pus *(wound)*; rotten *(fruit etc.)*

ሞቅሟቃ *moqmʷaqqa* adj. swollen, full of pus *(wound)*; rotten *(fruit etc.)*

ሞቅሟቃ ዐይን *moqmʷaqqa ayn* n. adj. rheumy-eyed *(person)*

አሞቀሞቀ *amoqämmoqä* v.i. became morbid, infected *(of wound; became rotten (fruit etc.)*

ሞተ *motä* v.i. died

ሙት *mut* adj. dead; adv. Truly! Certainly! *(col.)*

አባቴ ይሙት *abbate yəmut* I give you my word of honour

የሙት ልጅ *yämut ləǧ* n. orphan

የሞት ቅጣት *yämot qəṭat* death penalty

—ፍርድ *—fərd* death sentence

ይሙት በቃ ፍርድ *yəmut bäqqa fərd* capital punishment

ሙትቻ *mutəčča* adj. inactive, lazy, lacking initiative

ሞት *mot* n. death

ሞኖፖል *monopol* n. monopoly

ሞኛ *moñña* adj. fool, silly, foolish

ሞከረ *mokkärä* v.t. tried, tested, attempted

ሞካሪ *mokkari* n/adj. *(one)* who tries, tests

ሙከራ *mukkära* n. trial, test

ተሞከረ *tämokkärä* v.t. made a trial, test *(often of strength, skill etc.)* between one another

ተሟከረ *tämʷakkärä* v.t. tried each other out, had a test of strength

ተሞካከረ *tämokakkärä* v.i. tried each other out, put each other to the test

አሞካከረ *ammokakkärä* v.t. caused *(s/o)*, *(s/t)* to be tested, tried out

አሟከረ *ammʷakkärä* v.t. caused *(people)* to have a mutual test *(strength etc.)*

አስሞከረ *asmokkärä* v.t. had *t/s* tried out

ሞከተ *mokkätä* v.t. fattened up *(sheep, goat)*

ሞካች *mokkač* n. adj. *(one)* who fattens up *(sheep goat)*

ሙክት *mukkət* n. animal which is fattened up *(sheep, goat)*

ተሞከተ *tämokkätä* v.t. was fattened up *(sheep, goat)*

አስሞከተ *asmokkätä* v.t. had *(sheep, goat)* fattened up

ሞከከ *mokkäkä also* ሟከከ *mʷakkäkä* v.i. was overcooked, overripe, overfed *(flabby)*

ሙክክ አለ *mukəkk alä* v.i. be extremely overcooked, overripe, overfed *(flabby)*

ሞክሼ *mokše* n. namesake

ሞዘዘ *mozzäzä* v.i. became unbearably boring, oppressive *(speech behaviour)*; became importunate

ሞዛዛ *mozaza* adj. importunate, boring, oppressive *(speech, behaviour)*

ሞዛዛነት mozazannät n. tiresomeness, importunity, quality of being boring, dullness

ሙዝዝ አለ muzəzz alä v.i. became boring, tiresome

ሞያ moya or ሙያ muya n. special, ability, craft, profession

ሞያተኛ moyatäñña n. daily labourer

ባለሞያ balämoya adj. n. (one) who is skilled well-trained, who has wide experience, expert

ሞዴል model n. design, model

ሞጀረ moǧǧärä v.t. overfilled, filled to excess

ሙጅጅር አደረገ muǧǧərr adärrägä v.t. overfilled hastily, pour in more than one wanted to (by mistake)

ተሞጀረ tämoǧǧärä v.t. poured in too great a quantity

*ሞገሰ *moggäsä

ሞገስ mogäs n. appreciation, liking

ግርማ ሞገስ gərma mogäs n. dignity, high esteem

አሞገሰ amoggäsä v.t. spoke well (of s/o)

አሞጋሽ amoggaš n/adj. (one) who speaks well of another

አሞጋገሰ amogaggäsä v.t. spoke well of s/o often, frequently

ተሞገሰ tämoggäsä v.t. was spoken of, praised

ተሞጋሽ tämoggaš n. adj. (one) who is praised, honoured

ተሞጋገሰ tämogaggäsä v.t. praised, spoke well of each other

ሞገተ moggätä v.t. made a case against s/o (incourt); disputed, argued

ሞጋች moggač n/adj. (one) who makes a case against s/o (in court); (one) who disputes argues

ሙግት muggət n. argument, dispute (e.g. before a judge)

ተሟገተ tämʷäggätä v.t. made a case against s/o; disputed, argued

ተሟጋች tämʷagač n. s/o who represents another in court (not necessarily a lawyer); one skilled in presenting legal cases

አሟገተ ammʷaggätä v.t. arbitrated

አሟጋች ammʷagač n. arbitrator (legal)

አስሞገተ asmoggätä v.t. caused s/o to be accused before the court

ሞገደ moggädä v.t. made trouble; caused a storm; made difficulties

ሞገደኛ mogädäñña n. trouble maker

ሞገድ mogäd n. wave, tide

ሞገገ moggägä v.i. became emaciated, wasted away

ሞጋጋ mogaga adj. emaciated, thin cheecked, thin faced

ሙግግ ያለ mugəgg yalä v.i. very thin faced, extremely emaciated, ugly

ሞግዚት mogzit n. nurse (for children); guardian, trustee

*ሞጠሞጠ *moṭämmoṭä

ሞጠሞጥ moṭämoṭ adj. agressive in speech and facial expression

ሞጥሟጣ moṭmʷaṭṭa adj. agressive in speech, having a tendency to thrust the fact at one's opponent in argument

ሙጢ አፍ muṭṭ af adj. agressive in speech and facial expression

አሞጠሞጠ *amoţämmoţä* v.t. had protruding lips; was insulting, attacked s/o with words

ሞጨለፈ *močälläfä* v.t. grabbed, snatched by force, ravished *(with the extra meaning of, «grabbed and ran off»)*

ሞጭላፊ *močlafi* n. thief

ሙጭለፋ *mučläfa* n. robbery

ተሞጨለፈ *tämočälläfä* v.i. was robbed, stolen, snatched

አስሞጨለፈ *asmočälläfä* v.t. had s/t stolen

ሞጨሞጨ *močämmočä also* መጨመጨ *mäčämmäčä* v.i. streamed, were runny *(of the eyes only)*

ሞጭማጫ *mocmʷačča or* መጭማጫ *mäčmačča* adj./n. *(one)* who is rheumy-eyed

ሞፈር *mofär* n. beam of plough
ሞፈር ዘመት እርሻ *mofär zämmät əršа* cultivated land far away from the farmer's house

ሟለጠ *mʷalläţä* v.i. slipped from the hand, was slippery, *also* አሟለጠ

ሟሟ *mʷammʷa* v.i. was dissolved in water

ሟጠጠ *mʷaţţäţä* v.t. scraped

ሟጨረ *mʷaččärä* v.t. scratched

ሠ

ሠለሰ *sälläsä* v.t. did *(s/t)* on alternate days; made sauce thinner by adding water

ሣልስ *saləs* n. the third order of the Amharic vowel system

ሥሉስ *səllus* adj. threefold, triple

ሥላሴ *səllase* n. the Holy Trinity

ሠለስት *säläst or saləst* ሣልስት n. third day after funeral *(in Ethiopia obligatory day to visit bereaved)*

ሦስት *sost* adj. three

አሠለሰ *asälläsä* v.t. did s/t on alternate days

ሠለጠ *sälläţä* v.t. meddled in everyone's affairs; had a finger in every pie

ሠላጤ *sällaţe* n. bay

ሥሉጥ *səlluţ* adj. meddlesome, interfering, nosey

ሠለጠነ *säläţţänä* v.i. became skilled, was well trained; acquired power; became civilised

ሡልጣን *sulţan* n. Sultan

ሥልጡን *səlţun* adj. well trained; highly competent

ሥልጣን ሰጠ *səlţan säţţä* v.t. authorized, gave power

ባለሥልጣን *baläsəlţan* n. authority, official

ባለሥልጣኖች *baläsəlţanočč* n. authorities

ባለሙሉ ሥልጣን *balä mulu səlţan* plenipotentiary

ሥልጣኔ *səlləţţane* n. civilisation

አሠለጠነ *asäläţţänä* v.t. trained *(s/o)*, coached *(for sport)*; made *(s/o)* civilised

አሠልጣኝ *asälţaññ* n. trainer, coach

ሠሌዳ *säleda* n. wooden board
የመኪና— *yämäkina*–n. car plate

የማስታወቂያ— *yämastawäqiya* — n. notice board, bulletin board

ጊዜ— *gize* — n. multiplication table

ጥቁር— *ṭəqur* — n. blackboard

ሠመረ *sämmärä* v.i. reached successful conclusion *(work, scheme, plan etc.)*

አሠመረ *asämmärä* v.t. ruled *(e.g. line, margin)*

ማሥመሪያ *masmäriya* n. rule, ruler

መሥመር *mäsmär* line,

—መክፈቻ *—mäkfäča* n. area code number *(telephone)*

—ዳኛ *—daňňa* n. linesman

አሠማመረ *asämammärä* v.t. ruled a line ; put things in order

ተሠመረ *täsämmärä* v.i. was ruled *(line)*

ሠረሠረ *särässärä* v.t. bored *(a hole)*

ሠርሣሪ *särsari* n. burglar

መሠርሠሪያ *mäsärsäriya* n. borer *(tool)*

ተሠረሠረ *täsärässärä* v.i. was *bored*

ሠረገ *särrägä* v.i. sank, went down; penetrated infiltrated; permeated

ሠርጎ ገባ *särgo gäbba* v.i. infiltrated

—ገብ *—gäbb* n. infiltrator

ሠረገ *särrägä* v.t. prepared a wedding

ሠራጊ *särragi* n. / adj. s/o who prepares a wedding

ሠርግ *särg* n. wedding

ተሠረገ *täsärrägä* v.i. were bride and bridegroom

ሠራ *särra* v.t. made, worked, did, manufactured, operated; built; have an effect *(medicine)*

ሠሪ *säri* n. one who does s/t, e.g ቤት ሠሪ one who builds a house

ሠራተኛ *särratäňňa* n. worker, labourer, employee

የመንግሥት— *yämängəst*—n. civil servant

መሥሪያ ቤት *mäsriya bet* n. office, department *(of government)*

ሥራ *səra* n. work, job occupation, labour, task, act, deed; action, employment

—በዛበት *—bäzzabbät* was too busy

—ያዘ *—yazä* v.i. was busy was employed

—ገባ *—gäbba* got work, was employed

—ፈታ *—fätta* was out of work

—ፈት *—fätt* adj. unemployed, jobless

በሥራ ላይ አዋለ put into practice, used

የሥራ ቀን *yäsəra qän* n. weekday

—ጓደኛ *—guʷaddäňňa* n. colleague

የቤት ሥራ *yäbet səra* n. home work, house work

የእጅ— *yä'əǧǧ*—n. handicraft

ሠርግ *särg* n. wedding

ሠቀሠቀ *säqässäqä* v.i. levered up; lifted (e.g. *bread, eggs from cooking plate with slice)*

መሠቅሠቂያ *mäsäqsäqiya* n. lever; cooking slice etc. *(anything used to lift off, lever s/t up)*

ተሠቀሠቀ *täsäqässäqä* v. i. was levered up

ተንሠቀሠቀ *tänsäqässäqä* v.i, cried ones heart out, sobbed bitterly

ሠቀቀ säqqäqä v.t. horrified shocked s/o *(i.e. a cruel, abhorent act or sight)*

ሠቀቀን säqäqän n. deep sadness, desolation, melancholy

ሠቀቀናም säqäqänam adj. pessimistic, melancholic *(of person)*

ሥቅቅ አለ səqəqq alä v.i. was shocked, was horrified

ሠቀጠጠ säqäṭṭäṭä v.t. grated, squeaked, screeched *(e.g. of harsh noise such as chalk on blackboard, of rusty hinges)*

ሠወረ säwwärä v.t. concealed kept out of sight, hid

ሠዋራ säwwarra n/adj. hidden out of sight *(place etc.)*

ሥውር səwwər adj. hidden, out of sight, concealed

ዐይነ— aynä— adj/n: blind, sightless

ሠወርዋራ säwärwarra adj. very hidden, inaccessible *(place, road etc.)*

ዕፀ መሠውር əṣä mäsäwwər n. magical plant said to be used to make objects disappear

ተሠወረ täsäwwärä v.t. was concealed, hidden, kept out of sight

ተሠዋሪ täsäwwari adj. liable to disappear

ሠዋ säwwa v.t. sacrificed

ሠዊ säwwi n./adj one who sacrifices

መሥዋዕት mäswa'ət n. sacrifice

መሥዋዕትነት mäswa'ətənnät n. act of sacrificing, of being sacrificed, sacrifice

መሠዊያ mäsäwwiya n. place of sacrifice; an altar

ተሠዋ täsäwwa v.i. was sacrificed, was offered as a sacrifice

አሠዋ assäwwa v.t. had s/o sacrificed

ሠየመ säyyämä v.t named, gave *(s/o)* a name

ሠያሚ säyyami n adj. one who gives names

ሥያሜ səyyame, n nomenclature, terminology

ተሠየመ täsäyyämä v t. was given a name, was assigned to a particular court *(for judges)*

አሠየመ assäyyämä v.t. had s/o given a name

ሠደቃ sädäqa n basketwork table, ənǧära stand; muslim commemoration of the dead

ሠገረ säggärä v. t. trotted *(of mules only)*

ሠጋር säggar adj. trotting, which can trot

ሠጋሪ sägari n/adj. trotting

አሠገረ asäggärä v t. made *(a mule)* to trot

አሥጋሪ asgari n adj *(one)* who makes a mule trot

ዓሣ— asa- n. a fisherman

አሠጋገር assägagär n. style of trotting *(for mule)*

ሠጋ sägga v. t. was, became anxious, uneasy in mind

ሥጉ səgu n/adj. anxious

ሥጋት səgat n. anxiety, apprehension, fear, worry

አሠጋ asägga v.t. made anxious, caused fear, caused apprehension,

አሥጊ asgi n/adj. worrying; causing fear, critical, serious, alarming, dangerous

አሠጋ assägga v.t, worried *(s/o,)* made *(s/o)* anxious

ሢሶ siso adj. one third

—አራሽ -araš a tenant that pays one third of his farm yield to the land owner

ሣለ salä v.t. drew, painted *(pictures)*

ሠዓሊ *sä'ali* n/adj. one who draws pictures, artist

ሠዓሊነት *sä'alinnät* n. art (*the state of being artist*)

ሥዕል *sə'əl* n. picture, drawing

መሣያ *mäsaya* n. brush, pencil (*any painting or drawing instrument*)

ተሣለ *täsalä* v.t. was drawn (*picture*)

አሣለ *assalä* v.t. had (*a picture*) drawn, painted

sassa v.i. grew thin; became greedy

ሥሡ *səssu* n/adj. greedy

ሥሥ *səs* adj. thin; fine (*cloth etc.*)

ሥሥነት *səsənnät* n. thinness

ሥሥት *sassət* n. greed, cupidity

አሣሣ *asassa* v.. made thin, thinned out (*plants*); had sentimental value for (*s/o*)

ሣር *sar* n. grass

ሣርማ *sarəmma* adj. grassy

ሣር ቅጠል *sar qəṭäl* (*pron.*) everyone

ሣጥን *saṭən* n. box, chest

ቁም— *qum*— n. cupboard; wardrobe

ሥራ *səra* n. work; duty; job; profession

ሥር *sər* n. root; source

ቀይ— *qäyy*—n. beet root

ሥራሥር *sərasər* n. various roots

ሥርቻ *sərəčča* n. nook along the wall

ሥርዓት *sər'at* n. order; etiquette, procedure, formality, discipline, system, regulation

—አልባ *—alba* n. anarchist

ሥርዓት አልባነት *sər'atä albannät* n. anarchism

—ትምህርት *-təmhərt* n. curriculum

ነጥብ *—näṭəb* n. punctuation

ሥርዓት የሌለው *—sər'at yälelläw* adj. unmannerly, disorganized

ሥርው *in* ሥርወ መንግሥት *sərwä mängəst* n. dynasty

ሥርወ ቃል *sərwä qal* n. stem (*of a word*)

ሥን *sən* n. (*G.*) beauty

ሥነ ልቡና *sənä ləbbuna* n. psychology

— ሕይወት *—həywät* biology

— ምግባር *məgbar* n. ethical behaviour, virtue, good deeds

— ምግብ *—məgəb* n. nutrition (*the science of food value*)

— ሥርዓት *—sər'at* n. ceremony; protocol; order, procedure

— ጥበብ *—ṭəbäb* n. fine arts

— ጽሑፍ *—ṣəhuf* n. literature, belles lettres

— ፈለክ *—fäläk* n. astronomy

— ፍጥረት *—fəṭrät* n. nature, natural sciences

ሥጋ *səga* n. meat

—ሻጭ *səga šač̣* n. butcher

—በል *—bäll* adj. carnivorous

ሥጋዊ *səgawi* adj. carnal

ሥጋ ዘመድ *səga zämäd* n. blood relative

—አምላክ *—amlak* n. Host; Holy Communion

—ደዌ *—däwe* n. leprosy

—ወደሙ *—wädämu* n. Host; Holy Communion

ኀፍረተ— *hafrätä*— n. genitals

ጥሬ— *ṭəre*— n. raw meat

ሦስት *sost* adj. three

ሦስተኛ *sostäñña* adj. third

ረ

ረመጠ *rämmäṭä* v. t. baked *(by putting into hot ashes of fire)*

ረመጥ *rämäṭ* n. hot ashes

ርሚጦ *rəmmiṭo* n. bread *(baked in hot ashes)*

ርምጥምጥ *rəməṭməṭ* n. slattern *(person who is never really clean)*

ተርመጠመጠ *tärmäṭämmäṭä* v. i. was always engaged in dirty work; was always too busy in the kitchen

አርመጠመጠ *armäṭämmaṭä* v.t. did *(s/t)* in a slovenly way

ረሞጫ *rämoča* adj. hot, burning *(of ashes)*

ረሰረሰ *räsärräsä* v.t. mowed down *(grass, men in war etc.)*

ርስርስ *rəsrəs* adj. mown flat

ርስራሽ *rəsərraš* n/adj. *s/t* lying flat

ረሳ *rässa* v.i. forgot, left *s/t, s/o* behind

ሞት የረሳው *mot yärässaw* n. a very old man

ረሺ *räši* n/adj. forgetful *(person)*

ተረሳ *tärässa* v.i. was forgotten, left behind

ተረሳሳ *täräsassa* v.i. became forgotten *(due to the passage of time)*, forgot each other

አረሳሳ *arräsassa* v.t. distracted; took *(s/o's)* attention from *(s/t)*

አስረሳ *asrässa* v.t. made *(s/o)* forget

ረሸነ *räšsänä* v.t. executed by shooting, gunned down

ረሽ *räš* n. shot gun

ረቀቀ *räqqäqä* v.i. grew thin; was drafted *(letter, agreement etc.)*

ረቂቅ *räqiq* adj. thin; fine, delicate *(of fabrics;* draft *(of letter etc.*

ረቂቅነት *räqiqənnät* n. thinness, fineness

ርቀት *rəqqät* n. fineness depth *(of thinking)* subtlety

አረቀቀ *aräqqäqä* v.t. drafted *(piece of writing)*

ተራቀቀ *täraqqäqä* v.. was subtle, deep *(in thought)*; was casuistic, casuistical

ተራቃቂ *täraqaqi* adj/n. *(one who is)* subtle deep; casuistic

አስረቀቀ *asräqqäqä* v.t. caused *(letter etc.)* to be drafted

ረበረበ *räbärräbä* v.t. stacked corded *(wood)*; laid set *(fire, ready for lighting)*

ርብራብ *rəbrab* n. lattice framework; scaffold

ርብርብ *rəbrəb* or ርብራብ *rəbrab* adj./n. piled corded *(wood)*

ተረበረበ *täräbärräbä* v.i. was stacked, laid *(of wood*

ተረባረበ *täräbarräbä* v.i. piled on each other *(of children playing)*: rushed in

አስረበረበ *asräbärräbä* v.t. had *(s/t)* piled up, stacked

ረበሸ *räbbäšä* v.t. disturbed annoyed

ረብሻ *räbša* n. riot, brawl

ረብሸኛ *räbsäñña* n. rioter, riotous

ረበበ *räbbäbä* v.i. hovered

ረባቢ *räbabi* adj. hovering

ረቡዕ *räbu'ə or* ሮብ *rob* n. Wednesday

ረባ *räbba* v.i. multiplied *(of animals etc.)*; be profitable; be useful, be fertile *(cattle)*

ረብ — *rāb* n. gain profit, usefulness

(እ)ርባታ — *(ə)rbata* n. animal husbandry; conjugation *(gram.)*

እርባና — *ərbana* n. usefulness

ርቢ — *rəbbi* n. animal husbandry; cattle breeding

መርቢያ — *märbiya* n. breeding ground

አረባ — *arābba* v. t. bred, caused to breed, multiply; engaged in animal husbandry

ግሥ— — *gəss*—v.t. conjugated a verb

የግሥ እርባታ — *yägəss ərbata* n. conjugation of a verb

እርቢ — *arbi usually preceeded by* ከብት *kābt* n. cattle breeder, animal breeder, cattleman

አይረባም — *ayrābam* he is good for nothing, he is useless

የማይረባ ነገር — *yämmayrāba nāgār* nonsense, trifle

ተራባ — *tārabba* v. multiplied, increased *(of animals)*

መራቢያ — *märrabiya* n. breeding ground

አራባ — *arraba* v.t. crossed, cross bred

ማራቢያ — *märrabiya* n. place where breeding is carried on

ረባዳ — *rābbadda* adj/n. low lying *(land)*

ረታ — *rātta* v. t. won *(argument, court case, wager* etc.)

ረቺ — *rāči* n. winner *(of argument etc.)*

(እ)ርታታ — *(ə)rtata* n. victory *(in argument etc.)*

ተረታ — *tārätta* v. t. lost *(case, bet, argument)* ; lost hope *(of recovery from disease e.g.)*

ረኃብ — *see* ራብ

ረከሰ — *räkkäsä* v.i. was cheap; was impure, was defiled

ርኩስ — *rəkus also* እርኩስ *ərkus* adj. impure unclean; vicious

ርካሽ — *rəkkaš* adj. cheap, inexpensive; of low quality

አረከሰ — *aräkkäsä* v.t. profaned, defiled, debased; devaluated

*ረከበ — **räkkäbä*

ተረከበ — *täräkkäbä* v.t. took over, received

አስረከበ — *asräkkäbä* v. t. delivered, handed over

*ረከፈከፈ — **see* እርከፈከፈ

ረካ — *räkka* v.i. was satisfied,

አረካ — *aräkka* v.t. satisfied, made contented; gave *(s/o)* his fill *(e.g. food, drink)*

ረኻጥ — *rähāṭ* adj. lazy, dull bovine, stupid, slovenly *(usually of a women)*

ረኻጥነት — *rähāṭənnät* n. laziness, slovenliness, stupidity

ረዘመ — *räzzämä* v.i. lengthened out, became extended

ረዥም — *räžžəm or räggəm* adj. long, tall

እርዝማኔ — *ərzəmane* n. length

እርዝመት — *ərzəmät or* ርዝመት *rəzmät* n. length

አረዘመ — *aräzzämä* v.t. prolonged, made longer

ረዘረዘ — *räzärräzä* v.i. dripped out; flowed slowly *(e.g. oil)*

ርዝራዥ — *rəzərraž* n. leftovers, remains *(food, drink etc.)*

ረዘቀ — *räzzäqä* v.t. donated

ርዝቅ — *rəzq* n. bounty, abundance *(God given)*

ረዳ — *rädda* v.t. helped, assisted

ረጂ — *räği* n. assistant, helper

ረዳት — *räddat* n. helper,

assistant

ረድእ *räd'ə* n. assistant: pupil

ተረዳ *tärädda* v.i. was helped, got help

ተረዳዳ *tärädadda* v.i. gave mutual help; helped each other, cooperated

*ረዳ *rädda*

መርዶ *märdo* n. announcement of death *(of relative or close friend)*

ተረዳ *tärädda* v.t. understood, ealized, was convir·:d, was aware; was i/ ormed of the deat) of a near relativ· or a close friend

ተረጂ *tärä i* n. one who get help

መረጃ *m·: räğa* n. infor- п ion department c public security

ተረዳዳ *t ädaddu* v.i. helped, ded each other

መረዳጃ ማህበር *ıärrädağa mahəbär* ı. mutual help association

አረዳ *arädda* v.t. broke the news of some one's death *(relative, close friend)*

አስረዳ *asrädda* v.t. explained, informed, persuaded, convinced, proved

ማስረጃ *masräğğa* n. proof, evidence, example

ረድእ *räd'ə* n. assistant. *see also* ረዳ

ረድፍ *rädf* n row line *(of people)*, queue

ረገመ *räggämä* v.t. cursed

ረጋሚ *rägami* n, adj. cursing

ርጉም *rəgum or* እርጉም *ərgum* adj. cursed, wicked

እርግማን *ərgəman* n. curse, cursing

ተረገመ *täräggämä* v.i. was cursed

ተራገመ *täraggämä* v.t. cursed, wished evil on *(s/o)*

ተራጋሚ *täragami* n/adj. *(one who)* curses, or rails

አስረገመ *asräggämä* v.t. made s/o be cursed

ረገበ *räggäbä* v.i. went slack; became rumpled *(rope, sheet, etc.)*, sagged

ረገብ አለ *rägäbb alä* v.i. became a little slack, rumpled, sagged

ርግበት *rəgbät* n. sagging

አረገበ *aräggäbä* v.t. caused to become slack, rumpled

አራገበ *arraggäbä* v.t. fanned

ማራገቢያ *marragäbiya* n. fan, anything used to fan fire, chaff etc.

*ረገረገ *see* እረገረገ

*ረገበገበ **rägäbäggäbä*

(እ)ርብግብ *(ə)rgəbgəb* adj. kind hearted; motherly; compassionate

(እ)ርግብግቢት *ərgəbgəbit* n. propeller; fontanel adj. kind-hearted, motherly, compassionate *(fem.)*

ተርገበገበ *tärgäbäggäbä* v.i. switched, quavered *(eye lids;)* vibrated *(string instrument;)* fluttered *(birds wings, flag, curtain etc.)*: was kind-hearted, motherly, compassionate

ተርገብጋቢ *tärgäbgabi* adj. switching, quivering *(eye lids)*: vibrating: fluttering

አርገበገበ *argäbäggäbä* v.t. waved *(hand, piece of cloth etc.)*; blocked *(eyes)*: fluttered *(wings, piece of cloth etc.)*: vibrated *(string instrument)*

አርገብጋቢ *argäbgabi* adj/n. one *(who waves hands piece of cloth etc.)*

ረገድ *rägäd* n. aspect, point of view, manner *(way)*

ረገጠ *räggäṭä* v.t. trod; kicked; inked a rubber stamp by a blow; adjudicated land dispute *(by treading bounds)*; went over s/o's head *(complaint)*; practised foot drill *(mil.)*

ርጋጭ *rəggaç* n. trampled earth; footprint; adj. down trodden

እርግጫ *ərgəçça* n. kick

መርገጫ *märgäça* n. treadle, foot pedal; inking pad

ረጋገጠ *rägaggäṭä* v.t. trampled on

ተረገጠ *täräggäṭä* v.i. was trodden on; was kicked

መረገጫ *märrägäça* n. foothold

ተራገጠ *täraggäṭä* v.t., v.i. kicked out *(horse etc.)*, kicked each other *(children fighting)*; recoiled *(firearm)*

ተራጋጭ *täragaç* n. animal which kicks; boy who plays too much

መራገጫ *märragäça* n. play ground, play area

ተረጋገጠ *tärägaggäṭä* v.i. was trampled on; was certain, was confirmed

መረጋገጫ *märrägagäça* n. foothold

አረጋገጠ *arrägaggäṭä* v.i. became sure of, ascertained

አስረገጠ *asräggäṭä* v.t. had s/o kicked, beaten; drilled *(soldiers)*; assured s/o

ረገፈ *räggäfä* v.i. fell, dropped *(fruit etc. when tree is shaken)*; cleared up *(smallpox eruptions, rashes on body)*; died *(person)*

ረጋፊ *rägafi* adj. likely to drop, fall; mortal

ርጋፊ *rəggafi* n. dus shaken from *s/t*; detritus; riff-raff, low people, leftovers, scraps of food from table

አረገፈ *aräggäfä* v.t. caused fruit, leaves, etc. to drop from tree

አረጋገፈ *ärrägaggäfä* v.t. shook out *(clothes, bedsheets, etc.)*

ተራገፈ *täraggäfä* v.i. was unloaded; was shaken out

አራገፈ *arraggäfä* v.t. shook out; unloaded

አራጋፊ *arragafi* n. one who unloads; shakes out

አስረገፈ *asräggäfä* v.t. made *s/o* drop *s/t (from his hand)*

ረጋ *rägga* v.i. became calm, quiet; became coagulated; became peaceful

እርጎ *argo* n. yoghourt

እርጋታ *argata* n. calmness, quiet; peacefulness

አረጋ *arägga* v.t. curdled, made yoghourt

ተረጋጋ *tärägagga* v.i. became quiet, peaceful, settled *(of country or state, or disturbed person)*

አረጋጋ *arrägagga* v.t. quietened down, made peaceful, soothed, pacified

ረግረግ *rägräg* n. marshland, marshy, swamp

ረጠበ *räṭṭäbä* v.i. contributed money to a needy man *(due to sudden misfortune etc.)*

ረጣቢ *räṭabi* adj. n. contributor *(money)*

አርጥባን *arṭaban* n. money given as contribution *(to a needy man)*

ረጠበ *räṭṭäbä* v.i. got wet, was moist, was wet

አረጠበ *aräṭṭäbä* v.t. wetted, moistened, dampened

እርጥብ *ərṭəb* adj. wet, moist,

damp

እርጥበት *arṭəbät* or ርጥበት *rəṭbät* n. moisture, dampness

ረጨ *räččä* v.t. sprinkled

ረጪ *räči* n. one who sprinkles

ተረጨ *tärräččä* v.i. was sprinkled; widespread *(news)*

ተራጨ *täraččä* v.t. splashed *(water)* about

ተረጫጨ *tärräčaččä* v.t. splashed one another

አስረጨ *asräččä* v.t. had s/o sprinkle *(e.g. holy water)*

ረፈረፈ *räfärräfä* n.t. littered

ረፈደ *räffädä* v. got late *(in the morning time)*

ረፋድ *räffad* n. late morning, half a day

የረፋድ መንገድ *yäräffad mängäd* n. half day's journey

አረፈደ *aräffädä* v.i. got late in the morning *(person)*

ማርፈጃ *marfäǧa* n. morning's business, affairs

አረፋፈደ *aräfaffädä* v.i. became a little late in the morning *(person)*

አስረፈደ *asräffädä* v.t. delayed *(s/o)* in the morning

ሩማን *ruman* or ሮማን *roman* n. pomegranate

ሩር *rur* n. wooden, skin ball *(e.g. for the "gänna" game or polo)*

ሩሲያ *rusəya* a. Russia

ሩስኛ *rusəñña* n. Russian *(language)* also መስኮብኛ *mäskobəñña*

ሩስያዊ *rusyawi* n. Russian

ሩብ *rub* adj. a quarter

—ጉዳይ *-gudday* quarter to

ከሩብ *kärub* quarter past

ሩካቤ *rukabe* n. *(G.)* n. sexual intercourse

ሩካቤ ሥጋ *rukabe səga* n. sexual intercourse

ሩዝ *ruz* n. rice

ሩጫ *ruččа* see ሮጠ

ሪሕ *rih* n. rheumatoid arthritis

ሪቅ *riq* n. thatched grain store, *(usually of wood)*

ሪዝ *riz* n. moustache, sideburns

ራራ *rarra* v.i. was compassionate merciful, kind

ርኅሩኅ *rəhruh also* ሩሩ *rurru* adj. compassionate merciful, kind

ርኅራኄ *rəhrahe* n. kindness, compassion

—የለለው *-yälelläw* adj. cruel, savage

አራራ *ararra* v. made s/o kind, compassionate

ራሰ *rasä* v.i. got wet, soaked

አራሰ *arasä* v. t. made s/t wet; soaked s/t, drenched, moistened

ራስ *ras* n. head; self; title *(e.g. duke, lord)*

ራሰ በራ *rasä bära* adj. bald, hairless

ራሱ ዞረ *rasu zorä* v.i. was dizzy, was perplexed

ራሱን ሳተ *rasun satä* v.t. fainted, lost consciousness

—ቻለ *-čalä* v. t. was independent, was self-supporting

—ዐወቀ *-awwäqä* v.t. recovered consciousness

—ገታ *-gätta* v.t. controlled oneself

ራሳም *rasam* adj. having a large head

ራስ ምታት *ras mətat* n. headache

—ቅል *-qəl* n. skull

—ወዳድ *-wäddad* adj. selfish

ራስጌ *rasge* n. in the direction of the head; head of bed

ርእስ *rə'əs* n. title *(subject)*

ርእሰ ብሔር *rə'sä bəher* n. head of state

—አንቀጽ *-anqäṣ* n. editorial *(news paper)*

የራስ ንብረት *yäras nəbrät* n. one's own property

ራቀ *raqä* v.i. got far away;

went away

ሩቅ *ruq* adj. far

ርቀት *rəqät* n. distance

አራቀ *'uraqä* v.t. removed; took far away; disliked *(s/o)*

ተራራቀ *täraraqä* v.i. became, got separated; split up

አራራቀ *arraraqä* v.t. put at a distance *(two or more persons, things)*

አስራቀ *asraqä* v.t. put at a distance; got rid of

*ራቈተ *raqquʷätä*

(እ)ራቁት *(ə)raqut* adj. naked

እርቃን *ərqan* n. nakedness, nudity

እርቃነ ሥጋ *ərqanä səga* n. nakedness, nudity

ተራቈተ *täraquʷätä* v.i. became naked, nude; became barren; became very poor

አራቈተ *arraquʷätä* v.t. denuded; laid bare; made poor

ራበ *rabä* v.i. was hungry *(no person indicated)*

ራብ *rab or* ረኀብ *rähab* n. hunger

ዘመነ ረኀብ *zämänä rähab* n. famine *(particular occasion)*

ራብተኛ *rabtäñña or* ረኀብተኛ *rähabtäñña* n. hungry person

ተራበ *tärabä* v.i. was hungry

አስራበ *asrabä* v.t made *(s/o)* hungry

ራብዕ *rab'ə* n. fourth form in the Amharic vowel system

ራት *rat* or እራት *ərat* n. supper, dinner *(evening meal)*

የሳት እራት *yäsat rat* n. moth

ራኬት *raket* n. racket

ራዕይ *ra'əy* n. vision, apparition, *(revelation as in Bible)*

ራደ *radä* v.i. trembled, shook

አራደ *aradä* v.t. caused to tremble, shake; frightened

ራድዮ *radyo or* ሬድዮ *redyo* or ራድዮን *radyon* n. radio, wireless, radio set

ሬሳ *resa* n. corpse, dead body

የሬሳ ሳጥን *yäresa satən n.* coffin

ሬስቶራንት *restorant* n. restaurant

ሬብ *reb* or እሬብ *əreb* n buttocks, bottom *(coll).*

ሬት/ እሬት *ret/ əret* n. aloes; bitter

እንደ ሬት የመረረ *əndä ret yämärrärä* bitter as aloes

እሬት እሬት አለ *əret əret alä* was bitter; was harmful

ሬንጅ *renǧ* n. asphalt cf. ቅጥራን

ሬኮማንዴ *rekumande* n. registered letter

ሬፑብሊክ *republik* n. republic

ሬፑብሊካዊ *republikawi* adj. republican

ርሳስ *rəsas also* እርሳስ *ərsas* n. lead; pencil

* ርስ *in* የርስ በርስ *yärs bärs* adj. mutual

ርስት *rəst* n. property *(land)* see ወረሰ

ርቀት see ራቀ

ርቱዕ *in* ርቱዕ *and* ኢርቱዕ ተሳቢ *rətu', irətu' täsabi* n. direct and indirect object

ርችት *rəččət* n. fireworks,

ርኅሩኅ see ራራ

ርእስ see ራስ

ርእዮተ ዓለም *rə'əyotä aläm* n. idiology

ርካብ *rəkab* n. stirrup *also* እርካብ

ርኮት *rəkot* or እርኮት *ərkot* n. water skin, wineskin

ርዝራዥ *rəzərraž* n. remnant, fall out, leftovers

ርግብ *rəgb or* እርግብ *ərgəb* n. pigeon, turtle-dove; adj. kind-hearted

ዐይነ ርግብ *aynä rəgb* n. veil

ርጭ አለ *rəčč alä* v.i. was calm,

still *(surroundings)*

ሮማ *roma* n. Rome, Italy

ሮማዊ *romawi* n. Roman, Italian *(person)*

ሮማውያን *romawəyan* n. pl. Romans, Italians

ሮማይስጥ *romayəsṭ* n. Latin

ሮማን *roman*, *or* ሩማን *ruman* n. pomegranate

ሮሮ *rorro* n. remorse

—አሰማ *—assammu* v.t. made s/o feel remorseful; rebuked

ሮብ *rob* n. Wednesday, *also* ረቡዕ

ሮጠ *roṭä* v.i. ran

ሮጥ አለ *roṭṭ alä* v.i. jogged along

ሩጫ *ruč̣a* n. running

የሩጫ ውድድር *yäruč̣a wədəddər* n. race

ሯጭ *rwač̣* n. runner

መሮጫ *märoč̣a* n. track, running field

አሮጠ *aroṭa* v.t. chased, made s/o run

ተሯሯጠ *tärwarwaṭä* v.i. chased each other, ran about

አሯሯጠ *arrwarwaṭä* v.t. chased, hurried

አስሮጠ *asroṭä* v.t. made s/o run

ሰሀ *säha* n. fault, error, mistake

ሰለለ *sällälä* v.i. acted as a spy, spied

ሰላይ *sällay* n. spy, secret agent

ስለላ *səllälä* n. espionage, spying

ተሰለለ *täsällälä* v.i. was spied upon

አሰለለ *assällälä* v.t. had someone spied upon

አሰላይ *assällay* n. one who employs spies

ሰለለ *sällälä* v.i. became paralized, lame; was thin

ሰላላ *sälala* adj. paralised, crippled, lame

—መላላ *—mälala* thin and long

—ድምፅ *—dəmṣ* thin voice

ሰለመ *sällämä* v.t. greeted

ሰላም *sälam* interj. "peace", "greetings" "Hallo!"

—ነሣ *—nässa* v.t. disturbed, agitated *(disturbed)*

የሰላም ጓድ *yäsälm gu̇add* n. Peace Corps

ሰላማዊ *sälamawi* adj. peaceful

ሰልፍ *—sälf* n. demonstration *(political)*

—ውቅያኖስ *—wəqyanos* n. Pacific Ocean

ሰላማዊነት *sälamawinnät* n. peacefulness

ሰላምታ *sälamta* n. greetings

—ሰጠ *—säṭṭä* v.t. greeted saluted

—ነሣ *—nässa* v.i. ignored *(to greet s/o)*

—አቀረበ *—aqärräbä* v.t. greeted, saluted

መስለም *mäsläm* inf. to become Muslim

አሰለመ *asällämä* v.t. converted s/o to Islam

እስላም *əslam* n. Islam

እስልምና *əsləmənna* n. Islamic religion

ተሳለመ *täsallämä* v.t. acknowledged by bowing

ቤተክርስቲያን— *betäkrəstian—* went to the church

—ተሳላሚ *—täsalami* n. church-goer

መሳለሚያ *mässalämiya* n. church porch

ሰለሰለ *sälässälä* v.i. lost weight, became thin

አሰለሰለ *asäläsšälä* v.t. caused s/o to become thin

*ሰለሰለ **sälässälä*

አሰላሰለ *assälassälä* v.i. contemplated, pondered

ሰለቀ *sälläqä* v.t. ground fine *(as with millstone)*; beat s/o soundly

ስልቅ *səlləq* adj. fine ground

መሰለቂያ *mäsälläqiya* n. fine-grinding millstone

ተሰለቀ *täsälläqä* v.i. was ground fine

* ሰለቀ **sälläqä*

ተሳለቀ *täsalläqä* v.i. ridiculed, laughed at

መሳለቂያ *mässaläqiya* n. laughing stock

ሰለቀጠ *säläqqäṭä* v.t. swallowed whole

ሰለበ *sällábä* v.t. cut off s/o's genitals; cheated *(in weighing produce etc.)*; plundered in war

ሰላቢ *salābi* n. one who cheats in the measure, etc.

ሰለባ *sälaba* n. spoils of war, plunder

ስልብ *səlb* n. eunach

ተሰለበ *täsälläbä* v.i. was castrated

አሰለበ *assälläbä* v.t. had s/o castrated

ሰለተ *sällätä* v.t. put in order: arranged according to category

ስላች *səllač* n. diagonal cut

ስልት *səlt* n. way, manner, style, mode

ስልተ ምርት *səltä mərt* n. mode of production

የጦር ስልት *yäṭor səlt* n. strategy, tactics *(mil.)*

ሰቸ *säläččä* v.i. became bored

ሰልቺ *sälči* n. one who easily gets bored

ስልቹ *səlču* n. one who is easily bored

አሰለቸ *asäläččä* v.t. bored s/o; nagged s/o

አሰልቺ *asälči* n. bore; shrew; nagger; adj. boring, wearisome, nagging

የሚያሰለች *yämmiyasäläčč* adj. irksome, boring, wearisome

ተሰለቸ *täsäläččä* v.i. got bored with

ተሰልቺ *täsälči* n. boring person, thing

ተሰላቸ *täsälaččä* v.i. got bored with each other, tired of each other

ተሰለቻቸ *täsäläčaččä* v.i. got bored with each other

ሰሊጥ *säliṭ* n. sesame *(grain)*

ሰላ *sälla* v.i. turned out well; was sharpened *(knives, etc.)*; improved in speech, became eloquent

ስል *səl* adj. sharp

ስለት *səlät* n. sharpness; cutting edge, blade; vow

ሰላ see ሰሌት

ሰላጣ *sälaṭa* n. salad, lettuce

ሰሌን *sälen* n. straw mat

ሰልካካ *sälkakka* adj. clean cut *(feature)*

ሰልፍ *sälf* n. demonstration, parade; procession line *(row of persons)*, queue

ሰልፈኛ *sälfaññä* n. demonstrator

ሰላማዊ ሰልፍ *sälamawi sälf* n. demonstration *(political)*

ሰመመ *sämmämä* v.i. day dreamed, got lost in thought

ሰመመን *sämämän* n. day dreaming, a brown study

ሰመጠ *sämmäṭä* or ሰጠመ *säṭṭämä* v.i. got drowned, sank

ስምጠት *səmṭät* or ስጥመት *səṭmät* n. depth *(liquids)*

ስምጥ *səmṭ* n. depression *(geographical)*

—ሸለቆ *-šäläqo* n. rift valley

ሰማ *sämma* v.t. heard, listened: understood

(*a language*); became hot enough *(oven)*
ለይስሙላ *läyəsmulla* only for show
የሰሚ ሰሚ *yäsämi sämi* n. hearsay
ስሜት *səmmet* n. feeling, feelings
ስሞታ *səmota* n. complaint
መስሚያ *mäsmiya* n. hearing aid; headphones, etc.
አሰማ *asämma* v.t. made hot enough *(oven, pan etc.)*
አሰማ *assämma* v.t. announced, voiced, uttered made oneself heard; urged a plea
ተሰማ *täsämma* v.i. was heard
ተሰሚ *täsämi* adj. influential; authoritative
ተሰማማ *täsämamma* v.t. paid attention to each other
ተስማማ *täsmamma* v.i. agreed with each other, reached an agreement; bargained; got along; corresponded *(agreed)*; was consonant with
አስማማ *asmamma* v.t. reconciled, harmonized
ሰማዕት *säma'ət* n. martyr
ሰማዕትነት *säma'ətənnät* n. martyrdom pl. ሰማዕታት
ሰማንያ *sämanya* adj/n. eighty; legal marriage document
ሰማይ *sämay* n. sky, heaven
ሰማያዊ *sämayawi* adj. of the heavens, heavenly; light blue
ሰሜን *sämen* n/adj. north
ሰሜናዊ *sämenawi* adj. northern
—ዋልታ *—walta* n. North Pole
ሰም *säm* n. beeswax
ሰምና ወርቅ *sämənna wärq* metaphor
ሰምበሌጥ *sämbäleṭ* n. grass, straw for thatching; long grass
ሰምበር *sämbär* or ሰንበር *sänbär* n. stripe *(from a whip stroke)*, bruise
—አወጣ *—awäṭṭa* v.t. bruised
ሰሞን *sämon* n. week
ሰሞነኛ *sämonäñña* n. deacon during week of duty
ሰረረ *särrärä* v.t. had sexual intercourse *(of animals)*, mated
ሰራሪ *särari* n. animal who has sexual intercourse
ስርያ *sərrya* n. sexual intercourse *(animals)*, mating
ተሰረረ *täsärrärä* v.i. was served, mated *(animal)*
ተሳረረ *täsarrärä* v.i. had intercourse *(animals)*
አሳረረ *assarrärä* v.t. caused *(animals)* to breed; overbid, competed in bidding
አሳራሪ *assarari* n. one who bids competitively
አሰረረ *assärrärä* v.i caused *(animals.)* to breed
ሰረሰረ *särässärä* v.t. bored a whole
ሰርሳሪ *särsari* n. burglar
መሰርሰሪያ *mäsärsäriya* n. drill *(tool)*, auger
ተሰረሰረ *täsärässärä* v.i. was bored
ሰረቀ *särräqä* v.t. stole
ሰራቂ *säraqi* n. one who steals
ስርቅታ *sərrəqta* n. hiccup, hicough
ስርቆሽ *sərqoš* n. stealing
—በር *—bärr* n. secret door
ስርቆት *sərqot* n. stealing
ተሰረቀ *täsärräqä* v.i. was stolen
ተሰርቆ ሄደ *täsärqo hedä* left secretly
ተሳረቀ *täsarräqä* v.i. stole from each other
ተሰራረቀ *täsärarräqä* v.t. stole repeatedly from each other
አሰረቀ *assärräqä* v. had s/o robbed, caused s/o to be robbed
ሰረዘ *särräzä* v.t. cancelled

ሰረዝ sāräz n. *(punct. mark)* dash, hyphen
ነጠላ— *näṭäla*—n. comma(፣)
ድርብ— *dərrəb* — n. semicolon (፤)
ሰረዛ *sərräza* n. cancellation
ስርዝ *sərrəz* adj. cancelled
—ድልዝ *—dəlləz* adj. full of cancellation *(manuscript)*, deletion
ሰራረዘ *sārarräzä* v. crossed out heavily
ተሰረዘ *täsärräzä* v.i. was cancelled
አሰረዘ *assärräzä* v.i. had s/o crossed off a list
ሰረገ *see* ሠረገ
ሰረገላ *särägälla* n. chariot, wagon, coach, carriage
ሰረጐደ *särägg"ädä* v.t. poked a hole in, made an indentation in, indented.
ስርጉዳት *sərgudat* adj. hole, depression, indentation
ተሰረጐደ *täsärägg"ädä* v.i. was pushed in
*ሰረጨ *see* ተሰራጨ
ሰርን *särn* n. nostrils
ሰርክ *särk* adv. always, often, frequently
ሰርጣን *särṭan* n. crab
ሰሰነ *ˀəssänä or* ሴሰነ *sessänä* v.t. lusted *(sexual)*; had sexual desire for s/o
ሴሰኛ *sesäñña* adj. lustful
ሴሰኛነት *sesäññannät or* ሴሰኝነት *sesäññənnät* n. lustfulness
ሰስ *säs* n. klipspringer
ሰቀለ *säqqälä* v.t. hanged s/t; crucified s/o
ሰቃይ *säqay* adj/n. hangman
ሰቀላ *säqäla* n. cottage *(of rectangular shape)*
ስቅለት *səqlät* n. crucifixion
ስቅላት *səqqəlat* n. hanging *(punishment)*
መስቀያ *mäsqäya* n. hanger scaffold
ልብስ — *ləbs*—n. clotheshanger
መስቀል *mäsqäl* inf. to hang; n. cross
መስቀለኛ ጥያቄ *mäsqäləñña ṭəyyaqe* n. cross examination
መስቀለያ መንገድ *mäsqäləyya mängäd* n. cross-roads
ተሰቀለ *täsäqqälä* v. i. was hanged, was crucified
ተሰቃይ *täsäqqay* adj/n s/o who is to be hanged
አሳቀለ *assaqqälä* v.t. helped s/o hang s/o or s/t
አሰቀለ *assäqqälä* v. t. had s/t hanged, had s/o crucified
ተመሳቀለ *tämäsaqqälä* v.i. became interwoven, intermingled, confused
ተመሰቃቀለ *tämäsäqaqqälä* v.i. was confused, lost order
ምስቅልቅል *məsqəlqəl* n. confusion, disorder, haphazardness
አመሳቀለ *ammäsaqqälä* v.t. crossed one's hands; threw into disorder, confusion
አመሰቃቀለ *ammäsäqaqqälä* v.t. threw into constant disorder, confusion
ሰቀቀ *säqqäqä* v.i. felt uneasy, on edge
ሰቀቀኝ *säqqäqäññ* v.i. made me uneasy
ሰቃቂ *säqaqi* n. s/t which causes uneasiness
ተሳቀቀ *täsaqqäqä* v. i. was greatly disappointed
አሰቀቀ *assäqqäqä* v.i. made s/o greatly disappointed
አሰቃቂ *assäqqaqi* adj. horrible, horrifying
አሳቀቀ *assaqqäqä* v.t. disappointed s/o greatly
ስቅቅ አለ *səqəqq alä* v.t. was grieved very deeply indeed
ስቅቅ ብሎ አለቀሰ *səqəqq bəlo aläqqäsä* v.i. grieved deeply and wept bitterly
ሰቀቀን *säqäqän* n. great disappointment, deep sadness

ሰቀቀናም *säqäqänam* adj. deeply unhappy; greatly disappointed

ሰቀዘ *säqqäzä* v.t. gripped, seized with sharp pain

*ሰቀየ **säqäyyä*

ስቃይ *səqay* n. torment, agony, torture, plague

አሰቃየ *assäqayyä* v.t. tortured, plagued

ተሰቃየ *täsäqayyä* v. i. was tortured, was plagued

ሰቅ *säqq* n. girdle, belt

ሰበረ *säbbärä* v.t. broke, broke in

ዜማ *zema*— sang false notes

ሰብሮ ከፈተ *säbro käffätä* v.t. broke open

-ገባ —*gäbba* v. t. broke into a house

ሰባሪ *säbari* adj/n person or thing which breaks s.t

ሰባራ *säbara* adj. broken, broken down

ስባሪ *səbbari* n. broken piece

ስብርባሪ *səbərbari* n. fragments, broken pieces, fractions

ስብራት *səbbərat* n. fracture

ሰባበረ *säbabbärä* v.t. broke into pieces

ተሰበረ *täsäbbärä* v.i. was broken

ተሰባሪ *täsäbbari* adj. fragile, breakable

ተሰባበረ *täsäbabbärä* v.i. was broken into pieces

አሳበረ *assabbärä* v. t. found a short cut, shorter way *(on journey)*; raised the bid *(at auction)*

አሳባሪ መንገድ *assabari mängäd* n. short cut

አሰበረ *assäbbärä* v.t. had s.t broken

ሰበሰበ *säbässäbä* v.t. gathered, accumulated, assembled; harvested

አፉን— *afun*—v.t kept quiet *(through fear)*

ልብሱን— *ləbsun*—v.t. gathered up one's clothes

ሰብሳቢ *säbsabi* adj/n. gatherer accumulator; chairman

ስብስብ *səbsəb* n. a set, a group, collection

ስብሰባ *səbsäba* n. gathering, meeting, assembly, session, conference, congress, convention

—አደረገ —*adärrägä* v.t. held a conference

ሰባሰበ *säbussäbä* v.t. heaped up; gathered randomly

ስብስብ አለ *səbsəbb alä* v.i. gathered together; contracted

ተሰበሰበ *täsäbässäbä* v.i. was gathered, accumulated, assembled

ተሰብሳቢ *täsäbsabi* n. participating member

መሰብሰቢያ *mässäbsäbiya* n. meeting place

አሰባሰበ *assäbassäbä* v.t. helped in gathering s.t; organized *(people)*

ሰበቀ *säbbäqä* v.t. beat up *(eggs etc.)*; rubbed fire-stick; kindled

ሰባቂ *säbaqi* n. backbiter, tale-bearer

ሰብቅ *säbq* n. backbiting, sneaking

ስብቀት *səbqät* n. backbiting, tale-bearing, sneaking

አሳበቀ *assabbäqä* v.t. passed on gossip, told tales on s/o

አሳባቂ *assabaqi* n. sneak, tale-bearer, one who makes malicious reports on others

ሰበብ *säbäb* n. pretext, trumped up excuse

ሰበበኛ *säbäbäñña* n. malingerer, one who makes occasion of an injury, who takes advantage of a pretext

አሳበበ *assabbäbä* v. found a pretext, made a pretext of

ተሳበበ *täsabbäbä* v. i. was used as a pretext

ሰበከ *säbbäkä* v.t. preached; flattered

ሰባኪ *säbaki* adj/n. preacher; flatterer

ሰበካ *säbäka* n. parish

ስብከት *səbkät* n. preaching

ተሰበከ *täsäbbäkä* v.i. was preached; flattered

ተሰባኪ *täsäbaki* adj/n. s/o who is easily convinced, easily flattered

አሰበከ *assäbbäkä* v.t. had s/o preach

ሰባ *säbba* v.i. became fat *(animals)*

ስባት *səbat* n. fatness

ስብ *səb* n. fat

አሰባ *asäbba* v.t. fattened

አስቢ *asbi* adj/n. one who fattens *(cattle)* to sell

ሰባ *säba* adj/ n. seventy

ሰባኛ *säbaňňa* adj. seventieth

ሰባት *säbatt* adj/ n. seven

—እጅ *—əǧǧ* adj/adv. sevenfold

ሰባተኛ *säbattäňňa* adj. seventh

ሱባኤ *suba'e* n. retreat *(religious,)* time allocated to prayer and fasting

ሰብእ *säb'ə* n. *(G.)* man, human being

ኅብረተሰብ *həbrätä säb* n. society, the public

ቤተሰብ *betä säb* n. family

ሰብአዊ *säb'awi* n. humanist, philanthropist

—መብት *--mäbt* n. human rights

ኅብረተሰብአዊ *həbrätä säb'awi* adj. socialist

ሰብል *säbl* n. harvest, crop

ሰበዝ *säbäz* n. raffia grass

ሰበጠረ *see* አሰባጠረ

ሰተረ *sättärä* v. t. put in order, put neatly together

ስታራ *sättara* adj/n. reserved

ስትር *səttər* adj./n. orderly, neat

ተሰተረ *täsättärä* v. i. was put in order

ሰተት አለ *sätätt alä* v.i. passed through freely

* ሰተፈ *see* ተሳተፈ

ሰታቴ *sätate* n. large earthware stewpot

ሰነቀ *sännäqä* v.i. prepared provisions for travel

ስንቅ *sənq* n. provisions, food for journey

ተሰነቀ *täsännäqä* v. i. was prepared *(provisions)*

አሰነቀ *assännäqä* v.t. had provisions prepared

ሰነቀረ *sänäqqärä* v. t. forced into *(a tight place)*

ተሰነቀረ *täsänäqqärä* v.i. was forced into

ሰነበተ *sänäbbätä* v.i passed the week; lived quite long

ሰንበት *sänbät* n. Sabbath; Sunday

መሰንበቻ *mäsänbäča* n. week

አሰነበተ *asänäbbätä* v.t. delayed for one week, delayed for sometime

ተሰናበተ *täsänabbätä* v.i. came to say goodbye, bade farewell; resigned *(from job)*

ተሰነባበተ *täsänäbabbätä* v.t. bade farewell to each other

አሰናበተ *assänabbätä* v.t. released *(s/o)* from duty; sacked *(an employee)*

ሰነበጠ *sänäbbäṭä* v.t. slit, nick *(as with razor blade)*

ስንባጭ *sənəbbač̣* peel, rind *(e.g. citrus fruits)*, quarters *(of citrus fruit)*

ሰነኘ *sänäňňä* v.i. rhymed

ሰንኝ *sənəññ* n. rhyme

ሰነከለ *sänäkkälä* v. t. hobbled *(horse, donkey etc.)*; crippled *(with a blow on the leg)*

ሰንካላ *sänkalla* n/adj. limping, one who limps

ሰንኩል *sənkul* n/adj. cripple; handicapped person

አካለ-- *akalä* — adj. cripple

መሰናክል *mäsänakəl* n. hindrance, stumbling block

ተሰነከለ *täsänäkkälä*. v.i. was hobbled, was crippled

ተሰናከለ *täsänakkälä* v.i. was hindered

አሰናከለ *assänakkälä* v.t. hindered

አሰናካይ *assänakay* n. one who hinders s/o

አሰነካከለ *assänäkakkälä* v.t. threw everything into confusion

ሰነዘረ *sänäzzärä*. v.t. directed at *(accusation etc.)*. reached out, stretched out one's arm; measured a span *(with the hand)*

ሰንዝር *sənzər* n. a span, a hand's span

ተሰናዘረ *täsänazzärä* v.i. was stretched out; was directed at

መሰናዘሪያ *mässänazäriya* n. elbow-room, space to relax

ሰነድ *sänäd* n. document

*ሰነጸ *see* አሰናጸ

ሰነገ *sännägä* v. t. ringed the nose *(of a bull esp.)*; pierced beak *(of broody hen)* with feather

ሰንግ *sənnəg* adj/n. having nose ringed *(esp. bull)*; having beak pierced with feather *(broody hen)*

ተሰነገ *täsännägä* v.i. was ringed; had feather poked up nose

ሰነገ *sänäggä* v. t. stuffed *(green pepper with tomato and onions etc.)*

ሰነጠረ *sänäṭṭärä* v.t. split *(wood)* finely *(e. g. to make split, tooth pick etc.)*

ስንጣሪ *sənnəṭṭari* n. fine splinter

ስንጥር *sənṭər* n. fine splinter, tooth pick

ሰነጣጠረ *sänäṭaṭṭärä* v.t. split into many pieces

ተሰነጠረ *täsänäṭṭärä* v.t. was split finely

ሰነጠቀ *sänäṭṭäqä* v.t. split *(wood etc.;)* splintered; cracked,cleaved

ስንጣቂ *sənəṭṭaqi* n. chip of wood, splinter, split-off piece

ስንጥቅ *sənṭəq* n. a split, crack rift, fissure

መሰንጠቂያ *mäsänṭäqiya* n. saw, axe etc.

እንጨት— *ənčät* -- saw mill

ሰነጣጠቀ *sänäṭaṭṭäqä* v. t. split into many pieces

ተሰነጠቀ *täsänäṭṭäqä* v.i. was split, cracked

አሰነጠቀ *assänäṭṭäqä* v.t. had s/t split, cracked

ሰነፈ *sännäfä* v.i. became lazy

ሰነፍ *sänäf* adj. lazy, idle; feeble, indolent

--ምርት *—mərt* n. threshed crop *(still not winnowed*

ስንፍና *sənfənna* n. laziness, idleness, inaction, indolence

አሰነፈ *asännäfä* v. t. encouraged s/o to be lazy

አሳነፈ *assannäfä* v.t. caused s/o to be lazy

ሰነፈጠ *sänäffäṭä* v.t. tickled the nose *(of mustard)*

ሰናድር *sänadər* n. Schneider *(type of firearm)*

ሰናፍጭ *sänafəčč* n. mustard *see* ሰነፈጠ

ሰኔ *säne* n. June

ሰንሰለት *sänsälät* n. chain

ሰንከሎ *sänkällo* n. bucket, *also* ሸንከሎ *šänkällo*

ንኮፍ *sänkof or* ሸንኮፍ *šänkof* n. scab; flesh around of burst boil

ንደል *sändäl* n. joss-stick

—ጫማ *—čamma* n. sandals

ንደቅ ዓላማ *sändäq alama* n. flag

ንዱቅ *sänduq* n. chest, box

ንጋ *sänga* n. steer, bull fattened for slaughter

ንጠረዥ *sänṭäräž* n, chess; table *(mathematical)*

ንጢ *sänṭi* n. jack-knife

ሰኘ **säññä*

አሰኘው *assäññäw* he feels like, he feels up to

ኞ *säñño* n. Monday

—ማክሰኞ *-maksäñño* n. hopscotch

ሰኔና ሰኞ *sänennä säñño* unexpected coincidence

ከረ *säkkärä* v. i. became drunk, intoxicated

ሰካራም *säkkaram* n/adj. drunkard, drunken

ስካር *səkar* n. drunkeness

አሰከረ *asäkkärä* v.t. made s/o drunk, intoxicated

አስካሪ *askari* adj. alcholic

—መጠጥ *—mäṭäṭṭ* alcholic drink

ማስከሪያ *maskäriya* intoxicant, herb *(bərbirra)* used for stunning fish for catching

ተሳከረ *täsakkärä* v. i. got drunk together; got confused

አሳከረ *assakkärä* v.t. made drunk; confused

ሰከሰከ *säkässäkä* v.t. crammed, stuffed

ሰከነ *säkkänä* v.t. settled *(coffee grounds)*; became mature *(person)*

አሰከነ *asäkkänä* v.t. caused to settle *(coffee grounds)*

ሰካ *säkka* v.t. impaled, stick in, thrusted in

ስክ ሳሀን *sək sahən* n. triple canteen *(food container)*

መሰኪያ *mäsäkkiya* n. plug, *(usually with* የኤሌክትሪክ*)*

ተሰካ *täsäkka* v.i. was forced into, was pushed in

ተሳካ *täsakka* v.i. succeeded *(scheme, plan etc.)*

አሳካ *assakka* v. t. made s/t succeed

አሰካ *assäkka* v.t. had something pushed in, forced

ሰኮና *säkona or* ሸኮና *šäkona* n. hoof

ሰወጥ አለ *säwäṭṭ alä* v.t. lost the thread *(of speech, argument, brain of thought etc.)* for a brief moment

ሰዋሰው *säwasəw* n. grammar

ሰዋሰዋዊ *säwasəwawi* adj. grammatical

ሰው *säw* n. man, human being

—ሠራሽ *—särraš* adj. man-made, artificial

የሰው *yäsäw* adj. human; belonging to s/o else e.g. የሰው ቤት someone's house

—አገር *—agär* n. foreign country

ተራ— *tära—* n. layman, ordinary person

ሰውዬ *säwəyye* interj. you Mr. !

ሰውየው *säwəyyäw* the man, this, that man

ሰውነት *säwənnät* n. body, personality; constitution *(of a person)*

የሰው ልጅ *yäsäw ləǧ* n. human being; person of free condition *(not a slave)*

ሰዓት *sä'at* n. time, hour

—ቆጣሪ *—qoṭari* n. hour hand

—እላፊ *—əllafi* n. overtime: curfew

ከሰዓት በኋላ *käsä'at bähuʷala* in the afternoon

—በፊት *—bäfit* before noon

በሰዓቱ *bäsä'atu* on time, just at the right moment

በየሰዓቱ *bäyyäsä'atu* adv.

hourly from time to time

በሰዓት *bäsä'at* at noon

ያለ ሰዓት *yalä sä'at* adj. late

ዐቃቤ ሰዓት *aqqabe sä'at* n. minister of protocol *(palace official)*

ሰየመ *säyyämä* see ሠየመ

ሰየፈ *säyyäfä* v.t. beheaded

ሰያፊ *säyyafi* n. executioner *(for beheading)*

ሰያፍ *säyyaf* adj. diagonal

ሰይፍ *säyf* n. sword

ሰይፈኛ *säyfäñña* n. swordsman

ተሰየፈ *täsäyyäfä* v.i. was beheaded

አሰየፈ *assäyyäfä* v. t. had s/o beheaded

ሰይጣን *säyṭan* n. Satan, devil

ሰይጣናም *säyṭanam* adj. violent-tempered, hot-tempered

ሰይጣኑ መጣ *säyṭanu mäṭṭa* he was very angry

ሰደቃ *sädäqa* n. table *(arch.)*

ሰደበ *säddäbä* v.t. insulted, called by insulting names

ስድብ *sədəb* n. insult,

ተሰደበ *täsäddäbä* v.i. was insulted, called bad names

ተሳደበ *täsaddäbä* v.t. insulted, called bad names

ተሳዳቢ *täsadabi* n. slanderer, one who insults, s/o who calls bad names

ተሰዳደበ *täsädaddäbä* v.i. slandered, insulted each other, called each other bad names

አሰደበ *assäddäbä* v.t. incited to call s/o bad names

ሰደደ *säddädä* v.t. sent, let go

ሥር— *sər—* v.t. took root, was firmly established; became chronic

ስድ *sədd* adj. lawless, impolite, discourteous

ስደተኛ *səddätäñña* n. refugee

ስደት *səddät* n. exile

የሰደድ እሳት *yäsädäd əsat* n. wild fire

ተሰደደ *täsäddädä* v.i. was exiled

መሰደጃ *mässädäǧa* n. place of exile, refuge

ተሳደደ *täsaddädä* v.i. was chased away, ran away from, was persecuted

አሳደደ *assaddädä* v.t. chased away, followed in pursuit, persecuted

አሳዳጅ *assadaǧ* n. persecutor

ሰደፍ *sädäf* n. butt *(of gun)*

ሰገሌ *sägäle* n.adj. selfish, greedy *(person)*

ሰገራ in ሰገራ ቤት *sägära bet* n. latrine, w.c.

ሰገሰገ *sägässägä* v.t. stuffed in *(e.g. straw into sack)*; ate too much, forced together *(loose threads of hem to prevent fraying)*

ስግስግ *səgsəg* adj. stuffed in

ስግስግ አለ *səgsəgg alä* v.i. was overcrowded; were squeezed up together *(crowd of people)*, tucked in *(blankets of bed)*

ተሰገሰገ *täsägässägä* v.i. was stuffed, pushed in; squeezed up together, tucked in

*ሰገበገበ *sägäbäggäbä*

ስግብግብ *səgəbgəb* adj. greedy stingy, ravenous

ተስገበገበ *täsgäbäggäbä* v.i. was greedy, stingy, avid

ሰገባ *sägäba* n. sheath

ሰገነት *sägännät* n. balcony, grandstand

ሰገደ *säggädä* v.i. bowed, prostrated, genuflected, worshipped

ሰጋጅ *sägaǧ* n. one who bows, prostrates himself

ስጋጃ *səgaǧǧa* n. carpet, rug

ስግደት *səgdät* n. adoration

መስጊድ *mäsgid* n. mosque

መስገጃ *mäsgäğa* n. prayer mat, prayer rug

አሰገደ *assäggädä* v.t. made s/o bow, prostrate himself; made s/o submissive

ሰገገ *säggägä* v.t. stretched the neck out *(attacking, threatening posture)*

አሰገገ *asäggägä* v.t. ran full tilt *(at s/o)* charged *(e.g. rhinoceros)*

ሰጎን *sägon* n. ostrich

ሰጐደ *säggʷädä* v.t. depressed *(formed a depression)*, made an imprint of concavity

ሰጓዳ *sägʷadda* adj. depressed

ስጉዳት *səgudät* n. depression

ስጉዳት *səgguddat* n. dimple

ሰጠ *säṭṭä* v.t. gave

አሳልፎ— *asallafo*—v.t. betrayed

እጁን— *əğğun*— v.t. surrendered

ድምፅ— *dəmş*— v.t. voted, elected

አብሮ ይስጠን *abro yesṭänn* don't mention it!

እግዚአብሔር/እግዜር ይስጥልኝ *əgziabher/əgzer yəsṭəlləňň* thank you!

የሰጠ *yäsäṭṭä* adj. ideal, comfortable

ጤና ይስጥልኝ *ṭena yəsṭəlləňň* good morning, evening! etc., goodbye, hello!

ሰጪ *säči* adj. giver, bestower

ስጦታ *səṭota* n. gift, reward, endowment

ተሰጠ *täsäṭṭä* v.i. was given

ተሰጥዎ/ተሰጥኦ *täsäṭwo/täsäṭ'o* n. gift, talent

አሰጠ *assäṭṭä* v.t. had *s/t* given to s/o

አሳጣ *assaṭṭa* v.t. exposed *(s/o)*

ሰጠመ *saṭṭämä see also* ሰመጠ *sämmäṭä* v.i. sank

ሰጠጥ አለ *säṭäṭṭ alä or* ሲጢጥ አለ *siṭiṭṭ alä* v. i. squeaked

ሰጥ አለ *säṭṭ alä* v.i. was completely subdued

ሰጥ ለጥ አለ *säṭṭ läṭṭ alä* v.i. was utterly overcome and pacified

ሰፈረ *säffärä* v.i. camped; measured *(grain etc.)*

ሰፈረተኛ *säfärätäňňa or* ሰፈርተኛ *säfäriäňňa* n. district neighbour

ሰፈር *säfär* n. district, area *(of town)*

ሰፋሪ *säfari* n. settler; one who measures grain, etc.

ስፍራ *səfra* n. place

ስፍር *səfər* adj. measured out *(grain, etc.)*

—ቁጥር የሌለው *—quṭər yälelläw* adj. innumerable

መስፈሪያ *mäsfäriya* n. camping place; measuring aid *(e.g. bushel)*

እልቆ መሳፍርት *əlqo mäsafərt* adj. innumerable, immeasurable

ተሳፈረ *täsaffärä* v.i. got on board

ተሳፋሪ *täsafari* n. passenger, s/o on board

መሳፈሪያ ገንዘብ *mässafäriya gänzäb* n. fare

አሰፈረ *asäffärä* v.t. settled people in a given area; put on *(in writing)*

ማስፈሪያ *masfäriya* n. area of settlement

አሰፈረ *assäffärä* v.t. had grain etc. measured

አሳፈረ *assaffärä* v.t. put s/o on board, arranged s/o's departure

አሳፋሪ *assafari* n. one who accompanies s/o getting on board

ሰፈነ *säffänä* v.t. ruled over

መስፍን *mäsfən* n. ruler, aristocrat

መሳፍንት *mäsafənt* n. pl. aristocratic ruling class

ዘመነ— *zämänä* — n. time of the aristocratic rulers, barons *(18th century)*

ምስፍና *məsfənna* n. reign,

rule

ሰፈፈ *säffäfä* v.i. floated

ሰፋፊ *säfafi* adj. floating

ሰፈፍ *säfäf* n. unpurified bee wax *(as it floats in fermentation)*

ስፋፊ *səffafi* adj. buoyant

አሰፈፈ *asäffäfä* v.t. made s/t float

ሰፋ *säffa* v.i. became wide, broad

ሰፊ *säffi* adj. wide, broad, large, extensive

ሰፊው ሕዝብ *säffiw həzb* the broad masses

በሰፊው *bäsäffiw* adv. abundantly, extensively, widely

ሰፋ አለ *säfa alä* v.i. became rather wide, broad

ስፋት *səfat* n. width, breadth, area, size *(of room etc.)*

ተስፋፋ *täsfaffa* v.i. thrived, flourished, expanded, was wide, spread, developed

አሰፋ *asäffa* v.t. widened, broadened, increased in magnitude,

አስፋፋ *asfaffa* v.t. widened or broadened gradually, increased gradually in magnitude; developed, expanded; promoted

ሰፋ *säffa* v.t. served, sewed up;. stitched

ልብስ ሰፊ *ləbs säfi* n. tailor

ጫማ— *čamma—* n. shoemaker

ሰፌድ *säfed* n. basketwork disc *(for winnowing grain)*

ስፌት *səfet* n. sewing, stitching

ስፍ *səf* adj. sewn

ወስፌ *wäsfe* n. plaiting bodkin

ወሳፍጅ/ መሳፍጅ *wässafəčča also mässafəčča* n. leather work bodkin, awl

አሰፋ *assäffa* v.t. had tailored

ልብስ ማስ ፊያ ገንዘብ *ləbs massäfiya gänzäb* n. tailor's fee

ስፍሳፋ *säfsaffa* adj. ravenous, over-eager *see also* አሰፈሰፈ

ስፍነግ *säfnäg* n. sponge

ሱማሌ *sumale* n. Somalia, Somali

ሱረት *surrät* n. snuff

ሱሪ *surri* n. trousers

ሱስ *sus* n. addiction

ሱሰኛ *susäñña* adj/n. addicted, addict

ሱቅ *suq* n. shop

—በደረቴ *—bädäräte* n. peddler

ባለሱቅ *baläsuq* n. shopkeeper

ሱባዔ *suba'e* n. retreat *(religious)*

ሱቲ *suti* n. richly coloured cloth, hangings *(for church use)*

ሱካር *sukkar* n. sugar

—በሽታ *—bäššəta* n. diabetes

—በሽተኛ *—bässətäñña* n. diabetic

—ድንች *—dənnəčč* n. sweet potato

ሱዳን *Sudän* n. the Sudan; Sudanese, *also* ሱዳናዊ

ሱፋጭ *suffač* n. obsidian, cutting stone

ሱፍ *suf* n. wool; sunflower seed

—ልብስ *—ləbs* n. woollen dress

ሲል አለ *sill alä* v.i. choked to death

ሲሚንቶ *siminto* n. cement, mortar, concrete

ሲር *sir* n. shoe-lace

ሲሳይ *sisay* n. daily bread; fortune *(money, possessions etc.)*

ሲቃ *siqa* n. sob

ሲባጎ *sibago* n. string

ሲኒ *sini or* ስኒ *səni* n. cup

ሲኒማ *sinima* n. cinema, movie

ሲናር *sinar* n. tare, weed

ሲኖዶስ *sinodos* n. synod

ሲኦል *si'ol* n. hell

ሲዳሞ *sidamo* n. one of the Administrative Regions, Southern Ethiopia

ሲጋራ *sigara also* ሲጃራ *sigara* n. cigarettes

ሲጥ አለ *sitt alä* v.i. squeaked *(door, mouse etc.)*

ሳ— *sa*—imperfect verb prefix, without e.g. ሳያስብ ተናገረ *sayassəb tänaggärä* he spoke without thinking

ሳ - —*ssa* a pro-phrase indicating a question e.g. ከበደ ሄደ እኔሳ *Käbbädä hedä ənessa* Kebede has gone; what about me? cf. ስ

ሳለ *salä* v.t. coughed

ሳላም *salam* adj n. *(one)* who coughs frequently

ሳለ *salä* v.t. sharpened

ስለት *səlät* n. blade of a knife cutting edge

መሳል *mäsal* inf. to sharpen n. whetstone, sharpening stone

መሳያ *mäsaya* n. whetstone strop, file

ተሳለ *täsalä* v.i. was sharpened; made a vow

አሳለ *assalä* v.t. had s/o sharpen blade etc.

ሳላ *sala* n. oryx

ሳሌ *salle* n. crock

ሳሎን *salon* n. salon

ሳሕን *sahən* n. dish, plate

ጎድጓዳ— *godguʷadda*— bowl, basin

ሳመ *samä* v.t. kissed

ቤተክርስቲያን ሳሚ *betäkrəstian sami* n. church goer

ተሳመ *täsamä* v. i. was kissed

ተሳሳመ *täsasamä* v.i. kissed each other

አሳሳመ *assasamä* v.t. made kiss each other

አሳመ *assamä* v.i. made s/o kiss s/o s.t, *(e.g.* priest's cross)

ሳሙና *samuna* n. soap; adj. deceitful *(coll.)*

ሳማ *samma* n. stinging nettle

ሳምባ *see* ሳንባ

ሳምንት *sammənt* n. week

ሳምንታዊ *samməntawi* adj. weekly

ባለሳምንት *balä sammənt* n. one on duty for a given week

ሳቀ *saqä* v.i. laughed

ሳቂታ *saqqitta* adj. jocund

ሳቅ *saq* n. laughter

ሳቅ አለ *saqq alä* v.i. chuckled, smiled

አሳቀ *assaqä* v.t. amused *(caused to laugh)*, evoked a laughter

አሳሳቀ *assasaqä* v.t. flirted with

አስቂኝ *assəqiññ* adj. funny, humorous, laughable, amusing, comic

የሚያስቅ *yämmiyassəq* adj. ridiculous

ሳበ *sabä* v.t. pulled, attracted, lead *(a horse etc.)*

ሳቢ *sabi* adj. /n *(one)* who pulls

ሳቢ ዘር *sabi zär* n. noun of manner *(gram.)*

ስበት *səbät* n. gravity, gravitation

ሳቢያ *sabbiya* n. reason

ተሳበ *täsabä* v.i. was pulled; crawled, creeped

ተሳቢ *täsabi* n. trailer; object *(gram.)*

ተስቦ *täsəbo* n. epidemic

ተሳሳበ *täsasabä* v.t. pulled each other, attracted each other

አሳሳበ *assasabä* v.t. had *(people)* pull each other

አሳበ *assabä* v.t. had s/o or s/t pulled

ሳቢሳ *sabisa* n. gull, seagull; pelican

ሳብዕ *sab'ə* adj. seventh order of Amh. vowel system

ሳተ *satä* v.i. erred; missed

ስተት *sətät or* ስሕተት *səhtät* n. mistake, fault

ስተተኛ *sətätäñña* adj/n. faulty, wrong-doer

ተሳተ *täsatä* v.i. was missed *(target)*

ተሳሳተ *täsasatä* v.i. erred, made mistake

አሳሳተ *assasatä* v.t. caused s/o make a mistake, misled

አሳሳች *assasač* adj./n. misleading, one who misleads

አሳተ *assatä* v.t misled

አሳቻ *assačča* adj. misleading, deceptive *(person, road etc.)*

አሳች *assač* adj. misleading

ሳንቃ *sanqa* n. board *(wood)*

ሳንባ *sanba also* ሳምባ *samba* n. lung

ሳንባማ *sanbamma* adj. buff-coloured

ሴንቲሜትር *sentimetər* n. centimetre

ሳንቲም *santim* n. cent

ሳንጃ *sanǧa* n. bayonet

ሳይንስ *sayəns* n. science

ሳይንሰኛ *sayənsäñña* n. scientist

ሳይንሳዊ *sayənsawi* adj. scientific

ሳዱላ *sadulla* n. young girl

ሳድስ *sadəs* n./adj. sixth order of Amh. vowel system

ሳገ *sagä* v. t. forced in, packed in tightly

ሳጋ *saga* n. roofing slats, sticks *(to support thatch)*

ሳጠራ *saṭara* n. rush matting, wicker fencing

ሳጥን *saṭən* n. chest, box

ሳጥናኤል *saṭna'el* n. Satan

*ሳፈፈ **safäffä*

ተንሳፈፈ *tänsaffäfä* v.i. floated; drifted *(of logs in the river)*

አንሳፈፈ *ansaffäfä* v.t. floated, got afloat

ሳፋ *safa* n. tub

ሴም *sem* n. shem *(Bibl.)*

ሴማዊ *semawi* adj. Semitic

ሴራ *sera* n. plot, conspiracy

ሴረኛ *seräñña* n. plotte conspirator

አሴረ *aserä* v.t. plotted, conspired

ሴሰነ *sessänä see* ሰሰነ

ሴት *set* n. woman

ሴተኛ አዳሪ *setäñña adari* n. prostitute

ሴታሴት *setaset* adj. womanish, effemina

ሴቴ *sete* adj. female *(of species)*

ሴት ልጅ *set ləǧ* n. daughter

የሴት ልጅ *yäset ləǧ* adj. rude unmannerly child

ሴትነት *setənnät* n. femininity, womanly qualit

ሴኮንድ *second* n. second *time, also* ሰከንድ

ስ— *sə*—verbal pref. denoting time e.g. ስመ *səmaṭa* when I com

—ስ —*s* nominal suff., What about? as for e.g.

እኔስ *əness* What about me?

ስለሱስ ግድየለኝም *səlässus gəddelläññəm* as for hin I have nothing t worry

ስለ— *səlä*—conj. because, due to the fact that et

ስለምን *səlämən* int. adv. why? because of what

ስለዚህ *səläzzih* because *(of this)*

ስለዚያ *səläzziya* because *(of that)*

ስሌት *səllet* n. calculation

ስልም አለ *səlləmm alä* v.i. lost consciousness

ስልምልም አለ *sələmləmm alä* v.i. lost consciousness completely

ስልሳ *səlsa* adj. sixty

ስልባቦት *səlbabot* n. cream; skim on boiled mil

ስልት *səlt* n. manner, mode knack

ስልተ ምርት *səltä mərt* n. mod of production

ስልቻ *səlləčča* n. leather pouch, sack

ስልክ *səlk* n. telephone, telephone wire
ስልከኛ *səlkäñña* n. telephone operator
ስልክ ቤት *səlk bet* n. telegraph office
ስልጆ *səlgo* n. dip (*bean flour, oil, mustard and spices*)
ስሕተት *see* ሳተ
ስሙኒ *səmuni* n. quarter (*of a birr*)
ስማ በለው *səma bäläw* interj. oyez! oyez!
ስም *səm* n. name
ስመኛ *səmäñña* n. one who blames others for his own faults
ስም አወጣ *səm awäṭṭa* v.t. named (*a child*)
—አጠፋ *—aṭäffa* v.t. blackened ones's name, ruined one's reputation .
—አጥፊ *—aṭfi* adj. slanderous
—ማጥፋት ወንጀል *—maṭfat wänǧäl* n. defamation crime
—ጠራ *—ṭärra* v.t. called the roll
ስመ ጥሩ/ጥር *səmä ṭəru/ṭər* adj. reputable, prestigious, celebrity, famous
የሐሰት ስም *yähassät səm* n. alias
የነገር— *yänägär—* n. abstract noun (*gram.*)
የተጸውዖ *yätäṣäwwə'o—* n. proper noun (*gram.*)
የቁሳቁስ— *yäqusaqus—* n. material noun (*gram.*)
የወል— *yäwäl—* n. common noun (*gram.*)
የክርስትና— *yäkərəstənna—* n. Christian name
የጥቅል— *yäṭəqəll—* n. collective noun (*gram.*)
ተውላጠ— *täwlaṭä—* n. pronoun
ስያሜ *səyyame* n. nomenclature, naming
ስያሜ ቃላት *səyyame qalat* n. coinage (*of terms*)
ስምም *səməmm* n. agreement
ስምምነት *səməmənnät* n. agreement, accord, consent, treaty, *see also* ስማ
ስምንት *səmmənt* adj./n. eight
ስምንተኛ *səmäntäñña* adj. eighth
ስሞታ *səmota* n. complaint, grumble
ስሞተኛ *səmotäñña* adj./n. complaining
ስርቅታ *sərrəqta* n. hiccup
ስርቅ አለ *sərrəq alä* v.i. hiccupped
ስርየት *səryät* n. absolution
ስርጥ መንገድ *sərṭ mängäd* n. narrow path
ስቅጥጥ አለ *səqṭəṭṭ älä* v.i. be horrified, cringed with horror
ስብሐት *səbhat* n. praise
ስንት *sənt* int. adv. how much? how many
ስንት ጊዜ *—gize* how often? how long?
በስንት ሰዓት *bäsənt sä'at* when? at what time?
ከስንት አንዴ *käsənt ände* once in a blue moon
ስንተኛ *səntäñña* intr. adv. in what order? which number?
ባለስንት *balä sənt* intr. adv. at which price?
ስንኝ *sənəññ* rhyme
ስንኳ *sənkʷa or* እንኳ *ənkwa* adv. even, not even, "no!"
ስንደዶ *səndädo* n. thick plaiting reed
ስንዴ *sənde* n. wheat
ስንድድ *səndəd* n. bracelet (*of glass beads*)
ስዊድን *swidən* n. Sweden, Swedish
ስድሳ *sədsa or səlsa* ስልሳ adj n. sixty
ስድሳኛ *sədsañña or* ስልሳኛ *səlsañña sixtieth*
ስድስት *səddəst* adj/n. six
ስድስተኛ *səddəstäñña* adj. sixth
አንድ— *and—* adj. one sixth
ስፖርት *sport* n. sport
ሶለግ ውሻ *solăg wəšša* n. pointer (*kind of dog*)
ሶመሶመ *somässomä* v. cantered
ሶምሶማ *somsoma* n. canter

ሶማሌ *somale* n. somali
ሶማልያ *somalya* n. Somalia
ሶረን *sorän* type of partridge
ሶሻሊዝም *sošalizm* n. socialism
ሶሻሊስታዊ *sošlalistawi* n. socialist

ሸ

ሸለለ *šällälä* v.t. chanted war-chant; v.i. was very smartly dressed; boasted
ሸላይ *šällay* n. chanter of war chant; smartly dressed person; boaster
ሽለላ *šəllala* n. war chant; boast
አሸለለ *aššällälä* v.t. had s/o give war-chant; got s/o smartly dressed
ሸለመ *šällämä* v.t. decorated; gave present to
ሸላሚ *šällami* n. decorator; one who gives present
ሽልማት *šəlləmat* n. present, prize
ሽልም *šəlləm* adj. decorated
ሸላለመ *šälallämä* v.t. decorated over-elaborately
ተሸለመ *täšällämä* v.i. was given a present, prize; was decorated
ተሸላሚ *täšällami* n. prize winner, one who receives a present
ተሸላለመ *täšälallämä* v.i. exchanged presents
አሸለመ *aššällämä* v.t. had s/o given a present, prize
ሸልምልም *šələmləm* adj. black and white stripped; zebra stripped
ሸለምጥማጥ *šälämətmat* n. genet *(geneta abyssinica)*
ሸለሸለ *šäläššälä* v.t. weeded young crops *(with plough between rows)*
ሽልሻሎ *šəlšalo* n. weeding of young crops *(with plough between rows)*
ሸለቀቀ *šäläqqäqä* v.t de-husked *(maize)*
ሽልቅቅ *šəlqəq* adj. de-husked *(maize)*
ሽልቃቃ *šəlqäqa* n. action of de-husking
ተሸለቀቀ *täšäläqqäqä* v.t. was *maize*
አሸለቀቀ *aššäläqqäqä* v.t. had maize de-husked
ሸለቆ *šäläqo* n. valley
ሸለብ አደረገ *šälläbb adärrägä* v.i. dozed off
ሸለብታ *šäläbta* n. doze
አሸለበ *ašälläbä* v.i. dozed, took a nap
ሸለተ *šällätä* v.t. sheared
ሸላች *šällač* n. shearer
ሽልት *šəllət* adj. sheared
መሸለቻ *mäšälläča* n. shearing aid, shears
ተሸለተ *täšällätä* v.i. was sheared
አሸለተ *aššällätä* v.t. had *(a sheep etc.)* sheared
ሸለገ *šällägä* v.t. drew in one's stomach
ሽልግ *šəlləg* adj. drawn in
ሸለፈት *šäläfät* n. foreskin
ሸመቀ *šämmäqä* v.i. had grudge, ill will, resentment; plotted
ሸማቂ *šämmaqi* adj./n. grudging; plotting, ill willed
ሽመቃ *šəmmäqa* n. grudging, ill will, resentment; plotting
ሸመቀቀ *šämäqqäqä* v.t. drew tight *(belt, noose etc)*
ሽምቃቅ *šəmqaq* n. drawstring
ሸምቃቃ *šämqaqqa* n. jumpy, nervous *(person)*
ሸምቀቆ *šämqäqqo* n. noose, lasso
ተሸመቀቀ *täšämäqqäqä* v.i. was drawn tight

ተሸማቀቀ *täšämaqqäqä* v.i. was jumpy, nervous; cringed

ሸመተ *šämmätä* v.t. bought commodities *(especially grain)*

ሸማች *šämmač* n. consumer

ሸመታ *šämmäta* n. market price of grain

ተሸመተ *täšämmätä* v.i. was bought *(grain)*

አሸመተ *aššämmätä* v.t. had bought *(grain)*

ሸመደደ *šämäddädä* v.t. crammed *(commit facts to memory)*

ሸመድማዳ *šämädmaddа* adj./n. *(one)* who walks awkwardly *(usually through bad injury)*

ሽምድምድ *šəmədməd* adj. walking awkwardly, crippled

ተሽመደመደ *täšmädämmädä* v. i. walked awkwardly

ሸመገለ *šämäggälä* v.i. grew old; acted as mediator

ሸምጋይ *šämgay* adj. peacemaker, reconciler

ሽምግልና *šəmgələnna* n. old age; act of mediation

ሽማግሌ *šəmagəlle* n. old man; a peace-maker, reconciler, mediator

አሸመገለ *ašämäggälä* v.t. made *s/o* old. *(work etc.)*

ሸመጠጠ *šämäţţäţä* v.i. galloped furiously; stripped leaves from branch; told complete lies

ሽምጥ *šəməţţ* n. bunch of stripped twigs

ሽምጠጣ *šəmţäţa* n. furious gallop, run

አሸመጠጠ *aššämäţţäţä* v. had *(twig)* stripped

ሸሚዝ *šämiz* n. shirt

*ሸማ *see* ተሻማ *and* ሸም

ሸማ *šämma* n. tunic

ሸማኔ *šämmane* n. weaver

የሸማኔ እቃ *yäšämmane əqa* n. loom

ሸምበቆ *šämbäqqo* n. cane

(material)

ሸረሞጠ *šärämmöţä* v.i. prostituted

ሽርሙጣ *šärmuţa* n. harlot, prostitute; promiscuous person *(male)*

ሽርሙጥና *šərmuţənna* n. prostitution

አሸረሞጠ *ašärämmöţä* v.t. pandered, pimped

ሸረሪት *šärärit* n. spider

የሸረሪት ድር *yäšärärit dər* n. spider web

ሸረሸረ *šäräššärä* v.t. eroded *(with water)*

ሽርሽር *šəršər* adj. eroded

ተሸረሸረ *täšäräššärä* v.i. was eroded

*ሸረሸረ *see* ተንሸረሸረ

*ሸረተተ *see* ተንሸራተተ

ሸረኛ *šärräñña* adj. wicked, mischievous

ሸር *šärr* n. wickedness, mischief

ሸረኝነት *šärräññənnät* n. wickedness, mischievousness

ሸረከተ *šäräkkätä* v.t. ripped, tore apart; ground coarsely

ሽርክት *šərkət* adj. ripped, torn apart; coarsely grounded

ሸረካከተ *šäräkakkätä* v. gashed, tore to shreds

ተሸረከተ *täšäräkkätä* v.t. was ripped, torn; was ground coarsely

ተሸረካከተ *täšäräkakkätä* v.i. was torn to pieces

ሸረደደ *šäräddädä* v.t. derided, talked behind *s/o's* back, mocked

ሸርዳጅ *šärdaǧ* n. backbiter, mocker

ሽርዳዳ *šərdäda* n. backbiting, gossipping *(behind s/o's back)*

ሸረፈ *šärräfä* v.t. broke off *(a piece of s/t)*, pulled out *(milk tooth)*, lost *(tooth)*; changed *(into small money)*

ሸራፋ	*šarafa* n/adj. *(one)* who has lost some teeth
ሽራፊ	*šərrafi* n. segment, piece *(broken off)*
ሽርፋት	*šərrəfat* n. main part *(after piece is broken off)*
ሸራረፈ	*šärarräfä* v.t. broke off *(several pieces)*
ተሸረፈ	*täšärräfä* v.i. was broken off; pulled out; changed *(money)*
ተሸራፊ	*täšärrafi* adj. likely to break off
ተሸራረፈ	*täšärarräfä* v.i. be chipped, broken in several places
አሸረፈ	*aššärräfä* v. i. caused *(s/t)* to be chipped, broken off
ሸራ	*šära* n. canvas
ሸሸ	*šäššä* v.i. ran away
ሸሺ	*šäši* n. fugitive
ሽሽት	*šəššət* n. running away
መሸሻ	*mäšaša* n. place of refuge
አሸሸ	*ašäššä* v.t. took into safety, harboured
አሸሸ	*aššäššä* v.t. helped *(s/o)* run away
ሸሸገ	*šäššägä* v.t. hid *(s/t)*
ሸሻጊ	*šäššagi* n. one who hides
ሽሹግ	*šəššəg* adj. hidden
መሸሸጊያ	*mäšäššägiya* n. hiding place *(for s/t or s/o)*
ተሸሸገ	*täšäššägä* v. i. was hidden
መሸሸጊያ	*mäššäšägyia* n. hiding place *(for oneself)*
አሸሸገ	*aššäššägä* v. t. help s/o hide himself
ሸቀለ	*šäqqälä* v. i. worked, toiled *(manual work, occasionally)*
ሸቃይ	*šäqqay* n. occasional worker, toiler
ሽቀላ	*šəqqäla* n. working, toiling
አሸቀለ	*äššäqqälä* v. t. had s/o work, toil
ሸቀሸቀ	*šäqäššäqä* v. t. poked repeatedly *(e.g. with stick)*
መሸቅሸቂያ	*mäšäqšäqiyä* n. stick, etc. *(used to poke s/t)*
ሸቀበ	*šäqqäbä* v. i. predicted bad luck; rigged a balance *(to give short measure)*
ሸቃቢ	*šäqqabi* n. pessimist; one who falsifies balance *(to give short measure)*
ሽቀባ	*šəqqäba* n. predicting bad luck; rigging a balance
ተሸቀበ	*täšäqqäbä* v.i. was rigged *(scales, balance)*; was wished bad luck
*ሸቀበ	see አሻቀበ
ሸቀን	*šäqän* n. filth
ሸቀናም	*šäqänam* adj filthy
ሸቀጠ	*šäqqäṭä* v.t. retailed
ሸቀጣ ሸቀጥ	*šäqäṭa šäqäṭ* n. retail-goods
ሸቃጭ	*šäqqač̣* n. retailer
መሸቀጫ ገንዘብ	*mäšäqqäč̣a gänzäb* n. retailer's capital
ሸበለለ	*šäbällälä* v. t. rolled up *(carpet, etc.)*
ሽብልል	*šəbləl* adj. rolled up
*ሸበለበለ	**šäbäläbbälä*
ተሸበለበለ	*täšbäläbbälä* v. i. curled
ሸበላ	*šäbäla* adj. tall and handsome
*ሸበረ	see ተሸበረ
ሸበረቀ	**šäbärräqä*
ሽብረቃ	*šäbraqqa* adj. elaborately decorated *(e.g. cloth embroidery)*
አሸበረቀ	*ašäbärräqä* v.t./v.i. adorned, decorated; sparkled *(with decorations)*; was elegant
አሸብራቂ	*ašäbraqi* adj/n. *(one)* who is elaborately dressed, *(place)* which is elaborately decorated
ሸበሸበ	*šäbäššäbä* v.t. ruched,

pleated, *(tailoring)*; wrinkled *(forehead)*

ሽብሽብ *šəbšəb* adj. pleated *(cloth)*

ሽብሽቦ *šəbšəbo* n. pleated dress

አሻበሸበ *ašäbäššäbä* v. swayed gracefully *(dancing)*

ሸበበ *šäbbäbä* v.t. haltered; muzzled

መሸበቢያ *mäšäbbäbiya* n. halter; muzzle

ተሸበበ *täšäbbäbä* v.i. was haltered; muzzled

አሸበበ *äššäbbäbä* v.i. had *(an animal)* haltered, muzzled

ሸበተ *šäbbätä* v.i. got grey *(hair)*

ሽበት *šəbät* n. grey hair

ሽበታም *šəbätam* adj. very grey *(hair)*

ሸበቶ *šäbbäto* adj. grey haired

አሸበተ *ašäbbätä* v.t. caused *s/o* to go grey

ሽብ አደረገ *šäbb adärrägä* v.t. hitched, tied loosely

ሸ·ተ *šätä or* አሸተ *ašätä* v.t. became partly ripe *(peas, beans, maize etc. soft enough to eat)*

እሸት *əšät* n/adj. *(s/t)* just ripe enough to eat *(peas etc.)*

እሸትነት *əšätətnnät* n. part-ripeness *(soft, edible stage)*

ሸተተ *šättätä* v.t. smelt bad, stank

ሽታ *šətta* p. smell

መጥፎ— *mäṭfo*—unpleasant odour

ሽቶ *šətto or* ሽቱ *šəttu* n. perfume

አሸተተ *ašättätä* v.t. smelt

አሸተተ *aššättätä* v.t. got s/o to smell *s/t*

ሸተት አደረገ *šätätt adärrägä* v.t. slid along

ሸተትያ *šätätəyya* n. slide *(smooth slope)*

ሸታታ *šätata* adj. sloping

—መሬት *—märet* n. slopy ground

ሸነሸነ *šänäššänä* v.t. divided up *(land)*; cut into equal slices, parts; pleated *(cloth)*

ሽንሸና *šənsäna* n. division cutting up

ሽንሽን *šənšən* adj. divided, cut up; pleated

ተሸነሸነ *täšänäššänä* v.i. was divided up *(land)*, was cut into equal pieces; was pleated, ruched

አሸነሸነ *aššänäššänä* v.t. had *s/o* divide up, cut up, pleat

ሸነቀረ *šännäqqärä* v.t. forced in, jammed in

ሸነቈረ *šänäqqʷärä* v.t. bored *(hole)*

ሽንቍር *šənqʷər* n. small bored hole

ሸነቀጠ *šänäqqäṭä* v.i. kept fit

ሸንቃጣ *šänqaṭṭa* adj. fit *(in good athletic condition)*

ሸነቈጠ *šänäqqʷäṭä* v.t. whipped, lashed

ሸነተረ *šänättärä* v.t. made rows *(in earth for cultivation)*; made grooves*(water erosion)*

ሽንትር *šəntər* n. groove

ሽንትራት *šəntərat* n. row *(of earth for cultivation)*

ሸነታተረ *šänätattärä* v.t. made many rows; severely eroded

ተሸነተረ *täšänättärä* v.i. was cultivated in rows; was eroded

ሸነከፈ *šänäkkäfä* v.t. hobbled

ሸንካፋ *šänkaffa* adj. hobbled

ሸነደረ *šänäddärä* v.i. was cross-eyed

ሸንዳራ *šändarra* adj. cross-eyed

ሸነገለ *šänäggälä* v.t. comforted *(e.g. child with promises of gifts etc.)*

ሸንጋይ *šängay* n./adj. *(one)* who gives false reassurance

ሽንገላ *šəngäla* n. giving false reassurance; cajolery

ሸነጠ *šännäṭä or* ነሸጠ *näššäṭä* v.t. inspired, aroused great enthusiasm, made excited

ሸና *šänna* v.t. urinated

ሽንት *šənt* n. urine

—ቤት *—bet* n. lavatory

ሽንታም *šəntam* adj./n. incontinent, cowardly *(person)*

መሽኛ *mäšniya* n. chamber pot, container for passing urine

አሸና *aššänna* v.t. had s/o urinate *(child, a sick person)*

ሸንበቆ *šänbäqqo also* ሸምበቆ *šämbäqqo* n. cane *(plant)*

ሸንተረር *šäntärär* n. ridge; escarpment

ሸንተረርማ *šäntärärəmma* adj. ridge like

ሸንኮሎ *šänkällo* n. bucket

ሸንኮር አገዳ *šänkor agäda* n. sugar cane

ሸንዳ *šända also* አሸንዳ *ašända* n. water container; gutter *(spout of roof)*

ሸንጎ *šängo* n. assembly, meeting *(e.g. of village elders)*; parliament

ሸንጎበት *šängobät* n. side of the face

ሸኘ *šäññä* v.t. showed out, saw *s/o* on his way

ሸኚ *šäññi* n. one who shows out, sees *s/o* on his way

መሸኛ *mäšäñña* adj. covering *(letter)*

የመሸኛ ግብዣ *yämäšäñña gəbža* n. farewell party

ተሸኘ *täšäññä* v.i. was shown out, seen on one's way

አሸኘ *aššaññä* v.t. had *s/o* shown out

አሸኛኘት *aššäñañät* n. farewell ceremony

* ሸከመ *see* ተሸከመ

* ሸከረከረ **šäkäräkkärä*

ሽከርክሪት *šəkrkərit* n. hoop wheel, *see also* ተ ከረከረ • አሽከረከረ

ሸካሸከ *šäkäššäkä* v.t. de-husked *(grain etc. in a mortar)*; crushed *(e.g. hops, in a mortar)*

ተሸካሸከ *täšäkäššäkä* v.i. was de-husked, crushed *(in a mortar)*

አሸካሸከ *aššäkaššäkä* v.t. helped another to de-husk, crush *(in a mortar, two-man operation)*

ሸከፈ *šäkkäfä* v.t. arranged neatly, put in order

ሸካፋ *šäkkaffa* n. orderly methodical person

ሽክፍ *šəkkəf* adj. orderly methodical *(e.g. good housewife)*

* ሸካካ *see* አሸካካ

ሸክላ *šäkla* n. clay

—ሠሪ *—särri* n. potter

—ቀለም *—qäläm* adj. light brown

የሸክላ እቃ *yäšäkla əqa* n. earthenware

ሸክሌ *šäkle* n. mule of light brown colour

ሸክም *šäkəm* n. load

*ሸኮረመመ *see* ተሸኮረመመ

ሸኰተ *šäkkʷätä* v.t. scuffed, grazed; *(made hand movement for "stone," "scissors" and "paper" game)*

ተሸኰተ *täšakkʷätä* v.i. played "*stone*, "*scissors*" and "*paper*" hand game

ሸኮና *šäkona* n. hoof

*ሸወረረ **šäwärrärä*

ሸውራራ *šäwrarra* adj. cross-eyed

መንሸዋረር *mänšäwarär* inf. to go cross-eyed

ሸዋ *šäwa* n. Shewa *(name of one of the fourteen Administrative Regions of Ethiopia)*

ሸዬ or ሸዌ ሸየኛ *šäyäňňa* n. Shewan dialect
ሸውሻዋ *šäwšawwa* n. adj. *(one)* who has shallow affections
ሸገሸገ see አሸጋሸገ
ሸጐረ *šägg*ʷ*ärä* v.t. bolted *(e.g. door)*, locked up *(animals in byre, stable)*
  ሽጉር *šəggur* adj. bolted; locked in
  መሸጐሪያ *mäšägg*ʷ*äriya* n. bolt
  ተሸጐረ *täšägg*ʷ*ärä* v.i. was bolted; was locked up
ሸጐጠ *šägg*ʷ*äṭä* v.t. holstered, tucked into *(belt or armpit as gun or knife)*
  ሽጉጥ *šəgguṭ* n. revolver, pistol
  ሽጉጥ አለ *šəgguṭ alä* v.t. hid *o/s* in a confined space
  —አደረገ *—adärrägä* v.t. hid *(s/o, s/t in a confined space)*
  ተሸጐጠ *täšägg*ʷ*äṭä* v.t. hid *o/s*
ሸጠ *šäṭä* v.t. sold
  ሸጠኝ *šäṭäňň* he fooled me
  ሻጭ *šač̣* n. seller, vendor
  ሽያጭ *šəyyač̣* n. sale
  መሸጫ *mäšäč̣a* n. selling place
  ሻሸጠ *šašaṭä* v.t. sold out, sold quickly
  ተሸጠ *täšäṭä* v.i. was sold
  አሻሻጠ *aššašaṭä* v.t. helped in selling, acted as a broker
  አሻሻጭ *aššašač̣* n. broker; salesclerk, salesman
  አሸጠ *aššäṭä* v.t. had s/t sold
ሸፈተ *šäffätä* v.i. rebelled
  ሸፋች *šäffač* adj/n. rebellious, one who rebels
  ሽፍታ *šəfta* n. a rebel
  ሽፍትነት *šəftənnät* n. rebellion
  መሸፈቻ *mäšäffäčä* sanctury, hideout *(for escaped rebels)*
  አሸፈተ *aššäffätä* v.t. had *s/o* rebel
ሸፈነ *šäffänä* v.t. covered, concealed; veiled *(of fog)*
  ዓይን— *ayn—* v.t. blindfolded
  ሽፋን *šəfan* n. cover *(of book etc.)*; cover *(pretence)*; wrapper, casing
  የዓይን— *yä'ayn—* n. eyelid
  ሽፍን *šəffən* adj. covered
  ሽፍንፍን *šəfənfən*. adj. covered, concealed
  መሸፈኛ *mäšäffäňa* n. cover, lid
  ሸፋፈነ *šäfaffänä* v.t. put cover on; tried to conceal, tried to evade the issue
  ተሸፈነ *täšäffänä* v.i. was covered
  ተሸፋፈነ *täšäfaffänä* v.t. wrapped oneself, covered oneself *(with cloak)* etc.; was concealed
  አሸፈነ *aššäffänä* v.t. had s/t covered, wrapped
ሸፈጠ *šäffäṭä* v.t. denied falsely, deceived; broke out afresh *(wound)*
  ሸፋጭ *šäffäč̣* adj. dishonest
  ሸፍጥ *šäfṭ* n. false denial, deception
  ሸፍጠኛ *šäfṭäňňa* n. perfidious
ሸፈፈ *šäffäfä* v.i. had splay-feet
  ሸፋፋ *šäfafa* adj. splay-footed
  መንሻፈፍ *mänšafäf* inf. to be splay-footed, to warp
  አንሻፈፈ *anšaffäfä* v.t. turned one's feet out
  ተንሻፈፈ *tänšaffäfä* v.i. was splay-footed
ሹልዳ *šuluda or* ሹልዳ *šuləda* n. thigh-muscle
ሹሩባ *šurrubba* n. hair style *(tightly plaited)*
ሹርቤ *šurrubbe* n. ṭäg flask *(bərəlle)*
ሹራብ *šurrab* n. sweater
  የግር— *yägər*—n. socks, stockings
  የጅ— *yäğğ*—n. gloves
ሹሮ *šuro* n. thickening *(powdered bean or chick pea, used in wäṭ)*
ሹሮፕ *šurop* n. syrup

ሹካ *šukka* n. fork
ሹክ አለ *šukk alä* v.t. whispered *(in s/o 's ear)*
ሹክክ አለ *šukəkk alä* v.i. acted stealthily, was furtive *(manner)*
ሾካካ *šokaka* n. tell-tale, tale-bearer
አንሿከከ *anšʷakkäkä* v. t. gossiped; bore bad report about s/o
አንሿካኪ *anšʷakaki* adj/n.*(one)* who gossips; tells tales
አንሾካሾከ *anšokäšokkä* v.t. gossiped
ሹዋ አለ *šwa alä* v.i. whooshed *(e.g. grain poured from container)*
ሹጥ *šuṭ* n. tapeworm *(a detached piece)*
ሹጣም *šuṭam* adj. n. one who has tapeworm *(insult)*
ሺ *ši or* ሺህ *ših* adj thousand
ሺህኛ *šihəňňa* adj. thousandth
ሻለቃ *šaläqa or* ሻቃ *šaqa* n. major *(title)*
—ጦር *—ṭor* n. battalion
ሻምበል *šamball* n. captain
—ጦር *—ṭor* n. company
ሺል *šil* n. embryo
ሻ *ša* v.t. wanted, wished
ምን ትሻለህ? *mən təšalləh* what do you want?
ምንም አልሻ *mənəmm alša* I want nothing
ሻለቃ *šaläqa see* ሺ
*ሻለ **šalä*
ተሻለ *täšälä* v.i. improved, was better ,was preferable, was advisable
ተሻለው *täšaläw* felt better; preferred
ተሻሻለ *täšašalä* v.i. improved ameliorated
አሻለ *aššalä* v.t. improvd; ameliorated
አሻሻለ *aššäšalä* v.t. improved, ameliorated; amended, reformed
ማሻሻያ *in* የማሻሻያ ሐሳብ *yämaššašaya hassab* amendment
ሻማ *šama* n. candle,
ሻሞ *šamo* struggle *(to obtain s/t desirable)*
ሻምበል *see* ሺ
ሻምላ *šamla* n. rapier
ሻረ *šarä* v.t dismissed *(from office)*; reversed *(a decision)* impeached; cured *(wound)*
ከሹመት— *käšumät—* v.t impeached; dismissed from office
በዓል— *bä'al—* v.i worked on a holiday
ሹምሽር *šumšər n.* re-shuffle, shake up *(government, administration)*
ሽረት *šərät* n. cure
አሻረ *ašarä* v.t cured; cured of tapeworm
ተሻረ *täšarä* v.i was impeached
የማይሻር የማይለወጥ *yämmayəššar yämmayəlläwwäṭ* hard and fast *(rule)*
አሻረ *aššarä* v.t. had s/o impeached
ሻሽ *šaš* n. head scarf *(usually of fine gauze)*, gauze
ሻሸ *šašc* adj. white in colour *(e.g. cow, horse, clothes)*
ሻቀለ *šaqqälä* v.i. worried, tormented with anxieties, bothered
ሻንቅላ *šanqəlla* n. negro
ሻንቆ *šanqo* n. *nickname for a very dark person*
ሻንጣ *šanṭa* n. suitcase
ሻኛ *šaňňa* n. hump
ሻከረ *šakkärä* v.i. got coarse, rough *(in texture,)* rough, harsh *(sound)*
ሻከር አለ *šakärr alä* v.i. got rather coarse *(in texture)*
ሻካራ *šakara* adj. coarse *(in texture)*
አሻከረ *ašakkärä* v.t. made coarse, rough
ሆድ— *hod —* v.t. disappointed, antagonised,

	caused *(s/o)* to bear a grudge
ሻኩራ	*šakʷəra* n. censer decoration *(usually small bells)*
ሻይ	*šay* n. tea
—ቤት	*—bet* n. tea house
*ሻገረ	*see* ተሻገረ
ሻገተ	*šaggätä* v.i. went mouldy
ሻጋታ	*šagata* n. mould; caries
አሻገተ	*ašaggätä* v.t. caused *s/t* to go mouldy
ሻግያ	*šagəyya* adj. extremely dark *(person, insult)*
ሻጠ	*šaṭä* v.t. forced in *(bayonet etc.)*
ተሻጠ	*täšaṭä* v.i. was forced in
ሻፈደ	*šaffädä* v.i. felt aroused *(sexually)*
ሻፋዳ	*šafada* adj. highly aroused *(sexually)*
አሻፈደ	*ašaffädä* v.t. aroused *(sexually)*
ሼክ	*šek* n. sheik
ሽሀር	*šəhar* n. heifer
ሽል	*šəl also* ሺል *šil* n. embryo
ሽልጦ	*šəlləṭo* n. black bread
ሽመላ	*šəmäla* n. stork
ሽመል	*šəmäl* n. bat *(stick)*; bamboo, cane
ሽምብራ	*šəmbərra or* ሽንብራ *šənbəra* n. chick-pea
—ዱቤ	*dubbe* n. chick-pea *(large)*
ሽር አለ	*šərr alä* was smartly dressed
ሽሩሩ	*šəraru or* ሹሩሩ *šururu or* እሹሩሩ *əššəruru* n. lullaby
ሽርሽር	*šərrəšərr* n. walk *(for pleasure)*; pleasure trip
ሽርጥ	*šərraṭ* n. apron
አሸረጠ	*äšärräṭä* v.t. put on, wore *(apron)*
ሽርካ	*šərka* n. partner, associate, *also* ሸሪክ
ሽባ	*šəba* adj. lame
ሽብልቅ	*šəbälləq* n. wedge *(used in splitting logs)*
ሽብር	*šəbbər* n. terror
ሽቦ	*šəbo* n. wire
ሽንብራ	*šənbra or* ሽምብራ *šəmbəra* n. chick-pea
ሽንት	*šənt* n. urine *see* ሸና
ሽንኩርት	*šənkurt* n. onion
ቀይ—	*qäyy—* n. onion
ነጭ—	*näčč—* n. garlic
ሽንጥ	*šənṭ* n. waist-line
ሽንጣም	*šənṭam* adj. long-waisted
ሽንፍላ	*šənfəlla* n. rumen *(second stomach of ruminating animals)*
ሽክና	*šəkkənna* n. drinking gourd
ሽክ አለ	*šəkk alä* v.i. was smartly dressed *(chic)*
ሽኮኮ	*šəkokko* n. rock hyrax
ሽው አለ	*šəww alä* v.i. whispered *(light breeze, wind)*
ሽውታ	*šəwwəta* n. sudden attack of sickness
ሽፋል	*šəfal* n. eye-brow
ሽፍ አለ	*šəff alä* v.i. came out in a rash
ሽፍታ	*šəffəta* n. rash
ሾለ	*šolä* v.i. tapered, grew to a point
ሹል	*šul* adj. pointed
ሹልአፍ	*šul'af* adj. talkative
አሾለ	*äšolä* v.t. sharpened, made tapered
ሾለከ	*šolläkkä* v.t. passed through; found one's way out
ሾላካ	*šollaka* n. adj. inquisitive *(person)*; nosey-parker
መሿለኪያ	*mäšʷaläkiya* n. opening
አሾለከ	*ašolläkä* v.i. helped *s/o* squeeze out *(through narrow opening)*; smuggled *s/t* out
መሹለኪያ	*mäšuläkiya* n. bolt-hole; escape hole
አሾለከ	*aššolläkä* v.t. smuggled *(s/t.)* helped *(s/o)* out
ተሹለከለከ	*täšuläkälläkä* v.t. wriggled out, through
ሾላ	*šola* n. fig tree, fig *(fucus sycomorus)*
ሾመ	*šomä* v.t. promoted, gave rank

ሿሚ *šʷami* n. one who promotes
ሹመት *šumät* n. promotion, rank
ሹም *šum* n. superior, official
ሹምሽር *šumšər* n. re-shuflle, shake-up
ተሾመ *täšomä* v.i. was appointed, was given rank
ተሿሚ *täšʷami* adj./ n candidate for rank, promotion
ተሿሿመ *täšʷašʷamä* v. t. honoured each other, promoted each other
አሾመ *aššomä* v.t. had *(s/o)* appointed, promoted
ሾርባ *šorba* n. soup, bouillon
ሾቀ *see* አሾቀ
ሾተል *šotäl* n. sword
ሾከከ *šokkäkä* v.i. acted stealthily cf. ሹክክ አለ
ሾካካ *šokaka* adj. tell-tale, tale-bearer
ሾጠጠ *šoṭṭäṭä* v.i. was wedge-shaped, tapered
ሾጣጣ *šoṭaṭa* adj. wedge-shaped
ሾጥ አደረገ *šoṭṭ adärrägä* v.t. whipped, struck sharply
*ሾረ *see* አሾረ

—ቀ—

ቀለህ *qäläh* n. cartridge *(spent)*
ቀለለ *qällälä* v.i. became light, lost weight; acted disrespectfully
ቀለል አለ *qäläll alä* v.i. became rather light
ቀላል *qällal or* ቀሊል *qälil* adj. light; disrespectful
ቅሌት *qəllet* n. disrespect, scandal
ቅሌታም *qəlletam or* ቅሌተኛ *qəletäñña* adj. disrespectful, scandalous
አቀለለ *aqällälä* v.t. made lighter, simplified
ተቃለለ *täqullälä* v.i. was made lighter, was simplified; became notorious
አቃለለ *aqqällälä* v.t. oversimplified, made completely light
ቀለመ *qällämä* v.i. became coloured, tinted
ቀለም *qäläm* n. colour, tint; ink
ኅብረ— *həbrä—* n. colour harmony
የቀለም አባት *yäqäläm abbat* n. teacher. Master
ቀለም ነከረ *qäläm näkkärä* v.t. dyed
—ቀባ *—qäbba* v.t. painted
—አገባ *—agäbba* v.t. dyed
አቀለመ *aqällämä* v.t. coloured dyed, tinted
ማቅለሚያ *maqlämiya* n.dye, tint
ቀለሰ *qälläsä* v.t. stooped, bent down
ቤት— *bet—* v.t. built a small house
ቅልስልስ *qəlsləs* adj. bashful
ቀላለሰ *qälalläsä* v.t. erected a small house in haste
ተቀለሰ *täqälläsä* v.i. was erected *(a house)* hastily
አስቀለሰ *asqälläsä* v.t. had a small house erected in haste
ቀለበ *qälläbä* v.t. fed *(people)*, provided board
ቀለብተኛ *qälläbtäñña* n. boarder
ቀለብ *qälläb* n. board, full-board; provisions *(for journey)*
ቀላቢ *qällabi* n. landlady; housekeeper
ቅልብ *qəlləb* adj. fattened up *(animals)*

ቀሰሰ *qässäsä* be ordained priest, become a priest
[See ቄስ, ቀሲስ, ቅስና]

ቀለበ *qälläbä* catch in midair (ball or a falling object)

ቀለበ *qälläbä* (B) feed (oxen), provide support, nourish
ቀለብ *qälläb* food supplies, rations, stipend
የቤት ፡ ቀለብ supplies (of food)
የቤት ፡ ቀላቢት *yäbet qällabit* housekeeper

ቀልብ *qälb* mind, intelligence, power of reasoning
ቀልበ ፡ ቢስ scatterbrain
ቀልባም *qälbam* prudent

ቃሊብ *qalib* mold (casting)

ቀለበሰ *qäläbbäsä* turn down (the collar)

ቀለበት *qäläbät* ring (finger ring), loop
የቀለበት ፡ ጣት ring finger

ቃልቻ *qalləčča* magician

ቆለኛ, see ቈላ

ቀላዋጭ *qälawač̣* one who goes from house to house to get food, parasite

ቀለደ *qällädä* (B) joke, have fun, play a joke on, make fun of, trifle, kid, tease
ተቃለደ *täqallädä* joke with each other, joke with people
ቀልድ, see below

ቀላድ *qälad* rope serving to measure land, land that is measured

ቀልድ *qäld* joke, fun, jest, mockery, farce, wit, humor (see ቀለደ)
ቀልደኛ *qäldäñña* joker, witty, jocular
ቀልደኛ ፡ ነህ no kidding, are you kidding?
ቀልደኛነት *qäldäññannät* sense of humor

ቀለጠ *qälläṭä* melt, vi. (of butter, of metal), liquefy, vi. (of butter), be animated (applause), to be in quantity (of an item)
አቀለጠ *aqälläṭä* liquefy, vt. (butter), smelt (ore), melt (vt.), thaw (the ice), cause to resound
የቀለጠ *yäqälläṭä* molten (metal)
የቀለጠ ፡ ሀብታም very rich
ማቅለጫ *maqläč̣a* melting pot
መቅለጫ *mäqläč̣a*, in የብረት ፡ መቅለጫ foundry

ቅልጥም *qəlṭəm* marrow, shin, shinbone, shank

ቀለጠፈ *qäläṭṭäfä* hasten (vi.), hurry (vi.), make haste, be quick in doing something
አቀለጠፈ *aqäläṭṭäfä* make to hasten, hasten (vt.)
ቀልጣፋ *qälṭaffa* quick, rapid, fast, swift, supple, deft, nimble (acrobat), agile, dexterous, handy, skillful, efficient, expeditious, facile (writer)
ቅልጥፍና, see below
አቀላጥፎ *aqqälaṭfo* fluently
የቀለጠፈ *yäqäläṭṭäfä* limber (piano player)

ቅልጥፍና *qəlṭəfənna* dispatch (promptness), dexterity, efficiency, skill (facility); see ቀለጠፈ
ቅልጥፍና ፡ ጐደለው be clumsy
በቅልጥፍና skillfully

ቁልጭ ፡ ቁልጭ ፡ አለ *qulləč̣č̣ qulləč̣č̣ alä* light up (of eyes); see *ቈለጨለጨ

*ቈለጨለጨ, ተቍለጨለጨ *täqʷläč̣älläč̣ä* blink repeatedly (of eyes); see ቁልጭ

*ቀላፋ, አንቀላፋ *anqälaffa* doze, fall asleep
እንቅልፍ *ənqəlf* sleep (n.)

ቁልፍ *qulf* key, button, snap (of dress); see ቈለፈ
ቁልፍ ፡ ሠራተኛ locksmith
ቁልፍ ፡ ያዥ custodian, guard (see ያዘ)

የቁልፍ ፡ ቀዳዳ keyhole
የቁልፍ ፡ እናት lock
የቁልፍ ፡ ጋን lock
መርፌ ፡ ቁልፍ safety pin
የእጅጌ ፡ ቁልፍ cuff link

ቈለፈ *qʷälläfä* (B) lock (vt.), close with a key, buckle, button, hook (a dress), fasten
ተቈለፈ *täqʷälläfä*, passive of the preceding; lock (vi.)
ተቈላለፈ *täqʷälalläfä* be locked together (bumpers)
አቈላለፈ *aqqʷälalläfä* interlace (vt.), couple together (two cars)
ቁልፍ, see above
መቈለፊያ ፡ ጋን *mäqʷälläfiya gan* lock

ቀማ *qämma* (B) rob, take by force, carry away by force, snatch from the hand
†ቀማኛ *qämmaňňa* brigand, robber

*ቀማ, አቅማማ *aqmamma* falter (hesitate), play with the idea of doing something

ቁም *qum*, see ቆመ
ቁም ፡ ለቁም lengthwise
ቁም ፡ ሣጥን cupboard, cabinet, wardrobe (closet)
(ባለመሳቢያ ፡ ቁም ፡ ሣጥን chest of drawers)
ቁም ፡ ነገር worthwhile thing, important matter, significance, serious matter, basic thing, essential thing
ቁም ፡ ነገር ፡ አለው carry weight
ቁም ፡ ነገረኛ trustworthy (person), dutiful (person)
ቁም ፡ ጸሐፊ scribe, calligrapher
(የ)ቁም ፡ ጽሕፈት calligraphy
በቁሙ in his lifetime
በቁሙ ፡ ቀረ be unchanging, be constant

ቂም *qim* resentment, grudge, rancor, ill feeling, revenge (see *ቀየመ)
ቂም ፡ በቀል vengeance, feud
ቂም ፡ ያዘ nurse a grudge

ቂመኛ *qimäňňa* vindictive, person who holds a grudge

ቃመ *qamä* swallow without chewing, eat powdery things (roasted grain, sugar) from the hand

ቆመ *qomä* stop (vi.), be erected, stand, stand up, halt (vi.), come to a halt, cease, land (of a ship), be under way (of market)
(ቆማ ፡ ቀረች she is an old maid)
አቆመ *aqomä* stand something up, erect (a monument), raise, bring to rest, arrest (stop), put an end to, stop (vt.), bring to a stop, halt (vt.), park (a car), settle (an argument)
ተቃወመ *täqawwämä* be against, oppose, be opposed to, hinder, protest, resist, object, raise an objection, contradict, dissent, disapprove, take issue with, defy (the authority)
ተቋቋመ *täqʷaqʷamä* be established, be founded, be set up, be constituted, come into being, withstand (oppose), defy, resist, fight against, counter, cope with, come to grips with (a problem)
አቋቋመ *aqqʷaqʷamä* establish, set up (a business), situate, build (a factory), found (a bank), organize (a committee)
ቆም ፡ አለ *qomm alä* pause (v.)
ቁም, see above
ቋሚ *qʷami* permanent, steady (work), salaried (employee), skeleton (of building)
(ቋሚ ፡ ሥራ career)
(ቋሚ ፡ ንብረት immovable property
ቁመት, see below
አቋም *aqʷam* stand (position), standpoint, approach (attitude), structure (of human body, of organization), makeup, framework, bearing (manner)
ተቃዋሚ *täqawami* opponent, dissident
ተቃውሞ *täqawmo* opposition, ob-

jection, protest, resistance, disapproval (expression against)
(ካላንዳች ፡ ተቃውሞ unopposed; see አንዳች)
መቃወም mäqqawäm opposition
(በመቃወም against, in opposition)
መቋቋም mäqqʷaqʷam, in የመቋቋም ፡ ኀይል resistance (power of resisting)
መቋሚያ mäqʷamiya prayer stick
መቆሚያ, see above

ቀመለ *qämmälä* be filled with lice; (B) remove lice
ቅማል *qəmal* louse

ቀመመ *qämmämä* (B) add condiments, add spices, season (v.)
ቀማሚ *qämmami*, in መድኀኒት ፡ ቀማሚ druggist, pharmacist
ቅመም, see below

ቅመም *qəmäm* spice, condiment, seasoning (see ቀመመ)
ቅመማ ፡ ቅመም *qəmäma qəmäm* all kinds of spices, ingredients, seasoning
ቅመም ፡ የሌለው bland (food)
ቅመም ፡ የበዛበት —*yäbäzzabbät* spicy

ቀመረ *qämmärä* reckon (time)

ቁማር *qumar* gambling, game of chance
ቁማር ፡ ተጫወተ gamble (v.); see *ጫወተ
ቁማርተኛ *qumartäñña* gambler

ቀመሰ *qämmäsä* taste, take a taste, eat a little
(ኑሮ ፡ ቀመሰ experience life)
አቀመሰ *aqämmäsä* give someone something to taste

ቀሚስ *qämis* gown, dress (of woman)
ጉርድ ፡ ቀሚስ skirt

ቀመቀመ *qämäqqämä* hem (v.)
ቅምቅማት *qəmqəmat* hem (n.)

ቀምበር, see ቀንበር

ቁመት *qumät* size (of a person), height (of man), stature (see ቆመ)

ቀማኛ *qämmañña* robber, brigand (see ቀማ)
ቀማኛነት *qämmaññannät* robbery
ቂመኛ, see ቂም

*ቀመጠ, ተቀመጠ *täqämmäṭä* (B) sit, sit down, seat oneself, settle (vi.), sojourn, mount (a horse, mule), ascend (the throne), be put away (set apart), be set aside
አስቀመጠ *asqämmäṭä* place, seat, make to sit, lay, set apart, set aside, save, put aside, keep (reserve), store, deposit, purge (of medicine)
የቅምጥ *yäqəmməṭ* sitting, seated
መቀመጫ *mäqqämäča* seat
ማስቀመጫ *masqämmäča* container, depository, repository, saucer
ተቅማጥ, see below
ተቀማጭ *täqämmač* resident, reserve (saved money), savings deposit
አቀማመጥ *aqqämamäṭ* manner of sitting, seating, location, placement, situation (position), layout
የሚያስቀምጥ ፡ መድኀኒት *yämmiyasqämməṭ mädhanit* purgative

ቁምጣ *qumṭa* shorts, short trousers

ቆመጥ *qomäṭ* cudgel

ቆማጣ *qomaṭa*, ቈማጣ *qʷämaṭa* leper, leperous, maimed by leprosy
ቁምጥና *qumṭənna* leprosy

ቀረ *qärrä* be left, remain, be missing, be absent, absent oneself, stay away, be cancelled (meeting), be omitted, be no longer in existence, go out of use, die out (of custom), be called off
(ኋላ ፡ ቀረ stay behind)
(ወደ ፡ ኋላ ፡ ቀረ be slow (of watch), be backward, lag)
(እንደወጣ ፡ ቀረ he never returned, he is still missing)

አስቀረ *asqärrä* make remain, leave, leave out, abolish, exclude, cancel, omit (details), deprive, prevent (keep from happening), keep out (vt.), keep aside (vt.), hold back (vt.), put an end to, waive
(ወደ ፡ ኋላ ፡ አስቀረ cause to lag behind)
ቀርቶ *qärto* let alone, leaving aside
(ሌላው ፡ ቀርቶ to say nothing of others)
ቢቀረው *biqäräw*, in አንድ ፡ ቀን ፡ ቢቀረው one day before
ቢቀር *biqär*, in ሌላው ፡ ቢቀር let alone
ሳይቀር *sayqär*, in አንድም ፡ ሳይቀር without exception
ቀሪ *qäri* balance, remainder, residual
ቀሪ ፡ ገንዘብ balance
ቅሬት, see below
የቀረ *yäqärrä* absent (adj.), extinct, rest (remaining), remnant
የቀረው ፡ ቢቀር at least, at worst
የማይቀር *yämmayəqär* unavoidable
ል + imperfect + ምንም ፡ አልቀረውም come to the point of doing something, almost, nearly
ስ + negative imperfect + አይቀርም be liable to, most probably (as in ሳይመጣ ፡ አይቀርም he will most probably come, he may come)
[See also በቀር, በተቀር, በስተቀር, ይቅር, ይቅርታ]

*ቀራ, see ቀራራ

ቁራ *qura* crow, raven

ቁር *qur*, in የራስ ፡ ቁር helmet

ቃር *qar* heartburn

ቄራ *qera* slaughterhouse

ቅር ፡ አለ(ው) *qərr alä(w)* be discontented, be disappointed, be sore (vexed), feel amiss, have misgivings, have ill will
ቅር ፡ አሰኘ *qərr assäññä* disappoint, be disappointing, dissatisfy, hurt one's feelings, irk, make gloomy, slight, chagrin, depress, make resentful
ቅር ፡ ተሰኘ *qərr täsäññä* be dissatisfied, be disenchanted, feel aggrieved, be chagrined, be resentful
ቅሬታ, see below

ቃረመ *qarrämä* glean, pick up (information)

*ቀራራ, አቅራራ *aqrarra* sing a battle song
ቀረርቶ *qärärto* war cry, battle song

ቁርስ, see ቈረሰ

ቅርስ *qərs* heritage, heirloom, legacy, relic

ቈረሰ *q*ʷ*ärräsä* tear off a portion (of bread and other things), cut bread
ቁርስ *qurs* breakfast
ቁራሽ *qurraš* piece (of bread)

*ቀረሸ, አቀረሸ *aqäräššä* regurgitate

ቁራሽ, see ቈረሰ

ቅርሽም ፡ አለ *qəršəmm alä* crack, vi. (of branch)

ቀረቀረ *qäräqqärä* bolt (the gate), bar (the gate)
ተቀረቀረ *täqäräqqärä* be wedged, be lodged (be caught), get stuck (get caught), be jammed

ቈረቈረ *q*ʷ*äräqq*ʷ*ärä* found (a city), establish (a city)

ቈረቈረ *q*ʷ*äräqq*ʷ*ärä* cause discomfort (e.g. lumpy bed)

*ቈረቈረ, ተንቈረቈረ *tänq*ʷ*äräqq*ʷ*ärä* exude, pour down (of sweat)
አንቈረቈረ *anq*ʷ*äräqq*ʷ*ärä* pour water in a thin stream, decant
ማንቈርቈሪያ *manq*ʷ*ärq*ʷ*äriya* pitcher

ቆርቆሮ *qorqorro* tin, tin can, corrugated iron
ቆርቆሮ ፡ መክፈቻ can opener
ቆርቆሮ ፡ ቤት house with tin roof

በቆርቆሮ ፡ አሸገ can (food)
የቆርቆሮ ፡ ምግብ canned food

ቀረቀበ *qäräqqäbä* join two packs into a single load before putting them on the pack animal, tie up a load
ቅርቃብ *qərqab* load, pack

ቅራቅንቦ *qəraqənbo* odds and ends

ቈረቈዘ *qʷäräqqʷäzä* fail to grow (of grain), be dwarfed, be stunted
አቈረቈዘ *əqʷäräqqʷäzä* dwarf, vt. (of diet), stunt

ቀረበ *qärräbä* approach, come close, come near, be near, appear (stand before an authority), come forward, be presented to, be served (food), be submitted (bill, resolution)
አቀረበ *aqärräbä* present, offer, bring near, put forward, serve (dinner), convey (greetings), introduce (a bill), submit (a proposal), bring to the attention of (see also ሐሳብ)
ተቃረበ *täqarräbä* near (vi.), come near, approach, approximate
አቃረበ *aqqarräbä* bring together
ተቀራረበ *täqärarräbä* be in close vicinity, be about the same
አቀራረበ *aqqärarräbä* bring together, cause to come to a rapprochement
†ቅርብ *qərb* near (adj.), shallow
መቀራረብ *mäqqäraräb* affinity
ማቅረቢያ *maqräbiya* tray, serving tray
አቀራረብ *aqqäraräb* presentation
አቅራቢያ, see below

ቅርብ *qərb* near (adj.), shallow (see ቀረበ)
በቅርብ recently, close by, closely
በቅርቡ before long, recently, lately, shortly, soon, closely
በቅርብ ፡ ጊዜ recently, shortly, soon
ከቅርብ ፡ ጊዜ ፡ ወዲህ lately, recently
የቅርብ recent, close (friend), intimate (friend)
(የ)ቅርብ ፡ ዘመድ close relative
የቅርብ ፡ ጊዜ recent
ቅርብነት *qərbənnät* neighborhood (nearness), vicinity

ቈረበ *qʷärräbä* receive holy communion
አቈረበ *aqʷärräbä* administer the communion
ቍርባን, see below

ቍርበት *qurbät* tanned hide used as a sleeping mat

ቍርባን *qurban* holy communion, eucharist (see ቈረበ)
የቍርባን ፡ ሥነ ፡ ሥርዓት sacrament of communion

ቅርብነት, see ቅርብ

ቅሪት *qərrit* remainder (see ቀረ)
ቅሪት ፡ አካል fossil

ቅሬታ *qərreta* discontent, resentment, displeasure, disappointment, chagrin, grievance, breach (in friendship); see ቅር ፡ አለ
የቅሬታ reproachful

*ቀረነ, ተቃረነ *täqarränä* go against, clash (of stories), be irreconciliable, contradict, conflict with
ተቃራኒ *täqarani* opponent, opposite, contrary (term), conflicting, converse, inverse, reverse, counterpart, antipode, antithesis
ተቃራኒነት *täqaraninnät* contradiction, opposition, discrepancy (between two accounts)
መቃረን *mäqqarän* contradiction

ቅርንጫፍ *qərənčaf* bough, branch (of tree, of a company), subsidiary (of a company), chapter (of an association)

ቅርንፉድ *qərənfud* clove
የቅርንፉድ ፡ ምስማር screw

ቈረኘ *qʷäräññä* bind, attach, shackle
አቈራኘ *aqqʷäraññä* tie (prisoner to guard), bind (to a job)
ተቈራኘ *täqʷäraññä* be tied (prisoner to guard)
(በካቴና ፡ ተቈራኘ be shackled)
(ከአልጋ ፡ ተቈራኘ be bedridden)

ቁራኛ *quraňňa*, in በዓይን ፡ ቁራኛ ፡ ተመለከተ keep an eye on
በዓይን ፡ ቁራኛ ፡ ጠበቀ keep under surveillance
የመጽሐፍ ፡ ቁራኛ bookworm
የአልጋ ፡ ቁራኛ bedridden

ቀርከሃ *qärkäha* wicker cane (plant)

ቃሬዛ *qareza* stretcher, litter (stretcher)

ቃሪያ *qariya* green pepper, immature (person)

ቀረጠ *qärräţä* tax (v.), make pay custom duties
ቀረጥ, see below

ቀረጠ, see ቀረጸ

ቀረጥ *qäräţ* tax, taxation, tariff, custom duties (see ቀረጠ)
ቀረጥ ፡ ጣለ tax (v.)
ቀረጥ ፡ ተቀባይ tax collector

ቁርጥ *qurţ* cut, definite, decided, explicit, just like (see ቈረጠ)
ቁርጥ ፡ ሐሳብ resolution, determination, decision
ቁርጡን ፡ ቃል ፡ ልንገርህ let me tell you once and for all
ቁርጠኛ *qurţäňňa* definite, resolute

ቁርጥ ፡ ቁርጥ ፡ አለ *qurrəţţ qurrəţţ alä* come in gasps (breath), be abrupt (speech, words); see ቈረጠ
ቁርጥ ፡ ያለ *qurrəţţ yalä* decisive, downright (answer), firm (price), terse, positive, categorical

ቈረጠ *qʷärräţä* cut, cut down, chop (wood), chop off, hew (logs), cut loose, clip, amputate, disconnect, slice (bread, onions), rupture, determine, decide, fix, make a resolution, make up one's mind, be determined
(ሆዱን ፡ ቈረጠ gripe (of unripe fruit)
(ሐሳቡን ፡ ቈረጠ set one's mind, decide on, resolve)
(ተስፋ ፡ ቈረጠ despair, give up hope, be discouraged, be disheartened)
(ቲኬት ፡ ቈረጠ sell tickets)
(ቈርጦ ፡ ተነሣ *qʷärţo tänässa* set oneself to, have one's mind set on)
(በነፍሱ ፡ ቈርጦ at the risk of his life)
አስቈረጠ *asqʷärräţä*, causative of the preceding
(ተስፋ ፡ አስቈረጠ discourage, deject, dishearten)
(ቲኬት ፡ አስቈረጠ buy a ticket)
ተቈረጠ *täqʷarräţä* discontinue (vi.), be interrupted, cease (vi.), go dead (of telephone)
አቋረጠ *aqqʷarräţä* cut off, break off (relations), cut short (interrupt), discontinue, cease, sever (relations), terminate, cross (a street, border), take a short cut, cut across (a field), traverse
ቈራረጠ *qʷärarräţä* mutilate
ቁርጥ, see above
ቈራጥ *qʷärraţ* resolute, strongminded, determined (person), firm (attitude)
(ሐሳበ ፡ ቈራጥ determined, resolute)
ቈራጥነት, see below
ቁርጠት, see below
ቈራጭ *qʷäraç* one who cuts
(ቲኬት ፡ ቈራጭ ticket seller)
ቁራጭ *qurraç* piece, slice, slab, stub (of pencil), slip (of paper), clipping, butt
ማቋረጥ *maqqʷaräţ* interruption
(ያለማቋረጥ *yalämaqqʷaräţ* perpetually, continuously, regularly, on and on)
መቍረጫ *mäqʷräça* clippers
ማቋረጫ *maqqʷaräça* crossing
ማቋረጫ ፡ ስፍራ crosswalk
ተቋራጭ *täqʷaraç*, in ሥራ ፡ ተቋራጭ contractor
አቋራጭ *aqqʷaraç* cutoff, short cut
የማይቋረጥ *yämmayəqqʷarräţ* constant (ceaseless), continual, perpetual (clatter), persistent
ሳይቋረጥ *sayəqqʷarräţ* constantly, steadily, regularly, without interruption

nation, coherence

ተቀነባበረ *täqänäbabbärä* v.i. was accumulated, compiled, was synthesised *(ideas)*; was coordinated, was organized

አቀናበረ *aqqänabbärä* v.t. accumulated, synthesized, compiled; coordinated; organized *(work)*

አቀነባበረ *aqqänäbabbärä* v.t. accumulated, synthesized, compiled; coordinated; re-organized

አቀነባባሪ *aqqänäbabari* n. compiler; coordinator, organizer

ቀነተ *qännätä* v.t. girded up

ቅናት *qənat* n. girdle

መቀነቻ *mäqännäča* n girth band *(animals)*

መቀነት *mäqännät* n. cloth waist-band

ቀነዘረ *qänäzzärä* v.t. committed fornication, adultery

ቅንዝረኛ *qənzəräñña* n. fornicator, adulterer

ቅንዝር *qənzər* n. fornication, adultery

ቀነደበ *qänäddäbä* v.t. beat, struck *(with stick)*; drank off, drank down

ቀነጠሰ *qänäṭṭäsä* v.t. broke off *(e.g. twig)*

ቅንጠሳ *qənṭäsa* n. breaking off *(e.g. twig)*

ቅንጣሽ *qənəṭṭaš* n. piece broken off

ተቀነጠሰ *täqänäṭṭäsä* v.i. was broken off

አስቀነጠሰ *asqänäṭṭäsä* v.t. had *(s/t)* broken off

ቀነጠበ *qänäṭṭäbä* v.t. cut off *(small piece, e.g. meat)*; brought *(meat)* in small quantities

ቅንጣቢ *qənəṭṭabi* n. small piece *(which is cut off)*

ቅንጥብጣቢ *qənṭəbṭabi* n. pl. small pieces of meat *(cut off)*

ቀነጣጠበ *qänäṭaṭṭäbä* v.t. cut off several small pieces

ተቀነጣጠበ *täqänäṭaṭṭäbä* v.i. was cut off

*ቀነጣ **qänäṭṭä*

ቅንጡ *qənṭu* n./adj. *(one who is)* abandoned, free living, without principle; spendthrift

ቅንጦት *qənṭot* n. free living, luxury

የቅንጦት ዕቃ *yäqənṭot əqqa* n. luxury item

ተቀናጣ *täqänaṭṭa* v.i. felt free *(to do as one pleased)*

ቀነጨረ *qänäččärä* v.i. was stunted *(in growth or development)*

ቀንጫራ *qänčära* adj. stunted

ቀነጨበ *qänäččäbä* v.t, got a story wrong; passed on only part of piece of gossip, information

ቀነፈ *qännäfä* v.t. put between brackets, in parentheses

ቅንፍ *qənnəf* n. brackets, parentheses

ተቀነፈ *täqännäfä* v.i. was put in parentheses, brackets

ቀና *qänna* v.i. straightened up

ቀና *qänna* adj. cooperative, agreeable, good, honest

መልከ— *mälkä—* adj. handsome, good looking

ቀና አለ *qäna alä* v.i. straightened up a little

ቅን *qən* adj. straightforward; good-hearted good-willed

ቅኝ *qəññ* n. colony

—ግዛት *—gəzat* n. colony

ቅንነት *qənənnät* n. straightforwardness, good-heartedness

ይቅናህ *yəqnah* good luck

ቀና አለ *qäna alä* v.i. straight

ened up, looked up

—አደረገ —*adärrägä* v.t. held up *(the head)*; held erect

ተቀና *täqänna* v.i. was sold *(grain etc.)*

ተቃና *täqanna* v.i. was made straight; was successful

እድሉ— *əddəlu*—v.t. was lucky

ተቀናና *täqänanna* v.i. envied each other

አቀና *aqänna* v.t. straightened; raised *(the head)*; colonized

እህል— *əhəl*—v.t. sold *(grain)*

አገር አቀና *agär aqänna* v.t. settled and developed *a country*

አቅኚ *aqňi* n. settler, developer

አገር— *agär*— colonizer *(a country)*, settler

አቃና *aqqana* v.t. rectified, straightened

ቀና *qänna* v.i. became jealous, was envious

ቅናት *qənat* n. jealousy

ቀናተኛ *qännatäňňa* adj. jealous, envious

ቀናኢ *qäna'i* adj. jealous

ተቀናና *täqännana* v.i. envied each other

አስቀና *asqänna* v.t. made *(s/o)* jealous

ቀን *qän* n. day; time

የቀን መቁጠሪያ *yäqän mäquṭäriya* n. calendar

ሁል ቀን *hull qän* adv. daily

በቀን *bäqän* during the day

ቀን አለፈበት *qän alläfäbbät* was out of date

—ወጣለት —*wäṭṭallät* it has seen its days

ባለቀን *baläqän* n. one having his "day" *(time of success, power)*

ቀን በቀን *qän bäqän* n. in broad day light, every day, daily

በዐል ቀን *bä'äl qän* n. holiday

ከቀን ቀን *käqän qän* day after day

ከቀን ወደ ቀን *käqän wädä qän* from day to day

ከፉ ቀን *kəfu qän* n. bad time; time of famine

አዘቦት ቀን *azäbot qän* n. working day

በየቀኑ *bäyyäqänu* n. every day

እኩለ ቀን *əkkulä qän* n. mid-day

ቀንበር *qänbär* n. yoke; burden

ቀንበጥ *qänbäṭ or* ቀምበጥ *qämbäṭ* n. tendril, shoot

ቀንዲል *qändil* n. candle stick; annointing of the sick *(unction)*

ቀንድ *qänd* n. horn *(animal)*

ቀንደኛ *qändäňňa* n. ring leader

ቀንድ አውጣ *qänd awṭa* n. snail

ቀንዳም *qändam* n/adj. *(one)* having large horns

የቀለም ቀንድ *yäqäläm qänd* n. inkstand; intellectual

የቀንድ ከብት *yäqänd käbt* n. horned cattle, cattle

ቀንጃ *qänǧa* n. harness mate *(plough oxen)*

ቀኖና *qännona* n. canon *(church)*, repentance

ቀኝ *qäňň* n. right *(direction)*

—እጅ — *əǧǧ* n. right hand; collaborator

ቀኛዝማች *qäňňazmač* n. leader of the right flank

*ቀወለለ *see* ተንቀዋለለ

*ቀወሰ *see* ተቃወሰ

ቀዘቀዘ *qäzäqqäzä* v.i. got cool, cooled down; dropped off *(business)*, was lifeless *(town)*

ቀዘቀዘው *qäzäqqäzäw* felt cold

ቀዝቃዛ *qäzqazza* adj. cold, cool

ቅዝቃዜ *qəzəqqaze* n. coolness

አቀዘቀዘ *aqäzäqqäzä* v.t. cooled, cooled down

ማቀዝቀዣ *maqäzqäža* n. refrigerator

ተቀዛቀዘ *täqäzaqqäzä* v.i. was cool, was chilly

አቀዛቀዝ *aqqäzaqäz* n. coolness

ቀዘነ *qäzzänä* v.t. produced stool, faeces, diarrhea *(small child)*; had loose bowel movement *(adults)*; was extremely cowardly

ቅዘን *qəzän* n. loose faeces, loose stool

ቅዘናም *qəzänam* adj./n. *(one)* who is very cowardly

መቅዘኛ *mäqzäña* n. chamber pot

አስቀዘነ *asqäzzänä* v.t. encouraged *(e.g. child)* to defecate; frightened *(s/o)* extremely

ቀዘዘ *qäzzäzä* v.i. was low-spirited

ቅዝዝ አለ *qəzəzz alä* v.i. felt depressed, uneasy, melancholic

ቀዘፈ *qäzzäfä* v. t. rowed *(a boat)*

ቀዛፊ *qäzafi* adj./n. rower, oarsman

መቅዘፊያ *mäqzäfiya* n. oar

ተቀዘፈ *täqäzzäfä* v.i. was rowed

አስቀዘፈ *asqäzzäfä* v.t. had *(a boat)* rowed

*ቀየመ *see* ተቀየመ

ቀየሰ *qäyyäsä* v.t. surveyed *(land)*; planned, put up a scheme

ቀያሽ *qäyyaš* n. surveyor

ቅየሳ *qəyyäsa* n. surveying *(land)*

መቀየሻ *mäqäyyäša* n. surveyor's measure

ተቀየሰ *täqäyyäsä* v.i. surveyed, planned

አስቀየሰ *asqäyyäsä* v.t. had *(land)* surveyed; had *(s/t)* planned

ቀየረ *qäyyärä* v.t. changed; relieved *(changed)*

ቅያሪ *qəyyari* adj. change

—ልብስ —*ləbs* n. change of clothes

ቀያየረ *qäyayyärä* v.t. changed *(one's clothes, suits)*

ተቀየረ *täqäyyärä* v.i. was relieved *(by a substitute)*; was transferred *(of post)*

አቀያየረ *aqqäyayyärä* v.t. interchanged

ቀየደ *q iyyädä* v.t. hobbled *(an animal)*

ቅይድ *qəyyəd* adj. hobbled

ተቀየደ *täqäyyädä* v.i. was hobbled

አቀያየደ *aqqäyayyädä* v.t. hobbled *(two animals or more together)*

አስቀየደ *asqäyyädä* v.t. had *(an animal)* hobbled

ቀየጠ *qäyyäṭä* v.t. mixed; adulterated

ቅይጥ *qəyyəṭ* adj./n. mixed, adulterated

ቀያየጠ *qäyayyäṭä* v.t. mixed in small quantity; adulterated slightly

ተቀየጠ *täqäyyäṭä* v.i. was mixed; adulterated

አቀያየጠ *aqqäyayyäṭä* v.t. mixed, adulterated *(completely)*

አስቀየጠ *asqäyyäṭä* v.t. had *(s/t)* mixed, adulterated

ቀይ *qäyy* adj. red, *see also* ቀላ

ቀደመ *qäddämä* v.t. overtook, passed s/o in a course of action

ቀደም ሲል *qädämm sil* adv. previously, prior, before

—ብሎ —*bəlo* adv. earlier, previously, prior

ቀደምትነት *qäddämtənnät* n. priority

ቀዳሚ *qädami* adj./n. foremost; overtaker, first *(in rank)*

ቀዳሚነት *qädaminnät* n. priority

ቀዳማዊ *qädamawi or* ቀዳማይ *qädamay* adj. first *(m.)*

ቀዳሚት *qädamawit* adj. first *(f.)*

ቅዳሜ *qədame* n. Saturday

ቀድሞ *qädmo* adv/n. earlier; formerly, in olden times

በቀድሞ ዘመን *bäqädəmo zamän* in former days
ቅደም ተከተል *qədäm täkättäl* priority, one after the other
በቅደም ተከተል *bäqədäm täkättäl* in sequence, one after the other
ቅድሚያ *qədmiya* n. priority
—መንገድ *—mängäd* right of way
በቅድሚያ *bäqədmiya* in advance
ቅድም *qəddəm* adv. earlier
ቅደመ ታሪክ *qədmä tarik* n. pre-history
—አያት *—ayat* n. great grand mother/father
—ዓለም *—aläm* n. before the creation of the world
መቅድም *mäqdəm* n. preface
በቀደም *bäqäddäm* the other day
ተቀደመ *täqäddämä* v.t. was overtaken; was passed in a course of action
ተቀዳሚ *täqäddami* adj./n first, prior
ተቀዳደመ *täqädaddämä* v.t. competed in running
ተሽቀዳደመ *täšqädaddämä* v.t. competed in running
ተሽቀዳዳሚ *täšqädadami* n. competitor *(in running)*
አሽቀዳደመ *ašqädaddämä* v.t. had *(s/o)* compete in running
እሽቅድድም *əšqədəddəm or* እሽቅድምድም *ešqədəmdəm* n. running competition
አስቀደመ *asqäddämä* v. t. gave priority to
አስቀድሞ *asqäddəmo* adv. in advance, previously; already; beforehand
ከሁሉ— *kähullu—* first of all

ቀደሰ *qäddäsä* v.t. sanctified, blessed; said the mass *(liturgy)*
ቀዳሽ *qäddaš* adj./n. officiating priest, deacon
ቅዱስ *qəddus* adj. holy, saint
—ዮሐንስ *—yohannəs* New year *(St. John's Day)*
መንፈስ— *mänfäs—* n. Holy Ghost, Spirit
መጽሐፍ— *mäṣ'haf—* Bible
ቅዱስነት *qəddusənnät* n. holiness, sanctity
ቅዳሴ *qəddase* n. liturgy, Mass
ቅድስት *qəddəst* adj. holy *(f.)*
ቅድስተ ቅዱሳን *qəddəstä qəddusan* n. the Holy of Holies
ቅድስት ሥላሴ *qəddəst səllase* n. Holy Trinity
ንዋየ ቅድሳት *nəwayä qəddəsat* n. church furniture
ቅድስና *qəddəsənna* n. holiness, righteousness, piety
መቅደስ *mäqdäs* n. sanctuary *(of church)*
ቤተ መቅደስ *betä mäqdäs* n. temple
ተቀደሰ *täqäddäsä* v.i. was sanctified, blessed
የተቀደሰ *yätäqäddäsä* adj. sacred, venerable, blessed
አስቀደሰ *asqäddäsä* v.t. had *(s/o)* say the mass; attended the mass
አስቀዳሽ *asqäddaš* adj./n. church goers

ቀደደ *qäddädä* v.t. tore; cut out *(tailor)*; ripped *(clothes)*
ጎህ ሲቀድ *goh siqädd* at dawn
ቀዳጅ ሐኪም *qädağ hakim* n. surgeon
ቀዳዳ *qädada* n. hole, opening
ቀዶ ጥገና *qäddo ṭəggäna* n. operation, surgery
ቅድ *qədd* adj. cut, torn; style of cut *(clothes)*
ቅዳጅ *qəddağ* n. rent
ተቀደደ *täqäddädä* v.i. was torn; told lies
ተቀዳደደ *täqädaddädä* v.i. was torn up
አስቀደደ *asqäddädä* v.t. had *(s/t)* torn; had *(a dress, suit)* cut off

ቀዳ *qädda* v.t. hauled *(water)*; drew water copied from

ቀጂ *qäǧi* adj./n. one who hauls water; one who copies; imitates

ቅጅ *qəǧǧ* adj./n. copy; imitation

ተቀዳ *täqädda* v.i. was hauled *(water;)* was copied

አስቀዳ *asqädda* v.t. had *(s/o)* haul water; had *(s/o)* copy from

ቀጠለ *qäṭṭälä* v.t. continued; joined interconnecting parts together; came next in a series

ቀጣይ *qäṭṭay* adj./n. continuing; next in a series

ቅጣይ *qəṭṭay* n. extension, part connected to, annexed to

ቅጥል *qəṭṭəl* n. extension, part connected to, annexed to

ቅጥልጥል *qəṭəlṭəl* adj. articulated, made up of connecting parts *(e.g. chain, train)*

ቀጣጠለ *qäṭaṭṭälä* v.t. joined several parts together

ተቀጠለ *täqäṭṭälä* v.i. was joined together *(main part to a subsidiary part e.g. extension to cord or wire)*

ተቀጣይ *täqäṭṭay* n. extension piece

ተቀጣጣለ *täqäṭaṭṭälä* v.i. were joined to each other; caught fire *(spreading from one place to another)*

አስቀጠለ *asqäṭṭälä* v.t. had *(s/t)* joined on, connected

ቀጠረ *qäṭṭärä* v.t. employed *(in a job)*, gave appointment *(to meet)*

ቀጣሪ *qäṭari* adj./n. employer

ቀጠሮ *qäṭäro* n. appointment *(for meeting)*

ቅጥረኛ *qəṭräñña* n. employee

ቅጥር *qəṭər* n. employee

ተቀጠረ *täqäṭṭärä* v.i. was employed; was given appointment *(meeting)*

ተቀጣሪ *täqäṭṭari* n. employee

ተቃጠረ *täqaṭṭärä* v.t. made an appointment *(to meet)*

መቃጠሪያ *mäqqaṭäriya* n. rendezvous *(place)*

ተቀጣጠረ *täqäṭaṭṭärä* v.i. made an appointment *(to meet)*

አቃጠረ *aqqaṭṭärä* v.t. acted as a pimp

አቃጣሪ *aqqaṭari* n. pimp

አቀጣጠረ *aqqäṭaṭṭärä* v.t. *have (s/o)* made a rendezvous, appointment *(with s/o)*

አስቀጠረ *asqäṭṭärä* v.t. had *(s/o)* employed

አስቀጣሪ *asqäṭṭari* n. job broker

ቀጠቀጠ *qäṭäqqäṭä* v.t. hammered; bruised, struck repeatedly

ቀጥቃጣ *qäṭqaṭṭa* adj. shivering *(with fear)*; coward

ቀጥቃጭ *qaṭqač̣* adj./n. black smith *(derogatory)*

ቅጥቅጥ *qəṭqəṭ* adj. bruised;

ቅጥቀጣ *qəṭqäṭa* n. hammering, bruising repeated striking

ተቀጠቀጠ *täqäṭäqqäṭä* v.t. was hammered, bruised struck repeatedly

አስቀጠቀጠ *asqäṭäqqäṭä* v.t. had *(iron etc.)* forged; had *(s/o)* beaten repeatedly

ቀጠነ *qäṭṭänä* v.i. became thin; was diluted

ቀጠና *qäṭäna* n. famine

ቀጣና *qäṭana* n. zone, region

ቀጭን *qäč̣č̣ən* adj. thin, slender

ቅጥነት *qəṭnät* n. thinness

አቀጠነ *aqäṭṭänä* v.t. made thin; diluted

አቀጣጠን aqqäṭaṭän n. thinness
ቀጠፈ qäṭṭäfä v.i. told lies
ቀጣፊ qäṭafi n./adj. (one) who tells lies
ቀጣፊነት qäṭafinnät n. lying. perfidy
ቅጥፈት qəṭfät n. lying, perfidy
ቀጠፈ qäṭṭäfä v.t. plucked (e.g. fruit, flowers)
ተቀጠፈ täqäṭṭäfä v.i. was plucked
አቃጠፈ aqqaṭṭäfä v.t. helped (s/o) to pluck
አስቀጠፈ asqäṭṭäfä v.t. had (s/t) plucked
ቀጣ qäṭṭa v.t. punished, chastised, took disciplinary action
ቅጣት qəṭat n. punishment, chastisement, disciplinary action, fine, penalty
ተቀጣ täqäṭṭa v.i. was punished, chastised had disciplinary action taken against
ተቀጪ täqäči n. s/o against whom disciplinary action is taken
መቀጫ mäqqäča n. fine. penality
መቀጮ mäqqäčo n. fine, penalty
መቀጣጫ mäqqäṭača n. exemplary punishment
አስቀጣ asqäṭṭa v.t. had (s/o) punished
*ቀጨለጨለ see ተቅጨለጨለ
ቀጨመ qäččämä v.t. grimaced;
ቅጫም qəčam n. louse eggs. nits
ቅጫማም qəčamam adj./n.(one) infested with nits
አቀጨመ aqäččämä v.t. made (face) grimace
ቀጨሞ qäčämo n. tree (Myrsina Africana) fruit of which is a cure for tape-worm
ቀጨቀጨ qäčäqqäčä v.t. crunched (with teeth), chewed noisily
ቀጨጨ qäččäčä v.t. wasted away, became very thin
ቀጫጫ qäčača adj. skinny (insult)
አቀጨጨ aqäččäčä v.t. made (s/o) very thin, caused (s/o) to waste away
ቀጭኔ qäččəne n. giraf
*ቀጸበ qäṣṣäbä
ቅጽበት qəṣbät n. instant
ከመ— kämä—adv. instantly
ቀፈረረ qäfärrärä v.i. disarranged (hair)
ቀፍራራ qäfrarra adj. disarranged (hair)
ቅፍር qəfərr adj. disarranged (hair)
ቅፍርር አለ qəfrərr alä v.i. became dishevelled, disarranged (hair)
ተቀፈረረ täqäfärrärä v.i. was rumpled, rufiled (hair)
ቀፈቀፈ qäfäqqäfä v.t. hatched
ተቀፈቀፈ täqäfäqqäfä v.i was hatched
አስቀፈቀፈ asqäfäqqäfä v.t. had a hen hatch eggs; had too many children (irony)
ቀፈት qäfät n. belly
ቀፈታም qäfätam adj. big bellied (insult)
ቀፈደደ qäfäddädä v.t. tied very tightly
ተቀፈደደ täqäfäddädä v.i. was tied very tightly
አስቀፈደደ asqäfäddädä v.t. had (s/o) tied; bound very tightly; caused (s/o) to be imprisoned
ቀፈፈ qäffäfä v.t. aroused (people's) suspicion; projected an atmosphere of fear or distaste
ቀፋፊ qäfafi adj. causing fear, suspicion, distate in others
ቀፈፈ qäffäfä v.t. scraped (as in preparing leather); went collecting scraps (begging)
ቀፈፋ qäfäfa n. begging (from house to

house for scraps)

መቅፈፊያ *mäqʃäʃiya* n. scrapping instrument *(e.g. for skins, leather)*

ተቀፈፈ *täqäʃʃäʃä* v.i. was scrapped *(leather)*

ቀፎ *qäʃo* n. bee-hive

ቁልቋል *qulquʷal* n. euphorbia

ቁልፍ *see* ቁለፈ

ቁማር *qumar* n. gambling

ቁማርተኛ *qumartäñña* n. gambler

ቁምጣ *qumʃa* n. shorts *(usually* ቁምጣ ሱሪ *qumʃa surri)*

ቁራ *qura* n. crow

ቁር *qurr* n. helmet

ቁር *qurr* n. frost

ቁርበት *qurbät* n. skin, hide

ቁርበተ አሊም *qurbätä alim* n. umber

ቁርንጫጭ *qurənčʼačʼ* n./adj. kink; kinky

ቁርጥማት *see* ቆረጠመ

ቁቅ አደረገ *quqq adärrägä* v.i. farted, popped off

ቁባት *qubat* n. concubine, mistress

ቁና *qunna* n. grain measure *(straw, holding about 10 kilos)*

- -ተነፈሰ - *-tänäffäsä* v. panted

ቁንዶ በርበሬ *qundo bärbärre* n. black pepper

ቁንጣን *qunʃän* n. over-eating pains

ቁንጣናም *qunʃanam* adj./n. *(one)* who is sick from overeating

ቁጢጥ አለ *quʃiʃʃ alä* v.i. squated

*ቁጣ *see* ተቆጣ

ቁጫጭ *qučʼačʼ* n. black ant *(small, house variety)*

ቁጭ አለ *qučʼčʼ alä* v.i. sat down

ቂል *qil* adj. fool

ቂላቂል *qilaqil* adj. foolish

ቂም *qim* n. grudge

ቂመኛ *qimäñña* n./adj. *(one)* who holds a grudge

ቂም በቀል *qim bäqäl* n. vengeance

ቂም ያዘ *qim yazä* v.t. held a grudge against

አቄመ *aqemä* v.t. held a grudge against

ቂንድ *qind* n. seed pod, bed *(as in maize core)*

ቂንጥር *qinʃər* n. clitoris

ቂጣ *qiʃʃa* n. pan cake, unleavened bread

ቂጥ *qiʃ* n. buttock, bottom

ቂጥኝ *qiʃʃəññ* n. syphilis

ቃል *qal* n. word

ቃለ ጉባኤ *qalä guba'e,* n. minutes *(of a meeting)*

—አጋኖ —*agganno* n. interjection

ቃል ሰጠ *qal säʃʃä* v.i. made solemn declaration, made an affidavit; promised

—ገባ —*gäbba* v.t. gave promise

ቃሉ ተዘጋ *qalu täzzägga* v.i. lost o/s voice

ቃሊብ *qalib* n. mold *(casting)*

ቃልቻ *qalləčʼčʼa* n. soothsayer *(Moslem)*

ቃመ *qamä* v.t. tossed into the mouth; chewed čʼat

አቃመ *aqamä* v.t. gave s/o mouthful

ቃረመ *qarrämä* v. t. gleaned

ቃራሚ *qarami* n. gleaner

ቃርሚያ *qarmiya* n. gleanings

ቀራረመ *qärarrämä* v.t. gleaned; gathered here and there

ተቃረመ *täqarrämä* v.i was gleaned

አቃረመ *aqqarrämä* v.t. helped *(s/o)* to glean

አስቃረመ *asqarrämä* v.t. had *(s/o)* glean

ቃረነ *see* ተቃረነ

ቃሪያ *qariya* n. green pepper

ቃሬ *qarre* n. crest *(of hair, traditional for small boys)*

ቃሬዛ *qareza* n. stretcher

ቃር *qar* n. heart burn

*ቃሰተ *see* አቃሰተ

ቃበዘ *abbäzä* v.t. searched about, looked here and there, got lost, lost o/s way

ቃባዥ *qabaž* n./adj. *(one)*

who gets lost

ቃብድ *qabd* n. down payment, deposit, *also* ቀብዱ *qäbdu*

ቃተተ *qattätä* v.t tried in vain

ቃታ *qata* n. chamber *(gun)*

ቃና *qana* n. taste, flavour *(beverage)*, aroma

—ቢስ — *bis* n. flavourless, non-aromatic

ቃኘ *qaññä* v.t. tuned up; looked around; surveyed

ቅኝት *qəññət* b. tuning up; surveying

ተቃኘ *täqaññä* v.i. was tuned up; was surveyed

ቃዠ *qažžä* v.t. had a nightmare

ቅዠት *qəžät* n. nightmare

ቅዠታም *qəžätam* n./adj. *(one)* who has nightmares; *(one)* who talks nonsense

አቃዠ *aqažžä* v.t. was given nightmares; had nightmares

ቃዲ *qadi* n. a Muslim judge *(for religious affairs)*

*ቃጠለ *see* ተቃጠለ

ቃጣ *qaṭṭa* v.t. pretended, threatened to hit *(s/o)*; made as if to do *(s/t)*

ቃጫ *qaččа* n. sisal

ቃጭል *qačəl* n. small bell *(e.g. mass bell in church)*

ቃፊር *qafir* n. scout *(military)*

ቄራ *qera* n. abattoir, slaughter house

ቄስ *qes* n. priest

ቄሰ ገበዝ *qesä gäbäz* n. church administrator

ቅስና *qəssənna* n. ministry *(of priest)*, priesthood

ቄብ *qeb* n. pullet

ቄንጥ *qenṭ* n. style, fashion, savoir faire *(be—haviour)*

— አወጣ *—awäṭṭa* v.t. mocked *(by imitating)*, mimicked

ቄንጠኛ *qenṭäñña* n./adj. stylish *(person)*

ቄጠማ *qeṭäma or* ቀጤማ *qäṭema* n. sedge

ቅሉ *qəlu in* ቢሆንም ቅሉ *bihonəmm qəlu* adv. nevertheless

ቅሌት *qəllet* n. scandal; loss of face *(dignity)*,

ቅሌተኛ *qəlletäñña* adj. /n. *(one)* who loses face *(dignity)*

ቅሌታም *qəlletam* adj./n *(one)* who loses face *(dignity)*, scandalous

ቅል *qəl* n. gourd

የራስ ቅል *yäras* — n. skull

ቅልሽልሽ አለ *qələšləšš alä* v.i. felt sick

አቅለሸለሸ *aqläšälläšä* v.t. caused *(s/o)* to feel sick

ቅልብጭ አለ *qəlbəčč alä* v.i. was easy to hold, use, was handy

ቅልጥም *qəlṭəm* n. shin; marrow *(of bone)*

ቅመም *see* ቀመመ

ቅማያት *qəmäyat or* ቅድማያት *qədmayat* n. great-grandfather, great-grandmother

ቅምምጦሽ *qəmənməṭoš* n. pick-a-back, piggy-back

ቅምቡርስ *qəmburs* n. blow-fly larva, rootworm

ቅምባጫ *qəmbəčča* n. wicker pot storage pot

—ሆድ *—hod* n. small pot belly

ቅምጫና *qəmčana* n. gourd *(dried for use as container)*

ቅሪላ *qərilla* n. processed hide; adj. shabby *(person)*

ቅርስ *qərs* n. heritage, legasy, relic, antiquity

ቅር አለ *qərr alä* v.i. became discontented

-አሰኘ *-asäññä* v.t. disappointed, hurted *(s/o's)* feeling

ቅሬታ *qərreta* n. discontent

ቅርንጫፍ *qərənčaf* n. branch

ቅርንፉድ *qərənfud* n. clove

ቅርጫት *qərčat* n. basket

ቅርፊት *see* ቀረፈ

ቅስም	*qəsm* n. spirit, vigour
ቅስሙ ተሰበረ	*qəsmu täsäbbärä* v.i. broke *(s/o's)* spirit
ቅስና	*see* ቀሰሰ
ቅባኑግ	*qəbanug* n. noug oil
ቅቢ	*see* ቀባ
ቅብጥ	*qəbṭ* adj. Coptic *(lang.)*
ልሳነ ቅብጢ	*ləssanä qəbṭi* n. the Coptic language
ቅኔ	*qəne* n. poetry
ተቀኘ	*täqäññä* v.t. composed *(poetry)*
ባለቅኔ	*balä qəne* n. poet
ቅን	*qən* adj. good-hearted, straight-forward, good-natured, *see also* ቀና
ቅንቅን	*qənqən* n. moth
ቅንቅናም	*qənqənam* adj. moth-eaten; stingy, mean
ቅንጂላ	*qəndilla* n. loop
ቅንድብ	*qəndəb* n. eyebrow, eyelashes
ቅንጣት	*qənṭat* n. grain *(ear of corn, grain of sand etc.)*
ቅነፍ	*see* ቀነፈ
ቅዝዝ አለ	*qəzzəz alä* v. felt low, melancholic
ቅዝዝታ	*qəzəzta* n. depression, lethargy
ቅዳሜ	*qədame* n. Saturday
ቅድሚያ	*see* ቀደመ
ቅጠል	*qəṭäl* n. leaf
ቅጠልያ	*qəṭäləyya* adj. greenish
ቅጥ	*qəṭ* n. manner, method, system
—የለሽ	*—yälläš* adj. unsystemic
መላ—	*mäla—* n. *usually followed by a negative verb e. g.*
መላ ቅጥ የሌለው	*mäla qəṭ yälelläw* haphazard
ውጥንቅጥ	*wəṭənqəṭ* n. hodgepodge
ቅጠቢስ	*qəṭäbis* n. mishmash
ቅጥራን	*qəṭran* n. tar cf. ሬንጅ
ቅጥር	*qəṭər* n. enclosure, encircle
—ግቢ	*—gəbbi* n. campus
ቅጽ	*qəṣṣ* n. volume
ቅጽበት	*qəṣbät* n. wink
ቅጽል	*qəṣṣəl* n. adjective
ቆለለ	*qollälä* v.t. heaped
ቁለላ	*qulläla* n. heaping up
ተቆለለ	*täqollälä* v. was heaped; pounced on
አስቆለለ	*asqollälä* v.t. had *(s/o)* heaped up
ቆለመመ	*qolämmämä* v.t. bent round
ቆልማማ	*qolmamma* adj. bent-round
ቆላ	*qolla* n. lowland
ቆለኛ	*qolläñña* n. low-lander
ቆላ	*qolla* v.t. roasted *(coffee etc.)*
ጅራቱን—	*ǧəratun—* v.t. wagged the tail
ቁሌት	*qullet* n. degree of roasting
መቍሊያ	*mäqʷəliya* n. pan *(for ensuring coffee etc. roasts evenly)*
ተቆላ	*täqolla* v.i. was roasted
ተቋላ	*täqʷalla* v.t. shot at each other
አስቆላ	*asqolla* v.t. had *(s/t)* roasted, *(coffee etc.)*
አቁላላ	*aqulalla* v.t. stirred up *(onion, fat for wäṭ)*
ማቁላያ	*maqulaya* n. ingredients *(onions, fat, spices)*
ቆሌ	*qolle* n. guardian spirit
—ቢስ	*—bis* adj. undignified
—የራቀው	*—yäraqäw* adj. undignified
ቆሎ	*qolo* n. roasted grain *(e.g. peas, beans, barley, wheat etc.)*
ቆመ	*qomä* v.i. stood up; stopped; halted, came to a halt; ceased, was under way *(of market)*
ቆማ የቀረች	*qoma yäqärräč* an old maid
ቋሚ	*qʷami* n. usher *(banquet etc.:)* adj. permanent, steady *(work)*; skeleton *(of building)*

—ተጠሪ *—täṭäri* n. permanent secretary
—ንብረት *—nəbrät* n. immovable property
ቁም *qum* adj. standing; stopping; head *(of cattle)*
ቁምሳጥን *qum saṭən* n. cupboard, wardrobe, locker
ቁምስቅል አሳጣ *qum səqəl asaṭṭa* v.t. got *(s/o)* mixed up, confused
ቁም ነገር *—qum nägär* n. serious matter
—ነገረኛ *-nägärräñña* n. a serious person
ቁመት *qumät* n. stature, height
ቁመታም *qumätam* adj. tall
ቆም አለ *qomm alä* v.i. paused
መቋሚያ *mäqʷamiya* n. staff *(support, prayer stick)*
አቆመ *aqomä* v.t. erected; stopped *(s/t;)* brought to rest; put an end to, halted; parked *(a car)*
ማቆሚያ *mäqomiya* n. parking place
አቋም *aqʷam* n. standing, status, condition; standpoint; approach *(attitude)*
ተቋቋመ *täqʷaqʷämä* v.t. was established, well-established; resisted *(enemy etc.)*
መቋቋሚያ *mäqqʷaqʷamiya* n. means of resistance
ተቃወመ *täqawwämä* v.i. opposed, objected, protested, resisted, disapproved
ተቃዋሚ *täqawami n.* opponent, dissident
ተቃውሞ *täqawəmo* n. opposition, objection, protest; resistance, disapproval
አቋቋመ *aqqʷaqʷamä* v.t. established, set up *(a business)*, founded *(an organization)*
አስቆመ *asqomä* v.t. had *(s/o)* stand up; stopped *(s/o)*; interrupted
ቆመጠ *qommäṭä* v.t. amputated, cut off
ቁምጣ *qumṭa* adj./n. cut off
-ሱሪ *-surri* n. shorts
ቁምጥና *qumṭənna* n. leprosy
ቁምጥ አለ *qumməṭṭ alä* v.i. fell off; became detached
ቆመጥ *qomäṭ* b. baton, truncheon, stick, cudgel
ቁማጭ *qummač* n. cut-off piece, clip *(cigarette)*, butt
ቁምጥምጥ *quməṭməṭ* adj. cut into many pieces
ቆማጣ *qomaṭa* interj. leper *(gross insult)*
ቆሞስ *qomos* n. elder priest; vicar
ቆረጠ *see* ቈረጠ
ቆረጠመ *qoräṭämä* v.t. crunched
-ቁርጥማት *qurṭəmat* n. rheumatism
ቆሪ *qori* n. wooden mixing bowl
ቆርቆሮ *qorqorro* n. tin; corrugated iron, tin can
ቆርኪ *qorke* n. bottle top *(crown type)*
ቆርኪ *qorke* n. tora harte-beest
ቆሸሸ *qoššäšä* v.i. was dirty
ቆሻሻ *qošaša or* ቁሻሻ *qušaša* n./adj. dirt, rubbish filth, waste matter, litter, dirty, filthy, unclean, impure
አቆሸሸ *aqoššäšä* v.t. made dirty, filthy, littered
አንቋሸሸ *anqʷaššäšä* v.t. belittled, disdained, scorned
ቆሽማዳ *qošmadda* adj. weak; having a small appetite
ቆሽት *qošt* n. rectum
ቆሽታም *qoštam* n./adj. *(one)* who has a small appetite
ቆቅ *qoq* n. partridge
ቆብ *qob* n. skull cap; cap
—ጫነ *—čanä* v.i. became

a monk

ጣለ —*ṭalä* v.t. renounced *(o.s.)* habit *(monk)*

ቆነጀ *qonäǧǧä* v.i. became beautiful

ቆንጆ *qonǧo* adj. beautiful

ቁንጅና *qunǧənna* n. beauty

አቆነጀ *aqonäǧǧä* v.t. beautified, adorned

ቆነጠረ *qonäṭṭärä* v.t. took a pinch of

ቆንጥር *qonṭər* n. bur(r)

ቁንጣሪ *qunəṭṭari* n. pinch, small amount of

ቆነጣጠረ *qonaṭṭaṭṭärä* v.t. took several pinches of

ተቆነጠረ *täqonäṭṭärä* v.t. was pinched, had small pinch taken from

ተቆናጠረ *täqonaṭṭärä* v.i was in ill humor, was grouchy

አስቆነጠረ *asqonäṭṭärä* v.t. had *(s/o)* take a pinch *(of s/t)*

ቆንሲል *qonsil* n. consul

ቆንስላ *qonsəla* n. consulate

ቆየ *qoyyä* v.i. waited, awaited, lingered, remained, was late; lasted; lived long

ቆይታ *qoyyəta* n. prolonged appointment, engagement

መቆያ *mäqoyya* n. snack

ቆይቶ in ቆይቶ መጣ *qoyəto mäṭṭa* he came late

የቆየ *yäqoyyä* adj. old *(food)*; long standing, ancient

አቆየ *aqoyyä* v.t retarded; delayed; kept *(s/t)* back *(for s/o)*; kept waiting, detained *(kept in)*; spared *(put aside)*, preserved

አስቆየ *asqoyyä* v.t. had *s/o* delayed; kept *s/o (waiting)*

ቆዳ *qoda* n. leather, hide

የቆዳ በሽታ *yäqoda bäššəta* n. dermatosis, skin disease

ቆዳው ቂል *qodaw qil* adj., n. apparently naïve *(person)*; *(one)* clever than he seems

—ደንዳና —*dändanna* adj. brave, unassailable *(person)*

ቆጠቆጠ *qoṭäqqoṭä* v.i. smarted, burned

ቆጥቋጣ *qoṭquʷaṭṭa* adj. mean, stingy, tight-fisted

*ቆጠቆጠ **qoṭäqqoṭä*

ቍጥቋጦ *quʷṭqʷäṭo* n. bush

አቆጠቆጠ *aqoṭäqoṭṭä* v.t. sprouted new leaves, sent out fresh shoots

ቆጠበ *qoṭṭäbä* v.t. saved *(money)* economised; was thrifty

ቆጣቢ *qoṭṭabi* n. one who saves; thrifty

ቁጥብ *quṭṭəb* adj. reserved, shy

ቁጠባ *quṭṭäba* n. savings

ተቆጠበ *täqoṭṭäbä* v.t. was saved *(e.g. money)*; refrained

ተቆጣቢ *täqoṭṭabi* adj. refraining

ቆጥ *qoṭ* n. roost, nesting box

ቆፈረ *qoffärä* v.t. dug

ቆፋሪ *qoffari* adj./n. *(one)* who digs

ቁፍር *quffər* adj. dug-out *(place)*

ቁፈራ *quffära* n. digging

ቁፋሮ *quffaro* n. digging

ቁፋሪ *quffari* n. excavated earth

መቆፈሪያ *mäqoffäriya* n. digging aid *(e.g. spade)*

ቆፋፈረ *qofaffärä* v.t. dug here and there

ተቆፈረ *täqoffärä* v.i. was dug

አቋፈረ *aqqʷaffärä* v.t. helped in digging

አስቆፈረ *asqoffärä* v.t. had *(s/t)* dug; had *(s/o)* dig

ቆፈነነ *qofännänä* v.t. became stiff with cold

ቆፈን *qofän* n. stiffness due to cold

ቆፈናም *qofänam* n. one who is stiff with cold; frozen stiff

ቈለመመ *qʷälämmämä* v.t. bent over

ቁልመማ *qulmäma* n. twisting, wringing

ቁልም *quləmm* adj. bent over, round

ተቈለመመ *täqʷälämmämä* v.t. was twisted, wrung

አስቈለመመ *asqʷälämmämä* v. t. had s/t bent round

ቈለቈለ *qʷäläqqʷälä* v. i. went down

ቁልቁል *qulqul* adj. sloping down; adv. downward

ቍልቍለት *qʷulqʷəlät* adj. sloping; n. slope

ቈልቋላ *qʷälqʷalla* adj. inclined, down-ward sloping

አቈለቈለ *aqʷäläqqʷälä* v. i. went downwards,

ቈለፈ *qʷälläfä* v.t. closed, locked; buttoned up

ቈላፋ *qʷällaffa* adj. hook-shaped

ቈላፍ *qʷällaf* adj. uncircumcised *(arch.)*

ቍልፍ *qʷuləf* n. botton; key; padlock

ባልና ሚስት- *balənna mist* —n. press-stud

—ያዥ *—yaž* n. guard, custodian

የቍልፍ ቀዳዳ *yäqʷulf qädada* n. keyhole

መርፌ ቍልፍ *märfe qʷulf* n. safety pin

ቍልፍ *qʷulləf* adj. locked up

ቍልፍ አደረገ *qʷulləff adärrägä* v.t. locked *(s/t)* up

ቈላለፈ *qʷälalläfä* v.t. locked up *(all round house etc.)*

ተቈለፈ *täqʷälläfä* v.i. was locked up, bottoned

ተቋለፈ *täqʷalläfä* v.i. became interlocked

አቋለፈ *aqqʷalläfä* v.t. interlocked, intertwined

አቈላለፈ *aqqʷälalläfä* v.t. intertwined *(in a complex way)*

አስቈለፈ *asqʷälläfä* v.t. had *(s/t)* locked

ቈረመደ *qʷärämmädä* v.i. shrivelled up

ቈርማዳ *qʷärmadda* adj. shrivelled up

ቍርምድምድ *qʷurmədməd* adj. extremely shrivelled up

አቈራመደ *aqqʷärammädä* v.t. caused *(s/t)* to shrivel up

ተቈራመደ *täqʷärammädä* v.i. was caused to shrivel up, was stricken

ቈረሰ *qʷärräsä* v.t. broke off *(bread)*; took breakfast

ቍራሽ *qʷərraš* n. morsel of bread

ቁርስ *qurs* n. breakfast

ቁርስራሽ *qurəsraš* n. left-overs *(food)*

ቆራረሰ *qorarräsä* v.t. broke into pieces *(bread etc.)*

ተቆረሰ *täqorräsä* v.i. was broken into pieces

ተቆራረሰ *täqorarräsä* v.i. was crumbled, broken into many small pieces

አስቆረሰ *asqorräsä* v.t. had *(s/t)* broken into pieces

ቈረቈረ *qʷäräqqʷärä* v.t. hammered; knocked on; tapped; sprang to mind *(s/t bad)*; established *(a town etc.)*

መቈርቈሪያ *mäqʷärqʷäriya* n. hammer, *(s/t)* used as a hammer

ተቈረቈረ *täqʷäräqqʷärä* v. t. was disturbed *(about maltreatment of oneself or others)*; was founded *(town etc.)*

ተቈርቋሪ *täqʷärqʷari* n. sympathiser

አስቈረቈረ *asqʷäräqqʷärä* v.t. had

(a town etc.) founded

ረቈሰ qʷäräqqʷäsä v.t. bullied off *(hockey, polo, gännä.)*

ቈረቋሽ qʷärqʷaš n. first striker of ball

ተቈራቈሰ täqʷäraqqʷäsä v. t. striked simultaneously *(in ball games)*

ርቈዘ qʷäräqqʷäzä v. i. become feeble, emaciated *(through ill health)*, wasted away

ቈርቋዛ qʷärqʷazzä adj. feeble, emaciated

አቈረቈዘ aqʷäräqqʷäzä v. t. cause *(s/o)* to become feeble, emaciated;

አቈርቋዥ aqʷärqʷaž n. exploiter

ረበ qʷärräbä v.i. took Holy Communion

ቆራቢ qorabi n. communicant

የቆራቢ ራት yäqʷärabi rat n. food *(in payment for saying of special Mass)*

ቍርባን qʷərban n. Holy Communion

አቈረበ aqwärräbä v.t. made (s/o) take the Holy Communion

አስቈረበ asqʷärräbä v.t. had (s/o) take Holy Communion

ረኘ *see* አቈራኘ

ረጠ qʷärräṭä v.t. cut, amputated

ሐሳቡን— hassabun— set ones mind, decided on, resolved

ተስፋ— täsfa— lost hope, gave up hope; was discouraged, was disheartened

ቲኬት— ticket— sold ticket

—አስቈረጠ —asqʷärräṭä bought ticket

ቈርጦ ተነሳ quʷärṭo tänässa had one's mind set on

በነፍሱ ቈርጦ bänäfsu quʷärṭo at the risk of his life

ቈራጭ qʷärač adj. n. one who cuts

እንጨት— ənčät— n. s/o who fetches wood

ቈራጣ qʷäraṭa adj. amputated

ቍርጥ qʷuərṭ n. cut off piece; row meat *(dish)*; adj. definite

ቍርጠት qʷərṭät n. stomach-ache

ቍራጭ qurrač n. piece, slice, stub, slab

ቈራጥ qʷärraṭ adj. decisive, daring, resolute, strongminded, determined

ቈረጣ qʷäräṭa n. cutting *(action)*

መቈረጪት mäquračit n. scissors

ቍርጠት quʷrṭät n. stomach ache

መቈረጫ mäquräča n. cutting aid

ቈራረጠ qʷärarräṭä v.t. cut into pieces, chopped down

ቍርጥ ቍርጥ አለ quʷərraṭ quʷərreṭ alä was v.i. abrupt *(speech)*, came in gasps *(breath)*

ተቈረጠ täqʷärräṭä v.i. was cut; was decided

ተቈራጭ täqʷärrač n. maintenance money *(for family while absent taken from salary)*

ተቋረጠ täqʷarräṭä v.i. was discontinued, was interrupted

ተቋራጭ täqʷarrač n. contractor usually with ሥራ—

ተቈራረጠ täqʷärarräṭä v.t. was cut into pieces; was broken off *(relationship)*

አቋረጠ aqqʷarräṭä v.t. interrupted, discontinued used a short cut *(road)*

አቋራጭ aqqʷarač n. short cut *(road)*

አቈራረጠ aqqʷärarräṭä v.t. in-

duced *(s/o)* to break off *(relationship)*
አስቈረጠ *asqwärräṭä* v.t. had *(s/t)* cut, decided
ቈረጠመ *qʷäräṭṭämä* v.t. crunched
ቍርጥማት *qʷərṭəmat* n. rheumatism
ቍርጥምጥም አደረገ *qʷərṭəmṭəmm adärrägä* v.t. chewed to pulp
ቈረጣጠመ *qʷäräṭaṭṭämä* v. t. chewed, ground *(teeth)*
ተቈረጠመ *täqʷäräṭṭämä* v. i. was chewed, was, ground
ቈረፈደ *qʷäräffädä* v.t. became covered with goose pimples; was chapped
ቈርፋዳ *qʷärfadda* adj. covered with goose pimples
አቈረፈደ *aqʷäräffädä* v.t. caused *(skin)* to become goose-pimply
ቈሪ *qʷäri* n. wooden bowl
ቈራ *qʷärra* v.t. made a cut *(wound on skin)*, made a groove
ቁር *qur* n. cut *(wound)*
ተቈራ *täqʷärra* v.i. was cut *(wound)*
አስቈራ *asqʷärra* v.t. had *(s/o)* cut *(e.g. for tribal markings)*
ቈሰለ *qʷässälä* v.i. was wounded
ቍስል *qʷəsəl* n. wound
ቍስለ ሥጋ *qʷəsllä səga* n. body sores
የቈላ ቍስል *yäqolla qʷəsəl* n. running sore; infected wound; ulcer *(external)*
ቍስለኛ *qʷəsläñña* adj. /n. *(one)* who's wounded
አቈሰለ *aqʷässälä* v.t. wounded
ልብ አቁስል *ləbb aqusəl* adj. incorrigible; pestering
አቈሳሰለ *aqʷäsassälä* v.t. wounded a little
ቈሰቈሰ *qʷäsäqqʷäsä* v.i. poked *(the fire)*; started trouble
ቈስቋሽ *qʷäsqʷaš* adj./n. trouble-maker
ነገር— *nägär—* n. trouble-maker; agitator
መቈስቈሻ *mäqʷäsqʷäša* n. poker *(for the fire)*
ተቈሰቈሰ *täqʷäsäqqʷäsä* v.i. was poked *(fire)*
ቈነሰ *qʷännäsä* v.i. stank
ቍናስ *qʷənas* n. stink
ቍናሳም *qʷənasam* adj. stinking
አቈነሰ *aqʷännäsä* v.t. caused to stink
*ቈነቈነ *qʷänäqqʷänä*
ቈንቋና *qʷänqʷanna* adj./n miser*(ly)*
ቈነነ *qʷännänä* v.t. allocated *(rations)*
መቈነን *mäqʷənän* n. ration *(soldiers, monks etc.)*
ተቈነነ *täqʷännänä* v.i. was rationed; looked extremely proud, haughty
ተቈናኝ *täqʷännaññ* adj./n. *(one)* who receives ration; *(one)* who is exteremly proud, haughty
ቈነደደ *qʷänäddädä* v.t. struck
ተቈነደደ *täqʷänäddädä* v.i. was struck
ቈነጐለ *qʷonäggʷälä* v.t. sprouted
ቍንጒል *quʷəngʷəl* n. sprouting beans *(food)*
አቈነጐለ *aquʷänäguʷälä* v.t. sprouted
ቈነጠለ *see* ቆነጸለ
ቈነጠጠ *qʷänäṭṭäṭä* v.t. pinched *(with fingers)*; punished *(children)*
ቍንጢጥ *qʷənṭiṭ* n. pinching
ቍንጠጣ *qʷənṭäṭa* n. pinching
መቈንጠጫ *mäqʷänṭäča* n. pincers, tongs
ተቈነጠጠ *täqʷänäṭṭäṭä* v.i. was pinched; was punished
ተቈናጠጠ *täqʷänaṭṭäṭä* v.t. pinched; had a steady job
አስቈነጠጠ *asqʷänäṭṭäṭä* v.t. had s/o pinched

ቊነጸለ qu"änäṣṣälä v.t. tore, ripped (paper etc.)
ቍንጽል qu"ənṣəl adj. torn up
ቈጠረ q"äṭṭärä v.t. counted, (number)
ቈጣሪ q"äṭari adj./n. (one) who counts; (water eletric-gasmetre) etc.
ቈጠራ qo"äṭära n. counting, calculation
ሕዝብ— həzb— n. census
ቍጥር q"əṭər adj./n. number; knot (e.g. in string
መደበኛ— :nädäbäññu— n. cardinal number
ቁጥር አለ quṭṭərr alä v.i. huddled together
ቁጥርጥር quṭərṭər n. tangle
ቁጥጥር quṭəṭṭər n. supervision
ቈጣጠረ q"äṭaṭṭärä v.t. counted (not accurately), made a rough calculation
ተቈጠረ täq"äṭṭärä v.i. was counted
ተቈጣሪ täq"äṭṭari adj. countable
መቍጠሪያ mäqq"əṭärya n. rosary, prayer beads
ተቆጣጠረ täq"äṭaṭṭärä v.i. supervised; superintended; was entangled (rope, string)
ተቈጣጣሪ täq"äṭaṭari n. supervisor, superintendant
አቈጣጠረ aqq"äṭaṭṭärä v.t. interlocked
አስቈጠረ asq"äṭṭärä v.t. had (s/t) counted; scored (made points in game)
ቈጨ q"äččä v.i. regretted, had feeling of remorse
ቍጭት q"əččət n. regret, remorse
ተቈጨ täq"äččä v.i. had regret, remorse
አስቈጨ asq"äččä v.t. caused s/o to feel remorse
ቍላ q"əla n. penis; clapper (of bell)
ቍልጭ አለ qu"əlləčč alä v.i. was visible, clear lighted up (eyes)
ቍልቋል q"əlq"al n. euphorbia, cactus
ቍረንጮ q"ərän̆čo n. untanned hide, worn out leather
ቍርንጫጭ q"ərənčač n. kink adj. kinky
ቍርጭምጭሚት q"ərčəmčəmit n. ankle
ቍባት q"əbat n. concubine, also እቁባት
ቍንጣን q"ənṭan n. stomach-ache (through over eating)
ቍንጫ q"ənəčča n. flea
ቍንጮ q"ənčo n. pinnacle, summit
ቋሊማ q"alima n. sausage
ቋመጠ q"ammäṭä v.i. was tantilized; had fervent desire
ቋማጭ q"amač adj. tantalized, full of fervent desire
አቋመጠ aq"ammäṭä v.t. tantalized
ቋ አለ q"a alä v.i. made sudden noise, went "crash"
ቋቅ አለ q"aqq alä v.t. felt sick; felt nausea
ቋቅታ q"aqqəqtta n. vomit
ቋቍቻ q"aq"əčča n. impetigo
ቋቋቴ q"aq"ate n. knuckle-cracking
ቋቋቴያም q"aq"äteam adj./n. bony "bag of bones", (thin person)
ቋት q"at n. flour bin (i.. grinding mill)
ቋንቋ q"anq"a n. language
ቋንጃ q"anǧa n. achilles tendon
ቋንጣ q"anṭa n. dried meat; thin person
ቋያ q"ayya n. bush fire, forest fire
ቋድ q"ad n. plaited necklet (cloth, leather for pendent cross etc.)
ቋጠረ q"aṭṭärä v.t. made a knot, stowed away (in pocket etc.); swelled with pus, liquid; blistered
ቋጥኝ q"aṭṭəññ n. rock
ቋጨ q"aččä v.t. plaited, twisted (fringe of šämma)

በ— *bä*— pro. prefix in, at, on, etc. adv. prefix.+ simple imperfect, when, if; +perfect+ ጊዜ when

በሀ ድንጋይ *bäha dənigay* n. limestone

በለስ *bäläs* n. euphorbia, cactus

በለቀጠ *bäläqqäṭä* v.t. prised open, prised apart *(eyelids)*

ባልቃጣ *bälqaṭṭa* adj./n. *(insult)* legs akimbo; immodest *(in posture way of sitting)*

ብልቅጥቅጥ *bəlqəṭqəṭ* adj. legs spread apart, immodest in posture

ተበለቀጠ *täbäläqqäṭä* v.i. was prised open

ተበላቀጠ *täbälaqqäṭä* v.i. sat legs akimbo *(immodesty)*

*በለበለ *see* ተንበለበለ

በለተ *bällätä* v.t. cut up *(animal)*

ብልት *bəllət* n. portion of meat; genitals *(polite)*

—አውጪ *—awči* n. meat cutter; skilled butcher

በለዘ *bälläzä* v.i. tarnished

ብልዝ *bəlz* n. tarnish

ብልዝ አለ *bəlləzz alä* v.i. was tarnished

አበለዘ *abälläzä* v.t. caused *(s/t)* to become tarnished

በለገ *bällägä* v.i. rained *(small rains)*

ብላጊ *bəllagi* n. little rains

በልግ *bälg* n. little rains *(April-May)*; small rainy season

በለጠ *bälläṭä* v.t. exceeded; surpassed

በለጥ አለ *bäläṭṭ alä* v.t. exceeded, surpassed *(somehow)*

በላጭ *bälač̣* adj./n. exceeding, surpassing

ቢበልጥ *bibälṭ* at the most

ብልጥ *bəlṭ* adj. cunning, shrewd, smart, astute, crafty

ብልጣ— *bəlṭa*— adj. cunning, crafty, smart aleck

ብልጠት *bəlṭät* n. cunning, subtlety

ብልጫ *bəlča* n. excess; superiority

የበለጠ *yäbälläṭä* adj. adv. best

ከሁሉ— *kähullu*— more than

ተበለጠ *täbälläṭä* v.i. was fooled

ተበላለጠ *täbälalläṭä* v.i. competed with each other; surpassed one other; was unequal in status; varied; was not of the same height or age

ተበላላጭ *täbälalač̣* adj. surpassing one another

ተብለጠለጠ *täbläṭälläṭä* v.i. acted cunningly; tried to fool others

ተብለጥላጭ *täbläṭlač̣* n. slick, smart, cunning *(person)*

አበለጠ *abälläṭä* v.i. caused excess, increased; preferred

አባለጠ *abballäṭä* v.t. measured *(s/t)* against *(s/t)* else

አብልጦ *abləṭo* adv. best, more

ከሁሉ— *kähulu*— adv. more than

አበላለጠ *abbälalläṭä* v.t. compared *(two things with other)*; made great difference between, favoured

አስበለጠ *asbälläṭä* v.t. preferred

በለጠገ *bäläṭṭägä* or በለፀገ *bäläṣṣägä* v.i. became rich

ባለጠጋ *baläṭägga* or ባለፀጋ

baläṣägga adj./n. rich; a rich man

ብልጥግና *bəlṭəggənna or* ብል ፅግና *bəlṣəgənna* n. richness, riches

አበለጠገ *abäläṭṭägä* v.t. made rich

በለጠጠ *bäläṭṭäṭä* v.t. prised open cf. በለቀጠ

በልጣጣ *bälṭaṭṭa* adj. staring open, open-eyed; shameless

ብልጥጥ *bəlṭəṭ* opened wide, staring

ተበለጠጠ *täbäläṭṭäṭä* v.t. was prised open

*በለጨለጨ **bäläčälläčä*

ተብለጨለጨ *täbläčälläčä* v.i. sparkled, glittered

ብልጭልጭ *bələčləč* adj flashy, showy, flamboyant

በሉጥ *bälluṭ* n. oak

በላ *bälla* v.t. ate; consumed; won *(gambling)*

ብል *bəl* n. cloth eating vermin

በል *in* ሥጋ በል *səga bäll* adj. carnivorous, carnivore

በሊታ *bällitta* n. big eater አደራ በሊታ *adära bällitta* embezzler

ተበላ *täbälla* v.i. was eaten; wore away

መበያ *mäbbäya* n. an item of food that complements another *(e.g. ənǧära and wäṭ, bread and cheese etc.)*

መብል *mäbəl* n. food

አብላላ *ablalla* v.t. digested *(took into the mind)*

ይብላኝ *yəblaññ* interj. "I'm sorry for!"

በላተኛ *bällatäñña* n. regular customer *(hotel or restaurant)*

ብሎት *bəllot* n. non-fasting day

ብልት አደረገ *bəllətt adärrägä* v.t. ate up *(everything)*

ተበላ *täbälla* v.i. was eaten up; was corroded

መበላት *mäbbälat* inf. to be eaten; n. corrosion

ተበይ *täbäyi* adj.n. edible; loser *(gambling)*

መበያ *mäbbäya* n. that which accompanies a dish *(sauce etc.)*, appetizer

አበላ *abälla* v.t. fed

ተበላላ *täbälalla* v.i. backbited against each other

ተብላላ *täblalla* v.i. was fermented; was digested *(idea)*

ተባላ *täballa* v.i. backbited against each other

ተባይ *täbay* n. insect

አባላ *abbälla* v.t. accompanied at table

አስበላ *asbälla* v.t. had s/o eat

አብላላ *ablalla* v.t. pondered, digested *(idea, plan etc.)*

በረሐ *bäräha* n. desert, wilderness

በረኸኛ *bärähäñña* n. desert traveller

በረሐማ *bärähamma* adj. desert

በረረ *bärrärä* v.i. flew; piloted

በራሪ *bärari* adj./n. flying; that which flies; express *(bus)*

በረራ *bärära* n. flight *(of bird, plane)*

አበረረ *abärrärä* v.t. piloted, navigated *(air craft)*

አብራሪ *abrari* n. pilot *(aircraft)*

ተባረረ *täbarrärä* v.i. was chased away, driven away

ተባራሪ *täbarari* n. fugitive

—ወሬ *—wäre* n. gossip

—ጥይት *—ṭəyyəṭ* n.

stray bullet

አባረረ *abbarrärä* v.t. chased away, drove away; dismissed, fired

አባራሪ *abbarari* adj./n. *(one)* who chases s/o

በረሮ *bäräro* n. cockroach

በረቀ *bärräqä* v.i. struck *(lightning) see also* ባረቀ

ብራቅ *bəraq* n. lightning

ብርቅ *bərq* n. rare pleasure adj. rare, precious, unique

ተብረቀረቀ *täbräqärräqä* v.i. glittered, shimmered

አብረቀረቀ *abräqärräqä* v.i. sparkled

አብረቅራቂ *abräqraqi* adj. sparkling

በረቀሰ *bäräqqäsä* v.i. forced in *(usually s/t which is tender)*; broke *(virginity, maidenhead)*

ብርቅስ *bərqəs* n. gash, tear

ብርቅስቅስ አደረገ *bərqəsqqəss adärrägä* v.t. forced into violently

በረቃቀሰ *bäräqaqqäsä* v.t. pushed into; forced a way into *(virginity, maidenhead)*

ተበረቀሰ *täbäräqqäsä* v.t. was forced into

ተበረቃቀሰ *täbäräqaqqäsä* v.i. was forced into *(by s/t)*

አስበረቀሰ *asbäräqqäsä* v.t. had *s/o* force a way into *s/t*

በረበረ *bäräbbärä* v.t. searched around; went through o/s pockets, etc.

በርባሪ *bärbari* n. thief, one who searches around

ብርበራ *bərbära* n. searching

ተበረበረ *täbäräbbärä* v.i. was searched; had o/s pockets etc. gone through

አስበረበረ *asbäräbbärä* v.t. had s/o searched; had s/o's pockets gone through

በረታ *bärätta* v.i. became strong; was in good shape *(person)*; succeeded through difficulties

ብርቱ *bərtu* adj. strong; in good shape *(person)*

ብርታት *bərtat* n. strength, success

አበረታ *abärätta* v.t. strengthened, encouraged

በረት *bärät* n. byre, barn

በረንዳ *bärända* n. verandah

በረከተ *bäräkkätä* v.i. was plentiful; became abundant

በርካች *bärkač* adj. abundant, plentiful, surplus

በርካታ *bärkatta* adj. plentiful, surplus

ብርካቴ *bərəkkate* n. abundance, plenty, surplus

በረከት *bäräkät* n. abundance, plenty; prosperity; blessing

ገጸ— *gäṣṣä*— n. present

አበረከተ *abäräkkätä* v.t.gave present, offered a gift *for s/o* who is higher in rank

ተበራከተ *täbärakkätä* v.i. was more than sufficient; was abundant, multiplied

አበራከተ *abbärakkätä* v. t. caused to be plentiful; managed supply efficiently *(e.g. housewife)*

*በረከከ *see* ተንበረከከ

በረዘ *bärräzä* v.t. mixed with water; infiltrated *(political)*

በራዥ *bärraž* n. infiltrator *(political)*

ብርዝ *bərz* n. a drink which is a mixture of honey and water, unfermented mead

በራረዘ *bärarräzä* v.t. mixed with some water

ተበረዘ *täbärräzä* v.i. was

mixed with water

አስበረዘ *asbärräzä* v.t. had *(s/t)* mixed with water

በረደ *bärrädä* v.t. became cold, cool, chilly

በረደኝ *bärrädäňň* I feel cold

ብርድ *bərd* n. cold

—ልብስ *bərd ləbs* n. blanket

ብርዳም *bərdam* adj. cold

ብርዳማ *bərdamma* adj. cold *(month)*

በራድ *bärrad* adj. chilly; n. tea pot *(metal, oriental type)*

በረዶ *bärädo* n. hail

አበረደ *abärrädä* v.t. cooled; cooled down, appeased *(anger)*, calmed down

ማብረጃ *mabräǧa* n. serving jug

ተባረደ *täbarrädä* v.i. was cold

አስበረደ *asbärrädä* v.t. had *(s/t)* cooled, made (s/o) feel cold

በረገደ *bäräggädä* v.t. opened by force, burst open *(door etc.)*

ብርግድ አለ *bərgədd alä* v.t. made burst open

—አደረገ *—adärrägä* v.t. burst open

በረጋገደ *bärägaggädä* v.t. threw *(everytning)* open *(e.g. all doors etc.)*

ተበረጋገደ *täbärägaggädä* v.i. was burst, thrown open

አስበረገደ *asbäräggädä* v.t. had *(s/t)* burst, thrown open

በረገገ *bäräggägä* v.t. shied, bolted *(e.g. horse, with fright)*

በርጋጊ *bärgagi* adj./n. bolting, extremely emotional, fearful

ብርገጋ *bərgäga* n. bolting

አበረገገ *abäräggägä* v.t. caused *(s/o)*, *(s/t)* to bolt

አስበረገገ *asbäräggägä* v.t. caused *(s/t)*, *(s/o)* to shy, bolt; frightened

በራ *bära* adj. bald-headed; n. bald-head

በራ *bärra* v.i. lit *(light only)*

ብራ *bərra* n. sunny day, clear weather, bright weather

ብርሃን *bərhan* n. light

መብራት *mäbrat* inf.to become light n. light, electric light; lamp

አበራ *abärra* v.t. lit, put on light

ማብሪያ *mabriya* n. light switch

ተብራራ *täbrarra* v.i. was clarified, was made clear *(idea etc.)*; was elucidated, elaborated

አብራራ *abrarra* v.t. clarified, made clear, elucidated, explained, elaborated

አስበራ *asbärra* v.t. had light put on

በራፍ *bärraf* n. doorway

በሬ *bäre* n. ox; adj. stupid

በር *bärr* n. gate, door

በረኛ *bärräňňa* n. porter, gate-keeper

በርሚል *bärmil or* በርሜል *bärmel* n. barrel *(for liquids)*, drum

በርበሬ *bärbärre* n. red pepper, chilli

በርኖስ *bärnos* n. burnous, woollen cloak

በርጩማ *bärčumma* n. stool

በሰለ *bässälä* v.i. was cooked enough, was ripe; aged *(wine)*; reached maturity; was mature

በሳይ *bäsay* adj. easy to cook

በሳል *bässal* adj. easy to cook

ብስል *bəsəl* adj. mature *(youngster)*; well-cooked

አበሰለ *abässälä* v.t. cooked enough

አብሳይ *absay* n. cook

ማብሰያ *mabsäya* n. cooking

pot, cooking utensil

ተብሰለሰለ *täbsälässälä* v.t. was too pre-occupied *(with s/t)*; was obsessed

አብሰለሰለ *absälässälä* v.t. was obsessed

አስበሰለ *asbässälä* v.t. had *s/t* cooked enough

*በስረ *see* አበሰረ

በሰበሰ *bäsäbbäsä* v.i. rotted, was rotten

በስባሽ *bäsbaš* adj. liable to rot

በስባሳ *bäsbassa* adj. rotten; filthy; ill-mannered

አበሰበሰ *abäsäbbäsä* v.t. let *(s/t)* to get rotten; get rotten, get completely soaked *(clothes etc.)*; mixed flour with water

ተበሳበሰ *täbäsabbäsä* v.i. became completely dirty; overdid *(s/t)*; became a nuisance

በሳ *bässa* v.t. made a hole drilled; bored

በሺ *bäši* adj. borer, drill

ብስ *bəs* n. hole *(drilled)*

መብሻ *mäbša* n. s/t used to drill, bore, drill

ተበሳ *täbässa* v.i. was bored, drilled

ተበሳሳ *täbäsassa* v.i. was drilled, riddled *(with many holes)*

አስበሳ *asbässa* v.t. had *s/t* riddled with holes

*በሳጨ *see* ተባሳጨ

በስተ— *bästä*—prefix; towards

በስቲያ *bästya* adv. suffix; after

ተነገ— *tängä*—n. the day after tomorrow

በሶ *bässo* n. food from roasted barley flour

—ብላ *—bəla* n. sacred basil

በሸቀ *bäššäqä* v.i. was very angry

ብሽቅ *bəšq* adj. very angry putrified; deteriorated in character *(person)*

አበሸቀ *abäššäqä* v.t. made very angry, annoyed seriously

አብሻቂ *abšaqi* adj./n. annoying

ተባሸቀ *täbaššäqä* v.t. annoyed each other *(seriously)*

በሸቀጠ *bäšäqqäṭä* v.i. putrefied; got soaked *(with mud)*

በሽቃጣ *bäšqaṭṭa* adj. putrefied; muddied; ill-mannered, grumbling

ብሽቅጥቅጥ *bəšqəṭqəṭ* adj. hopelessly jumbled, mixed up

አበሸቀጠ *abbäšäqqäṭä* v.t. soaked; soaked with mud

ተበሻቀጠ *täbäšaqqäṭä* v.i. behaved badly; was over demanding, over critical

አበሻቀጠ *abbäšaqqäṭä* v.t. treated *(s/o)* badly

በሽታ *bäššəta* n. disease, illness

ተላላፊ— *tälalafi* —epidemic, contageous disease

የሚጥል— *yämmiṭəl—also* የባርያ በሽታ epilepsy

በሽተኛ *—bäššətäñña* n. patient, sick person

የእንቅልፍ በሽታ *yä'ənqəlf bäššəta* sleeping sickness

በቀለ *bäqqälä* v.i. grew, sprouted

ቂም በቀል *qim bäqäl* n. vengeance, revenge

ብቅል *bəqəl* n. malt

በቁልት *bäqqʷält* n. germinating seeds,

ቡቃያ *buqayya* n. fresh green shoots, sprouting grain

በቃል *bäqqal* adj. growing

አበቀለ *abäqqälä* v.t. grew, raised *(crops)*; grew *(hair)*

ተበቀለ *täbäqqälä* v.t. re-

venged
ተበቃይ *täbäqqay* adj. avenger
በቀተ *bäqqätä* v. i. went into exile, took refuge
በቀት *bäqat* n. flight, taking refuge
በቃ *bäqqa* v. i. was sufficient sufficed, was enough; was qualified, was competent; was righteous; interj. enough !stop!
የሚበቃ *yämmibäqa* adj. sufficient, adequate
የማይበቃ *yämmaybäqa* adj. insufficient, inadequate
በቂ *bäqi* adj. sufficient, adequate enough, satisfactory
በቃኝ *bäqqaňň* I have enough
የበቃ የነቃ *yäbäqqa yänäqqa* adj. holy, righteous
ብቃት *bəqat* n. holiness, righteousness;
ብቁ *bəqu* adj. efficient,
ብቁነት *bəqqunnät* n. efficeency, competency
ተባቃ *täbaqqa* v.i. got a small portion *(each one)*
አበቃ *abäqqa* v.t. finished, completed, terminated, brought to an end, was adjourned

የሱ ነገር *yässu nagar* it is all over with him, he is hopeless
አባቃ *abaqqa* v.t. distributed evenly and sufficiently
አበቃቃ *abbäqaqqa* v.t. distributed evenly and sufficiently
አብቃቃ *abqaqqa* v.t. distributed evenly and sufficiently; used economically
በቅሎ *bäqlo* n. mule
በቅበቃ *baqbäqqa* n. parrot, parakeet

በቆሎ *bäqqollo* n. *also* **የባሕር ማሽላ** *yäbahər mašəla* n. maize
ፈኪ- *fäki*--- n. popcorn
በተለይ *bätäläyy* adv. especially, specially, chiefly
በተረፈ *bätärräfä* adv. besides, apart from
በተነ *bättänä* v.t. scattered, dispersed; broke up *(a meeting)*, cast about *(by handfuls;*
ብትን *bəttən* adj. scattered, dispersed; cast *(in handfuls)*;
—ወረቀት —*wäräqät* n. loose paper
—ጨርቅ —*čärq* n. material *(cloth)*
--በርበሬ --*bärbäre* n. ground red pepper
ብትንትን *bətəntən* n. s/t that is scattered all over, dispersed
በታተነ *bätattänä* v.i. scattered all over, dispersed all over
ተበተነ *täbättänä* v.i. was scattered, dispersed, cast about; was adjourned, broke up *(meeting)*
ተበታተነ *täbätattänä* v.i. was scattered, dispersed all over
አበታተነ *abbätattänä* v.t dispersed
አስበተነ *asbättänä* v.t. had scattered, dispersed all over
በተኅ *bätäha* n. unfermented *(e.g. mead.)*
-ጠጅ *ṭäǧǧ* unfermented "*ṭäǧǧ*" *(mead)*
በትረያርክ *bäträyark* n. patriarch
በትረያርካ *bäträyarka* n. patriarchate
በትር *bättər* n. bat, stick
በትረ መንግሥት *bäträ mängəst* n. mace, sceptre
በነነ *bännänä or* **በነነ** *bənnänä* v.i raised *(dust)*.in the air
ብናኝ *bənnaňň* adj. raised

(in the air, dust); n. particle of dust
አቦነነ *abonnänä* v.t. made *(dust, smoke)* fill the air
በከለ *bäkkälä* v.t. stained; implicated *(s/o in a crime)*; contaminated
በካይ *bäkkay* adj./n. one who stains; one who puts the blame on another
ብክለት *bəklät* n. contamination
ብክል አደረገ *bəkkəll adärrägä* v.t. stained heavily
ተበከለ *täbäkkälä* v.i. was implicated *(in a crime)*
ተበካከለ *täbäkakkälä* v.i. stained each other; implicated each other *(in a crime)*
አስበከለ *asbäkkälä* v.t. had *(s/o)* stained; had *(s/o)* implicated
በከተ *bäkkätä* v.i. died from natural causes *(animal therefore not edible)*; became completely dirty
ብክት አለ *bəkkət alä* v.i. became very dirty; filthy
በክት *bäkt* adj. dirty *(insult)*, filthy
ብካች *bəkkač* adj. dirty, filthy
አበከተ *abäkkätä* v.t. made completely dirty, filthy
በኩል *bäkkul* adv. in the direction of; towards
በኩር *bäkʷər or* በሁር *bähər* n. first born
ዐሥራት በኩራት *asrat bäkʷərat* n. tithe
ብኩርና *bəkʷərənna* n. status of being heir; birthright
በወዘ *bäwwazä* v.t. shuffled *(cards)*
በዐል *bä'al* n. festival
በዘበዘ *bäzäbbäzä* v.t. plundered; exploited
በዝባዥ *bazbäž* n. plunderer; exploiter
ብዝበዛ *bəzbäza* adj. plundering; exploiting
ተበዘበዘ *täbäzäbbäzä* v.i. was exploited
ተበዝባዥ *täbäzbaž* adj. plundered; exploited
አስበዘበዘ *asbäzäbbäzä* v.t. had *(s/o)* plundered; had *(s/o)* exploited
በዚህ *bäzzih* adv. here; in this place; this way
በዚያ *bäzziya* adv. there; over there; that way
በዛ *bäzza* v.i. multiplied; exceeded; was too much
ብዙ *bəzu* adj. many, much
—ጊዜ *—gize* adv. often, many times
ብዛት *bəzat* n. quantity, excess; abundance
በብዛት *bäbəzat* in large quantities; adv. frequently
በጊዜ ብዛት *bägize bəzat* in the course of time
እምብዛም *əmbəzamm* adv. not so much; not that much
አበዛ *abäzza* v.t. multiplied; made to exceed; was numerous, abundant; increased; was much
አብዛኛው *abzaññaw* adj. most, the majority
ተባዛ *täbazza* v.i. was multiplied *(math.)*
ተባዢ *täbaži* n. multiplicand *(math.)*
አባዛ *abbazza* v.t. multiplied *(math.)*
አባዥ *abbaž* n. multiplier *(math.)*
በየነ *bäyyänä* v.t. passed judgement
በያኝ *bäyyäññ* n. one who judges
ብይን *bəyyən* n. judgement
ብያኔ *bəyyane* n. judgement
ተበየነ *täbäyyänä* v.t. was given *(verdict)*
አስበየነ *asbäyyänä* v.t. had

(a judgement) passed, given

በየደ *bäyyädä* v,t. welded *(metal etc.)*
  በያጅ *bäyyağ* n. welder
  ብየዳ *bəyyädda* n. welding
  ብይድ *bəyyəd* adj. welded
  መበየጃ *mäbäyyäğa* n. welding tool
  ተበየደ *täbäyyädä* v.t. was welded
  ተበያጅ *täbäyyağ* n. *(s/t)* to be welded
  አስበየደ *asbäyyädä* v.t. had *s/t* welded

በደለ *bäddälä* v.t. did *(s/o)* wrong; mistreated, treated ill
  በዳይ *bädday* n. *(one)* who does wrong to s/o
  በደል *bäddäl* n. hurt, wrong
  በደለኛ *bädäläñña* n/adj. one who does wrong to *(s/o)*
  ተበደለ *täbäddälä* v.i. was done wrong to
  ተበዳይ *täbädday* n. one who is wronged
  አስበደለ *asbäddälä* v.t. had wrong done *to (s/o)*

• በደረ *see* ተበደረ

በደው *bädäw* n. Bedouin
  በደዊ *bädäwwi* adj. Bedouin

በዳ *bäda* adj. desolate
  ምድረ— *mədrä—* n. desert

በዳ *bädda* v.t. copulated *(human beings, impolite)*
  በጂ *bäği* n/adj. *(one)* who copulates
  ብድ *bəd* n. copulation
  ብዳታም *bədatam* adj. n. *(one who)* is excessive in sexual intercourse *(woman)*
  ተበዳ *täbädda* v.i. had sexual intercourse
  አባዳ *abbada* v.t. had *(s/o)* have sexual intercourse
  አስበዳ *asbädda* v.t. had s/o fucked *(woman)*
  አስበጂ *asbäği* n. pimp

በድረጃን *bädrağan* n. egg-plant

በድን *bädən* n. dead body
  —ሆነ *—honä* v.i. became or went numb

በጀ *bäğğä* v.t. was of benefit to; interj. all right! *(yes! go on!)*
  አበጀ *abäğğä* v.t. mended, repaired; adv. well done
  አበጃጀ *abäğağğä* v.t. repaired somehow, fixed up roughly; ridiculed, made fun of (irony)
  ተበጀ *täbäğğä* v·i. was repaired, mended; ransomed, saved
  ተበጃጀ *täbäğağğä* v.i. was repaired, mended; adorned oneself

በጅሮንድ *bäğərond or* በዥሮንድ *bäžərond* n. government treasurer

በገነ *bägganä* v.i. burned with rage; was enraged
  አበገነ *abägganä* v.t. enraged; burned with rage

በገና *bägäna* n. harp *(Ethiopian, large variety)*
  —ደረደረ *—däräddärä* v.t. played the harp

በጋ *bäga* n. summer

በግ *bäg* n. sheep
  የበግ ጠቦት *yäbäg ṭäbbot* n. lamb
  —ጠጉር *—ṭägur* n. wool
  ሴት በግ *set bäg* n. ewe

በጎ *bäggo* adv. well; in a good way
  —ሆነ *—honnä* v.i. became well *(after sickness)*
  —አድራጊ *—adragi* adj.charitable, benevolent
  —አድራጎት *—adragot* n. charitable deeds; welfare; foundation *(for the needy)*
  —ሥራ *—səra* n. charitable work
  በጎነት *bäggonnät* n. well-being

በጠረ *see* አበጠረ

በጠሰ *bäṭṭäsä* v.t. snapped *(rope)*, tore off *(button)*

ብጥስ አለ *bəṭṭəs alä* v.i. was torn off *(by itself)*, snapped *(by itself)*

ብጣሽ *bəṭṭaš* n. adj. torn-off piece

ብጣሻም *bəṭṭašam* adj./n. arrogant; (s/o) with superiority complex *(insult)*

ብጥስጥስ *bəṭəsṭəs* adj. ragged; arrogant; snobbish

በጣጠሰ *bäṭaṭṭäsä* v.t. snapped; tore into pieces

ተበጠሰ *täbäṭṭäsä* v.i. was snapped; was torn off *(button)*

ተበጣጠሰ *täbäṭaṭṭäsä* v.i. was snapped, torn to pieces; acted arrogantly

ተበጣጣሽ *täbäṭaṭaš* adj. snobbish, arrogant

አስበጠሰ *asbäṭṭäsä* v.t. had *(s/t)* torn off, snapped

በጠበጠ *bäṭäbbäṭä* v.t. mixed together; beat up *(cooking)*; caused disturbance, confusion

በጥባጭ *bäṭbač̣* adj./n. trouble-maker, mischievous

ብጥበጣ *bəṭbäṭa* n. disturbance, confusion

ብጥብጥ *bəṭəbbəṭ* n. disturbance, uproar, confusion, rebellion, crises, violence

መበጥበጫ *mäbäṭbäč̣a* n. mixing-bowl, anything used for mixing

ተበጠበጠ *täbäṭäbbäṭä* v.i. was mixed together; was disturbed

ተበጣበጠ *täbäṭabbäṭä* v.i. quarrelled with each other; to be disturbed

ተበጣባጭ *täbäṭabač̣* adj. quarrelling

አበጣበጠ *abbäṭabbäṭä* v.t. incited quarrel, commotion, uproar

አበጣባጭ *abbäṭabač̣* n. one who incites quarrel, commotion, uproar, trouble-maker

አስበጠበጠ *asbäṭäbbäṭä* v.t. had *(s/t)* mixed together

በጢኅ *bäṭṭih* n. water melon, *also* ከርቡሽ

በጣ *bäṭṭa* v.t. made an incision, cut *(in skin, e.g. for tribal markings)*

ብጥ *bəṭ* n. incision

ብጣት *bəṭat* n. incision

ተበጣ *täbäṭṭa* v.i. was incised

አስበጣ *asbäṭṭa* v.i. had *s/o* or *s/t* incised

በጣም *bäṭam* adv. very, much greatly, considerably; too *(much, very)*

በጣጢስ *bäṭaṭis or* መጣጢስ *mäṭaṭis* n. sweet potato

ቡሃቃ *buhaqa* n. dough pot

ቡሄ *buhe* n. festival of transfiguration of Christ

ቡሆ *buho* n. dough *(fermented) see also* ቡኮ

ቡላ *bulla* adj. grey

ቡልቅ አለ *bulləqq alä* v.i. puffed out *(smoke)*

—አደረገ *—adärrägä* v.t. puffed out *(smoke)*

ቡልቅታ *bulləqta* n. jet. *(of water)* puff *(of smoke)*

ቡሎን *bulon* n. nut *(of metal)*

ቡራቡሬ *burraburre* adj. coloured, spotted *(in black and white or black and red, only for animal)*

ቡሬ *burre* adj. piebald *(black and white)*

ቡሬማ *burremma* adj. particoloured

ቡሽ *buš* n. cork

ባርኔጣ *burnєṭa* n. pith helmet
ቡቃ *buqa* n. appendicitis
ቡቃያ *buqayya* n. shoots *(of crops)*
ቡችላ *buččəlla* n. puppy, whelp
የወርቅ *yäwärq* n. gold-bar, bullion
ቡና *bunna or* ቡን *bun* n. coffee
-ቁርስ *—qurs* n. any snack taken while drinking coffee
-ቤት *—bet* n. bar, coffee bar
ቡናማ *bunnamma* adj. brown
ቡንኝ *bunnəññ* n. short seasoned crop *(especially ṭef)*
ቡን አለ *bunn alä* v.i. filled the air, was blown by the wind into the air cf ቦነነ
ቡከን *bukän* adj. extremely cowardly
ቡጢ *buṭṭi* fist, punch
በቡጢ መታ *bäbuṭṭi mätta* v.t. punched, boxed
ቧምቧ *bʷambʷa or* ቧንቧ *bʷanbʷa* n. pipe *(water etc.)*
ቧገተ *bʷaggätä* v.i. begged shamelessly
ቧጋች *bʷagač* n. low beggar
ቧጠጠ *bʷaṭṭäṭä* v.t. clawed *(animals)*
መቧጠጫ *mäbʷäṭäča* n. claw, rake *(tool)*
ተቧጠጠ *täbʷaṭṭäṭä* v.i. was clawed
አስቧጠጠ *asbʷaṭṭäṭä* v.t. had *(s/t)* clawed; had throat scraped *(for tonsilitis)*
ቧጨረ *bʷaččärä* v. scratched
ቧጫሪ *bʷačari* n. scratching, liable to scrach
ቦጫጨረ *bočaččärä* v.t. scratched all over
ተቧጨረ *täbʷaččärä* v.i. was scratched
ተቦጫጨረ *täbočaččärä* v.i. was scratched all over
ቡጭርጭር *bučərčər* adj. scratched; n. scribbling, scribble
አስቧጨረ *asbʷaččärä* v. t. had *(s/o)* scratched
ቡዳ *buda* adj./n. evil eye,
ቡዳንነት *budannät or* ቡድንነት *budənnät* n. evil influence, having the evil eye
ቡድን *budən* n. team
ተቧደነ *täbʷaddänä* v.t. formed a team
አቧደነ *abbʷaddänä* v.t. had a team formed
ቡግ አለ *bugg alä or* ቦግ አለ *bogg alä* v.i. flared uq; glared *(light)*
ቡጢ *buṭṭi* n. fist; boxing
ቡጭ ቡጭ አለ *bučč bučč alä or* ቦጭ ቦጭ አለ *bočč bočč alä* v.i. slopped around *(liquids)*
ሆዴ— *hode—* I am moved *(affected with pity)*
ቦጭቧጫ *bočbʷačča* adj. slopping; cowardly
ቡፍ አለ *buff alä* ,v.i. stiffened with rage; was swollen *(dough etc.)*
ቢላዋ *billawa or* ቢላዎ *billawo* n. knife
ቢልቢላ *bilbilla* n. propeller
ቢል ቢል አለ *bill bill alä* v.i. propelled
ቢልቃጥ *bilqaṭ or* ብልቃጥ *bəlqaṭ* n. ink pot, tube; small bottle
ቢራ *bira* n. beer
ቢራቢሮ *birrabirro* n. butterfly
ቢሮ *biro* n. office
ቢስ *bis* prefix/suffix adj. bad;—less
—ገላ *—gäla* n. leprosy
ጥላ— *ṭəla—* adj./n. *(one)* who is undignified
መቅኖ— *mäqno—* adj/n not durable, not long-lasting
ገዳ— *gäddä—* adj./n.

	(one who is) ill-starred, born unlucky
በቅሙ	*aqmä* -n. weakling
ቢስክሌት	*bisklet* n. bicycle
ቢጤ	*bițe* or ብጤ *bəțe* n. double *(one who bears close resemblance)*, of the same kind
የኔ ቢጤ	*yäne bițe* n. beggar *(polite)*
ባህል	*bahəl* n. custom, tradition
ያገር	*yagär*-- n. national custom
ባለ	*balä* –pref. possessing, owner of
ባለሟል	*baläm*ʷ*al* n. confidant, courtier
ባለሞያ	*balamoya* adj/n. skilled, qualified in a certain skill; expert
ባላልጋ	*balalga* n. of the royal line; rightful monarch
ባለቤት	*baläbet* n. owner; husband, wife
ባለኩል	*baläkkul* n. one who shares with s/o, a fifty per cent share holder
ባለ ነገር	*balä nägär* n. plantiff; one who brings legal action
ባለዕዳ	*balä'əda* or ባለዳ *baläda* n. borrower, debtor
ባለእጅ	*balä'əǧǧ* or ባለጅ *baläǧǧ* n. blacksmith
ባለጠጋ	*balä țägga* adj. rich, wealthy, *also* ባለፀጋ
ባላጋራ	*balagaru* adj. enemy, foe
ባለቤት	*see* ባለ
ባለገ	*ballägä* v.t. behaved badly; lacked breeding, politeness
ባለጌ	*baläge* adj. rude, implolite
ባለጌነት	*balägennät* n. rudeness; impoliteness
ብልግና	*bəlgənna* n. rudeness; impoliteness
ብልግ አለ	*bəlləgg alä* v.i. became very rude, impolite
አባለገ	*aballägä* v. t. made rude, impolite *(usually for children by parents)*
ባላ	*balla* n. forked stick; "Y" shaped stick
ባላምባራስ	*balambaras* Ethiopian title
ባላባት	*balabbat* n. aristocrat, landlord
ባላባትነት	*balabbatənnät* n. aristocracy
ባላንጣ	*balanța* n. foe
ባላንጣነት	*balanțannät* n. enmity, hostility
ባላገር	*balagär* n. rural person, country fellow, peasant; adj. rough
ባላገሬ	*balagäre* adj. rural; rustic
ባሌ	*bale* n. one of the Administrative Regions, Southern Ethiopia *(Bale)*
ባሌስትራ	*balestra* n. spring *(of a truck)*
ባል	*bal* n. husband; festival
ባልና ሚስት ቁልፍ	*balənna mist qulf* n. press stud
ባለባል	*baläbal* adj. n. married; married woman
ባለቤት	*baläbet* n. owner; husband, wife
ባልቦላ	*balbola* n. fuse [It.]
ባልትና	*baltənna* n. household management; home economics
ባልቴት	*baltet* n. elderly lady
ባልንጀራ	*balənǧära* n. friend; regular companion
ባልንጀርነት	*balənǧärənnät* n. friendship
ባልደረባ	*baldäräbä* n. companion; courtier entrusted by a king with responsibility for another's case
ባልደራስ	*baldäras* n. commander

of cavalry

ባልዲ *baldi* n. bucket

ባልጩት *balčutt* n. flint *(stone)*, crystal

ባሐ *bäha* adj/b. bald; limestone

—ራስ *—ras* adj· bald-headed

ባሕር *bahər* n. sea; lake

—ማሽላ *—mašəlla* or ባርማሽላ *bar mašəlla* n. maize cf. በቆሎ

—ማዶ *—mado* n. abroad

—ሸሽ *—šäšš* n. regression of the sea

—ዐረብ *—aräb* n. piece of coloured goatskin

—ነጋሽ *—nägaš* n. ruler of the sea coast *(ancient Ethiopian title)*

—ዛፍ *—zaf* n. eucalyptus

—ዳር *—dar* n. sea-shore; lake shore

—ሰላጤ *—sällaṭṭe* n. bay

—ኃይል *—hail* n. navy

—ወሽመጥ *—wäšmäṭ* n. channel

ባሕርይ *bahrəy* n. nature: character

የሥጋ — *yäsəga*—n. animal instinct

የነፍስ — *yänäfs*—n. spiritual nature

ባሕታዊ *bahətawi* n. ascetic

ብሕትውና *bəhtəwənna* n. asceticism

ተባሕትዎ *täbahtəwo* n. asceticism

ባረቀ *barräqä* n. went-off by itself *(fire arms)*; flashed *(lightning)*

ብራቅ *bəraq* n. lightning

መብረቅ *mäbräq* n. thunder-bolt

አባረቀ *abarräqä* v. t. fired unintentionally *(firearms)*

ባረከ *barräkä* v.t. blessed, sanctified

ባራኪ *baraki* adj./n. one who blesses, sanctifier

ቡራኬ *burrake* n. blessing, sanctification

ቡሩክ *buruk* adj. blessed, sanctified

ተባረከ *täbarräkä* v.i. was blessed, sanctified

አስባረከ *asbarräkä* v.t. had *s/o* blessed, sanctified

ባሩድ *barud* n. gun-powder

ባር *bar* n. bar *(drinking house)*

ባርባር አለ *bar bär alä* v.t. felt unsettled, uneasy

ባርኔጣ *barneṭa* n. hat

ባሪያ *barya* n. slave

ባርነት *barənnät* n. slavery

ባሪያ ፈንጋይ *bärya fängay* n. slave trader

የባሪያ በሽታ *yäbariya bäššəta* n. epilepsy

ባርዳ *barda* n. tare *(weight)*

ባሰ *basä* v.i. was aggravated, worsened, deteriorated

ሆደ ባሻ *hodä bašša* adj./n. touchy, over-sensitive

የባሰ *yäbasä* adj. worst, worse

የባሰበት *yäbasäbbät* adj./n. even worse *(person)*

ብሶት *bəsot* n. grievance

አባሰ *abasä* v.t. aggravated

አብሶ *abəso* adj. especially

ተባባሰ *täbabasä* v.i. went from bad to worse; was very much aggravated; reached point of no return *(dispute)*

አባባሰ *abbabasä* v.t. caused *(situation)* to aggravate

ባሻ *bašša* n. *Pasha*, Ethiopian title

ባቄላ *baqela* n. horse bean

ባቡር *babur* n. train; mill

—መንገድ *—mängäd* n. street, avenue, boulevard *(only those used by vehicles)*

የባቡር ሐዲድ *yäbabur hadid* n. rail-road

የምድር ባቡር *yämdər babur* n. train

የሰማይ — *yäsämay*— n. airplane *(arch.)*

ባባ *babba* v.i. felt anxious *(for s/o's safety)*
ቡቡ *bubbu or* ብቡ *bəbbu* adj. anxious *(about s/o)*
አባባ *ababba* v.t. caused s/o to be anxious *(about s/o)*
ባጠ *batä* v.i. started, began *(of month)*
በአታ *bä'ata* n. 3rd day of the month
መባቻ *mäbača* n. first day of the month
አባተ *abatä* v.t. moved into the month of...
ባተሌ *batäle* adj. busy, industrious
—ሆነ *—honä* v.i. became busy, industrious
ባት *bat* n. calf *(of leg)*
ባታም *batam* adj. n. having chubby calves *(legs)*
ባትሪ *batri* n. battery; flash-light
ባነነ *bannänä* v.i. woke up suddenly
አባነነ *abannänä* v.t. awakened suddenly
ባና *bana* n. coarse woolen blanket
ባኞ *baňňo* n. bath-tub
ባንክ *bank* n. bank *(institution)*
ባንኮኒ *bankoni* n. counter *(in a café)*
ባንዲራ *bandira* n. flag
ባንድነት *bandənnät* adv. together, in a body, *see* አንድ
ባከነ *bakkänä* v.i. was wasted; was very busy
ብኩን *bəkun* adj. wasteful
ብኩንነት *bəkunənnät* n. wastefulness
አባከነ *abakkänä* v.t. wasted *(money etc.)*
አባካኝ *abakaňň* adj. wasteful
አበካከነ *abäkakkänä* v.t. wasted here and there *(money)*
ባውዛ *bäwza* n. search light
ባዕድ *ba'əd* adj. /n. stranger, foreigner; unrelated *(family)*
—መነሻ *—männäša* n. prefix *(gram.)*
—መድረሻ *—mädräša* n. suffix *(gram.)*
ባዘተ *bazzätä* v.t. made cotton wool
ባዘቶ *bazäto* n. cotton wool
ባዘቀ *bazzäqä* v.i. laboured in vain; searched in vain; wasted *(o/s)* journey
ባዜቃ *bazeqa* n. mercury
ባዝራ *bazra* n. mare
ባዳ *bada* adj. unrelated *(family)*
ባዶ *bado* adj. empty, vacant; unoccupied *(house, seat, land)*; blank *(sheet of paper, space, bullet)*
—ለባዶ *—labädo* nil nil *(o–o)*
—ባዶውን አስቀረ *—badowən asqärrä* v.t. denuded
ባዶ እጅ *bado əǧǧ* adj. penniless, empty-handed
—እግር *—əgər* adj. barefooted
—ኪስ *—kis* adj. broke
ባጀት *baǧät or* በጀት *bäǧät* n. budget
የበጀት ወር *yäbäǧät wär* n. fiscal month
—ዓመት *—amät* n. fiscal year
ባጥ *baṭ* n. king-post
ቤሳ *besa* n. coin
ቤት *bet* n. house
ቤተልሔም *betä ləhem* n. Bethlehem; sacristy
ቤተመቅደስ *betä mäqdäs* n. temple
ቤተክርስቲያን *betäkrəstiyan* n. church
ቤተክህነት *betäkəhnät* n. clergy; church *(administration)*
ቤተመንግሥት *betä mängəst* n. palace
ቤተ መዛግብት *betä mäzagəbt or* መዝገብ ቤት *mäzgäb bet* n. archives
ቤተ መጻሕፍት *betä mäṣahəft* n. library
ቤተሰብ *betä säb* n. family,

house-hold

ቤተኛ *betäňňa* n. friend of the family

ቤተዘመድ *betä zämäd* * n. family, relations, kin

ቤተ እግዚአ ብሔር *betä əgziabəher* n. church, temple

ቤት ለቤት *bet läbet* around the house

—መታ *—mätta* v.t. rhymed

የቤት ሥራ *yäbet səra* n. house work; home-work

እመቤት *əmmäbet* n. lady

የቤት እቃ *yäbet əqa* n. furniture

—ጫማ *čamma* n. slippers

ቡና ቤት *bunna bet* n. bar, pub

ከቤት ቤት *käbet bet* from *door* to door, from house to house

ጠጅ ቤት *ṭäǧǧ bet* n. täǧ house

ብ— *bə— with simple imperfect*, if, when

ቤንዚን *benzin* n. petrol, gasoline

ቤዛ *beza* n. ransom

የጣት— *yäṭat—* n. thimble

ብሆር *bəhor* n. reedbuck

ብሉይ ኪዳን *bəluy kidan* n. Old Testament

ብሉያት *bəluyat* n. books of the Old Testament

ብላሽ *bəlaš* adj. useless, valueless

በብላሽ *bäbəlaš* n. gratis, free of charge

ብልሹ *bələššu* adj. corrupt, *see also* ተበላሸ

ብላታ *bəlatta* n. title *(Ethiopian)*

ብላቴና *bəlattena* n. boy *(arch.)*

ብላቴን ጌታ *bəlatten geta* n. title *(Ethiopian)*

ብሌን *bəlen* n. iris *(of eye)*

ብሌ *see* በላ

ብልሀ *bələh* adj. prudent, intelligent

ብልሃት *bəlhat* n. prudence, intelligence, know-how

ብልሃተኛ *bəlhatäňňa* adj. prudent, intelligent, wise

ብልኮ *bəlləkko* n. heavy cotton blanket

ብልጭታ *bəlləčta* n. flash, dazzling

ብልጭ አለ *bəlləčč alä* v.i. dazzled, glittered, *see* *ብልጨለጨ

ብሔር *bəher* n. country, nation

ብሔረሰብ *bəheräsäb* n. nationality

ብሔራዊ *bəherawi* n. national

—ስሜት *—səmmet* n. nationalism

—ሸንጎ *—šängo* n. parliament

—በዓል *—bä'al* n. national holiday

ጠባብ ብሔረተኛ *ṭäbbab bəherätäňňa* n. tribalist

—ብሔረተኛነት *—bəherätäňňannät* n. tribalism

እግዚአብሔር *əgzi'abəher* n. God

የፍትሐ ብሔር ሕግ *yäfətha bəher həgg* n. Civil Code, Civil Law

ብረት *bərät* n. iron, steel, metal

ብረታ ብረት *bəräta bərät* n. metals

ብረት ሠሪ *bərät säri* n. smith

—ለበስ *—läbbäs* adj. armoured

—ድስት *—dəst or* ብረድስት *bəräddəst* n. saucepan

እግር ብረት *əgər bərät* n. fetters

ዐረብ— *aräb—* n. steel

ብሩሽ *see* ቡሩሽ

ብራቢሮ *bərrabirro or* ቢራቢሮ *birrabirro* n. butterfly

ብራና *bəranna* n. parchment

—ፋቂ *—faqi* n. parchment-maker

ብራኳ *bərakkʷa* n. shoulder-blade

ብር *bər* n. reed *(once used as pen)*; stalk

ብር — *bərr* n. silver; dollar
  ባለብር — *balä bərr* adj. wealthy, rich
ብርሃን — *bərhan* n. light, illumination, *see also* በራ
ብርሌ — *bərəlle* n. täğ flask *(for drinking)*
ብርቅ — *bərq* adj. rare, scant, precious
ብርቱካን — *bərtukan* n. orange
  —ቀለም — *—qäläm* n. orange *(colour)*
ብርት — *bərt* n. hand-washing basin
ብርንዶ — *bərəndo* n. raw meat. *(not fat)*
ብርኩማ — *bərkumma* n. head-rest *(usually of wood)*; hand crutch *(for legless cripple)*
ብርጭቆ — *bərčəqqo* n. glass *(drinking)*
  —ወረቀት — *—wäräqät* n. sand-paper
ብስ — *see* በሳ
ብስና — *bəsna* n. eructation *(of person)*
  ብስናት — *bəsnat* n. eructation *(of person)*
  ብስናታም — *bəsnatam* n. *s/o* who habitually eructates *(insult)*
ብሶል — *bəsol* n. compass
ብቅ አለ — *bəqq alä* v.i. popped out, suddenly appeared
  ብቅ ጥልቅ አለ — *bəqq ṭəlləqq alä* n. popped up and down
ብብት — *bəbbət* n. arm-pit
ብትቶ — *bətətto* n. tattered clothes
  ብትቷም — *bətəttʷam* adj. ragged
ብቻ — *bəčča* adv./adj. only; but; however; alone
  ቆይ— — *qoy—* just wait, I will show you
  ለብቻ — *läbbəčča* adv. separately, in private; adj. secluded
  —ለብቻ — *—läbəčča* adv. separately
  ለየብቻ — *läyyäbəčča* adv. separately, apart
  ብቸኛ — *bəččäñña* adj. lonely, lone, lonesome, solitary
  ብቸኝነት — *bəččäññənnät* n. loneliness
ብው አለ — *bəww alä* v.i. was set ablaze; raged
  ብው ብሎ ሰከረ. — was extremely intoxicated
ብይ — *bəyy* n. marbles (toy)
ብዙ — በዛ *see*
ብድግ አለ — *bədəgg alä* v.i. stood up *(suddenly)*
  —አደረገ — *—adärrägä* v.t. lifted
ብጉር — *bəgur* n. pimple
  ብጉራም — *bəguram* adj. pimply
ብጉንጅ — *bəgunǧ* n. boil
ብጣሪ — *see* አበጠረ
ብጫ — *bəča or bıča* adj. yellow
  ብጫ ወባ — *bəča wäba* n. yellow fever
ብጭጭ አለ — *bəčəčč alä* v.i. was very light *(complexion)*
ብፁዕ — *bəṣu'* adj. beatitude
ቦላሌ — *in* ቦላሌ ሱሪ *bolale surri* n. wide trousers *(i.e. not jodhpurs)*
ቦሎቄ — *bolloqe* n. haricot bean
ቦረቀ — *borräqä* v.i. gambolled
  ቦረቂ — *borraqi* n. gambolling
  ቡረቃ — *burräqä* n. gambolling
ቦረቦረ — *boräbborä* v.t. bored *(hole)*; channeled its way *(river)*; eroded *(soil)*
  ቦርቧሪ — *borbʷari* n. borer
  መቦርቦሪያ — *mäborborlya* n. boring machine
  ተቦረቦረ — *täboräbborä* v.i. was bored; was eroded *(soil)*
ቦራ — *bora* n. white starred horse
ቦርሳ — *borsa* n. purse; hand-bag
ቦርጭ — *borč* n. large belly
  ቦርጫም — *borčam* adj. big-bellied
ቦቃ — *boqa* adj. red-polled *(animal)*
  ቦቃማ — *boqamma* adj. red-polled
ቦተረፈ — *botärräfä* v.t. bit lump

— out of *(as hyena)*

ቡትርፍ አደረገ *butr.ff adärrägä* v.t. bit lump out of

ተቦተረፈ *täbotärräfä* v.i. had lump bitten out of

ቦታ *bota* n. place, space, area, spot, site; position, status; role

--ያዘ *--yazä* v.t. occupied *(a place;)* reserved a place

—ያዙ *—bota yazu* they were seated

ቦት/ቡት *in* ቦት ጫማ *bot čamma* n. high boat

ቦነነ *bonnänä or* በነነ *bännäna* v.i. rose up into the air *(dust etc.)*

ቡናኝ *bunnaññ* n. dust mote

ቡን አለ *bunn alä* v.i. rose up suddenly *(dust cloud)*

ቦና *bona* n. dry season

ቦንዳ *bonda* n. hoop *(band of wood or metal)*

ቦከቦከ *bokäbbokä* v.i. got *(soft, mushy e.g. (overripe fruit)*

ቡክቡክ *bukbuk* adj. soft, mushy

ቦክቧካ *bokbʷakka* adj. soft, mushy

ቦካ *bokka* v.i. became fermented *(dough)*

ቡኮ *buko* n. dough, *also* ቡሆ

አቦካ *abokka* v.t. kneaded

አቡኪ *abuki* n. one who kneads

ማቡኪያ *mabukiya* n. kneading trough, pan; batch mixer

ተቦካ *täbokka* v.i. was kneaded

ቡሃቃ *buhaqä* n. dough pan

ቦዘ *bozä* v.i. became lifeless, imbecilic

ቦዝ አንቀጽ *boz ãnqäṣ* n. gerund, *(gram.)*

አቦዘ *abozä* v.t. caused *(s/o)* to become lifeless, imbecile

ቦዘነ *bozzänä* v.i. became idle

ቦዘንተኛ *bozäntäñña* n. idle

ቦዜኔ *bozäne* n. lumpen proletariat

አቦዘነ *abozzänä* v.t. made idle

ቦይ *boy* n. canal, waiter

ቦደሰ *boddäsä* v.t. cut a chunk off

ቡድስ *buddəs* n. lump, chunk which is cut off; place from which lump, chunk is cut off

ተቦደሰ *täboddäsä* v.t. was cut off *(lump)*

*ቦገቦገ *bogäbbogä*

ተንቦገቦገ *tänbogäbbogä* v.i flamed, burned

አንቦገቦገ *anbogäbbogä* v.t. made *s/t* flame

ቦግ አለ *bogg alä* v.i. flamed, flared up suddenly

—አደረገ *--adärrägä* v.t. ignited, lit up

ቦግታ *boggəta* n. flame

ቦጨቀ *bočč̣äqä* v.t. ripped, clawed, seized *(as prey)*

ቡጫቂ *bučč̣aqi* n. ripped off, clawed off piece

ቦጨቅ አደረገ *bočč̣äq adärrägä* v.t. ripped, clawed a little

ቦጫጨቀ *bočač̣č̣äqä* v.t. clawed, ripped all over; torn up *(paper etc.)*

ተቦጨቀ *täbočč̣äqä* v.i. was clawed, ripped all over; torn up *(paper)*

ተቧጨቀ *täbʷač̣č̣äqä* v.t. scrambled over *(meat, etc. e.g. dogs, vultures)*

ተቦጫጨቀ *täbočač̣č̣äqä* v.i. was torn up *(paper)*

ቦጭ ቦጭ አለ/ ተንቦጫበጨ *bočč̣ bočč̣ alä/ tänbočäbbočä* v.i. slopped about *(liquids)*

ቧልት *bʷalt* n. jokes

ተ

ተለመ *tällämä* v.t. ploughed *(furrow)*

ትልም *təlm* n. furrow

ተለቀ *tälläqä* v.i. became big, great

ትልቅ *təlləq* adj. big, great,

ተለቃለቀ *täläqalläqä* v.t. rinsed off *(o/s)*; smeared *(o/s)*

አለቃለቀ *alläqalläqä* v.t. had *(s/o)* rinse off; hand *(s/o)* smear *(himself)*

ተለተለ *tälättälä* v.t. cut into stripes *(longitudinally)*

ትልትል *təltəl* adj. cut in strips

ተተለተለ *tätälättälä* v.i. was cut in strips

አስተለተለ *astälättälä* v.t. had *(s/t)* cut in strips

ተላ *tälla* v.i. became full of maggots *(meat)*

ትል *təl* n. maggot, worm

የሐር— *yäharr—* n. silkworm

አተላ *atälla* v.t. caused *(s/t)* to get maggot ridden

ተላለፈ *tälallläfä* v.t. passed each other; was postponed; broke the law, *see* አለፈ

ተላላፊ *tälallafi* adj. contageous; n. passers-by

—በሽታ *—bäššəta* n. contageous disease

መተላለፊያ *mättälaläfiya* n. passage, way through

ተላጋ *see* ለጋ

ተልባ *tälba* n. linseed

የተልባ እግር *yätälba əgər* linen

ተልከሰከሰ *tälkäsäkkäsä* v.t. sniffed around *(e.g. dog)*; went around unsavoury places

ልክስክስ *ləkəskəs* adj. frequenting unsavoury places; dirty, filthy

አልከሰከሰ *alkäsäkkäsä* v.t. treated lightly *(serious matter)*

ተልከፈከፈ *tälkäfäkkäfä* v.t. sniffed around *(dog)*

ተልካሳ *tälkassa* adj. lazy, sluggish; n, lazy bones

ተልፈሰፈሰ *tälfäsäffäsä* v.i. tired *(e.g. of burden)*, weakened

ልፍስፍስ *ləfəsfəs* adj.n. weakening, tiring; weakling, one lacking stamina

አልፈሰፈሰ *alfäsäffäsä* v.t. worked feebly, half heartedly

ተሐዋስያን *tähawasəyan* n. insects

ተመለሰ *see* መለሰ

ተመለከተ *tämäläkkätä* v.t. looked at, observed, *see* *መለከተ

ተመልካች *tämälkač* n. observer, watcher, spectator

አመለከተ *amäläkkätä* v.t. applied *(for job)*; turned one's attention to

አመልካች *amälkač* n. applicant

ማመልከቻ *mamälkäča* n. application *(for job)*

አስመለከተ *asmäläkkätä* v.t. felt the inclination *(to do s/t)*

ተመላለሰ *see* መለሰ

ተመመ *tämmämä* v. walked in step *(quietly)*

ተመሠጠ *tämmässäṭä* v.i. was absorbed *(attention)*

ተመሥጦ *tämässəṭo* n. absorption *(attention)*

ተመሳጠረ *tämäsaṭṭärä* v.t. shared secrets *see* ምስጢር

ተመረረ *tämärrärä* v.i. was bitter about; resented bitterly *see* also መረረ

አማረረ — ammarrärä v.t. complained (bitterly, resentfully)

ተመረኰዘ — tämäräkkʷäzä v.t. bent on, supported (o's with a stick); have evidence

ምርኩዝ — mərkʷəz n. staff (stick)

ተመሰቀለ — tämäsäqqälä v.i. was confused, mixed up see also ሰቀለ

ተመሰቃቀለ — tämäsäqaqqälä v.i. was thrown into great confusion

አመሰቃቀለ — ammäsäqaqqälä v.t. was made very confused

ተመተመ — tämättämä v.t. patted down, tamped down

ትምትም — təmtəm adj. well tamped down

ትምትም አደረገ — təmtəmm adärrägä v.t. patted, tamped down firmly

ተተመተመ — tätämättämä v.t. had (s/t) tamped down firmly

አስተመተመ — astämättämä v.t. was tamped down firmly

ተመቸ — tämäččä v.i. was comfortable

ምቹ — məčču adj./n. comfortable; saddle cushion

ምቾት — məččot adj. comfort

ተመቻቸ — tämäčaččä v.i. kept comfortable; sat comfortably

ተመነ — tämmänä v.t. set a price, evaluated

ተመን — tämän n. price

ተተመነ — tätämmänä v.i. was evaluated and a price put on

አስተመነ — astämämänä v.t. had (s/t) evaluated, had (s/o) set a price on

ተመኘ — tämäññä v.i. wished (for)

ምኞት — məññot n. wish

አስመኘ — asmäññä v. t. wished (for)

ተመካ — tämäkka v.i. was proud of, relied on

ትምክህት — təmkəhət n. bragging boast, arrogance

ትምክህተኛ — təmkhətäñña adj. boastful, braggard

ተመጻደቀ — tämäṣaddäqä v.i. boasted put o/s forward see also ጻደቀ

ተመጻዳቂ — tämäṣadaqi n. boaster

አመጻደቀ — ammäṣaddäqä v.t. encouraged (s/o) to boast

ተማረ — tämarä v.i. studied, learned

ተማሪ — tämari n. student, pupil, learner

ተማሪ ቤት — tämari bet n. school cf. ትምህርት ቤት

የተማረ — yätämarä adj. educated, learned

ትምህርት — təmhərt n. study; subject; lesson

—ሚኒስቴር — —minister n. Ministry of Education

ኅብረ— — həbrä— social studies

ትምህርታዊ — təmhərtawi adj. educational; scholastic

ትምህርት ቤት — təmhərt bet n. school cf. ተማሪ ቤት

ሁለተኛ ደረጃ— — hulätäñña däräǧa— n. secondary school

መሠረተ ትምህርት — mäsärätä təmhrt n literacy

—ትምህርት ዘመቻ — —təmhərt zämäča n. literacy campaign

መምህር — mämhər n. teacher

ምሁር — məhur adj. learned, scholarly, intellectual

አስተማረ — astämmarä v.t. taught, instructed

አስተማሪ — astämari n. teacher, instructor

ተማረ — tämarä v.i. was pardoned, forgiven see also ማረ

ምህረት *məhrät* n. pardon, forgiveness

ተማማረ *tämamarä* v.i. forgave each other; taught each other

አስማረ *asmarä* v.t. had *(s/o)* forgiven, pardoned

ተማሰለ *tämassälä* v.i. resembled each other; was stirred *(food)*

ማማሰያ *mammasäya* n. stick used to stir food

ተምር *tämər* n. date *(fruit)*

ተምታታ *tämtatta* v.i. was confused *see also* መታ

አምታታ *amtatta* v.t. confused, put in disorder; deceived *(by confusing)*

ተምች *tämč* n. hairy caterpillar

ተምነሸነሸ *tämnäšännäšä* v.i. dressed showily

አምነሸነሸ *amnäšännäšä* v.t. adorned *s/o;* dressed *(s/o)* in finery

ተምዘገዘገ *tämzägäzzägä* v.i./t. ran full tilt; hurled forcefully

አምዘገዘገ *amzägäzzägä* v.t. threw *(e.g. stick)* forcefully

ተሞላቀቀ *tämolaqqäqä* v.i. became spoiled *(child);* be over-demanding

ሞልቃቃ *molqaqqa* adj. spoiled; over demanding

አሞላቀቀ *ammolaqqäqä* v.t. spoiled *(child)*

*ተረመሰ *see* አተራመሰ

ተረተ *tärrätä* v.t.told tales *(to entertain)*

ተራች *tärrač* n. story-teller

ተረት *tärät* n. story, tales

መተረቻ *mätärräča* n. subject of gossip; butt *(person)*

ተረተረ *tärättärä* v.t. uncoiled; slit open; unzipped

ትርትር *tərtər* adj. slit open; uncoiled

ተተረተረ *tätärättärä* v.i. was uncoiled; was slit open; was unzipped

አተራተረ *attärattärä* v.i. helped to uncoil or slit open

አስቷረተር *astärattärä* v.t. had *(s/t)* uncoiled, slit open

ተረተር *tärätär* n. eroded *(uneven)* ground

ተረከ *tärräkä* v.t. narrated *(history)*

ተራኪ *tärraki* n. historian, narrator

ታሪክ *tarik* n. history

ታሪከኛ *tarikäñña* adj. marvellous

ታሪክ ነገሥት *tarikä nägäst* n. chronicles of the kings

ታሪካዊ *tarikawi* adj. historical, historic

መተረኪያ *mätärräkiya* n. butt of gossip

ተተረከ *tätärräkä* v.i. was related *(history)*

ተረከበ *täräkkäbä* v.i. was handed over, received, took over

ተረካቢ *täräkkabi* adj./n. *(one)* who takes over, recipient

ርክክብ *rəkəkkəb* n. handing over *(formality)*

ተረካከበ *täräkakkäbä* v.t. handed-over

አረካከበ *arräkakkäbä* v.t. supervised handing over

አረካካቢ *arräkakabi* n. supervisor of handingover

አስረከበ *asräkkäbä* v.t. handed over; turned over *(s/t in one's possession;)* surrendered *(arms)*

ተረከከ *täräkkäkä* v.i. split *(s/ds)* skull

ትርክክ አደረገ *tərkəkk adärrägä* v.t. split open *(s/o's)* skull

ተተረከከ *tätäräkkäkä* v.i. was split open *(skull)*

ተረከዝ *täräkäz* n. ankle

ባለተረከዝ ጫማ *balä täräkäz čamma* n. high-heeled shoe

ተረኰሰ *täräkkʷäsä* v.t. stubbed out *(e.g. cigarette)*

ትርኳሽ *tərakkʷaš* n. ember, extinguished brand

መተርኰሻ *mätärkʷäša* n. *in* የሲጃራ— *yäsiǧara* — n. ash-tray

ተተረኰሰ *tätäräkkʷäsä* v.i. was stubbed out, extinguished

ተረገረገ *tärägärrägä* v.t. walked with rolling gait, challenged vehemently

ተረግራጊ *tärägragi* n. one who walks with rolling gait

አረገረገ *arägärrägä* v.i. was springy *(bed)*

አረግራጊ *arägragi* adj. springy *(bed etc.)*

ተረጐመ *täräggʷämä* v.t. translated, interpreted

ተርጓሚ *tärgʷami* adj./n. translator, interpreter

ትርጉም *tərgʷum* n. translation, interpretation

ትርጓሜ *tərgʷame* n. commentary

—መጻሕፍት *—mäṣahəft* n. commentary of the Bible

ትርጁማን *tərǧuman* n. interpreter *also* ትርጉማን

ተተረጐመ *tätäräggʷämä* v.i. was translated, interpreted

አስተረጐመ *astäräggʷämä* v.t. had *(a book)* translated; used an interpreter

ተረፈ *tärräfä* v.i. escaped danger; was saved; remained; was surplus, was in excess

ከዳጋ— *kadäga* — v.t. was out of danger

ተራፊ *tärafi* adj. *(that)* which remains, rest remainder

ትራፊ *tərrafi* n. left over *(food)*

ትርፍ *tərf* n. gain, profit

—አንጀት *—anǧät* n. appendix *(medicine)*

—ጊዜ *—gize* n. free time, leisure

በተረፈ *bätärräfä* adv. moreover, apart from, what else

አተረፈ *atärräfä* v.t. saved *(s/o)* from danger; made a profit

አትራፊ *atrafi* adj./n. *(one)* who makes profit; profit maker, merchant

አተራረፈ *atärarräfä* v.t. made small profit

ተትረፈረፈ *täträfärräfä* v.t. was superfluous, was abundant; was copious, overflew

ተራ *tära* adj./n. ordinary, common; mediocre quality; turn *(order)*

—ሕዝብ *—həzb* n. mass, crowd

—ሰው *—säw* n. ordinary person, insignificant person

—ቁጥር *—quṭər* n. cardinal number

—ወታደር *—wättaddär* n. private *(soldier)*

—ጠበቀ *—ṭäbbäqä* v.t. waited one's turn

ከተራ የተወለደ *kätära yätäwällädä* adj. of humble birth

ተረኛ *täräňňa* adj./n. *(one)* who is on duty; one whose turn it is

ባለተራ *balätära* n. one whose turn it is

በተራ *bätära* adv. by turn

ተራ በተራ *tära bätära* adv. turn by turn

በየተራ *bäyyätära* adv. turn by turn

ተራመደ *tärämmädä* v.i. stepped forward, walked; progressed.

ተራማጅ *täramaǧ* adj. progressive

እርምጃ *ərməǧǧa* n. steps *(walking)*; progress
ተረማመደ *tärämammädä* v.t. stepped over; walked over
መረማመጃ *märrämamäǧa* n. spring-board *(abstract)*; stepping stone
አራመደ *arrammädä* v.t. made *(s/o)* step over, made *(s/o,s/t)* progress; advocated
ተራራ *tärara* n. mountain
የተራራ ሰንሰለት *yätärara sänsälät* n. mountain-chain
ተራራማ *täraramma* adj. mountainous
ተራቢ *tärrabi* n. clown
ተራኰተ *tärakkʷätä* v.t. struck each other vehemently
ተራዳ *tärada* n. tent-pole, centre-pole *(of bell tent)*
ተራዳ *see* ረዳ
ተርመሰመሰ *tärmäsämmäsä* v.i. wriggled about, crawled about
ትርምስ *tərəmməs* n. disturbance, disorder *(crowd of people)*
ተተራመሰ *tätärammäsä* v.t. jostled, became mixed up *(crowd of people)*
ተተረማመሰ *tätärämammäsä* v.i. jostled, became mixed up *(crowd of people)*
አተራመሰ *attärammäsä* v.t. caused *(people)* to mingle, jostle about; disturbed *(people)*
አተረማመሰ *attärämammäsä* v.t. mixed up *(everything)*; threw into confusion
ተርመጠመጠ *tärmäṭämmäṭä* v.i. got cluttered up, got dirtied; got very busy *(e.g. in kitchen)*
እርምጥምጥ *ərməṭməṭ* adj. cluttered, dirty
አርመጠመጠ *armäṭämmäṭä* v.t. worked in a slovenly way
ተርበተበተ *tärbätäbbätä* v.i. shivered, trembled with fear, was terrorized
እርብትብት *ərbətbət* adj. shivering *(with fear)*
አርበተበተ *arbätäbbätä* v.t. made *s/o* shiver, tremble with fear, terrorized
ተርበደበደ *tärbädäbbädä* v.i. jumped nervously *(in answer to question)*
እርብድብድ *ərbədbəd* adj. jumpy, nervous
ተርበድባጅ *tärbädbaǧ* adj./n. *(one)* who is nervous, jumpy
አርበደበደ *arbädäbbädä* v.t. caused *(s/o)* to jump, nervously
ተርብ *tärb* n. wasp
ተርታ *tärta* n. row *(line)*
በተርታ *bätärta* adv. in a row
ተርታውን *tärtawən* adv. in a row, continuously
ተርገበገበ *tärgäbäggäbä* v.i. waved about *(e.g. in wind)*; was troubled about *(s/o)*; fluttered *(eyelids)*, flapped
እርግብግቢት *ərgəbgəbit* n. propeller *(child's toy)*; fontanelle *(of child)*
እርግብግብ *ərgəbgəb* adj. extremely hospitable; kindhearted, humane
ተርገብጋቢ *tärgäbgabi* adj. flapping, waving *(in wind)*
አርገበገበ *argäbäggäbä* v.t. waved *(hand)*
ተሰለፈ *täsälläfä* v.i. went in file; got prepared; got straight, in order *(to begin some action)*
ተሰላፊ *täsällafi* n. one who goes in file; gets prepared *(for task)*
ሰልፍ *sälf* n. parade, procession
ሰላማዊ— *sälamawi*—n. peaceful demonstration
አሰለፈ *assälläfä* v.t. had *s/o* parade; supervised procession, marching

አሰላፊ *assällafi* n. supervisor of parade; drill, marching supervisor

—መኰንን *—mäkonnən* n. officer in charge of parade, procession

ተሰማ *täsämma* v.i. was heard; was obeyed, venerated, see *also* ሰማ

ተሰሚ *täsämi* adj. respectful

ተሰሚነት *täsäminnät* n. respect, veneration

ተሰረነቀ *täsärännäqä* v.t. stick in *(o/s)* throat

ተሰራጨ *täsäraččä* v.i. was broadcast; was circulated

ስርጭት *sərəččət* n. distribution, circulation

ተሰረጫጨ *täsäräčaččä* v.i. was circulated all over *(also of blood)*

አሰራጨ *assäraččä* v.t. circulated *(news)*, propagated *(news)*

አሰረጫጨ *assäräčaččä* v.t. caused to be broadcast; circulated

ተሰቀቀ *täsäqqäqä* or ተሳቀቀ *täsaqqäqä* v.i. winced, shied away from *(s/t unpleasant)*; was embarrassed *(e.g. to receive)*

ስቅቅ አለ *səqq alä* v.i. was actually embarrassed; shied away from; was set on edge *(e.g. by grating sound)*

አሰቀቀ *assäqqäqä* v.t. caused *s/o* to be actually embarrassed; horrified *(s/o)*

አሰቃቂ *assäqqaqi* adj. horrifying abhorrent

ተሰወጠ *täsäwwäṭä* v.t. slipped from (*o/s*) mind

ተሳተፈ *täsattäfä* v.t. participated; partook, had a share of

ተሳታፊ *täsatafi* adj./n. (*one*) who participates, partakes, (*one*) who has a share of

አሳተፈ *assattäfä* v.t. caused to participate, partake

ተሳነ *täsanä* v.t. failed, was unable to

ተሳካ *täsakka* v.i. was successful, was accomplished; was interlocked *see also* ሰካ

አሳካ *assakka* v.t. made *(s/t)* successful, accomplished; interlocked

ተስለመለመ *täslämällämä* v.i. felt faint, dizzy, overcome *(by heat fumes etc.)*

ስልምልም አለ *səlləmləmm alä* v.i. felt faint, dizzy

ተስለከለከ *täsläkälläkä* v.i. wriggled, slithered *(e.g. snakes)*

ተስቦ *täsəbo* n. contagious disease, epidemic *see also* ሳበ

ተስፋ *täsfa* n. hope, promise

—ሰጠ *—säṭṭä* v.t. gave hope; promised

—ቆረጠ *—qorräṭä* v.t. despaired, lost hope, was discouraged

—አስቆረጠ *—asqorräṭä* v.t. discouraged, disheartened

—አደረገ *—adärrägä* v.i. made hope, hoped

—አጣ *—aṭṭa* v.t. despaired

ተሽቀዳደመ *see* ቀደመ

ተሸበረ *täšäbbärä* v.i. was panic-stricken, was alarmed, was terrorized

ሽብር *šəbbər* n. terror, panic, commotion

አሸበረ *aššäbbärä* v.t. filled with panic, terrorized, alarmed, reduced to chaos

ተሸከመ *täšäkkämä* v.t. carried

ተሸካሚ *täšäkkami* adj./n. *(one)* who carries, bearer

ሸክም *šäkəm* n. load

ተሸካከመ *täšäkakkämä* v.i. caried each other

አሸከመ *aššäkkämä* v.t. had *(s/o)* carry; helped *(s/o)* to carry

ተሸጋሸገ *täšägaššägä* v.t. moved up, closed up space *(e.g. in file)*

መሸጋሸጊያ *mäššägašəgiya* n. gap *(in file)*

አሸጋሸገ *aššägaššägä* v.t. had a space closed up *(e.g. in file, row etc.)*

ተሻለ *täšalä* v.t. felt better, recovered; became better

የተሻለ *yätäšalä* adj. better, best; preferable

ምን ይሻላል *mən yəššalal* what should be done?

ተሻሻለ *täšašalä* v.i. was improved, got better, became a little better

አሻለ *aššalä* v.t. made to feel better, made to recover a little

አሻሻለ *aššašalä* v.t. improved, ameliorated

ማሻሻያ ሐሳብ *mašašaya hassab* n. amendment

ተሻማ *täšamma* v.t. scrambled for *(e.g. children among themselves for thrown sweets etc.)*

ሽሚያ *šəmmiya* n. scrambling for

አሻማ *aššamma* v.t. caused *(people)* to scramble for

ተሻረከ *täšarräkä* v.i. became partners; became close associates, friends

ሸሪክ *šärik* n. partner, friend

ሽርካ *šərka or* ሽርክና *šərkənna* n. partnership, friendship

አሻረከ *aššarräkä* v.t. made partners, friends

ተሻገረ *täšaggärä* v.t. crossed *(a river etc.)*

መሻገሪያ *mäššagäriya* n. crossing place *(bridge etc.)*

ተሸጋገረ *täšägaggärä* v.t. crossed, passed over; passed from one year to another

ተሸጋጋሪ *täšägagari* adj. intersecting *(beam etc.)*

አሻገረ *aššaggärä* v.t. had *(s/o)* cross *(a river etc.)*

አሸጋገረ *aššägaggärä* v.t. had *(s/o)* cross

ተሽቆጠቆጠ *täšqoṭäqqoṭä* v.t. trembled with fear; was submissive

ተሽቆጥቋጭ *täšqoṭq*ʷ*aç* adj./n. *(one)* who is submissive

ሽቁጥቁጥ *šəquṭquṭ* adj. submissive

አሽቆጠቆጠ *ašqoṭäqqoṭä* v.t. caused *(s/o)* to be servile, to make *(s/o)* shake in his shoes

ተሽከረከረ *täškäräkkärä* v.i. rolled over *(e.g. wheel)*

ተሽከርካሪ *täškärkari* n. motor vehicle

ሽከርክሪት *skərkərit* n. wheel, hoop

አሽከረከረ *aškäräkkärä* v.t. rolled; drove *(a car)*

አሽከርካሪ *aškärkari* adj./n. *(one)* who drives, a driver

ተሽኮረመመ *täškorämmämä* v.i. shrank with embarassment *(e.g. young girl)*

ተሽኮርማሚ *täškormami* n. shy, retiring *(woman or girl)*

አሽኮረመመ *aškorämmämä* v.t. flirted

ተቀመጠ *täqämmäṭä* v.t. sat down; sat in a meeting

ተቀማጭ *täqämmaç* adj./n. *(one)* who sits; one who is alive; saving *(money)*

ተቅማጥ *täqmaṭ* n. diarrhoea

ቅምጥ *qəmməṭ* n. concubine *(polite)*

መቀመጫ *mäqqämäça* n. sitting place; stool;

bottom *(part of body)*

አቀማመጥ *aqqämamäṭ* n. sitting position

አስቀመጠ *asqämmäṭä* v.t. put down; put aside; kept aside; had diarrhoea

ተቀማጠለ *täqämaṭṭälä* v. i. lived lavishly, luxuriously

ቅምጥል *qəmaṭṭəl* adj. high living *(person)*

አቀማጠለ *aqqämaṭṭälä* v.t. treated *(s/o)* lavishly; spoilt *(e.g. o/s child)*

ተቀበለ *täqäbbälä* v.t. received, took over; accepted

አቀበለ *aqäbbälä* v.t. passed *s/t* over, handed over

ተቀባበለ *täqäbabbälä* v.i. passed over to each other

ቅብብል *qəbəbbəl* n. pass *(foot-ball, etc.)*

—ሩጫ *—ručča* n. relay race

አቀባበለ *aqqäbabbälä* v.t. passed from hand to hand; cocked *(e.g. rifle)*

አቀባባይ ከበርቴ *aqqäbabay käbbärte* n. middle-man; comprador-bourgeois

ተቀነባበረ *täqänäbabbärä* v.i. was compiled, set in orderly manner

ተቀናበረ *täqänabbärä* see above

አቀነባበረ *aqqänäbabbärä* v.t. compiled; *(from various sources)*

አቀነባባሪ *aqqänäbabbari* n. compiler

ተቀናቀነ *täqänaqqänä* v.t. acted as rival competitor

ተቀናቃኝ *täqänaqañ* adj./n rival, competitor

ተቀናጣ *täqänaṭṭa* v.i. felt too much at home; abused hospitality

ቅንጦት *qənṭot* n. abuse of hospitality; lavish, luxurious life

ተቀየመ *täqäyyämä* v.t. held a grudge, took offense

ቅያሜ *qəyyame* n. rancour, grudge, ill-feeling

ቂም *qim* n. resentment, grudge, ill-feeling, rancour,

አስቀየመ *asqäyyämä* v.t. hurt one's feeling, offended

አስቀያሚ *asqäyyami* adj. offensive, ugly, grotesque

ተቀዳጀ *täqädaǧǧä* v.i. was crowned *(success)*

አቀዳጀ *aqqädaǧǧä* v.t. had *(s/o)* crowned; invested with *(s/t)*

ተቃረነ *täqarränä* v.t. went against, contradicted,

ተቃራኒ *täqarani* n. opponent, conflicting, opposite

ተቃርኖ *taqarəno* n. conflict, opposition

ተቃና *täqanna* v.i. was successful; was straightened *see also* ቀና

አቃና *aqqanna* v.t. straightened

ተቃወመ *täqawwämä* v.t. objected, opposed, *see also* ቆመ

ተቃውሞ *täqawəmo* n. opposition, objection

ተቃዋሚ *täqawami* adj./n. *(one)* who objects, opposes

ተቃወሰ *täqawwäsä* v.i. was disrupted; got out of order

ቀውስ *qäws* n. disruption, disorder

የአእምሮ— *yä'a'əmməro—* n. mental disorder

አቃወሰ *aqqawwäsä* v.t. disrupted, made disordered

አቃዋሽ *aqqawaš* adj. disrupter

ተቃጠለ *täqaṭṭälä* v.i. was burnt, caught fire, was on fire

በንዴት— *bänəddet—*was filled with fury

ቃጠሎ *qaṭälo* n. blaze, burning

አቃጠለ *aqqaṭṭälä* v.t. burnt, set on fire

ተቀጣጠለ *täqäṭaṭṭälä* v.i. caught fire; was tied together

see ቀጠለ

ተቅለሰለሰ *täqläsälläsä* v.i. was submissive *(person)*

ቅልስልስ *qələsləs* adj. submissive ; shy

ተቅለስላሽ *täqläslaš* n. submissive person

ተቅለበለበ *täqläbälläbä* v.i. was too voluble, excitable

ተቅለብላቢ *täqläblabi* n. voluble, excitable person

ቅልብልብ *qələbləb* adj. voluble, over excited

ቀለብላባ *qäläblabba* adj. voluble, over exicted

አቅለበለበ *aqläbälläbä* v.t. rushed *(s/o.)* hurried *(s/o)* into forgetting things

ተቅለጠለጠ *täqläṭälläṭä* v.i. became greasy, oily, shiny with fat, sweat etc, *see also* ቀለጠ

ተቅበዘበዘ *täqbäzäbbäzä* v.i. run wild despairingly

ተቅበዝባዥ *täqbäzbaž* n. wild, fugitive

ቀበዝባዛ *qäbäzbazza* adj. running away wildly, despairingly

ቅብዝብዝ *qəbəzbəz* adj. running away wildy, despairingly

አቅበዘበዘ *aqbäzäbbäzä* v.t. caused *(s/o)* run-away wildly

ተቅነዘነዘ *täqnäzännäzä* v.i. became impatient

ቅንዝንዝ *qənəznəz* adj. impatient

አቅነዘነዘ *aqnäzännäzä* v.t. caused *(s/o)* to be impatient

ተቅዋም *täqwam* n. institute

ተቅጨለጨለ *täqçäläççälä* v.i. clinked, jingled *(of bells)* *see also* ቃጨለ

ተቆረቆረ *täqoräqqorä* v.i. was very much concerned *(for s/o)*

ተቆርቋሪ *täqorqʷari* adj./n. *(one)* who is very much concerned *(for s/o)*

ተቈራመደ *täqʷärammädä* v.i. lived without hope *(dragged out desperate existence)*

ተቈነነ *täqʷannänä* v.i. walked disdainfully, proudly

ተቈናኝ *täqʷännañ* n. disdainful, proud *(person)*

ቍንን *qʷənnən* adj. disdainful, proud

—አለ *—alä* v.i. was overbearingly disdainful

ተቆጣ *täqoṭṭa* v.i. was angry, enraged; v.t. rebuked

ተቆጪ *täqoççi* adj./n. *(one)* who gets easily angry; *(one)* who rebukes

—የለለው *—yälelläw* adj. undisciplined

ቁጡ *quṭṭu* adj. bad tempered, surly

ቁጣ *quṭṭa* n. wrath, anger

አስቆጣ *asqoṭṭa* v.t. made angry, enraged; stirred up trouble for (s/o)

ተቆጣጠረ *täqoṭaṭṭärä* v.t. controlled, supervised, superintended *see also* ቆጠረ

ተቆጣጣሪ *täqoṭaṭari* controller, supervisor, superintendant

መቆጣጠሪያ *mäqqoṭaṭäriya* n. means of controlling, supervising

ቁጥጥር *quṭəṭṭər* n. controlling, supervison

ተቍለጨለጨ *täqʷəläçälläçä* v.t. stared with surprise

ቍልጭልጭ *qʷələçləç* adj./n. *(one)* who blinks, flinches, stares with astonishment

አቍለጨለጨ *aqʷəläçälläçä* v.t. blinked, flinched *(o/s eyes)*

እንቍልልጭ *ənqʷələləç* *or* እንቍልልጮ *ənqʷələləço* n. gloating *(over possesson of s/t)*

ተቍነጠነጠ *täqʷənäţännäţä* v.i. become restless *(to go, do s/t else)*

ቍንጥንጥ *qʷənəţnəţ* adj. restless (to go, do s/t else)

አቍነጠነጠ *aqʷənäţännäţä* v.t. caused *s/o* to be restless

ተቋቋመ *täqʷaqʷamä see also* ቆመ *qomä* v.i. was established, was well established was erected; v.t. resisted *(enemy)*

አቋቋመ *aqqʷaqʷamä* v. t. established; made well established; erected

ተበላሸ *täbälašša* v.i. was spoiled, deteriorated, went wrong

አበላሸ *abbälašša* v.t.damaged, spoiled, deformed,

ተበሳጨ *täbäsaččä* v.i. was annoyed, disturbed

ብስጩ *bəsəččuadj.* annoyed, disturbed

ብስጭት *bəsəččət* n. disturbance, annoyance

ብስጭትጭት አለ *bəsčəččəčatt alä* v.i. was very much annoyed, disturbed

አበሳጨ *abbäsaččä* v.t. annoyed, disturbed

ተበሻቀጠ *täbäšaqqäţä* v.i. behaved badly; was over demanding, over-critical, *see also* በሸቀጠ

ብሽቅጥቅጥ አለ *bəšqəţqəţţ alä* v.i. behaved very badly, was umbearably over-critical

ተበተበ *täbättäbä* v.t. tied up roughly; put *(s/o)* in bad terms *(with superior)*

ተብታቢ *täbtabi* n. *(one)* who makes trouble with o/s superior bv gossip

ተብታባ *täbtabba* adj. stammerer

ትብትብ *təbtəb* adj. trouble-making *(with superior)*

ትብትብ አደረገ *təbtəbb adärrägä* v.t. tied roughly *(inextricably)* but firmly, complicated matters unnecessarily

ተተበተበ *tätäbättäbä* v.i. was tied up roughly inextricably

ተበታተነ *täbätattänä* v.i. was scattered, dispersed, *see also* በተነ

ተበደረ *täbäddärä* v.t. borrowed, got a loan

ተበዳሪ *täbäddari* adj. borrower

ብድር *bəddər* n. loan

መበደሪያ *mäbbädäria* n. loan agency, security for loan; collateral

አበደረ *abäddärä* v.t. gave loan, lent

አበዳሪ *abäddari* n. lender

ተበዳደረ *täbädaddärä* v.i. borrowed from each other, lent each other

ተበገረ *täbäggärä* v.i. yielded, gave in

የማይበገር *yämmayəbbäggär* adj. unyielding invulnerable; obstinate, invincible

ተበጠረ *täbäţţärä* v.i. was combed

ብጥር *bəţţər* adj. combed

ብጣሪ *bəţţari* n. chaff, etc. *(left after threshing)*

አበጠረ *abäţţärä* v.t. combed: sifted grain

አበጣሪ *abäţţari* n. thresher, sifter

ማበጠሪያ *mabäţţäriya* n. comb; grain cleaning, sifting machine

አበጣጠረ *abäţaţţärä* v.t. combed a little; cleaned *(grain)* a little

አስበጠረ *asbäţţärä* v.t. had *(s/o)* comb, clean grain

ተባ *täbba* v.i. became strong; was annealed, tempered

ተባረደ *täbarrädä see also* በረደ

chilly *(weather)*

ተባበረ *täbabbärä see also* አበረ v.i. unified, associated *(for a common cause)*, was coordinated

ተባባሪ *täbabari* adj/n *(one)* who is an associate; *(s/o)* who is implicated in a crime

ትብብር *təbəbbər* n. unification; support

አስተባበረ *astäbabbärä* v.t. had *(people)* unified, coordinated

አስተባባሪ *astäbabari* n. co-ordinator

ተባባሰ *täbabasä see also* ባሰ *basä* v.i. went from bad to worse; was very much aggravated; reached a point of no return *(dispute)*

ተባት *täbat or* ተባዕት *täba'ət* adj. male, masculine *(gram.)*

ተባታይ *täbatay* adj. masculine *(gram.)*

ተባይ *täbay* n. insect, vermin *(parasitic insect,)* see *also* በላ

ተብለጠለጠ *täblätällätä* v.i. acted cunningly, tried to fool others, *see* በለጠ

ተብለጥላጭ *täblätlač* n. slick, smart, cunning

ተብረቀረቀ *täbräqärräqä* v.i. glittered, shimmered, *see also* በረቀ

ተብረከረከ *täbräkärräkä* v.i. wobbled *(knees;)* trembled with fear

አብረከረከ *abräkärräkä* v.t. made *(s/o)* tremble; terrified *(s/o)*

ተብከነከነ *täbkänäkkänä* v.i. was preoccupied, was deep in thought

ተቧደነ *täbʷaddänä* v.t. formed a team *(sport mainly)*, *see also* ቡድን

ተቻ *täččä* v.i. criticized; gave one's opinion, commented on *(s/t, s/o)*

ተቺ *täčči* n. critic; commentator

ትችት *təččət* n. comment, criticism

ተተቻ *tätäččä* v.i. was criticized, commented on

አስተቻ *astäččä* v.t. had *(s/o)* criticized, had *(s/o)* give comment on *(s/o, s/t)*

ተነሣ *tänässa* v.i. rose up, stood up, got up *(from bed; started a journey)*

መነሻ *männäšä* n. starting point

መነሾ *männäšo* n. cause

ትንሣኤ *tənsa'e* n. Easter

አነሣ *anässa* v.t. lifted; took up; withdrew *(legal charge)*

ክርስትና— *kərəstənna* — v.t. christened

ተነሣሣ *tänässassa* v.i. was inspired, instigated, aroused; was agitated

አነሣሣ *annäsässa* v.t. inspired instigated, aroused; agitated

አነሣሽ *annäsaš* adj/n *(one)* who inspires, instigates; agitator

አስነሣ *asnässa* v.t. had *(s/t)* lifted; aroused *(from sleep)*; had *(s/o)* removed *(from position)*; agitated

ተነቃነቀ *tänäqannäqä* v.i. was shaken, moved, see *also* ነቀነቀ

አነቃነቀ *annäqannäqä* v.t. shook, moved

ተነበየ *tänäbbäyä* v.t. prophesied

ተንባይ *tänbay* n. prophet; one who prophesies

ትንቢት *tənbit* n. prophecy

ትንቢተኛ *tənbitäñña* adj/n. *(one)* who tells

prophecies

ነቢይ *näbiyy* n. prophet

ነባይ *näbay* adj. truthful (*opposite* አባይ *abay*) adj. falseful

ተነተነ *tänättänä* v.t analysed

ትንተና *tənt̤äna* n. analysis

ተንታኝ *täntañ* adj./n. (*one*) who analyses

ተተነተነ *tätänättänä* v.i. was analysed

አስተነተነ *astänättänä* v.t. had (*s/t*) analysed

ተነተገ *tänättägä* v.t. burned

ትንታግ *təntag* n. ember, brand

ተነነ *tännänä* n. vapoured

ተን *tänn* n. vapour

ተናኝ *tänañ* adj./n. (*that*) which evaporates

ተተናኮለ *tätänakkolä* v.t. provoked

ተተናኳይ *tätänakʷay* adj. provocative

ተንኮል *tänkol* n. provocation

ተንኮለኛ *tänkoläñña* adj./n. (*one*) who provokes

ተነኰሰ *tänäkkʷäsä* v.t. prodded, provoked by prodding

ተንኳሽ *tänkʷaš* adj./n (*one*) who provokes by prodding

ተነጣጠረ *tänäṭaṭṭärä* v.i. compared; defended (*o/s*) in court

ተነጣጣሪ *tänäṭaṭari* n. plaintiff, defendant in lawcourt

ተነጫነጨ *tänäčannäčä* v.t. cried over nothing; complained pointlessly

ነጭናጫ *näčnačča* adj/n (*one*) who complains pointlessly, grouchy

ተነጫናጭ *tänäčanač* adj/n. (*one*) who complains pointlessly

አነጫነጨ *annäčannäčä* v.t. caused (*s/o*) to complain pointlessly

ተነጻጸረ *tänäṣaṣṣärä* v.i. was compared with *s/t*, see *also* ተነጣጠረ

ተነጻጻሪ *tänäṣaṣari* adj./n. s/t which is compared with s/t else

አነጻጸረ *annäṣaṣṣärä* v.t. compared

ተነፈሰ *tänäffäsä* v.t. breathed; formed relief (*from s/t arduous*) *see also* ነፈሰ

ጎማው--- *gommaw*— the tyre is flat

ትንፋሽ *tənfaš* n. breath

ተንፈስ አለ *tänfäss alä* v. found slight relief

አስተነፈሰ *ästänäffäsä* v.t let air out; gave rest

ተነፈገ *tänäffägä* v.i. gave off noxious condensation

ትንፋጋን *tənfagän* n. noxious condensation

ትንፋግ *tənfag* n. noxious condensation

ተነፋ *tänäffa* v.i. v.i. was inflated; became extremely proud, *see also* ነፋ

ተናፋ *tänaffa* v.i. boxed each other (*coll.*)

ተነፋፋ *tänäfaffa* v.i. was extremely inflated

አናፋ *anaffa* v.t. brayed (*donkey*)

ወናፍ *wänaf* n. bellows; liar

ተነፋነፈ *tänäfannäfä* v.i. grumbled; obeyed with bad grace

ነፍናፋ *näfnaffa* adj./n (*one*) who obeys with bad grace

ተናነቀ *tänannäqä* v.i. v.t. gripped (*s/o*) firmly; was on the verge of tears *see* አነቀ

ትንቅንቅ *tənaqnəq* n. grabbing, gripping (*firmly*)

ተናዘዘ *tänazzäzä* v.t. made (*o/s*) will, confessed (*to a priest*)

ተናዛዥ *tänazaž* adj./n. (*one*) who makes his will, (*one*) who confesses

ኑዛዜ *nuzaze* n. will (*on*

property) confession, testament

የኑዛዜ ቃል — yänuzaze qal n. last will

አናዘዘ — annazzäzä v.t. had (s/o) make his will

አናዛዥ — annazaž n. priest who officiates at dying man's last testament

ተናደደ — tänaddädä v.i. became furious, vexed, see also ነደደ

ተናዳጅ — tänadağ adj./n. (one) who is easily irritated, furious

ተናጠበ — tänattäbä v.i. was hindered, stopped

አናጠበ — annattäbä v. t. hindered, stopped

ተናፈጠ — tänaffätä v.i. blew one's nose

ንፍጥ — nəft n. mucus

ንፍጡን ጠረገ — nəftun tärrägä wiped one's nose, sniffed

ተንሰቀሰቀ — tänsäqässäqä v.i. sobbed, wept bitterly

ስቅስቅ ብሎ አለቀሰ — səqsəqq bəlo aläqqäsä v.i. sobbed, wept bitterly

ተንሰፈሰፈ — tänsäfässäfä v.i. treated (s/o) extremely kindly; was importunate; felt very sharp pain

ተንሰፍሳፊ — tänsäfsafi adj./n. (one) who is importunate

ስፍስፍ አለ — səfsəff alä v.i. treated (s/o) extremely well; was importunate

አንሰፈሰፈ — ansäfässäfä v.t. gave very sharp pain (e.g. wound)

ተንሶለሶለ — tänsolässolä v.t. scrounged, cadged everywhere

ተንሸረሸረ — tänšäräššärä v.i. had a walk, a ride (for pleasure)

ሽርሽር — šərrašərr n. walk, ride (for pleasure)

መንሸርሸሪያ — mänšäršäriya n. place for walk

ተንሸራሸረ — see ተንሸረሸረ

መንሸራሸሪያ — mänšärašäriya n. walking place (for pleasure)

አንሸረሸረ — anšäräššärä v.t. took (s/o) for a walk, a ride

ተንሸራተተ — tänšärattätä v.i. slided glided, slipped

ተንሸዋረረ — tänšäwarrärä v.i. went cross-eyed

ሸውራራ — šäwrarra adj. cross-eyed

አንሸዋረረ — anšäwarrärä v.i. had cross-eyes

ተንቀለቀለ — tänqäläqqälä v.i. was over-hasty, over-excited

ቀልቃላ — qälqalla adj. over-hasty, over-excited

አንቀለቀለ — anqäläqqälä v.t. caused (s/o) to be over-hasty, over-excited

ተንቀረበበ — tänqäräbbäbä v.i. was slightly open, crookedly placed (e/g cover, lid)

አንቀረበበ — anqäräbbäbä v.t. put on crookedly (lid, cover)

ተንቀረፈፈ — tänqäräffäffä v.i. had slack posture; was very slow at work

ቀርፋፋ — qärfaffa adj. slack, slow at work

ቅርፍፍ አለ — qərfəff alä v.t. was very sluggish, slack

አንቀረፈፈ — anqäräffäfä v.t. handled awkwardly

ተንቀሳቀሰ — see ቀሰቀሰ

ተንቀበቀበ — tänqäbäqqäbä v.i. was extremely mean, miserly

ቀብቃባ — qäbqabba adj. extremely mean, miserly

ተንቀበደደ — tänqäbäddädä v.i. was very pregnant, very stout; was puffed up with rage

ተንቀባደደ — tänqäbaddädä v.i. became extremely proud

ተንቀባረረ — tänqäburrärä v.i. was

over-demanding

ቀብራራ *qäbrarra* adj. spoilt *(child)*; over-demanding

አንቀባረረ *anqäbarrärä* v.t. spoiled *(children)*

ተንቀዋለለ *tänqäwallälä* v.i. loitered around, walked aimlessly; grew tall *(youth)*

ቀውላላ *qäwlalla* adj. extremely tall; loitering about

አንቀዋለለ *anqäwallälä* v.t. made *(s/o)* loiter around, walk aimlessly *(through unemployment)*

ተንቀዠቀዠ *tänqäžäqqäžä* v.i. was unsettled; fussed about

ቀዥቃዣ *qäžqažža* adj. messing about, fussing around

ቅዥቅዥ አለ *qəžqəžž alä* v.i. was very unsettled; kept on fussing about

ተንቀጠቀጠ *tänqäṭäqqäṭä* v.i. trembled; shook *(with fear)*; was coward

ቀጥቃጣ *qäṭqaṭṭa* adj. shivering *(with fear)*; coward

ቅጥቃጤ *qəṭəqqaṭe* n. tremor

አንቀጠቀጠ *anqäṭäqqäṭä* v. t. shook, made *(s/o)* tremble

አንቅጥቃጤ *ənqəṭəqqaṭe* n. shaking, trembling

የመሬት— *yämäret*—n. earthquake

ተንቍራጠጠ *tänqʷäraṭṭäṭä* v.i. paced up and down *(nervously)*

አንቍራጠጠ *anqʷäraṭṭäṭä* v.t. caused *(s/o)* to pace up and down *(nervously)*

ተንበለበለ *tänbäläbbälä* v.i. flared up *(of fire)*

አንበለበለ *anbäläbbälä* v.i. flared up *(of fire)*; read fluently

ተንበረከከ *tänbäräkkäkä* v.i. kneeled of kneeling

መንበርከኪያ *mänbärkäkiya* n. kneeling place *(e/g. in a church)*

አንበረከከ *anbäräkkäkä* v.t. made *(s/o)* kneel; subdued

ተንበሸበሸ *tänbäšäbbäšä* v.i. was abundant

አንበሸበሸ *anbäšäbbäšä* v.t. offered in abundance

ተንቦለቦለ *tänboläbbolä* v.i. flowed in abundance

አንቦለቦለ *anboläbbolä* v.t. caused to flow abundantly

ተንቦረቀቀ *tänboräqqäqä* v. flowed, wore over-large *(of clothes)*

ቦርቃቃ *borqaqqa* adj. flowing, over-large *(of clothes)*

ተንቦራቀቀ *tänboraqqäqä* v.i. flowed, wore over-large *(clothes)*

አንቦራቀቀ *anboraqqäqä* v.t. caused to look baggy, ill-fitting

ተንቦገቦገ *tänbogäbbogä* v.i. blazed, flared up

አንቦገቦገ *anbogäbbogä* v.t. set ablaze

ተንቦጨቦጨ *tänbočäbbočä* or **ተንቦጫቦጨ** *tänbočabbočä* v.i. slopped about *(liquids)*

ሆዱ— *hodu* — felt pity

ቦጭቧጫ *bočbʷačča* n. coward; sloppy food

አንቦጨቦጨ *anbočäbbočä* or **አንቦጫቦጨ** *anbočabbočä* v.t. caused to slop about

ተንተረከከ *täntäräkkäkä* v.i. glowed incandescently, *see* **ተረከከ**

ተርካካ *tärkakka* adj. glowing incandescently

አንተረከከ *antäräkkäkä* v.t. caused to glow incandescently

ተንተራሰ *täntärasä* v.t. laid one's head on a pillow

ትራስ *təras* v. pillow

አንተራሰ *antärasä* v.t. slide a

pillow under; slide one's arm under *(as pillow)*

ተንተባተበ *täntäbattäbä* v.t. stammered, *see also* ተበተበ

ተንተከተከ *täntäkättäkä* v.i. simmered

አንተከተከ *antäkättäkä* v.t. let *(s/t)* simmer

ተንቶሰቶሰ *täntosättosä* v.i. wandered about aimlessly; was busy to no purpose

ተንቶስቷሽ *täntostʷaš* adj. purposely over-active

ቶስቷሳ *tostʷassa* adj. needlessly busy

ተንቻቻ *tänčaččа* v.i. made hubbub *(background noise of large crowd)*

ቻቻታ *čačata* n. hubbub. noise *(of crowd)*

ተንከላወሰ *tänkälawwäsä* v.i. messed about; was busy to no purpose

ተንከረፈፈ *tänkäräffäfä* v.i. became shabby

ከርፋፋ *kärfaffa* adj. shabby

ከርፍፍ አለ *kərfəff alä* v.i grew extremely shabby

አንከረፈፈ *ankäräffäfä* v.t. carried *(s/t)* awkwardly

ተንከባለለ *tänkäballälä* v.i. rolled

ተንከባላይ *tänkäbalay* adj. rolling

እንክብል *ənkəbəll* n. tablet *(aspirin, etc.)*

ክብልል አለ *kəbləll alä* v.i rolled over *(suddenly)*

አንከባለለ *ankäballälä* v.t rolled *(s/t)*

ተንከተከተ *tänkätäkkätä* v.i cackled *(laughter)*

አንከተከተ *ankätäkkätä* v.t. caused *(s/o)* to burst out laughing

ተንከፈረረ *tänkäfärrärä* v.i. became frizzy, unkempt *(hair)*

ክፍራራ. *käfrarra* aj. frizzy. unkempt *(hair)*

አንከፈረረ *ankäfärrärä* v.t caused to be unkempt *(hair)*

ተንኮል *tänkol* n. mischief, trick, malice

ተንኮለኛ *tänkoläñña* adj. mischievous, malicious crafty

ተንኳፈፈ *tänkʷaffäfä* v.i. rose *(dough)*

ተንዘረጠጠ *tänzäräṭṭäṭä* v.i. was big-bellied.

ዘርጣጣ *zärṭaṭṭa* aj. big-bellied. pot bellied

አንዘረጠጠ *anzäräṭṭäṭä* v.t stuck out, thrust out one's belly

ተንዘረፈጠ *tänzäräffäṭä or* ተንዘራፈጠ *tänzäraffäṭä* v.i. sat at one's ease, flopped down

አንዘረፈጠ *anzäräffaṭä* v.t. sprawled one's body out

ተንዘረፈፈ *tänzäräffäfä* v.i. dressed untidliy, carelessly; was ill-fitting *(clothes etc)*; hung loose

ዘርፋፋ *zärfaffa* adj. ill-fitting; untidily dressed, droopy

አንዘረፈፈ *anzäräffäfä* v.t. dressed untidily, hung loose

ተንዘፈዘፈ *tänzäfäzzäfä* v.t. shuddered; shook oneself

አንዘፈዘፈ *anzäfäzzäfä* v.t. made*(s/o)* shudder shake, tremble

ተንዛዛ *tänzazza* v.i. was superfluous, excessive

አንዛዛ *anzazza* v.i. caused superfluity, excess

ተንደላቀቀ *tändäluqqäqä* v.i lived lavishly; indulged in luxury, *see also* ደለቀቀ

ተንዠረገገ *tänžäräggägä* v.i was over-laden *(e.g tree with fruit)*

ዠርጋጋ *žärgagga* adj. over-laden tree with fruit

ተንደረበበ *tändäräbbäbä* v.i was heaped full; was reserved, patient, serene *(person)*

ድርበብ	dərbäb adj. heaped full
ደርባባ	därbabba adj. serene, reserved
ተንደረከከ	tändäräkkäkä v.i was over-laden *(e.g fruit) tree*; heaped up *(fire)*
ተንደቀደቀ	tändäqäddäqä v.i made gulping sound *(liquid emptying from bottle)*
አንደቀደቀ	andäqäddäqä v.i sipped *(from bottle)*
ተንደበደበ	tändäbäddäbä *or* ተንደባደበ tändäbaddäbä v.i came up in a rash *(e.g skin from insect bite)*
አንደበደበ	andäbäddäbä v.i caused *(skin)* to come up in a rash
ተንደፋደፈ	tändäfaddäfä v.i had death throes *(spasms)*
አንደፋደፈ	andäfaddäfä v.t caused to writhe
ተንገበገበ	tängäbäggäbä v.i was very avaricious, miserly; felt unberable pain
ገብጋባ	gäbgabba adj. avaricious, miserly
አንገበገበ	angäbäggäbä v.t caused unbearable pain
ተንገፈጠጠ	tängäfäṭṭäṭä v.i was inflated, swollen up *(e.g in pregnancy)*
አንገፈጠጠ	angäfäṭṭäṭä v.t caused to be swollen up
ተንገፈገፈ	tängäfäggäfä v.i was fed up *(with s/t)*, was completely tired of
አንገፈገፈ	angäfäggäfä v.t caused *s/o* to be fed up, tired of *(s/t)*
ተንጋለለ	tängallälä v.t laid oneself down *(on the back)*
አንጋለለ	angallälä v.t made s/o lie down *(on his back)*
ተንጋጋ	tängagga v.t rushed, gathered *(in a disorderly crowd)*
ጋጋታ	gagata n. disorderly rushing; confused noise *(of crowd)*
አንጋጋ	angagga v.t drove a crowd *(people, cattle)*
ተንጐራደደ	täng^wäraddädä v.i went to and for; paced up and down
ጐርዳዳ	g^wärdadda adj. well-knit; attractive in shape *(body)*
ጐርደድ አለ	g^wärdädd alä v.i walked up and down *(a little)*
በዱላ አንጐራደደ	bädulla ang^wäraddädä v.t beat into a corner; beat *(about the room etc.)*
ተንጠራራ	tänṭärarra v.i had a stretch, stretched up *(arms)*; reached up; aspired *(desperately)*
አንጠራራ	anṭärarra v.i stretched *(arms)*
ተንጠራወዘ	tänṭärawwäzä v.i was debilitated, weakened *(by disease, etc.)*
አንጠራወዘ	anṭaräwwäzä v.t weakened *(s/o)*, enfeebled
ተንጠፈጠፈ	tänṭäfäṭṭäfä v.i dripped off *(e.g water from wet clothes)*
አንጠፈጠፈ	anṭäfäṭṭäfä v.t squeezed out, squeezed dry
ላቡን—	labun — v.t sweatend
ተንጣለለ	tänṭallälä v.i spread out, spread over *(e.g flood, water, grain etc.)*
ተንጣጣ	tänṭaṭṭa v.i made a cracking sound; chattered excessively; farted continuously

with red-hot needles *(traditional cure for headache etc.)*

አንጣጣ *anṭaṭṭa* v. caused a cracking sound

ተንፈራገጠ *tänfäraggäṭä* v.i had leg convulsions *(e.g death throes)*

አንፈራገጠ *anfäraggäṭä* v.t caused leg convulsions

ተንፈራፈረ *tänfäraffärä* v.i had complete bodily convulsions

አንፈራፈረ *anfäraffärä* v.t caused bodily convulsions

ተንፈቀፈቀ *tänfäqäffäqä* v.i bubbled up; snivelled *(childern)*

አንፈቀፈቀ *anfäqäffäqä* v.t made *(s/t)* bubble up

ተንፏፏ *tänfʷaffʷa* v.i made a rushing noise *(e.g waterfall)*

ፏፏቴ *fʷafʷate* n. waterfall

ተኛ *täñña* v.i slept

ተኛት *täññat* had sexual intercource with her

ሆስፒታል ተኛ *hospital täñña* he was in the hospital

ጎማህ ተኝቷል *gommah täññətuʷal* you have a flat tyre

ተኝቶ አረፈደ *täññəto aräffädä* he overslept

መኝታ *mäññəta* or መተኛ *mätäñña* n. sleeping *(place)*

—ቤት *—bet* n. bed-room

አተኛኝ *attäññañ* or አተኛኘት *attäññañät* n. sleeping posture

አስተኛ *astäñña* v.t made *(s/d)* sleep, lie down

የሚያስተኛ መድኃኒት *yämmiyastäñña mädhanit* anesthetic

ተአምር *tä'ammər* or ታምር *tammər* n. miracle, pl. ተአምራት ፥ ታምራት

ተአምረኛ *tä'ammäräñña* adj. miraculous

ተከለ *täkkälä* v.t planted; forced into the ground *(spear etc.)*

ተካይ *täkay* adj/n *(one)* who plants

ትክለኛ *təkläñña* n. settler

ትክል *təkl* adj. planted

—አለ *—alä* v.i. was forced into the ground *(spear etc.)*

ተካከለ *täkkakkälä* v.i. planted here and there; became equal to

ተተከለ *tätäkkälä* v.i. was planted; was forced in; was made to settle *(at a specific place)*

ተተካይ *tätäkkay* n. settler

መተከያ *mättäkäya* n. settling place

አታከለ *attakkälä* v.t. helped to plant

አታክልት *atakəlt* or አትክልት *atkəlt* n. vegetables

ያትክልት ቦታ *yatkəlt bota* n. garden

አትክልተኛ *atkəltäñña* n. gardener

ተከላከለ *täkälakkälä* v.i. defended *see also* ከለከለ

ተከላካይ *täkälakay* n. defender

መከላከያ *mäkkälakäya* n. means of defending

—ሚኒስቴር *—minister* n. Ministry of Defense

አከላከለ *akkälakkälä* v.t. hindered; stood in the way

ተከማቸ *täkämaččä* v.i was gathered, accumulated agglomerated

ክምቹ *kəmačču* adj. gathered, accumulated, agglomerated

ክምችት *kəmaččət* n. accumulation, concentration

መከማቻ *mäkkämača* n. place of accummulation

አከማቸ *akkämaččä* v.t. gathered, accummulated, agglomerated

ተከሠተ *täkässätä* v.i. was manifested, became clear in the mind, *(see also* ከሠተ*)*

ተከራየ *täkärayyä* v. t. hired *(a boat etc.)* rented *(a house)*, v.i. was rented, hired *(a house a boat etc.)*

ተከራይ *täkäray* n. tenant

አከራየ *akkärayyä* v.t. let, rent out

አከራይ *akkäray* n. one who rents out a house etc.

ተከተለ *täkättälä* v.t followed

ተከታይ *täkättay* n. follower; that which follows, continuation

ቅደም ተከተል *qədäm täkättäl* n. sequence

ተከታተለ *täkätattälä* v.t followed each other was ordered in a sequence watched closely

ተከታታይ *täkätatay* adj. sequential; graded *(books etc.)*, following each other

አከታተለ *akkätattälä* v.t had *(s/t)* followed

አስከተለ *askättälä* v.t had *(s/o, s/t)* follow; brought as a result of

ተከተከ *täkättäkä* v.t pecked at

ተከነ *täkkänä* v.i got overcooked; became extremely angry

አተከነ *atäkkänä* v.t caused *(s/t)* to get over-cooked; caused *(s/o)* to get very angry

ተከናነበ *täkänannäbä* v.t covered one's head *(with cloth, etc.)*

ከንብንብ *kənəbnəb* n. head-covering

መከናነቢያ *mäkkänanäbiya* n. head-covering

አከናነበ *akkänannäbä* v.t had *(s/o)* cover his head

ተከዘ *täkkäzä* v.i was lost in thought *(sadness)* was melancholic; was sad, was pensive

ተካዥ *täkkaž* adj/n. melancholic *(person)*

ትካዜ *təkkaze* n. melancholy

ትክዝ አለ *təkkəzz alä* v.i was deeply melancholic

መተከዣ *mätäkkäža* n. cause of melancholy, snack, nibble *(nuts etc.)*

አስተከዘ *astäkkäzä* v.t caused *(s/o)* to be sad

ተካ *täkka* v.t substituted; re- imbursed

ምትክ *mətəkk* n. substitute; reimbursement; deputy

ተተካ *tätäkka* v.i was substituted; was reimbursed

ተተኪ *tätäki* n. substitute *(person or thing)*

ተካለለ *täkallälä* v.t demarcated borders *(see also* ከለለ*)*

ተካላይ *täkalay* n. member of a boundary commission

አካለለ *akkällälä* v.t supervised in border demarcation

አስካለለ *askällälä* v.t had border demarcated

ተካሰሰ *täkassäsä* v. v.i accused each other, litigate each other *see also* ከሰሰ

ተካሳሽ *täkässaš* n. defendant

አካሰሰ *akkassäsä* v.t caused *(people)* to litigate against each other

አስካሰሰ *askässäsä* v.t had *(s/o)* accused

ተካነ *täkanä* v.i. was ordained as a priest, deacon etc. *see also* ካነ

ክህነት *kəhənät* n. priesthood

ቤተ ክህነት *betä kəhnät* n. clergy, the Church

ተክህኖ *täkhəno* n. priestliness

ልብሰ— *ləbsä* — n. vestment *(ecclesiastical)*

አስካነ *askanä* v.t had *(s/o)* ordained

ተካፈለ *täkaffälä* v.t shared, participated, divided *(s/t)* between, among *see also* ከፈለ

ተካፋይ *täkafay* n. participant, one who shares

ተከፋፈለ *täkäfaffälä* v.i divided *(s/t)* between, among each other; divided in opinion

አካፈለ *akkaffälä* v.t shared with another, divided

አካፋይ *akkafay* adj/n. *(one)* who divides *(s/t)* equally between, among people etc.

የጋራ— *yägara*— n. common denominator

አከፋፈለ *akkäfaffälä* v.t distributed equal shares

አከፋፋይ *akkäfafay* n. distributor *(equally)*

ተክለፈለፈ *täkläfälläfä* v.i meddled, interfered, was busy-body

ተክለፍላፊ *täkläflafi* adj/n meddler, busy-body

ክልፍልፍ *kələfləf* adj / n. meddler, busy-body

አክለፈለፈ *äkläfälläfä* v. t. hustled, harried

ተክሊል *täklil* n. church marriage

ሥርዓተ— *sər'atä*—n. nuptial ceremony *(church)*

ተክበሰበሰ *täkbäsäbbäsä* v.i put on airs, was pretentious

ተክበስባሽ *täkbäsbaš* adj / n pretentious *(person)*

ክብስብስ *kəbəsbəs* adj. pretentious

ተኮማተረ *täkomattärä* v.i contracted, wrinkled

ኩምትርትር አለ *kumtərtərr alä* v.i. was contracted, wrinkted up

አኮማተረ *akkomattärä* v.t. contracted, wrinkled

ተኮረ *see* አተኮረ

ተኮረተመ *täkorättämä* v.i. sat hunched up *(e.g with sadness)*

ኩርትም አለ *kurtəmm alä* v.i. hunched up, curled up

ኩርትምትም አለ *kurtəmtəmm alä* v. hunched up

ተኮራመተ *täkorammätä* v.t. curled up one'slimbs *(thruogh illness)*

ኮርማታ *kormatta* adj. curled up, contorted

ኩርምት አለ *kurmətt alä* v.i. was extremely contorted

ኩርምትምት አለ *kurmətmətt alä* v.i was extremely contorted

አኮራመተ *akkorammätä* v. t. made *(s/o)* curl up

ተኮሳተረ *täkosatärrä* v.i frowned, looked serious *see also* ኮስተረ

ኮስታራ *kostarra* adj/n serious looking *(person)*

ተኮናተረ *täkonatä-ä* v.t. made a contract with

ተኮናታሪ *täkonatari* n. contractor, *also* ሥራ ተቋራጭ

ኮንትራት *kontrat* n. contract

ተኮፈሰ *täkoffäsä* v.i. dressed elegantly, impressively

ተኮፋሽ *täkoffaš* adj/n *(one)* who is dressed impressively

ተኰሰ *täkkwäsä* v.t. fired *(gun)*; became hot; had a fever; branded *(animal)*

ልብስ— *ləbs*— v. t. ironed *(clothes)*

ተኳሽ *täkkwaš* adj./n *(one)* who fires *(a shot)*; who brands *(animal)*

ጥሩ— *ʈəru*—n. marksman

ተኩስ *täkkws* n. firing

ተኳሽነት *täkuwašənnät* n. marksmanship

ትኩስ *təkkwəs* adj. fresh *(vegetables)*, warm *(food)*

ትኩሳት *təkkusat* n. fever

አተኰሰ *atäkkwäsä* v.t. had fever

ተኳኰሰ *täkwakkwäsä* v.t fired here and there

(*gun*); ironed slightly
ተተኰሰ *tätäkkʷäsä* v.i was fired (*gun*), was ironed; was branded (*animal*)
ተታኰሰ *tätäkkʷäsä* v.i fired at each other (*gun*), fought each other with firearms
ተታኳሽ *tätakʷaš* adj. fighting (*with arms*)
አስተኰሰ *astäkkʷässä* v.t had (*s/o*) *fire* (*gun*); had (*animal branded*); had clothes etc. ironed
ተኩላ *täkʷəla* n. wolf
ተኰረፈረፈ *täkʷəräfärräfä* v.i purred (*cats*); shrank (*washed cloth*)
ተኰነሰነሰ *täkʷənäsännäsä* v.t dressed ostentatiously
ተኰነስናሽ *täkʷənäsnaš* adj/n. (*one*) who is ostentatiously dressed
ተወ *täwä* v.t left; dropped (*a case*); stopped (*doing s/t.*) gave up, left off
ተው እባክህ *täw əbakkəh* be quiet; is it really so; come now!
ተተወ *tätäwä* v.i was left; was dropped (*a case*); was stopped
አስተወ *astäwä* v.t had (*s/o*) leave (*s/t*), drop (*a case*); had (*s/o*) stop
ተወላመመ *täwälammämä* v.i bent out of shape
አወላመመ *awwälammämä* v.t caused to bend out of shape
ወልግማ *wälgmamma* adj. bent out of shape
ወለምታ *wälämta* n. dislocation (*limbs*)
ወለም ዘለም አለ *wälämm zälämm alä* v.i was unreliable; shilly-shallied; was changeable in mind
ተወላከፈ *täwälakkäfä* v.i stumbled; was hindered stammered, stuttered, was lost for words
ወልካፋ *wälkaffa* adj. twisted; dishonest in (*character*)
አወላከፈ *awwälakkäfä* v.t hindered, tripped (*s/o*), got in (*s/o's*) way
አወላካፊ *awwäläkafi* n. (*s/t*) which trips one up
ተወላገደ *täwälaggädä* v.i twisted, bent out of shape
ወልጋዳ *wälgadda* adj. twisted, bent out of shape; twisted in (*character*)
ውልግድግድ *wəlgədgəd* adj. extremely twisted, contorted; messed up
አወላገደ *awwälaggädä* v.t caused s/t to be twisted, bent, messed up
ተወሐደ *täwähadä* or ተዋሐደ *täwahadä* v.i was unified
ተዋሕዶ *täwahədo* n. Monophysitism
አዋሐደ *awwahadä* v.t unified
ተወራረደ *täwärarrädä* v.i bet, made a wager *see also* ወረደ
ተወራራጅ *täwäraraǧ* n. one who bets
ውርርድ *wərərrəd* n. bet
አወራረደ *awärarrädä* v.t. made (*s/o*) bet; cut meat in lumps
ተወራጨ *täwäraččä* v.i. tossed and turned (*in bed*)
አወራጨ *awwäraččä* v.t. made (*s/o*) toss and turn
ተወሰወሰ *täwäsäwwäsä* v.i. was sewn (*with tacking stitches*); pedalled (*sewing machine*) *see also* ወሰወሰ
ተወናፈለ *täwänaffälä* v.i. participated in communal labour (*agriculture*)
አወናፈለ *awwänaffälä* v.t. gave one's oxen to a communal labour
ተወዳጀ *täwädaǧǧä* v.t. was befriended, *see also* ወደደ
ተወዳደረ *täwädaddärä* v.t. com

peted

ተወዳዳሪ *täwädädari* n. competitor

—የሌለው *—yälelläw* adj. matchless, incomparable, unequalled

ውድድር *wədəddər* n. competition

አወዳደረ *awwädaddärä* v.t.made to compete with each other; made comparison

ተወገደ *see* ወገደ

ተወጠረ *täwäṭṭärä* v.i. was stretched tight *(e.g. canvas)*; was disdainful, over-proud, *see also* ወጠረ

ተወጣጠረ *täwäṭaṭṭärä* v.i. was disdainful, over-proud; was stretched too tightly

ተወጫመደ *täwäčammädä* v.i. was rumpled up, wrinkled up

ወጭማዳ *wäčmadda* adj. scrawny, scraggy, skinny-legged

ውጭምድምድ *wəčmədməd* adj. skinny, scrawny

ተዋሰ *täwasä* v.t. borrowed *(an object)*; was a bondage, was a guarantor

ተዋሽ *täwaš* n. borrower

ውሰት *wəsät* n. borrowing

አዋሰ *awasä* v.t. lent

ተዋዋሰ *täwawasä* v.i. borrowed from each other

ዋስ *was* n. guarantor

ዋስትና *wastənna* n. guarantee

ተዋበ *täwabä* v.i. was beautiful, v.t. beautified oneself

ተዋጋ *täwagga* v.t. fought *(war)*; engaged in combat, *see also* ወጋ

ተዋጊ *täwagi* n. fighter *(war)*; combatant

—መኰንን *—mäkʷännən* officer in charge of operations

አዋጋ *awwagga* v.t. made *(s/o)* fight, combat

ተዋጣ *täwaṭṭa* v.i. was contributed *(money)*; succeeded *(scheme)*, *see* ወጣ

መዋጮ *mäwwačo* n. contribution

አዋጣ *awwaṭṭa* v.t. contributed *(money)*

ተውለበለበ *täwläbälläbä* v.i. waved *(flag up on flag pole)*

አውለበለበ *awläbälläbä* v.t. waved *(flag or one's hand)*

ተውላጠ ስም *täwlaṭä səm* n. pronoun

ተውረገረገ *täwrägärrägä* v.i. walked with a swaying gait *(usually for tall person)*

ተውረግራጊ *täwrägragi* n. one who walks with a swaying gait

ተውሳክ *täwsak* n. filth; parasite

ተውሳካም *täwsakam* adj. filthy

ተውሳከ ግሥ *täwsakä gəss* n. adverb

ተውዘገዘገ *täwzägäzägä* v.i. zoomed *(air craft)*

ተውዘግዛጊ *täwzägzagi* adj. zooming *(air craft)*

ተውተበተበ *täwtäbättäbä* v.i was entangled *(knot)*

ውትብትብ *wətəbtəb* adj. entangled *(knot)*

ተዘረከተ *täzäräkkätä* v.t. was cut open, laid open *(e.g. entrails) see also* ዘረከተ

ተዘረካከተ *täzäräkakkätä* v.i. was cut open in many places

ተዘረፈጠ *täzäräffäṭä* v.i. slumped down; plumped down, lounged about idly

ዝርፍጣ *zərfaṭṭa* adj. *(one)* who sprawls about, lounges idly

ተዘባነነ *täzäbannänä* vi. was over proud *see* ዘበነ

ተዘነጠለ *täzänäṭṭälä* v.t. was wrenched off, torn off, *see* ዘነጠለ

ተዘንጣይ *täzänṭay* adj. likely to become detached

ተዘናከተ *täzänakkätä* v.i. lived comfortably, lavishly;

took ones' ease

አዘናከተ *azzänakkätä* v. t. kept *(s/o)* in great style, state

ተዘከረ *täzäkkärä* v.t. helped *(s/o with food or money)*

ተዘካሪ *täzäkkari* n. benefactor, alms - giver

ተዝካር *täzkar* n. memorial feast for the dead

መዘከር *mäzäkkər* n. museum *also* ቤተ መዘከር

አዘከረ *azäkkärä* v.t. commemorated *(with feast for dead relative)*

ተዘዋወረ *täzäwawwärä* v.i. went around from place to place *see* ዘወረ

ተዘገረረ *täzägärrärä* v.i. fell flat, *see* ዘገረረ

ተዛመተ *täzammätä* v.i. spread gossip *see also* ዘመተ

ተዛማች *täzamač* adj. infectious, contagious

አዛመተ *azzammätä* v.t. caused, was the instrument of spreading *(s/t)*

አዛማች *azzamač* adj. carrying, spreading

ተዛመደ *täzammädä* v.i. was related to *(s/o)*, became very close to, friendly with *(s/o) see also* ዘመድ

አዛመደ *azzammädä* v.t. brought *(people)* together, unified

አዛማጅ *azzamağ* adj/n *(one)* who unifies, brings together

ተዛባ *täzabba* v.t. went out of balance, became detached

የተዛባ ዐረፍተ ነገር *yätäzabba aräftä nägär* ungrammatical sentences

አዛባ *azzaba* v.t. caused *(s/t)* to get out of balance

ተዛነቀ *täzannäqä* v.i was pressed together, was squeezed in tightly *(e.g. bus passengers)*

ተዛነፈ *täzannäfä* v.i. was uneven, not properly placed

አዛነፈ *azzannäfä* v.t. made *(s/t)* uneven, badly positioned

ተዛና *täzanna or* ተዝናና *täznanna* v.i. was relaxed

ተዛወረ *täzawwärä* v.t. changed one's job; was transferred; was moved else where, *see* ዘወረ

ተዛዋሪ *täzawari (one)* who is due for transfer

አዛወረ *azzawwärä* v.t. transferred *(s/o)* to another job; moved *(s/t)* elsewhere

ተዝለገለገ *täzlägällägä* v.i. was jellified, drawn out *(e.g spittle)*

ዝልግልግ *zələgləg* adj. jellied, drawn out, semi-liquid

አዝለገለገ *azlägällägä* v.t. caused to become jellified, drawn out

ተዝለፈለፈ *täzläfälläfä* v.i. fainted, swooned, fell unconscious; was exhausted, tired out

ተዝለፍላፊ *täzläflafi* adj./n swooning, fainting

ዝልፍልፍ *zələfləf* adj. fainting; exhausted, tired out

ተዝረበረበ *täzräbärräbä* v.i. dribbled *(saliva)*

አዝረበረበ *azräbärräbä* v.t. dribbled

ተዝረከረከ *täzräkärräkä* v.i. was messy, untidy *(esp. in work or the home)*; was unthrifty

አዝረከረከ *azräkärräkä* v.t. cause *(s/t)* to be messy, untidy

ተዝረጠረጠ *täzräṭärräṭä* v.i. lagged behind *(through fatigue)*; farted continuously

አዝረጠረጠ *azräṭärräṭä* v.t. terrified *(s/o)*

ተዝረፈረፈ *täzräfärräfä* v.t. dropped off *(e.g. pieces of s/t carried)*; dropped and flapped about (*clothing*)

ተዥጎረጎረ *täžgoräggorä* or ተዠጐረጐረ *täzguʷäräggu"ärä* v.i. was patterned in black or dark brown and white (*e.g. zebra, leopard*)

ዥጉርጉር *žəgurgur* adj. patterned in black or dark brown and white

አዥጐረጐረ *ažguʷäräggu"ärä* v.t. patterned (*s/t*) in black or dark brown and white

ተደለደለ *tädäläddälä* v.i. was made level (*ground*); was allocated to specific job, *see also* ደለደለ

ተደላደለ *tädäladdälä* v.i. was established firmly (*e.g. job*); sat comfortably; got an equal share; was in order; was pacified

አደላዳይ *addäladay* n. one who allocates, distributes

ተደራጊ *tädärragi* adj./n. passive (*gram.*) *see* *ደረገ

ተደራረገ *tädärarrägä* v.t. had sexual intercourse (*polite*)

አደራረግ *addäraräg* n. method, way of doing (*s/t*)

ተደናቀፈ *see* ደነቀፈ

ተደናበረ *tädänabbärä* felt one's way, felt about (*through shortsightedness, bad light etc.*) *see* ደነበረ

አደናበረ *addänabbärä* v.t. caused (*s/o*) to feel about, feel his way

ተደናገረ *tädänaggärä* v.i. was perplexed; lost the thread (*of one's discourse*)

ተደናገጠ *tädänaggäṭä* v. . was surprised, taken aback *see* ደነገጠ

ተደናጋጭ *tädänagač̣* adj. surprised, taken aback

አደናገጠ *addänaggäṭä* v.t. caused (*s/o*) to be surprised, taken aback

ተዳረቀ *tädarräqä* v.i. wasted effort, time (*in teaching or debate*)

ተዳራ *tädarra* v.t. flirted

ተዳቀቀ *tädaqqäqä* v.i. was bowed, crushed by sickness, *see olso* ደቀቀ

አዳቀቀ *addaqqäqä* v. . caused s/o to be bowed, crushed by sickness

ተዳበለ *tädabbälä* v.t. shared flat, house etc.) *see also* ደባል

ተዳባይ *tädabay* n. flat-sharer and co-tenant

አዳበለ *addabbälä* v.t. had s/o share (*flat or house*)

አዳባይ *addabay* n. one who lets (*s/o*) share (*house, flat*)

ተገን *tägän* n. shelter, protection, cover (*protection*)

ተዳፋ *tädaffa* v.i. went down hill, *see also* ደፋ

ተጋ *tägga* v.i. was diligent, persevered

ትጉ *təgu* adj. diligent, vigilant, assiduous

ትጋት *təgat* n. diligence, perserverance

ተጋለጠ *tägalläṭä* v.i. was exposed (*crime, wrongdoing*), *see also* ገለጠ

አጋለጠ *aggalläṭä* v.t. exposed (*s/o's crime etc.*)

ተጋባ *tägabba* v.i. got married; was passed from one container to another, *see also* ገባ

ተጋፈጠ *tägaffäṭä* v.t. faced danger bravely

አጋፈጠ *aggaffäṭä* v.t. put (*s/o*) in danger, jeopardy

ተግባር *tägbar* n. duty, action,

task, occupation, function

ተግባራዊ *tägbarawi* adj. functional

በተግባር *bätägbar* adv. practically

ተግ አደረገ *tägg därrägä* v.t. flashed (*e.g. torch etc.*) for a moment

ተግተረተረ *tägtärättärä* v.i. staggered, tried one's best

ተግተርታሪ *tägtärtari* adj. staggering n. one who tries one's best

ግትርትር *gətərtər* adj. staggering

ግትርትር አለ *gətərtərr alä* v.i. staggered heavily

ተግፈለፈለ *tägfäläffälä* v.i. bubbled up (*e.g. boiling ənğära and wäṭ*)

ግፍልፍል *gəfəlfəl* n. wäṭ with small pieces of *ənğära* added (*common for breakfast*)

አግፈለፈለ *agfäläffälä* v.t. boiled up (*wäṭ and ənğära*)

ተጎናጠፈ *tägonaṭṭäfä or* ተጎናጸፈ *tägonaṣṣäfä* v.i. wrapped šämma around (*o/s shoulders*)

መጎናጠፊያ *mäggonaṭäfiya* n. large kind of šamma

አጎናጠፈ *aggonaṭṭäfä* v.i. wrapped (*s/o*) in a šämma

ተጎራበተ *see* ጎረበተ

ተጐለተ *täg*ʷ*ällätä* v.i. sat idly, *see* ጐለተ

ተጉመጠመጠ *täg*ʷ*mäṭämmäṭä* v.t. rinsed out (*o/s mouth*)

መጉመጥመጫ *mäg*ʷ*mäṭmäča* n. rinsing water for the mouth

ተጕረበረበ *täg*ʷ*räbärräbä* v.i. became uneven, bumpy came up in lumps (*skin*)

ጕርብርብ *g*ʷ*ərəbrəb* adj. uneven; bumpy: covered in bumps (*skin*)

ጕርብርብ አለ *g*ʷ*urəbrəbb alä* v.i. became extremely uneven, bumpy; came up in many lumps (*skin*)

ተጓዘ *täg*ʷ*azä* v.i. travelled, made a journey, *see also* *ጓዘ

ተጠለለ *see* ጠለለ

ተጠለፈ *see* ጠለፈ

ተጠበበ *täṭäbbäbä see also* ጠበበ v.i became over-preoccupied

መጨነቅ መጠበብ *mäččanäq mäṭṭäbäb* extreme worry and preoccupation

ተጠናወተ *täṭänawwätä or* ተጸናወተ *täṣänawwätä* v.i was antagonistic towards (*s/o*)

ተጠጋ *täṭägga* v.i came near was under (*s/o's*) patronage, *see* *ጠጋ

መጠጊያ *mäṭṭägiya* n. shelter, refuge

ተጠጋጋ *täṭägagga* v.i came close to each other; were put close together

አጠጋጋ *aṭṭägagga* v.i caused to come close to each other; put close together

አስጠጋ *asṭägga* v.t sheltered (*protected*), harboured; brought close

ተጣረረ *täṭarrärä also* ተጻረረ *täṣarrärä* v.i was antagonistic, *see* ጠር *and* ጸር

ተጣራሪ *täṭarari* adj. antagonistic

ተጣራ *täṭarra see also* ጠራ *ṭärra* v.t called out to (*s/o*); v.i. was purified, distilled

ተጣበቀ *täṭabbäqä* v.t *see also* ጠበቀ *ṭäbbäqä* stuck to

ተጣደፈ *täṭaddäfä* v.i hurried *see* *ጠደፈ

ተጣመመ *täṭammämä* v.i was crooked, twisted, *see*

ጠመመ

ተጣፋ *täṭaffa* v.t destroyed each other, *see* ጠፋ

ተጥመለመለ *täṭmälämmälä* v.t writhed, shrivelled *(e.g dying snake)*

ጥምልምል *ṭəməlməl* adj. writhed, shrivelled, feeble, weakling

ጥምልምል አለ *ṭəmelməll alä* v.i withered, shrivelled *(to an extreme degree)*

አጥመለመለ *aṭmälämmälä* v.t made *(s/o, s/t)* writh, shrivel up

ተጥመሰመሰ *täṭmäsämmäsä* v.t made a rustling noise

ተጨለጠ *täčällätä* v.t was drunk to the last drop *see* ጨለጠ

ተጫማ *täčamma* v.t put shoes on *see* ጫማ

ተፈተለከ *täfätälläkä* v.i dashed off, *see* *ፈተለከ

ተፋ *täffa* v.t spat; vomited

ትፋት *təfat* n. vomit

ትፋታም *təfatam* adj. prone to vomit *(e.g habitual drunker)*

እትፍ አለ *əttəff alä* v.t spat

መትፊያ *mätfiya* n. spittoon

ተታፋ *tätaffa* v.t spat playfully *(of children)*

አስተፋ *astäffa* v.t retrieved one's possessions by force

ተፋለመ *see* ፈለመ

ተፋለሰ *see* ፈለሰ

ተፋቀደ *see* ፈቀደ

ተፋተገ *see* ፈተገ

ተፋዘዘ *see* ፈዘዘ

ተፋጠጠ *see* ፈጠጠ

ተፋፋመ *see* ፋመ

ተፍ ተፍ አለ *täff täff alä* v.i was busy in several places at once, was busy here and there

ተፌ *täffe* n. conscientious, keenworker

ተፍለቀለቀ *täfläqälläqä* v.i bubbled *(boiling liquids) see* ፈለቀለቀ

ተፍለከለከ *see* *ፈለከለከ

ተፍረቀረቀ *see* *ፈረቀረቀ

ተፍረጠረጠ *see* *ፈረጠረጠ

ተፍገመገመ *see* ፈገመ

ተፎካከረ *see* ፎከረ

ቱምቢ *tumbi* n. plumb line

ቱሪስት *turist* n. tourist

ቱር አለ *turr alä* v.i was chic, smartly dressed; flew off *(bird)*

ቱርክ *turk* adj / n. Turkey; Turkish

ቱስ ቱስ አለ *tuss tuss alä* v.i scuttled along *(scurried)*

ቱስ አለ *tuss alä* v.i hissed *(of air in a leak)*

ቱሽ አለ *tušš alä* v.t made a farting sound; whispered, gossiped to *(s/o)*

ቱባ *tubba* n. coil of yarn, hank

ቱቦ *tubbo* n. pipe, tube

ቱታ *tutta* n. overall

ቱግ አለ *tugg alä* v.i flared up exploded with rage

ቱግ ባይ *tugg bay* adj. easily made angry

ቱፋሕ *tuffah* n. apple

ቲማቲም *timatim* n. tomato

የቲማቲም ድልህ *yätimatim dəlləh* n. tomato paste

ቲአትር *tiy'atər or* ቴአትር *te'atər or* ቲያትር *tiyatər* n theatre

ቲኬት *tiket* n. ticket

—ቆራጭ *—qorač* n. ticket seller

ደርሶ መልስ— *dərso mäls—*n. roundtrip-ticket

ቲዮሪ *tiyori* n. theory

ታላቅ *tallaq or* ትልቅ *təlləq* adj large, big, grand *see* ተለቀ

*ታለለ *tallälä

ተላላ *tälala* adj. thoughtless, forgetful

ተታለለ *tätallälä* v.i. was deceived, cheated

ታመመ *tammämä* v.i. was sick was unwell *see* ሕመም *or* ሕመመ

ታመነ *tammänä* v.i. was believed, was reliable *see* አመነ

ታምር *tammər or* ተአምር *tä'ammər* n. miracle

ታምረኛ *tamməräñña or* ተአምረኛ *tä'ammərañña* adj. miraculous

ታምራታዊ *tamməratawi or* ተአምራታዊ *tä'ammərawi* adj. miraculous

ታምቡር *tambur* n. drum *(It.)*

ታረቀ *tarräqä* v.i. was reconciled; was corrected *(behaviour)*

ታራቂ *taraqi* n. one who is reconciled *(to s/o)*

መታረቂያ *mättaräqiya* n. pledge of re-conciliation *(damages etc.)*

እርቅ *ərq* n. reconciliation

አስታረቀ *astarräqä* v.t reconciled

አስታራቂ *astaraqi* n. peacemaker

ታረዘ *tarräzä* v.i was raggedly dressed

ታሪክ *see* ተረከ

ታሪፍ *tarif* n. tariff

ታርጋ *targa* n. license plate

ታበየ *tabbäyä* v.i was overbearing, conceited

ትቢት *təbit or* ትእቢት *tə'əbit* n. inordinate pride

ትቢተኛ *təbitäñña or* ትእቢተኛ *tə'bitäñña* adj. inordinately proud

ታቦት *tabot* n. Ark of the Tabernacle

ታቦተ ጽዮን *tabotä ṣəyon* n. Ark of Covenant

ታተረ *tattärä* v.t did one's best, tried one's hardest

ታታሪ *tatari* adj/n *(one)* who tries his best; energetic, ambitious

ታታ *tatta* v.t intertwined, interlaced

ታኅሣሥ *tahəsas or* ትሣሥ *təsas* n. December

ታኒካ *tanika* n. can *(for oil, paraffin etc.)*

ታናሽ *tannaš* n.young *(brother, sister)*; rump *(animals buttocks)*

ታንክ *tank* n. tank *(military)*

ታንከኛ *tankäñña* n. member of tank corps

ታንኳ *tankʷa* n. canoe *(esp. reed pith boat of lake Tana)*

ታከተ *takkätä* v.i was overworked, became exhausted

ትክት አለ *təkkətt alä* v.i was extremely exhausted

ታካች *takač* n/ adj. slothful, lazy *(person)*

አታከተ *atäkkätä* v.t bored *(s/o)*

አታካች *atakač* adj/n. bore, boring *(person)*

ታከከ *takkäkä* pushed against *see also* አከከ

ታወረ *tawwärä* v.i went blind *see also* ዕውር *əwwər*

ታክሲ *taksi* n. taxi

ታዘበ *tazzäbä* v.t was disappointed in *(s/o)*, changed one's view of *(s/o)* for the worst; took critical note of *(s/o's)* work, habits, etc.

ታዛቢ *tazzabi* n.one who is disappointed in *(s/o's)* work, one who takes critical note of *(s/o's)* work, habits etc.; political commentator.

ትዝብት *təzzəbt* v. unfavourable opinion, comment, view *(of behaviour, work etc.)*

ተዛዘበ *täzazzäbä* v.t was disappointed, have critical view of one another

አስተዛዘበ *astäzazzäbä* v.t created a mutually unfavourable opinion

ታዘዘ *tazzäzä* v.i obeyed, received orders, was ordered, *see also* አዘዘ

ታዛ *taza* n. shelter *(under the eaves of house)*, porch

ታደለ *taddälä* v.i was well favoured by fortune; was well endowed by birth, *see also* አደለ

ታደገ *taddägä* v.i had

	mercy on *(s/o)*
ታዳጊ	*taddagi* adj./n merciful *(person);* developing *(country)*
—አገር	*--agär* n. developing country
ታዲያ	*tadiya* interj. well then!
ታዲያሳ	*tadiyassa or* ታዲያስ *tadiyass* interj. so what next!
ታገለ	*taggälä* v.i wrestled with; struggled
ትግል	*təgəl* n. struggle; wrestling
ትግያ	*təgəyya* n. wrestling
ታጋይ	*tagay* n. wrestler; one who takes part in a struggle *(e.g political)*
አታገለ	*attaggälä* v.t had *(people wrestle, struggle)*
አታጋይ	*attagay* n. referee *(wrestling)*
ታገሠ	*taggäsä* v.i was patient
ታጋሽ	*taggaš* adj/n. patient *(person)*
ትግሥት	*təgəst or* ትዕግሥት *tə'əgəst* n. patience
ትግሥተኛ	*təgəstäñña or* ትዕግሥተኛ *tə'əgəstäñña* adj/n patient *(person)*
አስታገሠ	*astaggäsä* v.i calmed *(s/o)* down
አስታጋሽ	*astagaš* n/adj. *(s/o,s/t)* that calms *(s/o)* down
ማስታጋሻ	*mastagäša* n . means of calming down *(sedative)*, tranquilizer
ታጠቀ	*taṭṭäqä* v.i belted, girded *(o's)* up; was armed
ትጥቅ	*təṭq* n. equipment *(military)*
ትጥቅና ስንቅ	*təṭqənna sənq* n. provisions and supplies *(mil.)*
መታጠቂያ	*mättaṭäqiya* n. girdle, belt
አስታጠቀ	*astaṭṭäqä* v.t supplied with arms *(mil.)* ; helped in fastening belt, girdle
ታጠበ	*see* አጠበ
ታፈነ	*see* አፈነ
ታፈገ	*taffägä* v.i was crammed in *(people)*, *see also* አፈገ
ታፋ	*tafa* n. hip *(body)*
ቴሌስኮፕ	*teleskopp* n. telescope
ቴሌግራም	*telegram* n. telegram
ቴሌግራፍ	*telegraf* n. telegraph
ቴምብር	*tembər* n. stamp *(postage)*
የቀረጥ—	*yäqäräṭ—* n. revenue stamp
ቴኒስ	*tenis* n. tennis
ቴፕ	*tepp* n. tape
ትሉግሉግ አለ	*təluglugg alä* v.i billowed *(smoke)*
ትላንት	*təlant or* ትናንት *tənant* n. yesterday
ትላንትና	*təlantənna or* ትናንትና *tənantnna* n. yesterday
ትል	*təl* n. worm, insect
የሐር—	*yäharr—* n. silkworm
የኮሶ—	*yäkoso—*n. tapeworm
የሥጋ—	*yäsəga—*n. maggot
ትልቅ	*təlləq* adj. big, large, *see also* ተለቀ
ትልቅነት	*təlləqənnät* n. size; bigness; respectability
ትሑት	*təhut* adj. meek, humble, modest
ትሕትና	*təhətənna* n. modesty, humility
ትምህርት	*see* ተማረ
ትምቡሽ አለ	*təmbušš alä* v.i gave, sank in *(to the touch)*
ትምክህት	*see* ተመካ
ትምባሆ	*təmbaho* n. tobacco
ትሩፋት	*tərufat* n, charity, good deeds *see also* ተረፈ
ትራም	*təram* n. tram - car, streetcar
ትራስ	*təras* n. pillow
ትራፊክ	*tərafik* n. traffic police, traffic
ትርምስ	*tərəmməs* n. confusion, disarray
ትር ትር አለ	*tərr tərr alä* v.i. pulsed, beat *(heart)*
ትርታ	*tərrata* n. pulse, beat *(heart beat)*

ትርንጎ *tərəngo* n. citron

ትርኢት *tər'it* n. scene, show *(e.g on television)*

ትርኪ ምርኪ *tərki mərki* n. hodge-podge, junk, nonsense, rubbish

ትርጁማን *tərǧuman* n. interpreter

ትስብእት *təsbə'ət* n. incarnation

ትናጋ *tənnaga* n. palate

ትቢያ *təbbiya* n. dust.

ከትቢያ መነሣት *kätəbbiya männäsat* to rise from obscurity

ትንሽ *tənnəš* adj. small, little, a. bit, some of, a few

—ትንሽ — *tənnəš* adv. just a little

—በትንሽ — *bätənnəš* adv. gradually, bit by bit

ትንቢት *tənbit* n. prophecy

ትንታግ *təntag* n. spark, shoot of flame, flash

ትንኝ *tənəññ* n. gnat

የወባ— *yäwäba*—n. mosquito

ትንኩሽት *tənkušt* adj/n. aggressive *(child)*

ትንግርት *təngərət* n. s/t strange, unusual

ትከሻ *təkäšša* n. shoulder

ትከሻማ *təkäššamma* adj. big-shouldered, broad-shouldered

ትከሻም *təkäššam* adj/n broad-shouldered *(person)*

ትኋን *təhu*ʷ*an* n. bug

ትክትክ አለ *təkk təkk alä* v.i had a dry cough

ትዕቢት *tə'əbit* n. conceit *see* ታበየ

ትዕይንት *te'əyyənt* n. scene, scenery

ትዕይንተ ሕዝብ *tə'əyəntä həzb* n. demonsration *(political)*

ትዕግሥት *see* ታገሠ

ትዝ አለ *təzz alä* v.i came to mind

ትዝታ *təzzəta* n. nostalgia; memory, remembrance; recollection; memories

ትይዩ *təyəyyu* adj. apposite to, vis a-vis *see* አየ

ትዳር *tədar* n. married life, *see* አደረ

ባለትዳር *balä tədar* adj./n married *(person)*

ትጉህ *see* ተጋ

ትግሬ *təgre* adj. Tigrean

ትግራይ *təgray* n. Tigray, Administrative Region, north eastern Ethiopia

ትግርኛ *təgrəñña* n. Tigray language

ቶሎ *tolo* adv. qiuckly, soon at once

—ቶሎ —*tolo* adv. rapidly

—በል —*bäl* imp. hurry! come on!

ቶስቋሳ *tost*ʷ*assa* adj/n busy-body

አቶስቶሰ *atosättosä* v.i was a busy-body

አቶስቋሽ *atost*ʷ*aš* adj/n busy-body

*ቶፈቶፈ **tofättofä*

አቶፈቶፈ *atofättofä* v.i curried favour *(with superior by gossipping about colleagues)*

አቶፍቷፊ *atoft*ʷ*afi* adj/n *(one)* who curries favour through tale-bearing

ቶፋ *tofa* n. clay cooking pot

ቸል አለ *čäll alä* v.t ignored, paid no attention to, neglected

ቸልታ *čälləta* n. negligence

ቸልተኛ *čällətäñña* adj./n negligent *(person)*

ቸለል አለ *čäläll alä* v.i was neglectful

ቸለሰ *čälläsä* v.t emptied over *(s/o)*; emptied out *(e.g bucket of water)*

ተቸለሰ *täčälläsä* v.i was thrown out over s/o *(e.g bucket of water)*

ቸረ *čärä* v.i was open-handed, generous

ቸር *čär* adj. open-handed, generous

ችሮታ *čərota* n. generosity, open-handedness; financial assistance

ቸርነት *čärənnät* n. generosity

ቸረቸመ *čäräččämä* v.t chipped *(esp. blade, axe etc.)*, dented

ቸርቻማ *čärčamma* adj. chipped, dented

ችርችም *čərčəm* adj. chipped, dented

ቸረቸረ *čäräččärä* v.t retailed

ቸርቻሪ *čärčari* n. retailer

ችርቻሮ *čərčaro* n. retailing

አስቸረቸረ *asčäräččärä* v.t had *(s/t)* retailed

ቸርኪዮ *čärkiyo* n. rim *(of tyre)*

ቸሰሰ *čässäsä* v.*t* sizzled

ችስ አለ *čəss alä* v. sizzled

ቸበቸበ *čäbäččäbä* v.i sold in quantity; sold like hot cakes

ተቸበቸበ *täčäbäččäbä* v.i sold at a great rate

ቸብቸቦ *čabčäbbo* n. bob *(hair style)*

ቸነከረ *čänäkkärä* v.t nailed

ችንካር *čənkar* n. cleat, large nail

ተቸነከረ *täčänäkkärä* v.i was nailed

አስቸነከረ *asčänäkkärä* v.t had *(s/t)* nailed

ቸነፈር *čänäfär* n. epidemic, plague

ቸከ *čäkä* v.i became boring

ችኮ *čəkko* adj/n. boring *(person)*

ችክ አለ *čəkk alä* v.i was boring

መንቻካ *mänčakka* adj./n. boring *(person)*; persistent *(of stains in cloth)*

አቸከ *ačäkä* v.t rinsed perfunctorily *(did not wash s/t thoroughly)*

ቸከለ *čäkkälä* v. drove in a peg, stake

ችካል *čəkal* n. stake, peg

ችክል አለ *čəkkəll alä* v.i was driven n. *(stake)*

ተቸከለ *täčäkkälä* v.i was driven in *(stake, peg)*

አስቸከለ *asčäkkälä* v.t had *(s/o)* drive in *(stake, peg)*

ቸኰለ *čäkkʷälä* c.i hastened, was in a hurry

ቸኳይ *cäkkʷay* adj./n.*(one)* who is in a hurry

ችኰላ *čəkkʷäla* haste, hurry

ችኩል *čəkkul* adj./n hasty

ተቻኰለ *täčakkʷälä* v.i was in a hurry

አቻኳይ *aččakʷay* n. one who hurries *(s/o)*; adj. urgent

አስቸኰለ *asčäkkʷälä* v.t had *(s/o)* hurry, hasten

አስቸኳይ *asčäkkʷay* adj. urgent

ቸገረ *čäggärä* v.t lacked *(s/t)* had difficulty with *(s/t)* *(usually with pron. suff.)* e.g ቸገረኝ *čagäräññ* I am in difficulty, I am in need of

ችግር *čəggər* n. difficulty lack, handicap; problem

ያለ- ችግረኛ *yalä-* adv. easily *čəggəräñña* adj. n. needy *(person)*

ተቸገረ *täčäggärä* v.i. was in need, trouble; had a problem; was needy

አስቸገረ *asčäggärä* v.i. was nuisance, was importunate

አችግር ላይ ጣለ *əčəggər lay ṭalä* got one in trouble

—ወደቀ —*wäddäqä* he is in trouble

አስቸጋሪ *asčäggari* adj. difficult; importunate; causing problems

ቸፈቸፈ *čäfäččäfä* v.t cut into small pieces, chopped up

ችፍቻፊ *čəfəččafi* n. offcut, wood cuttings

መቸፍቸፊያ *mäčäfčäfiya* n. hatchet, hand-axe

ተቸፈቸፈ *täčäfäččäfä* v.i was chopped up; was cut into small pieces

ቸፈገ *čäffägä* or ችፍግ አለ *čəffəgg alä* v.i. grew thick, bushy *(forest, thicket etc.)*

ችፍግ *čəffəg* *adj.* bushy, thickly grown

ተቸፈገ *täčäffägä* v.i was bushy, thickly grown

ቻለ *čalä* v.i was able, capable

ቻይ *čay* adj. tough, resilient, forbearing, patient

ችሎታ *čəlota* n. ability, cleverness

ችሎት *čəlot* n. court session

ተቻለ *täčalä* v.i. was possible

አቻቻለ *aččačalä* v.t. made do *(with what little one had)*; stretched out *(resources)*

አስቻለ *asčalä* v.t. presided over *(court)*; was patient, forbearing *(with pron. suff.)* e.g. አስቻለው *he was patient*

ቻቻታ *čacata* n. noise, hum, buzz, *(of crowds)*

ቻይና *čayna* n. China

ቻይናዊ *čaynawi* n. Chinese

ቼ *če* gee-up

ቼክ *ček* n. check *(money)*

የቼክ ደብተር *yäček däbtär* n. check-book

ችላ አለ *čəlla alä* v.t, ignored, paid no attention *(to)* see also ቸል አለ

ችላ ባይ *čəlla bay* adj. indifferent

ችሎት *čəlot* n. session of court, tribunal, law court

ችቦ *čəbbo* n. torch

ችግኝ *čəggəññ* n. seedling, shoot

ችፌ *čəfe* n. eczema *(itching skin disease)*

ችፍ አለ *čəff alä* v.i was covered with boils, spots, had a rash; rained very lightly

ችፍርግ *čəfrəgg* n. *sida (small bush)*

ኀ

ኁለመና *hullämäna* n. whole body *(anatomical)*

ኀላፊ *see* አለፈ

ኀሙስ *hamus* n. Thursday

ኀምሳ *hamsa* adj. fifty *also* አምሳ

የኀምሳ አለቃ *yähamsa aläqa also* ያምሳ አለቃ *yamsa aläqa* n. sergeant

ኀምስ *hamǝs* n. fifth order of the Amharic vowel system

ኀይል *hayl* n. force, power, strength, vehemence

የባሕር— *yabāhǝr*— n. navy

የአየር— *yä'ayyär* — air force

ኀይለ ቃል *haylä qal* n. strong words; reproof, main point *(of paragraph)*

ኀያል *hayyal* adj. powerful, almighty, omnipotent

ኀይለኛ *hayläñña* adj. strong, powerful, mighty; violent, terrific, sharp *(pain)*

ኀይለኛነት *hayläññannät* n. strength, potency

ኀጋይ *hagay* n. little dry season *(December-March)*

ኀጢአት *haṭi'at* n. sin

ኀጢአተኛ *haṭi'atäñña* adj/n sinful *(person)*

ኀጢአተኛነት *haṭiatäññannät* n. sinfulness

ኀጥእ *haṭ'* n. sinner

ኀፍረት *hafrät* n. shame

ኀፍረተ ሥጋ *hafrätä sǝga* n. sexual organs *(polite)*, *see also* አፈረ

ኅብረት *hǝbrät* n. union, cooperation, solidarity, alliance, unity

ኅብረተሰብ *hǝbrätä säb* n. society

ኅብረተሰባዊ *hebrätä säbawi* adj. socialistic

ኅብረተ ሰብአ ዊነት *hǝbrätä säb'awinnät* n. socialism

ኅብር *hǝbr* n. metaphor

ኅብረ ትርኢት *hǝbrä tǝr'it* n. variety show

—ቀለማት —*qälämat* n. colour harmony

ማኅበር *mahǝbär* n. society, association

ማኅበርተኛ *mahǝbärtäñña* n. member *(of society, association)*

ማኅበርተኛነት *mahǝbärtäññannät* n. membership

ማኅበራዊ *mahǝbärawi* adj. sociable, social

—ኑሮ —*nuro* n. social life

ኅብስት *hǝbǝst* n. Host *(in Eucharist)*; loaf *(Ethiopian-bread)*

ኅዳር *hǝdar* n. November

ኅዳግ *hǝddag* n. margin *(of book)*

ኅፀፅ *hǝṣäṣ* n. defect

ኋላ *hʷala* adj. after n. behind, back *(part)*

ኋለኛ *hʷaläñña* adj. latter

የኋላ ኋላ *yähʷala hʷala* adv. later on; at the end

ነ

ነህ *näh* pron. you are *(sing m.)*

ነሐሴ *nähase* n. August

ነምር *nämǝr* n. leopard, *also* ነብር

ነሣ *nässa* v.t prevented; refused to give

እጅ— *ǝǧǧ nässa* v.t greeted

—መንሻ — *mänša* n. present, gift *(usually to superior)*

ተነሣ *tänässa* v.i stood up; got up *(in the morning)*

መነሻ *männäša* n. point of departure
መነሾ *männäšo* n. source, origin *(of an incident)*
ትንሣኤ *tənsa'e* n. Easter
ተነሣሣ *tänäsassa* v.i was induced, stirred, motivated to do *(s/t)*
አነሣሣ *annäsassa* v.t induced, stirred, motivated *(s/o)* to do *s/t*
አስነሣ *asnässa* v.t woke *(s/o)*; aroused, initiated *(s/t)*, *(s/o)*: agitated *(politcal)*
አስነሺ *asnäšši* n. agitator, arouser, incitor
ነረተ *närrätä* v.t beat severely *(e.g with baton)*
አስነረተ *asnärrätä* v.t had *(s/o)* beaten
ነርስ *närs* n. nurse
ነሰረ *nässärä* v.t bled through the nose
ነስር *näsər* nose-bleed
አነሰረ *anässärä* v.t had a nose-bleed
ነሰነሰ *näsännäsä* v.t sprinkled, spread about *(e.g powder, hay etc.)*; swished *(e.g horses tail)*
ነሳነሰ *näsannäsä* v.t sprinkled, spread here and there
አስነሰነሰ *asnäsännäsä* v.t had *(s/t)* sprinkled, spread about
ተነሰነሰ *tänäsännäsä* v.t was sprinkled, spread about
ነሸጠ *näššätä* v.i suddenly burst out *(talking, singing etc.)*, was enthusiastic
ነሽ *näš* pron. you are *(sing f.)*
ነቀለ *näqqälä* v.t uprooted pulled out; dispossessed, evicted *(tenant from land)*
ነቃይ *näqay* n. one who uproots; evicts
ንቃይ *nəqqay* adj. uprooted
ነቀላ *näqäla* n. action of. uprooting
መንቀያ *mänqäya* n. tool. etc. used to uproot *(s/t)*
ንቅል አለ *nəqqəl alä* v.i was suddenly uprooted, completely uprooted
ንቅልቅል አለ *nəqlqəll alä* v.i was completely uprooted
ተነቀለ *tänäqqälä* v.i was uprooted; was evicted
ነቃቀለ *näqaqqälä* v.t plucked up here and there
አናቀለ *annaqqälä* v.t helped *(s/o)* to pluck, uproot
አስነቀለ *asnäqqälä* v.t. had *(s/t)* uprooted; had *(s/o)* evicted
ነቀርሳ *näqärsa* n. scrofula; chronic ulcer *(of skin)*
የሳምባ— *yäsamba*—n. tuberculosis,
ነቀሰ *näqqäsä* v.i was tattooed; v.t. made a discount
ነቃሽ *näqaš* n. one who tattoos
ንቃሽ *nəqqaš* n. discount
ንቅሳት *nəqqəsat* n. tattoo
ንቃሳታም *nəqqəsatam* adj. tattooed
መንቀሻ *mänqäša* n. tattooing intrument
ተነቀሰ *tänäqqäsä* v.i. was tattooed
አስነቀሰ *asnäqqäsä* v.t. had *(s/o)* tattooed; had a discount made
ነቀነቀ *näqännäqä* v.t. shook *(tree, o/s head etc.)*
ንቅናቄ *nəqənnaqe* n. uprising *(political)*; motion
ንቅነቃ *nəqnäqa* n. agitation *(the liquids in container etc.)*
ተነቀነቀ *tänäqännäqä* v.i was shaken, agitated
ተነቃነቀ *tänäqannäqä* v.i was shaken up, agitated
ተነቃናቂ *tänäqanaqi* adj. moving, having motion; mobile
አነቃነቀ *annäqannäqä* v.t shook *(physically)*, agitated *(pols.)*

አንቃናቂ *annäqanaqi* n. agitator; one who shakes s/t

ነቀዘ *näqqäzä* v.i got weevilly, worm-infested *(grain)*

ንቀዝ *näqäz* n, weevil

ነቃዥ *näqaž* adj. liable to get weevils

ነቀዛም *näqäzam* adj. full of weevils

አነቀዘ *anäqqäzä* v.t caused *(s/t)* to be full of weevils

ነቃቀዘ *näqaqqäzä* v.i. had a few weevils in

ነቀፈ *näqqäfä* v.t criticized *(adversely)*, found fault, blamed

ነቃፊ *näqafi* n. critic, fault-finder

ነቀፋ *näqäfa* n. criticism *(adverse)*, fault-finding

ነቃቀፈ *näqaqqäfä* v.t criticised, blamed *(mildly)*

ተነቀፈ *tänäqqäfä* v.i was criticised, blamed

ተነቃቀፈ *tänäqaqqäfä* v.t criticised, blamed each other

አስነቀፈ *asnäqqäfä* v.i. had *(s/o)* criticised, blamed

አስነቃፊ *asnäqqafi* adj. liable to be criticised, improper *(deed etc.)*

ነቃ *näqqa* v.i got up, woke up; became lively, quick, agile; was full of cracks *(e.g wall)*

ንቁ *nəqu* adj. wide awake, quick, agile, active

ንቃት *nəqat* n. agility, activeness; crack *(e.g. in wall)*

ንቃተ ኅሊና *nəqatä həllina* n. consciousness

ነቃቃ *näqaqqa* v.i revived, came alive

ተነቃቃ *tänäqaqqa* v.i was made active, agile, was encouraged to be active, agile

አነቃ *anäqqa* v.t woke *(s/o)* up; revived *(s/o)*; made conscious

አነቃቃ *annäqaqqa* v.t. made *(s/o)* active, agile; encouraged *(s/o)* to be active, agile

አነቃቂ *annäqaqi* n. one who encourages *(s/o* to be active, agile

ነቈጠ *näqqʷäṭä* v.i was blotted, blotted *(e.g with ink)*

ነቍጥ *näqʷṭ* n. blot, splotch, spot

ነበልባል *näbälbal* n. flame, flare

ነበረ *näbbärä* v. was

ነባር *näbbär* n. *(gram.)* substantive, old-timer; adj. permanent

ንብረት *nəbrät* n. possessions belongings

መንበር *mänbär* n. throne; altar

ወንበር *wänbär* n. chair

ነበራርት *näbärart* n. lynx

*ነበበረ **näbäbbärä*

ንብብር *nəbəbbər* adj. heaped, superimposed, stratum *(layer of s/t)*

ነበበ *näbbäbä* v. resonated *(drum)*, *see also* አነበበ

ነባቢ *näbabi* adj. resonating

ንባብ *nəbab* n. reading

ምንባብ *mənbab* n. reading-book, reader, primer

አነበበ *anäbbäbä* v.t. read

አንባቢ *anbabi* n. reader

ተነበበ *tänäbbäbä* v.i was read

ተነባቢ *tänäbbabi* adj. legible

ተናበበ *tänabbäbä* v.i. compared two versions of a book etc.

ተናባቢ *tanabbabi* n. consonant

አናበበ *annabbäbä* v.t. checked *(one written version against another)*

አናባቢ *annababi* n. vowel

አስነበበ *asnäbbäbä* v.t had *(s/o)* read

*ነበነበ **näbännäbä*

አነበነበ *anäbännäbä* v.i mumbled, gabbled; droned *(of bees)*,

ነበዘ *näbbäzä* v.t changed colour *(dyed cloth)*;

looked drawn, wasted, exhausted *(about the face)*

ንብዝ አለ *nəbbəzz alä* v.i lost colour *(dyed cloth)*

ንብዝብዝ አለ *nəbəzbəzz alä* v.i completely changed colour; was completely changed *(colour)*; was completely drawn, pale *(about the face)*

አነበዘ *anäbbäzä* v.t caused to lose colour; caused to look pale, drawn

ነባ *näbba* v.i wept, cried

አነባ *anäbba* v.i wept, cried

እንባ *ənba* n. tears, teardrops

ነብር *näbər* n. leopard

ነብርማ *näbrəmma* adj. spotted *(animals)*

ነብሮ *näbro* n. biceps *(meat)*

ነቦጨ *näbboč̣ä* v.i splattered out, exploded *(from smashed vessel)*

ነተረከ *nätärräkä* v.i nagged, bickered, quarrelled

ነትራኪ *nätraki* adj. nagging, bickering, quarrelling

ንትርክ *nətərrək* n. action of nagging, bickering, quarrelling

ተነታረከ *tänätarräkä* v.i nagged each other

ተነታራኪ *tänätaraki* adj/n *(one)* who constantly nags

አነታረከ *annätarräkä* v.t caused people to nag, bicker

ነተበ *nättäbä* v.i was raged *(clothes)*

ነት *nät* n. sleeping mat *(of decorated leather)*

ነኈለለ *nähuʷällälä* v.i. grew simple-minded, imbecile

ነኋላላ *nähuʷlalla* adj. imbecile

ነኋለል *nähʷäläl* n/adj. imbecile

አነኈለለ *anähʷällälä* v.t stupefied

nän n. pron. we are

ነኝ *näññ* pron. I am

ነከረ *näkkärä* v.t soaked

ንክር *nəkər* adj. soaked

መንከሪያ *mänkäriya* n. basin, vesssel *(for soaking)*

ተነከረ *tänäkkärä* v.i. was soaked

አስነከረ *asnäkkärä* v.t had *(s't)* soaked

ነከሰ *näkkäsä* v.t bit

ነከስ አደረገ *näkäss adärrägä* v.t nibbled, bit a little

ንክሳት *nəkkəsat* n. bite *(place on skin)*

ንከሻ *nəkəša* n. bite *(place on skin)*

ንክስ አደረገ *nəkkəs adärrägä* v.t. bit hard, severely

ነካከሰ *näkakkäsä* v.t nibbled here and there

ተነከሰ *tänäkkäsä* v.i was bitten

ተነካከሰ *tänäkakkäsä* v.t bit each other; hated each other bitterly

አናከሰ *annakkäsä* v.t set at each other *(dogs)*; created animosity

ተናከሰ *tänakkäsä* v.t bit *(dog)*; had a severe grudge against each other

ተናካሽ *tänakaš* adj. liable to bite *(dog)*

አስነከሰ *asnäkkäsä* v.t had *(s/o)* bitten *(by a dog)*; was turned against one *(superior etc. through gossip)*

ነከተ *näkkätä* v.i was broken, smashed

ነካ *näkka* v.t touched; had sexual intercourse *(polite)*

ንክ *nək* adj. slightly unbalanced, mentally touched

ንክኪት *nəkəkkit* n. contamination *(by touching)*; contact

ንክክ *nəkəkk* n. contamination *(by touching)*; contact

ነካካ *nākakka* v.t touched lightly; felt with the hands; provoked slightly, teased

ተነካ *tänäkka* vi was touched; was distressed, moved *(by s/t)*

ተነካካ *tänäkakka* v.t contaminated s/o *(by touch)*

አናካ *annakka* v.i caused *(s/o)* to be contaminated; caused *(people)* to quarrel

አናኪ *annaki* n. trouble-stirrer, malicious gossipper

አነካካ *annäkakka* v.t caused s/o to be contaminated; caused *(people)* to quarrel

አነካኪ *annäkaki* n/adj. *(one)* who stirs up trouble between people by malicious gossip

አስነካ *asnäkka.* v.t had *(s/t, s/o)* touched

ነኰተ *näkkʷätä* v.i was broken into pieces

ንኳች *nəkkəʷač* n. broken fragments

እንኩቶ *ənkʷəṭo* n. roasted beans, peas, lentils *(etc.)* in shell; riff—raff

አነኰተ *anäkkʷätä* v.t roasted, *(peas, beans etc.)*

አንኳኰተ *anäkʷakkʷätä* v.t broke into pieces, smashed up

ነወር አለ *näwär alä* v.i stood up *(politely on entrance of guest etc.)*

ነውረኛ *näwräñña* adj/n. impolite, indecent

ነውር *näwər* adj/n. impolite, indecent

አስነወረ *asnäwwärä* v.i was shameful, indecent, impolite

አስነዋሪ *asnäwwari* adj. shameful, indecent

ነው *näw* v.*t*. it is

ነው እኮ *näw əkko excl.* indeed, it is!

ነዘረ *näzzärä* v.i throbbed gave pain *(wound)*; tingled *(limb after cramp)*; vibrated

ንዝረት *nəzzərat* n. throbbing, tingling vibration

ነዛነዘ *näzännäzä* v.t was importunate, nagged

ነዝናዛ *näznazza* adj. importunate, nagging

ነዝናዥ *näznaž* adj. importunate, nagging

ንዝነዛ *nəznäza* n. importuning, nagging

ተነዛነዘ *tänäzännäzä* v.i was bothered, nagged *(by s/o)*

ተነዛነዘ *tänäzannäzä* v.t bothered, nagged

ተነዛናዥ *tänäzanaž* adj. bothersome, nagging

ነዛ *näzza* v.t spread *(news, gossip)*; laid out *(money)*

ጉራውን— *gurrawən*—v.t was boastful

ተነዛ *tänäzza* v.i was spread *(news)*

ነደለ *näddälä* v.t perforated, poked a hole in

ነዳደለ *nädäddälä* v.t pierced here and there

አስነደለ *asnäddälä* v.t had s/t pierced, perforated

ነደደ *näddädä* v.i burned

ነዳጅ *nädaǧ* n/adj. *(petrol, diesel etc.)* inflammable

—ማደያ ጣቢያ *—maddäya ṭabiya* n. fueling station

ንዴት *nəddet* n. great anger, rage, fury, vexation

ንዴተኛ *nəddetäñña* adj. touchy, easily angered

ንዴታም *nəddetam* adj. touchy, easily angered

ንዳድ *nədad* n. malaria; high fever

ተናደደ *tänaddädä* v.i became furious, vexed

got angry, mad, was indignant

ተናዳጅ *tänadağ* ad. adj/n (*one*) who is easily irritated

አናደደ *annaddädä* v.t incited fury, vexation; angered, infuriated, enraged

አናዳጅ *annadağ* adj/n. (*s/t*) that incites fury, vexation

ነደፈ *näddäfä* v.t. stung (*e.g bee*); bit (*snake*); drew a sketch; carded, teased cotton

ነዳፊ *nädafi* adj./n. biting, stinging

ንድፍ *nədəf* n. sketch, design; carded, teased cotton

መንደፊያ *mändäfiya* n. bow (*for teasing out cotton*); sketching, designing instrument

ነዳደፈ *nädaddäfä* v.t stung in several places; drew a rough sketch

ተነደፈ *tänäddäfä* v.i was stung; was sketched; was teased, carded (*cotton*)

ተነዳደፈ *tänädaddäfä* v.t. stung each other

አናደፈ *annaddäfä* v.t. helped to sketch

አስነደፈ *asnäddäfä* v.t had (*s/o*) sketch (*s/t*); had (*s/o*) tease out (*cotton*)

ነዳ *nädda* v. drove (*car, animals etc.*)

ነጂ *näği* n. driver

መንጃ *mänğa* n. goad, stick for driving (*animals*)

—ፈቃድ — *fäqad* n. driving license

ተነዳ *tänädda* v.i was driven

አነዳድ *annädad* v.i way, manner of driving

አናዳ *annadda* v.t helped (*s/o*) to drive (*cattle*)

አስነዳ *asnädda* v.t had s/o drive (*cattle*); rustled, took away (*cattle*)

ነዶ *nädo* n. sheaf (*grass, hay etc.*)

ነገ *see* ነጋ

ነገሠ *näggäsä* v.i. reigned

ነጋሢ *nägasi or* ነጋሽ *nägaš* n. sovereign, ruler

ንጉሥ *nəgus* n. king

አፈ ንጉሥ *afä nəgus* n. title (*equivalent to lord chamberlain*)

ንጉሠ ነገሥት *nəgusä nägäst* n. emperor

ንግሥ *nəgs* adj. reigning

ሥርዓተ— *sər'atä* –n. coronation

ንግሥት *nəgəst* n. queen

ንግሥተ ነገሥታት *nəgəstä nägästat* n. empress

መንግሥት *mängəst* n. government

መንግሥተ ሰማያት *mängəstä sämayat* n. Kingdom of Heaven

በትረ መንግሥት *bäträ mängəst* n. royal staff (*of office*)

መናገሻ *männagäša* n. capital city

አነገሠ *anäggäsä* v.t. made (*s/o*) king

አንጋሽ *angaš* n.king-maker

ነገረ *näggärä* v.t told

ነጋሪ *nägari* n.teller

ነጋሪት *nägarit* n.large ceremonial drum

—ጋዜጣ —*gazeta* n.official gazette

ነገር *nägär* n. thing, case, word, matter, affair etc.

ነገረኛ *nägäräňňa* n. trouble-maker, trouble-stirrer; party to legal case

ቁም— *qum* — adj. trustworthy, dutiful, responsible

በነገሬ ላይ *bänägäre lai* by the way

ነገር ግን *nägär gən* adv. but

ንግር *nəggər also* ንግርት *nəggərt* n. sooth saying, prophecy

ንግርተኛ *nəggərtäñña* n. sooth sayer, prophet

ንግግር *nəgəggər* n. talk, speech, dialogue, discourses etc.

ተነጋገረ *tänägaggärä* v.i talked to each other, held a dialogue, chatted with each other

ተናገረ *tänaggärä* v.t said, talked

ተናጋሪ *tänagari* n/adj. good speaker, eloquent *(person)* orator; talkative

አነጋጋሪ *annägagari* n. interpreter

አነጋገር *annägagär* n. way, manner of talking

ትንግርት *təngərt* adj. unbelievable, amazing

አናገረ *annaggärä* v.t talked to *(s/o)*; made *s/o* talk; gave an audience to

አናጋሪ *annagari* n. *(person)* who leads *(s/o)* on, makes *(s/o)* talk

ነጋገረ *nägaggärä* v.t advised, warned

ተነጋገረ *tänägaggärä* v.t talked to each other; held a dialogue; chatted with each other

አስነገረ *asnäggärä* v.t had *(s/t)* told to *(s/o)*

* ነገተ *see* አነገተ

ነገደ *näggädä* v.t traded

ነጋዴ *näggade* n. merchant

የነጋዴዎች ምክር ቤት *yänäggadewočč məkər bet* chamber of commerce

ንግድ *nəgd* n. trade

የንግድ ምልክት *yänəgd mələkkət* n. trade mark

—ፈቃድ *—fäqad* trade-licence

ንገዳ *nəggäda* n. trading.

ነጋድራስ *näggadras* n. great merchant *(arch.)*

ነጋገደ *nägaggädä;* v.i traded a little *(as a sideline)*

ተነጋገደ *tänägaggädä* v.t bartered, traded, with each other

አስነገደ *asnäggädä* v.t had *(s/o)* engage in trade *(on o/s behalf)*

ነጋ *nägga* v.i dawned, became morning

—ጠባ *ṭäbba* adv. persistently, always, day in day out

በበነጋው *bäbänägaw* the following day, on the morrow

ንጋት *nəgat* n.dawn

ነገ *nägä* n. tomorrow

ለነገ የማይል *länägä yämmayəl* adj. unsparing

ነጋጋ *nägagga* v.i got light *(in the morning)*

አነጋ *anägga* v.i stayed up all night

አነጋጋ *anägagga* v.i stayed up all night

አስነጋ *asnägga* v.t had s/o stay all night

* ነጋ *see* አናጋ

ነጋሪት *nägarit* n ceremonial drum, *see also* ነገረ

ነጐረ *nägg^{w}ärä* v.i was clarified *(butter, by boiling)*

ንጉር *nəg^{w}ur* n. boiled, clarified *(butter)*

አነጐረ *anägg^{w}ärä* v.t clarified, boiled *(butter)*

አስነጐረ *asnägg^{w}ärä* v.t had *(butter)* clarified, boiled

ነጐደ *näg^{w}ädä* v.i thundered off; marched off determinedly

ነጐዴ *näg^{w}äde* n. any migrant bird

አነጐደ *anägg^{w}ädä* v.t hit heavily with a stick; hastened to finish work

ነጠለ *näţţälä* v.i split up a double sheet
ነጠላ *näţäla* adj. single; singular *(gram.)*; kind of shawl-like garment made of a single layer of cloth
—ሠረዝ *—säräz* comma ፣
—ጫማ *—čamma* n. sandals
—ቁጥር *—quţər* n. singular *(gram.)*
ንጣይ *nəţţay* n. one taken from a pair
ንጥል *nəţţəl* n. one taken from a pair
ነጣጠለ *näţaţţälä* v.t split up *(group)*; scattered, separated up
ተነጠለ *tänäţţälä* v.i was taken *(from a pair)*; stood out *(from a group, i.e. by disagreeing with majority)*
ተነጣይ *tänäţţay* n. one who stands out in a group
ተነጣጠለ *tänäţaţţälä* v.i split up *(group)*
አነጣጠለ *annäţaţţälä* v.t caused to split up
አስነጠለ *asnäţţälä* v.t had *(a group)* split up
ነጠረ *näţţärä* v.t bounced *(ball)*; refined *(by melting, e.g gold)*
ነጣሪ *näţari* n. bouncing
ንጥር *nəţər* adj. refined
ጥንተ— *ţəntä—* n. element *(chemical)*
ንጥር ቅቤ *nəţər qəbe* n. refined butter
—ወርቅ *—wärq* n. refined gold
ተነጠረ *tänäţţärä* v.i was refined
አነጠረ *anäţţärä* v.t refined; bounced
አንጣሪ *anţari* n. refiner
ወርቅ— *wärq—* n. goldsmith
አንጥረኛ *anţəräñña* n. silversmith
ማንጠሪያ *manţäriya* n. refining flux
አናጠረ *anäţţärä* v.i acted flamboyantly
አስነጠረ *asnäţţärä* v.t had *(s/t)* refined
ነጠቀ *näţţäqä* v.t snatched, took by force
ነጣቂ *näţaqi* n. robber
ንጥቂያ *nəţqiya* n. robbery
መንጠቆ *mänţäqqo* n. angling, fishing rod
ነጣጠቀ *näţaţţäqä* v.t robbed, snatched *(s/t)* from several people
ተነጠቀ *tänäţţäqä* v.i was snatched; was robbed
ተናጠቀ *tänaţţäqä* v.t struggled over, fought *(over s/t)*
ተናጣቂ *tänaţaqi* n. one who takes things by force, robber, thief
ተነጣጠቀ *tänäţaţţäqä* v.t struggled over, fought *(over s/t)*
አናጠቀ *annaţţäqä* v.t caused to quarrel over, fight over *(s/t)*
አስነጠቀ *asnäţţäqä* v.t had *s/o* robbed
ነጠበ *näţţäbä* v.i. dripped; blotted, blotched, *(e.g with ink)*
ነጥብ *näţəb* n. point, dot
ነጠብጣብ *näţäbţab* n. dots *(...)*
አነጠበ *anäţţäbä* v.t blotted, blotched
ነጠፈ *näţţäfä* v.i dried up *(spring etc.)*; went dry *(i.e stopped giving milk, cow)*
ነጣፊ *näţafi* v.t likely to be dry, go dry
አነጠፈ *anäţţäfä* v.t caused *(s/t)* to dry up, go dry; spread mat, carpet, made *(bed)*
አንጣፊ *anţafi* n. chambermaid, room boy

አስነጠፈ *asnäṭṭäfä* v.t had bed made; had *(s/t)* spread on floor

ምንጣፍ *mənṭaf* n. carpet, rug, mat

ነጣ *näṭṭa* v.i became white, pale *(face)*. became clean

ነጭ *näčč* adj. white; n. white *(person)*

ንጣት *nəṭat* n. whiteness

ነጣጣ *näṭaṭṭa* v.i became lighter, whitish

አነጣ *anäṭṭa* v.t made *(s/t)* white, clean

አነጣጣ *anäṭaṭṭa* v.t cleaned up a little, made whiter

አስነጣ *asnäṭṭa* v.t had *(s/t)* whitened, cleaned

ነጥር *näṭər* n. pound *(measure of weight)*

ነጨ *näččä* v.t plucked out *(hair, grass etc.)* by the roots

ነጫጨ *näčaččä* v.t plucked up here and there

ተነጨ *tänäččä* v.i was plucked up

ተነጫጨ *tänäčaččä* v.i plucked out each other's *(hair etc.)*

አስነጨ *asnäččä* v.t had *(s/t)* plucked up

*ነጨነጨ *see* ተነጫነጨ

ነጸብራቅ *see* *ጸበረቀ *and* አንጸባረቀ

ነጻ *näṣṣa* v.i became clean, *see also* ነጣ

ንጹሕ *nəṣuh* adj. clean

ንጻት *nəṣat* n. cleanliness

ንጹሕነት *nəṣuhənnät* n. cleanliness

ንጽሕና *nəṣəhənna* n. cleanliness

አነጻ *anäṣṣa* v.i cleaned

ነጻነት *näṣannät* n. freedom, liberty,independence

*ነጸጸረ *see* አነጻጸረ

ነፈለለ *näfällälä* adj. acted foolishly, idiotically, became imbecilic

ነፈላል *näfäläl* adj. idiot-like, imbecilic, moronic

ነፍላላ *näflalla* adj. idiot-like

ነፈረ *näffärä* v.i was overcooked, overboiled: boiled furiously *(water)*

ንፍር *nəfər* adj. overcooked, overboiled; furiously boiling *(water)*

ንፍሮ *nəfro* n. boiled beans, peas, chickpeas etc.

አነፈረ *anäffärä* v.t overcooked, overboiled

ነፈረቀ *näfärräqä* v.i suppurated *(boil, wound)*; sobbed bitterly *(child)*

ነፍራቃ *näfraqqa* adj. who sobs bitterly *(child)*

ተነፋረቀ *tänäfarräqä* v.i. cried, wept constantly; nagged *(child of its parents)*

ተነፋራቂ *tänäfaraqi* adj. *(child)* who cries excessively, nags

አነፋረቀ *annäfärräqä* v.t. spoiled *(child)*

ነፈሰ *näffäsä* v.t blew, wind, breathed

ግራም-ቀኝ *gəramm–qäññ* what ever may be, be that as it may

ነፈሰበት *näffäsäbbät* he is out of favour

ነፋሽ *näfaš* adj. breathing, blowing

ነፋሻ *näffašša* n. airy place, open area

ነፋስ *näfas* n. wind, air, fresh air

ዐውሎ — *awlo—* n. whirlwind, dust-devil, tornado

ነፍስ *näfs* n. spirit, soul

ነፍሰ ቢስ *näfsä bis* adj. hectic *(without rest)*

—ገዳይ *—gäday* n. assassin, murderer

ነፍሱን ሳተ *näfsun satä* v.t fainted, lost consciousness

ነፍስ ዐወቀ *näfs awwäqä* v.t. was mature

ነፍሱን— *näfsun*—v.t. recovered consciousness

ነፍስ ዘራ *näfs zärra* v.t regianed consciousness.

በነፍሱ ደረሰ *bänäfsu därräsä* he came to his rescue *(on time)*

ነፍሰጡር *näfsäṭur* n. pregnant woman *(polite)*

በነፍስ ወከፍ *bänäfs wäkkäf* adv. one each, individually

ንፋሽ *naffaš* n. chaff, dirt *(from winnowing)*

ነፍሳት *näfsat* n. germs, insects

መንፈስ *mänfäs* inf. to blow, breathe. n. ghost, spirit

—ቅዱስ —*qəddus* n. Holy Spirit

መንፈሳዊ *mänfäsawi* adj. spiritual

መንፈሳዊነት *mänfäsawinnät* n. spirituality

ነፋፈሰ *näfaffäsä* v.t blew, breathed *(slightly, lightly)*

ተነፈሰ *tänäffäsä* v.t breathed; exhaled, was winnowed; rested a little; licked *(of a tyre)*

ጎማው— *gommaw*—the tyre is flat

ትንፋሽ *tənffaš* adj. breathing

ተነፋፈሰ *tänäfaffäsä* v.i. breathed lightly; had a short rest; went out for fresh air

ትንፋሽ *tənfäš* n. breath

ተናፈሰ *tänaffäsä* v.i. went out for fresh air

መናፈሻ *männafäšä* n. open-air place, airy place

አነፈሰ *anäffäsä* v.t winnowed, threw grain up in to the wind,

ወሬ— *wäre*—talked gossip

ማንፈሻ *manfäšä* n. winnowing fan, basket

አነፋፈሰ *anäfaffäsä* v.t winnowed a little

አናፈሰ *annaffäsä* v.t aerated, aired out, ventilated

አስነፈሰ *asnäffäsä* v.t exposed to air *(with bad result)*

አስተነፈሰ *astänäffäsä* v.i lost air *(tyre)*; gave *(s/o)* a break *(from work)*

ነፈነፈ *näfännäfä* v.t enjoyed eating *(with good appetite)*

ነፍናፋ *näfnaffa* n. one having nasal speech defect

ተነፋነፈ *tänäfannäfä* v.i spoke nasally; grumbled *(obeyed with bad grace)*

ተነፋናፊ *tänäfanafi* n. one who speaks nasally; one who grumbles *(orders)*

አነፈነፈ *anäfännäfä* v.t sniffed, nosed about *(dog etc.)*

ነፈገ *näffägä* v.i was miserly, stingy; denied

ነፋጊ *näfagi* n. miser

ንፉግ *nəfug* adj. miserly, stingy

ንፍገት *nəfgät* n. miserliness, avarice

ተነፈገ *tänäffägä* v.i was prevented from doing *(s/t)*, having *(s/t)*

ተነፋፈገ *tänäfaffägä* v.i prevented each other from doing, having *(s/t)*

*ነፈጠ *see* ተናፈጠ

ነፋ *näffa* v.t blew *(s/t)*

ነፊ *näffi in* ጥሩምባ ነፊ *tərumba näfi* n. trumpeter

ንፍ *nəf* adj. inflated

ንፊት *nəffit* n. blowing,

blowing up
መንፊያ *mänfiya* n. air pump
ወንፊት *wänfit* n. seive, strainer
ወናፍ *wänaf* n. leather bellows
ነፋፋ *näfaffa* v.t inflated slightly, blew a little air
ተነፋ *tänäffa* v.i was in- flated, blown; was extremely proud
ተነፋፋ *tänäfaffa* v.i was blown-out, over inflated
ተናፋ *tänaffa* v.t hit each other, boxed, each other *(coll.)*
አናፋ *anaffa* v.t. brayed *(donkey)*
አስነፋ *asnäffa* v.t. had *(s/t)* inflated
ነፍጥ *näft* n. gun, firearm
ነፍጠኛ *näftäñña* n. rifle- man, sniper, armed retainer
ኑር see ናረ
ኑዛዜ *nuzaze* n. will, testa- ment
ተናዘዘ *tänazzäzä* v.t. made *(o/s)* will
ተናዛዥ *tänazaž* n. one who makes his will *(usually dying man)*
አናዘዘ *anazzäzä* v.t had *(s/o)* make his will
አናዛዥ *annazaž* n. s/o *(priest, elder)* who orders s/o to make his will
ኑግ *nug* n. niger seed
ቅባ ኑግ *qəba nug* n. oil- niger
ኒሻን *nišan or* ሊሻን *lišan* n. medal
ኒኬል *nikel or* ንኬል *nəkel* n. nickel
ና *na* imp. come!
—ና —*nna or* እና *ənna* suff. and
ናላ *nala* n. brain
ናሙና *namuna* n. sample, specimen

ናስ *nas* n. brass, *also* ነሐስ
ናረ *narä* v.i inflated *(raise of price)*
ንረት *in* የዋጋ ንረት *yäwaga nərät* n.inflation*(price)*
ናቀ *naqä* v.t looked down on; ignored, be- littled
ንቀት *nəqät* n. looking down on; despising, ignoring, belittling
ተናቀ *tänaqä* v.i was looked down on; de- spised
ተናናቀ *tänanaqä* v.t despised each other
አስናቀ *asnaqä* v.i was outstanding, excellent, incompar- able; degraded
ናኘ *naññä* v.t scattered
ተናኘ *tänaññä* v.i was scat- tered
ናቸው *naččäw pron.* they are
ናችሁ *naččəhu* you are *(pl.)*
ናወዘ *nawwäzä* v.i was rest- less; wandered around
ናውዥ *nawwaž* v.i restless person
ናዘዘ see ተናዘዘ
ናዝራዊ *nazrawi* adj/n. ascetic *(person)*
ናደ *nadä* v.t demolished, broke up, crumbled
ናዳ *nada* n. boulder, land slip, land slide
ተናደ *tänadä* v.i was broken up, de- molished
አስናደ *asnadä* v.t had *(s/t)* demolished
ናጠ *naṭä* v.t churned *(to make butter)*
ናጭ *nač̣* n. butter- churner
መናጫ *mänač̣a* n. churn
ተናጠ *tänaṭä* v.i was churned
አስናጠ *asnaṭä* v.t had *(butter churned)*
ናፈቀ *naffäqä* v.t yearned

for, longed for; had nostalgia, missed

ናፋቂ *nafaqi* adj. nostalgic *(person)*

ናፍቆት *nafqot* n. yearning, longing, nostalgia

ተናፈቀ *tänaffäqä* v.i was longed for, missed

ተናፋቂ *tänafaqi* adj. longed for, yearned for, missed

ተነፋፈቀ *tänäfaffäqä* v.t lónged, missed each other

ተነፋፋቂ *tänäfafaqi* adj. !onging for *(each other)*

—ን —*n (gram.)* direct object marker

ንስሐ *nəssəha* n. repentance

—ገባ —*gäbba* v.t repented

የንስሐ አባት *yänəssəha abbat* n. father–confessor

ንስር *nəsər* n. eagle

ንብ *nəb* n. bee

የንብ ዕጭ *yänəb əč̣* n. bee larva

ንብረት *nəbrät* n. property

ባለ ንብረት *balä nəbrät* n. owner

የአየር ንብረት *yä'ayyär nəbrät* n. climate, weather

ንዋይ *nəway* n. money *(G.)*

ንዋየ ቅድሳት *nəwayä qəddəsat* n. church equipment

ንዑስ *nə'us* adj. small; sub- e.g ንዑስ ኮሚቴ sub-committe, ንኡስ ሐረግ subordinate clause

ንጉሥ *see* ነገሠ

ንፍር *see* ነፈረ

ኖረ *norä* v.i lived

ኗሪ *nʷari or* ነዋሪ *näwari* adj/n. alive, living, inhabitant

ኑሮ *nuro* n. life; way of living

መኖሪያ *mänoriya* n. dwelling place, domicile

ተኖረ *tänorä* v.i was lived *(a life)*

ተኗኗረ *tänʷanʷarä* v.i co-existed; accomodated, bore with *(each other)*

አኖረ *anorä* v.t. placed *(s/t)*, set *(s/t,)* down; put *(s/o)* up

ማኖሪያ *manoriya* n. place for storing, putting things

ኖር አለ *nor alä, or* ነወር አለ *näwär alä* v.i. stood up *(politely on entrance of a guest etc.)*

አሁን *ahun* adv. now, right now presently, at persent, soon

—ለታ —*läta* some days ago

አሁንም *ahunəmm* adv. yet, even now, still

—ይማራል —*yəmmaral* he is still learning

አሁን ባሁን *ahun bahun* adv. how quickly! here and now, at this very moment

አሁንም አሁንም *ahunəmm ahunəmm* adv. constantly, repeatedly

—ሆነ ኋላ —*honä huʷala* sooner or later

አሁንስ *ahunəss* but now

አሁኑኑ *ahununu* adv. right away, at once, inmediately

አሁን ካሁን *ahun kahun* at any moment

—ገና *—gäna* just now, just this moment

ላሁኑ *lahun* just this once; for the time being

ባሁኑ ጊዜ *bahun gize* adv. now a days, currently

እስካሁን *əskahun* up to now, thus far; still

ካሁን ጀምሮ *kahun gämməro* from now on

ገና አሁን *gäna ahun* just now

አሄ *ahe or* አሄሄ *ahehe* excl. oh, no! *(disapproval of, e.g. course of action)*

አህያ *ahəyya* n. donkey, ass

የሜዳ-- *yämeda*-n. zebra, wild ass

አለ *alä* v.t said, spoke

ይበል *imperfect* ይል ፣ ይላል *jussive* ይበል *imp.* በል

ይላል *yəlal* he says;

ማር ማር ይላል *mar mar yəlall* it is sweet *(it has the taste of honey)*

በል *bal* say; come on, well then

በለው *bäläw* let him have it, hit him

ለ... ብሎ *lä...bəlo* for the sake of

ለ...ሲል *la...sil* for the benefit of

ሲል ሲል *sil sil* gradually, little by little

እንበል *ənbäl* let us suppose

ማን ልበል *man ləbäl* may I ask what your name is? whom shall I say? who is speaking ?

ባይ *bay* adj. *(one)* who speaks, says *(s/t)*

አልባሌ *aləbbale* adj.ordinary, unremarkable

ማለት *malät* inf. to say, speak; to mean; that is to say

አሉታ *aluta* negative *(gram.)*

አሉባልታ *alubalta* n. gossip

ተባለ *täbalä* v.i was said, spoken

ተባባለ *täbabalä* v.t said to each other; hit each other; agreed together *(on a price)*

አባባለ *abbabalä* v.t brought *(parties)* to an agreement

አባባል *abbabal* n. way of explaining, saying *(s/t)*, expression

አለ *allä* v.i there is

አለሁ አለሁ ባይ *allähu allahu bay* adj. pretentious, boastful

አለበት *alläbbät* he must e.g. መናገር-*männagär*—he has to speak

ማን አለብኝ ባይ *mann alläbbəññ bay* despot

ምን አለብኝ *mən alläbbəññ* how much money do I owe you

በሌለበት *bälelläbät* in his absence

በያለበት *bäyyalläbbät* everywhere

ከያለበት *käyyalläbbät* from all over

አለኝታ *alläñta* n. mainstay, reason for living

የለም *yälläm* v.i there not *(any)*; adv. no

ያለ የሌለ *yallä yälellä* in full force, all imaginable *(things)*

አለለ *allälä* v.i was frisky, aroused *(mating donkey)*

አለሌ *aläle* adj. frisky, aroused *(mating donkey)*; playboy, womaniser

አለል ዘለል አለ *aläll zäläll alä* v.i wandered about aimlessly

አለሎ *alällo* n. pestle, round stone *(used for crushing grain etc.)*

አለመ *allämä* v.t dreamed

አላሚ *allami* n. dreamer, one who has dreams

አልም *əlm or* ሕልም *həlm* n. dream
አለመጠ *alämmäṭä* v.i slowed down *(work)*; mocked *(s/o) see also* ለመጠ
አልማጭ *almač* n. one who slows down *(at work)*; mocker
አለቀ *alläqä* v.i finished; was consumed, terminated
አላቂ *alaqi* adj. consumable
—እቃ *—əqa* n. consumable goods
እላቂ *əllaqi* n. remnants; tattered clothes
እልቂት *əlqitt* n. extermination *(of people)*
እልቅ *əlq* n. all or nothing *(as a bet, wager)*
እልቅ አለ *əlqq alä* v.i was completely used up, finished
ተላለቀ *tälalläqä* v.t killed each other off
አስተላለቀ *astälalläqä* v.t caused to kill each other
አለቀሰ *aläqqäsä* v.i wept, cried, *see* ልቅሶ
አልቃሽ *alqaš* n. professional mourner
አልቃሻ *alqašša* n/adj. *(child)* who cries continuously
ለቀስተኛ *läqqästäñña* n. mourner
ልቅሶ *ləqso* n. mourning, lamentation, crying
ማልቀሻ *mälqaša* n. reliques *(dead person's effects displayed at funeral)*
አለቃቀሰ *aläqaqqäsä* v.i cried a little
አላቀሰ *allaqqäsä* v.t consoled, visited *(bereaved person)*
አላቃሽ *allaqaš* n. visitors *(to bereaved)*
ተላቀሰ *tälaqqäsä* v.i mourned for s/o
አስለቀሰ *asläqqäsä* v.t caused s/o cry, weep
አስለቃሽ *asläqqaš* n. s/t which causes grief, weeping
አለቃ *aläqa* n. chief, head
አለቅነት *aläqənnät* chiefdom
እልቅና *əlqənna* n. chiefdom
አለበ *alläbä* v.t milked; left marker *(in book)*
አላቢ *alabi* n. milkmaid, milker
እልባት *ələbat* n. bookmark
ማለቢያ *malläbbiya* n. milking pail
ማለቢያ *maläbiya* n. s/t used as bookmark
ታለበ *talläba* v.i was milked
ታላቢ *talabi* n. milk cow, dairy cow
አሳለበ *asalläbä* v.i had *(cow, goat etc.)* milked
አለበለዚያ *aläbälläzziya* adv. otherwise, *also* አለዚያ
አለት *alät* n. rock, hard stone
አለንጋ *alänga* n whip
አለኝታ *alläññəta* n. moral support
አለከለከ *aläkälläkä* v.i panted
አለክላኪ *aläklaki* adj. panting
አለጐመ *alägg^wämä* v.t worked slowly
አልጓሚ *alg^wami* n.slow worker
አለጠ *alläṭä* v.i was thin, flavourless *(food, wäṭ)*
አልጫ *alləčča* n. pepperless wäṭ
አለፈ *alläfä* v.t passed by; guaranteed *(s/o)*
አላፊ *alafi* n/adj. passer-by; passenger; responsible
አላፊነት *alafinnät* n. responsibility
እልፊት *əlfitt* n. transgression, contempt *(of court)*
ማለፊያ *mäläfiya* n. passage, corridor etc.; adj. acceptable, good

ታለፈ	*talläfä* v.i was passed, was ignored
ተላለፈ	*tälalläfä* v.i passed each other *(on the way)*; was postponed; trespassed, broke a law
ተላላፊ	*tälalafi* n. passer-by; traffic
—በሽታ	*—bäššəta* n. contagious disease
መተላለፊያ	*mättälaläfiya* n. way through; passageway
አሳለፈ	*asalläfä* v.t allowed to pass; acted as usher, a waiter
አሳላፊ	*asallafi* n. waiter
አስተላለፈ	*astälalläfä* v.t postponed; directed *(traffic, e.g policeman)*
አለፋ	*see* ለፋ
አለፋጨቀ	*alläfaččäqä* v.t squeezed out, squashed *(in the hand)*
አሉባልታ	*alubalta* n. gossip, hearsay, *see also* አለ
አሉማ	*aluma* n. amaranth
አሉታ	*aluta* n. negative, negation
አላመጠ	*allammäṭä* v.t chewed
ተላመጠ	*tälammäṭä* v.i was chewed
አላሰ	*alasä* v,i have s/o lick something *(e.g from fingers)*; diluted *ṭäǧ* with honey, *see* ላሰ
አላሸቀ	*see* ላሸቀ
አላባ	*alaba* n. produce, income *(from land)*
—ገለባ	*—gäläba* n. farm products
አላድ	*alad* n. half bərr *(arch.)*
አል—	*al—*pref. gram. negative marker
አልማዝ	*almaz* n. diamond
አልባሌ	*aləbbale* adj. ordinary, unremarkable *(person)*; *see also* አለ
አልቦ	*albo* n. spacing bead *(annular, usu. silver)*
አልኮል	*alkol* n. alcohol
አልኮሰኮሰ	*alkosäkkosä* v.i worked haphazardly
አልኮስኳሽ	*alkoskʷaš* n. slovenly worker
አልጋ	*alga* n. bed; kingship
—ወራሽ	*- wäräš* n. crown-prince
ድንክ-	*dənk-* n. truckle bed
ያልጋ ልብስ	*yalga ləbs* n. bed clothes
ባላልጋ	*balalga* n. occupant of the throne monarch
አልጐመጐመ	*algʷämäggʷämä* v.i grumbled *(over work)*
አልጐምጓሚ	*algʷämgʷami* n. grumbler
አልሜ	*see* አለጠ
አሎሎ	*alollo* n. pestle *(round stone for crushing grain)*, iron ball
አመለመለ	*amälämmälä* v.t rolled *(cotton in palms for ease of spinning)*
አመልማሎ	*amälmalo* n. wad of raw cotton *(rolled for spinning)*
አመለከተ	*amäläkkätä* v.t pointed at; applied *(e.g for work)*; turned ones attention, notified signifed *see also* ተመለከተ
አመልካች	*amälkač* n. applicant *(e.g. for work)*
—ተውላጠ ስም	*—ṭäwläṭä səm (gram.)* demonstrative pronoun
—ቅጽል	*—qəṣṣəl* n. *(gram.)* demonstrative adjective
ማመልከቻ	*mamälkäča* n. application *(for work)*
ምልክት	*mələkkət* n. sign mark; indication trace, symptom; signal
የንግድ—	*yänəgd—*n. trade mark
አስመለከተ	*asmäläkkätä* v.t felt the inclination *(to do s/t)*
አመለከ	*amälläkä* v.t worshipped

አምላኪ amlaki n. worshipper
ጣዖት— ṭa'ot—n. idolater
አምላክ amlak n. God
አምልኮ amləko a. woship
—ጣዖት —ṭa'ot n. idolatry
ተመለከ tāmällākā v.i was worshipped
ተመላኪ tāmällaki n. object of worship
አመለጠ see መለጠ
አመላለሰ see መለሰ
አመል amäl n. habit, character, bad temper
አመለኛ amäläñña adj. moody, bad-tempered
ላመል lamäl adv. barely, slightly, lightly, only
አመመ ammämä v.i was sick, ill (usu.with pronominal suffix) e.g አመመኝ amämäññ I feel sick, I feel ill
እመም əmäm or ሕመም həmäm n. disease, sickness
እመምተኛ əmämtäñña n. patient sick person
አማመመ amammämä v.i had slight pain, felt a little ill
ታመመ tammämä v.i was sick, ill
ታማሚ tamami n. sick person, patient
አሳመመ asammämä v.t hurt (s/o)
አመረረ see መረረ
አመረቀዘ see መረቀዘ
አመራ see መራ
አመሰ ammäsä v.t shuffled (e.g coffee beans on griddle); stirred (people up), agitated
አማሽ ammaš n. one who stirs up trouble
እምስ əmməs adj. lightly roasted (grain)
ማመሻ mammäša n. spatula (stick) for turning, roasting grain etc.
ታመሰ tammäsä v.i was turned, shuffled (roasting grain etc.); was troubled
አሳመሰ asammäsä v.t had (s/t) turned, shuffled (roasting grain etc.)
አመሰቃቀለ ammäsäqaqqälä v.t put into disorder, disarranged
አመሰቃቃይ ammäsäqaqay n. one who causes disorder, confusion
አመሰኳ amäsäkkʷa v.t chewed (cud)
የሚያመሰኳ እንስሳ yämmiyamäsäkkkʷa ənsəsa n. ruminant
አመሰገነ amäsäggänä v.t praised, thanked
አመስጋኝ amäsgañ n. one who is thankful, gives praise
ምስጋና məsgana n. thanks, praise
ተመሰገነ tämäsäggänä v.i was praised, was thanked
አመሰጋገነ amäsägəggänä v.t thanked, praised sparingly
አስመሰገነ asmäsäggänä v.t had (s/o) praised, thanked; did praiseworthy work
አመሳቀለ see አመሰቃቀለ
አመቀ ammäqä v. forced by pressing, compressed
አመት amät n. year also ዓመት
አመተ ምሕረት amätä məhərät A.D
አመቸ amäččä v.i was comfortable; was obliging, honest (character)
አመቺ amäčči adj. comfortable; convenient (time)
ምቹ məčču adj. comfortable
ምቹነት məččunnät n. comfortability
ምቾት məččot n. comfort

ተመቸ *tämäččä* v.i was convenient; was comfortable

ተመቻቸ *tämäčaččä* v.i sat comfortably

አመቻቸ *ammäčaččä* v.t set in order, arranged neatly, packed neatly

አመነ *ammänä* v.t believed, trusted

አማኝ *amañ* n. believer, one who believes,

እምነት *əmnät* n. belief, trust; reliance, faith

ታመነ *tammänä* v.i was trustworthy; was believed

ታማኝ *tammañ* adj. loyal, trustworthy

መታመኛ *mättamäña* n.guarantee

ተማመነ *tämammänä* v.t trusted each other

መተማመኛ *mättämamäña* n. guarantee

አስተማመነ *astämammänä* v.t convinced, proved *(s/t)* genuine; established the truth *(in a dispute, by third party)*

ማስተማመኛ *mastämamäña* n. evidence *(to settle dispute)*

አሳመነ *asammänä* v.t convinced (s/o)

አሳማኝ *asammañ* n. one who convinces *(s/o)*

ማሳመኛ *masammäña* n. convincing reason, fact

አመነታ *amänätta* v.t doubted, wavered

አመንቺ *amänči* adj. wavering, doubtful

አመነታታ *amänätatta* v.i became a little doubtful

አስመነታ *asmänätta* v.t caused *(s/o)* to doubt

አመነዘረ *ammänäzzärä* v.i committed adultery

አመንዛሪ *amänzari* n. adulterer; adj. adulterous

አመንዝራ *amänzəra* n. adulterer

አመናቀረ *ammänaqqärä* v.t treated rudely, impolitely *see also* መነቀረ

አመነቃቀረ *ammänäqaqqärä* v.t put into complete disorder

ተመናቀረ *tämänaqqärä* v.i behaved rudely

ተመነቃቀረ *tämänäqaqqärä* v.i behaved rudely;was put into complete disorder

አመዛዘነ *ammäzazzänä* v.t weighed up *(in o/s mind)* evaluated, *see* መዘነ

አመዛዛኝ *ammäzazañ* adj. intelligent, perspicacious

አመካኘ *ammäkaññä* v.i used as an excuse or pretext

ምክንያት *məknəyat* n. reason, cause, excuse, justification

አመድ *amäd* n. ashes, cinder

አመዳም *amädam* adj. pale *(complexion)*

አመድ አደረገ *amäd adärrägä* v.t turned to rubble, wrecked, destroyed completely

አመዳይ *amäday* n. frost

አመገ *ammägä* v.t crammed together

አመገለ *ammäggälä* v.t squeezed out *(pus)*. *see also* መገለ

አመጠጠ *amäṭṭäṭä* v.t blotted; dried out a little, *see also* መጠጠ

ማምጠጫ *mamṭäča* n. blotting paper

አሙስ *amus, also* ኀሙስ *hamus* Thursday

አሚና *amina* n. itinerant singer

አሚዶ *amido* starch (stiffening)

አማ *amma* v.t gossipped against *(s/o)*, backbited

አሜት *amet or* ሐሜት *hamet* n. malicious

gossip

አሜታ *ameta* or **ሐሜታ** *hameta* n. malicious gossip, backbiting

አሜተኛ *ametäñña* or **ሐሜተኛ** *hametäñña* n. backbiter

ታማ *tamma* v.i was gossipped against

ተማማ *tämamma* v.t spread tales about each other

አማረ *amarä* v.i was beautiful, attractive;

አምሮት *amrot* n. desire, appetite, pleasure; whim

አማራ *amara* n. Amhara

አማርኛ *amarəñña* n. Amharic; indirect suggestion

አማሰለ *see* **መሰለ**

አማን *aman* n. peace, tranquility

አማተበ *ammattäbä* v.i crossed oneself, made the sign of the cross

አማታ *see* **መታ**

አማት *amat* n. mother-in-law, father-in-law

አማካኝ *ammakañ* n. average

አማካይ *amakay* adj. central, middle

አማች *amač* n. brother-in-law; relative by marriage

አማጠ *amaṭä* v.i was in labour, *see also* **ምጥ**

አሜሪካ *amerika* n. America

አሜሪካዊ *amerikawi* American

አሜን *amen* intej. Amen.

አሜከላ *amekäla* n. thistle

አምላክ *amlak* n. God, *see* **አመለከ**

አምሳ *amsa* n. fifty

—አለቃ *—aläqa* n. sergeant

—እግር *—əgər* n. centipede

አምሳኛ *amsañña* adj. fiftieth.

አምሳል *amsal* n. resemblance *see also* **መሰለ**

አምሳያ *amsayya* n. resemblance

አምስት *amməst* adj. five

አምስተኛ *amməstäñña* adj. fifth

አምበል *ambäll* n. captain *(sport)*

ሻምበል *šambäll* n. captain *(mil.)*

አምቡላ *ambulla* n. sediment *(of ṭäǧ)*

አምቡላንስ *ambulans* n. ambulance

አምቧቧ *ambʷabbʷa* v.t allowed to pour, gush out *(e.g from pipe)*

አምባ *amba* n. flat-topped mountain *(with village settlement)*; quarter, district *(of town)*

—ገነን *—gännän* n. demagogue

አምባጓሮ *ambaguʷaro* skirmish, affray, fight, fracas

አመባጋሮኛ *ambäguʷaroñña* adj. quarrelsome

አምባረቀ *ambarräqä* v.t shouted, roared like thunder; thundered *see also* **ባረቀ**

አምባራይሌ *ambarayle* n. lesser kudu

አምባር *ambar* or **አንባር** *anbar* n. bracelet

አምባሳደር *ambasadär* n. ambassador

ባለሙሉ ሥልጣን— *balämulu səlṭan—*n. ambassador plenipotentiary

ኤምባሲ *embasi* n. embassy

አምባሻ *ambašša* n. flat bread *(decorated)*

አምባጓሮ *see* **አምባ**

አምባዛ *ambbazza* n. catfish,

አምቦልክ *amboləkk* n. envelope *also* **አምቦጦል** *and* **አንቦልክ**

አምቦረቀቀ *amboräqqäqä* v.t was made to look baggily dressed

አምቦጫቦጫ *amboč̣äbboč̣a* v.t slopped about *(e.g half-full water pot)*

ተምቦጫቦጫ *tämboč̣abboč̣ä* v.t slopped about

(*liquid*), *also* ተንበጫበጫ

አምታታ *see* መታ

አምና *amna* n. last year

አምፑል *ampul* n. electric bulb

አሟረተ *see* ሟርት

አሟሸ *amʷašša* v.t treated with oil and fat (*new clay cooking utensils*)

ተሟሸ *tämʷašša* v.i was treated (*new cooking pot, with oil*)

አምዘገዘገ *amzägäzzägä* v.t flew shudderingly (*e.g spear*)

ተምዘገዘገ *tämzägäzzägä* v.i was hurled shudderingly (*spear*)

አሞለጨ *see* ሞለጨ

አሞሌ *amole* n. bar of salt (*used as currency previously*), rock-salt

አሞራ *amora* n. bird of prey (*eagle, kite, crow etc.*)

አሞቀሞቀ *amoqämmoqä* v.i swollen with moisture (*e.g grain*); was inflamed and watery (*e.g diseased eye*)

አሞት *amot also* ሐሞት (*hamot*) n. bile; courage

አሞተቢስ *amotäbis* adj. cowardly

አሞት የሌለው *amot yälelläw* adj. cowardly

አሞቱ የፈሰሰ *amotu yäfässäsä* adj. apathetic, lacking in spirit, fire

አሞኘ *amoňňä* v.t fooled, made a fool of, *see also* ሞኝ

ማሞኛ *mamoňňa* n. placebo, means of distracting, fooling a child

አሞጭ *amoč* n. arisaema

አሠመረ *asämmärä* v.t ruled (*a line*); did well, *see* ሠመረ

ማስመሪያ *masmäriya* n. ruler, (*straight edge*)

አሠማመረ *asämammärä* v.t drew (*several lines*) with a ruler

አሳማ *asama* n. pig (*domestic*)

አሠሠ *assäsä* v.i wiped round *ənǧära məṭad with oil*); swept (*an area, military*)

አሠሣ *asäsa* n. sweeping (*military operation*)

ማሰሻ *massäša* n. wiping cloth (*for ənǧära məṭad*)

ታሠሠ *tassäsä* v.i was wiped round; was swept (*military*)

አሠረ *assärä* v.t tied, tied up; imprisoned

አሳሪ *asari* n. jailor

አሳር *asar* n. trials, troubles, tribulation

አሳረኛ *asaräňňa* adj trouble-prone

እሥረኛ *əsräňňa* n. prisoner

እሥራት *əssərat* n. imprisonment

እሥር *əssər* n. bundle; imprisonment

—ቤት *-bet* n. jail

ተሳሠረ *täsassärä* v.i was entangled; was entangled with each other; had (*s/t*) in common

ታሠረ *tassärä* v.i was imprisoned, tied up

ታሳሪ *tasari* adj. condemned, sentenced

መታሠሪያ *mättasäriyä* n. place of confinement

አሳሠረ *asassärä* v.t had s/o imprisoned, had s/t, s/o tied up

አስተሳሠረ *astäsassärä* v.t had (*people, things*) roped, chained together

አሠር *asär* n. dregs; excrement

አሠገረ *asäggärä* v.t fished; trotted (*horse, mule*), *see also* ሠገረ

አሥጋሪ *asgari* n. fisherman, *also* ዓሣ አሥጋሪ

ማሥገሪያ *masgäriya* n. bait (for fishing)

አረህ *aräh* n. spur, slope, side of a mountain

አረሆ *aräho or* አረሖ *aräho* n. chanteuse

አረመ *arrämä* v.t weeded; corrected, marked *(e.g school exercises)*

አረም *aräm* n. weed

አራሙቻ *arramuččä* n. discarded weeds

አራሚ *arrami* n. one who weeds; one who corrects, marks *(papers)*

እርማት *ərrəmat* n correction *(papers, exercises)*

ታረመ *tarrämä* v.i was weeded; was corrected

ተራረመ *tärarrämä* v.t corrected each other

አሳረመ *asarrämä* v.t had *(s/t)* corrected; had *(s/t)* weeded

አረመኔ *arämäne* adj. heathen; cruel

አረመኔነት *arämänennät* n. heatheness; cruelty

አረሚ *arämi* adj. heathen,

አረማዊ *arämawi* n. pagan

አረረ *arrärä* v.i burnt black *(by cooking)*

አረር *arär* n. bullet, ball *(of cartridge)*

እራሪ *ərrari* n. very short and thin person

አሳረረ *asarrärä* v.t caused burn black *(by cooking)*

አረሰ *arräsä* v.t ploughed; tended a woman after giving birth

አራስ *aras* newly born baby

አራሽ *araš* n. ploughman, farmer

እራሽ *ərraš* n. ploughed land

እርሻ *ərša* n. farming, tillage, agriculture

ማረሻ *maräša* n. plough

አራረሰ *ararräsä* v.t ploughed here and there

ታረሰ *tarräsä* v.t was ploughed; cultivated; was tended *(woman after giving birth)*

አሳረሰ *asarräsä* v.t had *(land)* cultivated

አሳራሽ *asarraš* n. gentleman farmer

አስተራረሰ *astärarräsä* v.t helped *(s/o)* cultivate, plough

አረቀ *arräqä* v.t trained, moulded *(s/o's character)*; straightened out *(an affair)*

ታረቀ *tarräqä* v.i was reconciled; was sraightened

አስታረቀ *astarräqä* v.t reconciled

አረበደ *arräbbädä* v.i. busied o/s *(to curry favour with s/o)*

አረባጅ *aräbbaǧ* adj. n, one who busies himself *(to curry favour)*

እርባጅ *arbaǧ* adj. n, *(one)* who busies himself *(to curry favour)*

ተርበደበደ *tärbädäbbädä* v.i shivered with fear

ተርበድባጅ *tärbädbaǧ* adj. fearful, shaking

አረንጓዴ *arängʷade* adj. green

አረደ *arrädä* v.t slaughtered

አራጅ *araǧ* n. slaughterer

እርድ *ərd* n. slaughtered animal; turmeric

ታረደ *tarärrdä* v.i was slaughtered

ታራጅ *taraǧ* n. animal for slaughter

ተራረደ *tärarrädä* v.t killed each other *(with knives, swords)*;

fooled, cheated each other

አሳረደ *asarrädä* v.t had *(an animal)* slaughtered

•

አረዳ *arädda* v.t broke bad news

አርጂ *arği* n. bringer of bad news

መረጃ *märrăğa* n. evidence, intelligence *(secret information)*

መርዶ *mărdo* n. announcement of death

ተረዳ *tärădda* v.i was given, had bad news; was helped

አስረዳ *asrădda* v.t explained, clarified, enlightened

አስረጅ *asrăğğ* n. informant

ማስረጃ *masrăğğa* n. evidence, proof; explanation

አረዳ *in* አረዳ መሬት *arădda măret* cultivated land *(several times)*

አረጀ *arăğğä* v.i grew old

አሮጌ *aroge* adj. old

አሮጊት *arogit* old woman

እርጅና *ərğənna* n. old age

አስረጀ *asrăğğä* v.t aged, caused to age

አረገዘ *arăggäzä* v.i was pregnant

እርጉዝ *ərguz* adj. pregnant

እርግዝና *ərgəzanna* n. pregnancy

ተረገዘ *tärăggäzä* v.i grew in the womb

አስረገዘ *asrăggäzä* v.t made s/o pregnant

አረገደ *arăggädä* v.i moved rhythmically, swayed *(in mourning)*

አርጋጅ *argağ* n. mourner *(who sways rhythmically)*

ማርገጃ *margăğa* n. mourning area *(in church yard)*

አረገረገ *arăgărrăgä* v.i swayed rhythmically *(priests etc.)*

አረግራጊ *arăgragi* n. swaying in rhythm

አረጋዊ *arăgawi* n. old man. *see also* አሮጌ and አረጀ

አረግ *arăg* n. creeper, shoot

አረጠ *arrăṭä* v.i was sterile *(human or animal)*

አረጠረጠ *arăṭărrăṭä* v.i loitered about aimlessly

አረጥራጭ *araṭrač* n. loiterer

አረፈ *see under* ዐረፈ

አረፈደ *see* ረፈደ

አረፋ *arăfa* n. froth, lather

አሪትሜቲክ *aritmetik* n. arithmetic

አራ *arra* v.t shitted, defecated, excreted *(not polite)*

አር *ar* n. shit, excrement; sediment *(not polite)*

አራስ *aras* woman in childbed

—ልጅ — *ləğ* n. new-born baby

አራት *aratt* adj. four

አራተኛ *arattăñña* adj. fourth

አራዊት *see* አውሬ

አራጣ *araṭa* n. usury, unlawful interest

—አበዳሪ —*abăddari* n. usurer

አሬራ *arera* n. skimmed milk

አርማ *arma* n. badge, emblem, insignia

አርመን *armăn* n. Armenia, Armenian

አርሲ *arsi* n. one of the Administrative regions, central Ethiopia *(Arsi)*

አርሸብ *aršəb or* አርሺብ *aršib* n. archive

አርበኛ *arbăñña* n. warrior, patriot, partisan

አርበኝነት *arbaññənnät* n. guerrilla warfare

አርባ *arba* adj. forty

አርባኛ *arbañña* adj. fortieth

አርቲቡርቲ *artiburti* n. hocus-pocus

አርነት *arənnät* n. freedom

—ወጣ — *wäṭṭa* v.i became free

አርአያ *ara'ya* n. good example

አርአያነት *ara'yannät* n. good example

አርእስት *ar'əst* n. title *(of book etc.)*; headline, heading
አርከፈከፈ *arkäfäkkäfä* v.t sprinkled, watered *(seedlings etc.)*
ማርከፍከፊያ *markäfkäfiya* n. watering can
ተርከፈከፈ *tärkäfäkkäfä* v.i was sprinkled, watered
አርኪዮሎጂ *arkiyoloği* n. archaeology
አርዘ ሊባኖስ *arzä libanos* n. cedar
አርድእት *ardə'ət* n. disciples
አርጃኖ *arǧano* n. nile lizard
አርገበገበ *argäbäggäbä* v.t fanned o/s, waved *(hand)*
እርግብግብ *ərgəbgəb* adj. soft-hearted
ተርገበገበ *tärgäbäggäbä* v.i fluttered; was soft-hearted
አርጋኖን *arganon* n. organ *(musical instrument)*
አርጩሜ *arčumme* n. lath, cane *(for beating children)*
አርጌ *see* አረጀ
አሰላ *asälla* v.i thought deeply, calculated see *also* ስሌት
አሰሰ *assäsä* v.t scoured the town; greased *(a griddle)*
አሰሳ *ässäsa* n. search
አሰረ *see* አሠረ
አሰበ *assäbä* v.i thought, calculated
አሳቢ *assabi* adj. thoughtful, considerate
አሳብ *assab* n. thought
—የለሽ *—yälläš* adj. inconsiderate; devil-may-care
ሒሳብ *hisab* n. arithmetic, calculation bill *(e.g in restaurant)*
አሳሰበ *asassäbä* v.t reminded *(s/o)*
አሳሳቢ *asassabi* n. reminder, one who reminds; adj. critical, serious
—ጉዳይ *—gudday* serious matter

ታሰበ *tassäbä* v.i was thought—
ታስቦ ዋለ *tassəbo walä* was commemorated
መታሰቢያ *mättasäbiya* n. commemoration
ያልታሰበ *yaltassäbä* adj. sudden; unexpected
ተሳሰበ *täsassäbä* v.t made the reckoning; thought of each other
ተሳሳቢ *täsasabi* n. creditor
አስተሳሰበ *astäsassäbä* v.t had *(s/o)* made up the reckoning *(third party)*
አሰባጠረ *assäbaṭṭärä* v.t got people together; laid *(s/t)* crosswise
አሰበጣጠረ *assäbäṭaṭṭärä* v.t mixed together; caused to get together
አሰት *assät* n. lie, falsehood *also* ሐሰት
አሰነበተ *see* ሰነበተ
አሰናከለ *see* ሰነከለ
አሰናዳ *assänadda* v.t prepared *(food, room, house)*, arranged
አሰናጅ *assänaǧ* n. one who prepares *(s/t)*
አሰነዳዳ *assänädadda* v.t busied o/s with preparation, arrangement
ተሰናዳ *täsänadda* v.i was arranged, prepared
መሰናዶ *mässänado* n. preparation, arrangement
ተሰነዳዳ *täsänädadda* v.i was arranged, prepared; got ready
አሰኘ *assäññä* v.i *(used. with pronominal suffix)* felt the urge to do s/t; e.g ወደ ቤቴ መሄድ አሰኘኝ *wädä bete mähed assäññäññ* I feel going home
ተሰኘ *täsäññä* v.i was named, called
አሰገገ *see* ሰገገ
አሰጣ *asäṭṭa* v.t spread out in sun *(grain, clothes*

etc. to dry)

ስጥ *səṭ* n. s/t spread out to dry

ማስጫ *masč̣a* n. place or thing where s/t is spread out to dry

አሰፈሰፈ *asäfässäfä* v.i was ravenous, anxious to have *(s/t)*

አሰፍሳፊ *asäfsafi* adj. ravenous, over-eager

አሰፋ *see* ሰፋ

አሲድ *asid* n. acid

አሲዳም *asidam* adj. quickly used up; insubstantial

አሳለፈ *asalläfä* v.t let *(s/t)* pass by, *see* አለፈ

አሳማ *asama* n. pig

ያሳማ ሥጋ *yasama səga* n. pork

አሳረረ *asarrärä* v.t caused to be burned black, *see.* አረረ

አሳሰበ *see* አሰበ

አሳሳ *see* ሣሣ

አሳቀ *see* ሣቀ

አሳሳቀ *see* ሣቀ

አሰቀቀ *see* ሰቀቀ

አሳበረ *see* ሰበረ

አሳበቀ *see* ሰበቀ

አሳበበ *see* ሰበበ

አሳነሰ *see* አነሰ

አሳንሰር *asansär* n. elevator, lift

አሳከረ *see* ሰከረ

አሳዘነ *see* አዘነ

አሳደረ *see* አደረ

አሳጣ *assaṭṭa* v.t betrayed *(confidence, friendship, trust etc.)*

አሳጪ *assač̣i* n. one who betrays *(confidence, trust, friendship etc.)*

አሴረ *see* ሴራ

አስ— *as—(gram.)* causative *pref.*

አስመጣ *see* መጣ

አስማ *asma* n. asthma

አስማት *asmat* n. spell, witchcraft, sorcery

አስማተኛ *asmatäñña* n. master of spells, sorcerer

አስረከበ *asräkkäbä* v.t delivered, handed over

አስረካቢ *asräkkabi* n. deliverer

ተረከበ *täräkkäbä* v.i received

ተረካቢ *täräkkabi* n. one who receives, receiver

ተረካከበ *täräkakkäbä* v.t handed over *(post, keys, equipment etc.)*

ተረካካቢ *tärăkakabi* n. participants in a hand-over

አረካከበ *arräkakkäbä* v.i took part in hand-over

አረካካቢ *arräkakabi* n. participant in hand-over

ርክክብ *rəkəkkəb* n. process of handing-over

አስቀረ *see* ቀረ

አስተማረ *astämarä* v.t. taught *see also* ተማረ

አስተማሪ *astämari* n. teacher, instructor

ማስተማሪያ *mästämariya* n. teaching aid, place

አስተባበለ *see* አበለ

አስተናገደ *astänaggädä* v.t. entertained *(guests)*; treated *(customers)*

አስተናጋጅ *astänagaǧ* n. steward, host, hostess

አስተናበረ *astänabbärä* v.t. looked after *(guests)*

አስታረቀ *see* *አረቀ

አስተዋለ *astäwalä* v.i. paid attention, took note of

አስተዋይ *astäway* adj. wise, intelligent, thoughtful, observant, prudent

አስታወሰ *astawwäsä* v.t. remembered

ማስታወሻ *mastawäša* n. memorandum; remembrance; note

አስታጐለ *astaggʷälä* v.i. hindered interrupted

አስከሬን *askären* n. corpse, body

ያስከሬን ሳጥን *yaskären saṭən* n. coffin

አስኰነነ *see* ኰነነ

አስኳል *askʷal* n. yolk

አስወደደ *see* ወደደ

አስደረገ *asdärrägä* v.t. had *(s/t)* made, *see*

አደረገ and *ደረገ

አስደራጊ *asdärragi* n. one who has s/t made

አስገባ *see* ገባ

አስገነዘበ *asgänäzzäbä* v.t. made s/o understand; called attention to

አስገኘ *asgäññä* v.t. discovered caused to be found, *see also* አገኘ

አስገኚ *asgäñi* n. discoverer, finder

አስፋልት *asfalṭ* n. asphalt

አሶመሰመ *asomässomä* v.i cantered *(a horse)*, *see also* *ሶመሶመ

አሶምሷሚ *asomsuʷami* adj. cantering

አሸ *aššä* v.t rubbed massaged, kneaded; rubbed between the palms *(i.e grain)*

ማሻ *maša* n: kneading trough; embrocation, balm

አሻሸ *ašaššä* v.t rubbed lightly, a little

አሽታ *aššəta* n. physiotherapy

ታሸ *taššä* v.i was rubbed, massaged kneaded; was sluggish in work

መታሻ *mättaša* n. ointment, balm *(for rubbing into skin)*

ተሻሸ *täšaššä* v.t snuggled up to: brushed against

አሳሸ *asaššä* v.t had s/o rubbed, massaged

አስተሻሸ *astäšaššä* v.t brought close to each other

አሸመ *aššämä* v.t trimmed *(hair)* perfectly

እሽም *əššəm* adj. perfectly trimmed *(e.g Afro hair style)*

ታሸመ *taššämä* v.i was perfectly trimmed

አሸረጠ *ašärräṭä* v.t hitched up *(i.e towel round waist)*, *see also* ሸርጥ

አሸር ባሸር *ašär bašär* adj. poor *(food)*

አሸበረ *aššäbbärä* v.t caused panic, disturbance, terrorized *see also* ሽብር

አሸባሪ *aššabbari* n. one who causes uproar. disturbance

አሸበረቀ *ašäbärräqä* v.i was decorated, adorned up *(person)*

አሸበሸበ *ašäbäššäbä* v.t swayed *(priests in ritual dancing)*

አሸብሻቢ *ašäbšabi* n. one who sways gracefully *(priestly dance)*

አሸተ *ašätä* v.i began to ripen, was nearly ripe *(just edible)*

እሸት *əšät* n. unripe form *(peas, bean etc.)*

አሸተተ *see* ሸተተ

አሸነፈ *aššännäfä or* አቸነፈ *aččännäfä* v.i/t. beat, won, triumphed over, was victorious, conquered

አሸናፊ *aššännafi* n. winner

ተሸነፈ *täšännäfä* v.i was beaten, lost *(game etc.)*, was conquered

ተሸናፊ *täšännafi* n. loser, defeated *(one)*

ተሸናነፈ *täšänannäfä* v.t beat each other

አሸንክታብ *ašänkətab* n. amulet

አሸንዳ *ašända* n. gargoyle, rainspout; drinking trough *(animals)*

አሸዋ *ašäwa* n. sand

አሸዋማ *ašäwamma* adj. sandy

አሸዋነት *ašäwannät* n. sandiness

አሸገ *aššägä* v.t packed: sealed

እሽግ *əššəg* adj. sealed; packed up

ማሸጊያ *maššägiya* n. glue, tape, paper etc. *(used for packing)*

ታሸገ *taššägä* v.i was sealed, packed up

አሳሸገ *asaššägä* v.t had *(s/t)* sealed wrapped up, packed

አሸጋሸገ *aššägaššägä* v.t packed *(s/t)* closer, closed up *(ranks, people etc.)*

ተሸጋሸገ *täšägaššägä* v.t was packed up closer

አሹራ *ašura* n. land sale tax

አሻራ *ašara* n. fingerprint

የራስ— *yärus*–n. light curls

የጅ— *yäǧǧ*–n. lines *(of palm of hand)*

አሻለ *aššalä* v.t improved, ameliorated *see also* *ሻለ

አሻሻለ *aššašalä* v.t improved ameliorated

አሻቀበ *ašaqqäbä or* አሻቀበ *ašäqqäbä* v.t went uphill, upwards

ሽቅብ *šəqqəb* adj. uphill, upwards

አሻንጉሊት *ašangullit* n. doll

አሻፈረኝ *ašafJäräññ* excl. definitely no; definitely not

አሽሙር *ašmur* n. veiled insult

አሽሙረኛ *ašmuräñña* n. one who gives a veiled insult

አሽሟጠጠ *ašmʷaṭṭäṭä* v.t insulted tacitly, criticised *(esp. behind s/o's back)*

አሽሟጣጭ *ašmʷaṭač̣* n. one who criticises, insults *(especially in a hidden way or behind s/o' back)*; point of curved sword; decorative ball on scabbard tip

አሽሟጣጭነት *ašmʷaṭač̣ənnät* n. veiled criticism

አሽቀነጠረ *ašqänäṭṭärä* v.t thrust aside

ተሽቀነጠረ *täšqänäṭṭärä* v.i was thrust aside

አሽቆለቆለ *see* አቆለቆለ

አሽበለበለ *ašbäläbbälä* v.t tumbled over, rolled away *(e.g whirlwind)*

ተሽበለበለ *täšbäläbbälä* v.i was whirled away, rolled away

አሽከረከረ *aškäräkkärä* v.t bowled along *(e.g child's hoop or wheel)*, drove *(vehicle)*

አሽከርካሪ *aškärkari* n. driver; one who bowls. *(hoop etc.)*

(እ)ሽክርክሪት *(ə)škərkərit* n. hoop *(child's)*

ተሽከረከረ *täškäräkkärä* v.i was rolled, bowled along.

ተሽከርካሪ *täškärkari* n. vehicle; s/t which is rolled along

አሽከር *aškär* n. servant *(male)*

አሽከርነት *aškärənnät* n. domestic service

አሽካካ *aškakka* v.t clucked *(laying hen)*

አሽካኪ *aškaki* adj. clucking *(hen)*

አሽኮረመመ *aškorämmämä* v.t flirted with, courted, made up to

አሽኮርማሚ *aškormami* n. flirt

ተሽኮረመመ *täškorämmämä* v.t was seductive, agreeable to flirtation, coy

ተሽኮርማሚ *täškormami* adj. coy, flirtatious

አሽጓጠጠ *ašgʷaṭṭäṭä also* አንጓጠጠ *angʷaṭṭäṭä* v.i was uncouth, vulgar *(in expession or speech)*

አሾለ *ašolä* v.t sharpened, made tapered, *see also* ሾላ

አፉን— *afun* – v.i was over-talkative

አሾለቀ *ašolläqä* v.i peeped at, round, through

አሾላቂ *ašollaqi* n. peeper

ማሾለቂያ *mašolläqiya* n. peep-hole

አሾለከ *see* ሾለከ

አሾቀ *aśoqä* v.t parboiled and sauted *(peas, beans etc.)*

አሹቅ *aśuq* n. sauted and parboiled *(beans etc.)*

አሾከሾከ *aśokäššokä* v.t gossipped against *(s/o)*

አሾክሿኪ *aśokšʷaki* n. gossipper

አሾፈ *aśofä* v.t mocked, laughed at

አሿፊ *aśʷafi* n. mocker

አቀለለ *see* ቀለለ

አቀለጠ *see* ቀለጠ

አቀላጠፈ *see* ቀለጠፈ

አቀመሰ *see* ቀመሰ

አቀማጠለ *aqqämaṭṭälä* v.t entertained royally, mangnificently

ቅምጥል *qəmaṭṭəl* adj. treated lavishly, indulged

ተቀማጠለ *täqämaṭṭälä* v.i was entertained royally, lavishly

አቀረሸ *aqärässä* v.t brought up *(vomitted a little, e.g babies)*

ቅርሻት *qəršat* n. vomit *(of children, small amount)*

አቀረቀረ *aqäräqqärä* v.t lowered one's gaze, looked away, bowed one's head

አቀረበ *see* ቀረበ

አቀበለ *aqäbbälä* v.t passed to *(s/o)*

ቅበላ *qəbbäla* n. Shrove Tuesday

ቅብብሎሽ *qəbəbbəloš* n. playing at "catch," playing ball

አቀባይ *aqäbbay* n. one who passes *(s/t)* to s/o

አቀባበለ *aqäbabbälä* v.t cocked *(fire-arm)*

ተቀበለ *täqäbbälä* v.t received

ተቀባይ *täqäbbay* n. recipient

ተቀባበለ *täqäbabbälä* v.t passed around, passed hand to hand, passed to each other

አስቀበለ *asqäbbälä* v.t had *(s/o)* receive *(s/t)*

አቀነበጠ *aqänäbbäṭä* v.t threw out shoots *(plant)*, *see also* ቀንበጥ

አቀና *aqänna* v.t straightened developed *(barren country)*; *see also* ቀና

አቅኚ *aqñi* n. settler, developer *(of land country)*; seller of grain *(usu. farmer)*

አቃና *aqqanna* v.t straightened

አቀናበረ *aqqänabbärä* v.t compiled *(literature)*; edited texts into one *see also* ቀነበረ

አቀናባሪ *aqqänabari* n. literary editor, compiler

አቀነባበረ *aqänäbabbärä* v.t compiled, edited, *see also* ቀነበረ

አቀነባባሪ *aqqänäbabari* n. compiler

አቀፈ *aqqäfä* v.t embraced; cradled *(a child in the arms)*; brooded *(hen)*

ዓለም አቀፍ *aläm aqqäf* adj. international

አቃፊ *aqafi* adj. embracing

እቅፍ *əqqəf* n. bundle *(sticks, hay, grass)*

ያበባ— *yabäba*–n. bunch of flowers

ማቀፊያ *maqäfiya* n. swaddling cloth, *(for child)*

ታቀፈ *taqqäfä* v.t cradled *(a child in o/s arms)*; held, caught *(s/t)* in o/s arms

መታቀፊያ *mätaqäfiya* n. swaddling cloth, shawl *(for child)*

ተቃቀፈ *täqaqqäfä* v. t embraced each other

አሳቀፈ *asaqqäfä* v.t gave a hen eggs to hatch

አስታቀፈ *astaqqäfä* v.t gave child to *(s/o)* to

mind, hold

አቁማዳ *aqumada also* አቅማዳ *aqmada* n. leather grain bag

አቃረ *aqarä* v.i *(usu. with pron. suffix)* had indigestion, *see also* ቃር

አቃሰተ *aqassätä* v.i groaned, moaned *(with pain);* puffed, panted *(due to over weight)*

አቃቂር *aqaqir* n. criticism, review *(of a book)*

—ማውጣት – *mawṭat* to criticize to *(find fault with)*

አቃተ *aqatä* v.t *(usu. with pron. suffix)* become difficult e.g መራመድ አቃተው *märramäd aqatäw* he could not walk

አቃጠረ *äqqaṭṭärä* v.t pimped acted as a pimp,

አቃጣሪ *aqqaṭari* n. pimp

ተቃጠረ *täqaṭṭärä* v.i had an appointment

አቃጨለ *aqaččälä or* አንቃጨለ *anqaččälä* v.t rang *(handbell), see also* ቃጭል

አቄለ *aqelä* v.t treated *(s/o)* like a fool, *see also* ቂል

አቄመ *aqemä* v.i had a grudge, *see also* ቂም

አቅለሸለሸ *aqläšälläšä* v.i felt sick *(nauseous),* nauseated

አቅለሽላሽ *aqläšlaš* adj. causing one to feel sick

አቅማማ *aqmamma* v.i felt uncertain, hesitated

አቅማሚ *aqmami* adj. uncertain, hesitant

አቅጣጫ *aqṭačča or* አግጣጫ *agṭačča* n. direction *(towards s/t)*

አቆለቆለ *aqoläqqolä* v.t went down-hill

አቆላለፈ *aqqolalläfä* v.t entangled, *see also* ቆለፈ

አቆላመጠ *aqqolammäṭä* v.t flattered

ቁልምጫ *qulməčča* n flattery

አቆላማጭ *aqolamač* n. flatterer

አቆመ *aqomä* v.t halted *(s/t, s/o)*, erected *(s/t)*, made *(s/o, s/t)* to stand up, *see also* ቆመ

አቆጠቆጠ *aqoṭäqqoäṭä* v.i developed shoots *(plant)*, sprouted; took successfully

አቆራኘ *aqqoärañña* v.t tied *(prisoner to guard)*

ተቆራኘ *täqorañña* v.i. was tied (prisoner to guard)

አቋረጠ *aqqʷarräṭä* v.t interrupted; disturbed; made a short-cut, *see* ቈረጠ

አቋራጭ *aqʷarač* n/adj. *(one)* who interrupts; disturbs

—መንገድ —*mängäd* n. a short-cut

አገር— *agär*—n. globe-trotter

ማቋረጫ *maqqʷaräča* n. a short-cut

ተቋረጠ *täqʷarräṭä* v.i was stopped; was discontinued

ሥራ— *səra* – v.t undertook a contract

ተቋራጭ *täqʷarač* n. contractor

የሥራ— *yäsəra*– n. contractor

አቋቋመ *aqqʷaqʷamä* v.t. established, set up; instituted; attended memorial, christening service, *see* ቆመ

አቋቋሚ *aqqʷaqʷami* n/adj. *(one)* who establishes, sets up, institutes

ተቋቋመ *täqʷaqʷamä* v.i was established, set up, instituted; was on firm grounds *(business)*

አበለ *abbälä* v.i. told lies;

denied

አባይ *abay* n. liar

አባይነት *abayənnät* n. untruthfulness

ታበለ *tabbälä* v.i. was denied

አስተባበለ *astäbabbälä* v.t. denied, declared untrue, rejected

አስተባባይ *astäbabay* n. one who denies s/t

ማስተባበያ *mästäbabäya* n. disclaimer

አበል *abäll* n. stipend, salary, allowance, *see also* በላ

የውሎ— *yäwəlo*— n. per diem, *also* የቀን አበል

የጡረታ— *yäṭurätä*— n. pension, social security

አበረ *abbärä* v.t collaborated stood with; conspired against

አበ[illegible] *in* ግብረ አበር *gəbrä abbär* collaborator, accomplice

አባሪ *abari* n. enclosure *(s/t enclosed)*, attachment *(document)*

አብሮ *abro* adv. together, along with

ተባበረ *täbabbärä* v.i. was united, cooperated, allied oneself, joined forces

ተባባሪ *täbabari* adj. cooperative, associate

ትብብር *təbəbbər* n. co-operation, co-ordination

አስተባበረ *astäbabbärä* v.t. co-ordinated

አስተባባሪ *astäbabari* n. co-ordinator

አበሰ *abbäsä* v.t. wiped, cleaned *(with a rag)*

አበሰረ *abässärä* v.t. announced good news, heralded

ብስራት *bəsrat* n. good news

አበሳ *abäsa* n. sin; misfortune

አበበ *abbäbä* v.i. blossomed flowered, bloomed

አበባ *abäba* n. flower, bloom

—ጎመን *–gommän* n. cauliflower

አበባማ *abäbamma* adj.flowery *(full of flowers)*

ያበባ ማስቀመጫ *yabäba masqämmäč̣a* n. vase

እቅፍ አበባ *əqqəf abäba* n. bouquet

አበባ ጉንጉን *abäba gungun* n. garland, wreath

አበጀ *abäǧǧä* v.t mended repaired, did well *see also* በጀ

አበጃጀ *abäǧaǧǧä* v.t. put in order; repaired, mended

አበጋዝ *abägaz* n. Ethiopian title *(leader)*

የጦር— *yäṭor–* n. war leader

አበጠ *abäṭä* v.i was swollen

እበጥ *əbäṭ* n. swelling

እባጭ *əbbač̣* n. swelling

እብጠት *əbṭät* n. swelling

አባጣ *abaṭa* adj. swollen

—ጎባጣ —*gobaṭa* n. uneven land, broken ground, undulating *(land)*

አባበጠ *ababbäṭä* v.t. got slightly swollen

አሳበጠ *asubbäṭä* v.t. made *(s/t)* swell

አበጠረ *abäṭṭärä* v.t. combed; winnowed, see በጠረ

አበጣሪ *abäṭṭari* n. winnower

ማበጠሪያ *mabäṭṭäriya* n. comb; winnowing basket

አበጣጠረ *abäṭaṭṭärä* v.t. combed slightly

አስበጠረ *asbäṭṭärä* v.t. had *(s/o)* comb, winnow

ተበጠረ *täbäṭṭärä* v.i. was combed; was winnowed

ተበጣጠረ *täbäṭaṭṭärä* v.i. combed each other's hair

ብጣሪ *bəṭṭari* n. chaff

አቡን *abun* n. bishop, archbishop, patriarch *(title of respect given to such people)*

አቡጀዲ *abuǧädid* n. cotton *(cloth)*, calico

አቡጊዳ *abugida* n. alphabet

አባ *abba* n. title of respect given to priests, monks

አባወራ *abba wärra* n. husband

አባጨጓሬ *abba čäggʷarre* n. caterpillar *(insect)*

አባል *abal* n. member *(of group, committee etc.)*

  አባለዘር *abaläzär* n. sperm; genital organ

  አባልነት *abalənnät* n. membership

አባረረ *abbarrärä* v.t drove away, *see also* በረረ

  አባራሪ *abbarari* adj/n. *(one)* who drives s/o away

አባራ *abarra* v.i stopped raining

አባበለ *ababbälä* v.t cajoled

  አባባይ *ababay* adj/n. *(one)* who cajoles

አባባ *see* ባባ

አባባ *abbabba* interj. father! daddy!

አባት *abbat* n. father

  ክርስትና— *kərəstənna* – n. God Father *cf.* ክርስትና እናት

  ጡት— *ṭut* – n. adoptive father

  የእንጀራ— *yä'ənǧära*—n. step father

አባከነ *abakkänä* v.t squandered, wasted, *see also* ባከነ

  አባካኝ *abakañ* adj. squanderer, wasteful

አባያ *abaya* adj. slothful, sluggardly

አባዬ *abbayye* interj. father! daddy!

አቤት *abet* interj. yes! yes sir!

አቤቱታ *abetuta* n. complaint, appeal *(to superior)*

አብረቀረቀ *abräqärräqä* v.i sparked; shone, became luminous, *see* በረቀ

  አብረቅራቂ *abräqraqi* adj. sparkling, luminous

አብሲት *absit* n. proving dough

  --መጣል *—mäṭal* inf. to make proving dough

አብሶ *abəso* adj. especially

አብሽ *abəš* n. fenugreek

አብቃቃ *see* ብቃ

አብነት *abənnät* n. example

አቧለተ *abuʷallätä* v.i made jokes, *see also* ቧልት

አቦሬ *abore* n. gourd, water scoop

  —አፍ *—af* adj. wide-mouthed

አቦካ *see* ቦካ

አቧራ *abʷara* n. dust

  አቧራማ *abʷaramma* adj. dusty

አቦሸማኔ *abbošämmane* n. cheetah, *also* ወቦሸማኔ

አተላ *atäla* n. sediment *(in beer)*, lees, dregs

አተመ *attämä* v.t stamped; printed

  አታሚ *attami* n. printer

  እትም *əttəm* n. printing; issue *(magazine etc.)*, edition

  ማተሚያ *mattämiya* n. printing device, machine

  —ቤት *—bet* n. printing press

  ማኅተም *mahətäm* n. seal, rubber stamp

  አሳተመ *asattämä* v.t had *(s/t)* printed, stamped

  አሳታሚ *asattami* n. publisher

  ማሳተሚያ *masattämiya* n. printing cost

  ታተመ *tattämä* v.i was stamped; printed

አተመተመ *atämättämä* v.t scooped up *(with bread)*, *see also* ተመተመ

  ማተምተሚያ *matämtämiya* n. ground red pepper

አተራመሰ *attärammäsä* v.t threw into disorder, messed up; disturbed *(people)*

  ትርምስ *tərəmməs* n. disturbance, disorder, chaos

አተራማሽ — *attäramaš* n. disturber
አተር — *atär* pea
አኩሪ— — *akuri—* n. soya bean
አተበ — *attäbä* v.t cut the ambilical cord
አታቢ — *attabi* n. one who cuts the ambilical cord *(professional)*
እትብት — *ətəbt* n. ambilical cord
እትብቱ የተቀበረበት — *ətəbtu yätäqäbbäräbbät* n. one's birthplace
አተተ — *attätä* v.i discussed at length
አተታ — *atäta* n. discussion *(lengthy)*
ታተተ — *tattätä* v.i was discussed at length
አተኮረ — *atäkkorä* v.t stared fixedly, gazed at
አታለለ — *attallälä* v.t deceived, cheated
አታላይ — *attalay* swindler, cheater, cheat
አታሞ — *atamo* n. small drum
አቴና — *atena* n. rush matting
አትሮንስ — *atronəs* n. bookstand, lectern
አቶ — *ato* n. Mr.
አቶሰቶሰ — *atosätosä* v. was inquisitive, interfering
ቶስቷሳ — *tostʷassa* adj. inquisitive, interfering
አቶስቷሽ — *atostʷaš* adj. inquisitive, interfering
አቻ — *ačča* adj. peer, of the same rank, of the same status
—ለአቻ — *—lä'ačča* matching pair, equals
አቻምና — *aččamına* year before last *also* ሀቻምና
አኀዜ ዓለም — *ahaze aläm* adj. all-powerful *(God)*
አነሣ — *anässa* v.t took up, lifted; withdrew *(a charge)*; was very absorbent *(grain for brewing)*
ፎቶግራፍ አንሺ — *fotograf anši* n. photographer
—ማንሻ — *—manša* n. camera
ማንሻ — *manša* n. lifting device
አነሣሣ — *annäsassa* v.t encouraged, incited to action, inspired confidence in. *see also* ተነሣ
አነሣሽ — *annäsaš* n/adj. *(one)* who encourages, incites to action, inspires confidence in
አነር — *anär* n. stray, wild cat, serval
አነሰ — *annäsä* v.i diminished; became smaller; was reduced, *see also* ትንሽ
አነስተኛ — *anästäñña* adj. medium, rather small
አሳነሰ — *asannäsä* v.t made smaller, reduced
አነቀ — *annäqä* v.t choked, strangled
ማነቆ — *manäqo* n. **drawback, stumbing-block**
ታነቀ — *tannäqä* v.i was choked, strangled, hanged oneself
አሳነቀ — *asannäqä* v.t had *(s/o)* choked, strangled
ተናነቀ — *tänannäqä* v.t gripped at each other
እንባ ተናነቀው — *ənba tänannäqäw* v.t was in melting mood
ትንቅንቅ — *tənəqnəq* n. struggle, fight
አነቀፈ — *anäqqäfä or* አደናቀፈ *addänaqqäfä* v.t caused *(s/o)* to stumble
አንቃፊ — *anqafi* n. stumbling-block
እንቅፋት — *ənqəfat* n. stumbling-block
አነቃ — *anäqqa* v.t awoke, wake *(s/o)* up, *see also* ነቃ
አንቂ — *anqi* adj/n *(one)* who awakes; stimulant, refreshing
ማንቂያ — *manqiya* n. stimulant; refreshing

አነቃቃ *annäqaqqa* v.t stirred *(s/o)* into action
አነቃቂ *annäqaqi* n. *(s/t), (s/o)* that stirs to action
ማነቃቂያ *mannäqaqiya* n. means of stirring *(s/o)* up
አነቈረ *anäqqʷärä* v.t plucked out *(eye, boil etc.)*
አነበበ *anäbbäbä* v.t read, *see also* ነበበ
አንባቢ *anbabi* adj/n. *(one)* who reads, reader
ምንባብ *mənbab* n. passage *(of reading)*
አነባበበ *anäbabbäbä* v.t read a few lines
አናባቢ *annababi* n. vowel
ማናበቢያ *mannabäbiya* n. vowel
አስነበበ *asnäbbäbä* v.t had *(s/o)* read
ተነበበ *tänäbbäbä* v.i was read
ተነባቢ *tänäbbabi* n. consonant
ተናበበ *tänabbäbä* v.t followed a reading *(for comparison)*
ተናባቢ *tänabbabi* adj. compounded *(word)*
አነበነበ *anäbännäbä* v.t murmmured
አነብናቢ *anäbnabi* adj/n. *(one)* who murmurs
አነባበረ *annäbabbärä* v.t superimposed
አነባበሮ *annäbabäro* n. *ənǧära* sandwich
ተነባበረ *tänäbabbärä* v.i was superimposed
አነባ *anäbba* v.t wept
እንባ *ənba or* እምባ *əmba* n. tears
—አድርቅ *—adrəq* n. hypocritical mourner
አነከሰ *anäkkäsä* v.i limped
አንካሳ *ankassa* adj. limping
አንካሴ *ankasse* n. stick with pointed metal end
ማንከሻ *mankäša* n. stick to support a limp
አነካከሰ *anäkakkäsä* v.t limped slightly
አስነከሰ *asnäkkäsä* v.t made *(s/o)* limp

አነከተ *anäkkätä* v.t broke; ate up voraciously, cf. ነኰተ
አነካከተ *anäkakkätä* v.t broke into pieces
አነኰረ *anäkkʷärä* n. broke up *(cake, pancake etc. in pan)*
እንኩሮ *ənkʷuro* n. flour mix *(for brewing)*
ማንኰሪያ *mankʷäriya* n. stirring stick *(for brewing flour)*
አነኰተ *änäkkʷätä* v.t roasted beans, peas etc. *(in shell)*
እንኰቶ *ənkʷəto* n. roasted beans, peas etc. *(in shell)*; riff-raff
ተነኰተ *tänäkkʷätä* v.i was roasted *(in shell)*
አነወረ *anäwwärä* v.t blamed
ነውር *näwər* n. indecency
አስነወረ *asnäwwärä* v.t, was indecent, impolite
አስነዋሪ *asnäwwari* n. indecency; impoliteness
አነዘረ *anäzzärä* v.i became numb, cramped, *see also* ነዘረ
አነደደ *anäddädä* v.i burned *(s/t)*; lit, *see also* ነደደ
አነገሠ *anäggäsä* v.t crowned as king, *see also* ነገሠ
አነገበ *anäggäbä* v.t carried on one's shoulder
አንጋቢ *angabi* adj./n. *(one)* who carries *(s/t)* on his shoulder
እንግብ *əngəb* n. s/t carried on one's shoulder
አነገተ *anäggätä* v.t carried on one's shoulder, round one's neck, *see* አንገት
አንጋች *angač* n. bodyguard
ማንገቻ *mangäča* n. shoulder-strap
አስነገተ *asnäggätä* v.t had s/o shoulder *(s/t)*
ተነገተ *tänäggätä* v.i was

shouldered.

አነኈረ *anägg^wärä* v.t refined *(butter)*

ንኈር *nəgwər* adj. refined *(butter)*

ተነኈረ *tänägg^wärä* v.i was refined

አነገ·ተ *anägg^wätä* v.t baked small *əngära (e.g for child)*

እንጐቻ *əng^wäčča* n. small *əngära*

አነጠ *annäṭä* v.t did carpentry

አናጢ *anaṭi* n. carpenter

አናጢነት *anaṭinnät* n. wood work

አሳነጠ *asannäṭä* v.t had some carpentry done; had s/o build *(house)*

ታነጠ *tannäṭä* v.i was built

አነጠረ *anäṭṭärä* v.t refined; bounced *(ball)*, *see also* ነጠረ

አንጣሪ *anṭari* adj/n. *(one)* who refines; works metal

ብር-- *bərr-* n. silver smith

ወርቅ-- *wärq-* n. gold smith

አንጥረኛ *anṭəräñña* n. -smith

ማንጠሪያ *mänṭäriya* n. refining device

አነጠሰ *anäṭṭäsä* v.i sneezed

አነጠነጠ *anäṭännäṭä* v.i showed thriving health *(person)*

አነጠፈ *anäṭṭäfä* v.t spread carpet *(on floor)*; made up a bed, *see also* ነጠፈ

ንጣፍ *nəṭaf* n. floor-covering

አንጣፊ *anṭafi* n. master of the Bedchamber

ምንጣፍ *mənṭaf* n. carpet

አነጣጠፈ *anäṭaṭṭäfä* v.t had rugs etc. spread about

አስነጠፈ *asnäṭṭäfä* v.t had s/o lay carpet

አናጠፈ *annaṭṭäfä* v.t helped *(s/o)* to spread carpets, make up beds

ተነጠፈ *tänäṭṭäfä* v.t was spread *(with carpets)*; was made up *(bed)*

አነጣ *anäṭṭa* v.t whitened *see also* ነጣ

አነጣጠረ *annäṭaṭṭärä* v.i aimed at *(target)*; made a comparison, *also* አነጻጸረ

አነጣጣሪ *annäṭaṭari* n. marksman

አነጸ *see* አነጠ

አነጻ *anäṣṣa* v.t. cleaned. *see also* ነጻ

አነጻጸረ *annäṣaṣṣärä* v.t compared *also* አነጣጠረ

ተነጻጸረ *tänäṣaṣṣärä* v.i was compared

ተነጻጻሪ *tänäṣaṣari* adj comparable

አነፈረ *anäffärä* v.t over-cooked, over boiled, *see also* ነፈረ

አነፈሰ *anäffäsä* v.t winnowed, *see also* ነፈሰ

አንፋሽ *anfaš* adj/n *(one)* who winnows

አነፈረቀ *anäfärräqä* *see* ነፈረቀ

አነፈነፈ *anafännäfä* v.i sniffed, nosed about *(of dog)*

አናረ *annarä* *see* ናረ

አናበበ *annabbäbä* v.t made a comparative reading; acted as a vowel *see* ነበበ

አናት *anat* n. head, top, summit of. ቁንጮ

አናካ *annakka* v.t caused *(s/o)* to be contaminated *see* ነካ

አናዘዘ *annazzäzä* v.t took *(s/o's)* will, *see also* ተናዘዘ

አናዛዥ *annazaž* adj/n *(one)* who takes *(s/o's)* will

ተናዘዘ *tänazzäzä* v.i made one's will

ተናዛዥ *tänazaž* adj/n *(one)* who makes his will

ኑዛዜ *nuzaze* n. will *(before death)*

ቃለ— *qalä*—n. testament *(document of one's will)*

አናደደ annaddädä v.t vexed, enraged, maddened see ነደደ
  አናጅ annadaǧ adj/n. (one, s/t) that causes rage
  ተናደደ tänaddädä v.i was vexed, maddened
  ተናጅ tänadaǧ adj/n one who is easily enraged, vexed
አናገሠ annaggäsä v.t exaggerated, see also ነገሠ
  አናጋሽ annagaš adj/n (one) who exaggerates
  ተናገሠ tänaggäsä v.i was exaggerated
አናገረ nagggarä v.t made s/o speak ; talked to s/o, gave s/o an audience; had (s/o) on see ነገረ
አናጋ annagga v.t shook (upset); disrupted
  አናጊ annagi adj/n (one) who shakes. disrupts
  ተናጋ tänagga v.i was shaken, disrupted
አናጠረ anaṭṭärä v.i acted flamboyantly see also ነጠረ
አናጠበ annaṭṭäbä v.t thwarted, frustrated; hindered
አናፋ anaffa v.t brayed, (donkey), made a strident noise, see ነፋ
አን— an—pref. of active verb
አንስታይ ጾታ anəstay ṣota n. female gender
አንሸተተ anšattätä v.i slipped
  አንሻታች anšatač adj. slippery
  ተንሸተተ tänšattätä v.i slipped
  ተንሻታች tänšatač adj. slipping
አንቀላፋ anqälaffa v.i fell asleep
  እንቅልፍ ənqəlf n. sleep
  እንቅልፋም ənqəlfam adj. sleepy; inactive
አንቀልባ anqälba n. small leather for carrying infants on the back
አንቀሳቀሰ anqäsaqqäsä v.t set (s/t) into motion; reactivated; moved, see also ቀሰቀሰ
  አንቀሳቃሽ anqäsaqaš adj/n one who moves, sets into motion; reactivates
  ማንቀሳቀሻ manqäsaqäša n. means for setting (s/t) into motion
  ተንቀሳቀሰ tänqäsaqqäsä v.i moved; was set into motion ; was reactivated
  ተንቀሳቃሽ tänqäsaqäš adj. moving ; movable, mobile
አንቀጠቀጠ anqäṭäqqäṭä v.t caused to tremble; frightened quivered
  አንቀጥቃጭ anqäṭqač adj. shaking; frightening; quivering
  ተንቀጠቀጠ tänqäṭäqqäṭä v.i trembled ; was frightened
  ተንቀጥቃጭ tänqäṭqač adj. shaking; quivering
  ቀጥቃጣ qäṭqaṭṭa adj. coward; fearful; stingy, miserly
አንቀጽ anqäṣ n. verb ; paragraph
  ርእሰ— rə'əsä—n. editorial (newspaper)
  ቀዳማይ— qädamay—n. perfect (verb)
  ካልአይ— kalə'ay—n. imperfect (verb)
  ሣልሳይ— saləsay—n. subjunctive (verb)
  ትእዛዝ— tə'əzaz—n. imperative (verb)
  ንዑስ— nə'us—n. infintive (verb)
  ቦዝ— boz—n. gerund
አንቃር anqar n. soft palate
አንቆረቆረ anqoräqqorä poured water in a thin stream
  ማንቆርቆሪያ manqorqoria n. pitcher
አንበሪ anbäri n. whale
  ዓሣ— asa—n. whale
አንበሳ anbässa n. lion
አንበጣ anbäṭä n. locust
አንቧተረ anbuʷaṭṭärä v.t splashed
አንተ antä pron. (you sing.m.)
አንተላከሰ antälakkäsä v.t muddled through, did one's job slovenly

አንተገተገ *antägättägä* v.t burnt brightly; glittered

አንቱ *antu* pron. you *(polite)*

አንቱታ *antuta* n. addressing in a polite form

አንቴና *antena* n. antenna

አንቺ *anči* pron. you *(f.)*

አንቺዬ *ančiyye* pron. you! *(f. exclamatory)*

አንከራተተ *ankärattätä* v.t. made to wander from place to place

አንከረፈፈ *änkäraffäfä* v.t. carried *(s/t)* slugishly, awkwardly, clumsily

ከርፋፋ *kärfaffa* adj. sluggish, awkward, clumsy

ተንከረፈፈ *tänkäraffäfä* v.t. behaved slugishly, awkwardly, clumsily

አንከበከበ *ankäbäkkäbä or* አንከባከበ *ankäbakkäbä* v.t. handled carefully, affectionately, kindly, cherished *(treat with affection)*, took under one's wings *see* *ከበከበ

እንክብካቤ *ənkəbəkkabe* n. careful handling, fostering

ተንከባከበ *tänkäbakkäbä* v.i. fostered, cherished *(treated with affection)*; took care of

አንካላ *ankalla* adj. lame *(person)*, one who limps

አንካሴ *ankasse* n. stick *(with pointed metal end)*, *see also* አንከሰ

አንኮላ *ankola* n. large drinking vessel made of gourd; adj. fool, moron

አንኳር *ankʷar* n. cube *(of sugar)*, lump *(of sugar)*

አንኳኳ *ankuʷakkuʷa* v.t. tapped at, knocked

አንዠቀዠቀ *anžaqäžžäqä* v.t. made to gush, run freely *(liquid)*, emitted a copious stream

አንዠት *anžät* አንጀት *anǧät* n. intestine; inner feeling, sympathy

አንዠተ ቢስ *anžätä bis* adj. indecisive; cruel

አንዣበበ *anžabbäbä* አንጃበበ *anǧabbäbä* v.i hovered

አንዣባቢ *änžabbäbi* v.i hovering

አንደላቀቀ *andälaqqäqä* v.t spoiled *(a child)*; indulged; treated sumptuously, lavishly, *see also* *ደለቀቀ

አንደላቃቂ *andälaqaqi* adj/n *(one)* who spoils *(a child)*

ድልቃቃ *dälqaqqa* adj. spoilt *(child)*

ተንደላቀቀ *tändälaqqäqä* v.i lived sumptuously, lavishly

ተንደላቃቂ *tändälaqaqi* adj/n *(one)* who lives sumptuously, lavishly

አንደረበበ *andäräbbäbä* v.t caused to become almost full, *see also* ደረበበ

አንደበት *andäbät* n. style of speech, language

አንደበተ ቀና *adäbätä qänna* adj. eloquent *(speaker)*

አንደፋደፈ *andäfaddäfä* v.t caused to writhe, *see also* *ደፋደፈ

ተንደፋደፈ *tändäfaddäfä* v.i writhed

አንድ *and* adj. one

—ሁለቴ *or* አንዴ ሁለቴ —*hulätte, ande hulätte* n. a couple of times, a few times

—ላይ —*lay* adv. together

—ሰው —*säw* pron. somebody, someone

—ቀን —*qän* n. some day, one day

—ባንድ —*band* adv. singly, point by point, in detail, one by one, one at a time

—ነገር —*nägär* n. something, one thing

—አደረገ —*adärrägä* v.t unified

—ጋ —*ga* adv. together

—ጊዜ —gize adv. once, sometime
ባንድ band adv. together
—ጊዜ —gize adv. at once
አንዱጋ anduga adv. somewhere
አንደኛ andäññä adj. first
አንዴ ande adv. once
አንዲት andit adj. one (f.)
አንዳች andačč n. s/t
አንዳንድ andand adj. some
አንዳፍታ andafta adv. one moment
አንድላንድ andland n. one to one
አንድላይ andəlay adv. together
አንድም andəmm pron. nobody, no one, either conj. or, also
አንድነት andənnät adv. together
እያንዳንዱ əyyandandu n. each one, everyone, everybody
ባንድነት bandənnät adv. together

አንጀት anǧät አንዠት anžät intestine; heart (feeling), sympathy,
አንጀተ ቢስ see አንዠት

አንጃ ግራንጃ anǧa gəranǧa n. malicious remarks
አንጃ anǧa n faction
አንጆ anǧo adj. tough meat
አንገራገረ angäraggärä v.i faltered; behaved, spoke hesitantly, was indecisive
አንገራጋሪ angäragari adj. faltering, hesitant, indecisive

አንገት angät n. neck
አንገተ ሰባራ angätä säbara adj. timid, shy, humble, submissive, meek
—ደንዳና —dändanna adj. obstinate
አንገት የሌለው angät yälelläw adj. selfish, inconsiderate
አንገትጌ angätge n. collar

አንገዋለለ angäwallälä v.t looked down upon s/o, belittled
አንገዋላይ angäwalay n. one who looks down upon s/o

አንገደገደ angädäggädä v.t caused (s/o, s/t) to totter, staggered
ተንገደገደ tängädäggädä or ተንገዳገደ tängädaggädä v.i tottered, staggered
ተንገድጋጅ tängädagaǧ adj. tottering, staggering
ገድጋዳ gädgadda adj. tottering, staggering

አንገፈገፈ angäfäggäfä v.t caused to be fed up, disgusted
አንገፍጋፊ angäfgafi adj. disgusting, repulsive
ተንገፈገፈ tängäfäggäfä v.i was fed up, disgusted

አንጋሬ angarre n. dry skin (sheeps, goats)

አንጋደደ angaddädä v.t slanted, deviated (line etc.) bent, curved, see also ገደደ
ተንጋደደ tängaddädä v.i tottered, staggered

አንጋጋ angagga v.t drove (cattle etc.) enmass
ተንጋጋ tängagga n. v.i was driven (cattle etc.) enmass
ጋጋታ gagata n. clamour, uproar

አንጋፋ angaffa n. first-born (son)

አንጎል angʷäl n. brain
አንጎላም angʷälam adj. intelligent
አንጎለቢስ angʷäläbis n. thoughtless, selfish

አንጎራጎረ angʷäraggʷärä v.t murmured, grumbled; hummed (a song)
አንጎራጓሪ angʷäragʷari adj/n (one) who murmurs, grumbles
እንጉርጉሮ əngʷərgʷəro n. humming song

አንጎደጎደ angʷädäggʷädä v.t poured abundantly, caused to gush

አንጓ anguʷa n. joint (finger), small separating point in sugar-cane and bamboo stalks

አንጓለለ *angʷallälä* አንገዋለለ *angäwallälä* v.t looked down upon s/o, belittled

አንጓላይ *angʷalay* n. one who looks down upon s/o, one who belittles others

አንጠለጠለ *anṭäläṭṭälä* v.t suspended, hung

ማንጠልጠያ *manṭälṭäya* n. hanger, support from which s/t can be hanged, handle

ተንጠለጠለ *tänṭäläṭṭälä* v.t was suspended, hung

ተንጠልጣይ *tänṭälṭay* adj. hanging, suspended

ተንጠላጠለ *tänṭälaṭṭälä* v.i climbed *(a tree etc.)*

አንጠበጠበ *anṭäbäṭṭäbä* አንጠባጠበ *anṭäbaṭṭäbä* v.t dropped

ተንበጠበ *täntäbäṭṭäbä* or ተንጠባጠበ *tänṭäbaṭṭäbä* v.i dripped

አንጣጣ *anṭaṭṭa* v.t caused to fizzle; snapped *(break with a sharp crack)*

ተንጣጣ *tänṭaṭṭa* v.i fizzled; snapped, crackled; farted

አንጦርጦስ *anṭorəṭos* n. abyss, inferno

አንጫጫ *ančaččа* v.t caused to make a loud noise; squealed

ተንጫጫ *tänčačča* v.i was noisy, cried in disagreement

ጫጫታ *čačata* n. noise

አንጸባረቀ *anṣäbarräqä* v.i reflected *see also* *ጸበረቀ

አንጸባራቂ *anṣäbaraqi* adj. reflecting

ተንጸባረቀ *tänṣäbarräqä* v.i was reflected

አንጻር *anṣar* n. direction *(of thought)*; *aspect*

አንጻር ላንጻር *anṣar lanṣar* facing one another, vis-a-vis

ከ... አንጻር *kä...anṣar* in contrast to, in the direction of

አንፈራጠጠ *anfäraṭṭäṭä* v.i sat with legs outstretched

አኖረ *anorä* v.t put down, placed; kept *(s'o)* in one's house etc. *see also* ኖረ

አኘከ *aññäkä* v.t chewed, masticated

ታኘከ *taññäkä* v.i was chewed, masticated

አእምሮ *a'əmməro* n. knowledge, mind, thought, wit

—ሳተ *—satä* v.i became insane

—ቢስ *—bis* adj. thoughtless, inconsiderate

—አጣ *—aṭṭa* v.i was shameless, inconsiderate, selfish

—ው ረጋ *—w rägga* v.i relaxed, was tranquilized

—አወቀ *—awwäqä* v.i matured *(mentaly)*, reached the state of reasoning

—ደካማ *—däkamma* adj. feeble-minded

የአእምሮ ሕመም *yäa'əməro həmäm* n. mental disease

—ሕመምተኛ *—həmämtäñña* adj. insane, mad

—ሐኪም *—hakim* n. psychiatrist

—ሕክምና *—həkkəmənna* n. psychiatry

አከለ *akkälä* v.t put more, gave more; became equal to

እኩል *əkkul* n. half; adj. equal

እኩለ ሌሊት *əkkulä lelit* n. midnight

—ቀን *—qän* n. midday

እኩል አደረገ *əkkul adärrägä* v.t equated

እኩሌታ *əkkuleta* adj/n half

እኩያ *əkkuyya* adj. of the same age, the same rank or position, peer

ታከለ *takkälä* v.i was put more; was given more

ተካከለ *täkakkälä* v.i was

equalized; had the same status

አሳከለ *asakkälä* v.t caused to be put more; caused to be given more; changed the form of e.g **ትልቅ አሳከለ** made big

አስተካከለ *astäkakkälä* v.t equalized; put into order; gave uniformity; trimmed; set *(a watch)*; rectified

ጠጉር አስተካካይ *ṭägur astäkakay* n. hair-dresser; barber

አከመ *akkämä* v.t treated *(patient)*

አካሚ *akkami* adj/n *(one)* who treats *(patient)*

አኪም *akim* **ሐኪም** *hakim* n. physician, doctor

—ቤት *—bet* n. hospital

ህክምና *həkkəmənna* n. treatment *(medical)*

ታከመ *takkämä* v.i was treated *(patient)*

ታካሚ *takkami* n. patient

አሳከመ *asakkämä* v.t had *(s/o)* treated

አሳካሚ *asakkami* n. one who cares for the treatment of a patient

አከምባሎ *akämbalo* n. lid of a *məṭad (clay oven for baking ənǧära)*

አከረረ *see* **ከረረ**

አከርካሪ *akärkari* n. back-bone

አከሰለ *see* **ከሰለ**

አከሰመ *see* **ከሰመ**

አከበረ *akäbbärä* v.t honoured, respected, revered, *see* **ከበረ**

አከበደ *akabbädä* v.t made heavy; difficult *see* **ከበደ**

አከተ *akkätä* v.t packed *(for journey)*

ታከተ *takkätä* v.i was packed

አሳከተ *asakkätä* v.t had *(s/t)* packed

አከተመ *akättämä* v.i reached an end; ended

ማከተሚያ *maktämiya* n. climax

አከናነበ *akkänannäbä* v.t covered s/o's head with the *šämma*

ተከናነበ *täkänannäbä* v.i covered one's head with the *šämma* *see also* * **ከናነበ**

ከንብንብ *kənəbnəb* n. covering *(of the head with the šämma)*

አከናወነ *akkänawwänä* v.t completed

ተከናወነ *täkänawwänä* v.i was completed; was perfectly done

ከንውን *kənəwwən* n. completion; perfectly done work

አከከ *akkäkä* v.t scratched *(one's body)*

እከክ *əkäk* n. itch

እከካም *əkäkam* adj. full of itches, full of scratches *(human being)*; wretched

ታከከ *takkäkä* v.i leaned, rested against *(s/o, s/t)*

ታካኪ *takaki* adj. leaning, resting, resting against *(s/o, s/t)*

አካከከ *akakkäkä* v.t scratched slightly

አስታከከ *astakkäkä* v.t made to rest against *(s/o, s/t)*; hinted

አሳከከ *asakkäkä* v.t itched

አከፈለ *akäffälä* v.i fasted *(for three days before Easter)*, *see* **ከፈለ**

አከፋይ *akfay* n. one who fasts *(for three days)*

አከፍሎት *akfəlot* n. fasting *(of three days)*

ማከፈያ *makfäya* n. present for *(s/o)* who has fasted

አካል *akal* n. body; organ; member

አካላት *akalat* n. members of the body

አካላዊ *akalawi* adj. pertaining to the body

አካለ መጠን *akalä mäṭän* n. manhood, full growth

—ጎደሎ *—godälo* adj. invalid, crippled

አካበተ *akabbätä* v.t accumulated *(usually wealth illegally)*

አካባች *akubač* adj/n. *(one)* who accumulates *(e.g wealth)*

አካፈለ *akkafälä see* ከፈለ

አካፋ *akafa* n. spade

አካፋ *akaffa* v.i drizzled

ካፍያ *kaffya* n. drizzle, shower *(of rain)*

አክሊል *aklil* n. crown

አክምባሎ *akəmbalo* n. cover of the griddle on which እንጀራ is made

አክ አለ *akk alä* v.i cleared one's throat

አክታ *akkəta* n. phlegm

አክ መባያ *akk mäbaya* spittoon

አክርማ *akərma* n. kind of grass from which baskets etc. are made

አክስት *akəst* n. aunt

አክሲዮን *aksion* n. share, stock

አኮላሸ *akkolaššä* v.t castrated *(animal)*, emasculated

ኩልሸት *kuləššət* n. castration

ተኮላሸ *täkolaššä* v.i was castrated, emasculated

አስኮላሸ *askolaššä* v.t had *(an animal)* castrated, emasculated

አኮማተረ *akkomattärä* v.t wrinkled, creased

ተኮማተረ *täkomattärä* v.i was wrinkled, creased

ኩምትርትር *kumtərtər* adj. severely wrinkled, creased

አኮመታተረ *akkomätattärä* v.t wrinkled, creased severely

አኮረፈ *akorräfä* v.i snored; was sulky; v.t foamed, produced foam, lathered

አኩራፊ *akurafi* adj/n. *(one)* who snores; irascible

ኩርፊያ *kurfiya* n. snoring; irascibility, sulking

ተኮረፈ *täkorräfä* v.t became irascible, sulky, *see also* ኮረፈ

ተኮራፊ *täkorrafi* adj. irascible, sulky

ተኳረፈ *täkʷarräfä* v.t became in unspeaking terms with *(s/o)*

አስኮረፈ *askorräfä* v.t angered

አኮራመተ *akkorammätä* v.t shrivelled; became crippled *(with disease)*

ኮርማታ *kormatta* adj. crippled, shrivelled

ኩርምትምት *kurmətmət* adj. crippled, shrivelled

ተኮራመተ *täkorammätä* v.i was shrivelled, crippled

አኮፋዳ *akofada* n. satchel, knapsack

አኰረተ *akʷärrätä* v.t produced bulb *(e.g onion)*

አኩራች *akʷərač* adj. bulbing *(plants e.g onion)*

ኰረት *kʷärät* n. pebble

አኰሰሰ *akʷässäsä* v.t made meagre, lean, thin; *see also* ኰሰሰ

አኰበኰበ *akʷäbäkkʷäbä* v.t ran with short paces;

አኰቴት *akkʷätet* n. consecrated bread *(sacrament)*, Host

አኹን *ahun also* አሁን *ahun* adv. now

አኹኑኑ *ahununu* adv. immediately

አወለቀ *awälläqä* v.t undressed, took off one's clothes, dismantled, *see also* ወለቀ

ልብ አውላቂ *ləbb awlaqi* adj. pestering, vexatious

ኪስ— *kis*—n. pick pocket

አወላለቀ *awälalläqä* v.t undressed completely; dismantled

አወለወለ *awäläwwälä* v.i had shining complexion,

see also ወለወለ
 አወላወለ *see* * ወላወለ
አወላገደ *see* * ወለገደ
አወረደ *awärrädä* v.t took down, unloaded; *see also* ወረደ
አወራ *awärra* v.t narrated, told, informed
 አውሪ *awri* n. narrator
 ተወራ *täwärra* v.i was told, narrated
 አዋራ *awwarra* v.t made s/o speak, made s/o divulge a secret
 አስወራ *aswärra* v.t caused to be talked about s/t
*አወሰ **awwäsä*
 ታወሰው *tawwäsäw* he thought of, he remembered
 አወሳ *awässa* v.t mentioned
 ተወሳ *täwässa* v.i was mentioned
አወቀ *see* ዐወቀ
አወናበደ *see* *ወነበደ
አወን *awän* adv. interj. yes
 አወንታ *awänta* n. affirmative, positive
አወከ *awwäkä* v.t troubled, disturbed; became difficult
 አዋኪ *awwaki* adj. troublesome, disturbing; difficult
 እውከት *əwkät* or ሁውከት *həwkät* n. trouble, disturbance; difficulty
 ታወከ *tawwäkä* v.i was disturbed, was put in difficult situation
አወካ *awäkka* v.i shouted *(commotion)*, uproared
 ዋካታ *wakata* n. shout, *(commotion)*, uproar
 ውካታ *wəkata* n. shout *(commotion)*, uproar
አወዛወዘ *see* ወዘወዘ
አወደ *awwädä* v.t perfumed
አወደሰ *see* ወደሰ
አወዳደረ *awwädaddärä* v.t caused to compete; compared
 ውድድር *wədəddər* n. competition
 አወዳዳሪ *awwädadari* adj/n. one who supervises a competion
 ተወዳደረ *täwädaddärä* v.i competed
 ተወዳዳሪ *täwädadari* n. competitor; resemblance, equal
አወጋ *awägga* v.i narrated, told stories, reported over *(s/t)*
 ወግ *wäg* n. tradition; narration, lore; usage
 በወግ *bäwäg* adv. properly
 የወግ ልብስ *yäwäg ləbs* n. regalia, uniform cf. የደንብ ልብስ
 ወገኛ *wägäñña* adj. conceited, vein
 አውጊ *awgi* adj. n *(one)* who narrates
አወጣ *see* ወጣ
አዋለ *see* ዋለ
አዋለደ *see* ወለደ
አዋልደጌሻ *awaldägešša* n. aardvark
 አዋሐደ *awwahädä* made one; mixed *(s/t)*; caused to digest
 ምግብ ማዋሐጃ *məgəb mawwahaga* n. food digestive
 ተወሐደ *täwahadä* v.i became united, unified; was digested *(food)*
አዋረደ *see* ወረደ
አዋራ *awara* n. dust, *also* አቧራ
አዋራ *see* አወራ
አዋሰ *awasä* v. lent, *see also* ዋሰ *was*
 አዋሽ *awaš* adj/n. *(one)* who lends
 ውሰት *wəsät* n. lending
 ተዋሰ *täwasä* v.t acted as guarantor; v.i borrowed
 ተዋዋሰ *täwawasä* v.i lent from each other guaranteed each other
አዋሽከ *awwaššäkä* v.t told tales
አዋዋለ *awwawalä* v.t helped in drawing a contract, agreement,

	see also ዋለ
አዋዋይ	*awwaway* adj/n *(one)* who helps drawing contract, agreement
ውል	*wəl* n. contract, agreement
ተዋዋለ	*täwawalä* v.i drew a contract, agreement
ተዋዋይ	*täwaway* n. contractor
አዋዜ	*awaze* n. a mixture of red pepper and other spices used for eating raw meat
አዋየ	*awwayyä* v.t consulted, asked for advice
አዋደደ	*see* ወደደ
አዋጣ	*see* ወጣ
አውላላ	*awlalla* n. open ground
አውሎ ነፋስ	*awlo näfas* n.whirl wind
አውራ	*awra* n. main, leader chief, head
—መንገድ	—*mängäd* n. main road
— ጎዳና	—*godana* n. highway
—ዶሮ	—*doro* n. cock
—ጠላት	—*ṭälat* n. mortal enemy
—ጣት	—*ṭat* n. thumb
አውራሪስ	*awraris* n. rhinoceros
አውራጃ	*awrağğa* n. district, ወረደ
አውሬ	*awre* n. ferocious animal; adj. inhuman, cruel, *pl.* አራዊት
አውሬነት	*awrennät* n. ferocity, savagery
አውሮፕላን	*awroppəlan* n. airplane
አውሮፓ	*auroppa* n. Europe, *also* አውሮጳ
አውተረተረ	*awtärättärä* v.t. meddled through, did *(s/t)* imperfectly, slovenly
አውተርታሪ	*awtärtari* adj/n *(one)* who meddles through, does his job imperfectly, slovenly
ተውተረተረ	*täwtärättärä* v.i. staggered, walked unsteadily, tottered
አውተፈተፈ	*awtäfättäfä* v.t. did one's job slovenly, imperfectly, *see* ወተፈ
ተውተፈተፈ	*täwtäfättäfä* v.i. was done slovenly, imperfectly; pocked one's nose in every business
ተውተፍታፊ	*täwtäftafi* adj/n *(one)* who acts slovenly: dirty *(mannerless)*
አውታር	*awtar* n. cord of lyre
የድምጽ—	*yädəmṣ*—n. vocal cords
አውቶቡስ	*awtobus* n. bus
አውደለደለ	*awdäläddälä* v.i. vagabonded; roamed
አውደልዳይ	*awdälday* adj vagabond, tramp, roamer
አውድማ	*awdəmma* n. threshing floor
አዎ	*awo* particle, yes ! *also* አዎን *awon*
አወንታ	*awänta* n. affirmative
አዕማድ	*a'əmad* n. pillars; derived forms *(of verb)*
አዘለ	*azzälä* v. t. carried *(child)* on the back; carried fruits *(tree)*
ማዘያ	*mazäya* n s/t used for carrying a child on the back *(cloth, tanned leather)* cf. እንቀልባ
ታዘለ	*tazzälä* v.t. was carried *(child)* on the back
አዘመመ	*see* ዘመመ
አዘመረ	*see* ዘመረ
አዘመተ	*see* ዘመተ
አዘረጠ	*azärräṭä* v.t farted
አዘረፈ	*see* ዘረፈ
አዘራ	*see* ዘራ
አዘነ	*äzzänä* v.i was sad, sorry; was sorrowful; mourned, deplored, had regrets, was in low spirit
አዛኝ	*azañ* adj. compassionate
አዘንተኛ	*azäntäñña* ሐዘንተኛ *hazäntäñña* n. mourner
አዛዘነ	*azazzänä* v.i was

somewhat sad

ተዛዘነ *tāzazzänä* v.i had mutual compassion

አሳዘነ *asazzänä* v.t aroused compassion, was pitiable, pathetic

አሳዛኝ *asazzaññ* adj. pitiable, pathetic

አዘወተረ *see* * ዘወተረ

አዘዘ *azzäzä* v.t ordered, commanded

አዛዥ *azzäž* adj/n commander, *(one)* who gives orders

ማዘዣ *mazäža* n. order *(written direction)*

የመድኃኒት— *yämädhanit*—n. prescription

የገንዘብ— *yägänzäb*—n. voucher

የፍርድ ቤት— *yäfərd bet*—n. warrant

ታዘዘ *tazzäzä* v.i. was ordered; obeyed

ታዛዥ *tazzaž* adj. obedient

ትእዛዝ *tə'zaz* n. order

ጸሐፊ- *ṣähfe*—n. minister of pen

አሳዘዘ *asazzäzä* v.t. had *(s/o, s/t)* ordered

አዘገመ *azäggämä* v.i. walked slowly, paced

ማዝገሚያ *mazgämia* n. *(s/t* that keeps *(s/o)* busy

አዘጋገመ *azägaggämä* v.i. walked rather slowly, paced rather slowly, did one's work very slowly

አዘጋጀ *azzägaǧǧä* v.t. prepared, made ready; *see also* under *ዘገጀ

አዘጠዘጠ *see* *ዘጠዘጠ

አዙሪት *azurit* n. whirlpool, *also* አዘዋሪት

አዛባ *azaba* n. dung

አዛባ *azzabba* v.t. made incompatible, created disharmony *(between two things)*, made incoherent *(sentence etc.)*

ተዛባ *tāzabba* v.i. was incompatible, was in disharmony, was incoherent

አዛውንት *azawənt* n. dignified elderly man

አዛጋ *azzagga* v.t/v.i. helped in closing; yawned, *see also* ዘጋ

አዜመ *azemä* v.i. chanted intoned, *see also* ዜማ

አዝሙድ *azmud* n. *in*

ጥቁር— *ṭəqur*— n. black cumin

ነጭ— *näčč*— n. bishops weed

አዝራር *azrar* n. button *(of clothes)*

አዝዋሪ *see* ዞረ

አዞ *azzo* n. crocodile; mixture of beans, peas etc. flour and powdered mustard used as appetiser

አዞረ *see* ዞረ

አዠ *ažžä* v.i. oozed

አየ *ayyä also* ዐየ v.t. saw, looked at

አየለ *ayyälä* v.i became strong, over-powered, was predominant, was prevalent *see also* ኀይል

አየር *ayyär* n. weather, air

—መንገድ *—mängäd* n. airline

—ወለድ *—wälläd* n. airborne

— —ወታደር *— —wättaddär* n. paratrooper

—ኃይል *—hail* n. Air Force

የአየር ሁኔታ *yä'ayyär huneta* n. weather condition

—መልእክት *—mälə'əkt* n. airmail, airletter

—ንብረት *—nəbrät* n. climate

—ወረራ *—wärära* n. air raid

—ጠባይ *—ṭäbay* n. weather, climate

—ፖስታ *—posta* n. airmail

አያ *ayya* n. title of respect for an elderly person *(male)*

አያሌ *ayyale* adj. much, adv. very much, a

good deal

አያት ayat n. grandfather, grandmother

አያያ ayyayya n. title of respect to an elder brother

አዬ aye interj. oh ! *(exclamation of astonishment)*

—ጉድ —gud interj. what a pity ! oh my goodness !

አይ ay interj. oh! *(exclamation of surprise)*

አይል *in* ምንም አይል mənəmmayəl it is tolerable, it is not bad

አይሁዳዊ ayhudawi adj. Jewish

አይሁድ ayhud n. Jew, Jews

አይብ ayb n. fresh cheese

አይቦ aybo n. white wheat

አይዞህ ayzoh don't be afraid, be courageous, take it easy, never mind

አይድረስ aydräs interj. that is awful !

አይደለም aydälläm v.t it is not

አይጥ ayṭ n. mouse

አይጠ በላ ayṭä bälla adj. mouse eater

አይጥማ ayṭəmma adj. greyish, having the colour of a rat

አይጠ መጎጥ ayṭä mägoṭ n. rat

አይጠዳሽ ayṭädaš adj. gloomy *(person)*, melancholic

አደለ addälä v.t distributed; had good luck e.g ታድያለሁ tāddəyyallähu I am lucky

አዳይ adday adj/n *(one)* who distributes

እድል əddəl n. luck

እድለ ቢስ əddəlä bis adj. unlucky, unfortunate *(person)*

ታደለ taddälä v.i was distributed ; became lucky

ማደያ *in* የነዳጅ ማደያ yänädag maddäya n. filling station, gas station.

አዳደለ adaddälä v.t distributed here and there *(in small quantity)*

አሳደለ asaddälä v.t had *(s/t)* distributed

አደላ adälla v.t was biased in favour of, treated with undue partiality

አዳይ adday adj/n *(one)* who treats with undue partiality

አድላዊ adlawi n. one who treats with undue partiality, adj. biased

አድሎኛ adloñña adj. biased *(in favour of)*

አደላደለ *see* ደለደለ

አደመ addämä v.t plotted, conspired

አዳሚ addami adj/n. *(one)* who takes part in a plot, conspiracy

አድመኛ admäñña n. conspirator, plotter,

አድማ adma n. plot conspiracy

እድመኛ ədmäñña n. guests *(in a wedding)*

ታደመ taddämä v.i was plotted conspirated; was invited to a wedding *(arch.)*

አደመጠ adämmäṭä v.t listened to ; followed an event carefully *see also* *ደመጠ

አድማጭ admač adj/n *(one)* who listens; follows an event attentively

አዳመጠ addammäṭä v.t listened to

ማዳመጫ maddamäča n. receiver *(telephone)*

አደረ addärä v.t passed the night

ያደረ መሬት yaddärä märet fallow land

ለጌታ አደረ lägeta addärä v.t entered into the service of a master

ሠርቶ አደር *sərto addär* n. the working people

እንዴት አደ ርክ *əndet addärk* good morning

ደኅና እደር *dähna ədär* good night

አዳሪ *adari* adj/n *(one)* who passes the night at a place

—ተማሪ *—tämari* n. boarding student

—ትምህርት ቤት *—təmhərt bet* n. boarding school

ሴተኛ አዳሪ *setäñña adari* n. prostitute

በረንዳ— *bärända—* n. vagabond, tramp

ዱር— *dur*—n. vagabond, brigand, tramp

እዳሪ *əddari* n. fallow land

—ወጣ *—wäṭṭa* v.i went to the W.C

አዳር *adar* n. an over night

አድሮ *adro* adv. finally

ውሎ— *wəlo*—adv. in the long run, eventually, at last

አድር ባይ *adər bay* adj. opportunist, servile

እድር *əddər* n. communal self-help organization

እድርተኛ *əddərtäñña* n. member of a self helping organization

ማደርያ *madärya* n. lodging, place to pass the night; military serivice land

ተዳደረ *tädaddärä* v.i was administered; *(institution etc.)*; lived in harmony with others

መተዳደሪያ *mättädadäriya* n. means of subsistence

—ሕግ *—həgg* n. constitution

አስተዳደረ *astädaddärä* v.t administered *(institution)*; passed the night together *(as companion)*

አስተዳዳሪ *astädadari (m)*. adj administrator; *(one)* who passes the night with *(s/o as companion)*

አደረሰ *see* ደረሰ

አደረቀ *see* ደረቀ

አደረገ *see* * ደረገ

አደራ *adära* n. *(s/t)* entrusted to *(s/o)*

የአደራ ደብዳቤ *yadära däbdabbe* n. letter of recommendation; registered letter

ባለ አደራ *balä'adära* n. trustee

አደራ *adärra* v.t formed webs

አደሰ *addäsä* v.t renewed

አዳሽ *addaš* adj. n. *(one)* who renews, renewer

አዲስ *addis* adj. new

—አበባ *—ababa* n. Addis Ababa *(capital of Ethiopia)*

—ኪዳን *—kidan* n. New Testament

እደሳ *əddäsa* n. renewing, renewal

አዳደሰ *adaddäsä* v.t renewed slightly

ታደሰ *taddäsä* v.i was renewed; was refreshed; was renovated

አሳደሰ *asaddäsä* v.t had *(s/t)* renewed

አደቀቀ *see* ደቀቀ

አደበ *addäbä* n. became polite, refrained from becoming mischievous

አደብ *addäb* n. politeness, good manners

—ግዛ *—gəza* be polite

አደበነ *see* ደበነ

አደባ *adäbba* v.i lurked, stalked

አደባባይ *addäbabay* n. open public place, square *(city)*; court *(judicial)*; formal gathering place of sovereign

አደባየ *adäbayyä* v.t hit force fully

አደነ *addänä* v.t hunted

አደን *addän* n. hunt, hunting

አዳኝ *addañ* n. hunter

አደነቀ *see* ደነቀ

አደነቆረ *adänäqqorä* v.t deafened, annoyed *(s/o)* by a loud voice or sound, made one's intelligence or faculties dulled, *see* ደነቆረ

አደናገረ *see* * ደነገረ

አደነገዘ *see* ደነገዘ

አደንጓሬ *adänguʷarre* n. haricot beans

አደዘደዘ *adäzäddäzä* v.t roamed, wandered aimlessly

አደዝዳዥ *adzdaž* adj. n. *(one)* who roams aimlessly

አደይ አበባ *adäy abäba* n. maskel flower *(wild flower that grows during the month of September, species of the ox-eye daisy)*

አደገ *addägä* v.i grew up, became taller, developed physically; rose *(in rank)*

አብሮ አደግ *abro addäg* n. childhood friend

ስድ አደግ *sədd addäg* adj. impertinent *(child)*, rude, impolite

ማደጎ *madägo* n. fosterchild

እድገት *ədgät* n. growth; promotion

አሳደገ *asaddägä* v.t fostered, promoted *(in rank)*

አሳዳጊ *asaddagi* n. foster-parent

አስተዳደግ *astädadäg* n. upbringing; breeding; education

አደገደገ *see** ደገደገ

አደፈ *addäfä* v.i become dirty, filthy, was soiled

አደፍ *adäf* n. menstruation

—ወረዳት *—wärrädat* v.t menstruated

እድፍ *ədəf* n. dirt, filth, stain

አሳደፈ *asaddäfä* v.t polluted. made dirty

አደጋ *adäga* n. danger, accident, peril

—ላይ ወደቀ *—lay wäddäqä* v.i was exposed to danger

—ጣለ *—ṭalä* v.t exposed to danger, imperilled

—ጣለ *—ṭalä* v.t attacked by surprise

አደገኛ *adägäñña* n. dangerous, unsafe, hazardous, perilous

የእሳት አደጋ *yä'sat adäga* n. fire hazard

———መከላከያ *———mäkkälakäya* n. firebrigade

አዱኛ *adduñña* n. world, wealth

ባለ— *balä—*adj. wealthy

አዳም *addam* n. Adam

አዳምና ሔዋን *addamənna hewan* n. Adam and Eve

አዳራሽ *see* ደረሰ

አዳበለ *see* ደባለ

አዳበረ *see* ዳበረ

አዳከመ *see* ደከመ

አዳገተ *see** ዳገተ

አዳጠ *see* ዳጠ

አዳፈነ *see* ደፈነ

አዳፋ *see* ደፋ

አድማስ *admas* n. horizon

አድባር *adbar* n. guardian spirit *(G. mountains)*

አዶ *addo* n. elephant hunter

አጀለ *aǧǧälä* v.t soaked *(for a prolonged time)*

ታጀለ *taǧǧälä* v.i was soaked

አሳጀለ *asaǧǧälä* v.t had *(s/t)* soaked

አጀንዳ *aǧända* n. agenda

አጅሬ *aǧǧire* adj. ingenious, smart, high spirited

አጀበ *aǧǧäbä* v.t escorted *(to give honour to s/o)*

አጀብ *aǧäb* n. entourage, suite, escort

አጃቢ *aǧǧabi* n. entourage, suite, escort

ታጀበ *taǧǧäbä* v.i was escorted

አሳጀበ *asaǧǧäbä v.t had (s/o) escorted*

አጃ *aǧǧa* n. oats

አገለለ *see* *ገለለ

አገለገለ see *ገለገለ

አገለደመ see *ገለደመ

አገለባበጠ see ገለበጠ

አገላገለ see ገላገለ

አገመ aggämä v.t cupped

 አጋሚ *aggami* adj/n *(one)* who performs cupping operation

 ዋገምት *wagämt* n. cupping instrument

አገሳ *agässa* v.i. roared *(lion)*; belched, *see also* ገሳ

 ግሳት *gəsat* n. roar *(lion)*; belch

አገር *agär* country; native land

 አገሬ *agäre* n. natives, indigenous people

 አገር ቤት *agär bet* n. countryside

 —አስተዳዳሪ *—astädadari* provincial administrator

 አገረ ገዥ *agärä gäž* n. governor

 ያገር ልጅ *yagär ləǧ* n. compatriot

 አገር አስተዳደር ሚኒስቴር *agär astädädär minister* n. ministry of interior

 —ውስጥ *—wəsṭ* adj. domestic, local

 —ግዛት ሚኒስቴር *—gəzat* ministry of interior *(arch.)*

 —ፍቅር *—fəqər* n. patriotism

 ቅኝ አገር *qəňň agär* n. colony

 ውጭ— *wəčč—* n. abroad

 የውጭ—ሰው *yäwəčč— säw* n. foreigner

 የሰው— *yäsaw agär* n. foreign country

 የትውልድ— *yätəwlədd*—n. native country

 ባላገር *balagär* n. countryman ; country *(countryside)*

አገረረ *see* ገረረ

አገሸሸ *agäššäšä also* ገሸሽ አደረገ *gäšäšš adärrägä* v.t got rid of; ignored *(intentionally)*

አገባ *see* ገባ

 አገባብ *aggäbab* n. syntax ; procedure, *see also* ገባ

አገባደደ *aggäbadäddädä* v.t brought to completion *(work etc.)*, made nearly completed

አገተ *aggätä* v.t. sequestrated *(cattle for grazing in one's land)*

አገነፈለ *see* ገነፈለ

አገነፋ *see* ገነፋ

አገናኘ *see* አገኘ *and* *ገኘ

 አገናዘበ *aggänazäbä* v.t. authenticated, verfied, *see* ገንዘብ

 አገናዛቢ *aggänazabi* adj. possessive *(gram.)*

 ተገናዘበ *tägänazzäbä* v.i. possessed, made one's own property; was authenticated, verified

 አስገነዘበ *asgänäzzäbä* v.t. drew the attention of, made s/o understand *(an issue)* ; clarified

አገኘ *agäňňä* v.t. found, got

 ግንኙነት *gənəňňunnät* n. relation

 ተገኘ *tägäňňä* v.i. was found

 ተገናኘ *tägänaňňä* v.i. met each other; had sexual intercourse *(polite)*

 አገናኘ *aggänaňňä* v.t caused to meet each other; made to encounter each other; let a calf suck

 አገናኝ መኰንን *aggänaň mäkʷännən* n. liaison officer

አገዘ *aggäzä* v.t helped, aided

 አጋዥ *aggaž* adj/n *(one)* who helps, aids

 ራስ አገዝ *ras aggäz* adj. self-helping

 እገዛ *əggäza* n. helping

 ተጋገዘ *tägaggäzä* v.i helped each other

 ተጋጋዥ *tägagäž* adj. helping each other, supporting each other

አገደ *aggädä* v.t obstructed

stopped, hindered, blocked; made inactive, tended domestic herd

ወለድ አገድ *wälläd aggäd* n. mortgage

አጋጅ *aggaǧ* n. herdsman

እግድ *əggəd* adj. stopped, hindered, blocked

ማገጃ *maggäǧa* n. pasture; obstruction

ታገደ *taggädä* v.i was obstructed, stopped, hindered blocked; was tendea *(domestic herd)*

አሳገደ *asaggädä* v.t caused to be obsructed, stopped etc; caused domestic herd to be tended

አገደመ see * ገደመ

አገደደ see * ገደደ

አገደፈ see ገደፈ

አገዳ *agäda* n. cane, stalk, stem

መሀል— *mähal*—n. shin

ሸንኮር— *šänkor*—n. sugar cane

አገገመ *agäggämä* v.t recovered *(from prolonged illness)*, convalesced

አገጋሚ *agäggami* adj/r convalescent

አገጠጠ *see* ገጠጠ

አገጭ *agač̣* n. chin

አገጯም *agäč̣am* adj/n one with big chin

አጋለ *see* ጋለ

አጋለጠ *see* *ገለጠ

አጋም *see* *ጋመ

አጋመሰ *see* ገመሰ

አጋም *agam* n. carisa edulis, hawthorn

አጋራ *aggarra* v.t shared *(s/t)* to *(s/o)*

አጋሪ *aggari* adj/n *one who shares (s/t) to (s/o)*

ተጋራ *tägarra* v.i shared *(s/t)* with *(s/o)* *see also* ጋራ

አጋር *aggar* n. helper; alliance

አጋሰስ *agassäs* n. pack-horse

አጋሰሰ *agassäsä* v.t collected, gathered indiscriminately

አጋበሰ *agabbäsä* v.t gathered collected indiscriminately

አጋተ *see* *ጋተ

አጋነነ *see* ገነነ

አጋና *agana* n. price, bid

አጋንዱራ *agandura* n. rough, coarse person, one lacking finesse

አጋዘ *see* * ጋዘ

አጋዘን *agazän* n. greater kudu

አጋደመ *aggaddämä* laid down horizontally

አግዳሚ *agdami* adj. horizontal

—ወንበር —*wänbär* n. bench

ጋድም *gadəm* adj. horizontal

አጋደደ *agaddädä* v.t became of good service, became useful

አጋጠመ *see* ገጠመ

አጋፈረ *aggafärä* v.t ushered

አጋፋሪ *aggafari* n. usher

አጋፈፈ *see* ገፈፈ

አጌጠ *see* ጌጥ

አግባብ *see* ገባ

እግተለተለ *see* * ገተለተለ

አጎለመሰ *see* ጎለመሰ

አጎበር *agobär* n. canopy *(covering over a bed)*

አጎት *aggot* n. uncle

ያጎት ልጅ *yaggot ləǧ* n. cousin

አጎነበሰ *see* *ጎነበሰ

አጎዛ *agoza* n. dried sheep's skin *(used for sitting on)*

አጎጠጠ *agoṭṭäṭä* v.t made grimaces *(to cause laughter)*, *also* አን ጓጠጠ

አጉጣጭ *aguṭač̣* adj/n *(one)* who makes grimaces

አጉለ *see* አስታጉለ

አጉላ *see* ጉላ

አጉለመሰ *see* ጎለመሰ

አጉረ *agguʷarä* v.t packed in *(an enclosure)*; stuffed, crowded together, huddled; penned up

ታጐረ *taggu"ärä* v.i was packed in, stuffed, crowded together

  አሳጐረ *asaggu"ärä* v.i had *(s/t)* stuffed packed, crowded together

አጐረሰ *see* ጎረሰ

አጐረበ *see* ጎረበ

አጐራ *agu"ärra* v.t cried, moaned in agony *(usually s/o possessed by evil spirit)*

አጐሳቀለ *see* ጐሰቈለ

አጐበር *see* አጎበር

አጓራ *see* አጐራ

አጓት *aggu"at* n. whey

አጓደደ *aggu"addädä* v.t caused to relax, caused to depend with confidence

  ተጓዳጅ *tägu"adağ* adj/n *(one)* who relaxes, takes easy, slow in action

አጓጓ *see* ጓጓ

አጠለለ *see* ጠለለ

አጠለቀ *see* ጠለቀ

አጠመቀ *see* ጠመቀ

አጠመደ *see* ጠመደ

አጠማ *see* ጠማ

አጠረ *aṭṭärä* v.t became short; was brief; shrank

  አጠረኝ *aṭṭäräññ* I am short of

  እጥረት *əṭrät* n. shortage

  አጭር *aččər* adj. short

  አሳጠረ *asaṭṭärä* v.i abridged, cut short, shortened

አጠረ *aṭṭärä* v.i made a fence around s/t, enclosed *(with a fence)*

  ታጠረ *taṭṭärä* v.i was fenced; was surrounded

  አጥር *aṭər* n. fence

    ግቢ *—gəbbi* n. courtyard, compound, campus

አጠራ *see* ጠራ

አጠራቀመ *see* *ጠረቀመ

አጠራጠረ *see* ጠረጠረ

አጠቀሰ *see* ጠቀሰ

አጠቃ *see* *ጠቃ

አጠቃለለ *see* ጠቀለለ

አጠበ *aṭṭäbä* v.t washed; bathed; developed *(a film)*; eroded *(soil by water)*

  አጠባ *aṭäba* n. washing

  አጣቢ *aṭabi* n. laundry man

  እጣቢ *əṭṭabi* n. wash *(kitchen liquid with waste food)*

  እጥበት *əṭbät* n. washing

  በደረቁ— *bädäräqu—*n. dry laundry

  እጥቤ *əṭṭəbbe* usually followed by ሌባ n. shameless thief

  ተጣጠበ *täṭaṭṭäbä* v.i washed oneself *(rashing)*

  ታጠበ *taṭṭäbä* v.t washed oneself; was washed; was eroded

  ታጣቢ *taṭabi* adj. washable

  መታጠቢያ *mättaṭäbiya* n. basin *(for washing)*

  —ቤት *—bet* n. bathroom, W.C

  አጣጠበ *aṭaṭṭäbä* v.t washed slightly

  አሳጠበ *asaṭṭäbä* v.t had *(s/t)* washed

  አስታጠበ *astaṭṭäbä* v.t poured water on *(s/o)* while washing

አጠበቀ *see* ጠበቀ

አጠበበ *see* ጠበበ

አጠባ *see* ጠባ

አጠነ *aṭṭänä* v.t fumigated

  አጣኝ *aṭañ* adj/n *(one)* who fumigates

  እጣን *əṭan* n. incense

  እጥነት *əṭnät* n. fumigation

  እጥን *əṭṭən* adj. fumigated

  ማእጠንት *ma'əṭänt* n. fumes of incense

  ማጠኛ *maṭäña* n. herb used in fumigation

  ታጠነ *taṭṭänä* v.i was fumigated

  አሳጠነ *asaṭṭänä* v.t had *(s/o)* fumigate *(place etc.)*

አጠነከረ *see* ጠነከረ

አጠነዛ *see* ጠነዛ

አጠንጠነ see *ጠንጠነ
አጠንፈፈ see ጠንፈፈ
አጠና see ጠና
አጠየቀ see ጠየቀ
አጠደቀ see ጠደቀ *and* ጸደቀ
አጠዳ see ጠዳ *and* ጸዳ
አጠገብ *aṭägäb* adv. close to

በ... *bä*...adv. by, near, beside

እ... *ə*...adv. by, near, beside

አጠጣ see ጠጣ
አጠፈ *aṭṭäfä* v.t folded; doubled

ቃሉን— *qalun aṭṭäfä* v.t retracted one's statement, broke one's word

አጠፌታ *aṭäfeta* adj. twofold
እጥፍ *əṭəf* n. doublefold, times
እጥፋት *əṭṭəfat* n. crease
ማጠፊያ *mäṭäfiya* n. hinge
ታጠፈ *taṭṭäfä* v.i was folded, doubled
ታጣፊ *taṭṭafi* adj. folding
—ወንበር *—wänbär* n. folding chair
መታጠፊያ *mättaṭafiya* n. curve *(of a road)*, bend of road)
አጣጠፈ *aṭaṭṭäfä* v.t folded *(clothes)*, folded up *(a letter)*, rolled up *(bed-clothes etc.)*

አጣ *aṭṭa* v.i became needy, poor; failed to find

እጦት *əṭot* n. poverty, need, lack, shortage
ታጣ *taṭṭa* v.i was absent, was not to be found
አሳጣ *asaṭṭa* v.t deprived *(s/o)* of one's possessions, wealth etc.

አጠለቀ see ጠለቀ
አጣመመ see ጠመመ
አጣመረ see ጠመረ
አጣሪ *aṭari* n. one who sells spices
አጣራ see ጠራ
አጣበቀ see ጠበቀ

አጣና *aṭana* n. rather thin stem of eucalyptus tree *(used as fuel or for building)*
አጣደፈ see ጠደፈ
አጣጣመ see ጣመመ
አጣጣረ see ጣረ
አጣጥ *aṭaṭ* n. thorny bush
አጣፈረ see ጠፈረ
አጣፈጠ see ጣፈጠ
አጤ see አፄ
አጤቀ *aṭeqä* v.t mocked at; was scornful
አጤነ *aṭenä* v.i pondered, thought deeply *(about)*

አጥያኝ *aṭyañ* adj. n *(one)* who thinks deeply *(about)*

አጥለቀለቀ see *ጠለቀለቀ
አጥመለመለ see *ጠመለመለ *and* ተ?መለመለ
አጥሚት *aṭmit* n. gruel
አጥቅ *aṭq* n. fringe *(of rug or shawl)*
አጥበረበረ *aṭbäräbbärä* v.t dazzled
አጥበርባሪ *aṭbärbari* adj. dazzling
አጥቢያ *aṭbiya* n. quarter *(division of a town or village)*

—ኮከብ *—kokäb* n. morning star
—ዳኛ *—dañña* n. magistrate, Justice of the Peace

አጥናፍ *aṭnaf* n. edge, boarder *(for the world)*

አጥናፈ ዓለም *aṭnafä aläm* n. the far end of the world

አጥወለወለ *aṭwäläwwälä* v.t nauseated

አጥወልዋይ *aṭwälway* adj. nauseous

አጦለ *aṭolä* v.t husked *(using a fan)*

ማጦያ *maṭoya* n. fan *(used for husking grain)*

አጦዘ *aṭozä* v.t hit *(s/o)* with a heavy blow
አጩ see ዐጩ
አጨለጨለ *ačäläččälä* v.i became green
አጨለገ *ačällägä* v.t looked at

(s/t) stealthily; stole (coll.)
አጭላጊ *ăčlagi* adj/n *(one)* who looks at *(s/t)* stealthily; a thief *(coll.)*
አጩማተረ *aččämattärä* v.t wrinkled *(one's face, cloth etc.)*, *see* ጨመተረ
አጨሰ *see* ጨሰ
አጨቀ *ačäqa* v.t made swampy; soaked
አጨቀ *aččäqä* v.t stuffed *(push, thrust)*, crammed
አጨበጨበ *see* ጨበጨበ
አጨነቈረ *ačänäquʷärä* v.t peeped at *(looked slyly)*
አጨደ *aččädä* v.t mowed
  አጨዳ *aččäda* mowing
  አጫጅ *ačaǧ* adj/n *(one)* who mows
  ታጨደ *taččädä* v.i was mowed
  ታጫጅ *tačaǧ* n. s/t ready for mowing
  ማጭድ *mačəd* n. sickle
  —እግር *—əgər* adj. bow-legged
  አጫጨደ *ačaččädä* v.t mowed here and there
  እጭድ አደረገ *əččəd adärrägä* v.t mowed completely, entirely
  አሳጨደ *asaččädä* v.t had *(grass, hay etc.)* mowed
አጫረተ *see* * ጨረተ
አጫወተ *see* * ጫወተ
አጫፈረ *see* ጨፈረ
አጭር *see* አጠረ
አጭበረበረ *ačbäräbbärä* v.t ; swindled, cheated, defrauded, embezzled, *see also* *ጨበረበረ
አጸፋ *aṣäfa* n. reprisal, retaliation; *(s/t)* done in return *(good or bad)*
  አጸፋውን መለሰ *aṣäfawən mälläsä* n. did *(s/t)* by way of reprisal
  አጸፋ ተውላጠ ስም *aṣäfa täwlaṭä səm* n. reflexive pronoun
አጽቅ *aṣq* n. joint *(finger, bamboo, sugar cane etc.)*; knuckle
አጼ *aṣe* n. title of former Emperors of Ethiopia
አፈላ *see* ፈላ
አፈላማ *afälama* n. money paid by a cattle owner for damages done by his cattle
አፈሙዝ *afämuz* n. muzzle *(of fire-arm)*
አፈረ *affärä* v.i was ashamed; became embarassed; became modest; remained fruitless *(farm land)*: backed out, went back on one's word, escaped from an agreement
  አፋሪ *afari* adj./n. *(one)* who is shy, embarassed
  አፋር *affar* adj. shy, embarassed
  አፋራም *affaram* adj./n. one who backs out
  እፍረት *əfrät* n. embarassment, shyness, shame, humiliation
  አፍረተ ስጋ *afrätä səga, or* ሐፍረት ሥጋ *hafrätä səga* n. genital organ *(pol.)*
  ታፈረ *taffärä* v.i was respected, honoured, revered
  ታፋሪ *taffäri* adj./n *(one)* who is respected, honoured, revered
  አሳፈረ *asaffärä* v.t disgraced, embarassed, humiliated
  አሳፋሪ *asaffari* adj. shameful, disgraceful
አፈረሰ *see* ፈረሰ
አፈረጠ *see* ፈረጠ
አፈረጠመ *see* ፈረጠመ
አፈር *afär* n. soil, earth
  —በላ *—bälla* v.i died
  —ብላ *—bəla* go to hell!
  —ይብላኝ *—yəblaññ* what a pity !
  የብረት— *yäbərät—* n. iron ore, ore
አፈሰ *affäsä* v.t scooped *(with the hands or with*

a scoop)

አፈሳ *afäsa* n. mass arrest

እፋሽ *əffaš* n. grain scooped from the ground *(usually mixed with dirt)*

ታፈሰ *taffäsä* v.i was scooped up

አሳፈሰ *asaffäsä* v.t had grain etc. scocped up; had mass arrested

አፈሰሰ *see* ፈሰሰ

አፈቀረ *see* * ፈቀረ

አፈተለከ *see* * ፈተለከ

አፈታ *see* ፈታ

አፈነ *affänä* v.t choked, suffocated; kidnapped: kept as a strict secret

አፍኖ ያዘ *affəno yazä* v.t suppressed *(a smile)*

—ገደለ *—gäddälä* v.t smothered

አፈና *afäna* n. kidnappping

አፋኝ *affañ* n. kidnapper

እፍኝ *əffəñ* n. handful, fistful

ማፈኛ *maffäña* n. gag, clip

ተፋፈነ *täfaffänä* v.i was overcrowded, congested; thronged

ታፈነ *taffänä* v.i was choked, suffocated, muffled *(the nose)*; was kidnapped; was kept as a strict secret

አሳፈነ *asaffänä* v.t had *s/o* kidnapped

አፈነገጠ *afänäggäṭä* v.i retreated, withdrew, receded

አፈንጋጭ *afängač̣* n. secessionist

አፈናጠጠ *see* ፈነጠጠ

አፈዘዘ *afäzzäzä see* ፈዘዘ

አፈገ *affägä* v.t cramped

እፍግ *əffəg* cramped, stuffed together

ታፈገ *taffägä* v.i was cramped, was stuffed together

ተፋፈገ *täfaffägä* v.t huddled together *(due to narrow space)*

እፍግፍግ አለ *əfəgfəgg alä* v.i was very much cramped, huddled, congested, became over—crowded

እፍግፍግ አደረገ *əfəgfəgg adärrägä* v.t cramped, huddled, congrsted

አፈገመ *see* ፈገመ

አፈገፈገ *see* ፈገፈገ

አፈጠነ *see* ፈጠነ

አፈጠጠ *see* ፈጠጠ

አፈፈ *affäfä* v.t trimmed *(edges of book)*; scraped, *(skin, hide)*

እፋፊ *əffafi* n. scraping *(small bits produced by scraping)*

አፈፍ አለ *afäff alä* v.i stood up abruptly

አፈፍ አደረገ *afäff adärrägä* v.t seized *(s/t)* abruptly, grabbed

አፉዋጨ *afuʷaččä* v.t whistled, *see also* ፉጨት

አፋለሰ *see* ፈለሰ

አፋረደ *see* ፈረደ

አፋደሰ *afaddäsä* v.i loitered around; wandered; vagabonded

አፋዳሽ *afadaš* adj. loiterer; wanderer; vagabond

አፋፋ *see* ፋፋ

አፋፍ *afaf* n. edge of a mountain, cliff, hill top, summit

አፍ *af* n. mouth; opening, inlet; language

አፈ ልስልስ *afä ləsləs* adj. polite, courteous, unruffled

አፈሙዝ *afämuz* n. muzzle *(of gun)*

አፈማር *afämär* n. glib; suave

አፈቅቤ *afäqəbe* adj. glib, suave

አፈታሪክ *afätarik also* ያፍ ታሪክ *yaf tarik* n. legend, mythology

አፈኛ *afäñña* adj. talkative

አፈንጉሥ *afänəgus* n. President of the Supreme Court

አፈጮሌ *afäčolle* adj. smart aleck

አፈጮማ *afäčoma* adj. glib,

suave

አፍለኛ *afläñña* n. unleavened *ənǧära*

•

ሙጢ አፍ *muṭi af* ad. talkative

እሾህ አፍ *əšoh af* n. one who makes malicious remarks

አፍላ *afla* n. prime, youthfulness, youth, vigour

አፍላል *aflal* n. large clay pot for boiling meat etc.

አፍሪቃ *afriqa* n. Africa

አፍሪቃዊ *afriqawi* n. African

አፍርንጅ *afrənǧ* n. ground pepper *(appetizer)*

አፍታታ see ፈታ

አፍንጫ *afənča* n. nose

አፍንጫማ *afənčamma* adj. long-nosed

አፍንጮ *afənčo* adj. long-nosed

አፍአ *afəʼa* n. external *(G.)*

አፍአዊ *afʼawi* adj. external

አፎት *afot* n. sheath

አፎቄ *afoqe* n. lance

አፍዮን *afyon* n. opium

አፓርትማ *appartma* n. apartment

ኡኡ አለ *ʼuʼu alä* v.i cried for help

ኡጋንዳ *uganda* n. Uganda

ኢሉባቦር *illubbabor* n. one of the Administrative Regions, western Ethiopia *(Ilubbabor)*

ኢምንት *imənt* n. nothing, not worth mentioning, unimportant

ኢትዮጵያ *itəyoppəya* n. Ethiopia

ኢትዮጵያዊ *ityoppəyawi* n. Ethiopian *(m.)*

ኢትዮጵያዊት *itəyoppəyawit* n. Ethiopian *(f.)*

ኢንሹ *inšu* n. Gunther's dikdik

ኢየሩሳሌም *iyyärusalem* n. Jerusalem

ኢየሱስ *iyyäsus* n. Jesus

ኢየሱሳዊ *iyyäsusawi* n. Jesuit

ኢዮቤልዩ *iyyobeləyu* n. jubilee

ኢጣሊያ *iṭaləya* n. Italy

ኢጣሊያንኛ *iṭalyanəñña* n. Italian *(language)*

ኢጣልያዊ *iṭalyawi* Italian *(person)*

ኤሊ *eli* n. tortoise

ኤርትራ *erətra* n. Eritrea

ኤርትራዊ *erətrawi* n. Eritrean

ባሕረ ኤርትራ *bährä erətra* n. Red Sea

ኤክዌተር *ekkwetär* n. equator *also* የምድር ሰቅ *yämədər säqq*

ኤጭ *eč̣č̣* interj. exclamation of abhorence

ኤጲስ ቆጶስ *epis qoppos* n. bishop

ኤጲፋንያ *epifanəya* n. epiphany

እህ *əh* interj. well *(expression of astonishment)*, well! *(expression of relief)*; well *(expression of consent)*, e.g well go ahead; oh, yes!

እህል *əhəl* n. grain, crops, food

እህላም *əhlam* adj. rich in grain, full of crops

እህት *əhət* n. sister, *also* እት *ət*

እህትማማች *əhətəmmamač* n. sisters

እልም አለ *əlləm alä* v.i disappeared, vanished

እልቅት *əlləqt* n. Adam's apple

እልቅና see አለቃ

እልባት *əlləbat* n. book-mark

እልክ *əllək* n. obstinacy, stubbornness *also* እልህ

እልከኛ *əlləkäñña* adj, stubborn, obstinate *also* እልከኛ

እልፍ *əlf* adj. ten thousand *(arch.)*

እልፍኝ *əlfəññ* n. living-room; porlour

—አስከልካይ *—askälkay* n. chamberlain

—አሽከር *—aškär* n. butler

እሑድ *əhud* n. Sunday

እመ ምኔት *əmmä mənet* n. abbess; Mother Superior

እመር አለ *əmmärr alä* v.i hopped, crossed *(a ditch etc.)* by hopping

እመቤት *əmmäbet* n. lady, lady of the house

እመቤታችን *əmmäbetaččən* Our Lady, the Virgin Mary

የቤት እመቤት *yäbet əmmäbet* n. housewife

እሙት *əmmät* interj./n yes

(answer given when a woman is called by s/o or when s/o calls her)

እመጫት *əmmäčat* n. nursing mother

—ጽሕፈት —*ṣəhfät* n. insertion *(writing)*

እማሆይ *əmmahoy* n. term used to address a nun *(such as "mother! etc.")*

እሜቴ *əmmete* interj. my lady!

እምር *əmmər* adj. tiny, minute

—ታህል —*tahəl* n. tiny thing

እምስ *əms* n. vagina, vulva

እምቡሽቡሽ *əmbušbuš* n. unfermented beer

እምቧ አለ *əmbuʷa alä* v.i lowed *(cow)*

እምቧይ *əmbuʷay* n. solanum incanum, solanum indicum

እምቡጥ *əmbuṭ* n. pad, shell

እምቢልታ *əmbilta* n. large wind instrument like a fife

እምቢልተኛ *əmbiltäñña* n. one who plays the እምቢልታ; *also* እምቢልታ ነፊ

እምቢ አለ *əmbi alä* v.i refused; became difficult to run, manipulate *(machine, gadget)*

እምቢተኛ *əmbitäñña* adj. disobedient, refractory, recalcitrant

እምቢታ *əmbita* n. refusal

እምብርት *əmbərt* n. navel; centre, core *(most important part of anything)*

እምብዛም *əmbəzamm (followed by a negative verb)* adv. seldom, not often rarely, scarcely

እምቦሳ *əmbossa* n. calf *(newly born)*

እምዬ *əmməyyä* interj. mother; *(lit. my mother)*

እምፍርፍር *əmfərfər or* እንፍርፍር *ənfərfər* n. boiled dry *ənǧära* with *wäṭ* cf. ፍንፍል

እሰይ *əssäy* interj. hurrah well done

እሴት *əsset* n. wage, value

እረኛ *ərräñña* n. shepherd herdsman; impolite rude, boorish, ill-mannered, vulgar

አረኝነት *ərräññənnät* n. herdsmanship

እረኝነት *ərräññənnät* n. impoliteness, rudeness, etc

(እ)ሩር *see* ሩር

(እ)ሩዝ *see* ሩዝ

(እ)ሩቅ *see* ራቀ

(እ)ሬዝ *see* ሬዝ

እሪያ *ərya* n. wild boar

እራሪ *ərrari* adj. dwarfish

(እ)ራስ *see under* ራስ

(እ)ራቁት *see* ራቁት

እርሱ *ərsu* pron. he, it

(እ)ርሳስ *see* ርሳስ

እርስዎ *ərsäwo* pron. you *(pol.)*

(እ)ርስት *see* ርስት *and* ወረሰ

እርሾ *əršo* n. leaven, yeast

እርቃን *in* እርቃን ሥጋ *ərqanä səga* n. nakedness

እርባና *see* ረባ

እርቦ *ərbo* n. one fourth *(product of land paid to landlord)*

እርኩም *ərkum* n. stork

እርኩስ *see* ረከሰ

እርከን *ərkän* n. degree *(solar measurement)*; staircase: terrace *(levelled area of sloping land)*

እርካብ *ərkab* n. stirrup

እርኮት *ərkot* n. water container *(made of hard leather)*

እርያ *ərya* n. wild boar *also* እሪያ

እርዬ አለ *ərrəy alä* v.i cried for help, *also* እሪ አለ

እርድ *ərd* turmeric; slaughtered animal *see also* እረደ

(እ)ርግብ *see* ርግብ

እርግብግቢት *ərgəbgəbit* n. propeller; fontanelle *see also* *ረገበገበ

እርግጥ *ərgəṭ* adj. sure; without any doubt, for granted *see* ረጋጠ

እርግጠኛ *ərgəṭäñña* adj. sure;

	without any doubt, for granted
እሮምታ	*ərromta* n. barrage *(continuous gunfire)*
እሰይ	*əssäy* interj. *(exclamation of joy, welcome, approval,)* hurrah;
እሳ	*əssa* interj. oho!; *(exclamation of surprise or triumph)*
እሳት	*əsat* n. fire; adj. brilliant, intelligent
እሳተ ገሞራ	*əsatä gämora* n. volcano
እሳታዊ	*əsatawi* adj. pertaining to fire
እሳት አፍ	*əsat af* adj. talkative, chatty
—አደጋ	*—adäga* n. fire-hazard; fire brigade
እሳቸው	*əssaččäw* pron. he, she *(polite)*
እስላም	*əslam* n. Mohammedan, Muslim *see also* ሰለመ
እስራኤል	*əsra'el* n. Israel
እስራኤላዊ	*əsra'elawi* n. Israelite
እስስት	*əsəst* n. chameleon; adj. spiteful, vicious
—አፍ	*—af* n. back-biting, slanderer
እስተ	*or* እስከ *əstä, əskä* prep. conj. until, till
እስከዚህ	*əskäzzih* prep. until here
እስከዚያ	*əskäzziya* prep: until there; till then
እስከየት	*əskäyät* prep. until where?
እስካሁን	*əskahun* conj. until now
እስቲ	*or* እስኪ *əsti, əski* well now, please ?
—ልየው	*—ləyäw* please let me see it *(him)*
—አሳየኝ	*—assayyäññ* please show me !
—ልሂድ	*—ləhid* let me go
—ትሄድና	*—təhedənna* let me see you dare go
እስትንፋስ	*əstənfas* n. breath, breathing; mere words not tangible, *see also* ነፈሰ
እስከ	*see* እስተ
እስክስታ	*əskəsta* n. shoulder dance *(typical Ethiopian)*
—ወረደ	*—wärrädä* v.t. danced *(with shoulders)*
እስክንድርያ	*əskəndərəya* n. Alexandria
እስያ	*əsya* n. Asia
ትንሹ—	*tənnəšu*—Asia Minor
እስፓንያ	*əspanəya* n. Spain
እስፓንኛ	*əspanəñña* n. Spanish
(እ)ስፖርት	*əsport* n. sport
እሸት	*see* ሼት
እሺ	*əšši* yes, all right, O.K.
—አለ	*—alä* v.i. complied, agreed, consented
—ባይ	*—bay* adj. submissive, compliant
እሽ	*əšš* interj. hush! silence keep calm!
—አለ	*əšš alä* v.t. shooed *(flies, birds, chickens etc)*
እሽሩሩ	*əššəruru* n. lullaby
እሽኮለሌ	*əškoläle* n. altercation, squabble
እሾኽ	*əšoh* n. thorn *also* እሾህ
እሾሃም	*əšoham* adj. thorny
(እ)ቀጭ አለ	*əqäčč alä* v.i. snapped *(break with a sharp crack)*
እቀጭታ	*əqqäččəta* n. snap *(sound of breaking)*
እበት	*əbbät* n. dung
እቡይ	*əbbuy* adj. wicked, evil minded, bad-hearted
እባብ	*əbab* n. serpent, snake
እባባም	*əbabam* adj. full of serpents, snakes
እባክህ	*əbakkəh* v.i. please? do me a favour?
እባክዎን	*əbakkäwon* v.i. please do me a favour? *(polite)*
እባካችሁ	*əbakkaččəhu* pl. of the above
እባክሽ	*əbakkəš* f. of the above
እብስ አለ	*əbbəss alä* v.i. left for good, disappeared

vanished (out of sight)

እብሪት *əbrit* n. arrogance, conceit

 እብሪተኛ *əbritäñña* adj. arrogant, conceited

እብነ በረድ *əbənä bäräd* n. marble

እብነ አድማስ *əbənä admas* n. diamond

እቴቴ *ətete* n. expression used to address an elder sister or an elder female relative

እቴዋ *ətewwa* my sister (*expression used to address a female aquaintance or a sister*)

እቴጌ *ətege* n. Empress

እት *or* እኅት *ət, əhət* n. sister

 እትማማች *ətəmmamač* n. sisters

 እትማማችነት *ətəmmamačənnät* n. sisterhood

 እትዬ *ətəyyä* n. my sister (*when addressing an elder sister or an elder acquaintance*)

እትፍ አለ *əttəf alä or* እንትፍ አለ *əntəff alä* v.t spat

እቶን *əton* n. furnace

እነ *ənnä* plural marker pref. እነማ *ənnäma* who ?

 እነኛ *ənnäñña or* እነዚያ *ənnazziya* pron. adj. those

 እነዚህ *ənnäzzih* pron. adj. these

እነኋት *ənnähuʷat* here she is (*arch.*)

እነሆ *ənnäho* v.t behold here he is! here it is!

እና *ənna* conj. and, and then, *see* ና *na*

እናት *ənnat* n. mother

 እናትነት *ənnatənnät* n. motherhood

 እናትና አባት *ənnatənna abbat* n. parents

 እናት አገር *ənnat agär* n. motherland

 የእንጀራ እናት *yäʾənǧära ənnat* n. stepmother

 የክርስትና— *yäkərəstənna*—n. godmother

እንስላል *ənsəlal* n. anise

እንሰት *ənsät* n. false banana

እንስራ *ənsəra* n. large water jar (*made of clay*)

እንስሳ *ənsəsa* n. adj. animal

 እንስሳነት *ənsəsannät* n. animality

 እንስሳት *ənsəsat* n. fauna

 እንስሳዊ *ənsəsawi* adj. animal

 የቤት እንስሳ *yäbet ənsəsa* n. domestic animal

እንስት *ənəst* adj. female

 እንስትነት *ənəstənnät* n. femininity

እንሽላሊት *ənšəlalit* n. lizard

እንሽርት ውኃ *ənsərt wəha* n. amniotic fluid

እንቃቅላ *ənqaqəlla* n. small poisonous lizard

እንቅርት *ənqərt* n. goitre

 እንቅርታም *ənqərtam* adj. goitrous

እንቅብ *ənqəb* n. large basket for measuring grain

እንቆቅልሽ *ənqoqəlləš* n. puzzle, riddle

እንቆቆ *ənqoqqo* n. seed of a a plant used against tapewarm

እንቁላል *ənqʷəlal* n. egg

 —ጣለ (ች) *ənqulal ṭallä(čč)* v.t laid an egg

እንቁራሪት *ənqʷərarit* n. frog

እንቁጣጣሽ *ənqʷəṭaṭaš* n. New Year's festival (*first of Mäskäräm*)

እንቡዋይ *see* እምቡዋይ

እንቢልታ *see* እምቢልታ

እንባ *or* እምባ *ənba, əmba* n. tears

 እንባም *ənbam* adj. easily irritated to weep

 እንባ አዘለ *ənba azzälä* v.t was tearful, was teary

 እንባ በእንባ ተራጩ *ənba bänba täraččä* v.i lamented (*in group*)

እንተን *or* እንትና *əntän, əntənna* n. what is his name? (*used when failing to remember s/o's name*)

እንትን *əntən* what is the name?

	(used when failing to remember the name of s/t)
እንትፍ አለ	*ənt*ə*ff alä.* or እትፍ አለ *ət*ə*ff alä* v.t spat
እትፍታ	*ətt*ə*fta* n. spitting
እንቶ ፈንቶ	*ənto fänto* n. nonsense
እንቺ	*ənči* imp. take, here you have *see* እንኪ
እንከን	*ənkän* n. defect, blemish *(of reputation)*
እንከናም	*ənkänam* adj. full of defect, imperfect
እንከን የማያጣው	*ənkän yämayatəw* adj. inacurrate, erroneous *(perpetually)*
እንክፍ	*ənkäf* adj. idiotic, imbecile, senile
እንካ	*ənka* imp. take! here you have *(m.)*
—በንካ	*—bänka* give and take
እንኪ	*ənki* or እንቺ *ənči* imp. take, here you have *(f.)*
እንክርት	*ənkərrit* n. brazier
እንክርዳድ	*ənkərdad* n. tares
እንክርዳዳም	*ənkərdadam* adj. full of tares
እንክብል	*ənkəbəll* n. tablet, pill, *see also* ተንከባለለ
እንኮኮ አለ	*ənkokko alä* v.t carried *(child)* on the shoulders
እንኮኮ	*ənkokko* n. carrying *(a child)* on the shoulders
እንኮይ	*ənkoy* n. plum
እንኳ	*ənkʷa* adv. even
እንኳን	*ənkʷan* *(with negative verb)* adv. not even
እንዘጥ አለ	or እንዝጭ አለ *ənzätt alä, ənzzäčč alä* v.i flopped *(on the bottom)*
እንዚራ	*ənzira* n. Ethiopian harp
(እ)ንዝህላል	*(ə)nzəhlal* adj. slack, careless
(እ)ንዝህላልነት	*(ə)nzəhlalənnät* n. slackness, carelessness
እንዝርት	*ənzərt* n. spindle
እንዝዝ	*ənzəz* n. type of beeltle
ጥቁር—	*təqur—*n. hornet
እንደ—	*əndä—*adj. prep. adv. like, as, according to, in accordance with
እንደልብ	*əndäləbb* as one wishes
እንደኔ	*əndäne* adv. according to me
እንደገና	*əndäggäna* adv. again
እንዲሁ	*əndihu* adv. and also, likewise
እንዲሁም	*əndihumm* adv. thus, likewise
እንዲህ	*əndih* adj. like this, such
እንዴታ	*əndeta* adv. surely
እንዴት	*əndet* adv. how?
እንዶድ	*əndod* n. phytolaca dodecandra *(a plant whose fruit is used as a detergent, soap tc.)*
እንጀራ	*ənǧära* n. bread *(usually Ethiopian)*
እንጀራ አባት	*ənǧära abbat* n. stepfather
—እናት	*—ənnat* n. stepmother
የንብ እንጀራ	*yänəb ənǧära* n. honeycomb
የንጀራ ልጅ	*yänǧära ləg* n. stepchild
እንጂ	*ənǧi* adv. conj. but, on the contrary,
ይሁን እንጂ	*yəhun ənǧi* adv. nevertheless
እንጃ	*ənǧa* adv. I have no idea, I dont know, I wouldn't know
እንጃለት	*ənǧallät* adv. I h ave no idea about him, I woudn't know about him *(expression of indifference)*
እንጃልህ	*ənǧalləh* adv. I have no idea about you, I wouldn't know about you; *(don't nag me)*
እንጃልሽ	*ənǧalləš* adv. *(f. of the above)*
እንጃልኝ	*ənǧalləññ* adv. woe

me!

እንጃባቱ *ənǧabbatu* adv. to Hell with him; I wouldn't know about him

እንጆሪ *ənǧorri* n. raspberry

እንገር *əngär* n. colstrum

እንጉዳይ *ənguday* n. mushroom

እንግሊዝ *əngəliz* n. Englishman, English

እንግሊዛዊ *əngəlizawi* n. Englishman

እንግሊዝኛ *əngliz əñña* n. English *(language)*

እንግሊዝ አገር *əngəliz agär* n. England

እንግልጣር *angltar* n. England *(arch.)*

እንግዲህ *əngədih* adv. therefore; hence, thus, now

እንግዲያማ *əngədiyamma* adv. well then, if that is the case

እንግዲያስ *əngədiyass* adv. *(same as above)*

ከእንግዲህ *kängədih* adv. hereafter

—ወዲህ *—wädih* adv. henceforth, from this time onward

—ወዲያ *—wädiya* adv. from this time on

እንግዳ *əngəda* n. guest, stranger; adj. odd, queer, unusual

—ነገር *–nägär* n. unusual thing

—ደራሽ *—däraš* n. sudden occurrence, unexpected happening

እንጎቻ *əngočča* n. small *ənǧära* *(specially baked for children) see* እንጎቶ

እንጣጥ አለ *ənṭaṭṭ alä* v.i sprang

እንጥል *ənṭəl* n. uvula, tonsil

እንጨት *ənčät* n. wood

የእንጨት *yä'ənčät* adj. wooden

እንጭጭ *ənčəč* n. unripe, green

እንፋሎት *ənfalot* n. vapour, steam

እንፍሌ *ənfəlle* n. lightly boiled meat

እንፍ አለ *ənf alä* v.i blew one's nose *(pol.)*

እኛ *əñña* pron. we

እኝኝ ብላ *əññəññ bəla* n. a three days' continuous rain sometimes at the beginning of September

እከሌ *əkäle, or* እገሌ *əgäle* n. so-and-so, such-and-such

እከክ *əkäk* n. itch, *see also* እኸክ

እከድዩ *əkkädəyyä* interj. oh no! *(exclamation of surprise, astonishment, stupefaction)*

እኩል *əkkul* adj/n equal, alike, half, uniform *see also* እክል

እክል *əkkəl* n. problem *(personal)*, obstacle

እክላም *əkkəlam* adj. full of problems

እኮ *əkko* adv. indeed! yes; of course! exactly, truly

እኸ *əhə* adv. yes! imp. go on *(i.e I am listening)*

እውልኝ *əwəlləñña* imp. see, look *(what is happening)*

እውነት *əwnät* n. truth, reality; adj. true, real

እውነተኛ *əwnätäñña* adj. truthful

እውነታ *əwnäta* n. reality

እውነተኛነት *əwñätäññaññät* n. truthfulness

እውነትም *əwnätəmm* adj. indeed, certainly, as a matter of fact

እውን *əwn* n. reality, truth

እዚህ *əzzih* adj. here

እዚያ *əzziya* adj. there

—እየ *—əyyä* pref. *(used both with nouns)* each, every *(with a perfect verb)* while, all the time that

እየቅሉ *əyyäqəlu* adj. different from one another

እያደር *əyyaddär* adv. later on, as time passes

እያንዳንዱ *əyondandu* adj. each

ones, every one

እየመጣ *əyyämäṭṭa* v.i he is coming

እዳ *əda* n. debt

ባለዳ *balädа* also ባለእዳ *balä'əda* n. creditor, debtor

እድመኛ *ədmäňňa* n. invited guests *(at a wedding feast), see also* እደመ

እድሜ *ədme* n. age

እድሞ *ədmo* n. fence *(of church);* churchyard

እጅ *əğğ* n. hand

እጀ ሰፊ *əğğä säffi* adj. generous

—በላህ *—bəlәh* adj. highly skilled *(in manual work)*

—ጠባብ *—ṭäbbab* n. tunic *(loose narrow sleeved shirt reaching the knees)*

እጀታ *əğğäta* n. handle *(of an axe)*

እጅ ለጅ *əğğ läğğ* hand in hand

—መንሻ *—mänša* n. present *(to higher man in rank or position)*

—ሰጠ *—säṭṭä* v.i. capitulated; surrendered

—በጅ *—bäğğ* n. cash *(payment);* act of working together to complete a piece of work quickly

—ቢዛ *—beza* n. thimble

—ነሳ *—nässa* v.i bowed down *(to greet)*

—አደረገ *—adärrägä* v.i took over, took control over *(/st),* possessed

—ና እግር *—na əgər* n. limbs

—እጅ አለ. *—əğğ alä* v.i got fed up with; loathed

—ከፍንጅ ተያዘ *—käfənğ täyazä* was caught red-handed

ሁለት እጅ *hulätt əğğ* twice as much

ባለጅ *baläğğ* n. blacksmith, craftsman

የእጅ ሥራ *yä'əğğ səra* n. manual work, handicraft

—ሰዓት *—sä'at* n. wristwatch

—ሹራብ *—šurrab* n. glove

—ቦምብ *—bomb* n. grenade

—ጥበብ *—ṭəbäb* n. handicraft

—ጽሕፈት *—ṣəhəfät* n. handwriting, penmanship

እጅጌ *.əğğəge* n. sleeve

እጅግ *əğəgg* adv. very much

—በጣም *—bäṭam* adv. extremely, very much

እጅጉን *əğğəgun* adv. very well ? *(after having greeted s/o to ask such a question as "are things going very well ?*

አገሌ *əgäle* n. so-and-so *also* እከሌ

አገሊት *əgälit* n. *(f)* so-and-so

እግር *əgər* n. foot

እግረ መንገድ *əgrä mängäd* n. on one's way

የእግር— *yä'əgər—* n. path, trail, track, footpath

እግረ ሙቅ *əgrä muq* n. tight shackle

እግረኛ *əgräňňa* n. pedestrian; adj. restless

እግር በግር *əgər bägər* adv. one after the other

—ብረት *—bərät* n. fetter, shackle

ልጅ እግር *ləğ əğər* n/adj. young man, young woman ; young

እጅና እግር *əğğənna əgər* n. limbs

እግዚአብሔር *əgzi'äbəher* n. God

እግዚእነ *əgzi'ənä* Our Lord

እግዚኦታ *əgzi'ota* n. name of prayer *(God have mercy upon us)*

እግዝእት *əgzə't* n. Our Lady

እግዝእትነ ማርያም *əgzə'tənä mariyam* n. Our Lady Mary

እጢ *əṭi* n. gland

እጣን *əṭan* n. incense

እጥቢ *see* አጠበ

እጭ *əčč* n. larva

እፉኝት *əfuňňit* n. viper

እፊያ *əffiya* n. lid *(of a cooking pot, basket)*

እፍ አለ	*əff alä* v.t blew on the fire; lived high
እፍ እፍ አለ	*əff əff alä* v.t blew on the fire repeatedly; lived in each others pocket
አፍላ	*afla* n. time of full vigour, prime
—ጐረምሳ	*afla gorämsa* n. in the prime of youth
እፎይ አለ	*əffoy alä* v.i sighed in or with relief, felt relief
እፎይታ	*əffoyta* n. relief
ኦሪት	*orit* n. pentateuch; biblical times
ኦሪታዊ	*oritawi* adj. pertaining to the Old Testament; old fashioned
ሕገ ኦሪት	*həggä orit* n. laws of Moses
ኦርቶዶክስ	*ortodoks* n. orthodox *(belief)*
ኦርቶዶክሳዊ	*ortodoksawi* n. orthodox *(believer)*
ኦርቶዶክሳዊት	*ortodoksawit* n. Orthodox *(church, or female Orthodox)*
ኦቶማቲክ	*otomatik* adj. automatic
ኦቶሞቢል	*otomobil* n. automobile
ኦፔራሲዮን	*operasiyon* n. surgery, *also* ቀዶ ጥገና

ከ

ከ—	*kä* prep. from, at, out of
ከመጣ	*kämätta* if he comes
ከልመጣ	*kalmätta* unless he comes
ከሀዲ	*see* ከደ.
ከለለ	*källälä* v.i tinkled *(ringing loud of a bell)*
ከለለ	*källälä* v.i screened, protected from view; staked out *(a plot of land)*, appropriated *(land for special purpose)*
ከለላ	*käläla* n. screen, cover *(protecting from view)*
ከላይ	*kälay* adj/n *(s/t)* that screens, covers
ክለላ	*kəlläla* n. demarcation, appropriation *(of land)*
ክልል	*kəlləl* n. boundary, confines, zone
ብሔራዊ—	*bəherawi*—n. national park
ተከለለ	*täkällälä* v.i was screened, protected from view ; was staked out; was appropriated *(land for special purpose)* demarcated, appropriated
ተካለለ	*täkullälä* v.t demarcated *(land border between neighbours or rivals)*
ተካላይ	*täkalay* adj/n *(one)* who participates in solving border disputes
አስከለለ	*askällälä* v.t had *(s/t or s/o)* screened, protected from view; had *(land, border)*
ከለሰ	*källäsä* v.t diluted *(a strong drink)*, added water *(in a stew)*; reviewed *(a lesson)*
ከላሽ	*källaš* n. revisionist
ክለሳ	*kəlläsa* n. reviewing *(a lesson)*, revision
ክልስ	*kəlləs* n. mulatto, half-caste
መከለሻ	*mäkälläša* n. hot water added to stew
ተከለሰ	*täkälläsä* v.i was diluted; was reviewed
ተካለሰ	*täkalläsä* v.i crossbred *(with each other)*
አካለሰ	*akkalläsä* v.t caused

to crossbreed

ከለበ *källäbä* v.i became restless, bustled, hustled

ከላባ *källabba* adj. graceless; busy-body

ከልብ *kälb* n. dog *(Ar.)*

ከለበሰ *källäbbäsä* v.t threw water at s/o, tossed out water

ተከለበሰ *täkäläbbäsä* v.i was tossed out *(water)*

አስከለበሰ *askäläbbäsä* v.t had water thrown at s/o

ከለቻ *källäčča* n. helmet

ከለከለ *käläkkälä* v.t prevented, hindered, forbade prohibited, impeded

ከልካይ *kälkay* adj/n who prevents, hinders, forbids, impedes

ክልክል *kəlkəl* adj. forbidden, prohibited, prevented

ተከለከለ *täkäläkkälä* v.t was prevented, hindered, forbidden,

ተከላካይ *täkälakay* adj/n *(one)* who defends, resists, withstands, defender, resistant

መከላከያ ሚኒስቴር *mäkkäläkäya minister* Ministry of Defence

አከላከለ *akkälakkälä* v.t caused to be prevented, forbidden, hindered, impeded

አስከለከለ *askäläkkälä* v.t caused to be prevented, hindered, impeded

እልፍኝ አስከልካይ *əlfəññ askälkay* n. chamberlain

ከለፈ *källäfä* v.t became restless, nuisance

*ከለፈለፈ **käläfälläfä*

ከለፍላፋ *käläflaffa* adj. mischievous, arch

ክልፍልፍ *kələfləf* adj. mischievous, arch

ክልፍልፍ አለ *kələfləff alä* v.i became too mischievous, arch

ተክለፈለፈ *täkläfälläfä* v.i become mischievous, arch

ተክለፍላፊ *täkläflafi* adj. mischievous, arch

አክለፈለፈ *akläfälläfä* v.t hustled, disturbed s/o's tranquility, serenity

ከል *käll* n. mourning dress *(black, blue or yellow, usually white dress dyed in such colours)*

ከመረ *kämmärä* v.t piled up stacked, put in a heap

ከማሪ *kämmari* adj/n *(one)* who piles up, stacks, puts in a heap

ክመራ *kəmmära* n. piling, stacking, heaping

ክምር *kemmər* n. pile, heap *(usually of stones, etc.)*

አከመረ *akkammärä* v.t helped *(s/o)* in piling up *(s/t)*

አስከመረ *askämmärä* v.t had *(s/t)* piled up, stacked, heaped

*ከመቸ * *kämäčča*

ክምቹ *kəməčču* adj. assembled; collected, concentrated; self-sufficient

ክምችት *kəməččət* n. collection, concentration

ተከማቸ *täkämaččä* v.i was assembled, gathered, concentrated

ተከመቻቸ *täkämäčaččä* v.i became gradually gathered, assembled, collected, concentrated

አከመቻቸ *äkkämäcaččä* v.t assembled, collected, gathered, concentrated *(gradually)*

ከመከመ *kämäkkämä* v.t patted into shape *(hair)*; raked together *(heap of hay)*

ክምክም *kəmkəm* n. well-shaped Afro hairstyle

ተከመከመ *täkämäkkämä* v.i was patted into shape *(hair)*; was raked together *(hay)*

ከሙን *kämun* n. cumin *(spice)*

ከምሱር *kämsur* n. primer *(of cartridge)*

ከሠተ *kässätä* v.t made clear, manifested, revealed

ክሥተት *kəstät* n. phenomenon

ተከሠተ *täkässätä* v.i was clear, manifested, revealed

ከረመ *kärrämä* v.i spent the year, spent the rainy season, spent a certain time of the year

ከራሚ *kärami* adj/n. *(one)* who spends a year or part of the year at a certain place, one who lives long; s/t that lasts long

ከርሞ *kärmo* n. next year

ክረምት *kərämt* n. rainy season

መከረሚያ *mäkrämiya* n. place, supply etc. for passing a year or part of a year

አከረመ *akärrämä* v.t kept for a year, delayed for a year or a part of a year, kept for a long time

አካረመ *akkarrämä* v.t lived with s/o *(e.g friend, relative)* for a year, or part of the year

ከረረ *kärrärä* v.i was twisted tightly *(rope, string)*; became acute *(situation, crises etc.)* became grave *(quarrel)*

ከራራ *kärara* adj. undersized, dwarfish *(person, animal)*

ክራር *kərar* n. Ethiopian lyre *(with six strings)*

ክር *kərr* n. thread; wick, ribbon *(typewriter)*

ተካረረ *täkarrärä* v.i came to a head *(quarrel)*; was aggravated *(from both sides)*, reached a crisis

አከረረ *akärrärä* v.t twisted tightly *(rope, string)*, made acute, grave *(situation, crisis quarrel)*

አክራሪ *akrari* adj/n radical *(political)*; *(one)* who aggravates situations, quarrel

ቀኝ— *qäññ—* n. right extremist

ግራ— *gəra—* n. left extremist

ከረበተ *käräbbätä* v.t knocked down *(with a blow or in wrestling)*

ተከረበተ *täkäräbbätä* v.i was knocked down

ከርቡሽ *kärbuš* n. water-melon

ከርቤ *kärbe* n. myrrh

*ከረተተ **kärättätä*

ከርታታ *kärtatta* n. adj wanderer, roamer; wandering, roaming, vagrant

ተንከራተተ *tänkärattätä* v.i wandered around, roamed, roved, became a vagrant

ተንከራታች *tänkäratač* adj/n *same as* ከርታታ

አንከራተተ *ankärattätä* v.t caused to wander around, roam, rove

ከረተፈ *kärättäfä* v.t hewed,

ተከረተፈ *täkärättäfä* v.i was hewed

አስከረተፈ *askärättäfä* v.t had *(s/t)* hewn

ከረከመ *käräkkämä* v.t trimmed, shortened *(to give good shape)*; cut *(s/o's)* hair

ክርክማት *kərkəmat* n. edge *(out of which the cut is made)*

ክርክም *kərkəm* adj/n trimmed; cut *(hair)*; edge *(out of which the cut is made)*

ክርክም አደ *kərkkəm adärrägä*

ረገ v.t trimmed well; gave good shape; *(by shortening)*

ተከረከመ *täkäräkkkämä* v.i was trimmed; was shortened *(to give good shape)*; was cut *(hair)*

አስከረከመ *askäräkkümä* v.t had *(s/t)* trimmed, cut short; had *(s/o's)* hair cut

ከረከረ *käräkkärä* v.i was acrid *(sharp stinging)*, sawedl

ማሲንቆ— *masinqo*— played the *masinqo*

ከርከር *kärkər* n. chancroid

ክርክር *kərkər* n. groove level *(of liquid measure)*

ተከረከረ *täkäräkkärä* v.i was sawed

ተከራከረ *täkärakkärä* v.i argued, debated contended, contested *(challenge)*

ዋጋ— *waga*—v.i bargained, haggled

ተከራካሪ *täkärakari* n. disputant n. litigant

አከራካሪ *akkärakari* adj. controversial, debatable

የሚያከራክር *yämmiyakkärakkər* adj. controversial, debatable

የማያከራክር *yämmayakkärakkər* adj. unquestionable, beyond dispute

ከረደደ *käräddädä* v.i became kinky; became coarse *(material, flour)*

ከርዳዳ *kärdadda* adj. kinky; coarse *(material, flour, powder etc.)*

ክርዳድ *kərdad or* እንክርዳድ *ənkərdad* n. tares

ክርድ *kərədd same as* ከርዳዳ

ክርድድ *kərdəd* adj. *same as* ከርዳዳ

ከረጢት *käräṭit* n. small bag, pouch

ከረፈፈ *see* ተንከረፈፈ

ከረፋ *käräffa* v.i stank, have a horrid and offensive smell

ክርፋታም *kərfatam* adj. stinking

ክርፋት *kərfat* n. stink

አከረፋ *akäräffa* v.t caused to stink, stank

ከራማ *kärama* n. respectability *(Ar.)*, charisma

ከርስ *kärs* n. belly, stomach

ከርሠ ባሕር *kärsä bahr* n. bottom of the sea

—ምድር —*mədər* n. bottom of the earth

ከርሳም *kärsam* adj. gluttonous

ከርከሮ *kärkärro* n. warthog

ከሰለ *kässälä* v.i became charcoal; was sunburnt, became extremely dark *(pigmentation)*

ከሰልማ *käsäləmma* adj. darkish, blackish

ከሰል *käsäl* n. charcoal

ከሳይ *käsay* adj. easily carbonized *(type of wood)*

—እንጨት —*ənččät* n. wood that can easily be transformed into charcoal

ክሳይ *kəssay* adj. carbonized

አከሰለ *akässälä* v.t made charcoal; sunburnt, darkened completely *(pigmentation)*

አክሳይ *aksay* adj/n *(one)* who makes charcoal

አስከሰለ *askässälä* v.t had *(s/o)* make charcoal

ከሰመ *kässämä* v.i dried *(wound)*; withered, faded *(plant)*, became sunburnt

አከሰመ *akässämä* v.t dried *(wound)*; faded, withered *(plant)*

ከሰረ *kässärä* v.i became bankrupt ; went broke

ኪሳራ *kässara* n. bankruptcy

ኪሳራ *kisara* n. expend-

	iture, expenses; costs; deficit
አከሰረ	*akässärä* v.t bankrupted; brought deficit, incurred unnecessary costs
አክሳሪ	*aksari* adj. bankrupting *(business deal)*
ከሰሰ	*kässäsä* v.t accused, brought a law suit,sued *(s/o)*, brought a charge against *(s/o)*
ከሳሽ	*käsaš* n. plaintiff, accuser
ክስ	*kəss* n. charge *(legal)*; accusation, suit *(in court of law)*
ተከሰሰ	*täkässäsä* v.i was charged *(in a court of law)*, was sued
ተከሳሽ	*täkässaš* n. defendant, accused
ተካሰሰ	*täkassäsä* v.t accused each other, brought charges against each other, sued each other
ተካሳሽ	*täkasaš* n. parties accusing each other
አካሰሰ	*akkassäsä* v.t caused to accuse each other etc.
አስከሰሰ	*askässäsä* v.t had, *(s/o)* accused, sued, charged
ሰበ	*kässäbä* v.t earned *(money in trade)*, profited; tilled *(land)*
ከሰብ	*käsäb* n. earning, profit
ሰከሰ	*käsäkkäsä* v.t harrowed *(ploughed ground)*; dashed to bits
ገንዘብ—	*gänzäb* — v.t squandered *(money)*
መከስከሻ	*mäkäskäša* n. harrow
ተከሰከሰ	*täkäsäkkäsä* v.t was harrowed; was dashed to bits
ተከሳከሰ	*täkäsakkäsä* v.t hit up each other; rained blows at each other
አከሰከሰ	*akäsäkkäsä* v.t gave plenty of food and drink
አስከሰከሰ	*askäsäkkäsä* v.t had *(ground)* harrowed; had *(s/t)* dashed to bits
ከሳ	*kässa* v.i became thin, became emaciated, lost weight, became skinny
ከሲታ	*kässitta* adj. thin, skinny
ክሳት	*kəsat* n. thinness, loss of weight.
አከሳ	*akässa* v.t made thin, made skinny
ከሸነ	*käššänä* v.t made excellent *(usually for ወጥ)*, garnished
ከሸፈ	*käššäfä* v.i misfired *(gun)*; became abortive *(plan, revolution)*
*ከበለለ	*see* ተንከባለለ
ከበረ	*käbbärä* v.i was honoured, revered; was precious, became wealthy; got rich, was celebrated *(holiday)*
የከበረ ድንጋይ	*yäkäbbärä dəngay* n. precious stone, gem
ከበሬታ	*käbäreta* n. honour, reverence
ከበርቴ	*käbbärte* adj. wealthy
የመሬት—	*yämäret*—n. land lord
ክቡር	*kəbur* adj. respectful; His honour, excellency
ክቡራን	*kəburan* gentlemen, your excellencies
ክቡራት	*kəburat* ladies
ክብረት	*kəbrät* n. wealth; riches
ክብር	*kəbr* n. honour, reverence, respect, prestige
ክብርና	*kəbrənna* n. virginity; celibacy
ክብረ በዓል	*kəbrä bä'al* n. celebration
ክብር ዘበኛ	*kəbr zäbäñña* n. bodyguard
ክብርና ገሠሠ	*kəbrənna' gässäsä*

	v.t deflowered
ተከበረ	*täkäbbärä* v.i was honoured; was venerated, commanded respect, became celebrated *(holiday)*
ተከባበረ	*täkäbabbärä* v.i gave mutual respect, respected each other
ተከባባሪ	*täkäbabari* adj. respecting each other
አከበረ	*akäbbärä* v.t honoured, venerated, gave respect to; celebrated *(holiday)*
ቃሉን—	*qalun*—he kept his word
አክባሪ	*akbari* adj. honouring, respecting
ቀጠሮ—	*qäṭäro*—adj. punctual
አከባበር	*akkäbabär* n. way of celebration, ceremony, celebration
አክብሮት	*akbərot* n. veneration, respect, honour
አከባበረ	*akäbabbärä* v.t gave pretentious honour, respect etc.
አስከበረ	*askäbbärä* v.t had *(s/o, s/t)* honoured, respected
ሕግ አስከባሪ	*həgg askäbbari* n. public prosecutor
ሥነ ሥርዓት —	*səna sər'at*—n. master of ceremonies; policeman
ፀጥታ—	*ṣäṭṭəta*—n. security man
ከበሮ	*käbäro* n. drum
—መታ	—*mätta* v.t played the drum
ከበሰ	*käbbäsä* v.i tied a big turban around the head
ከበበ	*käbbäbä* v.t encircled, surrounded, besieged, encompassed, crowded around *(s/t)*
ከበባ	*käbäba* n. encirclement, surrounding
ከባቢ	*käbabi* adj. surrounding
—አየር	*ayyär* n. atmosphere
—ግፊት	—*gəffit* n. atmospheric pressure
ክበብ	*kəbäb* n. club, circle *(geometrical)*
የሙዚቃ—	*yämuziqa*— n. glee club
የክበብ አጋማሽ	*yäkəbäb aggamaš* n. semi-circle
ክብ	*kəbb* adj. round, circular
ክብነት	*kəbbənnät* n. roundness
ክብብ አደረገ	*kəbəbb adärrägä* v.t encircled completely
ተከበበ	*täkäbbäbä* v.t was encircled, surrounded besieged completely
አካበበ	*akkabbäbä* v.t surrounded
አካባቢ	*akkababi* n. surrounding
አስከበበ	*askäbbäbä* v.t caused to be surrounded, encircled, besieged
ከበተ	*käbbätä* v.t accumulated *(wealth)*; hid one's ill-will
አካበተ	*akabbätä* v.t accumulated *(wealth)*
አካባች	*akabač* adj/n *(one)* who accumulates wealth
ከበደ	*käbbädä* v.i was heavy; was grave, was difficult, became serious *(situation)*; was severe *(punishment)*; was pregnant *(animal)*
ከባዳ	*käbbada* adj. heavy
ከባድ	*käbbad* adj. heavy; difficult; serious, grave; severe *(injury)*
ተካበደ	*täkabbädä* v.t was heavy
ተካባጅ	*täkabağ* adj. heavy
አከበደ	*akäbbädä* v.t made difficult, serious
*ከበከበ	*käbäkkäbä
ተንከባከበ	*tänkäbakkäbä* v.t treated well, cherished, yielded to the wishes of, took under one's wing

አንከባከበ *ankäbakkäbä* v.t *same as above*
ከብት *käbt* n. animal, livestock; adj. imbecile
—አርቢ *—arbi* n. breeder *(cattle)*
—እርባታ *—ərbata* n. breeding *(cattle)*
የጋማ— *yägamma* n. equines *(horses, donkeys, mules)*
የቀንድ— *yäqänd*— n. cattle, bovines
የጭነት— *yäčənät* — n. pack animal
*ከተለ **kättälä*
ክትትል *kətəttəl* n. keeping an eye on, watching, supervison
ምክትል *məkəttəl* n. vice–, acting *(for another)*
—ሚኒስትር *—ministr* n. vice-minister
ከተል አለ *kättäll alä* v.t followed *(s/o)*
ከተል አደረገ *kättäll adärrägä* v.t brought next
ተከተለ *täkättälä* v.t followed; resulted from
ተከታይ *täkättay* adj. following, follower, entourage
ተከታተለ *täkätattälä* v.t kept an eye on; kept up with; pursued; followed each other; happened in succession
ተከታታይ *täkätatay* adj/n. successive, consecutive; *(one)* who keeps *(an eye on)*
አስከተለ *askättälä* v.t caused to follow; incurred *(cost etc)*; resulted in, gave rise to
አከታተለ *akkätattälä* v.t caused to happen one after the other, gave rise to
ከተለበ *kätälläbä* v.t snatched *(thief)*
ተከተለበ *täkätälläbä* v.i was snatched

ከተመ *kättämä* v.t founded a city
ከተሜ *kätäme* n. city dweller, metropolitan
ከተማ *kätäma* n. city
—ቀመስ *—qämmäs* adj / n. *(one)* who is exposed to city life
መሀል— *mähal*—n. city centre
ከተረ *kättärä* v.i diked; harnessed *(a water fall)*, concentrated, gathered
ከተራ *kätära* n. eve of Epiphany *(lit. gathering)*
ክትር *kəttər* adj. diked; concentrated, gathered
ተከተረ *täkättärä* v.i was diked; was gathered was concentrated
አስከተረ *askättärä* v.t had a dike built up
ከተበ *kättäbä* v.t vaccinated; enrolled *(s/o)* in the army
ከታቢ *kätabi* adj/n *(one)* who vaccinates; *(one)* who enrolls people *(in the army)*
ክታብ *kətab* n. talisman, amulet *(charm)*
አሸን— *ašän*— n. talisman *(amulet)*
ክትባት *kəttəbat* n. vaccination
ተከተበ *täkättäbä* v.i was vaccinated, was enrolled *(in the army)*
አስከተበ *askättäbä* v.t had *(s/o)* vaccinated, had *(s/o)* enrolled *(in the army)*
ከተተ *kättätä* v.t put *(into a bag, satchel etc.)*
ከቶ *kätto* adv. absolutely, completely, fully; never
ከቶውንም *kättowənəmm* adv. never
ክተት *kətät* n. mobilization *(troops)*
ክት *kətt* n. *with* ልብስ e.g የክት ልብስ *yäkətt ləbs*

n. sunday best

ተከተተ *täkättätä* v.i was put in; was inserted; was stored; came to an end

አካተተ *akkattätä* v.t helped in putting *(s/t)* into a bag etc.; included

አካቴ *akkate in* እስከናካቴው *əskännakkattew* adv. never, at all

አስከተተ *askättätä* v.t had *(s/t)* put into a bag, satchel etc; had *(troops)* mobilized

ከተከተ *kätäkkätä* v.t chopped *(wood, meat etc.)*; inflicted *(with sharp pain)*

ክትካች *kətəkkač* n. splinters

ተንከተከተ *tänkätäkkätä* v.i shrieked with laughter, howled with laughter

ተንከታከተ *tänkätakkätä* v.i crumbled *(broke into pieces)*

ተከተከተ *täkätäkkätä* v.i was chopped *(wood, meat etc.)*

ተከታከተ *täkätakkätä* v.t bit each other fiercely

አንከተከተ *ankätäkkätä* v.t caused to shriek, howl with laughter

አንከታከተ *ankätakkätä* v.t. crumbled, crushed

አስከተከተ *askätäkkätä* v.t had *(s/t)* chopped

ከተፈ *kättäfä* v.t cut in little pieces *(meat)*; minced meat, onions etc; chopped

ክትፎ *kətfo* n. a dish of minced meat with butter flavoured with chilli *(served usually raw)*

መክተፊያ *mäktäfiya* n. chopping board *(meat onion etc.)*

ተከተፈ *täkättäfä* v.i was minced, chopped *(meat, onion etc.)* minced, chopped

ከት ብሎ ሳቀ *kätt bəlo saqä* v.i burst into laughter

ከቶ *see* ከተተ.

ከቸረ *käččärä* v.i dried *(bread)*

ከቻሮ *käčäro* adj. dwarfish *(person)*; dry *(humour)*, dull

ከቻራ *käčarra* adj. dwarfish *(person)*, dry *(humour)*

ከቸቸ *käččäčä* v.i became dry *(bread etc.)*, became dull *(conversation, speech etc.)*

ከቻቻ *käčača* adj. dry *(uninteresting)*, dull

ክችች አለ *kəččəč alä* v.i dried to excess; became extremely boring

ከች አለ *käčč alä* v.i arrived suddenly, arrived unexpectedly

ከነ— *kännä*—prep. including, with

ከነቤተሰቡ *kännä betäsäbu* with his family, including his family

ከነአካቴው *känn'akkattew* adv. in spite of these *(circumstances)*

ከነበለ *känäbbälä* v.t caused to tumble off, tipped up *(container)*

ከነተረ *känättärä* v.t tied fast; gave a stunning blow

ከነነ *kännänä* v.i became bone-dry

አከነነ *akännänä* v.i. made bone-dry

ከነከነ *känäkkänä* v.t. tickled *(pepper in the nostrils)*, vexed *(caused anxiety in one's mind)*

*ከነወነ * *känäwwänä*

ክንውን *kənawwen* n. accomplishment

ተከናወነ *täkänawwänä* v.i. was accomplished; was successful *(an undertaking)*

አከናወነ *akkänawwänä* v.t. accomplished; brought to success

ከነዳ *känädda* v.t. measured by cubits *(length of arm)*

ክንድ *kənd* n. arm, forearm; cubit

አስከነዳ *askänädda* v.t. had s/o measure by cubits

ከነፈ *kännäfä* v.t. bustled; fluttered about *(moved from place to place aimlessly)*

ክንፋም *kənfam* adj. winged

ክንፍ *kənf* n. wing

አከነፈ *akännäfä* v.t caused to move quickely, bustled

*ከናነበ • *känannäbä*

ተከናነበ *täkänannäbä* v.i. covered one's head *(with a šämma)*, pulled a blanket over one's head

አከናነበ *akkänannäbä* v.t. covered with a *šamma*, pulled blanket over s/o head

ከንቱ *käntu* vain, futile, useless

ከንቱነት *käntunnät* n. vanity, uselessness

ከንቲባ *käntiba* n. mayor

ከንች *känč* n. beams *(in building)*, rafters

ከንፈር *känfär* n. lip

ከንፈራም *känfäram* adj. thick-lipped

ከንፈር ወዳጅ *känfär wädağ* n. boy fiiend, girl fiiend

ከካ *käkka* v.t. ground *(coarsely)*

ክካም *kəkkam* adj. untidy, dirty

ክክ *kəkk* n. split-peas, beans etc. *(used for wäṭ)*

ተከካ *täkäkka* v.i was ground coarsely

አስከካ *askäkka* v.t had peas, beans eto. ground coarsely

ከውታታ *käwtatta* n. roamer, wanderer

ከውትት አለ *käwtätt alä* v.i roamed, wandered

ተንከዋተተ *tänkäwattätä* v.i roamed, wandered

ከውር *käwr* n. crucible, melting-pot

ከውካዋ *käwkawwa* adj. light, frivolous, not serious

ከዘራ *käzära* n. walking-stick, cane

ከዚህ *käzzih* adv. from here

— በኋላ —*bähuʷala* adv. after this

ከዚያ *käzziya* adv. from there

—በኋላ —*bähuʷala* adv. after that

—ወዲያ —*wädiya* adv. since then, ever since

ከይሲ *käysi* n. devil; cruel mischievous person, imp

ከደነ *käddanä* v.t covered with a lid; thatched house with grass;

ክዳን *kədan* n. cover, covering; thatch; cap *(pen)*

ቤት— *bet*—n. thatch

ተከደነ *täkäddänä* v.i was covered; thatched

አከደነ *akkaddänä* v.t helped in covering *(s/t)*; helped in thatching a house

አስከደነ *askäddänä* v.t had s/t covered; had a house thatched

ከዳ *kädda* v.t betrayed, deserted; abandoned; denied

ከዳተኛ *kädatäñña* n. traitor, deserter

ከጂ *käği* n. traitor

ክዳት *kədat also* ክሕደት *kəhdät* n. denial, betrayal; desertion

አስከዳ *askädda* v.t had s/o desert *(the army etc.)*; caused s/o to deny a friend etc. abandon etc.

ከጀለ *käğğälä* v.t coveted, had the inclination to do, to like s/t

ክጀላ *kəğğäla* n. inclination

to do, to have s/t

ከፈለ *käffälä* v.t paid out; divided

ከፊል *käfil* n. partial

በከፊል *bäkäfil* adv. partially

ከፋይ *käfay* n. payer

ክፋይ *kəffay* n. segment

ክፍል *kəfəl* n. portion; room *(in a house)*; class-room; division; grade *(class in school)*

ክፍለ ሀገር *kəflä hagär* n. administrative region

—ቃል *—qal* n. syllable

—ዓለም *—aläm* n. hemisphere, continent

—ዘመን *—zämän* century

—ጊዜ *—gize* n. period, session *(in class)*

—ጦር *—ṭor* n. division *(army)*

ክፍያ *kəfəyya* n. payment, pay, share

የመጀመሪያ— *yämäǧämmäriya*—n. down-payment

መክፈልት *mäkfält* n. meal served to the clergy after service

መክፈያ *mäkfäya* n. bed urinal

ከፋፈለ *käfaffälä* v.t divided up, divided, classified, distributed

ከፋፍለህ ግዛ *käfafläh gəza* divide and rule

ክፍልፋይ *kəfəlfay* n. fraction

ክፍልፍል *kəfəlfəl* adj. divided, allotted

ተከፈለ *täkäffälä* v.i was paid out; was divided

ተከፋይ *täkäffay* n. adj. payee; divisible

ተከፋፈለ *täkäfaffälä* v.i divided between each other; was divided into many parts; was segmented; was divided *(in opinion)*

ተካፈለ *täkaffälä* v.i took a share, participated, divided *(s/t)* with *(s/o)*, shared with another; split *(profit etc.)*

ተካፋይ *täkafay* adj. n one *(who)* participates in *(s/t)*, one *(who)* takes part in *(s/t)*

አከፋፈለ *akkäfaffälä* v.t distributed; apportioned, portioned out

አከፋፋይ *akkäfafay* n. distributor

ማምረቻና ማከፋፈያ *mamräčanna makkäfafäya* n. production and distribution

አካፈለ *akkaffälä* v.t divided *(total)*; distributed, allotted; imparted *(one's ideas)*

አካፋይ *akkafay* adj/n one *(who)* divides *(a total)*; one *(who)* distributes, allots

የጋራ — *yägara*—n. common denominator

ማካፈል *makkafäl* n. division *(arithmetic)*

አስከፈለ *askäffälä* v.t charged with a payment; made s/o pay charges

ከፈተ *käffätä* v.t opened; unlocked; got brighter *(colour)*

ክፍት *kəft* adj. open; bright *(colour)*

ልበ ክፍት *ləbbä kəft* adj. frank

ክፍት አፍ *kəft af* adj. talkative

መክፈቻ *mäkfäča* n. key, opener *(instrument)*

ቆርቆሮ— *qorqorro*—n. tin opener

ከፋፈተ *käfaffätä* v.t threw *(doors, windows etc.)* open

ክፍት አደረገ *kəffət adärrägä* v.t opened suddenly

ተከፈተ *täkäffätä* v.t was opened; started *(meeting)*

ተከፋች *täkäffač* n. s/t that can be opened

ተካፈተ *täkaffätä usually preceded with* አፍ *eg.* አፍ ተካፈተ *af täkaffätä* v.i insulted at each other.

blamed each other

ተከፋፈተ *täkäfaffätä* v.t was wide open

ከፈነ *käffänä* v.t wrapped up a corpse for burial

ከፈን *käfän* n. shroud

መከፈኛ *mäkäffäña* n. shroud

ተከፈነ *täkäffänä* v.i was wrapped up *(corpse)*

አስከፈነ *askäffänä* v.t had *(a corpse)* wrapped

ከፈከፈ *käfäkkäfä* v.t compacted the thatch roof, raked together *(thatch, heap of hay)*

ክፍክፍ *kəfkəf* adj. well raked and trimmed

ተከፈከፈ *täkäfäkkäfä* v.i was compacted well *(thatch, heap of hay)*, was raked together

አስከፈከፈ *askäfäkkäfä* v.t had *(thatch etc.)* compacted well, *(heap of hay etc. raked together)*

ከፈይ *käfäy* n. velvet

ከፈፈ *käffäfä* v.t trimmed the edges of s/t *(usually leather, edge of book etc.)*

ክፈፍ *kəfäf* n. edge *(trimmed)*

ተከፈፈ *täkäffäfä* v.i was trimmed *(edges of s/t)*

አስከፈፈ *askäffäfä* v.t had *(the edges of s/t)* trimmed

ከፋ *käfa* n. one of the Administrative Regions, south western Ethiopia *(Kafa)*

ከፋ *käffa* v.i became worse, wicked, became bad

ክፉ *kəfu* adj. wicked, evil, vicious, mean

—ቀን —*qän* n. hard time

ክፉኛ *kəfuñña* adv. awfully, gravely, badly; seriously

ክፋተኛ *kəfatäñña* adj. wicked, evil, bad

ክፋት *kəfat* n. wickedness, evil

ምን ከፋኝ *mən käffañ* I have no objection, I agree, I am willing

ከፋ አለው *käfa aläw* v.i was rather sad, became somewhat offended

ተከፋ *täkäffa* v.i became offended, sad, was hurt *(feeling)*

ተከፊ *täkäfi* adj/n *(one)* who is easily offended

አከፋ *akäffa* v.t worsened

አስከፋ *askäffa* v.t displeased, angered *(s/o)*; caused to dislike

አስከፊ *askäffi* adj. disgusting, offensive, repulsive; ugly

ከፍ አለ *käff alä* v.i was elevvated, high, raised

ከፍተኛ *käffətäñña* adj. higher, high, advanced *(course)*; important *(matter, rank etc.)*; maximum

—ፍርድ ቤት —*fərd bet* n. High Court

ከፍታ *käffəta* n. high *(mountain)*, altitude

ከፍ ከፍ አለ *käff käff alä* v.i was raised, elevated gradually, grew higher gradually

ኩሊ *kuli* n. coolie, porter

ኩሊነት *kulinnät* n. work of a coolie, porter

ኩላሊት *kulalit* n. kidney

ኩል *kul* n. antimony dust, *see also* ኳል

ኩልል አለ *see* ኩለለ

ኩምቢ *kumbi* n.trunk *(elephant)*

ኩራዝ *kurraz* n. small kerosene lamp; dwarf

ኩሬ *kure* n. pool, pond

ኩርማን *kurman* n. one fourth of an *ənǧära*

ኩርሲ *kursi* n. chair (Harar)

ኩርትም አለ *see* ኩረተመ

ኩርፋድ *kurfad* adj. pug-nosed and small-faced *(person)*

ኩስ *kus* n. excrement *(fowl)*

ኩሽ *kuš* n. Cush *(country in the Nile Valley)*
  ኩሻዊ *kušawi* n. Cushitic *(a sub-family of the Afro-Asiatic language)*
ኩበት *kubät* n. dry cow dung *(used as fuel)*
ኩባያ *kubbayya* n. cup, mug *(of metal)*
ኩብ ሜትር *kubb metər also* ሜትር ኩብ *metər kubb* cubic metre
ኩብኩባ *kubkubba* n. young locust
ኩታ *kuta* n. toga *(white cotton loose garment)*
ኩታራ *kutara* n. nipper *(small child)*
ኩክ *kuk* n. earwax
ኩክኒ *kukni* n. mange
  ኩክኒያም *kukniyam* adj. mangy
ኩይሳ *kuyyəsa* n. termite hill
ኩዳዴ *kudade also* ሁዳዴ *hudade* n. Lent
ኩዳድ *kudad also* ሁዳድ *hudad* n. plantation
ኩፍ አለ *kuff alä* v.i rose *(of dough)*
  ኩፍ ኩፍ አለ *kuff kuff alä* v.i became sullen *(person)*
ኩፍኝ *kuffənn* n. measles, chicken-pox
ኩፍ ጫማ *kuf čamma* n. shoes
ኪሎ *kilo* n. kilo
  —ሜትር *—metər* n. kilometer
  —ግራም *—gram* n. kilogramme
  —ዋት *—wat* n. kilowatt
ኪራይ *kiray* n. rent *(house, car etc. see also* ተከራየ*)*
  ኪራየተኛ *kirayätäññä* n. lessee
ኪስ *kis* n. pocket; drawer *(box-like container)*
  የኪስ ገንዘብ *yäkis gänzäb* n. pocket-money
ኪን *kin* n. skill
  ኪነት *kinät* n. art
  ኪነ ጥበብ *kinä ṭəbäb* n. work of art
ኪንታሮት *kintarot* n. wart
  ኪንታሮታም *kintarotam* adj. infested with warts
  የአህያ ኪንታሮት *yä'ahəyya kintarot* n. hemorrhoids
ኪያር *kiyar* n. cucumber
ኪዮስክ *kiyosk* n. kiosk, booth
ኪዳን *kidan* n. treaty, pact, covenant *(Biblical)*
  ሐዲስ— *haddis*—n. New Testament
  ብሉይ— *bəluy*—n. Old Testament
  ቃል— *qal*—n. agreement, pact, covenant; promise
ካህን *kahən* n. priest, pastor, clergyman *(pl.* ካህናት *see also* ካነ*)*
ካልእ *kalə'* adj. second *(G.)*
ካሉስ *kalos* n. satin
ካሜራ *kamera* n. camera
ካሚዮን *kamiwon* n. lorry, truck
ካም *kam* n. Ham
  ካማዊ *kamawi* adj. Hamite
ካምፉር *kamfur* n. camphor
ካራ *karra* n. curved knife *(large)*
ካርቦን *karbon* n. carbon
ካርታ *karta* n. map; title deed *(land)*; playing cards
ካርቶን *karton* n. cardboard
ካርኒ *karni* n. receipt
ካሮት *karot* n. carrot
ካሰ *kasä* v.t compensated, paid damages, indemnified
  ካሳ *kasa* n. compensation, indemnity, restitution, reparation
  ተካሰ *täkasä* v.i was compensated, indemnified, paid damage
    ተካካሰ *täkakasä* v.i compensated, indemnified each other; equalized
  አካካሰ *akkakasä* v.t caused damage to be paid, had compensation paid, equalized
  አስካሰ *askasä* v.t had compensation, damage paid
ካስማ *kasma* n. tent peg, stake *(for tent)*
ካበ *kabä* v.t piled up *(stones etc.)*; praised

(s/o) unduly

ኩብ *kab* n. pile *(of stones etc.)*

ክቦሽ *kəboš* n. piling

ተኻኸበ *täkakabä* v.i praised each other unduly

ኣካኸበ *akkakabä* v.t helped *(s/o)* in piling up *(stones etc.)*

ኣስከበ *askabä* v.t had *(stones etc.)* piled up

ካባ *kaba* n. quarry

ካባ *kabba* n. mantle, cloak cape

ካቤላ *kabella* adj. long-footed

ኩብት *see* ሀብት

ካቦ *kabbo* n. foreman *(It.)*

ካቲካላ *kati kala* n. arrack *(strong colourless alcoholic drink)*

ካታሎግ *katalog* n. catalogue

ካቶሊክ *katolik* n. catholic

ካቶሊካዊ *katolikawi* n. a catholic *(m.)*

ካቶሊካዊት *katolikawit* n. a catholic *(f.)*

ካች *kačč see also* ሀች *hačč* adj/adv. yonder, over there

ካቻምና *käččamna also* ሀቻምና *haččamna* n. the year before

ካነ *kanä* v.t ordained *(as a priest or deacon)*

ካህን *kahən* n. priest, pastor, clergyman

ክህነት *kəhnät* n. ordination

ቤተ— *betä*—n. clergy, the Church

ተካነ *täkanä* v.i was ordained; became an expert in a field

ኣስካነ *askanä* v.t had s/o ordained *(as a priest or deacon)*

ካንዴላ *kandella* n. spark-plug *(It.)*

ካኪ *kaki* n. khaki

ካካ *kakka* n. excrement *(a word used with children)*, adj. bad

ካውያ *kawəyya* n. iron *(for clothes)*

ካዕብ *ka'əb* n. second order of the alphabet *(e.g.* ሁ*)*

ካደ *kadä* v.t forsook, denied, renounced, repudiated *(a statement)*

ካጂ *kaǧi* adj/n *(one)* who forsakes, denies renounces, repudiates a statement

ክደት *kədat* also ክህደት *kəhdät* n. denial, forsaking renouncement, repudiation *(of a statement)*

ተካደ *täkadä* v.i was denied, renounced, repudiated *(a statement)*, forsaken

ኣስካደ *askadä* v.t caused to forsake, deny, renounce, repudiate *(a statment)*

ካደመ *kaddämä* v.t served *(coffee etc.)*

ካዳሚ *kaddami* adj/n *(one)* who serves *(coffee etc.)*

ካፊር *kafir* n. Christian *(word used by Moslems, meaning irreligious, unbelieving)*

*ካፋ **kaffa*

ካፊያ *kaffiya* n. drizzle, shower *(of rain)*

ኣካፋ *akaffa* v.i drizzled

ካፖርት *kapport* n. overcoat

ኬላ *kella* n. toll station

ኬሻ *keša* n. sack *(cloth, bag)*

ኬንትሮስ *kentros* n. longitude

ኬንያ *kenya* n. Kenya

ኬክሮስ *kekros* n. latitude

ክሊኒክ *klinik* n. clinic

ክላሰር *klasär* n. file *(folder)*

ክላክስ *klaks* n. hoot

ክልብሽ ኣለ *kəlbəšš alä* v.t nauseated

ክልብሽታ *kəlbəšta* n. nausea

ክልትው ኣለ *kəltəw alä* v.i collapsed *(for persons due to a hard blow or heavy sleep)*

ክረምት *kərämt* n. rainy season *see also* ክረመ

ክራር *see* ክረረ

ክራቫት *kravat* n. necktie

ክር *see* ክረረ

ክርስቲያን *kərəstiyan* n. Christian

ቤተክርስትያን *betäkrəstəyan* Church

ክርስትና *kərəstənna* n. Christianity

—አነሣ *—anässa* n. christened *(for godparents)*

ክርስቶሳዊ *krəstosawi* n. Christian

ክርስቶስ *krəstos* n. Christ

ክርታስ *kərtas* n. card board; membrane

ክርን *kərn* n. elbow

ክርክር *see* ከረከረ

ክሳድ *kəsad* n. collar

ክስ *see* ከሰሰ

ክብር *see* ከበረ

ክብሪት *kəbrit* n. matches

ክብርና *see* ከበረ

ክታብ *kətab* n. charm *(amulet)*

አሸን— *ašän*–amulet, talisman

ክው አለ *kəww alä* v.i was stunned, was caught by surprise; dried very much

ክፉ *see* ክፋ

ክፍ አለ *kəff alä word used to chase away a cat*

ክፍል *see* ከፈለ

ኮሚቴ *komite* n. committee

ኮመተረ *see* አኮማተረ

ኮምፓስ *kompass* n. compass

ኮረመተ *see* አኮረመተ

ኮረሪማ *korärima* n. cardamon

ኮረሸመ *koräššämä* v.t gormandised

ኮረብታ *koräbta* n. hill

ኮረብታማ *koräbtamma* adj. hilly

ኮረጀ *korräğä* v.t corrected *(exam. papers)*; cheated *(exams)*

ኩረጃ *kurräğa* n. cheating *(exams.)*

ተኮረጀ *täkorräğä* v.i was corrected *(exams)*

አስኮረጀ *askorräğä* v.t had *(s/o)* correct one's exam. papers; helped *(s/o)* cheat *(exams)*

ኮረጆ *koräğo* n. satchel

ኮረጠ *korräṭä* v.i was piquant *(food)*

ኮራ *korra* v.i became proud, showed off

ኩሩ *kuru* adj. proud; gentle, high-spirited

ኩራተኛ *kuratäñña* adj. proud; conceited

ኩራት *kurat* n. pride, conceit

ተኩራራ *täkurarra* v.i showed off, was boastful

አኮራ *akorra* v.t caused to become self-sufficient, independent

ኮርማ *korma* n. bull

ኮርቻ *korəčča* n. saddle

ኮርፋ ኮርፋ አለ *korfa korfa alä* v.i became somewhat angry; moody, bad-tempered

ኮሰመነ *kosämmänä* v.i became emaciated, lean, skinny

ኮስማና *kosmanna* adj. thin lean, skinny

አኮሰመነ *akosämmänä* v.t emaciated, made lean, skinny

ኮሶ *koso* n. tape-worm; taenia; taeniacide

—ታየው *—tayyäw* v.i became infested with tapeworms

—ጠጣ *—ṭäṭṭa* v.t took taeniacide

ኮሽሽ አለ *košäšš alä* v.i rustled

ኮሽም *košəm* n. rumex abyssinica *(kind of fruit with sweet and sour taste)*

ኮበለለ *kobällälä* v.i deserted *(the army etc.)*, ran away; eloped

ኩብለላ *kubläla* n. desertion; elopement

ኮብላይ *koblay* n. deserter, fugitive

አኮበለለ *akobällälä* v.t caused *(s/o)* to desert, run away; caused to elope

አስኮበለለ *akobällälä* v.t *see* አኮበለለ

አስኮብላይ *askoblay* adj/n *(one)*

who causes *(s/o)* to desert *(the army)*, run away

ኮባ *koba* n. false banana

ኮተኮተ *kotäkkotä* v.t hoed up weed

ኩትኳቶ *kutkuʷato* n. hoeing

ኩትኮታ *kutkota* n. hoeing

መኮትኮቻ *mäkotkoča* n. hoe

ተኮተኮተ *täkotäkkätä* v. was hoed

አስኮተኮተ *askotäkkotä* v.t had *(garden)* hoed

ኮቴ *kotte* n. hoof

የኮቴ ገንዘብ *yäkotte gänzäb* n. embarkation fee

ኮት *kot* n. coat

ኮትቻ *kotačča usually* ኮትቻ መሬት *kotačča märet* n. black cotton soil

*ኮነሰነሰ • *konäsännäsä*

ኩንስንስ *kunəsnəs* adj. stilted, unnatural, artifical *(behaviour)* pretentious

ተኮነሰነሰ *täkunäsännäsä* v.t behaved unnaturally, artifically, pretentiously

ተኩንስናሽ *täkunsnaš* adj. stilted, unnatural, artificial

ኮንትራት *konirat* n. contract

ኮንትሮባንድ *kontroband* n. contraband

ኮከብ *kokäb* n. star *(pl.* ከዋክብት *käwakəbt)*

—ቆጠራ *qoṭära* n. astrology, horoscope

—ቆጣሪ —*qoṭari* n. astrologer

አጥቢያ— *aṭbiya*—n. morning star

ኮከን *kokän* n. cockscomb *(red crest of cock)*

ኮክ *kok* n. peach

*ኮደደ • *koddädä*

ኩዳድ *kudad also* ሁዳድ *hudad* n. plantation

ኮዳ *kodda* n. water-bottle *(metal flask)*, canteen *(USA)*

ኮፈኮፈ *kofäkkofä* v.i errupted

ኵለለ *kuʷällälä* v.i became crystal clear

ኵለል አለ *kuʷälläl alä* v.i became crystal clear

*ኵለተፈ • *kuʷälättäfä*

ኵልታፋ *kuʷältaffa* adj. lisping

ኵልትፍ *kuʷəltəf* adj. lisping

ተኰላተፈ *täkuʷälattäfä* v.i lisped, stuttered

ኰለኰለ *kuʷäläkuʷälä* v.t tickled; lined up *(caused to be in line)*; spurred

ኵልኰላ *kuʷlkuʷäla* n. tickling; lining up; spurring

ኵልኵል *kuʷəlkuʷəl* adj. lined-up

—መስመር —*mäsmär* n. parallel lines

ተኰለኰለ *täkuʷäläkuʷälä* v.i was tickled; was lined up; was spurred

አስኰለኰለ *askuʷäläkuʷälä* v.t caused to line up

ኰላ *kuʷälla* v.t polished, made lustrous *(metal etc.)*

ኵልኵሎ *kuʷälkuʷällo* n. lock *(hair)*

ኰመኰመ *kuʷämäkkuʷämä* v.t relished *(food, drink)*; gormandized

ኰረተ *see* አኰረተ

ኰረት *kuʷärät* v. gravel

ኰረተመ *kuʷärättämä* v.t squatted *(on ones legs)*; crippled

ኰረታተመ *kuʷärätattämä* v.i squeezed *s/t* together; crippled

ተኰረተመ *täkuʷärättämä* v.i squatted

ተኰረታተመ *täkuʷärätattämä* v.i squatted down

ኰረኰመ *kuʷäräkkuʷämä* v.t chipped off; rapped on the head with the knuckles

ኵርኰማ *kuʷərkuʷäma* n. chipping off

ኵርኵም *kuʷərkuʷəm* n. blow

with knuckles

ኰረኰረ *kuʷäräkkuʷärä* v.t tickled, spurred *(a horse)*; cleaned the ears of wax

ኰረዳ *kuʷaräddä* n. maiden

ኰረፈ *kuʷärräfä* v.i bubbled, foamed

ኰረፌ *kuʷäräfe* adj. sparkling *(of wines and other drinks)*

ኩርፈኛ *kuʷərfäñña* n. one with whom one is not on speaking terms

ኩርፍተኛ *kurrəftäñña* adj. moody

ኩርፊያ *kuʷərfiya* n. snoring; grimace, sulks

ኩርፍ *kuʷərf* n. not on speaking terms

ኰሩ *see* ኮሩ

ኰሰሰ *kuʷässäsä* v.i emaciated, was lean and weak

ኰሳሳ *kuʷäsasa* a.dj emaciated, lean and weak

ኰሳሳነት *kuʷäsasannät* n. emaciation, weakness

አኰሰሰ *akuʷässäsä* v.t emaciated; belittled

አኳሰሰ *akuʷassäsä, or* እንኳሰሰ *ankuʷassäsä* v.t belittled

ኰሰተረ *kuʷäsättärä* v.t made a horrible face; trimmed *(wick of a lamp candle)*, snuffed

ኰስታራ *kuʷästarra* adj. serious, thoughtful; not given to pleasure seeking; daring

መኰስተሪያ *mäkuʷästäriya* n. snuffers

ሲጃራ— *sigara*—n. ash-tray

ተኰሰተረ *täkuʷäsättärä* v.i was trimmed *(wick of lamp etc.)*

ተኰሳተረ *täkuʷäsattärä* v.i frowned at, made a horrible face

ኰሰኰሰ *kuʷäsäkkuʷäsä* v.t itched *(of wool etc.)*; caused discomfort *(cloth)*

ኰስኳሳ *kuʷäskuʷassa* adj. uncomfortable *(cloth)*

ኰሳ *kuʷässa* v.t excreted *(waste matter)*

ኵሳም *kuʷəsam* adj. dirty

ኵስ *kuʷəs* n. excrement

ኰበለለ *see* * ኮበለለ

ኰነሰነሰ *see* *ኮነሰነሰ

ኰነነ *kuʷännänä* v.t condemned

ኰናኝ *kuʷännañ* adj. n *(one* who condemns

ኵነኔ *kuʷənäne* n. damnation, condemnation

ተኰነነ *täkuʷännänä* v.i was condemned

አስኰነነ *askuʷännänä* v.t showed pity for *(s/o)*, became pitiful, abject, pathetic

አስኰናኝ *askuʷännañ* adj. pathetic, much to be pitied

ኰከ *see* ኮከ

ኵርንችት *kuʷərənčət* n. small thorny bush

ኵስኵስት *kuʷəskuʷəst* n. ewer, coffee, teapot

*ኰበኰበ *see* አኰበኰበ

ኳ አለ *kuʷa alä* v.i knocked *(short, sharp sound of metal etc.)*

ኳኳቴ *kuʷakuʷate* n. repeated sound of knocks

ተንኳኳ *tänkuʷakkuʷa* v.i tinkled; produced repeated sounds of knocks

አንኳኳ *ankuʷakkuʷa* v.t knocked at a door

ኳለ *kuʷalä* v.t made up one's eyelashes with antimony

ኩል *kul* n. antimony *(powder)*

ተኳኳለ *täkuʷakuʷalä* v.t painted one's eyelashes with antimony

ኳስ *kuʷas* n. ball

ኳተ *kuʷatä* v.t cultivated

መኳቻ *mäkuʷača* n. small pick or cultivtor *(instrument)*

ኳንክ *kuʷank* n. cockscomb, crest

ኹለት *see* ሁለት

ኹሉ *see* ሁሉ

ኾነ *or* ሆነ *honä* v.i became

ወ

ወሀ *wäha also* ውሀ *wəha* n. water

—ሆነ *—honä* v.i was converted into liquid; was caught by surprise, was stunned

—ቋጠረ *—quʷaṭṭärä* v.t formed blisters

—በላው *—bällaw* v.i was drowned; became useless, vain

—ወሀ አለ *—wäha alä v.t.* became thirsty

—አጠጣ *—aṭäṭṭa* v.t watered *(plants)*

—ወረደ *—wärrädä* v.t went to fetch water

ወሀማ *wähamma* adj. watery

የወሀ ልክ *yäwäha ləkk* n. water-level; spirit-level

—ማጠራቀሚያ *—maṭṭäraqämiya* n. water res:rvoir

—ተርብ *—tärb* n. dragon-fly

እሀል ወሀ *əhəl—*n. food and drink

የቧምቧ— *yäbuʷambuʷa—*n. running water

የእንቁላል— *yä'ənqulal—*n. white *(of an egg)*

የግብር— *yägəbr—*n. douche *(of women)*

ፈረሰኛ— *färäsäñña—*n. torrent *(sudden)*

ፍልወሃ *fəlwäha* n. thermal springs

ወሀኒ *wähni* n. jail, penitentiary

—ቤት *—bet* n. jail, penitentiary

ወለላ *wälläla* n. honey *(separated from wax)*

ወለል አለ *wäläll alä* v.i became clear, brilliant

—አደረገ *—adärrägä* v.t caused to become clear, brilliant *(light etc.)*; opened wide

ወለም አለ *wälämın alä* v.t sprained

ወለምታ *wälämta* n. sprain, wrench

ወለም ዘለም አለ *wälämm zälämm alä* v.i wavered, hesitated, became indecisive

ወለቀ *wälläqä* v.i became disjointed, slipped off *(got free from)*, was put out of joint; was pulled out *(tooth)*

ወላቂ *wälaqi* adj. not fast enough, loose, easily disjointed

ውላቂ *wəllaqi* n. s/t disjointed

ውልቃት *wəlləqat* n. sprain, wrench

ወላለቀ *wälalläqä* v.i became disjointed completely, was taken to pieces was dismantled

ውልቅልቅ *wəlqələq* adj. dismantled, disjointed

ወለቅ አደረገ *wäläqq adärrägä* v.t disjointed slightly; undressed *(oneself suddenly)*

ውልቅ አለ *wəlləqq alä* v.t became disjointed suddenly, slipped off suddenly

ውልቅ አደረገ *wəlləq adärrägä* v.t disiointed suddenly;

caused to slip off suddenly; took off clothes etc. *(suddenly)*

ተዋለቀ *täwalläqä* v.i bit each other severely

አወለቀ *awälläqä* v.t dismantled, disjointed; pulled out, took off *(one's clothes)*

ልብ አውላቂ *ləbb awlaqi* adj. nagging, tiresome, wearing

ኪስ— *kis* — n. pick-pocket

አወላለቀ *awälalläqä* v.t dismantled completely; took off one's clothes; took to pieces

አስወለቀ *aswälläqä* v.t had s/t dismantled ,had s/t taken into pieces; had s/o take off clothes

ወለወለ *wäläwwälä* v.t mopped up, wiped; polished

መወልወያ *mäwälwäya* n. mop

ወላወለ *wälawwälä* v.i hesitated

ወላዋይ *wälaway* adj. hesitating, hesitant

አወላወለ *awwälawwälä* v.t help s/o in mopping up, in wiping; hesitated

አወላዋይ *awwälaway* adj. hesitant, hesitating

ወለወልዳ *wäläwälda* n. backbiter, dishonest, deceitful

ወለደ *wällädä* v.t gave birth to ; deliverd *(child)*; engendered; accrued interest

ወለድ *wälläd* n. interest *(bank etc.)*

ወላድ *wällad* n. fertile *(woman)*, fecund

ወላጅ *wälağ* n. parent

ውላጅ *wəllağ* adj. half-caste, bastard

ውልድ *wəld in* የቤት ውልድ *yäbet wəld* n. slave, born in his master's house

ልደት *lədät* n. Christmas; birth, birthday

ልጅ *ləğ* n. child, boy,

ወላለደ *wälallädä* v.t gave birth to a few offspring

ተወለደ *täwällädä* v.i was born

ተወላጅ *täwällağ* n. blood relation, kin

ትውልድ *təwlədd* n. generation

ተዋለደ *täwallädä* v.i intermarried *(thus producing offspring)*, multiplied *(human being)*; produced several shoots *(plant)*; was related through marriage

አዋለደ *awwallädä* v.t acted as midwife

አዋላጅ *awwalağ* n. midwife

አስወለደ *aswällädä* v.t caused to give birth to a child

ወለገደ **wäläggädä*

ወልጋዳ *wälgadda* adj. twisted bent, distorted, twisted out of shape

ተወላገደ *täwälaggädä* v.i. became twisted, crooked

ተወለጋገደ *täwälägaggädä* v.t became completely twisted, crooked

አወላገደ *awwälaggädä* v.t twisted, crooked

አወለጋገደ *awwälägaggädä* v.t twisted, distorted completely

ወለጋ *wällägga* n. one of the Administrative Regions western Ethiopia *(Wollega)*

ወላንሳ *wälansa* n. velvet; adj. amiable

ወላይታ *wälayətta* n. Wolayitta *(nationality, living in Sidamo)*

ወላይትኛ *wälayətəñña* n. the Wolayitta language

ወላፈን *wälafän* n. blazing fire

ወል *wäl* adj. common

የወል ስም — *yäwäl səm* n. common noun

ወሎ — *wällo* n. one of the Administrative Regions, north-eastern Ethiopia *(Wollo)*

ወመቴ — *wämmäte* adj. riff-raff, vagabond, vagrant

ወምፈል — *wämfäl also* ወንፈል *wänfäl* n. work *(farming)* carried out by helping each other

ወምበር — *wämbär also* ወንበር n. *wänbär* n. chair; judge

ወረሀ — *wäräha* n. cripple; adj. bow-legged

ወረረ — *wärrärä* v.t invaded *(army)*, infested *(vermin, insects etc.)*

ወረራ — *wärära* n. invasion; infestation

ወረርሽኝ — *wäräršəññ* n. plague, epidemic

ወራሪ — *wärari* adj/n invading *(army)*

ወሮበላ — *wärro bälla* adj. vagbond, vagrant, tramp, *hooligan*

ውርር አደረገ — *wərrər adärrägä* v.t invaded completely; infested completely *(vermin, insect)*

ተወረረ — *täwärrärä* v.i was invaded *(by an army)*; was infested *(with vermin, insects etc.)*

ፊት አውራሪ — *fit awrari* n. an Ethiopian title *(general)*

አስወረረ — *aswärrärä* v.t caused to be invaded; caused to be infested

ወረሰ — *wärräsä* v.t inherited; confiscated

ወራሽ — *waraš* n. heir

አልጋ— — *alga*—n. crown prince, princess

ዋርሳ — *warsa* n. brother-in-law *(term used among Muslims, since one can marry his sister-in-law after his brother's death)*

ርስት — *rəst* n. owned land

ያባት— — *yabbat*—n. heritage *(of land)*

ተወረሰ — *täwärräsä* v.i was inherited; was confiscated

ተወራሽ — *täwärraš* adj/n *(one)* whose property is confiscated

ተወራረሰ — *täwärarräsä* v.t was recorded *(e.g bills, vouchers etc. in a cash register)*

አወረሰ — *awärräsä* v.t gave one's property as an inheritance

አወራረሰ — *awärarräsä* v.t recorded *(bills, vouchers etc. in a cash register)*

ወረቀት — *wäräqät* n. paper; letter

ወረብ — *wäräb* n. chant (church)

ወረቦ — *wäräbbo* n. small antelope

ወረት — *wärät* n. capital *(money)*; liquid *(finance)*; stook; temporal friendship; vogue

ወረተኛ — *wärätäññä* adj. inconsistent *(in objectives, in wishes, in friendship)*; capricious *(in personal behaviour)*; fickle

ወረንጦ — *wäränto* n. tweezers

—አፍ — *—af* n. s/o who uses biting words

ወረክራካ — *wäräkrakka* adj. shaky, unsteady

ወረወረ — *wäräwwärä* v.t threw; bolted *(fastened with a bolt)*

ውርወራ — *wərwära* n. throwing

መወርወሪያ — *mäwärwäriya* n. bolt; shuttle *(in a loom)*

ተወረወረ — *täwäräwwärä* v.i was thrown; spurted *(in race)*; leaped

ተወርዋሪ — *täwärwari* adj. spurting, leaping

ተወራወረ *täwärawwärä* v.i threw s/t at each other

አስወረወረ *aswäräwwärä* v.t had s/o throw s/t

ወረዛ *wäräzza* v.t oozed through, moisted

አወረዛ *awäräzza* v.t caused to ooze, moist

ወረደ *wärrädä* v.i descended, went down, came down ; got off, dismounted

ትከሻ— *təkäšša*— v.i suffered from shoulder cramp

ወረዳ *wäräda* n. district, zone

ምክትል— *məkəttəl*— n. subdistict

ወራዳ *wärradda* adj. disgraceful, dishonourable, ignoble

ወራዳነት *wärraddannät* n. dishonour, shamefulness

ወራጅ *wärağ* adj. flowing, descending

—ውሀ —*wäha* n. flowing water

ወርድ *wärd`* n. breadth, width

ወርደ ሰፊ *wärdä säffi* adj. wide, broad *(cloth, garment etc.)*

—ጠባብ —*ṭäbbab* adj. narrow

ወርድና ስፋት *wärdənna səfat* dimensions

ወርዳም *wärdam* adj. wide, broad

ውርዴ *wərde* n. s/o cured of V.D. (syphilis)

ውራጅ *wərrağ* n. rags, old clothes, worn-out

ውርደት *wərdät* n. humiliation, indignity, disgrace, degradation

ውርድ *wərd in* ውርድ ንባብ *wərd nəbab* n. quicker style of reading *(of pupil's thus trained)*

—ከራሴ —*kärase* n. *(expression used to declare that grave consequences are inevitable)*

I warn you !

ውርጃ *wərğa* n. abortion

ውርጅብኝ *wərğəbbəňň* n. a sudden disaster ; stream of invectives

ወራረደ *wärarrädä* v.i descended gradually

ውርርድ *wərərrəd* n. bet, wager

ተወረደ *täwärrädä* v.i accomplished one's duties, became contented

ተወራጅ *täwärrağ* adj. inferior

ተወራረደ *täwärarrädä* v.i made a bet

ተዋረደ *täwarrädä* v.i was humiliated, debased dishonoured

አወረደ *awärrädä* v.t brought down ; caused to descend; led a choir

አውራጃ *awrağğa* n. province

አውራጅ *awrağ* n. choir leader, song leader

አወራረደ *awärarrädä* v.t brought down repeatedly

አወራረደ *awwärarrädä* v.t helped s/o bring down s/t; caused to bet; cut meat in lumps

አዋረደ *awwarrädä* v.t humiliated, despised, dishonoured ; helped s/o bring s/t down

አስወረደ *aswärrädä* v.t aborted ; had s/t brought down

ወረገኑ *wärrägänu* n. Royal Herdsmen

*ወረጨ *see* ተወራጨ

ወረፈ *wärräfä* v.t despised, scoffed at, taunted

ወራፊ *wärrafi* adj/n *(one)* who despises, scoffs at etc.

ወሬ *wäre* n. news, rumour gossip ; story, *see also* አወራ

የመንደር— *yämändär*— n. gossip the talk of the towr

ወሬኛ *wäreňňa* adj/n talkative, *(one)* who

has a loose tongue

ወር *wär* n. month

የወር መባቻ *yäwär mäbača* n. first day of the month

—አበባ *—abäba* n. menstruation

ወርቅ *wärq* n. gold

ወርቃማ *wärqamma* adj. golden; precious *(especially for time)*

ወርቃ ወርቅ *wärqawärq* adj. yellowish

ወርቅ አንጣሪ *wärq anṭari* n. goldsmith

የወርቅ ቡችላ *yäwärq buččəlla* n. gold-bar, bullion

መሶበ ወርቅ *mäsobä wärq* n. decorated mäsob

ራሰ— *rasä*—n. crown

ሰምና— *sämənna*—n. metaphorical speech, sentence, etc.

ወርች *wärč* n. thigh

ወርቸ ከንበል *wäräčä känbəl* adj. slanting *(landscape)*

ወርካ *wärka* n. sycamore

ወሰለተ *wäsällätä* v.i idled about; broke one's faith; prevaricated

ወስላታ *wäslatta* n. dishonest, liar; rogue

ውስልትና *wəslətənna* n. dishonesty, lie

አወሰለተ *awäsällätä* v.t caused to become idle, dishonest

ወሰነ *wässänä* v.i decided; limited, made a resolution

ወሰን *wässän* n. boundary; limit

—የሌለው *—yälelläw* adj. limitless, unlimited, boundless

ክብረ— *kəbrrä*—n. record *(score not reached before)*

ወሰንተኛ *wäsäntäñña* n. bordering *(country)*; neighbour *(of land)*

ወሳኝ *wässañ* adj. decisive; limiting

ውሳኔ *wəssane* n. resolution; decision

መወሰኛ *mäwässäña in* የሕግ መወሰኛ ምክር ቤት *yähəgg mäwässäña məkr bet* n. senate

ተወሰነ *täwässänä* v.i was decided; was limited

የተወሰነ *yätäwässänä* adj. limited, definite, specific

ያልተወሰነ *yaltäwässänä* adj. unristricted, unlimited, indefinite

ተዋሰነ *täwassänä* v.i demarcated, bordered with s/o, s/t, shared a common border

ተዋሳኝ *täwasañ* n. demarcating parties; bordering one another

አዋሰነ *awwassänä* v.t demarcated; bordered

አዋሳኝ *awwasañ* adj. bordering

አስወሰነ *aswässänä* v.t had s/t decided; had resolution passed

* ወሰከ **wässäkä*

ተውሳክ *täwsak* n. filth, dirt, parasite

ወሰካ *wäsäka* n. stretcher

ወሰወሰ *wäsäwwäsä* v.i pedalled *(e.g bicycle, sewing mechine)*; put stitches in

ወስዋሳ *wäswassa* adj. restless; undependable

ውስውስ *wəswəs* adj. stitched

ውስወሳ *wəswäsa* n. pedaling

መወስወሻ *mäwäswäša* n. pedal

ወሰደ *wässädä* v.t took

እንቅልፍ ወሰደው *ənqəlf wässädäw* v.i fell asleep

ወሰድ አደረገው *wäsädd adärrägäw* v.t became slightly crazy

ተወሰደ *täwässädä* v.i was taken

አዋሰደ *awwassädä* v.t helped s/o in taking s/t away

አስወሰደ *aswässädä* v.t had s/t taken away; let

s/t be stolen

ወሳፍቻ *see* ሰፋ

ወስከምቢያ *wäskämbia* n. cover *(of basket, pot etc.)*

ወስፈንጥር *wäsfänṭər* n. bow

ወስፋት *wäsfat* n. hookworm

ወስፋታም *wäsfätam* adj. lean, emaciated

ወስፋት ቋራጭ *wäsfat quʷäraç̌* adj. disgusting, repelent

ወስፌ *see* ሰፋ

ወሸለ *wäššälä* v.i did s/t slovenly, loosely

ወሻላ *wäšäla* adj. uncircumcized; coward

ውሻል *wəšal* n. wedge

ወሸመ *wäššämä* v.t took a woman as a mistress; took a man as a lover

ውሽማ *wəšəmma* n. mistress, lover, concubine

ወሸቀ *wäššäqä* v.t inserted, stuffed

ወሻቃ *wäššaqqa* adj. dependant, not self-supporting; lazy, sluggish

ወሻባ *wäšäba* n. carded cotton ready for spinning

ወሸከተ *wäšäkkätä* v.i told lies, told made-up stories

ወሻከት *wäšäkät* adj. liar

ወሽካታ *wäškatta* adj. liar

ወሽ *wäš* n. breast of a cow

ወሽመላ *wäšmälla* n. loquat

ወሽመጥ *wäšmäṭ* n. gusset

ወሽመጡ ተቆረጠ *wäšmäṭu täqorräṭä* was demoralized, frustrated, thwarted

የባሕር ወሽመጥ *yäbähər wäšmäṭ* n. gulf

ወቀረ *wäqqärä* v.t chiselled carved *(stone; millstone)*; tattooed

ውቅራት *wəqqərat* n. tattoo

ውቅራታም *wəqəratam* adj. tattooed

መዋቅር *mäwaqər* n. structure, framework

ላእላይ— *la'əlay*–n. superstructure

ታሕታይ— *tahtay*–n. infrastrcture

ተዋቀረ *täwaqqärä* v.i was erected *(building)*

አስወቀረ *aswäqqärä* v.t had stone etc. chiselled, carved; had s/o tattooed

ወቀሰ *wäqqäsä* v.t reprimanded, reproached, criticized

ወቀሳ *wäqqäsa* n. reprimand, reproach, criticism

ወቃሽ *wäqaš* adj. n. *(one)* who reprimand's reproaches, criticizes

ተወቀሰ *täwäqqäsä* vi was reproached, criticized

ተወቃቀሰ *täwäqaqqäsä* v.i reproached, critici ed each other

ተዋቀሰ *täwaqqäsä* v.i reproached criticized each other

ወቀጠ *wäqqäṭä* v.t pounded, crushed to powder, pestled *(with mortar)*; castrated *(animal)*

ወቀጣ *wäqäṭa* n. pounding, crushing *(with mortar)*

ውቃጭ *wəqqaç̌* n. left–over of a thing pounded

ውቅጥ *wəqṭ* adj. powdered; castrated

—በርበሬ *—bärbärre* n. pounded pepper

—ወይፈን *—wäyfän* n. castrated bull

ሙቀጫ *muqäç̌ç̌ä* n. mortar

—ግልገል *—gəlgäl* n. pestle

ተወቀጠ *täwäqqäṭä* v.i was pounded, crushed to powder; was castrated *(animal)*

አዋቀጠ *awwaqqäṭä* v.t helped s/o in pounding, in crushing s/t to powder

አስወቀጠ *aswäqqäṭä* v.t had s/t pounded, crushed to powder, had *(an animal)* castratec

ወቃ *wäqqa* v.t threshed; beat
ውቂያ *wəqqiya* n. threshing
መውቂያ *mäwqiya* n. thresher, threshing-machine
ተወቃ *täwäqqa* v.i was threshed, was beaten
አዋቃ *awwäqqa* v.t helped in threshing
አስወቃ *aswäqqa* v.t had grain threshed
ወቄት *wäqet* n. ounce
ወቅት *wäqt* n. time, season, period
ወቅቱ አይደለም *wäqtu aydäləm* it is untimely
በወቅቱ *bäwäqtu* adv. on time
በየወቅቱ *bäyyäwäqtu* adv. periodically, frequently
ወበራ *wäbärra* v.i blustered *(of persons)*
ወበቀ *wäbbäqä* v.i became excessively hot
ወበቅ *wäbäq* n. excessive heat
አወበቀ *awäbbäqä* v.i felt excessive heat
ወባ *wäba* n. malaria; adj. skinny
ወባማ *wäbamma* adj. malaria district
የወባ ትንኝ *yäwäba tənəňň* n. mosquito
ብጫ ወባ *bəča wäba* n. yellow fever
ወቦ ሸማኔ *wäbbo šämmane* n. cheetah, *also* አቦሸማኔ
ወተት *wätät* n. milk
ወተታም *wätätam* n. full of milk *(of cow)*
ወተት አንጀት *wätät angät* n. intestine *(of an animal)*
ወተወተ *wätäwwätä* v.t pestered s/o with requests, importuned
ወትዋታ *wä...atta* adj. importunate
ወትዋች *wätwač* adj. importunate
ወተፈ *wättäfä* v.t plugged *(a leak, a bottle etc.)*
ወታፋ *wättaffa* adj. inactive, lazy
ውታፍ *wətaf* n. plug, cork, stopper
ውትፍ *wəttəf* adj. inactive, lazy
ተወተፈ *täwättäfä* v.i was plugged; became inactive, lazy
አስወተፈ *aswättäfä* v.t had a leakage plugged
ወተፍታፋ *wätäftaffa* adj. dirty, untidy; *see* አወተፈተፈ
ወታቦ *wätabo* adj. tottery
ወታደር *wätaddär* n. soldier
ወታደራዊ *wättaddärawi* adj. military
ወታደርነት *wätaddärənnät* n. military profession
ወትሮ *wätro* adv. long ago
እንደወትሮው *əndä wätrow* as always, as usual
ያለወትሮው *yalä wätrow* adv. unusually
ወነበደ *wänäbbädä* v.i became a brigand
ወንበዴ *wänbäde* n. brigand
ውንበዳ *wənbäda* n. brigandage
ውንብድና *wənbədənna* n. brigandage
ተወነባበደ *täwänäbabbädä* v.i deceived, deluded each other
ተወናበደ *täwänabbädä* v.i was deceived, deluded
አወናበደ *awwänabbädä* v.t deluded, misled s/o
አወናባጅ *awwänabağ* adj/n misleading, charlatan
ወነከረ *wänäkkärä* v.t entangled
አወናከረ *awwänakkärä* v.t entangled; did one's work slovenly
ወነወነ *wänäwwänä in* ጅራቱን ወነወነ *ğəratun wänäwwänä* v.t wagged the tail
ወነጀለ *wänäğğälä* v.t incriminated, accused s/o of wrong doing
ወንጃይ *wänğay* adj/n *(one)* who incriminates,

accuses s/o of wrong doing

ወንጀል *wänğäl* n. crime

ወንጀለኛ *wänğäläññä* adj/n criminal

ውንጀላ *wənğäla* n. act of incriminating, accusation

ተወነጀለ *täwänäğğälä* v.i was incriminated, was accused of wrong doing

ተወነጃጀለ *täwänäğağğälä* v.i incriminated each each other of wrong doing

አስወነጀለ *aswänäğğälä* v.t had s/o accused of wrong doing

ወነጨፈ *wänäččäfä* v.t slung *(threw a stone with a sling)*

ወንጭፍ *wänčəf* n. sling *(for throwing stones)*

የላስቲክ— *yälastik*—n. catapult

ወና *wäna* adj. deserted *(house)*

ወናፍ *wänaf* n, bellows

ወንበር *wänbär* *also* ወምበር *wämbär* chair; judge

ታጣፊ— *taṭṭafi*—n. folding stool

ወንዝ *wänz* n. river

የወንዜ ልጅ *yäwänze ləğ* n. compatriot, fellow country-man

ወንዛወንዝ *wänza wänz* n. riverside

ወንድ *wänd* adj. male; brave, daring

ወንደ ላጤ *wändä laṭṭe* n. bachelor

ወንዳወንድ *wändawänd* adj. tomboy; manly

ወንዳገረድ *wändagäräd* adj. hermaphrodite

ወንዴ *wände'* adj. male *(plants etc.)*

ወንድነት *wändənnät* n. bravery, daring

ወንድም *wändəmm* n. brother

ታላቅ— *tallaq*—n. elder brother

ወንድማማችነት *wändəmmamačənnät* n. brotherhood, fraternity

የወንድም ልጅ *yäwändəmm ləğ* n nephew, niece

ወንጌል *wängel* n. Gospel

ወንጌላዊ *wängelawi* adj. Evangelist

ወንጠፍት *wänṭäft* n. small strainer

ወንፈል *wänfäl* n. communal labour *see* ጂጊ *and* ደቦ

ወንፊት *wänfit* n. sieve *see* ነፋ

ወከለ *wäkkälä* v.t represented *(s/o)*, acted on behalf; appointed s/o as one's representative; delegated

ወኪል *wäkkil* n. representative, delegate

ወካይ *wäkkay* adj/n *(one)* who delegates s/o

ውክላ *wəkkäla* n. mandate

ውክልና *wəkkələnna* n. representation, mandate

ተወከለ *täwäkkälä* v.i was delegated, mandated acted as s/o's agent *(trade)*

ተወካይ *täwäkkay* n. representative delegate

ወዘተ. *wäzätä* abbreviation *for* ወዘተርፈ *wäzätärfä* etcetera

ወዘተ *wäzzätä* v.t put a can on an oven *(for boiling water)*

ወዘና *wäzäna* n. beauty, charm, gloss

ወዘናም *wäzänam* adj. beautiful, charming

ወዘወዘ *wäzäwwäzä* v.t shook, waved *(hand etc.)*

ውዝወዛ *wəzwäza* n. skaking, waving

ውዝዋዜ *wəzəwwaze* n. dance, sway

ተወዛወዘ *täwäzawwäzä* v.i was shaken, waved, swayed

ተወዛዋዥ *täwäzawaž* adj. shaking, waving *(swaying hand etc.)*

አወዛወዘ *awwäzawwäzä* v.t shook, waved
ወዘፈ *wäzzäfä* v.t put aside *(work)*, made indolent
ውዝፍ *wəzzəf* adj. *used with* እዳ *'əda* overdue *(payment)*
ተወዘፈ *täwäzzäfä* v.i sat idly
ወዛ *wäzza* v.i transpired *(face)*; brightened, had a lively look
ወዛም *wäzzam* adj. bright *(face)*, lively
ወዛደር *wäzaddär* n. proletariat, worker
ወዝ *wäz* n. transpiration; brilliance*(face)*, sweat
ውዛት *wəzat* n. brilliance
አዋዛ *awwazza* v.t treated subtly, tried to convince subtly
ወዠብ *wäžäb* n. windy torrent
ወየበ *wäyyäbä* v.i became yellowish *(tooth, nail etc.)*; became tainted
ወይባ *wäyba* adj. yellowish, tainted
ውይባት *wəyyəbat* n. taint
ወየው *wäyyäw* interj. oh my God ! oh dear !
ወያኔ *wäyäyane* n. occasional tribal war *(in Wollo)*
ወይ *wäy* adv/conj. either ; or; interj; yes! *(in response to s/o calling)*
ወይም *wäyəmm* adv. or, either
ወይራ *wäyra* n. olive tree
ወይስ *wäyəss* adv. or
ወይን *wäyn* n. grape ; wine
ወይንማ *wäynəmma* adj. violet
ወይናደጋ *wäynadäga* n. region with mild weather, temperate zone
ወይን ጠጅ *wäyn ṭägg* n. wine; adj. violet
ወይኖ *wäyno* adj. violet
ወይዘሮ *wäyzäro* n. Madam, Mrs.

ወይጉድ *wäygud* interj. oh !
ወይጉዴ *wäygude* interj. oh me !
ወይፈን *wäyfän* n. bull
ወዮ *wäyyo* interj. alas !
ወዮታ *wäyyota* n. lamentation
ወደ *wädä* prep. to, towards
ወዲህ *wädih or* ወደዚህ *wädäzzih* adv. here
ወዲያ *wädiya or* ወደዚያ *wädäzziya* adv. there; interj. away with it! away with you!
ወዲያልኝ *wädyalləññ* interj. alas!
ወዴት *wädet* adv. where
ወዲያው *wädyaw* adv. immediately, soon after
ወደለ *wäddälä* v.i became stout, fat, corpulent
ወደላ *wädälla* adj. corpulent, fat, stout
ወደል *wädäl* adj. fat, stout, corpulent
—አህያ *—ahəyya* n. jackass
አወደለ *awäddälä* v.t made fat, stout, corpulent
ወደመ *wäddämä* v.t was completely destroyed, annihilated
ውድማ *wədma* n. forest, uninhabited, deserted place, desert
አወደመ *awäddämä* v.t destroyed, annihilated
አውድማ *awdəmma* n. threshing ground
*ወደረ **wäddärä*
ወደር *wädär* n. of the same kind, resemblance
—የለሽ *—yälläš* adj. incomparable
ወደረኛ *wädäräñña* adj. competitor, rival
ተወዳደረ *täwädaddärä* v.i competed; was compared
ወደሮ *wädäro* n. rope
*ወደሰ **wäddäsä*
ውደሳ *wəddäsa* n. praising
ውዳሴ *wəddase* n.. praise, laudation, eulogy

—ከንቱ *—käntu* or ከንቱ— *käntu*—n. cajolery, flattery

አወደሰ *awäddäsä* v.t praised

ወደቀ *wäddäqä* v.i fell down; was killed in battle ; failed *(exam. etc.);* committed fornication

ውዳቂ *wəddaqi* n. scum *(people)*, riff-raff; leftovers, rubbish

ውድቀት *wədqät* n. sin

ውድቅ *wədq* adj. overruled *(claim, objection)*

ተዋደቀ *täwaddäqä* v.i killed each other *(in battle-field)*

ወደብ *wädäb* n. harbour, haven, port

ወደደ *wäddädä* v.i loved, liked; desired; was in love with

ወዳድ *wäddad* adj/n *(one)* who likes s/o, s/t

አገር— *agär*—n. patriot, nationalist

ወዳጅ *wädaǧ* n. friend, lover

ወዳጅነት *wädaǧənnät* n. friendship

ወዶ ዘማች *wäddo zämač* n. volunteer *(soldier)*

—ገባ *gäbba*—n. dog *(who seeks refugee in s/o house)*

ውድ *wədd* adj. dear; expensive

ውድነት *wəddənnät* n. expensiveness

ወደድ አለ *wäddäd alä* v.i became somewhat expensive

ተወደደ *täwäddädä* v.i was loved, liked; became expensive

ተወዳጅ *täwäddaǧ* adj. dear *(person)*

ተዋደደ *täwaddädä* v.i loved, liked each other; was fixed *(e.g spade, pickaxe etc. with the handle)*

አዋደደ *awwaddädä* v.t made to love, like each other; fixed instrument with handle

አስወደደ *aswäddädä* v.t made expensive; caused to like s/o, s/t

ወጀብ *wäǧäb* n. storm, tide

ወገረ *wäggärä* v.t stoned

ወጋሪ *wägari* adj/n *(one)* who stones

ውግረት *wəgrät* n. stoning

ተወገረ *täwäggärä* v.i was stoned

አስወገረ *aswäggärä* v.t had s/o stoned

ወገብ *wägäb* n. waist

—መሞከር *—mämokkär* go to the toilet *(pol.)*

ወገን *wägän* n. side, way, direction; party section

ባለወገን *bäläwägän* adj. belonging to the high class, influential

*ወገደ **wäggädä*

ተወገደ *täwäggädä* v.i was eliminated, was fired *(from work)*

አስወገደ *aswäggädä* v.t eliminated, discarded, got rid of

ወግድ *wägəd* imp. get out of the way, go away

ወገግ አለ *wägägg alä* v.i dawned, began to grow light

ወገግታ *wäggägta* n. early dawn illumination

ውጋገን *wəgagän* n. irradiation

ወገጠ *see* ወቀጠ

ወጋ *wägga* v.t pierced; stabbed; pricked; gave an injection to; combated

ወጊ *wägi* in መርፌ ወጊ n. one who gives an injection to s/o

ውጋት *wəgät* n. sharp pain *(stomach, back etc.)*

ወጋጋ *wägagga* v.i felt occasional pain *(stomach, back etc.)*

ተወጋ *täwägga* v.i was pierced; was pricked was given an injection

ተዋጋ *täwagga* v.i fought, combated, fought, each other; gored

ተዋጊ *täwagi* n. fighter, warrior

—አውሮፕላን *—auroppəlan* n. fighter plane

አዋጋ *awwagga* v.t conducted war; caused to quarrel

አዋጊ *awwagi* adj/n *(one)* who conducts war; *(one)* who incites a quarrel

—መኰንን *—mäkonnən* n. combatant officer

አስወጋ *aswägga* v.t had s/o stabbed; had s/o given an injection

ወጋግራ *wägagra* n. beam *(in a building)*

ወጌሻ *wägešša* n. s/o trained in physiotherapy, masseur; surgeon

ወግ *wäg* n. custom; short story; chat, talk

ወገኛ *wägäñña* adj. braggart, assuming, presumptuous

—አክራሪ *wäg akrari* adj. conservative

—አጥባቂ *aṭbaqi* adj. conservative

ባለወግ *baläwäg* n. dignitary, man of rank, peer

ልብስ *yäwäg ləbs* n. uniform

ወጠረ *wäṭṭärä* v.t stretched, tightened

ወጣራ *wäṭṭarra* adj. puffed up

ውጥረት *wəṭrät* n. dilemma, pressure *(compelling force)*, tension

ውጥር *wəṭṭər* adj. conceited

ውጥርጥር *wəṭərṭər* adj. puffed up

ተወጠረ *täwäṭṭärä* v.i was stretched, tightened; was conceited, puffed up

ተወጣጠረ *täwäṭaṭṭärä* v.i was completely stretched, tightened

አዋጠረ *awwaṭṭärä* v.t helped s/o in stretching s/t tightly

አስወጠረ *aswäṭṭärä* v.t had s/t stretched

ወጠቀ *wäṭṭäqä* v.t stuffed *(oneself with food)*

ተወጠቀ *täwäṭṭäqä* v.i was stuffed *(with food)*

ወጠነ *wäṭṭänä* v.t started, began, commenced

ወጣኝ *wäṭṭañ* n. beginner

ውጥን *wəṭṭən* adj. s/t started; unfinished

ተወጠነ *täwäṭṭänä* v.i was started,, began, commenced

አስወጠነ *aswäṭṭänä* v.t had s/t started, began, commenced

ወጠጤ *wäṭäṭe* n. young goat(m.)

ወጣ *wäṭṭa* v.i went up, ascended, climbed

ወጣት *wäṭṭat* n. adj. young man; youth

ወጣትነት *wäṭṭatənnät* n. youth

ወጣ ገባ *wäṭṭa gäbba* adj. uneven *(esp. landscape)*

ወጥ *wäṭṭ in* አንድ ወጥ *and wäṭṭ* adj. uniformed

ወጭ *wäč* n. expenses

ውጤት *wəṭṭet* n. result, outcome; output; effect; mark *(examination)*

የእንስሳት— *yä'ənsəsat*—n. animal pruducts

ውጭ *wəčč* n. outside

—አገር *—agär* n. abroad

መዋጮ *mäwwačo* n. contribution *(of money)*

መውጫ *mäwča* n. outlet

ወጣ አለ *wäṭa alä* v.i went out

ወጣጣ *wäṭaṭṭa* v.i went out frequently

ተወጣጣ *täwäṭaṭṭa* v.i was contributed *(money etc.)*, was raised *(money, manpower)*

ተዋጣ *täwaṭṭa* v.i was

raised *(money, man-power etc.)*; became successful *(enterprise, scheme)*

አወጣ *awäṭṭa* v.t made go out, took out; issued *(coin, magazine)*, expelled; saved (s/o); spent *(money)*

እጅ— *əǧǧ*—raised one's hand

እጁን— *əǧǧun*—saved himself

ምሥጢር— *məsṭir*—v.t divulged a secret

ገንዘብ— *gänzäb*—v.t spent money; drew money

ራሱን— *rasun*—v.t saved oneself

ቀንድ— *qänd*—v.t became very old; was infuriated

—አውጣ —*awṭa* n. snail

ዓይን— *ayn* — ad,. thick-skinned, shameless

አውጫጭኝ *awčaččəňň* n. judicial inquiry of a community for offence committed by one of its members

ማውጫ *mawča* n. table of contents

አወጣጣ *awwäṭaṭṭa* v.t convinced, cajoled s/o to speak the truth

አዋጣ *awwaṭṭa* v.t raised, contributed money; became enterprising *(business)*

አዋጪ *awwač* n. contributor *(money etc.)*

አስወጣ *aswäṭṭa* v.t made to go out; chased out, drove away

አስተዋጽኦ *astäwaṣə'o* n. contribution

ወጥ *wäṭ* n. sauce

—ቤት —*bet* n. kitchen; cook

ወጭት *wäčit* n. dish *(container)*

ወፈረ *wäffärä* v.i became thick, fat, voluminous

ወፍራም *wäfram* adj. fat, thick; voluminous

ውፍሬ *wəffare* n. fatness; thickness

ውፍረት *wəfrät* n. fatness, thickness

ወፈር አለ *wäfärr älä* v.i became slightly fat, thick

ወፋፈረ *wäfaffärä* v.t got fat

አወፈረ *awäffärä* v.t fattened, thickened

ወፈፈ *wäffäfä* v.i with a pronominal suffix e.g ወፈፈው v.i became slighty insane, eccentric

ወፈፌ *wäfäffe* adj. eccentric, neurotic

ወፈፍተኛ *wäfäftäňňa* adj. eccentric, neurotic

ወፍ *wäf* n. bird

የሌት— *yälet*–n. bat

ወፈ ያሬድ *wäfä yared* n. bird of paradise

ወፍ ዘራሽ *wäf zärraš* n. wild *(of plants)*

—አራሽ —*arraš* n. wild *(of plants)*

የወፍ በሽታ *yäwäf bäššəta* n. jaundice

—ቤት —*bet* n. cage ,nest

—ጎጆ —*goǧǧo* n. nest

ወፍጮ *see* ፈጨ

ዉርዴ *see* ወረደ

ዋለ *walä* v.i passed, spent the day; did a favour to s/o

እንዴት ዋልክ *əndet walk* how are you? good afternoon, good day

ውለታ *wəläta* n. favour

ባለውለታ *bäläwəläta* n. one who is indebted to s/o, one who has one's gratitude

ውለታ ቢስ *wəläta bis* adj. thankless, ungrateful

—ቢስነት —*bisənnät* n. ingratitude

ውል *wəl* n. agreement, pact; knot

ውለኛ *wəläňňa* adj. trustworthy, dependable

ውሎ *wəlo*. n. a full day *(12 Hrs.)*

—አበል —*abäll* n. per diem

—አድሮ —*adro* adv. in the long run, sooner or later

—ገባ መንገድ —*gäbba mängäd* n. a day's journey

ሙያ *muya* n. special skill

ሙያተኛ *muyatäñña* n. labourer

ባለሙዋል *balä mu*ʷ*al* n. favourite *(person)*

ባለሙያ *balä muya* adj/ n highly skilled *(person)*

ደኅና ዋል *dähna wal* have a good day, bye-bye

ተዋዋለ *täwawalä* v.i made a pact, agreed with one another

አዋለ *awalä* v.t kept s/o, s/t for the whole day; used s/t for a particular purpose

በሥራ ላይ— *bäsəra lay*— put into practice, executed *(a plan)*

አዋዋለ *awwawalä* v.t helped to make an agreement, a pact; spent the day with s/o *(as a company)*

አዋዋይ *awwaway* adj/n one who helpes in making an agreement, a pact

ዋለለ *wallälä* v.i wavered, bacame unsteady, vacillated, became inconstant; hesitated

ዋላላ *walala* adj. wavering, unsteady

ዋልያ *waliya* n. walia ibex

ዋልታ *walta* n. pole; a round disc of wood in the inner top of a round roof where the rafters join together

የሰሜን— *yäsämen*— n. North Pole

የደቡብ— *yädäbub*— n. South Pole

ዋልካ *walka* n. black cotton soil

ዋርሳ *warsa* n. brother-in-law *(for a female)* see also ወረሰ

ዋርዳ *warda* n. black mule

ዋስ *was* n. guarantor

ዋሸ *waššä* v.i told lies, lied; told a falsehood promise

ዋሾ *wašo* adj liar

ውሸት *wəšät* n. lies

ውሸታም *wəšätam* adj. liar

ዋሻ *wašša* n. cave, den, cavern

ዋሽንት *walənt* n. flute, fife

—ነፊ —*näfi* n. flute player

ዋቢ *wabi* n. guarantor

—መጽሐፍት —*mäṣahəft* n. bibliography

*ዋበ **wabä see* ተዋበ

ዋተተ *wattätä* v.i roamed, wandered *(hence became very tired)*

አውታታ *awtatta* adj/n *(one)* who wanders, roams

ዋነስ *wanäs* n. turtle-dove

ዋና *wana* n. swimming *see also* ዋኘ

የዋና ልብስ *yäwana ləbs* n. bathing suit

ዋናተኛ *wanätäñña* n. swimmer

ዋና *wanna* adj. main essential, major, principal proprietor; capital investment

—አዛዥ —*azzaž* n. commander-in-chief

—ከተማ —*kätäma* n. capital city

—ዲሬክተር —*direktär* n. general director

—ፀሐፊ —*ṣähafi* n. secretary general; executive secretary

—ገንዘብ —*gänzäb* n. capital investment

ዋነኛ *wannäñña* n. proprietor; chief

ዋኔ *wane* n. turtle-dove cf. ዋንስ

ዋንዛ *wanza* n. cardia africana

ዋንጫ *wänča* n. a drinking-horn, goblet

ዋኘ *waññа* v.i swam

ዋና *wana* n. swimming

የዋና ልብስ *yäwana ləbs* n. bathing suit

ዋነተኛ *wanätäñña* n. swimmer

ዋኚ *wäññi* n. swimmer

መዋኛ *mäwaña* n. swimming pool

አስዋኘ *aswaññä* v.t had s/o swim

ዋከታ *wakata also* ውካታ *wəkata* n. uproar, commotion, *see* ኣወከ

ዋዌ *wawe* n. copula, conjunction *(gram.)*

ዋዛ *waza* n. jest, scoff

—ፈዛዛ *—fäzaza* n. joke, not serious, jest

ዋዜማ *wazema* n. eve

ዋድያት *wadyat* n. large shallow basin

ዋጀ *wağğä or* ዋዠ *wažžä* v.t ransomed

ዋገምት *see* አገመ

ዋጋ *waga* n. price, cost, value ; reward ; fee

በምንም— *bämənəmm—* at any price

የጉልበት— *yägulbät—*n. labour cost

ዋጋ ነሳ *waga nässa* v.t discredited

—ቈረጠ *—quʷärrätä* v.t fixed a price

—ሰበረ *—säbbärä* v.t cheapened *(the price of s/t)*

—ሰጠ *—sättä* v.t appreciated

—ቢስ *—bis* adj. worthless

—አለው *—alläw* is worthwhile, is important is of value

—አሳረረ *—assarrärä* v.t bid against s/o

—አጣ *—atta* v.t became discredited, useless

—ያለው *—yalläw* adj. worthy, important, worth considering

—የለሽ *—yällaš* n. worthless, useless ; priceless

የዋጋ ዝርዝር *yäwaga zərzər* n. invoice, price-list

ዋግ *wag* n. rust *(plant disease)*

ዋግሹም *wagšum* n. title of former governors of Lasta

ዋጠ *watä* v.t swallowed, gulped

ምራቁን የዋጠ *məraqun yäwatä* adj. mature *(person)*, serious

ተዋጠ *täwatä* v.t was swallowed, gulped

አዋጠ *awatä* v.t gave s/o, s/t to swallow

አስዋጠ *aswatä* v.t gave s/o, s/t to swallow

ውሃ *see* ውሀ

ውለታ *see* ዋለ

ውላጅ *see* ወለደ

ውል *wəl* n. contract, agreement, *see also* ተዋዋለ *and* አዋዋለ

ውል አለ *wəll alä* v.t had a sudden desire, nostalgia

ውልታ *wəlləta* n. sudden desire, nostalgia, ardour

ውልምጥምጥ *wəlmətmət* adj. irresolute, unsteady; subservient, bootlicking

ውልብ አለ *wəlləbb alä* v.t caught a glimpse of

ውልብልቢት *wəlbləbit* n. propeller; tip of the tongue

ውልክፍክፍ አለ *wəlkəfkəff alä* v.i. became entangled, *see also* ተወሳከፈ

ውሪ *wəri* n. kid *(child)*

ውራ *wərra* n. last *(in competition; examination etc.)*

—ወጣ *—wätta* he became last *(in his class, contest etc.)*

ውርባ *wərba* n. dew

ውር ውር አለ *wərr wərr alä* v.i

fluttered, flew here and there; moved here and there suddenly in small numbers

ውርውርታ warwarta n. sudden movement in small numbers

ውርንጭላ waranč̣alla ውርንጫ waranč̣a n. young donkey

ውርዶ see ወረደ

ውርጅብኝ see ወረደ

ውርጋጥ wargaṭ n. whipper-snapper

ውርጭ warč̣ n. frost

ውስጥ wasṭ n/prep, interior, inside

ወደ— wädä– adv. inside, in

ውስጥ አዋቂ wasṭä awaqi adj. well-informed

ውስጠ ደምብ wasṭä dämb n. by-law

—ዘ —zä n. verbal adjective; adj. mysterious

ውስጣዊ wasṭawi adj. internal

ውስጥ ለውስጥ wasṭ läwasṭ adv. secretly, stealthily

—ውስጡን —wasṭun adv. secretly

—እግር —agar n. sole (human foot)

እውስጥ awasṭ adv. inside

ከውስጥ käwasṭ adv. underneath, inside

የውስጥ yäwasṭ adj. internal

በ...ውስጥ ba...wasṭ prep, in, inside

ከ...ውስጥ kä...wasṭ out of, from

እ...ውስጥ a...wasṭ prep. in, inside

ውሻ wašša n. dog

ውሻነት waššannät n. filthiness, dishonourable behaviour

ውሽልሽል wašalšal adj. slovenly made, cf. ወሸለ

ውሽንፍር wašanfar n. rain accompanied by a strong wind

ውቃቢ waqabi n. guardian spirit

ውቃቤ ቢስ waqabe bis adj. graceless

—አምላክ —amlak n. guardian spirit

—የራቀው —yäraqäw adj. graceless

ውቅያኖስ waqyanos n. ocean

ውነት wanät also እውነት awnät n. truth, reality

ውነተኛ wanä täñña adj. truthful, trustworthy

ውነታ wanäta n. reality

ውን wan እውን awan adj. real

ውንድቢ wandabbi n. eland (taurotragus oryx)

ውካታ wakata n. uproar, commotion, see አወካ

ውዳሴ see ወደሰ

ውዴላ waddella n. saddle-blanket

ውድማ wadma n. forest, uninhabited, deserted place, desert, see ወደመ

ውድድር wadaddar n. competition see አወዳደረ

ውጅምብር wağambar ውዥምብር n. choas, utter confusion

ውጥን see ወጠነ

ውጥንቅጥ waṭanqaṭ n. jumble, medley

ዎፍ see ወፍ

ዐ

ዐልቅት allqatt n. leech (small blood-sucking worm)

ዐመል amäl n. habit, character

ዐመላም amälam adj. n. moody; s/o with bad disposition

ዐመለኛ amälämña adj/n. moody, s/o with a bad disposition; vicious (horse, mule etc.)

ዐመለቢስ amäläbis adj/n bad-tempered; disagreeable, mannerless *(person)*

ላመል *lamäl* adv. barely

ዐመቀ *ammäqä* v.t. stuffed, crammed, forced in by pressing

ዕምቅ *əmməq* n. stuffed, crammed

ታመቀ *tammäqä* v.i was stuffed, crammed, forced in by pressing

አሳመቀ *asammäqä* v.t had s/t stuffed, crammed etc.

ዐመጠ *ammäṭä* or ዐመፀ *ammäṣä* v.i revolted, rebelled

ዐመጥ *amäṭ* also ዐመፅ *amäṣ* n. revolution uprising, mutiny

ዐመጠኛ *amäṭäñña also* ዐመፀኛ *amäṣäñña* n. rebel, insurgent, lawless, criminal

ዐምድ *amd* n. column, pillar

ዐምደ ወርቅ *amdä wärq* n. arcade

ዐሞሌ *amole* n. salt bar *(used as currency in earlier days)*

ዐሣ *asa* n. fish

ዐሣነባሪ *asanäbari* n. whale

ዐሣ አጥማጅ *asa äṭmäǧ* n.— አሥጋሪ— *asgari* n. fisherman

ዐሥር *assər* adj. ten

ዐሥረኛ *assəräñña* adj. tenth

ዐረቀ *arräqä* v.t straightened out *(branch, back of a person etc.)*; molded *(character)*

ዐረበ *arräbä* v.t tanned *(of animal skin)*

ዐራቢ *arrabi* n. tanner

ዐረብ *arab* n. an Arab

ባሕር— *bahər*—n. leather *(tanned)*

—ብረት *—bərät* n. steel

—አገር *—agar* n. Arabia

ዐረብኛ *aräbəñña* n. Arabic language

ዐረብያ *aräbəya* n. Arabia

ዐረንቋ *aränqʷä* ዐርንቃ *aronqa* n. marshy, boggy land

ዐረዘ *see* ታረዘ

ዐረገ *arrägä* v.t ascended

ዕርገት *ərgät* n. Ascension

ዐረፈ *arräfä* v.i rested, became quiet, reposed, landed *(plane)*; was housed; died, passed away

ዐረፍተ ነገር *aräftä nägär* n. sentence

ዕረፍት *əräft* n. break, rest, repose, vacation, recess, pause, interval

ዕርፍ *ərf* n. plow handle

ዕርፈ መስቀል *ərfä mäsqäl* n. spoon for administering the Eucharist

ማረፊያ ቤት *maräfiya bet* n. custody *(imprisonment)*

ምዕራፍ *mə'əraf* n. chapter

አሳረፈ *asarräfä* v.t had s/o rested, paused; landed *(airplane)*

ዐረፋ *aräfa* n. lather

ዐርብ *arb* n. Friday; weaver's frame

ዐቀበት *aqäbät* n. steep, upward slope

—ቁልቁለት *—qulqulät* n. ups and downs

ዐቃቢት *aqqabit* n. woman who grinds the wheat for Eucharistic bread

ዐቃቤ ሕግ *aqqabe həgg* n. prosecutor

—መጻሕፍት *—mäṣahəft* n. librarian

ዐቀደ *aqqädä* v.t planned, thought of a plan; projected, designed *(a plan)*

ዐቅድ *aqd* n. plan, scheme

ዕቀዳ *əqqəda* n. planning, scheming, projecting

ዕቅድ *əqqəd* n. plan, scheme; project

ታቀደ *taqqädä* v.t was planned; was projected etc.

አሳቀደ *asaqqädä* v.t had s/t planned, schemed, projected

ዐቅል *aql* n. mind; sense, brain

ዐቅም *aqm* n. force, power; ability, capacity; measure

ዐቅመ ቢስ *aqmä bis* adj./n weak, weakling

ዐበደ *abbädä* v.i went mad, became crazy, became insane; became frenzied

ዕብደት *əbdät* n. madness; insanity, lunacy

ዕብድ *əbd* adj. mad, crazy, insane, lunatic

—ውሻ —*wəšša* n. rabid dog

አሳበደ *asabbädä* v.t maddened, drove crazy

ዐወቀ *awwäqä* v.i knew, was familiar with, recognized, realized; had sexual intercourse with *(a woman)*

ዐውቆ ዐበድ *awqo abbäd* n. eccentric person

ዐዋቂ *awaqi* adj. knowledgeable, intelligent, wise; full-grown

ዕውቀት *əwqät* n. knowledge

ዕውቀተኛ *əwqatäñña* adj. knowledgeable, well-informed

ዕውቅ *əwq* adj. well-known

ዕውቂያ *əwqiya* n. acquaintance

ተዋወቀ *täwawwäqä* v.i became acquainted with one another, was introduced to each other

ታወቀ *tawwäqä* v.i was known, became famous

ታዋቂ *tawaqi* adj. known, famous

መታወቂያ *mättawäqiya* n. identification

—ወረቀት —*wäräqät* n. indentity card

አሳወቀ *asawwäqä* v.i made s/t known, informed

አስተዋወቀ *astawäwwäqä* v.t introduced *(people)*

አስታወቀ *astawwäqä* v.t informed, notified, announced, declared

ማስታወቂያ *mastawäqiya* n. notice, information

—መለጠፊያ —*mäläṭṭäfiya* n. notice-board

ዐውደ ዓመት *awədä amät* n. festival *(lit. turn of the year)*

ዐዘቅት *azäqt* n. abyss, difficult, grave situation

ዐየ *ayyä* v.t saw; observed, looked at

ተያየ *täyayyä* v.i looked at each other; saw one another

ታየ *tayyä* v.i was seen, appeared, was shown; was displayed, was visible

አሳየ *asayyä* v.t showed demonstrated, displayed, exhibited; presented *(a play)*

አስተያየ *astäyayyä* v.t. compared

አስተያየት *astäyayät* n. observation, judgement, attitude, opinion, point of remark

—አደረገ —*adärrägä* took into consideration

ዐይን *ayn* n. eye

—ለዐይን —*läyn* face to face

ዐይነ ማዝ *aynämaz* n conjunctivitis

—ምድር —*mədr* n. excrement *(human)*; a little hole in the ground used as water closet

—ርግብ —*rəgb* n. veil

—ሰባራ —*säbara* adj. shy; timid

—ስብ —*səb* n. eye-orbit

—ስውር —*səwwər* adj. blind

—ሸውራራ —*šäwrarra* adj. squint-eyed

—ኅሊና —*həllina* n. thought

—ደረቅ —*däräq* adj. impudent, shameless, cheeky

—ገመድ —*gämäd* n. approximate estimation

ዐይናማ *aynamma* adj. beautiful, pretty

ዐይናር *ayniar* n. eye-discharge
ዐይን ለዐይን *ayn lä'ayn* adv. face to face
—ዐዋጅ *—awaǧ* adj. be at loss in selecting one thing among many others
—አውጣ *—awṭa* adj. impudent, saucy
—አፋር *—affär* adj. shy, timid, bashful
—የሌለው *—yälelläw wəšät* *adj.*out-and-out (lie),complete *(lie)*
ለዐይን ሲይዝ *lä'ayn siyəz* adv. in the dusk
ቅጽበተ ዓይን *qəṣbätä ayn* n. moment, a split second
በዐይኑ ቁራኛ *bä'aynä quraňňa* keeping an eye on
ባንድ ዐይን ዐየ *band ayn ayyä* treat alike, was impartial
የዐይን ምስክር *yä'ayn məsəkkər* n. eye-witness
—ቆብ *— qob* n. eyelid
—ብሌን *—bəlen* n. pupil of the eye
አንዳይና *andayna* adj. one-eyed
ዐይነት *aynät* n. type, sort, kind, quality; colour
ዐጤ *aṭe* ዐጼ *aṣe* n. title of a king *(e.g emperor)*
ዐጥንት *aṭənt* n. bone; ancestry
ባለ ዐጥንት *balä aṭənt* adj. bony; of good parentage
ዐጥንት የሌለው *aṭənt yälelläw* adj weak *(person, morally)*
ዐጨ *aččä* v.t was engaged, betrothed; recommended *(s/o to a position)*
ዕጩ *əču* n. candidate
—መኰንን *—mäkkonən* n. cadet
—መምህር *—mämhər* n. teacher training school student
ዕጮኛ *əčoňňa* n. fiancée;
ማጫ *mača* n. dowry
ተጫጨ *täčaččä* v.i engaged to one another *(for marriage)*
ታጨ *taččä* v.i was engaged betrothed; was recommended *(to a position)*
መታጫ *mättača* n. dowry
አሳጨ *asaččä* v.t caused s/o to be engaged *(to marry)*; had s/o recommended
ዐጽም *aṣm* n. skeleton, remains *(dead body)*
ዐጽመ ርስት *aṣmä rəst* n. family land
ዒላማ *ilama* n. aim, target
ዔሊ *eli* n. tortoise
ዓለም *aläm* n. world
ዓለመኛ *alämäňňa* adj/n comfortable person *(free from pain, anxiety etc.)*, euphoric, relieved; living luxuriously
ዓለማዊ *alämawi* adj/n worldly *(person)*; sensuous; secular
ዓለማዊነት *alämawinnät* n. worldliness
ዓለሙን አየ *alämun ayyä* enjoyed life
ዓለም አቀፍ *aläm aqqäf* adj. international
ክፍለ ዓለም *kəfla aläm* n. hemisphere
ዘለዓለም *zälä'aläm* adv. forever ; always, eternally
ዘለዓለማዊ *zälä'alämawi* adj. eternal
ዓጼ *see* ዐጤ
ዓላማ *alama* n. aim, goal, target, purpose, objective, intent
—ቢስ *—bis* adj. aimless, purposeless
—የለሽ *—yälläš* adj. aimless purposeless
ዓመት *amät* n. year
ዐውደ— *awdä—*n. holiday *(religious)*
ዓመተ ምሕረት *amätä məhrät* n. A.D, year of grace
ዓመታዊ *amätawi* adj. annual
ዓመት በዓል *amät bä'al* n. holiday anniversary

በየዓመቱ *bäyyä amätu* adv. yearly, annually

ከዓመት ዓመት *kä'amät amät* year in, year out

ዕለት *əlät* n. day

ዕለታዊ *əlätawi* adj. daily

ዕልል አለ *ələll alä* v.i uttered cries of joy, jubilation

ዕልልታ *ələlta* n. cries of joy, jubilation

ዕርፈ መስቀል *ərfä mäsqäl* n. spoon for administering the Eucharist

ዕቃ *əqa* n. goods, thing, object, article; luggage; vessel, instrument; genital organs (*pol.*)

—ማጠቢያ *—maṭäbiya* n. sink

—ቤት *—bət* n. store-house; storekeeper

—አዟሪ *—azuʷari* n. peddler

ሆድ ዕቃ *hod əqa* n. entrails, guts

የሸክላ— *yäškla—* n. earthenware

የበቅሎ— *yäbäqlo—* n. harness

የቤት— *yäbet—* n. furniture, utensil

የወንድ— *yäwänd—* n. penis (*pol.*)

የሴት— *yäset—*n. vagina(*pol.*)

ጥሬ— *ṭəre—* n. raw material

ዕንቍ *ənquʷ* n. precious stone, jewelry

ዕንቍጣጣሽ *ənquʷəṭaṭaš* n. New Year's Day

ዕውር *əwwər* adj. blind

ዕጓለ ማውታ *əguʷalä mawta* n. orphan

ዕጣ *əṭa* n. lot, chance (*of lottery*); fate, destiny

—አወጣ *—awäṭṭa also* ዕጣ ጣለ *əṭa ṭalä* v.t cast lot

—ደረሰው *—därräsäw* v.t drew the winning lot

ዕጨጌ *əč̣äge* n. title of the Abbot of the monastery of Däbrä Libanos

ዕፁብ ድንቅ *əṣ̣ub dənq* adj. marvellous, astonishing, breath-taking

ዕፅ *əṣ̣* n. herb (*used as medicine*); plant

ዕፀ በል *əṣ̣ä bäll* adj. herbivorous

ዕፀዋት. *əṣ̣äwat* n. flora

ዘ

ዘሆን *zähon also* ዝሆን *zəhon* n. elephant

ዘሆኔ *zähone* n. elephantiasis

የዘሆን ኩምቢ *yäzəhon kumbi* n. tusk

—ጆሮ ይስጠኝ አለ *yäzəhon ǧoro yəsṭäññ alä* lend a deaf ear

—ጥርስ *yäzəhon ṭərs* n. ivory

ዘለለ *zällälä* v.i jumped; leaped, climbed over; skipped over (*a word etc.*), left aside; gambolled; dissolved the must of beer with water

ዘላይ *zälay* n. jumper (*sport*)

ዝላይ *zəllay* n. jumping, leaping

ዝሊያ *zəlliya* n. jump, leap

ዝልል *zəlləl* n. beer must dissolved with water

መዝለያ *mäzläya* n. spring-board

ተዘለለ *täzällälä* v.i was skipped over (*a word etc.*); was left aside; was dissolved with water (*beer must*)

ተዛለለ *täzallälä* played cheerfully, gambolled

አዘለለ *azzälällä* v.i had s/o jump, leap

ዘለላ *zäläla* n. bunch (*grapes, strawberries etc.*), cluster

የእንባ— *yä'ənba–* n. teardrops

የወይን— *yäwäyn–* n. cluster, bunch of grapes

ዘለሰ *zällăsä* v.t stooped *(one's head)*

ዘለሰኛ *zäläsäňňa* n. type of poetry causing sadness or low spirit

ዝልስ *zəlləs* adj. stooped

ዘለቀ *zälläqä* v.i penetrated *(water)*; completed *(study, book reading)*; went through *(difficulties etc.)*; appeared; lasted *(ration etc.)*

ዘለቄታ *zäläqeta* n. continuity, lasting, perpetuity, permanence

ዘላቂ *zälaqi* adj. perpetual, continuous, lasting

ተዘለቀ *täzälläqä* v.i was completed

የሚዘለቅ አይደለም *yämizzälläq aydälläm* it is unbearable, very difficult

አዘለቀ *azälläqä* v.t brought to the end; caused to survive *(difficulties)*, brought into view

አዛለቀ *azzalläqä* v.t lasted long

የማያዛልቅ ክርክር *yämmayazzalləq kərəkkər* weak argument

ዘለበት *zäläbät* n. buckle *(of belt)*

ዘለዓለም *zälä'aläm* adv. forever see ዓለም

ዘለዘለ *zäläzzälä* v.t cut meat in small strips

ዘልዛላ *zälzalla* adj. careless, lax, unguarded

ዘልዛላነት *zälzallannät* n. carelessness, laxity

ዝልዝል *zəlzəl* n. meat cut into small strips

—ጥብስ *—ṭəbs* n. roasted meat cut into small strips

ተንዘላዘለ *tänzälazzälä* v.i was careless, lax; was untidy, slovenly

እንዘላዘለ *anzälazzälä* v.t carried s/t awkwardly

ዘለግ አለ *zälägg alä* v.i was high in stature, was tall, able-bodied, of manly appearance

ዘለግላጋ *zäläglagga* adj. tall, of manly appearance

ዘለፈ *zälläfä* v.t rebuked, blamed, reproached, reprimanded

ዘለፋ *zäläfa* n. rebuke blame, reproach, reprimand

ዝልፈት *zəlfät* n. rebuke, blame, reproach, reprimand

ዝልፊያ *zəlfiya* n. rebuke, blame, reproach, reprimand

ተዛለፈ *täzalläfä* v.t rebuked blamed, reproached, reprimanded

ተዛላፊ *täzalafi* adj/n *(one)* who rebukes, blames, reproaches

አዘለፈ *azzälläfä* v.t have s/o rebuked, blamed, reproached, reprimanded

ዘለፍላፋ see ተዘለፈለፈ

ዝልፍልፍ *zəlfləf* adj. fainting; exhausted, tired out

ዘላለም see ዓለም

ዘላበደ *zälabbädä* v.i babbled, jabbered

ዘላባጅ *zälabaǧ* adj/n *(one)* who jabbers

ዘላን *zällan* n/ adj nomad; impolite, lawless *(of person)*

ዘመመ *zämmämä* v.t curved down, lent, inclined

አዘመመ *azämmämä* v.t curved down, lent, inclined

አዝማሚያ *azmammiya* n. inclination; tendency, direction

ዘመሚት *zämämit* n. a kind of red ant

ዘመረ *zämmärä* v.t sang *(bird)*; sang a song, chanted

ዝመራ *zəmmāra* n. singing
ዝማሬ *zəmmare* n. song, hymn
መዘምር *mäzämmər* n. singer *(church)*, cantor
መዘምራን *mäzämmərān* n. pl. choir
መዝሙር *mäzmur* n. hymn, song
ብሔራዊ— *bəhərawi*—n. national anthem
መዝሙረ ዳዊት *mäzmurä dawit* n. Psalms of David
ደቀ መዝሙር *däqqä mäzmur* n. disciple pl: ደቀ መዛሙርት
አዘመረ *azämmärä* v.t sang a song, sang a hymn
ዘመተ *zämmätä* v.i went on a military mission, expedition; made a raid; campaigned; migrated
ዘመቻ *zämäča* n. raid, military expedition; campaign, fight
ዘማች *zämač* n. compaigner *(soldier, raider, fighter in war*, etc.)
—ወፍ —*wäf* n. migrating bird
ተዛመተ *täzammätä* v.i became rampant *(disease)*; spread *(news, disease, fire)*
አዘመተ *azämmätä* v.t led a campaign, a raid, led army to the front, led an expedition *(war)*
አዝማች *azmač* n. leader of an expedition *(war)*; refrain *(of a song)*
ቀኛ— *qäññ*—n. old Ethiopian title *(lit. commander of the right wing)*
ግራ— *gəra* – n. old Ethiopian title *(commander of the left wing)*
አዛመተ *azzammätä* v.t spread *(news, disease)*
አዘመተ *azzämmätä* v.t led an army *(to war)*
ዘመን *zämän* n. date, epoch, period, era
ዘመናዊ *zämänawi* adj. modern, fashionable, up-to-date; sophisticated
ዘመናይ *zämänay also* ዘበናይ *zabänay* adj. sophisticated; up-to-date; parvenu
ዘመን አመጣሽ *zämän amäṭṭaš* adj vogue; latest *(fashion)*
ዘመዘመ *zämäzzämä* v.t embroidered *(needlework)*
ዝምዘማ *zəmzämä* n. needle-work
ዝምዝማት *zəmzəmat* n. embroidery
ተዘመዘመ *täzämäzzämä* v.i was embroidered
ዘመድ *zämäd* n. relative, relation, kinsman, family, friend *see under* ተዛመደ
ሁሉ ዘመዴ *hullu zämäde* adj. popular *(person)*
ቅርብ ዘመድ *qərb zämäd* n. close relative
ቤተ— *betä* — n. relations *(relatives)*
ዘመዳሞች *zämädamočč* n. relatives
ዘመድ አዝማድ *zämäd azmad* n. relations *(relatives)*
የሥጋ ዘመድ *yäsəga zämäd* n. blood relation
የዘመድ አውራ *yäzämäd awra* n. chief of a clan, a family
ዘማ *zämma* n. adulteress; *see also* ዝሙት
ዘማዊ *zämmawi* adj. adulterous, fornicator
ዝሙተኛ *zəmmutäñña* adj. adulterous, fornicator
ዘምቢል *zämbil* n.- basket *(of woven palm leaves)*
ዘምባባ *zämbaba* n. palm tree
ዘረረ *zärrärä* v.t stretched s/t in full length;

knocked s/o down; knocked out

ተዘረረ *täzärrärä* v.i was stretched at full length; was knocked-down, was knocked out

ዘረነቀ *zärännäqä* v.t stuffed in, forced in; inserted

ተዘረነቀ *täzärännäqä* v.i was stuffed in, forced in, was inserted

ዘረከተ *zäräkkätä* v.t tore away *(made a rent in s/t)*; tore open s/o's belly *(with a knife etc.)*

ዘርካታ *zärkatta* adj. fattish

ዝርክት *zərəkt* adj. torn

ዝርክት አለ *zərkkətt alä* v.i was suddenly torn way

ዝርክት አደረገ *zərkkətt adärrägä* v.t tore s/t away suddenly

ተዘረከተ *täzäräkkätä* v.i was torn away suddenly

ዘረክራካ *zäräkrakka* adj. messy, untidy *see* ተዝረከረከ

ዝርክርክ ያለ *zərəkrəkk yalä* adj. messy, untidy

ዝርክርክ አደረገ *zərəkrəkk adärrägä* v.t made messy, untidy

ዘረዘረ *zäräzzärä* v.i .v.t developed ears *(of corn etc.)*; changed money *(into small denominations)*; enumerated; itemized; discussed in detail

ዘርዛራ *zärzarra* adj. loose *(sieve, wire-netting etc.)*

ዝርዛሪ *zərəzzari* n. change *(small dénominations)*

ዝርዝር *zərzər* n. change

ተዘረዘረ *täzäräzzärä* v.i was changed *(money into small denominations)*; was itemized, was enumerated

አዘረዘረ *azzäräzzärä* v.t had money changed into small denominations

ዘረገፈ *zäräggäfä* v.t poured out, emptied, tipped out

ዝርግፍ ወርቅ *zərgəf wärq* n. necklace *(golden)*

ዝርግፍ አለ *zərgəff alä* v.i was emptied; was tipped out

ዝርግፍ አደረገ *zərgəff adägärrä* v.t poured out; emptied; tipped out *(quickly)*

ተዘረገፈ *täzäräggäfä* v.i was emptied; was tipped out; flooded in

አዘረገፈ *azzäräggäfä* v.t had s/t emptied, s/t tipped

ዘረጋ *zärägga* v.t stretched out, spread out, extended; unrolled *(carpet etc.)*

ዝርግ *zərg* adj. flat

—ሳሕን *— sahən* n. flat dish

ዝርግነት *zərgənnät* n. flatness

ተዘረጋ *täzärägga* v.i was spread; was extended

አዘረጋ *azzärägu* v.t caused s/t to be spread, extended

አዘረጋጋ *azzärägagga* v.t caused s/t to be spread extensively

*ዘረጠ **zärräṭä*

ዘረጦ *zäräṭo* adj. coward, weakling

ዝራጭ *zərraç̣* adj. coward, weakling

አዘረጠ *azärräṭä* v.t farted *(vulgar, impolite)*

በዱላ— *bädulla*—hit severely with a stick

ዘረጥራጣ *zäräṭraṭṭa* adj. coward, weakling

ዝርጥርጥ *zərəṭrəṭ* adj. coward

ተዝረጠረጠ *täzräṭärräṭä* v.i was a coward, withdrew frightened

አንዛረጠ *anzarräṭä* v.t lived a vagabond life

አዝረጠረጠ *azräṭärräṭä* v.t caused fear, panic

ዘረጠጠ *zäräṭṭäṭä* v.t caused to

fall by pulling s/o's legs; degraded s/o by not using a polite form of address

ዘረጠጥ *zäräṭäṭṭ* adj. stout *(person)*, pot-bellied

ዘርጣጣ *zärṭaṭṭa* adj. stout *(person)*, pot-bellied

ዝርጥጥ *zərṭəṭ* adj. stout *(person)*

ተንዘረጠጠ *tänzäräṭṭäṭä* v.t. grew too stout

ተዘረጠጠ *täzäräṭṭäṭä* v.i. was made to fall by pulling s/o's legs

አንዘረጠጠ *anzäräṭṭäṭä* v.t. grew too stout

ሆዱን— *ሆዱን* — he had a stout belly

አዘረጠጠ *az zäräṭäṭä* v.t had s/o fell by pullng his legs

* ዘረፈጠ * *zäräffäṭä*

ዘርፋጣ *zärfaṭṭa* adj. idle, lazy

ተንዘራፈጠ *tänzäraffäṭä* v.i. occupied a large space by sitting idly

ተዘረፈጠ *täzäräffäṭä* v.i. sat idly

ዘረፈ *zärräfä* v.t. plundered, ransacked; composed poetry impromptu

ዘረፋ *zäräfa* n. plundering, ransacking

ዘራፊ *zärafi adj/n* (one) who plunders

ቅኔ ዘራፊ *qəne zärafi* n. one who composes poetry impromptu

ዘራፍ *zärraf* n. pillager

ዝርፊያ *zərfiya* n. pillage, plundering

ተዘረፈ *täzärräfä* v.i. was plundered, ransacked

ተዘራረፈ *täzärarräfä* v.i plundered, ransacked each other

አዘረፈ *azzärräfä* v.t. had s/t plundered, ransacked

*ዘረፈ * *zärräfä*

ዘርፍ *zärf* fringe of dress, garment

ዘርፍና ባለቤት *zärfənna balābet* n. constructive state *(gram.)*

* ዘረፈረፈ * *zäräfärräfä*

ዘረፍራፋ *zäräfraffa* adj. untidy

ዝርፍርፍ *zərəfrəf* adj. slovenly

አዝረፈረፈ *azräfärräfä* v.t. put one's clothes on carelessly

*ዘረፈፈ * *zäräffäfä*

ዘረፈፍ *zäräfäf* adj. untidy

ዘርፋፋ *zärfaffa* adj. untidy

ተንዘረፈፈ *tänzäräffäfä* v.i hung loosely

አንዘረፈፈ *anzäräffäfä* v.t. hung loosely, carried s/t clumsily

ዘራ *zärra* v.t sowed, seeded, grew *(wheat etc.)*

ዘሪ *zäri* adj./n.*(one)* who sows

ዘራም *zäram* adj. blessed with many descendants

ዘር *zär* n. seed; noun

ጎመን— *gomənän* – n. rapeseed

ዘረ መልካም *zärä mälkam* adj. of a decent family

—መጥፎ *—mäṭfo* adj. from a bad family

—ቢስ *—bis* adj. of low class

—ቡሩክ *—buruk* adj. from a blessed family

—ብዙ *—bəzu* adj. rich in progeny

—ከፉ *—kəfu* adj. from bad family

—ደግ *—dägg* adj. from a decent family

—ጥሩ *—ṭəru* adj. from good family

ዘር ቆጣሪ *zär qoṭari* adj. of blue blood

የዘር ግንድ *yäzär gənd* n.family tree

ጥሬ ዘር *ṭəre zär* n. noun *(derived from a verb)*

ተዘራ *täzärra* v.i was sown

አዘራ *azära* v.t winnowed

ማዝሪያ *mazriya* n. winnowing implement, tool

አዘራ *azzära* v.t had seed

sown

ዘርፍ — see ዘረፈ

ዘቀዘቀ — *zäqäzzäqä* v.t turned up-side-down, overturned

ዘቅዛቃ — *zäqzaqqa* adj. sloping *(area)*

ዝቅዝቅ — *zəqzəq* adv. downwards

ተዘቀዘቀ — *täzäqäzzäqä* v.i hung up-side-down, was overturned

አዘቀዘቀ — *azäqäzzäqä* v.t went down, went downwards

ፀሀይ—ች — the sun went down

አዘቀዘቀ — *azzäqäzzäqä* v.t made s/t go down

ዘቀጠ — *zäqqäṭä* v.i settled to the bottom of a liquid; sank

ዝቃጭ — *zəqqač̣* n. sediment, residue

ዝቅጥቃጭ — *zəqəṭqač̣* n. sediment, residue

አዘቀጠ — *azäqqäṭä* v.i went down *(as residue, sediment)*

አዘቅት — *azäqt* n. abyss

ዞቃቅቤ — *ẓäqaqəbe* n. kind of aromatic plant, basil

ዘበለለ — *zäbällälä* v.t emptied the bowels in great quantity

ዘበተ — *zäbbätä* v.i derided, laughed scornfully at

ዘበት — *zäbät* n. banter, firvolity

ተዘባበተ — *täzäbabbätä* v.i derided ,laughed scornfully at each other

መዘባበቻ — *mäzzäbqbäča* n. laughing - stock, ridicule

ዘበነ — *zäbbänä* v.i became sophisticated; modernized *(people)*

ዘበናይ — *zäbänay* ዘመናይ *zämänay* adj/n. sophisticated, modern, parvenu

ዘበናይነት — *zäbänayənnät* n. sophistication

ዘበን — *also* ዘመን *zäbän* n. time, era, epoch

ተዘባነነ — *täzäbannänä* v.i became extremely self-confident, snobbish, conceited

ተዘባናይ — *täzäbanay* adj. snobbish, conceited

አዘባነነ — *azzäbannänä* v.t. treat s/o lavishly, sumptuously, treated s/o in grand style

ዘበዘበ — *zäbäzzäbä* v.t was verbose, dwelt upon a subject

ነገር ዘብዛቢ — *nägär zäbzabi* adj. importunate

ዘብዛባ — *zäbzabba* adj. impotunate

ዝብዘባ — *zəbəzzəb* n. dwelling upon a subject, importunity

ዘበጠ — *zäbbäṭä* v.i sloped downward

ዘባጣ — *zäbaṭa* n. depression *(surface)*

ዘብጥ — *zäbṭ* n. depression

ዘቢብ — *zäbib* n. raisin, dried grape

ዘባ — *zäbba* v.i warped, was bent

ተዛባ — *täzabba* v.i. became incoherent *(sentence)*; was out of order; was distorted

አዛባ — *azzabba* v.t. made incoherent *(sentence)*; distorted *(information etc.)*

ዘባረቀ — *zäbarräqä* v.i. talked nonsense, confused an issue, rambled on, wandered in one's talk

ዘባራቂ — *zäbaraqi* adj/n *(one)* who talks nonsense, confuses an issue

ዘበራረቀ — *zäbärarräqä* v.t. made messy, put in

a disorderly manner, confused an issue, disorganized

ዝብርቅርቅ zəbrəqrəq n. mess

ተዘበራረቀ täzäbärarräqä v.t. was made completely messy, was put in a disorderly manner, was completely confused

ተዘባረቀ täzäbarräqä v.i. was made messy, was put in a disorderly manner, was confused

አዘበራረቀ äzzäbärarräqä v.t. made completely messy, put in a disorderly manner, confused completely

አዘባረቀ äzzäbarräqä v.t. made messy, put in a disorderly manner, confused

ዘባተሎ zäbatälo n. ragged-clothes

ዘብ zäb n. sentry

ዘበኛ zäbäñña n. watchman, guard

ዘቦ zäbo in ወርቅ-warqä- n. cloth interwoven with gold thread

ዘነቀ zännäqä v.t. inserted forcefully

ተዘነቀ täzännäqä v.i. was forcefully inserted

በአእምሮዬ ሐሳብ ተዘነቀብኝ an uneasy feeling sneaked into my mind

ዘነቆለ zänäqqolä v.t. poked s/o's eye *(with a finger)*

ተዘነቆለ täzänäqqolä v.i. was poked with a finger *(eye)*

ዘነበ zännäbä *also* ዘነመ v.i. rained

ዝናብ zənab n. rain

ሌባ— leba— n. brief rain

ወጨፎ— wäčäfo—n. rainstorm

ዶፍ— dof—n. heavy rain

የዝናብ ልብስ yäzənab ləbs n. raincoat

—መለኪያ —mäläkkiya n. rain gauge

ዝናባም zənabam adj. rainy

አዘነበ azännäbä v.*. caused to rain

* ዘነበለ *zänäbbälä

ዘንባላ zänballa adj. slanting

ዝንባሌ zənəbbale n. inclination, tendency, preference, trend

አዘነበለ azänäbbälä v.i. slanted; stooped, inclined

ዘነተረ zänättärä v.t. snatched with the teeth

ተዘነተረ täzänättärä v.i. was snatched with the teeth

ዘነነ zännänä v.i. slanted

ዘነን ያለ zänänn yalä adj. slanting

ዘናና zänana adj. slanting

* ዘነከተ zänäkkätä

ዘንካታ zänkatta adj. graceful, exuberant

ተዘናከተ täzänakkätä v.i. behaved gracefully

ዘነዘና zänäzäna n. pestle

ዘነጋ zänägga v.i forgot, became absent-minded

ዝንጉ zəngu adj. forgetful, scatter-brained

ዝንጋታ zəngata n. forgetfulness

ተዘነጋ täzänägga v.i. was forgotten

ተዘነጋጋ täzänägagga v.i. was forgotten; forgot each other

ተዘናጋ täzänagga v.i. felt confident

አዘነጋ azänägga v.t. caused to forget

አዘናጋ azzänagga v.t. caused to forget *(with the intention of doing harm to s/o.)*

ዘነጠ zännätä v.i. became chic; showed an air of superior excellence *(behaviour)*

ዘናጭ *zännač* adj. stylish; dandified

ዜንጥ *zenṭ* n. chic; air of superior excellence

ዜንጠኛ *zenṭäñña* adj. stylish

ዝንጣ *zənnäṭa* n. chic; air of superior excellence

ዘነጠለ *zänäṭṭälä* v.t. cut s/t away *(branch from a tree etc.)*; cut s/t open *(e.g belly of an animal by a hyena)*; mispronounced a syllable *(esp. its pitch)*

ዝንጥል *zənṭəl* n. branch *(of tree freshly cut)*

ዘነጣጠለ *zänäṭaṭṭälä* v.t. cut s/t away in pieces; cut s/t open repeatedly

ተዘነጠለ *täzänäṭṭälä* v.i. was cut away ; was cut open

ተዘነጣጠለ *täzänäṭaṭṭälä* v.t. was cut into pieces; was ragged *(clothes)*

አዘነጠለ *azzänäṭṭälä* v.t. had s/t cut into pieces

ዘነጠፈ *zänäṭṭäfä* v.t. cut away *(branch from a tree)*

ዝንጣፊ *zənəṭṭafi* n. twig, bough

ተዘነጠፈ *täzänäṭṭäfä* v.i. was cut away *(branch)*

ዘነፈ **zännäfä*

ዝንፋት *zənnəfat* n. overlapping

ተዛነፈ *täzannäfä* v.i became of uneven length, overlapped

ተዛናፊ *täzanafi* adj. of uneven length; overlapping

አዛነፈ *azzannäfä* v.t. caused to be of uneven length, caused to overlap

ዘንፋላ *zänfalla* adj. graceful, glamorous, exuberant

ተዘናፈለ *täzänaffälä* v.i. behaved gracefully

ዘና *zänna* v.i. relaxed, felt at ease

መዝናኛ *mäznaña* n. means of amusement, en tertainment

—ቦታ *—bota* n. place of amusement, entertainment, recreation

ተዛና *täzanna* v.i. felt at ease

ተዝናና *täznanna* v.i. felt at home

አዝናና *aznanna* v.t. entertained

አዝናኝ *aznañ* adj. entertaining

ዘንቢል *zänbil* n. basket

ዘንካታ *zänkatta* adj. graceful

ዘንድ *zänd* adv. near, besides, t

እኔው ዘንድ ነው he is near me, beside me , he is at my place *(with simple imperfect, that... may)* ይመጣ ዘንድ ነገርኩት I told him that he might come; prep. from ከእግዚአብሔር ዘንድ from God, adv since ከመጣ ዘንድ እኔ አነጋግረዋለሁ since he has come I shall talk to him

ዘንድ አንቀጽ *zänd anqäṣ* n. jussive *(gram.)*

ዘንዶ *zändo* n. larg snake

ዘንጋዳ *zängada* n. sorghum

ዘንግ *zäng* n. road, axis, goad, shaft *(of spear)*

የፈረስ ዘንግ *yäfäräs zäng* n. kind of shrub

ዘከረ *zäkkärä* v.t. commemorated *(religious occasion)* with a feast

ዝክር *zəkər* n. commemoration with a banquet *(in a religious occassion)*

ዝክረ ነገር *zəkrä nägär* n. memorabilia

መዘክር *mäzäkkər* n. *in* ቤተ መዘክር museum

ተዘከረ *täzäkkärä* v.i. gave alms to s/o

ተዝካር *täzkär also* ተዝካር n. feast or banquet in commemoration of a dead relative

—አወጣ *—awäṭṭa* v.t. gave a feast or banquet in commemoration of a dead relative

አዘከረ *äzäkkärä* v.t. prayed on at a feast or banquet in commemoration of a dead person

ዘከዘከ *zäkäzzäkä* v.t. poured out in quantity; emptied completely

ምሥጢር— *məsṭir—* v.t. divulged a secret, had a loose tongue

ዝክዝክ *zäkzakka* adj. extravagant

—ወንፊት *—wänfit* n. loose sieve

ዝክዝክ *zəkzək* adj. loose *(fabrics)*

ዝክዝክ አደረገ *zəkzəkk ädärrägä in* ምስጢሩን ዝክዝክ አድርጎ አወጣ divulged all secrets

ተዘከዘከ *täzäkäzzäkä* v.i. was poured out in quantity, was emptied completely

አዘከዘከ *azzäkäzzäkä* v.t. had s/t emptied completely ምስጥሬን ሁሉ አዘከዘከኝ he made me tell him all my secrets

ዘካ(ት) *zäka(t)* n. alms *(used by Moslems only)*

ዘኬ *zäkke* n. food collected by church students from begging; meal eaten at church after mass service *(brought by believers)*

—ለቃሚ *—läqami* adj. beggar *(insult to students)*

—ተማሪ *—tämari* n. student who supports himself by begging

ዘወረ *zäwwärä* v.t. turned a wheel

ዘዋራ *zäwwarra in* —ቦታ *—bota* n. an out-of-the way place

ዘወርዋራ *zäwärwarra* adj. roundabout way

ዝውውር *zəwəwwər* n. transfer

መዘውር *mäzäwwər* n. pulley

ተዘወረ *täzäwwärä* v.i. was turned *(wheel)*

ተዘዋወረ *täzäwawwärä* v.i. moved around, travelled about; circulated *(blood)*

ተዘዋዋሪ *täzäwawäri* adj. circulating, migrant, wandering, errant, mobile

—ክሊኒክ *—klinik* n. mobile clinic

ተዛወረ *täzawwärä* v.i. was transferred

ተዛዋሪ *täzawäri* adj. transferable, mobile

አዘወረ *azzäwwärä* v.t. had a wheel turned

አዛወረ *azzawwärä* v.t. had s/o tranferred

ዘወተረ *zäwwättärä*

ዘውትር *zäwätər* adv. always constantly, regularly

ተዘወተረ *täzäwättärä* v.t. has become usual, habitual

አዘወተረ *azäwättärä* v.t. frequented *(a place)*; did s/t regulary, continued to do s/t constantly

አዘውታሪ *azäwtari* adj/n one who frequently does s/t

ዘው አለ *zäww alä* v.i. came in suddenly, entered abruptly

ዘው ዘው አለ *zäww zäww alä* v.i. entered here and there

ዘውድ *zäwd* n. crown

—አማካሪ *—ammakari* n. crown counselor

—አገዛዝ *—aggäzaz* n. kingdom

—ደፋ *—däffa* v.t. was crowned, became a king, an emperor

—ጫነ —čanä v.t. see ዘውድ ደፋ
ባለ— balä — n. legitimate heir to the throne
ዘዌ zäwe n. angle
ዘየረ zäyyärä v.t. greeted *(used by Moslems only)*
ዝየራ zəyyära n. greeting
ተዘያየረ täzäyayyärä v.i. greeted each other
ዘየነ zäyyänä v.t. embelished, decorated
ዝየና zəyyäna n. embelishment, decoration
ዘየደ zäyyädä v.i. was tactful, prudent
ዘያጅ zäyyaǧ adj. tactful, prudent
ዝየዳ zəyyäda n. tact, prudence
ዘዬ zäye n. tact, prudence
—አዋቂ —awaqi adj. prudent, tactful
ዘይቤ zäyəbe n. figure of speech, expression
ዘይት zäyət n. oil
የምግብ— yäməgəb—n. edible oil
የሞተር— yämotor—n. motor oil
የተልባ— yätälba—n. linseed oil
የኑግ— yänug— noug oil
የወይራ— yäwäyra— n. olive oil
የጉሎ— yägulo— n. castor oil
ዘዴ zäde n. method, way of doing *s/t*, ways and means of doing s/t
—አዋቂ —awaqi adj. tactful, prudent
ዘዴኛ zədeñña adj. tactful, prudet, resourceful
በዘዴ bäzäde adv. carefully, artfully
ዘገመ zäggämä
ዘገምተኛ zägämtäñña adj./n *(one)* who walks slowly
ዘገምታ zägämta n. walking slowly
አዘገመ azäggäma v.i. walked; did s/t slowly plodded, made slow headway
አዝጋሚ azgami n. plodder
ዘገረረ zägärrärä v.t. knocked s/o down
ዘገበ zäggäbä v.t. aimed, took aim
ዘገባ zägäba n. report
ዘጋቢ zägabi n. reporter
መዝገብ mäzgäb n. register, roster, ledger, record
መዝገበ ቃላት mäzgäbä qalat n. dictionary, lexicon
መዝገብ ቤት mäzgäb bet n. archives, record office, registry
መዝጋቢ mäzgabi n. registrar
ምዝገባ məzgäba n. registration
ተመዘገበ tämäzäggäbä v.i. was registered
መመዝገቢያ mämmäzgäbiya n. registration fee, place
ተመዝጋቢ tämäzgabi n. registering candidate
አስመዘገበ asmäzäggäbä v.t. had s/o registered
ዘገነ zäggänä v.t. took handful *(grain etc.)*
ዝግን zəgən n. highly seasoned dish of minced meat cooked in butter
አዘገነ azzäggänä v.t. had s/o take a handful *(grain etc.)*
ዘገነነ zägännänä used with pronominal suffix such as -ኝ-ው etc. e.g
ዘገነነው zägännänäw v.i. was disgusted *(by a horrible scene)*, was horrified
ዘግናኝ zägnañ n. horrifying scene
ዘገየ zägäyyä v.i. was late, was delayed
ዘግየት አለ zägyätt alä v.i. came a little late
አዘገየ azägäyyä v.t. delayed, detained, postponed, kept late
ዘግይቶ መጣ zägyəto mäṭṭa he was late
ቢዘገይ ቢዘገይ bizägäy bizägäy at the latest
ቢዘገይም bizägäyyəm however

late he/ it is

*ዘገጀ zägäǧǧä

ዝግጁ zəgəǧǧu adj. ready, prepared *(to do s/t)*

ዝግጅት zəgəǧǧət n. preparation, arrangement

ተዘገጃጀ *täzägäǧǧaǧǧä* v.i. was prepared, was arranged

ተዘጋጀ *täzägaǧǧä* v.i. was ready, was prepared; prepared oneself; was put in order

አዘገጃጀ *azzägäǧaǧǧa* v.t. prepared, arranged, put in order

አዘጋጀ *azzägaǧǧä* v.t. prepared, arranged, put in order

አዘጋጅ *azzägaǧ* adj/ n. *(one)* who prepares, arranges, puts in order

መጽሔት— *mäṣəhet—* n. editor of a periodical

ማዘጋጃ *mazägaǧa in* ማዘጋጃ ቤት municipality, a city hall

ዘጋ *zägga* v.t. closed, blocked, shut off, obstructed, blocked up

ዝግ *zəg* adj. closed, blocked

መዝጊያ *mäzgiya* n. door, gate, entrance

ዝግ ችሎት *zəg čəlot* n. closed session of a court of law

ተዘጋ *täzägga* v.i. was closed

ተዘጊ *täzägi* adj. easy to close

አዘጋ *azzägga* v.t. had s/t *(door, opening)* closed

አዛጋ *azzagga* v.t. yawned

*ዘጎረጎረ *zägorägorä

ዘጎርጓራ *zägorgʷarra* adj. stripped, multicoloured

ዝጉርጉር *zəgurgur* adj. stripped, multicoloured

ተዝጎረጎረ *täzgoräggorä* v.i. became stripped, multicoloured

አዝጎረጎረ *azgorägorrä, also* አዥጎረጎረ *ažgoräggorä* v.t. made stripes, made multicoloured

ዘጎነ *zäggonä* v.i. was full of sores

ዘጠና *zäṭäna* adj/n ninety

ዘጠናኛ *zäṭänaňňa* adj/n ninetieth

ዘጠኝ *zäṭäňň* adj. nine

ዘጠነኛ *zäṭänäňňa* adj/n ninth

*ዘጠዘጠ * *zäṭäzzäṭä*

ዘጠዘጥ *zäṭäzaṭ* adj. tramp, bum *(U.S.)*

ዘጥ ዘጥ አለ *zäṭṭ zäṭṭ alä* v.i. loafed

አዘጠዘጠ *azäṭäzzäṭä* v.t. loafed, wandered about doing nothing, bummed

አዘጥዛጭ *azäṭzač̣* adj/n *(one)* who loafs, wanders about doing nothing, bum

ዘጭ አለ *zäč̣č̣ alä also* እንዘጭ አለ *ənzäč̣č̣ alä* v.i. fell down abruptly, slumped

ዘፈቀ *zäffäqä* v.i. dipped, soaked

ዝፍቅያ *zəfqiya* n. dipping *(boys in swimming)*

ተዘፈቀ *täzäffäqä* v.i. was dipped, soaked, plunged

ተዛፈቀ *täzaffäqä* v.i. dipped each other *(in swimming)*

አዘፈቀ *azäffäqä* v.t. had s/o dipped in water

ዘፈነ *zäffänä* v.t. sang

ዘፈን *zäfän* n. song

—አወረደ *—awärrädä* v.t. led a choir *(in singing)*

ዘፋኝ *zäfaň* n. singer

አዘፈነ *azzäffänä* v.t. had s/o sing

አዛፈነ *azzaffänä* v.t. accompanied s/o in singing

ዘፈዘፈ *zäfäzzäfä* v.t. soaked in water; *(clothes, grain etc.)*, put aside undone for a long time e.g. ስራውን ዘፈዘፈው he put his work aside for a long time

ዘፋዘፎ *zäfazäfo* adj. rounded, obese

ዝፍዝፍ *zəfzəf* adj. soaked *(in water)*; lazy

ተዘፈዘፈ *täzäfäzzäfä* v.i. was soaked in water

ዘፈዘፈ *zäfäzzäfä*

ተንዘፈዘፈ *tänzäfäzzäfä* v.i. writhed *(in pain)*; trembled *(in terror)*

አንዘፈዘፈ *anzäfäzzäfä* v.t. caused to tremble *(in terror)*, shiver with fear

ዘፈጠጠ *zäfäṭṭäṭä*

ዘፈጠጥ *zäfäṭäṭ* adj. pot-bellied

ዘፍጣጣ *zäfṭaṭṭa* adj. stout, pot-bellied

ተንዘፈጠጠ *tänzäfäṭṭäṭä* v.i had large prominent belly, became pot-bellied

አንዘፈጠጠ *anzäfäṭṭäṭa* v.t appeared with a large belly

ዘፍ አለ *zäff alä* v.i. slumped

ዙረት *see* ዞረ

ዙሪያ *see* ዞረ

ዙር *see* ዞረ

ዙጥ አደረገ *zuṭṭ adärrägä* v.i. broke wind, farted

ዙፋን *zufan* n. throne

—ለቀቀ *—läqqäqä* v.t. abdicated

—ቤት *—bet* n. throne room

—ወረሰ *—wärräsä* v.t. succeeded to the throne

—ላይ ወጣ *—lay wäṭṭa* v.t. came to the throne

ዚቀኛ *ziqäñña* n. an admirable person; a subtle person

ዛለ *zalä* v.i wearied *(body limb)*; was exhausted *(body, mind)*

ዝለት *zəlät* n. weariness

አዛለ *azalä* v.t. caused weariness, exhausted

ዛላ *zala* n. ear of corn; stature

ዛላው መልከም *zalaw mälkəm* adj. tall and handsome

ዛር *zar* n. kind of evil spirit that possesses people

ባለ— *balä—* n. s/o possessed by an evil spirit

ዛራም *zäräm* adj. possessed by «zar»; easily irritated

የዛር ፈረስ *yäzär färäs* n. person attacked by «zar»

ዛሬ *zare* n. adv. & n to-day; at this present age, period

—ነገ *—nägä* n. procrastination

——አለ *——alä* v. procrastinated, stalled

ዛሬውኑ *zärewənu* adv. this very day

እስከ ዛሬ *əskäzare* until today, to date

ዛቀ *zaqä* v.t. scooped up, shovelled; removed s/t e.g. grain, ashes, dung, flour in great quantity

ዝቆሽ *zəqoš* adj. very cheap e.g. ዋጋው ዝቆሽ ነው the price is very cheap

መዛቂያ *mäzaqiya* n. scoop

ተዛቀ *täzaqä* v.i. was scooped up, shovelled, removed in great quantity

አዛቀ *azzaqä* v.t. had s/t scooped up, shovelled etc.

ዛቢያ *zabiya* n. shaft *(handle of an axe)*

ዛተ *zatä* v.i. threatened

ዛቻ *začča* n. threat, menace

ተዛዛተ *täzazatä* v.i. threatened each other

ዛተለ *zättälä* v. became ragged

ዛተሎ *zatälo* n. rag

ዛኒጋባ *zanigabba* n. annex *(building)*

ዛዘነ *zazzänä* v.i. had a strong sexual desire *(lusted)*

ዛዛኝ *zazañ* adj. lustful

(after a woman)

• ዛዛ • zazza

ተንዛዛ *tänzazza* v.i. was superfluous

አንዛዛ *anzazza* v.t. made superfluous

ዛገ *zagä* v.i. corroded, rusted

ዝገት *zəgät* n. rust

አዛገ *azagä* v.t rusted

ዛጎል *zagol* n. shell, coral

ዛጎልማ *zagoləmma* adj. coral

ዛፍ *zaf* n. tree

ባሕር— *bahər*—n. eucalyptus

ዛፉ *zafu* n. dwarf *(ironical)*

ዜማ *zema* n. chant, song, tune; church song

ዜመኛ *zemäñña* n. person with a good voice, *also* ባለ ዜማ

ዜማ ሰበረ *zema säbbärä* v.t. sang false notes

—አወረደ —*awärädä* v.t. led a song

አዜመ *azemä* v.t. sang, chanted

ዜሮ *zero* n. zero; naught, nil; love *(in games)*

ዜሮ ለዜሮ *zero läzero* nil-nil

ዜና *zena* n. news

—መዋዕል —*mäwa'əl* n. chronicle

—አቀባይ —*aqäbbay* n. reporter

—አጠናቃሪ —*aṭṭänaqari* n. correspondent *(newspaper)*

—እረፍት —*əräft* n. obituary

አርእስተ— *arə'əstä*—n. headlines *(news)*

ዜጋ *zega* n. citizen, subject

የውጭ— *yäwəčč*—n. foreign national, expatriate

ዝሀ *zəha* n. hank, *also* ዛሃ

ዝሆን *zəhon also* ዛሆን *zähon* n. elephant

ዝሆኔ *zəhone* n. elephantiasis

የዝሆን ጥርስ *yäzəhon ṭərs* n. ivory

የ—ጆሮ ይስጠኝ አለ *yä—ǧoro yəsṭäññ alä* lend a deaf ear

ዝሙት *zəmmut* n. adultery, lust, fornication

ዝሙተኛ *zəmmutäñña* n. adulterer, fornicator

ዘማ *zämma* n. adulteress

ዝማም *zəmam* n. purified gold

ዝማሬ *see* ዘመረ

ዝም አለ *zəmm alä* v.i. kept quiet, remained still, held still; was indifferent

ዝምተኛ *zəmmətäñña* adj. quiet, still, silent; reserved

ዝምታ *zəmməta* n. silence

ዝም ብሎ *zəmm bəlo* adv. just so, without any reason ዝም ብሎ ይናደዳል he is irritated without any reason

ዝም አሰኘ *zəmm assäññä* v.t silenced, hushed

ዝምብ *zemb also* ዝንብ *zənb* n fly

ዝምቡን እሽ አለ *zəmbun əšš alä* v.t. swished away flies

ዝምባም *zəmbam* adj/n full of flies; inactive; a slowcoach

ዝምቦ *zəmbo* n. slowcoach

ዝምበ ከልከል *zəmbä kälkəl* n. mosquito-net

ዝር አለ *zərr alä* v.i. appeared, came around ወፍ ዝር የማይልበት ቦታ an abandoned place, a deserted place

ዝርክርክ አለ *zərəkrəkk alä* v.i. was littered, strewn, cluttered, untidy, messy

ዝረክራካ *zärkrakka* adj. untidy; extravagant

ዝርክርክ *zərəkrək* adj. messy; untidy

ተዝረከረከ *täzräkärräkä* v.i. was untidy, messy

አዝረከረከ *azräkärräkä* v.t. made untidy, messy; littered

ዝርግፍ አለ *see* ዘረገፈ

ዝቅ አለ *zəqq alä* v.i. lowered; sank *(price)*, declined, became inferior

ዝቅተኛ *zəqqətäñña* adj. inferior

ዝቅታ *zəqqəta* n. depression, condescension

ዝቅ ዝቅ አለ *zəqq zəqq alä* v.i. deteriorated

ዝቅ ዝቅ አደረገ *zəqq zəqq adärrägä* v.t. deteriotated
ዝባዝንኬ *zəbazənke* n. trifle
ዝባድ *zəbad* n. civet *(substance)*
ዝተት *zəttät* n. coarse woollen cloth
ዝተታም *zəttätam* adj. ragged, tattered, threadbare
ዝና *zənna* n. fame, reputation
ዝነኛ *zənnäñña* adj. famous, reputable, renowned, eminent, celebrated
ዝናማ *see* ዝነኛ
ዝናቢስ *zənna bis* adj. without fame, reputation
ዝና ወዳድ *zənna wäddad* adj. anxious for fame
ዝናር *zennar* n. cartridge belt
የዝናር ማፈኛ *yäzənnar maffäña* n. belt strap
ዝናብ ዘነበ *see* ዘነበ
ዝንባሌ *see* ዘነበለ
ዝንብ *see* ዝምብ
ዝንተ ዓለም *zentä aläm* adv. from time immemorial
ዝንጀሮ *zəngaro* n. monkey, ape, baboon
ተራ— *tära*—n. anubis baboon
ነጭ— *näčč*—n. hamadryas baboon
ጨላዳ— *čälada*—n. gelada baboon
ዝንጅብል *zənğəbəll* n. ginger
ዝንጉርጉር *zəngurgur* adj. spotted, striped, multicoloured
ዝንጥል *see* ዘነጠለ
ዝከር *see* ዘከረ
ዝይ *zəyy* n. goose, gander
ዝጉን *see* ዘጋነ
ዝግ *see* ዘጋ
ዝግባ *zəgba* podocarpo (*podocarpus gracilior*)
ዝግ አለ *zəgg alä* v.i. was slow, slowed down
ዝግተኛ *zəggətäñña* adj. slow, tardy, slow-moving
ዝግታ *zəggəta* n. slowness, tardiness
ዝግን *see* ዘገነ
ዝፍት *zəft* n. tar
ዞረ *zorä* v.i. turned around, rotated, went around, revolved
ዟሪ *zŭwari* n. vagabond wanderer, vagrant
ዙረት *zurät* n. wandering, vagrancy ስራው ዙረት ነው he is leading a vagrant life
ዙሪያ *zuria* n. circumference, circuit; surrounding area
ዙር *zur* n. round *(action)* በመጀመሪያው ዙር in the first round
ዙሮ ገጠም *zuro gäṭṭäm* adj. roundish
ዞሮ ዞሮ *zoro zoro* adv. at least, finally, in the end
ተዟዟረ *täzuʷazuʷarä* v.i. went around; misjoined
አዞረ *azorä* v.t.i took s/t around; was giddy ራሱን አዞረው he became giddy
አዟሪ *azuʷari* n. peddler *also* ሸቀጥ / እቃ አዟሪ
አዙሪት *azurit* n. whirlpool.
ማዞሪያ *mazoriya* n. telephone operator, switch board

ዠ

ዠለጠ *žälläṭä* v.t. hit *(with a stick)*
ተዠለጠ *täžälläṭä* v.i was hit (with stick)
አዠለጠ *ažžälläṭä* v.t. had s/o hit *(with a stick)*
ዠመረ *see* ጀመረ
ዠምበር *see* ጀምበር
ዠረር አለ *žärärr alä* v.i. flowed abundantly
ዠረገገ *žäräggägä* v.t stripped off *(the fruits from*

the branch)

ተንዠረገገ tänžäräggägä v.i. bore abundantly; flew down (of hair)

*ዠረገደ *žäräggädä

ዠርጋዳ žärgadda adj. graceful, elegant

ዠርባ see ጀርባ

ዠቀዠቀ žäqäžžäqä

ተንዠቀዠቀ tänžäqäžžäqä v.i. flowed abundantly, gushed

አንዠቀዠቀ anžäqäžžäqä v.t. caused to flow abundantly, caused to gush

*ዠበረረ *žäbärrärä

ዠበረር žäbärär adj. senile

ዠብራራ žäbrarra adj. senile, feeble-minded

ዠብረር አለ žäbrärr alä v.i. became senile, feeble-minded

ተንዠባረረ tänžäbarrärä v.i. became senile, feeble-minded

*ዠበበ/ጀበበ *žäbbäbä also ǧäbbäbä

ተንዣበበ tänžabbäbä v.i. hovered

አንዣበበ anžabbäbä v.i. hovered

አንዣባቢ anžababi adj. hovering

ዠበድ አደረገ žabbädd adärrägä v.t. hit slightly

ዠብዱ žäbdu also ጀብዱ ǧäbdu n. adventure

ዠንዲ see ጀንዲ

ዠገነ see ጀገነ

ዠጐረጐረ see * ዘጎረጎረ

*ዠጎደጎደ *žägodäggodä

ተዥጎደጎደ täžgodäggodä v.i. was plentiful

አዥጎደጎደ ažgodäggodä v.t. gave, brought s/t abundantly

ዠርት žart also ጀርት ǧart n. porcupine

ዣን— žan also ጃን ǧan used in ዣንሆይ žanhoy, n. His Majesty

ዣንጥላ ጃንጥላ žanṭəla also ǧanṭəla n. umbrella, parasol

ዣንጥራር also ጃንጥራር žanṭəraar, ǧanṭərar n. Old title of a Wollo feudal

ዣንደረባ also ጃንደረባ žandäraba, ǧandäräba n. eunuch

ዥማት also ጅማት žəmmat, ǧəmmat n. tendon

ዥረት also ጅረት žərät, ǧərät n. creek, brook, stream

ዥራት also ጅራት žərat, ǧərat n. tail

ዥራታም ኮከብ žəratam kokäb n. comet

ዥራፍ also ጅራፍ žəraf, ǧəraf n. whip (especially the kind used by men)

ዥብ also ጅብ žəb, ǧəb n. hyena

ዥንፎ also ጅንፎ žənfo, ǧənfo n. metal protection on the butt of a spear, walking-stick etc.

ዥዋዥዌ also ጅዋጅዌ žəwwažewwe, ǧəwwaǧəwwe n. swing, pendulum

ዥው ያለ ገደል žəww or ጅው ያለ ገደል ǧəww yalä gädäl n. precipice (of mountain)

ዥግራ also ጅግራ žəgra, ǧəgra n. guinea fowl

ዦሮ also ጆሮ žoro, ǧoro, n. ear

ዦፌ አሞራ also ጆፌ አሞራ žoffe, ǧoffe amora n. vulture

የ

የ— yä prep. of
የሰው ልጅ ታሪክ the history of mankind;
+personal pronoun
የኔ (የእኔ) my, mine
with perfect and imperfect verb who, that, which
የመጣው ሰው the man who came,
የሚመጣው ሰው the man who will come

የለ— *yällä—*
—የለሽ in *ləbb*—adj.
ልበ— absent-minded
ስመ— *səm*—adj. nameless
ቅርጸ— *qərṣ*—adj. shapeless, amorphous
አመል— *amäl*—adj. cranky, grouchy, moody

የሌለው *or* የለለው *yälelläw yälälläw* prep. without, free from, *suff.* less e.g ቤት የሌለው homeless ጥርጣሬ የሌለው doubtless

የለም *yällām* n. there is not; he is not around

የሌት ወፍ *yälet wäf* n. bat

የመን *yämän* n. Yemen

የመኒ *yamani* n. Yemenite

የሚ— *yämmi—with imperfect indicating third person sing & pl.*, which, who, that
የሚናገር ወፍ
a bird that talks

የማ— *yämma with imperfect indicating negation*, that... who...
not, which... not
የማይሰራ ሰው a man that does not work

የማን *yämann* pron. whose

የም— *yämm—with imperfect, indicating first person sing & pl.*, what, that
የምናገረውን አላውቅም
I don't know what I am talking about

የምስራች *yäməssəračč* n. good news, good tidings, hurrah !

የምር *yämərr* adv. seriously, earnestly

የሰራ አካላት *yässära akalat* n. the entire body
የሰራ አካላቴን ያመኛል
I feel pain in my entire body

የረር *yärär* n. name of a mountain east of Addis Ababa

የርሱ *also* የሱ *yärsu, yässu* pron. his

የርሳቸው *yärsaččäw, also* የሳቸው *yässaččäw* pron. their, theirs

የብስ *yäbs* n. mainland, dry land, land

የት *yät* pron. where
የቱ *yätu* pron. which, which one
የትም *yätəmm* adv. everywhere, anywhere, any place
የትና የት *yätənnayät* adj. long *(distance)*, inaccessible
የትኛው *yätəññäw* pron. which one
የትየለሌ *yätəyyäläle* adj. unattainable, beyond one's reach

የኔታ *yäneta, (for* የኔጌታ *yänegeta)* interj. master *(for a teacher or an elderly person)*

የንሹ *yänšu also* ኢንሹ *inšu* n. dikdik

የካቲት *yäkkatit* n. February

የክት *(see also under* ከተተ*)*
የክት ልብስ *yäkətt ləbs* n. Sunday best

የወል *yäwäl* adj. common

የዋህ *yäwwah* adj. innocent, simple, meek, harmless
የዋህነት *yäwwahənnät* n. innocence, simplicity

የዚያ *see* እዚህ

የየ— *yäyyä* pron. every/everyone የየሰውን ታሪክ ንገረኝ tell me the story of every man

የይ *yäyy* n. jackal

የዲያ *yädiya, also* ኧዲያ *ädiya (expression of abhorrence)* away with it

የግድ *see* *ገደደ

የፍጥኝ *yäfiṭṭəññ in* የፊጥኝ አሰረ tied the hands behind the back

—ዪቱ —*yitu* def. art. feminine marker e.g. ልጅ+ ዪቱ= ልጂቱ *ləgitu* the girl

ያ *ya* adj. pron. that
ያ ሌላ ይህ ሌላ that is a different thing

ያህል yahəl see .. o under አክለ adv. about, nearly, approximately ዋጋው ይህን ያህል ነው ለማለት አልችልም I cannot tell the price exactly

ያም yam adj. that

-ሆነ ይህ —honä yəh adv. nevertheless, in any case

—ቢሆን —bihon adv. whatever it is, even at that

ያኔ yanne, also ያን ጊዜ yangize adv. at that time; then

ያን yannən adj. acc. that

ያንማ yannəmma but that

ያንን yann adj. acc. that

ያኛው yaññaw the other one

ያች yačč pron/adj. f. that

ያቻትና yaččatənna there she is

ያው yaw there he is

ያውልህ yawəlləh here it is

ያውና yawənna there he is

ያውኮ yawəkko but there he/ it is !

ያዘ yazä v.t. caught; grasped, held, seized; started መናገር፡ ከያዘ አያቆምም after having started to talk he never stops

ይዘት yəzät n. content, volume

ይዞታ yəzota n. tenure የመሬት ይዞታ land tenure

ያዝ ለቀቅ yazz läqqäq not serious ሥራውን ያዝ ለቀቅ ያደርጋል He is not serious at his duty/work.

መያዣ mäyža n. container; pawn, mortgage; hostage

ተያዘ täyazä v.i. was caught, was arrested; was impounded; was occupied (place), was busy (telephone)

ተያዥ täyaž n. guarantor

ተያያዘ täyayazä v.i. was connected; was coherent; was inflamed, caught fire

አያያዘ ayyayazä v.t. joined together, connected, united; kindled

አያያዝ ayyayaz n. handling, management; behaviour

አስያዘ asyazä v.t. had s/o arrested, caught; impounded

ማስያዣ masyaža n. bail

ዬ —ye poss. pron. suff. used after nouns ending with vowels; e.g. በሬ+ዬ=በሬዬ my ox

—ዬ yye suff. pron. added to name of countries to denote birth place e.g. ወሎዬ Wolloyan, ጅሩዬ Gərruyan

—ዬው —yäw def. art. m. the, ሰውዬው the man

ዬጭ yečč, also ኤጭ ečč (expression of abhorence) away with it!

ይ— yə—pron. suff. imperfect marker e.g. ይ+verb + አል =ይመጣል he will come

ይሁዳ yəhuda n. Judea

ይሁዲ yəhudi n. Jew;

ይህ yəh adj. this

•ይህማ yəhamma but this, well, this

ይህም yəhəmm and this

ይህን yəhənn this

ይህን ያህል —yahəl this much, all these

ይህኛው yəhəññaw this one

ይኸው yəhäw here he/ it is

•ይሉኝታ yəluññta (see also under አለ) concern about public opinion

—ቢስ —bis adj. unscrupulous

ይሉኝ አይል yəluññ ayəl adj. unscrupulous

ይላማ yəlama, also ኢላማ ilama n. target, aim

ይልቅ yələq see also ላቀ adv. rather than, more

ይልቁን yələqun adv. rather

ይልቁንም yələqunəmm adv.

especially. on the contrary

ይልቁንስ *yəlqunəss* adv. rather, by preference or choice

ይልቅስ *yələqəss* adv. rather, by preference or choice

ይማም *yəmam*, *also* ኢማም *imam* n. Imam (*title of Muslim leader, especially of the one that leads the prayer in the forefront*)

ይቅርታ *yəqərta*, *see also under* ቀረ excuse, ይቅርታ አድርግልኝ excuse me, ይቅርታ ያድርጉልኝ excuse me (*pol.*)

ይበል *see* አለ

ይብላኝ ይብላኝ *see* በላ

ይብራ *yəbra* n. duck

ይብስ *see* ባሰ

ይቶት *yətot* n. title of an old widow

ይኸው *see* ይሀ

ይድረስ *see also under* ደረሰ used in የይድረስ የይድረስ done in a hurry, hastily done

ይግባኝ *yəgəbaňň see also* ገባ n. appeal (*in court*). petition

ይፋ *yəfa* n. s/t official

—ሆነ *—hona* v.i. became official

—ወጣ *—wäṭṭa* v.i. was declared officially

በይፋ *bäyəfa* adv. openly. publicly

—ዮ *-yyo* dem. pron. f. that, ያች ሴትዮ that woman

—ዮዋ *—yowa* def. art. f. the. ሴትዮዋ the woman

ዮርዳኖስ *yordanos* n. Jordan

ማየ ዮርዳኖስ *mayä*—n. sacred water of the River Jordan

—ዮሽ *yyoš* dis. adv. *used in* ሁለትዮሽ pairs, አራትዮሽ in fours etc.

ዮድ *yod* n. iodine

ደ

ደኸየ *dähäyyä* v.i. was impoverished, became poor

ደኻ ደኻ *däha* (*also* ድኻ፣ ደሀ ፣ ድሀ) adj./n poor

—ሰብሳቢ *—säbsabi* n. philanthropist

—አደግ *—addäg* n. orphan

ድኽነት *dəhənnät* n. poverty, penury

አመለ ደኻ *amälä däha* adj. of bad charcter, grouchy, sulky

አደኸየ *adähäyyä* v.t. impoverished

ደለለ *dällälä* v.t. cajoled. flattered

ደላላ *dällala* n. broker, middleman

ደላይ *dällay* n. flatterer

ድለላ *dəllala* n. flattering; brokerage

የድለላ ዋጋ brokerage

ድልል *dəlləl* adj. easily cajoled, flattered, persuadable, gullible

ተደለለ *tädällälä* v.i. was cajoled, flattered, persuaded

መደለያ *mäddäläya* n. bribe

መደለያ *mädälläya* n. blandishment

ደለል *däläl* n. alluvial soil, silt

ደለቀ *dälläqä* v.t. hit with the fist (*especially one's chest in a funeral*). ደረቱን ደለቀ he hit his chest with the fist

ድልቂያ *dəlqiya* n. dance (*with leaps*)

ተደለቀ *täddälläqä* v.i. danced (*with jumps*)

*ደለቀቀ **däläqqäqä*

ደለቀቅ *däläqäq* adj. spoilt (*usually child*)
ደልቃቃ *dälqaqqa* adj. spoilt: lavishly living
መንደላቀቂያ *mändälaqäqiya* n. lavish items
ተንደላቀቀ *tändälaqqäqä* v.i. lived lavishly
ተንደላቃቂ *tändälaqaqi* adj./n. one who lives lavishly, luxuriously
አንደላቀቀ *andälaqqäqä* v.t. lavished, treated s/o generously

ደለበ *dälläbä* v.i got fat (*ox*)
ድልብ *dəlb* adj. fatted (*ox*)
—ሠንጋ —*sänga* n. fatted (*ox*)
አደለበ *adälläbä* v.t. fattened (*ox*)
አድላቢ *in* ሰንጋ–n. one who fattens cattle

ደለኸ *dällähä* v.t. pounded red pepper with garlic, onion, salt and other spices
ድልኸ *dälləh* n. red pepper pounded with garlic, onion, salt and other spices

ደለዘ *dällázä* v.t. pounded soaked pepper; thrashed (*with a stick*); crossed out (*a line*), deleted
ድልዝ *dälləz* n. pounded soaked pepper; deletion

ደለደለ *däläddälä* v.t. leveled (*road, ground*); devided s/t into equal parts; assigned to various places (*pupils in class-rooms, soldiers to different posts etc.*)
ደልዳላ *däldalla* adj. well-built (*person*); well-established (*in life*); well - balanced (*scale*)
ድልደላ *dəldäla* n. distribution, assignment
ድልድል *dələddəl* n. distribution, assignment
ድልድይ *dəldəy* n. bridge
ተደለደለ *tädäläddälä* v.i. was leveled; was divided into equal parts; assigned in various places (*pupils in class-rooms, soldiers to different post*)
ተደላደለ *tädäladdälä* v.i was well settled (*in life*): sat comfortably;
አደላደለ *addäladdälä* v.t. helped s/o to settle well
አስደለደለ *asdäläddälä* v.t. had s/t leveled; had s/t divided into equal parts etc.

ደለፈሰ *däläffäsä* v.t. scooped out in great quantity

ደላ *dälla* v.i. was comfortable, agreeable, happy
ድሎት *dəlot* n. comfort, happiness, luxury, opulence
ድሎተኛ *dəlotäñña* adj/n (*one*) who lives a happy, luxurious, opulent life
ተድላ *tädla* n. pleasure
—ደስታ —*dästa* n. pleasure and happiness

*ደላ *dälla*
አደላ *adälla* v.t. was partial, showed favour, was biased
አድልዎ *adləwo* n. partiality, bias, favouritism
አዳላ *addalla* v.t. was partial, showed favour

ደላላ see ደለለ
ደላጎ *dälago* n. piece of discarded old leather; imbecile
—ለባሽ —*läbaš* adj. ragged

ደመመ *dämmämä* v.i. used with pron. suff. i.e. ደመመው he was astonished
ደማሚ *dämami* adj.- astonishing
ተደመመ *tädämmämä* v.i. was

astonished

ደመረ *dämmärä* v.t. added *(math.)*, summed up

ደመራ *also dämära,* ዳመራ *damära)* n. a heap of poles and sticks to be used as a bonfire at Mascal *cross)* feast

ድመራ *dəmmära* n. addition

ድማሪ *dəmmari* n. s/t that is added to .

ድምር *dəmmər* n. sum, total

ተደመረ *tädämmärä* v.i. was added, summed up; joined with s/o

ተደማሪ *tädämmari* n. s/t that is added to

ተዳመረ *tädammärä* v.i. was added together

ሶስቱ ቁጥሮች ተዳምረው ውጤታቸው ፴፪ ሆነ the three figures were added and the result was 32

አዳመረ *addammärä* v. t. added together

አስደመረ *asdämmärä* v.t. had s/t added toegther

ደመሰሰ *dämässäsä* v.t. destroyed, annihilated, exterminated; stamped out

ድምሰሳ *dəmsäsa* n. destruction, annihilation, extermination

ተደመሰሰ *tädämässäsä* v.i. was destroyed, annihilated, exterminated, stamped out

አስደመሰሰ *asdämässäsä* v.t. had s/t, s/o, destroyed, killed, exterminated

ደመቀ *dämmäqä* v.i. was brightened *(light, colour)*, became lively *(gathering, party, game etc.)*

ደማቃ *dämmaqa* adj. bright *(colour)*

ደማቅ *dämmaq* adj. bright *(colour)*; lively *(party, social occasion)*; gay or loud *(colour)*

ድምቀት *dəmqät* n. brightness *(colour, light)*

ድምቅ *dəmq* adj. bright

አደመቀ *adämmäqä* v.t. enlivened

አድማቂ *admaqi in.* ዘፈን— *zäfän—* n. a good leader of singing

አዳመቀ *addammäqä* v.t. enlivened

አዳማቂ *addamaqi* n. one who sings well

ደመነ *see* ዳመነ

ደመወዝ *dämäwäz* n. salary, wage, *(see also under* ደማ*)*

ደመወዝተኛ *dämäwäztäñña* n. salaried worker, employee

ባለደመወዝ *balädämäwäz* n. salaried worker, employee

ደመደመ *dämäddämä* v.t. finished, ended, terminated; *(a speech)*

ድምደማ *dəmdäma* n. conclusion *(of a speech)*

ድምድማት *dəmdəmat* n. upper parts of walls that are joined to the roof

መደምደሚያ *mädämdämya* n. conclusion *(of speech)*

ተደመደመ *tädämäddämä* v.t. was concluded; finished building the walls of a building

*ደመጠ *see also under* ድምጽ

ድምጥ *dəmţ* n. voice, sound

ድምጣም *dəmţam also* ድምጻም n. a good singer

ድምጠ መልካም *dəmţä mälkam* n. one with a sweet voice

—ሰላላ *—sälula* n. one with a thin voice

—ጎርናና *—gornnana* n. one with hoarse, rough voice

ድምጥማጥ *dəməţəmaţ* n. whereabouts

ድምጥማጡ ጠፋ *dəməţmaţu ţäffa* no one knows his whereabouts

ተደመጠ *tädämmäţä* v.i. was listened

ተደማጭ *tädämmaç* adj. influential, powerful

ተደማመጠ *tädämammäţä* v.i. list

ened to each other

አደመጠ *adämmäṭä* v.t. listened to

አዳመጠ *addammäṭä* v.t. listened to; waited for eagerly

ማዳመጫ *maddamäč̣a* n. receiver *(telephone)*

ደማ *dämma* v.i. bled

ድማት *dəmat* n. bleeding

ደም *däm* n. blood

ደመ መራራ *dämä märara* adj. offensive, allergic *(of person)*, unsympathetic

—መራር *—märrar (same as above)*

—በራድ *—bärrad* adj. cool, unexcited

—ቢስ *—bis* adj. cowardly

—ነፍስ *—näfs* n. instinct

ደመኛ *dämäñña* n. enemy, foe, mortal enemy

ደመ ከልብ *dämä kälb* adj/n *(one)* who dies a dog's death, s/o unprotected by the law

ደመወዝ *dämäwäz* n. salary, wage

ደመግቡ *dämä gəbu* adj. charming, handsome

ደማም *dämam* adj. charming, attractive

ደም መላሽ *dämmälaš* n. avenger *also* ደመላሽ

—መሰለ *—mässälä* v.i. turned red *(from anger)*; reddened

—ማነስ *—manäs* n. anaemia

የ—ስር *yä–sər* n. blood vessel, vein

—ሸተተው *—šättätäw* v.t. became agressive, became blood thirsty

—በደም ሆነ *—bädäm honä* v.i. was stained with blood

—ብዛት *—bəzat* b. high blood pressure

—ተበቀለ *—täbäqqälä* v.t. avenged

—ተቃባ *—täqabbä* v.i. was in enmity with

—አስተኔ *—astne* adj. reddish

—አስተፊ *—astäffi* n. inedible poisonous mushroom

—አፈላ *—afälla* v.t. vexed, provoked

—አፈሰሰ *—afässäsä* v.t. shed blood

—አፈታ *—afätta* v.i. bled continuously

—ወረዳት *—wärrädat* she had her menses *(irregularly)*

—ደም አለው *—aläw* v.i. was infuriated, was blood-thirsty

—ጋን *—gan* n. artery

—ግባት *—gəbat* n. good complexion

—ፍላት *—fəlat* n. blind anger

በደም ፍላት ገደለው he killed him in blind anger

አደማ *adämma* v.i. bled hurt, injured

ደማሚት *dämamit* n. dynamite

ደምበኛ *dämbäñña, also* ደንበኛ *dänbañña* n. client, customer; government soldiers that have settled in hostile areas of Ethiopia; adj. regular, correct

የደምበኛ ልጅ *yädämbäñña ləǧ* n. offspring of a ደምበኛ

ደምበጃን *dämbäǧan* n. demijohn *also* ደንበጃን

ደምባራ *see* ደንበረ

ደምብ *dänb (see also under* ደንብ*)* n. regulation, law, principle, rule, provision, procedure

ደምቦጭ አለ *dämboč̣č̣ alä* v.i. had round cheeks

ደረመን *därämän* n. itching skin disease *(such as dandruff, scurf)*

ደረመናም *därämänam* n. scruffy person

ደረሰ *därräsä* v.i. reached *(a place)*, arrived; happened; was ready *(food etc.)*; reached *(maturity)*

መጽሐፍ— *mäṣhaf* — v.t. wrote

a book

ደረሰለት *därräsällät* v.i. came to his help

ደረሰበት *därräsäbät* v.t. learnt *(found out)*; caught up with; befell him *(bad sense)*

ደረሰኝ *därräsäññ* n. receipt

ደራሲ *därasi* n. author, composer, writer

ደራሲነት *därasinnät* n. authorship

ደራሽ ውሃ *däraš wäha* n. flash flood

ደርሶ መልስ *därso mäls* n. round trip

—ቲኬት *—ticket* n. round-trip ticket

ድራሹ ጠፋ *dərrašu ṭäffa* v.i. no one knows his whereabouts

ድርሰት *dərsät* n. composition, essay, treatise

ድርሳን *dərsan* n. a homily book

ድርስ *dərs* adj. in—እርጉዝ *—ərguz* n. a pregnant woman whose days are near for delivery

መድረሻ *mädräša* n. arrival, time or place of arrival, destination; haven

—ቢስ *—bis* n. tramp, vagrant

ባዕድ መድረሻ *ba'əd—* n. suffix

ድርሽ አይልም *dərrəšš ayləm* he never shows up *(due to bad consequences)*

ተደረሰ *tädärräsä* v.i. was composed, was written *(book, essay etc.)*

ተዳረሰ *tädarräsä* v.i. was distributed, allocated *(to several people)*

አደረሰ *adärräsä* v.t. delivered *(consignment)*; brought forward *(message)*

ጸሎት— *ṣälot* — v.t. said his prayers

አያድርስ *ayadərs* interj. God save! God forbid!

አድራሻ *adrašša* n. address

አዳረሰ *addarräsä* v.t. has distributed, allocated *(to several people)*

አዳራሽ *addaraš* n. hall

የማዘጋጃ ቤት— *yämäzzägağa bet—* n. the Town Hall

ደረሰመ *därässämä* v.t. demolished *(building)*; sunk *(foundation)*

ተደረሰመ *tädärässämä* v.i. was sunk *(foundation)*

ደረቀ *därräqä* v.i. was dry, dried out; was stiffened; was stubborn, obstinate, persistent; got strong *(beverage)*

ደረቅ *däräq* adj. dry, dried; stiff; stubborn, obstinate, persistent; pigheaded

—ሌሊት *—lelit* n. midnight

—ምች *—məčč* n. disease with a severe headache and high temperature

—ትንቢት *—tənbit* n. an imminent prophesy.

—እንጀራ *—ənğära* n. ənğära without wäṭ ወጥ

—ወዝ *—wäz* n. dandruff

—ግንባር *—gəmbbar* adj. unlucky, chanceless

—ጉንፋን *—gunfan* n. dry influenza

—ጦር *—ṭor* n. emergency troop *(without provisions and heavy weapons)*

ደረቆት *däräqot* n. boiled and dried *(barely, wheat, etc. used in brewing ṭäla ጠላ)*

ደረቃ *däraqa* adj. lean, emaciated

ድርቀት *dərqät* n. dryness; stubbornness

ሆድ— *hod—*n. constipation

ድርቅ *dərq* n. drought

—ቀበሌ *—qäbäle* n. drought affected area

ድርቅ ብየ *dərrəqq bəyyä* adj.

obstinate, wilful, stubborn

ድርቅና *dərqənna* n. wilfulness

ድርቆሽ *dərqoš* n. hay; dried *ənğära*

ደረቅ ዐይን *däräq ayn* adj. shameless, immodest *(behaviour)*

ተዳረቀ *tädarräqä* v.t. tried to say or do s/t in vain

ተድረቀረቀ *tädräqärräqä* v.i. was obstinate, wilful

አደረቀ *adärräqä* v.t. dried

አስደረቀ *asdärräqä* v.t. had s/t dried

ደረበ *därräbä* v.t. put s/t on top of s/t ; put on a blanket, a sheet of cloth

ደርብ *därb* n. storey

ድርብ *dərrəb* adj. compound *(word)*; double

—ሰረዝ *—säräz* n. semi-colon (;)

—ኩታ *—kuta* n. double *kuta* ኩታ

ድርብርብ *dərəbrəb* adj. laminated

መደረቢያ *mädärrābiya* n. general name for ኩታ or blanket etc.

ተደረበ *tädärräbä* v.i. concurred, co-operated *(in inflicting harm to s/o)*

ተደራቢ *tädärrabi* n. accomplice

ተደራረበ *tädärarräbä* v.i. came one on the top of the other *(work incident)*; laminated; was redundant

ተደራራቢ *tädärarabi* adj. redundant

ደረበበ *däräbbäbä*

ደርባባ *därbabba* adj. gentle, graceful

ድርብብ *dərbäb* n. measure *(for grain)* not quite full

አንድ ቁና ተድርብብ a measure of grain and a second not quite full

ደርበብ አለ *därbäbb alä* v.i. was gentle, graceful; withdrew from the discussion bashfully

ተንደረበበ *tändäräbbäbä* v.i. was rather full, was rather quiet, calm

አንደረበበ *andäräbbäbä* v.t. caused to become almost full

ደረተ *därrätä* v.t. patched

ድሪቶ *dərito* n. patched material

ድሪቷም *dəritu"am* adj. ragged *(person)*

ድርት *dərrət* adj. patchy

ተደረተ *tädärrätä* v.i. was patched

አስደረተ *asdärrätä* v.t. had torn clothes patched

ደረት *därät* n. chest *(body)*, breast

ደረተ ሰፊ *därätä säfi* adj. strongly-built *(person)*

ደረታም *därätam* adj. *(one)* with a broad chest

ሱቅ በደረቴ *suq bädäräte* n. pedlar

*ደረከከ **däräkkäkä*

ደርካካ *därkakka* adj. glowing *(embers, charcoal)*

ተንደረከከ *tändäräkkäkä* v.i. glowed; fruited well

ደረደረ *däräddärä* v.t. set in rows, arranged in order. aligned; enumerated

በገና— *bägäna—* v.t. played the harp

ድርደራ *dərdära* n. setting in rows

ድርድር *dərdər* n. orderly arrangement

ድርድር *dərəddər* n. negotiation

በገና ድርደራ *bägäna dərdära* n. playing the harp

መደርደሪያ *mädärdäriya* n. shelf

ተደረደረ *tädäräddärä* v.i. was set in rows, was arranged in order

ተደራደረ *tädäradärä* v.i. negotiated

ተደራዳሪ *tädäradari* n. negotiator

ተንደረደረ *tändäräddärä* v.i.

dashed

መንደርደሪያ ሐሳብ — *mändärdäriya hassab* n. main idea

—አረፍተ ነገር — *—aräftä nägär* n. topic sentence

አደራደረ — *addäraddärä* v.t. conducted negotiation

አስደረደረ — *asdärädädärä* v.t. had things set in rows

ደረጀ — *däräǧǧä* v.t. developed *(financially, physically)*, prospered

ድርጁ — *dərəǧǧu* adj. stable *(financially)*

ድርጅት — *dərəǧǧət* n. organization, firm *(business)*, institution

ተደራጀ — *tädäraǧǧä* v.i. was organized, institutionalized

አደራጀ — *adäraǧǧä* v.t. developed, stabilized; made prosperous v.t. organized, institutionalized

አደራጅ ኮሚቴ — *addäraǧ comite* n. organizing committee

*ደረገ — **därrägä*

ድርጊት — *dərggitt* n. action, happening, episode, incident: behaviour

ተደረገ — *tädärrägä* v.i. was done, has happend, occurred

ተደራጊ ግሥ — *tädärragi gəss* n. passive verb

አደረገ — *adärrägä* v.t. has done, did

አድራጊ — *adragi* adj/n *(one)* who does s/t

—ግስ — *—gəss* n. active verb

—ፈጣሪ — *—fäṭari* adj. omnipotent, dictator

አድራጎት — *adragot* n. action, deed

በጎ— — *baggo—* n. philanthrophy, charity

——ድርጅት — *——dərəǧǧit* n. philanthropic institution, charitable institution

አድርጎ — *adrəgo—used (with a preceding adj.)* as

ደህና— — *dähna—well* e.g. ደህና አድርጎ መታው he bit him well

አደራረግ — *addäraräg* n. way, manner of doing, using things

አስደረገ — *asdärrägä* v.t. had s/t done

አስደራጊ ግሥ — *asdärragi gəss* n. causative verb

ደረገመ — *däräggämä* v.t. slammed *(door)*

ድርግም አለ — *dərgəmm alä* v.i. went out suddenly *(fire, light)*: went suddenly dark

ተደረገመ — *tädäräggämä* v.i. slammed *(door)*; went out suddenly *(fire, light)*, became suddenly dark

ደረፎጭ — *däräfoč̣č̣* adj. ugly

ደራ — *därra* v.i. was lively *(market)*; was successful *(marriage)* e.g. ትዳሩ ደርቷል his marriage was/is successful

የደራ ገበያ — *yädärrä gäbäyä* n. lively market

ድሪያ — *dərriya* n. flirtation

ተዳራ — *tädarra* v.t. flirted

*ደራ — **därra*

አደራ — *adärra* v.t. made webs

ድር — *dər* n. web; warp

ድርና ማግ — *dərənna mag* n. warp and weft

——ሆኑ — *——honu* v.i. they lived together in complete harmony

የሸረሪት ድር — *yäšärärit dər* n. spider's web

ደራጎን — *däragon* n. dragon

ደርቡሽ — *därbuš* n. Sudanese; the Mahdi's soldiers

ደርብ — *därb* n. storey, *see also* ደረብ

—ቤት — *—bet* n. storeyed building

ደርዝ — *därz* n. selvedge; hem; ደርዝ ያለው ሰው ነው he is a principled man

ደርግ — *därg* n. committee *(G.)*

ንኡስ— — *nə'us—* n. subcommittee

ደሰመ — *dässämä* v.t. made lunge

ደሰሰ *dässäsä* v.i. became squalid, shabbily *(hut)*

ደሳሳ *däsasa* adj. squalid, shabby *(hut)*

—ጎጆ *goǧǧo* n. a shabby hut

ደሴት [illegible] n. island

ደሴት —*akkäl* n. peninsula

ደስ አለ *däss alä* v.i. was pleasing, attractive, was charming

—ተሰኘ —*täsäññä* v.i. was happy, pleased

—አለው —*aläw* v.i. was contented, pleased

ደስታ *dässəta* n. pleasure, happiness, delight.

በ— *bä—* adv. with pleasure, gladly

ደስተኛ *dässətäñña* adj. joyful, happy

የደስደስ *yädäsdäss* n. charm, attraction

የደስደስ አላት she is charming, attractive

ተደሰተ *tädässätä* v. enjoyed oneself, was pleased, amused oneself

ተደሳች *tädässač* adj. cheerful, enjoying oneself, happy

መደሰቻ ቦታ *mädäsäča bota* n. place of entertainment

አስደሰተ *asdässätä* v.t. amused, made happy, entertained, pleased

አስደሳች *asdässač* adj. enjoyable, pleasing, lovely

*ደሸደሸ *däšäddäšä

ደሸደሽ *däšädäš* adj. loitering, dawdling

አደሸደሸ *adäšäddäšä* v.t. loitered around, bummed around

አደስዳሽ *adäsdaš* n. loiterer, bum

ደቀመዝሙር *däqqämäzmur* n. student, desciple, pl. ደቀ መዛሙርት *däqqä mäzamurt*

ደቀለ *däqqälä* v.t. had an illegitimate child

ዲቃላ *diqala* n/adj. bastard, illegitimate child; child *(euphemistically)*

ድቀላ *dəqäla* n. crossbreeding

ተዳቀለ *tädaqqälä* v.i. was crossbred

አዳቀለ *addaqqälä* v.t. crossbred

ደቀቀ *däqqäqä* v.i. was fine, minute

ደቂቃ *däqiqa* n. minute

ደቃቃ *däqaqa* adj. weak, feeble

ደቃቃ *däqqaqa* adj. fine

ደቃቅ *däqqaq* adj. fine, minute

ተዳቀቀ *tädaqqäqä* v.i. became weak *(body: due to exhaustion, disease)*

አደቀቀ *adäqqäqä* v.t. pounded; made weak *(fatigue, disease)*

አስደቀቀ *asdäqqäqä* v.t. had s/t pounded, powdered

ደቀነ *däqqänä* v.t. put under the tap *(bucket, kettle etc.)*

ድቅን *dəqqən* n. s/t put under the tap *(e.g. bucket, kettle)*

ድቅን አለ *dəqqənn alä* v.i. blocked s/o's way

ተደቀነ *tädäqqänä* v.i. blocked s/o's way

ደቀደቀ *däqäddäqä* v.t. ploughed virgin land; stamped *(repeatedly one's foot)*

ደቅደቂት *däqdäqqit* n. motorcycle

ዱቅዱቅ *duqduq* n. pounded pepper

ድቅድቅ *dəqdəq* n. ploughed virgin land

ተንደቀደቀ *tändäqäddäqä* v.i. produced a sound like that of a motor-cycle

ደቂቃ *däqiqa* *see* ደቀቀ

ደቃ *däqqa* v.t. hit severely

ደቆሰ *däqqosä* v.t. grounded, pounded

ድቁስ *dəqqus* n. powdered pepper

መደቆሻ *mädäqqoša* n. millstone
ደቋቆሰ *däqʷaqqosä* v.t. battered
ደቆስቋሳ *däqosqʷassa* adj. feeble, weak
ተደቆሰ *tädäqqosä* v.i. was powdered

ደበለለ *däbällälä* v.t. threw down *(in wrestling)*
ተደበለለ *tädäbällälä* v.i. was thrown down *(in wrestling)*
ተንደባለለ *tändänballälä* v.i. rolled *(in the dust like a donkey)*
አንደባለለ *andäballälä* v.t. rolled down, threw s/o down

*ደበለበለ *also* ዶቦለቦለ **däbäläbbälä*, **däboläbbolä*
ደበልባላ *däbälballa* adj. oval
ድቡልቡል *dəbulbul* adj. round *(ball-shaped)*
ድብልብል *dəbelbəl* adj. fat and roundish
ተድበለበለ *tädbäläbbälä* v.i. was fat and roundish; rounded out *(figure)*
አድበለበለ *adbäläbbälä* v.t formed into a ball

ደበለቀ *däbälläqä* v.t. mixed; confounded *also* ደባለቀ
ድብልቅ *dəbəlləq* n/adj. mixture, mixed; compound
ደበላለቀ *däbälalläqä* v.t. mixed up, amalgamated
ድብልቅልቅ *dəbləqləq* n. confusion; uproar; anarchism *(confusion)*
ተደበለቀ *tädäbälläqä* v.i. joined others, mixed with others
ተደባለቀ *tädäballäqä* v.i. was mixed; joined others
ተደበላለቀ *tädäbälalläqä* v.i. was thrown into utter confusion, was mixed up; was disorganized
አደባለቀ *addäballäqä* v.t. mixed; confused
አስደበለቀ *asdäbälläqä* v.t. caused to be mixed; caused s/o to join others
አስደባለቀ *asdäballäqä* v.t. caused to be mixed

ደበሎ *däbälo* n. tanned sheep skin *(worn by students of the traditional school and shepherds)*
—ለባሽ *—labaš* adj. of humble parents

ደበሰሰ *däbässäsä* v.i. faded *(colour)*, was dim
ደብሳሳ *däbsassa* adj. faded, dim

*ደበሰበሰ • *däbäsäbbäsä*
ደበስባሳ *däbäsbassa* adj ambiguous
ተድበሰበሰ *tädbäsäbbäsä* v.i. was ambiguous
አድበሰበሰ *adbäsäbbäsä* v.t. made ambiguous

ደበቀ *däbbäqä* v.t. hid, concealed; sheltered *(hide)*
ደባቃ *däbbaqqa* adj. out-of-the-way
ደባቃ ቦታ an out-of-the-way place
ድበቃ *dəbbäqa* n. concealment
ድብቅ *dəbbəq* adj. hidden, concealed; secret
በድብቅ ሄደ he left secretly
ድብብቆሽ *dəbəbbəqoš* n. hide-and-seek
ተደበቀ *tädäbbäqä* v.i. was hidden, concealed; was kept secret
ተደባበቀ *tädäbabbäqä* v.i. hid from each other
አስደበቀ *asdäbbäqä* v.t. had s/t hidden

ደበበ *däbbäbä* v.i. overhung
ድባብ *dəbab* n. large processional umbrella
ደበብ አለ *däbäbb alä* v.i. discoloured

ደበተ *dābbätä* v.t. depressed *(less active)*

ደባች *dābbač* adj. depressing *(less active)*

ድብት አደረገ *dəbbət adärrägä* v.t. made depressed *(inactive)*

ደበነ *dābbänä* v.i.;v.t. was over roasted; was infuriated; was tightly tied

ድባኖ *dəbbano* adj. dwarfish, undersized

ድብን ያለ እንቅልፍ *debbənn yalä ənqəlf* n. heavy, sound sleep

አደበነ *adäbbänä* v.t. infuriated, burnt with fury

ደበናንሳ *däbänansa* n. tanner; blacksmith

ደበዘዘ *däbäzzäzä* v.i. was dim; faded, tarnished *(lost lustre)*

ደብዛዛ *däbzazza* adj. dim, gloomy; blurred *(print)*, vague, indistinct

አደበዘዘ *adäbäzzäzä* v.t faded, blurred

ደበደበ *däbäddäbä* v.t beat, attacked, assaulted

ደባደቦ *däbadäbo* n. stitched rag

ድብደባ *dəbdäba* n. beating, striking, assaulting

ድብዳብ *dəbdab* n. pack saddle *(usually goat or sheepskin)*

ተንደበደበ *tändäbäddäbä* v.i. was full of inflammation *(body)*

ተደበደበ *tädäbäddäbä* v.i. was beaten, attacked assaulted

ተደባደበ *tädäbaddäbä* v.i. beat each other up

ተደባዳቢ *tädäbadabi* adj. quarrelsome, aggressive *(physically)*

ደቡብ *däbub* n. south

ደቡባዊ *däbubawi* n. adj. southern

ደቡብ ምሥራቅ *däbub məsraq* south-east

—ምዕራብ *—mə'rab* southwest

—ዋልታ *—walta* n. South Pole

ደባ *däba* n. intrigue

—ሠራ *—särra* v.t. intrigued

—ዋለ *—walä* v.t. intrigued

አደባ *adäba* v.i lurked

ደባለቀ *see* ደበለቀ

ደባል n. *däbbal* room-mate

ደብር *däbər* n. sanctuary *(church,)* pl. አድባራት *adbarat*

የደብር አለቃ *yädäbər aläqa* n. vicar

ደብተራ *däbtära* n. unordained but highly trained clergyman

ደብተር *däbtär* n. exercise book copy-book

ደብዳቤ *däbdabbe* n. letter

የሹመት— *yäšumät*— letter of accreditation *(diplomatic)*

ደብዛ *däbza* n. trace, whereabouts

ደብዛው ጠፋ *däbzaw ṭäffa* n. all trace was lost of him, no one knows his whereabouts

ደቦ *däbo see also* ጂጊ *and* ወንፈል n. communal labour

•ደቦለቦለ • *däboläbbolä*

ደቦልቧላ *däbolbuʷalla* adj. round

ድቡልቡል *dəbulbul* adj. round, ball-shape, spherical

ተድቦለቦለ *tädboläbbolä* v.i was made round, was rolled *(dough etc.)*

አድቦለቦለ *adboläbbolä* v.t rounded *(made round)*, rolled *(dough etc.)*

ደቦል *däbbol* n. cub

ያንበሳ— *yanbässa*— n. lion-cub

•ደኀረ •*däharä*

ደኀራይ *däharay* n. cantle *(of a saddle)*

አድኃሪ *adhari* n. reactionary

(የ)አድኅሮት ኃይላት *(yä) adhərot hailat* n. reactionary forces

ደነሰ *dännäsä* v.t. danced

ደናሽ *dännaš* n. dancer

ዳንስ *dans* n. dance
—ቤት *—bet* n. dance-hall
ዳንሰኛ *dansäñña* n. dancer
አስደነሰ *asdännäsä* v.t danced with s/o

ደነቀ *dännäqä* v.i with pronominal suffix e.g. ደነቀው was astonished, admired, surprised
ድንቅ *dənq* n/adj wonder, astonishment, marvel; wonderful, astonishing, marvellous
ድንቅ አለው *dənnəq aläw* v.i. was astonished; admired, surprised; was perplexed; was amused
ተደነቀ *tädännäqä* v.i. was astonished, wondered
ተደናቂ *tädännaqi* adj. astonishing, surprising; superb, marvellous
ተዳነቀ *tädannäqä* v.i was exaggerated
አደነቀ *adännäqä* v.t. admired, wondered, was impressed
አድናቂ *adnaqi* n. fan
አድናቆት *adnaqot* n. admiration, appreciation, astonishment
አስደነቀ *asdännäqä* v.t. astonished, surprised
አስደናቂ *asdännaqi* adj. impressive, admirable, magnificent

ደነቀረ *dänäqqärä* v.t. inserted forced in, knocked into, wedged in
ደንቃራ *dänqara* n. stumbling-block, nuisance, obstacle
ተደነቀረ *tädänäqqärä* v.i was inserted; acted as a stumbling block, an obstruction
ነገር ተደነቀረብኝ *nägär tädänäqqäräbbəññ* I was obstructed

ደነቀፈ **dänäqqäfä* *see also* ነቀፈ *and* አነቀፈ
ደንቃፋ *dänqaffa* adj. wobbly, staggering
ተደናቀፈ *tädänaqqäfä* v.i. stumbled, faltered, staggered; was interrupted, obstructed
አደናቀፈ *addänaqqäfä* v.t. made to stumble, interrupted, hampered the movement; thwarted, obstructed

ደነቆለ *dänäqqolä* v.t. poked s/o's eye *(with the finger)*

ደነቆረ *dänäqqorä* v.i. was deaf, was stupid *see also* አደነቆረ
ደንቆሮ *dänqoro* adj. deaf, ignorant, stupid
ድንቁርና *dənqurənna* n. stupidity, ignorance, deafness

ደነበረ *dänäbbärä* v.i. shied, bolted *(of a horse)*; jumped *(startled)*
ደንባሪ *dänbari* adj. shy, skittish
ደንባራ *dänbarra* adj. weak-sighted; excitable, restless
ተደናበረ *tädänabbärä* v.i. groped
አደናበረ *adänabbärä* v.i. caused to bolt *(horse)*
አደናባሪ *addänabari* n/adj. crook ; misleading
አስደነበረ *asdänäbbärä* v.t. caused to bolt *(horse)*; frightened, alarmed, stupefied
አስደንባሪ ወሬ alarming news

ደነባ *dänäbba* v.t. set rules and regulations, established procedures
ደንብ *dänb* n. rule, regulation, procedure, provision
የደንብ ልብስ *yädänb ləbs* n. uniform
ስለደንብ *səlä dänb* n. point of order
በደንብ *bädänb* adv. prop-

erly, perfectly

እንደ ደንቡ *əndä dänbu* as is the rule, according to the rules and regulations

ውስጠ ደንብ *wəsṭä dänb* n. by-law

ደንበኛ *dänbäñña* adj/n. regular, correct; genuine; customer, client

ደንብ ሠራ *dänb särra* v.t. set rules and regulations

—አልባ *—alba* adj. chaotic, disorderly

—አወጣ *—awäṭṭa* v.t. set rules and regulations

በደንቡ መሰረት *bädänbu mäsärät* according to the rules and regulations

ደነበዘ *dänäbbäzä* v.i. was discoloured

ደነበዝ *dänäbäz* adj. weak-minded

ደንባዛ *dänbazza* adj. weak-minded

ተደናበዘ *tädänabbäzä* v.i. was in a smoky haze

ደነነ *dännänä* v.i. slanted *(tree etc.)*

ደናና *dänana* adj. slanting

ደነዘ *dännäzä* v.i. became blunt *(blade)*; was dull *(intellect)*

ደነዝ *dänäz* adj. blunt *(blade)*; dull *(blade, intellect)*

አደነዘ *adännäzä* v.t. dulled; stupified *(with drinks)*

ደነዘዘ *dänäzzäzä* v.i grew numb; was dull *(intellect)*

አደነዘዘ *adänäzzäzä* v.t. made insensitive, stupefied, be numbed

ደነደነ *dänädännä* v.i. was plump, fat; was conceited

ደንዳና *dändanna* adj. plump, fat; sturdy

ደንዳኔ *dändanne* n. large intestine

*ደነገረ • *dänäggärä*

ደንጋራ *dängarra* adj. perturbed, perplexed; puzzled

ተደናገረ *tädännaggärä* v.i. was perturbed, perplexed

አደናገረ *addänaggärä* v.t. perturbed, perplexed, confused, puzzled

አደናጋሪ *addänagari* adj. perturbing, puzzling; fraudulent

አደነጋገረ *addänägaggärä* v.t. threw into utter confusion, disorder

ደነገዘ *dänäggäzä* v.i. became weak-sighted *(due to old age)*

ደንጋዛ *dängazza* adj. weak-sighted

ድንግዝግዝ አለ *dəngəzgəzz alä* v.i. became dusk

ደነገገ *dänäggägä* v.t. instituted, decreed by-law

ድንጋጌ *dənəggage* n. legislative decree, law, regulation

ደነገጠ *dänäggäṭä* v.i. was alarmed, startled, shocked, was taken aback

ደንጋጣ *dängaṭṭa* adj. shy, timid; amenable *(person)*

ድንጉጥ *dənguṭ* adj. shy, timid; amenable *(person)*

ድንጋጤ *dənəggaṭe* n. shock, alarm, fright

ተደናገጠ *tädänaggäṭä* v.i. was alarmed, startled, shocked

አስደነገጠ *asdänäggäṭä* v.t. startled, frightened, terrified, shocked

አስደንጋጭ *asdängač* adj. terrifying, shocking, frightening

ደነጎረ *dänäggorä* v.t. dug up land; brought an irrelevant topic into a discussion

ደንጎራ — *dängora* n. spear headed digging implement, *also* መደንጎሪያ

ድንጉርጉር መንገድ — *dəngurgur mängäd* n. rough road

ደነፈፈ — *dänäffäfä* v.i. was slow, stupid, obtuse

ድንፉፍ — *dənfäf* adj. slow, stupid, obtuse

ደነፋ — *dänäffa* v.i. bragged, boasted, blustered, vaunted

ደንፊ — *dänfi* adj. braggart, boastful, big-mouthed

ድንፋታ — *dənfata* n. bragging, boast

ደን — *dänn* n. forest, woods

ደናማ — *dännamma* adj. forested, wooded

ደንቃራ — *see* ደንቀረ

ደንበጃን — *dänbäğan* n. demijohn *also* ደምበጃን

ደንብ — *see* ደነባ

ደንታ — *dänta* n. care

—ቢስ — *—bis* adj. careless

—የለሽ — *—yälläš* adj./ careless

ደንደሮ — *dändärro* n. stupid fat woman

ደንደስ — *dändäss* n. backbone

ደንደሳም — *dänddässam* adj. strong, vigorous, sturdy *(physical)*

ደንዳኔ — *see* ደነደነ

ደንገላሳ — *dängälasa* n. trot *(horse)*

ደንገሎ — *dängällo* n. animal feed *(bread of impure flour)*

ደንገጡር — *dängäṭur* n. lady-in waiting, lady of the bed-chamber

ደኅና — *dähna* adj. good, safe, well, fine, all right *see also* ዳነ

በደኅና ያግባህ — *bädähəna yagbah* Bon Voyage!

ደኅና ሁን — *—hun* goodbye

—ሰንብት — *—sänbət* bye-bye!

—ቀን — *—qän* peaceful time

—አምሽ — *—amš* Good evening! *(when departing)*

—እደር — *—ədär* Good night

—ክረም — *—kəräm* Goodbye! *(for a longer time)*

—ዋል — *—wal* have a good day!

ደኅንነት — *dähnənnät* n. safety, well-being

የሕዝብ— — *yähəzb*-public security

ደከመ — *däkkämä* v.i. got tired, fatigued; was weak; strove, endeavoured

ደካማ — *däkama* adj. weak, feeble, weary

ድኩም — *dəkum* adj. handicapped pl. ድኩማን *dəkumman*

ድካም — *dəkam* n. exhaustion, weakness

ድክመት — *dəkmät* n. weakness, imperfection

ተደከመ — *tädäkkämä* v.i. exhausted all possibilities

ተዳከመ — *tädakkämä* v. i. became exhausted, was tired out

አደከመ — *adäkkämä* v.t. weakened, tired, fatigued

አዳከመ — *addakkämä* v.t. exhausted, fatigued

አድካሚ — *adkami* adj. exhausting

*ደከደከ — **däkäddäkä*

ተንደከደከ — *tändäkaddäkä* v. i. boiled *(thick liquid e.g polenta, pudding etc.)*

አንደከደከ — *andäkäddäkä* v.t. boiled *(thick liquid,*

ደኸየ — *dähäyyä* v.i. was poor was impoverished

ድኻ — *dəha* n./adj. poor

ድኅነት — *dəhənnät* n. poverty, penury

አደኸየ — *adahäyya* v.t. impoverished

ደወለ — *däwwälä* v.t. rang *bell)*; struck *(a clock)* dialled, called on the telephone; hit strongly

ደወል — *däwäl* n. bell

ደዋይ *däwway* n. bell ringer
ድወላ *dəwwäla* n. ringing
ተደወለ *tädäwwälä* v.i. was rung
አስደወለ *asdäwwälä* v.t. had a bell rung
*ደወረ **däwwärä*
ድውር *dəwwər* n. spool
አዳወረ *adawwärä* v.t wound on the spool
ማዳወሪያ *madawäriya* n. distaff
ደዌ *däwe* n. disease, sickness, illness
—ስጋ *—səga* n. leprosy
—ነፍስ *—näfs* n. sin
ድውይ *dəwwəy* n. midget, dwarf
*ደዘደዘ **däzäddäzä*
ደዘደዝ *däzädäz* n. tramp, wanderer
አደዘደዘ *adäzäddäzä* v.t. wandered, bummed
አደዝዳዥ *adäzdaž* adj. vagabond
ደይን *däyn* n. judgement
እለተ— *əlätä—* n. the Day of Judgement
ደደሆ *dädäho* n. juniper
ደደረ *däddärä* v.i. hardened, solidified
ድድር *dəddər* adj. hard, solid
ደደቀ *däddäqä* v.t. dug up land
ድድቅ *dəddəq* adj. dug up *(land)*
ደደበ *däddäbä* v.i. was dull, stupid, moron
ደደብ *däddäb* adj. dull, stupid, idiot
አደደበ *adäddäbä* v.t. dulled
ደጅ *däğğ* n. outside, out of doors, entrance
ደጃ ሰላም *däğğä sälam* n. gateway of a church compound; place where churchmen eat after services
—ጠኚ *—ṭäñi* n. applicant waiting for a certain post
ደጅ ጥናት *däğğ ṭənat* n. waiting patiently to be employed
ደጅ አዝማች also *däğğ azmač* governor of province, general of an army *(old usage)*
ደጃፍ *däğğaf* n. front of house, entrance, doorway
ደጀን *däğän* n. rearguard
—ጦር *—ṭor* n. rear of an army
ደጃች *däğğač* short form of ደጅ አዝማች *see above*
ደገመ *däggämä* v.t. repeated; recited *(a prayer)*, gave a second time
ደጊመ ፊደል *dägimä fidäl* n. repetitive letters e.g ደበበ, ጠበጠበ
ደግሞ *dägmo* adv. *also* ደግም moreover, besides furthermore, also, again
ዳግመኛ *dagmäñña* adv. again, another time, once again
ዳግማይ *dagmay, also* ዳግማዊ *dagmawi* adj. second *(preceding the name of a king) e.g* ዳግማይ/ዊ ዮሐንስ Yohannis II
ዳግማይ ትንሣይ *dagmay tänsai* n. the Sunday after Easter
ዳግማዊ *dagmawi see* ዳግማይ
ዳግም *dagəm* adj. second
—አረቄ *—aräqi* n. redistilled arrack
ዳግሞሽ *dagmoš* adv. second time
ድጋሚ *dəggami* adj. repeated
በድጋሚ *bädəggami* adv. repeatedly
ድግምት *dəgəmt* n. recitation *(charm)*
ተደገመ *tädäggämä* v.i. was recited
ተደጋገመ *tädägaggämä* v.i. was done, happened repeatedly, became

frequent

ተደጋጋሚ *tädägagami* adj. frequent

አስደገመ *asdäggämä* v.t. had s/t repeated

ደገሰ *däggäsä* v. t. gave a feast, made preparation for banquet

ድግስ *dəggəs* n. banquet, festive meal

ተደገሰ *tädäggässä* v.i. was prepared *(banquet)*; was in store *(of trouble)*

አስደገሰ *asdäggäsä* v.t. had a festive meal prepared

*ደገተ **däggätä*

ዳገት *dagät* n. uphill road, slope

አዳገተ *adaggätä* v.i. was difficult, was hard; was impossible

አዳጋች *adagač* adj. difficult, hard, arduous

ደገነ *däggänä* v.t. pointed *(a gun, an arrow)*

ደጋን *dägan* n. bow for carding cotton, wool

—እግር *—əgər* adj. bandy-legged

ድገና *dəggäna* n. pointing *(a gun etc.)*

ድግን *dəggən* adj. pointed *(gun, arrow)*

—መትረየስ *—mäträyyäs* n. tripoded - machine-gun

—መጋዝ *—mägaz* n. hack-saw

ተደገነ *tädäggänä* v.i. was pointed *(a gun, an arrow)*

ደገኛ ደጋ *see*

ደገደገ *dägäddägä* v.i. was weak-sighted; was weak, emaciated

ደግዳጋ *dägdagga* adj. lean, emaciated, feeble

አደገደገ *adägäddägä* v.t wore the *šämma* down over the shoulder and round the waist as a sign of respect

አደግዳጊ *adägdagi* adj. servile, subservient, obsequious

አስደገደገ *asdägäddägä* v.t. had complete control over others

ደገፈ *däggäfä* v.t. supported *(an opinion, a motion)*, favoured; backed

ደጋፊ *däggafi* n. partisan supporter; backer; benefactor

ደግፍ *däggəf in* ጆሮ ደግፍ *ǧoro däggəf* n. mumps

ድጋፍ *dəgaf* n. support, backing, endorsement

መደገፊያ *mädäggäfiya* n. support, buttress, bracket

ተደገፈ *tädäggäfä* v.i. was supported; leant on; propped oneself against

መደገፊያ *mäddägäfiya* n. arm *(of chair)*, s/t used to lean on

ተደጋገፈ *tädägaggäfä* v.i. supported, backed each other

ተደጋጋፊ *tädägagafi* adj. supporting each other, complementary to each other

አስደገፈ *asdägäfä* v.t. rested

ደጋ *däga* n. highland

ወይና— *wäina* — n. temperate zone

ደገኛ *dägäñña* n. highlander

ደጋን *see* ደገነ

ደግ *dägg* adj. good-hearted, kind, nice

ደጋደግ *däggadägg* adj. good-hearted, generous

ደግ ነው *dägg näw* interj. O.K! good!

—ሥራ *—səra* n. benevolence

ደግነቱ *däggənnätu* adv. luckily, fortunately e.g ደግነቱ አልሞተም luckily he did not die

ደግነት *däggənnät* n.

goodness, kindness

ደጎመ *däggomä* v.t. subsidized

ድጎማ *dəggoma* n. subsidy

መደጎሚያ *mädäggomiya* n. subsidy

ተደጎመ *tädäggomä* v.i. was subsidized

ደጎሰ *däggosä* v.t. decorated the cover of a book

ድጕስ *dəgʷs* n. leather decoration

ድጕሳት *dəggʷsat see* ድጕስ

ደጎባ *däggoba* adj. uneducated and servile; n. pupa, chrysalis *(of locust)*

ደፈረ *däffärä* v.i. was bold, dared; was disrespectful; violated; was courageous

ደፋር *däffar* adj. courageous, bold, fearless, adventurous; disrespectful, uncouth, rude; insolent

ድፍረት *dəfrät* n. courage, boldness; impudence, rudeness, insolence

ተደፈረ *tädäffärä* v.i. was violated, trespassed upon

ተዳፈረ *tädaffärä* v.i. took liberties with, treated with impudence; behaved rudely

ተዳፋሪ *tädafari* adj. impudent, rude, insolent

ተደፋፈረ *tädäfaffärä* v.i. took courage

አደፋፈረ *addäfaffärä* v.t. emboldened, encouraged

አስደፈረ *asdäffärä* v.t. had s/o violate s/t or s/o

ደፈረሰ *däfärräsä* v.i got muddy, became turbid

ድፍርስ *dəfrəs* adj. muddy, turbid

—አይን *—ayn* adj. bloodshot

—ጠላ *—ṭälla* n. unfiltered *ṭälla*

—ጠጅ *—ṭäǧǧ* n. unfiltered *ṭäǧǧ*

አደፈረሰ *addäfäräsä* v.t. stirred up, agitated *(liquid)*; disturbed, put in a state of chaos

ደፈቀ *däffäqä* v.t. dipped, dunked

አረፋ— *aräfa —* v.t. foamed

ድፍቂያ *dəfqiya* n. dipping *(boys in swimming)* cf. ዝፍቂያ

ተደፈቀ *tädäffäqä* v.i. was dipped

ተዳፈቀ *tädaffäqä* v.i. dipped each other *(in swimming)* cf. ተዛፈቀ

አስደፈቀ *asdäffäqä* v.t. had s/o dipped *(in swimming)*

ደፈነ *däffänä* v.t. filled up *(hole in the ground)*; stopped a leak; closed *(eyes)*

ደፈና *däfäna in* በደፈናው *bädäfänaw* adv. in general, by and large

ዳፈን *dafän* n. absence of a clergyman from a service

የዳፈን ገንዘብ *yädafän gänzäb* n. penalty paid by clergyman for absenting himself from a service

ድፍን *dəfən* adj. solid *(not hollow)*; entire

—ቅል *—qəl* n. *(lit.)* solid gourd; stupid, blockhead

—አበሻ *—abäša* n. the entire Ethiopian population

ደፈንፋና *däfänfanna* adj. vague, obscure, ambiguous

ድፍንፍን *dəfənfən* adj. vague, obscure, ambiguous

ዳፍንት *dafənt* n. hemeralopia

ዳፍንታም *dafəntam* n. s/o suffering from hemeralopia: adj. slow, sluggish
ተደፈነ *tädäffänä* v.i. was filled up *(hole in the ground)*, was stopped *(a leak)*; was closed *(eyes)*
ተዳፈነ *tädaffänä* v.i. was choked *(fire)*; did not take place *(church service)*
ተድፈነፈነ *tädfänäffänä* v.i. was kept secret
አዳፈነ *addaffänä* v.t. choked up fire
አዳፍኔ *addafne* n. mortar *(gun)*
አድፈነፈነ *adfänäffänä* v.t made ambiguous *(intentionally)*
አስደፈነ *asdäffänä* v.t.had a hole filled up

ደፈደፈ *däfäddäfä* v.t. mixed beer must with water
ድፍድፍ *dəfədəf* n. beer must
ተንደፋደፈ *tändäfaddäfä* v.i. writhed

*ደፈጠ *däffäṭa*
ደፈጣ *däfäṭa* n. ambush
—ተዋጊ *—täwagi* n. guerrilla fighter
አደፈጠ *adäffäṭä* v.t. lay in ambush, lurked
አስደፈጠ *asdäffäṭä* v.t. caused s/o to be in ambush

ደፈጠጠ *däfäṭṭäṭä* v.t. squashed flat, rolled *(made flat)*
ደፍጣጣ *däfṭaṭṭa* adj. flatly squashed
ድፍጥ *dəfəṭṭ* adj. flatly squashed
—አፍንጫ *—afənča* adj. flat-nosed
ተደፈጠጠ *tädäfäṭṭäṭä* v.t. was flatly squashed

ደፋ *däffa* v.t. spilt *(liquid)* bent *(the neck)* *made* s/o fall flat on his face; fornicated
ዘውድ— *zäwd*–v.t. was crowned
ዳቦ— *dabbo*–v.t. baked bread
አንገቱን— *angätun*–v.t. became meek, became mild and patient
ድፋት *dəfat* n. Ethiopian mark of low pitch of sound
ድፎ ዳቦ *dəfo dabbo* n. large baked loaf of bread
ዱፋ አለ *dāfa alä* v.i. died suddenly ; stooped
ዱፋ ቀና አለ *dāfa qāna alä* v.i. bustled about
ተዱፋ *tädäffa* v.i. was spilt; died suddenly
ተዳፋ መሬት *tädafa märet* n. sloping ground
ተዳፋት *tädāfat* n. slope
አዳፋ *addaffa* v.t. drove *(cattle)* downhill
አድፋፋ *adfaffa* v.t. spent money extravagantly
አድፋፊ *adfafi* adj. extravagant

ደፍ *däf* n. door-sill
ደፍ አለ *däff alä* v.i thudded to the ground

ዱለት *dulät* n. spiced dish of chopped sheep or goat's tripe and liver mixed with butter eaten as a first course; conspiracy

ዱለቻ *dulläčča* n. an old bull

ዱላ *dulla* n. club, stick
ዱለኛ *dulläñña* n. quarrelsome, aggressive, disposed to attack
ዱላ ቀረሽ *dulla qärräš in* ዱላ ቀረሽ ጥል fierce quarrel

ዱልዱም *see* ዱለዱም

ዱር *dur* n. forest, wood
ዱርዬ *durəyye* adj. hooligan, hoodlum, vagabond

ዱሮ *duro also* ድሮ *dəro* adv. in the past, in olden times, long ago

—ዘመን —*zämän* in olden times, long ago, in the past
ዱሽ *duš* n. stump *(of the limb)*.
ዱቄት *duqet, also* ዶቄት *doqet* n. flour, powder
ዱባ *dubba* n. pumpkin, squash
ዱቤ *dube* n. credit
ዱቤ *dubbe in* ዱቤ ባቄላ *dubbe baqela* n. broad beans
ዱብል *dubl adj.* double
ዱብ አለ *dubb alä* v.t. came suddenly; tumbled down
ዱብ ዱብ አለ *dubb dubb alä* v.i. trickled *(tears)*; toddled *(child)*
ዱብ እዳ *dubb əda* n. unexpected incident, a surprise
ዱካ *duka* n. trace, trail, track, footprint
ዱዳ *duda also* ድዳ *dəda* adj. dumb, mute
ዲቁና *see under* ዲያቆን
ዲቃላ *see under* ዶቀለ
ዲብ *dib* n. knoll
ዲናሞ *dinamo* n. dynamo
ዲናሚት *dinamit* n. dynamite
ዲካ *dikka* n. limit
ዲያብሎስ *diablos* n. devil
ዲዳ *dida* adj. dumb, mute, also ዱዳ ፣ ድዳ
ዲግሪ *digri* n. degree *(diploma)*
ዲፕሎማ *diploma* n. diploma
ዳለጠ *dalläṭä* v.i. slipped, slided
አዳለጠ *adalläṭä* v.t. slipped, slided
ዳለቻ *daləčča* adj. grey
ዳሌ *dalle* n. hips *(woman's)*
ዳልጋ አንበሳ *dalga anbäsa* n. caracal
ዳመነ *dammänä* v.i. was cloudy
ዳመና *dammäna* n. cloud
ዳመናማ *damännamma also* ዳመናም *dammänam* adj. cloudy
ዳመጠ *dammäṭä* v.t crushed *(with a roller)*, crushed cotton to separate the seeds
ዳመጦ *damäṭo* n. cotton whose seeds are separated
ዳምጠው *damṭäw* n. road-roller
መዳመጫ ብረት *mädamäča bərät* n. metal rod used to separate seeds from cotton
—ድንጋይ —*dəngay* n. smooth flat stone used for crushing cotton to separate seeds
ተዳመጠ *tädämmäṭä* v.i. was crushed *(with a roller)*
ዳማ *dama* n. checkers
ዳማ ፈረስ *dama färäs* n/adj reddish-brown horse; bay
ዳምጠው *see* ዳመጠ
ዳሞትራ *damotəra* n. big venomous kind of spider
ዳረ *darä* v.t. gave s/o in marriage, married, married off
ተዳረ *tädarä* v.i. was married.
ትዳር *tədar* n. married life, home life
—ያዘ —*yazä* v.t. was married, started a home
—ፈታ —*fätta* v.t. was divorced
ባለትዳር *balä tədar* n. married
ዳረገ *darrägä* v.t. donated
ዳረጎት *darägot* n. donation
ድርጎ *dərgo* n. endowment
ተዳረገ *tädarrägä* v.i. was donated
ዳሩ ግን *daru gən* adv. but, nonetheless, however
ዳር *dar* n. border, bank *(of lake, river)*, edge
ዳራገር *daragär* n. border countries, frontier
ዳርቻ *darəčča* adv. edge, end
ከዳር እዳር *kädar ədar* from end to end; throughout, entirely

ዳር ዳር አለ dar dar alä v.i. beat around the bush, hesitated

ዳርና ዳር darənna dar two extreme ends

ከዳር ዳር kädar dar from all sides, *also* ከዳር እስከዳር

ዳሰ dasä v.t. tramped upon, stamped s/t out

ተዳሰ tädasä v.i. was tramped upon, was stamped out

ዳሰሰ dassäsä v.t. touched; felt with the hands; caressed

ዳስ das n. booth, shelter *(hut)*

ዳሸቀ daššäqä v.i. was stamped, was stamped out

•ዳበለ • dabbälä n.

ደባል däbbal room-mate

ተዳበለ tädabbälä v.i. roomed with s/o

አዳበለ addabbälä v.t. let s/o room with s/o

ዳበረ dabbärä v.i. thrived, was enriched

አዳበረ adabbärä v.t. enriched, fertilized *(soil,* developed *(muscle)*

ማዳበሪያ madabäriya n. fertilizer

ዳበሰ dabbäsä v.t. touched lightly, felt *(touch),* felt one's way, groped

ዳበሳ dabbäsa n. groping

ደባበሰ däbabbäsä v.t. caressed, fondled, patted *(child)*

ዳቢት dabit n. sirloin

ጎድን ተዳቢት godən tädabit n. sirloin with ribs

ዳባ dabba n. yellowish tanned cow skin *(worn by monks and hermits etc. as an over coat)*

ባለዳባ balädabba adj. / poor, *usually used together with* በለዳባና ባለከባ the poor and the rich

ዳቦ dabbo n. bread *(of wheat),* loaf of bread

—ቆሎ —qollo n. small round dough balls roasted and eaten as provisions on a journey

ዶሮ— doro—n. large loaf of bread baked with chicken stew

ዳነ danä v.i. was cured, was healed, recovered, was saved

መድሃኒት mädhanit n. medicament; medicine; remedy; cure; drug; poison

የሚያስተኛ— yämiyastäñña- n. anesthetic

መድሃኒተኛ mädhanitäñña n. healer; poisoner *(person)*

መድሃኒታም mädhanitam n. poisoner

መድሃኒት ቀመሰ mädhanit qämmäsä v.t. took medicine; took a purgative

—ቀማሚ —qämmami n. pharmacist, druggist

—ቤት —bet n. pharm- drugstore

መድኃኔ ዓለም mädhane aläm n Saviour of the W *(Christ)*

መድን mädən n. guarantee, security; bail

የመድን ድርጅት yämädən dəraǧǧət n. insurance *(company)*

አዳነ adanä v.t. saved, rescued; cured, healed; redeemed

ዳተኛ datäñña adj. slack, remiss

ዳንሰ *see* ደነሰ

ዳንኪራ dankira n. dance *(hitting the ground with the feet),* war-dance

ዳንዴ dande adj. strong and stupid

ዳንግሌ dangəlle n. ram

ዳኘ daññä v.t judged, arbitrated

ዳኛ dañña n. judge; umpire

ዳኝነት daññənnät n. arbitration, judgeship, judgement

(*ability to judge*)

ዳኛ ረገጠ *daňňa räggäṭä* court defiance

—ተሰየመ *—täsäyyämä* v.i. acted as a judge

አጥቢያ ዳኛ *aṭbiya daňňa* n. Justice of the Peace

የውሃ ወራጅ ዳኛ *yäwəha wärag daňňa* n. temporary arbitrator

የዘመድ ዳኛ *yäzämäd daňňa* n. family arbitrator

ተዳኘ *tädaňňä* v.i. was brought to court (*person*)

ዳከረ *dakkärä* v.i. worked hard, fatigued

ዳክዬ *dakkəyye* n. duck

ዳኸ *dahä* v.i. crawled baby), walked on all fours (*like a baby*)

ዳዊት *dawit* n. David; the **Psalms of David**

—ደገመ *—däggämä* v.t. recited the psalter of David

መዝሙረ— *mäzmurä—* n. **Psalms** of David

ዳዋ *dawwa* n. undergrowth, shrub

—ለበሰ *—läbbäsä* v.t was full of shrubs

—በላው *—ballaw* v.t. was covered with shrubs, sank into oblivion

ዳውላ *dawəlla* n. twenty *qunnas (grain measure appr.* 100 *kg.)*

ዳዴ *dade* n. toddling (*child*)

—አለ *—alä* v.i. toddled (*child*)

ዳዶ *dado* n. nut

*ዳገተ **daggätä*

ዳገታም *dagätam* adj. sloping, hilly

ዳገት *dagät* n. slope, uphill road, ascent

አዳገተ *adaggätä* v.i. was difficult, was impossible

አዳጋች *adagač* adj. difficult, impossible

(*understanding*)

ዳጠ *daṭä* v.t. ran over, rolled over s/t; mashed (*vegetables etc.*)

ዳጣ *däṭa* n. slippery

ዳጥ *daṭ* n. slippery

ተዳጠ *tädaṭä* v.i. was run over *e.g.* በመኪና ተዳጠ he was run over by a car

አዳጠ *adaṭä* v.t. caused to slip

ዳጨ *daččä* v.t. ran over

ዳፈነ *see* ደፈነ

ዳፋ *dafa* used as በ...ዳፋ *bä... däfa* prep. because of, due to someones fault; በርሱ ዳፋ ተቀጣሁ I was punished due to his fault

ዳፍንት *däfnət* n. hemeralopia (*eye disease that causes visibility at night difficult*) *see also* ደፈነፈነ

ዳፍንታም *dafəntam* n. s/o suffering from hemeralopia; adj. slow, sluggish

ድል *dəl* n. victory, triumph

—ሆነ *—honä* v.i. was conquered, was defeated

—መታ *—mätta* v.t. defeated, vanquished, overcame, subdued

—ነሳ *—nässa see* ድልመታ

—አደረገ *—adärrägä see* ድል መታ and ድል ነሳ

ባለድል *balädəl* adj. victorious, triumphant

ድል ያለ *dəll yalä used with* ድግስ *dəggəs* n. sumptuous banquet

ድልኸ *dəlləh* n. sauce of spiced pepper

ድልድይ *see* ደለደለ

ድመት *dəmmät* n. cat

—ዓይን *—ayn* adj. blond-eyed

የድመት ግልገል *yädəmmät gəlgäl* n. kitten
ድንቡሎ *dənbullo* adj. pretty *(girl)*; 5 cents *(in rural areas)*
ድምቡሽ *dəmbuš* adj. plump *(woman)*
ድምቡሼ ገላ *dəmbušše gäla* adj. fat in a pleasant-looking way
ድምቡጭ አለ *dəmbuč̣č̣ alä* v.i. was plump, was rounded *(cheeks)*
ድምቢጥ *dəmbiṭ* n. type of small bird *(sylvia lugens)*
ድምብላል *dəmbəlal* n. coriander
ድምድማት *see* ደመደመ
ድምጥማጥ *dəmaṭmaṭ used as* ድምጥማጡ ጠፋ *dəmṭmatu ṭäffa* was annihilated, destroyed completely, disapeared completely
ድምጽ *dəmṣ* n. sound voice, tone; vote
—ማጉያ *—maguya* n. loud-speaker
—ሰጠ *—säṭṭä* v.t. voted
ድምፈፍ *also* ድንፈፍ see ደነፈፈ
ድሪ *dəri* n. necklace, string *(of pearls)*
ድሪቶ *see* ደረተ
ድራማ *dərama* n. drama
ድር *dər see also* ድሬ n. warp; web
ድርና ማግ *dərənna mag* n. warp and weft ድርና ማግ ሆኑ they agreed completely, they lived in complete harmony
ድርስ *see* ደረሰ
ድርብ *see* ደረበ
ድርጎ *see* ዳረገ
ድርጭት *dərč̣č̣ət* n. quail *(alanda cristata)*
ድሮ *dəro also* ዱሮ *duro* adv. in the past, formerly, in olden times, previously, long ago, already
ድስት *dəst* n. saucepan *(clay)*
ብረት— *bərät—* n. saucepan *(metal)*
ሰታቴ— *sätate—* n. large saucepan *(clay)*
አፈድስት ብርሌ *afädəst bərəlle* n. small bell-mouthed flask *(used for drinking mead and beer)*
ድቡላ *see* ደቡላ
ድቡሽት *dəbbušt* n. sand
ድብ *dəbb* n. bear *(animal)*
ድባብ *see* ደበበ
ድብኝት *dəbəññət* n. small cylindrical granary made of mud, earth
ድንበር *dənbär also* ድምበር *dəmbär* n. boundary, borderline, border
ድንበርተኛ *dənbärtäñña*, ድንበረተኛ *also dəmbärätäñña* n. one whose land is adjoining s/o's land
ድንቡሼ *see* ድምቡሽ
ድንቢጥ *see* ድምቢጥ
ድንች *dənnəč̣č̣* n. potatoes
ስኳር— *səkʷar—* n. sweet potatoes
ድንክ *dənk* n. dwarf; midget
—አልጋ *—alga* n. couch
ድንክዬ *dənkəyyä* adj. dwarfish
ድንኳን *dənkʷan* n. tent
—ተከለ *—täkkälä* v.t. pitched a tent
ድንገት *dəngät* adv. suddenly, by chance; perhaps, in case
ድንገተኛ *dəngätäñña* adj. sudden, unexpected; emergency
በድንገት *bädəngät* adv. suddenly, accidentally, unexpectedly
ድንጉላ ፈረስ *dəngulla* n. stallion
ድንጉል *dəngul* n. worker bee
ድንጋይ *dəngay, also* ድንጊያ *dängiya* n. stone
—ልብሱ *—ləbsu* n. tortoise
—ራስ *—ras* adj. stupid

—ሽበት —*šəbät also* የድንጋይ ሽበት *yädəngay šəbat* n. moss
—ወቃሪ —*wäqari* n. stone-mason
—ከሰል —*käsäl* n. coal
(የ)—ዘመን *(yä)—zämän* n. stone age
(የ) ኩላሊት— *(yä) kulalit*— n. stone in the kidney
በሀ— *bäha*— n. soapstone
ባሪያ— *bariya* — n. black stone
ወፍጮ— *wäfčo* — n. millstone
ድንግል *dəngəl* n. virgin
ድንግላይ *dəngəlay* adj/n celibate
ድንግላዊ *dəngəlawi* adj/n celibate
ድንግልና *dəngələnna* n. celibacy
ድኝ *dəññ* n. sulphur
ድኩላ *dəkkula* n. bushbuck *(tragelaphus scriptus)*
ድኻ *see* ደኸየ
ድው አለ *dəww alä* v.i. was perplexed, was in a stupor
ድዳ *dəda, also* ዱዳ adj. dumb, mute *(unable to speak)*
ድድ *dədd* n. gum *(of teeth)*
ድዳም *dəddam* n. one with protruding gums
ድድቅ *see* ደደቀ
ድጅኖ *dəǧano* n. crowbar *(used for moving out stones)*
ድጋፍ *see* ደገፈ
ድግ *dəg* n. long cloth band *(worn wrapped tightly around the waist)*, sash
ድግር *dəgər* n. ploughshare
ድግስ *see* ደገሰ
ድጓ *dəguʷa* n. Ethiopian hymn book
ድፋርሳ *dəfarsa* n. defassa waterbuck, common waterbuck *(kobus defassa, kobus ellipsiprymnus)*
ድፎ ድፎ *see* ደፋ
ዶለ *dolä* v.t. inserted, put in *(feeling)*
ዶለተ *dollätä* v.i. conspired, plotted, intrigued
*ዶለዶለ * *doläddolä*
ዶልዷላ *dolduʷalla* adj. generous
ዶልዷሌ *dolduʷalle* adj. generous
አባ— *abba*—adj. generous
ተንዶለዶለ *tändoläddolä* v.i. gushed
ዶለዘ *doläz* adj. dead *(to all feeling)*
ዶለዶመ *doläddomä* v.i. became blunt *(point, sharp edge)*; was dull
ዶልዷማ *dolduʷamma* adj. blunt *(point, sharp edge)*, dull *(pencil)*
ዱልዱም *duldum* adj. blunt, dull
አዶለዶመ *adoläddomä* v.t, made blunt, dull
ዶማ *doma* n. pickaxe
ዶመኛ *domäñña* n. one who uses a pickaxe for cultivating land *(not a plough)*
ዶሮ *doro* n. hen, chicken
—ወጥ —*wäṭ* n. stew made with chicken
—ዳቦ —*dabbo* n. large loaf of raised bread baked with chicken stew
—ጩኸት —*čuhät* n. early in the morning, cock-crow, dawn, day-break
ቄብ— *qeb*—n. pullet
አውራ— *awra*—n. cock, rooster
ዶቃ *doqa* n. glass bead
ዶቄት *doqet, also* ዱቄት *duqet* n. flour, powder
የፉርኖ— *yäfurno*— n. white flour
ዶኬ *dokke* n. ordinary powdered legume stew, *also* ዶዮ
ዶክተር *doktär, also* ዶክቶር *doktor* n. doctor, medical doctor, physician
ዶዮ *oyyo* n. ordinary powdered legume stew
ዶጮ *doččo* n. small glass or clay container

ዶፋር — *dofär* n. idoform

ዶፈዶፈ — *dofäddofä* v.t. became fat

ዶፈዶፍ — *dofädof* adj. fattish

ዶፍዷፋ — *dofdu"affa* adj. fattish

ዶፍ — *dof* used as ዶፍ ዝናብ

—ዝናብ — *—zənab* n. heavy rain

ጀ

*ጀለ — **ǧälä*

ጅላንጅል — *ǧəlanǧǧəl* adj. imbecile stupid, silly

ጅላጅል — *ǧəlaǧəl* adj. naive, silly

ጅል — *ǧəl* fool, imbecile, stupid, foolish, naive

ጅልነት — *ǧələnnät* n. stupidity, silliness, naivety

ተጃጃለ — *täǧaǧalä* v.i. behaved naively, stupidly

አጃጃለ — *aǧǧaǧalä* v.t. made fun of, ridiculed

*ጀለጀለ — **ǧäläǧǧälä*

ተንጀላጀለ — *tänǧälaǧǧälä* v.i. was poorly dressed, shabby

ጀለጠ — *see* ዠለጠ

ጀሌ — *ǧäle* n. combatant without firearms

ጀልባ — *ǧälba* n. small boat

ጀመረ — *ǧämmärä* v.t. started, commenced

ጀማሪ — *ǧämari* n. beginner; novice

ከ...ጀምሮ — *kä..ǧämməro* beginning from, since

ጅምር — *ǧəmmər* adj. started

በጅምር የቀረ — adj. incomplete

መጀመሪያ — *mäǧämmäriya* n. beginning, start, first, front

ተጀመረ — *täǧämmärä* v.i. was started

አስጀመረ — *äsǧämmärä* v.t. had s/t started

ጀምብ — *ǧämb* n. one of two parts of loads of an animal

ጀምበር — *ǧämbär also* ዠምበር n. sun

ጀረገገ — *ǧärägägä also* ዠረገገ v.t. stripped off *(fruits from branches)*

ተንጀረገገ — *tänǧäräggägä* v.i. bore abundantly *(fruit)*, bore a heavy crop

አንጀረገገ — *anǧäräggägä* v.t. bore abundantly *(fruit)*, bore a heavy crop *(fruit tree)*

ጀሶ — *ǧässo* n. gypsum

ጀርመን — *ǧärmän* n. German Germany, German Language

ጀበርቲ — *ǧäbärti* n. name given by Arabs to Ethiopian Moslems

ጀበና — *ǧäbäna* n. kettle, coffee pot

ጀበደ — *ǧäbbädä also* ዠበደ v.t. struck *(hit)* s/o with a stick

ጀባ — *ǧäba* word used when offering s/t to s/o, especially cup of coffee

ጀብዱ — *ǧäbdu* n. act of bravery, adventure, heroic act

ጀብደኛ — *ǧäbdäñña* adj. adventurous

ጀቦነ — *ǧäbbonä* v.t. covered s/o or oneself with a piece of cloth; muffled

*ጀነነ — **ǧännänä*

ጀናና — *ǧänana* adj. extremely proud

ጅንን — *ǧənnən* adj. proud, conceited

ተጀነነ — *täǧännänä* v.i. became proud, conceited

ጀንዲ *ǧändi* n. tanned hide of an ox or a cow *(used for sleeping on)*

ገጀነ *gäǧǧänä* v.i. was courageous,

ጀግና *ǧägna* adj. courageous, brave, hero gallant, valourous,

ጀግንነት *ǧägnənnät* n. courage bravery, valour

አጀገነ *aǧǧäggänä* v.t. emboldened, put heart to, made a man of

ጁህ *ǧuh* n. cloth made of soft wool

ጂኦሜትሪ *ǧiometry* n. geometry

ጂኦሜትራ *ǧiometra* n. land-surveyor

ጂኦግራፊ *ǧiografi* n. geography

ጂጌ *ǧige* n. communal labour

ጃል *ǧal* *exclamatory word marking agreement, joy, or surprise e.g* ንገረኝ እንጂ ጃል Oh! please tell me እንዲህ ነው እንጂ ጃል that is marvellous! ምንው ጃል! what is going around!

ጃርት *ǧart* n. porcupine

ጃንሆይ *ǧanhoy* n. title used in addressing a monarch

ጃንደረባ *ǧandarāba* n. eunuch

ጃንጥላ *ǧanṭəla* n. parasol, umbrella, parachute

ጃኖ *ǧano* n. tunic with broad red band *(näṭäla with broad red band)*

ጃኬት *ǧakket* n. jacket

ጃዊ *ǧawwi* n. piece of red cloth

ጃውሳ *ǧawwusa* n. highway robber, a lawless-man; uncouth person

ጃጀ *ǧaggä* v.i. became senile

ጃገሬ *in* ጋሻጃገሬ *gašša ǧagre* n. body-guard; shield-bearer

ጃፓን *ǧappan* n. Japan

ጃፓናዊ *ǧappanawi* n/adj. Japanese

ጄኔራል *ǧeneral* n. general

ጅማት *ǧəmmat* n. sinew, nerve, tendon

ጅማታም *ǧəmmatam* adj. skinny, bony

ጅምሩክ *ǧəmruk also* ጉምሩክ n. custom house

ጅምናስቲክ *ǧəmnastik* n. gymnastics, athletics

ጅራፍ *ǧəraf* n. plough-man's whip

ጅብ አለ *ǧəbb alä also* እጅብ አለ *əǧǧib alä* v.i. agglomerated, clustered

ጅብ *ǧəb* n. hyena

—አፍ *—af* n. s/o having a large mouth

ጅንጀሮ *see also* ዝንጀሮ *ǧənǧäro zənǧäro* monkey, ape, baboon

ጅንፎ *ǧənfo, also žənfo* ዥንፎ n. metal protection on the butt of a spear, a walking- stick

ጅዋጅዌ *ǧəwwaǧəwwe* n. swing

ጅዋጅዌ ተጫወተ *ǧəwwaǧəwwe täčawwätä* v.i. played on the swing, swung

ጅው *used as* ጅው አድርጎ ጠጣ *ǧəww adrəgo ṭäṭṭa* v.t. gulped down

—ያለ ገደል *—yalä gädäl* n. precipice

ጅጊ *ǧəgi* n. communal labour *cf.* ወንፈል፣ ደቦ

ጅግራ *ǧəgra* n. guinea hen

ጆሮ *ǧoro* n. ear ; handle of *(a cup)*

—ሰጠ *goro säṭṭä* v.i. listened attentively

—ደግፍ *—däggəf* n. mumps

—ግንድ *—gənd* n. area around the ears

—ጠቢ *—ṭäbbi* n. informer

ለምለም— *lämläm—* n. lobe

ጆንያ *ǧonəyya* n. sack

ጆፌ አሞራ *ǧoffe amora* n. vulture

ጆፍጆፌ *ǧofǧoffe* n. hair-tuft

ገሀነም gähannäm n. Gehenna, Hell

ገሀነመ እሳት gähannämä əsat n. inferno, Hell

ገሀድ gähad adj. open, clear, visible

ገሀዱ ዓለም gähadu aläm the visible world

በገሀድ bäghad adv. openly, evidently

*ገለለ *gällälä

ገለልተኛ gälältäñña adj. aloof secluded, isolated

—አገሮች —agäročč n. neutral states

ገለልተኛነት gälältäññannät n. neutrality, seclusion

ግል gəll adj. private exclusive; personal

በግል bägəll adv. privately

በየግል bäyyägəll adv. individually

ግለኛ gəllañña adj. individualistic, unsociable

ግላዊ gəllawi adj. private

—ሀብት —habt n. private property

ገለል አለ gäläll alä v.i. moved aside, stood aside, gave way; avoided situations

—አደረገ —adärrägä v.t. made to give way, got rid of; segregated

ተገለለ tägällälä v.i. was segregated, was made to give way; was excluded

አገለለ agällälä v.t. kept in the background, secluded, got rid of

ራሱን— rasun— v.t. secluded oneself, kept onself aloof, avoided situations

ገለማ gälämma v.i. became rancid *with pron. suff.*

ገለማኝ gälämmaññ I have had enough, I got fed up

ገለሞተ gälämmotä v.i. became a widower

ጋለሞታ galämota n. a widow

ግልሙትና gəlmutənna n. unmarried life *(after divorce)*

አገለሞተ agälämmotä v.t. gave shelter to a widow

ገለበ gälläbä v.t. denudated, stripped off *(s/o's or ones clothes)*

ግልብ gəlb adj. superficial

ግልብነት gəlbənnät n. superficiality

ገለበጠ gäläbbäṭä v.t. turned upside-down; poured liquid from one container to another; copied *(book)*; overthrew; turned over *(a page)*

ገልባጭ *in* አፈር ገልባጭ äfär gälbač dump-truck

ግልባጭ gəlləbbač n. copy *(of a book, a letter, a passage etc.)*

ተገለበጠ tägälälbbäṭä v. i. was turned upside-down, was overthrown, was copied *(book)*; was turned over, was tipped over; was capsized *(boat etc.)*

ተገለባበጠ tägäläbabbäṭä v. i. turned over *(changed position)*; changed one's mind *(frequently)*

ተገላበጠ tägälabbäṭä v.i. turned this way and that

አገላበጠ aggälabbäṭä v.t. turned this way and that; leafed through *(a book)*; scrutinized

ጉዳዩን በጥን ቃቄ አገላ ብጦ አየ he scrutinized the matter carefully

አስገለበጠ *asgäläbbäṭä* v.t had a book, article etc. copied

ገለባ *gäläba* n. straw, chaff, hull *(of peanut etc.)*; adj. shallow *(not serious)*

ገለታ *gäläta* n. favour, gratitude

—ቢስ *—bis* adj. ungrateful

*ገለወደ * *gäläwwädä*

ገልዋዳ *gälwadda* n. loafer

ተንገላወደ *tängälawwädä* v.i. loafed about

*ገለደመ * *gäläddämä*

ገልድም *gəldəm* n. skirt *(worn by men; similar to a kilt)*

አገለደመ *agäläddämä* v.t. wore a skirt

ገለጀጀ *gäläǧǧäǧä* v.i. became senile

ገለጀጅ *gäläǧäǧ* adj. senile; awkward

ገልጃጃ *gälǧaǧǧa* adj. senile; awkward

ተንገላጀጀ *tängälaǧǧäǧä* v.i. became senile; became awkward

*ገለገለ * *gäläggälä*

ግልጋሎት *gəlgalot* n. service

ተገለገለ *tägälägälä* v. i. was served; made use of, employed

ተገልጋይ *tägälgay* n. clientele

አገለገለ *agällägälä* v.t. served, rendered service; was valid, was in use

አገልጋይ *agälgay* n. servant

አገልግሎት *agälgəlot* n. service; use, benefit

አገልግል *agälgəl* n. a round basket for carrying food etc, during a journey

ያገለገለ *yagäläggälä* adj. second-hand, used *e.g* ያገለገለ መኪና second-hand car

ገለጠ *also* ገለጸ *gällätä* v.t. unveiled, uncovered; explained, opened *(a book)*

ገለጣ *also* ገለጸ *gäläṣa*, *gäläṣa* n. explanation

ገላጣ *gälaṭa* adj. open *(space without trees)*

ገላጭ *gälač in* ገላጭ ድርሰት *—gälač dərsät* n. expository composition

ግላጭ *in* በግላጭ *bägəllač* adv. openly

የደመና— *yädämmäna gəllač* n. clear sky *(after being cloudy)*

ግልጥ *gəlṭ* adj. clear, open; sincere *also* ግልጽ ግልጥነት *or* ግልጽነት *gəltənnät*, *gələṣənnät* n, clarity; sincerity

መግለጫ *mägläča* n. statement, declaration, communique;explanation, demonsration

—ሰጠ *—säṭṭä* he made a statement, he declared

—አወጣ *—awäṭṭa* he issued a statement

ገላለጠ *gälallätä* v.t. disclosed *(a secret)*; exposed

ተገለጠ *tägällätä* v.i. was unveiled, uncovered; was explained; was opened *(book)*; was disclosed;was declared

ተጋለጠ *tägallätä* v.i. was exposed *(by revealing the guilt or wrong doing)*; was exposed*(uncovered)*

አጋለጠ *aggallätä* v.t. exposed *(a plot,wrong doing)*

*ገለፈተ *gäläffätä*

ገለፈት *gäläfät* n. bark, rind

ገለፈታም *gäläfätam* adj. dirty,

untidy

ገለፈጠ *gäläffäṭä* v.i. smirked

ገለፈጥ *gäläfäṭ* n. smirker

ገልፋጭ *gälfač̣* n. smirker

ገለፈፈ *gäläffäfä* v.t. peeled, stripped

ግልፋፊ *gəläffafi* n. peel

ተገለፈፈ *tägäläffäfä* v.i. peeled, was stripped

ገላ *gäla* n. body

ገላ ነክ *gäla näkk* n. underwear

የገላ ሳሙና *yägäla samuna* n. toilet-soap

ገላመጠ *gälammäṭä* v.t. glared at ,stared fiercely

ግልምጫ *gəlməč̣č̣a* n. angry, fierce look

ተገለማመጠ *tägälämammäṭä* v. i. looked here and there *(due to fear)*

ተገላመጠ *tägälammäṭä* v.i. glared at, stared fiercely; looked here and there *(due to fear)*

*ገላታ * *gälatta*

ገልቱ *gältu* adj. unskilled, ignorant, lay

ተንገላታ *tängälatta* v.i. was maltreated, suffered *(hardship)*, was handled roughly

አንገላታ *angälatta* v.t. maltreated, handled roughly

እንግልት *əngələtt* adj. maltreated

ገላገለ *gälaggälä* v.t. intervened between two quarreling, fighting people; relieved from danger; arbitrated

ገላጋይ *gälagay* n. peacemaker

ግልግል *gələggəl* n. peacemaking; relief

መገላገያ ገንዘብ *mäggälagäya gänzäb* n. arbitration fee

ተገላገለ *tägälaggälä* v.i. was arbitrated; delivered (a child) ልጅዋን ያለ ችግር ተገላገለች she delivered her child without difficulty

ገል *gäl* n. piece of broken earthenware

ገመለ *gämmälä* v.t. baked a large loaf of unleavened bread

ግምል *gəmməl* n. large unleavened bread

ገመል *also* ግመል n. camel

ገመሰ *gämmäsä* v.t. divided into two; ploughed for the first time

ገመሳ *gämäsa* n. ploughing for first time

ገሚስ *gämis* adj. half

ግማሽ *gəmmaš* adj. half

ተገመሰ *tägämmäsä* v. was divided, split into two

ተጋመሰ *tägammäsä* v.i. was halfway finished

አስገመሰ *asgämmäsä* v.t had land ploughed for the first time; had divided into two

አጋመሰ *aggammäsä* v.t. reached halfway; did half of s/t

አጋማሽ *aggamaš* adj/n. half, middle; halfway

ገመተ *gämmätä* v.t. estimated, evaluated, rated; valued, assessed; assumed, presumed

ዝቅ አድርጎ— *zəqq adərgo*—v.t. underestimated

ከፍ አድርጎ— *käf adərgo*—v.t. overestimated

ገማች *gämmač* n. evaluator,

ግምት *gəmmət* n. estimation, assessment, evaluation; guess, assumption

በግምት *bägəmmət* adv. approximately, roughly

ያለግምት *yalägəmmət* without estimating; without proper thinking

ተገመተ *tägämmätä* v.i. was estimated, assessed, evaluated, assumed; have a low opinion of s/o

አስገመተ *asgämmätä* v.t. had s/t, s/o evaluated, rated, assessed

ገመና *gämäna* n. faults, mistakes

—ከታች —*kätač* one who hides the faults of others

ገመናው ተገለጠ *gämänau tägälläṭä* he was exposed *(his wrong doings were revealed)*

—ወጣ —*wäṭṭa* his villainy was exposed

ገመደ *gämmädä* v.t. twisted a rope, made a rope; entwined, made *(issue)* more diffcult

ነገር መገመድ ይወዳል he likes to make things more difficult

ገመድ *gämäd* n. rope

—አፍ —*af* adj. inarticulate

—ጣለ —*ṭalä* v.t. measured land *(by means of a rope)*

ገመደለ *gämäddälä* v.t. hacked

ተገመደለ *tägämäddälä* v.i. was hacked

ገመገመ *gämäggämä* v.t. evaluated, appraised, assessed

ገምጋሚ *gämgami* n. evaluator, assessor

ግምገማ *gəmgäma* n. evaluation, assessment, appraisal

ተገመገመ *tägämäggämä* v.i. was evaluated, appraised

አስገመገመ *asgämäggämä* v.t. had s/o, s/t, evaluated etc; came in torrents *(rain)*

ገመጠ *gämmaṭä* v.t. tore off a mouthful, tored chunk off

ግማጭ *gəmmač̣* n. chunk

ገማ *gämma* v.i. stank, smelt bad, was putrid

ግማት *gəmat* n. stink, bad smell

ግማታም *gəmatam* adj. stinking, having a bad smell, putrid

ግም *gəm* adj. stinking

ግማግም *gəmagəm* n. worthless fellow

ተጋማ *tägamma* v.i. mistreated each other; led a horrible life

ተግማማ *tägmamma* see ተጋማ

አገማ *agämma* v.t rot, caused to become putrid; put aside to be destroyed

ገምቦ *gämbo also* ገንቦ n. amphora, clay pot *(medium sized opposed to* ጋን *and* እንስራ*)*

የደም— *yädäm*—adj. pretty

ገሞራ *gamora in* እሳተ ገሞራ *əsatä gämora* n. volcano

ገሞራው *gämora*ʷ n. a tough person *(only used by braggarts)*

ገሠሠ *gässäsä in* ግሥ ገሠሠ *gəss gässäsä* v.t. conjugated a verb

ግሣዊ ስም *gəssawi səm* n. verbal noun

ማሠሪያ ግሥ *maśariya gəss* finite verb

ገሠጸ *gässäṣä* v.t. reprimanded, rebuked, reproved

ግሣጼ *gəssaṣe* n. reprimand, rebuke

ተግሣጽ *tägsaṣ* n. admonition, reproof, reprimand, *also* ገሥጣ

ገረመ *gärrämä* used with. suf. ገረመኝ *gärrämäññ* I was astonished, amazed, perplexed

ግሩም *gərum* adj. wonderful, marvellous, splendid, magnificient

—ድንቅ —*dənq* adj. splendid, marvellous

ግርማ *gərma* n. majesty, dignity

—ሌሊት —*lelit* dreadfulness of the night

—መለኮት —*mäläkot* n. divine power

—መንግሥት *—mängəst* n. stately condition

—ሞገስ *mogäs* n. respectability

ግርማዊ *gərmawi* adj. majestic

ግርማዊ ንጉሠ ነገሥት Imperial Majesty

ባለግርማ *balägərma* adj. respectable

ተገረመ *tägärrämä* v.i. was astonished, surprised, amazed, impressed

አስገረመ *asgärrämä* v.t. caused to be astonished, surprised, amazed, impressed

አስገራሚ *asgärrami* adj. astonishing, amazing, impressive

ገረመመ *gärämmämä* v.t. looked maliciously at, looked fiercely at

ገረረ *gärrärä* v.i. became scorching *(sun)*; became extremely heated *(oven)*

ገራራ *gärara* adj. scorching

*ገረሸ * *gäräššä*

ግርሻ *gərša* n. relapse

አገረሸ *agäräššä* v.i. relapsed

አገረሸበት *agäräššäbbät* suffered a relapse

*ገረበበ * *gäräbäbä*

ገርባባ *gärbabba* adv. ajar

ገርበብ አለ *gärbäbb alä* v.i. was ajar; kept quiet, withdrew from discussions

ተንገረበበ *tängäräbäbä* v.i. was ajar

ገረኑግ *gäränug* n. gerenuk *(litocranius walleri)*

ገረዘ *gärräzä* v.t. circumcised; grafted *(plant)*

አንደበቱ ያልተገረዘ *andäbätu yaltägärräzä* adj. ill-mannered, insolent, rude, vulgar

ግረዛ *gərräza* n. act of circumcising

ግርዛት *gərzät also* ግዝረት *gəzrät* n. circumcision

ግርዛት *gərrəzat* n. circumcision *(manner of)*

ተገረዘ *tägärräzä* v.i. was circumcised

አስገረዘ *asgärräzä* had s/o circumcised, had a plant grafted

ገረደፈ *gäräddäfä* v.t. pounded coarsely

ግርድፍ *gərddəf* adj./n. coarsely pounded *(flour)*

ገረድ *gäräd* n. maid-servant, house-maid

ልጃገረድ *ləğagäräd* n. girl

ወንዳገረድ *wändagäräd* n. hermaphrodite *(human being)*

የጭን ገረድ *yäçən gäräd* n. concubine, mistress

ግርድና *gərdənna* n. position of maidservant

ገረጀፈ *gäräğğäfä* v.i. grew old, aged ; became senile ; was tough *(meat)*

ገርጃፋ *gärğaffa* adj. aged: tough *(meat)*

*ገረገረ * *gäräggärä*

ገርጋራ *gärgarra* adj . restive *(horse)*; wilful, obstinate

ግርግር *gərrəgərr* n. disturbance, panic, turmoil ; riot; commotion; hustle and bustle

አንገራገረ *angäraggärä* v.t. became restive *(horse)*; was wilful, obstinate

አንገራጋሪ *angäragari* adj. wilful, obstinate

*ገረገበ * *gäräggäbä*

ግርግብ *gərgəb* adj. lightly boiled *(beans peas etc.)*

ተንገረገበ *tängäräggäbä* v.i. was lightly boiled *(beans, peas etc.)*; was *(morally)* tortured

አንገረገበ *angäräggäbä* v.t

boiled lightly *(beans)*; tortured *(morally)*

ገረገደ *gäräggädä* v.t. fenced; erected a wall *(wooden)*

ግርግድ *gərgəd* n. erected wooden wall

ገረፈ *gärräfä* v.t. whipped lashed, flagellated

ገራፊ *gärafi* n. flagellant

ግርፊያ *gərfiya* n. whipping, flagellating, lashing

ግርፋት *gərrəfat* n. skin eruption

ግርፍ *gərf in* አሸዋ ግርፍ n. *ašäwa gərf* cemented mud wall

ተገረፈ *tägärräfä* v.i. was whipped, lashed, flagellated

ገራ *gärra* v.t. tamed, trained a beast

ገሪ *gäri* n. animal-tamer

ገር *gär* adj. simple-hearted, good-natured

ገራገር *gäragär* adj. naive

ተገራ *tägärra* v.i. was tamed; trained *(beast)*

ያልተገራ *yaltägärra* adj. savage; ill-mannered, uncouth

አስገራ *asgärra* v.t. had a beast tamed, trained

ገራም *gärram* adj. pacific, peaceful; gentle *(horse)*

ገሰሰ *gässäsä* violated *in* መብቱ አይገሰስም *mäbtu ayəggäsässəm* his rights are not to be violated

ሕጓ ተገሰሰ *həggu^wa tägässäsä* she was deflowered

ገሰረ *gässärä* v.t. gulped *(liquid)*

ገሰገሰ *gäsäggäsä* v.i. hurried, walked rapidly, walked fast

ግስጋሴ *gəsəggase* n. rapid advance, fast walk *also* ግስገሳ

*ግሳ * *gässa*

ግሳት *gəsat* n. belch; roar *(lion)*

አገሳ *agässa* v.t. belched; roared *(lion)*

ገሸለጠ *gäšälläṭä* v.t. peeled off

ተገሸለጠ *tägäšälläṭä* v.i was peeled off

ገሸረ *gäššärä* v.t. dumped *(placed)*

ግሽር *gəššər* adj. conceited

ተገሸረ *tägäššärä* v.i. sat idle; was conceited

እንደ ድንጋይ አትገሸር don't sit over there like a stone

*ገሸገሸ *gäšäggäšä*

ተንገሸገሸ *tängäšäggäša* v.i. felt disgusted, disliked greatly; had an aversion to, had enough of

አንገሸገሸ *angäšäggäšä* v.t. loathed

ገበሎ *gäbälo* n. type of lizard

ገበረ *gäbbärä* v.t. paid tribute *(in kind and money)*

ገባር *gäbbar* n. tenant farmer

—ወንዝ —*wänz* n. tributary *(river)*

ግብረ ሥጋ *gəbrä səga* n. sexual relations

—መርፌ —*märfe* n. fine woollen carpet

—ሰዶም —*sädom* n. sodomy

—በላ —*bälla* n. dependants of a person of high rank

—አበር —*abbär* n. accomplice, partner in crime, confederate

—ገብ —*gäbb* n. morals

—ጠል —*ṭäll* n. land whose tax is not paid for several years and thus could be claimed for transfer by anyone

ግብር *gəbər* n. tax, income tax; banquet, feast

ግብር አበላ *gəbər abälla* v.t. feasted, gave a feast to

—ውሃ *—wäha* n. douche *(for women)*

—ከፋይ *—gəbər käfay* n. tax-payer

ምግባር *məgbar* n. virtue

ተግባር *tägbar* n. act, practice; occupation

በተግባር *bätägbar* adv. in practice, practically

ተግባራዊ *tägbarawi* adj. practical

ገበሬ *gäbäre* n. farmer, peasant

(የ)— ማኅበር *yä — mähəbär* farmers' association, peasants association

ግብርና *gəbrənna* n. agriculture, farming

የ— ሚኒስቴር *yä—minister* Ministry of Agriculture

ገበር *gäbär* n. lining of a garment

ገበርዲን *gäbärdin* n. gabardine

*ገበሰበሰ * *gäbäsäbbäsä*

ግብስብስ *gəbəsbəs* adj. trash *(material)*

አግበሰበሰ *agbäsäbbäsä* v.t. accumulated indiscriminately

ገበታ *gäbäta* n. large wooden bowl *(for kneading)*; dining-table

—ቀረበ *—qärräbä* the table is set

—አስደንጋጭ *—asdängač* n. big eater, *see* ደነገጠ

—ተነሣ/ ከፍ አለ *—tänässa/käff alä* the table is cleared

(የ)ገበታ ልብስ *yä/gäbäta ləbs* n. table-cloth

ገበታው ደነገጠ *gäbätaw dänäggäṭä* have little food on the table

ገበቴ *gäbäte* n. wooden bowl

ገበዝ *gäbäz* n. administrator of a church

ግብዝና *gəbəznna* n. the post of a *gäbäz* ገበዝ

ገበየ *gäbäyyä* v.t. shopped, went marketing; acquired

ገበያ *gäbäya* n. market; market-place

(የ) —ቀን *(yä)—qän* n. market-day

ገበያ ቆመ *gäbäya qomä* the market is underway

—ተበተነ *—täbättänä* v.t. the market is over

—አለው *—alläw* there is demand for *(goods)*; he does a good business

—ደራ *—därra* the market is in full swing

—ወጣ *—wäṭṭa* went to the market

ገበያተኛ *gäbäyatäñña* n. shopper

ገብዪ *gäbyi* n. shopper, customer

ተገበያየ *tägäbäyayyä* v.t. transacted; made a deal

*ገበደደ * *gäbäddädä*

ተገባደደ *tägäbaddädä* v.i. was almost completed *(assignment)*

አገባደደ *aggäbaddädä* v.t. has almost completed

*ገበገበ * *gäbäggäbä*

ገብጋባ *gäbgabbä* adj. greedy, stingy, parsimonious

ተስገበገበ *täsgäbäggäbä* v.i. was greedy, stingy

ተንገበገበ *tängäbäggäbä* v.i. was greedy, stingy; was scorched ; suffered *(morally)*

አንገበገበ *angäbäggäbä* v.t scorched ; caused to suffer *(morally)*; inflicted pain

አንገብጋቢ ጥያቄ (ጉዳይ) a burning question *(issue)*

ገበጣ *gäbäṭa* n. a game consisting of a board with

a double row of twelve holes played with pebbles or beads

ገባ *gäbba* v.i. entered, went in, came in, got in

ልብሱ ቀለም— *ləbsu qäläm*—have a dress dyed

ሽፍታው— *šəftaw* — the rebel submitted to the authorities

ቃል— *qal*— he made a promise, he pledged, he guaranteed

ቅዝቃዜ ገባው *qəzəqqaze gäbbaw* he froze *(felt very cold)*

ነገሩ— *nägäru*—he understood the issue

በነገሩ ገባ *bänägäru gäbba* he interfered in the matter

ትምህርት ገባው *təmhərt gäbbaw* he understood, followed, comprehended his subject, lesson

ንስሐ— *nəssəha* he repented

እሳት ገባው *əsat gäbbaw* was almost burnt *(by cooking or roasting)*

ከመንገድ ገባ *kämängäd gabba* he came home from a journey

ወዶ— *wäddo*— n. volunteer *(military)*

ድህነት ገባው *dəhnnät gäbbaw* he was impoverished

ገደል ገባ *gädäl gäbba* he was precipitated; he was lost *(had bad luck)*

ጉድጓድ ገባ *gudguʷad*—he fell into a ditch

ገራ ገባው *gəra gäbbaw* he was confused, perplexed, was in difficulty, was at a loss

ገበር ገባ *gəbər gäbba* meal is served *(in the palace or in homes of dignitaries)*

ጣልቃ— *ṭalqa*—he interfered, meddled

ፀሐይ ገባች *ṣähay gäbbačč* the sun has set

ገቢ *gäbi* n. income

—ሸቀጥ *—šäqäṭ* n. import

—ቀረጥ *—qäräṭ* n. income-tax

—ገንዘብ *—gänzäb* n. income

ገቢና ወጭ *gäbinna wäči* income and expenditure

ግባት *gəbat in* ግባተ መሬት *gəbatä märet.* burial

የደም ግባት *yädäm gəbat* n. good complexion

ገብ *gäbb in* ሁሉ ገብ *hullä gäbb* adj. comprehensive, versatile

ሰርጎ— *särgo*—n. infiltrator

ባሕረ— *bähra*—n. cape

ውሃ— መሬት *wəha–märet* land with irrigation canals

ውሎ — መንገድ *wəlo–mängäd* one day's roundtrip journey

ዐይነ— *aynä gäbb* adj. attractive; handsome

ግብረ— *gəbra gäbb* n. morals adj. polite

ጋብቻ *gabəčča* n. marriage, matrimony

ግቢ *gəbbi* n. palace; compound; enclosure; premises

ቅጥር— *qəṭər*—n. campus

ገቢ ነፍስ ውጪ ነፍስ be in great trouble

ግብ *gəb* n. score *(in a game)*, goal *(soccer)*; aim, objective

መግቢያ *mägbiya* n. entrance

ተገቢ *tägäbbi* adj. proper appropriate; right *(person)*, appropriate *(choice)*; fitting

ተጋባ *tägabba* v.i. married one another

ገራ— *gəra*—v.i. he was confused, was at a loss was perplexed

ተግባባ *tägbabba* v.i. reached an agreement, consented

ተግባቢ *tägbabi* adj. agreeable *(ready to agree)*

አገባ *agäbba* v.t. brought in, put into, inserted; scored *(a goal)*; paid back; married

ይግባኝ አለ *yəgbaññ älä* submitted an appeal *(to a law of court)*

አግቦ *agbo* n. veiled insult, sarcasm cf. አሽሙር

አጋባ *aggabba* v.t. emptied a container; arranged marriage, unpacked

ግራ— *gəra*—v.t. confused bedevilled, muddled

አስገባ *asgäbba* v.t. inserted; let in, admitted; put in; introduced *(bring s/t into use for the first time)*

አስተጋባ *astägabba* v.i. echoed, reverberated

ገባሬ ሠናይ *gäbare sännay* n. priest or deacon who plays major role during the Mass

ገባር *see* ገበረ

ገብር * *gäbr*

ገብረ ጉንዳን *gäbrä gundan* n. skilful type of ant

ገብስ *gäbs* n. barley

*ገተለተለ * *gätälättälä*

ግትልትል *gətəltəl* adj. jumbled, disordered

ተግተለተለ *tägtälättälä* v.i. came, went disorderly

አግተለተለ *agtälättälä* v.t. carried away or brought with disorderly

ገተረ *gättärä* v.t. pulled tight, stretched tight

ገታራ *gättara* adj. stubborn, obstinate

ግትር *gəttər* adj. stubborn, obstinate, persistent

ተገተረ *tägättärä* v.i. was stretched tight; stuck around

ተገታተረ *tägätattärä* v.i. was stretched tighly

ተጋተረ *tägattärä* v.ik. started one's duties seriously

አጋተረ *aggattärä* v.t. gave a serious assignment

*ገተገተ **gätäggätä* *in* ቁስሉ ገተገተው his wound throbbed with pain

ገትጋታ *gätgatta* adj. nagging

ገታ *gätta* v.t. reined a horse; constrained *(temper)*; repressed *(laughter)*

ራሱን— *rasun*-controlled oneself

ተገታ *tägätta* v.i. was constrained, repressed

ገነባ *gänäbba* v.t. built *(a house etc.)*,

ገንቢ *in* ገንቢ ሂስ *gänbi his* n. constructive criticism

ግንባታ *gənbata* n. bulding up

ግንብ *gənb also* ግምብ *gəmb*, stone wall

—ቤት *—bet* n. stone house, concrete building

ግንበኛ *gənbäñña also* ግምበኛ *gəmbäñña* n. mason, bricklayer

ገነተረ *gänättärä* v.i. became tougher or leathery *(meat for not being well-cooked)*

ገንታራ *gäntarra* adj. wilful

ግንትር *gəntər* leathery meat

ገነት *gännät* n. paradise

ምድረ— *mədrä*-earthly paradise

ገነነ *gännänä* v.i. was famous, grew *(of fame)*, became illustrious

ገነን *in* አምባ ገነን *amba gännän* n. dictator, tyrant

ገናና *gänana* adj. famous, illustrious

ተጋነነ *tägannänä* v.i. was exaggerated

አጋነነ *aggannänä* v.t. exaggerated; maximized, overstated

ቃለ አጋኖ *qalä agganno* n. exclamation

የ—ምልክት *yä-mələkkət* exclamation mark

ገነዘ *gännäzä* v.t. shrouded *(a corpse)*

ግንዘት *gənzät* n. putting in a shroud

መገነዣ *mägännäža* n. shroud

ገነዘበ **gänäzzäbä*

ግንዛቤ *gənəzzabe* n. realisation, awareness

ተገነዘበ *tägänäzzäbä* v.i. realized, was aware, perceived

አገናዘበ *agänazzäbä* v.t. compared, counter-checked

አገናዛቢ ተውላጠ ስም *aggänazabi täwlaṭä-səm* possessive pronoun

—አፀፋ *—aṣäfa* – reflexive pronoun

ገነደሰ *gänäddäsä* v.t cut down *(a big tree)*

ገነገነ *gänäggänä* v.i hesitated, was suspicious

ገንጋኝ *gängañ* adj. hesitant, suspicious

ገነጠለ *gänäṭṭälä* v.t. broke-off *(branches)*; detached *(the stub)*

ግንጣይ *gənəṭṭay* cut off branch

ግንጥል *gənəṭəl* n. stick *(freshly cut)*

—ጌጥ *—geṭ* n. not going with, not matching *(*clothes*)*

ገነጣጠለ *gänäṭaṭṭälä* v.t. cut in pieces

ተገነጠለ *tägänäṭṭälä* v.i. was broken off *(branch)*; seceded

ተገንጣይ *tägänṭay* n. sessesionist; faction

ተገነጣጠለ *tägänäṭattälä* v.i. fell into pieces

ገነፈለ *gänäffälä* v.i. boiled over

በቁጣ— *bäquṭṭa*–burnt out in anger, was filled with fury

ግንፍል *gənfəl* adj. boiled

ግንፍልፍል *(meat) gənfəlfəl* ənğära boiled in wäṭ

*ገነፋ **gänäffa*

ገንፎ *gänfo* n. porridge *(of wheat, barley oats etc.)*

አገነፋ *agänäffa* v.t. cooked porridge

ገና *gäna* adj. adv. still, yet, but

አሁን ገና መጣ *ahun gäna mäṭṭa* he came just now, he came at this very moment

እንደገና *əndägäna* adv. again

ገና ነው *gäna näw* it is early, it is not yet

—ነኝ *—näññ* I am not ready

—ለገና *längäna* on the pretext that s/t will happen

ገና ለገና ይመጣል ብለህ ቀኑን ሙሉ ተቀምጠህ ትውላለህ? Are you going to sit down all day on the pretext that he will come?

ገና ዘንቦ ተባርቆ there is still a long way to go *(not at this time)*

ገና ቆዶ *same as above*

ገና ገም *same as above*

ገና *gänna* n. Christmas; name of a game played during advent *(s/t like hockey)*; bat *(used in the game)*

ስብከተ— *səbkätä—* advent

ገንባሌ *also* ጋምባሌ *gänbale, gamballe* n. boot-tree, legging, puttee

ገንቦ *see* ገምቦ

ገንዘብ *gänzäb* n. money, currency, property *see* *ገነዘበ

—ሰብሳቢ *—säbsabi* n. money collector

—ቤት *—bet* n. treasurer

—ተቀባይ *—täqäbbay* n. cashier; receiving teller

—አወጣ *—awäṭṭa* spent money

—አይሆንም *—ayhonəm* he, it is useless

ልጁ ገንዘብ አይሆንም he is a useless boy

—አደረገ *—adärrägä* possessed, acquired

—አጠፋ —*aṭäffa* squandered money

—ከፋይ —*käfay* n. paying teller; payer, pay master

ተጠባባቂ ገንዘብ *täṭäbabaqi gänzäb* n. reserve fund

ዋና ገንዘብ *wanna gänäzb* n. capital

ጥሬ— *ṭəre—* cash

—ያዥ —*yaž* n. treasurer

ገንዳ *gända* n. trough (*for animals to drink from*)

ገንገበት *gängäbät* adj. miserly, stingy

• ገኘ • *gäññä*

ግንኙነት *gənəññunnät* n. relationship, contact, association; communication; intercourse

ግኝት *gəññət* n. discovery

ተገኘ *tägäññä* v.i. was found; was recovered

ተገናኘ *tägänaññä* v.i. met each other; was compatible; had sexual intercourse

አገናኘ *aggänaññä* v.t. brought together

አገናኝ መኰንን *aggänaññ mäkonnən* liaison officer

አገኘ *ägaññä* v.t. found, discovered; earned; came across, met; acquired

አስገኘ *asgäññä* v.t. brought in (*money, wealth*); produced, resulted in

• ገወለለ •*gäwällälä*

ተንገዋለለ *tängäwallälä* v.i. was looked down upon, was belittled

አንገዋለለ *angäwallälä* v.t. looked down, belittled

ገውዝ *gäwz* n. nut

ገዘረ *see* ገረዘ

ገዘተ *gäzzätä* v.t. anathematised; applied sanctions against

ግዝት *gəzzət* n. sanction, ban

ተገዘተ *tägäzzätä* v.i. swore gave one's words

አስገዘተ *asgäzzätä* v.t. had (s/o) swear

ገዘገዘ *gäzäggäzä* v.t. sawed; cut with difficulty (*with dull blade*); weakened (*of prolonged illness*)

ገዝጋዛ *gäzgazza* adj. stammering; stubborn, heavy-headed

ገዘፈ *gäzzäfä* v.i. was stout, was fat

ግዝፍ *gəzäf* n. stoutness, fatness, massiveness

ግዙፍ *gəzuf* adj. tall and fat; gigantic; massive

ግዝፈት *gəzfät* n. massiveness; stoutness, fatness

አገዘፈ *agäzäfä in* ልቡን— *ləbbun*–v.t. was conceited,

ገዛ *gäzza* v.t. bought, purchased; ruled over, dominated; hired a lawyer

ነፍስ— *näfs*–became conscious (*aware of*)

አደብ— *adäb*–became polite

ገዢ *gäž* n. buyer; master; ruler

ግዛት *gəzat* n. area of jurisdiction, territory of a state, realm

ቅኝ— *qəññ—* n. colony (*territory*)

የገዛ ልጁ *yägäzza ləğu* his own son

—ራሴ —*rase* I myself

በገዛ እጄ *bägäzza əğğe* by myself

—ፈቃዴ *bägäzza fäqade* on my own accord, by myself

ግዥ *gəžž* n. bargain, buy, transaction

ተገዛ *tägäzza* v.i. was ruled, was subdued

ተገዢ *tägäž* n. subject (*under s/o's rule*)

ተገዛዛ *tägäzzazza* v.i. transacted

ተጋዛ *tägazza* v.i. occupied land as a tenant, leased *(land as a tenant)*

ተጋዥ *tägaž* n. tenant

መጋዞ *mäggazo* n. rent *(of land)*

አጋዛ *aggazza* v.t. leased land to a tenant

ገደለ *gäddälä* v.t. killed, massacred, murdered, put to death

ራሱን— *rasun*— committed suicide

ገዳይ *gäday* n. killer

ነፍሰ— *näfsä* — n. murderer, killer

ገድል *gädl* n. saint's life *(acta sanctorum)*

ገድለኛ *gäläñña* adj. miraculous

ባለገድል *balägädl* adj. miraculous

ግዳይ *gədday* n. trophy; booty *(captured from the enemy)*

—ቆጠረ *—qoṭṭärä* displayed one's booty *(captured from the enemy)*

ግድያ *gədəyya* n. killing

ተገደለ *tägäddälä* v.i. was killed

ተጋደለ *tägaddälä* v.i. killed one another; fought

ተጋድሎ *tägadəlo* n. fighting; campaign *(against social evils)*

ተጋዳይ *tägaday* n. warrior

አስገደለ *asgäddälä* v.t. had s/o killed

ገደል *gädäl* n. precipice, cliff

ገደላማ *gädälamma* adj. precipitous

ገደላገደል *gädälagädäl* adj. full of precipices

ገደል ሰደደ *gädäl säddädä* v.t. got s/o into trouble

—ገባ *—gäbba see* ገባ

የገደል ማሚቶ *yägädäl mammito* n. echo

*ገደመ **gäddämä*

ገደማ *gädäma* adv. approximately, roughly; hereabout

እዚህ ገደማ hereabouts, round

ወደ ስድስት ሰዓት ገደማ towards 12 o'clock

ጋድም *gadəm in* ጋድም ወንበር *gadəm wänbär* n. bench

ግድም *gədəm* n/adv. area, place; near, around

ጋድሚያ *gadmiya* n. heavy sleeper

አገደመ *agäddämä* v.t. passed by

አግድመት *agdəmät* n. plane

አግድም *agdəm* adj. horizontal, transverse

አግድሞሽ *agdəmoš* adv. horizontally

አግድም አየው *agdəm ayyäw* he looked at him spitefully

አጋደመ *aggaddämä* v.t. laid (s/o), (s/t) down

አግዳሚ ወንበር *agdami wänbär* n. bench

—ጠረጴዛ *—ṭäräppeza* n. desk *(long)*

አላፊ አግዳሚ *alafi agdami* n. passers-by

*ገደረደረ **gädäräddärä*

ገደርዳራ *gädärdarra* adj. pretentious

ግድርድር *gədərdər* adj. pretentious

ተግደረደረ *tägdäräddärä* v.i. pretended *(not to want, or like s/t)*

ተግደርዳሪ *tägdärdari* adj. pretentious

ገደበ *gäddäbä* v.t. made a dam, dammed

ገደብ *gädäb* n. limit, limitation; probation

—አደረገ *—adärrägä* v.t. stipulated

—የሌለው *—yälelläw* absolute *(limitless)*

ያፍ— *yaf*—limit of what one should say

ግድብ — gəddəb n. dam, dike, barrage

*ገደደ — *gäddädä

ገዳዳ — gäddada adj. twisted, crooked, bent

ተንጋደደ — tängäddädä v.i. became twisted, bent

አንጋደደ — angaddädä v.t. twisted, bent

*ገደደ — *gäddädä with pron suff. in mən gäddädäññ ምን ገደደኝ I agree with, o.k., I have no objection

ግዳጅ — gəddaǧ n. duty, obligation

ግዴታ — gəddeta n. duty, obligation compulsory; condition (stipulation)

በግድ — bägədd adv. by force, unwillingly

ያለውድ በግድ — yaläwədd bägədd by force

ግድ ሆነበት — gədd honäbbät he was forced, he couldn't do otherwise

—የለም — —yällläm never mind

—የለውም — —yällläwəm he is careless, he does'nt mind

—የለሽ — —yällläš adj. careless

ምን ግዴ — mən gədde what do I care?

ተገደደ — tägäddädä v.i. was compelled, was forced; was obligated

አጋደደ — aggaddädä v.t. was useful, was helpful

ምን አገዶኝ — mən agəddoññ I am not against it

አስገደደ — asgäddädä v.t. forced, brought pressure on, compelled

ገደገደ — gädäggädä v.t. erected a wooden wall

ግድግዳ — gədgədda n. wall

*ገደገደ — *gädäggädä

ተንገዳገደ — tängädaggädä v.i. staggered

አንገዳገደ — angädaggädä v.t. staggered

ገደፈ — gäddäfä v.t. broke the fast; made a mistake omitted

ግድፈት — gədfät n. a non-fasting day; omission, error

አገደፈ — agäddäfä v.t. made s/o break the fast; had s/o err (while writing etc.)

አስገደፈ — asgäddäfä v. t. had s/o made a mistake (while writing etc.)

ገዴ — gädde n. buzzard (kind of falcon)

ገድ — gädd n. good luck, good omen

ገደ ቢስ — gäddä bis adj. ill-omened, unlucky

ገዳማ — gäddamma adj. lucky (things e. g. number)

ገዳም — gäddam adj. lucky (person)

ገድ በለኝ — gädd bäläññ wish me good luck

—የለሽ — —yällläš adj. ill-omened, unlucky

ገድል — see ገደለ

*ገገመ — * gäggämä

ገገምተኛ — also ገመምተኛ gämämtäñña n. convalescent

አገገመ — agäggämä v.i. convalesced

ገገረ — gäggärä v.i. became hard, solid (liquid)

ግግር — gəggər adj. hard, solid

ገጠመ — gäṭṭämä v.t. fitted together, joined together; fitted in, joined (bad people); fixed, repaired; matched (game); engaged (the enemy;) wrote poetry; rhymed

ገጠም — gäṭṭäm in ኩታ ገጠም መሬት plots of land adjoining one another

ገጣሚ — gäṭami in ግጥም— gəṭəm—poet

ግጥሚያ *gəṭmiya* n. match *(game)*; confrontation, engagement *(battle)*

ኳስ— *kuʷas*–football match

ግጥም *gəṭəm* n. poetry, poem

ግጥም አለ *gəṭṭəmm alä* died suddenly

ገጣጠመ *gäṭaṭṭämä* v.i. re-assembled *(machinery etc.)*

ግጥም— *gəṭəm*–scribbled poetry

ተጋጠመ *tägäṭaṭṭämä* v.i. was fitted together; was assembled *(car etc.)*; confronted each other

መገጣጠሚያ *mäggäṭaṭämiya* n. joint *(of body etc.)*

ተጋጠመ *tägaṭṭämä* v.i. met *(teams)*; confronted

ፊት ለፊት- *fit läfit*–was confronted with *(enemy)*; coincided *(events)*

ተጋጣሚ *tägaṭami* n. contestant, adversary *(in contest of any kind)*

አገጣጠመ *aggäṭaṭṭämä* v.t. assembled *(car etc.)*; made people confront each other *(to settle disagreements or misunderstandings)*

አጋጠመ *aggaṭṭämä* v.t. brought together

ምን አጋጠመህ! what has happened to you?

አንድ አንበሳ አጋጠመኝ! I ran across a lion

አጋጣሚ ነገር! an unexpected thing

በአጋጣሚ *bä'aggaṭami* adv. by chance, unexpectedly

የአጋጣሚ ነገር *yä'aggaṭami nägär* just by chance

ገጠር *gäṭär* n. rural area, countryside

የገጠር መሬት *yägäṭär märet* rural land

ገጠሬ *gäṭäre* n. countryman *(person living in rural land)*

ገጠበ *gäṭṭäbä* v.t wounded *(especially the back of a beast of burden)*

ገጣባ *gäṭaba* adj. wounded *(back of a beast of burden)*

ተገጣጠበ *tägäṭaṭṭäbä* v.i. was full of scratches and wounds

ገጠገጠ *gäṭäggäṭä* v.t. built houses close together

ግጥግጥ ያለ መንደር a dense village

ገጠጠ *gäṭṭäṭä in* ጥርሱ ገጠጠ *ṭərsu gäṭṭäṭä* had teeth too long

ገጣጣ *gäṭaṭa* adj. buck-toothed

ገጦ *in* ገጦ ለጣይ *gäṭṭo läṭay* one who cannot close his mouth because of his protruding teeth *(insult)*

ተንጋጠጠ *tängaṭṭäṭä* v.i. was bent

አንጋጠጠ *angaṭṭäṭä* v.i. looked upwards; lifted up one's eyes

ገጥ **gäṭṭ*

ገጥታ *gäṭṭəta* n. direction

ገጠ ቢስ *gäṭṭä bis* adj. graceless

ገጨ *gäččä* v.t. bumped, knocked against; run over *(vehicle)*

ገጨኀን *gäččähänn* adj. crude, coarse *(manners, person)*

ግጭት *gəččət* n. collision; crash, clash, friction conflict misunderstanding

ገጭ አለ *gäčč alä* v.i. came suddenly

ተገጨ *tägäččä* v.i. bumped on s/t

ተጋጨ *tägaččä* v.i. knocked, against, crashed had a conflict with, clashed *(be in disagreement)*

አገጫጨ *aggäčaččä in* ብርጭቆ አገጫጨ *bərčəqqo*

	aggäčaččä toasted *(raising glasses)*
አጋጨ	*aggaččä* v.t. clashed *(objects); hit s/o* violently; created a conflict, animosity between
*ገጨገጨ	*gäčäggäčä
ተንገጫገጨ	*tängäčaggäčä* v.i rattled, jerked along
አንገጫገጨ	*angäčaggäčä* v.t. rattled; jolted
ገጽ	*gäṣṣ* n. face *(of earth)*; page *(of book)*
ገጸ መልካም	*gäṣṣä mälkam* adj. beautiful, handsome
—ቢስ	—*bis* adj. ugly
—ባሕርይ	—*bährəy* n. character *(in a novel, short story)*
ገጽታ	*gaṣṣəta* n. appearance, look
ገፈተ	* *gäffätä*
ገፈት	*gäfät* n. scum
ገፈተረ	*gäfättärä* v.t. pushed s/o violently, shoved
ተገፋተረ	*tägäfättärä* v.i. pushed at
ገፈገፈ	*gäfäggäfä* v.t. spent a miserable life አስር ዓመት እስር ቤት ገፍ ግፎ ወጣ was released after ten miserable years in prison
ተንገፈገፈ	*tängäfäggäfä* v.i. was disgusted, had a strong aversion to
አንገፈገፈ	*ängäfäggäfä* v.t. had a strong dislike to, was filled with dismay; disgusted
*ገፈጠጠ	* *gäfäṭṭäṭä*
ገፈጠጥ	*gäfäṭäṭ* adj. protuberant
ገፍጣጣ	*gäfṭaṭṭa* adj. protuberant
ተንገፈጠጠ	*tängäfäṭṭäṭä* v.i. became big-bellied
አንገፈጠጠ	*angäfäṭṭäṭä* v.t. bellied
ገፈፈ	*gäffäfä* v.t. stripped off *(garment)*; divested *(an official of power and authority)* skimmed
ገፈፋ	*gäfäffa* n. exploitation, exorbitant *(price)*
ገፋፊ	*gäfafi* n. exploitin *(selfish)*
ተገፈፈ	*tägäffäfä* v.i. was stripped off; was skinned; was divested; was skimmed
ገፋ	*gäffa* v.t. pushed, shoved; mistreated
ሥራውን—	*sərawən*—he made good progress *(in ones duties)*
ትምህርት—	*təmhərt*—he advanced in studies
እድሜ—	*ədmew*—he has advanced in years
ወሰን—	*wäsän*-trespassed *(la*
ወተት—	*wätät*— v.t. churned
ቢገፋ ቢገፋ	*bigäfa bigäfa* utmost in
ገፊ	አፈር ገፊ *afär gäfi* peasant *(insult)*
በገፍ	*bägäf* adv. abundantly, in great quantity
ግፊት	*gəffit* n. pressure *(power)*, impulse
ግፊያ	*gffəya* n. crush *(persons; pushing, pressing)*
ግፋ ቢል	*gəfa bil* if the worst comes
ግፍ	*gəf* n. injustice, unfairness, violence, atrocity
—ሠራ	—*särra* did an injustice
—ዋለ	—*walä* committed evil
—ፈጸመ	—*fäṣṣämä* committed an atrocious crime
ግፈኛ	*gəfäñña* adj. wicked, cruel; atrocious
ገፋፋ	*gäfaffa* v.t. instigated, pressed strongly, motivated, put pressure

on

ተገፋ *tägäffa* v.i. went forward *(work)*; was maltreated

ተገፊ *tägäfi* adj. maltreated

ተጋፋ *tägaffa* v.i. shoved one another, pressed *(push)*

ሥልጣን — *səlṭan*— was disrespectful, he went over his head

ተጋፍቶ አለፈ *tägafto älläfä* he forced his way through

ተገፋፋ *tägäfaffa* v.i. was instigated, motivated

ጉላንጆ *gulunǧo* n. gristle tough *(meat)*; ugly

ጉልላት *gulləlat* n. dome, cupola

ጉልማ *guləmma* n. plot of land *(given to s/o)*

ጉልባን *gulban* n. thickly boiled beans and wheat *(served on Good Friday)*

ጉልት *see* ጎለተ

ጉሎ *gulo* n. castor plant

—ፍሬ *—fəre* n. castor bean

—ዘይት *—zäyət* n. castor oil

ጉማ *guma* n. blood money, ransom

—በላ *—bälla* took blood money

ጉማሬ *gumarre* n. hippopotamus

—አለንጋ *—alänga* lash made of hippopotamus skin

ጉም *gum* n. mist, fog

የጉም ሽንት *yägum šənt* n. drizzle

—ጅብ *—ǧəb* adj. stingy, niggardly

ጉማም *gumam* adj. foggy, misty

ጉምሩክ *gumruk* n. customs office, customs house

የጉምሩክ *yägumruk qäräṭ*

ቀረጥ duty paid at the customs

ጉም ጉም አለ *gumm gumm alä* v.i. grumbled *(complained)*; grumbled *(thunder)*

ጉምጉምታ *gumgumta* n. grumbling *(complaint; thunder)*

ጉረኖ *guränno* n. enclosure *(for sheep and goats)*

ጉራ *gurra* n. bragging, boasting, show-off

—ነዛ *—näzza* bragged, boasted

—ነፋ *—näffa* bragged, boasted

ጉረኛ *gurräñña* n. braggart, boaster

ጉራማይሌ *quramaile* n. type of black-bird, *(black and green coloured)*; tattoo *(of the gum of the teeth at intervals)*

ጉራቻ *gurračča* adj. black *(for horse)*

ጉራች *gurrač̌* name given to a black horse

ጉራንጉር *gurangur* adj. rugged, rough *(place)*

ጉራጌ *gurage* Gurage land, Gurage people

ጉሬ *gure, also gore* ጎሬ n. den, lair

ጉሬዛ *gureza* n. colobus monkey *(Colobus abysinicus)*

ጉሬዛማ *gurezamma* adj. black and white coloured

ጉርጥ *gurṭ* n. toad

ጉሮሮ *gurorro*; *also* ጉረሮ *gurärro* n. throat

ጉሽርጥ *gušrəṭṭ* n. plant with oblong tubers used by women for colouring their hands and feet

ጉበት *gubbät* n. liver

የጉበት በሽታ *yägubbät bäššita* n. liver cancer

ጉባኤ	*guba'e* n. conference, assembly, congregation
—ቃና	—*qana* ge'ez poem of two stanzas
—ነገረ	—*näggärä* taught the commentary of the Bible
ቃለ—	*qalä*— n. minutes *(of a meeting)*
—ተቀመጠ	—*täqämmäṭä* sat in a conference
—አደረገ	—*adärrägä* held a conference
አፈ—	*afä*—n. chairman *(arch.)*
ጠቅላላ—	*ṭäqlalla*—General Assembly
ጉብታ	*gubbəta* n. hillock
ጉብ አለ	*gubb alä* v.i. sat tight
ጉበኛ	*gubäñña* n. spy *(arch.)*
ጉቦ	*gubbo* n. bribe
—ሰጠ	—*säṭṭä* v.t. bribed
—በላ	—*bälla* v.t. took bribes
ጉቦኛ	*gubboñña* n. one who takes bribes
ጉትቻ	*gutəčča* n. ear-ring
ጉትያ	*gutəyya* n. crest *(of bird)*, tuft of hair on children's head
ጉቶ	*gutto* n. tree stump
ጉኒና	*gunina* n. cap *(head-covering)*
ጉንዳን	*gundan* n. ant
ጉንፋን	*gunfan* n. common cold
ጉንፋን ያዘው	*gunfan yazäw* he caught cold
ጉያ	*guyya* n. lap
ጉዳይ	*gudday* n. matter, business; problem
—የለኝም	*gudday yälläññəm* I don't care a pin
ጉዳዬ አይደለም	*guddaye aydälläm* it is not my business
ጉዳይ ፈጻሚ	*gudday fäṣṣami* solicitor, chargé d'affairs
ባለጉዳይ	*balägudday* person with a case in the court, person who has problem to be discussed with an official
ጉዳይ	*gudday* less, to ለሦስት አሥር ጉዳይ ten to three
ጉድ	*gud* adj. strange surprising, unusual
ወይ	*wäy*—what a strange thing, how strange, what a wonder
ጉደኛ	*gudäñña* adj. surprising strange
ጉድ አወጣ	*gud awäṭṭa* divulged
—አደረገ	—*adärrägä* deluded
—ፈላ	—*fälla* something strange has happened
ጉድ ጉድ አለ	*gudd gudd alä* v.i. bustled about
ጉድባ	*gudba* n. ditch
ጉዶ	*guddo* n. short curved sword, scimitar
ጉጉት	*guggut* n. owl ; anxiety
ጉጉት	*see* ጓጓ
ጉጉ	ጉጉ see ጓጓ
ጉግማንጉግ	*gugmangug* n. Gog and Magog
ጉግስ	*gugs* n. polo-type game
ጉጠት	*guṭät* n. pincers, pliers forceps cf. ፈቻል
ጉጥ	*guṭ* n. stump (of a branch)
ጉፍታ	*gufta* n. scarf *(hair-covering used by Moslem women)*
ጊንጥ	*ginṭ* n. scorpion
ጊዜ	*gize* n. time
—የወለደው	—*yäwällädäw* adj. recent, transitory; haphazard; modern
—ያለ —	—*yalä*–late at night
በጊዜ	*bägize* adv. on time, early
ጊዜው አይደለም	*gizew aydälläm* it is unseasonal, premature
ጊዜያዊ	*gizeyawi* adj. provisional, tentative,

interim, temporary

ሁልጊዜ *hullgize* adv. always

ሌላ— *lela*— adv. another time

ምን— *mən*— adv. when? at what time

—ጊዜም —*gizemm* adv. always, all along; at any time

በሆነ ጊዜ *bahonä gize* adv. at a certain stage; sometimes; any time

በቅርብ— *bäqərb*—adv. in the near future, shortly

በዛሬ— *bäzare*—adv. nowadays

በየጊዜው *bäyyägizew* adv. often, constantly, from time to time, regularly

ባሁኑ ጊዜ *bähunu gize* adv. nowadays

ባለ— *balä*—a man of the world; powerful, influential man

ባንድ— *band*—adv. at once; simultaneously; immediately

ብዙ— *bəzu*— adv. often

ብዙውን— *bəzuwən*— adv, most of the time

ትርፍ— *tərf*. spare time; leisure

ትንቢት— *tənbit*—future tense

ኀላፊ— *halafi*—perfect *(past)* tense

አለ— *alä*—adv. late, untimely

አንድ— *and*—adv. once

አብዛኛውን *abazññawən*—adv. most of the time

ከቅርብ— ወዲህ *käqərb—wädih* adv. in recent times

ከ—ወደ— *ka—wädä*—adv. from time to time

ክፉ ጊዜ *kəfu gize* n. famine

ክፍለ— *kəflä*—n. period

የዚህን— *yäzihən*—adv. at this time, then

የዚያን— *yäzziyan*–at that time, then

ያለ— *yalä*—untimely, inopportunely, prematurely

ያን— *yann*—adv. at tha. time, then

ጥቂት— *təqit*—adv. for a short while

ጊደር *gidär* n. heifer

ጋለ *galä* v.i. was hot, was red from heating *(metal)*; was heated *(discussion, argument)*.

የጋለ ብረት *yägalä bərät*. heated metal

—ስሜት *səmmet* enthusiasm, ardour, fervent desire

ግለት *gəlät* n. heat, hotness

የፀሐይ— *yäṣähay*—the heat of the sun

ተጋጋለ *tägagalä* v.i. was heated *(discussion, argument)*

አጋለ *agalä* v.t. made hot *(metal etc.)*

አጋጋለ *aggagalä* v.t. heated up *(discussion)*; instigated

ጋለበ *galläbä* v.t. rode *(a horse, bicycle etc.)*; made to gallop ሊጋ ልበኝ ፈለገ he wanted to have full control over me

ግልቢያ *gəlbiya* n. horse riding, galloping

ጋመ *gamä* v.i. heated up

ተጋጋመ *tägagamä* v.i. be on fire

አጋጋመ *aggagamä* v.t. fired *(caused to begin burning)*

ጋማ *gamma* n. mane *(of horse, mule)*

የጋማ ከብት *yägamma käbte* n. beast of burden

ጋሜ *gamme* n. hair-do of a girl

ጋሞ ጎፋ *gamogofa* n. one of the Administrative Regions ,southern Ethiopia

ጋረ *garä* v.i. toiled; tried

one's best
ጋር *gar* n. toil
በጋር በጣር *bagär bäṭar* with tremendous toil and agony
ግረት ጥረት *gərät ṭərät* toil and agony
ጋረደ *garrädä* v.t. veiled, covered, concealed, screened; curtained off; blinded
ግርዶሽ *gərdoš* n. screen, veil: eclipse
የጨረቃ— *yäčäräqa*—lunar eclipse
የፀሐይ— *yäṣähay*—solar eclipse
ተጋረደ *tägarrädä* v.i. was veiled, covered, concealed, screened, was covered by curtains
መጋረጃ *mäggaräǧa* n. curtain
ጋረጠ *garräṭä* v.t. pricked *(for thorns and stubs of pointed wood)*
ጋሬጣ *gareṭa* n. prickle *(of plants)*, thorns
ተጋረጠ *tägarräṭä* v.i. stood in one's way
ጋሪ *gari* n. carriage, horse-drawn car, cart
የእጅ— *yä'ǧǧ*--n. wheelbarrow
ጋሪ ነጂ *gari näǧi* n. carter
ጋራ *gara* n. mountain
ጋራማ *garamma* adj. mountainous
see ጋር
ጋራዥ *garaž* n. garage, hangar
ጋሬ *garre* n. ənǧera made out of flower of mixed grains *(inferior quality)*
ጋሸበ *gaššäbä* v.i. grew precociously *(plants)*
ጋሻ *gašša* shield
—ጃግሬ —*ǧagre* n. equerry
—መሬት —*märeṭ* land measuring appr. 40 hectares
ጋሼ/ጋሽዬ *gašše, or gaššəyye* term used by a younger brother or sister to address an older brother *(also used to address any person older than oneself) cf.* እትዬ
ጋበዘ *gäbbäzä* v.t. invited to a meal; treated to; offered *(drinks, cigarettes etc.)*
ጋባዥ *gabaž* n. host, hostess *(woman entertaining guests)*
ግብዣ *gəbža* n. invitation, reception, party, feast
ተጋበዘ *tägabbäzä* v.i. was invited; threatened to beat, kill s/o; bid defiance to
ጋተ *gatä* v.t. let a child drink out of the hand
ተጋተ *tägatä* v.i. made to drink *(unwillingly, e.g medicine)*
አጋተ *agatä* v.t. started having a larger udder
ጋኔን *ganen* n. demon, evil spirit adj. wicked *(pl.* አጋንንት *aganənt)*
ጋኔናም *ganenam* adj. moody, bad-tempered
ጋኔን ጎታች *ganen gottač* n. sorcerer
ጋን *gan* n. very large pitcher used in making beer
የደም— *yädäm*—n. artery
የጠምንጃ— *yäṭämänǧa* — n. chamber *(of gun)*
ጋንድያ *gandəyya* n. a fat lazy person
ጋንጢጥ *ganṭiṭ* adj. scornful, contemptuous, sniffy
*ጋዘ * *gazä*
ግዞት *gəzot* n. banishment, confinement
ግዞተኛ *gəzotäñña* person in banishment

ግዞት ቤት *gəzot bet* n. banishment *(place)*

መጋዣ *mägažža* n. beast of burden *(horse)*

ተጋዘ *tägazzä* v.i. was banished, was put in prison, was under house arrest

አጋዘ *agazä* v.t. banished, exiled; carried away, transported

ጋዝ *gaz* n. petroleum, kerosene, gas

ጋየ *gayyä* v.t. was set on fire

አጋየ *agayyä* v.t burnt off, set on fire

*ጋደለ * *gaddälä also* አጋደለ *agaddälä* v.i. leaned to one side, inclined

ጋዲ *gadi* n. strip of leather etc., for tying the hind legs of a cow when milking

ጋገረ *gaggärä* v.t. baked bread

ጋጋሪ *gagari in* ዳቦ ጋጋሪ *dabbo* — n. baker

እንጀራ— *ənǧära—ənǧära* baker

ዳቦ መጋገሪያ *dabbo mägagariya* n. oven; bakery

ተጋገረ *tägaggärä* v.i. baked formed a thick layer; was sticky

ጋጋ *gagga* v.i. slapped *(someone's face)*

*ጋጋ * *gagga*

ጋጋታ *gagata* n. uproar, clamour, haste

ተንጋጋ *tängagga* v.i. flocked together

አንጋጋ *angagga* v.t. drove flock

ጋጋኖ *gagano* n. water-hen

ጋጠ *gaṭä* v.t. grazed, pastured; gnawed a bone

ጋጠ ወጥ *gaṭä wäṭṭ* adj. impolite, rude

ግጦሽ *gəṭoš* n. pasture, grazing land

ግጠህ ውጣ *gəṭäh wəṭa* move heaven and earth, stick it out

ሰው መጋጥ ይወዳል he likes to backbite people

ራብ ጋጠኝ *rab gaṭäññ* I am terribly hungry

አጋጠ *agaṭä* v.t. pastured, grazed

መጋጫ *mägača* n. grazing land

ጋጠጠ *gaṭṭäṭä* v.t. cut s/t back; cut badly, cut very short

ጋጣ *gaṭa,* also ጋጥ *gaṭ* n. stable, pen *(cattle)*, stall *(horse)*

ጌሾ *gešo* n. a plant, the leaves of which are used in the preparation of beer and mead ጠጅ hop, buckthorn

ጌታ *geta* n. lord, master: owner; adj. rich *(having much money or property)*

ጌታው *getaw* n. Sir! Mr.!

ጌታዬ *getaye* My Lord!

ጌቶች *getočč* Master

ጌትነት *getənnät* wealthiness, richness

ለጌታ አደረ *lägeta addärä* was in someones service

የኔታ *yaneta* term used in addressing one's teacher, master

ጌጅ *geǧǧ* n. gauge, *gage*

ጌጥ *geṭ* n. decoration ornament, adornment, jewelery

ጌጠኛ *geṭäñña* adj. well decorated

ጌጣጌጥ *geṭageṭ* n. jewelery

ተጊያጊያጠ *tägiyagiyaṭä* n. put ornaments on, decorated oneself

አጌጠ *ageṭä* v.t. was decorated; well-dressed

ግላስ *gəlas* n. caparison *(of a horse)*

ግል *see* ገለለ

ግልገል *gəlgäl* n. lamb, kid, cub *(young of animals)*

ግልገል አንሣ *gəlgäl ansa* type of eagle that snatches kids, lambs

ግልባጭ *see* ገለበጠ

ግልምጫ *see* ገለመጠ

ግልድም *see* *ገለደመ

ግልጥ *see* ገለጠ

ግልፍ አለው *gəlləff alläw* v.i. he got mad *(suddenly)*

ግልፍተኛ *gələftäñña* adj. hot-blooded, ill-tempered, ill-natured

ግልፍታም *gəlləftam* adj. same as above

ግልጽ *see* ገለጠ *or* ገለጸ

ግመል *also* ገመል *gəmäl*, !*gämäl* n. camel

ግማደ መስቀል *gəmmadä mäsqäl* piece of the cross on which Christ was crucified

ግም *see* ገማ

ግምሩክ *gəmruk* ጉምሩክ *also gumruk* n. customs office, customs house

ግምባር *gəmbar*, *also* ግንባር *gənbar* n. forehead; brow; front *(military)*; luck

—ለግምባር *—lägəmbar* face to face, vis-a-vis cf. ፊት ለፊት

ግምባረ ቦቃ *gəmbarä boqa* adj. white spotted *(cow on the forehead)*

ግንባሩን ቋጠረ *gənbarun qʷäṭṭärä* v.i. frowned

ግምባሩ የማይታጠፍ *gəmbaru yämmayə-ttaṭṭäf* adj. daring, bold

ግምባራም *gəmbaram* adj. lucky

ግምባር የሌለው *gəmbar yälelläw* adj. unlucky, unfortunate

—ቀደም *—qäddäm* n. forefront, vanguard

—አስመታ *—asmätta* v.i. waited at someone's house or office for favour

ባለግምባር *balägəmbar* adj. lucky, fortunate

የጦር ግምባር *yäṭor gəmbar* front line; battle field

ግም ግም አለ *gəmm gəmm alä* v.i. thundered *(from a distance)*; started uprising, rebellion

ግምግምታ *gəmgəmta*, thunder; starting of an uprising, a rebellion

ግምት *see* ገመተ

ግምጃ *gəmǧa* n. silk or velvet cloth with embroidery; muslin

ግምጃ ቤት *gəmǧa bet* n. treasury, storehouse

ግሥ *see* ገሠሠ

ግሩም *see* ገረመ

ግራ *gəra* n. left adj. difficult

ግራም ነፈሰ ቀኝ whatever may happen

ግራ ቀመስ *gəra qämmäs* left oriented, tending left *(politically)*

—ቀኝ *—qäññ* n. drill *(military)*

—ቢስ *—bis* adj. clumsy, ungraceful

—አክራሪ *—akrari* ultra-leftist

ግራዝማች *gərazmač* commander of the left *(title)*

ግራ አጋባ *gəra aggabba* v.t. bewildered, puzzled, perplexed

—ክንፍ *—kənf* n. left-wing

—ወንበር *—wänbär* one of the three judges in a court sitting on the left side

—ገባው *—gäbbaw* v.i. was bewildered, puzzled, perplexed

—ጌታ *—geta* a church authority who stands in the outermost corridor of the

church
—ጎንደር —gondär n. slave (euphemism)
ገራኝ gərañ adj. left-handed
ገራማፎን gəramafon n. gramophone, phonograph
ግራም gram n. gramme
ኪሎ— kilo— n. kilogramme
ግራር gərar n. acacia abessinica
ግራዋ gərawwa n. vernonia mycrocephala
ግራጫ gəraċ̣ča adj. grey (only for donkeys and mules)
ግርማ see ገረመ
ግር አለ gərr alä v.i. was confused
ግር ግር አለ gərr gərr alä v.i was in a state of confusion
ግርኝ see ገረኘ
ግርዶሽ see ጋረደ
ግርጌ gərge n. foot (of bed)
በስተ— bästä— adv. at the foot of
ግርግር see * ገረገረ
ግስላ gəssəlla n. panther
ግስንግስ gəssangəs n. junk, hodge-podge, rubbish.
ግቢ see ገባ
ግቢር see ገበረ
ግብዝ gəbbəz n. hypocrite adj. not strong enough (construction)
ግብጥ see ገበጸ
ግብጽ gəbṣ n. Egypt
ግብጻዊ gəbṣawi n. Egyptian
ግትልትል see* ገተለተለ
ግትር see ገተረ
ግትት gəttät adj. naïve, foolish n. an old basket
ግትቻ gətəčča adj. stupid, inactive; worth nothing
ግጫ gəčča n. tuft of hard grass
ግን gən (sometimes) ግና adv. prep. rel. pron., conj. but, however
ነገር— nägər—but
ዳሩ— daru—but
ግንበኛ see ገነባ
ግንባር see ገምበር
ግንቦት gənbot n. May
ግንዘት see ገነዘ
ግንዲላ see ግንድ
ግንድ gənd n. trunk (of tree); block (of wood)
ግንደ ቆርቁር gəndä qorqur n. woodpecker
ግንዲላ gəndilla n. log (of tree)
የዘር ግንድ yäzär gənd n. genealogy
ጆሮ ግንድ ǧoro gənd n. temple
ግንጥል see ገነጠለ
ግንጭል gənčəl n. jaw
ግኡዝ gə'uz n. inanimate
—ፆታ —ṣota n. neuter gender
ግዕዝ gə'əz n. Geez language (a classical language of Ethiopia)
ግዞት see ጋዘ
ግዳይ see ገደለ
ግዳጅ see ገደደ
ግድግዳ see ገደገደ
ግግ gəgg n. milk-teeth (before they appear)
ግፍ see ገፋ
ግፍልፍል see ተገፈለፈለ
ጎህ goh n. dawn, daybreak
—ሲቀድ —siqädd adv. at daybreak
ጎለመሰ golämmäsä v.i. developed, matured (phsyically, mentally)
ጎልማሳ golmassa n. adult, youngman
የጎልማሶች ትምህርት yägolmasočč təmhərt adult education
አጎላመሰ agolammäsä v.t. complemented (gram.)
አጎላማሽ aggolamaš adj. complementary (gram.)
ጎለበተ golābätä v.i. became

strong

ጉልበት *gulbät* n. strength, energy ; knee

ጉልበተኛ *gulbätäñña* adj. strong, sturdy; aggressive

ጎምላላ *gomlalla* adj. graceful

ተጎማለለ *tägomallälä* v.i. walked gracefully

ጎመን *gommän* n. greens

—ዘር —*zär* n. rape seed

ጎመዘዘ *gämäzzäzä* v.i. tasted sour

ጎምዛዛ *gomzzaza* adj. sour

ተጎማዘዘ *tägomazzäzä* v.i. tasted sour

አጎመዘዘ *agomäzzäzä* v.t. turned sour

ጎመዠ *see* ጎመጀ

ጎመደ *gommädä* v.t. cut into chunks

ጉማጅ *gummağ* n. chunk

ጎመድ *gomäd* n. pole *(wood)*, cane *(used for beating s/o)*

ጎማዳ *gomada* adj. cut ugly

ጎመጀ *gomäğğä* v.i. had an appetite for; desired eagerly

አስጎመጀ *asgomäğğä* v.t. looked delicious and appetising; tempted *(attracted)*

ጎማ *gomma* n. tire; rubber; wheel *(vehicle)*

ጎረመሰ *gorämmäsä* v.i. reached adolescence *(male)*

ጉርምስና *gurməsənna* n adolescence

ጎረምሳ *gorämsa* n. adj. adolescent

ጎረሰ *gorräsä* v. t. took a mouthful; v.i. was loaded *(gun)*

ጉራሽ *gurraš* n. mouthful

ጉርሻ *gurša* n. mouthful; tip *(for service)*

አጎረሰ *agorräsä* v.t. gave a mouthful; loaded *(a gun)*; tipped

ጎረበ *gorräbä* v. i. crushed, wrinkled *(dress etc.)*

ተጉረበረበ *täguräbärräbä* v.i was wrinkled *(dress etc.)*

*ጎረበተ * *goräbbätä*

ጉርብትና *gurbətənna* n. neighbourhood

ጎረቤት *goräbet* n. neighbour

ጎረቤታም *goräbetam* n. neighbours

ተጎራበተ *tägorabbätä* v.i. lived in neighbourhood

ተጎራባች *tägorabač* adj. neighbouring

አጎራበተ *aggorabbätä* v.i. allowed s/o to be one's neighbour

ጎረበጠ *see* ጉረበጠ

ጎረደ *gorrädä* v.t. cut, chopped

ጉራጅ *gurrağ* n. stub *(of wood)*

ጉርድ *gurd* n. s/t cut off

—ቀሚስ n. skirt

ጎራዳ *gorada* n. ugly

ጎራጅ *gorağ in* ጉራጅ ቃል *gorağ qal* contracting word *(gram.)*

ጎራረደ *gorarrädä* v.t. cut into pieces, chopped

ጎረደመ *gorăddämä* v.t. munched

ጎረዶማን *gorädoman* n. driver of a merchants caravan *(beast of buraen)*

ጎራ *gora* n. mountain

ጎራ አለ *gora alä* v.i stopped over, dropped in *(on one's way)*

ጎራዴ *gorade* n. sword

ጎሬ *see* ጉሬ

ጎርምጥ *gormət* n. crab

ጎርደድ አለ *gordädd alä* v.i perambulated, walked to and fro

ተንጎራደደ *tängoraddädä* v.i perambulated, walked to and fro

ጎሳ *gosa* n. clan

ጎሽ *gošš* n. buffalo; interj. well done! bravo!

ጎበበ *gobbäbä* v.i. towered.

overtopped, overhanged

ጎባባ *gobaba* adj. towering, overtopping, overhanging

ጎበዘ *gobbäzä* v.i became successful; became smart, was brave

ጉብዝና *gubzənna* n. success; bravery, courage

ጎበዝ *gobäz* adj. successful; smart, brave; n. young man, fine young man

የጎበዝ አለቃ የጎበዝ አለቃ *yägobäz aläqa* n.leader of warriors

ጎተራ *gotära* n. granary, grain storage

—ሆድ *—hod* adj. big-bellied

ጎታ *gota* n. small granary

* ጎነጠፈ * *gonäṭṭäfä also* ተጎናጸፈ

ተጎናጠፈ *tägonaṭṭäfä, tägonaṣṣäfä* v.i. was wrapped up, wrapped oneself up *(with shawl, toga etc.)*

መጎናጠፊያ *also* መጎናጸፊያ *maggonaṭäfiya, mäggonaṣäfiya* n. shawl, toga

ጎነጸፈ *see* ጎነጠፈ

ጎን *gonn* n. side, flank *(of body)*; adv. by the side of, beside

እ... ጎን *ə...gonn* adv. beside

ከ... ጎን *kä...gonn* adv. close to, beside

ወደጎን *wädä gonn* adv. aside, abreast

ጎን ለጎን *gonn lägonn* adv. close to, beside, alongside

ጎንደር *gondär* n. one of the Administrative Regions, north-western Ethiopia *(Gondar)*

ጎንደሬ *gondäre* n. Gonderian

ጎንደርኛ *gondärəñña* n. the dialect of Gondar

ጎዘጎዘ *gozzäggozä* v.t. spread out s/t on the floor *(mattress, straw etc. as bedding)*

ጉዝጓዝ *guzguʷaz* n. bedding

ጎደለ *goddälä* v.i. subsided *(of flood water)*, diminished; decreased was incomplete; was short in; fell short

ጉድለት *guddlät* n. defect, deficiency, lack, shortcoming; fault, mistake

ጎደሎ *godälo* adj. not full; incomplete, lacking; weakling

—ቀን *—qän* evil day

—ቁጥር *—quṭər* odd number

የቀን ጎደሎ *yäqän godälo* evil day

ቀን የጎደለበት *qän yägoddäläbbät* adj. wretched, heart-broken

አካለ ጎደሎ *akalä*—n. crippled, invalid

እምነተ ጎደሎ *əmnätä* — adj. dishonest

ጉዳይ *gudday in* ሩብ ጉዳይ *rub gudday* quarter to

ተጓደለ *täguʷaddälä* v.i. failed to fulfil

አጎደለ *agoddälä* v.t. decreased; diminished; stood in need of

ጎዳ *goda* adj. plain *(not coloured, ordinary)*

—ሸማ *—šämma* plain šämma

—በሬ *—bäre* a bull of ordinary colour

ጎዳ *godda* v.t. harmed, injured, damaged, hurt; overcharged
e.g. በዋጋ ተጎዳን we are overcharged *(price)*

ጉዳት *gudat* n. harm, injury, damage; suffering; disadvantage

ጉዳተኛ *gudatäñña* adj. suffering, harmed, injured ill-conditioned

ጎጂ *goǧi* adj. harmful

ተጎዳ *tägodda* v.i. was harmed, injured, damaged, hurt; suffered; was overcharged

ጎዳኒሳ godanissa n. scar

ጎጆ goǧǧo *also* ጎዦ gožžo n. small hut; booth, cottage

ደሳሳ— däsasa — n. shack

—ቀለሰ —qälläsä v.t. built a small house

—ወጣ —wäṭṭa v.t. married

ጎጆና ጉልቻ goǧǧonna gulləčča married life

የወፍ ጎጆ yäwäf goǧǧo n. cage *(birds)* n. nest

ጎፈረ goffärä v.i. was large and bushy *(hair)*

ጎፈሬ gofäre n. Afro style *(hair-cut)*

ጎፈር goffär n. mane of a lion

ጎፈሪያም gofäriyam adj. bushy hair

አጎፈረ agoffärä v.t. grew large bushy hair

ጎፈነነ gofännänä v.t averted one's eyes from; was repellant *(food)*, was disgusting

*ጎፈፈ *goffäfä

ጎፋፋ gofafa adj. lubberly; blockhead

ጎፍላ gofla n. tuft of hair

*ጎለመመ *golämämä

ጉልማማ guʷälmamma adj. stately, graceful

ተጉላመመ täguʷälammämä v.i. walked gracefully

ጉለተ guʷällätä v.i. placed three stones above a fire-place in order to make the cooking pot rest; endowed *(land to a church)*

ጉልተኛ gultäñña n. big land owner

ጉልት *in* ርስተ ጉልት rəstä gult n. fief, land given by a ruler to an individual or to the church as an endowment

ጉልት guʷəllət n. back-street market

ጉልቻ guʷəlləčča n. three stones or earthen-ware tripod on which the cooking pot rests above the fire

ተጉለተ täguʷällätä v.i. sat idly *(for a long time)*

*ጉለደፈ *guʷäläddäfä

ጉልድፍ guʷəldəf adj. lisping lacking dexterity

ጉልዳፋ guʷäldaffa adj. lacking dexterity

ተጉላደፈ täguʷäladdäfä v.i. lisped

ጉለጉለ guʷäläggu ʷälä v.t. cleaned ploughed land of weeds; emptied out *(a sack, a suit-case)*

ምስጢር— məsṭir – let the cat out of the bag; let one into the secret

ጉልጓሎ guʷəlguʷalo n. cleaning ploughed land of weeds *also* ጉልጎላ

ጎላ guʷälla v.i. was magnified *(appeared larger)*, stood out; was clear

ጉልህ guʷələh adj. clear, evident, obvious; gross *(error)*

አጎላ aguʷälla v.t. magnified *(made to appear larger)*; amplified

ድምፅ ማጉያ dəmṣ maguʷya n. amplifier; megaphone

አጉሊ መነጽር agʷyi mänäṣṣər n. microscope

ጎመራ guʷämärra v.i. started ripening *(fruit, grain)*

ጎመተመተ *guʷämätämmätä

አጉመተመተ aguʷmätämmätä v.i. murmured *(complained in a murmur)*

*ጎመዘዘ *see* ኮመዘዘ

*ጎመጠመጠ *guʷämäṭämmäṭä

ተጉመጠመጠ täguʷmäṭämmäṭä v.i. rinsed *(the mouth)*

ጎማ *see* ኰማ

*ጎረመረመ *guʷärämärrämä

ጉርምርምታ guʷərəmrəmta n.

growling

አጕረመረመ *aguʷərämärrämä* v.t. murmured, grumbled; grunted, complained

አጕረምራሚ *aguʷərämrami* adj. grumbling, murmuring

***ጐረመሰ** *see* ጎረመሰ

ጕርምጥ *guʷärməṭ* n. incurable skin ulcer

ጐረሰ *see* ጎረሰ

ጐረበጠ *guʷäräbbäṭä* v.t. was uncomfortable, was hard *(sitting or sleeping place)*

ሆዴን ጐረበጠኝ *hoden guʷäräbbäṭäññ* I feel unwell in my stomach

ጐርባጣ *guʷärbaṭṭa* adj. uncomfortable, hard *(sitting, sleeping place)*

***ጐረነነ** **guʷärännänä*

ጐርናና *guʷärnanna* adj. rough *(voice)*

ጐረና *guʷäränna* v.i. tasted burnt

ጕርናት *guʷərnat* n. burnt taste

አጐረና *aguʷäränna* v.t. burnt *(the food)*

ጐረደመ *see* ጎረደመ

ጐረጐረ *guʷäräggʷärä* v.t. searched *(a house etc.)*; poked

አንጐራጐረ *anguʷäraggʷärä* v/t sang melancholy song

እንጕርጕሮ *ənguʷərgguʷəro* n. melancholy song

***ጐረጠ** **guʷärräṭä*

ጕርጥ *guʷərṭ also* ጐርጥ n. frog

ጕርጥ ዐይን *guʷərṭ ayn* adj. ox-eyed

ጐረጥራጣ *guʷäräṭraṭṭä* n. one with bulging eyes

አጕረጠረጠ *aguʷräṭärräṭä* v. t. looked furiously at s/o

አጕርጥ *aguʷərṭ* adj. sardonic, scornful

ጐረፈ *guʷärräfä* v.i. flooded, flew in abundance; gushed *(of tears)*; lathered

ጐርፍ *guʷärf* n. flood, torrent

***ጐራ** **guʷärra*

አጐራ *aguʷärra* v.t. groaned, screamed *(hysterically)*

አጓራ *aguʷarra* v.t. bellowed *(ox)* groaned; boomed *(cannons)*

ጐሰመ *guʷässämä, also* ጐሸመ *guʷäššämä,* v.t. thumped *(s/o on the side to bring s/t to his attention)*; jerked *(with sudden push)*; nudged

ነጋሪት— *nägarit—* v.t. drummed

ጕሰማ *guʷssäma* n. nudge

ጐሰረ *guʷässärä* v.t. stuffed into; stuffed *(oneself with food)*

ጐሰቈለ *guʷäsäqquʷälä* v.t. was in a miserable condition, was wretched

ጕስቈላ *guʷ əsqʷällä* n. wretchedness, misery

ጐስቋላ *guʷäsquʷalla* adj. miserable, wretched

ተጐሳቈለ *täguʷäsaqquʷälä* v.i suffered greatly; was mishandled

አጐሳቈለ *aguʷäsaqquʷälä* v.t mistreated, misused, mishandled; rendered haggard *(of suffering)*

ጐሰጐሰ *guʷäsäggʷäsä* v.t. crammed, stuffed into, stuffed *(oneself with food)*

***ጐሸ** **see* ጎሸ

ጐሸመ *see* ጎሰመ

ጐበኘ *guʷäbäññä* v.t. visited, toured; inspected, reviewed *(troops)*

ጕብኝት *guʷəbəññət* n. visit; tour

ጐብኚ — *guʷäbñi* n. visitor
አገር— — *agär–* n. tourist
አስጐበኘ — *asguʷäbäññä* v.t. showed around; guided *(visitors, tourists)*
አስጐብኚ — *asguʷäbñi* n. tourist guide

ጐበበ — *see* ጎበበ
ጐበዘ — *see* ጎበዘ

*ጐበደደ — * *guʷäbäddädä*
አጐበደደ — *aguʷäbäddädä* v.i. bowed to, demeaned onself, licked the boots
አጐብዳጅ — *aguʷäbdaǧ* adj. boot-licking

*ጐበጐበ — **gaʷäbäggu ʷäbä*
አጐበጐበ — *aguʷäbäggu ʷägbä* v.i. acted as a stooge for
አጐብጓቢ — *aguʷäbguʷabi* n. stooge

ጐበጠ — *guʷäbbäṭä* v.i. was bent; was humped, was curved
ጐባጣ — *guʷäbaṭa* adj. curved, hunched, bent
ጐቢጥ — *guʷäbiṭ* n. humpback *(insult)*
ጐብጠት — *guʷbṭät* n. bend
አጐበጠ — *aguʷäbbaṭä* v.t. bent, forced into a curve

ጐባን — *guʷäbban* n. one who has taken s/o's husband or wife

*ጐተመ — * *guʷättämä*
አጐተመተመ — *aguʷtämättämä* v.i. murmured *(complained)*

ጐተተ — *guʷättätä* v.t. pulled, dragged, drew toward, tagged on
ጕተታ — *guʷəttäta in* የገመድ ጕተታ *yägämäd guʷəttäta* tug of war
ጐታታ — *guʷätata* n/adj. sluggard, slacker, sluggish, slow *(in work)*
ጕትት — *guʷəttət* adj. slow
ጕትቻ — *guʷətəčča also yä-ğoro guʷətəčča* n. ear-ring
ተጐተተ — *täguʷattätä* v.i. was pulled, dragged; lagged behind
ተጐታች — *täguʷättač* n. trailer
ተጓተተ — *täguʷattätä* v.i. slackened; lagged behind, delayed *(work)*, took a long time

*ጐተነ — **guʷättänä*
ጕተና — *guʷətäna* n. bushy hair
አጐተነ — *aguʷättänä* v.t. grew bushy hair

ጐተጐተ — *guʷätäggu ʷätä* v.t. badgered, kept nagging
ጕትጐታ — *guʷətguʷäta* n. badgering, nagging

ጐነቈለ — *guʷänäqquʷälä* v.i. germinated
ጕንቊል — *guʷənqul* n. soaked and germinating beans used as food
አጐነቈለ — *aguʷänäqquʷälä* v.t. germinated

*ጐነበሰ — **guʷänäbbäsä*
ጐንበስ ቀና አለ — *guʷänbäss qäna alä* v.i. toiled *(at a task)*
አጐነበሰ — *aguʷänäbbäsä* v.i. bent, stooped; bowed to
አጐንባሽ — *aguʷänbaš* adj. boot-licking *also* አፋሽ አጐንባሽ
አስጐነበሰ — *asguʷänäbbäsä* v.t. subdued *(brought under control)*

*ጐነዘለ — **guʷänäzzälä*
ጐንዛላ — *guʷänzalla* adj. undulating *(field of wheat etc.)*
ተጐናዘለ — *täguʷänazzälä* v.i. undulated *(a field of wheat in the breeze)*

ጐነጐነ — *guʷänäggu ʷänä* v.t. plaited *(hair, rope)*, braided
ጐንጓኝ — *in* ነገር ጐንጓኝ *nägär guʷänguʷañ* n. schemer, intriguer
ጕንጕን — *guʷənguʷən* n. plait, braid

ያበባ— *yabäba*— n. wreath, garland

ተጐነጐነ *tägʷänäggʷänä* v.t. was plaited

ጐነጠ *gʷännäṭä* v.t. jerked cf. ጐሰመ

በነገር—ኝ *bänägär—ñ* passed rude remarks about me, that was a dig at me

ጕንጣ *gʷənnäṭa* n. jerk *(sudden push)*

*ጐነጨ *gʷänäč̣č̣ä*

ጕንጭ *gʷənč̣* n. cheek

—ሙሉ *—mulu* adj. mouthful

ጕንጫም *gʷənč̣am* s/o with fat cheeks

ተጐነጨ *tägʷänäč̣č̣ä* v.t. took a gulp, sipped

ጐነጠፈ *see* ጎነጠፈ

ጐነፈ *gʷännäfä* v.t. soaked in hot water

ጐደሪ *gʷädärri* n. taro

*ጐደኘ * *gʷädäññä*

ጓደኛ *gʷaddäñña* n. friend, companion, colleague

የሥራ— *yäsəra*—n. co-worker, colleague

የትምህርት ቤት— *yätəmhərt bet*—n. school mate

የክፍል— *yäkəfəl*—n. classmate

የጦር ጓድ *yäṭor gʷadd* n. ally

ጓደኞች *gʷaddäññamoč* n. pl. friends, companions, associates

ጓደኝነት *gʷaddäññənnät* n. friendship, fellowship

ጓድ *gʷadd* n. comrade

ተጐዳኘ *tägʷädaññä* v.i became friend to; joined

*ጐደደ **gʷäddädä*

ጐዳዳ *gʷädada* adj. graceful *(in movement)*

ተንጓደደ *tängʷaddädä* v.i. moved gracefully

ጐደጐደ *gʷädäggʷädä* v.i. became hollow, deep; sank in *(soil, road etc.)*

ጐድጓዳ *gʷädgʷadda* adj/n hollow, deep; depression

ጕድጓድ *gʷədgʷad* n. pit, hole, cavity; well, depression, ditch

—ማሰ *—masä* n.t. plotted, conspired, pulled wires

አጐደጐደ *agʷädäggʷädä* v.t. hollowed out, deepened

ጎጃም *gʷäğğam* n. one of the Administrative Regions western Ethiopia *(Gojam)*

ጐጃሜ *gʷäğğame* n. Gojamite

ጐፈየ *gʷäfäyyä* v.i. was lean *(meat)*; was thin *(ox)*

ጕፋያ *gʷfayya* adj. lean *(meat)*, thin

ጕቶ *see* ጉቶ

ጓ አለ *gʷa alä* v. i. banged *(made a loud noise)*

*ጓለለ **gʷallälä*

ጕላይ *gʷəllay* n. husk

ተንጓለለ *tängʷallälä* v.i. was raked

አንጓለለ *angʷallälä* v.t. raked; paid no attention to *(consciously)*

ጓል *gʷal* n. clod *(lump of earth)*

*ጓመጠ **gʷammäṭä*

አጓመጠ *agʷammäṭä* v.t. gormandized, devoured

ጓሮ *gʷaro* n. backyard

እምባ— *əmbba*—n. quarrel

እምባ ጓሮኛ *—gʷaroñña* adj. quarrelsome

*ጓሸ **gʷaššä*

ጕሽ *gʷəš* n. unfiltered beer

ጓነ *gʷanä* v.i. bonded, rebounded, bounced *(ball etc.)*

አጓነ *agʷanä* v. t. rebounded, bounced

*ጓዘ **gʷazä*

ጕዞ *gʷəzo* n. journey, trip, travel, voyage, itinerary

ጕዘኛ *gʷəzoñña* n. traveller

ተጓዘ *tägʷazä* v.i. travelled, journeyed

ተጓዥ *taguʷaž* n. traveller; passenger
ተጓጓዘ *tägʷaguʷazä* v. i. was transported
መጓጓዣ *mägguʷaguʷaža* n. means of transportation, vehicle
አጓጓዘ *agguʷaguʷazä* v. t transported
አስጓዘ *asguʷazä* v.t. had goods transported
ጓያ *guʷayya* n. vetch
*ጓደደ **guʷaddädä*
ተጓደደ *täguʷaddädä* v.i. was slow *(intentionally)*
ጓዳ *guʷada* n. store-room
—አዋቂ *—awwäq* adj. well informed, privy to, in the know
ጓድ *see* ጉዴኛ
ጓጐለ *guʷagguʷälä* v.i. clotted *(cream, soup etc.)*
ሰውነቱ— *säwənnätu*—have muscle-bound
ጓጓላ *guʷagguʷala* n. clot
አጓጐለ *aguʷagguʷälä* v.t. clotted
አጓጉል *aguʷagul* adj. improper, indecent, incorrect, unbecoming
—እምነት *—əmnät* n. superstition
ጓጐረ *guʷagguʷärä* v.t. groaned *(made a deep sound)*
ጓጐጠ *guʷagguʷäṭä* v.t. poked *(with a stick or finger)*; vomited
ጓጉንቸር *guʷaguncär* n. toad
ጓጓ *guʷagguʷa* v.i. wished strongly, have a fervent desire, was anxious, curious, eager; yearned; looked forward
ጉጉ *guʷəggu* adj. desirous, curious
ጉጉት *guʷggut* n. longing curiously, fervent desire
ጉንፋን *see* ጉንፋን
ጉድባ *see* ጉድባ

ጠ

ጠለለ *ṭällälä* v.i. was purified; was pure; was filtered
ጠላላ *ṭäläla* n. shelter, shed
ጠላላ *in* ጠላላ ሜዳ *ṭäläla meda* n. open landscape
ተንጣለለ *tänṭallälä* v.i. spread *(water on a flat land)*
አጠለለ *aṭällälä* v.t. purified, filtered; strained *(passed liquid through a cloth)*
ማጥለያ *maṭläya* n. sifter, filter, strainer
*ጠለለ **ṭällälä*
ጠል *ṭäll* n. dew; rain; verdure
ጥላ *ṭəla* n. shade. shadow umbrella
—ቢስ *—bis adj*. graceless, undignified; airy, light-hearted
—የሌለው *—yälelläw* adj. undignified
—የቀለለው *—yäqällälläw* adj. light-minded
ጥላማ *ṭəlamma* adj. shady
ዓይነ ጥላ *aynäṭəla* n. phobia, aversion
ተጠለለ *täṭällälä* v.i. took shelter; sought refuge; took cover
መጠለያ *mäṭṭäläya* n. shed, shelter; refugee camp
አስጠለለ *asṭällälä* v.t. gave shelter to, sheltered
*ጠለመ *see* ጽልመት
ጠለቀ *ṭälläqä* v.i. was deep; dived; sank; submerged, be profound

የጠለቀ ትምህርት *yäṭälläqä təmhərt* profound learning
—እውቀት —*əwqät* profound knowledge
ጠላቂ *ṭälaqi* n. diver
ጣልቃ *ṭalqa* adv. in between
—ገባ —*gäbba* v.t meddled, interfered; broke into conversation; intruded
—ገብ —*gäbb* n. meddler, intruder
—ገብነት —*gäbbənät* n. interference, intrusiveness
መጥለቂያ *mäṭläqiya* n. dipper
ጥልቀት *ṭəlqät* n. depth
—የሌለው —*yälelläw* adj. shallow
የፀሐይ/የጀንበር— *yäṣahay/yäǧänbär—* *ṭəlqät* n. sundown
ጥልቅ *ṭəlq* adj. deep, profound; expert *(knowledge)*
ጥልቅ አለ *ṭəlləqq alä* v.t. intruded, mixed in, interfered
ጥልቅ ብዩ *ṭəlləqq bəyyä* n. busy-body
ጥልቆ *ṭəlləqqo* n. small axe
መጥለቂያ *mäṭläqiya* n. bucket, can etc. for dipping water out
ተጣለቀ *täṭalläqä* v.i. ducked each other cf. ተዛፈቀ
ተጥለቀለቀ *täṭläqälläqä* v.i. was flooded, was overflowing, was overwhelmed
አጠለቀ *aṭälläqä* v.t. put on *(shirt, trousers etc.)*; wore *(a chain around the neck)*
ላብ አጠለቀው *lab aṭälläqäw* he was drenched with sweat
አጥለቀለቀ *aṭläqälläqä* v.t. flooded, overflowed; overwhelmed *(gratitude, joy etc.)*
ጠለዘ *ṭälläzä* v.t. hit, kicked strongly
ጆሮ የሚጠለዝ ሙዚቃ deafening music

*ጠለጠለ • *ṭäläṭṭälä*
ተንጠለጠለ *tänṭäläṭṭälä* v.i. was hung, was suspended; swung
የተንጠለጠለ *yätänṭäläṭṭälä*
—ጉዳይ *gudday* a pending case, issue
አንጠለጠለ *anṭäläṭṭälä* v.t. hung up; suspended
ማንጠልጠያ *manṭälṭäya* n. handle *(of suitcase)*, hook, peg *(for coat, hat)*; staple *(of padlock)*

ጠለፈ *ṭälläfä* v.t. tripped *(up)*; tied the legs of animal; entangled; kidnapped *(a girl, a slave)*; hijacked; embroidered; connected *(wire, rope)*
ጠለፋ *ṭäläfa* n. hijacking, kidnapping, abduction
ጠላፊ *ṭäläfi* n. hijacker, kidnapper
ጥልፊያ *ṭəlfiya* n. hijacking, abduction; catching and pulling s/o's leg
ጥልፍ *ṭəlf* n. needlework, embroidery
ጥልፍልፍ *ṭəlafləf* n. entanglement
መጥለፊያ *in* መጥለፊያ ቋንቋ *mäṭläfiya quʷanquʷa* a language from which translation is made
ተጠለፈ *täṭälläfä* v.i. was abducted, hijacked; was tripped *(up)*
ተጠላለፈ *täṭälalläfä* v.i. was entangled *(thread)*, interlocked; interlinked

ጠላ *ṭälla* n. common

Ethiopian beverage *(beer)*

ጉሽ ጠላ *guš*—young beer

ጠላ *ṭälla* v.i. hated, disliked

ጠላት *ṭälat* n. enemy, foe, adversary

ጥላቻ *ṭəlačča* n. hatred, dislike, hostility, antagonism, animosity

ጥል *ṭəl* n. quarrel, fight, enmity

ጥለኛ *ṭəläñña* n. person who is not on speaking terms with someone

ተጠላ *täṭälla* v.i. was hated, became unpopular

የተጠላ *yätäṭälla* adj. unpopular; hated

ተጣላ *täṭalla* v.i. quarreled with, fought with; disputed

አጣላ *aṭṭalla* v.t. set two people at variance

አጥላላ *aṭlalla* v.t. spurned, contemned

አስጠላ *asṭälla* v.t. disgusted

ማስጠሎ *masṭällo* adj. ugly, hideous

አስጠይ *asṭäyy* adj. disgusting, abhorrent

ጠልሰም *ṭälsäm* n. amulet *(with colourful designs)*

ጠሎት *see* ጸሎየ

*ጠመለመለ *see* ተጥመለመለ

ጠመመ *ṭämmämä* v.i. was crooked, twisted, curved, deformed was stubborn, played against, refused

ጠማማ *ṭämama* adj. crooked, bent, curved; uncooperative, stubborn

ተጣመመ *täṭammämä* v.i. was crooked, distorted

አጣመመ *aṭṭammämä* v.t. distorted; twisted, bent

*ጠመረ **ṭämmärä*

ጣምራ *in* ጣምራ ጠላት *ṭamra ṭälat* n. joint enemy

ጥምር *ṭəmmər* adj. **affixed**

—ቃል *—qal* affixed word; compounded word

ተጣመረ *täṭammärä* v.i. was combined, coupled

ተጣማሪ *täṭamari* n. noun in apposition *(gram.)*

አጣመረ *aṭṭammärä* v.t. combined, coupled; folded, crossed *(the arms)*, joined

መስተፃምር *mästäṣamər* n. conjunction *(gram.)*

ጠመረረ *ṭämärrärä* v.i. became exceedingly hot *(sun, fire)*; became very severe *(war)*

ጠመሰመሰ *see* ተጥመሰመሰ

ጠመሰሰ *ṭämässäsä* v.t. trampled *(crushed under the feet)*

ጠመቀ *ṭämmäqä* v.t. brewed beer; immersed in water, soaked *(clothes)*

ጥምቀት *ṭəmqät* n. baptism, Epiphany

ጥምቀተ ባሕር *ṭəmqätä bahər* open space where the feast of Epiphany is celebrated

ምጥማቅ *məṭmaq* n. baptismal font

ተጠመቀ *täṭämmäqä* v.i· was brewed *(beer)*; immersed oneself in water

ሰውነቴ በላብ ተጠመቀ I was in a sweat

አጠመቀ *aṭämmäqä* v.t. baptized, christened

ማጥመቂያ *mäṭmäqiya* n. baptismal font

ጠመኔ *ṭämäne* n. chalk *(for writing)*

ጠመንዣ/ጃ *ṭämänža /ǧa* n. gun, rifle

ጠመንጃ መፍቻ *ṭämänǧa mäfča* n. screw-driver

*ጠመዘመዘ **ṭämäzämmäzä*

ጠመዝማዛ *ṭämäzmazza* adj/n.

sinuous, zigzag

ተጥመዘመዘ *täṭmäzämmäzä* v.i. twisted *(road)*

አጥመዘመዘ *aṭmäzämmäzä* v.t. twisted

ጠመዘዘ *ṭämäzzäzä* v.t. wrung, twisted

ጠምዛዛ *ṭämzazza* adj/n tortuous *(road)*, winding, spiral; zigzag

ጥምዝ *ṭəməzz* adj. twisted

ተጠመዘዘ *täṭämäzzäzä* v.i. twisted

መጠምዘዣ *mäṭṭämzäža* n. curve, turn *(in a road)*

ተጠማዘዘ *täṭämazzäzä* v.i. bent, wound

ጠመዥ *ṭämäž* n. type of barley *(whose husk can be easily removed)*

ጠመደ *ṭämmädä* v.t. yoked *(oxen together)*; looked at s/o with hatred

ጥማድ *ṭəmmad* n. team *(of oxen)*

ጥንድ *ṭənd also* **ጥምድ** n. couple, pair

ወጥመድ *wäṭmäd* n. snare, trap *(for animals)*

—ገባ *—gäbba* v.t. was caught in a snare, was ensnared, was trapped

ተጠመደ *täṭämmädä* v.i. was yoked *(oxen)*; was looked at with hatred

በሥራ— *bäsəra*—was very busy

ተጣመደ *täṭammädä* v.i. have animosity against each other

አጠመደ *aṭämmädä* v.t. set traps, entrapped, laid snares; caught *(fish)*

አጥማጅ *in* ዓሣ አጥማጅ *asa aṭmaǧ* n. fisherman

ማጥመጃ *maṭmäǧa* n. snare, trap

አጣመደ *aṭṭammädä* v.t. joined up *(oxen)*

አጣማጅ *in* አጣማጅ በሬ *aṭṭamaǧ bäre* one of the pair of oxen

አስጠመደ *asṭämmädä* v.t. caused *(s/o)* to be looked at with hatred

ጠመጠመ *ṭämäṭṭämä* v.t. wrapped *(a scarf round the head)*; wound *(bandage)*; coiled up

ጠምጣማ *ṭämṭamma* adj. sturdy

ጠምጣሚ *ṭämṭami* n. priest, clergyman *(pejorative)*

ጥምጥም *ṭəmṭəm* n. turban, headband

ጥምጥም አለ *ṭəmṭəmm alä* v.i. became sturdy; v.t embraced *(forcefully)*; curled up

ጥምጥም ያለ *ṭəmṭəmm yalä* adj. sturdy

ተጠመጠመ *täṭämäṭṭämä* v.i. was entwined, clung to *(e.g. a child to his mother etc.)*; coiled

ጠማ(ው) *ṭämma(w)* v.i. was thirsty, had a thirst for

ጥማት *ṭəmat* n. thirst

ጥም *ṭəm* n. thirst

ተጠማ *täṭämma* v.i. was thirsty ; had a fervent desire to

አጠማ *aṭämma* v.t. blotted *(dried up wet ink)*

ማጥሚያ *maṭmiya* n. blotter

አስጠማ *asṭämma* v.t. made thirsty

ጠምበለል *ṭämbäläl* n. jasmine

ጠረመሰ *ṭärämmäsä* v.t. smashed down *(wall, door etc.)*

ተጠረመሰ *täṭärämmäsä* v.i. got smashed

ጠረረ *ṭärrärä* v.i. was very strong *(sun)*

ጠራራ *ṭärara* n. blazing

(sun)

የጠራራ ፀሐይ *yäṭärara ṣähay* mid-day sun

ጠረሰ *ṭärräsä* v.i. became blunt *(knife, razor)*

ጥርስ *ṭərs* n. tooth, tusk

የዝሆን— *yäzəhon*—n. tusk, ivory

—ሸረፈ *—šärräfä* v.i. lost one's milk-tooth

ጥርሰ በረዶ *ṭərsä bärädo* adj. with snow-white teeth

—ወላቃ *—wälaqa* adj. toothless

—ገጣጣ *—gäṭaṭa* adj. buck-toothed

ጥርሱን ነከሰ *ṭərsun näkkäsä* v.t. had patience, perseverance

—ነከሰብኝ *—näkkäsäbbəññ* he threatened me

ጥርሱን ነክሶ *ṭərsun näkso* adv. patiently, with perseverance

ጥርሳም *ṭərsam* adj. buck-toothed

ጥርስ አፋጨ *ṭərs afaččä* v.t. gnashed *(the teeth)*

—አወጣ *—awäṭṭa* v.t. cut a tooth

—ገባ *—gäbba* v.t. became antipathetic

አጠረሰ *aṭärräsä* v.t. dulled *(edge of a blade, razor)*

የጥርስ ሐኪም *yäṭərs hakim* n. dentist

—ሳሙና *—samuna* n. toothpaste

ጠረቀመ *ṭäräqqämä* v.t. slammed *(the door)*

ጥርቅም አድርጎ በላ *ṭərqəmm adərgo bälla* ate well

——አድርጎ አሰረ *——assärä* v.t. tied s/t fast

*ጠረቀመ *ṭäräqqämä*

ጥርቃሚ *ṭəraqqami* n. the riff-raff, the rubble

ጥርቃሞ *ṭərəqqamo* n. the riff-raff, the rubble

ጥርቅም *ṭərəqqəm* n. collection

ጥርቅምቅም *ṭərqəmqəm* n. rubble *(disorderly crowd)*; hotch-potch, jumble

ተጠረቃቀመ *täṭäräqaqqämä* v.i. gathered together, was gathered together

ተጠራቀመ *täṭäraqqämä* v.i. was collected; gathered *(people)*; accumulated

አጠራቀመ *aṭṭäraqqämä* v.t. collected, gathered accumulated; saved *(money)*

ጠረበ *ṭärräbä* v.t. carved, hewed *(shaped by chopping)*

ጠራቢ *in* ድንጊያ ጠራቢ *dängiya ṭärabi* n. stonemason

ጠርብ *ṭärb* n. lumber, board, plank

ጠርብ የሚያህል ሰው *tärb yämmiyahəl säw* a gigantic man

ጥራቢ *ṭərrabi* n. shavings

ጥርብ ድንጊያ *ṭərb dängiya* n. hewn stone

መጥረቢያ *mäṭräbiya* n. hatchet, axe

*ጠረበበ *ṭäräbbäbä*

ጠርባባ *ṭärbabba* adj. sulky

ተንጠረበበ *tänṭäräbbäbä* v.i. sulked

ጠረነቀ *ṭärännäqä* v.t tied firmly

ጠረን *ṭärän* n. odour

*ጠረወዘ *ṭäräwwäzä*

ተንጠራወዘ *tänṭärawwäzä* v.i. walked feebly

ጠረዘ *ṭärräzä* v.i. bound *(a book)*

ጠርዝ *ṭärz* n. fringe, hem, edge, border

ጥራዝ *ṭəraz* n. volume *(book)*; binding

—ነጠቅ *—näṭṭäq* adj. superficial, shallow, semi-learned

*ጠረዘዘ *ṭäräzzäzä*

ጠርዛዛ *ṭärzazza* adj. gloomy, depressed

ተንጠረዘዘ *tänṭäräzzäzä* v.i. was

gloomy, depressed

ጠረገ *ţärrägä* v.t. swept, wiped, cleaned; shined *(shoes)*; mopped *(the forehead)*

መንገድ— *mängäd*—v.t. opened a road to, cleaned a road to, paved the way for

ጠራጊ *in* ጫማ ጠራጊ *čamma ţäragi* n. shoeshine boy

ጥራጊ *ţərragi* n. rubbish, sweepings

ጥርጊያ *in* ጥርጊያ መንገድ *ţərgiya mängäd* n. cleared road *(not paved)*

ጥርጊያ ጎዳና *ţərgiya godana* *see* ጥርጊያ መንገድ

መጥረጊያ *mäţrägiya* n. broom, sweeper

ተጠረገ *in* ተጠርጎ ሄደ *täţärgo hedä* left for good *(only for an unwanted person)*

ተጠራረገ *in* ተጠራርጎ ጠፋ *täţärargo ţäffa* disappeared together completely *(only for unwanted person)*

ጠረጠረ *ţäräţţärä* v.i. suspected; mistrusted, doubted, had suspicions

ጠርጣሪ *ţärţari* adj. suspicious, doubtful; sceptic, distrustful

ጥርጣሬ *ţərəţţare* n. suspicion, distrust, doubt

ጥርጥር *ţərəţţər* n. doubt, suspicion

ያለ— *yalä*—adv. unquestionably, undoubtedly

ተጠረጠረ *täţäräţţärä* v.i. was suspected *(of being guilty)*

ተጠራጠረ *täţäraţţärä* v.i. was in doubt about, called into question, coudn't believe

አትጠራጠር *attəţţäraţär* be sure, take my word

ተጠራጣሪ *täţäraţari* adj. sceptical, distrustful

አጠራጠረ *aţţäraţţärä* v.t. was questionable, doubtful, equivocal

አጠራጣሪ *aţţäraţari* adj. questionable, doubtful, equivocal

ጠረጠረ *ţäräţţärä* c.t removed husks with the teeth *(of cooked beans etc.)*

ጥርጣሪ *ţərəţţari* n. husks removed in the above way

ጠረጠሰ *ţäräţţäsä* v.i. got blunt *(of sharp edge)*

ጥርጥስ *ţərţəs* adj. blunt

ተንጠራጠሰ *tänţäraţţäsä* v.t. got blunt *(sharp edge)*

ጠረጴዛ *ţäräppeza* n. table; desk

የጠረጴዛ ልብስ *yäţäräppeza ləbs* n. table-cloth

ጠረፍ *ţäräf* n. border *(line dividing two states or countries)*, coast, frontier

የጠረፍ ክልል *yäţäräf kəlləl* n. border line *(line dividing two countries)*

ጠረፍ ጠባቂ *ţäräf ţäbbaqi* n. border patrol

ጠራ *ţärra* v.t. called, called up; named; mentioned

ጋበዘ— *gəbža*—v.t. invited *(to a party, feast etc.)*

ሰም— *səm*—v.t. took attendance

—ጠሪ —*ţäri* one who takes the attendance

ጥሪ *ţərri* n. call, invitation

የፍርድ ቤት ጥሪ *yäfərd bet ţərri* n. summons *(order to appear before a judge or magistrate)*

የጥሪ ወረቀት *yäţərri wäräqät* n. invitation card

የናት አገር ጥሪ *yännat agär ţərri* call of the Motherland

ተጠራ *täţärra* v.i. was called, summoned

ሰሙ— *səmu*—v.i became famous, found recognition

ተጠሪ *täṭäri* n. representative, patron

ቋሚ— *quʷami*—n. permanent secretary

ተጣራ *täṭarra* v.i. called out (*summoned*)

አስጠራ *asṭärra* v.t. had (s/o) called, summoned

ስሙን— *səmmun*—won a good name for oneself

ጠራ *ṭärra* v.i. was pure, was clear; brightened (*sky*); cleared up (*weather*)

ጥራት *ṭərat* n. purity, pureness

ጥሩ *ṭəru* adj. good, fine, nice

ስመ— *səmä* — dj. famous, reputable

ጥር in ስመ ጥር *səmä ṭər* adj. famous, reputable

ተጣራ *täṭarra* v.i. was filtered, refined, purified; was verified; was sold out

ጉዳዩ— *guddayu*—the case was cleared up

የተጣራ ገቢ *yätäṭarra gäbi* net income

—ወሬ —*wäre* authentic news

አጠራ *aṭärra* v.t. cleaned, purified, made clear

አጣራ *aṭṭarra* v.t. purified distilled, filtered, clarified; cleared up; verified; sold out

ማጣሪያ *maṭṭarïa* n. filter; strainer

ጠራራ *ṭärara* n. blazing sun

የጠራራ ፀሐይ *yäṭärara ṣähai* mid-day sun

*ጠራራ **ṭärarra*

ተንጠራራ *tänṭärarra* v.i. reached out; streched one's arms (*legs, oneself*); aspired too much

አንጠራራ *in* አንጠራራኝ *anṭärarraññ* I felt like stretching myself

ጠር *see* ፀር

ጠርሙስ(ዝ) *ṭärmus (z)* n. bottle

ጠርቡሽ *ṭärbuš* n. tarboosh, fez

ጠሰቀ *ṭässäqä* v.t. tied tightly

ጥስቅ አድርጎ ይበላል *ṭəssəqq adərgo yəbälal* he is a big eater

ጠስቆ አሰረ *ṭässəqo assärä* he tied fast

ጥስቅ ያለ ሰውነት *ṭəssəqq yalä säwənnät* strongly built body

ጠቀለለ *ṭäqällälä* v.t. coiled; wrapped, wrapped up; (*a rug etc.*); enveloped

አገሪቱን ጠቅልሎ ገዛ he ruled over the entire country

ጓዙን ጠቀለለ *guʷazun ṭäqällälä* he packed up his things

ጠቅልሎ አገባት *ṭäqləlo agäbbat* he married her (*after having a woman as a mistress for a long time*)

ቁርበቱን ጠቅልሎ ሄደ *qurbätun ṭäqləlo hedä* he left for good

ጠቅላላ *ṭäqlalla* adj. total; overall: general; rough (*idea*)

—ድምር —*dəmmər* grand total, sum, total

—ጉባኤ —*guba'e* general assembly

ጠቅላላውን/ በጠቅላላው *ṭäqlallawən/ bäṭäqlallaw* adv. in general, generally

በጠቅላላ እነጋገር *bäṭäqlalla annägagär* generally speaking

ጠቅላይ *in* ጠቅላይ መምሪያ *ṭäqlay mämriya* headquarters

—ሚኒስቴር ጽሕፈት ቤት —*ministeṛ ṣəhfät bet* office of the Prime Minister

—ሚኒስትር —*ministər* n. Prime Minister, premier

—አቃቤ ሀግ —*aqqabe həgg* n. Procurator Genera

—አዛዥ — *azzaž* n. commander-in-chief

—ፍርድ ቤት — *fərd bet* Supreme Court

ጥቅል *ṭəqqəl* n. parcel, package, coil

—ጎመን — *gommän* n. head of a cabbage

የጥቅል ስም *yäṭəqqel səm* n. collective noun

ጥቅል ብራና *ṭəqəll bəranna* n. scroll *(of parchment)*

መጠቅለያ ወረቀት *mäṭäqläya wäräqät* n. wrapping paper

ተጠቃለለ *täṭäqallälä* v.i. was summed up, was concluded; was covered *(subject)*, was aggregated

ማጠቃለያ *maṭṭäqaläya* n. conclusion

አጠቃለለ *aṭṭäqallälä* v.t. concluded, brought to an end.

አጠቃላይ *aṭṭäqalay* adj, comprehensive, general, inclusive

—ሕግ — *həgg* n. universal law

ጠቀመ *ṭäqqämä* v.t. benefitted, rendered service; v.i. was beneficial, was useful, helpful; stitched *(clothes)*

ጠቀሜታ *ṭäqämeta* n. benefit, advantage

ጠቃሚ *ṭäqami* adj. useful, beneficial, advantageous, valuable; profitable important *(advice)*

ጥቅም *ṭəqəm* n. benefit, profit, use, usefulness

ተጠቀመ *täṭäqqämä* v.i. used, made use of; benefitted; took the advantage of; drove a profit

ተጠቃሚ *täṭäqqami* n. beneficiary; user

ተጠቃሚ ሕዝብ — *həzb* consumers

ጠቀሰ *ṭäqqäsä* v.t. winked at; cited, quoted; referred to; dipped a pen into ink

ሰማይ ጠቀስ *sämay ṭäqqäs* n. skyscraper

ጥቅስ *ṭəqs* n. citation, quotation

ትእምርተ— *tə'mərtä* — n. quotation mark

ጥቅሻ *ṭəqša* n. wink

ተጠቃሽ in ተጠቃሽ ተሳቢ *täṭäqqaš täsabi* n. direct object *(gram.)*

ተጠቃቀሰ *täṭäqaqqäsä* v.i. called by winking at each other

አጠቀሰ *aṭäqqäsä* v.t. dunked *(bread)*

አጣቀሰ *aṭṭaqqäsä* v.t. gave a comparative reference

ጠቀጠቀ *ṭäqäṭṭäqä* v.t. stuffed, pressed down ; compressed

ጠቃጠቆ *ṭäqaṭäqo* n. scar *(from smallpox)*; spots, speckle, freckle

ጥቅጥቅ *ṭəqṭəq* adj. compacted, compressed, stuffed

*ጠቃ *ṭäqqa

ጥቃት *ṭəqat* n. oppression, assault, maltreatment

ተጠቃ *täṭäqqa* v. i. was oppressed, assaulted, maltreated; mated *(for animals)*

ተጠቂ *täṭäqi* adj. oppressed, maltreated

አጠቃ *aṭäqqa* v.t. oppressed, assaulted, maltreated, mated *(for animals)*

ብቸኝነት ያጠቃዋል *bəččäññənnät yaṭäqqawal* he suffers from loneliness

አጥቂ *aṭqi* n. oppressor, aggressor

ጠቆመ *ṭäqomä* v.t. gave a hint, pointed out ; informed on; pointed at; nominated *(for election)*

ጠቋሚ *ṭäqʷami* n. informer, stool-pigeon *(person)*

ጥቆማ *ṭəqqoma* n. hint, information; nomination *(for election)*
ጥቁም *ṭəqqum* n. nominee
ተጠቆመ *täṭäqqomä* v.i. was nominated; was pointed out

ጠቆረ *ṭäqqorä* v.i. turned black; grew dark
ጠቋራ *ṭäqʷara* adj. dark *(skin)*, Negro
ጥቁሬ *in* ጥቁሬ ዝንጀሮ *ṭəqure zəngäro* n. kind of dark baboon
ጥቁር *ṭəqʷr* adj. dark *(skin)*, black, Negro
—ራስ *—ras* n. layman
—ሰሌዳ *—säleda* n. blackboard
—አባይ *—abbay* n. Blue Nile
—አዝሙድ *—azmud* n. cumin *(black)*
—እንግዳ *—əngəda* n. an unexpected special guest
—እንጨት *—ənčät* n. ebony
—ገበያ *—gäbäya* n. black market
አጠቆረ *aṭäqqorä* v.t. blackened, blacked, darkened
ገንዘብ— *gänzab—* v.t. bought or sold currencies in the black market
ፊቱን— *fitun—* v.i. frowned, looked black, made a face

ጠበል *ṭäbäl* n. holy water; mineral water
—ቀመሰ *—qämmäsä* partook in a ጠበል ceremony
—ተነከረ *—tänäkkärä* v.t. immersed oneself *(in holy water)*
—ተጠመቀ *—täṭämmäqä (same as above)*
—ጻድቅ *—ṣädiq* n. monthly celebration with food and drinks in honour of saints
ጠበልተኛ *ṭäbältäñña* n. people who immerse themselves in holy water

*ጠበረረ • *ṭäbärrärä*
ተንጠባራሪ *tänṭäbarari* adj. conceited

*ጠበረበረ * *ṭäbäräbbärä*
አጥበረበረ *aṭbäräbbärä* v.t. blinded *(by sun)* glared *(light)*, bedazzled

ጠበሰ *ṭäbbäsä* v.t. roasted *(meat, maize)*, fried, grilled; toasted; scorched
ጠባሳ *ṭäbasa* n. scar
ጥብስ *ṭəbs* n. fried, roast
—ሥጋ *—səga* n. roasted meat
—ወጥ *—wäṭ* n. stew
መጥበሻ *mäṭbäša* n. frying or roasting pan

ጠበሰቀ *ṭäbässäqä* v.t. hit violently *(with a stick)*

ጠበቀ *ṭäbbäqä* v.t. waited for; looked after, watched, took care of; expected; waited for; preserved
ቃሉን— *qalun—*he kept his promise
አፉን— *afun—*was cautious *(in expressing what one wants to say)*
ጊዜ— *gize—* waited for an opportune time
ጠበቃ *ṭäbäqa* n. advocate, lawyer, attorney
—ገዛ *—gäzza* n. hired a lawyer
ጠባቂ *ṭäbbaqi* n. keeper, guardian, custodian
በር— *bärr—* n. doorkeeper
በግ— *bäg—* n. shepherd
የበላይ— *yäbälay ṭäbbaqi* n. patron
ጥበቃ *ṭəbbäqa* n. watching, guarding; protection, conservation
የሕዝብ ጤና — ሚኒስቴር Ministry of Public Health
የሕዝብ ደህንነት—ሚኒስቴር Ministry of Public Security

ጥብቅ *ṭəbbəq* adj. acting; mistress *(concubine)*

ጥብቅና *ṭəbqənna* n. advocacy, power of attorney

ተጠበቀ *täṭäbbäqä* v.i. was expected; was kept; was looked after; was taken care of

ተጠባበቀ *täṭäbabbäqä* v.i. expected; awaited, looked forward to

ተጠባባቂ *täṭäbabaqi* adj. acting

—ሹም *—šum* n. acting head

ጠበቀ *ṭäbbäqä* v. t. was tightened, was firm, was fastened; was stressed *(syllable)*

ጠባቃ *ṭäbäqa* adj. tight, fast; firm

ጥብቅ *ṭəbq* adj. tight tied; severe, strict, rigid; drastic

—ማስጠንቀቂያ *—masṭänqäqiya* n. strict warning

—ማሳሰቢያ *—masassäbiya* n. cautionary notice

—ትእዛዝ *—tə'əzaz* n. strict order

ጥብቆ *ṭəbbəqo* n. long children's shirt

መጣብቅ *mäṭabq* n. glue

አጠበቀ *aṭäbbaqä* v.t. tightened, fastened; put emphasis

አጥባቂ *in* ወግ አጥባቂ *wäg aṭbaqi* adj. conservative

አጥብቆ *aṭbəqo* adv. strongly, very much

ተጣበቀ *täṭabbäqä* v.t. was glued, was stuck together, adhered to; clung to

አጣበቀ *aṭṭabbäqä* v.t. glued; stuck together

አጣብቂኝ *aṭṭabqiññ* n. very narrow passage *(way through)*

ማጣበቂያ *maṭṭabäqiya* n. glue, gum, adhesive

ጠበበ *ṭäbbäbä* v.i. was narrow; was tight *(clothes)*

ጠባብ *ṭäbbab* adj. narrow, tight

አስተሳሰበ— *astäsasäbä—* adj. narrow-minded

እጀ— *əggä*—n. long Ethiopian shirt

ጥበት *ṭəbbät* n. constriction *(for limited space)*

ተጠበበ *in* ተጨነቀ ተጠበበ *täčännäqä täṭäbbäbä* v.i. was preoccupied, worried, was careworn

ተጣበበ *täṭabbäbä* v.i. was crammed with; was crowded

አጠበበ *aṭäbbäbä* v.t. narrowed, tightened

አጣበበ *aṭṭabbäbä* v.t. crowded, jammed

•ጠበበ •*ṭäbbäbä*

ጠቢብ *ṭäbib* n. wise; artisan

ጠይብ *ṭäyib* n. one with the evil eye

ጥበበኛ *ṭəbäbäñña* adj. wise skillful, clever, sapient, sagacious

ጥበብ *ṭəbäb* n. wisdom, technique

ሥነ— *sənä* — n. fine arts

ኪነ— *kinä*—n. art, work of art, technology

የእጅ— *yä'əğğ*—n. handicraft

—ቀሚስ *—qämis* n. dress with a coloured hem

ጥበበ ፈለክ *ṭəbäbä fäläk* n. astrology

ጠበደለ *ṭäbäddälä* v.i. became fat

ጠብደል *ṭäbdäl* adj. fat, large

—እንጀራ *—ənğära* n. large ənğära

ጠበጠበ *ṭäbäṭṭäbä* v.t. patted, *(a ball)*, patted *(hit gently with the open hand)*

ጥብጠባ *ṭəbṭäba* n. act of patting a ball

ነጠብጣብ *näṭäbṭab* n. dots

ተንጠባጠበ *tänṭäbaṭṭäbä* v.i.

dripped, dribbled, trickled *(of water)*, was scattered

አንጠባጠበ *anṭäbaṭṭäbä* v.t. dribbled, dropped one by one, dripped, let fall one by one, scattered

ጠባ *ṭäbba* v.t. sucked, suckled,

መስከረም ሲጠባ *mäskäräm siṭäba* at the end of the rainy season, at the beginning of autumn

ነጋ ጠባ *nägga ṭäbba* adv. day in day out

ጠቢ *ṭäbi in* ጆሮ ጠቢ *goro ṭäbi* n. spy, stool–pigeon, nark, informant

ጥቢ *ṭəbbi* n. spring

ጥቦት *ṭəbbot, or* ጠቦት *ṭäbbot* n. lamb

ተጣባ *in* ኮሶ ተጣባ *kosso täṭabba* v.i have tapeworms

አጠባ *in* ጡት አጠባ *ṭut aṭäbba* v.t. adopted a child

አጥቢ *in* አጥቢ እንስሳት *aṭbi ənsəsat n.* mammals

ጠባይ *ṭäbay* n. charac er, conduct, behaviour, manners; nature *(character)*

ልዩ — *ləyyu*—n. peculiarity

ጠባየ መልካም *ṭäbayä mälkam* adj. good - natured, courteous

—መጥፎ *mäṭfo*—adj. ill-natured

ጠብ *ṭäb* n. quarrel

ጠበኛ *ṭäbäñña* adj. quarrelsome, quick-tempered

ጠብ አለ *ṭäbb alä* v.i. dripped,

ጠብ የማ ይለው *ṭäbb yämmayläw* adj. stingy, mean, niggardly

ሥራው ጠብ አይልም *səraw ṭäbb ayləmm* futile exercise, fruitless work

ጠብ in ጠብ እርግፍ አለ *ṭäbb ərgəff alä* v.i. toiled, hustled and bustled, was submissive

ጠብታ *ṭäbbəta* n. drop; speck

ጠቦት *see* ጠባ

ጠነሰሰ *ṭänässäsä* v.t. mixed hop and yeast for brewing beer

ጥንስስ *ṭənsəs* n. the mixture of the above

ጠነቆለ *ṭänäqqolä* v.t. engaged in sorcery, was a soothsayer; pricked some one's eye *(with the finger)*

ጠንቋይ *ṭänquʷay* n. wizard, magician, witch-doctor, sorcerer

ጥንቆላ *ṭənqola* n. witchcraft, magic, sorcery

ተጠናቆለ *täṭänaqqolä* v.i. was a dare-devil

*ጠነቀረ *ṭänäqqärä*

አጠናቀረ *aṭṭänaqqärä* v.i. compiled *(news report etc.)*

ጠነቀቀ *ṭänäqqäqä* v.t. took care *(in orthography)*

ጠንቃቃ *ṭänqaqqa* adj. careful, prudent, cautious, meticulous

ጥንቁቅ *ṭənquq* adj. careful; meticulous; cautious, thorough, scrupulous, prudent

ጥንቃቄ *ṭənəqqaqe* n. care, carefulness, precaution, prudence

ተጠነቀቀ *täṭänäqqäqä* v.i. was careful, took care, watched out, took precautions, was prudent

ተጠናቀቀ *täṭänaqqäqa* v.i. was completed, was finished, was brought to an end; was ready

አጠናቀቀ *aṭṭänaqqäqä* v.t. completed, finished, brought to an end; made ready

አስጠነቀቀ *asṭänäqqäqä* v.t. warned, alarmed, put on the alert, cautioned

ማስጠንቀቂያ *masṭänqäqiya* n. warning, alarm, notice *(warning)*

*ጠነበረ **ṭänäbbärä*

ጠንባራ *ṭänburra also* ጠምባራ adj. one-eyed, weak-sighted *(insult)*

*ጠነበሰ **ṭänäbbäsä*

ጠንባሳ *ṭänbassa* adj. weak-sighted *(insult)*

ጥንብስብስ *ṭənbəsbəs* adj. weak-sighted

ተጠናበሰ *täṭänabbäsä* v.i. was weak-sighted; walked unsteadily *(due to weak sight)*

ጠነበዘ *ṭänäbbäzä* v.i drunk oneself to death

እስኪ. ጠነብዘ ጠጣ he drunk far too much

ጠንባዛ *ṭänbäzzä* n. drunkard

ጠነባ *ṭänäbba* v.i. stank, became putrid

ጥንባት ጥምባት *ṭənbat, also ṭəmbat* n. stink

ጥንባታም *ṭənbaṭam* adj. stinking, fetid, malodorous

ጥንብ *also* ጥምብ *ṭənb, ṭəmb* adj. stinking, fetid; n. carcass, dead body *(of animal)*

-አንሣ *—ansa* n. vulture, scavenger

አጠነባ *aṭänäbba*, v.t. putrefied

ጠነነ *ṭännänä* v.i. became difficult

ጠነነኝ *ṭännännäññ* I found it diffiult *(to understand)*

አጠነነ *aṭännänä* v.t. made difficult

ጠነከረ *ṭänäkärä* v.i. was strong, rigorous; was hard, was solid, was tough

ጠንካራ *ṭänkkära* adj. strong, hard, solid: firm, tough, robust

ጥንካሬ *ṭənəkkare* n. strength, toughness, firmness

ተጠናከረ *täṭänakkärä* v.i. was reinforced, was envigorated, recuperated; was consolidated; was emphasized

ማጠናከሪያ *maṭṭänakäria* n. reinforcement

አጠነከረ *aṭänäkkärä* v.t. reinforced; fortified; consolidated

አጠናከረ *aṭṭänakkärä* v.t. reinforced; emphasized consolidated

*ጠነወተ **ṭänäwwätä*

ተጠናወተ *täṭänawwätä* v.t. attacked *(disease)*

ጠነዛ *ṭänäzza* v.i. burnt due to lack of water *(cooking food)*

ወሬው ጠነዛ *wärew ṭänäzza* the story became boring *(due to hearing repeatedly)*

ጠናዛ *ṭänaza* adj. feeble and ugly

*ጠነጋ **ṭänägga*

አጠናጋ *in* በጥፊ አጠናጋ *baṭəffi aṭṭänagga* v.t. slapped s/o's face violently

*ጠነጠነ **ṭänäṭṭänä*

ጥንጥን *ṭənṭən* adj. *(s/t)* coiled

ተጠነጠነ *täṭänäṭṭänä* v.i. was coiled

አጠነጠነ *aṭänäṭṭänä* v.t. coiled; pondered over, put one's thinking cap on

ጠነፈፈ *ṭänäffäfä* v.i. was sifted

አጠነፈፈ *aṭänäffäfä* v.t. sifted

ማጠንፈፊያ *maṭänfäfiya* n. sifter

*ጠና **ṭänna*

ጠኚ *see* ደጅ ጠኚ

ጥናት *ṭənat see* ደጅ ጥናት

ጠና *ṭänna* v.i. was strong was firm

ጥኑ — *ţənu* adj. strong, firm

ጥናት — *ţənat* n. strength, steadfastness; study, research; survey *(assessment)*

ተጠና — *täţänna* v. i. was studied, was surveyed, was considered

ጉዳዩ እየተጠና ነው — *guddayu əyyätäţänna näw* the case is being considered, studied

አጠና — *aţänna* v.t. made strong, hardened; studied; surveyed

ተጥናና — *täţnanna, also* ተጽናና *täşnanna* v.i. found solace, was encouraged

አጥናና — *aţnanna, also* አጽናና *aşnanna* v.t. consoled, gave comfort, encouraged, gave solace

አጥናኝ — *aţnañ* n. consoler

አስጠና — *asţänna* v.t. tutored

አስጠኚ — *asţäññi* n. tutor

ጠኔ — *ţänne* n. famished condition

—ይዞኛል — *—yəzoññal* I am famished for food

ጠኔያም — *ţännəyam* n. starveling

ጠንቅ — *ţänq* n. cause *(of s/t bad)*

ጠንቀኛ — *ţänqäñña* adj. harmful, disastrous, evil; vicious *(spiteful)*

ጠንበለል — *see* ጠምበለል

ጠንፍ — *ţänf* n. border, edge

•ጠወለወለ — •*ţäwäläwwälä*

አጥወለወለ — *aţwäläwwälä* v.t. felt giddy; nauseated

ጠወለገ — *ţäwällägä* v.i. faded, withered; fatigued, wearied; wilted

ጠውላጋ — *ţäwlaggu* adj. withered; fatigued; weary *(body)*

•ጠወረ — *see* ጦረ

ጠዘጠዘ — *ţäzäţţäzä* v.i. smarted *(sharp pain)*

[illegible] — *ţəzţäza* n. smart *(sharp pain)*

ጥዝጣዜ — *ţəzəţţaze* n. smart. *(sharp pain)*

ጠየመ — *ţäyyämä* v.i. became dark brown

ጠይም — *ţäyyəm* adj. dark-brown *(person's complexion)*

ጠየቀ — *ţäyyäqä* v.t. asked, inquired, demanded; entailed, questioned; paid a visit, called on someone

ጠያቂ — *ţäyyaqi in* በሽተኛ— *bäššəttäñña*— n. visitor *(of sick person)*

ጥየቃ — *ţəyyäqa* n. visiting; questioning

ጥያቄ — *ţəyyaqe* n. question, request, query, interrogation

የጥያቄ ምልክት — *yäţəyyaqe mələkkət* n. question mark

የቃል ጥያቄ — *yäqal ţəyyaqe* n. interview

መጠይቅ — *mäţäyyəq* n. questionnaire

ተጠየቀ — *täţäyyäqä* v.i. was asked

ተጠየቅ — *täţäyyäq* n. logic

ተጠያቂ — *täţäyyaqi* adj. responsible, accountable

መጠየቂያ ቅጽ — *mäţäyyäqiya qəşş* n. requisition form

ተጠያየቀ — *täţäyayyäqä* v.t. sought information

አጠየቀ — *aţäyyäqä* v.t. proved, gave evidence

አጠያየቀ — *aţţäyayyäqä* v. t. collected information; became doubtful

አጠያያቂ — *aţţäyayaqi* adj. doubtful

አጣየቀ — *aţţayyäqä* v.t. became questionable, disputable

•ጠየፈ — •*ţäyyäfä*

ጠያፍ — *ţäyyaf also* ጸያፍ *şäyyaf* adj. distasteful, unbecoming, repugnant; vulgar; taboo

ጥዩፍ *ṭəyyuf* adj. fastidious, squeamish *(easily disgusted)*

ጥይፍተኛ *ṭəyyəfṭäñña* adj. fastidious, squeamish *(easily disgusted)*

ተጠየፈ *täṭäyyäfä* v.i. abhorred; was fastidous, squeamish

ተጠያፊ *täṭäyyafi* adj. fastidious, squeamish

አጠያየፈ *aṭṭäyayyäfä* v. t. disliked, disrelished, distasted

አስጠየፈ *also* አጸየፈ *asṭäyyäfä aṣṣäyyäfä* v.t. was disgusting

አስጠያፊ *also* አጸያፊ *asṭäyyafi, aṣṣäyyafi* adj. disgusting, nasty *(remarks)*; vulgar, repellent

ጠያር ግመል *ṭäyyar gəmäl* n. dromedary

ጠይብ *ṭäyəb* n. cottage artisan *(used in derogatory sense)*

ጠደቀ *täddäqä see also* ጸደቀ v.i. took root *(transplated plant)*

ጠዲቅ *ṭädik* n. loaf of raised bread served on a Christian religious occasion

ጠበል— *ṭäbäl*—n. food and drinks served on a Christian religious occasion

*ጠደፈ *ṭädäffä

ጥድፊያ *ṭədfiya* n. haste, hurry, rush

ተጣደፈ *täṭaddäfä* v.i. hastened, hurried, rushed

አጣደፈ *aṭṭaddäfä* v.t. hastened, hurried, rushed

በጥያቄ አጣደፈው assailed him with questions

አጣዳፊ *aṭṭadafi* adj. urgent, pressing

አጣዳፊ ሥራ *aṭṭadafi səra* n.pressing business, urgent task

ጠዳ *ṭädda see also* ጸዳ v.i. was clean, was neat

ጥዱ *ṭədu* adj. clean, neat

የማይጠዳው *yämmayṭädaw* adj. gloomy, cheerless *(person)*

ተጣዳ *täṭadda* v.t. cleaned oneself

ጠድከል *ṭädkäl* n. a pair of compasses

ጠጅ *ṭäǧǧ* n. hydromel, mead

—ቤት — *bet* n. bar where ṭäǧǧ is served; person in charge of the distribution of ṭäǧǧ *(in a royal palace)*

—ጣለ —*ṭalä* v.t. prepared ṭäǧǧ

የወይን— *yäwäyən*— n. wine

ጠገራ *in* ጠገራ ምሳር *ṭägära məssar* n. hatchet, axe

—ብር —*bərr* n. thaler

ጠገበ *ṭäggäbä* v.i. was satiated, was full *(from food)*; was arrogant, conceited

ጥጋብ *ṭəgab* n. satiety; plenty; arrogance, conceit

ጥጋበኛ *ṭəgabäñña* adj. arrogant,conceited

አጠገበ *aṭäggäbä* v.t. satiated;

አጥጋቢ *aṭgabi* adj. satisfactory, adequate, convincing

—መልስ —*mäls* n. saisfactory answer

አጣገበ *aṭṭaggäbä* v.t. supplied plentifully

ጠገነ *ṭäggänä* v.t. repaired, mended, fixed, patched up, tr.atd a fracture or dislocation

ጠጋኝ *ṭäggañ* n. craftsman

ጥገና *ṭəggäna* repair, fixing

—ክፍል —*kəfəl* n. maintenance shop

ቀዶ— *qäddo*—n. opertion *(surgical)*, surgery

ጥግን *ṭəggən* adj. mended

ተጠጋገነ *täṭägaggänä* v.i. helped each other; backed each other up

አስጠገነ *astäggänä* v.t. had s/t repaired, mended

*ጠገገ *ṭäggägä* v.i. cicatrised, healed up, skinned over

ጠጉር *ṭəgur* n. hair

ጠጉረ ሉጫ *ṭägurä luçça* smooth-haired

—ከርዳዳ *—kärdadda* woolly haired

ጠጉራም *ṭäguram* adj. hairy

ጠጉር ቆራጭ *ṭägur qoraç* n. barber, hair-dresser

—አስተካካይ *—astäkakay* barber, hair-dresser

—ማስተካከያ ቤት *—mastäkakäya bet* n. barber-shop

—አሰራር *—assärar* n. hairdo,

የበግ— *yäbäg*— n. wool

ጠጋ *ṭäga see also* ፀጋ n. wealth; grace

ጠጋቢስ *ṭäggabis* adj. graceless

ባለጠጋ *baläṭägga* adj. wealthy

*ጠጋ **ṭägga*

ጥግ *ṭəgg* n. side; corner adv. close to; vicinity

—ያዘ *—yazä* v.t. took cover, cornred onself

ጥገኛ *ṭəggäñña* adj./n dependant, subject (*not independant*)

ጥገኝነት *ṭəggäññənnät* n. dependency

ጥገኛ ሀረግ *ṭəgäñña harăg* n. subordinate clause

—ሀገር *—hagär* n. protectorate

ባለጥግ *baläṭəgg* n. protègè

ተጠጋ *täṭägga* v.i. got near, advanced upon, drew close, approached; took sheltor, sought protection

መጠጊያ *mäṭṭägiya* n refuge, shelter

ተጠጋጋ *täṭägagga* v.i. came close to each other, was contiguous, were put close togther

አጠጋጋ *aṭṭägaga* v.t. cause to come close to each other, put close together

አስጠጋ *asṭägga* v.t. sheltered (*protected*); harboured (*gave shelter*); brought close

ጠጠረ *ṭäṭṭärä* v.i. hardened; solidified

ጠጠር *ṭäṭär* n. gravel, pebble

—ጣይ *—ṭay* n fortune teller (*using pebbles*)

ጥጥር *ṭəṭṭər* adj solid, hard

አጠጠረ *aṭäṭṭärä* v.t. hardened, solidified; made difficult

ጥያቄውን አጠጠረው *ṭəyyaqew̃ən aṭäṭṭäräw* he made the question difficult

*ጠጠተ **ṭäṭṭätä, see also* ጸጸተ *ṣäṣṣätä*, *with pronominal suffix* e.g. ጠጠተኝ *ṭäṭṭätäññ* I regreted; I was filled with remorse

ጠጠት *ṭäṭät* n. regret, remorse

ተጠጠተ *täṭäṭṭätä* v.i. regretted, repented, was sorry

ጠጣ *ṭäṭṭa* v.t. drunk; smoked (*cigarettes*)

እቁብ— *əqqub*—joined a money saving association

ጠጭ *ṭäçç* n. drinker, drunkard

መጠጥ *mäṭäṭṭ* n. beverage, drink, strong drink. liquor

ውሃ መጠጫ *wəha mäṭäççä* n. drinking vessel; tip

ተጣጣ *täṭaṭṭa* vi. was added to, was supplemented.

አጠጣ *aṭäṭṭa* v.t. gave to drink; irrigated, watered (*a plant*)

አጣጣ *aṭṭaṭṭa* v.t. joined s/o for a drink

አጣጭ *aṭṭaç* n. drinking partner

ጠፈረ ṭäffärä v.t. wrapped and tied tighty

ጠፍር ṭäfər n. leather, strip, thong

--ነካሽ --näkaš itinerant merchant (*who uses beast of burden for transporting goods; pejoraive*)

አጣፈረ *aṭṭafärä in* በጥፊ አጣፈረ *bäṭəfi aṭṭaffärä* slapped on the face

ጠፈር *ṭafär* n. firmament, space (*where the universe exists*)

ጠፈረተኛ *ṭäfärätäñña* n astronaut, cosmonaut

የጠፈር መንኩራኩር *yäṭäfär mänkorakur* n. space-ship

ጠፈጠፈ *ṭäfäṭṭäfä* v.t. levelled, flattened out

በጥፊ ጠፈጠፈው *bäṭəffi ṭäfäṭṭäfäw* he slapped him on the face repeatedly

ጠፍጣፋ *ṭäfṭaffa* adj. flat, level

ጥፍጥፍ *ṭəfṭəf* n. animal dung flattened with the hands in order to dry to be used as fuel

• ጠፈጠፈ • *ṭäfäṭäffä*

ጠፈጠፍ *ṭäfäṭäf* n. drips

ተንጠፈጠፈ *tänṭäfäṭṭäfä* v.t. dripped, trickled, streamed (*sweat*)

አንጠፈጠፈ *anṭäfäṭṭäfa* v.t dripped (*sweat*), dripped dry

ጠፈፈ *ṭäffäfä* v.t. started draining (*became less wet*)

ጠፍ አለ *ṭäff alä* v.i. became clean, neat, tidy, spruce

አጠፈፈ *aṭäffäfä* v.t. drained

ጠፋ *ṭäffa* v.i disappeared, was lost, went astray, vanished, was missing; was extinguished; go out (*of light, fire, electricity*); died (*of engine*), was eradicated; was spoilt (*child;*) was destroyed (*country*)

ጠፋኝ *in* ስሙ ጠፋኝ I forgot his name

ስሙ ጠፋ he was discredited

መንገድ ጠፋው he lost his way

ብልሃቱ ጠፋኝ I am at a loss

አገሪቱ ጠፋች the country was desroyed

የሚያደርገው ጠፋው he was puzzled, perplexed

ይዞ ጠፋ run away with (*absconded with*)

ገንዘብ ጠፋው ጠፋበት he lost money

ጠፍ ሆነ was abandoned, deserted (*country*)

መሬት --*märet* n. waste land, undeveloped land, unclaimed or abandoned land

ከብት --*käbt* n. strayed animal

ጨረቃ *ṭäräqa* n. moonless night

ጥፉ *in* መልከ ጥፉ *mälkä-ṭəfu* adj. ugly

ጥፋት *ṭəfat* n. mistake, fault; offense, guilt, damage, destruction

ምን ጥፋት አጠፋህ what wrong did you commit?

ጥፋተኛ *ṭəfatäñña* n. wrogdoer, offender, guilty

መጥፎ *mäṭfo* adj. bad, wicked, evil,

ሽታ *šətta* repugnant odour, bad smell

ተጠፋፋ *täṭäfaffa* v.. lost each other

ተጣፋ *täṭaffa* v.i. desroyed each other

አጠፋ *aṭäffa* v.t. committed a crime, did wrong, committed an offense; exterminatd, eradicated; extinguished, turned off (*light*), blew out (*candle*)

ራሱን አጠፋ did away with himself
ስም አጠፋ defamed *(s/o's reputation)*
ድንግል አጠፋ deflowered
ገንዘብ አጠፋ wasted money, squandered money
በላጲስ አጠፋ erased with a rubber
አጥፊ *aṭəfi* n. wrongdoer, offender, guilty
አጥፊና ጠፊ *aṭfinna ṭäfi* mortal enemies
አጣፋ *aṭṭaffa* v.t. robed oneself *(with šämma)*; exceeded in rank, character, achievment etc.
ጡሌ *ṭulle* n. gourd *(Bottle)*
ጡል ጡል አለ *ṭull ṭull alä* v.i. walked in a fast and graceless manner; meddled in
ጦልጧላ *ṭolṭuʷalla* adj. meddlesome
ተንጦለጦለ *tänṭoläṭṭolä* v.i. was meddlesome
ጡር *ṭur* n. wrongdoing
ነፍሰ — *näfsä—* adj. pregnant
—ጡርነት *—ṭurənnät* n. pregnancy
ጡረኛ *ṭuräñña* n. a wrongdoer
ጡር ሰሪ *ṭur säri* n. wrongdoer
ጡብ *ṭub* n. brick, tile
ጡብ ጡብ አለ *ṭubb ṭubb alä* v.i. hopped about *(children, birds etc.)*
ጡት *ṭut* n. breast, teat
የጡት ጫፍ *yäṭut čaf* n. nipple; spout
ጡት ተወ was weaned
ጡት አጠባ adopted a child
ጡት ጣለ was weand
ጡት አስጣለች weaned
የጡት ልጅ adopted child
የጡት አባት foster father
የጡት እናት foster mother
ጡንቻ *ṭunča* n. muscle
ጡንቸኛ *ṭunčäñña* aj. hefty, strong; quarrelsome
ጡንቻማ *ṭunčamma* adj. muscular *(having much muscle)*

ጡዋት *also* ጥዋት *ṭuwat, ṭəwat* n. morning
ነገ ጧት tomorrow morning
ዛሬ ጧት this morning
ጡዋትና ማታ everyday, always
ጡዋት ጡዋት every morning
ጡፍ አደረገ *ṭuff adärrägä* v.t. sent out wind *(farted)*
ጡጦ *ṭuṭo* n. baby's bottle,
የጡጦ ጫፍ nipple of baby's bottle
ጡጫ *ṭučča* n. fist, punch
በጡጫ መታ *bäṭučča mätta* gave a blow with the fist, punched
ጢም *ṭim also* ጺም *ṣim* n. beard
ባፍ ጢሙ ተደፋ fell on one's face
ጢም አለ *ṭimm alä* v.i. was filled to the brim, was filled to capacity
ጢም ብሎ ሞላ *ṭimm bəlo molla* v.i. was filled to capacity
ጢቅ አለ *ṭiqq alä* v.t. spat between the teeth *(as a sign of disgust or contempt)*
ጢቅታ *ṭiqqəta* n. spittle, spit
ጢን አለ *ṭinn alä* v.i. overflowed; was full; was conceited
ጢን ብሎ ሰከረ he was dead drunk
ጢንጦ *in* ጢንጦ መሬት *ṭinto märet* n. plot of land
ጣለ *ṭalä* v.t. threw away, threw out, threw down; dropped, lost; discarded
መልሕቅ— —anchored
መሠረት— —laid the foudation
ቀላድ— —measured land *(for distribution or to impose a land tax)*
ቀረጥ— imposed a tax
በረዶ— hailed
ተስፋ— placed hope
አደጋ ላይ— exposed to danger, imperiled
አደጋ— attacked by surprise

እጣ— drew lots
እምነት— placed confidence
እንቁላል—(ች) laid eggs
ዐይኑን— set eyes on, have an eye to
ዕቁብ— paid the *əqqub* money *(see ዕቁብ)*
ድንኳን— pitched *(a tent)*
ዳስ— erected a booth
ዝናብ— rained
ጠጅ— prepared hydromel
ጡት— was weaned
ጥሎሽ— gave a dowry *(by fiancé to his fiancée)*
ጥንቡን— hit rock bottom *(price)*
ጨርቁን— he was stark raving mad

ጣይ *in* ጣይ በሽታ *ṭay bäššəta* n. epilepsy *(also* የሚጥል በሽታ*)*
ጥለት *ṭəlät* n. embroidered fringe of dress
ጥሎ ማለፍ *ṭəlomaläf* n. knockout *(game)*
ጥሎሽ *ṭəloš* n. dowry *(money the fiancé gives to his fiancée)*
የእግዚአብሔር— *ya'əgziabəher* — the wrath of God
መጣያ *in* ቁሻሻ መጣያ *qušaša mäṭaya* n. dump
ተጣጣለ *in* እጣ ተጣጣለ *əṭa ṭäṭaṭalä* v. i. drew lots *also* እጣ ጣለ
ጣልቃ *see* ጠለቀ.
ጣመ *ṭamä* v.i. tasted pleasant, was savoury, was tasty
ጣም *ṭam* n. taste *also* ጣዕም
ጣመ ቢስ *ṭamä bis* adj . tasteless, crude *(not having grace, taste or rifinement)*
ጣም የለሽ *ṭam yälläš* adj. tasteless; crude *(not having grace, taste or refinement)*
—አጣ *—aṭṭa* v.i. was tasteless *(food)*
አጣመ *aṭamä* v.t. made tasty ; spiced
አጣጣመ *aṭṭaṭamä* v.t. tasted
ጣመን *ṭamän* n. muscular fatigue
ጣማ *ṭama* n.toil
—ገንዘብ — *gänzäb* n. hard earned money, property
ጣረ *ṭarä* v.i. tried hard, toiled, made an effort
—ሞት *—mot* n. death throes, agony
ጥረት *ṭərät* n. effort, endeavour
መጣር መጋር *mäṭar mägar* inf. to toil, work hard
ተጣጣረ *täṭaṭarä* v.. endeavoured, strove for, tried hard
ተጣጣሪ *täṭaṭari* adj. enterprising
አጣጣረ *aṭṭaṭari* v.t . was in death throes
ጣሰ *ṭasä* v. broke through *(a fence etc.)*; trespassed, breached, violated *(the law)*; pounded coarsely
ጥሻ *ṭəša* n. bush, thicket
የማይጣስ ህግ inviolable law
ጣሰሰ *ṭassäsä* v.t trampled down
ጣሳ *ṭasa* n. can, tin
በጣሳ አሸገ *bäṭasa aššägä* v.t. canned *(food)*
የጣሳ ምግብ *yäṭasa məgəb* n. canned-food
ጣቃ *ṭaqa* n. bolt of cloth
ጣባ *ṭaba* n. small clay dish *(container)*
ጣት *ṭat* n finger
ሌባ— *leba–.* index finger
ማሀል— *mahəl–*n. middle finger
ትንሽ— *ṭənnəš* – n. little finger
አውራ— *awra* – n. thumb
የቀለበት— *yäqäläbät* — n. ring finger
የእግር— *ya'əgər* – n. toe
የጣት ቤዛ *yäṭat beza* n. thimble
—አንጓ *—anguʷa* n. knuckle
ጣእም *ṭa'əm* n. taste, flavour
ጣእመ ቃል *ṭa'əmä qal* n. elo-

quence

—ዜማ *—zema* n. melody

ጣኦስ *ṭa'os* n. peacock

ጣኦት *ṭa'ot* n. idol

—አምላኪ *—amlaki* adj. idolatrous

—አምልኮ *—amləko* n. idolatry

ጣውንት *ṭawənt* n. one that has taken someone's wife or husband

ጣዝማ *ṭazma* n. bee-like insect

—ማር *—mar* n. honey of such an insect

ጣይ *see* ፀሀይ

ጣደ *ṭadä* v.t. put a cooking pot, a kettle, a pan etc. on the fire

ምጣድ *məṭad* n. griddle, disc *(of clay in which bread is made)*

ብረት ምጣድ *bərät* — n. disc *(of iron on which coffee etc. is roasted)*

ጣጣ *ṭaṭa* n. trouble, complication, nuisance

ጣጠኛ *ṭaṭäñña* adj. troublesome, problematic, complicated

ባለ ብዙ ጣጣ *balä bəzu ṭaṭa* full of problems

ጣጣ የለሽ *ṭaṭa yälläš* adj. irreproachable, perfect, unimpeachable

*ጣጣ *ṭaṭṭa

ጣጣቴ *ṭaṭate* n. talkative

ተንጣጣ *tänṭaṭṭa* v.i. snapped *(as of burning wood)*, crackled *(as of burning dry sticks)*; was loquacious

ጣፈ *ṭafä see also* ጻፈ v.t. wrote; patched/up *(a garment)*

ጥፈት *ṭəfät* n. writing

መጣፊያ *mäṭafiya* n. a patch *(piece of material put on a hole or damaged part of a garment)*

መጣፍ *mäṭaf* n. book *also* መጽሐፍ

ጣፈጠ *ṭaffäṭä* v.i. was sweet, was tasty; was delicious, was savoury

ጣፋጣ *ṭafaṭa* adj. sweet, tasty, delicious

ጣፋጭ *ṭafač̣* adj. sweet, tasty, delicious

መጣፈጥ *mäṭafäṭ* n. niggela seed, fennel-flower cf. አዝሙድ

ነጭ— *näčč—* n. bishop's weed. cf. ነጭ አዝሙድ

ጥቁር— *ṭəqur —* n. black cummin cf. ጥቁር አዝሙድ

አጣፈጠ *aṭaffäṭä* v.t. sweetened, flavoured, made tasty

ጣፊያ *ṭaffiya* n. spleen, milt

ጤሰ *ṭesä* v.i. smoked; was infuriated

ጢስ *ṭis* n. smoke, fume

የመርዝ— *yämärz—* n. poison gas

ጢሰኛ *ṭisäñña* n. tenant farmer

ጢሳም *ṭisam* adj. smoky

አጤሰ *aṭesä* v.t. smoked *(cigarettes)*

ቤቱን አጤስኩበት I have fumigated the house

አጢያሽ *aṭiyaš* n. smoker

ጤና *ṭena* n. health

የሕዝብ ጤና ጥበቃ ሚኒስቴር *yähəzb ṭena ṭəbbäqa minister* Ministry of Public Health

ጤና ቢስ *ṭena bis* adj. sick, ill; disturbing *(person)*

—ነሣ *—nässa* v.t. disturbed

—አዳም *—addam, or* ጤናዳም *ṭenaddam* n. rue *(ruta hortensis)*

—አጣ *—aṭṭa* v.t. was in poor health

ይስጥልኝ *—yəsṭəlləññ* how are you? good-bye, good morning, good evening, good night

የጤና ጠንቅ *yäṭena ṭänq* insanitary

ለጤናዎ *läṭenawo* to your health

ጤነኛ *ṭenäñña* adj. healthy *(person)*

ጤናማ *ṭenamma* adj. healthy

(body)

ጤዛ — *ṭeza* n. dew

ጤፍ — *ṭef* n. millet-like cereal whose flour is used for *ənǧära*

ማኛ— — *maňňa*— very white ṭef

ሰርገኛ — — *särrgäňňa*— *ṭef* of mixed colour

ቡንኝ — *bunnəňň*— rapidly growing *ṭef*

ጥቁር— — *ṭəqur ṭef* brown *ṭef*

ጥለት — *see* ጣለ

ጥላ — *ṭəla* n. umbrella; shade, shadow

ጥላማ — *ṭəlamma* adj. shady

ጥላ ቢስ — *ṭəla bis* adj. graceless

ጃን ጥላ — *ǧanṭəla* n. parasol

ዓይነ ጥላ — *ayənä ṭəla* n. phobia

ጥሎ ማለፍ — *see* ጣለ

ጥሞና — *ṭəmmona* n. calm

በጥሞና — *bäṭəmmona* adv. calmly

ጥሩምባ — *ṭərumba* n. trumpet, auto horn

ጥሩምበኛ — *ṭərumbäňňa* n. trumpeter

ጥሩምባ ነፋ — *ṭərumba näffä* v.t. played the trumpet; praised himself; bragged

ጥሪት — *ṭərit* n. property, possession

—ሰበሰበ — —*säbässäbä* v.t. accumulated wealth

ባለጥሪት — *balä ṭərit* n. a well-to-do person

ጥሬ — *ṭəre* n. green *(grain)*; crude

—ሥጋ — —*səga* n. raw meat

—እቃ — —*əqa* n. raw material

—ዘር — —*zär* n. verbal noun

—ዘይት — —*zäyət* n. crude oil

—ገንዘብ — —*gänzäb* n. cash

ጥራጥሬ — *ṭəraṭəre* n. cereals

ጥር — *ṭərr* n. January

ጥርስ — *see* ጠረሰ

ጥርኝ — *ṭərəňň* n. civet-cat

—ፈረስ — —*färäs* white spotted horse

ጥርጊያ — *see* ጠረገ

ጥሻ — *see* ጣሰ

ጥቀርሻ — *ṭəqärša* n. soot *(from chimney, or roof)*

ጥቁር — *see* ጠቆረ

ጥቂት — *ṭəqit* adj. some, a little, a few, small *(amount)*

ጥቃቅን — *ṭəquqqən* n. minute, minor, tiny

ጥቅል — *see* ጠቀለለ

ጥቅምት — *ṭəqəmət* n. October

ጥበብ — *see* ጠበበ

ጥብስ — *see* ጠበሰ

ጥብኛ — *ṭəbbəňňa* n. small round loaf of bread

ጥንት — *ṭənt* n. former days, ancient times, earlier days

ጥንታውያን — *ṭəntawəyan* n. people of the past

ጥንት የሌለው — *ṭənt yälelläw* that who or which has no beginning

የጥንት ሰው — *yäṭənt säw* n. early man

ጥንቸል — *ṭənčäl* n. rabbit, hare

ጥንዚዛ — *ṭənzizza* n. kind of beetle

ጥንድ — *see* ጠመደ

ጥንፍ — *also* ጽንፍ *in* አጥናፈ ዓለም *aṭnafä aläm* remotest part of the world

ከጥንፍ እስከ አጥናፍ — *käṭənf əskä aṭnaf* from here to eternity

ጥዋ — *see* ጽዋ

ጥዋት — *see* ጡዋት

ጥይት — *ṭəyyət* n. bullet, ammunition, cartridge; adj. intelligent, skillful

—የማይበሳው — —*yämmaybäsaw* adj. bullet- proof

ጥድ — *ṭəd* n. juniper tree

ጥጃ — *ṭəǧǧa* n. calf *(young of cow)*

ጥገት — *ṭəggäṭ* n. milking-cow

ጥግ — *see* ጠጋ

ጥጥ — *ṭəṭ* n. cotton

ጥጥፍሬ — *ṭəṭfəre* n. cotton seed, *also* ጥፍጥሬ

ጥፊ — *ṭəffi* n. slap

በጥፊ መታ — *bäṭəffi mätta* v.t. slapped

—ጠፈጠፈ — —*ṭäfäṭṭäfä* v.t. slapped repeatedly

ጥፍር *ṭəfər* n. fingernail, claw

ጥፍራም *ṭəfram* adj. impolite, insolent *(lit. one with uncut fingernails)*

*ጦላ *ṭolä

ጦለጦል *ṭolätol* adj. light-footed, fleet; inquisitive, meddlesome, nosey

ጦልጧላ *ṭoltuʷalla* adj. light-footed, fleet; inquisitive, meddlesome, nosey

ጦመ *ṭomä, also* ጾመ *ṣomä* v.i. fasted

ጦም *ṭom* n. fast

—ቀን *—qän* n. fast-day

ጦመኛ *ṭomäñña* n. one who fasts

ጧሚ *ṭuʷami* n. one who fasts

ጦም አደረ *ṭom addärä* v.t. went without supper

—አዳሪ *—adari* n. one living in wretched poverty

—ፈታ *—fätta* v.t. broke one's fast

ጦረ *ṭorä* v.t. cared for aged people *(especially for parents or relatives)*

ጡረታ *ṭuräta* n. pension, social security

—አስገባ *—asgäbba* v.t. pensioned off

—አወጣ *—awṭṭa* v.t. pensioned off

—ወጣ *—wäṭṭa* v.t. retired

—ገባ *—gäbba* v.i. retired

የጡረታ ቤት *yäṭuräta bet* n. home for the aged, old folks' home

—አበል *—abäll* n. pension, social security

ጦር *ṭor* n. war; army; spear, lance

—ኃይሎች *—hailočč* n. armed forces *(the army)*

—አዛዥ *—azzaž* n. army commander

—አዝማች *—azmač* n. commander of battle-field

የ—ካሣ *yä—kasa* n. war reparations

—ግምባር *—gəmbbar* n. war front *(military)*

የ—ጓደኛ *ya—guʷaddäñña* n. ally

ምድር — *mədər—* n. ground forces

አፍላ ጦር *afla* n. active army

ክፍለ— *kəflä—*n. division *(army unit)*

ደራቅ— *däräq—*n. emergency troop *(without provisions and heavy weaponry)*

ጦረኛ *ṭoräñña* n. warrior, fighter

ጦርነት *ṭorənnät* n. war, battle, warfare

የጦር መሣሪያ *yäṭor mässarlya* n. weapon, armament

ጦር መሪ *ṭor märi* n. commander *(military)*

የ—መርከብ *yä—märkäb* n. warship, fleet

—ሚኒስቴር *—minister* Ministry of War

—ሜዳ *—meda* n. battlefield

የጦር ሜዳ መነጽር *yäṭor meda mänäṣṣər* n. field-glasses, binoculars

ጦር ሠራዊት *särawit* n. army

—ሰፈር *säfär* n. military camp

—ስልት *—səlt* strategy, tactics

—ተፈታ *—täfätta* v.i. has surrendered, yielded *(army)*

*ጦስ *ṭos

በርሱ ጦስ ነው ከሥራ የወጣሁት it is due to him that I have been dismissed from my job

ጦሰኛ *ṭosäñña* adj. troublesome

ጦስኝ *ṭosəññ* n. wild thyme,

ጦሽ አለ *ṭoš alä* v.i. snapped

ጦቢያ *ṭobbiya* n. Ethiopia *(arch.)*

ጦጣ *ṭoṭa* n. ape, monkey

ጦጢት *ṭoṭit* n. word used

for calling an ape

ጦፈ ţofä v.i. flew into a rage; sky-rocketed *(of price)*

በንዴት— bänəddet—was enraged, flew into a temper

ጡፍ ţuʷaf n. candle *(rather thin type)*

ተጧጧፈ täţuʷaţţuʷafä in ጥሉ ተጧጧፈ the quarrel has been aggravated

ጧ አለ ţuʷa alä v.i. cracked

ጨ

ጨለመ çällämä v.i. got dark, was dark *(room)*

ጨለማ çälläma, *also* ጭለማ çəlläma n. darkness; night

—ፊት —fit adj. gloomy *(person)*

መጨለም *in* የፀሐይ መጨለም yäṣähai mäççälläm n. eclipse

አጨለመ *in* ፊቱን አጨለመ fitun açällämä he put on a long face

ጨለጠ çälläţä v.t. drank to the last drop

ጨላጭ çällaç n. drinker cf. ጠጪ

ጭላጭ çəllaç n. last drop *(of beverage)*

ጭልጥ ብሎ ሄደ çəlləţţ bəlo hedä he left for good, disappeared

—አድርጎ ዋሸ —adəgo waššä he told lies shamelessly

—ጠጣ —täţţa he drank to the last drop

አጫላጭ aççalaç n. drinking companion

ጨለፈ çälläfä v.t. ladled out, dipped out

ጭልፋ çəlfä n. ladle, dipper

ጨሌ çälle n. green *(area of land with growing grass)*; glass-bead, necklace

—ጣይ —ţai n. sorcerer

ጨሌ çälle n. roan antelope *(usually followed with* ባለጋሜ*)*

*ጨመለቀ *çämälläqä

ጨመለቅ çämälläq adj. filthy, bedraggled

ጨምላቃ çämlaqqa adj. filthy; bedraggled, slovenly; dirty *(unclean in thought or talk)*

ተጨመላለቀ täçämalälläqä v.i. was besmeared, was bismirched; was arrogant

ተጨማለቀ täçämalläqä v.i. was smeared, was bedraggled; was arrogant

አጨመላለቀ açämälalläqä v.t. besmeared, bismirched made a mess of

አጨማለቀ aççämalläqä v.t. smudged; made a mess of

ጨመረ çämmärä v.t. added, increased; gave, put, had some more; raised

ጭማሪ çəmmari n. increment, increase

የደመወዝ— yädämäwäz—n. salary increment

የዋጋ— yäwaga— n. price increase

ጭምር çəmmər adj. in addition, including

ተጨመረ täççämmärä v.i. was added, was included; was raised *(salary)*; joined others

ተጨማሪ täçämmari adj. extra, additional; more

በተጨማሪ bätäçämmari adv. moreover, furthermore, in addition, among other things

አስጨመረ *asçämmärä* v.t. has s/t added, increased had *(salary)* raised

ጨመቀ *çämmäqä* v.t. squeezed; wrung *(wet clothes)*; made a resume, made an abstract

ጭማቂ *çəmmaqi* n. juice

የብርቱካን— *yäbərtukan-* n. orange juice

የፍሬ ነገሩ— *yäfəre nägäru-* n. gist

መጭመቂያ *mäçmäqiya* n. mangle

ተጨመቀ *täçammäqä* v.t. was squeezed; was wrung

አስጨመቀ *asçämmäqä* v.t. had s/t squeezed; had wet clothes wrung

ጨመተ *çämmätä* v.i. became taciturn, reserved

ጭምት *çəmmət* adj. taciturn, reserved

*ጨመተረ **äçmättärä*

ጨምታራ *çämtarra* adj. wrinkled

ተጨመታተረ *täçämätattärä* v.i. was full of wrinkles

ተጨማተረ *täçämattärä* v.i. was wrinkled

አጨማተረ *in* ግምባሩን — *gəmbarun-* wrinkled ones forehead

ጨመደደ *çämäddädä* v.t. grabbed *(made a sudden snatch)*

ጨምዳዳ *çämdadda* adj. wrinkled, creased; dwarfish and lean

ተጨመዳደደ *täçämädaddädä* v.i. was completely creased, wrinkled cf. ተጨመታተረ

ተጨማደደ *täçämaddädä* v.i. creased, was wrinkled

አጨማደደ *aççämaddädä* v.t. creased, wrinkled

ግምባሩን— *gəmbarun-* — wrinkled one's forehead

ጨመጨመ *çämäççämä* v.t. kissed repeatedly

ተጨማጨመ *täçämaççämä* v.i. kissed each other repeatedly

*ጨረመመ **çärämmämä*

ጨርማማ *çärmamma* adj. deformed

ተጨራመመ *täçärammämä* v.i. was deformed

አጨራመመ *aççärammämä* v.t. deformed

*ጨረመተ **çarämmätä*

ጨርማታ *çärmatta* adj. deformed cf. ጨርማማ and ጨርማዳ

ተጨረማመተ *täçärämammätä* v.i. was deformed; creased

ተጨራመተ *täçärammätä* v.i. was deformed, creased

ጨረር *çärär* n. ray, stream of light

የፀሐይ— *yäṣähai-* n. sunbeam

*ጨረመደ **çärämmädä*

ጨርማዳ *çärmadda* adj. deformed, creased

ተጨራመደ *täçärammädä* v.i. was deformed; creased

አጨራመደ *äççärammädä* v. t. deformed; creased

ጨረሰ *çärräsä* v.t. finished completed, ended, terminated; consumed; exterminated; ate up; used up

ጨርሶ *çärrəso* adv. completely, quite; through and through

ጨርሶ አይገባኝም I don't quite understand

ጭራሽ *çərraš* adj. completely, altogether

እስከነ ጭራሹ *əskännä çərrašu* altogether, completely

በጭራሽ *bäçərraš* adj. absolutely not; never; not at all

ተጨረሰ *täçarräsä* v.i. was completed, was finished; was consumed

ተጫረሰ *täççarräsä* v.t. killed each other

አጫረሰ *aččarräsä* v.t. helped in finishing s/t
ጨረቂት *čäräqit* n. type of sorghum
ጨረቃ *čäräqa* n. moon
ሙሉ— *mulu—* n. full moon
ጠፍ— *ṭäf—* n. moonless night
የጨረቃ ግርዶሽ *yäčäräqa gərdoš* lunar eclipse
ጨርቋ *also* ጮርቃ *čärquʷa, čorqa* adj. immature *(crop)*
ጨረባ *in* የጨረባ ተዝካር *yäčäräba täzkar* full of confusion, full of turmoil
*ጨረተ **čärrätä* also *ጫረተ *čarrätä*
ጨረታ *čärräta* n. auction; tender
የጨረታ ዋጋ *yäčärräta waga* n. bid
ተጫረተ *täčarrätä* v.i. bid *(made bid)*
ተጫራች *täčarač* n. bidder
አጫረተ *aččarrätä* v.t. put s/t up to auction
አጫራች *aččarač* n. auctioneer
ጨረገደ *čäräggädä* v.t. cut *(with a spade or a sickle etc.)*
*ጨረጨረ **čäräččärä*
ተንጨረጨረ *tänčäräččärä* v.t. broiled
አንጨረጨረ *ančäräččärä* v.t. broiled
ጨረጨሰ *čäräččäsä* v.t. became very old
ጨርጫሳ *čärčassa* adj. very old
ጨረፈ *čärräfä* v.t. touched slightly
ጨረፍታ *čäräfta* n. glimpse
በጨረፍታ አየ *bäčäräfta ayyä* caught a glimpse of
*ጨረፈፈ **čäräffäfä*
አንጨረፈፈ *ančäräffäfä* v.i. *in* ጠጉሩን—had unkempt hair
ጨርቅ *čärq* n. cloth, fabric, rag
ጨርቃ ጨርቅ *čärqa čärq* n. textiles, fabrics
ጨርቁን ጣለ *čärqun ṭalä* v.i. became mad
ጨርቅ ሰፊ *čärq säfi* n. tailor
ጨሰ *see* ጤሰ
ጨቀየ *čäqäyyä* v.i. was muddy, was covered with mud
ጭቃ *čəqa* n. mud, mire
ጭቃማ *čəqamma* adj. muddy, miry
ጭቃ ሹም *čəqa šum* n. village headman
—ቤት *-bet* n. mud-house
—ጅራፍ *—ǧəraf* unexpected odd thing
አጨቀየ *ačäqäyyä* v.t. turned into mire
ጨቀጨቀ *čäqäččäqä* v.t. nagged, pestered
ጨቅጫቃ *čäqčaqqa* adj. pestering, nagging
ጭቅጭቅ *čəqəččəq* n. dispute, quarrel, argument
ተጨቃጨቀ *täčäqaččäqä* v.i. disputed; quarreled
ተጨቃጫቂ *täčäqačaqi* adj. pestering, nagging
አጨቃጨቀ *aččäqaččäqä* v.t. was disputable, caused quarrel
አጨቃጫቂ *aččäqačaqi* adj. problematic; insoluble *(problem)*
ጨቅላ *čäqla* n. baby, infant
ጨቅላነት *čäqlannät* n. babyhood, infancy
ጨቆነ *čäqqonä* v.t. oppressed domineered
ጨቋኝ *čäqquʷañ* n. oppressor, tyrant; domineering, cruel
ጭቁን *čəqqun* adj. oppressed
—መደብ *—mädäb* oppressed class
ጭቆና *čəqqona* n. oppression, tyranny
ተጨቆነ *täčäqqonä* v.i. was oppressed
ተጨቋኝ *täčäqquʷañ* adj. oppressed
—መደብ *—mädäb* oppressed class
*ጨበረረ **čäbärrärä*

ጨበረር *čäbärär* adj. unkempt

ጭብራራ *čäbrarra* adj. unkempt

*ጨበረበረ **čäbäräbbärä*

ተጭበረበረ *täčbäräbbärä* v.i was cheated, embezzled

አጭበረበረ *ačbäräbbärä* v.t.dazzled; cheated, swindled, embezzled

አጭበርባሪ *ačbärbari* n. cheat, swindler, crook, imposter

ጨበጠ *čäbbäṭä* v.t. squeezed, clutched, clenched *(the fist)*; clasped; grabbed; grasped

ጨበጣ in የጨበጣ ውጊያ *yäčäbäṭa wəggiya* hand-to-hand combat

ጨባጣ *čäbbaṭṭa* n. midget

ጨብጥ *čäbṭ* also ጨብጦ *čäbaṭo* n. gonorrhea

ጭባጭ *čəbbač* n. handful

ጭብጥ in የነገሩ ጭብጥ *yänägäru čəbṭ* the main point, the gist

ጭብጥ *čəbbəṭ* n. handful, fistful, bunch

ጭብጦ *čəbbəṭo* n. round, rather heavy loaf of bread *(carried as provisions)*

ተጨበጠ *täčäbbäṭä* v.i. was squeezed; was grabbed; grasped

ተጨባጭ *täčäbbač* adj. comprehensible; concrete

—ምክንያት *—məknäyat* n. concrete fact

ተጨባበጠ *täčäbabbäṭä* v.i. wrinkled, creased

እጅ ለእጅ ተጨባበጡ *əǧǧ läǧǧ täčäbabbäṭu* they shook hands

አጨባበጠ *ačč̣ababbäṭä* v.t. wrinkled, creased

ጨበደ *čäbbodä* v.t. grabbed

ጨብጥ see ጨበጠ

*ጨበጨበ **čäbäččäbä*

ጭብጨባ *čəbčäba* n. applause, hand clapping

አጨበጨበ *ačäbäččabä* v.t. clapped, clapped hands, applauded

አጨብጫቢ *ačäbčäbi* n. henchman

አስጨበጨበ *asčäbäččäbä*, or ተጨበጨበለት *täčäbäččäbällät* he was acclaimed, was received with applause

ጨበጨበ *čäbäččäbä* v.i. became verdant, sent forth leaves

ጨነቀ *čännäqä* with pron. suff. e.g ጨነቀኝ *čännäqäñ* I am at a loss, I am embarrassed, I am in a difficulty

ጭንቀት *čənqät* n. worry, concern, disturbance, anguish

ጭንቅ *čənq* n. worry, hardship, difficulty

ተጨነቀ *täčännäqä* v.i. showed concern, was embarassed, was in a dilemma

—ተጣበበ *—täṭäbbäbä* v.i. was in great straits, was puzzled

ተጨናነቀ *täčänannäqä* v.i. was crowded, was congested

አስጨነቀ *asčännäqä* v.t. molested, nagged, pestered; put s/o in a great difficulty, worry

አስጨናቂ *asčännaqi* adj. puzzling, full of difficulties, harrowing

*ጨነቆረ **čänäqqorä*

ጨንቋራ *čänquʷarra* adj. cross-eyed

አጨነቈረ *ačänäqquʷärä* v.i. peeped *(took a look at)*

*ጨነበሰ **čänäbbäsä*

ጨንባሳ *čänbassa*, also ጨምባሳ *čämbassa* adj. weak-sighted

ጨነገፈ *čänäggäfä* v.i. aborted *(miscarried)*; went wrong, was thwarted

ጭንገፍ *čəngaf* n. abortion *(creature produced by abortion)*

ተጨናገፈ *täčänaggäfä* v.i. miscarried *(plans etc.)*; was thwarted, failed

አጨናገፈ *aččänaggäfä* v.t. foiled, thwarted, hindered

*ጨንጎለ *čänäggolä

ተጨናጎለ *täčänaggolä* v.i. miscarried *(plans etc.)* was thwarted, failed, cf. ተጨናገፈ

አጨናጎለ *aččänaggolä* v.t. foiled, thwarted, hindered, cf. አጨናገፈ

ጨንገር *čängär* n. twig, stick *(for punishing children)*

ጨከነ *čäkkänä* v.i. was cruel, ruthless, severe, harsh

ጨካኝ *čäkkañ* adj. cruel, ruthless, merciless, brutal

ጭከና *čəkkäna* n. cruelty brutality, atrocity

ጭካኔ *čəkkane* n. cruelty, brutality, atrocity

በጭካኔ ገደለው *bäčəkkane gäddäläw* he killed him in cold blood

ተጨካከነ *täčäkakkänä* v.i. treated each other infavourably

ጨዋ *čäwa* n. person of good breeding, not a slave adj. well-behaved, well mannered, gentleman; illiterate, layman

ጨዋነት *čäwannät* n. good breeding, politeness, decency

የጨዋ ልጅ *yäčäwa ləǧ* n. free person *(not a slave)*

—ቤተ ሰብ *—betäsäb* n. of good family

ጨውናና *čäwnanna* adj. small-eyed

ጨገገ *with pron. suff.* e.g ጨገገኝ *čäggägäññ* I am feeling uneasy, I grew uneasy

ጭጋግ *čəgag* n. mist, haze, fog

ጭጋጋም *čəgagam* adj. misty, hazy, foggy

ጭጋግ ፊት *čəgag fit* adj. unpleasant, cheerless, gloomy *(person)*

ጨጨብሳ *čäččäbsa* n. unleavened bread cut into pieces and mixed with butter

ጨፈለቀ *čäfälläqä* v.t. crushed, squashed; ploughed virgin land for the second time; amalgamated *(business etc.)*

ጭፍለቃ *čəfläqa* n. ploughing virgin land for the second time

ጭፍልቅ *čəfləq* n. virgin land ploughed for the second time

ተጨፈለቀ *täčäfälläqä* v.i. was crushed, squashed; was ploughed for the second time *(virgin land)*

አስጨፈለቀ *asčäfälläqä* v.t. had s/t crushed, squashed; had virgin land ploughed for the second time; was amalgamated *(business)*

ጨፈረ *čäffärä* v.i. danced

ጨፋሪ *čäffari* n. dancer

ጭፈራ *čəffära* n. dance

ጭፍራ *čəfra* n. accompaniment; escort, suite; soldier, subbordinate

ተጫፈረ *täčaffärä* v.i. joined others, mixed with others

ተጫፋሪ *täčafari* n. accomplice

አጫፈረ *aččaffärä* v.t. mixed, brought together

አጫፋሪ *aččafari* n. suite, escort; accomplice

አስጨፈረ *asčäffärä* v.t. had s/o dance

*ጨፈረረ *čäfärrärä

ጨፈረር *čäfärär* adj. unkempt

ጨፍራራ *čäfrarra* adj. unkempt

ጨፈቃ *čäfäqa* n. bundle of wood

ተጨፋፈቀ *täčäfaffäqä* v.i. was overcrowded, was congested

ጨፈነ *čäffänä* v.t. shut *(the*

eyes)

ጨፋና *ç̌äffanna* adj. poor-sighted

ጭፍን *ç̌əffən* adj. with eyes shut

በጭፍን ሠራው *bäç̌əffən särraw* he did it blindly *(thoughtlessly)*

ጨፈገገ *ç̌äfäggägä* v.t. frowned

ጨፍጋጋ *ç̌äfgagga* adj. gloomy

—ቀን *—qan* n. muggy day

ጨፈጨፈ *ç̌äfäç̌ç̌äfä* v.t. cut into pieces, chopped off, cut down, lopped; exterminated

ጭፍጨፋ *ç̌əfç̌äfa* n. chopping off, cutting down; extermination

ጭፍጫፊ *ç̌əfəç̌ç̌afi* n. cut off pieces

ተጨፈጨፈ *täç̌äfäç̌ç̌äfä* v.i. was cut into pieces; was chopped off; was cut down; was exterminated

ተጨፋጨፈ *täç̌äfaç̌ç̌äffä* v.i. exterminated each other, killed each other

ጨፌ *ç̌äffe* n. lush meadow

ጡርርር አለ *ç̌urərr alä* v.i. trickled *(flowed as a little stream)*

መንጮረር *mänç̌orär* n. spout

ጩቅ *ç̌uq* adj. greedy

ጩቤ *ç̌ube* n. small dagger

ጩስ *see* ጢስ

ጫማ *ç̌amma* n. shoe, foot *(measurement)*; sole *(of foot)*

—ሰሪ *—säri* n. cobbler

—ሰፊ *—säfi* n. shoemaker

—ሳመ *—samä* v.t. kissed s/o's foot *(as a sign of respect or gratitude)*

—ጠራጊ *—ţäragi* n. shoeblack

ላስቲክ — *lastik—or* ጎማ *-gomma—*n. rubbers

ቡት— *but—*n. boots

ነጠላ— *näţäla—*n. sandals

ኩፍ— *kuf—*n. boots *(arch.)*

የቤት— *yäbet—*n. slippers

የጫማ ማሰሪያ *yäç̌amma mäsäriya* n. shoelace, shoestring

—ማንኪያ *—mankiya* n. shoe horn

—ቀለም *—qäläm* n. shoe cream shoe polish

ተጫማ *täç̌amma* v.t. put on shoes *(arch.)*

መጫሚያ *mäç̌ç̌amiya* n. shoes *(arch.)*

ጫረ *ç̌arä* v.t. scribbled; scraped; scratched; struck *(a match)*

እሳት— *əsat—* v.t. got fire from a neighbour

ጫር ጫር አደረገ *ç̌arr ç̌arr adärrägä* v.t. scraped out slightly

ጫጫረ *ç̌aç̌arä* v.t. scribbled, scrawled

ጭረት *ç̌ərät* n. scratch, stroke *(in writing)*, dash, accent *(accent mark)*

ንኡስ— *nə'us—n. hyphen*

ተጫጫረ *täç̌aç̌arä* v.i. was full of scratches

አጫረ *in* ጠብ አጫረ *ţäb aç̌ärä* v.t. started a fight

ጠብ አጫሪ *ţäb aç̌ari* adj. aggressive, troublemaker

ጫት *ç̌at* n. leaves with mild narcotic quality *(chewed mostly by Muslims)*

—ቃመ *—qamä* v.t. chewed *ç̌at*

ጫነ *ç̌anä* v.t. loaded *(beast of burden, truck)*, burdened; put the saddle on

ጫና *ç̌änna* n. burden *(fig.)*

ጭነት *ç̌ənät* n. load, burden, cargo, freight

የጭነት መርከብ *— märkäb* n. freighter

—መኪና *— mäkina* n. truck, lorry

—ከብት *—käbt* n. beast of burden, pack animal

መጫኛ *mäç̌aňňa* n. strap of leather used in fastening a load, thong

ጫን አለ *ç̌ann alä* v.t. pressed *(a button etc.)*; overcharged

ተጫነ *täç̌anä* v.t. was loaded; pressed *(a button)*;

depress *(the gas pedal)*; suppressed

ተጫጫነ *täçaçanä* v.i. oppressed *(of weather, sleep)*

ተጫጫነው *täçaçanäw* felt drowsy

አጫጫነ *äççaçanä* v.t. helped in loading

አስጫነ *asçanä* v.t. had s/t loaded

ጫንቃ *çanqa* n. shoulder

ጫካ *çakka* n. forest, woods, jungle

ጫካ ለጫካ ሄደ *çakka läçakka hedä* he went through the forest

ጫካማ *çakkamma* adj. wooded

*ጫወተ **çawwätä*

ጨዋታ *çäwata* n. play; entertainment, amusement; conversation

—ያዘ *—yazä* v.t. was engaged in conversation

የጨዋታ ሜዳ *yäçawata meda* n. playing field

ጭውውት *çəwəwwət* n. entertainment, friendly conversation, *(with a friend or friends)*

ተጫወተ *täçawwätä* v.t. played, chatted, had a friendly conversation

ተጫዋች *täçawač* adj. playful; sociable; player

መጫወቻ *mäççawäča* n. toy, plaything

ተጨዋወተ *täçäwawwätä* v.i. conversed, had a friendly discussion

አጫወተ *aççawwätä* v.t. entertained s/o, amused s/o, kept s/o company

አጫዋች *aççawač* n. referee *(in game)*; entertainer, jester

ተጫወተበት *täçawwätäbbät* he played tricks on him, he ridiculed him

ጫጉላ *çagula* n. nuptual house

ጫጩት *çaçutt* n. chick

የወፍ— *yäwäf—* n. baby bird

*ጫጫ **çaçça*

ጫጫታ *çaçata* n. noise, row

ተንጫጫ *tänçaçça* v.i. was noisy; made a loud noise, cried in disagreement

አንጫጫ *ançaçça* v.t. caused to make a loud noise, to squeal

ጫጫ *çaçça* v.i. stopped growing, was emaciated

አጫጫ *açaçça* v.t. emaciated

ጫፍ *çaf* n. top; edge, tip, summit; point *(knife)*; hem

ጫፍና ጫፍ *çafənna çaf* n. two ends of s/t

ጫፍ ጫፉን ነገረኝ *çaf çafun näggäräññ* He told me some part of the story. He gave me a hint.

ጭላት *çəlat* n. hawk, falcon cf. ጭልፊት

ጭላንጭል *çəlançəl* n. spark *(of light)*; gleam, glimmer

የተስፋ— *yätäsfa—* n. glimmer, ray *(of hope)*

ጭላዳ *çəlada*, *or* ጨላዳ *çälada* n. gelada baboon

ጭልፊት *çəlfitt* n. sparrow, hawk cf. ጭላት

ጭልፋ *see* ጨለፈ

ጭማሪ *see* ጨመረ

ጭማቂ *see* ጨመቀ

ጭምት *see* ጨመተ

ጭምጭምታ *çəmçəmta* n. rumour

—ሰማ *—sämma* v.t. got wind of

ስለሱ ምንም —የለ *sələssu mənemm —yällä* nothing has been heard about him

ጭረት *see* ጫረ

ጭራ *çəra* n. hair at the end of an animal's tail; fly-whisk, fly-swatter

—ቀረሽ *—qärräš* n. madcap

—ቆላ *—qolla* v.t. wagged *(the tail;)* licked the boots of

ጭራው ጮሌ *çəraw çolle* adj. cunning

ጭራሮ *çəraro* n. dry sticks

—እግር *—əgər* adj. thin-legged

ጭራቅ *çəraq* n. cannibal

ጭራቅነት *çəraqənnät* n. cannibalism

ጭር አለ	*čərr alä* v.i. was calm, still *(surrounding)*, was silent, deserted *(streets etc.)*
ጭርታ	*čərrəta* n. calmness, stillness
ጭርንቁስ	*čərənqus* n. rag *(piece of old and torn cloth)*
ጭርንቁሳም	*čərənqusam* adj. ragged
ጭስ	*see* ጢስ
ጭቁን	*see* ጨቆነ
ጭቅቅት	*čəqəqqət* n. dirt, filth *(on one's body and clothes)*
ጭቅቅታም	*čəqəqqətam* adj. dirty, filthy *(of people)*
ጭቃ	*see* ጨቀየ
ጭቅና	*čəqqənna* n. fillet, sirloin
የጭቅና ጥብስ	*yäčəqqənna ṭəbs* n. *fillet steak*
ጭብጥ	*see* ጨበጠ
ጭቦ	*čəbbo* n. injustice, unfairness
ጭበኛ	*čəbboñña* adj. unfair, unjust
ጭን	*čən* n. lap, thigh
የጭን ቅልጥም	*yäčən qəlṭəm* n. tibia
—ገረድ	*—gäräd* n. mistress *(concubine)*
ጭንቅ	*see* ጨነቀ
ጭንቅላት	*čənqqəlat* n. skull
ጭንቅላታም	*čənqəllatam* n. one with a small face and a big head
ጭንጫ	*čənča* n. stony ground
ጭኮ	*čəkko* n. flour made of roasted barley mixed with butter (usually taken with as provisions for a long journey)
ጭው አለ	*čəww alä* v.i. rang *(of the ear)*
ጭው አለብኝ	*čəww aläbbəññ* I feel dizzy
ጭው ያለ በረሃ	*čəww yalä bäräha* n. a vast expanse of desert
——ገደል	*——gädäl* n. precipice
ጭድ	*čəd* n. ṭef straw
እሳትና ጭድ	*əsatənna čəd* adj. irreconcilable, antagonistic *(lit. fire and straw)*
ጭገር	*čəgär* n. hair *(of a person)* other than that of the head
ጭገራም	*čəgäram* adj. hairy
ጭጭ አለ	*čəčč alä* v.i. hushed, remained dumb, lapsed into silence
ጭፍን	*see* ጨፈነ
ጮለ	*čolä* v.i. schemed, was crafty
ጮሌ	*čolle* n/adj schemer, crafty
*ጮለ	*čolä*
አጮለ	*in* በጥፊ አጮለ *bäṭəffi ačolä* smacked, slapped
ጮማ	*čoma* adj. fat *(meat)*
—ከብት	*—käbt* fat animal
አፈ—	*afä—* n. flatterer
ጮረረ	*čorrärä* v.i. trickled *(flowed as a small stream)* cf. ጨርር አለ
ጮራ	*čorra* n. ray of the sun
ጮርቃ	*čorqa* adj. immature *(crop)*
ጮቅ	*čoq* n. chap *(of the skin)*
ጮቤ	*in* ጮቤ መታ *čobbe mätta* v.t .leapt with joy
—ረገጠ	*—räggäṭä* v.t. leapt with joy
—ዘለለ	*—zällälä* v.t. leapt with joy
ጮኸ	*čohä* v.i. cried *(shouted)*, yelled, shouted in a loud voice; screamed, cried out; barked *(dog)*; appealed *(to a sovereign etc.)*
ጩኸት	*čuhät* n. shout, cry, scream, yell, noise howl; clamour, appeal
—ትርፉ	*—tərfu* adj. effort-wasting, futile
ዶሮ—	*doro—* n. early morning
ተጯጯኸ	*täčuʷačʷahä* v.i. made repeated demands; clamoured repeatedly
አጮኸ	*ačohä* v.t. cracked *(whip etc.)*
በጥፊ—	*bäṭəffi—* v.t. smacked, slapped the face
አስጮኸ	*asčohä* v.t. caused to cry, shout

ጰ

ጰልቃን — *pälqan* n. pelican

ጰራቅሊጦስ — *päraqlitos* n. the Paraclete, the Holy Spirit

ጰንጠቆስጤ — *pänṭäqosṭe* n. Pentecost, Whitsunday

ጳጉሜ(ን) — *pagume(n)* n. intercalary month *(5-10 September)*

ጳጳስ — *pappas* n. bishop

ሊቀ ጳጳስ — *also* ሊቀ ጳጳሳት *liqä pappas, liqä pappasat* n. archbishop

ጰጰሰ — *päppäsä* v.i. was ordained bishop

አጰጰሰ — *apäppäsä* v.t. ordained bishop

ጸ

*ጸለመ — **ṣällämä*

ጽልመት — *ṣəlmät* n. darkness

ጸለየ — *ṣälläyä* v.i. prayed, recited prayers

ጸሎት — *ṣälot* n. prayer, service

ጸሎተኛ — *ṣälotäñña* adj. religious, pious

የጸሎት ቤት — *also* ቤተ ጸሎት *yäṣälot bet, betä ṣälot* n. chapel

ጸሎት አደረሰ — *ṣälot adärräsä* v.t. prayed

ጸሎተ ሃይማኖት — *ṣälotä haimanot* n. the Creed

ጸሎተ ማእድ — *—ma'ədd* n. say grace

—ማኅበር — *—mähəbär* n. communal prayer

—ኀሙስ — *—hamus* n. Maundy Thursday

መታሰቢያ ጸሎት — *mättäsäbiya ṣälot* n. memorial service

ተጸለየ — *täṣälläyä* v.i. was prayed

አጸለየ — *aṣṣälläyä* v.t. had prayer made

ጸሐይ — *see* ፀሐይ

ጸር — *see* ፀር

*ጸበረቀ — **ṣäbärräqä*

ተንጸባረቀ — *tänṣäbarräqä* v.i. was sparkled, shimmered, was reflected

ነጸብራቅ — *näṣäbraq* n. glare; reflection

አንጸባረቀ — *anṣäbarräqä* v.t. sparkled, glittered, glared, glistened; reflected

አንጸባራቂ — *anṣäbaraqi* adj. glaring; brilliant

ጸነነ — *ṣännänä* v.i. was difficult

ጸና — *sänna see* ጠና

ጽኑ(እ) — *ṣənu(')* adj. stable, firm; acute, severe

—እሥራት — *—əssərat* n. hard labour

ጽኑአን ግሦች — *ṣənu'an gəssoč* n. strong verbs

ጽኑነት — *ṣənunnät* n. strength, firmness

ተጽናና — *täṣnänna* v.i. was consoled, found solace; was comforted; cheered up

አጸና — *aṣänna* v.t. ratified, put into effect

አጽናና — *aṣnanna* v.t. consoled, gave comfort, gave solace; encouraged

ጸናጽል — *ṣänaṣəl* n. sistrum

*ጸየፈ — **ṣäyyäfä*

ጸያፍ — *ṣäyyaf* adj. disgusting, base; gross *(language)*, obscene *(language)*

ተጸየፈ — *täṣäyyäfä* v.i. abhored, loathed

አጸየፈ — *aṣṣäyyäfä* v.t. was offensive, filled with disgust

አጸያፊ — *aṣṣäyyafi* adj. base,

dishonourable, disgusting, loathsome

ጸደቀ *ṣäddäqä* v.i. was declared righteous, was pious; was ratified *(bill)*; was approved

ጻድቅ *ṣadəq* adj. righteous, pious, just

ጽድቅ *ṣədq* n. righteousness

ተመጻደቀ *tämäṣaddäqä* v.i. behaved hypocritically; aggrandized oneself

ተመጻዳቂ *tämäṣadaqi* adj. hypocritical

መመጻደቅ *mämmäṣadäq* inf. self-aggrandizement

አጸደቀ *aṣäddäqä* v.t. ratified, approved

ጸደይ *ṣädäy* n. spring *(season)*

ጸዳ *ṣädda* v.i. was cleaned, was disinfected

ጽዱ *ṣədu* adj. clean

ጽዳት *ṣədat* n. sanitation, cleanliness

የጽዳት ዘመቻ *yäṣədat zämäča* sanitation campaign

ተጸዳዳ *täṣädadda* v.i. cleaned up; went to the lavatory

መጸዳጃ *mäṣṣädağa* n. lavatory

አጸዳ *aṣäddda* v.t. cleaned; cleaned up

ጸጉር *ṣägur* n. hair, fur, *also* ጠጉር

ጸጋ *ṣägga* n. grace

—ቢስ *—bis* adj. graceless

ባለ— *balä—* n. rich, wealthy, well-to-do

ጸጥ አለ *ṣäṭṭ alä* v.i. was silent, calm, quiet; quieted down *(wind, storm, wave etc.)*; was secure

ጸጥ ለጥ አለ *ṣäṭṭ läṭṭ alä* v.i. surrendered, was subdued, yielded, gave in, admitted, defeated

ጸጥተኛ *ṣäṭṭətäñña* adj. quiet *(gentle; not rough in disposition)*

ጸጥታ *ṣäṭṭəta* n. quiet, tranquility, calm, silence, stillness; security

—አስከበረ *askäbbära* restored order, kept peace; suppressed, subdued rebellion

—አስከባሪ *—askäbbari* security forces

በጸጥታ *bäṣäṭṭəta* adv. quietly

የጋራ ጸጥታ *yägara ṣäṭṭəta* collective security

የጸጥታ ምክር ቤት *yäṣäṭṭəta məkər bet* Security Council *(UNO)*

ጸጥ አሰኘ *ṣäṭṭ assäññä* v.t. quietened, silenced suppressed

—አደረገ *—adärrägä* quietened, suppressed, quelled

ጸጸተ *with pronominal suff.* e.g. ጸጸተኝ *ṣäṣṣätäññ* I felt sorry, I regretted

ጸጸት *ṣäṣät* n. remorse, sorrow, repentance, regret

ጸጸተኛ *ṣäṣätäñña* adj. sorrowful, remorseful

ተጸጸተ *täṣäṣṣätä* v.i. regretted, repented, was sorry

ጻፈ *ṣafä, also* ጣፈ *ṭafä* v.t. wrote, wrote down

ጸሐፊ *ṣähafi* n. writer, clerk, secretary, scribe; author

ጸሐፌ ትእዛዝ *ṣähafe tə'əzaz* n. Minister of the Pen

ልዩ ጸሐፊ *ləyyu ṣähafi* n. private secretary

ቁም— *qum—* n. calligrapher

ዋና— *wanna—* n. secretary general

ጽሑፍ *ṣəhuf* n. writing *(anything written)*

ሥነ— *sənä—* n. literature

አፋዊ ሥነ ጽሑፍ *afawi sənä ṣəhuf* n. oral literature

— ጽሑፋዊ *—ṣəhufawi* adj. literary

በራሪ ጽሑፍ *bärari ṣəhuf* n. leaflet

ጽሕፈት *ṣəhəfät* n. writing

ቁም— *qum—*n. calligrpahy

የቃል— *yäqal—* n. dictation

አጭር— *aččər —* n. stenograpy, short-hand

የእጅ— *yä'əǧǧ—* n. hand—

writing

የጽሕፈት መኪና *yäṣəhəfät mäkina* n. typewriter

መጽሐፍ *mäṣhaf* n. book

መጻሕፍት ቤት *mäṣahəft bet* n. library

መጽሐፍ ቅዱስ *mäṣhaf qədus* n. Bible, Scripture

ቤተ መጻሕፍት *betä mäṣahəft* n. library

(የ) መጻሕፍት ሱቅ/ መደብር *(yä) mäṣahəft suq/ mädäbbər* book-shop, book-store

ተጻፈ *täṣafä* v.i. was written, was recorded *(in writing)*

ተጻጻፈ *täṣaṣafä* v.i. corresponded with one another

አጻፈ *aṣṣafä* v.t. had a letter, a book written, dictated

ጻሕል *ṣahəl* n. paten

ጽላት *ṣəllat* n. tablet of wood or stone used as a *tabot*

ጽላተ ሙሴ *ṣəllatä muse* n. Tablet of the Law

ጽልመት *see* ጸለመ

ጽኑ *see* ጸና *and* ጠና

ጽንፍ pl. አጽናፍ *in* አጽናፈ ዓለም *aṣnafä aläm* remote place of the world

ጽዋ *ṣəwwa* n. chalice, cup

—አነሣ *—anässa* v.t. drank a toast

ጽዮን *ṣəyon in* አክሱም*—aksum* —the church of St. Mary in Axum

ጽዮናዊ *ṣəyonawi* adj. Zionist

ጽጌ ረዳ *ṣəgge räda* n. rose *(flower)*

ጾመ *see also* ጦመ *somä, ṭomä* v.t. fasted

ጸዋሚ *ṣəwami* ጹሚ *ṣuʷami* n. faster

ጾመኛ *ṣomäñña* n. faster

ጾም *ṣom* n. fast, fasting

—አደረ *—addärä* v.i. went without supper

—አዳሪ *—adäri* adj. very poor

—ገደፈ *—gäddäfä* v.t. broke one's fast

ጾታ *ṣota* n. gender, sex

ተባዕታይ— *täba'tay—* masculine gender

አንስታይ— *anstay—* feminine gender

የወል— *yäwäl—* common gender

ግዑዝ— *gə'uz—* neuter gender

ፀ

ፀሐይ *ṣähay* n. sun

ፀሐያማ *ṣähayamma* adj. sunny, bright *(day)*

ፀሐይ ወጣች *ṣähay wäṭṭač* the sun rose

—ጠለቀች *—ṭälläqäčč* the sun set

ብርሃነ ፀሐይ *bərhanä ṣähay* n. sunlight

የፀሐይ መነጽር/ መነጥር *yäṣähay mänäṣṣər/ mänäṭṭər* sun-glass

—ጨረር *—čärär* n. sun-beam

—ግርዶሽ *—gərdoš* n. eclipse

ፀር *ṣar* n. enemy

ፀረ— *ṣärä—* pref. against, anti—

ፀረ ሕዝብ *ṣärä həzb* adj. anti-people

—መርዝ *—märz* adj. antidote

—ማርያም *—maryam* n. protestant *(lit. anti-Mary)*

—ተባይ *—täbay* n. insecticide

—ታንክ *—tank* n. antitank

—አውሮፕላን *—auroppəlan* n. anti-aircraft

—ኢምፔሪያሊዝም *—imperialism* n. anti-imperialism

—ፊውዳል *—fiwdal* n. anti-feudal

ፀነሰ (ች) *ṣännäsäčč* v.t. became pregnant

ፅንስ *ṣəns* n. pregnancy, embryo

ፅንሰ ሐሳብ *ṣənsä hassab* n. meaning, connotation, concept

ፅንስ ማስወረድ *ṣəns maswärräd* n. abortion

ተፀነሰ *täṣännäsä* v.i. conceived *(of pregnancy*

ፀዳል *ṣädal* n. brilliance *(o light)*

ፈ

'ፈለመ •*fällämä*

ፍልሚያ *fəlmiya* n. duel *(any two-sided contest)*

ተፋለመ *täfallämä* v.i. fought duels

ተፋላሚ *täfalami* n. dueller

አፋለመ *affallämä* v.t. caused *(s/o)* to fight a duel

ፈለሰ *fälläsä* v. was uprooted *(plant)*; immigrated, migrated

ፈላሻ *fällaša* n. Ethiopian Jew

ፍልሰታ *fəlsäta* n. The Assumption *(of Mary)*

ፍልስልስ *fəlsləs* adj. destroyed, dilapidated

ፍልስልሱ ወጣ *fəlsləsu wäṭṭa* v.t. fell into pieces

ተፋለሰ *täfallä̈sä* v.i. went wrong, was disrupted

አፈለሰ *afälläsä* v.t. uprooted *(a plant)*

አፋለሰ *affalläsä* v.t. disrupted, destroyed; caused *(s/t)* to come to nothing

ፈለሰመ *see* ፈለሰፈ

•ፈለሰሰ •*fälässäsä*

ፈለሰስ *fäläsäs* adj/n. *(one)* who lives in luxurious surroundings

ፈልሳሳ *fälsassa* adj/n. *(one)* who lives in luxurious surroundings

ተንፈላሰሰ *tänfälassäsä* v.i. lived luxuriously

ፈለሰፈ *fälässäfä*, *also* ፈለሰመ *fälässämä* v.i. philosophized; made a discovery; invented

ፈላስፋ *fälasfa*, *or* ፈላስ *fälasma* n. philosopher

ፍልሰፋ *fəlsäfa* n. discovery invention

ፈልሳፊ *fälsafi* n. inventor discoverer

ፍልስፍና *fəlsəfənna* n. philosophy

ተፈላሰፈ *täfälassäfä* v.i. philosophised

ፈለቀ *fälläqä* v.i. sprung from gushed out *(liquid* originated *(idea)*

አፈለቀ *afälläqä* v.t. generate produced *(idea)*; caused to spring from

•ፈለቀለቀ •*fäläqälläqä*

ፍልቅልቅ *fələqləq* adj. jovial, smiling, cheerful

ተፍለቀለቀ *täfläqälläqä* v.i. bubbled *(boiling liquid)*

የፊቱ ወዝ ተፍለቀለቀ *yäfitu wäz täfläqälläq* had a glossy complexion

አፍለቀለቀ *afläqälläqä* v.t. cause to bubble

ፈለቀቀ *fäläqqäqä* v.t. broke loose

ጥጥ— *ṭəṭ*— v.t. treated cotton in a gin, or with the fingers

ፍልቃቂ *in* የጥጥ ፍልቃቂ *yäṭə fəlləqqaqi* n. cotton seed cf. ጥጥ ፍሬ

ጥጥ ፈልቃቂ ማኪና *ṭəṭ fälqaqi mäkina* n. gin *(for treating cotton)*

ፍልቃቂ *in* የወርቅ ፍልቃቂ *yäwärq fələqqaqi* n gold foil, gold lea

መፈልቀቂያ in የብረት መፈልቀቂያ *yäbərät mäfälqäqiya* n. crowbar

ተፈለቀቀ *täfäläqqäqä* v.i. broke loose

• **ፈለከለከ** / **ተፍለከለከ** • *fäläkälläkä* *täfläkälläkä* v.i. swarmed *(ants etc.)*

ፈለክ *fäläk* n. planet

ፈለገ *fällägä* v.t. wanted, desired, wished, liked; looked for, searched for, sought, expected; was interested in

ፈላጊ *fällagi* n. one who wants, desires; searcher

ዕቃው ፈላጊ የለውም *əqaw fällagi yälläwəm* the commodity has no demand

ፈለግ *fäläg* n. trail, trace track; path; example

ፍለጋ *fəllägä* n. search, quest

ፍላጎት *fəllagot* n. wish, desire, want *(need)*, will, interest; inclination

ተፈለገ *täfällägä* v.i. was sought, desired, wanted

ተፈላጊ *täfällagi* adj. necessary, essential, required, desirable

ተፈላለገ *täfälallägä* v.i. looked for one another; had a mutual interest

አፋለገ *affallägä* v.t. helped s/o in searching for s/t

አስፈለገ *asfällägä* v.t. was important, necessary, imperative

ማረፍ አስፈለገኝ *märäf asfällägäññ* I felt like resting

ፈለጠ *fällätä* v.t. split *(wood)*, quarry *(marble, stone etc.)*; v.i. feel a headache e.g. ራሴን ፈለጠኝ *rasen fällätäññ* I feel a headache. I have a headache.

ፈለጣ in እንጨት ፈለጣ *ənčät fälläta* act of splitting wood, wood chopping

ፈሊጥ *fälit* n. method, style, mode; sagacity

አዲስ— *addis—* n. new style

ፈሊጠኛ *fälitäñña* adj. sagacious; tactful, artful, resourceful, clever, ingenious *(in)*, adroit

ፈላጭ in እንጨት ፈላጭ *ənčät fälač* n. wood-chopper

ደንጊያ— *dängiya—*n. quarryman

ፈላጭ ቆራጭ *fälač qorač* n. dictator, authoritarian, absolute ruler, tyrant

ፍልጥ *fəlt* n. split wood

ተፈለጠ *täfällätä* v.i. was split *(wood)*, was chopped

ተፈላጭ *täfällač* adj. easily split *(wood)*

ፈለፈለ *fäläffälä* v.t. hatched *(chicken)*; bored into, hollowed out; shelled *(beans)*; husked *(corn)*

ፈልፈላ *fälfäla* adj. extremely wicked *(person)*

ፍልፈል in ፍልፈል አፈር *fəlfäl afär* n. mole

ፍልፍል *fəlfəl* adj. shelled *(beans etc.)*

መፈልፈያ in የቡና መፈልፈያ *yäbunna mäfälfäya* n. coffee pulper

ተፈለፈለ *täfäläffälä* v.i. was hatched; was hollowed, was shelled; was husked

አስፈለፈለ *asfäläffälä* v.t. had *(s/t)* shelled; hollowed, husked

ፈሊጥ *see* ፈለጠ

ፈላ *fälla* v.i. boiled; was fermented; swarmed *(moved in large numbers)*

ፍላት *fəlat* n. boiling

ፍል *fəl adj.* boiled

ፍል ውሃ *fəlwäha* n. hot spring, thermal springs

ተፈላ *täfällä* v.i. was boiled

አፈላ *afälla* v.t. boiled, made to boil

ጉድ— *gud*—v.t. created trouble

አፍላል *aflal* n. medium sized cooking pot

እንፋሎት *ənfalot* n. steam, vapour

አስፈላ *asfälla* v.t. had *(s/t)* boiled

ፈረመ *färrämä* v.t. signed *(a document)*; endorsed *(a check)*

ፈራሚ *färrami* adj./n. *(one)* who signs *(a document)*; one *(who)* endorses *(a check)*; signatory

ፊርማ *firma* n. signature

ተፈረመ *täfärrämä* v.i. was signed *(a document)*; was endorsed *(a check)*

ተፈራረመ *täfärarrämä* v.i. concluded an agreement, ratified *(on both sides)*

ተፈራራሚ *täfärarami* n. signatories

አስፈረመ *asfärrämä* v.t. had *(s/o)* signed

ፈረሰ *färräsä* v.t. fell in ruins, fell apart, collapsed; was destroyed; was violated *(pact)*; was abrogated *(contract)*

ፈራሽ *färaš* adj. liable to fall apart; legally invalid

ፈራሽ በስባሽ *färaš bäsbaš* dj. mortal

ፍራሽ *fəraš* n. mattress

ፍራሽ *fərraš* n. ruins, remains

ፈራረሰ *färarräsä* v.i. fell to pieces, fell in ruins

ፍርስራሽ *fərsraš* n. ruins, remains

ፍርስርስ *fərsrəs* adj. dilapidated

ፍርስርሱ ወጣ *fərsrəsu wäṭṭa* v.i. fell into pieces, was dilapidated

ተፋረሰ *täfarräsä* v.i. disagreed *(on price)*

አፈራረሰ *afärarräsä* v.t. wrecked, destroyed, ruined

ፈረሱላ *färäsulla* n. 17 kilos

ፈረስ *färäs* n. horse, stallion

— ሜዳ— *meda* — n. Greyer's zebra

ፈረሰኛ *färäsäñña* n. horseman, cavalry; cavalryman; torrent

ሌጣ ፈረስ *leṭa färäs* n. barebacked horse

(የ) ሰይጣን ፈረስ *yäsäyṭan färäs* adj moody

(የ) ፈረስ ጉልበት *yäfäräs gulbät* n. horse power

—ግልገል —*gəlgəl* n. colt

*ፈረቀ **färräqä*

ፈረቃ *färäqa* n. shift system *(in schools etc.)*

ፈርቅ *färq* n. difference *(price)*

*ፈረቀረቀ **färäqärräqä*

ተፍረቀረቀ *täfräqärräqä* v.i. suppurated; oozed with pus

ፈረንሳይ *färänsay* n. France

ፈረንሳዊ *färänsawi* adj. French, Frenchman

ፈረንሳይኛ *färänsayəñña* n. French *(language)*

*ፈረከረከ **färäkärräkä*

ፈረክራካ *färäkrakka* adj. falling apart

ፍርክርክ *fərəkrək* adj. falling apart

ተፍረከረከ *täfräkärräkä* v.i. fell apart; trembled with fear

*ፈረከሰ **färäkkäsä* v.t. cracked

ፍርክስ *fərkəs* n. a crack

ተፈረከሰ *täfäräkkäsä* v.i. was cracked

ፈረደ *färrädä* v.t. judged, pronounced sentence, rendered judgement

ፈረደለት *färrädällät* he ruled in his favour

ፈረደበት *färrädäbbät* he ruled against him

ፈራጅ *färaǧ* adj./n. one who judges, pronounces sentence

ፍርጃ *fərǧa* n. disaster, calamity; punishment

of God

ፍርድ *fərd* n. judgement; award *(decision given by a judge or arbitrator)*

ፍርደ ገምድል *fərdä gämdəl* n. biased judge

ፍርድ ሚኒስቴር *fərd minister* n. Ministry of Justice

—ሚኒስትር *—ministr* n. Minister of Justice

—ሸንጎ *—šängo* n. people's tribunal

—ቤት *—bet* n. court, tribunal, court of justice

አውራጃ ፍርድ ቤት *awrağğa fərd bet* n. awrağğa court *(provincial court)*

ከፍተኛ—— *käffətäñña* — n. high-court

ወረዳ—— *wäräda* — n. district-court

ወታደር—— *wättadär*— n. court-martial

ጠቅላይ—— *ṭäqlay*— n. supreme court

ተፈረደ *täfärrädä* v.i. was judged; was evaluated

ተፋረደ *täfarrädä* v.i. brought one's case to the court of justice

ተፋራጅ *täfarağ* adj./ n. *(one)* who brings his case to the court of justice

አፋረደ *affarrädä* v.t. arbitrated, saw the case of opponents

አስፈረደ *asfärrädä* was decided in his favour

•ፈረገረገ *°färägärrägä*

ፍርግርግ *fərəgrəg* adj. interwoven, n. grid, grating

•ፈረገጠ *•färäggäṭä*

ተንፈራገጠ *tänfäraggäṭä* v.i. wriggled

ፈረጠ *färräṭä* v.i. broke open, burst

ፈርጥ *färṭ* a stone in a setting

ፍርጥ አድርጎ ተናገረ *fərraṭṭ adrgo tänaggärä* he spoke bluntly, he spoke straight out

አፈረጠ *afärräṭä* v.t. broke open, squeeze *(the pus)*

ተፍረጠረጠ *täfräṭärräṭä* v.i. was squeezed out *(boil etc.)*

አፍረጠረጠ *in* አፍረጥርጦ ተናገረ *afräṭrəṭo tänaggärä* he spoke bluntly, he spoke straight out

ፈረጠመ *färäṭṭämä* v.i. became fleshy, strong

ፈርጣማ *färṭamma* adj. well-built, strong *(person)*, corpulent

አፈረጠመ *afäräṭṭämä* v.t. became fleshy, strong

ፈረጠጠ *färäṭṭäṭä* v.i. ran away *(horse)*; deserted

ፈርጣጭ *färṭač* n. deserter

ፍርጠጣ *fərṭäṭa* n. desertion

•ፈረጠጠ *•färäṭṭäṭä*

ተንፈራጠጠ *tänfäraṭṭäṭä* v.i. was stretched *(legs while sitting)*

አንፈራጠጠ *anfäraṭṭäṭä* v.t. stretched one's legs *(while sitting)*

ፈረፈረ *färäffärä* v.t. crumbled, broke into small pieces

ፍርፋሪ *fərəffari* n. crumbs

ፍርፍር *fərfər* n. crumbled ənğära mixed in wäṭ

ተፈረፈረ *täfäräffärä* v.i. crumbled

•ፈራፈረ *färaffärä*

ተንፈራፈረ *tänfäraffärä* v.i. flopped around, writhed

ፈሪሳዊ *färisawi* n. hypocrite, self-righteous person, Pharisee

ፈራ *färra* v.i. was afraid, feared, was fearful, was frightened

ፈሪ *färi* adj. coward, timid, fearful

ፈሪሀ እግዚአብሔር *färiha əgzi'abəhər* n. the fear of God

ፈሪነት *färinnät* n. cowardice

ፍራት *fərat* n. fright, fear, scare, ፍራት ፍራት አለው *fərat fərat aläw* v.i hesitated due to fear

ፍራቻ *fəračča* n. fear

ተፈራ *täfärra* v.i. was feared, respected, honoured

ተፈሪ *täfäri* adj./n. *(one)* who is feared, respectful, honourable

ተፈራራ *täfärarra* v. i. feared each other; had mutual respect

አስፈራ *asfärra* v.t. frightened, terrified, scared

አስፈሪ *asfärri* adj. fearful, fierce, ferocious

አስፈራራ *asfärarra* v.t. terrified, scared, threatened

ፈራ *färra*

ፍሬ *fəre* n. fruit, seed, berry

—ሰጠ *—säṭṭä* v.t. was productive; bore fruits *(of work)*

ፍሬያማ *fəreyamma* adj. fruitful

ፍራፍሬ *fərafəre* n. fruits *(of all kind)*

ፍሬ ቢስ *fəre bis* adj. useless, pointless, fruitless, absurd, futile, ridiculous

—ነገር *—nägär* n. gist, main point, central ideas; essence; summary *(of an article)*

የሥራ— *yäsəra —* n. output, result *(of one's activities)*

የብልት— *yäbəllət —* n. testicle

አፈራ *afärra* v.t. produced fruits, bore fruits

ፈር *fär* n. furrow *(of a —plough)*

—ለቀቀ *—läqqäqä* v.i. missed the point

—ያዘ *—yazä* v.t. stuck to the point

ፈርስ *färs* n. chyme and chyel

ፈርሳም *färsam* adj. big-bellied

ፈርጅ *färǧ* n. fringe, ruffle *(of skirt)*

ፈርጥ *see* ፈረጠ

ፈሰሰ *fässäsä* v.i. poured out, spilled over; flew

ሐሞቱ— *hamotu—* lost courage, lost hope

ሞልቶ— *molto—* v.i. overflew

ፈሰሴ *fäsäse* n. one with long hanging hair *(woman)*

ፈሰስ *fäsäs* n. gutter *(of a roof)*

—አደረገ *—adärrägä* reimbursed unspent goverment money to the central treasury

ፈሳሽ *fäsaš* n. liquid, fluid

—ውሃ *—wəha* n. running water

ፍሳሽ *fəssaš* n. sewage; leakage

የውሃና የፍሳሽ ባለ ስልጣን *yäwəhanna yäfəssaš baläsəlṭan* water and sewage authority

ፍስስ አለ *in* ልቡ ፍስስ አለ *ləbbu fəsəss alä* his heart sank; became lazy

ሰውነቱ ፍስስ አለ *säwənnätu fəsəss alä* felt sluggish

ተፋሰሰ *in* ደም ተፋሰሰ *däm täfassäsä* v.i. killed each other, injured each other

አፈሰሰ *affässäsä* v.t.spilled, leaked, poured

ደም— *däm—* shed blood

አፋሰሰ *affassäsä* v.t. spilled here and there

ፈሰከ *fässäkä* v.t. broke the fast

ፋሲካ *fasika* n. Easter

ፍስክ *fəssək* n. non-fasting day

ፈሰፈሰ *fäsäffäsä* v.t. thrashed soundly, gave a thorough beating

ፈሳ *fässa* v.t. broke wind, farted

ፈሳም *fäsam* n. farter; coward

ፈስ *fäs* n. fart

ፈሱን ጠበሰ *fäsun ṭäbbäsä* ran away quickly from;

(people) to be stupified

ፈየደ *fäyyädä* v.i. became useful

ፋይዳ *fayda* n. usefulness, value, importance

—ቢስ *—bis* adj. useless, worthless

—የለሽ *—yälläš* adj. uselsss, valueless

ፈጀ *fäǧǧä* v.t. consumed, ate up; exterminated; took *(time)*; burnt *(of hot liquid)*

ነገረ ፈጅ *nägärä fäǧǧ* n. representative *(in legal affairs)*

ፍጆታ *fəǧota* n. consumption; floor *(in a debate)*

—ይሰጠኝ *—yəssäṭäññ* May, I take the floor?

ፍጅት *fəǧǧət* n. massacre; uproar, disturbance, tumult

ተፈጀ *täfäǧǧä* v.t. was consumed, was eaten up

ተፋጀ *täfaǧǧä* v.i. destroyed one another; was hot *(pepper)*; burnt *(hot liquid)*

አፋጀ *affaǧǧä* v.t. caused to destroy one another

አስፈጀ *asfäǧǧä* v.t. had s/o destroyed

ፈገመ *fäggämä* v.i. tumbled down

ፍግም አለ *fəggəmm alä* v.i. tumbled down; died suddenly

አፈገመ *afäggämä* v.t. let s/o tumble down

ፈገገ *fäggägä* v.i. smiled

ፈገግታ *fägägta* n. smile

—ቢስ *—bis* adj. cheerless

•ፈገጠ *•fäggäṭä*

ፈገጠው *fäggəṭäw* to Hell with it

ፈገፈገ *fägäffägä* v.t. rubbed; scr ped

ፍግፋጊ *fəgəffagi* n. scrapings

ተፈገፈገ *täfägäffägä* v.i. was rubbed, scraped

•ፈገፈገ *•fägäffägä*

ተፈጋፈገ *täfägaffägä* v.i. pressed against

አፈገፈገ *afägäffägä* v.t. drew back; retreated; gave ground; withdrew

ፈጠመ *see also* ፈጸመ

ፍጥምጥም *fəṭəmṭəm* n. engagement *(agreement to marry)*

ተፈጠመ *täfäṭṭämä* v.i. gave a promise in front of a judge

ተፈጣጠመ *täfäṭaṭṭämä* v.i. became engaged *(to get married)*

ፈጠረ *fäṭṭärä* v.t. created, devised *(a scheme)*; invented

ፈጠራ *fäṭära* n. invention

የፈጠራ ወሬ *yäfäṭära wäre* fabrication *(false story of events)*

—ጽሑፍ *—ṣəhuf* creative writing

ፈጣሪ *fäṭari* n. creator

ፍጡር *fəṭur* n. creature, being *(creature)*

ፍጥረት *fəṭrät* n. creature

ሥነ— *sənä—* n. nature

ተፈጠረ *täfäṭṭärä* u.i. was created

ተፈጥሮ *täfäṭro* n. nature, natural state

የተፈጥሮ ሀብት *yätäfäṭro habt* n. natural resources

ፈጠነ *fäṭṭänä* v.i. was quick, hurried, went fast, was fast, speeded up

ፈጣን *fäṭṭan* adj. quick, swift, rapid

ፍጡን *in* ፍጡን ረድኤት *fəṭunä rädə'et* patron saint

ፍጥነት *fəṭnäṭ* n. speed, velocity, rapidity

—ጨመረ *—čämmärä* v.t. accelerated

በፍጥነት *bäfəṭnät* adv. immediately, rapidly,fast

ተፋጠነ *täfaṭṭänä* v.i. hurried

አፋጠነ *affaṭṭänä* v.t. speeded, quickened, hastened

አፋጣኝ *affaṭañ* adj. urgent

ፈታሽ *fättaš* n. inspector

ፍትሻ *fəttäša* n. inspection, search

ተፈተሸ *täfättäšä* v.i. was checked; was inspected; was searched

ተፈታተሸ *täfätattäšä* v.i. tried out one another

አስፈተሸ *asfättäšä* v.t. had *s/t*, s/o inspected; searched

ፈተነ *fättänä* v.t. examined, tested, experimented, put to the test; tempted

ፈተና *fätäna* n. examination, test; trial, temptation

ፈታኝ *fättan* n. examiner, invigilator

ፍቱን *fətun* adj. efficacious *(remedy)*, efficient *(e.g. way of teaching)*, tried

ፍቱንነት *fətunənnät* n. efficacy

መፈተኛ *mäfättäña* adj. experimental

ተፈተነ *täfättänä* v.i. was examined, tested; was put to the test

ተፈታኝ *täfättañ* n. candidate *(in an examination)*, examinee

ተፈታተነ *täfättatänä* v.i. tempted s/o, put temptation in somebody's way

ተፈታታኝ *täfätatañ* n. tempter

አፈታተነ *affätattänä* v.t. caused to compete against each other

አስፈተነ *asfättänä* v.t. had s/o examined, had s/t tested

ፈተገ *fättägä* v.t. rubbed, removed the hulls; scrubbed *(pans)*

ፍተጋ *fəttäga* n. rubbing

ፍትግ *fəttəg* n. wheat, barley etc. whose hulls are removed

ተፈተገ *täfättägä* v.i. was rubbed; was scrubbed

ተፋተገ *täfattägä* v.i. made friction *(by rubbing)*; quarrelled

አፋተገ *affattägä* v.t. caused to rub against each other

አስፈተገ *asfättägä* v.t. had the hulls removed; had s/t scrubbed

ፈተፈተ *fätäffätä* v.t. crumbled up s/t soft *(bread in sauce)*; was impertinent, was intrusive *in* ነገር ፈትፋች *nägär fätfač* adj. impertinent, intrusive

ፍትፍት *fətfət* n. scrambled bread *(ənğära)* mixed in pepper sauce

ፈታ *fätta* v.t. released, untied unfastened; undid *(a knot)*; divorced; solved; deciphered; gave absolution

ሥራ— *səra*— v.t. was idle, was out of work

ፈት *fätt* n. divorced *(mainly for woman)*

ፍታት *also* ፍትሐት *fətat*, *fəthat* n. prayer for the dead

ፍትሕ *fəth* n. justice

ፍትሐ ብሔር ሕግ *fətha bəher həgg* civil code

ፍች *fəčč* n. interpretation; solution; meaning; divorce

መፍትሔ *mäftəhe* n. solution; remedy

መፍቻ *mäfča* n. spanner; key

የጠመንጃ— *yätämänğa*— n. screwdriver

ፈታታ *fätotta* v.t. dismounted, dismantled

ዕድሜ ይፍታህ *ədme yəftah* n. life imprisonment

ተፈታ *täfätta* v.i. was released; was untied, was divorced; was solved

ጦር— *tor*— v.t. was routed *(for an army)*

ተፋታ *täfatta* v.i. divorced one another

ተፍታታ *täftatta* v.i. was disentangled *(a thread)*

አፍታታ *in* ሰውነቱን አፍታታ *säwənnätun aftatta* v.t. limbered up

እግሩን— *əgrun—* v.t. stretched one's legs

አፈታ *in* ደም አፈታበት *däm afättabbät* bled heavily

አፋታ *affatta* v.t. divorced *(of s/o pronouncing a divorce)*

አስፈታ *asfätta* v.t. had s/o released *(from prison, detention)*; had s/t untied, freed

ፈቻል *fäčäl* n. pincers

ፈነቀለ *fänäqqälä* v.t. pulled out, ripped out *(pulled out)*

መፈንቅል *in* መፈንቅለ መንግሥት *mäfänqəlä mängəst* n. coup d'etat

ተፈነቀለ *täfänäqqälä* v.i. was pulled out

ተፈናቀለ *in* ከሥራው ተፈናቀለ *käsəraw täfänaqqälä* he lost his job

አፈናቀለ *in* ከሥራ አፈናቀለ *käsəra affänaqqälä* caused s/o to lose his job

• ፈነቸረ • *fänäččärä*

ተፈነቸረ *täfänäččärä* v.i. died instantly

ፈነከተ *fänäkkätä* v.t. broke open, threw open, broke into pieces

ፍንካች *fənəkkač* n. moiety

ፍንክት *fənkət* adj. broken open; full of scars *(on the head)*

ፍንክች አለ *fənkəčč alä* v.i. flinched

ወይ ፍንክች *wäy fənkəčč* I will never flinch

ተፈነከተ *täfänäkkätä* v.i. was broken open

ተፈናከተ *täfänakkätä* v.t. hit each other's heads

ፈነደቀ *fänäddäqä* v.i. was jubilant, cheerful, vivacious

ፍንደቃ *fəndäqa* n. exaltation, ecstasy, spiritual uplift

ፍንድቅ አለ *fənddəqq alä* v.i. was jubilant, cheered up

• ፈነደደ *fänäddädä*

ፈንዳዳ *fändadda* adj. big-bottomed

አፈነደደ *afänäddädä* v.t. stooped *(immoral)*; lowered oneself morally

ፈነዳ *fänädda* v.i. exploded, blew up, burst; blew up *(of fire)*; erupted *(of volcano)*; was open *(of flower)*, bloomed

ፈንጂ *fänǧi* n. explosive dynamite, *also* ዲናሚት

ፍንዳታ *fəndata* n. out-break, irruption

ፈንዳ ፈንዳ አለ *fända fända alä* v.i. cheered up

አፈነዳ *afänädda* v.t. exploded, blew up, burst

ፈነገለ *fänäggälä* v.t. overthrew, overturned

ፈንጋላ *fängalla* adj. unsteady

ፈንጋይ *in* ባሪያ ፈንጋይ *barəya fängay* n. slave trader

ፍንገላ *in* ባሪያ ፍንገላ *bärəya fəngäla* n. slave trading

ተፈነገለ *täfänäggälä* v.i. was overthrown, overturned

• ፈነገጠ *see* አፈነገጠ

ፈነጠረ *fänäṭṭärä* v.t. flicked

ፈንጠር አለ *fänṭṭär alä* v.i. was secluded, kept oneself aloof, withdrew oneself

ፈንጣራ *in* ፈንጣራ ቦታ *fänṭarra bota* n. remote place

ፍንጣሪ *fənəṭṭari* n. spark *(given off by flint)*

ፍንጥር *fənṭər* n. drink after doing some business

ወስፈንጥር *wäsfänṭər* n. bow

ተፈናጠረ *täfänaṭṭärä* v.i. flipped

back

ተስፈንጠረ *täsfänäṭṭärä* v.i. was ejected, was projected *(shell)*

ተስፈንጣሪ *täsfänṭari* adj. extremist *(politics)*

አፈናጠረ *affänaṭṭärä* v.t. projected *(shell)*

አስፈንጠረ *asfänäṭṭärä* v.t. flipped; projected *(shell)*

ፈንጠቀ *fänäṭṭäqä* v.t. projected *(beam of light)*; splashed water

ፍንጣቂ *fənəṭṭaqi* n. spark; splotch *(of ink, sauce etc.)*

ተፈናጠቀ *täfänaṭṭäqä* v.i. was splashed; was plattered

አፈናጠቀ *affänaṭṭäqä* v.t. splashed

ፈንጠዘ *fänäṭṭäzä* v.i. was merry, was excited and happy, exalted

በደስታ— *bädässəta*— was full of joy

ፈንጠዝያ *fänṭäzəyya* n. merry-making, jubilance, exaltation

—በፈንጠዝያ ሆነ —*bäfänṭäzəyya honä* was in great joy and merriment

አስፈንጠዘ *asfänäṭṭäzä* v.t. treated s/o lavishly

•ፈንጠጠ •*fänäṭṭäṭä*

ተፈናጠጠ *täfänaṭṭäṭä* v.i. rode pillion

ተፈናጣጭ *täfänaṭač* n. pillion rider

አፈናጠጠ *affänaṭṭäṭä* v.t. had s/o ride pillion

ፈነጨ *fänäččä* v.i. gambolled; pranced *(of a horse)*; frolicked, capered

•ፈነፈነ •*fänäffänä*

ተፈናፈነ *täfänaffänä* v.i. got close to one another, huddled

መፈናፈኛ ቦታ *mäffänafäña bota* place to stand on

•ፈነፈነ •*fänäffänä*

አፈነፈነ *afänäffänä* v.t. smelt, sniffed *(of an animal)*

ፈንታ *also* ፋንታ *fänta, fanta* n. share, portion, turn

በ...— *bä*...—instaad of, in place of

በፈንታው *bäfäntaw* in his turn

ፈንዜ *fänze* n. curved sword

ፈንጣጣ *fänṭaṭa* n. small-pox

•ፈክፈከ •*fäkäffäkä*

አፈክፈከ *afäkäffäkä* v.t. erupted *(skin)*

ፈካ *fäkka* v.i. blossomed *(flower)*; brightened *(face, colour)*; brightened, was alight *(face)*, smiled; burst open *(popcorn)*

ፍካት *fəkat* n. brightness *(colour, face)*

ፍክ *fək* adj. bright *(colour)*

አፈካ *afäkka* v.t. animated; blossomed

ፈወሰ *fäwwäsä* v.t. healed, cured

ፈዋሽ *fäwwaš* n. healer

ፈውስ *fäws* n. healing

ፈውስ ቢስ *fäwsä bis* adj. incurable

ፈውስ የለሽ *fäws yällaš* adj. incurable

ተፈወሰ *täfäwwäsä* v.i. was healed, cured

አስፈወሰ *asfäwwäsä* v.t. had s/o healed, cured

ፈዘዘ *fäzzäzä* v.i. became dull *(eye)*; stared; was glassy *(eyes)*; was dazed *(by a blow)*; was numb *(limbs)*; was in a stupor

ፈዛዛ *fäzazza* adj. slow; feeble *(eye)*

ዋዛ— *waza*—aimless pursuit, lacking seriousness, trivial

ተፋዘዘ *täfazzäzä* v.i. gazed at each other

አፈዘዘ *afäzzäzä* v.t. dazed *(by a blow)*; made listless; bewitched *(charmed)*

አፋዘዘ *affazzäzä* v.t. caused

(people) to be stupified

ፈየደ *fäyyädä* v.i. became useful

ፋይዳ *fayda* n. usefulness, value, importance

--ቢስ *—bis* adj. useless, worthless

—የለሽ *—yälläš* adj. uselsss, valueless

ፈጀ *fäǧǧä* v.t. consumed, ate up; exterminated; took *(time);* burnt *(of hot liquid)*

ነገረ ፈጅ *nägärä fäǧǧ* n. representative *(in legal affairs)*

ፍጆታ *fəǧota* n. consumption; floor *(in a debate)*

—ይሰጠኝ *—yəssäṭäññ* May, I take the floor?

ፍጅት *fəǧǧət* n. massacre; uproar, disturbance, tumult

ተፈጀ *täfäǧǧä* v.t. was consumed, was eaten up

ተፋጀ *täfaǧǧä* v.i. destroyed one another; was hot *(pepper);* burnt *(hot liquid)*

አፋጀ *affaǧǧä* v.t. caused to destroy one another

አስፈጀ *asfäǧǧä* v.t. had s/o destroyed

ፈገመ *fäggämä* v.i. tumbled down

ፍግም አለ *fəggəmm alä* v.i. tumbled down; died suddenly

አፈገመ *afäggämä* v.t. let s/o tumble down

ፈገገ *fäggägä* v.i. smiled

ፈገግታ *fägägta* n. smile

—ቢስ *—bis* adj. cheerless

•ፈገጠ *•fäggäṭä*

ፈገጠው *fäggəṭäw* to Hell with it

ፈገፈገ *fägäffägä* v.t. rubbed; scraped

ፍገፋጊ *fəgəffagi* n. scrapings

ተፈገፈገ *täfägäffägä* v.i. was rubbed, scraped

•ፈገፈገ *•fəgäffägä*

ተፈጋፈገ *täfägaffägä* v.i. pressed against

አፈገፈገ *afägäffägä* v.t. drew back; retreated; gave ground; withdrew

ፈጠመ *see also* ፈጸመ

ፍጥምጥም *fəṭəmṭəm* n. engagement *(agreement to marry)*

ተፈጠመ *täfäṭṭämä* v.i. gave a promise in front of a judge

ተፈጣጠመ *täfäṭaṭṭämä* v.i. became engaged *(to get married)*

ፈጠረ *fäṭṭärä* v.t. created, devised *(a scheme);* invented

ፈጠራ *fäṭära* n. invention

የፈጠራ ወሬ *yäfäṭära wäre* fabrication *(false story of events)*

—ጽሑፍ *—ṣəhuf* creative writing

ፈጣሪ *fäṭari* n. creator

ፍጡር *fəṭur* n. creature, being *(creature)*

ፍጥረት *fəṭrät* n. creature

ሥነ— *sənä—* n. nature

ተፈጠረ *täfäṭṭärä* u.i. was created

ተፈጥሮ *täfäṭro* n. nature, natural state

የተፈጥሮ ሀብት *yätäfäṭro habt* n. natural resources

ፈጠነ *fäṭṭänä* v.i. was quick, hurried, went fast, was fast, speeded up

ፈጣን *fäṭṭan* adj. quick, swift, rapid

ፍጡን *in* ፍጡነ ረድኤት *fəṭunä rädə'et* patron saint

ፍጥነት *fəṭnänt* n. speed, velocity, rapidity

—ጨመረ *—čämmärä* v.t. accelerated

በፍጥነት *bäfəṭnät* adv. immediately, rapidly,fast

ተፋጠነ *täfaṭṭänä* v.i. hurried

አፋጠነ *affaṭṭänä* v.t. speeded, quickened, hastened

አፋጣኝ *affaṭañ* adj. urgent

ፈጠጠ *fäṭṭäṭä* v.i. popped *(of eyes)*
ፈጣጣ *fäṭaṭa* adj. pop-eyed
ፍጥጥ ብሎ አየ *fəṭəṭṭ bəlo ayyä* v.i. stared at, gazed at
ተፋጠጠ *täfaṭṭäṭä* v.i. were stupified; struck each other speechless; confronted each other
አፋጠጠ *affaṭṭäṭä* v.t. caught *(s/o)* out *(e.g. with difficult question)*; put *(s/o)* on the spot
ፈጠፈጠ *fäṭäffäṭä* v.t. squashed *(press out of shape)*
ፈጥርቅ መጠጥ *fäṭrəq mäṭäṭṭ* n. very strong drink
ፈጨ *fäččä* v.t. ground *(grain)*, milled flour, crushed *(rock)*
ፈጫይ *fäčay* n. grinder *(woman who earns her living by grinding grain for other people)*
ወፍጮ *wäfčo* n. mill, grinding slab
—ቤት *—bet* n. mill
ተፋጨ *täfaččä* v.i. was sharpened *(a knife against another knife)*
አፋጨ *affaččä* v.t. sharpened *(a knife against another knife)*; gnashed *(of the teeth)*
*ፈጨረጨረ **fäčäräččärä*
ተፍጨረጨረ *täfčäräčärä* v.i. floundered, made frantic efforts
ተፍጨርጫሪ *täfčärčari* a man of great enterprise
ፈጸመ *fäṣṣämä, see also* ፈጠመ *fäṭṭämä*, v.t. ended, fulfilled, finished, carried out, completed, accomplished
ፈጽሞ *fäṣṣəmo* adv. entirely, completely, utterly
—አልመጣም *—almäṭṭamm* he has never come
ፍጹም *fəṣṣum* adj. complete, absolute, perfect
በፍጹም *bäfəṣṣum* adv. absolutely, entirely
—አልመጣም *—almäṭṭamm* he has never come
ፍጹምነት *fəṣṣumənnät* n. perfection
ፍጻሜ *fəṣṣame* n. ending, end, completion, fulfilment
ተፈጸመ *täfäṣṣämä* v.i. came to an end, was completed; came true
አስፈጸመ *asfäṣṣämä* v.t. executed, carried out, got s/t finished
አስፈጻሚ *asfäṣami* n. executor
ጉዳይ— *gudday—* n. solicitor, barrister
አፈጻጸም *—affäṣaṣäm* n. procedure
ፈፋ *fäfa* n. rivulet, brook
ፉሎ *fulo* n. headstall
ፉርኖ *furno* n. bread *(European style)*
—ቤት *—bet* n. bakery
—ዱቄት *—duqet* n. white flour
ፉርጎ *furgo* n. car *(train)*
ፉትቦል *futbol* n. football *also* እግር ኳስ
ፉት አለ *futt alä* v.i. sipped
ፉንጋ *funga* adj. ugly
ፉካ *fuka* n. opening in a wall
ፉክክር *see* ፎከረ
ፉጨት *fučät* n. whistling *(with the mouth etc.)*
አፏጨ *afuʷaččä* v.t. whistled *(with the mouth)*
ፉጋ *fuga* n. cabinet-maker *(a derogatory word)*
ፊላ *fila* n. kind of grass, used as roof covering
ፊር ፊር አለ *firr firr alä* v.i. writhed helplessly
ፊሽካ *fiška* n. whistle
—ነፋ *—näffa* v.t. whistled
ፊት *fit* n. face, front; adv. at first, before
በ— *bä—* adv. before, early
ከ— *kä—* adv. infront of
እ— *ə—* adv. in front of
ከሁሉ በፊት *kähullu bäfit* first of all

ከፊት ለፊት *käfit läfit* in front of, opposite, face to face
ከሰዓት በፊት *käsä'at bäfit* n. forenoon
ከዚህ— *käzzih—* adv. previously, before
ወደ— *wädä—* in the future, later on
የፊት እግር *yäfit əgər* n. foreleg
—ጥርስ *—ṭərs* n. incisor
ፊተኛው *fitäññäw* the earlier one
ፊት ልሙጥ *fitä ləmuṭṭ* adj. plain *(ordinary, without ornament)*
—መጣጣ *—mäṭaṭa* adj. lean-faced
—ስልካካ *—sälkakka* adj. handsome *(good-looking*
—ከባድ *—käbbad* adj. with an unpleasant face
ፊቱ ተኮማተረ *fitu täkomattärä* v.i. frowned
—ደም መሰለ *—däm mässälä* v.i. blushed
—ደነገጠ *—dänäggäṭä* v.i. was disconcerted
—ገረጣ *—gäräṭṭa* v.i. became pale
—ጭር አለ *—čərr alä* v.i. was melancholy
ፊቱን ቋጠረ *fitun quʷaṭṭärä* v.t. frowned
—አዞረ *—azorä* v.t. ignored
—ኮሶ አስመሰለ *—koso asmässälä* v.t made a terrible face
—ኮሰተረ *—kosättärä* v.t. showed seriousness, frowned
ፊት ለፊት *fit läfit* adv. face to face, in front of, opposite to
ፊትና ኋላ *fitənna huʷala* one following the other
ፊት ነሣ *fit nässa* v.t. refused, treated s/o in an unfriendly way
ፊታውራሪ *fitawrari* old Ethoipian title
ኮሶ ፊት *koso fit* adj. making grimaces
ወደፊት *wädä fit* interj. forward! in the future

ጨጓራ ፊት *čäggʷarra fit* adj. pimply
የፊታችን *yäfitaččən* the coming *(e.g. Tuesday)*
ፊና *in* በየፊናው *bäyyäfinaw* in their various ways, each in his own way
ፊናንስ *finans* n. finance
የፊናንስ ዘበኛ *yäfinance zäbäñña* n. customs official
ፊን አለ *finn alä* v.i. spouted
ፊንጢጣ *finṭiṭṭa* n. anus
ፊኛ *fiñña* n. bladder; balloon
ፊውዳል *fiwdäl* adj. feudal
ፊደል *fidäl* n. alphabet, letter *(syllabary)*, character *(letter)*
—ለየ *—läyyä* v.t. mastered the alphabet
—ቆጠረ *—qoṭṭärä* v.t. mastered the alphabet
—አስቆጠረ *—asqäṭṭärä* v.t. taught the alphabet
ፊጥ አለ *fiṭṭ alä* v.t. mounted a horse, mule etc. quickly
ፊጥኝ *in* የፊጥኝ አሰረ *yäfiṭṭəñña assärä* v.t. tied the hands behind the back
ፋመ *famä* v.i. got red hot; became glowing, became live *(coals, fire)*
ፍም *fəm* n. ember, hot coals
ፊቱ— መሰለ *fitu—mässälä* v.i. blushed
ተፋፋመ *täfafamä* v.i. glowed, burnt up, flamed up; reached a climax; was in full swing; raged *(battle)*
አፋፋመ *affafamä* v.t: made *(s/t)* flare up; made *(s/t)* reach a climax
ፋረ *farä* v.t. hollowed out
ፋርማሲ *farmasi* n. pharmacy
ፋርስ *fars* n. Persia
ፋሮ *faro* n. white-tailed mongoose
ፋሲካ *also* ፋሲጋ *see* ፈሰከ
ፋስ *fas* n. axe
ፋሽኮ *fašco* n. flask

ፋቀ *faqä* v.t. scraped; tanned *(hide; rubbed (teeth);)* scaled *(a fish); wrote* off *(debt)*
ፋቂ *faqi* n. tanner
ፍቅፋቂ *fəqəffaqi* n. scrap
መፋቂያ *in* ጥርስ መፋቂያ *tərs mäfaqiya* n. stick of a particular tree used to brush the teeth
ፋብሪካ *fabrika* n. factory, plant
ባለ— *balä* — n. manufacturer
ፋታ *fata* n. moment of rest, lull
—ሰጠ *—sättä* v.t. gave time
—ነሣ *—nässa* v.t. kept busy
—የለውም *—yälläwəmm* v.i he is tied down *(by work)*
ፋነነ *fannänä* v.i. was led astray *(child etc.)*
ፋኖ *fanno* n. volunteer *(fighter arch.)*
ፋና *fana* n. torch
ፋንታ *fanta* n. portion, share; turn
በኔ— *bäne* — in place of me
ፋንድያ *fändəyya* n. excrement *(of horse, mule, donkey)*
ፋኖ *see* ፋነነ
ፋኖስ *fanos* n. lamp, lantern, oil lamp
ፋከልቲ *fakälti* n. faculty
ፋክቱር *faktur* n. receipt, bill, invoice
ፋይል *fail* n. file *(record)*
ፈየለ *fäyyälä* v.t. filed
ፋይዳ *fäyda* n. use, value, importance
—ቢስ *—bis* adj. useles
—የለሽ *—yälläš* adj. useless, unimportant
ፋደት *fadät* n. weasel
ፋገ *see* አፋገ
ፋጉሎ *fagullo* n. oil-cake, expeller
ፋፋ *faffa* v.i. thrived *(of children)*, grew fat
ፌቆ *feqo* n. oribi *(ourebia ourebi)*
ፌንጣ *fenṭa* n. grasshopper, cricket
ፌዝ *fez* n. joke, mockery, jest
ፌዘኛ *fezzäñña* adj./n.*(one)* who jokes, mocker
አፌዘ *afezä* v.i. joked, mocked, derided, made fun of
አፍያዥ *afyaž* adj./n. *(one)* who jokes, mocker
ፍላጻ *fəlaṣṣa* n. arrow
ፍሥሐ *fəssəha* n. joy, happiness
ፍሩስኪ *fruska* n. bran
ፍሪዳ *fərida* n. fattened bullock
ፍራሽ *fəraš* n. mattress
ፍሬት *see* ፈሬ
ፍሬ *fəre* n. fruit, berry, seed
—ሰጠ *—sättä* v.t. gave good results, bore fruit *(work)*
—ቢስ *—bis* adj. useless, pointless, fruitless; futile
—ነገር *—nägär* n. central idea, gist, summary, essence
የሥራ— *yäsəra—* n. output
የብልት— *yäbəllət—* n. testicle
ፍራፍሬ *fərafəre* n. fruits
ፍሬያማ *fəreyamma* adj. fruitful
ፍርምባ *fərəmbba* n. chest *(of animal)*
ፍትሐት *fəthat* n. absolution
ጸሎተ— *ṣälotä—* n. funeral ceremony
ፍትሕ *fəth* n. justice, judgement
ፍትሐ ብሔር ሕግ *fətha bəher həgg* n. civil code
ፍትወት *fətwät* n. lust *(sexual)*
ፍትወተ ሥጋ *fətwätä səga* n. the lusts of the flesh
ፍትወተኛ *fətwätäñña* adj. lustful
ፍናፍንት *fənafənt* n. hermaphrodite *also* ወንዳገረድ
ፍንከት *see* ፈነከተ
ፍንጃል *fənǧal* n. porcelain cup

ፍንጅ — ከ እጅ ከፈንጅ *kăfənğğ* adj. red-handed

ፍንጥር — *see* ፈነጠረ

ፍንጭ — *fənč* n. hint, clue, key *(to a mystery)*

ፍየል — *fəyyäl* n. goat

—መላስ — *—mälas* adj. talkative

የሜዳ— — *yämeda—* n. gazelle

ፍዳ — *fədda* n. hardship, misery, tribulation

ፍዳውን አየ — *fəddawən ayyä* he suffered greatly

ፍጆታ — *see* ፈጀ

ፍግ — *fəg* n. manure, dung

ፍጥረት — *see* ፈጠረ

ፎሌ — *folle* n. drinking vessel made of a dried gourd

ፎለፎል — *foläfol* adj. cheerful *(person)*, jovial vivacious

ፎልፏላ — *folfuʷalla* adj. cheerful *(person)*, jovial, vivacious

ፎረሸ — *forräšä* v.i. failed, was unsuccessful *(col.)*

ፉርሽ — *furš* n. failure *(col.)*

ፎረፎር — *foräfor* n. dandruff, scurf

*ፎቀቀ — **foqqäqä*

ፎቃቃ — *foqaqa* n. tattle-tale, informer

ፎቀቅ አለ — *foqqäq alä* v.i. stood aside, got out of the way; *also* ፈቀቅ አለ

ተንፏቀቀ — *tänfuʷaqqäqä* v.i. dragged oneself along the ground

አንፏቀቀ — *anfuʷaqqäqä* v.t. pushed a little

አንፏቃቂ — *anfuʷaqaqi* n. tattle-tale, informer

ፎቅ — *foq* n. storey

—ቤት — *—bet* n. a building with saveral storeys *(floors)*

ባለስድስት ፎቅ ቤት — *bäläsəddəst foq bet* a six-storeyed building

ፎነነ — *fonnänä* v.t. cut off someone's nose

ፎናና — *fonana* n. one with the nose cut; short-nosed

ፎከረ — *fokkärä* v.t. uttered war boasts, bragged, boasted

ፉከራ — *fukkära* n. bragging boasting

ፉክክር — *fukəkkər* n. competition, rivalry

መፈክር — *mäfäkkər* n. slogan

ተፎካከረ — *täfokakkärä* v.i. competed with each other

ተፎካካሪ — *täfokakari* n. competitor, rival

አፎካከረ — *affokakkärä* v.t. caused *(s/o)* to compete

ፎከተ — *fokkätä* v.t. scratched *(the body)*

ፎክት — *fokät* n. itch

ፎጣ — *foṭa* n. towel

ፏፏቴ — *fuʷafuʷate* n. waterfall, cataract, falls

*ፏጨ — **fuʷaččä*

ፉጨት — *fuččäṭ* n. whistling *(with the mouth)*

አፏጨ — *afuʷaččä* v.t. whistled *(with the mouth)*

ፐ

ፒራሚድ — *piramid* n. pyramid

ፒያኖ — *piyano* n. piano

ፒጃማ — *piǧama* n. pyjamas

ፓርላማ — *parlama* n. parliament

ፓርቲ — *parti* n. party

ፓትርያርክ — *patrəyark* n. patriarch

ፓኮ — *pakko* n. packet, box *(matches)*

ፓይለት — *pailät* n. pilot *(air plane)*

ፓፓዬ — *pappaye* n. papaya

ፔርሙዝ — *permuz* n. thermos flask

ፕላስተር — *plastär* n. adhesive tape

ፕላስቲክ *plastik* n. plastic

ፕላኔት *planet* n. planet

ፕላን *plan* n. plan

ፕሬስ *pres* n. press

ፕሬዚዴንት *prezident* n. president

ፕሮባ *proba* n. fitting *(by a tailor)*

ፕሮብሌም *problem* n. problem

ፕሮቶኮል *protokol* n. protocol

ፕሮጄ *prože* n. project

ፕሮግራም *program* n. programme

ፕሮፌሰር *profesär* n. professor

ፕሮፓጋንዳ *propagandda* n. propaganda

ፖሊቲካ *politika* n. politics

ፖሊቲከኛ *politikäñña* n. politician; liar

የፖሊቲካ ሰው *yäpolitika säw* n. statesman

—ቡድን *—budən* n. party *(political)*

ፖሊሲ *polisi* n. policy

ፖሊስ *polis* n. policeman, police

የፖሊስ ሠራዊት *yäpolis särawit* n. police force

ፖሊስ ጣቢያ *polis ṭabiya* n. police station

ፖምፓ *pompa* n. pump

ፖስታ *posta* n. letter, mail, envelope

ፖስተኛ *postäñña* n. postman, mailman

ፖስታ ሳጥን *posta saṭən* n. post-office box, mail box

—ቤት *—bet* n. post- office

English - Amharic Dictionary

Part II

ENGLISH - AMHARIC

a
'ኤይ.'ኧ -ያተሙ- አንድ

abandon
ኧ'ባንደን -ግ- እርግ'ፍ አርጎ መተው [ተወ] ፣ መክዳት [ከ'ዳ]

abandoned
ኧ'ባንደንድ -ቅ- የተተወ

immoral
-ቅ- ል'ቅ ፣ ስ'ድ (ለጠባይ)

abasement
ኧ'ቤይስመንት -ስ- ውርደት

abate
ኧ'ቤይት -ግ- ጸ'ጥ ማለት [አለ] (ለማዕበል ወዘተ) ፣ ማነስ [አ'ነሰ] ፣ መድከም [ደ'ከመ]

abbey
'አቢ -ስ- ገዳም ፣ ደብር

abbreviate
ኧብ'ሪቪዬይት -ግ- ማሳ'ጠር [አሳ'ጠረ] (ለቃላት)

abbreviation
ኧብሪቪ'ዬይሽን -ስ- ማሳ'ጠር (ለቃላት)

abdicate
'አብዲኬይት -ግ- ሹመት በፈቃድ መተው [ተወ]

abdomen
'አብደመን -ስ- ሆድ

abduct
ኧብ'ደክት -ግ- መጥለፍ [ጠ'ለፈ] ፣ መፈን ገል [ፈነ'ገለ] (ለሰው)

abet
ኧ'ቤት -ግ- ጥፋት እንዲሠሩ ማ'ደፋፈር [አ'ደፋ'ፈረ] ፣ መገፋፋት [ገፋ'ፋ]

abetter
ኧ'ቤተ -ስ- ለመጥፎ ሥራ የ'ሚገፋ'ፋ ፣ የ'ሚያ'ደፋ'ፍር

abeyance
ኧ'ቤየንስ -ስ- እሥራ ላይ እንዳይውል የተ ደ'ረገ ሕ'ግ

abhor
ኧብ'ሆር -ግ- መጥላት [ጠ'ላ] (ፈ'ጽሞ) ፣ መ' ጸየፍ [ተጸ'የፈ]

abide
ኧ'ባይድ -ግ- መኖር [ኖረ] ፣ ባንድ ሥፍራ መ'ቀመጥ [ተቀ'መጠ] ፣ መ'ታገሥ [ታ'ገሠ]

abiding
ኧ'ባይዲንግ -ቅ- ለረ'ጅም ጊዜ የ'ሚቆ'ይ

ability
ኧ'ቢሊቲ -ስ- ችሎታ

abject
'አብጀክት -ቅ- የተዋ'ረደ ፣ ወ'ራ'ዳ

ablaze
ኧብ'ላይዝ -ቅ- የ'ሚ'ቃ'ጠል ፣ የ'ሚንበለ'በል (ቤት ወዘተ)

able
'ኤይበል -ቅ- ችሎታ ያ'ለው ፣ የሠለ'ጠነ ፣ የ'ሚችል

abnormal
አብ'ኖ:መል -ቅ- ያልተለ'መደ ፣ እንግዳ (ለነ ገር)

aboard
ኧ'ቦ:ድ -ቅ- በመርከብ ፣ በባቡር ፣ በአውሮ' ፕላን ላይ (ተሣፍሮ)

abode
ኧ'በውድ -ስ- መኖሪያ ቦታ

abolish
ኧ'ቦሊሽ -ግ- መደምሰስ [ደመ'ሰሰ] ፣ መሠ' ረዝ [ሠ'ረዘ]

abolition
አበ'ሊሽን -ስ- መደምሰስ

abominable
ኧ'ቦሚነበል -ቅ- አ'ሥ'ቃቂ ፣ የ'ሚያስጠ'ላ ፣ አ'ጸ'ያፊ

abomination
ኧቦሚ'ኔይሽን -ስ- አ'ሥ'ቃቂ ነገር

aboriginal
አበ'ሪጂነል -ቅ- ጥንታዊ ነዋሪ (ያንድ አገር የመሠረት ሕዝብ)

aborigine
አበ'ሪጂኒ -ስ- ያንድ አገር ጥንታዊ ነዋሪ ሰው

abortion
ኧ'ቦ:ሽን -ስ- ልጅ ማስወ'ረድ

abound
ኧ'ባውንድ -ግ- መትረፍረፍ [ተትረፈ'ረፈ]
about
ኧ'ባውት -ተግ- ገደማ ፣ ያህል ፤ ወዲያ'ና ወዲህ (መሄድ)
above
ኧ'በቭ -ተግ- ላይ ፣ በላይ
abrasion
ኧብ'ሬይዥን -ስ- መፋቅ
abreast
ኧብ'ሬስት -ተግ- ጐ'ን ለጐ'ን
abridge
ኧብ'ሪጅ -ግ- ማሳ'ጠር [አሳ'ጠረ] (መጽሐፍ)
abridgement
ኧብ'ሪጅመንት -ስ- ማሳ'ጠር ፤ ያ'ጠረ ጽሑፍ
abroad
ኧብ'ሮ:ድ -ተግ- በው'ጭ አገር ፣ ባሕር ማዶ
abrupt
ኧብ'ረፕት -ቅ- ቁ'ር'ጥ ቁ'ር'ጥ ያለ (ለንግ'ግር) ፤ ድንገተ'ኛ (ለነገር) ፣ ያልታ'ሰበ
abruptness
ኧብ'ረፕትነስ -ስ- ቁ'ር'ጥ ቁ'ር'ጥ ማለት (ለንግ'ግር) ፤ ድንገተ'ኛ'ነት (ለነገር)
abscess
'አብሴስ -ስ- እ'ባጭ ፣ እበጥ (መግል የጸ'ጠረ)
abscond
ኧብስ'ኮንድ -ግ- መሸሽ [ሸ'ሸ] ፣ መ'ደበቅ [ተደ'በቀ] (ጥፋት አጥፍቶ ቅጣት እን'ዳይደርስ'በት)
absence
'አብሰንስ -ስ- አለመ'ገኘት ፣ መቅረት
absent
'አብሰንት -ቅ- ያልተገ'ኘ (እሥራ ላይ) ፣ ቀሪ፣ የሌ'ለ
vague
-ቅ- ሐ'ሳብ ብኩ'ን
absentee
አብሰን'ቲ: -ስ- እሥራ ያልተገ'ኘ
absolute
'አብሰሉ:ት -ቅ- ፍ'ጹም ፣ የተሟ'ላ (ለጠባይ ወዘተ)
absolution
አብሰ'ሉ:ሽን -ስ- መንጻት (ከኀጢአት) ፣ ሥርየት
absolve
ኧብ'ዞልቭ -ግ- ማንጻት [አነ'ጻ] ፣ ነጻ ማው ጣት [አወ'ጣ] (ከወንጀል ተግባር)
absorb
ኧብ'ሶ:ብ -ግ- መምጠጥ [መ'ጠጠ] (እንደ ስፋ ነግ)
absorbent
ኧብ'ሶ:በንት -ቅ- መጣጭ ሳቢ (ፈሳ ወዘተ)
absorbing
ኧብ'ሶ:ቢንግ -ቅ- መጣጭ ፤ አስተያየት ማራ
abstain
ኧብስ'ቴይን -ግ- ራስን መከልከል [ከለ'ከለ] አንድ ነገር ከማድረግ ራስን ማገ'ድ [አ'ገደ]
abstemious
ኧብስ'ቲምየስ -ቅ- ራሱን ከብዙ መብል'ና መጠ'ጥ የ'ሚገታ
abstinence
'አብስቲነንስ -ስ- በመጠኑ መኖር
abstract
'አብስትራክት -ቅ- የ'ማይ'ጨ'በጥ ፣ የ'ማያ 'ዳ'ሰስ ፣ ረቂቅ
summary
-ስ- አሕጽሮተ ጽሑፍ
abstract
ኧብስት'ራክት -ግ- ማውጣት [አወ'ጣ] ፤ ካን ድ ነገር ወይን'ም ከሐ'ሳብ መውሰድ [ወ'ሰደ]
abstruse
ኧብስት'ሩ:ስ -ቅ- አዳጋች ፤ በቀ'ላሉ የማ'ይ ገባ ፤ ጥልቅ ፣ የተሸ'ሸገ
absurd
ኧብ'ሰ:ድ -ቅ- የ'ማይመስል ፣ የተጃጃለ
abundance
ኧ'በንደንስ -ስ- ብዛት ፣ የተትረፈ'ረፈ
abundant
ኧ'በንደንት -ቅ- ብዙ
abuse
ኧብ'ዩ:ዝ -ግ- ለመጥፎ ነገር ማዋል [አዋለ] (ሥልጣንን ፣ መብትን ወዘተ)
curse
-ግ- መ'ሳደብ [ተሳ'ደበ]
abusive
ኧብ'ዩ:ሲቭ -ቅ- ተሳዳቢ ፣ ጸረፊ ፣ አ'ዋራጅ (በመ'ሳደብ)

abysmal
ኧ'ቢዝመል -ቅ- በጣም መጥፎ (ለነገር፣ለሁናቴ)
abyss
ኧ'ቢስ -ስ- ከል'ክ ያ'ለፈ ጥልቀት ፣ አንጦር ጦስ ፣ ጅ'ው ያለ ገደል
academic
አክ'ዴሚክ -ቅ- የቀለም (ትምህርት ወዘተ) ፣ የምሁራን (ማኅበር)
not practical
-ቅ- በሥራ ላይ ያልዋለ (ዕውቀት)
academy
ኧ'ካደሚ -ስ- ከ'ፍተ'ኛ ትምህርት ቤት የሙዚቃ ከ'ፍተ'ኛ ትምህርት ቤት
accede
ኦክ'ሲይድ -ግ- መስማማት [ተስማ'ማ] ፣ ከ'ፍተ'ኛ ሥራ መያዝ [ያዘ]
accelerate
ኧክ'ሴለሬይት -ግ- ፍጥነት መጨ'መር [ጨ'መረ]
acceleration
ኧክሴለ'ሬይሽን -ስ- ፍጥነት መጨ'መር ፣በጣም መፍጠን
accent
'አክሴንት -ስ- ያ'ነጋገር ፣መንገድ (ጐንደር'ኛ፣ ሸዋ'ኛ ፣ ጐ'ጃም'ኛ ወዘተ)
stress
-ስ- በቃላት ላይ የ'ሚ'ደ'ረግ ይዘት
accept
ኧክ'ሴፕት -ግ- መ'ቀበል [ተቀ'በለ]
acceptable
ኧክ'ሴፕትበል -ቅ- የ'ሚ'ቀ'በሉት ፣ ተስማሚ
access
'አክሴስ -ስ- ሊያደርስ የ'ሚያስችል መንገድ፣ ዘዴ
accessory
ኧክ'ሴሰሪ -ስ- የጥፋት ረ'ዳት
car
-ስ- የተሽከርካሪዎ'ች መለ'ዋወጫ
jewellery
-ስ- የሴቶ'ች ጌጣ ጌጥ
accident
'አክሲደንት -ስ- ድንገት
unpleasant
-ስ- አደጋ
accidental
አክሲ'ደንተል -ቅ- ድንገተ'ኛ
accidentally
አክሲ'ደንትሊ -ተግ- በድንገት
acclaim
ኧክ'ሌይም -ግ- በእልልታ መ'ቀበል [ተቀ'በለ]
acclamation
አክለ'ሜይሽን -ስ- የደ'ስታ አ'ቀባበል
accommodate
ኧ'ኮመዴይት -ግ- ማረፊያ ማ'ዘጋጀት [አ'ዘጋ'ጀ] ፣ መርዳት [ረ'ዳ]
accommodation
ኧኮመ'ዴይሽን -ስ- ማረፊያ (በሆቴል)
accompaniment
ኧ'ከምፐኒመንት -ስ- አብሮ መ'ጫወት (ሙዚቃ ፣ ዘፈን)
accompanist
ኧ'ከምፐኒስት -ስ- አብሮ ተጫዋች
accompany
ኧ'ከምፐኒ -ግ- ለዘፋኝ ሙዚቃ መምታት [መ'ታ]
go with
-ግ- አብሮ መሄድ [ሄደ]
accomplice
ኧ'ከምፕሊስ -ስ- የጥፋት ረ'ዳት ፣ ግብረ አ'በር
accomplish
ኧ'ከምፕሊሽ -ግ- ፍ'ጻሜ ማድረስ [አደ'ረሰ] ፣ መፈ'ጸም [ፈ'ጸመ]፣ማ'ከናወን [አ'ከና'ወነ]
accomplished
ኧ'ከምፕሊሽድ -ቅ- የተፈ'ጸመ ፣ የተከና'ወነ፣ ባለሞያ
accomplishment
ኧ'ከምፕሊሽመንት -ስ- ክን'ውን ፣ ሞያ ፣ ስጦታ ፣ ተውህቦ
accord
ኧ'ኮ፡ድ -ስ- ስምም'ነት
accordingly
ኧ'ኮ፡ዲንግሊ -ተግ- በ . . . መሠረት ፣ ስለ'ዚህ

accost

ኧ'ኮስት -ግ- ማ'ነጋገር [አ'ነጋ'ገረ] (የ'ማያ ውቁትን ሰው)

rudely

-ግ- በጉ'ሽማ መጥራት [ጠ'ራ]

account

ኧ'ካውንት -ስ- ሒሳብ

credit

-ስ- ዱቤ

story

-ስ- ታሪክ

accountable

ኧ'ካውንተበል -ቅ- ኀላፊ (ተወ'ቃሽ ሊሆን የ'ሚችል)

accountant

ኧ'ካውንተንት -ስ- የሒሳብ መዝገብ ያዥ

accumulate

ኧክ'ዩምዩሌይት -ግ- መሰብሰብ [ሰበ'ሰበ] ፣ ማ'ከማቸት [አ'ከማ'ቸ] ፣ እ'ጠራ'ቀመ [ማ'ጠራቀም]

accumulator

ኧክ'ዩምዩሌይተ -ስ- በኤሌክትሪክ የ'ሚ'ሞ'ላ ባትሪ

accuracy

'አክዩረሲ -ስ- ፍ'ጹም'ነት ፣ ል'ክ'ነት

accurate

'አክዩረት -ቅ- ል'ክ ፣ ፍ'ጹም

accursed

ኧ'ከ፡ስት -ቅ- የተረ'ገመ ፣ እርጉም ፤ የ'ማይሳ'ካ'ለት

accusation

አክዩ'ዜይሽን -ስ- ክ'ስ

accusative

ኧክ'ዩ፡ዘቲቭ -ቅ- ተሳቢ (ሰዋስው)

accuse

ኧክ'ዩ፡ዝ -ግ- መክሰስ [ከ'ሰሰ] ፣ መወንጀል [ወን'ጀለ]

accustom

ኧ'ከስተም -ግ- መልመድ [ለ'መደ] ፣ ራስን ማልመድ [አለ'መደ]

ace

'ኤይስ -ስ- በካርታ ጨዋታ አንደ'ኛው ቁጥር

very good

-ቅ- በጣም ጥሩ ፣ የሠለ'ጠነ (ለአው'ሮ'ፕላን ነጂ ፣ ለሽቅድ'ድም መኪና ነጂ)

ache

'ኤይክ -ስ- ውጋት ፣ ሕመም

head-

-ስ- ራስ ምታት

achieve

ኧ'ቺይቭ -ግ- ያ'ሰቡትን ማግኘት [አገ'ኘ] ፣ ወ'ዳ'ቀዱት ግብ መድረስ [ደ'ረሰ]

achievement

ኧ'ቺይቭመንት -ስ- የሥራ ክን'ውን ፣ አንድ ተግባር መፈ'ጸም

acid

'አሲድ -ስ- አሲድ ፣ አቺዶ

-ቅ- መጣጣ ፣ ኮምጣ'ጣ

acidity

አ'ሲዲቲ -ስ- ቃር ፤ የአቺዶ'ነት ጣዕም ፣ ጠባይ ያ'ለው

acknowledge

ኧክ'ኖለጅ -ግ- ዋጋ መስጠት [ሰ'ጠ] (ለሥራ ፣ ለአድራጐት) ፤ ራስ በመነቅነቅ ሰላምታ መስጠት [ሰ'ጠ] ፤ የተላከ ዕቃ መድረሱን ማ'ረጋገጥ [አ'ረጋ'ገጠ]

acknowledgement

ኧክ'ኖለጅመንት -ስ- ያንድ ሰው ድርሰት እንዲታ'ወቅ ማድረግ

greeting

-ስ- ሰላምታ

acoustics

ኧ'ኩስቲክስ -ስ- የድምፅ ጥናት ፤ ባን'ድ ሕንፃ ውስጥ የድምፅ ማስተጋባት ሁናቴ

acquaint

ኧክ'ዌይንት -ግ- ሰው ማስተዋወቅ [አስተዋ'ወቀ] ፣ ማ'ለማመድ [አ'ለማ'መደ] (ካንድ ሁናቴ ጋር)

acquaintance

ኧክ'ዌይንተንስ -ስ- የ'ሚያውቁት ሰው ፣ ዕውቂያ ፤ ዕውቀት

acquiesce

አክዊ'ዬስ -ግ- መስማማት [ተስማ'ማ] (ያለ መ'ጠራጠር)

acquiescence
ኧክዊ'ዬሰንስ -ስ- ስምም'ነት (በፈቃደ'ኛ'ነት)

acquire
ኧክ'ዋየ -ግ- ማግኘት [አገ'ኘ]

acquisition
አክዊ'ዚሽን -ስ- አ'ዲስ ንብረት

acquit
ኧክ'ዊት -ግ- ነጻ መልቀቅ [ለ'ቀቀ] (በፍርድ ቤት)

acquittal
ኧክ'ዊተል -ስ- ነጻ የመልቀቅ ሥርዓት

acre
'ኤይከ -ስ- ፬ሺ፶፯ ሜትር ካሬ (የመሬት ስፋት ል'ክ)

acrid
'አክሪድ -ቅ- የ'ሚሰነ'ፍጥ (ሽ'ታ)

acrimonious
አክሪ'መውኒየስ -ቅ- መራራ ፣ ኀይለ'ኛ (ክ ር'ክር)

across
ኧክ'ሮስ -ተግ- በማዶ ፣ በአ'ሻጋሪ

act
'አክት -ግ- ማድረግ [አደ'ረገ]
drama
-ስ- የቲያትር ክፍል ፣ ገቢር

acting
'አክቲንግ -ቅ- ተጠባባቂ ፣ እንደራሴ (ያንድ ሥራ)
theatre work
-ስ- በቲያትር ተካፋይ መሆን

action
'አክሽን -ስ- ግብር ፣ ሥራ

active
'አክቲቭ -ቅ- ጉበዝ ፣ ንቁ (ሠ'ራተ'ኛ)

activity
አክ'ቲቪቲ -ስ- ሥራ

actor
'አክተ -ስ- የቴአትር ተጫዋች (ተባዕት) ፣ ተዋናይ

actress
'አክትረስ -ስ- የቴአትር ተጫዋች (እንስት) ተዋናዪት

actual
'አክቹል -ቅ- ል'ክ'ኛ ፣ እውነተ'ኛ (ለትር ጉም ፣ ለፍ'ች) ፤ በአሁኑ ጊዜ ያ'ለ

actually
'አክቹሊ -ተግ- በውነቱ

acumen
'አክዮሜን -ስ- ጉበዝ ነ'ጋዴ የመሆን ችሎታ
mental acuteness
-ስ- ማስተዋል

acute
ኧክ'ዩ፡ት -ቅ- ኀይለ'ኛ (ሕመም) ፤ አስቸ'ጋሪ (ጉ'ዳይ)

adamant
'አደመንት -ቅ- ጽኑእ (የው'ሳኔ)

Adam's apple
አደምዝ 'አፐል -ስ- ማንቁርት

adapt
ኧ'ዳፕት -ግ- እንዲስማ'ማ ማድረግ [አደ'ረገ] (በመለዋወጥ) ፣ ለአ'ዲስ ሁናቴ እንዲ'መ'ች አመል ፣ ጠባይ ፣ ሁናቴ መለወጥ [ለ'ወጠ]

adaptability
ኧዳፕተ'ቢሊቲ -ስ- ራስን የማስማማት ችሎታ ፣ ሁናቴ

add
'አድ -ግ- መጨ'መር [ጨ'መረ]
mathematical
-ግ- መደ'መር [ደ'መረ]

addiction
ኧ'ዲክሽን -ስ- ሱስ ፣ መጥፎ ልማድ (ሜት ፡ ሲጃራ ፣ መጠ'ጥ ወዘተ)

addition
ኧ'ዲሽን -ስ- ድ'ምር

address
ኧድ'ሬስ -ግ- መ'ናገር [ተና'ገረ] (በስብሰባ ውስጥ)
-ስ- አድራ'ሻ

adept
ኧ'ዴፕት -ቅ- ሥልጡን ፣ ባለሞያ

adequate
'አደከወት -ቅ- በቂ ፣ ተመጣጣኝ

adhere
ኧድ'ሒየ -ግ- መ'ጣበቅ [ተጣ'በቀ] ፣ መደ ገፍ [ደ'ገፈ] (ሐሳብ ፣ ዐላማ)

adherent
ኧድ'ሒረንት -ስ- ተከ'ታይ (ለፖለቲካ ክፍል)
adhesion
ኧድ'ሂዠን -ስ- መ'ጣበቅ (አንድ ነገር ከሌላው ጋር በመጣበቅ)
adhesive
ኧድ'ሂዚቭ -ቅ- ተጣባቂ ፣ መጣብቅ
adjacent
ኧ'ጀይሰንት -ቅ- ቅርብ ፣ ጉ'ን ፣ ቀ'ጥሎ ያ'ለ
adjective
'አጀክቲቭ -ስ- ቅ'ጽል (ሰዋስው)
adjoining
ኧ'ጆይኒንግ -ቅ- ቀ'ጥሎ ያ'ለ ፣ ቅርብ
adjourn
ኧ'ጀ፡ን -ግ- መቅ'ጠር [ቀ'ጠረ] (ስብሰባ ፣ ጉባኤ ፣ ሳልተወ'ሰነ ጊዜ)
adjournment
ኧ'ጀ፡ንመንት -ስ- ቀጠር (የስብሰባ ፣ የጉባኤ)
adjudicate
ኧጁ'ዩዲኬይት -ግ- መፍረድ [ፈ'ረደ] (ለውድ'ድር)
adjust
ኧ'ጀስት -ግ- ማስተካከል [አስተካ'ከለ] ፣ በደምብ ማድረግ [አደ'ረገ]
administer
ኧድ'ሚኒስተ -ግ- መግዛት [ገ'ዛ] (ሳገር) ፣ ማስተዳደር [አስተዳ'ደረ]
-to
-ግ- መስጠት [ሰ'ጠ]
administration
አድሚኒስት'ሬይሽን -ስ- አገር አ'ገዛዝ ፣ የአስተዳደር ሥራ
admirable
'አድሚረበል -ቅ- አስገ'ራሚ ፣ አስደ'ናቂ ፣ ድንቅ ፣ ግሩም
admiral
'አድሚረል -ስ- የባሕር ኀይል ከ'ፍተ'ኛ መኰ'ንን
admiration
አድመ'ሬይሽን -ስ- አድናቆት
admire
ኧድ'ማየ -ግ- ማድነቅ [አደ'ነቀ] ፣ መ'ገረም [ተገ'ረመ]

admissible
ኧድ'ሚሰበል -ቅ- የ'ሚ'ቀ'በሉት ፣ ነውር ያልሆነ
admission
ኧድ'ሚሽን -ስ- የሠ'ሩትን በደል አምኖ መ'ቀበል
entry
-ስ- መግባት
-fee
-ስ- የመግቢያ ዋጋ
admit
ኧድ'ሚት -ግ- ማመን [አ'መነ] (ጥፋትን) ፣ እን'ዲገቡ መፍቀድ [ፈ'ቀደ]
admonish
አድ'ሞኒሽ -ግ- መገ'ሠፅ [ገ'ሠፀ] ፣ መቆ'ጣት [ተቆ'ጣ] (ሰውን ፣ ልጅን ወዘተ)
adolescence
አደ'ሌሰንስ -ስ- የጉርምስ'ና ጊዜ
adolescent
አደ'ሌሰንት -ስ- ጉረምሳ
adopt
ኧ'ዶፐት -ግ- ጉ'ዲፈ'ቻ መውሰድ [ወሰደ] ፣ ማደጉ ማሳ'ደግ [አሳ'ደገ] ፣ የሰውን ልጅ እንደ ልጅ አድርጎ ማሳ'ደግ [አሳ'ደገ] ፣ የጡት ልጅ ማድረግ [አደ'ረገ] ፣ የሌላውን ሰው ነገር ፣ ሐ'ሳብ ወስዶ እሥራ ላይ ማዋል [አዋለ]
adoration
አደ'ሬይሽን -ስ- በጣም መውደድ ፣ በጣም ማፍቀር (እግዚአብሔርን ወዘተ) ፣ ው'ዳሴ
adore
ኧ'ዶ፡ -ግ- በጣም መውደድ [ወ'ደደ] (እንደ እግዚአብሔር) ፣ ማወ'ደስ [አወ'ደሰ]
adorn
ኧ'ዶ፡ን -ግ- ማስጌጥ [አስጌጠ] ፣ መሸ'ለም [ሸ'ለመ]
adrift
ኧድ'ሪፍት -ቅ- የሚዋ'ልል ፣ ቁጥ'ጥር የሌ'ለ'በት (መርከብ በባሕር)
adroit
ኧድ'ሮይት -ቅ- ቅልጥፍ ፣ ቀልጣ'ፋ ፣ ሥልጡን
adult
ኧ'ደልት -ቅ- ጉልማ'ሳ
adult
'አደልት -ስ- ጉልማ'ሳ

adulterate
ኧ'ደልተሬይት -ግ- መጥፎ ነገር በንጹሕ ላይ መደባለቅ [ደባለ'ቀ]፣ በክ'ለሳ ጥራት መቀ'ነስ [ቀ'ነሰ]

adultery
ኧ'ደልተሪ -ስ- ዝ'ሙት

advance
ኧድ'ቫ:ንስ -ግ- ወደፊት መግፋት [ገ'ፋ] (ለ ወ'ታ'ደር) ፤ መ'ራመድ [ተራ'መደ]

advancement
ኧድ'ቫ:ንስመንት -ስ- መ'ራመድ (የማዕረግ ዕድገት)

advantage
ኧድ'ቫ:ንቲጅ -ስ- ትድሚያ ፣ ከ'ፍ ያለ ቦታ ፤ ጥሩ ዕ'ድል

advent
'አድቬንት -ስ- መድረስ ፤ ምጽአት
festival
-ስ- ከልደት በፊት ያ'ሉት ሳ'ምንቶ'ች፣ ሱብከተ ገ'ና

adventure
ኧድ'ቬንቸ -ስ- አደገ'ኛ ሁናቴ ፤ አደጋ ያ'ለ'በት ጉዞ

adverb
'አድቨብ -ስ- ተውሳከ ግ'ሥ (ሰዋስው)

adversary
'አድቨሰሪ -ስ- ጠላት ፣ ባላንጣ

adverse
'አድቨ:ስ -ቅ- አ'ዋኪ ፣ ም'ቹ ያልሆነ (ሁናቴ)

adversity
ኧድ'ቨ:ሲቲ -ስ- ማጥፎ ጊዜ ፣ የች'ግር ጊዜ

advertisement
ኧድ'ቨ:ቲስመንት -ስ- ማስታወቂያ (የንግድ ሸቀጣሸቀጥ)

advertiser
'አድቨታይዘ -ስ- ማስታወቂያ አውጪ (የንግድ ሸቀጣሸቀጥ)

advertise
'አድቨታይዝ -ግ- ማስታወቅ [አስታ'ወቀ] (የንግድ ዕቃ)

advice
ኧድ'ቫይስ -ስ- ምክር

advisable
ኧድ'ቫይዘበል -ቅ- የተሻለ (ቢያደርጉት ጥሩ ው'ጤት የ'ሚያስገ'ኝ)

advise
ኧድ'ቫይዝ -ግ- መምከር [መ'ከረ]

advisory
ኧድ'ቫይዘሪ -ቅ- መካሪ

advocate
'አድቮኬይት -ግ- መደ'ገፍ [ደ'ገፈ] (ሐሳብ)
-ስ- ጠበቃ

aerial
'ኤሪየል -ስ- አንቴና

aerodrome
'ኤረድረውም -ስ- የአውሮ'ፕላን ማረፊያ ፣ የአውሮ'ፕላን ማቢያ

aeronautics
ኤረ'ኖ:ቲክስ -ስ- የአውሮ'ፕላን በረራ ትምህርት

aeroplane
'ኤረፕሌይን -ስ- አውሮ'ፕላን

afar
ኧ'ፋ: -ተግ- በሩቅ

affable
'አፈበል -ቅ- ፈገግተ'ኛ

affair
ኧ'ፌየ -ስ- ጉ'ዳይ
love-
-ስ- ውሽ'ም'ነት ፣ ድ'ብቅ ፍቅር (በ ወንድ'ና በሴት መካ'ከል)

affect
ኧ'ፌክት -ግ- መንካት [ነ'ካ] (ጉ'ዳይ ወዘተ)፣ የሰውን ልማድ መገልበጥ [ገለ'በጠ]

affected
ኧ'ፌክተድ -ቅ- የተለ'ወጠ ፤ የ'ሚገ'ደው
exaggerated
-ቅ- ነ'ኝ ባይ ፣ ከመጠን የበ'ለጠ

affection
ኧ'ፌክሽን -ስ- ፍቅር ፤ ዝን'ባሌ

affiliate
ኧ'ፊሊዬይት -ግ- ግን'ኙ'ነት ማድረግ [አደ'ረገ]

affinity
ኧ'ፊኒቲ -ስ- የቀ'ረበ ግንኙ'ነት ፤ ተመሳሳይ'ነት

affirm
ኧ'ፈ:ም -ግ- ማ'ረጋገጥ [አ'ረጋ'ገጠ]

affirmation
አፈ'ሜይሽን -ስ- ማ'ረጋገጥ

affirmative
ኧ'ፈ:መቲቭ -ቅ- የእውንታ

affix
ኧ'ፊክስ -ግ- መለ'ጠፍ [ለ'ጠፈ] (በግድግ'ዳ ላይ)

afflict
ኧፍ'ሊክት -ግ- ማ'ሠቃየት [አ'ሠቃ'የ]

affliction
ኧፍ'ሊክሽን -ስ- ክ'ባድ ሕመም ፣ ክ'ባድ መከራ

affluent
'አፍሉወንት -ቅ- ሀብታም ፣ ባለጸ'ጋ

afford
ኧ'ፎ:ድ -ግ- መቻል [ቻለ] (ለመክፈል፣ለማድረግ ፣ ለማለት)

affray
ኧፍ'ሬይ -ስ- ጥል ፣ ብጥ'ብጥ

affront
ኧፍ'ረንት -ስ- ስድብ ፣ ሰውን የ'ሚያስቀ'ይም ተግባር

aflame
ኧፍ'ሌይም -ቅ- የ'ሚንበለ'በል

afloat
ኧፍ'ሎውት -ቅ- የ'ሚንሳ'ፈፍ ፣ ተንሳፋፊ

afore-said
አ'ፎ:ሴድ -ቅ- ቀደ'ም ብሎ የተነ'ገረ (ለጽሑፍ)

afraid
ኧፍ'ሬይድ -ግ- መፍራት [ፈ'ራ]

afresh
ኧፍ'ሬሽ -ተግ- እንደገና (መጀ'መር)

after
'አ:ፍተ -መዋ- ከ . . . በኋላ

aftermath
'አ:ፍተማሰ -ስ- ያንድ አደጋ ፣ መቅሠፍት ፣ መዐት ው'ጤት (ፍርሰራሽ ፣ ብጥ'ብጥ ወዘተ)

afternoon
አ:ፍተ'ኑ:ን -ስ- ከሰዓት ፣ ከቀትር በኋላ

afterwards
'አ:ፍተወድዝ -ተግ- በኋላ

again
ኧ'ጌን -ተግ- እንደገና

against
ኧ'ጌንስት -መዋ- (ተቃውሞን መግለጫ)፤በ . . . አጠገብ ፣ ከ . . . ጋር (ጦር'ነት)

age
'ኤይጅ -ስ- ዕድሜ ፤ ዘመን

aged
'ኤይጅድ -ቅ- በዕድሜ ገፋ ያለ ፣ ሽማግ'ሌ

agency
'ኤይጀንሲ -ስ- ውክል'ና ፣ ያንድ ወኪል ሥራ ፣ ቢሮ ወዘተ

agenda
ኧ'ጀንደ -ስ- ዝርዝር (በስብሰባ ላይ የ'ሚ'ወያ'ዩ'ባ'ቸው ጉ'ዳዮ'ች)

agent
'ኤይጀንት -ስ- ወ'ኪል

agglomeration
ኧግሎመ'ሬይሽን -ስ- መ'ከማቸት ፣ መ'ሰብሰብ

aggravate
'አግረቬይት -ግ- ማባስ [አባሰ]

aggregate
'አግረጊይት -ቅ- ድ'ምር (ጠቅላ'ላ)

aggression
ኧግ'ሬሽን -ስ- የጠላት'ነት ስ'ሜት ፣ ጥል (ያለምክንያት)

aggressive
ኧግ'ሬሲቭ -ቅ- ጥለ'ኛ ፣ ጦገደ'ኛ

aggressor
ኧግ'ሬሰ -ስ- ጥል ያ'ነሣ'ሣ ፣ ጠብ አጫሪ ወዘተ

agile
'አጃይል -ቅ- ፈ'ጣን ፣ ቀልጣ'ፋ

agility
ኧ'ጂሊቲ -ስ- ፍጥነት

agitate
'አጂቴይት -ግ- መነቅነቅ [ነቀ'ነቀ] (ለመደባለቅ)
make trouble
-ግ- መበጥበጥ [በጠ'በጠ] ፣ ማ'ወክ [አ'ወከ]

aglow
ኧግ'ሎው -ቅ- የፋመ ፣ የተጋጋለ ፣ የተንተረ'ከከ (ከሰል ፣ እሳት)

ago
ኧ'ገው -ተግ- ከ . . . በፊት

agony
'አገኒ -ስ- ሕማም (ታ'ላቅ) ፣ ሥቃይ

agrarian
ኧግ'ሬሪየን -ቅ- የእርሻ

agree
ኧገ'ሪ: -ግ- መስማማት [ተስማ'ማ]

agreeable
ኧግ'ሪየበል -ቅ- ተስማሚ

agreement
ኧግ'ሪ:መንት -ስ- ውል ፣ ስምም'ነት

agriculture
'አግሪከልቸ -ስ- እርሻ ፣ ግብር'ና

ahead
ኧ'ሔድ -ተግ- ወደፊት

aid
'ኤይድ -ግ- መርዳት [ረ'ዳ]

ail
'ኤይል -ግ- መ'ታመም [ታ'መመ]

ailment
'ኤይልመንት -ስ- ሕመም ፣ በ'ሽታ

aim
'ኤይም -ግ- ማ'ነጣጠር [አ'ነጣ'ጠረ]
-ስ- ግብ ፣ ተምኔት

air
'ኤየ -ስ- አ'የር

aircraft
'ኤክራ:ፍት -ስ- አውሮ'ፕላን

airfield
'ኤፊይልድ -ስ- ያውሮ'ፕላን ማረፊያ (በተለ'ይ ለጦር አውሮ'ፕላን)

air force
'ኤፎ:ስ -ስ- ያ'የር ኀይል

airline
'ኤላይን -ስ- ያ'የር መንገድ (የንግድ)

airmail
'ኤሜይል -ስ- ያ'የር ደብዳ'ቤ ፣ በአውሮ'ፕላን የ'ሚ'ላክ ደብዳ'ቤ

airman
'ኤመን -ስ- ያ'የር ኀይል ወ'ታ'ደር ፣ የግ'ል አውሮ'ፕላን ነጂ

airport
'ኤፖ:ት -ስ- ያውሮ'ፕላን ማረፊያ

airtight
'ኤታይት -ቅ- አ'የር የ'ማያስገ'ባ

airy
'ኤሪ -ቅ- ነ'ፋ'ሻ

aisle
'አይል -ስ- ትኔ ማሕሌት ፣ በተደረ'ደሩ ወንበሮ'ች መሀል ጠ'ባብ መ'ተላለፊያ

ajar
ኧ'ጃ: -ቅ- በከፊል ክፍት ፣ ገርበ'ብ ያለ

akin
ኧ'ኪን -ቅ- የ'ሚ'መሳ'ሰል

alacrity
ኧ'ላክሪቲ -ስ- ፍጥነት (ለሥራ)

alarm
ኧ'ላ:ም -ግ- ማስደንገጥ [አስደነ'ገጠ]
-ስ- ምል'ክት (ያደጋ)

alas
ኧ'ላስ -ቃአ- ወይኔ

album
'አልበም -ስ- ፎቶግራፍ ፣ ቴምብር ወዘተ የ'ሚ'ሰበ'ሰብ'በት ደብተር

alcohol
'አልከሆል -ስ- አልኮል (አስካሪ መጠ'ጥ)

alcove
'አልከውቭ -ስ- ት'ንሽ ቅ'ሥት (በግርግ'ዳ ውስጥ)

ale
'ኤይል -ስ- ጠ'ላ (መጠ'ጥ)

alert
ኧ'ለ:ት -ቅ- ንቁ
-ስ- ማስጠንቀቂያ

alias
'ኤይሊየስ -ስ- የተለ'ወጠ ስም (በወንጀለኞ'ች ዘንድ)

alibi
'አለባይ -ስ- ወንጀል በተደ'ረገ'በት ቦታ አለመኖርን ለማ'ረጋገጥ የ'ሚ'ሰጥ ማስረ'ጃ

alien
'ኤይሊየን -ስ- እንግዳ ፣ የው'ጭ አገር ሰው ፣ ባዕድ

alight
ኧ'ላይት -ቅ- የ'ሚ'ቃ'ጠል ፣ የተያያዘ (በሳት)
-ግ- መውረድ [ወ'ረደ] (ካንድ ነገር ላይ)

align
አ'ላይን -ግ- ማስተካከል [አስተካ'ከለ]
alike
አ'ላይክ -ት- መሳይ
alimentary
አሊ'ሜንትሪ -ት- ምግብነ'ት ያ'ለው
alive
አ'ላይቭ -ት- በሕይወት ያ'ለ ፣ ነዋሪ
all
'ኦ:ል -ት- ሁ'ሉ
all right
ኦ:ልራይት -ተግ- መልካም ፣ ጥሩ ፣ ደኅና
allay
አ'ሌይ -ግ- ማ'ረጋጋት [አ'ረጋ'ጋ] (ጥር'ጣሬ፣ ፍርሐት)
allegation
አለ'ጌይሽን -ስ- ክ'ስ (ገና ማስረ'ጃ ያልቀ'ረ በ'በት)
allege
አ'ሌጅ -ግ- መ'ናገር [ተና'ገረ] (ያለማስረ'ጃ)
allegiance
አ'ሊይጀንስ -ስ- ታማኝ'ነት መያዝ ፤ በጦር'ነት ጊዜ ለማገልገል ውለታ መግባት ፣ ግ'ዴታ መግባት
allegory
'አሌጎሪ -ስ- ምሳ'ሌያዊ ተረት (በሰው ፣ በእንስሳት አስመ'ስሎ የ'ሚ'ነ'ገር)
alleviate
አ'ሊ:ቪዬይት -ግ ሥቃይን መቀ'ነስ [ቀ'ነሰ] ፣ ሕመምን ማሳ'ነስ [አሳነ'ሰ]
alley
'አሊ -ስ- ጠ'ባብ መንገድ ፣ ስርጥ መንገድ
alliance
አ'ላየንስ -ስ- የጦር ጓ'ድ አገር'ች ፤ የመ'ረዳዳት ቃል ኪዳን (በአገር'ች መካ'ከል)
allied
'አላይድ -ት- የተስማ'ማ ፣ የተባ'በረ
alligator
'አሊጌይተ -ስ- ዐ'ዞ ፣ አርጃኖ
allocate
'አለኬይት -ግ- መስጠት [ሰ'ጠ] ፣ መቆ'ነን [ቆ'ነነ] ፣ ማ'ካፈል [አ'ካ'ፈለ] ፣ መደልደል [ደል'ደለ]
allot
አ'ሎት -ግ- ማ'ካፈል [አ'ካ'ፈለ] ፣ ማ'ደል [አ'ደለ]
allotment
አ'ሎትመንት -ስ- መቆነን ፤ እ'ጻፊ ፣ እቤት አጠገብ የ'ሚ'ገ'ኝ ቦታ
allow
አ'ላው -ግ- መፍቀድ [ፈ'ቀደ]
allowance
አ'ላወንስ -ስ- የኪስ ገንዘብ ፤ ል'ዩ ወጭ
alloy
'አሎይ -ስ- ቅል'ቅል (ማዕ'ድን)
allude
አሉ'ዩ:ድ -ግ- ማውሳት [አወ'ሳ] ፣ መጥቀስ [ጠ'ቀሰ]
alluring
አል'ዩ:ሪንግ -ት- አስተያየት ማራኪ
allusion
አ'ሉዠን -ስ- ማውሳት ፣ መጥቀስ
ally
'አላይ -ስ- ጓ'ድ ፣ ተባባሪ (በጦር'ነት ጊዜ)
almighty
ኦ:ል'ማይቲ -ት- ሁ'ሉን የ'ሚችል (ለእግዚአብሔር)
almond
'አ:መንድ -ስ- ለውዝ
almost
'ኦ:ልመውስት -ተግ- ል ፣ ሊ . . . ነበ.
alms
'አ:ምዝ -ስ- ምጽዋት ፣ ለበ'ጎ አድራጎት የ'ሚ'ሰጥ ገንዘብ
aloft
አ'ሎፍት -ተግ- በላይ
alone
አ'ለውን -ተግ- ብ'ቻ
along
አ'ሎንግ -ተግ- ከ . . . ጋር
-መዋ- በ . . .
alongside
አሎንግ'ሳይድ -ተግ- ቀ'ጥሎ
aloof
አ'ሉ:ፍ -ት ፣ ተግ- ገለልተ'ኛ (ከሰዎ'ች በመራቅ ወዘተ) ፤ በሩቅ ፤ ከሩ

aloud
ኧ'ላውድ -ተግ- በጩኸት ፣በከ'ፍተ'ኛ ድምፅ
alphabet
'አልፈቤት -ስ- ፊደል
alphabetical
አልፈ'ቤቲከል -ቅ- በፊደል ተራ
already
ኦ:ል'ሬዲ -ተግ- ቀድሞ ፣ ቦሬት (ከተወ'ሰነ ጊዜ)
also
'ኦ:ልሰው -ተግ- ደግሞ ፣ ደ'ሞ
-መዋ- -ም ፣ እ'ና
altar
'ኦ:ልተ -ስ- መንበር ፣ ምሥዋዕ
alter
'ኦ:ልተ -ግ- መለ'ወጥ [ለ'ወጠ]
alteration
ኦ:ልተ'ሬይሸን -ስ- ለውጥ
altercation
ኦ:ልተ'ኬይሸን -ስ- ክር'ክር
alternate
'ኦ:ልትኔይት -ግ- መ'ለዋወጥ [አ'ፈራ'ረቀ]
alternate
ኦ:ል'ተ:ነት -ቅ- [illegible] የ'ሚመጣ፣ የ'ሚያሠ'ልስ
alternative
ኦ:ል'ተ:ነቲቭ -ስ- [illegible] (ከሁ ለት ነገር)
although
ኦ:ል'ዘው -መዋ- ምን'ም እን[illegible]
altitude
'አልቲትዩድ -ስ- ከ'ፍታ'ነት ፣ ከ'ፍታ
altogether
ኦ:ልተ'ጌዘ -ተግ- በፍ'ጹም ፣ ፈ'ጽሞ ፣ በሙ'ሉ
aluminium
አሉ'ሚንየም -ስ- አ'ሉሚንየም
always
'ኦ:ልዌይዝ -ተግ- ሁ'ል ጊዜ ፣ ዘወትር ፣ ሥርክ
amalgamate
ኧ'ማለገሜይት -ግ- ማ'ዋሐድ [አ'ዋሐደ]
amass
ኧ'ማስ -ግ- መሰብሰብ [ሰበ'ሰበ] ፣ ማ'ከማቸት [አ'ከማ'ቸ] ፣ ማግበስበስ [አግበሰ'በሰ]

amateur
'አመተ -ቅ- የ'ማይ'ከ'ፈለው ሙዚቀ'ኛ ፣ ስፖርተ'ኛ ወዘተ
amaze
ኧ'ሜይዝ -ግ- መ'ገረም [ተገ'ረመ]
ambassador
አም'ባሰደ -ስ- የመንግሥት መልእክተ'ኛ (ወደ ሌላ መንግሥት የ'ሚ'ላክ) ፣ አም'ባሳደር
amber
'አምበ -ስ- ሙ'ጫ (ደረቅ) ፣ ጠቆር ያለ ብጫ ቀለም ፣ ል'ባልማ (ል'ብ-አልማ) ቋሎል ፣ የዛጐል'ነት ባሕርይ ያ'ለው
ambidextrous
አምቢ'ዴክስትረስ -ቅ- ግራ'ኝ'ና ቀ'ኝ የሆነ፣ በግራው በቀ'ኙ'ም መሥራት የ'ሚሆን'ለት
ambiguity
አምቢግ'ዩዊቲ -ስ- አ'ጠራጣሪ ትርጉም ፣ ግልጽ ያልሆን'ና በሁለ'ት መንገድ ሊ'ፈታ የ'ሚችል ነገር ፣ ሁናቴ
ambiguous
አም'ቢግዩወስ -ቅ- አ'ሻሚ ፣ ግልጽ ያልሆነ (ለትርጉም)
ambition
አም'ቢሽን -ስ- የጋለ ፍ'ላጐት ፣ ል'በ ት'ልቅ'ነት ፣ ተምኔት
ambulance
'አምብዩለንስ -ስ- የሕመምተ'ኞ'ች ማ'መላለሻ መኪና
ambush
'አምቡሽ -ግ- አደጋ ለመጣል ማድፈጥ [አደ'ፈጠ]
amelioration
አሚሊየ'ሬይሸን -ግ- ማ'ሻሻል [አ'ሻሻለ]
amenable
ኧ'ሚነበል -ቅ- ተቀ'ባይ (ትእዛዝ) ፣ ሐ'ሳብ ፣ ትእዛዝ የ'ማይ'ቃ'ወም
amend
ኧ'ሜንድ -ግ- ማስተካከል [አስተካ'ከለ]
amendment
ኧ'ሜንድመንት -ስ- ማ'ሻሻል (ሕ'ግ ወዘተ
amenity
ኧ'ሜንቲ -ስ- ባንድ ቀበሌ የ'ሚ'ገ'ኝ ጠቅላላ የሕዝብ አገልግሎት
amiable
'ኧይሚየበል -ቅ- ተወ'ዳጅ ፣ ሰው ወዳጅ

amicable
'አሚከበል -ቅ- ተወ'ዳጅ ፣ ሰው ወዳጅ ፣ የመ'ዋደድ ስ'ሜት

amid(st)
አ'ሚድ (ስት) -ተግ- በመካ'ከል

amiss
አ'ሚስ -ቅ- የተበላ'ሸ ፣ ብል'ሹ ፣ በስሕተት የተሠ'ራ

ammunition
አምዩ'ኒሽን -ስ- ጥ'ይት

amnesty
'አምንስቲ -ስ- ምሕረት (ለእስረ ኛ)

among(st)
አ'መንግ (ስት) -ተግ- በመካ'ከል

amorous
'አመረስ -ቅ- የፍቅር'ና የመውደድ ስ'ሜት የያዘው (በፍትወተ ሥጋ)

amount
አ'ማውንት -ስ- መጠን
-ግ- መድረስ [ደ'ረሰ] ፣ ማ'ከል [አ'ከለ] (ለመጠን ፣ ለብዛት)

amphibious
አም'ፊቢየስ -ቅ- በየብስ'ም በውሃ'ም ውስጥ መኖር የ'ሚችል ፍጡር

ample
'አምፐል -ቅ- በቂ ፣ ሰ'ፊ

amplify
'አምፐሊፋይ -ግ- ማጉላት [አጉ'ላ]

amplifier
'አምፐሊፋየ -ስ- ማጉያ

amputate
'አምፐዩቴይት -ግ- መቁረጥ [ቈ'ረጠ] (እ'ጅ፣ እግር)

amuse
አም'ዩ፡ዝ -ግ- ማስደ'ሰት [አስደ'ሰተ]

an
'አን -ያተመ- አንድ

analogy
አ'ናለጂ -ስ- ተመሳሳይ'ነት (ባን'ዳንድ ሁኔቱ በሁለ'ት ነገር'ች መካ'ከል) ፣ በከፊል ተመሳሳ ይ'ነት

analyse
'አነላይዝ -ግ- መተንተን [ተነ'ተነ]

analysis
አ'ናለሲስ -ስ- ትንተና

anatomy
አ'ናተሚ -ስ- አናቶሚ (የሰው'ነት ክፍሎ'ች ጥናት) ፤ አካል ፣ ሰው'ነት

ancestors
'አንሰስተዝ -ስ- ትውል'ድ ፣ አያት ቅድመ ያት ፣ ዘር ማንዘር

anchor
'አንከ -ስ- መልሕቅ

ancient
'ኤይንሸንት -ቅ- ጥንታዊ

anecdote
'አኔክደውት -ስ- በንግ'ግር ውስጥ እንደም' ሳሌ የ'ሚ'ጠ'ቀስ ታሪክ (የ'ሚያ'ሥቅ)

and
'አንድ -መዋ- እ'ና - ና - ም

angel
'ኤይንጀል -ስ- መልአክ

anger
'አንገ -ስ- ቁ'ጣ

angle
'አንገል -ስ- ማዕዘን

angry
'አንግሬ -ቅ- ቁ'ጡ

anguish
'አንገዊሽ -ስ- ታ'ላቅ ሐዘን ፣ ት'ልቅ ሥቃይ

angular
'አንግዩለ -ቅ- ቀ'ጭን ፣ መንግ'ና (ለሰው) ፣ የማዕዘን መ'ታጠፊያ ነጥብ

animal
'አኒመል -ስ- እንስሳ ፣ አውሬ

animosity
አኒ'ሞሲቲ -ስ- ጠላት'ነት ፣ ጥላ'ቻ

ankle
'አንክል -ስ- ቁርጭምጭሚት

annex
'አኔክስ -ግ- የሌሎ'ችን አገር ከግዛት ጋር ማ'ዋሐድ [አ'ዋሐደ]

annexe
አ'ኔክስ -ስ- ቅ'ጥያ (ለቤት)

annihilate
አ'ናየሌይት -ግ- መደምሰስ [ደመ'ሰሰ] ፣ ማጥ ፋት [አጠ'ፋ]

nniversary
አኒ'ቨ:ሰሪ -ስ- ዓመት በዐል ፤ ክበረ በዐል
nnotate
'አነቴይት -ግ- ትርጉም መስጠት [ሰ'ጠ] (ለ መጽሐፍ) ፤ መግለጽ [ገ'ለጸ] ፤ ማብራራት [አብራ'ራ]
nnounce
ኧ'ናውንስ -ግ- ማስታወቅ [አስታ'ወቀ] ፤ ማ' ወጅ [ዐ'ወጀ]
nnouncement
ኧ'ናውንስመንት -ስ- ማስታወቂያ ፤ ዐዋጅ
nnoy
ኧ'ኖይ -ግ- ማስቆ'ጣት [አስቆ'ጣ] ፤ ማ'በሳ ጨት [አ'በሳ'ጨ]
nnual
'አንዩወል -ቅ- ዓመታዊ
nnuity
ኧን'ዩዊቲ -ስ- በ'ያመቱ የ'ሚ'ከ'ፈል የተወ' ሰነ ገንዘብ
nnul
ኧ'ነል -ግ- ሕ'ግን መሠ'ረዝ [ሠ'ረዘ]
nnunciation
ኧ'ነንሲ'ዬይሽን -ስ- ብሥራት
noint
ኧ'ኖይንት -ግ- በዘይት ራስን መቀ'ባት [ቀ'ባ] (በተለ'ይ ለክህነት፣ ለንጉሥ ፤ ለክርስቶስ)
nomaly
ኧ'ኖመሊ -ስ- ከልምድ'ና ከሥርዓት ው'ጭ መሆን ፤ ሕ'ግ አለማክበር
nonymous
ኧ'ኖነመስ -ቅ- ስም የሌለ'በት መጽሐፍ ፤ ደብዳ'ቤ ፤ ስጦታ ፤ ወዘተ
nother
ኧ'ነዘ -ቅ ፤ ተስ- ሌላ
nswer
'አ:ንሰ -ግ- መልስ መስጠት [ሰ'ጠ]
-ስ- ም'ላሽ ፤ መልስ (የጥ'ያቄ)
nt
'አንት -ስ- ጉንዳን ፤ ገብረ ጉን'ዳን ፤ ቁጫጭ
nteater
'አንቲተ -ስ- ወልደጌ'ሣ
ntagonism
አን'ታገኒዘም -ስ- ጠላት'ነት ፤ ባላንጣ'ነት

antagonist
አን'ታገኒስት -ስ- ተቃዋሚ ፤ ባላን'ጣ
antelope
'አንተለውፕ -ስ- አጋዘን ፤ ሚዳ'ቋ ወይን'ም የሚዳ ፍ'የል የ'ሚመስሉ እንስሳት
antenna
አን'ቴና -ስ- አንቴና ፤ የራዲዮ'ና የቴሌቪዥን ማዕበል መ'ቀበያ
anterior
አን'ቲሪየ -ቅ- ቀደም ብሎ የመ'ጣ
anthem
'አንሰም -ስ- የቤተ ክርስቲያን መዝሙር ፤ መዝሙር (ያንድ አገር)
anthology
አን'ሶለጂ -ስ- ምርጥ ምንባቦ'ች ፤ የምንባብ መድበል
antic
'አንቲክ -ስ- አ'የዘ'ለሉ መጮኽ ፤ መቦ'ረቅ ፤ ጅላጅል
anticipate
አን'ቲሲፔይት -ግ- ይሆናል ብሎ መጠ'በቅ [ጠ'በቀ] ፤ ሳይሆን አይቀር'ም ብሎ መሥራት [ሠ'ራ]
antidote
'አንቲደውት -ስ- የመርዝ ማርከሻ
antipathy
አን'ቲፐሢ -ስ- ጥላ'ቻ
antique
አን'ቲይክ -ቅ- ጥንታዊ ፤ ታሪካዊ
antiquity
አን'ቲክዊቲ -ስ- የጥንት ጊዜ (በታሪኩ የታ ወ'ቀ)
antiseptic
አንቲ'ሴፕቲክ -ስ- የቁስል መድኃኒት
antler
'አንትለ -ስ- የሚዳ'ቋ፣ የሚዳ ፍ'የል ወይን'ም ያጋዘን ቀንድ
anus
'ኤይነስ -ስ- የሰገራ መውጫ ቀዳዳ ፤ (የሰው ፤ የእንስሳት ወዘተ) ፤ ፊንጢ'ጣ ፤ ሙ'ኒ
anvil
'አንቪል -ስ- ብረት የ'ሚ'ቀጠቀጥ'በት ብረት፣ መስፍ
anxiety
አንግ'ዛየቲ -ስ- መሥጋት ፤ ሥጋት ፤ ጭንቀት

anxious
'አንክሸስ -ቅ- የተጨ'ነቀ ፣ ሥጉ

any
'ኤኒ -ቅ- ማ'ን'ኛው'ም ፣ አንዳ'ች

anybody
'ኤኒቦዲ -ተስ- ማ'ን'ኛው'ም ሰው

anyhow
'ኤኒሀው -ተግ- በማ'ን'ኛው'ም ሁናቴ ፣ ያ'ም
ሆነ ይህ
-ቅ- እንደነገሩ

anyone
'ኤኒወን -ተስ- ማ'ን'ኛውም ሰው

anything
'ኤኒሲንግ -ተስ- ማ'ና'ቸውም ነገር

anyway
'ኤኒዌይ -ተግ- በማ'ና'ቸውም ሁናቴ

anywhere
'ኤኒዌየ -ተግ- የት'ም

apart
ኧ'ፓ:ት -ተግ- ተለ'ይቶ ፣ በተለ'ይ

apartment
ኧ'ፓ:ትመንት -ስ- አ'ፓርትማ ፣ ብዙ ቤተሰብ
የ'ሚያኖር ሕንፃ

apathetic
አፐ'ሴቲክ -ቅ- የ'ማይገ'ደው

apathy
'አፐሲ -ስ- የስ'ሜት ማጣት ፣ ግ'ዴ'ለሽ መሆን

ape
'ኤይፕ -ስ- የዝንጀሮ'ና የጦጣ ዐይነት እን
ስሳ ነገር ግን ጅራት የሌ'ለው

aperient
ኧ'ፔሪየንት -ስ- የ'ሚያስቀ'ምጥ መድኃኒት

aperitif
ኧ'ፔሪቲፍ -ስ- ከምግብ በፊት የ'ሚ'ጠ'ጣ
መጠ'ጥ (እንዲያስርብ) ፣ ከሣቴ ከርሥ

aperture
'አፐቸ -ስ- ት'ንሽ ቀዳዳ ፣ ብስ

apex
'ኤይፔክስ -ስ- ጫፍ

apiary
'ኤይፒየሪ -ስ- የንብ ቀፎዎ'ች ቦታ

apologetic
ኧፖለ'ጀቲክ -ቅ- ይቅርታ ጠ'ያቂ ፣ ተፀ'ፃች

apologize
ኧ'ፖለጃይዝ -ግ- ይቅርታ መጠ'የቅ [ጠ'የቀ]

apology
ኧ'ፖለጂ -ስ- ይቅርታ

apostle
ኧ'ፖሰል -ስ- ደ'ቀ መዝሙር ፣ ሐዋርያ

apostrophe
ኧ'ፖስትረፊ -ስ- ጭረት (የንጥብ ዓይነት) (')

appal
ኧ'ፓ:ል -ግ- ማስደንገጥ [አስደን'ገጠ] ፣ ማ'ጸ'
የፍ [አ'ጸ'የፈ]

appalling
ኧ'ፓ:ሊንግ -ቅ- አስደንጋጭ ፣ አ'ጸ'ያፊ

apparatus
'አፐሬይተስ -ስ- መ'ቀላጠፊያ መ'ሣሪያ (በሳ
ይንስ ላቦራትሪ)

apparel
ኧ'ፓረል -ስ- ልብስ

apparent
ኧ'ፓረንት -ቅ- ግልጽ ፣ የ'ማያ'ጠራ'ጥር

apparently
ኧ'ፓረንትሊ -ተግ- በግልጽ

apparition
አፐ''ሪሽን -ስ- የተከ'ሰተ መንፈስ

appeal
ኧ'ፒይል -ግ- ይግባኝ መጠ'የቅ [ጠ'የቀ]
-ስ- ቁንጅ'ና ፣ ደማም'ነት ፣ የተራድኦ
ገንዘብ ስብሰባ

appear
ኧ'ፒየ -ግ- ብ'ቅ ማለት [ብ'ቅ አለ] ፣ መም
ሰል [መ'ሰለ] ፣ መ'ታየት [ታ'የ]

appease
ኧ'ፒይዝ -ግ- ማስደ'ሰት [አስደሰተ] ፣ ማ
በያ መስጠት [ሰ'ጠ] ፣ ማስታገሥ ፣ [አስታ
ገሠ] ፣ መ'ለማመጥ [ተለማ'መጠ]

appellant
ኧ'ፔለንት -ስ- ባለይግባ'ኝ ፣ ይግባ'ኝ ባይ

append
ኧ'ፔንድ -ግ- መቀ'ጠል [ቀ'ጠለ]

appendicitis
አፔንዲ'ሳይቲስ -ስ- የትርፍ አንጀት ሕመም

appertain
አፐ'ቴይን -ግ- መ'ገናዘብ [ተገና'ዘበ]

appetite
'አፐታይት -ስ- የመብላት ፍ'ላጎት

applaud
ኧፐ'ሉ:ድ -ግ- ማጨብጨብ [አጨበ'ጨበ]

applause
ኧፐ'ሉ:ዝ -ስ- ጭብጨባ

apple
'አፐል -ስ- ፖም (የፍራፍሬ ዓይነት)

appliance
ኧፕ'ላየንስ -ስ- መ'ሣሪያ

applicable
ኧፕ'ሊከበል -ቅ- ተ'ጻፂ የ'ሚ'መለ'ከተው

applicant
'አፕሊከንት -ስ- ጠ'ያቂ (የሥራ) ፣ አመልካች

application
አፕሊ'ኬይሽን -ስ- ማመልከቻ ፤ እሥራ ላይ ማዋል

apply
ኧፕ'ላይ -ግ- መጠ'የቅ [ጠ'የቀ] (ሥራ) ፡ ማመልከት [አመለ'ከተ]

appoint
ኧ'ፖይንት -ግ- መቅጠር [ቀ'ጠረ] ፤ መሾም [ሾመ]

appointment
ኧ'ፖይንትመንት -ስ- ሥራ ፣ ማዕረግ

apportion
ኧ'ፖ:ሽን -ግ- መቆ'ነን [ቆ'ነነ]

apposite
'አፐሲት -ቅ- ተስማሚ (ለንግ'ግር)

appraise
ኧፕ'ሬይዝ -ግ- መመርመር [መረ'መረ] ፡ መገ'መት [ገ'መተ]

appreciate
ኧፕ'ሪሺዬይት -ግ- መውደድ [ወ'ደደ] ፣ ደ'ስ መ'ሰኘት [ተሰ'ኘ]

apprehend
አፕሪ'ሄንድ -ግ- መያዝ [ያዘ]
understand
-ግ- መ'ረዳት [ተረ'ዳ]

apprehension
አፕሪ'ሄንሽን -ስ- መፍራት ፣ መ'ጨነቅ (ለመጪ ሁኔታ)

'apprentice
አፕ'ሬንቲስ -ስ- ሞያ ተማሪ (የእ'ጅ)

approach
ኧፕ'ረውች -ግ- መቅረብ [ቀ'ረበ]
-ስ- መንገድ (ያ'ቀራረብ)

approbation
አፕረ'ቤይሽን -ቅ- መስማማት ፣ ማመስገን ፡ አበ'ጀህ ማለት

approve
ኧፕ'ሩ:ቭ -ግ- መስማማት [ተስማ'ማ] ፡ ማጽደቅ [አጸ'ደቀ]

approximate
ኧፕ'ሮክሲመት -ቅ- አቅራ'ቢያ ፣ ያህል ፡ ገደማ
-ግ- መቅረብ [ቀ'ረበ]

appurtenance
ኧ'ፐ:ተነንስ -ስ- ንብረት ፣ የግ'ል ዕቃ ፣ ያንድ ነገር አባሪ የሆነ

April
'ኤይፕረል -ስ- ሚያዝያ

apron
'ኤይፕረን -ስ- ሽ'ርጥ

apt
'አፕት -ቅ- ተስማሚ ፣ ትክ'ክል ፣ ደምበ'ኛ

aptitude
'አፕቲትዩ:ድ -ስ- ችሎታ ፤ ተስማሚ'ነት ፣ የተፈጥሮ ችሎታ

aquarium
ኧክ'ዌሪየም -ስ- ዓሣ ማስቀ'መጫ ገንዳ (ሰው ሠ'ራሽ)

aquatic
አክ'ዋቲክ -ቅ- የውሃ (ወገን)

aqueduct
'አክዊደክት -ስ- የመጠ'ጥ ወሃ የ'ሚሄድ'በት ቦይ

aquiline
'አክወላይን -ቅ- ንሥር መ'ሰል ፤ ቀ'ጭን'ና ጎባጣ (ለአፍንጫ)

arable
'አረበል -ቅ- ለእርሻ ተስማሚ (መሬት)

arbiter
'አ:ቢተ -ስ- ሽማግ'ሌ ፣ አስታራቂ

arbitrary
'አ:ቢትረሪ -ቅ- በጣም ያልታ'ሰበ'በት ፣ በች ኮ'ላ የተደ'ረገ (ው'ሳኔ) ፣ ያለ በቂ ምክንያት የተወ'ሰነ (ው'ሳኔ) ፤ ተቀናቃኝ የሌ'ለው (በሥ ልጣኑ)

arbitrate
'አ:ቢትሬይት -ግ- መሸምገል [ሸመ'ገለ] (ማስ ታረቅ)

arbitration
አ:ቢት'ሬይሽን -ስ- ሽምግላ

arbitrator
'አ:ቢትሬይተ -ስ- ሽማግ'ሌ ፣ አስታራቂ

arbour
'አ:በ -ስ- ጥላ'ማ ቦታ (አዛፍ ሥር ወዘተ)

arc
'አ:ክ -ስ- ቅ'ሥት (ቅርፅ)

arch
'አ:ች -ስ- ቅ'ሥት

archaic
አ:'ኬይክ -ቅ- ጥንታዊ ፣ ታሪካዊ

archangel
'አ:ኬንጀል -ስ- ሊቀ መላእክት

archbishop
አ:ች'ቢሸፕ -ስ- ሊቀ ጳ'ጳሳት

archaeology
አ:ኪ'ዮለጂ -ስ- በመሬት ውስጥ የተቀ'በሩ የታሪክ ቅርሶ'ች ጥናት

archer
'አ:ቸ -ስ- ቀስተ'ኛ ፣ በቀስት'ና በፍላ'ፃ የ'ሚ' ዋ'ጋ

archipelago
አ:ቺ'ፔለገው -ስ- የተሟ'ፈሩ ደሴቶ'ች

architect
'አ:ኪተክት -ስ- አርኪቴክት (የቤት ፕላን ነ ዳፊ)

archives
'አ:ካይቭዝ -ስ- ሰነዶ'ች (አሮጌ)
office
-ስ- ቤተ መዛግብት

ardent
'አ:ደንት -ቅ- በጉ'ዳዩ በጣም የ'ሚያ'ስብ'በት ፣ ስ'ሜቱ በጉ'ዳዩ የተቀሰ'ቀሰ ፣ ጥልቅ ስ'ሜት ያ'ለው (ስለአንድ ጉ'ዳይ)

ardour
'አ:ደ -ስ- ፍቅር ፣ ጥሩ ስ'ሜት ፣ ጥልቅ ስ'ሜት

arduous
'አ:ድዩወስ -ቅ- አስቸ'ጋሪ ፣ አሰልቺ ፣ አ'ቀኪ (ሥራ)

area
'ኤሪየ -ስ- ቦታ (የተወ'ሰነ) ፣ ሠፈር
measure
-ስ- ስፋት

arena
ኧ'ሪ:ነ -ስ- ሰፊ ክ'ብ ቦታ (የስፖርት ወዘተ)

argue
'አ:ጊዩ -ግ- መ'ከራከር [ተከራ'ከረ]

argument
'አ:ግዮመንት -ስ- ክር'ክር

arid
'አሪድ -ቅ- ደረቅ

arise
ኧ'ራይዝ -ግ- መ'ነሣት [ተነ'ሣ]

aristocracy
አሪስ'ቶክረሲ -ስ- ባላ'ባቶ'ች

arithmetic
ኧ'ሪስመቲክ -ስ- ሒሳብ

ark
'አ:ክ -ስ- ታቦት
ship
-ስ- የኖሕ መርከብ

arm
'አ:ም -ስ- ክንድ

armament
'አ:መመንት -ስ- የጦር መ'ሣርያዎ'ች ፣ ትጥቅ

armchair
አ:ም'ቼየ -ስ- ባለመ'ደገፊያ ወምበር (የእ'ጅ መ'ደገፊያ ያ'ለው)

armistice
'አ:ሚስቲስ -ስ- ጦር'ነት ለጊዜው ለማቆም መስማማት

armour
'አ:መ -ስ- የብረት ልብስ ፣ ጥሩር

armpit
'አ:ምፒት -ስ- ብ'ብት

arms
'አ:ምዝ -ስ- የጦር መ'ሣሪያ

army
'አ:ሚ -ስ- ጦር ሠራዊት ፣ ወ'ታ'ደር
aroma
ኧ'ረውመ -ስ- መዐዛ
aromatic
አረ'ማቲክ -ቅ- መዐዛ ያ'ለው
around
ኧ'ራውንድ -ተግ- ባ'ካባቢ
arouse
ኧ'ራውዝ -ግ- ማስነ'ሣት [አስነ'ሣ]
arrange
ኧ'ሬይንጅ -ግ- ማ'ዘጋጀት [አ'ዘጋ'ጀ]
array
ኧ'ሬይ -ስ- ሰልፍ
arrears
ኧ'ሪየዝ -ስ- የተወ'ዘፈ ፣ ያልተከ'ፈለ የቤት ፣ የመሬት ፣ የሥራ ወዘተ እዳ
arrest
ኧ'ረስት -ግ- መያዝ [ያዘ] (ለፖሊስ)
arrive
ኧ'ራይቭ -ግ- መድረስ [ደ'ረሰ]
arrogant
'አረገንት -ቅ- ዘባቻ ፣ ደ'ፋር ፣ እብሪተ'ኛ
arrow
'አረው -ስ- ፍላ'ጻ ፣ ወስፈን'ጥር
arsenal
'አ:ሰነል -ስ- የጦር መ'ሣሪያ ዕቃ ቤት ፣ የመ' ሣሪያ ፋብሪካ
arsenic
'አ:ሰኒክ -ስ- አሰኒክ (ኀይለ'ኛ መርዝ)
arson
'አ:ሰን -ስ- የሰው ቤት ማ'ቃጠል
art
'አ:ት -ስ- ጥበብ ፣ አንድ ነገር የማድረግ ችሎታ ፣ አንድ ነገር የመፍጠር ተሰጥዎ
creative
-ስ- ኪነ ጥበብ
arterial
አ:'ቲሪየል -ቅ- ዋ'ና ፣ አውራ ፣ የደም ሥር ወገን
artery
'አ:ተሪ -ስ- ት'ልቅ የደም ሥር
artful
'አ:ትፉል -ቅ- ብልኀተ'ኛ ፣ ዘዴ'ኛ ፣ ሎ'ሌ
article
'አ:ቲክል -ስ- ዕቃ
literary
-ስ- ጽሑፍ(ጋዜጣ)
grammatical
-ስ- መስተአ'ምር (ሰዋስው)
articulate
አ:'ቲክዩሌይት -ግ- ግልጽ አድርጎ መ'ናገር [ተና'ገረ]
articulate
አ:'ቲክዩለት -ቅ- ጥሩ ተናጋሪ ፣ ነገር ዐዋቂ
artificial
አ:ቲ'ፊሸል -ቅ- ሰው ሠ'ራሽ
artillery
አ:'ቲለሪ -ስ- መድፈ'ኛ
artisan
'አ:ቲዛን -ስ- በእ'ጅ ሥራ ዕውቀት የሠለ'ጠነ
artist
'አ:ቲስት -ስ- ሠዓሊ ፣ የኪነ ጥበብ ሰው
as
'አዝ -መዩ- እንደ
as...as
-መዩ- ከሆነ
ascend
ኧ'ሴንድ -ግ- መውጣት [ወ'ጣ] (ወደላይ)
ascendancy
ኧ'ሴንደንሲ -ስ- ድል ፣ ሥልጣን፣የበላይ'ነት ፣ መግዛት ፣ የመግዛት ኀይል (ሥልጣን)
ascendant
ኧ'ሴንደንት -ቅ- ወጪ (ወደላይ)
ascension
ኧ'ሴንሽን -ስ- ዕርገት
ascent
ኧ'ሴንት -ስ- መውጣት
ascertain
አሰ'ቴይን -ግ- ማ'ረጋገጥ [አ'ረጋ'ገጠ]
ascetic
አ'ሴቲክ -ቅ- ባሕታዊ
ascribe
ኧስክ'ራይብ -ግ- ማ'ሳበብ [አ'ሳ'በበ] ፣ አንድ ነገር የሌላ መሆኑን መግለጽ [ገ'ለጸ]

ash
’አሽ -ስ- አመድ ፤ የዛፍ ዓይነት
Ash Wednesday
-ስ- የጾመ አርባ መጀ'መሪያ ቀን
ashamed
ኧ’ሼይምድ -ቅ- ያ'ፈረ
ashen
’አሸን -ቅ- የገረ'ጣ (መልክ)
ashore
አ’ሾ፡ -ተግ- በወደብ ላይ ፣ በባሕር ዳር
ash-tray
’አሽ-ትሬይ -ስ- መተርኮሻ (የሲጃራ)
aside
ኧ’ሳይድ -ተግ- በስተጐ'ን
-ስ- የምሥጢር ንግ'ግር
ask
’አ፡ስክ -ግ- መጠ'የቅ [ጠ'የቀ]
askance
ኧስ’ካንስ -ተግ- በመ'ታዘብ
askew
ኧስክ’ዩው -ቅ ፣ ተግ- ጐባጣ
asleep
ኧስ’ሊይፕ -ቅ- የተ'ኛ
aspect
’አስፔክት -ስ- አቅጣ'ጫ ፣ አግጣ'ጫ፤ ትር እይት
aspersion
ኧስ’ፐ፡ሽን -ስ- ስድብ ፣ ሰውን ባልሠ'ራው ሥራ ማ'ዋረድ
asphalt
’አስፎልት -ስ- የሬንጅ'ና የጠጠር ድብ'ልቅ (ለመንገድ መሥሪያ)
asphyxia
ኧስ’ፊክሲየ -ስ- መ'ታፈን (የመ'ታፈን ሞት)
aspirant
’አስፒረንት -ቅ- ከ'ፍ ወዳለ ማዕርግ ለመድ ረስ የ'ሚ'መኝ
-ስ- ከ'ፍ ያለ ም'ኞት ያ'ለው
aspiration
አስፒ’ሬይሽን -ስ- ከ'ፍ ያለ ተስፋ
aspire
አስ’ፓየ -ግ- ከ'ፍ ወዳለ ማዕረግ ፣ ም'ኞት ለመድረስ መ'መኘት [ተ'መኘ]

ass
’አስ -ስ- አህ'ያ
assail
ኧ’ሴይል -ግ- መግጠም[ገ'ጠመ] (ለጦር'ነት) ፤ መ'ጨነቅ [ተጨ'ነቀ] (ፍርሃት)
assailant
ኧ’ሴይለንት -ስ- በኀይል አደጋ የ'ሚጥል ጠ ላት ፣ ተከራካሪ ጠላት
assassin
ኧ’ሳሲን -ስ- ነፍሰ ገዳይ (ሹምን)
assassinate
ኧ’ሳሲኔይት -ግ- መግደል [ገ'ደለ] (ሹምን)
assassination
ኧሳሲ’ኔይሽን -ስ- መግደል (ሹምን)
assault
ኧ’ሶልት -ግ- አደጋ መጣል [ጣለ]
assay
አ’ሴይ -ግ- መሞ'ከር [ሞ'ከረ]
gold
-ግ- መፈ'ተን [ፈ'ተነ] (ወርቅ)
assemble
ኧ’ሴምበል -ግ- መ'ሰብሰብ [ተሰበ'ሰበ]
assembly
ኧ’ሴምብሊ -ስ- ስብሰባ
assent
ኧ’ሴንት -ግ- መስማማት [ተስማ'ማ]
-ስ- ስምም'ነት
assert
ኧ’ሰ፡ት -ግ- መብት እንዲ'ጠ'በቅ'ለት መ'ና ገር [ተና'ገረ]
say
-ግ- ማለት [አለ]
assess
ኧ’ሴስ -ግ- መመርመር [መረ'መረ] ፣ ማ'መ ዛዘን [አ'መዛ'ዘነ]
assets
’አሴትስ -ስ- የተቀ'መጠ ገንዘብ ፣ ዋጋ ያ'ላ' ቸው ንብረቶ'ች
assignment
ኧ’ሳይንመንት -ስ- ተግባር (የ'ሚ'ፈ'ጸም)
assimilate
ኧ’ሲሚሌይት -ግ- መ'ዋሐድ [ተዋሐደ] (እነ ስተ'ኛው ከከ'ፍተ'ኛው)

assist
ኧ'ሲስት -ግ- መርዳት [ረ'ዳ]
associate
ኧ'ሰውሲዩይት -ግ- መ'ተባበር [ተባ'በረ]
-ስ- ጓ'ደ'ኛ ፣ የሥራ ጓ'ደ'ኛ
association
ኧ'ሰውሲዩይሽን -ስ- ማኅበር
assorted
አ'ሶ፡ቲድ -ቅ- ል'ዩ ል'ዩ
assume
ኧስ'ዩ፡ም -ግ- ማ'ሰብ [አ'ሰበ] ፣ መገ'መት [ገ'መተ] ፣ መምሰል [መ'ሰለ]
assurance
ኧ'ሾ፡ረንስ -ስ- ዋስት'ና ፣ መጽናናት
assure
ኧ'ሾ፡ -ግ- ማ'ረጋገጥ [አ'ረጋ'ገጠ]
asterisk
'አስተሪስክ -ስ- ኮከባዊ ምል'ክት (በጽሑፍ)
asthma
'አስመ -ስ- አስም ፣ መተንፈስ የ'ሚያ'ግድ በ'ሽታ
astonish
ኧስ'ቶኒሽ -ግ- መ'ገረም [ተገ'ረመ] ፣ መ'ደነቅ [ተደ'ነቀ]
astonishment
ኧስ'ቶኒሽመንት -ስ- መ'ገረም ፣ መ'ደነቅ
astound
ኧስ'ታውንድ -ግ- መገ'ረም [ተገ'ረመ] ፣ መ'ደነቅ [ተደ'ነቀ]
astray
ኧስት'ሬይ -ተግ- በመጥፋት ፣ በመኰብለል
astride
ኧስት'ራይድ -ተግ- እንፈራ'ጠ (መሄድ ፣ መ'ቀመጥ)
astrology
ኧስት'ሮለጂ -ስ- ኮከብ ቆጠራ
astronomy
ኧስት'ሮነሚ -ስ- የፈለክ ጥናት
astute
ኧስት'ዩ፡ት -ቅ- ብልህ ፣ ሥ'ሉ
asunder
ኧ'ሰንደ -ተግ- ለያይቶ ፣ ተለያይቶ

asylum
ኧ'ሳይለም -ስ- መ'ጠጊያ ፣ መ'ሰደጃ
mental-
-ስ- የእብዶ'ች ሐኪም ቤት
at
'አት -መዋ- በ...
-two o'clock
በሁለ'ት ሰዓት
-home
በቤት ፣ እቤት
-last
በመጨ'ረሻ
-once
ባንድ ጊዜ ፣ ወዲያውኑ
atheism
'ኤይቢይዝም -ስ- ክሂዶተ እግዚአብሔር
atheist
'ኤይቢይስት -ስ- በእግዚአብሔር መኖር የ'ማያምን ሰው
athlete
'አስሊይት -ስ- የስፖርት ሰው ፣ እስፖርተ'ኛ
atlas
'አትለስ -ስ- አትላስ ፣ የዓለምን ካርታ የ'ያዘ መጽሐፍ
atmosphere
'አትመስፊየ -ስ- አ'የር ፣ ነፋስ
atone
ኧ'ተውን -ግ- መ'ታረቂያ መስጠት [ሰ'ጠ] ፣ መካሥ [ካሠ] ፣ መዋገዝት [ዋ'ገዘ]
atrocious
ኧት'ረውሸስ -ቅ- አ'ሠ'ቃቂ
atrocity
ኧት'ሮሲቲ -ስ- አ'ሠ'ቃቂ ወንጀል ወይን'ም ሥራ
attach
ኧ'ታች -ግ- ማ'ጣበቅ [አ'ጣ'በቀ] ፣ ማ'ያያዝ [አ'ያያዘ]
attachment
ኧ'ታችመንት -ስ- የማ'ያያዝ ተግባር ፣ ማ'ያያዝ ፣ አባሪ ጽሑፍ

attack
ኧ'ታክ -ግ- አደጋ መጣል [ጣላ] ፣ መግጠም [ገ'ጠመ] (ጦር'ነት)
of sickness
-ግ- በሽታ መያዝ [ያዘ]
-ስ- አደጋ ፣ መ'ያዝ (በበ'ሽታ)
attain
ኧ'ቴይን -ግ- መድረስ [ደ'ረሰ] (ም'ኞት)
attempt
ኧ'ቴምት -ግ- መሞ'ከር [ሞ'ከረ]
attend
ኧ'ቴንድ -ግ- አተ'ኩሮ ማ'ሰብ [አ'ሰበ]
be present
-ግ- መ'ገኘት [ተገ'ኘ]
wait for
-ግ- መጠ'በቅ [ጠ'በቀ]
function
-ግ- ማሳ'ለፍ [አሳ'ለፈ] (ምግብ ፣ ገብ ኀ)
attendance
ኧ'ቴንደንስ -ስ- በስብሰባ የነ'በረ (ሕዝብ)
attendant
ኧ'ቴንደንት -ስ- አሳ'ላፊ ፣ ቋሚ
attention
ኧ'ቴንሸን -ስ- አተ'ኩሮ ማ'ሰብ
-ግ- ተጠንቀቅ (ትእዛዝ ፣ ለወ'ታ'ደር)
attentive
ኧ'ቴንቲቭ -ቅ- ጥንቁቅ ፣ ንቁ
attenuated
ኧ'ቴንዩዌይተድ -ቅ- መንማ'ና ፣ የከ'ሳ (በበ'ሽታ ምክንያት)
attest
ኧ'ቴስት -ግ- መ'ረጃ መስጠት [ሰ'ጠ] (በፍርድ ቤት)
attic
'አቲክ -ስ- ት'ንሽ ክፍል (ከጣራ በታ'ች)
attire
ኧ'ታየ -ስ- ልብስ
attitude
'አቲትዩ:ድ -ስ- የሰው'ነት አ'ቋቋም ፣ አስተያየት ፣ አስተሳሰብ
attorney
ኧ'ተ:ኒ -ስ- ወ'ኪል (ያንድን ድር'ጅት ጉ'ዳይ የ'ሚፈ'ጽም) ፣ ጠበቃ

attract
ኧት'ራክት -ግ- መሳብ [ሳበ] ፣ አስተያየትን መውሰድ [ወ'ሰደ] ፣ መማረክ [ማ'ረከ]
attribute
'አትሪብዩት -ስ- መ'ታወቂያ ፣ ጠባይ
credit
ኧት'ሪብዩት -ግ- መስጠት [ሰ'ጠ] (የሚ'ገ'ባው መሆኑን በማመን)
auction
'ኦ:ክሸን -ስ- ሀ'ራጅ
auctioneer
ኦ:ክሸ'ኒየ -ስ- ዕቃ በሀ'ራጅ የ'ሚሸጥ
audacious
ኦ:'ዴይሸስ -ቅ- ደ'ፋር ፣ ጉበዝ
audacity
ኦ:'ዳሲቲ -ስ- ድፍረት ፣ ጉብዝ'ና
audible
'ኦ:ዲበል -ቅ- የ'ሚ'ሰ'ማ
audience
'ኦ:ዲየንስ -ስ- ተመልካች (ሕዝብ)
audit
'ኦ:ዲት -ግ- መ'ቆጣጠር [ተቆጣ'ጠረ]
audition
ኦ:'ዲሸን -ስ- መፈ'ተን (ቲያትር ሠ'ራተ'ኞን)
auditor
'ኦ:ዲተ -ስ- ሒሳብ ተቆጣጣሪ
auditorium
ኦ:ዲ'ቶ:ሪየም -ስ- ታ'ላቅ አ'ዳራሽ (የሙዚቃ የንግ'ግር)
augment
ኦ:ግ'ሜንት -ግ- ማብዛት [አበ'ዛ] ፣ ከ'ፍ ማድረግ [አደ'ረገ] (በመጠን ፣ በቁጥር)
august
ኦ:'ገስት -ቅ- የተከ'በረ ፣ ባለግርማ
August
'ኦ:ገስት -ስ- ነሐሴ
aunt
'አ:ንት -ስ- አክስት
auspices
'ኦ:ስፒሲዝ -ስ- ተጠባባቂ'ነት ፣ መሪ'ነት ፣ ረዳት'ነት
auspicious
ኦ:ስ'ፒሸስ -ቅ- ባለተስፋ

austere
አስ'ቲየ -ቅ- ያላጌጠ ፣ ተራ
authentic
አ:'ፁንቲክ -ቅ- እውነተ'ኛ ፣ ማ'ታለል የሌ'ለ'በት
author
'አ:ሷ -ስ- ደራሲ
authoritative
አ:'ሮረተቲቭ -ቅ- ሥልጣን የተመረ'ኰዘ ፣ ባለሥልጣን ፣ እምነት የ'ሚ'ጣል'በት
authority
አ:'ሮረቲ -ስ- ሥልጣን
authorize
'አ:ሷራይዝ -ግ- ሥልጣን መስጠት [ሰ'ጠ]
autobiography
አ:ተባ'ዮግረፊ -ስ- በባለቤቱ የተጻፈ የራስ ታሪክ
autocracy
ኦ'ቶክረሲ -ስ- ለሥልጣኑ ወሰን የሌ'ለው ያንድ ሰው አስተዳደር (የመንግሥት)
autograph
'አ:ተግራፍ -ስ- ፊርማ ፣ ያንድ ሰው የራሱ የእ'ጅ ጽሑፍ
automatic
አ:ተ'ማቲክ -ቅ- አውቶማቲክ ፣ በራሱ የ'ሚ ሠራ
autonomous
አ:'ቶነመስ -ቅ- ነጻ (መንግሥት)
autonomy
አ:'ቶነሚ -ስ- ነጻ'ነት ያ'ለው (መንግሥት)
autumn
'አ:ተም -ስ- መፀው (በእንግሊዝ አገር መስከረም'ና ጥቅምት) ፣ በልግ (በኢትዮ'ጵያ)
auxilliary
አ:ክ'ዚልየሪ -ቅ- ረዳ ፣ አባሪ ፣ መ'ጠባበቂያ
avail
አቬይል -ግ- መርዳት [ረ'ዳ] ፣ ራስን ለርዳታ ማ'ዘጋጀት [አ'ዘጋ'ጀ]
available
አ'ቬለበል -ቅ- የ'ሚ'ገ'ኝ ፣ ለማግኘት የ'ማያስቸ'ግር
avarice
'አቨሪስ -ስ- የገንዘብ ጉ'ጉት ፣ ንፍገት

avenge
አ'ቬንጅ -ግ- መ'በቀል [ተበ'ቀለ]
avenue
'አቬንዩ -ስ- ጐዳና
average
'አቨረጅ -ስ- መካ'ከለኛ ፣ እማካ'ኝ ፣ ል'ዩ ል'ዩ ቁጥሮ'ች ተደ'ምረው በብዛታ'ቸው ሲ'ከ'ፈል የ'ሚደርሰው (ምሳሌ፣ 4+5+9=18÷3=6)
averse
አ'ቨ:ስ -ቅ- የሚጠላ ፣ ጠዬ
aversion
አ'ቨ:ሽን -ስ- ጥላ'ቻ
avert
አ'ቨ:ት -ግ- ማ'ገድ [አ'ገደ] (ለአደጋ) ፣ ማስወ'ገድ [አስወ'ገደ]
aviary
'ኤይቪየሪ -ስ- የተሰበ'ሰቡ ሕይወት ያ'ላ'ቸው ወፎ'ች ፣ የወፍ ጎ'ጆ
aviation
ኤይቪ'ዬይሽን -ስ- አቪያሲዮን ፣ የመብረር ጥበብ
avid
'አቪድ -ቅ- ጉ'ጉ ፣ ጠንካ'ራ ምኞ'ት ያ'ለው
avoid
አ'ቮይድ -ግ- ራስን መከልከል [ከለ'ከለ] ፣ በጉ'ዳዩ አለመግባት [-ገ'ባ] አንድ ነገር እንዳ ይደርስ ገለ'ል ማለት [አለ]
avow
አ'ቫው -ግ- በሐሳብ ድ'ርቅ ማለት [አለ] ፣ አንድ ነገር ለመተው መ'ሣል [ተሣለ] ፣ መማል [ማለ]
await
አ'ዌይት -ግ- አንድ ነገር መጠ'በቅ [ጠ'በቀ] (ይደርሳል ብሎ)
awake
አ'ዌይክ -ግ- መ'ነሣት [ተነ'ሣ] ፣ መንቃት [ነ'ቃ] (ከመ'ኝታ)
-ቅ- ንቁ
award
አ'ዎ:ድ -ግ- መሸ'ለም [ሸ'ለመ]
aware
አ'ዌየ -ቅ- የ'ሚያውቅ ፣ የተጠነ'ቀቀ
away
አ'ዌይ -ተግ- ወዲያ

awe
'አ፡ -ስ- አክብሮት
awful
'አ፡ፉል -ቅ- አስፈ'ሪ ፣ የ'ሚያስጠ'ላ
awfully
'አ፡ፈሊ -ተግ- በጣም ፣ ከፉ'ኛ
awhile
አ'ዋይል -ተግ- ጥቂት ጊዜ ፣ እንዳፍታ
awkward
'አ፡ክወድ -ቅ- አ'ዋኪ ፣ አስፈ'ሪ (ለሁኔቱ)
awl
'አ፡ል -ስ- መብሻ ፣ መሰርሰሪያ ብረት

awning
'አ፡ኒንግ -ስ- ዳስ ፣ ከለላ
awry
አ'ራይ -ቅ- ዝብርቅርቅ
axe
'አክስ -ስ- መጥረቢያ ፣ ጥ'ል'ቆ ፣ ፋስ
axle
'አክሰል -ስ- መንኮራኩሮ'ች የ'ሚይዝ ጋድ ሚያ ብረት
azure
'አዠዩር -ቅ- ሰማያዊ

B

babble
'ባበል -ግ- መለፍለፍ [ለፈ'ለፈ] ፤ ማልጎም ጎም [አልጎመ'ጎመ]
baboon
በ'ቡን -ስ- ግመሬ ዝንጀሮ
baby
'ቤይቢ -ስ- ሕፃን
babyish
'ቤይቢይሽ -ቅ- ያልበ'ሰለ (ለሰው)፣ የልጅ 'ነት ጠባይ ያ'ለው
baby-sitter
'ቤይቢ ሲተ -ስ- ሕፃናት ጠ'ባቂ (ወላጆ'ች በሌ'ሉ ጊዜ)
bachelor
'ባቸለ -ስ- ያላገ'ባ ፣ ወንደላ'ጤ
back
'ባክ -ስ- ጀርባ
-ተግ- ወደ ኋላ
-ቅ- የኋላ ፤ ዘመናዊ ያልሆነ ፤ ወደኋላ የቀ'ረ ፤ ዝ'ቅተ'ኛ
backbite
'ባክባይት -ስ- ሐሜት
backbone
'ባክበውን -ስ- ደንደ'ስ ፤ የ'ማያወላ'ውል ጠባይ፣ ያንድ ነገር ዋ'ናው ክፍል

background
'ባክግራውንድ -ስ- በስተኋላ ያ'ለ ነገር (የሥ ዕል ፣ የፎቶግራፍ) ፤ ቤተሰብ ፣ አስተዳደግ ወዘተ
backward
'ባክወድ -ቅ- ያልሠለ'ጠነ ፣ ወደኋላ የቀ'ረ
backwards
'ባክወድዝ -ተግ- ወደኋላ ፣ የኋሊት
backwater
'ባክዎ፡ተ -ስ- በወንዝ አጠገብ የ'ሚ'ገ'ኝ የረ '.ጋ ኩሬ (ወንዙ የ'ማይደርስ'በት)
bacon
'ቤይከን -ስ- በእንፋሎት የደ'ረቀ ያሣማ ሥጋ
bacteria
ባክ'ቲሪየ -ስ- በ'ሽታ የ'ሚያመጡ ጥቃ'ቅን ፍጥረቶ'ች
bad
'ባድ -ቅ- መጥፎ ፣ ክፉ
badge
'ባጅ -ስ- የመ'ለያ ምል'ክት ፣ መ'ለ'ዮ (በል ብስ ላይ ፣ በባርኔጣ ላይ ወዘተ)
badger
'ባጀ -ግ- መጨቅጨቅ [ጨቀ'ጨቀ] ፣ መጎት ጎት [ጐተ'ጐተ]
baffle
'ባፈል -ግ- ማስቸ'ገር [አስቸ'ገረ] ፣ ማ'ወክ [አ'ወከ] ፣ መጽነን [ጸ'ነነ]
-ስ- ክል'ል ፣ ጋርዶሽ

bag
'ባግ -ስ- ከረጢት ፣ አቅማዳ

baggage
'ባጊጅ -ስ- የጉዞ ዕቃ

bail
'ቤይል -ግ- በመ'ዋስ ማስለ'ቀቅ [አስለ'ቀቀ] (እስረ'ኛን) -ስ- መ'ተማመኛ ገንዘብ

bait
'ቤይት -ስ- የሀሣ ማጥመጃ ምግብ ፣ ወጥመድ (ሥዕላዊ)

bake
'ቤይክ -ግ- መጋገር [ጋ'ገረ]

baker
'ቤይከ -ስ- ዳ'ቦ ፣ እንጀራ ጋጋሪ

bakery
'ቤይከሪ -ስ- ዳ'ቦ መጋገሪያ (ሱቅ ፣ ቦታ)

balance
'ባለንስ -ግ- መመ'ዘን [መ'ዘነ]
-ስ- ሚዛን

balcony
'ባልከኒ -ስ- ሰገ'ነት

bald
'ቦ:ልድ -ቅ- መላጣ ፣ በራ ራስ ፣ ራሰ በራ

baldness
'ቦ:ልድነስ -ስ- መላጣ'ነት ፣ በራ'ነት

baleful
'ቤይልፉል -ቅ- በጥላ'ቻ የተመ'ላ

baulk
'ቦ:ልክ -ግ- ማ'ደናቀፍ [አደና'ቀፈ]
-ስ- የተቆ'ረጠ ግንድ

ball
'ቦ:ል -ስ- ኳስ

ballad
'ባለድ -ስ- ከጥንት የመ'ጣ ዘፈን ፣ ግጥም ፣ ተረት (በግጥም መልክ)

ballet
'ባሌ -ስ- በውዝ'ዋዜ የ'ሚ'ገ'ለጽ ቲያትር (በሙዚቃ የታ'ጀበ)

balloon
በ'ሉ:ን -ስ- የተነ'ፋ ቆዳ ወይን'ም ላስቲክ

ballot
'ባለት -ስ- የምርጫ ካርድ ፣ ወረቀት

ballpoint
'ቦ:ልፖይንት -ስ- እስክሪፕቶ ፣ የጭቃ ብዕር

balm
'ባ:ም -ስ- የእበጥ ፣ የቁስል ቅባት

balustrade
'ባሉስትሬይድ -ስ- በግራ'ና በቀ'ኝ ያ'ለ የመ'ወጣጫ መ'ደገፊያ ፣ በሰገ'ነት ላይ ያ'ለ መ'ደገፊያ

bamboo
ባም'ቡ: -ስ- ሸመል ፣ ቀርከሃ

ban
'ባን -ግ- ማቆም [አቆመ] ፣ መከልከል [ከለ'ከለ] (አንድ ድር'ጅት ፣ ነገር ወዘተ እንዳይቀ'ጥል)
-ስ- ማ'ገጃ ሕ'ግ

banal
በ'ናል -ቅ- ተራ ፣ ል'ዩ ያልሆነ ፣ አስተያየት የ'ማይማ'ርክ

banana
በ'ና:ነ -ስ- ሙዝ

band
'ባንድ -ስ- ስብስባ ፣ የሙዚቃ ጓ'ድ ፣ መጠቅለያ (የወረቀት ፣ የሻሽ)

bandage
'ባንዲጅ -ስ- የቁስል መጠቅለያ ፣ የቁስል ማሰሪያ (ሻሽ)

bandit
'ባንዲት -ስ- ሽፍታ ፣ ወምበዴ ፣ ቀ'ማ'ኛ

baneful
'ቤይንፉል -ቅ- ክፉ ፣ መጥፎ ፣ ጐጂ

bang
'ባንግ -ግ- ድ'ም ማለት [አለ]
-ስ- ከ'ፍ ያለ ድምፅ

bangle
'ባንገል -ስ- አምባር

banish
'ባኒሽ -ግ- ማጋዝ [አጋዘ] (እሥር ቤት)

banishment
'ባኒሽመንት -ስ- ግዞት

banister
'ባኒስተ -ስ- የቤት ደረ'ጃ ገደብ

bank
'ባንክ -ስ- በወንዝ ዳር'ቻ ያፈር ፣ ያሸዋ ቁ'ልል
money
-ስ- ባንክ (የገንዘብ)

bankrupt

'ባንክረፕት -ስ- መክሰሩን ሕ'ግ ያ'ረጋ'ገጠ'ለት ሰው ፣ ንብረቱ ተሸጦ ለእዳ እንዲ'ከፈ'ል የተወ'ሰነ'በት ሰው

-ቅ- እዳውን መክፈል የ'ማይችል

bankruptcy

'ባንክረፕሲ -ስ- ክሳራ ፣ መክሰር

banner

'ባነ -ስ- ሰን'ደቅ ዓላማ ፣ የጨርቅ ምል'ክት (በሰልፍ)

banquet

'ባንክዊት -ስ- ግብር (ግብዣ)

bantam

'ባንተም -ስ- ል'ዩ ዓይነት ትን'ንሽ ዶሮ

banter

'ባንተ -ስ- ቀልዳቀልድ

baptism

'ባፕቲዝም -ስ- ጥምቀት (ሥርዓቱ)

baptize

ባፕ'ታይዝ -ግ- ማጥመቅ [አጠ'መቀ] ፣ ክርስት'ና ማንሣት [አነ'ሣ]

bar

'ባ: -ግ- መከልከል [ከለ'ከለ] ፣ ማ'ገድ [አ'ገደ]

pole

-ስ- ማ'ገጃ ብረት

drinking

-ስ- መጠጥ ቤት ፣ መሸታ ቤት ፣ ቡ'ና ቤት

barb

'ባ:ብ -ስ- የመንጠ'ቆ ፣ የፍላ'ፃ ጫፍ (ወደኋላ የተመ'ለሰው ስለት)

barbarian

ባ:'ቤሪየን -ስ- አረመኔ (ሰው)

barbaric

ባ:'ባሪክ -ቅ- አረመኔ\(ተግባር)

barbarity

ባ:'ባሪቲ -ስ- አረመኔ'ነት

barbarous

'ባ:በረስ -ቅ- ያልሠለ'ጠነ ፣ ጨ'ካኝ

barbecue

'ባ:ቢክዩ -ስ- የፍም ጥብስ (ከቤት ው'ጭ የ'ሚ'ጠ'በስ)

barber

'ባ:በ -ስ- ጠጉር ቆራጭ ፣ ጠጉር አስተካካይ ፣ ጢም ላጭ

bare

'ቤየ -ቅ- ባዶ ፣ የተራ'ቆተ ፣ ያልተሸ'ፈነ ፣ ገላጣ ፣ ለች'ግር ያህል የ'ሚበቃ

barely

'ቤሊ -ተግ- በጥቂቱ ፣ በጭረፍታ ፣ በግልጥ ፣ በይፋ

bargain

'ባ:ጊን -ግ- ዋጋ መ'ከራከር [ተከራ'ከረ] በዋጋ ውጣ ውረድ ማለት [አለ]

-ስ- የዋጋ ክር'ክር ፣ የዋጋ ውጣ ውረድ

barge

'ባ:ጅ -ስ- ታንኳ ፣ ት'ንሽ መርከብ .

bark

'ባ:ክ -ግ- መጮኸ [ጮኸ] (ለው'ሻ)

-ስ- የው'ሻ ጩኸት

of tree

-ስ- ልጥ (የዛፍ)

barley

'ባ:ሊ -ስ- ገብስ

barn

'ባ:ን -ስ- ጎተራ

barometer

በ'ሮመተ -ስ- ባሮሜትር (ያ'የር መለ'ኪያ መ'ሣሪያ)

baron

'ባረን -ስ- «ባሮን» (ዝ'ቅተ'ኛ የሹመት ስም)

barrack

'ባረክ -ስ- የወ'ታ'ደር'ች መኖሪያ ቤት ፣ የወ'ታ'ደር ሠፈር

heckle

-ግ- መበጥበጥ [በጠ'በጠ] ፣ ማ'ወክ [አ'ወከ] (በንግ'ግር ጊዜ)

barrage

'ባራ:ጅ -ስ- የተፋፋመ ተኩስ (ወደ አንድ አቅጣ'ጫ የ'ሚ'ተ'ኮስ)

river

-ስ- ግ'ድብ (የውሃ)

barrel

'ባረል -ስ- በርሜል (በተለ'ይ የእንጨት) ፣ አፈሙዝ (ጠመንጃ)

barren
'ባረን -ት- ድርቅ (አገር)
of female
-ት- መሃን ፣ መ'ካን

barricade
ባሪ'ኬይድ -ስ- መ'ሸሸጊያ ፣ መ'ከላከያ ፣ መሰ ናከል (ለጦር'ነት)

barrier
'ባሪየ -ስ- ማ'ገጃ

barrister
'ባሪስተ -ስ- የሕ'ግ ጠበቃ

barter
'ባ:ተ -ግ- መ'ላወጥ [ተላ'ወጠ] (ለንግድ ፣ ም'ሳሌ ዕቃ በቃ)

base
'ቤይስ -ስ- መሠረት ፣ መሥፈሪያ ቦታ ፣ ሠፈር
low
-ት- ወ'ራ'ዳ

baseless
'ቤይስለስ -ት- መሠረተቢስ ፣ መሠረት የሌ 'ለው

basement
'ቤይስመንት -ስ- ከፎቅ ቤት በታ'ች ያ'ለ ክፍል

baseness
'ቤይስነስ -ስ- ወ'ራ'ዳ'ነት

bashful
'ባሽፉል -ት- ተሽኮርማሚ ፣ አ'ፋር

basic
'ቤይሲክ -ት- መሠረታዊ

basin
'ቤይሰን -ስ- ጎድጓ'ዳ ሳሕን ፣ ገበታ (ማቡ ኪያ) ፣ ገንዳ

basis
'ቤይሲስ -ስ- መሠረት

bask
'ባ:ስክ -ግ- መ'ዘረር [ተዘ'ረረ] (እፀሐይ ላይ)

basket
'ባ:ስኪት -ስ- ቅርጫት

bass
'ቤይስ -ት- ዝ'ቅተ'ኛ (ለድምፅ)፣ ዝ'ቅተ'ኛ የድ ምፅ ስልት

bastard
'ባ:ስተድ -ስ- ዲቃላ
colloquial
-ስ- የታ'ባ'ከ

baste
'ቤይስት -ግ- ቅባት ማፍሰስ [አፈ'ሰሰ] (በጥ ብስ ሥጋ ላይ)

bat
'ባት -ስ- ገ'ና (ለጨዋታ)
animal
-ስ- የሌሊት ወፍ

batch
'ባች -ስ- ስብስብ ፣ ቁ'ልል

bath
'ባ:ሰ -ግ- ሰው'ነትን መ'ታ'ጠብ [ታ'ጠበ]
-ስ- መ'ታጠቢያ ክፍል ፣ ባ'ኞ

bathe
'ቤይዘ -ግ- በውሃ ማጠብ [አ'ጠበ] ፣ መዋ ኘት [ዋ'ኘ]

bather
'ቤይዘ -ስ- ዋኝ ፣ ዋነተ'ኛ

bathroom
'ባ:ሰሩም -ስ- የመ'ታጠቢያ ክፍል ፣ መ'ታጠ ቢያ ቤት

baton
'ባተን -ስ- አ'ጭር በ'ትር

battalion
በ'ታልየን -ስ- የሻለቃ ጦር

batter
'ባተ -ግ- መቀርቀር [ቀረ'ቀረ] ፣ መምታት [መ'ታ] (ለበ'ር)
-ስ- የዕንቁላል'ና የዱቄት ድብ'ልቅ

battery
'ባተሪ -ስ- የኤሌክትሪክ ኀይል የተከማ'ቸ'በት ዕቃ ፣ የባትሪ ደንጊያ

battle
'ባተል -ስ- ጦር'ነት ፣ ው'ጊያ

bawl
'ቦ:ል -ግ- መጮኽ [ጮኸ] ፣ ማልቀስ [አለ'ቀሰ] (በከ'ፍተ'ኛ ድምፅ)

bay
ቤይ -ግ- መጮኽ [ጮኸ] (ለእንስሳት)
geographical
-ስ- የባሕር ወሽመጥ

bayonet
'ቤየኔት -ስ- ሳንጃ

bazaar
በ'ዛ፡ -ስ- የገበያቦታ ፣ ሱቆ'ች የ'ሚ'ገ'ኙ'በት የከተማ ክፍል ፤ የብዙ ል'ዩ ል'ዩ ዕቃዎ'ች ር'ካሽ ሽ'ያጭ

be
'ቢይ -ግ- መሆን [ሆነ]

beach
'ቢይች -ስ- የባሕር ፣ የሐይቅ ዳር

beacon
'ቢይከን -ስ- በተራራ ጫፍ ላይ ያ'ለ እሳት (ለምል'ክት)

bead
'ቢይድ -ስ- ዶቃ ፣ ማርዳ (እንዱ እንክብ'ል)፣ ጤ'ሎ

beak
'ቢይክ -ስ- የወፍ አፍ

beaker
'ቢይከ -ስ- ት'ልቅ ብርጭ'ቆ (ከፉ ላይ ባንድ ወገን ወጣ ያለ ከንፈር ያ'ለው)

beam
'ቢይም -ስ- አግዳሚ ፣ ተሸካሚ ፣ ወፍራም አራት ማዕዘን'ነት ያ'ለው እንጨት

bean
'ቢይን -ስ- ባቄላ

bear
'ቤየ -ስ- ድ'ብ
carry
-ግ- መ'ሸከም [ተሸ'ከመ]

bearable
'ቤረበል -ቅ- የ'ማያ'ውክ ፣ ቀ'ላል

beard
'ቢየድ -ስ- ጢም

bearer
'ቤረ -ስ- ተሸ'ካሚ ፣ ኩሊ ፣ ሽ'ቃይ ፣ ሐ'ማል

bearing
'ቤሪንግ -ስ- አቋ'ቋም ፤ ጠባይ ፤ ተሸ'ካሚ ብረት ፣ ኩሺኔ'ታ (የመኪና)

beast
'ቢይስት -ስ- አውሬ

beastly
'ቢይስትሊ -ቅ- ያውሬ'ነት ጠባይ ያ'ለው ፣ አስቀ'ያሚ

beat
'ቢይት -ግ- መምታት [መ'ታ]
at sport
-ግ- ማ'ሸ'ነፍ [አ'ሸ'ነፈ]

beautiful
ብ'ዩቲፉል -ቅ- ቆንጆ'፣ ውብ ፣ ያማረ

beauty
ብ'ዩ፡ቲ -ስ- ቁንጅ'ና

because
ቢ'ኮዝ መዩ ፣ ተግ- ስለ ፣ በ . . . ምክንያት

beckon
'ቤከን -ግ- መጥቀስ [ጠ'ቀሰ] (በእ'ጅ ፣ በራስ)

become
በ'ከም -ግ- መሆን [ሆነ]

becoming
በ'ከሚንግ -ቅ- ቆንጆ ፣ ውብ

bed
'ቤድ -ስ- አልጋ

bedding
'ቤዲንግ -ስ- ያልጋ ልብስ

bedeck
በ'ዴክ -ግ- ማስጌጥ [አስጌጠ]

bedroom
'ቤድሩም -ስ- መ'ኝታ ቤት

bee
'ቢይ -ስ- ንብ

beef
'ቢይፍ -ስ- የበሬ ፣ የላም ሥጋ

beehive
'ቢሐይቭ -ስ- የንብ ቀፎ

beer
'ቢየ -ስ- ጠ'ላ ፣ ቢራ

beeswax
'ቢይዝዋክስ -ስ- የማር ሰፈፍ

beetle
'ቢይትል -ስ- ጢንዚ'ዛ

befall
በ'ፎ፡ል -ግ- መሆን [ሆነ] ፣ መድረስ [ደ'ረሰ] (ሁኔቱ)

before
በፎ፡ -ተግ- በፊት ፤ አስቀ'ድሞ
in time
-መዋ- ከ . . . በፊት

befriend
በፍ'ሬንድ -ግ- መ'ወዳጀት [ተወዳ'ጀ]
beg
'ቤግ -ግ- መለመን [ለ'መነ] ፥ መቧገት [ቧ'ገተ]
beggar
'ቤገ -ስ- ለ'ማኝ ፥ ቧጋች
begin
ቢ'ጊን -ግ- መጀ'መር [ጀ'መረ]
beginner
ቢ'ጊነ -ስ- ጀ'ማሪ ፥ አላዋቂ
beginning
ቢ'ጊኒንግ -ስ- መጀ'መርያ
begrudge
ቢገ'ረጅ -ግ- መ'መቅኘት [ተመቀ'ኘ] ፥ መንቆጥቆጥ [ተንቆጠ'ቆጠ] (ለመስጠት)
beguile
ቢ'ጋይል -ግ- ማ'ታለል [አ'ታ'ለለ] ፥ ማ'ወና'በድ [አ'ወና'በደ]
behalf
ቢ'ሃ፡ፍ -ስ- ፈንታ
behave
ቢ'ሄይቭ -ግ- ራስን መምራት [መ'ራ] ፥ ራስን ከክፉ ሥራ ማራቅ [አራቀ]
behaviour
ቢ'ሄቭየ -ስ- ጠባይ
behead
ቢ'ሄድ -ግ- መሰ'የፍ [ሰየፈ] (የሰውን ራስ)
behind
በ'ሃይንድ -ተግ- ወደኋላ
-መዋ፣ ከ . . . ኋላ
behold
በ'ሆውልድ -ግ- መ'መልከት [ተመለ'ከተ]
exclamation
-ቃአ- እ'ነሆ
being
'ቢይንግ -ስ- ሕያው ፍጡ'ር
belch
'ቤልች -ግ- ማገሳት [አገ'ሳ] (ከመጥገብ የተነ'ሣ)
-ስ- ግሳት
belief
በ'ሊይፍ -ስ- እምነት ፥ ሃይማኖት

believe
በ'ሊይቭ -ግ- ማመን [አ'መነ]
bell
'ቤል -ስ- ደወል ፥ ቃጭል
belligerent
በ'ሊጀረንት -ቅ- ጠበ'ኛ ፥ በጥባጭ
bellow
'ቤለው -ግ- እንደ በሬ ማገሳት [አገ'ሳ] ፥ በቁ'ጣ መጮኸ [ጮኸ]
bellows
'ቤለውዝ -ስ- ወናፍ
belly
'ቤሊ -ስ- ሆድ ፥ ከርስ
belong
በ'ሎንግ -ግ- መ'ገናዘብ [ተገና'ዘበ]
belongings
በ'ሎንጊንግዝ -ስ- ንብረት ፥ ዕቃ
beloved
በ'ለቭድ -ቅ- ው'ድ ፥ የተወ'ደደ
below
በ'ለው -ተግ- በታ'ች
belt
'ቤልት -ስ- ቀበ'ቶ ፥ መ'ታጠቂያ
bench
'ቤንች -ስ- ረ'ጅም ወምበር ፥ አግዳሚ ወምበር
bend
'ቤንድ -ግ- መጉበጥ [ጎ'በጠ]
of road
-ስ- መ'ጠምዘዣ መንገድ ፥ ትክ'ክል ያልሆነ ፥ ጎባጣ መንገድ
beneath
በ'ኒይስ -ተግ- በታ'ች
benediction
ቤኔዲክሽን -ስ- ቡራኬ ፥ ጸሎተ ቡራኬ
benefactor
'ቤነፋክተ -ስ- ቸር ሰው ፥ መጽዋች (ገንዘብ የ'ሚሰጥ) ፥ በ'ጎ አድራጊ
beneficial
ቤነ'ፊሽል -ቅ- ደ'ግ ፥ ጥሩ
benefit
'ቤነፊት -ግ- ማትረፍ [አተ'ረፈ] ፥ መ'ጠቀም [ተጠ'ቀመ]
-ስ- ጥቅም

benevolent
በ'ኔቨለንት -ቅ- ለሌሎ'ች በ'ጎ አድራጊ

benign
በ'ናይን -ቅ- ርኅሩኅ ፣ ቸር

benzine
'ቤንዚን -ስ- ቤንዚን ፣ ነዳጅ

bequeathe
ቢክ'ዊይዝ -ግ- ማውረስ [አወ'ረሰ]

bequest
ቢክ'ዌስት -ስ- ውርስ ዕቃ ፣ ገንዘብ

bereaved
በ'ሪቭድ -ቅ- ሐዘንተ'ኛ
-ስ- ሐዘንተ'ኛ

berry
'ቤሪ -ስ- እንጆ'ሪ

berth
'በ፡ስ -ስ- መ'ኝታ ቦታ (በመርከብ ላይ)

beseech
ቢ'ሲይች -ግ- መለ'መን [ለ'መነ]፣ መ'ለማመጥ [ተለማ'መጠ]

beside
በ'ሳይድ -መዋ- በ . . . አጠገብ
-me
በኔ አጠገብ

besides
በ'ሳይድዝ -ተግ- ደግሞ ፣ ከ'ዚህ በላይ

besiege
ቢ'ሲይጅ -ግ- መከበብ (ለጦር'ነት)

best
'ቤስት -ቅ- የበ'ለጠ ፣ ተወዳዳሪ የሌ'ለው

bestial
'ቤስቲየል -ቅ- አረመኔ ፣ ጨ'ካኝ ፣ ሰብአዊ ስ'ሜቱን የተገ'ፈፈ ፣ እራዊት መሰ'ል

bestow
በስ'ተው -ግ- መስጠት [ሰ'ጠ] (ከበላይ)

bet
'ቤት -ግ- መ'ወራረድ [ተወራ'ረደ]
-ስ- ውር'ርድ

betray
በት'ሬይ -ግ- መክዳት [ከ'ዳ] ፣ አሳ'ልፎ መስጠት [ሰ'ጠ] (ለጠላት)

betrayal
በት'ሬየል -ስ- ክዳት ፣ አሳ'ልፎ መስጠት

betroth
በት'ረውዝ -ግ- ማጨት [አ'ጨ]

betrothal
በት'ረውዝል -ስ- ማጨት ፣ ቀለበት ማድረግ (ለእጮ'ኛ)

better
'ቤተ -ቅ- የተሻለ

between
በት'ዊይን -መዋ- በ . . . መካ'ከል

bevel
'ቤቨል -ስ- በሰ'ያፍ የተቆ'ረጠ ነገር

beverage
'ቤቨሪጅ -ስ- መጠ'ጥ (ሙቅ)

bevy
'ቤቪ -ስ- ስብሰባ (በተለ'ይ የሴቶ'ች)

bewail
ቢ'ዌይል -ግ- ማልቀስ [አለ'ቀሰ]፣ ወይ ማለት [አለ]

beware
ቢ'ዌየ -ግ- መ'ጠንቀቅ [ተጠነ'ቀቀ]

bewilder
ቢ'ዊልደ -ግ- ማስጨ'ነቅ [አስጨ'ነቀ] ፣ ማ'ደናገር [አ'ደና'ገረ]

bewitch
ቢ'ዊች -ግ- በአስማት ማደንዘዝ [አደነ'ዘዘ]

beyond
ቢ'ዮንድ -መዋ- በስተኋላ ፣ አልፎ

bias
'ባየስ -ስ- ማዘንበል ፣ ወዳንድ ወገን ማድላት ፣ ጠማማ ፍርድ ፣ አድልዎ

bib
'ቢብ -ስ- በሕፃናት አንገት ላይ የ'ሚ'ታ'ሰር ፎጣ ወይን'ም መሐ'ረም

Bible
'ባይበል -ስ- መጽሐፍ ቅ'ዱስ

biblical
'ቢብሊክል -ቅ- የመጽሐፍ ቅ'ዱስ

bibliographical
ቢብሊዮግ'ራፊክል -ቅ- የመጻሕፍት ዝርዝር

bibliography
ቢብሊ'ዮግረፊ -ስ- የመጻሕፍት ዝርዝር

biceps
'ባይሴፕስ -ስ- ጡንቻ (የእ'ጅ)

bicker
'ቢከ -ግ- ላ'ረባ ነገር መጨ'ቃጨቅ [ተጨ ቃ'ጨቀ]

bicycle
'ባይሲክል -ስ- ቢስኪሌት

bid
'ቢድ -ግ- ዋጋ መንገር [ነ'ገረ]
-ስ- መግገር ዋጋ

bier
'ቢየ -ስ- ቃሬዛ

big
'ቢግ -ቅ- ት'ልቅ ፣ ታ'ላቅ

bigamy
'ቢገሚ -ስ- ሁለ'ት ሴት ማግባት ፣ በሚስት ላይ ሁለ'ተ'ኛ ሴት የማግባት ወንጀል

bigoted
'ቢገተድ -ቅ- ዐዋቂ ነ'ኝ ባይ ፣ ጠ'ባብ አስተ ያየት ያ'ለው ፣ ች'ኮ

bilateral
ባይ'ላተረል -ቅ- ከሁለ'ት ወገን ፣ ሁለ'ቱን ወገን የ'ሚነካ

bile
'ባይል -ስ- ሐሞት ፣ ቋ'ጣ

bilingual
ባይ'ሊንግዮወል -ቅ- ሁለ'ት ቋንቋዎ'ች አስተ ካክሎ የ'ሚ'ና'ገር

bill
'ቢል -ስ- ደ'ረሰ'ኝ ፣ ሒሳብ

billet
'ቢለት -ስ- የወ'ታ'ደር ቤት፣የንጨት ቁ'ራጭ

billion
'ቢልየን -ስ- ቢልዮን (ሚሊዮን ጊዜ ሚሊ ዮን)

billow
'ቢለው -ስ- ማዕበል

billy-goat
'ቢሊ ገውት -ስ- ወንድ ፍ'የል

bin
'ቢን -ስ- የእንጀራ ፣ የጥራጥሬ ወዘተ ማስቀ 'መጫ በርሜል

bind
'ባይንድ -ግ- ማሰር [አ'ሰረ]

binder
'ባይንደ -ስ- ጠ'ራዥ ፣ ደ'ጓሽ ፣ የመ'ገ'ረዣ ዕቃ

binding
'ባይንዲንግ -ስ- ጥራዝ

biography
ባ'የግረፊ -ስ- የሕይወት ታሪክ

biology
ባ'የለጂ -ስ- ሕይወት ያ'ላ'ቸው ፍጡሮ'ች ጥናት ፣ ባዮሎጂ

birch
'በ:ች -ስ- ል'ምጭ

bird
'በ:ድ -ስ- ወፍ

birth
'በ:ዝ -ስ- ልደት

birthday
'በ:ዝዴይ -ስ- የልደት በዓል

birthmark
'በ:ዝማ:ክ -ስ- ማርያም የሳመ'ችው ምል'ክት (በሰው'ነት ላይ)

birthplace
'በ:ዝፕሌይስ -ስ- የተወ'ለዱ'በት አገር

biscuit
'ቢስኪት -ስ- ብስኩት

bisect
'ባይ'ሴክት -ግ- ለሁለ'ት ትክ'ክል ክፍሎ'ች መክፈል [ከ'ፈለ] (በመቁረጥ)

bishop
'ቢሸፕ -ስ- ጳ'ጳስ

bit
'ቢት -ስ- ቁ'ራሽ
horse's
-ስ- ልጓም

bitch
'ቢች -ስ- ሴት ው'ሻ

bite
'ባይት -ግ- መንከስ [ነ'ከሰ]፣ መንደፍ [ነ'ደፈ]

biting
ባ'ይቲንግ -ቅ- ብርዳም ነፋስ
of comment
-ቅ- የ'ሚያሳ'ዝን ነቀፌታ

bitter
'ቢተ -ቅ- መራራ

black
ብ'ላክ -ቅ- ጥቁር

black-beetle
ብ'ላክቢተል -ስ- ጥቁር ጢንዚ'ዛ

blackboard
ብ'ላክቦ:ድ -ስ- ጥቁር ሰሌዳ

blackmail
ብ'ላክሜይል -ግ- ገንዘብ ለመውሰድ ማስ ፈራራት [አስፈራ'ራ] (ስም አጠፋ'ለሁ፣ ምስ ጢር አወጣ'ለሁ በማለት)

blacksmith
ብ'ላክስሚᎀ -ስ- ብረት ሠሪ ፣ ቀጥቃጭ ፣ ባለ'ጅ

bladder
ብ'ላደ -ስ- ፊ'ኛ

blade
ብ'ሌይድ -ስ- ስለት ፣ ምላ'ጭ

blame
ብ'ሌይም -ግ- ጥፋተ'ኛ ማድረግ [አደ'ረገ] ፣ ማ'መካኘት [አመካ'ኘ]

blank
ብ'ላንክ -ቅ- ንጹሕ ፣ ባዶ

blanket
ብ'ላንኬት -ስ- ብርድ ልብስ

blasphemy
ብ'ላስፈሚ -ስ- በእግዚአብሔር ላይ መጥፎ መ'ናገር ፣ እግዚአብሔርን መድፈር

blast
ብ'ላ:ስት -ስ- ኀይለ'ኛ ነፋስ ፣ የመፈንዳት ድምፅ

blatant
ብ'ሌይተንት -ቅ- ሐፍረተ ቢስ

blaze
ብ'ሌይዝ -ግ- መንበልበል [ተንበለ'በለ] (ለእሳት)

bleach
ብ'ሊይች -ግ- ማንጣት (አነ'ጣ)
-ስ- ማንጫ ዱቄት

bleak
ብ'ሊይክ -ቅ- ገላጣ ፣ ባዶ ፣ ድርቅ (ለመሬት)

bleat
ብ'ሊይት -ግ- መጮኽ [ጮኸ] (ለበግ'ና ለፍ'የል)

bleed
ብ'ሊይድ -ግ- መድማት [ደ'ማ]

blemish
ብ'ሌሚሽ -ስ- መጥፎ ምል'ክት ፣ (መልክ የ'ሚያጠፋ)

blend
ብ'ሌንድ -ግ- ማ'ደባለቅ [አ'ደባ'ለቀ]

bless
ብ'ሌስ -ግ- መባረክ [ባ'ረከ]

blessed
ብ'ሌስድ -ቅ- የተባ'ረከ ፣ ቡሩክ፣ የተቀ'ደሰ

blight
ብ'ላይት -ስ- የአትክልት በ'ሽታ (እንዲጠወ 'ልግ የ'ሚያደርግ)

blind
ብ'ላይንድ -ግ- ዓይን ማጭበርበር [አጭበረ' በረ]
-ቅ- ዕ'ውር
-ስ- መ'ጋረጃ

blindfold
ብ'ላይንድፎልድ -ግ- የሰው ዓይን በጨርቅ ጠዝቶ መሸ'ፈን [ሸ'ፈነ]

blink
ብ'ሊንክ -ግ- ዓይን ማርገብገብ [አርገበ'ገበ]

bliss
ብ'ሊስ -ስ- ታ'ላቅ ደስታ

blister
ብ'ሊስተ -ስ- ውሃ የቋ'ጠረ ቁስል

blithe
ብ'ላይᎀ -ቅ- ደ'ስ ያለው ፣ የተደ'ሰተ

blizzard
ብ'ሊዘድ -ስ- ኀይለ'ኛ ነፋስ (በረዶ የያዘ)

blob
ብ'ሎብ -ስ- ት'ንሽ ን'ጣቢ ፣ ት'ንሽ ጠ'ብታ

block
ብ'ሎክ -ግ- ማ'ገድ [አ'ገደ]
-ስ- የንጨት ጉ'ማጅ ፣ የደንጊያ ፍን'ካች

blockade
ብሎ'ኬይድ -ግ- አንድ ቦታ መክበብ [ከ'በበ] (ጠላትን ግንኙ'ነት ለማሳ'ጣት) ፣ ማ'ገድ [አ'ገደ] (ግንኙ'ነት ለመከልከል)

blockhead
ብ'ሎክሄድ -ስ- ደ'ደብ ሰው

blonde
ብ'ሎንድ -ቅ- ወርቅ'ማ ጠጉር ያ'ለው፣ያ'ላት
blood
ብ'ለድ -ስ- ደም
bloodthirsty
ብ'ለድሰስቲ -ቅ- ደም ለማፍሰስ የ'ሚቸ'ኩል፣ ጨ'ካኝ
bloom
ብ'ሉ:ም -ግ- ማ'በብ [አ'በበ]
blossom
ብ'ሎሰም -ግ- ማ'በብ [አ'በበ]
-ስ- አበባ
blot
ብ'ሎት -ስ- የቀለም እንገብ'ጣቢ
blotch
ብ'ሎች -ስ- በቆዳ ላይ ያ'ለ መጥፎ ምል'ክት
blouse
ብ'ላውዝ -ስ- ብሉዝ ፣ የሴቶ'ች ሸሚዝ
blow
ብ'ለው -ግ- መንፋት [ነ'ፋ]
-ስ- ጡ'ጫ
blubber
ብ'ለበ -ስ- የዓሣ አንበሪ ሞራ
-ቅ- ያ'በጠ (ለከንፈር)
bludgeon
ብ'ለጀን -ስ- ዱ'ላ (የበረት ፣ የንጨት)
blue
ብ'ሉ: -ቅ- ሰማያዊ
bluff
ብ'ለፍ -ግ- ማንጓለል [አንጓ'ለለ] (የሰውን ሐሳብ)
blunder
ብ'ለንደ -ግ- ሥራ አልኩስኩሶ መሥራት [ሠ'ራ] ፣ ሥራ ማ'ጨማለቅ [አ'ጨማ'ለቀ]
blunt
ብ'ለንት -ቅ- ደነዝ ፣ ዱልዱም ፣ ደ'ፋር
blur
ብ'ለ: -ስ- ጭረፍታ ፣ ው'ልብታ
blurt
ብ'ለ:ት -ግ- ሳያ'ስቡ በድንገት መ'ናገር [ተና'ገረ]
blush
ብ'ለሽ -ግ- ከሀፍረት የተነ'ሣ ፊት መቅላት [ቀ'ላ]

bluster
ብ'ለስተ -ግ- መፎ'ከር [ፎ'ከረ]፣ መዛት [ዛተ]፣ መደንፋት [ደነ'ፋ]
-ስ- ድንፋታ ፣ የንፋስ ቶጪት
boar
'ቦ: -ስ- ወንድ ዐሣማ (ያልተኮላ'ሸ) ፣ ኮርማ ዐሣማ
board
'ቦ:ድ -ስ- ጠፍጣ'ፋ የንጨት ቁ'ራጭ ፣ ማንቀ ship, train etc.
-ግ- መውጣት [ወ'ጣ] ፣ መ'ሣፈር [ተሣ ፈረ]
-and lodging
-ስ- የመኖሪያ'ና የቀ'ለብ ዋጋ
-card
-ስ- ወፍራም ካርቶን
boarder
'ቦ:ደ -ስ- እሰው ቤት ለምግቡ'ና ለመኖርያው እ'የከ'ፈለ የ'ሚኖር ፣ ቀ'ለብተ'ኛ
boarding-house
'ቦ:ዲንግ 'ሃውስ -ስ- በኪራይ የ'ሚ'ታ'ደር' በት ቤት
boarding-school
'ቦ:ዲንግ ስ'ኩ:ል -ስ- አዳሪ ተማሪ ቤት
boast
'በውስት -ግ- መፎ'ከር [ፎ'ከረ] ፣ ጉ'ራ መን ዛት [ነ'ዛ] ፣ መ'መካት [ተመ'ካ]
boat
'በውት -ስ- ጀልባ
bobbin
'ቦቢን -ስ- በከራ ፣ ማጠንጠኛ እንጨት ፣ እን ከር'ት
body
'ቦዲ -ስ- ሰው'ነት ፣ አካል
bodyguard
'ቦዲጋ:ድ -ስ- የክብር ዘበ'ኛ ፣ የግ'ል ጠ'ባቂ ፣ አሽከር
bog
'ቦግ -ስ- አሮንቃ
bogus
'በውገስ -ቅ- ግ'ብዝ
boil
'ቦይል -ግ- መቀ'ቀል [ቀ'ቀለ]
-ስ- ብጉንጅ

bold
'ቦልድ -ቅ- ደ'ፋር ፥ ጎበዝ ፥ ጀግና
bolster
'ቦልስተ -ግ- መደ'ገፍ [ደ'ገፈ] ፥ መርዳት [ረ'ዳ]
pillow
-ስ- ትራስ
bolt
'ቦልት -ግ- መደንበር [ደነ'በረ]
food
-ግ- መጉስጉስ [ጉሰ'ጉሰ] (ምግብ)
lock
-ስ- መቀርቀሪያ ፥ መደንቀሪያ
bomb
'ቦም -ስ- ቦም'ብ ፥ ፈንጂ
bombastic
ቦም'ባስቲክ -ቅ- ትዕቢተ'ኛ ፥ የ'ሚ'ነ'ፋ ፥ ጉ'ረ'ኛ
bombard
ቦም'ባ:ድ -ግ- ቦምብ መጣል [ጣለ] (ከአ'የር) ፥ በቦምብ መደብደብ [ደበ'ደበ]
bomber
'ቦመ -ስ- ቦምብ ጣይ አውሮ'ፕላን
bond
'ቦንድ -ስ- ሕ'ጋዊ ስምም'ነት ፥ ስለወ'ሰዱት ገንዘብ የ'ሚ'ሰጥ ፊርማ ያ'ለ'በት ደ'ረሰኝ
tying rope
-ስ- ማሠሪያ
bondage
'ቦንዲጅ -ስ- ባር'ነት ፥ ግዞት
bone
'በውን -ስ- ዐጥንት
bonfire
'ቦንፋየ -ስ- ደመራ ፥ የቁሻሻ ቃጠሎ
bonnet
'ቦነት -ስ- የሴት ባርኔጣ
bonus
'በውነስ -ስ- ጉርሻ (ገንዘብ)
book
'ቡክ -ስ- መጽሐፍ
-ግ- አስቀ'ድሞ በመክፈል ፥ በመንገር ቦታ መያዝ [ያዘ] (በባቡር በአውሮ'ፕላን ፥ በቴያትር ወዘተ)
booking
'ቡኪንግ -ስ- አስቀ'ድሞ በመክፈል፥ በመንገር ቦታ ቀድሞ መያዝ (በቴያትር ፥ በባቡር ወዘተ)
bookish
'ቡኪሽ -ቅ- መጻሕፍት በብዛት የ'ሚያ'ነብ ፥ መጻሕፍት በብዛት መጥቀስ የ'ሚ'ወ'ድ
book-keeper
'ቡክኪፐ -ስ- መዝገብ ያዥ (የገንዘብ)
booklet
'ቡክለት -ስ- ት'ንሽ መጽሐፍ
boom
'ቡ:ም -ግ- ድ'ም ማለት [አለ] (አንድ ነገር ሲወድቅ)
-ስ- የኤኮኖሚ ደረጃ መጻበር ፥ ድ'ምታ (ድምፅ) ፥ ረ'ጅም ግንድ
boon
ቡ:ን -ስ- ቡራኬ ፥ ማመስገኛ ነገር
-ቅ- የተደ'ሰተ ፥ ደ'ስተ'ኛ
-ስ- ውለታ
boot
ቡ:ት -ስ- ቦት ጫ'ማ
booth
ቡ:ስ -ስ- ኪዮስክ
booty
'ቡ:ቲ -ስ- በጦር'ነት ላይ የተዘ'ረፈ ዕቃ ፥ ስለ ባ ፥ ማርጣ ፥ የምርኮ ንብረት
booze
'ቡ:ዝ -ግ- ብዙ መጠጣት [ጠ'ጣ] (እስኪሩ መጠ'ጠ'ች)
-ስ- መጠ'ጥ ፥ አልኮል
border
'ቦ:ደ -ስ- ወሰን
bore
'ቦ: -ግ- መፈልፈል [ፈለ'ፈለ] ፥ መብሳት [በ'ሳ] ፥ መንገፍገፍ [ተንገፈ'ገፈ] ፥ መሰልቸት [ሰለ'ቸ]
boredom
'ቦ:ደም -ስ- መንገፍገፍ ፥ መሰልቸት
boring
'ቦ:ሪንግ -ቅ- አሰልቺ ፥ አንገፍጋፊ
born
'ቦ:ን -ቅ- የተወ'ለደ
borough
'በረ -ስ- ሠፈር ፥ የከተማ ክፍል

borrow
'ቦረው -ግ- መ'በደር [ተበ'ደረ]
bosom
'ቡዘም -ስ- ደረት ፣ የጡት አ'ካባቢ
boss
'ቦስ -ስ- አለቃ ፣ ሹም ፣ የጋ'ሻ ጉጥ
both
'በውስ -ቅ- ሁለ'ቱም
bother
'ቦዘ -ግ- ማስቸ'ገር [አስቸ'ገረ] ፣ ማስጨ'ነቅ [አስጨ'ነቀ] ፣ ማ'ወክ [አ'ወከ]
bottle
'ቦተል -ስ- ጠርሙዝ ፣ ጠርሙስ
bottom
'ቦተም -ስ- ሥር ፣ መ'ቀመጫ (ቂጥ) ፣ ዳ'ሌ
-ቅ- ታ'ች
bough
'ባው -ስ- ቅርንጫፍ (የዛፍ)
boulder
'ቦልደ -ስ- ታ'ላቅ ቋጥ'ኝ
bounce
'ባውንስ -ግ- ማንጠር [አነ'ጠረ] (ኳስ)
bound
'ባውንድ -ግ- እ'መ'ር እ'መ'ር ማለት [አለ] ፣ ማንጠር [አነ'ጠረ]
limit
-ስ- ወሰን
forced
-ቅ- የተገ'ደደ
on the way to
-ቅ- ዝግ'ጁ (ለመሄድ)
tied up
-ቅ- የታ'ሠረ (በገመድ ፣ በሰንሰለት ወዘተ)
boundary
'ባውንደሪ -ስ- ወሰን(ያገር)
bountiful
'ባውንቲፉል -ቅ- ለ'ጋስ ፣ ቸር
bounty
'ባውንቲ -ስ- ለ'ጋስ'ነት ፣ ቸር'ነት
bout
'ባውት -ስ- የቦክስ'ና የትግል ጨዋታ ውድ'ድር ፣ የተወ'ሰነ ጊዜ (አንድ ሥራ የተፈ'ጸመ'በት)

bow
'ባው -ግ- እ'ጅ መንሣት [ነ'ሣ]
of ship
-ስ- የመርከብ ፊት
bow
'በው -ስ- ባለውል እስር (ቱርጋሳ)
weapon
-ስ- ቀሥት
bowel
'ባውል -ስ- ደንዳ'ኔ (እሥር የ'ሚ'ጠራ'ቀም'በት የአንጀት ክፍል)
bowl
'በውል -ስ- ሰ'ፊ ሳሕን
box
'ቦክስ -ግ- በጡጫ መምታት [መ'ታ]
container
-ስ- ሣጥን ፣ ካርቶን
boxer
'ቦክስ -ስ- ቦክሰ'ኛ
boxing
'ቦክሲንግ -ስ- የቦክስ ጨዋታ
boy
'ቦይ -ስ- ልጅ (ወንድ)
brace
ብ'ሬይስ -ግ- በንጨት ማጠንከር [አጠነ'ከረ]፣ ማጥበቅ [አጠ'በቀ]
tool
-ስ- መሰርሰሪያ (መ'ሣሪያ)
bracelet
ብ'ሬይስለት -ስ- አም'ባር
bracket
ብ'ራከት -ስ- ቅ'ንፍ ፣ ድጋፍ ፣ ማስደ'ገፊያ (የዕቃ መደርደሪያ ወዘተ)
brackish
ብ'ራኪሽ -ቅ- ከ'ባድ (ለውሃ ጣዕም)
brag
ብ'ራግ -ግ- መፎ'ከር [ፎ'ከረ]
braid
ብ'ሬይድ -ስ- የወርቅ ፣ የብ'ር ጥልፍ
brain
ብ'ሬይን -ስ- አንጎል ፣ አእምሮ

brake
ብ'ሬይክ -ግ- ማገታት [ገ'ታ] ፣ ፍሬን መያዝ [ያዘ]
-ስ- ፍሬን ፣ ሎጋም
branch
ብ'ራ:ንች -ስ- ቅርንጫፍ
brand
ብ'ራንድ -ግ- ምል'ክት ማድረግ [አደ'ረገ] (በ ጋለ ብረት ፣ ለእንስሳት)
animals
-ስ- ምል'ክት (የእንስሳት)
trade mark
-ስ- ምል'ክት (የንግድ)
brandish
ብ'ራንዲሽ -ግ- መቃጣት [ቃ'ጣ] (ዱ'ላ)
brass
ብ'ራ:ስ -ስ- ነሐስ
brave
ብ'ሬይቭ -ቅ- ጎበዝ ፣ ጀግና
brawl
ብ'ሮ:ል -ግ- እም'ባጓሮ ማንሣት [አነ'ሣ]
bray
ብ'ሬይ -ስ- የአህ'ያ ጩኸት
braze
ብ'ሬይዝ -ግ- መበ'የድ [በ'የደ]
breach
ብ'ሪይች -ግ- መጣስ [ጣሰ] (ሉሕ'ግ)
bread
ብ'ሬድ -ስ- ዳ'ቦ
breadth
ብ'ሬድስ -ስ- ስፋት
break
ብ'ሬይክ -ግ- መስበር [ሰ'በረ]
bad news
-ግ- ማርዳት [አረ'ዳ]
rest
-ስ- ዕረፍት
breakdown
ብ'ሬይክዳውን -ግ- መ'ሰበር [ተሰ'በረ] ፣ መ 'ሰናከል [ተሰና'ከለ] (ለመኪና ወዘተ)
mental
-ስ- የአእምሮ ፣ የሰው'ነት ጤና ድንገ ተ'ኛ መ'ናወጥ

breakfast
ብ'ሬክፈስት -ስ- ቁርስ
breast
ብ'ሬስት -ስ- ጡት
bosom
-ስ- ደረት
breath
ብ'ሬስ -ስ- ትንፋሽ ፣ እስትንፋስ
breathe
ብ'ሪይዝ -ግ- መተንፈስ [ተነ'ፈሰ]
breeches
ብ'ሪቺዝ -ስ- ጠ'ባብ ሱ'ሪ
breed
ብ'ሪይድ -ግ- መርባት [ረ'ባ] (ለእንስሳት)
breeder
ብ'ሪይደ -ስ- ከብት አርቢ
breeze
ብ'ሪይዝ -ስ- ነፋስ (ቀ'ላል) ፣ የነፋስ ሽ'ውታ
breezy
ብ'ሪይዚ -ቅ- ነፋሳም (ሳይበዛ ሽ'ው የ'ሚል)
brethren
ብ'ሬዘረን -ስ- ወን'ድ'ም'ች ፣ ወን'ድ'ማማ ቾ'ች
brevity
ብ'ሬቪቲ -ስ- አ'ጭር'ነት (ለንግ'ግር)
brew
ብ'ሩ: -ግ- መጥመቅ [ጠ'መቀ] (መጠ'ጥ)
brewery
ብ'ሩወሪ -ስ- መጥመቂያ (ቦታ)
bribe
ብ'ራይብ -ግ- ጉ'ቦ መስጠት (ሰ'ጠ)
-ስ- ጉ'ቦ
bribery
ብ'ራይበሪ -ስ- ጉ'ቦ መስጠት
brick
ብ'ሪክ -ስ- ጡብ ፣ ሸክላ
bridle
ብ'ራይደል -ስ- ልጓም
bridegroom
ብ'ራይድግሩም -ስ- ወንድ ሙሽ'ራ
bridesmaid
ብ'ራይድዝሜይድ -ስ- ሴት ሚዜ

bridge
ብ'ሪጅ -ግ- ድልድይ መሥራት [ሠ'ራ]
-ስ- ድልድይ

brief
ብ'ሪይፍ -ቅ- አ'ጭር (ንግ'ግር)
legal
-ስ- መ'ረጃ ወረቀት (የክ'ስ)

briefcase
ብ'ሪይፍኬይስ -ስ- የ'ጅ ቦርሳ

brigade
ብሪ'ጌይድ -ስ- ቢሪጌድ

brigand
ብ'ሪገንድ -ስ- በመዝረፍ'ና ሰውን እያ'ፈነ በመያዝ ገንዘብ የ'ሚያገ'ኝ ወንበዴ

bright
ብ'ራይት -ቅ- ብሩህ ፣ ያልጨ'ለመ ፣ ፀሐያ'ማ

brilliant
ብ'ሪልየንት -ቅ- የ'ሚያበራ ፣ የ'ሚያንጸባ'ርቅ፣ ብልኅ

brim
ብ'ሪም -ስ- የዕቃ ፣ የስኒ አፍ

brine
ብ'ራይን -ስ- ጨው ያ'ለ'በት ውሃ ፣ የጨው ውሃ

bring
ብ'ሪንግ -ግ- ማምጣት [አመ'ጣ]

brink
ብ'ሪንክ -ስ- ዳር

brisk
ብ'ሪስክ -ቅ- ፈ'ጣን

bristle
ብ'ሪሰል -ግ- መገንፈል [ገነ'ፈለ] (በቁ'ጣ)
-ስ- ያቀመ'ቀመ ጠጉር

British
ብ'ሪቲሽ -ቅ- ብሪጣንያዊ ፣ ብሪታንያዊ

brittle
ብ'ሪተል -ቅ- ተሰ'ባሪ ፣ በቀ'ላሉ የ'ሚ'ሰ'በር

broach
ብ'ረውች -ግ- መክፈት [ከ'ፈተ] (ጠርሙዝ ፣ በርሜል) ፣ ውይ'ይት ፣ ንግ'ግር መጀ'መር [ጀ'መረ]

broad
ብ'ሮ:ድ -ቅ- ሰ'ፊ

broadcast
ብ'ሮ:ድካ:ስት -ግ- በራዲዮ መ'ናገር [ተና'ገረ]
-ቅ- የተበታ'ተነ ጥራጥሬ

broaden
ብ'ሮ:ደን -ግ- ማስፋት [አሰ'ፋ]

brocade
ብረ'ኬይድ -ስ- ጥልፍ (ልብስ)

broken
ብ'ረውከን -ቅ- የተሰ'በረ

broker
ብ'ረውከ -ስ- ደ'ላላ ፣ አ'ሻሻጭ
stock-
-ስ- የአክሲዮን አ'ሻሻጭ

bronze
ብ'ሮንዝ -ስ- ነሐስ

brooch
ብ'ረውች -ስ- የልብስ ፈርጥ (ጌጥ)

brood
ብ'ሩ:ድ -ግ- መተ'ከዝ [ተ'ከዘ]
-ስ- ጫጩ'ቶ'ች

brook
ብ'ሩክ -ስ- ጅረት

broom
ብ'ሩም -ስ- መጥረጊያ (የቤት)

broth
ብ'ሮስ -ስ- ቀ'ጭን ሾርባ ፣ መረቅ

brothel
ብ'ሮሰል -ስ- የሴተ'ኛ አዳሪ ቤት (የሸርሙጣ ቤት)

brother
ብ'ረዘ -ስ- ወን'ድ'ም

brotherhood
ብ'ረዘሁድ -ስ- ወን'ድ'ም'ነት ፣ ወን'ድ'ማማ ች'ነት

brother-in-law
ብ'ረዘሪንሎ: -ስ- አማች ፣ የሚስት ወንድ'ም

brow
ብ'ራው -ስ- ግምባር

brown
ብ'ራውን -ቅ- ቡ'ና'ማ

bruise
ብ'ሩ:ዝ -ስ- ሰም'በር (ከተመ'ቱ በኋላ እሰው'ነት ላይ የ'ሚ'ታ'ይ ምል'ክት)

brush
ብ'ረሽ -ግ- መጥረግ [ጠ'ረገ] ፣ መቦ'ረሽ [ቦ'ረሸ]
-ስ- ብሩሽ
brutal
ብ'ሩ፡ተል -ቅ- ጨ'ካኝ ፣ አረመኔ ፣ አውሬ (ለጠባይ)
brute
ብ'ሩ፡ት -ስ- አውሬ ፣ ጨ'ካኝ ሰው
bubble
'በበል -ግ- መፍለቅለቅ [ተፍለቀ'ለቀ] (ለፍላት)
-ስ- የአረፋ ኳስ
buck
'በክ -ስ- ወንድ አጋዘን
bucket
'በኪት -ስ- ባልዲ ፣ ሸንከ'ሎ
buckle
'በከል -ስ- ዘለበት
bud
'በድ -ስ- እምቡጥ
budge
'በጅ -ግ- መንቀሳቀስ [ተንቀሳ'ቀሰ] ፣ ገለ'ል ማለት [አለ]
budget
'በጂት -ስ- ባጀት ፣ የመንግሥት ገቢ'ና ለ'የመሥሪያ ቤቱ የሚ'ደለ'ደል የገንዘብ ድርሻ
buff
'በፍ -ግ- መወልወል [ወለ'ወለ] (ወርቅ ፣ ብረታብረት)
-ቅ- ነጣ ያለ ብጫ
buffalo
'በፈለው -ስ- ጎ'ሽ (እንስሳ)
buffer
'በፈ -ስ- ከ'ብ በባቡር ፊት ያ'ለ የግ'ጭት መ'ከላከያ ብረት ፣ ፓራውልት (የባቡር)
buffoon
በ'ፉ፡ን -ስ- ቂል ፣ በሁኔቱው የ'ሚያ'ሥቅ ሰው
bug
'በግ -ስ- ትን'ንሽ ነፍሳት (ትኋን፣ተባይ ወዘተ)
bugbear
'በግቤየ -ስ- የ'ሚፈሩት ነገር
bugle
ብ'ዩ፡ገል -ስ- ጥሩምባ (የወ'ታ'ደር)

bugler
ብ'ዩ፡ግለ -ስ- ጥሩምባ ነፊ (ወ'ታ'ደር)
build
'ቢልድ -ግ- መገንባት [ገነ'ባ]
builder
'ቢልደ -ስ- ቤት ሠሪ ፣ ተቋራጭ (ቤት ለመሥራት)
building
'ቢልዲንግ -ስ- ግንብ ፣ ሕንፃ
bulb
'በልብ -ስ- አምፑል
plant
-ስ- ሥር (ያትክልት)
bulge
'በልጅ -ግ- መ'ወጠር [ተወ'ጠረ] ፣ መ'ነፋት [ተነ'ፋ]
-ስ- የተወ'ጠረ ፣ የተነ'ፋ ነገር
bulk
'በልክ -ስ- ክብደት
bull
'ቡል -ስ- በሬ
bullet
'ቡለት -ስ- ጥ'ይት
bullion
'ቡለየን -ስ- የወርቅ የብ'ር ነዶ
bullock
'ቡለክ -ስ- ወይፈን (የተኮላ'ሸ)
bully
'ቡሊ -ስ- ደካማ አጥቂ ፣ በጥባጭ ጠበ'ኛ
bump
'በምፕ -ግ- በኀይል መውደቅ [ወ'ደቀ] ፣ ዱ'ብ ማለት [አለ]
-ስ- እበጥ
bumper
'በምፐ -ቅ- በጣም ት'ልቅ
of car
-ስ- የግ'ጭት መ'ከላከያ (የመኪና) ፣ ፓራውልት
bumptious
'በምሸስ -ቅ- ኩሩ
bun
'በን -ስ- ክ'ብ ኬክ
bunch
'በንች -ስ- እ'ቅፍ (በተለ'ይ የአበባ)

bundle
'በንደል -ስ- እሥር ፣ ረብጣ
bung
'በንግ -ስ- ውታፍ ፣ መወ'ተፊያ
bungalow
'በንገለው -ስ- ጎ'ጆ
bungle
'በንገል -ግ- አድበስብሶ መሥራት [ሠራ']
bunk
'በ'ንክ -ስ- የንጨት አልጋ (ከመርከብ ፣ በባቡር ላይ)
bunting
'በንቲንግ -ስ- ል'ዩ ል'ዩ ቀለም ያ'ለው ሰንደቅ ዓላማ የ'ሚ'ሠ'ራ'በት ብ'ትን ጨርቅ ፣ ሰንደቅ ዓላማ ፣ ሰንደቅ ዓላማ'ዎ'ች
buoy
'ቦይ -ስ- አደጋ ለማስጠንቀቂያ በባሕር ላይ የ'ሚ ንሳ'ፈፍ ነገር (የጉ'ዞ አቅጣጫ የ'ሚያመ ለ'ክት)
buoyant
'ቦየንት -ቅ- ተንሳፋፊ
happy
-ቅ- ደ'ስተ'ኛ
burden
'በ:ደን -ስ- ሸክ:ም
-ግ- መጫን [ጫነ]
burglar
'በ:ግለ -ስ- ቤት ሰርሳሪ ፣ ሌባ
burglary
'በ:ግለሪ -ስ- ቤት ሰርሳሪ'ነት ፣ ሌብ'ነት ቤት ሥርሠራ
burial
'ቤሪየል -ስ- ሥርዓተ ቀብር
burly
'በ:ሊ -ቅ- ኀይለ'ኛ ፣ ደልዳ'ላ
burn
'በ:ን -ግ- ማ'ቃጠል [አ'ቃ'ጠለ] ፣ መፍጀት [ፈ'ጀ] (ለእሳት)
burnish
'በ:ኒሽ -ግ- መወልወል [ወለ'ወለ] (ብረት)
burr
'በ: -ስ- ጨጎጎት (ልብስ የ'ሚይዝ)
burrow
'በረው -ግ- ጉድጓድ መቆ'ፈር [ቆ'ፈረ]
-ስ- ጉድጓድ (የጥንቸል መኖሪያ)
burst
'በ:ስት -ግ- መፈንዳት [ፈነ'ዳ]
-ስ- ድንገተ'ኛ ድምፅ (የጠመንጃ ወዘተ)
bury
'ቤሪ -ግ- መቅበር [ቀ'በረ]
bus
'በስ -ስ- አውቶቡስ
bush
'ቡሽ -ስ- ቁጥቋጦ
bushel
'ቡሸል -ስ- የእህል መሥፈሪያ
bushy
'ቡሺ -ቅ- ች'ፍ'ግ ያ'ለ
business
'ቢዝነስ -ስ- ንግድ ፣ ሞያ ፣ ድር'ጅት
businesslike
'ቢዝነስላይክ -ቅ- የተሟ'ላ ፣ ሥርዓት ተከ'ታይ ፣ ብቁ
bustle
'በሰል -ግ- መ'ቻኰል [ተቻኰ'ለ]
-ስ- ዋካታ
busy
'ቢዚ -ቅ- ሠ'ራተ'ኛ ፣ ባለ ብዙ ሥራ ፣ ሥራ ያልፈ'ታ ፣ ባተሌ
but
'በት -መዋ- ግን ፣ ነገር ግን
butcher
'ቡቸ -ስ- ከብት አራጅ ፣ ሉካን'ዳ ነ'ጋዴ
butler
'በትለ -ስ- የልፍ'ኝ አሽከር
butt
'በት -ስ- የወሃ በርሜል
of gun
-ስ- ሰደፍ (ጠመንጃ)
of goat
-ግ- መውጋት [ወ'ጋ] (ለቀንድ ከብት)
butter
'በተ -ስ- ቅቤ
butterfly
'በተፍላይ -ስ- ቢ'ራቢ'ሮ

buttock
'በተክ -ስ- መ'ቀመጫ (ቂጥ) ፣ ዳ'ሌ
button
'በተን -ስ- ቁልፍ (የልብስ)
buttonhole
'በተንሆውል -ስ- የቁልፍ (መግቢያ) ቀዳዳ
-ግ- መነዝነዝ [ነዘ'ነዘ] ፣ ማስለቀት [አስለ'ቀ]
buttress
'በትረስ -ግ- መደ'ገፍ [ደ'ገፈ]
-ስ- ድጋፍ (ለቤት)
buy
'ባይ -ግ- መግዛት [ገ'ዛ]
buzz
'በዝ -ግ- ጥ'ዝ ማለት [አለ] (ለንብ)

by
'ባይ -መዋ- በ . . .
near-
በ . . . አጠገብ
-car
በመኪና
bygone
'ባይጎን -ቅ- ያ'ለፈ
bystander
'ባይስታንደ -ስ- ተመልካች ፣ ታ'ዛቢ
byway
'ባይዌይ -ስ- ጠ'ባብ መንገድ

C

cab
'ካብ -ስ- ታክሲ
cabbage
'ካቢጅ -ስ- ጎ'መን
cabin
'ካቢን -ስ- ጐጆ
of ship etc.
የተሳፋሪዎ'ች መ'ቀመጫ (በአውሮ'ፕላን ፣ በመርከብ ወዘተ)
cabinet
'ካቢኔት -ስ- የሚኒስቴር'ች ምክር ቤት
furniture
-ስ- ት'ንሽ ቁም ሣጥን ፣ (የጌጣጌጥ፣ የስኒና የሳሕን ወዘተ ማስቀ'መጫ)
cable
'ኬይበል -ስ- የብረት ገመድ
telegram
-ስ- ቴሌግራም
cackle
'ካክል -ግ- መንጫጫት [ተንጫ'ጫ] (ለሚጤ'ት)
cadet
ክ'ዴት -ስ- እጩ መኰ'ንን

cadge
'ካጅ -ግ- መለ'መን [ለ'መነ] (ገንዘብ)
cafe
'ካፌ -ስ- ቡ'ና ቤት
cafeteria
ካፌ'ቲሪየ -ስ- ተመ'ጋቢዎ'ች ራሳ'ቸው ምግ'ባ'ቸውን የ'ሚያነሡ'በት የምግብ ቤት
cage
'ኬይጅ -ስ- የወፍ ፣ ያንበሳ ወዘተ ቤት (ከብረት ወይን'ም ከሽቦ የተሠ'ራ)
cajole
ክ'ጆውል -ግ- ማባበል [አባ'በለ]
cake
'ኬይክ -ስ- ኬክ ፣ ዳ'ቦ
calamity
ክ'ላሚቲ -ስ- መቅሠፍት ፣ ጥፋት ፣ መከራ
calculate
'ካልክዩሌይት -ግ- ማ'ሰብ [አ'ሰበ] ፣ መቁ'ጠር [ቆ'ጠረ]
calculation
ካልክዩ'ሌይሽን -ስ- ሒሳብ
calendar
'ካለንደ -ስ- ቀን መቍጠሪያ

calf
'ካ:ፍ -ስ- ጥ'ጃ
call
ኮ:ል -ግ- መጥራት [ጠ'ራ] (ሰው እንዲመጣ ማን:ረግ)
caller
ኮ:ለ -ስ- ጎብኚ ፣ ጠ'ያቂ
calling
ኮ:ሊንግ -ስ- ሞያ
callous
'ካለስ -ስ- የደ'ረቀ ቆዳ
-ቅ- ጨ'ካኝ ፣ ርኅራኄ የሌ'ለው
callow
'ካለው -ቅ- ያልሠለ'ጠነ ፣ ልምድ የሌ'ለው
calm
'ካ:ም -ቅ- ዝ'ምተ'ኛ ፣ ጸ'ጥተ'ኛ
calumny
'ካለምኒ -ስ- የውሸት ሐሜት ፣ የውሸት ክ'ስ
camel
'ካመል -ስ- ግመል
camera
'ካምረ -ስ- ፎቶግራፍ ማንሻ
camouflage
'ካመፍላ:ጅ -ስ- ማ'ለሳፇ (የጠላትን ወ'ታ'ደ ር'ች) ፣ ማስመ'ሰያ
camp
'ካምፕ -ስ- ሠፈር
campaign
ካም'ፔይን -ግ- መ'ዋጋት [ተ'ዋጋ] ፣ መ'ወ ዳ'ደረ] (ለምርጫ)
-ስ- የተደጋ'ገመ ው'ጊያ ፣ ውድ'ድር (ለምርጫ)
camp-bed
'ካምፕ'ቤድ -ስ- የመንገድ አልጋ
camping
'ካምፒንግ -ስ- በአንድ ቦታ ላይ መሥፈር
campus
'ካምፐስ -ስ- የዩኒቨርስቲ ግ'ቢ
can
'ካን -ስ- ቆርቆ'ሮ
-ግ- መቻል [ቻለ]
canal
ክ'ናል -ስ- ቦይ ፣ መስኖ

cancel
'ካንሰል -ግ- መፋቅ [ፋቀ] ፣ ማጥፋት [አጠ 'ፋ]
cancer
'ካንሰ -ስ- ነቀርሳ
candid
'ካንዲድ -ቅ- ግልጥ ፣ እውነተ'ኛ (ለሰው)
candidate
'ካንዲዴይት -ስ- እጩ
candied
'ካንዲድ -ቅ- በሱ'ካር የተሸ'ፈነ
candle
'ካንደል -ስ- ሻማ
candlestick
'ካንደልስቲክ -ስ- መቅረዝ
candour
'ካንደ -ስ- ግልጥ'ነት ፣ እውነተ'ኛ'ነት
candy
'ካንዲ -ስ- ከረሜ'ላ
cane
'ኬይን -ስ- አገዳ
walking stick
-ስ- በ'ትር ፣ ምርኩዝ
canine
'ኬይናይን -ቅ- የው'ሻ ዘር ፣ ው'ሻ የ'ሚመ ስል
tooth
-ስ- የው'ሻ ከራንቻ ፣ ቀንጠ'ጤ
canker
'ካንከ -ስ- አጣቆ (የተክል በ'ሽታ)
canned
'ካንድ -ቅ- የታ'ሸገ (ቆርቆ'ሮ)
cannibal
'ካኒበል -ስ- ጭራቅ
cannon
'ካነን -ስ- መድፍ
cannon-ball
'ካነን'ቦ:ል -ስ- የመድፍ ጥ'ይት
canoe
ክ'ኑ: -ስ- ታንኳ
canon
'ካነን -ስ- የቤተ ክርስቲያን ሕ'ግ ፣ ሥርዓተ ቤተ ክርስቲያን

canopy
'ካነፒ -ስ- ዳስ ፣ ክለላ ፣ አጎበር

canteen
ካን'ቲይን -ስ- የምግብ አ'ዳራሽ (በፋብሪካ ፣ በዩኒቨርስቲ ወዘተ)

canter
'ካንተ -ግ- ደንገላሳ መምታት [ሠ'ታ]
-ስ- ደንገላስ

canvas
'ካንቨስ -ስ- ሸራ

cap
'ካፕ -ስ- ቆብ

capable
'ኬይፐበል -ቅ- ሬ ፆቂ ፣ የ'ሚችል

capacious
ከ'ፔይሸስ -ቅ- ሰ'ፊ ፣ ብዙ ቦታ ያ'ለው

capacity
ክ'ፓሲቲ -ስ- አንድ ነገር የ'ሚይዘው መጠን
ability
-ስ- ችሎታ

cape
'ኬይፕ -ስ- ካ'ባ
geographical
-ስ- ርእሰ ምድር

caper
'ኬይፐ -ስ- ሚጥሚ'ጣ
trick
-ስ- ማ'ታለያ
-ስ- የሕፃናት ጠባይ በጨዋታ (ቀዛ ፣ ፌዛዛ) ፣ መ'ዛለል

capital
'ካፒተል -ቅ- በሞት ፍርድ የ'ሚ'ቀ'ጣ (ወን ጀል)
city
-ስ- ዋ'ና ከተማ ፣ መዲና
money
-ስ- ተቀ'ማጭ ገንዘብ ፣ መ'ነሻ ገንዘብ (የሥራ ፣ የንግድ ወዘተ)
very good
-ቅ- በጣም ጥሩ ፣ ድንቅ

capitulate
ክ'ፒትዩሌይት -ግ- ድል በመ'ነሣት ምክን ያት ለባለድሉ አገር እ'ገዛዙን ማስረ'ከብ [አስ ረ'ከበ]

caprice
ከፕ'ሪይስ -ስ- አምሮት (ጥቃ'ቅን'ና የ'ማይ ረባ ፣ ም'ሳሌ ፣ የርጉዝ ሴት)

capricious
ከፕ'ሪሸስ -ቅ- ስለጥቃ'ቅን ነገር ለጥብቆ አ 'ሳቢ

capsize
ካፕ'ሳይዝ -ግ- መ'ገልበጥ [ተገለ'በጠ] (ለመ ርከብ ፣ ለጀልባ)

capsule
'ካፕሱል -ስ- ደረቅ እምቡጥ ፣ የመድኃኒት ሙልሙል ቢልቃጥ

captain
'ካፕቲን -ስ- ሻምበል

caption
'ካፕሽን -ስ- ከሥዕል በግርጌ የ'ሚ'ጻፍ መግ ለጫ ፣ ከሥዕል በታ'ች የተመለ'ከተ ጽሑፍ (በጋዜጣ ወዘተ)

captive
'ካፕቲቭ -ስ- ምርኮ'ኛ

captivity
ካፕ'ቲቪቲ -ስ- ምርኮ

capture
'ካፕቸ -ግ- መማረክ [ማ'ረከ] ፣ መያዝ [ያዘ]

car
'ካ፡ -ስ- መኪና ፣ አውቶሞቢል

carbon
'ካ፡በን -ስ- ጥላት ፣ ጥላሸት ፣ ከሰል (የንጨት)

carbon-paper
'ካ፡በን 'ፔይፐ -ስ- የካርቦን ወረቀት

carbuncle
'ካ፡በንከል -ስ- እበጥ (ት'ልቅ) ፣ ቀ'ይ የ'ሚ ያብረቀ'ርቅ ዕንቍ

carcass
'ካ፡ከስ -ስ- ጥምብ (በድን ፣ የእንስሳ)

card
'ካ፡ድ -ስ- ካርድ ፣ ወረቀት

cardboard
'ካ፡ድቦ፡ድ -ስ- ካርቶን

cardigan
'ካ፡ዲገን -ስ- የሱፍ ኮት (ጨርቁ በእ'ጅ የተ ሠ'ራ)

care
'ኬየ -ግ- መ'ጠንቀቅ [ተጠነ'ቀቀ]
-ስ- ጥን'ቃቄ
career
ከ'ሪየ -ስ- ሥራ (የሕይወት ሙሉ)
careful
'ኬፉል -ቅ- ጥንቁቅ
careless
'ኬለስ -ቅ- የ'ማይ'ጠነ'ቀቅ ፣ ንዝህላል'፣ ዝርክርክ (በሥራው)
caress
ከ'ሬስ -ግ- መዳሰስ [ዳ'ሰሰ] ፣ መዳበስ [ዳ'በሰ] ማሻሸት [አሻ'ሸ] (በፍቅር)
caretaker
'ኬቴይከ -ስ- ቤት ጠ'ባቂ (ባለቤቱ በሌ'ለ'በት ጊዜ) ፤ ያንድ ሕንፃ ኀላፊ ፤ ጊዜያዊ አስተዳዳሪ (ለመንግሥት)
cargo
'ካ:ገው -ስ- ጭነት (የአውሮ'ፕላን ፣ የመርከብ)
carnal
'ካ:ነል -ቅ- ሥጋዊ (መንፈሳዊ'ነት የሌ'ለው)
carnivorous
ካ:'ኒቨረስ -ቅ- ሥጋ ተመ'ጋቢ ፣ ሥጋ በ'ል
carol
'ካረል -ስ- የልደት መዝሙር (የክርስቶስ) ፣ የገ'ና መዝሙር
carpenter
'ካ:ፐንተ -ስ- አናጢ
carpentry
'ካ:ፐንትሪ -ስ- አናጢ'ነት
carpet
'ካ:ፐት -ስ- ምንጣፍ ፣ ስጋ'ጃ
carriage
'ካሪጅ -ስ- ሰረገ'ላ
carrier
'ካሪየ -ስ- ተሸ'ካሚ ፣ ኩሊ ፣ ዕቃ በመኪና አ'ጓጓዥ
carrot
'ካረት -ስ- ካሮት
carry
'ካሪ -ግ- መ'ሸከም [ተሸ'ከመ]
cart
'ካ:ት -ስ- ጋሪ
cart-horse
'ካ:ት'ሆ:ስ -ስ- ጋሪ ጎ'ታች ፈረስ
carton
'ካ:ተን -ስ- የካርቶን ማጥን
cartoon
ካ:'ቱ:ን -ስ- የ'ሚያ'ሥቅ የጋዜጣ ሥዕል
cartridge
'ካ:ትሪጅ -ስ- ቀለሀ
carve
'ካ:ቭ -ግ- መቅረፅ [ቀ'ረፀ] (ድንጊያ ፣ እንጨት ፣ እብነ በረድ ወዘተ)
meat
-ግ- መቁረጥ [ቈ'ረጠ] (ለሥጋ)
cascade
ካስ'ኬይድ -ስ- የውሃ ፏፏቴ
case
'ኬይስ -ስ- ሻንጣ
legal
-ስ- ክ'ስ
example
-ስ- ም'ሳሌ
cash
'ካሽ -ስ- ጥሬ ገንዘብ
cashier
ካ'ሺየ -ስ- ገንዘብ ተቀ'ባይ ፣ ከፋይ ፣ መንዛሪ
cask
'ካ:ስክ -ስ- የንጨት በርሚል
cast
'ካ:ስት -ግ- [መጣልጣል] ፣ መወርወር [ወረ'ወረ] ፤ ለቴያትር ሠ'ራተ'ኞ'ች የ'ሚሠሩትን ድርሻ ማ'ደል [አ'ደለ]
plaster
-ስ- ጂፕስ
theatrical
-ስ- ቴያትር ተጫዋቾ'ች ፣ ተዋናዮች
-ግ- ፈሳሽ ማዕ'ድን ቅርፅ እን'ዲይዝ በጉድጓድ ውስጥ ማፍሰስ [አፈ'ሰሰ]
castigate
'ካስቲጌይት -ግ- መቅጣት [ቀ'ጣ] (በመምታት)

casting
'ካ፡ስቲንግ -ስ- መጣል
theatrical
-ስ- በፊልም ፣ በቲያትር የ'ሚሠሩ ሰዎ'ች ም'ደባ

castle
'ካ፡ሰል -ስ- ግንብ ፣ ም'ሽግ

castor
'ካ፡ስተ -ስ- ተሽከርካሪ (ለወንበር ፣ ለቁም ሣጥን ወዘተ)

casual
'ካዥዩወል -ቅ- ድንገተ'ኛ ፣ ሳይ'ጠባ'በቁት የሆነ ፣ እንደፈ'ቀደው ይሁን የ'ሚል ፣ የ'ማይ'ጠነ'ቀቅ ፣ ደንታ ቢስ

casualty
'ካዠዩወልቲ -ስ- በከ'ባድ አደጋ የተጎ'ዳ ሰው ፣ በጦር'ነት የቆ'ሰሉ ፣ የሞቱ ወ'ታ'ደሮ'ች

cat
'ካት -ስ- ድ'መት

catalogue
'ካተሎግ -ስ- በቤተ መጻሕፍት ያ'ሉ የመጻሕፍት ዝርዝር ፣ ለሽ'ያጭ የቀ'ረበ የዕቃ ዝርዝር ፣ እሱቅ ውስጥ የዕቃውን ዓይነት የ'ሚገልጽ ዝርዝር ጽሑፍ

cataract
'ካተራክት -ስ- የውሃ ፏፏቴ
disease
-ስ- ዓይንን የ'ሚያለብስ በ'ሽታ ፣ ዓይን ሞራ

catarrh
ከ'ታ፡ -ስ- አ'ክታ'ና ንፍጥ በብዛት እንዲወጣ የ'ሚያደርግ በ'ሽታ ፣ ጉንፋን

catastrophe
ከ'ታስትረፊ -ስ- መቅሠፍት ፣ ድንገተ'ኛ አደጋ

catch
'ካች -ግ- መያዝ [ያዘ] ፣ መቅለብ [ቀ'ለበ]

catching
'ካቺንግ -ቅ- ተላላፊ (ለበ'ሽታ)

catechism
'ካተኪዝም -ስ- ምስጢረ ሥ'ላሴ ፣ ትምህርተ ክርስቲያን (ከመ'ጠመቅ በፊት የ'ሚ'ማሩት)

categorical
ካተ'ጎሪከል -ቅ- እርግጠ'ኛ ፣ ፍ'ጹም (የ'ማያ'ጠራ'ጥር)

category
'ካተግሪ -ስ- መደብ ፡ የወል መ'ታወቂያ (ለብዙ ነገሮ'ች)

cater
'ኬይተ -ግ- ምግብ ማ'ዘጋጀት [አ'ዘጋ'ጀ]

caterpillar
'ካተፒለ -ስ- አ'ባ ጨ'ጓ'ሬ ፣ የጎ'መን ትል

catgut
'ካትገት -ስ- የደ'ረቀ አንጀት ፣ ጅ'ማት

cathedral
ከ'ቲድረል -ስ- ት'ልቅ ደብር (ጳ'ጳስ የ'ሚ'ቀመጥ'በት)

cattle
'ካተል -ስ- ከብት

cauliflower
'ኮሊፍላወ -ስ- አበባ ጎ'መን

cause
'ኮ፡ዝ -ግ- እንዲሆን ማድረግ [አደ'ረገ]
reason
-ስ- ምክንያት

cauterize
'ኮ፡ተራይዝ -ግ- መተ'ኮስ [ተ'ኮሰ] (በው'ነት በጋለ መ'ሣሪያ)

cautious
'ኮ፡ሸስ -ቅ- ጥንቁቅ ፣ ሥጉ

cavalry
'ካቨልሪ -ስ- ፈረሰ'ኛ ወ'ታ'ደር

cave
'ኬይቭ -ስ- ዋ'ሻ

cavity
'ካቪቲ -ስ- ጎድጓ'ዳ ነገር ፣ ጉድጓድ ፣ ሥር ሥር

cease
'ሲይስ -ግ- ማቆም [አቆመ] (ሥራን ፣ ንግ'ግርን ወዘተ)

cedar
'ሲይደ -ስ- አርዘ ሊባኖስ (የዛፍ ዓይነት)

cede
'ሲይድ -ግ- መልቀቅ [ለ'ቀቀ] (ለመብት) ፡ ማመን [አ'መነ] ፣ መ'ቀበል [ተቀ'በለ] (አስተያየት)

ceiling
'ሲይሊንግ -ስ- ጣራ (የውስጡ ክፍል)

celebrate
'ሴለብሬይት -ግ- በዓል ማክበር [አከ'በረ]
celebration
ሴለብ'ሬይሽን -ስ- ክብረ በዓል
celebrity
ሲ'ሌብረቲ -ስ- ባለዝ'ና ፣ የታ'ወቀ ፣ የተከ'በረ
celestial
ሰ'ሌስቲየል -ቅ- ሰማያዊ ፣ የሰማይ
celibacy
'ሴለበሲ -ስ- ምንኩስ'ና ፣ ንጽሕ'ና (ለወን'ድ ብ'ቻ)
celibate
'ሴለበት -ቅ- የመነ'ኩሰ ፣ በንጽሕ'ና የ'ሚ ኖር
cell
'ሴል -ስ- ት'ንሽ ክፍል (የእስረ'ኛ ፣ የመነ ኩሴ)
battery
-ስ- የባትሪ ደንጊያ
cellar
ሴለ -ስ- የዕቃ ቤት (ከወለል በታ'ች የ'ሚ'ገ'ኝ)
cement
ሰ'ሜንት -ስ- ሲሚንቶ
cemetery
'ሴመትሪ -ስ- መቃብር (ቦታ)
censor
'ሴንሰ -ግ- መ'ቆጣጠር [ተቆጣ'ጠረ]
person
-ስ- ተቆጣጣሪ ፣ ሳንሱር
censorship
'ሴንሰሺፕ -ስ- ተቆጣጣሪ'ነት
censure
'ሴንሸ -ግ- መ'ቃወም [ተቃ'ወመ]
-ስ- አለመስማማት
census
'ሴንሰስ -ስ- የሕዝብ ቆጠራ
cent
'ሴንት -ስ- ሳንቲም (የብ'ር አንድ መቶ'ኛ)
centenarian
ሴንተ'ኔሪየን -ስ- መቶ ዓመት ዕድሜ ያ'ለው
centenary
ሴን'ቲነሪ -ስ- የመቶ'ኛ ዓመት በዓል
centimetre
'ሴንቲሚተ -ስ- ሳንቲሜትር
centipede
'ሴንቲፒይድ -ስ- አምሳ እግር (የትል ዓይነት)
central
'ሴንትረል -ቅ- ማዕከላዊ ፣ ጠቅላይ
centralize
'ሴንትረላይዝ -ግ- ማማከል [አማ'ከለ] ፣ ማ እከላዊ ማድረግ [አደ'ረገ] ፣ መጠቅለል [ጠቀ' ለለ]
centre
'ሴንተ -ስ- መካ'ከል ፣ መሀል
century
'ሴንቸሪ -ስ- አንድ መቶ ዓመት
ceramic
'ሴራሚክ -ቅ- የሸክላ ሥራ
cereal
'ሲሪየል -ስ- እሀል (ስንዴ ፣ ጤፍ ፣ ገብስ ወዘተ)
ceremonial
ሴረ'ሞኒየል -ቅ- የክብረ በዓል ፣ በዓላዊ ፣ ሥነ ሥርዓታዊ
-ስ- በዓል
ceremony
'ሴረመኒ -ስ- በዓላዊ ሥነ ሥርዓት
certain
'ሰ፡ተን -ቅ- እርግጥ
certainly
'ሰ፡ተንሊ -ተግ- በርግጥ
certainty
'ሰ፡ተንቲ -ስ- እርግጠ'ኛ'ነት ፣ እርግጠ'ኛ'ነት
certificate
ሰ'ቲፊከት -ስ- የምስ'ክር ወረቀት
certify
'ሰ፡ቲፋይ -ግ- መመስከር [መሰ'ከረ] ፣ ማ'ረጋ ገጥ [አ'ረጋ'ገጠ]
cesspool
'ሴስፑ፡ል -ስ- የሰገራ መ'ጠራቀሚያ ጉድጓድ
chafe
'ቼይፍ -ግ- እ'ጅ ማ'ፋተግ [አ'ፋ'ተገ](ሙ ቀት ለማግኘት)
be impatient
-ስ- አለመ'ታገሥ ፣ ትዕግሥት ማጣት
chaff
'ቻፍ -ስ- እ'ብቅ ፣ ት'ቢያ

chagrin
'ቻግሪን -ስ- ማዘን ፣ ደ'ስ አለመ'ሰኘት
chain
'ቼይን -ስ- ሰንሰለት
chair
'ቼ: -ስ- ወንበር
chairman
'ቼ:መን -ስ- አፈ ጉባኤ ፣ ሊቀ መንበር
chalice
'ቻሊስ -ስ- ጽ'ዋ (የሥጋ ወደሙ)
chalk
'ቾ:ክ -ስ- ጠመኔ ፣ (ቾክ) አስተማሪ በጥቁር ሰሌዳ ላይ የ'ሚጽፍ'በት
challenge
'ቻለንጅ -ግ- መ'ቋቋም [ተቋቋመ] ፣ መ'ወዳደር [ተወዳ'ደረ]
-ስ- መ'ቋቋም ፣ ውድ'ድር
chamber
'ቼይምበ -ስ- አ'ዳራሽ ፣ ምክር ቤት
chambermaid
'ቼይምበሜይድ -ስ- ሴት አገልጋይ (አልጋ አንጣፊ ወዘተ)
champion
'ቻምፒየን -ስ- አ'ሸ'ናፊ (የ ' ድር)
chance
'ቻ:ንስ -ስ- ዕ'ድል
change
'ቼይንጅ -ግ- መለ'ወጥ [ለ'ወጠ]
money
-ስ- ለውጥ ፣ ምን'ዛሪ
channel
'ቻነል -ስ- ቦይ ፣ ጠ'ባብ የባሕር መ'ተላለፊያ ፣ ወሃ መ'ተላለፊያ ፈረፈር
chant
'ቻ:ንት -ግ- ማሕሌት መቆም [ቆመ]
chaos
'ኬዮስ -ስ- ብጥ'ብጥ ፣ ሕ'ገ ወ'ጥ'ነት
chapel
'ቻፐል -ስ- የጸሎት ቤት ፣ ት'ንሽ ቤተ ክርስ ስቲያን
chaperon
'ሻፐረውን -ስ- የደ'ረሰ'ች ልጅ ጠ'ባቂ ሴት (ሞግዚት)
chapter
'ቻፐተ -ስ- ምዕራፍ (የመጽሐፍ)
char
'ቻ: -ስ- ቤት ጠራጊ ሴት
character
'ካረክተ -ስ- ጠባይ ፣ መ'ለያ
letter
-ስ- ፊደል
charcoal
'ቻ:ኮውል -ስ- ከሰል (የንጨት)
charge
'ቻ:ጅ -ግ- መ'ክሰስ [ከ'ሰሰ]
fee
-ስ- ክ'ስ
battle
-ስ- ግጥሚያ ፣ መግጠም (ለጦር'ነት)
fire-arm
-ግ- ማጉረስ [አጎ'ረሰ] (መ'ሣርያ)
money
-ግ- ማስከ'ፈል [አስከ'ፈለ]
fill
-ግ- የ'ሚችለውን ያህል መሙላት [ሞ'ላ]
charitable
'ቻሪተበል -ቅ- ቸር ፣ ለ'ጋስ
charity
'ቻሪቲ -ስ- በ'ጎ አድራጎት
charm
'ቻ:ም -ስ- ውበት ፣ የደስ ደ'ስ
charming
'ቻ:ሚንግ -ቅ- አስደ'ሳች ፣ ውብ ፣ የደስ ደ'ስ ያ'ለው
chart
'ቻ:ት -ስ- የባሕር ካርታ (ለመርከብ ጉዞ የ'ሚ ያገለ'ግል) ፣ ሠንጠረዥ
charter
'ቻ:ተ -ስ- ንጉሣዊ ትእዛዝ (አንድ ነገር ለመ ፍቀድ)
hire
-ግ- በሙሉ መ'ከራየት [ተከራ'የ] (አው ሮ'ፕላን ፣ መርከብ ወዘተ)
charwoman
'ቻ:ውመን -ስ- ቤት ጠራጊ ሴት

chase
’ቼይስ -ግ- ማ'ሳደድ [አሳ'ደደ]
chasm
'ካዝም -ስ- ጥልቅ'ና ጠ'ባብ ሸለቆ
chaste
’ቼይስት -ቅ- ድንግል'ና ፣ ንጽሕ'ና ያ'ለው (ለሴት)
chastise
ቻስ’ታይዝ -ግ- መቅጣት [ቀ'ጣ] (በመምታት ፣ በመገረፍ) ፣ መቅሠፍ [ቀ'ሠፈ]
chastity
’ቻስቲቲ -ስ- ድንግል'ና ፣ ንጽሕ'ና (ከፈቃደ ሥጋ)
chat
’ቻት -ግ- መ'ጫወት [ተጫ'ወተ] ፣ ማውራት [አወ'ራ]
chatter
’ቻተ -ግ- መለፍለፍ [ለፈ'ለፈ] ፤ ጥርስ ማንቀጥቀጥ [አንቀጠ'ቀጠ] (ከብርድ ፣ ከፍርሃት የተነ'ሣ)
chauffeur
’ሸውፈ -ስ- ሾፌር ፣ ለሰው የተቀ'ጠረ አውቶሞቢል ነጅ
cheap
’ቺይፐ -ቅ- እር'ካሽ
cheat
’ቺይት -ግ- ማ'ታለል [አ'ታ'ለለ]
check
’ቼክ -ግ- መ'ቆጣጠር [ተቆጣ'ጠረ] ፣ ማቆም [አቆመ] ፣ መግታት [ገ'ታ] (ፈረስ ወዘተ)
cheek
’ቺይክ -ስ- ጉንጭ
cheekbone
’ቺይክበውን -ስ- የጉንጭ አጥንት
cheeky
’ቺይኪ -ቅ- ባለጌ ፣ ያልታ'ረመ ፣ ለበላይ አክብሮት የ'ማያሳ'ይ
cheer
’ቺየ -ግ- በደ'ስታ መጮኽ [ጮኸ]
cheerful
’ቺየፉል -ቅ- ደ'ስተ'ኛ ፣ ደ'ስ ያለው ፣ ተደ'ሳች
cheese
’ቺይዝ -ስ- የደ'ረቀ አይብ (ፎርማጅ)
chef
’ሼፍ -ስ- በሆቴል ውስጥ የወጥ ቤቶ'ች አለቃ
chemical
'ኬሚክል -ስ- ጥንተ ንጥር
-ቅ- ጥንተ ንጥራዊ
chemist
'ኬሚስት -ስ- ቀ'ማሚ (መድኃኒት ፣ ጥንተ ንጥር)
chemistry
'ኬሚስትሪ -ስ- ጥንተ ንጥር ት'ምህ (ኬሚስትሪ)
cheque
’ቼክ -ስ- አንድ ባንክ ላንድ ሰው ገንዘብ እን ዲከፍል የ'ሚ'ታ'ዘዝ'በት ወረቀት ፣ ቼክ
cherish
’ቼሪሽ -ግ- ማፍቀር [አፈ'ቀረ] ፣ መ'ከባከብ [ተከባ'ከበ]
chest
’ቼስት -ስ- ደረት ፤ ት'ልቅ ሣጥን
chew
ችʼዩ -ግ- ማ'ላመጥ [አ'ላ'መጠ] ፣ ማ'ኘክ [አ'ኘከ]
chicken
’ቺከን -ስ- ጫጩ'ት
chicken-pox
’ቺከን ፖክስ -ስ- ጉድፍ (በ'ሽታ)
chick-pea
’ቺክፒ -ስ- ሽምብራ
chief
’ቺይፍ -ስ- አለቃ ፣ ዋ'ና
chieftain
’ቺይፍተን -ስ- አለቃ ፣ ሹም (የነገድ ፣ የጎሳ)
child
’ቻይልድ -ስ- ሕፃን
childhood
’ቻይልድሁድ -ስ- ሕፃን'ነት ፣ ልጅ'ነት
childish
’ቻይልዲሽ -ቅ- የልጅ ሥራ ፣ ፍሬ ቢስ
chill
’ቺል -ስ- ብርድ
a cold
-ስ- ጉንፋን
chilli
’ቺሊ -ስ- ሚጥሚ'ጣ (በርበ'ሬ)

chilly
'ቺሊ -ቅ- ብርዳም ፣ ቀዝቃ'ዛ
chime
'ቻይም -ስ- የደወል ድምፅ
chimney
'ቺምኒ -ስ- የጢስ መውጫ (ለቤት)
chin
'ቺን -ስ- አገጭ
chink
'ቺንክ -ስ- ጭላን'ጭል
chip
'ቺፕ -ስ- ስ'ባሪ ፣ ስን'ጣሪ (የንጨት)
potato
-ስ- የድ'ን'ች ጥብስ
chirp
'ቸ፡ፕ -ስ- የወፍ ድምፅ
chisel
'ቺዘል -ስ- መሮ
chivalrous
'ሺቨልረስ -ቅ- የተቀ'ጣ ፣ የታ'ደበ (ለሴት) ፣ የደካሞ'ች ፣ የተጠ'ቁ ረ'ዳት
chock
'ቾክ -ስ- ወፍራም እንጨት (ያንድ ነገር ማቆሚያ)
chocolate
'ቾክለት -ስ- ቾ'ኮላታ
choice
'ቾይስ -ስ- ምርጫ
choir
ክ'ዋየ -ስ- መዘ'ምራን
choke
'ቾውክ -ግ- ማነቅ [አነ'ቀ] ፣ ጉሮ'ሮን ፈርጥቆ መያዝ [ያዘ]
choose
'ቹ፡ዝ -ግ- መምረጥ [መ'ረጠ]
chop
'ቾፕ -ግ- መከተፍ [ከ'ተፈ] ፣ መቆራረጥ [ቆ ራ'ረጠ]
chopper
'ቾፐ -ስ- ት'ንሽ መጥረቢያ ፣ ፋስ
chorus
'ኮ፡ረስ -ስ- መዘ'ምራን ፣ ዘፋኞ'ች
Christ
ክ'ራይስት -ስ- ክርስቶስ ፣ መሲሕ
christen
ክ'ሪሰን -ግ- ማጥመቅ [አጠ'መቀ] ፣ ክርስ ት'ና ማስነ'ሣት [አስነ'ሣ]
christian
ክ'ሪስትየን -ቅ- ክርስቲያን
Christmas
ክ'ሪስመስ -ስ- የገ'ና በዓል፣ ገ'ና
chronic
ክ'ሮኒክ -ቅ- ብዙ ጊዜ የ'ሚቆይ (በ'ሽታ)
chronicle
ክ'ሮኒክል -ስ- ዜና መዋዕል
chubby
'ቸቢ -ቅ- ክ'ብ ፊት'ና ጉንጫም (ሰው)
chuckle
'ቸክል -ግ- በቀ'ስታ መንከትከት [ተንከተ 'ከተ] (ለሣቅ)
chunk
'ቸንክ -ስ- ት'ልቅ ቁ'ራጭ ፣ ሙ'ዳ
church
'ቸ፡ች -ስ- ቤተ ክርስቲያን ፣ ቤተ እግዚአብ ሔር
churn
'ቸ፡ን -ግ- ወተት መገፋት [ገ'ፋ] ፣ መናጥ [ናጠ]
chute
'ሹ፡ት -ስ- መንሸራተቻ
cigar
ሲ'ጋ፡ -ስ- ሲጋር (ጥቅ'ል ትምባሆ)
cigarette
ሲገ'ሬት -ስ- ሲጋራ ፣ ትምባሆ
cinder
'ሲንደ -ስ- ረመጥ
cinema
'ሲነማ -ስ- ሲኒማ
cinnamon
'ሲነመን -ስ- ቀረፋ
circle
'ሰ፡ክል -ስ- ክበብ ፣ ክ'ብ ነገር
circular
'ሰ፡ክዩለ -ቅ- ክ'ብ
circulate
'ሰ፡ክዩሌይት -ግ- ማ'ደል [አ'ደለ] ፣ መዞር [ዞረ] ፣ ከቦታ ወደ ቦታ በነጻ መ'ዘዋወር [ተዘ ዋ'ወረ]

circumcise
'ሰ:ከምሳይዝ -ግ- መግረዝ [ገ'ረዘ]

circumference
' ሰ'ከምፈረንስ -ስ- ዙሪያ ፣ ክበብ (ያንድ ነገር)

circumstance
'ሰ:ከምስታንስ -ስ- ሁናቴ ፣ ሁኔታ

circumstantial
ሰከምስ'ታንሽል -ቅ- ቀጥተ'ኛ ማስረ'ጃ የሌ'ለው (ምስክር'ነት በፍርድ ቤት)፣ምክንያታዊ ወይን'ም አ'ሳባቢ ማስረ'ጃ

circus
'ሰ:ከስ -ስ- ሰርከስ ፣ የእንስሳት ጨዋታ ትርኢት

cite
'ሳይት -ግ- መጥቀስ [ጠ'ቀሰ] (ለማስረ'ጃ ፣ ለማ'ረጋገጫ)፤እፍርድ ቤት ማቅረብ [አቀ'ረበ]

citizen
'ሲቲዘን -ስ- ዜጋ

city
'ሲቲ -ስ- ከተማ

civic
'ሲቪክ -ቅ- የማ'ዘጋጃ ቤት

civilian
ሲ'ቪልየን -ስ- ሲቪል ፣ (ወታ'ደር ያልሆነ)

civilization
ሲቪሊ'ዜይሽን -ስ- ሥ'ል'ጣኔ

claim
ክ'ሌይም -ግ- መብቱ ነው ብሎ መጠ'የቅ [ጠ'የቀ] ፣ የኔ ነው ማለት [አለ]
-ስ- ማመልከት (መብት ለመጠ'የቅ)

claimant
ክ'ሌይመንት -ስ- አመልካች ፣ አቤት ባይ

clamber
ክ'ላምበ -ግ- መንጠላጠል [ተንጠላ'ጠለ] ፣ መውጣት [ወ'ጣ) (ተራራ ፣ ዛፍ ወዘተ)

clammy
ክ'ላሚ -ቅ- እርጥብ (ከላብ የተነ'ሣ)

clamour
ክ'ላመ -ስ- ጩኸት

clamp
ክ'ላምፕ -ግ- ማ'ያያዝ [አ'ያያዘ]
-ስ- ማ'ያያዥ

clan
ክ'ላን -ስ- ጎሳ

clandestine
ክ'ላንደስታይን -ቅ- ምስጢራዊ

clap
ክ'ላፕ -ግ- ማጨብጨብ [አጨበ'ጨበ]

clarify
ክ'ላሪፋይ -ግ- ጉልህ ማድረግ [አደ'ረገ] ፣ መግለጽ [ገ'ለጸ] ፣ ንጹሕ ማድረግ (አደ'ረገ) ፣ ማብራራት [አብራ'ራ]

clarity
ክ'ላሪቲ -ስ- ግልጽ'ነት ፣ ጉልህ'ነት

clash
ክ'ላሽ -ግ- መ'ላተም [ተላ'ተመ] ፣ መ'ጋጨት [ተጋ'ጨ] ፣ መ'ከራከር [ተከራ'ከረ]

clasp
ክ'ላ:ስፕ -ግ- መጨ'በጥ [ጨ'በጠ] ፣ መቆ'ለፍ [ቆ'ለፈ] ፣ ማ'ያያዝ [አ'ያያዘ]

class
ክ'ላ:ስ -ስ- ክፍል (በትምህርት ቤት)
category
-ስ- ደረጃ ፣ መደብ (በማኅበራዊ ኑሮ)

classify
ክ'ላሲፋይ -ግ- በደምብ መከፋፈል [ከፋ'ፈለ] (በ'ያይነቱ ፣ በ'የወገኑ)

clatter
ክ'ላተ -ስ- ኳኳቴ (ድምፅ)

clause
ክ'ሎ:ዝ -ስ- አንቀጽ (የውል)
grammatical
-ስ- ዐረፍተ ነገር (አንድ ማሰሪያ አንቀጽ ብ'ቻ ያ'ለው)

claw
ክ'ሎ: -ስ- ጥፍር (የእንስሳት)

clay
ክ'ሌይ -ስ- ሸክላ

clean
ክ'ሊይን -ግ- ማጽዳት (አጸ'ዳ) ፣ መጥረግ [ጠ'ረገ] (ለቤት)
-ቅ- ንጹሕ ፣ የጸ'ዳ

cleanliness
ክ'ሌንሊኔስ -ስ- ንጽሕ'ና ፣ ጽዳት

clear
ክ'ሊየ -ቅ- ግልጽ
liquid
-ቅ- በውስጡ የ'ሚያሳ'ይ
cleft
ክ'ሌፍት -ስ- ስንጥቅ
clemency
ክ'ሌመንሲ -ስ- ምሕረት ፣ በጥፋት ላይ ልል መሆን ፣ ጥፋትን አክብዶ አለማየት
clench
ክ'ሌንች -ግ- መጨ'በጥ [ጨ'በጠ] (እ'ጅን)
clergy
ክ'ለ:ጂ -ስ- ካህናት
clergyman
ክ'ለ:ጂመን -ስ- ካህን
clerical
ክ'ሌሪክል -ቅ- የጸሓፊ (ሥራ)
priestly
-ቅ- የካህን
clerk
ክ'ላ:ክ -ስ- ጸሓፊ
clever
ክ'ሌቨ -ቅ- ብልኅ
cleverness
ክ'ሌቨነስ -ስ- ብልኀተ'ኛ'ነት
click
ክ'ሊክ -ስ- ቀ'ጭታ (ድምፅ)
client
ክ'ላየንት -ስ- ደምበ'ኛ (የገበያ)
clientele
ክላየን'ቴል -ስ- ደምበ'ኞ'ች
cliff
ክ'ሊፍ -ስ- ገደል ፣ ኸ'ው ያለ ገደል
climate
ክ'ላይመት -ስ- ያንድ ቦታ ጠቅላ'ላ ያ'የር'ና የነፋስ ሁናቴ
climax
ክ'ላይማክስ -ስ- አንድ ታሪክ ፣ ድርጊ'ት ፣ ሁናቴ እስተያየት የ'ሚግ'ርክ'በት ደረጃ
climb
ክ'ላይም -ግ- መውጣት [ወ'ጣ] ፣ መንጠላ ጠል [ተንጠላ'ጠለ]
cling
ክ'ሊንግ -ግ- መያዝ [ያዘ] (አጥብቆ)

clinic
ክ'ሊኒክ -ስ- ክሊኒክ ፣ የጤና ጣቢያ
clip
ክ'ሊፕ -ስ- ትን'ንሽ ዕቃዎ'ች ማ'ያያዣ ነገር
clique
ክ'ሊይክ -ስ- እርስ በእርሳ'ቸው የ'ሚ'ደጋ'ገፉ የግ'ል ግን'ኙ'ነት ያ'ላ'ቸው ሰዎ'ች
cloak
ክ'ለውክ -ስ- ካ'ባ
cloakroom
ክ'ለውክሩም -ስ- ልብስ ማስቀ'መጫ ክፍል (ካ'ፖርት ፣ ባርኔጣ ወዘተ)
clock
ክ'ሎክ -ስ- የጠረ'ጴዛ ሰዓት
clog
ክ'ሎግ -ግ- መ'ደፈን [ተደ'ፈነ] (በቆሻሻ)
close
ክ'ለውስ -ቅ- ቅርብ ፣ የተጠ'ጋ
close
ክ'ለውዝ -ግ- መዝጋት [ዘ'ጋ] (በበ'ር) ፣ ማ ጠፍ [አ'ጠፈ] (መጽሐፍ)
cloth
ክ'ሎፏ -ስ- ብ'ትን ጨርቅ
clothe
ክ'ለውዧ -ግ- ማልበስ [አለ'በሰ]
clothes
ክ'ለውዧስ -ስ- ልብስ
cloud
ክ'ላውድ -ስ- ደ'መና
cloudy
ክ'ላውዲ -ቅ- ደ'መና'ማ
clove
ክ'ለውቭ -ስ- ቅርንፉድ
clown
ክ'ላውን -ስ- አ'ሣቂ ሰው ፣ ሰውን ባ'ነጋገሩ'ና በመ'ላ ሁናቴው የ'ሚያ'ሥቅ ሰው
club
ክ'ለብ -ስ- ክበብ ፣ ማኅበር
stick
-ስ- ዱ'ላ ፣ በ'ትር
clue
ክ'ሉ: -ስ- ፍንጭ ፣ ምል'ክት

clumsy
ክ'ለምዚ -ቅ- አ'ረማመዱ የ'ሚያስጠ'ላ ፣ ቀር
ፋ'ፋ
roughly made
-ቅ- ጥሩ ሆኖ ያልተሠ'ራ ፣ የ'ማያምር

coach
'ኮውች -ግ- ማሠልጠን [አሠለ'ጠነ] (ለስፖ
ርት)
trainer
-ስ- አሠልጣኝ
vehicle
-ስ- ሠረገ'ላ

coagulate
ኮ'ዋግዩሌይት -ግ- መርጋት [ረ'ጋ] (ለፈሳሽ)

coal
'ኮውል -ስ- ከሰል (የድንጊያ)

coarse
'ኮ:ስ -ቅ- ሻካራ ፣ ኮስኳ'ሳ ፣ ግርድፍ'፤ ያ'ላ
መ
behaviour
-ቅ- ያልታ'ረመ (ለጠባይ)

coast
'ኮውስት -ስ- የባሕር ዳር

coat
'ኮውት -ስ- ካ'ፖርት ፣ ኮት

coax
'ኮውክስ -ግ- ማባበል [አባ'በለ] ፣ ማግባባት
[አግባ'ባ]

cobbler
'ኮብለ -ስ- ጫ'ማ አ'ዳሽ

cobra
'ኮብረ -ስ- እ'ፉ'ኝት

cock
'ኮክ -ስ- አውራ ዶሮ

cockerel
'ኮክረል -ስ- አውራ ዶሮ (በእድሜ አነ'ስ ያለ)፥
ስ'ራን ዶሮ

cockroach
'ኮክረውች -ስ- በረሮ

cocoa
'ኮውኮው -ስ- ካካዎ

code
'ኮውድ -ስ- ሕ'ገ መንግሥት፤ በልምድ ፣ በባ
ህል ላይ የተመሠ'ረቱ ሕ'ጎ'ች
secret writing
-ስ- ምስጢራዊ ጽሑፍ

coffee
'ኮፊ -ስ- ቡን ፣ ቡ'ና

coffee-pot
'ኮፊ ፖት -ስ- ጀበና ፣ ቡ'ና ማፍያ ፣ መከረጅ

coffin
'ኮፈን -ስ- የሬሳ ሣጥን

coherent
ኮ'ሂረንት -ቅ- የተያያዘ (ለንግ'ግር)

coil
'ኮይል -ግ- መጠምጠም [ጠመ'ጠመ] ፣ መጠ
ቅለል [ጠቀ'ለለ]
-ስ- ጥምጥም ነገር ፣ ጥ'ቅል

coin
'ኮይን -ስ- መሐ'ለቅ ፣ ዝርዝር ፍራንክ

coincide
ኮዊን'ሳይድ -ግ- በአንድ ጊዜ መሆን [ሆነ]
(ለሁለ'ት ነገር'ች)

coincidence
ኮ'ዊንሲደንስ -ስ- ድንገተ'ኛ ድርጊ'ት ፣ ድን
ገተ'ኛ አ'ጋጣሚ

cold
'ኮልድ -ስ- ብርድ
-ቅ- ብርዳም ፣ ቀዝቃ'ዛ
sickness
-ስ- ጉንፋን

collaborate
ከ'ላበሬይት -ግ- መ'ረዳዳት [ተረዳ'ዳ] ፣ ተጋ
ግዞ መሥራት [ሠ'ራ]
with enemy
-ግ- ከጠላት ጋር መ'ተባበር [ተባ'በረ]

collapse
ከ'ላፕስ -ግ- መ'ደምሰስ (ተደመ'ሰሰ] ፣ መፍ
ረስ [ፈ'ረሰ]፤ ተዝለፍልፎ መውደቅ [ወ'ደቀ]

collar
'ኮለ -ስ- አንገትጌ ፣ ከሳድ

colleague
'ኮሊይግ -ስ- የሥራ ጓ'ደ'ኛ

collect
ክ'ሌክት -ግ- መሰብሰብ [ሰበ'ሰበ] ፣ ማ'ከማ
ቸት [አ'ከማ'ቸ]

collection
ክ'ሌክሽን -ስ- የተሰበ'ሰበ ፣ የተከማ'ቸ ነገር

collector
ክ'ሌክተ -ስ- ሰብሳቢ ፣ አ'ከማች

college
'ኮለጅ -ስ- ኮ'ሌጅ ፣ ከ'ፍተ'ኛ ትምህርት ቤት

collide
ክ'ላይድ -ግ- መ'ጋጨት [ተጋ'ጨ] ፣ መ'ላ
ተም [ተላ'ተመ]

collision
ክ'ሊዠን -ስ- ግ'ጭት ፣ መ'ላተም

colloquial
ክ'ለውክዊየል -ቅ- የተራ ሰው ፣ የመንገድ
ቋንቋ ፣ (የጽሑፍ ያልሆነ)

colloquialism
ክ'ለውክዊየሊዝም -ስ- ተራ አ'ነጋገር ፣ ተራ
ቃል

colon
'ኮውለን -ስ- ሁለ'ት ነጥብ (፡)

colonel
'ከ፡ነል -ስ- ኮሎኔል

colony
'ኮለኒ -ስ- ቅ'ኝ ግዛት ፣ ቅ'ኝ አገር

colossal
ኮ'ሎሰል -ቅ- ታ'ላቅ ፣ በጣም ት'ልቅ ፣ በጣ
ም ግዙፍ

colour
'ከለ -ስ- ቀለም

colouring
'ከለሪንግ -ስ- አ'ቀባለም ፣ መልክ

colt
'ኮልት -ስ- የፈረስ ግልገል

column
'ኮለም -ስ- ረ'ጅም ዐምድ
of house
-ስ- ምሰ'ሶ
of newspaper
-ስ- ዐምድ (የጋዜጣ)

comb
'ከውም -ግ- ማበ'ጠር [አበ'ጠረ] (ለጠጉር)
-ስ- ማበ'ጠሪያ ፣ ሚዶ

combat
'ኮምባት -ግ- መ'ዋጋት [ተዋ'ጋ] ፣ መግጠም
[ገ'ጠመ] (ለጦር'ነት)
-ስ- ው'ጊያ ፣ ጦር'ነት

combatant
ከም'ባተንት -ስ- ተዋጊ

combination
ኮምቢ'ኔይሽን -ስ- መ'ጣመር ፣ መ'ገናኘት
(የሁለ'ት ነገር'ች)

combine
ከም'ባይን -ግ- ማ'ጣመር [አ'ጣመረ]

combine
'ኮምባይን -ስ- ያንድ'ነት ማኅበር ፣ ኅብረት
(የንግድ)

combustion
ከም'በስቸን -ስ- መ'ቃጠል

come
'ከም -ግ- መምጣት [መ'ጣ]

comedian
ከ'ሚይዲየን -ስ- አ'ሣቂ ፣ ቀ'ላጅ (ሰው)

comedy
'ኮመዲ -ስ- አ'ሣቂ ፣ ቀላ'ጅ ቴያትር ፣ አ'ሥ
ቂ'ኝ ቴያትር (ፍጻ'ሜው የደ'ስታ የሆነ)

comely
'ከምሊ -ቅ- መልከ ቀ'ና ፣ ውብ ፣ ቆንጆ (ለል
ጃገረድ)

comet
'ኮመት -ስ- ጂራታም ኮከብ

comfort
'ከምፈት -ስ- ም'ቾት ፣ ድሎት

comfortable
'ከምፈተበል -ቅ- ም'ቹ ፣ ድሎት ያ'ለው

comical
'ኮሚከል -ቅ- አ'ሥቂ'ኝ

comma
'ኮመ -ስ- ነጠላ ሠረዝ (’)

command
ክ'ማ፡ንድ -ግ- ማዘዝ [አ'ዘዘ]

commander
ክ'ማ፡ንደ -ስ- አ'ዛዥ

commanding
ክ'ማ፡ንዲንግ -ቅ- አ'ዛዥ
impressive
-ቅ- ባለግርማ ፣ ግርማ ሞገስ ያ'ለው

commandment
ከ'ማ፡ንድመንት -ስ- ትእዛዝ
commemorate
ከ'ሜመሬይት -ግ- የማስታወሻ በዓል ማድ ረግ [አደ'ረገ]
commence
ከ'ሜንስ -ግ- መጀ'መር [ጀ'መረ]
comment
'ኮሜንት -ግ- አስተያየት መስጠት [ሰ'ጠ]
-ስ- አስተያየት
commentary
'ኮመንትሪ -ስ- ትርጓሜ ፣ አስተያየት (ስለአ ንድ ሁናቴ ፣ ድርጊ'ት)
radio
-ስ- ስለአንድ ድርጊ'ት በራዲዮ የ'ሚ 'ሰጥ ሐተታ ፣ ት'ችት (ስፖርት ወዘተ)
commentator
'ኮመንቴይተ -ስ- አስተያየት ሰጭ ፣ መፈ'ከር
commerce
'ኮመ፡ስ -ስ- ንግድ
commercial
ከ'መ፡ሸል -ቅ- የንግድ
commission
ከ'ሚሽን -ግ- ማዘዝ [አ'ዘዘ] ፣ አንድ ነገር እንዲፈ'ጽሙ ሥልጣን መስጠት [ሰ'ጠ]
payment
-ስ- የደ'ላል'ነት ዋጋ ፣ ለደ'ላላ የ'ሚ'ከ 'ፈል ገንዘብ
commit
ከ'ሚት -ግ- መፈ'ጸም [ፈ'ጸመ] ፣ ማድረግ [አ'ደረገ] (መጥፎ ...ራ)
to prison
-ግ- እሥር ቤት ማስገ'ባት [አስገ'ባ] (ለዳ'ኛ)
committee
ከ'ሚቲ -ስ- ደርግ (ጉባኤ)
commodity
ከ'ሞደቲ -ስ- የንግድ ዕቃ ፣ ሸቀጣሸቀጥ ፣ የርሻ'ና የማዕ'ድን ው'ጤት
common
'ኮመን -ቅ- ተራ ፣ የጋራ ፣ የተለ'መደ ፣ እን ግዳ ያልሆነ
low class
-ቅ- ዝ'ቅተ'ኛ (በማኅበራዊ ኑሮ) ፣ ባለጌ ፣ ስ'ድ

commonplace
'ኮመንፕሌይስ -ቅ- ተራ የሆነ
commotion
ከ'መውሽን -ስ- ብጥ'ብጥ ፣ ሁከት ፣ ፀ'ጥታ መንሣት
communal
'ኮምዩነል -ቅ- ኅብረ ሰብአዊ
communicate
ከም'ዩኒኬይት -ግ- መ'ገናኘት [ተገና'ኘ] ፣ ማ'ገናኘት [አ'ገና'ኘ] ፣ ማስተላለፍ [አስተ'ላ ለፈ] (በሽታ ፣ መልእክት)
communication
ከምዩኒ'ኬይሽን -ስ- መ'ገናኛ
communion
ከም'ዩንየን -ስ- ቁርባን
community
ከም'ዩኒቲ -ስ- ኅብረተ ሰብ
compact
'ኮምፓክት -ቅ- ደኅና ሆኖ የታ'ሸገ ፣ የተ ጠጋ'ጋ
companion
ከም'ፓንየን -ስ- ጓ'ደ'ኛ ፣ ባልንጀራ
company
'ከምፐኒ -ስ- ኩ'ባን'ያ ፣ ሽሪካ
social
-ስ- በኅብረተ ላይ ያ'ሉ ሰዎ'ች ፣ እንግ ዶ'ች
compare
ከም'ፔየ -ግ- ማ'ወዳደር [አ'ወዳ'ደረ] ፣ ማ'ነ ፃፀር (አ'ነፃ'ፀረ)
comparison
ከም'ፓሪሰን -ስ- ማ'ነፃፀር ፣ ማ'ወዳደር
compartment
ከም'ፓ፡ትመንት -ስ- ክፍል ፣ በባቡር ውስጥ የተሣፋሪዎ'ች መ'ቀመጫ ክፍል
compass
'ከምፐስ -ስ- ኮም'ፓስ ፣ ያቅጣ'ጫ መምሪያ መ'ጣሪያ (ጠድክል)
compassion
ከም'ፓሽን -ስ- ርኅራኄ
compatible
ከም'ፓቲበል -ቅ- አንድ ላይ መኖር የ'ሚ ችል ፣ ተስማሚ ፣ ከሌላ ሰው ጋር በደ'ስታ መኖር የ'ሚችል

compel
ክም'ፔል -ግ- ማስገ'ደድ [አስገ'ደደ]

compensate
'ኮምፐንሴይት -ግ- መካሥ [ካሠ]፣ መተ'ካት [ተ'ካ] (ባጠ'ፉት በወ'ሰዱት ዕቃ ፋንታ)

compete
ክም'ፒይት -ግ- መ'ወዳደር [ተወዳ'ደረ]

competent
'ኮምፐተንት -ቅ- ችሎታ ያ'ለው ፣ ለሥራ ተገቢ የሆነ ሰው

competition
ኮምፐ'ቲሽን -ስ- ውድ'ድር

competitor
ኮም'ፔቲተ -ስ- ተወዳዳሪ

compile
ክም'ፓይል -ግ- ማ'ዘጋጀት [አዘጋ'ጀ] (ለመ ጽሐፍ)

complain
ክምፕ'ሌይን -ግ- መ'ነጫነጭ [ተነጫ'ነጨ]፣ አቤቱታ ማቅረብ [አቀ'ረበ] ፤ በሰው ላይ ስሕ ተት ማግኘት [አገ'ኘ]

complaint
ክምፕ'ሌይንት -ስ- አቤቱታ ፣ ክ'ስ

complete
ክምፕ'ሊይት -ግ- መጨ'ረስ [ጨ'ረሰ]፣ መፈ 'ጸም [ፈ'ጸመ]
-ቅ- ሙሉ ፣ ፍ'ጹም

complex
'ኮምፕሌክስ -ቅ- የተወሳ'ሰበ ፣ ድብልቅልቅ፣ አስቸ'ጋሪ ፣ ዘንቅ

complexion
ክምፕ'ሌክሽን -ስ- የመልክ ቀለም ፣ መልክ

complicate
'ኮምፕሊኬይት -ግ- ማ'ጣመም [አ'ጣ'መመ] አ'ዋኪ ማድረግ [አደ'ረገ]፣ የተወሳ'ሰበ ማድረግ [አደ'ረገ]

complicated
'ኮምፕሊኬይተድ -ቅ- አ'ዋኪ ፣ አስቸ'ጋሪ

complication
ኮምፕሊ'ኬይሽን -ስ- የተወሳ'ሰበ ፣ የተዘባ 'ረቀ ነገር (ሁናቴ)

compliment
'ኮምፕሊሜንት -ግ- ማመስገን [አመሰ'ገነ]
-ስ- ምስጋና ፤ መሞገስ (ለሞገሰው)

comply
ክምፕ'ላይ -ግ- መስማማት [ተስማ'ማ] ፤ እ ንዱ በጠ'የቀው ነገር ታ'ዛዥ መሆን [ሆነ]

compose
ክም'ፖውዝ -ግ- መድረስ [ደ'ረሰ] (መዚቃ መጽሐፍ ፣ ቅኔ)

composer
ክም'ፖውዘ -ስ- መዚቃ ደራሲ

composition
ኮምፐ'ዚሽን -ስ- ድርሰት (የጽሑፍ ፣ የሙ ዚቃ)

compound
'ኮምፓውንድ -ስ- አጥር ግ'ቢ
chemical mixture
-ስ- የተደባ'ለቀ ጥንተ ንጥር

comprehend
ኮምፕሪ'ሄንድ -ግ- መ'ረዳት [ተረ'ዳ] ፣ ማስ ተዋል [አስተዋለ]

comprehension
ኮምፕሪ'ሄንሽን -ስ- ማስተዋል ፣ መ'ረዳት

comprehensive
ኮምፕሪ'ሄንሲቭ -ቅ- አ'ጠቃላይ ፣ ብዙ ነገር የያዘ

compress
ክምፕ'ሬስ -ግ- መ'ጫን [ተጫነ] ፣ መጠቅ ጠቅ [ጠቀ'ጠቀ]

compromise
'ኮምፕረማይዝ -ግ- ሁለ'ት ወገኖ'ች በ'የበ 'ኩላ'ቸው አንዳንድ ነገር በመተው እለመ ግባባትን ማስወ'ገድ [አስወ'ገደ]

compulsion
ኮም'ፓልሽን -ስ- ግ'ዴታ ፣ ያለ ው'ድ

compulsory
ክም'ፓልሰሪ -ቅ- የ'ሚያስገ'ድድ

compute
ክምፕ'ዩት -ግ- ማ'ስብ [አ'ሰበ] (ለሒሳብ)

comrade
'ኮምራድ -ስ- ጓ'ደ'ኛ ፣ ባልንጀራ

comradeship
'ኮምረድሺፕ -ስ- ጓ'ደ'ኛ'ነት ፣ ባልንጀር'ነት

conceal
ክን'ሲይል -ግ- መ'ሸሸግ [ተሸ'ሸገ] ፣ መደ 'በቅ [ደ'በቀ]

concede
ኮን'ሲይድ -ግ- መ'ሸነፍን መግለጽ [ገ'ለጸ]

conceive
ኮንሲ'ይቭ -ግ- ማርገዝ [አረ'ገዘ]
think
-ግ- ማሰብ [አ'ሰበ]

concentrate
ኮንሰንትሬይት -ግ- ባንድ ነገር ላይ አተ'ኩሮ ማ'ሰብ [አ'ሰበ] ፤ ማ'ከማቸት [አ'ከማ'ቸ]

concentration
ኮንሰንት'ሬይሽን -ስ- አተ'ኩሮ ማ'ሰብ
gathering
-ስ- ስብሰባ ፣ ባንድ ሥፍራ መ'ሰብሰብ፣ መ'ከማቸት

concept
ኮንሴፕት -ስ- ሐ'ሳብ

conception
ኮን'ሴፕሽን -ስ- ሐ'ሳብ
pregnancy
-ስ- እርግዝ'ና ፣ መፅነስ

concern
ኮን'ሰርን -ስ- የ'ሚገ'ድ ፣ የ'ሚያሳ'ስብ ነገር ፣ ቸ'ል የ'ማይሉት ጉ'ዳይ ፣ የ'ሚያገባ ጉ'ዳይ

concert
ኮንሰት -ስ- ኮንሰርት (ሙዚቃዊ ትርኢት)

concise
ኮን'ሳይስ -ቅ- የተመ'ጠነ ፣ አ'ጭር'ና ግልጽ (ለንግ'ግር)

conclude
ኮንክ'ሉ:ድ -ግ- መደምደም [ደመ'ደመ] ፣ መጨ'ረስ [ጨ'ረሰ)
decide
-ግ- መ'ወሰን [ወ'ሰነ]

conclusion
ኮንክ'ሉ:ዠን -ስ- መደምደሚያ ፣ ማሠሪያ
decision
-ስ- ው'ሳኔ

concord
ኮንኮ:ድ -ስ- ስምም'ነት ፣ ሰላማዊ ግን'ኙ'ነት

concrete
ኮንክሪይት -ቅ- ግዑዝ የ'ሚ'ጨ' በጥ ፣ የ'ሚ 'ዳ'ሰስ
building material
-ስ- ሲሚንቶ

condemn
ኮን'ዴም -ግ- መፍረድ [ፈ'ረደ] ፣ ጥፋተ'ኛ ነው ማለት [አለ] ፣ ማውገዝ [አወ'ገዘ]

condense
ኮን'ዴንስ -ግ- ማሳ'ጠር [አሳ'ጠረ] (ለጽሑፍ)
scientific
-ግ- ወደ ፈሳሽ'ነት መ'ለወጥ [ተለ'ወጠ]

condition
ኮን'ዲሽን -ስ- ሁናቴ ፣ ሁኔታ ፣ አ'ኳኋን

condole
ኮን'ደውል -ግ- ማስተዛዘን [አስተዛ'ዘነ]

conduct
ኮንደክት -ስ- አመል ፣ ጠባይ

conduct
ኮን'ደክት -ግ- መምራት [መ'ራ]

cone
ኮውን -ስ- ድፍ ቀንጫ

confectioner
ኮን'ፌክሽን -ስ- ጣፋጭ ምግብ ሠሪ

confectionery
ኮን'ፌክሽነሪ -ስ- ጣፋጭ ምግብ

confer
ኮን'ፈ: -ግ- መስጠት [ሰ'ጠ] (ለማዕረግ) መ'መካከር [ተመካ'ከረ]

conference
ኮንፈረንስ -ስ- ጉባኤ ፣ ስብሰባ

confess
ኮን'ፌስ -ግ- ን'ስሐ መግባት [ገ'ባ] ፣ ጥፋትን ማመን [አ'መነ]

confide
ኮን'ፋይድ -ግ- ች'ግርን ማ'ዋየት [አ'ዋ'የ]፣ እምነት በሰው ላይ መጣል [ጣለ]

confidence
ኮንፊደንስ -ስ- እምነት
secret
-ስ- ምስጢር

confidential
ኮንፊ'ዴንሸል -ቅ- ምስጢራዊ ፣ ድ'ብቅ

confine
ኮን'ፋይን -ግ- ማጋዝ [አጋዘ] ፣ እሥር ቤት ማስገ'ባት [አስገ'ባ]

confinement
ከን'ፋይንመንት -ስ- ግዞት ፣ እ'ሥራት
birth of child
-ስ- የወሊድ ጊዜ
confirm
ከን'ፈ፡ም -ግ- ማጽደቅ [አጸ'ደቀ] ፣ ማ'ረጋገጥ [አ'ረጋ'ገጠ]
confirmation
'ኮንፈ'ሜይሽን -ስ- ማጽደቅ ፣ ማ'ረጋገጥ
confiscate
'ኮንፈስኬይት -ግ- መውረስ [ወ'ረሰ] (ሀብት በመንግሥት)
conflict
ከንፍ'ሊክት -ግ- መ'ጣላት [ተጣ'ላ] ፣ አለመግባባት [-ተግባ'ባ]
conflict
'ኮንፍሊክት -ስ- አለመስማማት ፣ ጥል ፣ አለመግባባት
conform
ከን'ፎ፡ም -ግ- ሌሎችን መምሰል [መሰለ] (በጠባይ ወዘተ) ፣ መ'ከተል [ተከ'ተለ]
confront
ከንፍ'ረንት -ግ- መግጠም [ገ'ጠመ] (እዴጋ ፣ ዛ'ቻ)
confrontation
ኮንፍረን'ቴይሽን -ስ- መግጠም (እዴጋ ፣ ዛ'ቻ)
confuse
ከንፍ'ዩ፡ዝ -ግ- ማ'ደናገር [አ'ደና'ገረ]፣ መ'ደናገር [ተደና'ገረ]
confusion
ከንፍ'ዩ፡ዠን -ስ- መ'ደናገር ፣ ድንገርገር ፣ ብጥ'ብጥ
congeal
ከን'ጂይል -ግ- መርጋት [ረ'ጋ] (ለፈሳሽ)
congenial
ከን'ጂይኒየል -ቅ- በምርጫ ፣ በስ'ሜት የ'ሚስማ'ማ ፣ ተስማሚ
congestion
ከን'ጀስቸን -ስ- መ'ተፋፈግ ፣ መ'ጨናቆን
congratulate
ከንግ'ራትዩሌይት -ግ- የምሥራ'ች ማለት [አለ]
congratulation
ከንግራትዩ'ሌይሽን -ስ- የም'ሥራ'ች ማለት

congregate
'ኮንግረጌይት -ግ- መ'ሰብሰብ [ተሰበሰ'በ]
congress
'ኮንግረስ -ስ- ስብሰባ ፣ ጉባኤ
conjecture
ከን'ጀክቸ -ስ- ግምት'ሽ የሌ'ለው ሐሳብ ፣ መላ
conjugation
ኮንጁዩ'ጌይሽን -ስ- እርባታ (የግ'ሥ) ፣ መ'ጣመር ፣ መ'ያያዝ
conjunction
ኮን'ጀንክሽን -ስ- መስተፃምር (ሰዋስው)
conjure
'ከንጀ -ግ- ምትሀት መሥራት [ሠ'ራ] (በእ'ጅ ቅልጥፍ'ና)
conjurer
'ከንጀረ -ስ- ምትሀተ'ኛ
connect
ከ'ኔክት -ግ- ማ'ገናኘት [አ'ገና'ኘ]
connection
ከ'ኔክሽን -ስ- ግን'ኙ'ነት
connive
ከ'ናይቭ -ግ- መደ'ለት [ደ'ለተ]
connubial
ከን'ዩ፡ቢየል -ቅ- የጋብ'ቻ
conquer
'ኮንከ -ግ- ማ'ሸ'ነፍ [አ'ሸ'ነፈ] ፣ ድል መንሣት [ነ'ሣ]
conqueror
'ኮንከረ -ስ- ድል ነሺ ፣ ባለድል ፣ አ'ሸ'ናፊ
conscience
'ኮንሸንስ -ስ- ኅ'ሊና ፣ ክፉ'ና ደ'ግን መለ'ያ ውሳጣዊ ስ'ሜት
conscientious
ኮንሺ'ዬንሸስ -ቅ- ሥራውን ዐውቆ የ'ሚሠራ ፣ ኀላፊ'ነት የ'ሚ'ሰ'ማው ፣ ጠንካ'ራ (ለሥራ)
conscious
'ኮንሸስ -ቅ- የነ'ቃ ፣ ንቁ ፣ ሊያ'ስብ ፣ ሊ'ረ'ዳ የ'ሚችል
conscript
'ኮንስክሪፕት -ግ- በግ'ዴታ ወ'ታ'ደር'ነት መ'መልመል [ተመለ'መለ]
-ስ- በግ'ዴታ የ'ሚያገለ'ግል ወ'ታ'ደር

consecutive
ከን'ሴክዩቲቭ -ቅ- ተከታታይ ፣ ቅደም ተከ'ተል'ነት ያ'ለው
consent
ከን'ሴንት -ግ- መስማማት [ተስማ'ማ]
-ስ- ስምም'ነት
consequence
ኮንሲክዌንስ -ስ- የ'ሚ'ገ'ባ መደምደሚያ ፣ መፈ'ጸሚያ
result
-ስ- ው'ጤት ፣ አንድ ሁኔቴ የ'ሚያስከ'ትለው ነገር
consequently
ኮንሲክዌንትሊ -ተግ- በኋላ
therefore
-ተግ ስለ'ዚህ ፣ በ'ዚህ ምክንያት
conservative
ከን'ሰ፡ቨቲቭ -ቅ- ለውጥ የ'ማይወ'ድ ፣ በጥ'ንቱ ልማድ የጸ'ና
conserve
ከን'ሰ፡ቭ -ግ- ማቆ'የት [አቆ'የ] (ዕቃ እንዳ ይ'በላ'ሽ በማድረግ)
consider
ከን'ሲደ -ግ- መመርመር [መረ'መረ] ፣ በነ ገሩ ፣ በጉ'ዳዩ ማ'ሰብ [አ'ሰበ]
considerable
ከን'ሲደረበል -ቅ- በጣም ት'ልቅ ፣ ሊያስተ ውሉት የ'ሚ'ገ'ባ
considerate
ከን'ሲደረት -ቅ- ርኅሩኅ ፣ ለሰው አ'ሳቢ
consideration
ከንሲደ'ሬይሽን -ስ- ሐ'ሳብ (ጥን'ቃቄ ያ'ለ'በት)
thoughtfulness
-ስ- ርኅራኄ ፣ ለሰው ማ'ሰብ
consign
ከን'ሳይን -ግ- ማስረ'ከብ [አስረ'ከበ]
entrust
-ግ- አደራ መስጠት [ሰ'ጠ]
send
-ግ- መላክ [ላከ]
consignment
ከን'ሳይንመንት -ስ- ጭነት (የተላከ)
consist of
ከን'ሲስት ኦቭ -ግ- ከ . . . መ'ሥራት [ተሠ'ራ]

consistent
ከን'ሲስተንት -ቅ- ተመሳሳይ ፣ (አንድ ዓይ ነት የሆነ) ፣ የ'ማይ'ለ'ወጥ ፣ የተወ'ሰነ
consolation
ኮንሰ'ሌይሽን -ስ- ማጽናኛ
consolidation
ከንሶሊ'ዴይሽን -ስ- ማጠንከር ፣ ማ'ዋሐድ ፣ የጠ'ና ማድረግ
consonant
ኮንሰነንት -ስ- ድምፅ ተ'ቀ'ባይ ፊደል (ሰዋ ሰው)
-with
-ቅ- የ'ሚስማ'ማ ፣ ኅብር'ነት ያ'ለው
conspicuous
ከንስ'ፒክዩወስ -ቅ- በቀ'ላሉ የ'ሚ'ታ'ይ ያልተሠ'ወረ ፣ ለዓይን ግልጽ የሆነ
conspiracy
ከንስ'ፒረሲ -ስ- መሸ'መቅ ፣ ሴራ
conspirator
ከንስ'ፒረተ -ስ- ሸ'ማቂ ፣ ሴረ'ኛ
constable
ኮንስተበል -ስ- ተራ የፖሊስ ወ'ታ'ደር
constant
ኮንስተንት -ቅ- የ'ማይ'ለ'ወጥ ፣ የተወ'ሰነ ፣ የ'ማያ'ቋ'ርጥ
constipation
ኮንስቲ'ፔይሽን -ስ- የሆድ ድርቀት (ሠገራ የ'ሚከለ'ክል በ'ሽታ)
constitution
ኮንስቲት'ዩ፡ሽን -ስ- ሕ'ገ መንግሥት ፣ አ'ቀን ባበር ፣ አ'መሠራረት ፣ የሰው'ነት ጤን'ነት
construct
ኮንስት'ረክት -ግ- መገንባት [ገነ'ባ] ፣ መሥ ራት [ሠ'ራ] (ቤት ወዘተ)
constructive
ኮንስት'ረክቲቭ -ቅ- ጠቃሚ ፣ መ'ሻሻል የ'ሚያመጣ ፣ አልሚ
consul
ኮንሰል -ስ- ቆንሲል (በው'ጭ አገር የአገሩን ጉ'ዳይ የ'ሚ'ጠባ'በቅ ሹም)
consult
ከን'ሰልት -ግ- ማ'ማከር [አ'ማ'ከረ] ፣ ምክር መጠ'የቅ [ጠ'የቀ]

consultant
ከን'ሰልተንት -ስ- አ'ማካሪ ፣ ምክር ሰጪ ፣ ምክር ተቀ'ባይ

consume
ከንስ'ዩ:ም -ግ- መጨ'ረስ [ጨ'ረሰ] ፣ መፍ ጀት [ፈ'ጀ] (ለምግብ ወዘተ)

consumer
ከንስ'ዩ:መ -ስ- ጆምበ'ኛ (የንግድ)
final user
-ስ- በ'ላተ'ኛ (ገዝቶ ለራሱ ጥቅም የ'ሚ ያውል)

consumption
ከን'ሰምሽን -ስ- መጨ'ረስ ፣ መፍጀት (ምግብ ፣ ነዳጅ ወዘተ)

contact
ኮን'ታክት -ግ- መ'ገናኘት [ተገና'ኘ] ፣ መ'ነ ካካት [ተነካ'ካ]
a person
-ስ- የ'ሚያውቁት ሰው (በሥልጣን ላይ ያ'ለ)

contagious
ከን'ቴይጀስ -ቅ- በመ'ነካካት የ'ሚ'ተላ'ለፍ፣ ተላላፊ (በ'ሽታ)

contain
ከን'ቴይን -ግ- መያዝ [ያዘ] (ለዕቃ)

container
ከን'ቴይነ -ስ- መያዣ (ለዕቃ)

contaminate
ከን'ታሚኔይት -ግ- መ'ነካካት [ተነካ'ካ]፣ በ 'ሽታ ማስተላለፍ [አስተላ'ለፈ]

contemplate
ኮንተምፕሌይት -ግ- ማ'ሰላሰል [አ'ሰላ'ሰለ]፣ አጥልቆ መመርመር [መረ'መረ]፣ማውጣት ማውረድ [አወ'ጣ አወ'ረደ]፣አተ'ኩሮ መ'መ ልከት [ተመለ'ከተ]

contemplation
ኮንተምፕ'ሌይሽን -ስ- ማ'ሰላሰል ፣ ጥልቅ ምርመራ

contemporary
ከን'ቴምፖራሪ -ቅ- በአንድ ዘመን አብሮ የኖረ (ሰው ወዘተ)

contempt
ከን'ቴምት -ስ- ማ'ዋረድ ፣ ማፌዝ ፣ ንቀት

content
ከን'ቴንት -ቅ- የተደ'ሰተ ፣ ያልከ'ፋው ፣ ቅ'ር ያላለው

content
'ኮንቴንት -ስ- ይዞታ

contest
'ኮንቴስት -ስ- ውድ'ድር

continent
'ኮንቲነንት -ስ- አህጉር

continual
ኮን'ቲንዩወል -ቅ- የ'ማያ'ቋ'ርጥ ፣ የ'ሚቀ 'ጥል

continuation
ከንቲንዩ'ዌይሽን -ስ- መቀ'ጠል ፣ የ'ሚ'ከ 'ተል ነገር

contingent
ከን'ቲንጀንት -ቅ- ሊደርስ የ'ሚችል ፣ እርግ ጠ'ኛ ያልሆነ
close to
-ቅ- ወደፊት ሊሆኑ ከ'ሚችሉ ነገሮ'ች ጋራ የተያያዘ
body of troops
-ስ- የጦር ክፍል

contortion
ከን'ቶ:ሽን -ስ- መ'ጠማዘዝ (የሰውነ'ት ወዘተ)

contour
'ኮንቱወ -ስ- ቅርፅ ፣ መልክ

contraband
'ኮንትረባንድ -ስ- ኮንትሮባንድ ፣ ቀረጥ ያልተ ከ'ፈለ'በት ሸቀጥ (በድ'ብቅ የ'ሚ'ሸጥ)

contraceptive
ኮንትረ'ሴፕቲቭ -ስ- የርግዝ'ና መ'ከላከያ

contract
'ኮንትራክት -ስ- ስምም'ነት ፣ ውል ፣ ኮንት ራት

contract
ከንት'ራክት -ግ- መ'ኮማተር [ተኮማ'ተረ]
a disease
-ግ- በ'ሽታ መያዝ [ያዘ]

contractor
ከንት'ራክተ -ስ- ተቋራጭ ፣ ተዋዋይ (የሥራ)

contradict
ኮንትረ'ዲክት -ግ- መ'ቃወም [ተቃ'ወመ] ፣ መ'ቃረን [ተቃ'ረነ]

contrary
'ኮንትረሪ -ቅ- ተቃራኒ
contrast
'ኮንትራስት -ግ- ል'ዩ'ነት ለማግኘት ማ'ነ ፃፀር [አ'ነፃ'ፀረ] ፣ ል'ዩ'ነት ማግኘት [አገ'ኘ]
-ስ- ጉልህ የሆነ ል'ዩ'ነት
contribute
ከንት'ሪብዩት -ግ- ገንዘብ ማ'ዋጣት[አ'ዋ'ጣ]፣ አንድ ነገር ለመኖሩ ፣ ለመ'ሠራቱ ምክንያት መሆን [ሆነ]
contribution
ኮንትሪብ'ዩሽን -ስ- እስተዋጽኦ ፣ መ'ዋጮ
contributor
ከንት'ሪብዩተ -ስ- ገንዘብ አ'ዋጭ ፣ መ'ዋጮ የ'ሚያደርግ ሰው
contrivance
ከንት'ራይቨንስ -ስ- ለል'ዩ ተግባር የተሠ'ራ መኪና ፣ መ'ቀላጠፊያ
control
ከንት'ሮል -ግ- ሥልጣን መያዝ [ያዘ]
controversial
ኮንትረ'ቨ፡ሸል -ቅ- የ'ማይስማ'ሙ'በት ፣ የ'ሚ ያ'ከራ'ክር
controversy
ከንት'ሮቨሲ -ስ- ክር'ክር ፣ የ'ማይስማ'ሙ'በ ት ጉ'ዳይ
convalescent
ኮንቨ'ሌሰንት -ቅ- አገ'ጋሚ ፣ ገመምተ'ኛ
convene
ከን'ቪይን -ግ- ጉባኤ መሰብሰብ [ሰበ'ሰበ]
convenient
ከን'ቪይኒየንት -ቅ- ተስማሚ ፣ ም'ቹ
convent
'ኮንቨንት -ስ- ገዳም (የሴቶ'ች)
convention
ከን'ቬንሽን -ስ- ት'ልቅ ስብሰባ
custom
-ስ- ባህል
conventional
ከን'ቬንሽነል -ቅ- ባህል' አክባሪ ፣ በባህል ላይ የተመሠ'ረተ ፣ የተለ'መደ ነገር
converge
ከን'ቨ፡ጅ -ስ- መ'ጋጠም [ተጋ'ጠመ] ፣ መ'ገና ኘት [ተገና'ኘ]

conversant
ከን'ቨ፡ሰንት -ቅ- ዐዋቂ ፣ ልምድ ያ'ለው
conversation
ኮንቨ'ሴይሽን -ስ- ንግ'ግር
converse
ከን'ቨ፡ስ -ግ- መ'ነጋገር
converse
'ኮንቨስ -ስ- ተቃራኒ ፣ ተቃዋሚ ነገር
conversion
ከን'ቨ፡ሽን -ስ- ሃይማኖት መለ'ወጥ
convertible
ከን'ቨ፡ተበል -ቅ- መ'ዛወር ፣ መ'ለወጥ የ'ሚ ችል
convey
ከን'ቬይ -ግ- ማ'ዘዋወር [አ'ዘዋ'ወረ] (ካንድ ቦታ ወደ ሌላው)
convict
ከን'ቪክት -ግ- መፍረድ [ፈ'ረደ] (ሲ'ፈ'ረድ 'በት)
convict
'ኮንቪክት -ስ- እሥረ'ኛ ፣ የተፈ'ረደ'በት ሰው
conviction
ከን'ቪክሽን -ስ- ጽኑ እምነት
convince
ከን'ቪንስ -ግ- ማሳ'መን [አሳ'መነ]
convivial
ከን'ቪቪየል -ቅ- የደ'መቀ (ግብዣ) ፣ ማኀበ ራዊ ፣ ሞቅ ያ'ለው (በመ'ጠጥ)
convoy
'ኮንቮይ -ስ- ሠልፍ (የጦር መኪናዎ'ች)
convulsion
ከን'ቨልሽን -ስ- ወፈ'ፍ ማድረግ (ድንገተ'ኛ የሰው'ነት) ፣ መባተት
cook
'ኩክ -ግ- ወጥ መሥራት [ሠ'ራ]
chef
-ስ- ወጥ ቤት (ሰው) ፣ ወጥ ሠሪ
cookery
'ኩከሪ -ስ- ወጥ አ'ሠራር
cooker
'ኩክ -ስ- ምድ'ጃ

cool
'ኩ:ል -ግ- ማቀዝቀዝ [አቀዘ'ቀዘ]
-ቅ- ቀዝቃ'ዛ

cooperate
ኮ'ዖፐሬይት -ቅ- መ'ተባበር [ተባ'በረ] ፣ መ'ረዳዳት [ተረዳ'ዳ]

cooperation
ኮዖፐ'ሬይሽን -ስ- ኅብረት ፣ ትራድኦ

coordinate
ኮ'ዖ:ዲኔይት -ግ- በትክ'ክለ'ኛ መንገድ እንዲ'ሠ'ራ ማስተባበር [አስተባ'በረ]

cope with
'ከውፕ ዊዝ -ግ- አንድ አስቸ'ጋሪ ሥራ ደኅና አድርጎ ማ'ካሄድ [አ'ካሄደ] ፣ ብቁ ሆኖ መ'ገኘት [ተገ'ኘ]

copious
'ከውፒየስ -ቅ- ብዙ ፣ የተትረፈ'ረፈ

copper
'ኮፐ -ስ- መዳብ

copulate
'ኮፐዩሌይት -ግ- መ'ገናኘት [ተገና'ኘ] (በፈቃደ ሥጋ)

copy
'ኮፒ -ግ- መገልበጥ [ገለ'በጠ] ፣ መቅዳት [ቀ'ዳ] (ጽሑፍ ወዘተ)
-ስ- ቅ'ጂ ፣ ግል'ባጭ

cord
'ኮ:ድ -ስ- ገመድ ፣ ሲባጎ

cordial
'ኮ:ዲየል -ቅ- ደ'ግ'ነት የተሞ'ላ ፣ ል'ባዊ

cordon
'ኮ:ደን -ስ- የማዕረግ ምል'ክት (እንደ መቀ'ነት ያ'ለ) ፣ መከበብ (በፖሊስ)

core
'ኮ: -ስ- ቡጥ ፣ ማእከላዊ ቦታ

co-respondent
ከውረስ'ፖንደንት -ስ- በዝ'ሙት የተከ'ሰሰ ሰው (ባና ካልታፈ'ታ'ች ከሰው ሚስት ጋር በመ'ገናኘት)

coriander
'ኮሪያንደ -ስ- ድምብላል

cork
'ኮ:ክ -ስ- ቡሽ

corkscrew
'ኮ:ክስክሩ -ስ- የቡሽ መንቀያ

corn
'ኮ:ን -ስ- የስንዴ ዓይነት እህል

coronation
ኮረ'ኔይሽን -ስ- የንግሥ በዓል ፣ በዓለ ንግሥ

corner
'ኮ:ነ -ስ- ማዕዘን

corps
'ኮ: -ስ- ጓ'ድ

corpse
'ኮ:ፐስ -ስ- ሬሳ ፣ በድን

corporal
'ኮ:ፐረል -ስ- ያ'ሥር አለቃ
-ቅ- የሰውነ'ት

corporation
ኮፐ'ሬይሽን -ቅ- የማ'ዘጋጃ ቤት መማክርት
company
-ስ- ኩ'ባን'ያ

correct
ከ'ሬክት -ግ- ማረም [አ'ረመ] (የተሳሳተውን)
-ቅ- ል'ክ ፣ ያልተሳሳተ

correction
ከ'ሬክሽን -ስ- እ'ርማት

correctness
ከ'ሬክትነስ -ስ- ሕ'ግ አክባሪ'ነት ፣ ትክ'ክለ'ኛ'ነት

correspond
ኮረስ'ፖንድ -ግ- መ'ጻጻፍ [ተጻጻፈ]
be equal
-ግ- መ'ተካከል [ተካ'ከለ] ፣ መ'መሳሰል [ተመሳ'ሰለ]

correspondent
ኮረስ'ፖንደንት -ስ- ደብዳ'ቤ የ'ሚ'ጻጻፉት ሰው
newspaper
ወ'ኪል (የጋዜጣ)

corridor
'ኮሪዶ: -ስ- መ'ተላለፊያ (የቤት)

corrode
ከ'ረውድ -ግ- መ'በላት [ተበ'ላ] (ብረታ ብረት)

corrosion
ከ'ረውዥን -ስ- መ'በላት ፣ መዛግ

corrugated iron
ኮረጌይተድ'አየን -ስ- የቤት ክዳን ቆርቆ'ሮ

corrupt
ከ'ረፐት -ግ- ማ'በላሸት [አ'በላ'ሸ] ፣ ማጥ
ፋት [አጠ'ፋ]
-ቅ- ብል'ሹ ፣ ጥፉ

cost
'ኮስት -ግ- ማውጣት [አወ'ጣ] (ለዋጋ)
በ . . . መ'ገዛት [በ . . . ተገ'ዛ]

costly
'ኮስትሊ -ቅ- ው'ድ

costume
'ኮስትዩም -ስ- ልብስ

cot
'ኮት -ስ- የሕፃን አልጋ

cottage
'ኮተጅ -ስ- ት'ንሽ የመኖሪያ ቤት (በባላገር) ፣
ዛኒጋ'ባ

cotton
'ኮተን -ስ- ጥጥ

couch
'ካውች -ስ- ድንክ አልጋ

cough
'ኮፍ -ግ- መሳል [ሳለ] (ለጉንፋን)

council
'ካውንሰል -ስ- መማክርት ፣ ደርግ

councillor
'ካውንሰለ -ስ- የደርግ ፣ የጉባኤ አባል

counsellor
'ካውንሰለ -ስ- አ'ማካሪ

count
'ካውንት -ግ- መቁጠር [ቆ'ጠረ] ፣ ማ'ሰብ
[አ'ሰበ] (ለሒሳብ)

countenance
'ካውንተነንስ -ስ- ፊት ፣ በፊት ላይ ያ'ለ ሲ'ሜ
ት (የሐዘን ፣ የደ'ስታ ወዘተ)

counter
'ካውንተ -ስ- ዕቃ ለሽ'ያጭ የ'ሚቀርብ'በት
ረ'ጅም የሱቅ ጠረ'ጴዛ
games
-ስ- ፊሽ (የመ'ጫወቻ)
mechanical
-ስ- መቁጠሪያ (መ'ሣሪያ)

counterfeit
'ካውንተፊት -ቅ- ትክ'ክለ'ኛ ያልሆነ ፣ ለማ
'ታለል እስመ'ስሎ የተሠ'ራ ገንዘብ

counterfoil
'ካውንተፎይል -ስ- ጉርድ (የካርኒ ወዘተ)

countless
'ካውንትሌስ -ቅ- ቁጥር የሌ'ለው ፣ በጣም
ብዙ ፣ ተቆጥሮ የ'ማያልቅ

country
'ከንትሪ -ስ- አገር

countryman
'ከንትሪመን -ስ- ባላገር (ሰው) ፣ ያገር ልጅ

countryside
'ከንትሪሳይድ -ስ- ባላገር (አገር)

couple
'ከፐል -ስ- ሁለ'ት የሆነ ነገር ፣ ጥንድ ፣ ባልና'
ሚስት
-ግ- ማ'ጣመር [አ'ጣ'መረ]

courage
'ከሪጅ -ስ- ድፍረት ፣ ጀግን'ነት

courageous
ከ'ሬይጀስ -ቅ- ደ'ፋር ፣ ጀግና ፣ ጎበዝ

courier
'ኩሪየ -ስ- መልክተ'ኛ

course
'ኮ:ስ -ስ- ትምህርት ፣ በተወ'ሰነ ጊዜ የ'ሚ'ማ
ሩት ትምህርት
race-
-ስ- የሽቅድ'ድም ሜዳ

court
'ኮ:ት -ስ- የታ'ጠረ ቦታ ፣ አጥር ግ'ቢ
legal
-ስ- ፍርድ ቤት
palace
-ስ- ቤተ መንግሥት
personnel
-ስ- በቤተ መንግሥት የ'ሚኖሩ ሰዎ'ች

courteous
'ኮ:ቲየስ -ቅ- የታ'ረመ ፣ ጥሩ ጠባይ ያ'ለው
ሰው አክባሪ ፣ ትሑት

courtesy
'ከተሲ -ስ- የታ'ረመ ጠባይ ፣ ትሕት'ና

court-martial
ኮ:ት'ማሸል -ስ- የወ'ታ'ደር ፍርድ ቤት

courtyard
'ኮ:ትያ:ድ -ስ- አጥር ግ'ቢ ፣ ቅጥር ግ'ቢ

cousin
'ከዝን -ስ- ያ'ጎት ፣ ያክስት ልጅ
cover
'ከቨ -ግ- መሸ'ፈን [ሸ'ፈነ] ፣ መክደን [ከ'ደነ]
-ስ- መሸ'ፈ'ኛ ፣ ክዳን
covet
'ከቨት -ግ- የሰው ንብረት ለመውሰድ መከ'ጀል [ከ'ጀለ] ፣ በሰው ንብረት መቅናት [ቀ'ና]፣ መሴ'ሰን [ሴ'ሰነ]
cow
'ካው -ስ- 'ላም
coward
'ካወድ -ስ- ፈሪ ፣ ቦቅቧ'ቃ
cowardice
'ካወዲስ -ስ- ፍርሀት
cowl
'ካውል -ስ- የመነኩሴ ቆብ ፣ ሽፋን (የራስ)
coy
'ኮይ -ቅ- ሲያሽኮረ'ምሙት ዓይነ አ'ፋር የ'ሚ መስል
crab
ክ'ራብ -ስ- ስ'ምንት እግር'ች ያ'ሉት ደንጊያ ለ'በስ ዐሣ
crack
ክ'ራክ -ግ- መንቃት [ነ'ቃ] (ግድግ'ዳ ፣ ዕቃ ወዘተ)
one's fingers
-ግ- ማንጸጸት [አንጸ'ጸ] (ጣት)
cracker
ክ'ራክ -ስ- መስበሪያ ፣ መፈርከሻ
biscuit
-ስ- ደረቅ ብስኩት
crackle
ክ'ራክል -ግ- መንጣጣት [ተንጣ'ጣ] ፣ መንጸጸት [ተንጸ'ጸ] (ለድምፅ)
cradle
ክ'ረይደል -ስ- የሕፃን አልጋ
craft
ክ'ራ፡ፍት -ስ- ጥበብ (የእ'ጅ)
ship
-ስ- መርከብ
craftsman
ክ'ራ፡ፍትስመን -ስ- የእ'ጅ ጥበብ ያ'ለው ፣ በተግባረ እድ የሠለ'ጠነ

crafty
ክ'ራ፡ፍቲ -ቅ- አ'ታላይ ፣ ሥ'ሌ ፣ ብልጥ ፣ ተንኰለ'ኛ
crag
ክ'ራግ -ስ- ጸጥ'ኝ ፣ የጸጥ'ኝ ጫፍ
cram
ክ'ራም -ግ- መጎስጎስ [ጎሰ'ጎሰ] ፣ ግ'መቅ [ዐ'መቀ]
cramp
ክ'ራምፕ -ስ- ድንዛዜ ፣ መ'ጨበጥ (የሰው'ነት)
crane
ክ'ሬይን -ስ- ረ'ጅም እግር'ና አንገት ያ'ለው ቁመታም ወፍ ፣ ክ'ባድ ሸክም የ'ሚያነሣ መኪና
crank
ክ'ራንክ -ስ- መዘ'ወር [ዘ'ወረ]
crash
ክ'ራሽ -ግ- ወድቆ መ'ሰበር [ተሰ'በረ]
-ስ- ወድቆ የተሰ'በረ ነገር ፣ ስብርባሪ (በመውደቁ ምክንያት)
crate
ክ'ሬይት -ስ- ት'ልቅ የእንጨት ሣጥን
crater
ክ'ሬይተ -ስ- ሰ'ፊ ጕድጓድ (አንድ ነገር በመፈንዳቱ የተቆ'ፈረ)
crave
ክ'ሬይብ -ግ- ለማግኘት መጓጓት [ጓ'ጓ]
crazy
ክ'ሬይዚ -ቅ- እብድ
creak
ክ'ሬይክ -ግ- ሲ'ጥ ሲ'ጥ ማለት [አለ] (ለበ'ር፣ ለወንበር ወዘተ)
cream
ክ'ሪይም -ስ- ቅባት ፣ ስልባቦት
crease
ክ'ሪይስ -ስ- እ'ጥፋት
create
ክሪ'ዩይት -ግ- መፍጠር [ፈ'ጠረ]
creation
ክሪ'ዩይሽን -ስ- ፍጥረት ፣ ፍጡር
creative
ክሪ'ዩይቲብ -ቅ- ፈጣሪ ፣ አንቂ (ለሐሳብ)
creator
ክሪ'ዩይተ -ስ- ፈጣሪ

creature

ክ'ሪይቸ -ስ- ፍጥረት

credence

ክ'ሪይደንስ -ስ- እምነት ፥ እውነት መሆኑን መቀ'በል

credentials

ክሪ'ዴንሽልዝ -ስ- መ'ታወቂያ ወረቀት

credible

ክ'ሬዲበል -ቅ- የ'ሚ'ታ'መን

credit

ክ'ሬዲት -ስ- ዱቤ

-ግ- ገንዘብ በሌላ ሒሳብ ማስቀ'መጥ [አስቀ'መጠ]

creditor

ክ'ሬዲተ -ቅ- አበ'ዳሪ

credulity

ክሬድ'ዩሊቲ -ስ- እምነት (ያለማ'ሰብ) ፥ በቂ ያልሆነ ማስረ'ጃ መ'ቀበል

credulous

ክ'ሬድዩለስ -ቅ- በቀ'ላሉ አማኝ

creed

ክ'ሪይድ -ስ- እምነት

liturgical

-ስ- ጸሎተ ሃይማኖት

creek

ክ'ሪይክ -ስ- ት'ንሽ ወንዝ ፥ ጅረት

creep

ክ'ሪይፕ -ግ- መዳኸ [ዳኸ]

creepy

ክ'ሪይፒ -ቅ- የ'ሚያስፈ'ራ ፥ የ'ሚያስደነ'ግጥ፥ የ'ሚዘገ'ንን

cremation

ክሪ'ሚይሽን -ስ- ከድን ማ'ቃጠል

crematoriu,

ክሬመ'ቶ:ሪየም -ስ- በድ', የ'ሚ'ቃ'ጠል'በት ቦታ

crescent

ክ'ሬስንት -ስ- ሙሉ ያልሆነ'ች ጨረቃ

shape

-ስ- ማጭድ ቅርፅ

cress

ክ'ሬስ -ስ- ጉ'ጉብሉ (እንደሰላጣ ያ'ለ በወንዝ ዳር የ'ሚበቅል ተክል)

crest

ክ'ሬስት -ስ ጉተና ፥ ተ'ራ ፥ ቁንጮ ፥ ኒ'ንክ

sign

-ስ- አርማ

crevasse

ክሪ'ቫስ -ስ- ሥንጥቅ (የመሬት)

crevice

ክ'ሬቪስ -ስ- ቀ'ጭን ሥንጥቅ (የተባይ መ'ሸሸጊያ) ፥ ንቃቃት

crew

ክ'ሩ: -ስ- በመርከብ በአውሮ'ፕላን ውስጥ የ'ሚሠሩ ሠራተኞ'ች

cricket

ክ'ሪከት -ስ- ክሪኬት (የእንግሊዝ ጨዋታ)

insect

-ስ- ዋዝንቢት

crime

ክ'ራይም -ስ- ወንጀል

criminal

ክ'ሪሚነል -ቅ- ወንጀለ'ኛ

crimson

ክ'ሪምዘን -ቅ- ብሩህ ቀ'ይ

cringe

ክ'ሪነጅ -ግ- በፍርሃት ማፈግፈግ [አፈገ'ፈገ]

crinkle

ክ'ሪንክል -ግ- መ'ጨማደድ [ተጨማ'ደደ] ፥ መ'ኮማተር [ተኮማ'ተረ]

cripple

ክ'ሪፐል -ቅ- አካለ ስንኩል ፥ ድ'ውይ

crisis

ክ'ራይሲስ -ስ- የብጥ'ብጥ ፥ የሁከት ጊ'

crisp

ክ'ሪስፕ -ቅ- ደረቅ'ና ቀ'ጭን

critical

ክ'ሪቲክል -ቅ- ስሕተት የ'ሚያገ'ኝ ፡ ··'ች፡

dangerous

-ቅ- አሥጊ ፥ አ'ሠ'ጊ

criticism

ክ'ሪቲሲዘም -ስ- ት'ችት ፥ ስሕተት ማግኘት ፥ ሂስ

criticize

ክ'ሪቲሳይዝ -ግ- ስሕተት ማግኘት [አገ'ኘ] ፥ መተ'ቸት [ተ'ቸ]፥በሰው ላይ መፍረድ [ፈ'ረደ]፥ አስተያየት መስጠት [ሰ'ጠ]

croak
ክ'ረውክ -ስ- የእንቁራሪት ጩኸት
crocodile
ክ'ሮከዳይል -ስ- ዐ'ዞ
crockery
ክ'ሮከሪ -ስ- ሳሕን ፥ ፊንጃል'ና የመሳ'ሰለው
crooked
ክ'ሩክድ -ት- ጠማማ (ለቅርፅ ፥ ለአመል)
crop
ክ'ሮፕ -ስ- ሰብል ፥ አዝመራ
whip
-ስ- አለንጋ
cross
ክ'ሮስ -ግ- መ'ሻገር [ተሻ'ገረ]
crucifix
-ስ- መስቀል
angry
-ት- ቁ'ጡ
crossbar
ክ'ሮስባ: -ስ- አግድም ብረት (በተለ'ይ በሁለ'ት ብረቶ'ች የቆም የተያዘ)
crossing
ክ'ሮሲንግ -ስ- መ'ሸጋገር ፥ አንድ መንገድ ሌላውን የ'ሚያ'ቋ'ርጥ'በት ቦታ
cross-roads
ክ'ሮስረውድዝ -ስ- መስቀል'ያ መንገድ
crouch
ክ'ራውች -ግ- በእግር ቁጢ'ጥ ብሎ መ'ቀመጥ [ተቀ'መጠ]፥ ተኰንብሶ መ'ቀመጥ [ተቀ'መጠ]፥ ማድባት [አደ'ባ]
crow
ክ'ረው -ግ- መጮኽ [ጮኸ] (ለዶሮ)
crow
ክ'ረው -ስ- ቁራ
cock
-ስ- የዶሮ ጩኸት
crowbar
ክ'ረውባ: -ስ- የማተን መክፈቻ ብረት
crowd
ክ'ራውድ -ስ- የተሰበ'ሰበ ሰው ፥ የሰው ክም'ችት
crowded
ክ'ራውዲድ -ት- የተሰበ'ሰበ ፥ የታ'ፈገ
crown
ክ'ራውን -ስ- ዘውድ
crucial
ክ'ሩ:ሸል -ት- በጣም አስፈ'ላጊ
crucible
ክ'ሩ:ሲበል -ስ- ማፍያ ዕቃ
crucifixion
ክሩ:ሲ'ፊክሽን -ስ- ስቅለት
crucify
ክ'ሩ:ሲፋይ -ግ- መስቀል [ሰ'ቀለ]
crude
ክ'ሩ:ድ -ት- ያልነ'ጠረ
of person
-ት- ባለጌ ፥ ያልተቀ'ጣ
roughly made
-ት- መና'ኛ
cruel
ክ'ሩወል -ት- ጨ'ካኝ ፥ አረመኔ (ርኅራኄ በማ ጣት)
cruelty
ክ'ሩወልቲ -ስ- ጭ'ካኔ ፥ አረመኔ'ነት (ርኅራኄ በማጣት)
cruet
ክ'ሩወት -ስ- የቅመም ቅመም መያዣ ዕቃ (እማዕ'ድ ላይ የ'ሚቀርብ)
cruise
ክ'ሩ:ዝ -ግ- በመርከብ መንሸራሸር [ተንሸራ'ሸረ]፤ የጠላት መርከብ መ'ከታተል [ተከታ'ተለ]
cruiser
ክ'ሩ:ዘ -ስ- ት'ልቅ የጦር መርከብ
crumb
ክ'ረም -ስ- ፍር'ፋሪ (የምግብ)
crumble
ክ'ረምበል -ግ- መፈርፈር [ፈረ'ፈረ]
crumple
ክ'ረምፕል -ግ- መጨባበጥ [ጨባ'በጠ]
crunch
ክ'ረንች -ግ- መኮረሻሸም [ኮረሻ'ሸመ] ፥ መቆርጠም [ቆረ'ጠመ]
crusader
ክሩ'ሴይደ -ስ- የመስቀል ጦር'ነት ወ'ታ'ደር
crush
ክ'ረሽ -ግ- ማድቀቅ [አደ'ቀቀ]

crust
ክ'ረስት -ስ- የዳ'ቦ ቅር'ፊት ፣ የደረቀ ዳ'ቦ ቁ'ራሽ

crusty
ክ'ረስቲ -ቅ- ደረቅ ፣ ቅርፊ'ት የሞ'ላ'በት

crutch
ክ'ረች -ስ- መ'ደገፊያ እንጨት (ለእግረ ሰባራ ሰው) ፣ ምርኩዝ

cry
ክ'ራይ -ግ- ማልቀስ [አለ'ቀሰ]
shout
-ስ- ጩኸት

crying
ክ'ራይንግ -ቅ- አልቃ'ሻ

crypt
ክ'ሪፕት -ስ- ከቤተ ክርስቲያን በታ'ች ያ'ለ የመቃብር ቦታ

cryptic
ክ'ሪፕቲክ -ቅ- በቀ'ላሉ የ'ማይገባ ፣ ምስ ጢር የሞ'ላ'በት

crystal
ክ'ሪስተል -ስ- መስተዋት (ዋጋው የከ'በረ) ፣ ብር'ሌ (ማዕ'ድን)
geological
-ስ- ባልጩ'ት

cub
'ከብ -ስ- ያንበሳ ግልገል

cube
ክ'ዩ፡ብ -ስ- ስ'ድስት ማዕዘን ያ'ለው ቅርፅ

cubic
ክ'ዩ፡ቢክ -ቅ- ኩ'ብ

cubicle
ክ'ዩ፡ቢክል -ስ- ባንድ ክፍል ውስጥ ትን'ንሽ ክፍሎ'ች

cucumber
ክ'ዩከምበ -ስ- ክያር

cud
'ከድ -ስ- እንስሳት የ'ሚያመነ'ዥኩት ሣር ፣ ምግብ

cuddle
'ከድል -ግ- አጥብቆ ማቀፍ [አ'ቀፈ]

cudgel
'ከጀል -ስ- 'ዱላ ፣ በ'ትር (መምቻ)

cue
ክ'ዩ፡ -ስ- የቢልያርድ መ'ጫወቻ ዘንግ
sign
-ስ- ምል'ክት (አንድ ነገር ለመ'መል ከት)

cuff
'ከፍ -ስ- እ'ጅጌ

culinary
'ከሊነሪ -ቅ- የወጥ ቤት ፣ ከወጥ ጋር ግን'ኙ 'ነት ያ'ለው

culminate
'ከልሚኔይት -ግ- መጨ'ረስ [ጨ'ረሰ]

culmination
ከልሚ'ኔይሸን -ስ- ተፍጻሜት ፣ መጨ'ረሻ

culpable
'ከልፐበል -ቅ- ሊ'ወ'ቀስ የ'ሚ'ገ'ባው ፣ ተወ 'ቃሽ

culprit
'ከልፕሪት -ስ- ጥፋተ'ኛ ሰው ፣ ወንጀለ'ኛ ፣ በወንጀል የተከ'ሰሰ ሰው

cult
'ከልት -ስ- አምልኮ (ጣዖት)

cultivate
'ከልቲቬይት -ስ- ማረስ [አ'ረሰ] ፣ ማሳ'ደግ [አሳ'ደገ] (ለእትክልት)

cultivation
ከልቲ'ቬይሸን -ስ- እርሻ

cultural
'ከልቸረል -ቅ- የትምህርት ፣ ባህል ነ'ክ

culture
'ከልቸ -ስ- ባህል ፣ ትምህርት

cumbrous
'ከምብረስ -ቅ- እ'ጅግ ከ'ባድ'ና ም'ቹ ያልሆነ (ለመ'ሸከም)

cumin
'ኩሚን -ስ- ከሙን

cumulative
ክ'ዩምዩለቲቭ -ቅ- የ'ሚያድግ ፣ እ'የጨ'መረ የ'ሚሄድ

cunning
'ከኒንግ -ቅ- ሎ'ሌ ፣ ብልጥ

cup
'ከፕ -ስ- ስኒ

cupboard
'ከበድ -ስ- ቁም ሣጥን

cupidity
ክዩ'ፒዲቲ -ስ- ሥ'ሥት

cur
'ከ፡ -ስ- ባለቤት የሌ'ለው ውሻ ፣ ልክስክስ

curable
ክ'ዩረበል -ቅ- ሊድን ፣ ሊ'ፈ'ወስ የ'ሚ'ቻል

curacy
ክ'ዩረሲ -ስ- ሰበካ (የንፍቅ ቄስ)

curate
ክ'ዩረት -ስ- ንፍቅ ቄስ (ረ'ዳት ቄስ)

curative
ክ'ዩረቲቭ -ቅ- መድኀኒት'ነት ያ'ለው

curator
ክዩ'ሬይተ -ስ- የምዩዚየም ኀላፊ

curb
'ከ፡ብ -ግ- መ'ቆጣጠር [ተቆጣ'ጠረ]
-ስ- ዛብ ፣ መግቻ (ለፈረስ ፣ ለበቅሎ)

curdle
'ከ፡ድል -ግ- መርጋት [ረ'ጋ] (ወተት)

cure
ክ'ዩወ -ግ- ማዳን [አዳነ] ፣ መፈ'ወስ [ፈ'ወሰ]

curfew
'ከ፡ፍዩ -ስ- ከተወ'ሰነ ጊዜ በኋላ መ'ዘዋወር የ'ሚከለ'ከል ትእዛዝ (የመንግሥት)

curio
ክ'ዩሪየው -ስ- ያንድ አገር ማስታወሻ ዕቃ

curiosity
ክዩሪ'ዮሰቲ -ስ- ሁ'ሉን የማወቅ ፍ'ላጎት ፣ ቸ'ኩልነ'ት

curious
ክ'ዩሪየስ -ቅ- ሁ'ሉን ለማወቅ የ'ሚቸ'ኩል ፣ እንግዳ ፣ ያልተለ'መደ

curl
'ከ፡ል -ግ- መጠቅለል [ጠቀ'ለለ]

currant
'ከረንት -ስ- ዘቢብ

currency
'ከረንሲ -ስ- ገንዘብ

current
'ከረንት -ቅ- ያሁን ጊዜ
of river
-ስ- ጐርፍ
electric
-ስ- ኮ'ሬንቲ ፣ ኤሌክትሪክ

curriculum
ክ'ሪክዩለም -ስ- ሥርዓተ ትምህርት

curse
'ከ፡ስ -ግ- መርገም [ረ'ገመ]
-ስ- እርግማን

cursed
'ከ፡ስት -ቅ- የተረ'ገመ

cursive
'ከ፡ሲቭ -ቅ- የተያያዘ (ጽሕፈት)

cursory
'ከ፡ሰሪ -ቅ- ች'ኩል ፣ ፍጥነት ያ'ለ'በት

curtail
ክ'ቴይል -ግ- ማሳ'ጠር [አሳ'ጠረ]

curtain
'ከ፡ተን -ስ- መ'ጋረጃ ፣ አጎበር

curtsy
'ከ፡ትሲ -ግ- እ'ጅ መንሣት [ነ'ሣ] (ለሴት)

curvature
'ከ፡በቸ -ስ- ቆልማ'ማ'ነት ፣ መ'ቆልመም፣ ቁልምም

curve
'ከ፡ብ -ስ- ቆልማ'ማ ፣ ጠማማ ነገር

cushion
'ኩሸን -ስ- መ'ከ'ዳ

custodian
ከሰ'ተውዲየን -ስ- ጠ'ባቂ ፣ ኀላፊ ፣ አሳ'ዳጊ

custody
'ከስተዲ -ስ- ጠ'ባቂ'ነት ፣ አሳ'ዳጊ'ነት

custom
'ከስተም -ስ- ልምድ ፣ ልማድ

customs
'ከስተምዝ -ስ- ጉምሩክ ፣ ኬ'ላ

customary
'ከስተመሪ -ቅ- የተለ'መደ

customer
'ከስተመ -ስ- ደምበ'ኛ (የገበያ)

custom-house
'ከስተም 'ሀውስ -ስ- ጉምሩክ

cut
'ካት -ግ- መቁረጥ [ቆረጠ]
-ስ- ቁርጥ ፣ ቁስል (በመ'ቁረጥ)

cute
ክ'ዩ:ት -ቅ- የ'ሚያምር ፣ ቆንጆ ፣ እ'ጥ'ር ም'ጥ'ን ያለ

cutlery
'ካትለሪ -ስ- ቢ'ላዋ ፣ ሹ'ካ'ና ማንካ ወዘተ

cutlet
'ካትሌት -ስ- የጎድን ሥጋ ፣ ኮትሌት

cutter
'ካተ -ስ- ሥለት ፣ ቆራጭ

cutting
'ካቲንግ -ስ- ተቆርጦ የ'ሚ'ተ'ከል ተክል
newspaper
-ስ- ከጋዜጣ ላይ ተቆርጦ የወ'ጣ ጽሑፍ

cycle
'ሳይክል -ስ- ተከታትሎ በተወ'ሰነ ጊዜያት የ'ሚ'ደጋ'ገም ነገር ፣ ዑደት
bicycle
-ስ- ቢስክሌት

cyclist
'ሳይክሊስት -ስ- ቢስክሌት ነጂ

cyclone
'ሳይክሎውን -ስ- ታ'ላቅ አውሎ ነፋስ

cylinder
'ሲሊንደ -ስ ክ'ብ ዐምድ

cylindrical
ሰ'ሊንድሪክል -ቅ- ባለክ'ብ ዐምድ

cymbals
'ሲምበልዝ -ስ- ከነሐስ የተሠ'ሩ ሁለ'ት ሰሐን መ'ሰል የሙዚቃ መ'ሣሪያዎ'ች

cynic
'ሲኒክ -ስ- የነ'ገሩትን የ'ማያምን ሰው ፣ ጠማማ ትርጉም የ'ሚሰጥ ሰው ፣ ተጠራጣሪ

cynical
'ሲኒክል -ቅ- የነ'ገሩትን የ'ማያምን ፣ ጠማማ ትርጉም ሰጭ

D

dab
'ዳብ -ግ- መተምተም [ተመ'ተመ]

dad
'ዳድ -ስ- አ'ባቴ ፣ አ'ባ'ዬ ፣ አ'ብ'ዬ

daft
'ዳፍት -ቅ- ቂል ፣ ደካማ አእምሮ ያ'ለው

dagger
'ዳገ -ስ- ጩቤ ፣ ጉ'ዶ

daily
'ዴይሊ -ተግ- በ'የቀኑ
-ቅ- የቀን

dainty
'ዴይንቲ -ስ- የ'ሚያስጐመ'ጅ ምግብ ፣ እ'ጅ የ'ሚያስቆረ'ጥም ምግብ
-ቅ- የ'ሚያስጐመ'ጅ ፣ እ'ጅ የ'ሚያስቆረ'ጥም (ምግብ) ፣ ሁ'ሉ ነገር የ'ማይጥመው
-ቅ- እ'ጥ'ር ም'ጥ'ን ያለ (ለሴት)

dairy
'ዴሪ -ስ- የወተት ፋብሪካ

dais
'ዴይስ -ስ- ሉዓላዊ ቦታ ፣ ት'ንሽ የእንጨት መድረክ ፣ ሉዓላዊ መድረክ

dam
'ዳም -ስ- የውሃ ግ'ድብ
animal
-ስ- ያረ'ገዘ'ች እንስሳ (ፈረስ ፣ በግ ወዘተ)

damage
'ዳሚጅ -ግ- ማ'በላሸት (አ'በላ'ሸ)
-ስ- ብል'ሽት

damn
'ዳም -ግ- መኰ'ነን [ኰ'ነነ]

damnation
ዳም'ኔይሸን -ስ- ጥፋት ፣ ኩነኔ

damp
'ዳምፕ -ቅ- እርጥብ

dance
'ዳ፡ንስ -ግ- እስክስታ መውረድ [ወ'ረደ] ፣ መደ'ነስ [ደ'ነሰ]

dancer
'ዳ፡ንስ -ስ- እስክስታ ወራጅ ፣ ደ'ናሽ ፣ ጨ'ፋሪ

dancing
'ዳ፡ንሲንግ -ስ- እስክስታ መውረድ ፣ ዳንስ ፣ ጭ'ፈራ

danger
'ዴይንጀ -ስ- አደጋ

dangerous
'ዴይንጀረስ -ቅ- አደገ'ኛ

dangle
'ዳንገል -ግ- ማንጠልጠል [አንጠለ'ጠለ] ፣ መንጠልጠል [ተንጠለ'ጠለ]

dare
'ዴየ -ግ- መድፈር [ደ'ፈረ]
challenge
-ግ- መ'ፎካከር [ተፎካ'ከረ]

daring
'ዴሪንግ -ቅ- ደ'ፋር

dark
'ዳ፡ክ -ስ- ጨ'ለማ
-ቅ- ጥቁር (የልብስ ፣ የሰው መልክ ወዘተ)

darken
'ዳ፡ከን -ግ- ማጥቆር (አጠ'ቆረ) ፣ መጨ'ለም [ጨ'ለመ]

darkness
'ዳክ፡ነስ -ስ- ጭ'ለማ ፣ ጨ'ለማ

darn
'ዳ፡ን -ግ- መጣቀም [ጣ'ቀመ] (በተለ'ይ ለሱፍ ልብስ)

dart
'ዳ፡ት -ግ- መ'ፈትለክ [ተፈተ'ለከ]
-ስ- በእ'ጅ የ'ሚ'ወረ'ወር በጣም ት'ን ሽ ፍላ'ፃ

dash
'ዳሽ -ግ- መሮጥ

dashing
'ዳሺንግ -ቅ- ሎጋ ፣ አስደ'ሳች ፣ መልከ መል ካም
running
-ቅ- ሩ'ጫ

date
'ዴይት -ስ- ቀን ፣ ዘመን (ም'ሳሌ ፣ መስከረም ፩ ቀን ፲፱፻፹'፯ ዓ ም)

daub
'ዶ፡ብ -ግ- መምረግ [መ'ረገ] (በጭቃ)

daughter
'ዶ፡ተ -ስ- ልጅ (ሴት)

daughter-in-law
'ዶ፡ተሪንሎ፡ -ስ- ምራት

dauntless
'ዶ፡ንትሌስ -ቅ- ደ'ፋር

dawdle
'ዶ፡ደል -ግ- ወደኋላ መቅረት [ቀ'ረ] ፤ በከ ንቱ ጊዜ ማባከን [አባ'ከነ] ፣ ያለ ዓላማ በመን ገድ ላይ መንከራተት [ተንከራ'ተተ]

dawn
ዶ፡ን -ስ- ንጋት

day
'ዴይ -ስ- ቀን

daylight
'ዴይላይት -ስ- የቀን ብርሃን

dazed
'ዴይዝድ -ቅ- የደነዘ'ዘው ፣ ለጊዜት ጊዜ ስ'ሜቱን ያ'ጣ (በመ'መታት ምክንያት)

dazzle
'ዳዘል -ግ- ዓይን ማንጸባረቅ [አንጸባ'ረቀ]

dazzling
'ዳዝሊንግ -ቅ- የ'ሚያንጸባ'ርቅ

deacon
'ዲይከን -ስ- ዲያቆን

dead
'ዴድ -ቅ- የሞተ ፣ ም'ውት

deaden
'ዴደን -ግ- ሕመም መቀ'ነስ [ቀ'ነሰ] ፤ ድም ፅን ማብረድ [አበ'ረደ]

dead-line
'ዴድ ላይን -ስ- የተወ'ሰነ ጊዜ (አንድ ሥራ የ'ሚ'ፈ'ጸም'በት)

deadly
'ዴድሊ -ቅ- ለሕይወት አሥጊ

deaf
'ዴፍ -ቅ- ደንቆሮ (ጆሮው የ'ማይሰማ)

deafen
'ዴፈን -ግ- ማደንቆር [አደነ'ቆረ] (በድምፅ)

deafness
'ዴፍነስ -ስ- ድንቊር'ና
deal
'ዲይል -ግ- መነ'ገድ [ነ'ገደ]
playing cards
-ግ- የመ'ጫወቻ ካርታ ማ'ደል [አ'ደለ]
dealer
'ዲይለ -ስ- ነ'ጋዴ
cards
-ስ- ካርታ አ'ዳይ
dear
'ዲየ -ቅ- የተወ'ደደ ፣ ው'ድ
price
-ቅ- ው'ድ (ለዋጋ)
dearest
'ዲይረስት -ቅ- እ'ጅግ የተወ'ደደ
death
'ዴፀ -ስ- ሞት
debar
ዲ'ባ: -ግ- ማ'ገድ [አ'ገደ] ፣ መከልከል [ከለ'ከለ]
debased
ዲ'ቤይስድ -ቅ- ዝ'ቅ ያለ ፣ የተዋ'ረደ
money
-ቅ- ሴላ ብረታብረት የተጨ'መረ'በት (መሐ'ለቅ)
debatable
ዲ'ቤይተበል -ቅ- የ'ሚያ'ከራ'ክር ፣ አ'ከራ ካሪ
debate
ዲ'ቤይት -ግ- መ'ከራከር [ተከራ'ከረ]
debauchery
ዲ'ቦ:ቸሪ -ስ- በግብረ ገ'ብ ዝ'ቅተ'ኛ'ነት ዝ'ሙት ፣ ምግብ'ና መጠ'ጥ ወዘተ ማብዛት
debility
ዲ'ቢሊቲ -ስ- ድካም (የሰው'ነት)
debris
'ዴብሪ -ስ- ፍርስራሽ (የቤት)
debt
'ዴት -ስ- እ'ዳ ፣ ብ'ድር
debtor
'ዴተ -ስ- ተበ'ዳሪ ፣ ባለዳ
decade
ዲ'ኬይድ -ስ- ዐ'ሥር ዓመት
decadent
'ዴከደንት -ቅ- ወ'ራ'ዳ
decapitate
ዲ'ካፒቴይት -ግ- የሰው አንገት መሠ'የፍ [ሠ'የ ፈ]
decay
ዲ'ኬይ -ግ- መሻገት [ሻ'ገተ] ፣ መ'በላት [ተበ'ላ]
deceased
ዲ'ሲይስት -ቅ- ሙት
deceit
ዲ'ሲይት -ስ- ማ'ታለል
deceitful
ዲ'ሲይትፉል -ቅ- አ'ታላይ
deceive
ዲ'ሲይቭ -ግ- ማ'ታለል [አ'ታ'ለለ]
December
ዲ'ሴምበ -ስ- ታኅሣሥ
decent
'ዲሰንት -ቅ- ጨዋ ፣ የተከ'በረ
deception
ዲ'ሴፕሽን -ስ- ማ'ታለል
deceptive
ዲ'ሴፕቲቭ -ቅ- አ'ታላይ
decide
ዲ'ሳይድ -ግ- መቁረጥ [ቈ'ረጠ] (ለሐሳብ)
decipher
ዲ'ሳይፈ -ግ- አ'ዋኪ ጽሑፍ ማንበብ [አነ 'በበ]
decision
ዲ'ሲዥን -ስ- ው'ሳኔ
decisive
ዲ'ሳይሲቭ -ቅ- የመጨ'ረሻ ፣ ጽኑእ (በው'ሳኔው)
of person
-ቅ- ቆ'ራጥ
deck
'ዴክ -ግ- ማስጌጥ [አስጌጠ]
of ship
-ስ- የመርከብ ወለል
declaim
ዲክ'ሌይም -ግ- በሕዝብ ፊት መ'ናገር [ተና 'ገረ]

declamation
ዴክለ'ሜይሽን -ስ- በሕዝብ ፊት ስ'ሜት የ'ሚቀሰ'ቅስ ንግ'ግር ማድረግ
declaration
ዴክለ'ሬይሽን -ስ- ንግ'ግር ፣ ዐዋጅ
declare
ዲክ'ሌየ -ግ- መግለጽ [ገ'ለጸ] ፣ ማ'ወጅ [ዐ'ወጀ]
decline
ዲክ'ላይን -ግ- ማነስ [አ'ነሰ]
refuse
-ግ- እም'ቢ ማለት [አለ]
decompose
ዲከም'ፖውዝ -ግ- መበስበስ [በሰ'በሰ]
decorate
'ዴከሬይት -ግ- ማጌጥ [አጌጠ]
house
-ግ- ቤት ቀለም መቀ'ባት [ቀ'ባ]
decoration
ዴክ'ሬይሽን -ስ- ጌጥ
medal
-ስ- ኒሻን
decorative
'ዴክረቲቭ -ቅ- ያጌጠ ፣ ያማረ
decorator
'ዴከሬይተ -ስ- ቤት የ'ሚቀ'ባ ሰው
decorous
'ዴከረስ -ቅ- የተከ'በረ ፣ ጥሩ ጠባይ የ'ሚያሳ'ይ
decoy
'ዲኮይ -ስ- መሳቢያ ፣ ወጥመድ ማግቢያ ነገር ፣ ማጥመጃ
decrease
ዲክ'ሪይስ -ግ- ማነስ [አ'ነሰ]
decree
ዲክ'ሪይ -ግ- ትእዛዝ ማውጣት [አወ'ጣ] (ንጉ ሣዊ)
-ስ- ትእዛዝ ፣ ዐዋጅ
decrepit
ዲክ'ሬፒት -ቅ- በዕድሜ ምክንያት ያረ'ጀ ፣ የተበላ'ሸ
decry
ዲክ'ራይ -ግ- መ'ቃወም [ተቃ'ወመ]
dedicated
'ዴዲኬይቲድ -ቅ- ሕይወቱን ላንድ ተግባር ያዋለ
dedication
ዴዲ'ኬይሽን -ስ- ሕይወትን ላንድ ተግባር ማዋል
deduce
ዲድ'ዩስ -ግ- በሁኔታው መሠረት ፍርድ መስ ጠት [ሰ'ጠ] (ስሐ'ሳብ)
deduct
ዲ'ደክት -ግ- መቀ'ነስ [ቀ'ነሰ] (ከደመወዝ ወዘተ)
deduction
ዲ'ደክሽን -ስ- የሒ'ሳብ ው'ጤት
money
-ስ- ቅ'ናሽ
deed
'ዲይድ -ስ- ሥራ ፣ ተግባር
deem
'ዲይም -ግ- ማሰብ [አ'ሰበ] ፣ ማመን [አ'መነ]
deep
'ዲይፕ -ቅ- ጥልቅ
deepen
'ዲይፐን -ግ- ማጥለቅ [አጠ'ለቀ] ፣ ጥልቅ ማድረግ [አደ'ረገ]
deer
'ዲየ -ስ- አጋዘን
deface
ዲ'ፌይስ -ግ- ቅርፅ ማጥፋት [አጠ'ፋ] ፣ ጽሑፍ እንዳይ'ነ'በብ መደ'ለዝ [ደ'ለዘ]
defamation
ዴፈ'ሜሽን -ስ- የስም ማጥፋት ወንጀል
default
ዲ'ፎልት -ግ- በቀጠሮ አለመ'ገኘት [-ተገ'ኘ] (በፍርድ ቤት)
in debt
-ግ- የተበ'ደሩትን ገንዘብ በጊዜ አለመ ክፈል [-ከ'ፈለ]
defaulter
ዲ'ፎልተ -ስ- በቀጠሮው ያልተገ'ኘ (በፍርድ ቤት)
defeat
ዲ'ፊይት -ግ- ማ'ሸ'ነፍ [አ'ሸ'ነፈ]
-ስ- ማ'ሸ'ነፍ

defect
'ዲፌክት -ስ- ጉድለት ፣ እንከን
defective
ዲ'ፌክቲቭ -ቅ- ጉድለት ያ'ለ'በት
defence
ዲ'ፌንስ -ስ- መ'ከላከያ
defend
ዲ'ፌንድ -ግ- ለራስ መ'ከላከል ፣ [ተከላ'ከለ]
defendant
ዲ'ፌንደንት -ስ- ተከ'ሳሽ
defender
ዲ'ፌንደ -ስ- ተከላካይ
defensive
ዲ'ፌንሲቭ -ቅ- የመ'ከላከያ (ዘዴ)
defer
ዲ'ፌ፡ -ግ- ማስተላለፍ [አስተላ'ለፈ] (ለሌላ ቀን)
deferential
ዴፈ'ሬንሽል -ቅ- ሥልጣን አክባሪ
defiant
ዲ'ፋየንት -ቅ- ተጻጻሚ ፣ መ'ካች
child
-ቅ- የ'ማይ'ታዘ'ዝ (ልጅ)
deficiency
ዲ'ፊሽንሲ -ስ- ጉድለት ፣ እንከን
deficient
ዲ'ፊሸንት -ቅ- የጎ'ደለው ፣ ሙሉ ያልሆነ ፣ እንከን ያ'ለ'በት
deficit
'ዴፊሲት -ስ- የገንዘብ ማነስ ፣ ከገቢ ወጪ መብዛት (በንግድ)
defile
ዲ'ፋይል -ግ- ማርከስ [አረ'ከሰ]
define
ዲ'ፋይን -ግ- መወ'ሰን [ወ'ሰነ] (የቃል ፍ'ች ለመስጠት)
definite
'ዴፊኒት -ቅ- የተወ'ሰነ ፣ ቁርጥ ፣ ግልጽ
definition
ዴፊ'ኒሽን -ስ- ው'ሳኔ ፣ ያንድ ነገር ሁናቴ ፣ ጠባይ መግለጫ
deformed
ዲ'ፎ፡ምድ -ቅ- ሰው'ነቱ የተበላ'ሸ ፣ ቅርፁ የጠ'ፋ
deformity
ዲ'ፎ፡ሚቲ -ስ- የሰው'ነት ፣ የቅርፅ መ'በላሸት
defraud
ዲፍ'ሮ፡ድ -ግ- ማ'ታለል [አ'ታ'ለለ] (ለገንዘብ)
defray
ዲፍ'ሬይ -ግ- መክፈል [ከ'ፈለ]
deft
'ዴፍት -ቅ- ቀልጣ'ፋ ፣ ባለሙያ
defunct
ዲ'ፈንክት -ቅ- የሞተ ፣ ም'ውት ፣ የ'ማይሠራ (ለማኅበር ወዘተ)
defy
ዲ'ፋይ -ግ- መ'ጻጻም [ተጻጻመ]
orders
-ግ- አለመ'ታዘዝ [-ታ'ዘዘ]
degenerate
ዲ'ጄነሬይት -ግ- መ'ዋረድ [ተዋ'ረደ]
degrade
ዲግ'ሬይድ -ግ- ማ'ዋረድ [አ'ዋ'ረደ] ፣ ዝ'ቅ ማድረግ [አደ'ረገ]
degrading
ዲግ'ሬይዲንግ -ቅ- አ'ዋራጅ ፣ ዝቅ አድራጊ
degree
ዲግ'ሪይ -ስ- ማዕርግ ፣ ደረጃ ፣ ተዋረድ
deity
'ዴይቲ -ስ- አምላክ'ነት ፣ አምላካዊ ጠባይ ወይን'ም ባሕርይ
dejected
ዲ'ጄክተድ -ቅ- ያ'ዘነ ፣ በፍ'ጹም ያልተደ'ሰተ
delay
ዲ'ሌይ -ግ- መዘግየት [ዘገ'የ]
-ስ- መዘግየት
delegate
'ዴሊጌይት -ግ- ሥልጣን ለበታ'ች እንዲሠ'ራ'በት መስጠት [ሰ'ጠ] ፣ መወ'ከል [ወ'ከለ]
delegate
'ዴለገት -ስ- በብዙ ሰዎ'ች ስም የተወ'ከለ መልእክተ'ኛ
delegation
ዴለ'ጌይሽን -ስ- መልእክተ'ኞች
delete
ዲ'ሊይት -ግ- መፋቅ [ፋቀ] (ቃላት ወዘተ)

deletion
ዲ'ሊይሽን -ስ- የተፋቀ ፣ የተደ'ለዘ ጽሑፍ

deliberate
ዲ'ሊበረት -ቅ- የታ'ሰበ'በት ፣ በማወቅ የተ ደ'ረገ ፣ ሆን ተብሎ የተደ'ረገ

deliberation
ዲሊበ'ሬይሽን -ስ- ውይ'ይት ፣ አንድ ነገር በጥን'ቃቄ ማጥናት ፤ በንግ'ግር ፣ በእንቅስ'ቃሴ መዘተ ፣ ዝ'ግተ'ኛ'ነት

delicacy
'ዴሊከሲ -ስ- ረቂቅ'ነት
food
-ስ- ጣዕም ያ'ለው ምግብ
politeness
-ስ- ጥን'ቃቄ

delicate
'ዴሊከት -ቅ- አስደ'ሳች ፤ በረቂቅ'ነት የተ ሠ'ራ ፤ አደጋ የ'ማይችል

delicious
ዲ'ሊሸስ -ቅ- ጣፋጭ ፣ ጣዕም ያ'ለው

delight
ዲ'ላይት -ግ- መ'ደሰት [ተደ'ሰተ] ፣ ማስደ 'ሰት [አስደ'ሰተ]
-ስ- ደ'ስታ

delightful
ዲ'ላይትፉል -ቅ- በጣም የተደ'ሰተ

delineate
ዲ'ሊኒዬይት -ግ- ሥዕል መንደፍ [ነ'ደፈ]

delinquency
ዲ'ሊንክወንሲ -ስ- ግ'ዳጅ አለመፈ'ጸም ፤ ሕ'ገ ወ'ጥ'ነት (ለወ'ጣቶ'ች) ፣ ብልግ'ና

delinquent
ዲ'ሊንክወንት -ቅ- ወንጀለ'ኛ (ለወ'ጣቶ'ች) ፣ ግ'ዳጁን የ'ማይፈ'ጽም ፣ ባለጌ

delirious
ዲ'ሊሪየስ -ቅ- ቅዠታም (በበ'ሽታ ምክንያት)

deliver
ዲ'ሊቨ -ግ- ማስረ'ከብ [አስረ'ከበ]

deliverance
ዲ'ሊቨረንስ -ስ- ድኅነት (የእግዚአብሔር) ፤ ነጻ መውጣት ፣ መዳን

delivery
ዲ'ሊቨሪ -ስ- ርክ'ክብ
of child
-ስ- መውለድ ፣ መ'ገላገል (ለሕፃን)

dell
'ዴል -ስ- ት'ንሽ ሸለቆ ብዙ ዛፍ ያ'ለ'በት

delude
ዲሉ'ዩ:ድ -ግ- ማ'ታለል [አ'ታ'ለለ] ፣ ማጭ በርበር [አጭበረ'በረ]

deluge
'ዴልዩጅ -ስ- ድንገተ'ኛ የውሃ ሙላት

delusion
ዲሉ'ዩ:ዠን -ስ- ማ'ታለል ፤ የተሳሳተ ስ'ሜት ወይን'ም እምነት (ከሕመም የተነ'ሣ)

de luxe
ዲ'ለክስ -ቅ- በጣም ያማረ ፤ በጣም ምቾት ያ'ለው

delve
'ዴልቭ -ግ- መቆ'ፈር [ቆ'ፈረ] (በአካፋ)

demagogue
'ዴመጎግ -ስ- በንግግሮ'ች ላይ ሕዝብ የ'ሚ ያሥነ'ሣ የፖሊቲካ መሪ

demand
ዲ'ማ:ንድ -ግ- መጠ'የቅ [ጠ'የቀ]

demeanour
ዲ'ሚ:ን -ስ- አመል ፣ ጠባይ ፣ ሁናቴ

demented
ዲ'ሜንቲድ -ቅ- ያ'በደ ፣ እብድ

demise
ዲ'ማይዝ -ስ- ሞት

democracy
ዲ'ሞክረሲ -ስ- ዲሞክራሲ ፣ የሕዝብ ግዛት

demolish
'ዶሞሊሽ -ግ- ማጥፋት [አጠ'ፋ] ፣ ማውደም [አወ'ደመ]

demolition
ዴመ'ሊሽን -ስ- መፍረስ (የቤት ፣ የሕንፃ)

demon
'ዲይመን -ስ- ርኩስ መንፈስ ፣ ሠይጣን

demonstrate
'ዴመንስትሬይት -ግ- ማሳ'የት [አሳ'የ] ፤ ማስ ረ'ጃ እ'ያቀ'ረቡ መግለጽ [ገ'ለጸ]
political
-ግ- ሰላማዊ ሠልፍ ማድረግ [አደ'ረገ]

demonstration
ዴመንስትˈሬይሽን -ስ- በምˈሳሌ ፣ በማስረˈጃ ማሳˈየት ፣ ወˈታˈደራዊ ሰልፍ
political
-ስ- ሰላማዊ ሠልፍ

demonstrative
ደˈሞንስትረቲቭ -ቅ- ገላጭ ፣ አመልካች (ሰዋ ሰው)

demonstrator
ˈዴመንስትሬይተ -ስ- አሳዪ ፣ ገላጭ (ሰው)
political
-ስ- ሰላማዊ ሠልፈˈኛ

demoralize
ደˈሞረላይዝ -ግ- ቅስም መስበር [ሰˈበረ]

demur
ዲˈመ: -ግ- መˈጠራጠር [ተጠራˈጠረ] (መˈልስ ለመስጠት)

demure
ዲምˈዩወ -ቅ- ዓይነ አˈፋር (በተለˈይ ለልጃገረድ ፣ ለሴት)

den
ˈዴን -ስ- ጉድጓድ ፣ መˈሸሸጊያ (ያውሬ)

denial
ዲˈናየል -ስ- ክህደት ፣ ተቃውሞ ፣ አለመˈቀበል (ሐˈሳብ) ፣ ማስተባበል

denomination
ዲኖሚˈኔሽን -ስ- በአንድ ሃይማኖት የˈሚያምኑ ሰዎˈች የሚˈጠሩˈበት ስም ፤ አንድ ዓይነት የሆኑ የˈሚˈጠˈሩበት (ምሳሌ ፣ ሃይማኖት ፣ ገንዘብ ፣ መለˈኪያ)
money, stamps
-ስ- የመሐˈለቅ ፣ የቴምብር ዋጋ

denominator
ዲˈኖሚኔተ -ስ- የጋራ አˈካፋይ (በሒሳብ)

denote
ዲˈነውት -ግ- ማመልከት [አመለˈከተ]

denounce
ዲˈናውንስ -ግ- [ከˈሰሰ] ፣ በሕዝብ መሀል መወንጀል [ወነˈጀለ] ፤ የስምምˈነት ውል ለማፍረስ ማˈሰብን ማስታወቅ [አስታˈወቀ]

dense
ˈዴንስ -ቅ- ጥቅጥˈቅ ያለ ፣ ችˈፍˈግ ያለ

density
ˈዴንሲቲ -ስ- ውፍረት (ለፈሳሽ)
population
-ስ- በአንድ ቀበሌ የነዋሪ ሕዝብ ብዛት

dent
ˈዴንት -ስ- ሥርጉዳት

dental
ˈዴንተል -ቅ- የጥርስ

dentifrice
ˈዴንቲፈሪስ -ስ የጥርስ ሳሙና

dentist
ˈዴንቲስት -ስ- የጥርስ ሐኪም

denture
ˈዴንቸ -ስ- ሰው ሠˈራሽ ጥርስ

denunciation
ዲነንሲˈዬይሽን -ስ- መወንጀል ፣ በሰው ላይ መˈናገር

deny
ዲˈናይ -ግ- መካድ [ካደ] ፣ ማስተባበል [አስተባˈበለ]

depart
ዲˈፓ:ት -ግ- መሄድ [ሄደ] ፣ መተው [ተወ] ፣ መሞት [ሞተ]

department
ዲˈፓ:ትመንት -ስ- ክፍል ፣ ቅርንጫፍ ፣ ንኡስ ክፍል

departmental
ዲፓ:ትˈሜንተል -ቅ- የክፍል (የአስተዳደር)

departure
ዲˈፓ:ቸ -ስ- ጉዞ ፣ ጉዞ መጀˈመር

depend (on)
ዲˈፔንድ -ግ- መˈመካት [ተመˈካ] ፣ ሐˈሳብ እሰው ላይ መጣል [ጣለ]

dependable
ዲˈፔንደበል -ቅ- የˈሚˈመˈኩˈበት ፣ የˈሚያምኑት ፣ እምነት የˈሚˈጣልˈበት

deplore
ዲፕˈሎ: -ግ- በጣም ማዘን [አˈዘነ] ፤ ዋይ ማለት [አለ] ፤ አለመስማማት [-ተ ስማˈማ]

deploy
ዲፕˈሎይ -ግ- ወˈታˈደር በˈየጦር ግምባር ማˈሰለፍ [አˈሰˈለፈ] ፤ ቦታ ቦታ መስጠት [ሰˈጠ]

deport
ዲ'ፖ:ት -ግ- ካገር ማስወ'ጣት [አስወ'ጣ] (ወ ዳገሩ ወይን'ም ወደ ሌላ አገር እንዲሄድ)

deportation
ዲፖ'ቴይሽን -ስ- ካገር ማስወ'ጣት ፣ እንዲን ሕዝብ በኀይል ካገር ማ'ባረር

deportment
ዲ'ፖ:ትመንት -ስ- ያ'ረማመድ ሁናቴ ፣ ጠባይ

depose
ዲ'ፖውዝ -ግ- ከዙፋን ማውረድ [አወ'ረደ]

deposit
ዲ'ፖዚት -ግ- ማስቀ'መጥ [አስቀ'መጠ] (ለገ ንዘብ)
bank account
-ስ- ተቀ'ማጭ ገንዘብ (በባንክ ወዘተ)
guarantee
-ስ- መያዣ ገንዘብ ፣ ቀብድ

depositor
ዲ'ፖዚተ -ስ- አስቀ'ማጭ (ገንዘብ በባንክ)

depository
ዲ'ፖዚትሪ -ስ- ዋጋ ያ'ላ'ቸው ዕቃዎ'ች የ'ሚ 'ቀ'መጡ'በት ቤት ፣ ያደራ ዕቃ ማስቀ'መጫ ቤት

depot
'ዴፖው -ስ- ግምጃ ቤት (የወ'ታ'ደር ወዘተ)

depraved
ዲፕ'ሬይቭድ -ቅ- ፍ'ጹም ሕ'ገ ወጥ ፣ የተበ ላ'ሸ ፣ ብል'ሹ

depravity
ዲፕ'ራቪቲ -ስ- ሕ'ገ ወ'ጥ'ነት ፣ ብል'ሹ'ነት ፣ ከግብረ ገ'ብ'ነት መራቅ

depreciate
ዲፕ'ሪሺዬይት -ግ- ማርጀት [አረ'ጀ] (ለዕቃ) ፣ ዋጋ መቀ'ነስ [ቀ'ነሰ]

depreciation
ዲፕሪሺ'ዬይሽን -ስ- ዋጋ መቀ'ነስ (በእርጅ'ና ምክንያት)

depredation
ዴፕሪ'ዴይሽን -ስ- ዘረፋ

depression
ዲፕ'ሬሽን -ስ- ረ'ባ'ዳ አገር
mood
-ስ- ጭፍግ'ግ ማለት (ለስ'ሜት)

deprive
ዲፕ'ራይቭ -ግ- መ'ከልከል [ተከለ'ከለ]

depth
'ዴፕስ -ስ- ጥልቀት

deputation
ዴፕዩ'ቴይሽን -ስ- ወ'ኪል'ነት ፤ አቢት ዓዮ 'ች (የተወ'ከሉ)

depute
ዲፕ'ዩውት -ግ- አንድ ሥራ እንዲሠራ ሰው መወ'ከል [ወ'ከለ]

deputize
'ዴፕዩታይዝ -ግ- መ'ወከል [ተወ'ከለ]

deputy
'ዴፕዩቲ -ስ- ረ'ዳት (ምንድ ሹም)
parliament
-ስ- የሕዝብ እንደራሴ

derailment
ዲ'ሬይልመንት -ስ- የባቡር ሐዲድ ለ'ቆ መ'ገልበጥ

deranged
ዲ'ሬይንጅድ -ቅ- እብድ ፣ አእምሮው የተና 'ወጠ ፤ የተማ'ታ'በት

derangement
ዲ'ሬይንጅመንት -ስ- እብደት ፣ የአእምሮ መ 'ናወጥ ፤ መ'ማታት

derelict
'ዴሬሊክት -ቅ- የተተወ ፣ ለመ'በላሸት የደ 'ረሰ ፤ የተረ'ሳ

deride
ዲ'ራይድ -ግ- ለማፌዝ መሣቅ [ሣቀ] ፣ መ'ሣ ለቅ [ተሣ'ለቀ]

derision
ዲ'ሪዠን -ስ- የፌዝ ሣቅ

derisive
ዲ'ራይሲቭ -ቅ- ፌዘ'ኛ

derivation
ዴሪ'ቬይሽን -ስ- የወ'ጣ ፣ ከአንድ ነገር

derivative
ዲ'ሪቨቲቭ -ቅ- የወ'ጣ ፣ ከአንድ ነገር የተገ'ኘ

derive
ዲ'ራይቭ -ግ- መውጣት [ወ'ጣ] ፣ ካንድ ነገር ሌላ ነገር ማግኘት [አገኘ] (ም'ሳሌ ፣ ቃላት ከቃል ማውጣት)

derogatory
ደ'ሮገትሪ -ቅ- አ'ዋራጅ ፣ ክብር የ'ሚነካ

descend
ዲ'ሴንድ -ግ- መውረድ [ወ'ረደ] ፣ ማቆልቆል [አቆለ'ቆለ]

descendant
ዲ'ሴንደንት -ቅ- የልጅ ልጅ ፣ ሲወር'ድ ሲ'ዋ'ረድ የመ'ጣ

descent
ዲ'ሴንት -ስ- ወደታ'ች መውረድ ፣ ማቆልቆል

heredity
-ስ- ትውል'ድ ፣ ዘር

describe
ዲስክ'ራይብ -ግ- ስለአንድ ነገር ሙሉ መግለጫ መስጠት [ሰ'ጠ]

description
ደስክ'ሪፕሽን -ስ- ሙሉ መግለጫ

desert
'ዴዘት -ስ- ምድረ በዳ ፣ ሰው የ'ማይኖር'በት ክፍለ ሀገር

desert
ዲ'ዞ:ት -ግ- መተው [ተወ] ፣ መክዳት [ከ'ዳ] (ለወ'ታ'ደር)

deserter
ዲ'ዞ:ተ -ስ- የከ'ዳ ወ'ታ'ደር ወይን'ም መርከ በ'ኛ

deserve
ዲ'ዞ:ቭ -ግ- የተገ'ባው መሆን [ሆነ]

design
ዲ'ዛይን -ስ- ዕ'ቅድ ፣ ፕላን
-ግ- ዕ'ቅድ መሥራት [ሠ'ራ]

designate
'ዴዚግኔይት -ግ- ማመልከት [አመለ'ከተ] ፣ መወሰን [ወ'ሰነ] ፣ ለአንድ ሥራ መሾም [ሾመ]

desirable
ዲ'ዛይረበል -ቅ- ሊመርጡት የ'ሚ'ገ'ባ ፣ አስተያየት ማራኪ ፣ አስደ'ሳች ፣ ከል'ብ የ'ሚ'ፈ'ለግ

desire
ዲ'ዛየ -ግ- መ'መኘት [ተመ'ኘ] ፣ በጣም መፈ'ለግ [ፈ'ለገ] ፣ ከል'ብ መፈ'ለግ [ፈ'ለገ]

desk
'ዴስክ -ስ- የማንበቢያ'ና የጽሕፈት ጠ'ረ'ጴዛ

desolate
'ዴዘለት -ቅ- ሰው የ'ማይኖር'በት ፣ በጣም ያ'ዘነ (በብ'ቸ'ኝ'ነት ምክንያት)

despair
ዲስ'ፔየ -ግ- ተስፋ መቁረጥ [ቆ'ረጠ] ፣ ያለ ተስፋ መቅረት [ቀ'ረ]

despatch
ዲስ'ፓች -ግ- መላክ [ላከ] (ዕቃ)

desperate
'ዴስፐረት -ቅ- ተስፋ ቢስ ፣ ተስፋ የቆ'ረጠ

despicable
ዲስ'ፒክበል -ቅ- ፍ'ጹም ክብር የ'ማይ'ገ'ባው

despise
ዲስ'ፓይዝ -ግ- መዝለፍ [ዘ'ለፈ] ፣ መንቀፍ [ነ'ቀፈ]

despite
ደስ'ፓይት -መዋ- ም'ንም እንኳ(ን) . . . በ

despoil
ደስ'ፖይል -ግ- ሀብት ፣ ገንዘብ መቀ'ማት [ቀ'ማ] ፣ መዝረፍ [ዘ'ረፈ]

despondency
ደስ'ፖንደንሲ -ስ- ማዘን ፣ መ'ከፋት

despondent
ደስ'ፖንደንት -ቅ- ያ'ዘነ ፣ የከ'ፋው

despot
'ዴስፖት -ስ- ተቀናቃኝ የሌ'ለው ጨ'ቋኝ ገዥ

dessert
ዲ'ዞ:ት -ስ- ከዋ'ና ምግብ በኋላ የ'ሚቀርብ ጣፋጭ ምግብ ፣ ፍራፍሬ ወዘተ

destination
ዴስቲ'ኔይሽን -ስ- የ'ሚ'ጓዙ'በት ፣ የ'ሚሄ ዱ'በት ቦታ

destined (for)
'ዴስቲንድ -ቅ- ለ . . . የታ'ሰበ

destiny
'ዴስቲኒ -ስ- ተምኔት ፣ አንድ ሰው ወደፊት የ'ሚገጥመው ዕ'ድል (ጥሩ ወይን'ም መጥፎ)

destitute
'ዴስቲትዩ:ት -ቅ- ያ'ጣ ፣ የቸ'ገረው ፣ በጣም የደኸ'የ

destroy
ዲስ'ትሮይ -ግ- መደምሰስ [ደመ'ሰሰ] ፣ ማፈራረስ [አፈራ'ረሰ] ፣ መግደል [ገ'ደለ] ፣ መፍጀት [ፈ'ጀ] (መግደል)

destroyer
ዲስት'ሮየ -ስ- የ'ሚደመ'ስስ ሰው ፣ የ'ሚያፈራ'ርስ ሰው ፣ የጦር መርከብ (መካ'ከለ'ኛ መጠን ያ'ለው)

destruction
ዲስት'ረክሽን -ስ- ጥፋት ፣ መፈራረስ ፣ እልቂት ፣ ፍርስራሽ

destructive
ዲስትክ'ረቲቭ -ቅ- አጥፊ ፣ አፍራሽ ፣ አ'በላሽ

detach
ዲ'ታች -ግ- መነጣጠል [ነጣ'ጠለ] ፣ መፍታት [ፈ'ታ]

detached
ዲ'ታችት -ቅ- የተነጣ'ጠለ ፣ ለብ'ቻው ተለ'ይቶ ያ'ለ

detail
'ዲቴይል -ግ- ስለአንድ ነገር ጥቃ'ቅን ጠባይ ሁሉ መ'ናገር [ተና'ገረ]
-ስ- ዝርዝር ነገር

detain
ዲ'ቴይን -ግ- እን'ዳይሄድ መከልከል [ከለ'ከለ] ፣ ማቆ'የት [አቆ'የ] ፣ በእስር ቤት ማቆ'የት [አቆ'የ]

detect
ዲ'ቴክት -ግ- ፈ'ልጎ ማግኘት [አገ'ኘ]

detective
ዲ'ቴክቲቭ -ስ- መርማሪ (በተለ'ይ የወንጀል)
-story
-ስ- የወንጀለ'ኛ'ና የምር'ምሩ ታሪክ ያ'ለ'በት መጽሐፍ

detention
ዲ'ቴንሽን -ስ- እሥር ቤት ማቆ'የት

deter
ዲ'ተ፡ -ግ- የ'ሚመጣውን ፈርቶ ከመሥራት (ሰው ማ'ገድ [አ'ገደ]

detergent
ዲ'ተ፡ጀንት -ስ- ዱቄት ወይን'ም ፈሳሽ የሆነ ማጽጃ ፣ ንጹሕ ማድረጊያ

deteriorate
ዲ'ቲሪየሬይት -ግ- እ'የከ'ፋ ፣ እ'የተበላ'ሸ መሄድ [ሄደ]

determination
ዲተ፡ሚ'ኔይሽን -ስ- ቁርጥ ሐሳ'ብ

determine
ዲ'ተ፡ሚን -ግ- መቁረጥ [ቆ'ረጠ] (ሐ'ሳብን)

deterrent
ዲ'ተረንት -ስ- ከፍርሃት የተነ'ሣ የ'ሚ'ሠ'ራን የሚያ'ግድ ነገር

detest
ዲ'ቴስት -ግ- አጥብቆ መጥላት [ጠ'ላ] ፣ መ'ጸየፍ [ተጸ'የፈ]

dethrone
ዲθ'ረውን -ግ- ከአልጋ ማውረድ [አወ'ረደ] (ንጉሥ)

detonate
'ዴተኔይት -ግ- ማፈን'ዳት [አፈነ'ዳ] ፣ በኀይል መፈን'ዳት [ፈነ'ዳ]

detour
'ዲቱወ -ግ- ከዋ'ናው መንገድ መውጣት [ወ'ጣ] (ዋ'ናው መንገድ ስለታ'ገደ ወይን'ም እስኪ'ሠ'ራ)
-ስ- ተለ'ዋጭ ሌላ መንገድ (ዋ'ናው መንገድ ስለታ'ገደ ወይን'ም እስኪ'ሠ'ራ)

detract
ዲት'ራክት -ግ- ማሳ'ነስ [አሳ'ነሰ] ፣ መቀ'ነስ [ቀ'ነሰ] (የሰው ስም ፣ ዕቃ ፣ ዋጋ ወዘተ)

detrimental
ዴትሪ'ሜንተል -ቅ- ጎጂ

devaluation
ዲቫልዩ'ዌይሽን -ስ- ዋጋ ማ'ውረድ (በተለ'ይ የገንዘብ)

develop
ዲ'ቬለፕ -ግ- እንዲያድግ ማድረግ [አደ'ረገ] ፣ ማስፋፋት [አስፋ'ፋ]

development
ዲ'ቬለፕመንት -ስ- እድገት ፣ መስፋፋት

deviate
'ዲቪዬይት -ግ- ከተለ'መደው ሥርዓት መውጣት [ወ'ጣ]

device
ዲ'ቫይስ -ስ- መ'ቀላጠፊያ መ'ሣሪያ ፣ ዕ'ቅድ፡ አንድ ነገር ለመሥራት የታ'ሰበ ዘዴ ወይን'ም የተሠ'ራ መ'ሣሪያ

devil
'ዴቭል -ስ- ዲያብሎስ ፣ ሰይጣን

devil-may-care
ዲ'ቨል ሜይ'ኬየ -ቅ- ግ'ዴ'ለሽ
devilry
'ዴቨልሪ -ስ- የሰይጣን ሥራ
devious
'ዲቪየስ -ቅ- ጠምዛ'ዛ
person
-ቅ- ል'ቡ የ'ማይ'ገ'ኝ
devise
ዲ'ቫይዝ -ግ- መፈልሰፍ [ፈለ'ሰፈ] (መ'ሣ ሪያ ፣ ዕ'ቅድ)
devoid
ዲ'ቮይድ -ቅ- ባዶ ፣ የተራ'ቆተ ፣ የሌ'ለ'በት
devote
ዲ'ቮውት -ግ- ጊዜን ፣ ኀይልን ፣ ሕይወትን ላንድ ተግባር ማዋል [አዋለ]
devoted
ዲ'ቮውተድ -ቅ- ጊዜውን ፣ ኀይሉን ፣ ሕይወ ቱን ላንድ ተግባር ያዋለ
loving
-ቅ- በጣም የ'ሚያፈቅር
devotion
ዲ'ቮውሽን -ስ- ጊዜን ፣ ኀይልን ፣ ሕይወትን ላንድ ተግባር ማዋል
devour
ዲ'ቫወ -ግ- መዋጥ [ዋጠ] (ለታላ'ላቅ እንስ ሳት) ፣ መስልቀጥ [ሰለ'ቀጠ]
devout
ዲ'ቫውት -ቅ- ሃይማኖተ'ኛ
dew
ድ'ዩ: -ስ- ጤዛ
dexterity
ዴክስ'ቴሪቲ -ስ- ቅልጥፍ'ና (የእ'ጅ ፣ የሰው 'ነት)
dexterous
'ዴክስትረስ -ቅ- እ'ጀ ቀልጣ'ፋ
diabetes
ዳየ'ቢቲዝ -ስ- የሱ'ካር በ'ሽታ
diabolical
ዳየ'ቦሊክል -ቅ- ሰይጣናዊ ፣ በጣም ክፉ
diagnose
'ዳየግኖውዝ -ግ- መመርመር [መረ'መረ] (ሐ ኪም በ'ሽታ)

diagnosis
ዳየግ'ኖውሲስ -ስ- ምርመራ (በ'ሽታ ለማወቅ በሐኪም)
diagonal
ዳ'ያገነል -ስ- አ'ገናኝ መሥመር (ከማዕዘን ማዕ ዘን የ'ሚያ'ገና'ኝ
-ቅ- አ'ገናኝ (ለመሥመር ፣ ከማዕዘን ማዕዘን)
diagram
'ዳየግራም -ስ- ንድፍ (የማስረ'ጃ ሥዕል)
dial
'ዳየል -ስ- ክበብ ፣ የሰዓት ወይን'ም የሌላ መሣ'ሪያ ክ'ብ መልክ
telephone
-ስ- የቴሌፎን ማዞሪያ (ቁጥር ያ'ለበ'ት)
-ግ- የቴሌፎን ጥ'ሪ ለማድረግ. ቁጥር ማዞር [አዞረ]
dialect
'ዳየሌክት -ስ- የቋንቋ ዲታላ ፣ ባንድ ቋንቋ ውስጥ ያንድ ወገን ሕዝብ ወይን'ም ቀበሌ የ'ሚ 'ና'ገር'በት የቋንቋ ዘየ (ም'ሳሌ ፣ ጎንደር'ኛ፣ ሸዋ'ኛ ፣ ወሎ'ኛ ወዘተ)
dialectic
ዳያ'ሌክቲክ -ስ- በክር'ክር መልክ እውነትን ለማግኘት መ'መራመር
dialogue
'ዳየሎግ -ስ- ንግ'ግር ፣ በንግ'ግር መልክ የተዘጋ'ጀ ጽሑፍ ፣ ውይ'ይት
diameter
ዳ'ያሚተ -ስ- ክበብን ለሁለ'ት የ'ሚከፍል መሥመር (ዲያሜትር)
diamond
'ዳየመንድ -ስ- አልማዝ
diaper
'ዳየፐ -ስ- የቅዘን ጨርቅ (የሕፃን) ፣ የሕፃን የንጽሕ'ና ጨርቅ
diarrhoea
ዳየ'ሪየ -ስ- ተቅማጥ ፣ ቅዘን
diary
'ዳየሪ -ስ- ማስታወሻ መያዣ ደብተር (የየቀ ኑን ሁናቴ ጽፈው የ'ሚይዙ'በት)
dice
'ዳይስ -ስ- ዛሀራ

dictate
ዲክ'ቴይት -ግ- የቃል ጽሕፈት ማ'ጻፍ [አ'ጻፈ] ኀይል ሥልጣን ተመርኩዞ ማዘዝ [አ'ዘዘ]

dictation
ዲክ'ቴይሽን -ስ- የቃል ጽሕፈት ፤ ኀይል ፣ ሥልጣን የተመረ'ኮዘ ትእዛዝ

dictator
ዲክ'ቴይተ -ስ- ተቀናቃኝ የሌ'ለው ገዥ

dictatorial
ዲክተ'ቶሪየል -ቅ- ትእዛዝ አብዛኛ ፣ ማዘዝ የ'ሚወ'ድ ፣ ተቀናቃኝ የሌ'ለው (ገዥ) ፣ ኀይል ሥልጣን የተመረኮ'ዘ

diction
'ዲክሽን -ስ- የአ'ነጋገር ግልጽ'ነት ፤ የቃላት አ'መራረጥ (በንግ'ግር)

dictionary
'ዲክሽነሪ -ስ- መዝገበ ቃላት

die
'ዳይ -ግ- መሞት [ሞተ]

diet
'ዳየት -ስ- ምግብ
regimen
-ስ- ል'ዩ ምግብ (የሕመምተ'ኛ)

differ
'ዲፈ -ግ- መ'ለየት [ተለ'የ]

difference
'ዲፈረንስ -ስ- ል'ዩ'ነት

different
'ዲፈረንት -ቅ- ል'ዩ (የተለ'የ)

differentiate
ዲፈ'ሬንሺዬይት -ግ- መለ'የት [ለ'የ] ፣ ለ'ቶ ማወቅ [ዐ'ወቀ]

difficult
'ዲፊከልት -ቅ- አስቸ'ጋሪ ፣ አ'ዋኪ

difficulty
'ዲፊከልቲ -ስ- ች'ግር ፣ መከራ ፣ ሁከት

diffuse
ዲፈ'ዩስ -ቅ- የተበታ'ተነ ፣ የተሰራ'ጨ የተደባ'ለቀ (በመ'ዋሐድ)

diffusion
ዲፈ'ዩዥን -ስ- መ'በታተን ፣ መ'ሰራጨት መ'ደባለቅ (በመ'ዋሐድ)

dig
'ዲግ -ግ- መቆ'ፈር [ቆ'ፈረ]

digest
ዳይ'ጀስት -ግ- ማንሸራሸር [አንሸራ'ሸረ] (ለምግብ)

digestible
ደ'ጀስተበል -ቅ- የ'ሚንሸራ'ሸር ፡ በቶ ከሰው'ነት የ'ሚስማ'ማ (ምግብ)

digestion
ደ'ጀስቾን -ስ- ማንሸራሸር (ምግብ)

digestive
ደ'ጀስቲቭ -ቅ- ምግብን ለማንሸራሸር የ'ረዳ

digit
'ዲጂት -ስ- አንድ አኀዝ
finger
-ስ- ጣት

dignified
'ዲግኒፋይድ -ቅ- የተከ'በረ ፣ ክብሩን ጠ'ባ

dignify
'ዲግኒፋይ -ግ- ማክበር [አከ'በረ] ፣ በማዕረ ከ'ፍ ማድረግ [አደ'ረገ]

dignitary
'ዲግኒተሪ -ስ- ት'ልቅ ሹመት ያ'ለው ሰ (በተለ'ይ በቤተ ክህነት)

dignity
'ዲግኒቲ -ስ- ክብር ፣ የታ'ላቅ'ነት ስ'ሜት ታ'ላቅ ሹመት ፣ ማዕረግ

digress
ዳይግ'ሬስ -ግ- ከመንገድ ማግለል [አገ'ለለ] ፣ ከአርእስት መውጣት [ወ'ጣ] (ለንግ'ግር)

dike
'ዳይክ -ስ- ያፈር ቁ'ልል (ውሃን የ'ሚይዝ ፣ የ'ሚገ'ድብ)
dam
-ስ- ግ'ድብ

dilapidated
ዲ'ላፒዴይተድ -ቅ- የተለያ'የ ፣ የፈራ'ረሰ ፣ የወ'ላለቀ (ለሕንፃ ፣ ለቤት ዕቃ ወዘተ)

dilate
ዳይ'ሌይት -ግ- በሰ'ፊው መ'ከፈት [ተከ'ፈተ] ፣ ማስፋት [አሰ'ፋ] ፤ በረ'ጅም መጻፍ [ጻፈ] ወይን'ም መ'ናገር [ተና'ገረ]

dilatory
'ዲለተሪ -ቅ- ጊዜ አባካኝ ፣ የ'ሚያዘገ'ይ ፣ ዝ'ግተ'ኛ

diligence	ትጋት	u. ct,	መራ አሳየ አዘዘ
diligent	ትጉ ትጉህ ተጋ		ተቈጣጠረ ቀጥተኛ
dilute	አቀጠነ	direction	አቅጣጫ መሪነት ተቈጣ
dim	ቀነሰ ደብዛዛ		ጣሪነት መመሪያ
dimensions	ውርድና ስፋት	directive	መምሪያ መሪ ፡ ቃል
diminish	ቀነሰ አሳነሰ ተቀነሰ	directly	በቀጥታ
	አነሰ ጉደለ	director	ዲሬክተር አስኪያጅ
diminution	ቅነሳ	directory	ማውጫ የስም ፡ ማውጫ
dine	እራት ፡ በላ	dirge	ሙሾ
ding)	ቆሸሽ ፡ ያለ	dirt	ቆሻሻ እድፍ ጉድፍ
dining room	መብል ፡ ቤትየም ግብ ፡ ቤት		መበሎ ፡ ታየ
dinner	ራት እራት	dirty	ቆሻሻ አደፈ
dip	አጠለቀ አጠ ቀሰ	disability	ጉድለት
Jiploma	የምስክር ፡ ወረቀት	disable	ሰነከለ
diplomacy	ዲፕሎማሲ		
diplomatic	ዘዴኛ የዲፕሎማሲ		

disabled
ዲ'ሴይበልድ -ቅ- አካለ ስንኩል
disadvantage
ዲሰድ'ቫ:ንቲጅ -ስ- እንቅፋት ፣ መሰናክል
disagree
ዲሰግ'ሪ: -ግ- አለመስማማት [-ተስማ'ማ]
disagreeable
ዲሰግ'ሪየበል -ቅ- የ'ማይስማ'ማ ፣ ደ'ስ የ'ማ ያ'ሰ'ኝ ፣ ደወዳጅ'ነት ስ'ሜት የ'ማያሳ'ይ ፣ ቁ'ጡ
disagreement
ዲሰግ'ሪ:ሜመንት -ስ- አለመስማማት
disallow
ዲሰ'ላው -ግ- መከልከል [ከለ'ከለ] ፣ አለመ 'ቀበል [-ተቀ'በለ]
disappear
ዲሰ'ፒየ -ግ- መጥፋት [ጠ'ፋ] ፣ መ'ሠወር [-ተሠ 'ወረ]
disappearance
ዲሰ'ፒረንስ -ስ- መጥፋት ፣ መ'ሠወር
disappoint
ዲሰ'ፖይንት -ግ- ማሳ'ዘን [አሳ'ዘነ] ፣ የሰ'ጡ ትን ተስፋ አለመፈ'ጸም [-ፈ'ጸመ]
disappointment
ዲሰ'ፓይንትመንት -ስ- አለመ'ደሰት ፣ ማዘን (የፈ'ለጉትን ነገር ባለማግኘት)
disapprove
ዲሰፕ'ሩ:ቭ -ግ- አለመስማማት [-ተስማ'ማ]
disarm
ዲ'ሳ:ም -ግ- መ'ሣሪያ ፣ መ'ከላከያ መቀ'ማት [ቀ'ማ]
disaster
ዲ'ዛ:ስተ -ግ- መዓት ፣ ጥፋት
disastrous
ዲ'ዛ:ስትረስ -ቅ- ድንገተ'ኛ ጥፋት የ'ሚያ ስከ'ትል
disband
ዲስ'ባንድ -ግ- ማኅበር መፍታት [ፈ'ታ] ፣ ማኅበር መበ'ተን [በ'ተነ] ፣ ከወ'ታ'ደር አገል ግሎት ማ'ሰናበት [አ'ሰና'በተ]
disbelieve
ዲስበ'ሊይቭ -ግ- አለማመን [-አ'መነ]
disburse
ዲስ'በ:ስ -ግ- ገንዘብ መክፈል [ከ'ፈለ]
disbursement
ዲስ'በ:ስመንት -ስ- መክፈል
disc
'ዲስክ -ስ- ክ'ብ ጠፍጣ'ፋ ነገር
record
-ስ- የሙዚቃ ሸክላ
discard
ዲስ'ካ:ድ -ግ- መጣል [ጣለ] ፣ የ'ማይፈ'ልጉ ትን የመ'ጫወቻ ካርታ እመሬት ላይ መጣል [ጣለ] ፣ ማስወ'ገድ [አስወ'ገደ]
discern
ዲ'ሰ:ን -ግ- መለ'የት [ለ'የ] (በማየት)
discerning
ዲ'ሰ:ኒንግ -ቅ- ክፉ'ና ደ'ጉን መለ'የት የ'ሚ ችል ፣ አስተዋይ
discharge
ዲስ'ቻ:ጅ -ግ- መልቀቅ [ለ'ቀቀ] ፣ መፍታት [ፈ'ታ] (እሥረ'ኛ) ፣ ከሥራ ማስወ'ጣት [አስ ወ'ጣ]
disciple
ዲ'ሳይፐል -ስ- ደ'ቀ መዝሙር ፣ ተማሪ
discipline
'ዲሲፕሊን -ስ- ሥርዓት ፣ ሥነ ሥርዓት
disclose
ዲስክ'ለውዝ -ግ- መግለጽ [ገ'ለጸ] ፣ (የተደ 'በቀ ነገር)
disclosure
ዲስክ'ለውዠ -ስ- መግለጽ ፣ የተደ'በቀውን ይፋ ማድረግ
discolour
ዲስ'ከለ -ግ- ማደብዘዝ [አደበ'ዘዘ] (ለቀለም)፣ ቀለም መለ'ወጥ [ለ'ወጠ] ፣ መበ'ከል [በ'ከለ] (በቀለም)
discomfiture
ዲስ'ከምፈቸ -ስ- ማፈር
discomfort
ዲስ'ከምፈት -ስ- ደ'ስ አለመ'ሰኘት ፣ ቀ'ላል ሕመም
disconcert
ዲስከን'ሰ:ት -ግ- ማሳ'ፈር [አሳ'ፈረ] ፣ ማ'ደና ገር [አ'ደና'ገረ]
disconnect
ዲስከ'ኔክት -ግ- መለያየት [ለያ'የ]
disconsolate
ዲስ'ኮንሰለት -ቅ- ያልተደ'ሰተ ፣ የ'ማይጽና'ና

discontented
ዲስከን'ቴንተድ -ቅ- ያልተ'ደ'ሰተ፣ቅ'ር ያለው
discontinue
ዲስከን'ቲንዩ -ግ- ማ'ቋረጥ [አ'ቋ'ረጠ] ፣ አለ መቀ'ጠል [-ቀ'ጠለ]
discord
'ዲስኮ:ድ -ስ- አለመስማማት ፣ ኅብረት ማጣት
discordant
ዲስ'ኮ:ድንት -ቅ- የ'ማይስማ'ማ
discount
'ዲስካውንት -ስ- የዋጋ ቅ'ናሽ ፣ እ'ጅ በ'ጅ ለ'ሚከፍል የ'ሚ'ደ'ረግ የዕዳ ፣ የብ'ድር ቅ'ናሽ
discourage
ዲስ'ከሪጅ -ግ- ማስፈራራት [አስፈራ'ራ] ፣ አለማ'ጃገን [-አ'ጃ'ገነ]፣ ተስፋ ማስቆ'ረጥ [አስ ቆ'ረጠ]
discourse
'ዲስኮ:ስ -ስ- ንግ'ግር
discover
ዲስ'ከቨ -ግ- ማግኘት [አገ'ኘ] ፣ ቀድሞ ያል ታ'ወቀ ነገር መፈልሰፍ [ፈለ'ሰፈ]
discovery
ዲስ'ከቨሪ -ስ- ፍልስፍ'ና ፣ ቀድሞ ያልታ'ወቀ ነገር ማግኘት
discredit
ዲስክ'ሬዲት -ግ- ዋጋ ማሳ'ጣት [አሳ'ጣ]
discreet
ዲስክ'ሪይት ጠንቃ'ቃ (በንግ'ግር)
discrepancy
ዲስክ'ሬፐንሲ -ስ- የሒሳብ ጉድለት፣ጉድለት
discretion
ዲስክ'ሬሽን -ስ- ጠንቃ'ቃ'ነት (በሥራ ፡ በአ'ነጋገር) ፣ ነጻ'ነት (አእምሮ የፈረ'ደውን ለመሥራት)
discriminate
ዲስክ'ሪሚኔይት -ግ- ለ'ይቶ ማወቅ [ዐ'ወቀ]
socially
-ግ- የዘር ል'ዩ'ነት ማድረግ [አደ'ረገ]
discrimination
ዲስክሪሚ'ኔይሽን -ስ- ል'ዩ'ነት ፣ በነገር ፡ በሁኔቴዎ'ች መካ'ከል ያ'ለውን ጥቃ'ቅን ል'ዩ'ነት የማወቅ ችሎታ
racial
-ስ- የዘር ል'ዩ'ነት

discuss
ዲስ'ከስ -ግ- መ'ወያየት (ተወያ'የ] ፣ አንድ ጉ'ዳይ መመርመ'ር'ና ማጥናት [አጠ'ና]
discussion
ዲስ'ከሽን -ስ- ውይ'ይት
disdain
ዲስ'ዴይን -ግ- ማንቋሸሽ [አንቋ'ሸሸ] ፡ በን ቀት ዓይን መ'መልከት [ተመለ'ከተ]
disease
ዲ'ዚይዝ -ስ- በ'ሽታ ፣ ሕመም
disembark
ዲሴም'ባ:ክ -ግ- (ከመርከብ ከውሮ'ፕላን) መው ረድ [ወ'ረደ]
disengage
ዲሴን'ጌይጅ -ግ- ወደኋላ መ'መለስ [ተመ'ለሰ] (በጦር'ነት) ፣ ራስን ነጻ ማድረግ [አደ'ረገ] (ከገ ቡ'በት ነገር)
disentangle
ዲሴን'ታንገል -ግ- መፈታታት [ፈታ'ታ] ፣ መለያየት [ለያ'የ] (ለተወሳ'ሰበ ነገር)
disfigure
ዲስ'ፊገ -ግ- መልክ ቅርፅ ማጥፋት [አጠ'ፋ] (በማቁሰል ፡ በማ'በላሸት)
disgorge
ዲስ'ጎ:ጅ -ግ- ማስታወክ [አስታ'ወከ] (ለእን ስሳት) ፣ በ'ሚ'ገባ ያልተገ'ኘ ትርፍ መመ'ለስ [መ'ለሰ]
disgrace
ዲስግ'ሬይስ -ስ- ነፍረት ፡ በሰዎ'ች ዘንድ መ'ከበርን ማጣት (ከመጥፎ አመል የተነ'ሣ)
disgraceful
ዲስግ'ሬይስፉል -ቅ- ነፍረተ'ኛ ፣ አሳ'ፋሪ
disguise
ዲስ'ጋይዝ -ግ- መልክን ድምፅን መለ'ወጥ [ለ'ወጠ] (እንዳ'ይታ'ወቁ)
-ስ- መልክን ድምፅን መለ'ወጥ (እንዳ ይ'ታወቁ)
disgust
ዲስ'ገስት -ግ- መጥላት [ጠ'ላ] ፡ መ'ጸየፍ [ተጸ'የፈ]
-ስ- ጥላ'ቻ ፡ መ'ጸየፍ
disgusting
ዲስ'ገስቲንግ -ቅ- አ'ጸ'ያፊ ፡ ማስጠ'ሎ

dish

'ዲሽ -ስ- የምግብ ማቅረቢያ ሳሕን (ጎድጓ'ዳ)

food

-ስ- ምግብ

dishcloth

'ዲሽክሎፅ -ስ- የሳሕን መወልወያ ጨርቅ

dishearten

ዲስ'ሀ፡ተን -ግ- ማስፈራራት [አስፈራ'ራ]

dishonest

ዲ'ሶኔስት -ቅ- የ'ማይ'ታመን ፣ አ'ታላይ ፣ አጭበርባሪ ፣ ወስላ'ታ

dishonour

ዲ'ሶነ -ግ- አለማክበር [-አከ'በረ] ፣ ማ'ዋረድ [አ'ዋ'ረደ]

dishonourable

ዲ'ሶነረበል -ቅ- የ'ማይ'ከ'በር ፣ ነፍረተ ቢስ

disinfect

ዲሲን'ፌክት -ግ- በ'ሽታ ከ'ሚያመጡ ነፍሳት ነጻ ማድረግ

disinfectant

ዲሲን'ፌክተንት -ስ- የተባይ መግደያ መድኃኒት

disinherit

ዲሲን'ሄሪት -ግ- ልጅ ከውርስ መከልከል [ከለ'ከለ] ፤ መካድ [ካደ]

disintegrate

ዲ'ሲንቲግሬይት -ግ መ'ሰባበር [ተሰባ'በረ]

disintegration

ዲሲንቲግ'ሬይሽን -ስ- መ'ሰባበር

disinterested

ዲ'ሲንትሬስተድ -ቅ- የ'ማያ'ዳ'ላ ፤ አድልዎ የ'ሌ'ለ'በት

dislike

ዲስ'ላይክ -ግ- አለመውደድ [-ወ'ደደ]

dislocate

'ዲስለኬይት -ግ- መለያየት [ለያ'የ] ፣ ከቦታ ማ'ናወጥ [አ'ና'ወጠ] (ለሰው'ነት መ'ገጣጠሚያ)

dislocation

ዲስለ'ኬይሽን -ስ- መለያየት

dislodge

ዲስ'ሎጅ -ግ- ቦታ ማስለ'ቀቅ [አስለ'ቀቀ]፡ ካ'ሉ'በት ቦታ በኀይል ማስለ'ቀቅ [አስለ'ቀቀ]

disloyal

ዲስ'ሎየል -ቅ- የ'ማይ'ታ'መን ፣ እምነት የ'ማይ'ጣል'በት ፣ ከሓዲ

dismal

'ዲዝመል -ቅ- የ'ማያስደ'ስት ፤ የጨፈ'ገገው ፤ ያ'ዘነ

dismantle

ዲስ'ማንተል -ግ- መፈታታት [ፈታ'ታ] ፣ መበታተን [በታ'ተነ] ፣ መለያየት [ለያ'የ] (መ'ሣሪያ)

dismay

ዲስ'ሜይ -ስ- አለመ'ደሰት

dismiss

ዲስ'ሚስ -ግ- ማስወ'ገድ [አስወ'ገደ] ፣ ማ'ባረር [አ'ባ'ረረ]፣ማስወ'ጣት [አስወ'ጣ] (ከሥራ)

dismount

ዲስ'ማውንት -ግ- መውረድ [ወ'ረደ] (ከፈረስ ወዘተ)

disobedience

ዲሰ'ቢዲየንስ -ስ- አለመ'ታዘዝ ፡ እም'ቢተ'ኛ'ነት

disobedient

ዲሰ'ቢዲየንት -ቅ- የ'ማይ'ታ'ዘዝ ፡ እምቢተ'ኛ ፣ አሻ'ፈረኝ ባይ

disobey

ዲሰ'ቤይ -ግ- አለመ'ታዘዝ [-ታ'ዘዘ]

disorder

ዲ'ሶ፡ደ -ስ- ሕ'ገ ወ'ጥ'ነት ፣ ብጥ'ብጥ ፡ የሕዝብን ፀ'ጥታ ማ'ወክ

disorderly

ዲ'ሶ፡ደሊ -ቅ- ሕ'ገ ወጥ ፡ በጥባጭ

disorganize

ዲ'ሶ፡ገናይዝ -ግ- ያለሥርዓት ማስቀ'ረት [አስ'ቀረ] ፡ መደበላለቅ [ደበላ'ለቀ] ፡ ሥርዓት ማሳ'ጣት [አሳ'ጣ]

disown

ዲ'ሰውን -ግ- ከውርስ ማ'ገድ [አ'ገደ] ፡ ኀላፊ'ነትን ማስወ'ረድ [አስወ'ረደ]

disparage

ዲስ'ፓረጅ -ግ- ማንቋሸሽ [አንቋ'ሸሸ] ፡ ማ'ቃለል [አ'ቃ'ለለ] (ሰውን)

disparity

ዲስ'ፓረቲ -ስ- ል'ዩ'ነት ፡ አለመ'መሳሰል

dispatch
ዲስ'ፓች -ግ- መላክ [ላከ] ፣ ፈጥኖ መላክ [ላከ] ፣ በፍጥነት መጨ'ረስ [ጨ'ረሰ]

dispel
ዲስ'ፔል -ግ- መበታተን [በታ'ተነ]

dispensable
ዲስ'ፔንሰበል -ቅ- ሊቀር የ'ሚችል ፣ ቢቀር የ'ማይጎዳ

dispensary
ዲስ'ፔንሰሪ -ስ- የመድኃኒት ቤት (በሆስፒታል)

dispensation
ዲስፔን'ሴይሽን -ስ- መስጠት ፣ ማ'ደል ፣ የ'ሚ'ታ'ደል ነገር

dispense
ዲስ'ፔንስ -ግ- መስጠት [ሰ'ጠ] ፣ ማ'ደል [አ'ደለ] (መድኃኒት ፣ ምፅዋት (ወዘተ)
medicine
-ግ- መድኃኒት መቀ'መም [ቀ'መመ]

dispersal
ዲስ'ፐ:ሰል -ስ- መ'በታተን ፣ የተበታ'ተነ መሆን

disperse
ዲስ'ፐ:ስ -ግ- መበታተን [በታ'ተነ] ፤ መ'በታተን [ተበታ'ተነ]

displace
ዲስፕ'ሌይስ -ግ- ከቦታ ማ'ቃወስ [አ'ቃ'ወሰ] ፤ ያለቦታው ማስቀ'መጥ [አስቀ'መጠ]

display
ዲስፕ'ሌይ -ግ- ማሳ'የት [አሳ'የ] (ለዕቃ)
-ስ- ትርኢት ፤ ለመ'ታየት የተዘረ'ጋ ዕቃ

displease
ዲስፕ'ሊይዝ -ግ- ማስከ'ፋት [አስከ'ፋ] ፤ ማስቀ'የም [አስቀ'የመ]

disposal
ዲስ'ፖውዘል -ስ- መጣል (ቆሻሻ ፤ ጉድፍ)
order
-ስ- ትእዛዝ

disposition
ዲስፖ'ዚሽን -ስ- ጠባይ ፤ ዝን'ባሌ ፣ አ'ቀማመጥ

dispossess
ዲስፖ'ዜስ -ግ- ይዞታ ፤ ንብረት በተለ'ይ መሬት ማስለ'ቀቅ [አስለ'ቀቀ]

disproportionate
ዲስፕረ'ፖ:ሽነት -ቅ- ያልተመዛ'ዘነ ፣ ብልጫ ያ'ለው

disprove
ዲስፕ'ሩ:ቭ -ስ- ልክ' አለመሆኑን ማስረ'ዳት [አስረ'ዳ]

disputable
ዲስፕ'ዩ:ተበል -ቅ- የ'ሚያ'ከራ'ክር ፣ የ'ሚያ'ጠራ'ጥር

dispute
ዲስፕ'ዩ:ት -ስ- ጥል ፣ ክር'ክር

disqualify
ዲስክ'ዎሊፋይ -ግ- ያንድ ሰው ችሎታ በቂ አለመሆኑን መግለጽ [ገ'ለጸ] ፤ ከውድ'ድር ማስወ'ጣት [አስወ'ጣ] (ለስፖርት)

disquiet
ዲስክ'ዋየት -ግ- ማ'ወክ [አ'ወከ] ፣ መበጥበጥ [በጠ'በጠ] ፤ ሰላም መንሣት [ነ'ሣ]
-ስ- ጭንቀት ፣ ሁከት ፣ ብጥ'ብጥ(የፖለቲካ ወዘተ)

disregard
ዲስረ'ጋ:ድ -ግ- ቸ'ል ማለት [አለ] ፤ ዋጋ አለመስጠት [-ሰ'ጠ]

disreputable
ዲስ'ሬፕዩተበል -ቅ- ወ'ራ'ዳ ፤ ክብር የ'ማይ'ሰ'ጠው

disrespect
ዲስረስ'ፔክት -ስ- አለማክበር ፣ ብልግ'ና

disrespectful
ዲስረስ'ፔክትፉል -ቅ- ባለጌ ፤ ያልተቀ'ጣ ፣ አመለቢስ

disrupt
ዲስ'ረፕት -ግ- መበጥበጥ [በጠ'በጠ] (ዕ'ቅድን) ፤ ሕ'ግ'ና ሥርዓት የሌ'ለው ማድረግ [አደ'ረገ]

disruption
ዲስ'ረፕሽን -ስ- ብጥ'ብጥ ፤ ሁከት ፤ ሕ'ግ'ና ሥርዓት ማጣት

dissect
ዲ'ሴክት -ግ- መበ'ለት [በ'ለተ]

dissection
ዲ'ሴክሽን -ስ- ብ'ልት ማውጣት (በደን ወዘተ በሕ'ክምና)

disservice
ዲ'ሰ:ቪስ -ስ- ጉዳት ቢስ ሥራ

dissipate
'ዲሲፔይት -ግ- ማባከን [አባ'ከነ] (ጊዜ ፣ ገን ዘብ) ፣ ማስወ'ገድ [አስወ'ገደ] (ፍርሃት ፣ ድን ቁር'ና ወዘተ)

dissipated
'ዲሲፔይተድ -ቅ- ኑሮው በመጥፎ ልምድ የተበላ'ሸ ፤ ብኩን ፣ የተበታ'ተነ

dissolute
'ዲሰሉት -ቅ- አውደልዳይ ፣ እንዳ'ሻው የ'ሚ ኖር (መሸተ'ኛ ፣ ቅንዝረ'ኛ)

dissolution
ዲሰ'ሉሽን -ስ- የምክር ቤት መ'ዘጋት ፤ መ'ለ ያየት

dissolve
ዲ'ዞልቭ -ግ- መሟሟት [ሟ'ሟ] ፣ ማሟሟት [አሟ'ሟ]

dissonant
'ዲሰነንት -ቅ- ጣዕመ ዜማ የሌ'ለው ፣ ሻካራ (ድምፅ)

dissuade
ዲስ'ዌይድ -ግ- አንድ ነገር እንዳያደርጉ መም ከር [መ'ከረ] ፣ መገፋፋት [ገፋ'ፋ]

distance
'ዲስተንስ -ስ- ርቀት

distant
'ዲስተንት -ቅ- ሩቅ

distasteful
ዲስ'ቴይስትፉል -ቅ- ለ'ዛ ቢስ ፣ ጣዕመ ቢስ

distend
ዲስ'ቴንድ -ግ- መ'ነፋት [ተነ'ፋ] ፣ መንፋት [ነ'ፋ]

distil
ዲስ'ቲል -ግ- ማ'ጣራት [አ'ጣ'ራ] (ለውሃ በሙቀት)

distillation
ዲስቲ'ሌይሽን -ስ- ማ'ጣራት

distiller
ዲስ'ቲለ -ስ- አ'ጣሪ

distillery
ዲስ'ቲለሪ -ስ- ማ'ጣሪያ ቦታ

distinct
ዲስ'ቲንክት -ቅ- የተለ'የ ፤ የ'ማያ'ሳስት ፣ ተለ 'ይቶ የ'ሚ'ታ'ወቅ

distinction
ዲስ'ቲንክሽን -ስ- ል'ዩ'ነት ፣ የተለ'የ መ'ታ ወቂያ (ለማዕረግ)

distinctive
ዲስ'ቲንክቲቭ -ቅ- ል'ዩ

distinguish
ዲስ'ቲንግዊሽ -ግ- ለ'ይቶ ማወቅ [ዐ'ወቀ]

distinguished
ዲስ'ቲንግዊሽት -ቅ- የተለ'የ ፤ የተከ'በረ

distort
ዲስ'ቶ:ት -ግ- ማ'ጣመም [አ'ጣ'መመ] ፣ ማ'በ ላሸት [አ'በላ'ሸ] ፣ ማ'ወላገድ [አ'ወላ'ገደ]

distortion
ዲስ'ቶ:ሽን -ስ- ማ'ጣመም ፣ ማ'ወላገድ ፣ ማ'በ ላሸት

distract
ዲስት'ራክት -ግ- ሐ'ሳብ ወደ ሌላ አቅጣ'ጫ መግረክ [ማ'ረከ] ፤ አተ'ኩረው እንዳያ'ስቡ ማ'ሰናከል [አ'ሰና'ከለ] ፤ ሐ'ሳብ ማባከን [አባ 'ከነ]

distraction
ዲስት'ራክሽን -ስ- ሐ'ሳብ የ'ሚወስድ ነገር ፣ ሐ'ሳብ አባካኝ ነገር

distress
ዲስት'ሬስ -ስ- ጭንቅ ፣ ሐዘን

distribute
ዲስት'ትሪብዩት -ግ- ማ'ደል [አ'ደለ]

distribution
ዲስትሪብ'ዩሽን -ስ- ማ'ደል

district
'ዲስትሪክት -ስ- ወረዳ ፣ ክፍለ ሀገር

distrustful
ዲስት'ረስትፉል -ቅ- ሰው የ'ማያምን ፣ ተጠ ራጣሪ

disturb
ዲስ'ተ:ብ -ግ- ማ'ወክ [አ'ወከ] ፣ መበጥበጥ [በጠ'በጠ]

disturbance
ዲስ'ተ:በንስ -ስ- ብጥ'..ጥ ፣ ሁውከት

disunite
ዲስዩ'ናይት -ግ- መለያየት [ለያ'የ] ፣ ኅብረት ማሳ'ጣት [አሳ'ጣ]

disused
ዲስ'ዩ:ዝድ -ቅ- ከአገልግሎት ው'ጭ የሆነ ፣ የ'ማይ'ሠ'ራ'በት

ditch

'ዲች -ስ- ቦ'ይ ፣ ረ'ጅም ቁ'ፍር (ለመ'ከላከያ፣ ለውሃ መውረጃ)

dive

'ዳይቭ -ግ- መጥለቅ [ጠ'ለቀ] (ራስን አስቀ'ድሞ እውሃ ውስጥ)

diver

'ዳይቨ -ስ- ጠላቂ ሰው (እውሃ ውስጥ)

diverge

ዳይ'ቨ:ጅ -ግ- ወደ ል'ዩ ል'ዩ አቅጣ'ጫ መሄድ [ሄደ] ፣ ከባህል ፣ ከአስተያየት የተለ'የ መሆን [ሆነ]

diverse

ዳይ'ቨ:ስ -ቅ- ል'ዩ ል'ዩ (በጠባይ ፣ በዐይነት)

diversion

ዳይ'ቨ:ሽን -ስ- አቅጣ'ጫ መለ'ወጥ [ለ'ወጠ] (ለም'ሳሌ መንገድ ሲ'ዘ'ጋ)

divert

ዳይ'ቨ:ት -ግ- አስተያየት ፣ አቅጣጫ መለወጥ [ለ'ወጠ] ፣ ማስደ'ሰት [አስደ'ሰተ]

divide

ዲ'ቫይድ -ግ- መክፈል [ከ'ፈለ] ፣ መከፋፈል [ከፋ'ፈለ]

dividend

'ዲቪዴንድ -ስ- ድርሻ ፣ ክፍ'ያ (ለባለአክሲዮኖ'ች የ'ሚ'ከፈል)

divination

ዲቪ'ኔይሽን -ስ- ወደፊት የ'ሚሆነውን መ'ና ገር ፣ መ'ንበይ

divine

ዲ'ቫይን -ቅ- መለኮታዊ ፡ የእግዚአብሔር

diving

'ዳይቪንግ -ስ- መስጠም

divinity

ዲ'ቪኒቲ -ስ- መለኮት ፣ አምላክ ፡ መለኮታዊ ኀይል

divisible

ዲ'ቪዚበል -ቅ- ሊ'ከ'ፈል የ'ሚችል

division

ዲ'ቪዠን -ስ- ክፍል ፡ ማ'ካፈል ፡ መ'ከፈል ፣ አለመስማማት ፣ በሐ'ሳብ መ'ለያየት

divorce

ዲ'ቮ:ስ -ግ- መፋታት [ፈ'ታ] (ሚስት ፣ ባል)

divulge

ዳይ'ቨልጅ -ግ- ምስጢር ማውጣት [አወ'ጣ]

dizziness

'ዲዚነስ -ስ- ራስ መክበድ ፣ ራስ መዞር ፣ ማጥወልወል

dizzy

'ዲዚ -ቅ- ራሱ የከ'በደው ፣ አእምሮው የታ'ወከ

do

'ዱ -ግ- መሥራት [ሠ'ራ] ፣ ማድረግ {አደ'ረገ

docile

'ደውሳይል -ቅ- በቀ'ላሉ ሊያስተምሩት ሊ'ቆጣ'ጠሩት የ'ሚ'ቻል

dock

'ዶክ -ስ- የመርከብ ወደብ (መርከብ የ'ሚ'ሠ'ራ'በት ቦታ)

docker

'ዶከ -ስ- የመርከብ ዕቃ አውራጅ

docket

'ዶኬት -ስ- ደ'ረሰ'ኝ

doctor

'ዶክተ -ስ- ሐኪም

academic

-ስ- ዶክተር

doctorate

'ዶክተረት -ስ- የዶክተር'ነት ማዕረግ

doctrine

'ዶክትሪን -ስ- የሃይማኖት ትምህርት ፡ የሕይወት ወይም የእምነት መምሪያ ትምህርት

document

'ዶክዩመንት -ስ- ማስረ'ጃ ጽሑፍ

documentary

ዶክዩ'ሜንትሪ -ቅ- ማስረ'ጃ'ነት ያ'ለው (የተጻፈ)

dodge

'ዶጅ -ግ- ማምለጥ [አመ'ለጠ] (ከአደጋ ም'ሳሌ ፣ ከተወረ'ወረ ነገር)

doe

'ደው -ስ- ሴት አጋዘን ፣ ሴት ጥንቸል

doe-skin

'ደውስኪን -ስ- ያጋዘን ቆዳ

dog

'ዶግ -ስ- ው'ሻ

dogged
'ዶገድ -ቅ- ችኮ ፤ ተስፋ የ'ማይቆርጥ

dogma
'ዶግመ -ስ- የሃይማኖት ሕ'ገጋት (ማስረ'ጃ የሌ'ለው፣ ለም'ሳሌ፣ ከሃይማኖት ሰዎ'ች የታ'ዘዘ)

doll
'ዶል -ስ- አሻንጉ'ሊት

dollar
'ዶለ -ስ- ብ'ር (ገንዘብ)

dolorous
'ዶለረስ -ቅ- በጣም ያ'ዘነ ፣ የ'ሚያሳ'ዝን ፣ የ'ሚያ'ም

dolt
'ዶልት -ቅ- ቂል ፣ ሞ'ኝ ፣ ደንቆሮ ፣ ደ'ደብ

domain
ደ'ሜይን -ስ- የመሬት ሀብት ፤ ግዛት

dome
'ደውም -ስ- ክ'ብ ጣራ

domestic
ደ'ሜስቲክ -ቅ- የቤት

domesticate
ደ'ሜስቲኬይት -ግ- እንስሳን ማልመድ [አለ'መደ]

domicile
'ዶሚሳይል -ስ- መኖርያ ቤት

dominant
'ዶሚነንት -ቅ- የ'ሚገዛ ፣ ባለሥልጣን ፣ የማዘዝ መብት ያ'ለው ፣ የሰ'ፈነ

dominate
'ዶሚኔይት -ግ- መግዛት [ገ'ዛ] (በሥልጣን)

domination
ዶሚ'ኔይሽን -ስ- ሥልጣን

domineer
ዶሚ'ኒየ -ግ- በኀይል ማሳ'ደር [አሳ'ደረ]

dominion
ደ'ሚንየን -ስ- ሥልጣን ፣ ኀይል ፣ ግዛት (አገር)

donate
ደ'ኔይት -ግ- መስጠት [ሰ'ጠ] ፣ መለ'ገሥ [ለ'ገሠ] (ለበ'ጎ አድራጎት)

donation
ደ'ኔይሽን -ስ- ስጦታ (የእርዳታ)

donkey
'ዶንኪ -ስ- አህ'ያ

donor
'ደውነ -ስ- ሰጪ ፣ ለ'ጋሽ (በተለ'ይ ደሙን ለሕመምተ'ኛ)

doom
'ዱ:ም -ስ- ዕ'ድል ፣ ፍርድ ፣ ጥፋት ፣ ሞት

doomsday
'ዱ:ምዝዴይ -ስ- የመጨ'ረሻ የፍርድ ቀን ፣ ምጽአት

door
'ዶ: -ስ- በ'ር ፣ ደ'ጃፍ

door-keeper
'ዶ:ኪፐ -ስ- በ'ረ'ኛ ፣ በ'ር ጠ'ባቂ

door-mat
'ዶ:ማት -ስ- የግር መጥረጊያ ጨርቅ (እበ'ር ላይ የ'ሚ'ነ'ጠፍ)

dormant
'ዶ:መንት -ቅ- እንቅልፋም (ለጊዜው ሥራ የ'ማይሠራ)

dormitory
'ዶ:መትሪ -ስ- የመ'ኝታ አ'ዳራሽ

dormouse
'ዶ:ማውስ -ስ- ዐይጠ መጐጥ

dose
'ደውስ -ስ- ል'ክ (ለአንድ ጊዜ የ'ሚሆን መድኃኒት)

dot
'ዶት -ስ- ነቁጥ ፣ ነጥብ

dotage
'ደውተጅ -ስ- የአእምሮ ድካም (ከእርጅ'ና የተነ'ሣ) ፣ መጃጀት

double
'ደበል -ቅ- እጥፍ

doubt
'ዳውት -ግ- መ'ጠራጠር [ተጠራ'ጠረ]
-ስ- ጥር'ጥር

doubtful
'ዳውትፉል -ቅ- የ'ሚያ'ጠራ'ጥር ፣ አ'ጠራጣሪ

doubtless
'ዳውትሌስ -ቅ- የ'ማያ'ጠራ'ጥር

douche
'ዱ:ሽ -ስ- ግብር ውሃ ፣ ግብር ውሃ መውጣት ፤ ከላይ እሰው'ነት ላይ የ'ሚፈ'ስ ውሃ (ሰው'ነት ለመታጠብ) ፤ ውሃውን የ'ሚያፈሰ'ው መ'ሣሪያ

dough
'ዶው -ስ- ሊጥ (የዳ'ቦ)
dove
'ዶቭ -ስ- እርግብ
dovecote
'ዳቭኮት -ስ- የርግብ ቤት
down
'ዳውን -ተግ- ወደ ታ'ች
downcast
'ዳውን'ካ:ስት -ቅ- ያ'ዘነ ፣ ያልተደ'ሰተ
downfall
'ዳውንፎ:ል -ስ- ድቀት ፣ ውድቀት ፣ ፍርስራሽ ከ'ባድ ዝናም
downpour
'ዳውንፖ: -ስ- ከ'ባድ ዝናም (የ'ማያ'ቋ'ርጥ)
downright
'ዳውንራይት -ቅ- ቀ'ጥተ'ኛ ፣ ግልጽ ፣ ጥን ቁቅ
downward(s)
'ዳውንወድ(ዝ) -ተግ- ወደታ'ች
dowry
'ዳውሪ -ስ- ጥሎሽ (ሴት የም'ትሰጠው)
doze
'ዶውዝ -ግ- ማሸ'ለብ [አሸ'ለበ] (እንቅልፍ) ፣ ማንጎላጀት [አንጎላ'ጀ]
dozen
'ደዘን -ስ- ደርዘን ፣ ቁጥሩ በሥራ ሁ'ለት ዩሆን (ዕቃ)
drab
ድ'ራብ -ቅ- ብሩህ ቀለም የሌ'ለው ፣ የ'ማያምር (ለልብስ)
draft
ድ'ራ:ፍት -ስ- ረቂቅ (ጽሑፍ) ፣ ንድፍ (ሥዕል)
draftsman
ድ'ራፍ:ትስመን -ስ- ንድፍ ነዳፊ ፣ (የመሀን 'ዲስ)
drag
ድ'ራግ -ግ- መጎ'ተት [ጎ'ተተ]
dragon
ድ'ራገን -ስ- ደራጎን (ክንፍ ያ'ለው'ና እሳት የ'ሚተፋ ፍጡር)
dragonfly
ድ'ራገንፍላይ -ስ- የውሃ ተርብ

drain
ድ'ሬይን -ስ- የውሃ መሄጃ (በመንገድ ዳር ፣ የቆሻሻ'ና የእድፍ)
drainage
ድ'ሬይነጅ -ስ- የፍ'ሳሽ መሄጃ በዮ'ች
dramatic
ድረ'ማቲክ -ቅ- አስደ'ናቂ ፣ አስገ'ራሚ (ሕያው ታሪክ ፣ ቴያትር)
dramatist
ድ'ራመቲስት -ስ- የቴያትር መጽሐፍ ደራሲ
drape
ድ'ሬይፕ -ግ- ማልበስ [አለ'በሰ] ፣ መሸ'ፈን [ሸ'ፈነ] ፣ ማ'ጣፋት [አ'ጣ'ፋ] (ኩታ ወዘተ)
draper
ድ'ሬይፐ -ስ- ጨርቃ ጨርቅ ነ'ጋዴ
drapery
ድ'ሬይፐሪ -ስ- የግድግ'ዳ ልባስ ጨርቅ
drastic
ድ'ራስቲክ -ቅ- ከ'ባድ ው'ጤት የ'ሚያስከ 'ትል
draught
ድ'ራ:ፍት -ስ- ከሁ'ለት ትይ'ዩ አቅጣ'ጫ የ'ሚ ገባ ኀይለ'ኛ አ'የር ፣ መጎተት ፣ መሳብ
drink
-ስ- ባንድ ትንፋሽ የ'ሚ'ጠ'ጣ መጠ'ጥ
game (pl.)
-ስ- ዳማ (የጨዋታ ዓይነት)
draught board
ድ'ራ:ፍትቦ:ድ -ስ- የዳማ መ'ጫወቻ ገበታ
engineering
-ስ- የንድፍ መንደፊያ ገበታ (የመሀን ዲስ)
draughtsman
ድ'ራ:ፍትስመን -ስ- የሕንፃዎ'ችን ፕላን'ና ን ድፍ የ'ሚሠራ ሰው
draw
ድ'ሮ: -ግ- መሣል [ሣለ] (ለሥዕል)
pull
-ግ- መሳብ [ሳበ] ፣ መጎ'ተት [ጎ'ተተ] ፣ ውሃ መቅዳት [ቀ'ዳ] (ከጉድጓድ) ፣ መምዘዝ [መ'ዘዘ] (መ'ሣሪያ ከአፎት ወዘተ)
drawback
ድ'ሮ:ባክ -ስ- እንቅፋት ፣ መጥፎ ዕ'ድል

drawer
ድ'ሮ፡ወ -ስ- የጠረ'ጴዛ መሳቢያ
drawing
ድ'ሮ፡ዊንግ -ስ- ሥዕል
dread
ድ'ሬድ -ስ- ት'ልቅ ፍርሃት ፣ ጭንቅ
dreadful
ድ'ሬድፉል -ቅ- በጣም የ'ሚያስፈ'ራ ፣ በጣም የ'ሚያስጨ'ንቅ
dream
ድ'ሪይም -ግ- ማ'ለም [አ'ለመ]
-ስ- ሕልም
dreamy
ድ'ሪይሚ -ቅ- ሐ'ሳበ ብኩን ፣ እንዳ'ለመ የ'ሚኖር
dreary
ድ'ሪየሪ -ቅ- የ'ሚቀ'ፍ ፣ የ'ሚያሳ'ዝን ፣ የ'ሚሰለ'ች
dregs
ድ'ሬግዝ -ስ- አተላ ፣ ዝ'ቃጭ
dress
ድ'ሬስ -ግ- መልበስ [ለ'በሰ]
women's
-ስ- ቀሚስ
dresser
ድ'ሬሰ -ስ- አልባሽ ፤ የቀዳጅ ሐኪም ረ'ዳት
dribble
ድ'ሪበል -ግ- መላገግ [ላ'ገገ] ፣ ማንጠብጠብ [አንጠበ'ጠበ] (ለውሃ)፣ኳስ ደጋግሞ ማንጠር [አነ'ጠረ]
-ስ- ልጋግ
drift
ድ'ሪፍት -ስ- መዋለል [ዋ'ለለ] (እባሕር ላይ አቅጣ'ጫ ሳይጠ'ብቁ)
drill
ድ'ሪል -ግ- መብሳት [በ'ሳ] ፣ መሠርሠር [ሠረ'ሠረ]
-ስ- መሠርሠሪያ ፣ መብሻ መ'ሣሪያ
military
-ግ- ማሠልጠን [አሠለ'ጠነ] (ለወ'ታደር)
-ስ- የሰልፍ ትምህርት
material
-ስ- የጥጥ ጨርቅ

drink
ድ'ሪንክ -ግ- መጠጣት [ጠ'ጣ]
-ስ- መጠጥ
drip
ድ'ሪፕ -ግ- መንጠብጠብ [ተንጠበ'ጠበ]
-ስ- ጠ'ብታ
drive
ድ'ራይቭ -ግ- መንዳት [ነ'ዳ] (የመኪና ወዘተ)
-out
-ግ- ማስወ'ጣት [አስወ'ጣ] ፣ ማ'ባረር [አባ'ረረ]
driver
ድ'ራይቨ -ስ- መኪና ነጂ ፣ ሾፌር
droop
ድ'ሩ፡ፕ -ግ- መሸ'ነብ [ሸ'ነበ]
drop
ድ'ሮፕ -ግ- መጣል [ጣለ] ፣ መውደቅ [ወ'ደቀ]
-ስ- ጠ'ብታ
droppings
ድ'ሮፒንግዝ -ግ- ፍግ ፣ ፋንድ'ያ ወዘተ
drought
ድ'ራውት -ቅ- ድርቅ ፣ የዝናም ማነስ ፣ ጥም
drown
ድ'ራውን -ግ- መስጠም [ሰ'ጠመ]
drowsy
ድ'ራውዚ -ቅ- ያንቀላ'ፋ ፣ የ'ሚያንጎላ'ጅ
drudge
ድ'ረጅ -ስ- የተንገላ'ታ አገልጋይ ፣ ከ'ባድ የ'ሚያሰለ'ች ሥራ የ'ሚሠራ አሽከር
drug
ድ'ረግ -ስ- ለመድኃኒት'ነት የ'ሚያገለ'ግል ጥንተ ንጥር ፤ አስካሪ ቅጠላቅጠል (ጫት ፣ ሐሺሽ ፣ አፒየም ወዘተ)
drum
ድ'ረም -ስ- ከበሮ ፣ አታሞ ፣ ታምቡር
drummer
ድ'ረመ -ስ- ከበሮ መቺ ፣ አታሞ መቺ
drunk
ድ'ረንክ -ቅ- የሰ'ከረ
drunkard
ድ'ረንከድ -ስ- ሰ'ካራም
drunkenness
ድ'ረንከንኔስ -ስ- ሰ'ካራም'ነት ፣ ስካር

dry
ድ'ራይ -ግ- መድረቅ [ደ'ረቀ]
-ቅ- ደረቅ ፣ ድርቅ

duck
'ደክ -ስ- ዳ'ክ'የ
avoid
-ግ- በድንገት ራስን ወ'ይም ሰው'ነትን ማዘንበል [አዘን'በለ] (ከመ'ታየት ለመዳን)

dull
'ዶል -ቅ- ደ'ደብ ፣ በቶሎ የ'ማይገባው
weather
-ቅ- የ'ሚቀ'ፍ ፣ ጭፍግ'ግ ያለ (ቀን)

dumb
'ደም -ቅ- ድዳ

dump
'ደምፐ -ግ- መጣል [ጣለ]
-ስ- ቆሻሻ መጣያ ፣ አመድ ማፍሰሻ

dune
ድ'ዩ:ን -ስ- ያሸዋ ክ'ምር (በነፋስ የተከ'መረ)

dung
'ደንግ -ስ- እ'በት ፣ ፍግ

dungeon
'ደንጀን -ስ- ወህኒ ቤት ፣ ጨ'ለማ ክፍል (ምድር ቤት ያ'ለ)

dunghill
'ደንግሂል -ስ- የእ'በት ፣ የፍግ ቁ'ልል

duplicate
ድ'ዩፐሊኬይት -ግ- ጽሑፍ ማ'ባዛት [አ'ባ'ዛ] (በማ'ባዣ መኪና ወዘተ) ፣ በሁ'ለት ማ'ባዛት [አ'ባ'ዛ] ፣ በትክ'ክል መገልበጥ [ገለ'በጠ] (ጽሑፍ)

duplicate
ድ'ዩፐሊከት -ስ- የተበ'ዛ ጽሑፍ (አንድ ገል'ባጭ)

durable
ድ'ዩረበል -ቅ- ጠንካ'ራ ፣ ረ'ጅም እድሜ ያ'ለው

during
ድ'ዩሪንግ -መዋ- በ . . . ጊዜ ውስጥ

dusk
'ደስክ -ስ- ማምሻ (የጀምበር መጥለቂያ ጊዜ)

dust
'ደስት -ስ- አቧራ ፣ ት'ቢያ

duster
'ደስተ -ስ- አቧራ መጥረጊያ ፣ አቧራ ማ'ራገፊያ

dustpan
'ደስትፓን -ስ- የቆሻሻ መሰብሰቢያ ዕቃ

dusty
'ደስቲ -ቅ- አቧራ ያለ'በሰው ፣ ቡ'ላ

dutiful
ድ'ዩ:ቲፉል -ቅ- ታ'ዛዥ ፣ ሰው አክባሪ

duty
ድ'ዩ:ቲ -ሰ- ተግባር
customs
-ስ- ቀረጥ

duty-free
ድ'ዩ:ቲ ፍሪይ -ቅ- ከቀረጥ ነጻ የሆነ (ዕቃ ፣ ሸቀጣሸቀጥ)

dwarf
ድ'ዎ:ፍ -ስ- ድንክ ሰው ፣ እንስሳ ወዘተ

dwell
ድ'ዌል -ግ- መኖር [ኖረ]

dwelling
ድ'ዌሊንግ -ስ- መኖሪያ ቦታ

dwindle
ድ'ዊንደል -ግ- እ'ያ'ነሰ ፣ እ'የቀ'ነሰ መሄድ [ሄደ]

dye
'ዳይ -ግ- ቀለም መንከር [ነ'ከረ]
-ስ- ቀለም (ልብስ መንከሪያ)

dyer
'ዳየ -ስ- ቀለም ነካሪ

dying
'ዳይንግ -ቅ- የ'ሚሞት

dynamic
ዳይ'ናሚክ -ቅ- ንቁ ፣ ኀይል ያ'ለው ፡ እንቅስ'ቃሴ የ'ሚፈጥር

dynamite
'ዳይነማይት -ስ- ፈንጂ ፣ ዲናሚት

dynasty
'ዲነስቲ -ስ- የነገሥታት የዘር ሐረግ ፣ ሥርወ መንግሥት

each
'ኢይች -ቅ- እ'ያንዳን'ዱ
eager
'ኢይገ -ቅ- ጉ'ጉ
eagle
'ኢይገል -ስ- ንሥር
ear
'ኢየ -ስ- ጆሮ
early
'ኧሊ -ተግ- በማለዳ ፣ ቀደ'ም ብሎ ፣ ማልዶ
earn
'ኧን -ግ- ማትረፍ [አተ'ረፈ] (ገንዘብ) ፣ ማግ ኘት [አገኘ] (ዝ'ና ፣ ጥሩ ስም ወዘተ)
earnest
'ኧነስት -ቅ- ቁም ነገረ'ኛ ፣ በነገሩ ያ'ሰበ'በት ፣ የቆ'ረጠ (አንድ ነገር ለመሥራት)
earnings
'ኧኒንግዝ -ስ- ትርፍ ፣ ደመዎዝ
ear-ring
'ኢየሪንግ -ስ- ጉት'ቻ
earth
'ኧþ -ስ- መሬት
globe
-ስ- ዓለም
dust
-ስ- አፈር
earthenware
'ኧþንዌየ -ስ- የሸክላ ዕቃ
earthquake
'ኧþክዌይክ -ስ- የመሬት መንቀጥቀጥ
ease
'ኢይዝ -ስ- ም'ቾት ፣ መዝናናት ፣ የመንፈስ ፀ'ጥታ
easel
'ኢይዘል -ስ- ማስቀ'መጫ (የጥቁር ሰሌዳ ፣ የሥዕል መዘተ)
east
'ኢይስት -ስ- ምሥራቅ
Easter
'ኢይስተ -ስ- በዓለ ትንሣኤ

eastern
'ኢይስተን -ቅ- ምሥራቃዊ ፣ የምሥራቅ
easy
'ኢይዚ -ቅ- ቀ'ላል
eat
'ኢይት -ግ- መብላት [በ'ላ] ፣ መ'መገብ [ተመ 'ገበ]
ebony
'ኤበኒ -ስ- ጥቁር እንጨት ፣ ዞ'ጲ
eccentric
ኤክ'ሴንትሪክ -ቅ- የተለ'የ ጠባይ የ'ሚያሳ'ይ (ለሰው) ፣ ወፈ'ፌ
ecclesiastic
ኤክሊዚ'ያስቲክ -ስ- ካህን
echo
'ኤከው -ስ- የገደል ማ'ሚቶ (ነገር ግን ይሀ'ን ለመሳ'ሰለው ድምፅ ሁ'ሉ)
eclipse
ኢክ'ሊፕስ -ስ- የፀሐይ መጨ'ለም (ጨረቃ በር ፀ'ና በመሬት መካ'ከል በም'ትሆን'በት ጊዜ)
economics
ኤክ'ኖሚክስ -ስ- የአገር ሀብት ው'ጤት'ና የማ'ከፋፈል ጥናት ፣ ኢኮኖሚክስ
economical
ኤክ'ኖሚክል -ቅ- ቆ'ጣቢ ፣ ር'ካሽ
economize
ኢ'ኮነማይዝ -ግ- በቁ'ጠባ መኖር [ኖረ] ፣ ወጪን መቀ'ነስ [ቀ'ነሰ]
ecstasy
'ኤክስተሲ -ስ- ታ'ላቅ ደስታ ፣ ሐ'ሤት
edge
'ኤጅ -ስ- ጠርዝ ፣ ዳር'ቻ
edible
'ኤደበል -ቅ- የ'ሚ'በ'ላ
edifice
'ኤዲፊስ -ስ- ታ'ላቅ ሕንፃ
edit
'ኤዲት -ግ- ለማ'ተም የሌላውን ሰው ጽሑፍ ማ'ዘጋጀት [አዘጋጀ] (አ'ርሞ አስተካክሎ ወዘተ)

editor
'ኤዲተ -ስ- ጋዜጣ አ'ዘጋጅ ፣ መጽሐፍ አ'ቀና ባሪ ፣ መጽሐፍ አ'ጠናቃሪ

educate
'ኤጅዮኬይት -ግ- ማስተማር [አስተማረ] ፣ ማሠልጠን [አሠለ'ጠነ]

education
ኤጅዮ'ኬይሽን -ስ- ትምህርት ፣ አስተዳደግ (በዕውቀት በግብረ ገ'ብ'ነት)

effect
ኢ'ፌክት -ስ- ው'ጤት ፣ በአእምሮ ላይ የቀ'ረ ስ'ሜት

effective
ኢ'ፌክቲቭ -ቅ- ው'ጤት ሊያስገ'ኝ የ'ሚችል ብቁ ፣ በአእምሮ ላይ ት'ልቅ ስ'ሜት የ'ሚተው

effeminate
ኢ'ፌሚነት -ቅ- ሴታ ሴት

efficient
ኢ'ፊሽንት -ቅ- በቂ ችሎታ ያ'ለው ፣ አጥጋቢ ው'ጤት የ'ሚሰጥ ፣ የሠለ'ጠነ

effigy
'ኤፊጂ -ስ- ምስል (የሰው ፣ በደንጊያ በእን ጨት ላይ ወዘተ)

effort
'ኤፈት -ስ- ጥረት ፣ ትግል (አንድ ነገር ለመ ፈ'ጸም) ፣ሙ'ከራ

effrontery
ኤፍ'ረንተሪ -ስ- ማንጓጠጥ ፣ የ'ማይ'ገ'ባ ድፍ ረት

egg
'ኤግ -ስ- እንቁላል

egoistic
ኤጎ'ዊስቲክ -ቅ- ራሱን ወ'ዳድ

eight
'ኤይት -ቅ- ስምንት

eighteen
ኤይ'ቲይን -ቅ- ዐሥራ ስ'ምንት

eighteenth
ኤይ'ቲንስ -ቅ- ዐሥራ ስ'ምንተ'ኛ

eighth
'ኤይትስ -ቅ- ስምንተ'ኛ

eightieth
'ኤይቲየስ -ቅ- ሰማንያ'ኛ

eighty
'ኤይቲ -ቅ- ሰማንያ

either
'አይዘ -መዋ- ወይን'ም
-ቅ- ከሁለ'ት አንዱ

ejaculate
ኢ'ጃክዩሌይት -ግ- ሰውን ጩሆ መ'ጣራት [ተ ጣ'ራ] ፣ በድንገት መ'ናገር ፣ [ተና'ገረ]፤በድ ንገት ማስፈንጠር [አስፈነ'ጠረ]
-ስ- ድንገተ'ኛ ዋይታ

eject
ኢ'ጀክት -ግ- ማስፈን'ጠር [አስፈነ'ጠረ] ፣ ገፍትሮ ማስወ'ጣት [አስወ'ጣ]

elaborate
ኢ'ላበረት -ቅ- በብዙ ጥን'ቃቄ'ና በተሟ'ላ ሁናቴ የተሠ'ራ ፣ ጌጣ ጌጥ የበ'ዛ'በት
-ግ- በዝርዝር መግለጥ [ገ'ለጠ]

elapse
ኢ'ላፕስ -ግ- ማለፍ [አ'ለፈ] (ለጊዜ)

elastic
ኢ'ላስቲክ -ስ- ላስቲክ
expanding
-ቅ- የላስቲክ
-ቅ- የ'ሚ'ለ'ጠጥ

elated
ኢ'ሌይተድ -ቅ- በጣም የተደ'ሰተ (አንድ ተግባር በመፈ'ጸም)

elbow
'ኤልበው -ስ- ክርን

elder
'ኤልደ -ስ- በዕድሜ የበ'ለጠ (በቤተ ሰብ ውስጥ)

elect
ኢ'ሌክት -ግ- መምረጥ [መ'ረጠ] (ድምፅ በመ ስጠት)

election
ኢ'ሌክሽን -ስ- ምርጫ

elector
ኢ'ሌክተ -ስ- መራጭ

electorate
ኢ'ሌክትረት -ስ- መራጮ'ች

electricity
ኤሌክት'ሪሲቲ -ስ- ኤሌክትሪክ

electrician
ኤሌክት'ሪሽን -ስ- ኤሌክትሪክ ሠ'ራተ'ኛ

eleven
ኢ'ሌቨን -ቅ- ዐሥራ አንድ
eleventh
ኢ'ሌቨንθ -ቅ- ዐሥራ አንደ'ኛ
elegant
'ኤሌገንት -ቅ- ያማረ'በት (ለልብስ)
element
'ኤለመንት -ስ- ጥንተ ነገር (ያልተከፋ'ፈለ እንደተፈ'ጠረ ያ'ለ ነገር)
elementary
ኤለ'ሜንትሪ -ቅ- ቀ'ላል ፣ የ'ማያ'ውክ
education
-ስ- የአንደ'ኛ ደረጃ ትምህርት
elephant
'ኤለፈንት -ስ- ዝሆን
elevate
'ኤለቬይት -ግ- ከ'ፍ ማድረግ [አደ'ረገ]
elevator
'ኤለቬይተ -ስ- አሳንሰር
elicit
ኢ'ሊሲት -ግ- ነገር ማ'ዋጣት [አዋ'ጣ] (እውነት ፣ ምስጢር ፣ ወሬ ወዘተ)
eligible
'ኤሊጀበል -ቅ- ላንድ ሥራ የደ'ረሰ ፣ የተገ'ባ ፣ መ'መረጥ የ'ሚችል
for marriage
-ቅ- ሊጋብ'ቻ የደ'ረሰ
eliminate
ኢ'ሊመኔይት -ግ- ማስወ'ገድ [አስወ'ገደ] መፋቅ [ፋቀ] (ስም)
elite
ኤ'ሊይት -ስ- በማዕረግ ፣ በትምህርት ፣ በሀብት እ'ጅግ የላቁ ሰዎ'ች
elongate
'ኢሉንጌይት -ግ- ማስረ'ዘም [አስረ'ዘመ]
elope
ኢ'ለውፕ -ግ- መኰብለል [ኰበ'ለለ] (ሴት ከወዳጅ ጋር ለመ'ጋባት)
eloquence
'ኤለከወንስ -ስ- ል'ሳን ቅን'ነት ፣ እንደበተ ርቱዕ'ነት
eloquent
'ኤለከወንት -ቅ- ል'ሳን ቅን ፣ እንደበተ ርቱዕ
else
'ኤልስ -ቅ- ሌላ
otherwise
-ተግ- አለበለ'ዚያ ፣ ያለ'ዚያ
elsewhere
ኤልስ'ዌየ -ተግ- በሌላ ቦታ
elucidate
ኢል'ዩሲዴይት -ግ- ያንድ ነገር ፍ'ች ጉልህ እድርጎ መግለጽ [ገ'ለጸ] ፣ ማስረ'ዳት [አስረ'ዳ]
elude
ኢል'ዩ:ድ -ግ- ማምለጥ [አመ'ለጠ] (ከመያ'ዝ ፣ ከመታ'የት ወዘተ በማ'ታለል)
elusive
ኢል'ዩ:ሲቭ -ቅ- ለመያዝ የ'ሚያ'ውክ ፣ ለመ'ረዳት'ና ለማስ:ታወስ የ'ሚያ'ውክ
emaciated
ኢ'ሜይሲዩይተድ -ቅ- የመነ'መነ ፣ እ'ጅግ የከ'ሳ
emancipate
ኢ'ማንሲፔይት -ግ- ነጻ ማውጣት [አወ'ጣ] ፣ ከባር'ነት እር'ነት ማውጣት [አወ'ጣ]
embalm
ኢም'ባ:ም -ግ- በድን እን'ዳይበሰ'ብስ መድኃኒት ማድረግ [አደ'ረገ]
embankment
ኢም'ባንክመንት -ስ- ያፈር ቁ'ልል (ለውሀ መገ'ደቢያ)
embargo
ኤም'ባ:ገው -ስ- የንግድ ግን'ኙ'ነት ካንድ አገር ጋር ማ'ቋረጥ
embark
ኤም'ባ:ክ -ግ- መ'ሣፈር [ተሣ'ፈረ] (በመርከብ ፣ በአውሮ'ፕላን ፣ በባቡር)
embarrass
ኤም'ባረስ -ግ- ማሳ'ፈር [አሳ'ፈረ]
embarrassment
ኤም'ባረስመንት -ስ- ኀፍረት
embassy
'ኤምበሲ -ስ- ኤም'ባሲ ፣ በው'ጭ አገር ያገሩ መልክተ'ኛ የሆነ ሰው መሥሪያ ቤት
embellish
ኤም'ቤሊሽ -ግ- ማጌጥ [አጌጠ] (አንድ ነገር)
ember
'ኤምበ -ስ- ፍም

embezzle
ኤም'ቢዘል -ግ- ገንዘብ ማጭበርበር [አጭበ ረ'በረ] ፣ ገንዘብ ማጉደል [አጎ'ደለ] (አደራ የተሰ'ጠውን ፣ መዝገብ በማ'ቃወስ)

embitter
ኤም'ቢተ -ግ- ማስመ'ረር [አስመ'ረረ]

emblem
'ኤምብለም -ስ- አርማ (የቤተ ሰብ ፣ የድር 'ጅት)

embody
ኤም'ቦዲ -ግ- ጨ'ምሮ መያዝ [ያዘ] ፣ እሥራ ላይ መዋል [አዋለ]

embrace
ኤምብ'ሬይስ -ግ- ማቀፍ [አ'ቀፈ]

embroider
ኤምብ'ሮይደ -ግ- ጥልፍ፡ መጥለፍ [ጠ'ለፈ]

embryo
'ኤምብሪየው -ስ- ፅንስ ፣ ሽል

emerald
'ኤመረልድ -ስ- በ'ሉር
colour
-ቅ- አረንጓዴ

emerge
ኢ'መ:ርጅ -ግ- ብ'ቅ ማለት [አለ] (ከተደ'በቀ 'በት)

emergency
ኢ'መ:ርጀንሲ -ስ- ያልጠ'በቁት አደገ'ኛ ሁናቴ ፣ አስቸ'ኳይ ው'ሳኔ የ'ሚያ'ሻው

emery-cloth
'ኤመሪ ክሎሰ̲ -ስ- የብርጭ'ቆ ወረቀት

emetic
ኢ'ሜቲክ -ስ- የሚያስታ'ውክ መድኃኒት

emigrant
'ኤሚግረንት -ስ- አገሩን ለ'ቆ ወደሌላ አገር የ'ሚሄድ ሰው (ለመኖር)

emigration
ኤሚግ'ሬይሽን -ስ- አገር ለ'ቆ ወደሌላ አገር ለመኖር መሄድ

eminent
'ኤሚነንት -ቅ- ከ'ፍተ'ኛ ፣ ባለ ክብር ፣ ስመ ጥር (ሰው)

emissary
'ኤሚሰሪ -ስ- መልእክተ'ኛ

emit
ኢ'ሚት -ግ- ከራሱ ማውጣት [አወ'ጣ] (ፀሐይ ብርሃን) ፣ ማሥረጽ [አሠ'ረጸ]

emotion
ኢ'መውሽን -ስ- ኀይለ'ኛ ስ'ሜት (ውስጣዊ)

emperor
'ኤምፐረ -ስ- ንጉሠ ነገሥት

emphasise
'ኤምፈሳይዝ -ግ- የበ'ለጠ ዋጋ መስጠት [ሰ'ጠ] (ለቃል ፣ ለሐ'ሳብ ወዘተ)

emphatic
ኤም'ፋቲክ -ቅ- የበ'ለጠ ዋጋ ሰ'ቶ የተገ'ለጠ (ቃል ፣ ሐ'ሳብ ወዘተ)

empire
'ኤምፓየ -ስ- የንጉሠ ነገሥት ግዛት

employ
ኤምፕ'ሎይ -ግ- መቅጠር [ቀ'ጠረ] (ለሥራ)

employee
ኤምፕ'ሎይ -ስ- ተቀጣሪ ፣ ሠ'ራተ'ኛ

employer
ኤምፕ'ሎየ -ስ- ቀጣሪ

employment
ኤምፕ'ሎይመንት -ስ- ሥ'ራ

empower
ኤም'ፓወ -ግ- ሥልጣን መስጠት [ሰ'ጠ]

emptiness
'ኤምፕቲነስ -ስ- ባዶ'ነት

empty
'ኤምቲ -ቅ- ባዶ

emulate
'ኤምዩሌይት -ግ- ለመ'ተካከል መሞ'ከር [ሞ 'ከረ] ፣ የበ'ለጠ አድርጎ ለማሥራት መሞ'ከር [ሞ'ከረ]

enable
ኤን'ኤይበል -ግ- ማስቻል [አስቻለ] (ችሎታ)

enamel
ኢ'ናመል -ስ- ብርጭ'ቆ የ'ሚመስል ነገር ፣ ብ ረት፣ሰሐን ወዘተ የ'ሚ'ቀ'ባ'በት (ለጌጥ ወዘተ)

enchant
ኤን'ቻ:ንት -ግ- ከል'ክ በላይ ማስደ'ሰት [አስ ደ'ሰተ]

enchantment
ኤን'ቻ:ንትመንት -ስ- ከል'ክ ያ'ለፈ ደ'ስታ

enchantress
ኤን'ቻ:ንትረስ -ስ- ሴት ጠንቋይ
encircle
ኤን'ሰ:ክል -ግ- መክበብ [ከ'በበ]
enclose
ኤንክ'ለውዝ -ግ- ማጠር [አ'ጠረ]
shut in
-ግ- ባንድ ነገር ውስጥ መዝጋት [ዘ'ጋ]፣ ማ'ጎር [አ'ጎረ]
enclosure
ኤንክ'ለውዠ -ስ- ግ'ቢ፣ የታ'ጠረ ቦታ
encounter
ኤን'ካውንተ -ግ- መግጠም [ገ'ጠመ] (ያል ጠ'በቁትን ነገር)
encourage
ኤን'ከሪጅ -ግ- ማ'በረታታት [አ'በረታ'ታ]
end
'ኤንድ -ግ- መጨ'ረስ [ጨ'ረሰ]፣ ማብቃት [አበ'ቃ]
-ስ- መጨ'ረሻ
endanger
ኢን'ዴይንጀ -ግ- አደጋ ላይ መጣል [ጣለ]
endeavour
ኤን'ዴቨ -ግ- በጣም መሞ'ከር [ሞ'ከረ]
-ስ- ሙ'ከራ
ending
ኤን'ዲንግ -ስ- መጨ'ረሻ፣ ማቆሚያ፣ ባዕድ መድረሻ (ሰዋሰው)
endless
ኤንድ'ሌስ -ቅ- ማለቂያ የሌ'ለው
endorse
ኤን'ዶ:ስ -ግ- በፊርማ ማ'ረጋገጥ [አ'ረጋ'ገጠ]፣ መፈ'ረም [ፈ'ረመ] (ለቼክ ወዘተ)፣ መደ'ገፍ [ደ'ገፈ] (ያንድ ሰው ሐ'ሳብ ወዘተ)
endow
ኤን'ዳው -ግ- መስጠት [ሰ'ጠ] (ገንዘብ፣ ሀብት፣ መስጠት [ሰ'ጠ] (ተውሀቦ፣ የተፈጥሮ ስጦታ ወዘተ)\
endurance
ኢንድ'ዩ:ረንስ -ስ- ትዕግሥት፣ ቻይ'ነት (መከራ)
endure
ኤን'ድዩወ -ግ- መ'ታገሥ [ታ'ገሠ]፣ መቻል [ቻለ] (መከራ)

enemy
'ኤነሚ -ስ- ጠላት፣ ባላንጣ
energy
'ኤነጂ -ስ- ኀይል
enforce
ኤን'ፎ:ስ -ግ- ማስገ'ደድ [አስገ'ደደ]
engaged (become)
ኤን'ጌይጅድ -ግ- ማጨት [አ'ጨ]
engagement
ኤን'ጌይጅመንት -ስ- መ'ተጫጨት
work
-ስ- ሥራ
appointment
-ስ- ቀጠሮ
engine
'ኤንጂን -ስ- መኪና
locomotive
-ስ- ባቡር ሳቢ መኪና
engineer
ኤንጂ'ኒየ -ስ- መሀንዲስ
engineering
ኤንጂ'ኒየሪንግ -ስ- መሀንዲስ'ነት
English
'ኢንግሊሽ -ቅ- እንግሊዛዊ
language
-ስ- እንግሊዝ'ኛ ቋንቋ
Englishman
'ኢንግሊሽመን -ቅ- እንግሊዛዊ (ሰው)
engrave
ኤንግ'ሬይቭ -ግ- ስም፣ ቅርፅ ወዘተ በወርቅ፣ በብ'ር ላይ ፈልፍሎ መጻፍ [ጻፈ]
enjoy
ኤን'ጆይ -ግ- በአንድ ነገር መ'ደሰት [ተደ'ሰተ]
enjoyment
ኤን'ጆይመንት -ስ- ደ'ስታ
enlarge
ኤን'ላ:ጅ -ግ- ማስፋት [አሰ'ፋ]፣ ማሳ'ደግ [አሳ'ደገ] (ለፎቶግራፍ)
enlighten
ኤን'ላይተን -ግ- ማብራራት [አብራ'ራ]፣ ማስረ'ዳት [አስረ'ዳ]

enormous
ኢ'ኖ፡መስ -ቅ- በጣም ት'ልቅ ፣ በጣም ሰ'ፊ
enough
ኢ'ነፍ -ቅ- በቂ
enquire
ኢንክ'ዋየ -ግ- መጠ'የቅ [ጠ'የቀ] (ስለአንድ ነገር ለማወቅ)
enrich
ኤን'ሪች -ግ- ማበልጸግ [አበለ'ጸገ] ፣ ማዳበር [አዳ'በረ]
enrol
ኤን'ሮል -ግ- መ'መዝገብ [ተመዘ'ገበ]
enrolment
ኤን'ሮልመንት -ስ- ስም ማስመዝገብ
ensure
ኤን'ሾ፡ -ግ- ማ'ረጋገጥ [አ'ረጋ'ገጠ] ፣ ካደጋ የራቀ ማድረግ [አደ'ረገ]
entail
ኤን'ቴይል -ግ- መጠ'የቅ [ጠ'የቀ] (አንድ ሥራ የ'ሚያስፈ'ልገው ጊዜ ፣ ድካም ገንዘብ ወዘተ)
entangle
ኤን'ታንገል -ግ- ማ'ወሳሰብ [አ'ወሳ'ሰበ] ፣ እች'ግር ላይ መጣል [ጣለ]
enter
'ኤንተ -ግ- መግባት [ገ'ባ]
enterprise
'ኤንተፕራይዝ -ቅ- ዕ'ቅድ (የሥራ) ፣ ሊያ 'ዋ'ጣ ወይን'ም ላያ'ዋ'ጣ የ'ሚችል የሥራ ዕ'ቅድ
enterprising
'ኤንተፕራይዚንግ -ቅ- ባለ ዕ'ቅድ (የሥራ) ፣ ያ'ዋ'ጣ'ኛል ብሎ ሥራ የ'ሚጀ'ምር
entertain
ኤንተ'ቴይን -ግ- እንግዳ ማ'ጫወት [አ'ጫ'ወተ] ፣ ማስተናገድ [አስተና'ገደ]
enthusiasm
ኤንቱ'ዩዚያዝም -ስ- ታ'ላቅ ፍ'ላጎት ፣ ጽኑእ ም'ኞት
enthusiastic
ኤንቱዩዚ'ያስቲክ -ቅ- ጽኑእ ም'ኞት ያ'ለው
entice
ኤን'ታይስ -ግ- ለመሳብ ፣ ለማ'ሳሳት ፣ ለማባበል መሞ'ከር [ሞ'ከረ]
entire
ኤን'ታየ -ቅ- ጠ'ላ ፣ ሙሉ ፣ ድፍን

entrails
'ኤንትሬይልዝ -ስ- ሆድ ዕቃ
entrance
'ኤንትረንስ -ስ- መግቢያ ፣ በ'ራፍ ፣ በ'ር
entrance
ኤንት'ራ፡ንስ -ግ- በጣም ማስደ'ሰት [አስደ'ሰተ]
entreat
ኤንት'ሪይት -ጉ- መ'ለማመጥ [ተለማ'መጠ]፣ መ'ለማመን [ተለማ'መነ]
entrust
ኤንት'ረስት -ግ- ኀላፊ'ነት መስጠት [ሰ'ጠ]፣ አደራ ማለት [አለ]
envelope
'ኤንቨለውፐ -ስ- አንቦል'ፕ
envious
'ኤንቪየስ -ቆቅ- ቀ'ናተ'ኛ ፣ ቀናኢ
environment
ኤን'ቫይረንመንት -ስ- አ'ካባቢ (አንድ ፍጡር የ'ሚኖር'በት)
envoy
'ኤንቮይ -ስ- መልእክተ'ኛ (የመንግሥት)
envy
'ኤንቪ -ስ- ም'ቀ'ኝ'ነት ፣ ቅናት
epic
'ኢፒክ -ቅ- ታሪካዊ (ጀግና)
poem
-ስ- ያንድ ጀግና ገብዝ'ና የ'ሚተ'ርክ ረ'ጅም ግጥም
epidemic
ኤፒ'ዴሚክ -ስ- ተላላፊ በ'ሽታ (ተስቦ ፡ ወረርሽ'ኝ)
epilepsy
'ኤፒሌፕሲ -ስ- የ'ሚጥል በ'ሽታ ፡ የባሪያ በ'ሽታ
episode
'ኤፒሰውድ -ስ- ከተከታታይ ሁናቴ'ዎ'ች አንዱ
epistle
ኢ'ፒሰል -ስ- መልእክት ፡ ደብዳ'ቤ (የመጽሐፍ ቅ'ዱስ)
epitaph
'ኤፒታፍ -ስ- ለሞተ ሰው የ'ሚ'ደ'ረግ ንግ'ግር ፡ በሞተ ሰው መቃብር ላይ የ'ሚ'ጻፍ ጽሑፍ

epoch
'ኢ.ፖክ -ስ- ዘመን ፣ ጊዜ (ታሪካዊ ፣ የሕይወት ወዘተ)

equal
'ኢይክወል -ቅ- ተመሳሳይ ፣ ትክ'ክል ፣(አ'ቻ (በብዛት ፣ በመጠን በማሰረግ)

equality
ኢክ'ዎሊ.ቲ -ስ- ተመሳሳይ'ነት ፣ ትክ'ክል'ነት

equalize
'ኢይክወላይዝ -ግ- ማስተካከል [አስተካ'ከለ]፣ እ'ኩል ማድረግ [አደ'ረገ]

equanimity
ኢክወ'ኒሚ.ቲ -ስ- የመንፈስ ጸ'ጥታ

equation
ኢክ'ዌይዥን -ስ- ማስተካከል ፣ መ'ተካከል

equator
ኢክ'ዌይተ -ስ- የምድር ወገብ

equine
'ኢክዋይን -ቅ- የፈረስ ፣ ፈረስ የ'ሚመስል

equip
ኢክ'ዊፕ -ግ- የ'ሚያስፈ'ልግ ዕቃ ማ'ዘጋጀት [አ'ዘጋ'ጀ] ፣ የጦር ትጥቅ ማቅረብ [አቀ'ረበ]

equipment
ኢክ'ዊፕመንት -ስ- የ'ሚያስፈ'ልግ ዕቃ ማ'ዘጋጀት ፣ ለሥራ የ'ሚያስፈ'ልጉ ዕቃዎ'ች ፣ የጦር መ'ሣሪያዎ'ች ወዘተ

equivalent
ኢክ'ዊቨለንት -ቅ- ተመሳሳይ ፣ ተወዳዳሪ (በዋጋ ፣ በመጠን ፣ በትርጉም)

equivocal
ኢክ'ዊቮክል -ቅ- ግልጽ ያልሆነ ፣ ትርጉሙ ግልፅ ያልሆነ ፣ እ'ጠራጣሪ ትርጉም ያ'ለው

era
'ኢረ -ስ- ዘመን ፣ ጊዜ (በታሪክ)

eradicate
ኢ'ራዲኬይት -ግ- ነቅሎ ማጥፋት [አጠ'ፋ] ፣ ማስወ'ገድ [አስወ'ገደ] ፣ መደምሰስ [ደመ'ሰሰ]

erase
ኢ'ሬይዝ -ግ- መፋቅ [ፋቀ] ፣ ማጥፋት [አጠ'ፋ] (በላ'ጲስ)

eraser
ኢ'ሬይዘ -ስ- ላ'ጲስ

erect
ኢ'ሬክት -ግ- ቀ'ጥ ማድረግ [አደ'ረገ] ፣ ማቆም [አቆመ] (ለሕንጻ ወዘተ)

erection
ኢ'ሬክሽን -ስ- መቆም ፣ ቀ'ጥ ማለት ፣ ሕንጻ

erosion
ኢ'ረውዠን -ስ- የመሬት በጐርፍ መ'ሸርሸር ፣ እ'የ'ለቀ መሄድ (የመሬት)

err
'ኧ፡ -ግ- መ'ሳሳት [ተሳሳተ] ፣ ጥፋት መሥራት [ሠ'ራ]

erratic
ኢ'ራቲክ -ቅ- እምነት የ'ማይጣል'በት ፣ ጠባዩ የ'ሚ'ለዋ'ወጥ

error
'ኤረ -ስ- ስሕተት ፣ ግድፈት

eruption
ኢ'ረፕሽን -ስ- መፈንዳት (ለእሳተ ገሞራ)

escape
ኧስ'ኬይፕ -ግ- ማምለጥ [አመለ'ጠ]

escort
'ኢስኮት -ግ- ማ'ጀብ [አ'ጀበ]

especially
ኢስ'ፔሸሊ -ተግ- በተለ ይ ፣ ይልቁንም

espionage
'ኢስፒየናዥ -ስ- ስ'ለላ

essay
'ኢሴይ -ስ- ጽሑፍ (ብዙ ፣ ያልበለጠን ጊዜ አጠ'ር ያለ)

essential
ኢ'ሴንሸል -ቅ- አስፈ ላጊ

establish
ኢስ'ታብሊሽ -ግ- መመሥረት [መሠ'ረተ] ፣ ማቆም [አቆመ]

estate
ኧስ'ቴይት -ስ- እርስት

esteem
ኢስ'ቲይም -ግ- ማክበር [አከ'በረ]

estimate
'ኢስቲሚይት -ግ- መገ'መት [ገ'መተ] ፣ መገምገም [ገመ'ገመ]

estuary
'ኢስትዩወሪ -ስ- ወንዝ ወደ ባሕር የ'ሚፈ'ስ'በት በታ

eternal
ኢ'ተ:ንል -ቅ- ዘለዓለማዊ ፣ መጨ'ረሻ የሌ'ለው

ethical
'ኤቲክል -ቅ- ግብረ ገ'ባዊ (ለጠባይ) ፣ ከግብረ ገ'ብ'ነት ጋር ግን'ኙ'ነት ያ'ለው

ethics
ኢቲክስ -ስ- የግብረ ገ'ብ'ነት ጥናት

Ethiopia
ኢቲ'የውፒያ -ስ- ኢትዮ'ጵያ

Ethiopian
ኢቲ'የውፒየን -ቅ- ኢትዮ'ጵያዊ

eucalyptus
ዩክ'ሊፕተስ -ስ- ባሕር ዛፍ

Eucharist
'ዩ:ክሪስት -ስ- ሥጋ ወደሙ ፡ ቁርባን

eunuch
'ዩነክ -ስ- ጃንደረባ ፡ ስልብ

European
ዩረ'ፒየን -ቅ- አውሮ'ጳዊ

evade
ኢ'ቬይድ -ግ- ማምለጥ [አመ'ለጠ] ፡ ገለል ማለት [አለ] ፡ መልስ ለመስጠት አለመፈ'ለግ [-ፈለ'ገ]

evacuate
ኢ'ቫክዩዌይት -ግ- ማስለ'ቀቅ [አስለ'ቀቀ] (ሕዝብ ከሥፍራ)

evaluate
ኢ'ቫልዩዌይት -ግ- መገ'መት [ገ'መተ]

evaporate
ኢ'ቫፐሬይት -ግ- መትነን [ተ'ነነ]

evasive
ኢ'ቬይዚቭ -ቅ- ማምለጫ ፡ ከንድ ሁናቴ መራቂያ (መልስ ወዘተ)

eve
'ኢይቭ -ስ- ዋዜማ

even
'ኢይቨን -ተግ- እንኳን ፡ በ . . . ም
-ቅ- ለ'ጥ ያለ ፡ የተስተካ'ከለ ፡ የተመ'ዛ'ዘነ ፣ ለሁለ'ት በትክ'ክል ሊ'ከ'ፈል የ'ሚ'ቻል

evening
'ኢይቭኒንግ -ስ- ምሽት

event
ኢ'ቬንት -ስ- ድር'ጊት ፣ ሁናቴ

eventful
ኢ'ቬንትፉል -ቅ- አዳ'ዲስ ነገር ያ'ለ'በት ፣ አስደ'ሳች

ever
'ኤቨ -ተግ- መ'ቸም ፣ ምንጊዜም ፣ ሁል ጊዜ

everlasting
ኤቨ'ላ:ስቲንግ -ቅ- መ'ጨ'ረሻ የሌ'ለው ፣ ዘለዓለማዊ

every
'ኤቭሪ -ቅ- 'ሰ ያንዳንዱ

everybody
'ኤቭሪቦዲ -ስ- እ'ያንዳንዱ ሰው

everyday
ኤቭሪ'ዴይ -ቅ- በ'የቀኑ ፣ የ'የቀኑ

everyone
'ኤቭሪወን -ስ- እ'ያንዳንዱ ሰው

everything
'ኤቭሪሲንግ -ስ- ማ'ን'ኛው'ም ነገር ፣ ሁ'ሉ'ም ነገር

everywhere
'ኤቭሪዌየ -ተግ- የት'ም

evict
ኢ'ቪክት -ግ- ማስወ'ገድ [አስወ'ገደ] (በሕ'ግ)፣ መንቀል [ነ'ቀለ] (ሰውን ከርስት)

evidence
'ኤቪደንስ -ስ- ማስረ'ጃ

evil
'ኢይቭል -ስ- ክፋት

ewe
'ዩው -ስ- ሴት በግ

exact
ኤግ'ዛክት -ቅ- በትክ'ክል ፡ ል'ክ

exactly
ኤግ'ዛክትሊ -ተግ- በትክ'ክል
-ቃአ- ል'ክ እንደ'ዚሁ

exaggerate
ኤግ'ዛጀሬይት -ግ- ማ'ጋነን [አ'ጋ'ነነ]፣ ከ'ሚ'ገ'ባ በላይ ስለአንድ ነገር መ'ናገር [ተና'ገረ]

examination
ኤግዛመ'ኔይሽን -ስ- ፈተና

examine

ኤግ'ዛመን -ግ- መፈ'ተን [ፈ'ተነ] ፣ መመርመር [መረ'መረ]

example

ኤግ'ዛ:ምፐል -ስ- ም'ሳሌ ፣ ማስረ'ጃ

excavate

'ኤክስከቬይት -ግ- መቆ'ፈር [ቆ'ፈረ] (የተደ'በቀ ነገር ለማግኘት)

exceed

ኤክ'ሲይድ -ግ- መብለጥ [በ'ለጠ] ፣ መላቅ [ላቀ]

excellent

'ኤክሴለንት -ቅ- በጣም ጥ'ሩ ፣ እ'ጅግ የላቀ

except

ኤክ'ሴፕት -ተግ- ከ . . . በስተቀር

exception

ኤክ'ሴፕሽን -ስ- ያልተለ'መደ ነገር ፣ ሁናቴ ፣ እ'ጠቃላይ ሕ'ግን የማይ'ከ'ተል ነገር ፣ ሁናቴ

exceptional

ኤክ'ሴፕሽነል -ቅ- ያልተለ'መደ ፣ በጣም ጥሩ

excerpt

'ኤክሰ:ፕት -ስ- እስተዋፅኦ ፣ አ'ጭር ምንባብ (የመጽሐፍ ፣ የፊልም ፣ የቴያትር ወዘተ)

excess

ኤክ'ሴስ -ስ- ከል'ክ ማ'ለፍ ፣ ማትረፍ ፣ ማትረፍረፍ

excessive

ኤክ'ሴሲቭ -ቅ- ከል'ክ ያ'ለፈ ፣ የተትረፈ'ረፈ

exchange

ኤክስ'ቼይንጅ -ግ- መ'ለዋወጥ [ተለዋ'ወጠ]

excise

'ኤክሳይዝ -ግ- መቅረጥ [ቀ'ረጠ] (በአገር ውስጥ የ'ሚ'ሸጡ ዕቃዎ'ችን)

tax

-ስ- ቀረጥ (በአገር ውስጥ በ'ሚ'ሸጡ ዕቃዎ'ች ላይ የ'ሚ'ጣል)

take out

-ግ- መቁረጥ [ቆ'ረጠ] (ከመጽሐፍ አንዱን ክፍል)

excite

ኤክ'ሳይት -ግ- ማስደ'ሰት [አስደ'ሰተ] ፣ ስ'ሜትን መቀስቀስ [ቀሰ'ቀሰ]

excitement

ኤክ'ሳይትመንት -ስ- ደ'ስታ ፣ የስ'ሜት ፣ መ'ቀስቀስ

exclaim

ኤክስክ'ሌይም -ግ- በድንገት መጮኸ [ጮኸ] (ከሥቃይ ፣ ከ'ቁጣ ፣ ከድን'ጋጤ ወዘተ የተ'ነ'ሣ)

exclamation

ኤክስክለ'ሜይሽን -ስ- የማ'ጋነን ጩኸት ፣ የእንክሮ ድምፅ

exclude

ኤክስክ'ሉ:ድ -ግ- ለ'ይቶ ማስቀ'ረት [አስቀ'ረ]

exclusive

ኤክስክ'ሉ:ሲቭ -ቅ- የተለ'የ ፣ ል'ዩ

excrement

'ኤክስክረመንት -ስ- ዓይነ ምድር ፣ ኩስ

excretion

ኤክስክ'ሪይሽን -ስ- የወ'ጣ ነገር (ከሰው'ነት ፣ እሰር ፣ አር ፣ ላቦት ወዘተ)

excruciating

ኤክስክ'ሩ:ሺዬይቲንግ -ቅ- በጣም የ'ሚያ'ም ፣ የ'ሚያ'ሠቃ'ይ

excursion

ኤክስ'ክ:ሸን -ስ- አ'ጭር የሽ'ርሽ'ር ጉዞ

excuse

ኤክስክ'ዩ:ዝ -ግ- ይቅር ማለት [አለ] ፣ ስኅተትን ቻ'ል ማለት [አለ]

excuse

ኤክስክ'ዩ:ስ -ስ- ይቅርታ ፣ ምክንያት (የሠ'ሩት ሥራ ል ክ መሆኑን ለማስረ'ዳት)

execute

'ኤክሲክዩ:ት -ግ- መፈ'ጸም [ፈ'ጸመ] (የተጠ'የቁትን ፣ የታ'ዘዙትን ነገር)

execution

ኤክሲክ'ዩ:ሽን -ስ- መፈ'ጸም (እንድ ጉ'ዳይ) ፣ መግደል (ሞት የተፈ'ረደ'በትን)

executive

ኤክ'ዜክዩቲቭ -ስ- ባለሥልጣን

exempt

ኤክ'ዜምፕት -ግ- ከግ'ዴታ ነጻ መሆን [ሆነ]

-ቅ- ሕ'ግ የማያስገ'ድደው

exercise

'ኤክሰሳይዝ -ስ- መልመጃ ፣ መ'ለማመጃ

-ግ- መሥራት [ሠ'ራ] ፣ ማድረግ [አደ'ረገ]

exert

ኤክ'ዘ:ት -ግ- በጣም መሥራት [ሠ'ራ] ፣ እሥራ ማዋል [አዋለ]

exhale
ኤክስ'ሄይል -ግ- መተንፈስ [ተነ'ፈሰ] (ወደ ውጭ)

exhaust
ኤግ'ዞ፡ስት -ግ- ማድከም [አደ'ከመ]
-ስ- የመኪና ጢስ መውጫ ቧም'ቧ

exhibit
ኤግ'ዚቢት -ግ- ማሳ'የት [አሳ'የ]

exhibition
ኤክሲ'ቢሽን -ስ- ኤክዚቢሽን ፣ ለመ'ታየት የቀ'ረቡ ዕቃዎ'ች ፣ ትርኢት (የዕቃዎ'ች)

exile
'ኤክሳይል -ግ- ማጋዝ [አጋዘ] (ለቅጣት)
-ስ- ግዞተ'ኛ ፣ የግዞት ቦታ

exist
'ኤግ'ዚስት -ግ- መኖር [ኖረ]

existence
ኤግ'ዚስተንስ -ስ- መኖር ፣ ህ'ላዌ

exit
ኤግዚት -ስ- መውጫ በ'ር

expand
ኤክስ'ፓንድ -ግ- መ'ለጠጥ [ተለ'ጠጠ] ፣ መ'ሳብ [ተሳበ]

expect
ኤክስ'ፔክት -ግ- መ'ጠባበቅ [ተጠባ'በቀ] (አንድ ሁናቴ ፣ ነገር ወዘተ እን'ደ'ሚሆን)

expectant
ኤክስ'ፔክተንት -ቅ- በጉጉ'ት በተስፋ የ'ሚጠ'ብቅ

expedition
ኤክስፔ'ዲሽን -ስ- የጥናት ፣ የምርመራ ጉዞ ፣ አንድ ዓላማ ያ'ለው ጉዞ

expel
ኤክስ'ፔል -ግ- ማስወ'ጣት [አስወ'ጣ] ፣ ማስወ'ገድ [አስወ'ገደ]

expend
ኤክስ'ፔንድ -ግ- ገንዘብ ፣ ጊዜ ፣ ጉልበት ወዘተ ላንድ ተግባር ማዋል [አዋለ]

expenditure
ኤክስ'ፔንዲቸ -ስ- ወጭ (የገንዘብ)

expense
ኤክስ'ፔንስ -ስ- ወጭ (የገንዘብ)

expensive
ኤክስ'ፔንሲቭ -ቅ- ው'ድ (ለዋጋ)

experience
ኤክስ'ፒሪየንስ -ስ- የሥራ ልም'ምድ (በማየት'ና ፣ በመሥራት የተገ'ኘ)

experiment
ኤክስ'ፔሪመንት -ግ- መፈ'ተን [ፈ'ተነ] (ያንድ ነገር ሁናቴ ለማጥናት)
-ስ- ሙ'ከራ (የጥናት)

expert
'ኤክስፐ፡ት -ቅ- ዐዋቂ ፣ ባለሙያ

expire
ኤክስ'ፓየ -ግ- ማለቅ [አ'ለቀ] (ለጊዜ)

explain
ኤክስፕ'ሌይን -ግ- መግለጽ [ገ'ለጸ] ፣ ማስረ'ዳት [አስረ'ዳ]

explanation
ኤክስፕለ'ኔይሽን -ስ- አ'ገላለጽ

explode
ኤክስፕ'ለውድ -ግ- መፈንዳት [ፈነ'ዳ] ፣ ማፈንዳት [አፈነ'ዳ]

exploit
ኤክስፕ'ሎይት -ግ- ያገር ሀብት እሥራ ላይ ማዋል [አዋለ] ፣ ያለ አግባብ የሰው ጉልበት መብላት [በ'ላ]

exploit
'ኤክስፕሎይት -ስ- የጉብዝ'ና ሥራ ፣ ተግባር (በጦር'ነት ወዘተ)

explore
ኤክስፕ'ሎ፡ -ግ- መርምሮ ማግኘት [አገ'ኘ]

explosion
ኤክስፕ'ለውዠን -ስ- መፈንዳት

export
'ኤክስፖ፡ት -ግ- የንግድ ዕቃ ወደው'ጭ አገር መላክ [ላከ]

exposed
ኤክስ'ፐውዝድ -ቅ- ግልጽ የሆነ ፣ ያልተሸ'ፈነ

exposure
ኤክስ'ፐውዠ -ስ- ተገልጦ መ'ታየት

expound
ኤክስ'ፖውንድ -ግ- ማስረ'ዳት [አስረ'ዳ]

express
ኤክስፕ'ሬስ -ግ- በድርጊት በቃላት ፣ በአ'መለካከት ማስረ'ዳት [አስረ'ዳ]
-ቅ- ፈ'ጣን

expression
ኤክስፐ'ሬሽን -ስ- መልክ ፣ ፊት ፣ የመልክ ሁናቴ (ቁ'ጣ ፣ ሐዘን ፣ ደ'ስታ ወዘተ)

extend
ኤክስ'ቴንድ -ግ- መዘርጋት [ዘረ'ጋ] ፣ ማር ዘም [አረ'ዘመ] ፣ ማስረ'ዘም [አስረ'ዘመ]

extension
ኤክስ'ቴንሽን -ስ- ተጨ'ማሪ ነገር

extensive
ኤክስ'ቴንሲቭ -ቅ- ት'ልቅ ፣ የተዘረ'ጋ ፣ ሰ'ፊ

extenuate
ኤክስ'ቴንዩዌይት -ግ- የሥ'ሩትን ጥፋት ቀ'ላል አድርጎ ማሳየ'ት [አሳ'የ] ፣ ጥፋትን ማቅለል [አቀለ'ለ]

exterior
ኤክስ'ቲሪየ -ቅ- የውጭ ፣ አፍኣዊ

exterminate
ኤክስ'ተ:ሚኔይት -ግ- መፍጀት [ፈ'ጀ] ፣ መ ጨ'ረስ [ጨ'ረሰ] ፣ መደምሰስ [ደመ'ሰሰ]

external
ኤክስ'ተ:ንል -ቅ- የው'ጭ ፣ አፍኣዊ

extinct
ኤክስ'ቲንክት -ቅ- ያ'ለቀ ፣ የጠ'ፋ ፣ ዘሩ የ'ማ ይ'ገ'ኝ (ለእንስሳት ዓይነት)

extinguish
ኤክስ'ቲንግዊሽ -ግ- ማጥፋት [አጠ'ፋ] (ለእ ሳት)

extort
ኤክስ'ቶ:ት -ግ- በዛ'ቻ ፣ በኀይል መውሰድ [ወ 'ሰደ] (ገንዘብ)

extra
'ኤክስትረ -ቅ- ሌላ ፣ ተጨ'ማሪ

extract
ኤክስት'ራክት -ግ- ማውጣት [አወ'ጣ] (በኀ ይል) ፣ መንቀል [ነ'ቀለ]

extraordinary
ኤክስት'ሮ:ዲንሪ -ቅ- ያልተለ'መደ ፣ እንግዳ የሆነ

extravagant
ኤክስት'ራቨገንት -ቅ- ገንዘብ አባካኝ

extreme
ኤክስት'ሪይም -ቅ- ከባድ (ለሕ'ግ ፣ ለድህ'ነት ወዘተ) ፣ ወደ አንድ ወገን ፈ'ጽሞ ያደ'ላ

exult
ኤክ'ዘልት -ግ- በጣም መ'ደሰት [ተደ'ሰተ]

eye
'አይ -ስ- ዓይን

eyebrow
'አይብራው -ስ- ቅንድብ

eyeglasses
'አይግላሲዝ -ስ- መነ'ጥር ፣ መነ'ጽር

eyelash
'አይላሽ -ስ- ሽፋሽፍት ፣ ሽፋል

eyelid
'አይሊድ -ስ- ያይን ቆብ

eyesight
'አይሳይት -ስ- ያይን ብርሃን

eye witness
'አይዊትነስ -ስ- ምስ'ክር ፣ ያይን ምስ'ክር

fable
'ፌይበል -ስ- ተረት

fabric
'ፋብሪክ -ስ- . አካል ፣ ቅርፅ (ያንድ ነገር) ጨርቃ ጨርቅ ፣ ድር'ና ማግ (የጨርቅ)

fabricate
'ፋብሪኬይት -ግ- መሥራት [ሠ'ራ] (ዕቃ) ፣ ፈጥሮ ማውራት [አወ'ራ]

face
'ፌይስ -ግ- መግጠም [ገ'ጠመ] (ዓይን ለዓ ይን)
-ስ- ፊት ፣ መልክ

facetious
ፈ'ሲሽስ -ቅ- ፌዝ የ'ሚያበዛ (ያለቦታው)

facilitate
ፈ'ሲሊቴይት -ግ- ቀ'ላል ማድረግ [አደ'ረገ] ፣ ችግር ማ'ቃለል [አ'ቃ'ለለ]

facility

ፈ'ሲሊቲ -ስ- ሥራ የ'ሚያ'ቀላ'ጥፍ መ'ሣሪያ ፡ አገልግሎት ወዘተ ፣ ሥራ ፣ ትምህርት ለማ'ከናወን የ'ሚረዳ ዘዴ

fact

'ፋክት -ስ- እውነት ፣ እርግጠ'ኛ ነገር

factor

'ፋክተ -ስ- ምክንያት ፡ የተለ'የ ው'ጤት ለማስገ''ኘት የነ'በረ ሁናቴ

factory

'ፋክትሪ -ስ- ፋብሪካ

faculty

'ፋክልቲ -ስ- ል'ዩ ስጦታ ፣ ተውህቦ ፣ ችሎታ ፣ በዩኒቨርስቲ ውስጥ ል'ዩ የትምህርት ክፍል ፣ የዩኒቨርስቲ መምህራን

fade

'ፌይድ -ግ- መደብዘዝ ፡ [ደበ'ዘዘ] ፡ ቀለም መልቀቅ [ለ'ቀቀ]

fail

'ፌይል -ግ- መውደቅ [ወ'ደቀ]፣ (ፈተና ወዘተ)፣ ማቋት [አቋተ] (እንድ ሥራ ፣ ሙ'ከራ)

faint

'ፌይንት -ግ- መዝለፍለፍ [ተዝለፈ'ለፈ]
-ቅ- ጉልህ ያልሆነ ፡ ደካማ

fair

'ፌየ -ቅ- ነጣ ያለ ፣ አድልዎ የሌ'ለ'በት ፣ የ'ማያ'ዳ'ላ ፣ ደረቅ'ና ጥሩ (ለአ'የር)

faith

'ፌይ<u>ስ</u> -ስ- እምነት

faithful

'ፌይ<u>ስ</u>ፉል -ቅ- ታ'ማኝ ፡ እሙን

fake

'ፌይክ -ስ- እውነተ'ኛ ያልሆነ ፡ ማስመ'ሰያ ነገር

fall

'ፎ:ል -ግ- መውደቅ [ወ'ደቀ]

fallacy

'ፋለሲ -ስ- ውሸት

fallow

'ፋለው -ቅ- ታርሶ ያ'ደረ መሬት

false

'ፎልስ -ስ-, ውሸት ፣ የተሳሳተ (ለንግ'ግር)

falter

'ፎ:ልተ -ግ- ፈ'ራ ተ'ባ ማለት [አለ] (በንግ'ግር ፣ በርም'ጃ ፣ በሥራ ወዘተ)

fame

'ፌይም -ስ- ዝ'ና ፣ ጥሩ ስም

familiar

ፈ'ሚልየ -ቅ- የታ'ወቀ ፣ የተለ'መደ ፣ ብዙ ጊዜ ያ'ዩት ፣ የሰ'ሙት ወዘተ

family

'ፋመሊ -ስ- ቤተ ሰብ

famine

'ፋሚን -ስ- ረኀብ (ባን'ድ አገር) ፣ ቀጠና

famous

'ፌይመስ -ቅ- ዝ'ነ'ኛ ፣ ስመ ጥሩ ፣ ስመ ጥር

fan

'ፋን -ስ- ማ'ራገቢያ

fanatic

ፈ'ናቲክ -ቅ- አንድ ነገር ፣ ሐ'ሳብ በመደ'ገፍ ፣ በመ'ቃወም የ'ሚ'መና'ቸክ ሰው ፣ እምነቱን (ሐ'ሳቡን) አለቅጥ የ'ሚያጤን ሰው

fancy

'ፋንሲ -ስ- ከእውነት የራቀ እምነት ፣ ሐ'ሳብ

fangs

'ፋንግዝ -ስ- የው'ሻ ክራንቻ ፣ እባብ መርዙን የ'ሚያስተላ'ልፍ'በት ጥርስ

fantastic

ፋን'ታስቲክ -ቅ- ድንቅ ፣ ሊሠሩት የ'ማይ'ቻል (ሰ'ቅድ ፡ ሐ'ሳብ)

fantasy

'ፋንተዚ -ስ- ከእውነት የራቀ እምነት ፣ በሐ'ሳብ እንጂ እሥራ ላይ ሊውል የ'ማይችል ነገር

far

'ፋ: -ቅ- ሩቅ

fare

'ፌየ -ስ- የጉዞ ዋጋ
food
-ስ- ምግብ

farewell

ፌ'ዌል -ቃአ- ደኅና ይሁኑ (ሁን)

farm

'ፋ:ም -ስ- እርሻ (ቦታ)

farmer

'ፋ:መ -ስ- ገበሬ ፣ አራሽ

farther

'ፋ:<u>ዘ</u> -ቅ- የራቀ ፣ ሩቅ

fascinate

'ፋሲኔይት -ግ- ማስደ'ነቅ [አስደ'ነቀ]

fashion
'ፋሽን -ግ- መቅረፅ [ቀ'ረፀ]
style
-ስ- ሞድ

fast
'ፋ:ስት -ግ- መጦም [ጦመ] ፣ መጸም [ጸመ]
-ስ- ጦም ፣ ጾም

fast
ፋ:ስት -ቅ- ፈ'ጣን ፤ የተጣ'በቀ ፣ በቀ'ላሉ የ ማ ይ'ነቃነ'ቅ

fasten
'ፋ:ሰን -ግ- ማጥበቅ [አጠ'በቀ]

fastener
'ፋ:ስነ -ስ- ማጥበቂያ

fat
'ፋት -ቅ- ወፍራም
of meat
-ስ- ስብ

fatal
'ፌይተል -ቅ- ሞት የ'ሚያስከ'ትል ፣ አደገ'ኛ

fate
'ፌይት -ስ- ዕ'ድል ፣ እጣ

father
'ፋ:ዘ -ስ- አ'ባት
father-in-law
-ስ- አማት (ለወንድ)

fatigue
ፈ'ቲይግ -ስ- የሰው'ነት ዝለት ፣ መድከም (በሥራ ምክንያት)

fatten
'ፋተን -ግ- ማወ'ፈር [አወ'ፈረ] ፣ መቀ'ለብ [ቀ'ለበ] (ለማስባት)

fault
'ፎልት -ስ- ስኅተት

faultless
'ፎልትሌስ -ቅ- እንከን የሌ'ለው

faulty
'ፎልቲ -ቅ- ስሕተት የመ'ላ'በት

favour
'ፌይቨ -ግ- መውደድ [ወ'ደደ]
-ስ- ውለታ

favourable
'ፌይቨረበል -ቅ- ጥሩ ፣ ተስማሚ

favourite
'ፌይቨሪት -ቅ- ተስማሚ ፣ አብልጠው የ'ሚ ወ'ዱት

fawn
'ፎ:ን -ግ- ጅራት መቁላት [ቆ'ላ] (ለውሻ') ፣ ማ'ቆላመጥ [አ'ቆላ'መጠ]
colour
-ቅ- ግራ'ጫ

fear
'ፊየ -ስ- ፍርሃት

fearful
'ፊየፉል -ቅ- ፈሪ ፣ አስፈሪ

fearless
'ፊየሌስ -ቅ- የ'ማይፈራ ፣ ደ'ፋር

feasible
'ፊይዘበል -ቅ- እሥራ ላይ ሊውል የ'ሚችል

feast
'ፊይስት -ግ- በዓል ማክበር [አከ'በረ]
-ስ- በዓል

feat
'ፊይት -ስ- ጀብዱ ፣ ከል'ክ ያ'ለፈ የጉብዝ'ና ሥራ

feather
'ፌዘ -ስ- ላባ (የወፍ ፣ የዶሮ ወዘተ)

features
'ፊይቸዝ -ስ- መልክ ፣ ያንድ ነገር የተለ'የ ጠባይ

February
'ፌብሩወሪ -ስ- የ'ካቲት

federation
ፌደ'ሬይሽን -ስ- ፌዴራሲዮን ፣ ባንድ ጠቅ ላይ አ'ገዛዝ የ'ሚ'ገ'ዙ ነጻ የውስጥ ደምብ ያ'ላ'ቸው ያንድ መንግሥት አገሮ'ች

fee
'ፊይ -ስ- ለማኅበርተ'ኛ'ነት ፣ ለትምህርት፣ለሕ'ክም'ና ወዘተ የ'ሚ'ከ'ፈል ያገልግሎት ዋጋ

feeble
'ፊይበል -ቅ- ደካማ

feed
'ፊይድ -ግ- መመ'ገብ [መ'ገበ] ፣ ማብላት [አበ'ላ]

feeder
'ፊይደ -ስ- መ'ጋቢ (እንስሳት ፣ አትክልት) ተከባካቢ ፤ መ'ጋቢ (መንገድ)

feel
’ፊይል -ግ- መዳሰስ [ዳ'ሰሰ]
emotion
-ግ- መ'ሰማት [ተሰ'ማ] (ለስ'ሜት)
felicity
ፈ’ሊሲቲ -ስ- ደ'ስታ ፣ ሐ'ሤት
feline
’ፊይላይን -ቅ- የድመት ወገን
fell
’ፌል -ግ- መቁረጥ [ቆ'ረጠ] (ለዛፍ) ፣ መጣል [ጣለ]
fellow
’ፌለው -ስ- ጓ'ደ'ኛ ፣ ሰው
fellowship
’ፌለውሺፕ -ስ- ጓ'ደ'ኛ'ነት ፣ ማኅበር
felon
’ፌለን -ስ- ወንጀለ'ኛ (ከ'ባድ)
felony
’ፌለኒ -ስ- ከ'ባድ ወንጀል
felt
’ፌልት -ስ- ወፍራም ጨርቅ
female
’ፊይሜይል -ቅ- እንስት
feminine
’ፌመኒን -ቅ- አነስታይ
fen
’ፌን -ስ- ረግረግ ፣ ጨቀጨቅ
fence
’ፌንስ -ስ- አጥር
ferment
ፈ’ሜንት -ስ- ብጥ'ብጥ ፣ ሁውከት (የፖሊቲካ)
ferment
’ፈ:ሜንት -ግ- መፍላት [ፈ'ላ] (ለጥንስስ) ፣ መቡካት [ቦ'ካ] (ለቡኮ ፣ ለሊጥ)
ferocious
ፈ’ረውሸስ -ቅ- ጨ'ካኝ ፣ ኀይለ'ኛ ፣ አውሬ
fertile
’ፈ:ታይል -ቅ- ለም (ለመሬት)
fertility
ፈ’ቲሊቲ -ስ- የመሬት ልማት ፣ መ'ራባት (ለሰው ፣ ለእንስሳ)
fertilizer
’ፈ:ቲላይዘ -ስ- የመሬት ማዳበሪያ
fertilize
’ፈ:ቲላይዝ -ግ- እንዲ'ራ'ባ ማድረግ [አደ'ረገ]
fervour
’ፈ:ቨ -ስ- ጥልቅ ስ'ሜት ፣ ታ'ላቅ ፍ'ላጎት ፣ የመንፈስ መ'ቃጠል
fester
’ፌስተ -ግ- መንፍረቅ [ነፈ'ረቀ] (ለቁስል)
festival
’ፌስቲቫል -ስ- በዓል ፣ ክብረ በዓል
fetch
’ፌች -ግ- ሄዶ ማምጣት [አመ'ጣ]
feud
ፍ’ዩ:ድ -ስ- ከ'ባድ የ'ቆየ ጥል (በሁለ'ት ቤተ ሰብ ፣ ሰዎ'ች መካ'ከል)
fever
’ፊይቨ -ስ- ት'ኩሳት (ሕመም)
few
ፍ’ዩው -ቅ- ጥቂት
fiance
ፊ’ያንሴ -ስ- እጮ'ኛ
fickle
’ፊክል -ቅ- እምነት የ'ማይ'ጣል'በት ፣ ከ'ዳ ተ'ኛ ፣ ተለዋዋጭ
fiction
’ፊክሸን -ስ- ል'ብ ወ'ለድ ታሪክ
fiddle
’ፊደል -ግ- መ'ጫወት [ተ'ጫ'ወተ] (አንድ ነገር በእ'ጅ ይዞ ባለማስተዋል)
cheat
-ግ- ማጭበርበር [አጭበረ'በረ]
fidget
’ፊጂት -ግ- መቁነጥነጥ [ተቁነጠ'ነጠ]
field
’ፊይልድ -ስ- ሜዳ ፣ መስክ ፣ የተወ'ሰነ የት ምህርት ዓይነት
fiend
’ፊይንድ -ስ- ሰይጣን ፣ ርኩስ መንፈስ ፣ በጣም ክፉ'ና ጨ'ካኝ ሰው
fierce
’ፊየስ -ቅ- አውሬ ፣ ጨ'ካኝ ፣ ኀይለ'ኛ
fifteen
ፊፍ’ቲይን -ቅ- ዐሥራ አ'ምስት
fifteenth
ፊፍ’ቲንθ -ቅ- ዐሥራ አ'ምስተ'ኛ

fifth
'ፊፍስ -ቅ- አ'ምስተ'ኛ
fiftieth
'ፊፍቲየስ -ቅ- አምሳ'ኛ
fifty
'ፊፍቲ -ቅ- አምሳ
fig
'ፊግ -ስ- የበለስ ፍሬ
fight
'ፋይት -ግ- መ'ዋጋት [ተዋ'ጋ] ፡ መ'ታገል [ታ'ገለ]
-ስ- ው'ጊያ ፡ ትግል
figure
'ፊገ -ስ- ቅርፅ ፡ መልክ ፡ አኀዝ
file
'ፋይል -ስ- ሞረድ ፡ ፋይል ፡ የሰልፍ መሥመር
filings
'ፋይሊንግዝ -ስ- ሙ'ራጅ ፡ ብ'ናኝ
fill
'ፊል -ግ- መሙላት [ሞ'ላ]
filling
'ፊሊንግ -ስ- በተሰ'በረ ጥርስ ውስጥ የ'ሚ'ሞ'ላ ነገር
filly
'ፊሊ -ስ- ያልተጠ'ቀ'ች ፈረስ
film
'ፊልም -ስ- ፊልም
layer
-ስ- ሥሥ ሽፋን
filter
'ፊልተ -ግ- ማ'ጣራት [አ'ጣ ራ] (ለፈሳሽ)
-ስ- ማ'ጣሪያ
filth
'ፊልስ -ስ- ተውሳክ ፡ እድፍ ፡ ቁሻሻ
filthy
'ፊልሲ -ቅ- እድፋም ፡ ቁሻሻ
filtration
ፊልት'ሬይሽን -ስ- ማ'ጣራት
fin
'ፊን -ስ- የዐሣ ክንፍ
final
'ፋይነል -ቅ- የመጨ'ረሻ
finance
ፋይ'ናንስ -ግ- በገንዘብ መርዳት [ረ'ዳ] ፡ ለአንድ ዕ'ቅድ ገንዘብ ማውጣት [አወ'ጣ]
-ስ- የመንግሥት ገንዘብ አስተዳደር
find
'ፋይንድ -ግ- ማግኘት [አገ'ኘ]
finding
'ፋይንዲንግ -ስ- ተፈ'ልጎ የተገ'ኘ ነገር ፡ ሕ'ጋዊ ው'ሳኔ(ዎ'ች)
fine
'ፋይን -ስ- መቅጣት [ቀ'ጣ]
punishment
-ስ- ቅጣት
thin
-ቅ- ረቂቅ ፡ ሥሥ
good
-ቅ- ጥሩ ፡ መልካም
finery
'ፋይነሪ -ስ- ጌጣ ጌጥ ያ'ለ'በት ልብስ
finger
'ፊንገ -ስ- ጣት
finger-print
'ፊንገፕሪንት -ስ- አሻራ
finish
'ፊኒሽ -ግ- መጨ'ረስ [ጨ'ረሰ]
fir
'ፈ፡ -ስ- የዛፍ ዓይነት (አርዘ ሊባኖስ የ'ሚመስል)
fire
'ፋየ -ስ- እሳት
dismiss
-ግ- ከሥራ ማስወ'ገድ [አስወ'ገደ]
fire brigade
'ፋየብሪጌይድ -ስ- የሳት አደጋ መ'ከላከያ ድር'ጅት
fireman
'ፋየመን -ስ- የእሳት አደጋ መ'ከላከያ ወ'ታ'ደር
stoker
-ስ- ማገዶ አቅራቢ (በባቡር ላይ)
fireplace
'ፋየፕሌይስ -ስ- ምድ'ጃ

fireproof
'ፋየፕሩ፡ፍ -ቅ- እሳት የ'ማያ'ቃ'ጥለው ፣ እሳት የ'ማይጎዳው
firewood
'ፋየውድ -ስ- ማገዶ
fireworks
'ፋየወ፡ክስ -ስ- ር'ችት
firm
'ፈ፡ም -ቅ- ጽኑእ ፣ ጠንካ'ራ
firmament
'ፈ፡መመ'ንት -ስ- ጠፈር ፣ ሰማይ
firmness
'ፈ፡ምኔስ -ስ- ጽኑእ'ነት ፣ ጠንካ'ራ'ነት
first
'ፈ፡ስት -ቅ- አንደ'ኛ ፣ የመጀ'መሪያ
firstborn
'ፈ፡ስትቦ፡ን -ስ- የበኲር ልጅ
fiscal
'ፊስከል -ቅ- የመንግሥት (ገንዘብ)
fish
'ፊሽ -ስ- ዐሣ
fisherman
'ፊሸመን -ስ- ዐሣ አጥማጅ ፣ ዐሣ አሥጋሪ
fishmonger
'ፊሽመንገ -ስ- ዐሣ ነ'ጋዴ
fishy
'ፊሺ -ቅ- ዐሣ ዐሣ የ'ሚሸ'ት
suspicious
-ቅ- የ'ሚያ'ጠራ'ጥር (ነገር ፣ ሁናቴ)
fissure
'ፊሸ -ስ- ስንጥቅ (በደንጊያ ወዘተ)
fist
'ፊስት -ስ- ቡ'ጢ
fit
'ፊት -ግ- መስማማት [ተስማ'ማ]
-ስ- የ'ሚጥል በ'ሽታ ፣ ድንገተ'ኛ ቁ'ጣ፣ ቅናት ወዘተ
fitness
'ፊትኔስ -ስ- መስማማት
fitter
'ፊተ -ስ- ገጣሚ (ዕቃ ፣ መኪና ወዘተ)
fitting
'ፊቲንግ -ስ- የ'ሚ'ገ'ጠም ነገር ፣ እቤት ውስጥ የ'ሚገባ ነገር
suitable
-ቅ- የ'ሚስማ'ማ
five
'ፋይቭ -ቅ- አ'ምስት
fix
'ፊክስ -ግ- መለ'ጠፍ [ለ'ጠፈ]
mend
-ግ- ማበ'ጀት [አበ'ጀ] ፣ መጠ'ገን [ጠ'ገነ]
fixed
'ፊክስት -ቅ- የተለ'ጠፈ
mended
-ቅ- የተበ'ጀ
fizz
'ፊዝ -ግ- መፍላት [ፈ'ላ] (የታ'ሸገ መጠ'ጥ ፣ ሲ'ከ'ፈት)
fizzy
'ፊዚ -ቅ- የ'ሚፈላ
flabby
ፍ'ላቢ -ቅ- የ'ሚዋ'ልል ፣ ጠንካ'ራ ያልሆነ ፣ ደካማ (ለሰውነት ሥጋ)
flag
ፍ'ላግ -ስ- ሰን'ደቅ ዐላማ
-ግ- ተስፋ መቁረጥ ፣ [ቈ'ረጠ] ፣ መደ'ከም [ደ'ከመ]
flagon
ፍ'ላገን -ስ- ት'ልቅ ጠርሙዝ (የመጠ'ጥ መያዣ)
flagrant
ፍ'ሌይግረንት -ቅ- ደ'ፋር ፣ የ'ማያፍር ፣ ዓይን ያረቀ
flagstaff
ፍ'ላግስታ፡ፍ -ስ- የሰን'ደቅ ዐላማ እንጨት ፣ ሰን'ደቅ
flail
ፍ'ሌይል -ግ- መውቃት [ወ'ቃ] (በበ'ትር)
-ስ- መውቂያ በ'ትር
flair
ፍ'ሌየ -ስ- የተፈጥሮ ስጦታ ፣ ተውህቦ
flamboyant
ፍላም'ቦየንት -ቅ- እዩ'ኝ እዩ'ኝ ባይ ፣ ጉ'ረ'ኛ ፣ ጌጣ ጌጥ የበ'ዛ'በት

flame
ፍ'ሌይም -ስ- ነበልባል
flange
ፍ'ላንጅ -ስ- ዘርፍ
flank
ፍ'ላንክ -ስ- ሽንጥ
flannel
ፍ'ላነል -ስ- ወፈ'ር ያለ የሱፍ ልብስ
flap
ፍ'ላፕ -ግ- መውለብለብ [ተውለበ'ለበ]
-ስ- ክዳን
flare
ፍ'ሌየ -ግ- ቡ'ግ ማለት [አለ] (ለጥቂት ጊዜ)
flash
ፍ'ላሽ -ግ- ቡ'ግ ማለት [አለ] ፣ ማብለጭለጭ [አብለጨ'ለጨ]
-ስ- ድንገተ'ኛ ብርሃን
flask
ፍ'ላ፡ስክ -ስ- ኮ'ዳ
flat
ፍ'ላት -ቅ- የተዘረ'ጋ ፣ አሰልቺ
-ስ- በፎቅ ላይ አንድ መኖሪያ ቤት
tyre
የፈነ'ዳ ፣ የተነ'ፈሰ ጎ'ማ
flatiron
ፍ'ላታየን -ስ- ካው'ያ
flatten
ፍ'ላተን -ግ- መጻመጥ [ጻ'መጠ]
flatter
ፍ'ላተ -ግ- ማ'ቆላመጥ [አ'ቆላ'መጠ] ፣ ማስደ'ሰት [አስደ'ሰተ]
flattery
ፍ'ላተሪ -ስ- ቁልም'ጫ
flaunt
ፍ'ሎ፡ንት -ግ- በግልጽ አለመ'ታዘዝ [-ታዘ'ዘ]
flavour
ፍ'ሌይቨ -ስ- መዓዛ ፣ ጣዕም
flaw
ፍ'ሎ፡ -ስ- እንከን
flaxen
ፍ'ላክሰን -ቅ- የገረ'ጣ (ለጠጉር)
flay
ፍ'ሌይ -ግ- ቆዳ መግፈፍ [ገ'ፈፈ] (ለቅጣት)

flea
ፍ'ሊይ -ስ- ቁን'ጫ
fleck
ፍ'ሌክ -ስ- ነቁጥ ፣ ጉድፍ
flee
ፍ'ሊይ -ግ- መሸሽ [ሸ'ሸ] ፣ መጥፋት [ጠ'ፋ]
fleece
ፍ'ሊይስ -ስ- የበግ ጠጉር
fleet
ፍ'ሊይት -ስ- የጦር መርከቦ'ች
-ቅ- በፍጥነት የ'ሚሮጥ
flesh
ፍ'ሌሽ -ስ- ሥጋ
fleshy
ፍ'ሌሺ -ቅ- ወፍራም
flex
ፍ'ሌክስ -ግ- ማጠፍ'ና መዘርጋት [አ'ጠፈ ፣ ዘረ'ጋ]
-ስ- የተሸ'ፈነ ሽቦ
flexibility
ፍሌክሲ'ቢሊቲ -ስ- የመታጠፍ ችሎታ ፣ ግ'ትር አለመሆን ፣ ሐ'ሳብን በቀ'ላሉ የመለ'ወጥ ችሎታ
flexible
ፍ'ሌክሲበል -ቅ- መ'ታጠፍ የ'ሚችል ፣ ግ'ትር ያልሆነ ፣ ሐ'ሳቡን በቀ'ላሉ የ'ሚለው'ጥ
flick
ፍ'ሊክ -ግ- በጣት ማስፈን'ጠር [አስፈነ'ጠረ] ፣ ጣት ማጮኽ [አጮኸ] (ለመጥራት)
flicker
ፍ'ሊከ -ግ- መደብዘዝ [ደበ'ዘዘ] (ጢፍ ፣ ሻማ)
flier
ፍ'ላየ -ስ- በራሪ ፣ አውሮ'ፕላን ነጂ
flight
ፍ'ላይት -ግ- ሽ'ሽት ፣ መብረር
flighty
ፍ'ላይቲ -ቅ- የ'ማይ'ታ'መን
flimsy
ፍ'ሊምዚ -ቅ- በጣም ቀ'ጭ'ን'ና ቀ'ላል ፣ በቀ'ላሉ ሊ'በላ'ሽ ፣ ሊ'ጎ'ዳ የ'ሚችል
flinch
ፍ'ሊንች -ግ- ወደኋላ ማፈግፈግ [አፈገ'ፈገ] (ከፍርሃት ፣ ከበ'ትር የተነ'ሣ)

fling
ፍ'ሊንግ -ግ- መወርወር [ወረ'ወረ]
flint
ፍ'ሊንት -ስ- ደን'ጊያ (የሲጃራ ማ'ቀጣጠያ ወ ዘተ)
flippant
ፍ'ሊፐንት -ቅ- የ'ማይገ'ደው ፣ ደንታ ቢስ
flirt
ፍ'ለ፡ት -ግ- ማሽኮርመም [አሽኮረ'መመ]
flirtation
ፍለ'ቴይሽ'ን -ስ- ማሽኮርመም
flit
ፍ'ሊት -ግ- ብ'ር ብ'ር ማለት [አለ]
float
ፍ'ለውት -ግ- መንሳፈፍ [ተንሳ'ፈፈ]
flock
ፍ'ሎክ -ስ- መንጋ (የበግ)
floe
ፍ'ለው -ስ- የ'ሚንሳ'ፈፍ የበረዶ ቁ'ራጭ
flog
ፍ'ሎግ -ግ- መግረፍ [ገ'ረፈ]
flood
ፍ'ለድ -ስ- ጎርፍ
floodlight
ፍ'ለድላይት -ስ- ት'ልቅ መብራት (በቤት ው'ጭ)
floor
ፍ'ሎ፡ -ግ- መጣል [ጣለ] (መ'ቶ)
-ስ- ወለል
storey
-ስ- ፎቅ ፣ ደርብ
floral
ፍ'ሎ፡ረል -ቅ- የአበባ
florid
ፍ'ሎሪድ -ቅ- የቀ'ላ (ለመልክ) ፣ በጣም ያጌጠ
florist
ፍ'ሎሪስት -ስ- አበባ ሻጭ
flotsam
ፍ'ሎትሰም -ስ- በወሃ ላይ የተንሳ'ፈፈ ነገር (ቆሻሻ ፣ የመርከብ ስ'ባሪ ወዘተ)
flour
ፍ'ላወ -ስ- ዱቄት

flourish
ፍ'ለሪሽ -ግ- ማማር [አማረ] ፣ መሥመር [ሠ'መረ]
flow
ፍ'ለው -ግ- መፍሰስ [ፈ'ሰሰ]
flower
ፍ'ላወ -ስ- አበባ
fluctuate
ፍ'ለክቹዌይት -ግ- መ'ለዋወጥ [ተለዋ'ወጠ] (ለእንቅስ'ቃሴ) ፣ መድከም [ደ'ከመ] ፣ መበርታት [በረ'ታ]
flue
ፍ'ሉ፡ -ስ- የጢስ መውጫ (በቤት ውስጥ)
fluent
ፍ'ሉወንት -ቅ- አንደበተ ቀ'ና
fluff
ፍ'ለፍ -ስ- የተጠቀ'ለለ የሱፍ፣ የጥጥ ወዘተ ብ'ናኝ
fluid
ፍ'ሉዊድ -ስ- ፈሳሽ (ውሃ ፣ ወተት ፣ ወዘተ)
fluke
ፍ'ሉ፡ክ -ስ- አ'ጋጣሚ ዕ'ድል
flurry
ፍ'ለሪ -ስ- ድንገተ'ኛ ሩ'ጫ ፣ መበርገግ ፣ ድንገተ'ኛ የነፋስ ሽ'ውታ
flush
ፍ'ለሽ -ግ- መቅላት [ቀ'ላ] (ቀለም)
wash away
-ግ- ጠርጎ መሄድ [ሄደ]
fluster
ፍ'ለስተ -ግ- ማ'ደናበር [አ'ደና'በረ] ፣ ማ'ደናገር [አ'ደና'ገረ]
flute
ፍ'ሉ፡ት -ስ- ዋሽንት
flutter
ፍ'ለተ -ግ- ብ'ር ብ'ር ማለት [አለ]
fly
ፍ'ላይ -ግ- መብረር [በ'ረረ]
-ስ- ዝምብ
foal
'ፎውል -ስ- የፈረስ ግልገል ፣ የአህ'ያ ውርንጫ ፣ ውርንጭ'ላ

foam
'ፎውም -ግ- አረፋ መድፈቅ [ደ'ፈቀ]
-ስ- አረፋ ፣ ኮረፋ

fodder
'ፎደ -ስ- የደ'ረቀ የእንስሳት ምግብ (ድርቆሽ፣ ገለባ ወዘተ)

foe
'ፈው -ስ- ጠላት ፣ ባላንጋራ

foetus
'ፊተስ -ስ- ሺል

fog
'ፎግ -ስ- ጉም ፣ ጭጋግ

foggy
'ፎጊ -ቅ- ጭጋጋም

foil
'ፎይል -ግ- ወንጀል እንዳይሠራ ማቆም [አ ቆመ]
tin-
-ስ- የብ'ር መልክ ያ'ለው ወረቀት

fold
'ፎልድ -ግ- ማጠፍ [አጠ'ፈ]

folder
'ፎልደ -ስ- ዶሴ

foliage
'ፈውሊየጅ -ስ- ቅጠላ ቅጠል

folk
'ፈውክ -ስ- ሕዝብ

folk-lore
'ፈውክሎ: -ስ- ያ'ባቶ'ች ተረት ፣ እምነት ፣ ባህል (ጥናት)

follow
'ፎለው -ግ- መ'ከተል [ተከ'ተለ]

follower
'ፎለወ -ቅ- ተከ'ታይ ፣ ደ'ጋፊ (የእምነት ወዘተ)

folly
'ፎሊ -ስ- ቂል'ነት ፣ ጅል'ነት

foment
ፈ'ሜንት -ግ- መፍላት [ፈ'ላ] (ጥንስስ) ፣ ብጥ 'ብጥ ማንሣት [አነ'ሣ]

fond
'ፎንድ -ቅ- አፍቃሪ ፣ የ'ሚወ'ድ

fondle
'ፎንደል -ግ- ማሻሸት [አሻ'ሸ] ፣ መደባበስ [ደባ'በሰ]

font
'ፎንት -ስ- ማጥመቂያ ገበታ (በቤተ ክርስቲ ያን ውስጥ)

food
'ፉ:ድ -ስ- ምግብ

fool
'ፉ:ል -ስ- ቂል ሰው ፣ ሞ'ኝ ሰው
-ግ- ማ'ታለል [አ'ታ'ለለ] ፣ ማቄል [አቄለ]

foolish
'ፉ:ሊሽ -ቅ- ቂል ፣ ሞ'ኝ

foot
'ፉት -ስ- እግር

foothold
'ፉትሀውልድ -ስ- የእግር መቆንጠጫ ፣ መ'ቆ ናጠጫ ቦታ

footman
'ፉትመን -ስ- አ'ጃቢ (ፈረሰ'ኛን ወዘተ) ፣ አገ ልጋይ (እንግዳ በማስገ'ባት'ና በማስተናገድ)

footpath
'ፉትፓ:ስ -ስ- የግር መንገድ

footprint
'ፉትፕሪንት -ስ- ዱካ

for
'ፎ: -መዋ- ለ . . .
-መየ- ስለ

forage
'ፎረጅ -ግ- ቀ'ለብ መሰብሰብ
-ስ- የእንስሳት ምግብ ፣ መ'ኖ

forbear
ፎ'ቤየ -ግ- አንድ ነገር ከመሥራት ራስን መግታት [ገ'ታ]

forbear
'ፎቤየ -ስ- አያት ቅድም አያት

forbid
ፈ'ቢድ -ግ- መከልከል [ከለ'ከለ]

force
'ፎ:ስ -ግ- ማስገ'ደድ [አስገ'ደደ]
-ስ- ኀይል

forceps
'ፎ:ሴፕስ -ስ- ወረንጦ

ford
'ፎ:ድ -ግ- ጥልቅ ባልሆነ ቦታ ወንዝ መ'ሻገር [ተሻ'ገረ]
-ስ- ወንዝ መ'ሻገሪያ ቦታ

forearm
'ፎ:ራ:ም -ስ- ክንድ

foreboding
ፊ'በውዲንግ -ስ- ሟርት (ስለ ሚመጣ ሁኔታ)

forecast
'ፎ:ካ:ስት -ግ- መ'ተንበይ [ተነ'በየ] ፥ ወደፊት የ'ሚያጋጥመውን ነገር መ'ናገር [ተ'ናገረ]

forefather
'ፎ:ፋ:ዘ -ስ- አያት ቅድም አያት

forefinger
'ፎ:ፊንገ -ስ- ሌባ ጣት

forehead
'ፎሪድ -ስ- ግንባር ፥ ግምባር

foreigner
'ፎረነ -ስ- የውጭ አገር ሰው

foreman
'ፎ:መን -ስ- የሠራተኞች ተቆጣጣሪ ፥ አለቃ

foremost
'ፎ:መውስት -ቅ- የመጀ'መሪያ ፥ በጣም አስፈ'ላጊ

forenoon
'ፎ:ኑ:ን -ስ- ጧት ፥ ከቀትር በፊት

forerunner
'ፎ:ረነ -ስ- መንገድ ጠራጊ (አንድ ነገር መምጣቱን የ'ሚነግር)

foresee
ፎ'ሲ -ግ- የ'ሚመጣውን ማወቅ [ዐ'ወቀ] ፥ ወደፊት ለ'ሚመጣው ሁኔታ መ'ዘጋጀት [ተዘጋ'ጀ]

foreshadow
ፎ'ሻደው -ግ- ቀድሞ ማስጠንቀቅ [አስጠን'ቀቀ] ፥ ማመልከት [አመለ'ከተ]

foresight
'ፎ:ሳይት -ስ- ለ'ሚመጣ ች'ግር አስቀ'ድሞ ማ'ሰብ ፥ ሁኔታዎ'ችን ቀድሞ የማየት ተግባር

forest
'ፎረስት -ስ- ደ'ን ፥ ዱር

forestall
ፎስ'ቶ:ል -ግ- አንድ ነገር ቀድሞ በመሥራት ሌላው እንዳይሠራው ማድረግ [አደረ'ገ]

forester
'ፎረስተ -ስ- ደ'ን ጠባቂ

forestry
'ፎረስትሪ -ስ- የደ'ን አ'ያያዝ ትምህርት

forewarn
ፎ:'ዎ:ን -ግ- በቅድሚያ ማስጠንቀቅ [አስጠ'ን'ቀቀ]

foreword
'ፎ:ወ:ድ -ስ- የመጽሐፍ መቅድም (ብዙ ጊዜ ከደራሲው ያልሆነ)

forfeit
'ፎፊት -ግ- በቅጣት መልክ አንድ ነገር ማጣት [አ'ጣ] (በሕ'ግ ፥ በስሕተት)
-ስ- ቃል የተገ'ባ'በትን ነገር ለመፈ'ጸም መያዣ ገንዘብ ፥ የቅጣት'ና ገንዘብ

forge
'ፎ:ጅ -ግ- ብረት መቀጥቀጥ [ቀጠ'ቀጠ] (ቅርፅ ለመስጠት) ፥ ለማ'ታለል አስመ'ስሎ መሥራት [ሠ'ራ] (ፊርማ ፥ ገንዘብ)

forgery
'ፎ:ጀሪ -ስ- ሐ'ሰ ወ'ረ ገንዘብ መሥራት ፥ ማስረ'ጃ ፥ መዝገብ ወዘተ ማ'ታለስ (ለማጭ በርበር)

forget
ፈ'ጌት -ግ- መርሳት

forgive
ፈ'ጊቭ -ግ- ይቅር ማለት [አለ]

forgo
ፎ'ገው -ግ- መተው [ተወ]

fork
'ፎ:ክ -ስ- ሹ'ካ ፥ ባ'ላ
pitch-
-ስ- መን'ሽ

forlorn
ፈ'ሎ:ን -ቅ- ያ'ዘነ ፥ የተ'ከዘ ፥ የከ'ፋው

form
'ፎ:ም -ስ- ቅርፅ

formal
'ፎ:መል -ቅ- የተወ'ሰነ ሕ'ግ የተከ'ተለ ፥ ሥነ ሥርዓታዊ ፥ ጠባዩ የ'ማይ'ለዋ'ወጥ

formality
ፎ'ማለቲ -ስ- ሥነ ሥርዓት ፥ ወግ

former
'ፎ:መ -ቅ- የቀድሞ

formerly
'ፎ:መሊ -ተግ- ባ'ለፈው ጊዜ
formidable
'ፎ:ሚደበል -ቅ- አስቸ'ጋሪ ፡ ኀይለ'ኛ ፡ መስ ናከል የበ'ዛ'በት
formulate
'ፎ:ምዩሌይት -ግ- መሥራት [ሠ'ራ] (ዕ'ቅድ)
forsake
ፈ'ሴይክ -ግ- መካድ [ካደ] ፡ መተው [ተወ]
forthcoming
ፎ:ብ'ከሚንግ -ቅ- ወደፊት የ'ሚመጣ
fortification
ፎ:ቲፊ'ኬይሽን -ስ- ም'ሽግ
fortify
'ፎ:ቲፋይ -ግ- መመ'ሸግ [መ'ሸገ]
fortitude
'ፎ:ቲትዩ:ድ -ስ- ጀግን'ነት ፡ ለች'ግር ለሥቃይ አለመ'በገር
fortnight
'ፎ:ትናይት -ስ- ሁለ'ት ሳም'ንት
fortress
'ፎ:ትረስ -ስ- ም'ሽግ ፡ አምባ
fortunate
'ፎ:ትዩነት -ቅ- ዕ'ድለ'ኛ
fortune
'ፎ:ትዩን -ስ- ዕ'ድል ፡ ሀብት ፡ ብዕል
forty
'ፎ:ቲ -ቅ- አርባ
forward
'ፎ:ወድ -ተግ- ወደፊት
fossil
'ፎስል -ስ- እመሬት ላይ የ'ሚ'ገ'ኝ የተደሞ ታሪክ ምል'ክት (የድ'ሮቹ ሕያውት የነ'በራ'ቸው ፍጥረቶ'ች)
foster
'ፎስተ -ግ- ማ'በረታታት [አ'በረታ'ታ] ፡ ማሳ'ደግ [አሳ'ደገ]
foster-father
'ፎስተፋ:ዘ ስ የጡት አ'ባት
foster-mother
'ፎስተመዘ ስ የጡት እ'ናት
foul
'ፋውል -ቅ- በጣም የቆ'ሸሸ ፡ አስቀ'ያሚ ፡ መጥፎ ሽ'ታ'ና ጣዕም ያ'ለው ፡ ሸ'ረ'ኛ
sport
-ስ- ስሕተት ፡ ጥፋት
found
'ፋውንድ -ግ- መመሥረት [መሠ'ረተ]
foundation
ፋውን'ዴይሽን -ስ- መሠረት
founder
'ፋውንደ -ስ- መሥራች
foundling
'ፋውንድሊንግ -ስ- ወድቆ የተገ'ኘ ሕፃን
foundry
'ፋውንድሪ -ስ- የብረት ማቅለጫ
fount
'ፋውንት -ስ- ምንጭ (የውሃ)
fountain
'ፋውንተን -ስ- ምንጭ (የውሃ)
four
'ፎ: -ቅ- አራ'ት
fourteen
ፎ:'ቲ:ን -ቅ- በሥራ አራ'ት
fourteenth
ፎ:'ቲ:ንስ -ቅ- በሥራ አራ'ተ'ኛ
fourth
'ፎ:ስ -ቅ- አራ'ተ'ኛ
fowl
'ፋውል -ስ- ወፍ ፡ ዶሮ
fox
'ፎክስ -ስ- ቀበሮ
fraction
ፍ'ራክሽን -ስ- ስ'ባሪ ፡ ያንድ ሙሉ ነገር ክፍል (ለሒሳብ)
fracture
ፍ'ራክቸ -ስ- ስ'ብረት (የአጥንት)
fragile
ፍ'ራጃይል ቅ በቀ'ላሉ የ'ሚ ሰ'በር
fragment
ፍ'ራግመንት ስ ስ'ባሪ
fragrance
ፍ'ሬይግረንስ ስ መዓዛ ፡ ጥሩ ሽ'ታ

fragrant
ፍ'ሬይግረንት -ቅ- ጥሩ ሽ'ታ ያ'ለው ፣ ሽ'ታው የ'ሚያ'ውድ

frail
ፍ'ሬይል -ቅ- ደካማ (በሰው'ነተ ጠባይ) ፣ በቀ'ላሉ የ'ሚ'ሰ'በር

frame
ፍ'ሬይም -ስ- ክፈፍ ፣ ሰው'ነት ፣ አካል

framework
ፍ'ሬይምወ:ክ -ስ- ቅርፅ በመስጠት ፣ ድጋፍ በመሆን የ'ሚያገለ'ግል መ'ዣሪያ ፣ ሥርዓት ፣ መሠረት (ለመንግሥት ፡ ለዕ'ቅድ ወዘተ)

franchise
ፍ'ራንቻይዝ -ስ- የመምረጥ ሙሉ መብት (የ ሕዝብን እንደራሴዎ'ች ወዘተ)

frank
ፍ'ራንክ -ቅ- ግልጽ ፡ እውነተ'ኛ ፡ ቀ'ጥተ'ኛ (ነገር የ'ማያድበሰ'ብስ)

frantic
ፍ'ራንቲክ -ቅ- የተደና'ገረው (ከሥቃይ ፡ ከሀ ፍረት ወዘተ የተነ'ሣ)

fraternal
ፍረ'ተ:ንል -ቅ- የወንድ'ም'ነት

fraternity
ፍረ'ተ:ነቲ -ስ- ወንድ'ም'ነት

fraternize
ፍ'ራተናይዝ -ግ- መ'ወዳጀት [ተወዳ'ጀ]

fraud
ፍ'ሮ:ድ -ስ- ማጭበርበር (ለገንዘብ)

fray
ፍ'ሬይ -ግ- መንተብ [ነ'ተበ]
fight
-ስ- ጥል ፡ ጭቅ'ጭቅ

freak
ፍ'ሪይክ -ስ- ያልተለ'መደ ቅርፅ ፡ መልክ ፡ ጸባይ ሐ'ሳብ ያ'ለው ሰው

freckles
ፍ'ሬክልዝ -ስ- በሰው'ነት ቆዳ ጥቋ'ቁር ምል'ክቶ'ች

free
ፍ'ሪይ -ግ- ነጻ ማውጣት [አወ'ጣ]
without payment
-ቅ- ነጻ ፡ ያለ ዋጋ

freedom
ፍ'ሪይደም -ስ- ነጻ'ነት

freeze
ፍ'ሪይዝ -ግ- ወደ በረዶ'ነት መ'ለወጥ [ተለ'ወጠ] ፣ ወደ በረዶ'ነት መለ'ወጥ [ለ'ወጠ]

freight
ፍ'ሬይት -ስ- በየብስ ፣ በመርከብ ፣ ባውሮ'ፕላን የ'ሚ'ላክ ጭነት ፣ ለጭነት የ'ሚከ'ፈል ኪራይ

French
ፍ'ሬንች -ቅ- ፈረንሳይ
language
-ስ- ፈረንሳይ'ኛ

frenzy
ፍ'ሬንዚ -ስ- የእብድ'ነት ሥራ

frequent
ፍረክ'ወንት -ግ- ማዘውተር [አዘወ'ተረ]
ፍ'ሪክወንት -ተግ- ሁል ጊዜ

fresh
ፍ'ሬሽ -ቅ- ት'ኩስ ፡ ቀዝቃ'ዛ (ለነፋስ)

freshman
ፍ'ሬሽመን -ስ- በዩኒቨርስቲ ያንደ'ኛ ዓመት ተማሪ

fret
ፍ'ሬት -ግ- ለት'ንሽ ነገር መጨ'ነቅ [ተጨ'ነቀ]

fretful
ፍ'ሬትፉል -ቅ- ያልተደ'ሰተ ፡ ቅ'ር ያለው

friar
ፍ'ራየ -ስ- መነኩሴ (የተለ'የ ሥርዓት ወገን የሆነ)

friction
ፍ'ሪክሽን -ስ- መ'ፋተግ
trouble
-ስ- አለመስማማት ፡ በሐ'ሳብ መ'ለያየት

Friday
ፍ'ራይደይ -ስ- ዓርብ

friend
ፍ'ሬንድ -ስ- ወዳጅ ፡ ጓ'ደ'ኛ ፣ ረ'ዳት

friendship
ፍ'ሬንድሺፕ -ስ- ወዳ'ጅ'ነት

fright
ፍ'ራይት -ስ- ፍርሃት (ትልቅ'ና ድንገተ'ኛ

frightful
ፍ'ራይትፉል -ቅ- በጣም የ'ሚያስፈ'ራ ፡ የ'ሚ ያስደነ'ግጥ

frigid
ፍ'ሪጂድ -ቅ- የቀዘ'ቀዘ (ለወዳጅ'ነት)
woman
-ቅ- ቀዝቃ'ዛ (ለአ'የር ፡ ለስ'ሜት)

frill
ፍ'ሪል -ስ- የልብስ ጌጥ (የሐርኮት ፡ ተጎርብ ርቦ የተሠ'ራ)

fringe
ፍ'ሪንጅ -ስ- ዘርፍ ፡ መርገፍ (የልብስ)

frisky
ፍ'ሪስኪ -ቅ- ሐሤ'ተኛ ፡ ፈንጣዥ

fritter
ፍ'ሪተ -ግ- መሰባበር [ሰባ'በረ] ፡ ማድቀቅ [አድ'ቀቀ] ፡ ቀስ በቀ'ስ ማባከን [አባ'ከነ] (ለገ ንዘብ ለጊዜ ወዘተ)

frivolous
ፍ'ሪቮለስ -ቅ- ዋጋ ቢስ ፡ አርባን የሌ ለው ሞ'ኝ ፡ ባዶ እንጉል

frock
ፍ'ሮክ -ስ- መ'ነኵሳጸፊያ ፡ ቀሚስ

frog
ፍ'ሮግ -ስ- እንቁራሪት

frolic
ፍ'ሮሊክ -ግ- መፈንጠዝ [ፈነ'ጠዘ]

from
ፍ'ሮም -ተግ- ከ . . .

front
ፍ'ረንት -ስ- ፊት

frontier
ፍ'ረንቲየ -ስ- ያገር ወሰን

frost
ፍ'ሮስት -ስ- ውርጭ

froth
ፍ'ሮስ -ስ- አረፋ

frown
ፍ'ራውን -ግ- ፊት ማኰሳተር [አኰሳ'ተረ]

frozen
ፍ'ረውዘን -ቅ- ውሃ በረዶ'ነት የተለ ወጠ

frugal
ፍ'ሩጋል -ቅ- ገንዘብ ቆ ጣቢ (ለምግብ)

fruit
ፍ'ሩ፡ት -ስ- ፍራፍሬ

fruitful
ፍ'ሩ፡ትፉል -ቅ- ፍሬ የ'ሚሰጥ ፡ ሊወልድ የ'ሚችል ፡ ዋጋ ያ'ለው

fruition
ፍሩ፡'ዊሽን -ስ- ፍሬ ማፍሪያ ጊዜ ፡ መ'ከናወን (ያ'ቀዱት ዕ'ቅድ) ፡ የሥ'ራ ክን'ውን

fruitless
ፍ'ሩ፡ትሌስ -ቅ- ፍሬ የ'ማይሰጥ

frustrate
ፍረስት'ሬይት -ግ- ማ'ደናቀፍ [አ'ደና'ቀፈ] ፡ (ለሥራ ፡ ለዕ'ቅድ) ፡ ማ'ጓተት [አ'ጓ'ተተ] ፡ ማ'ጨናገፍ [አ'ጨና'ገፈ]

frustration
ፍረስት'ሬይሽን -ስ- ተስፋ መቁረጥ ፡ መ'ደና ቀፍ ፡ መ'ጓተት

fry
ፍ'ራይ -ግ- መጥበስ [ጠ'በሰ]

frying-pan
ፍ'ራይንግ ፓን -ስ- መጥበሻ

fuel
ፍ'ዩወል -ስ- ማገዶ ፡ ነዳጅ

fugitive
ፍ'ዩ፡ጀቲቭ -ስ- የተሰ ደደ ፡ የተባ ረረ ሰው ፡ ኮብላይ

fulfil
ፉል'ፊል -ግ- ቃል ማክበር [አከ'በረ] ፡ ዕ ቅ ድ እሥራ ላይ ማዋል [አዋለ]

fulfillment
ፉል'ፊልመንት -ስ- መፈ'ጸም (ተስፋ ፡ ግ'ዴ ጅ ወዘተ) ፡ መፈጸም (ያ'ሰቡት ፡ የተመ'ኙት)

full
'ፉል -ቅ- ሙሉ

fully
'ፉሊ -ተግ- በሙሉ

fumble
'ፈምበል -ግ- መደባበስ [ደባ'በሰ] (አንድ ነገር ለመፈ ለግ) ፡ አንድ ነገር ደኅና አድርጎ በእ'ጅ መያዝ አለመቻል [ቻለ]

fume
ፍ'ዩ፡ም -ስ- ጢስ (ማ'ን'ኛው ም ዓይነት)

fumigate
ፍ'ዩ፡ሚጌይት -ግ- በጢስ ማጠን [አ'ጠነ] (ተ ባይ ለመግደል)

un
'ፈን -ስ- ደ'ስታ ፡ ጨዋታ ፡ ቀልድ
unction
'ፈንክሽን -ስ- ሥራ ፡ ተግባር
und
'ፈንድ -ስ- የተሰበ'ሰበ ገንዘብ (ላንድ ተግባር እንዲውል) ፡ በብዛት የ'ሚ'ገ'ኝ ነገር
undament
'ፈንደሜንት -ስ- መሠረት ፡ ቢጋር
undamental
ፈንደ'ሜንተል -ቅ- መሠረታዊ
uneral
ፍ'ዩነረል -ስ- ሥርዓተ ቀብር
ungus
'ፈንገስ -ቅ- የእንጉዳይ ዓይነት ተክል
funnel
'ፈነል -ስ- የጢስ መውጫ (የመርከብ ፡ የባቡር)፡ማንቆርቆሪያ (የደፍ ዋንጫ ቅርጽ ያ'ለው)
funny
'ፈኒ -ቅ- የ'ሚያ'ሥቅ
strange
-ቅ- የ'ሚያስገ'ርም
fur
'ፈ: -ስ- ለምድ ፡ ደበሎ
furious
ፍ'ዮ:ሪየስ -ቅ- ቁ'ጡ
furl
'ፈ:ል -ግ- መጠቅለል [ጠቀ'ለለ] (ለሰን'ደቅ ዓላማ ወዘተ)
furnace
'ፈ:ነስ -ስ- እቶን ፡ ከውር
furnish
'ፈ:ኒሽ -ግ- ቤት በዕቃ መሙላት [ሞ'ላ]
provide
-ግ- ፡ ማቅረብ [አቀ'ረበ]
furniture
'ፈ:ኒቸ -ስ- የቤት ዕቃ
furrow
'ፈረው -ስ- ትልም ፡ ፈር
further
'ፈ:ዘ -ቅ- ተጨ'ማሪ ፡ ራ'ቅ ያለ
-ተግ- ከ'ዚህ በላይ ፡ ደግሞ
furtive
'ፈ:ቲቭ -ቅ- ተንኰለ'ኛ ፡ የ'ሚያደርገውን የ'ሚደ'ብቅ
fury
ፍ'ዩ:ሪ -ስ- ቁ'ጣ ፡ ኃይለ'ኛ ን'ዴት
fuse
ፍ'ዩ:ዝ -ስ- ፊልሾላ (የኤሌክትሪክ)
fuss
'ፈስ -ግ- ለጥቃ'ቅን ነገር በጣም መ'ጨነቅ [ተጨ'ነቀ]
fussy
'ፈሲ -ቅ- በጣም ጠንቃ'ቃ (ለጥቃ'ቅን ነገር)
fusty
'ፈስቲ -ቅ- መጥፎ ሽ'ታ ያ'ለው
futile
ፍ'ዩ:ታይል -ቅ- እርባን የሌ'ለው ፡ ጥቅመ ቢስ
future
ፍ'ዩቸ -ስቅ- ተስፋት ፡ የ'ሚመጣ ጊዜ ፡ የወደፊቱ
fuzzy
'ፈዚ -ቅ- በእ'ጭር ጠጉር የተሸ'ፈነ ፡ ጠጉረ ከርዳ'ዳ ፡ ግልጽ ያልሆነ

G

gabble
'ጋበል -ግ- መለፍለፍ [ለፈ'ለፈ] ፡ መቀባጠር [ቀባ'ጠረ]
gadget
'ጋጀት -ስ- ት'ን'ሽ መ'ሣሪያ ወይን'ም የመ'ሣሪያ መለ'ወጫ
gag
'ጋግ -ግ- አፍ መ'ለጐም [ለ'ጐመ] (እንዳይና'ገሩ)
gaiety
'ጌየቲ -ስ- በደ'ስታ መፈንደቅ

gaily
'ጌይሊ -ተግ- በደ'ስታ ፣ በ'ሚያስደ'ስት ሁ ኔታ

gain
'ጌይን -ግ- ማትረፍ [አተ'ረፈ]
-ስ- ትርፍ

gait
'ጌይት -ስ- ያረ'ማመድ ሁኔታ ፣ ያ'ሯሯጥ ሁኔታ

galaxy
'ጋለክሲ -ስ- ባንድ'ነት የተሰበ'ሰቡ ከዋክብ ት ፣ የከዋክብት ክምች'ት

gale
'ጌይል -ስ- በጣም ጠንካ'ራ ነፋስ

gall
'ጎ:ል -ግ- ማቁሰል [አቆ'ሰለ] ፣ ማስቆ'ጣት [አስቆ'ጣ] ፣ ማ'ናደድ [አ'ና'ደደ]
bile
-ስ- ሐሞት

gallant
'ጋለንት -ቅ- ጎበዝ ፣ ጀግና ፣ ጨዋ ፣ ያማረ (ለመርከብ)

gall-bladder
'ጎ:ል ብ'ላደ -ስ- የሐሞት ከረጢት

gallery
'ጋለሪ -ስ- በፎቅ ላይ ያ'ለ ሰገ'ነት
picture-
-ስ- የሥዕል ማሳ'ያ አ'ዳራሽ

galley
'ጋሊ -ስ- በመርከብ ውስጥ ያ'ለ ወጥ ቤት

gallon
'ጋለን -ስ- ጋሎን (የፈሳሽ መለ'ኪያ)

gallop
'ጋለፕ -ግ- መጋለብ [ጋ'ለበ]

gallows
'ጋለውዝ -ስ- ሰው መስቀያ ዕንጨት

galore
ጋ'ሎ: -ተግ- በመትረፍረፍ ፣ በብዛት

gamble
'ጋምበለ -ግ- ቁማር መ'ጫወት [ተጫ'ወተ]

gambler
'ጋምብለ -ስ- ቁማርተ'ኛ

gambol
'ጋምበል -ግ- መፈንጨት [ፈነ'ጨ] ፣ በደ'ስታ መዝለል [ዘ'ለለ] ፣ መቦ'ረቅ [ቦ'ረቀ]

game
'ጌይም -ስ- ጨዋታ

gander
'ጋንደ -ስ- ወንድ ዳ'ክ'ዬ

gang
'ጋንግ -ስ- ወ'ሮበ'ላ ፣ ወንበዴዎ'ች

gangster
'ጋንግስተ -ስ- ኀይለ'ኛ ወንጀል ሠራ (መ'ሣ ሪያ የያዘ)

gangway
'ጋንግዌይ -ስ- ጠ'ባብ መ'ተላለፊያ

gaol
'ጄይል -ስ- እሥር ቤት

gailer
'ጄይለ -ስ- የወህኒ ቤት ፣ ዘበ'ኛ ፣ የወህኒ ቤት ኀላፊ

gap
'ጋፕ -ስ- ክፍት ቦታ (በሁለ'ት ነገሮ'ች መካ 'ከል ያ'ለ)

gape
'ጌይፕ -ግ- አፍ ከፍቶ ማየት [አ'የ] (በመ 'ደነቅ)

garage
'ጋራ:ዥ -ስ- ጋራዥ ፣ ተ'ሽከርካሪዎ'ች የ'ሚ ያርፉ'በት ቦታ

garb
'ጋ:ብ -ስ- የልብስ ስፌት ዓይነት ፣ ልብስ

garbage
'ጋ:ቢጅ -ስ- ው'ዳቂ ነገር ፣ ቆሻሻ ፣ ጥ'ራጊ

garden
'ጋ:ደን -ስ- ያትክልት ቦታ ፣ ዐፀድ

gargle
'ጋ:ገል -ግ- ጉሮ'ሮን ፣ አፍን በውሃ መጉመጥ መጥ [ተጉመጠ'መጠ]

garland
'ጋ:ለንድ -ስ- ያበባ ጌጥ

garlic
'ጋ:ሊክ -ስ- ነ'ጭ ሽንኩርት

garment
'ጋ:መንት -ስ- ልብስ

garnish
'ጋ:ኒሽ -ግ- ማስጌጥ [አስጌጠ] ፣ ምግብ ውስጥ ቅመማ ቅመም መጨ'መር [ጨ'መረ] ፣ መከ'ሽን [ከ'ሽነ]

garrison
'ጋሪሰን -ስ- አንድ ከተማ ወይን'ም ምሽግ የ'ሚጠ'ብቁ ወ'ታ'ደሮ'ች

garrulous
'ጋረለስ -ቅ- ለፍላፊ ፣ ስለጥቃ'ቅን ነገር መዘ ላበድ የ'ሚወ'ድ

garter
'ጋ:ተ -ስ- የግር ሹ'ራብ መወ'ጠሪያ ላስቲክ (የሴቶ'ች)

gas
'ጋስ -ስ- ጋዝ ፣ አ'የር

gaseous
'ጌይሲየስ -ቅ- ጋዝ የ'ሚመስል

gasoline
'ጋሶሊይን -ስ- ቤንዚን

gash
'ጋሽ -ስ- ጥልቀት ያ'ለው ቁስል ፣ የሰው'ነት ብጣት

gasp
'ጋ:ስፕ -ግ- ወደላይ ወደላይ መተንፈስ

gastric
'ጋስትሪክ -ቅ- የሆድ

gate
'ጌይት -ስ- በ'ር

gather
'ጋ<u>ዘ</u> -ግ- መሰብሰብ [ሰበ'ሰበ]
think
-ግ- ማ'ሰብ [አ'ሰበ]

gauge
'ጌይጅ -ግ- በጥን'ቃቄ መለ'ካት [ለ'ካ]
measure
-ስ- መለ'ኪያ.

gaunt
'ጎ:ንት -ቅ- በጣም ቀ'ጨን ፣ ከ'ሲ'ታ ፣ ማስ ጠ'ሎ

gauze
'ጎ:ዝ -ስ- የሕ'ክም'ና ጥጥ

gay
'ጌይ -ቅ- ደ'ስተ'ኛ ፣ የተደ'ሰተ

gaze
'ጌይዝ -ግ- አተ'ኩሮ መ'መልከት [ተመለ'ከተ]

gazelle
ገ'ዜል -ስ- ፌቆ

gear
'ጊየ -ስ- ማርሽ ፣ ፍጥነት መለ'ወጫ (የመ ኪና)

gearbox
'ጊየቦክስ -ስ- ካምቢዮ ፣ የፍጥነት መለ'ወጫ መ'ሣሪያ ያ'ለ'በት ሣጥን (በመኪና ሞቶር ውስጥ)

gem
'ጂም -ስ- ዕንቁ ፣ የተከ'በረ ድንጊያ (የተወለ'ወለ'ና የተቆ'ረጠ) ፣ ከ'ፍ ያለ ዋጋ ያ'ለው ዕቃ

gender
'ጂንደ -ስ- ጾታ

general
'ጂንረል -ቅ- ጠቅላ'ላ
military
-ስ- ጄኔራል (ደ'ጃዝማች ፣ ፊታውራሪ)

generally
'ጂንረሊ -ተግ- በጠቅላ'ላው
usually
-ተግ- ሁል ጊዜ

generate
'ጂነሬይት -ግ- ማውጣት [አወ'ጣ] ፣ ከለመ ኖር ወደ መኖር ማምጣት [አመ'ጣ]

generation
ጂነ'ሬይሽን -ስ- ትውል'ድ

generosity
ጀነ'ሮሲቲ -ስ- ል'ግሥ'ና ፣ ቸርነት

generous
'ጂንረስ -ቅ- ለ'ጋሥ ፣ ቸር

genesis
'ጂነሲስ -ስ- ፍጥረት ፣ ልደት ፣ አሬት ዘፍጥ ረት

genial
'ጂይኒየል -ቅ- ፈገግተ'ኛ ፣ ርኅሩኅ ፣ ገራገር ፣ ደ'ጋደ'ግ ፣ ተባባሪ

genius
'ጂይኒየስ -ስ- የላቀ የአእምሮ ፣ የኪነ ጥበብ ስጦታ ፣ የተፈጥሮ ተውህቦ

gentle

'ጀንትል -ቅ- ጨዋ ፣ የተከ'በረ ፣ ርኅሩኅ ፣ ተወ'ዳጅ

genuflect

'ጀንዩፍሌክት -ግ- ለጸሎት መንበርከክ [ተንበረ'ከከ]

genuine

'ጀንዩወን -ቅ- እውነተ'ኛ ፣ መ'ሳሳት የሌ'ለ'በት ፣ የታ'መነ

geography

ጂ'ዮግረፊ -ስ- መልከዐ ምድር

geology

ጂ'ዮለጂ -ስ- ጂኦሎጂ (የመሬት ሁኔቴ'ና ጠባይ ጥናት)

germ

'ጀ:ም -ስ- ጀርም ፣ በ'ሽታ የ'ሚያመጡ ጥቃ'ቅን ፍጥረቶ'ች

germicide

'ጀ:ሚሳይድ -ስ- የተባይ መግደያ መድኃኒት

germinate

'ጀ:ሚኔይት -ግ- ማቆንጐል [አቆነ'ጐለ] ፣ መብቀል [በ'ቀለ]

gesticulate

ጂስ'ቲክዩሌይት -ግ- ሲ'ና'ገሩ እ'ጅን ፣ አካልን ማ'ወዛወዝ [አ'ወዛ'ወዘ]

gesture

'ጀስቸ -ስ- የሰው'ነት የእ'ጅ ንቅናቄ (ሐ'ሳብ ለመግለጽ)

get

'ጌት -ግ- ማምጣት [አመ'ጣ]

obtain

-ግ- ማግኘት [አገ'ኘ]

geyser

'ጊይዘ -ስ- ፍልውሃ (ከመሬት የ'ሚፈልቅ)

ghastly

'ጋ:ስትሊ -ቅ- አስፈ'ሪ ፣ አስደንጋጭ

ghost

'ገውስት -ስ- የሙታን መንፈስ (ለሕያዋን የ'ሚ'ታ'ይ) ፣ መንፈስ

giant

'ጃየንት -ስ- በጣም ረ'ጅም ፍጡር ፣ ከሰው ቁመት የላቀ ርዝመት ያ'ለው ሰው ፣ ወይን'ም ሌላ ት'ልቅ ፍጡር

giblet

'ጂብለት -ስ- የዶሮ ወይን'ም የሌሎ'ች አዋፍ ሆድቃ (የ'ሚ'በ'ላው ክፍል)

giddy

'ጊዲ -ቅ- ራሱን የ'ሚያዞረው ፣ የ'ሚያጥለ'ውለው ፣ ኀላፊ'ነት የ'ማይ'ሰማው

gift

'ጊፍት -ስ- ስጦታ ፣ ሽ'ልማት

gifted

'ጊፍተድ -ቅ- ተውህቦ ያ'ለው

gigantic

ጃይ'ጋንቲክ -ቅ- ኀ'ያል (ሰው ፣ ከመጠበላይ የሆነ ፍጡር)

giggle

'ጊገል -ግ- እ'የተሽኮረ'መሙ መሣቅ [ሣ

gill

'ጊል -ስ- የዐሣ መተንፈሻ (ሳምባ)

gilt

'ጊልት -ቅ- ወርቅ ቅብ

gimlet

'ጊምለት -ስ- መሠርሠሪያ (መ'ሣሪያ)

gin

'ጂን -ስ- ጅ'ን (· ዛ'ጥ) ፣ የጥጥ መፈልቂያ መኪና

ginger

'ጂንጀ -ስ- ዝንጅብል

gipsy

'ጂፕሲ -ስ- በዘ-ረት የ'ሚኖር አንድ ነገ (በአውሮ'ጳ ውስጥ) ፣ ዘዋሪ ፣ ቤት የ'ለሽከርታ'ታ

giraffe

ጂ'ራፍ -ስ- ቀ'ጭኔ

girder

'ገ:ደ -ስ- ጠንካ'ራ የብረት ፣ የእንጨት ዘገ

girdle

'ገ:ደል -ግ- መ'ታጠቅ [ታጠ'ቀ] (በመ'ታቂያ)

-ስ- መ'ታጠቂያ

girl

'ገ:ል -ስ- ልጃገረድ

girth

'ገ:ስ -ስ- መቀ'ነቻ (የጭነት ፣ የኮር'ቻ)

gist

'ጂስት -ስ- ዋ'ና ሐ'ሳብ (የክር'ክር)

give
ጊቭ -ግ- መስጠት [ሰ'ጠ]

glacier
ግ'ላሲየ -ስ- የበረዶ ወንዝ

glad
ግ'ላድ -ስ- ደ'ስታ

glade
ግ'ሌይድ -ስ- በደ'ን መካ'ከል ያ'ለ ገላጣ ቦታ

glamour
ግ'ላመ -ስ- የ'ሚማ'ርክ ቁንጅ'ና ፣ ደማም'ነት

glance
ግ'ላ:ንስ -ግ- መልከ'ት ማድረግ

gland
ግ'ላንድ -ስ- እጢ

glare
ግ'ሌየ -ግ- አፍ'ጦ መ'መልከት [ተመለ'ከተ] (በቁ'ጣ)
strong light
-ስ- ዓይን የ'ሚያጭበረ'ብር (የ'ሚያጥበረ'ብር) ብርሃን

glass
ግ'ላ:ስ -ስ- ብርጭ'ቆ
material
-ስ- [illegible]

gleam
ግ'ሊይም -ስ- [illegible] የብርሃን ጭላንጭል ፣ የ'ሚያብለጨ'ልጭ ብርሃን (በተለ'ይ ብ'ል'ጭ ድር'ግ'ም የ'ሚል)

glean
ግ'ሊይን -ግ- መቃረም [ቃ'ረመ]

glee
ግ'ሊይ -ግ- ደ ስ:ታ ፣ ፈንጠ'ዝያ

glen
ግ'ሌን -ስ- በተራራ መሀ'ከል ያ'ለ ጠ'ባብ ሸለቆ

glib
ግ'ሊብ -ቅ- ቋንቋው የ'ሚገራ'ለት (ነገር ግን የ'ሚለው የ'ማይ'ታ'መን)

glide
ግ'ላይድ -ግ- መንሸራተት [ተንሸራ'ተተ]

glimmer
ግ'ሊመ -ግ- ጭ'ል ጭ'ል ማለት [አለ]
-ስ- ጭላንጭ'ል

glimpse
ግ'ሊምስ -ግ- ማየት [አ'የ] (ነገር ግን የታ'የው ነገር ቶሎ ሲጠፋ)
-ስ- ው'ልብታ

glisten
ግ'ሊሰን -ግ- ማንጸባረቅ [አንጸባ'ረቀ] (ለውሃ)

glitter
ግ'ሊተ -ግ- ማንጸባረቅ [አንጸባ'ረቀ] ፣ መንቆጥቆጥ [ተንቆጠ'ቆጠ] (ለጌጣጌጥ)

gloat
ግ'ለውት -ግ- በሰው ሥቃይ መ'ደሰት [ተደ'ሰተ]

globe
ግ'ለውብ -ስ- ድቡልቡል የሆነ ነገር ፣ መሬት፣ ሉል (መልከዐ ምድር)

globular
ግ'ሎብዩለ -ቅ- ድቡልቡል

globule
ግ'ሎብዩ:ል -ስ- ጠ'ብታ (የውሃ ፣ የደም ወ.ዘ.ተ)

gloom
ግ'ሉ:ም -ስ- ጨለምለ'ም ማለት ፣ ደብዘ'ዝ ማለት
sadness
-ስ- ሐዘን ፣ አለመ'ደሰት ፣ መ'ከፋት

gloomy
ግ'ሉ:ሚ -ቅ- ደብዛ'ዛ ፣ ጨለ'ም ያለ
sad
-ቅ- ያልተደ'ሰተ ፣ ያ'ዘነ ፣ የተከ'ፋ ፣ ጭፍግ'ግ ያለው

glory
ግ'ሎሪ -ስ- ክብር ፣ ስብሐት

glorious
ግ'ሎሪየስ -ቅ- ባለክብር ፣ ክቡር ፣ ስመ ጥር

gloss
ግ'ሎስ -ስ- የ'ሚያበራ የ'ሚያንጸባ'ርቅ ነገር

glossy
ግ'ሎሲ -ቅ- የ'ሚያበራ ፣ የ'ሚያንጸባ'ርቅ

glove
ግ'ለቭ -ስ- የእ'ጅ ሹ'ራብ ፣ ጓዋንቲ

glow
ግ'ለው -ግ- መፋም [ፋመ]

glow-worm
ግ'ለወ:ም -ስ- የ'ሚያበራ ትል ፣ ትለበ'ራ

glue
ግ'ሉ: -ስ- መጣብቅ ፣ ማ'ጣበቂያ ሙቅ ፣ ማ'ሸጊያ

glum
ግ'ለም -ቅ- ያ'ዘነ ፣ የተከ'ፋ

glut
ግ'ለት -ስ- የተትረፈ'ረፈ ነገር

glutton
ግ'ለተን -ስ- ሆዳም ሰው ፣ ከመጠን በላይ የ'ሚበላ ሰው

gnash
'ናሽ -ግ- ጥርስ መቆርጠም [ቆረ'ጠመ] ፣ ጥርስን ማ'ፋጨት [አ'ፋ'ጨ] (በቁ'ጣ)

gnat
'ናት -ስ- ቢምቢ ፣ የወባ ትን'ኝ

gnaw
'ኖ: -ግ- መጎርደም [ጎረ'ደመ]

go
'ገው -ግ- መሄድ [ሄደ]

goad
'ገውድ -ግ- መኰልኰል [ኰለ'ኰለ] (ለፈረስ ወዘተ)
-ስ- ከብት መንጃ ል'ም'ጭ

goal
'ጎውል -ስ- ግብ ፣ ዐላማ

goat
'ገውት -ስ- ፍ'የል

gobble
'ጎበል -ግ- በች'ኮላ መብላት [በላ] ፣ መስገብገብ [ተስገበ'ገበ] (ለምግብ)

go-between
'ገውበትዊይን -ስ- አ'ቃጣሪ (ሴት) ፣ አስታራቂ

goblet
'ጎብለት -ስ- ዋንጫ

god
'ጎድ -ስ- አምላክ

God
'ጎድ -ስ- እግዚአብሔር

godchild
'ጎድ ቻይልድ -ስ- የክርስት'ና ልጅ

goddess
'ጎደስ -ስ- እንስት አምላክ

godfather
'ጎ:ድፋ:ዘ -ስ- የክርስት'ና አ'ባት

godmother
'ጎድመዘ -ስ- የክርስት'ና እ'ናት

godsend
'ጎድሴንድ -ስ- ድንገተ'ኛ ዕ'ድል

goggles
'ጎገልዝ -ስ- የነፋስ ፣ የአቧራ መነ'ጥር (በተለ'ይ ቢሲክሌት ነጂዎ'ች የ'ሚያደርጉት)

goitre
'ጎይተ -ስ- እንቅርት

gold
'ጎውልድ -ስ- ወርቅ
colour
-ቅ- ብጫ

goldsmith
'ጎውልድስሚስ -ስ- ወርቅ አንጣሪ ፣ ወርቅ ሠሪ

good
'ጉድ -ቅ- ጥሩ ፣ መልካም

good-bye
ጉድ'ባይ -ቃአ- ደኅና ይሁኑ (ሁን)

goods
'ጉድዝ "-ስ- ሸቀጣ ሸቀጥ

goodwill
ጉድ'ዊል -ስ- በ'ጎ ፈቃድ

goose
'ጉ:ስ -ስ- ዝ'ዪ

gore
'ጎ: -ግ- መውጋት [ወ'ጋ] (በቀንድ)
-ስ- የ'ሚፈ'ስ ደም

gorge
'ጎ:ጅ -ግ- እ'የተስገበ'ገቡ መብላት [በ'ላ]
-ስ- ሸለቆ (በሁለ'ት ገደል መሀ'ከል ያ'ለ)

gorgeous
'ጎ:ጆስ -ቅ- በጣም የ'ሚያም: ፣ በቀለም ያሸበ'ረቀ

gospel
'ጎስፐል -ስ- ወንጌል

gossamer
'ጎሰመ -ስ- የሸረሪት ድር

gossip
’ጎሲፕ -ግ- ያልተረጋ'ገጠ ወሬ ማ'ዋራት [አ ዋ'ራ]
-ስ- ሐሜት ፣ ያልተረጋ'ገጠ ወሬ ፣ ጭምጭምታ

gouge
’ጋውጅ -ግ- መቦርቦር [ቦረ'ቦረ] ፣ መሰርሰር [ሰረ'ሰረ]

gourmand
’ጎ፡መንድ -ቅ- ሆዳም

govern
’ገቨን -ግ- መግዛት [ገዛ] (በሥልጣን)

government
’ገቨንመንት -ስ- ግዛት ፣ መንግሥት

governor
’ገቨነ -ስ- ገዥ

gown
’ጋውን -ስ- ረ'ጅም ቀሚስ

grab
ግ’ራብ -ግ- አፈ'ፍ አድርጎ መያዝ [ያዘ] ፣ ጠ'ፍሮ መያዝ [ያዘ] ፣ መንጠቅ [ነ'ጠቀ]

grace
ግ’ሬይስ -ስ- ረድኤት ፣ ውበት ፣ ያ'ረማመድ ማማር
prayer
-ስ- ከማዕ'ድ በፊት'ና በኋላ የ'ሚ'ጸ'ለይ ጸሎት

graceful
ግ’ሬይስፉል -ቅ- ረድኤት ያ'ለው ፣ ሲ'ራ'መድ የ'ሚያምር'በት ፣ ዠርጋ'ዳ

gracious
ግ’ሬይሸስ -ቅ- ቸር ፣ ለ'ጋሥ

grade
ግ’ሬይድ -ስ- ማዕረግ ፣ ደረጃ

gradient
ግ’ሬይዲየንት -ስ- ቁልቁለት'ነት ያ'ለው ቦታ

gradual
ግ’ራጁወል -ቅ- ዝ'ግተ'ኛ ፣ ቀ'ስ በቀ'ስ የ'ሚ'ደ'ረግ

graduate
ግ’ራጁዌይት -ግ- መ'መረቅ [ተመ'ረቀ] (በትምህርት)

graft
ግ’ራ፡ፍት -ግ- መከተብ [ከ'ተበ] (ለአትክልት)

grain
ግ’ሬይን -ስ- እህል ፣ ጥራጥሬ ፣ ቅንጣት

grammar
ግ’ራመ -ስ- ሰዋስው

granary
ግ’ራነሪ -ስ- የእህል ጎተራ

grand
ግ’ራንድ -ቅ- ት'ልቅ ፣ አስደ'ናቂ

grandeur
ግ’ራንድዩወ -ስ- ት'ልቅ'ነት ፣ ገናና'ነት

grandfather
ግ’ራንድፋ፡ዘ -ስ- ወንድ አያት

grandmother
ግ’ራንድመዘ -ስ- ሴት አያት

grange
ግ’ሬይንጅ -ስ- በትናን'ሽ ቤቶ'ች የተከ'በበ የባለቤቱ መኖሪያ (በባላገር) ፤ የእህል ጎተራ

granite
ግ’ራኒት -ስ- ጥቁር ድንጊያ

grape
ግ’ሬይፕ -ስ- ወይን

grant
ግ’ራ፡ንት -ግ- መስጠት [ሰ'ጠ] (የ'ጠ'የቁትን)

graphic
ግ’ራፊክ -ቅ- አ'ገላለጹ ሕያው የሆነ ፣ በ'ሚ'ታዩ ምል'ክቶ'ች የተገ'ለጸ ፣ የጽሑፍ ፣ የሥዕል ወዘተ

grapple
ግ’ራፕል -ግ- ጨ'ብጦ መያዝ [ያዘ] ፣ ለቀ'ም ማድረግ [አደ'ረገ] ፣ መ'ታገል [ታገለ]

grasp
ግ’ራ፡ስፕ -ግ- መያዝ [ያዘ] ፣ መጨ'በጥ [ጨ'በጠ]
understand
-ግ- መ'ረዳት [ተረ'ዳ]

grasping
ግ’ራ፡ስፒንግ -ቅ- ሥ'ሥታም (የገ'ንዘብ) ፣ ለሥልጣን ፣ ለገንዘብ ትርፍ የ'ሚ'ጓ'ጓ

grass
ግ’ራ፡ስ -ስ- ሣር

grasshopper
ግ’ራ፡ስሆፐ -ስ- ፌንጣ

grate

ግ'ሬይት -ግ- መፋቅ [ፋቀ] (ም'ሳሌ፣ፎርማጆ)
-ስ- እሳት የ'ሚነ'ድ'በት ፍርግርግ ብረት

grateful

ግ'ሬይትፉል -ቅ- ባለውለታ

grater

ግ'ሬይተ -ስ- መፋቂያ ፣ መፈርፈሪያ (መ'ጣሪያ)

gratify

ግ'ራቲፋይ -ግ- የፈ'ለጉትን መስጠት [ሰ'ጠ] ማስደ'ሰት [አስደ'ሰተ]

gratitude

ግ'ራቲትዩ:ድ -ስ- ምስጋና (ለተደ'ረገ'ለት ውለታ የ'ሚ'ደ'ረግ)

gratuity

ግ'ረትዩዊቲ -ስ- ጉርሻ ፣ ስጦታ ፣ ያገልግሎት ገንዘብ (ለወ'ታ'ደር'ች ያገልግሎታ'ቸው ጊዜ ሲ'ፈ'ጸም የ'ሚ'ሰ'ጥ)

grave

ግ'ሬይቭ -ስ- መቃብር

serious

-ቅ- ከ'ባድ ፣ አ'ሳኪ

gravedigger

ግ'ሬይቭዲገ -ስ- መቃብር ቆ'ፋሪ

gravel

ግ'ራቭል -ስ- ጠጠር

gravestone

ግ'ሬይቭስተውን -ስ- የመቃብር ድንጊያ (ጽሑፍ የ'ሚ'ጻፍ'በት)

graveyard

ግ'ሬይቭያ:ድ -ስ- የመቃብር ቦታ

gravity

ግ'ራቭቲ -ስ- የመሳብ ኀይል ፣ አስቸ'ጋሪ'ነት

gravy

ግ'ሬይቪ -ስ- ቅባት (የተጠ'በሰ ሥጋ)

gray

ግ'ሬይ -ቅ- ግራ'ጫ ፣ አመድ'ማ

graze

ግ'ሬይዝ -ግ- መጋጥ [ጋጠ] (ለእንስሳት)

wound

-ስ- ጭረት (ለቁስል)

grease

ግ'ሪይስ -ስ- የቀ'ለጠ ሞራ ፣ ቅባት

greasy

ግ'ሪይሲ -ቅ- ቅባታም ፣ አዳላጭ

great

ግ'ሬይት -ቅ- ት'ልቅ ፣ ታ'ላቅ

greatcoat

ግ'ሬይትከውት -ስ- ካ'ፖርት (ከበ'ድ ያለ)

greatly

ግ'ሬይትሊ -ተግ- በጣም ፣ በብልጫ

greatness

ግ'ሬይትነስ -ስ- ት'ልቅ'ነት

greed

ግ'ሪይድ -ስ- ሥ'ሥት (ለምግብ ፣ ለገንዘብ)

greedy

ግ'ሪይዲ -ቅ- ት'ቅታም ፣ ሥ'ሥታም (ለምግብ ፣ ለገንዘብ ወዘተ)

green

ግ'ሪይን -ቅ- አረንጓዴ ፣ ገና ያልበ'ሰለ ፣ ምርታ (ለአትክልት)

greet

ግ'ሪይት -ግ- ሰላምታ መስጠት [ሰ'ጠ]

greeting

ግ'ሪይቲንግ -ስ- ሰላምታ

grenade

ግረ'ኔይድ -ስ- የእ'ጅ ቦምብ

grey

ግ'ሬይ -ቅ- ግራ'ጫ ፣ አመድ'ማ

grid

ግ'ሪድ -ስ- የወንፊት መልክ ያ'ለው የብረት መ'ጣሪያ

grief

ግ'ሪይፍ -ስ- ሐዘን

grievance

ግ'ሪይቨንስ -ስ- የአቤቱታ ምክንያት ፣ አቤቱታ

grieve

ግ'ሪይቭ -ግ- ማዘን [አ'ዘነ]

grievous

ግ'ሪይቨስ -ቅ- አሳ'ዛኝ ፣ ከ'ባድ

grill

ግ'ሪል -ስ- ጥብስ ሥጋ ፣ መጥበሻ ፣ የወንፊት መልክ ያ'ለው የብረት መ'ጣሪያ (ለሥጋ መጥበሻ)

grim

ግ'ሪም -ቅ- የጨፈ'ገገው ፣ ጥላ'ቻ ያ'ደረ'በት

grimace
ግ'ሪመስ -ግ- ፊትን በጥላ'ቻ ማ'ኮፋተር [አ'ኮ ፋ'ተረ] ፣ መ'ኮሳተር [ተኮሳ'ተረ]

grime
ግ'ራይም -ስ- እንሽቅ ፣ እድፍ

grin
ግ'ሪን -ግ- ፈገ'ግ ማለት [አለ]

grind
ግ'ራይንድ -ግ- መፍጨት [ፈ'ጨ]

grindstone
ግ'ራይንድስተውን -ስ- የወፍጮ ደንጊያ

grip
ግ'ሪፕ -ግ- መጨ'በጥ [ጨ'በጠ] ፣ መያዝ [ያዘ]

gripe
ግ'ራይፕ -ስ- የሆድ ቁርጠት

gristle
ግ'ሪስል -ስ- እንጆ
ነት)

grit
ግ'ሪት -ስ- የደ'ቀቀ ጠጠር

groan
ግ'ረውን -ግ- መጓጉር [ጓ'ጉረ] ፣ ማቃሰት [አቃ'ሰተ]

grocer
ግ'ረውሰ -ስ- የምግብ ሸቀጥ ነ'ጋዴ

grocery
ግ'ረውሰሪ -ስ- የምግብ ሸቀጥ ሱቅ

groggy
ግ'ሮጊ -ቅ- ተንገድጋጅ ፣ ተንገዳጋጅ ፣ ለመ ውደቅ የደ'ረሰ

groin
ግ'ሮይን -ስ- ብሻ

groom
ግ'ሩ:ም -ግ- መጥረግ [ጠ'ረገ] (ፈረስን)
servant
-ስ- ፈረስ እጣቢ
well-ed
ልብሱ ያማረ'በትና ጠጉሩ'ም በደምብ የተ በ'ጠረ

groove
ግ'ሩ:ቭ -ስ- ስንጥቅ

grope
ግ'ረውፕ -ስ- መዳበስ [ዳ'በሰ] (እንደ ዕ'ውር ወዘተ)
-ቅ- ዶፊደፍ ፣ ወፍራም

gross
ግ'ረውስ -ቅ- ባለጌ ፣ ያልታ'ረመ ፣ ደ'ደብ
number
-ስ- ዐሥራ ሁ'ለት ደርዘን

ground
ግ'ራውንድ -ስ- መሬት

groundless
ግ'ራውንድለስ -ቅ- መሠረተ ቢስ ፣ በቂ ምክ ንያት የሌ'ለው

group
ግሩ:ፕ -ስ- የተሰበ'ሰበ (ሰው)

grouse
ግ'ራውስ -ግ- ማጉረምረም [አጉረመ'ረመ]

grove
ግ'ረውቭ -ስ- አነስተ'ኛ ደ'ን

grovel
ግ'ሮቨል -ግ- ራስን ዝ'ቅ ማድረግ [አደ'ረገ] (በትሕት'ና)

grow
ግ'ረው -ግ- ማደግ [አ'ደገ]
make-
-ግ- መትከል [ተ'ከለ] ፣ መዝራት [ዘ'ራ]

growl
ግ'ራውል -ግ- መጓጉር [ጓ'ጉረ] ፣ መጮኽ [ጮኸ]

growth
ግ'ረውዝ -ስ- እድገት

grub
ግ'ረብ -ስ- ትል (ወዲያው የተፈለ'ፈለ)
food
-ስ- ምግብ (ተራ ቃል)

grubby
ግ'ረቢ -ቅ- ያልጸ'ዳ ፣ ያ'ደፈ

grudge
ግ'ረጅ -ግ- መ'መቅኘት [ተመቀ'ኘ] ፣ መን ፈግ [ነ'ፈገ]

gruel
ግ'ሩ:ወል -ስ- መቅ ፣ እጥሚት

gruesome

ግ'ሩ፡ሰም -ቅ- አስቀ'ያሚ ፣ ለማየት የ'ሚያ 'ሠ'ቅቅ

gruff

ግ'ረፍ -ስ- ሸካራ'ነት ፣ ነጭና'ጫ'ነት ፣ አመ ለቢስ'ነት

grumble

ግ'ረምበል -ግ- ማጉረምረም [አጉረመ'ረመ]

grunt

ግ'ረንት -ስ- ማኩረፍ (በተለ'ይ ለዐሣማ ድ ም'ፅ)

guarantee

ጋረን'ቲ፡ -ግ- ተያዥ መሆን [ሆነ] ፣ ዋስ መሆን [ሆነ]

-ስ- ዋስት'ና ፣ ተያዥ'ነት

guarantor

'ጋረንቶ፡ -ስ- ዋስ ፣ ተያዥ ፣ ዋቢ

guard

'ጋ፡ድ -ግ- መጠ'በቅ [ጠ'በቀ] (እንዳያመልጥ)

-ስ- ጠ'ባቂ ፣ ዘበ'ኛ

guardian

'ጋ፡ድየን -ስ- አሳ'ዳጊ ፣ ኀላፊ (ለሕፃን)

guerilla

ገ'ሪለ -ስ- የደፈጣ ውጊ'ያ ፣ በደፈጣ የ'ሚ'ዋ 'ጉ ሰዎ'ች

guess

'ጌስ -ግ- ግ'ስብ [አ'ሰበ] (በግ'ምት) ፣ መገ ምገም [ገመ'ገመ]

-ስ- የግ'ምት ሐ'ሳብ

guest

'ጌስት -ስ- እንግዳ (ሰው)

guidance

'ጋይደንስ -ስ- አ'መራር ፣ የመምራት ሥራ

guide

'ጋይድ -ግ- መምራት [መ'ራ]

person

-ስ- መሪ

guile

'ጋይል -ስ- ተን'ኰል'ነት ፣ አታላይ'ነት

guilt

'ጊልት -ስ- ጥፋት ፣ ሕ'ግን የመጣስ ሁኔታ ፣ ስ'ሜት

guinea fowl

'ጊኒፋውል -ስ- ጅግራ

guinea-pig

'ጊኒ'ፒግ -ስ- መድኃኒት ወዘተ መፈ'ተኛ (ሰ ው፣እንስሳ ወዘተ)

guise

'ጋይዝ -ስ- ያልሆኑትን መስሎ መ'ታየት የልብስ ዓይነት ቅ'ድ ፣ ሞድ

gulf

'ገልፍ -ስ- የባሕር ሠ'ላጤ

gullet

'ገለት -ስ- የምግብ መ'ተላለፊያ ቧንቧ (ከጉ ሮ'ሮ እስከ ሆድ ያ'ለው)

gullible

'ገለበል -ቅ- የ'ዋህ ፣ በቀ'ላሉ የ'ሚ'ም'ኝ

gulp

'ገልፕ -ግ- መ'ጕንጨት [ተጕን'ጨ]

-ስ- ጉንጭ ሙሉ

gum

'ገም -ስ- ድ'ድ

adhesive

-ስ- መጣብቅ ፣ ማ'ጣበቂያ ፣ ማ'ሸጊያ

of a tree

-ስ- ሙ'ጫ

gumboil

'ገምቦይል -ስ- የድ'ድ እብጠት

gun

'ገን -ስ- ጠበንጃ (ጠመንጃ)

gunner

'ገነ -ቅ- መድፈ'ኛ

gunpowder

'ገንፓውደ -ስ- ባሩድ

gunsmith

'ገንስሚስ -ስ- ጠበንጃ ሠሪ

gurgle

'ገ፡ገል -ስ- የውሃ ድምፅ (ጠ'ባብ አፍ ካ'ለው ጠር'ሙዝ ሲ'ቀ'ዳ) ፣ መንዶቅዶቅ

gush

'ገሽ -ግ- በብዛት መፍሰስ [ፈ'ሰሰ] ፣ መጉረፍ [ጎ'ረፈ]

gust

'ገስት -ስ- የነፋስ ሽ'ውታ

gut

'ገት -ስ- አንጀት

cat-

-ስ- የከ'ረረ ጅ'ማት፣ጀግን'ነት፣ጉብዝ'ና

gutter
'ገተ -ስ- የውሃ መ'ተላለፊያ (በመንገድ ዳር) ፣ የውሃ መውረጃ ቧን'ቧ (ከጣራ ላይ)

guttural
'ገተረል -ቅ- የጉሮ'ሮ (ፊደል ወዘተ) ፣ የጉባበ ጉሮኛ

guy
'ጋይ -ስ- ሰው

guzzle
'ገዘል -ግ- መገ'ጠም [ገ'ጠመ] (ለመጠ'ጥ)

gymnastics
ጂም'ናስቲክስ -ስ- የሰው'ነት ማጠንከሪያ እን ቅስ'ቃሴ ፣ ጂምናስቲክ

habit
'ሀቢት -ስ- ልማድ
dress
-ስ- የመነኮሳት ል'ዩ ል'ዩ ልብስ

habitable
'ሀቢተበል -ቅ- በውስጡ ሊኖሩ'በት የ'ሚ ቻል

habitation
ሀቢ'ቴይሽን -ስ- መኖሪያ ቤት

habitual
ሀ'ቢቹውል -ቅ- የተለ'መደ፣በልማድ የተሠ'ራ

hack
'ሀክ -ግ- መቆራረጥ [ቆረ'ረጠ] ፣ መተፍ ተፍ [ተፈ'ተፈ]
horse
-ስ- ያረ'ጀ ፈረስ ፣ ጌ'ኛ፣ የ'ሚ'ከራ'ይ ፈረስ

hackneyed
'ሀክኒይድ -ቅ- የተለ'መደ ፣ ተራ (ለንግ'ግር ፣ ለጽሑፍ)

haemorrhage
'ሄመሪጅ -ስ- የደም ሥር መ'በጠስ'ና የደም በሰው'ነት መፍሰስ

haft
'ሀፍት -ስ- እ'ጀታ (የቢ'ለዋ ወዘተ)

haggard
'ሀገድ -ቅ- የጠወ'ለገ ፣ የደ'ከመው (ለሰው)

hail
'ሄይል -ግ- መ'ጣራት [ተጣ'ራ] (ሰው ሰላ ምታ ለመስጠት)
-ስ- በረዶ (የዝናብ)

hailstone
'ሄይልስተውን -ስ- በረዶ (እንደ ጠጠር)

hair
'ሄየ -ስ- ጠጉር

hairdresser
'ሄድሬስ -ስ- ጠጉር አስተካካይ ፣ ጠጉር ቆራጭ

hairy
'ሄረ -ቅ- ጠጉራም

hale
'ሄይል -ቅ- ጤና'ማ

half
'ሀ:ፍ -ስ- ግ'ማሽ ፣ እ'ኩል

hall
'ሆ:ል -ስ- አዳራሽ

hallmark
'ሆ:ልማ:ክ -ስ- የወርቅ'ነት'ና የብር'ነት ማ'ረጋገጫ ምል'ክት (እንጠራው የ'ሚጽፈው ጽሑፍ)

hallo
ሀ'ለው -ቃአ- እንደምን ነህ (ነሽ)

halo
'ሄለው -ስ- በራስ ዙሪያ የ'ሚታ'ይ የቅ ዱ ሳን ምል'ክት

halt
'ሆልት -ግ- መቆም [ቆመ] ፣ ማቆም [አቆመ]

halve
'ሀ:ቭ -ግ- ለሁለ'ት መቁረጥ [ቆረጠ] ፣ ለሁ ለ'ት መግመስ [ገ'መሰ]
-ቅ- ለሁለ'ት የተከ'ፈለ ፣ የተገ'መሰ

ham
'ሀም -ስ- በጨስ የደ'ረቀ'ና ጨው ያ'ለ'በት ያሣማ ወርች ሥጋ

hamlet
'ሀምለት -ስ- ት'ንሽ መንደር

hammer
'ሀመ -ስ- መዶሻ

hammock
'ሀመክ -ስ- በዛፍ'ና በዛፍ መካ'ከል የ'ሚን ጠለ'ጠል የ'ሚ'ተ'ኛ'በት ጨርቅ (እንደ አልጋ)

hamper
'ሀምፐ -ስ- ት'ልቅ ቅርጫት
handicap
-ግ- መግታት [ገ'ታ] ፣ እንዳይንቀሳ'ቀስ ማድረግ [አደ'ረገ]

hand
'ሀንድ -ስ- እ'ጅ

handbill
'ሀንድቢል -ስ- ለሕዝብ የ'ሚ'በ'ተን የንግድ ማስታወቂያ ወረቀት

handbook
'ሀንድቡክ -ስ- መምሪያ መጽሐፍ

handcuff
'ሀንድክፍ -ስ- የእ'ጅ እግር ብረት

handicap
'ሀንዲካፕ -ስ- እንቅፋት ፣ መሰናከል

handicraft
'ሀንዲክራ፡ፍት -ስ- የእ'ጅ ሥራ

handkerchief
'ሀንከቺፍ -ስ- መሐ'ረብ

handle
'ሀንደል -ግ- መያዝ [ያዘ] ፣ መ'ቆጣጠር መቻል [ቻለ]
-ስ- ማንጠልጠያ ፣ ጆሮ (የዕቃ)

handsome
'ሀንሰም -ቅ- ያማረ ፣ የተዋበ (ለወንድ)

handwriting
'ሀንድራይቲንግ -ስ- የእ'ጅ ጽሕፈት

handy
'ሀንዲ -ቅ- ተስማሚ ፣ ቅልጥ'ፍ ያለ (ለዕቃ)

hang
'ሀንግ -ግ- መስቀል [ሰ'ቀለ] ፣ ማንጠልጠል [አንጠለ'ጠለ]

hangar
'ሀንገ -ስ- ያውሮ'ፕላን ጋራዥ

hanger
'ሀንገ -ስ- የልብስ መስቀያ

hangman
'ሀንግመን -ስ- ሰቃይ (የተፈ'ረደ'በትን ሰው

hank
'ሀንክ -ስ- ጥ'ቅል ገመድ ፣ ጥ'ቅል ሱፍ ፣ ድ

hanker
'ሀንክ -ግ- መ'መኘት [ተመ'ኘ]

haphazard
ሀፕ'ሃዘድ -ቅ- በድንገት የሆነ፣ሳያ'ስ'ቡት የተ ደ'ረገ

happen
'ሀፐን -ግ- መሆን [ሆነ]

happiness
'ሀፒነስ -ስ- ደ'ስታ ፣ ፍ'ሥሐ

happy
'ሀፒ -ቅ- ደ'ስተ'ኛ ፣ ተደ'ሳች

harlot
'ሀ፡ለት -ስ- ሴተ'ኛ አዳሪ

harrass
'ሀረስ -ግ- በ'የጊዜው ማስፈራራት [አስፈ ራ'ራ] ፣ መነዝነዝ [ነዘ'ነዘ] ፣ ማልፋት [አለ'ፋ

harbour
'ሀ፡በ -ስ- ወደብ (የመርከብ ማቆሚያ)

hard
'ሀ፡ድ -ቅ- ጠንካ'ራ

harden
'ሀ፡ደን -ግ- ማጠንከር [አጠነ'ከረ]

hardly
'ሀ፡ድሊ -ተግ- በች'ግር ፣ በመ'ቸገር

hardship
'ሀ፡ድሺፕ -ስ- መከራ ፣ ች'ግር

hardware
'ሀ፡ድዌየ -ስ- የወጥ ቤት ቁሳቁስ (ብረታብረት)

hardy
'ሀ፡ዲ -ቅ- መከራ ቻይ ፣ ጀግና

hare
'ሄየ -ስ- ጥንቸል (የሜዳ)

harelip
'ሄየሊፕ -ስ- የተከ'ፈለ የላይ'ኛው ከንፈር

hark
'ሀ:ክ -ስ- ማ'ዳመጥ [አ'ዳ'መጠ]

harm
'ሀ:ም -ግ- መጉዳት [ጎ'ዳ]

harmonious
ሀ:'መውኒየስ -ቅ- ሲሰሙት የ'ሚያስደ'ስት ፣ ጣዕመ ዜማ ያ'ለው ፣ ስምም'ነት ያ'ለው

harness
'ሀ:ነስ -ስ- የፈረስ ዕቃ

harp
'ሀ:ፕ -ስ- በገና

harrow
'ሀረው -ስ- አፈር መከስከሻ መ'ሣሪያ (የእ ርሻ)

harsh
ሀ:ሽ '-ቅ- ሻካራ ፣ ያልተስማ'ማ I ኀይለ'ኛ (ለጠባይ)

sound

-ቅ- ሻካራ ድምፅ ፣ ጩ'ካኝ

harvest
'ሀ:ቨስት -ግ- ማምረት [አመ'ረተ] ፣ ሰብል መሰብሰብ [ሰበ'ሰበ[

-ስ- ምርት

hasp
'ሀ:ስፕ -ስ- ማጠፊያ (ለበ'ር ፣ ለሻንጣ ፣ ለሣ ጥን ወዘተ)

haste
'ሄይስት -ስ- ፍጥነት ፣ ች'ኩል'ነት ፣

-ግ- ማ'ጣደፍ [አ'ጣ'ደፈ] ፣ መቸ'ኰል [ቸ'ኰለ]

hat
'ሀት -ስ- ባርኔጣ

hatch
'ሀች -ስ- የመርከብ ክዳን (የዕቃ መጫ'ኛውን ክፍል የ'ሚከድነው)

-ግ- መፈልፈል [ፈለ'ፈለ] ፣ መ'ፈል 'ፈል [ተፈለ'ፈለ] (የዕንቁላል)

hatchet
'ሀቸት -ስ- ጥ'ልቆ ፣ ት'ንሽ መጥረቢያ

hate
'ሄይት -ግ- መጥላት [ጠ'ላ]

haughty
'ሆ:ቲ -ስ- ኩሩ ፣ ሰው ናቂ ፣ ደ'ፋር (በን ግ'ግር)

haul
'ሆ:ል -ግ- መጎ'ተት [ጎ'ተተ]

haunch
'ሆ:ንች -ስ- ዳ'ሌ

haunt
'ሆ:ንት -ግ- በርኩስ መንፈስ መ'ባረር [ተባ 'ረረ]

-ስ- ሁልጊዜ የ'ሚሄዱ'በት ቦታ ፣ ቤት

have
'ሀቭ -ግ- መ'ገናዘብ [ተገና'ዘበ] ፣ መኖር [አ'ለ]

haven
'ሄይቨን -ስ- የረ'ጋ ወደብ ፣ መ'ጠጊያ ቦታ

havoc
'ሀቨክ -ስ- ብጥ'ብጥ ፣ ሽ'ብር

hawk
'ሆ:ክ -ስ- ጭል'ፊ'ት

-ግ- ከቦታ ቦታ እ'የተዘዋ'ወሩ ዕቃ መነ'ገድ [ነ'ገደ]

hay
'ሄይ -ስ- ድርቆሽ

haystack
'ሄይስታክ -ስ- የድርቆሽ ክ'ምር

hazard
'ሀዘድ -ስ- አደጋ ፣ ዕ'ድል

hazardous
'ሀዘደስ -ቅ- አደገ'ኛ

haze
'ሄይዝ -ስ- ብርሃን የ'ሚሸ'ፍን ቀለ'ል ያለ ደ'መና ፣ ጭጋግ

he
'ሂይ -ተስ- እርሱ ፣ እርሳ'ቸው ፣ እ'ሱ ፣ እ'ሳ ቸው

head
'ሄድ -ስ- ራስ

chief

-ስ- አለቃ ፣ ሹም

headache
'ሄዴይክ -ስ- ራስ ምታት

headland
'ሄድለንድ -ስ- ወደ ባሕር ውስጥ ገባ ያለ ገደል

headlight
’ሄድላይት -ስ- የመኪና የፊት መብራት ፣ በመርከብ እናት ላይ ያ'ለ መብራት

headmaster
ሄድ’ማ፡ስተ -ስ- የትምህርት ቤት ዲሬክተር

headquarters
ሄድክ’ዎ፡ተዝ -ስ- ጠቅላይ መምሪያ (የወ'ታ'ደር) ፤ ያንድ ድር'ጅት ጠቅላይ መሥሪያ ቤት

headstrong
’ሄድስትሮንግ -ቅ- በፍ'ላጐቱ የ'ሚ'መ'ራ ፣ ች'ኮ ፤ መንቻ'ካ

headway
’ሄድዌይ -ስ- ወደፊት የመሄድ እንቅስ'ቃሴ (በተለ'ይ የመርከብ)

heal
’ሂይል -ግ- መፈ'ወስ [ፈ'ወሰ] ፤ ማዳን [አዳነ]

health
’ሄልስ -ስ- ጤና

healthy
’ሄልሲ -ቅ- ጤና'ማ

heap
’ሂይፕ -ግ- መቆ'ለል [ቆ'ለለ]
-ስ- ቁ'ልል

hear
’ሂየ -ግ- መስማት [ሰ'ማ]

hearsay
’ሂየሴይ -ስ- ወሬ (አፈ ታሪክ)

hearse
’ኸ፡ስ -ስ- የሬሳ መኪና

heart
’ሀ፡ት -ስ- ል'ብ
good-ed
-ቅ- ርኅሩኅ

heartbeat
’ሀ፡ትቢይት -ስ- የልብ ት'ርታ

heartburn
’ሀ፡ትበ፡ን -ስ- ቃር

hearten
’ሀ፡ተን -ግ- ማጽናናት [አጽና'ና] ፣ ማ'በረታታት [አ'በረታ'ታ] ፤ ማ'ደፋፈር [አ'ደፋ'ፈረ]

hearth
’ሀ፡ስ -ስ- ምድ'ጃ

heartily
’ሀ፡ተሊ -ተግ- ከል'ብ

heartless
’ሀ፡ትለስ -ቅ- ጨ'ካኝ ፤ የርኅራኄ ስ'ሜት የሌ'ለው

heat
’ሂይት -ግ- ማሞቅ [አሞቀ]
-ስ- ሙቀት

heath
’ሂይስ -ስ- የከብት ማ'ሠማሪያ ቦታ (የማ'ንም ያልሆነ)

heathen
’ሂይዘን -ቅ- አረመኔ

heave
’ሂይቭ -ግ- መጎተት [ጎ'ተተ] ፣ ማንሣት [አ ነ'ሣ] ፤ መግፋት [ገ'ፋ]

heaven
’ሄቨን -ስ- ሰማይ
religious
-ስ- መንግሥተ ሰማያት

heavy
’ሄቪ -ቅ- ከ'ባድ

hectic
’ሄክቲክ -ቅ- ሥራ የ'ማያስፈ'ታ ፣ ፋታ የ'ማ ይሰጥ ፤ የተፋ'ጠነ

hedge
’ሄጅ -ስ- በድ'ንበር ዙሪያ የ'ሚ'ገ'ኝ ተክል

heed
’ሂይድ -ግ- ማስተዋል [አስተዋለ]
-ስ- ጥን'ቃቄ ፤ ማስተዋል

heel
’ሂይል -ስ- ተረከዝ

hefty
’ሄፍቲ -ቅ- ጠፍ'ራም ፣ ከ'ባድ'ና ኀይለ'ኛ

heifer
’ሄፈ -ስ- ጊደር

height
’ሀይት -ቅ- እርዝማኔ

heighten
’ሀይተን -ግ- የበ'ለጠ ማድረግ [አደ'ረገ] ፣ ከ'ፍ ማድረግ [አደ'ረገ]

heir
’ኤየ -ስ- ወራ'ሽ (ወንድ)

heiress
’ኤየሬስ -ስ- ወራ'ሽ (ሴት)

hell
'ሄል -ስ- ሲኦል
helm
'ሄልም -ስ- የመርከብ መሪ (መ'ሣሪያ) ፤ ጥሩር
help
'ሄልፕ -ግ- መርዳት [ረ'ዳ]
helpful
'ሄልፕፉል -ቅ- ረጂ ፣ ለመርዳት የተዘጋ'ጀ
helpless
'ሄልፕለስ -ቅ- ደካማ ፣ ረ'ዳት የሌ'ለው
hem
'ሄም -ስ- የልብስ ጠርፍ ፣ የልብስ ጠርዝ (በተ ለ'ይ ታጥፎ የተሰ'ፋ)
hemisphere
'ሄመስፊየ -ስ- የዓለም አ'ጋማሽ
hemp
'ሄምፕ -ስ- አእምሮ የ'ሚያደነ'ዝዝ መድኃ ኒት የ'ሚወጣ'በት ተክል ፣ ቃ'ጫ የ'ሚወ ጣ'በት ተክል
hen
'ሄን -ስ- ዶሮ
hence
'ሄንስ -ተግ- ስለ'ዚህ ፡ ከ'ዚህ የተነ'ሣ
her
'ኸ: -ተስ- እርሷ ፣ የርሷ
herald
'ሄረልድ -ስ- የንጉሥ መልእክተ'ኛ ፡ በዋጅ ነጋሪ
herb
'ኸ:ብ -ስ- የሚ'በ'ላ ቅጠላቅጠል ፣ የምግብ ማጣፈጫ ተክል
herd
'ኸ:ድ -ስ- መንጋ
herdsman
'ኸ:ድዝመን -ስ- ከብት አ'ጋጅ ፣ ከብት ጠ'ባቂ
here
'ሂየ -ተግ- እ'ዚህ
hereafter
ሂየ'ራ:ፍተ -ተግ- ከ'ዚህ በላይ ፡ ከእንግዲህ ወዲህ ፡ ወደፊት
hereby
ሂየ'ባይ -ተግ- በ'ዚህ
hereditary
ኸ'ረዲትረ -ቅ- የተወ'ረሰ (ጠባይ ወዘተ)
heresy
'ሄረሲ -ስ- ጥር'ጣሬ (የሃይማኖት) ፤ ሐራጥ ቃ'ነት
herewith
ሂየ'ዊዝ -ተግ- ከ'ዚህ ጋር
heritage
'ሄሪተጅ -ስ- ከ'ባቶ'ች የተወ'ረሰ ነገር
hermit
'ኸ:ሚት -ስ- ባሕታዊ
hermaphrodite
ኸ'ማፍሮዳይት -ስ- ፍናፍንት
hernia
'ኸ:ኒያ -ስ- እበጥ (የሆድ)
hero
'ሂረው -ቅ- ጀግና (ለወንድ)
heroine
'ሄረዊን -ቅ- ጀግና (ለሴት)
heroism
'ሄረዊዝም -ስ- ጀግን'ነት
herself
ኸ'ሴልፍ -ተስ- እርሷ እራሷ ፣ እ'ሷ ራሷ
hesitate
'ሄዘቴይት -ግ- መ'ጠራጠር [ተጠራ'ጠረ] ፈ'ራ ተ'ባ ማለት [አለ]
hew
ሀ'ዩው -ግ- መፈልፈል [ፈለ'ፈለ] ፡ መጥረብ [ጠ'ረበ] (ለድ'ንጋይ)
hibernate
'ሃይበኔይት -ግ- ማንቀላፋት [አንቀላ'ፋ] (የክ ረምትን ጊዜ ፡ ለእንቁራሪት ወዘተ)
hidden
'ሂድን -ቅ- የተሸ'ሸገ ፡ የተደ'በቀ
hide
'ሀይድ -ግ- መደ'በቅ [ደ'በቀ]
hideous
'ሂዲየስ -ቅ- መልከ ጥፉ ፡ ማስጠ'ሎ ፡ አስቀ 'ያሚ
high
'ሀይ -ቅ- ከ'ፍ ያለ
highly
'ሀይሊ -ተግ- በት'ልቁ ፡ በብዙው
highness
'ሀይነስ -ስ- ልዑል'ነት

highway
'ሀይዌይ -ስ- አውራ ጎዳና
hike
'ሃይክ -ግ- በግር ረ'ጅም መንገድ መንሸራሸር [ተንሸራ'ሸረ]
hilarious
ሂ'ሌሪየስ -ቅ- በጣም አስደ'ሳች [ጊዜ] ፣ ሣቅ'ና ደ'ስታ የሞ'ላ'በት ፦
hilarity
'ሂላሪቲ -ስ- ደ'ስታ
hill
'ሂል -ስ- ዐቀበት ፣ ኮረብታ
hillock
'ሂለክ -ስ- ጉ'ብታ ፣ ት'ንሽ ኮረብታ
hilt
'ሂልት -ስ- የጐራዴ ፣ የጩቤ እ'ጀታ
him
'ሂም -ተስ- እርሱን ፣ እ'ሱን
himself
ሂም'ሴልፍ -ተስ- እርሱ ራሱ ፣ እ'ሱ ራሱ
hind
'ሀይንድ -ስ- ኋላ (ጀርባ)
hinder
'ሂንደ -ግ- ማ'ወክ [አ'ወከ] ፣ መከልከል [ከለ'ከለ]
hindrance
'ሂንድረንስ -ስ- እንቅፋት ፣ መሰናክል
hinge
'ሂንጅ -ስ- ማጠፊያ (የበ'ር ፣ የመስኮት ወዘተ)
hint
'ሂንት -ስ- አ'ጭር ጠቋሚ ምክር
hip
'ሂፕ -ስ- ዳ'ሌ
hippopotamus
ሂፐ'ፖተመስ -ስ- ጉማ'ሬ
hire
'ሀየ -ግ- መ'ከራየት [ተከራ'የ]
employ
-ግ- መቅጠር [ቀ'ጠረ]
hireling
'ሀየሊንግ -ስ- በገንዘብ የተቀ'ጠረ ሞያተ'ኛ ፣ ለገንዘብ ሲል የ'ሚ'ዋ'ጋ ወ'ታ'ደር
his
'ሂዝ -ተስ- የርሱ ፣ የ'ሱ
hiss
'ሂስ -ስ- እ'ስ ማለት (እንደ እባብ) ፣ አለመስማማትን ለመግለጽ "እ'ስ" ማለት
historian
ሂስ'ቶ:ሪየን -ቅ- ባለታሪክ ፣ ታሪክ ዐዋቂ ፣ ታሪክ ጸሓፊ ፣ የታሪክ ሊቅ
historic
ሂስ'ቶሪክ -ቅ- ታሪካዊ
history
'ሂስተሪ -ስ- ታሪክ
hit
'ሂት -ግ- መምታት [መ'ታ]
hitch
'ሂች -ግ- አንድ ነገር ላይ ማሰር [አ'ሰረ] ፣ ወደ ላይ ከ'ፍ ማድረግ [አደ'ረገ]
hitherto
ሂዘ'ቱ: -ተግ- እስካሁን ድረስ
hive
'ሀይቭ -ስ- የንብ ቀፎ
hoard
'ሆ:ድ -ግ- ማ'ከማቸት [አ'ከማ'ቸ] ፣ ማድለብ [አደ'ለበ] (ገንዘብ ፣ ምግብ ወዘተ)
hoarse
'ሆ:ስ -ቅ- ጎርና'ና (ለድምፅ)
hoax
'ሆውክስ -ስ- ማሞ'ኘት (በቀልድ'ና በጨዋታ)
hobble
'ሆበል -ግ- እያነ'ከሱ በዝ'ግታ መ'ራመድ [ተራ'መደ] ፣ መቀ'የድ [ቀ'የደ]
hobby
'ሆቢ -ስ- የትርፍ ጊዜ ሥራ (ገንዘብ የ'ማይ'ከ'ፈሉ'በት ለመ'ደሰት ፣ የ'ሚሠሩት ሥራ)
hoe
'ሆው -ስ- መኰትኰቻ
hog
'ሆግ -ስ- የተኰላ'ሸ ዐሣማ (ለእርድ የ'ሚ'ቀ'ለብ)
hoist
'ሆይስት -ስ- እየተንገዳ'ገዱ ማንሣት [አነ'ሣ]
hold
'ሆውልድ -ግ- መያዝ [ያዘ]
holder
'ሆውልደ -ስ- መያዣ

hole
'ሆውል -ስ- ቀዳዳ ፣ ሽንቁር

holiday
'ሆለዴይ -ስ- በዓል ፣ የዕረፍት ቀን ፣ ሀውደ ዓመት

hollow
'ሆለው -ቅ- ውስጡ ባዶ የሆነ ፣ ቡርቡር

holy
'ኸውሊ -ቅ- ቅ'ዱስ.

homage
'ሆመጅ -ስ- አክብሮት ፣ የበታ'ች'ነትን ፣ ታ'ዛ ዥ'ነትን መግለጽ

home
'ኸውም -ስ- መኖሪያ ቤት ፣ የተወ'ለ'ዱበት ቦታ ፣ የትውል'ድ አገር

homeless
'ኸውምለስ -ቅ- ቤት የሌ'ለው

homely
'ኸውምሊ -ቅ- እንግዳ ተቀ'ባይ ፣ ብሩኸ ገ'ጽ

homesick
'ኸውምሲክ -ቅ- አገሩ የና'ፈቀው

homespun
'ኸውምስፐን -ቅ- እቤት የተፈ'ተለ ፣ ተራ ፣ ግልጽ
-ስ- እቤት የተፈ'ተለ ጨርቅ

homestead
'ኸውምስተድ -ስ- ባለቤቱ የ'ሚያርሰው እር ስት ፣ በርሻ ቦታ ላይ ያ'ለ የመኖርያ ቤት

homicide
'ሆመሳይድ -ስ- ያንድ ሰው በሌላ መ'ገደል ፣ ነፍስ ግ'ዳይ

homogenous
ኸ'ሞጀነስ -ቅ- ተመሳሳይ ፣ ከመጀ'መሪያ እስከ መጨ'ረሻ አንድ ዓይነት የሆነ

honest
'ኦነስት -ቅ- ታ'ማኝ ፣ እውነተ'ኛ

honey
'ሀኒ -ስ- ማር

honeycomb
'ሀኒከውም -ስ- የማር እሸት

honeymoon
'ሀኒሙ:ን -ስ- የጫጉላ ጊዜ ፣ የመ'ሞሸሪያ ጊዜ (ጉዞ ወደሌላ አገር ፣ ከተማ)

honorary
'ኦነረሪ -ቅ- የ'ማይ'ከ'ፈለው (ያንድ ድር'ጅት አባል) ፣ የክብር አባል ወዘተ

honour
'ኦነ -ግ- ማክበር [አከ'በረ]
-ስ- ክብር

honourable
'ኦነረበል -ቅ- የተከ'በረ ፣ ክቡር

hood
'ሁድ -ስ- ከልብስ ጋር የተያያዘ ሾጣጣ ቆብ

hoodwink
'ሁድዊንክ -ግ- ማ'ታለል [አ'ታ'ለለ] ፣ ማ'ሳ ሳት [አ'ሳሳተ] ፣ ዓይን መሸ'ፈን [ሸ'ፈነ] (የፈ ረስ)

hoof
'ሁ:ፍ -ስ- ኮ'ቴ (እግር)

hook
'ሁክ . -ስ- ሜንጦ

hooligan
'ሁ:ሊገን -ስ- አ'ሸ'ባሪ ፣ በጥባጭ ፣ ወ'ሮበ'ላ

hoop
'ሁ:ፕ -ስ- ክ'ብ ነገር (የብረት ፣ የእንጨት)

hoot
'ሁ:ት -ስ- የክላክስ ድምፅ ፣ የመኪና ጡሩምባ ድምፅ

hooter
'ሁ:ተ -ስ- ክላክስ (የመኪና ጡሩም'ባ)

hop
'ሆፕ -ግ- ባንድ እግር እ'የዘ'ለሉ መሄድ [ሄደ] ፣ እንጣ'ጥ እንጣ'ጥ ማለት [አለ]

hope
'ኸውፕ -ግ- መ'መኘት [ተመ'ኘ] ፣ ተስፋ ማድረግ [አደ'ረገ]
-ስ- ም'ኞት ፣ ተስፋ

hopeful
'ኸውፕፉል -ቅ- ባለም'ኞት ፣ ሙሉ ም'ኞት ያ'ለው ፣ ባለተስፋ.

hopeless
'ኸውፕለስ -ቅ- ዋጋ ቢስ ፣ ተስፋ ቢስ ፣ መድ ኅን የሌ'ለው

horde
'ሆ:ድ -ስ- መንጋ ፣ መዐት (ም'ሳሌ ፣ የወ'ታ 'ደር መዐት)

horizon
ኸ'ራይዘን -ስ- አድማስ

horizontal
ሆረ'ዞንተል -ቅ- አግድም ፣ ገድሞሽ
horn
'ሆ:ን -ስ- ቀንድ
trumpet
-ስ- ቀንደ መለከት
car-
-ስ- ክላክስ
hornet
'ሆ:ነት -ስ- ተርብ
horrible
'ሆረበል -ቅ- አስፈ'ሪ ፣ አስደንጋጭ
horror
'ሆረ -ስ- ፍርሃት ፣ ድን'ጋጤ ፣ መ'ጸየፍ
horse
'ሆ:ስ -ስ- ፈረስ
horsecloth
'ሆ:ስክሎስ -ስ- ቀሚስ (የፈረስ)
horseman
'ሆ:ስመን -ስ- ፈረሰ'ኛ
horseradish
'ሆ:ስራዲሽ -ስ- ፍጅል
horseshoe
'ሆ:ሹ -ስ- የፈረስ ጫ'ማ
horticulture
'ሆ:ቲ:ከልቸ -ስ- ያበባ መትከል ሞያ ፣ ያትክ ልት ቦታ አ'ያያዝ
hose
'ኸውዝ -ስ- ያትክልት ማጠጫ ጉ'ማ ፣ ሸራ ፣ ፕላስቲክ (ቀ'ጭን ረጅ'ም ውስጡ ባዶ የሆነ ፣ የቧምቧ ዓይነት)
hospitable
ሆስ'ፒተበል -ቅ- እንግዳ ተቀ'ባይ
hospital
'ሆስፒተል -ስ- የሐኪም ቤት ፣ ሆስፒታል
hospitality
ሆስፒ'ታለቲ -ስ- እንግዳ ተቀ'ባይ'ነት
host
'ኸውስት -ስ- አስተናጋጅ ፣ እንግዳ ተቀ'ባይ (ወንድ) ፣ የሰው መዓት (ብዙ ሰው)
host
'ኸውስት -ስ- ኅብስት (ለሥጋ ወደሙ የ'ሚ ቀርብ) ፣ አ'ኮቴት
hostage
'ሆስቲጅ -ስ- መያዣ የ'ሚሆን የጦር እስረ'ኛ
hostel
'ሆስተል -ስ- ዘል'ዩ ድር'ጅት የ'ሚ'ሠ'ራ መኖርያ ቤት (የተማሪዎ'ች ፣ የሠ'ራተ'ኞ'ች ወዘተ)
hostess
'ሀውስተስ -ስ- እንግዳ ተቀ'ባይ (ሴት) ፣ ሴት አስተናጋጅ
hostile
'ሆስታይል -ቅ- ጠላት'ነት የ'ሚያሳይ ፣ የጠ ላት
hostility
ሆስ'ቲሊቲ -ስ- ጠላት'ነት
hot
'ሆት -ቅ- ሙቅ
hotel
ሀው'ቴል -ስ- ሆቴል
hound
'ሀውንድ -ስ- ው'ሻ (በተለ'ይ የአደን ፣ የሽቅ ድ'ድም)
hour
'አወ -ስ- ሰዓት ፣ ጊዜ
hourly
'አወሊ -ተግ- በ'የሰዓቱ (የተደ'ረገ ፣ የሆነ)
house
'ሀውስ -ስ- ቤት
household
'ሀውስ'ሆውልድ -ስ- ቤተሰብ
housekeeper
'ሀውስኪፐ -ስ- ገረድ (በዕድሜ የገ'ፋ'ች)
housemaid
'ሀውስሜይድ -ስ- ገረድ (በዕድሜ አነ'ስ ያለ'ች)
hovel
'ሆቨል -ስ- መና'ኛ ት'ን'ሽ ጎ'ጆ
hover
'ሆቨ -ግ- ማንዣበብ [አንዣ'በበ]
how
'ሀው -ተግ- እንዴት
however
ሀ'ዌቨ -ተግ- ቢሆን'ም ፣ ይሁን'ና ፣ በምን'ም ሁናቴ ፣ በምን'ም መንገድ

howl
'ሀውል -ግ- በከ'ፍተ'ኛ ድምፅ መጮኸ [ጮኸ] (ለው'ሻ ፣ ለቀበሮ)

hub
'ኸብ -ስ- የመንኰራኩር መካ'ከል ክፍል

hubbub
'ኸበብ -ስ- ዋካታ

huddle
'ኸደል -ግ- መ'ታፈግ [ታ'ፈገ] (እንደበግ) ፣ መ'ሸጋሸግ [ተሸጋ'ሸገ] (ለሙቀት)

hue
ሀ'ዩው -ስ- ቀለም ፣ መልክ (ቀ'ይ ፣ አረንጓዴ ፣ ብጫ'ና ፣ ሰማያዊ)

hug
'ኸግ -ግ- ማቀፍ [አ'ቀፈ]

huge
ሀ'ዩጅ -ቅ- በጣም ት'ልቅ

hum
'ኸም -ስ- ድምፅ (አፍን ዘግቶ የ'ሚ'ሰ'ማ) ሀ'ምታ ፣ ማንጐራጎር (ዘፈን)

human
ሀ'ዩ:መን -ቅ- ሰብአዊ
-ስ- ሰው

humane
ሀዩ'ሜይን -ቅ- ርኅሩኅ ፣ ሰብአዊ

humanity
ሀዩ'ማኒቲ -ስ- ሰብአዊ'ነት ፣ የሰው ልጅ ፣ ርኅራኄ

humble
'ኸምበል -ቅ- ትሑት

humdrum
'ኸምድረም -ቅ- አሰልቺ ፣ ተራ ፣ ትርኪምርኪ

humid
ሀ'ዩ:ሚድ -ቅ- እርጥብ

humidity
ሀዩ'ሚደቲ -ስ- እርጥበት

humiliate
ሀዩ'ሚሊዬይት -ግ- ማ'ዋረድ [አ'ዋ'ረደ] ማሳ'ፈር [አሳ'ፈረ]

humility
ሀዩ'ሚለቲ -ስ- ትሕት'ና

hummock
'ኸመክ -ስ- ት'ንሽ ጉ'ብታ

humour
ሀ'ዩመ -ስ- ሣቅ ፣ ቀልድ ፣ ቧልት

humourous
ሀ'ዩመረስ -ቅ- ሣ'ቂተ'ኛ ፣ ቀልደ'ኛ ፣ ቧል ተ'ኛ ፣ አ'ሥቂ'ኝ

hump
'ኸምፕ -ስ- ሻ'ኛ (የግመል ወዘተ)

humpback
'ኸምፕባክ -ስ- እጀርባው ላይ ጉ'በታ ያ'ለ'በት ሰው

hunch
'ኸንች -ግ- ሰው'ነትን ሽም'ቅቅ ማድረግ [አደ'ረገ] (ከብርድ የተነ'ሣ)
-ስ- ጥር'ጣሬ

hunchback
'ኸንችባክ -ስ- እጀርባው ላይ ጉ'ብታ ያ'ለ'በት ሰው

hundred
'ኸንድረድ -ቅ- መቶ

hundredth
'ኸንድረድስ -ቅ- መ'ቶኛ

hunger
'ኸንገ - ስ- ረኀብ

hungry
'ኸንግሪ -ቅ- ረኀብተ'ኛ ፣ የራበው

hunt
'ኸ:ንት -ግ- ማ'ደን [አ'ደነ]

hunter
'ኸንተ -ስ- አዳ'ኝ

hurl
'ኸ:ል -ግ- በኀይል መወርወር [ወረ'ወረ] ፣ በኀይል መ'ናገር [ተና'ገረ]

hurricane
'ሐሪከን -ስ- በጣም ኀይለ'ኛ ነፋስ (በሰዓት ከ፸፭ ኪ. ሜ በላይ ፍጥነት ያ'ለው)

hurry
'ኸሪ -ግ- መፍጠን [ፈ'ጠነ]

hurt
'ኸ:ት -ግ- መጉዳት [ጎ'ዳ] ፣ ማቁሰል [አቆ'ሰለ]

husband
'ኸዝበንድ -ስ- ባል ፣ ባለቤት (ተባዕት)

hush
'ኸሽ -ስ- ፀ'ጥታ ፣ (ትእዛዝ ፣ ፀ'ጥ በል)

husk
'ኸስክ -ስ- ሽፋን (የእህል) ፣ ልጣጭ (የፍራ ፍሬ)

husky
'ሀስኪ -ቅ- ወፍራም ጠንካ'ራ (ለሰው)
voice
-ቅ- ወፍራም ድምፅ

hustle
'ሀሰል -ግ- በፍጥነት መሄድ [ሄደ]

hut
'ሀት -ስ- ጎጆ

hutch
'ሀች -ስ- የትን'ንሽ እንስሳት ማስቀ'መጫ ሣጥን (ባንድ በ'ኩል የሽቦ ወንፊት ያ'ለ'በት)

hybrid
'ሀይብሪድ -ስ- ክ'ልስ (ለእንስሳት ፣ ለእትክ ልት)

hydrophobia
'ሀይድረ'ፎውቢየ -ስ- የው'ሻ በ'ሽታ ፣ ውሃ የ'ማያስጠ'ማ ፣ ውሃ የ'ሚያስፈ'ራ በ'ሽታ

hyena
'ሀይነ -ስ- ጅብ

hygiene
ሀይ'ጂይን -ስ- የጤና አ'ጠባበቅ ትምህርት ፣ የንጽሕ'ና መሠረታዊ ልምዶ'ች ፣ ንጽሕ'ና

hygienic
ሀይ'ጂይኒክ -ቅ- ጤና'ማ ፣ ንጹሕ ፣ ለጤና አ'ጠባበቅ ተስማሚ

hymn
'ሂም -ስ- መዝሙር (መንፈሳዊ) ፣ ማሕሌት

hyphen
'ሃይፈን -ስ- አግድም ሠረዝ (—)

hypnotise
'ሂፕነታይዝ -ግ- ማደንዘዝ [አደነ'ዘዘ] ፣ እእ ምሮ መሰ'ወር [ሰ'ወረ] ፣ ማፍዘዝ [አፈ'ዘዘ]

hypocrisy
ሂ'ፖክረሲ -ስ- ግ'ብዝ'ነት ፣ መ'መጻደቅ

hypocrite
'ሂፖክሪት -ቅ- ግ'ብዝ ፣ ተመጻዳቂ

hypothesis
ሃይ'ፖፀሲስ -ስ- መላ ምት ፣ የምናልባት ሐ'ሳብ

hysterical
ሂስ'ቴሪክል -ቅ- አንድ ነገር አእምሮውን ያ'ና'ወጠው ፣ ግ'ልፍተ'ኛ

ib.s
'አይቢስ -ስ- ጋጋኖ

ice
'አይስ -ስ- በረዶ (የረ'ጋ ውሃ)

ice cream
አይስክሬይም -ስ- አይስ ክሬም ጂላ'ቲ (ከበረዶ የተሠ'ራ ጣፋጭ ምግብ)

icy
'አይሲ -ቅ- በጣም ብርዳም

idea
አይ'ዲየ -ስ- ሐ'ሳብ

ideal
አይ'ዲየል -ቅ- የ'ሚስማ'ማ ፣ ፍ'ጹም የሆነ ፣ እንከን የሌ'ለ'በት

identical
አይ'ዴንተክል -ቅ- ተመሳሳይ ፣ በምን'ም ሁናቴ ል'ዩ'ነት የ'ማያሳ'ይ

identify
አይ'ዴንተፋይ -ግ- ለ'ይቶ ማወቅ [ዐ'ወቀ]

identity
አይ'ዴንተቲ -ስ- መ'ታወቂያ

idiom
'ኢድየም -ስ- ያ'ነጋገር ዘዩ ፣ ያ'ነባበር መን ገድ (ያገድ ቋንቋ)

idiot
'ኢድየት -ስ- ደ'ደብ ሰው

idiotic
ኢድ'ዮቲክ -ቅ- ደንቆሮ ፣ ደ'ደብ

idle
'አይደል -ቅ- ሥራ ፈ'ት ፤ ሰነፍ ፤ እሥራ ላይ ያልዋለ
idleness
'አይደልነስ -ስ- ሥራ ፈ'ት'ነት
idol
'አይደል -ስ- ጣኦት
idolize
'አይደላይዝ -ግ- ከ'ሚ'ገ'ባው በላይ መውደድ ፤ ግድነት'ና ክብር መስጠት [ሰ'ጠ]
if
'ኢፍ -መ፤- በ... ፤ ከ ፤ ...
ignite
ኢግ'ናይት -ግ- መለ'ኰስ [ለ'ኰሰ] ፤ ማ'ቃጠል [አ'ቃ'ጠለ]
ignition
ኢግ'ኒሽን -ስ- መለ'ኮስ ፤ ማ'ቃጠል
engine
-ስ- ሞቶር ማስነ'ሻ
ignoble
ኢግ'ነውበል -ቅ- ወ'ራ'ዳ ፤ ክብር የሌ'ለው
ignominy
'ኢግነመኒ -ስ- ውርደት (በሕዝብ መካ'ከል) ፤ የ'ሚያሳ'ፍር ሥራ
ignorance
'ኢግነረንስ -ስ- ድንቁር'ና ፤ አለማወቅ
ignorant
'ኢግነረንት -ቅ- ደንቆሮ ፤ አላዋቂ
ignore
ኢግ'ኖ: -ግ- 'ቸል ማለት [አለ]
ill
'ኢል -ግ- መ'ታመም [ታ'መመ]
illegal
ኢ'ሊይገል -ቅ- ሕ'ገ ወ'ጥ
illegible
ኢ'ሌጀበል -ቅ- የ'ማይ'ነ'በብ
illegitimate
ኢለ'ጂተመት -ቅ- ዲቃላ ፤ ሕ'ጋዊ ያልሆነ
illicit
ኢ'ሊሲት -ቅ- ሕ'ጋዊ ያልሆነ ፤ የ'ማይ'ፈ'ቀድ
illiteracy
ኢ'ሊተረሲ -ስ- ማንበብ'ና መጻፍ አለመቻል
illiterate
ኢ'ሊተረት -ቅ- ማንበብ'ና መጻፍ የ'ማይችል

illness
'ኢልነስ -ስ- ሕመም ፤ በ'ሽታ
ill-tempered
ኢል'ቴምፐድ -ቅ- የ'ማይ'ታ'ገሥ ፤ በቶ'ሎ የ'ሚ'ቆ'ጣ ፤ ግ'ልፍተ'ኛ
illuminate
ኢል'ዩ:መኔይት -ግ- ማብራት [አበ'ራ]
illusion
ኢ'ሉ:ዠን -ስ- ለዓይን የ'ሚመስል ነገር (ነገር ግን እውነት ያልሆነ) ፤ ምትሀት
illustrate
'ኢለስትሬይት -ግ- በሥዕላ ሥዕል ማስጌጥ [አስጌጠ] (ለመጽሐፍ)
use examples
-ግ- በም'ሳሌ ማስረ'ዳት [አስረ'ዳ]
illustration
ኢለስት'ሬይሽን -ስ- ሥዕል
example
-ስ- ም'ሳሌ
illustrious
ኢ'ለስትሪየስ -ቅ- ዝ'ነ'ኛ ፤ የታ'ወቀ ፤ ስሙጥር
image
'ኢመጅ -ስ- ቅርፅ ፤ ምስል
imaginary
ኢ'ማጀንሪ -ቅ- ሐ'ሳባዊ ፤ የ'ሚያ'ስቡት ነገር ግን እውነት ያልሆነ
imagination
ኢማጀ'ኔይሽን -ስ- ሐ'ሳብ ፤ ግ'ምት
imagine
ኢ'ማጀን -ግ- ማ'ሰብ [አ'ሰበ] ፤ ሊሆ ይችላል ብሎ መገ'መት [ገ'መተ]
imbecile
'ኢምበሲይል -ቅ- ነሁላ'ላ ፤ ደንቆሮ ፤ አእምሮ ደካማ
imbibe
ኢም'ባይብ -ግ- መጠ'ጣት [ጠ'ጣ] ፤ መቅሰም [ቀ'ሰመ] (ሐ'ሳብ)
imitate
'ኢመቴይት -ግ- አስመ'ስሎ መሥራት [ሠ ራ]
imitation
ኢመ'ቴይሽን -ስ- ማስመ'ሰል ፤ አምሳ'ያ
immaculate
ኢ'ማከዩለት -ቅ- ንጹሕ ፤ ያላ'ደፈ ፤ ጢእት ያልሠ'ራ ፤ ያልተበ'ከለ

immaterial

ኢመ'ቲሪየል -ቅ- አግባብ የሌ'ለው ፣ ከነገር ው'ጭ የሆነ ፣ አስፈ'ላጊ ያልሆነ

immature

ኢመ'ቺወ -ቅ- ያልበ'ሰለ (ለሰው)

immediate

ኢ'ሚይዲየት -ቅ- የአሁን ፣ በመካ'ከል ያል ተቋ'ረጠ ፣ ወዲያው

immemorial

ኢመ'ሞ:ሪየል -ቅ- የ'ማያስታ'ውሱት ፣ የጥ ንት ፣ የቀድሞ (ጊዜ)

immense

ኢ'ሜንስ -ቅ- ት'ልቅ ፣ በጣም ሰ'ፊ

immerse

ኢ'መ:ስ -ግ- መዝፈቅ [ዘ'ፈቀ] ፣ ማጥመቅ [አጠ'መቀ]

immersion

ኢ'መ:ሽን -ስ- ዝፍቀት ፣ ጥምቀት

immigrate

'ኢመግሬይት -ስ- ለመኖር አንድ አገር ውስጥ መግባት [ገ'ባ] (የራስን አገር ለ'ቆ)

immigration

ኢመግ'ሬይሽን -ስ- ፍልሰት ፣ አገር ለ'ቆ መሄድ (በሌላ አገር ለመኖር)

imminent

'ኢመነንት -ቅ- በቅርብ ጊዜ የ'ሚሆን፣መሆኑ የ'ማይቀር (በተለ'ይ ለአደጋ)

immobile

ኢ'መውባይል -ቅ- የ'ማይንቀሳ'ቀስ ፣ አንድ ቦታ ላይ የጸ'ና

immodest

ኢ'ሞደስት -ቅ- ደ'ፋር ፣ ዓይን አውጣ

immoral

ኢ'ሞረል -ቅ- ግብረ ገ'ብ'ነት የሌ'ለው ፣ ወ 'ራ'ዳ

immorality

ኢመ'ራለቲ -ስ- ግብረ ገ'ብ'ነት የሌ'ለው መ ሆን

immortal

ኢ'ሞ:ተል -ቅ- ሕያው ፣ ዘለዓለም ነዋሪ

immovable

ኢ'ሙቨበል -ቅ- የ'ማይንቀሳ'ቀስ ፣ አንድ ቦታ ላይ ቀዋሚ የሆነ

immune

ኢም'ዩ:ን -ቅ- ምን'ም ነገር የ'ማይነካው (በ'ሽታ)

imp

'ኢምፕ -ስ- ት'ንሽ ሠይጣን (ብዙ የ'ማይ ጐዳ) ፣ ቅልብልብ ልጅ

impact

'ኢምፓክት -ስ- ግ'ጭት

influence

-ስ- ተጽእኖ

impair

ኢም'ፔየ -ግ- ማድከም [አደ'ከመ] ፣ ዋጋ መቀ'ነስ [ቀ'ነሰ] ፣ መጉዳት [ጐ'ዳ]

impart

ኢም'ፓ:ት -ግ- ማ'ካፈል [አ'ካፈለ] ፣ መስ ጠት [ሰ'ጠ] (ለምክር ፣ ለዕውቀት)

impartial

ኢም'ፓ:ሸል -ቅ- የ'ማያ'ዳ'ላ ፣ አንዱን ወገን ከሌላው አብልጦ የ'ማያይ

impassable

ኢም'ፓ:ሰበል -ቅ- ሊ'ሻ'ገሩት የ'ማይ'ቻል ፣ ሊሄዱ'በት የ'ማያስችል (መንገድ ወዘተ)

impasse

'ኢፓስ -ስ- መውጫ መንገድ የሌ'ለ'በት ቦታ፣ ሁናቴ

impatience

ኢ'ፒይሸንስ -ስ- አለመ'ታገሥ ፣ መ'ቆጣት ፣ መ'ጣደ'ፍ

impeach

ኢም'ፒይች -ግ- መክሰስ [ከ'ሰሰ] (በታ'ላቅ ወንጀል) ፣ የጥር'ጣሬ ጥ'ያቄ መጠየ'ቅ [ጠ'የቀ] (ስለሰው ጠባይ ወዘተ)

impeccable

ኢም'ፒ:ሰበል -ቅ- ስሕተት የሌ'ለ'በት ፣ ጉድ ለት የ'ሌ'ለ'በት ፣ ኃጢአት የ'ማይሠራ

impede

ኢም'ፒይድ -ግ- ማ'ደናቀፍ [አ'ደና'ቀፈ] መከልከል [ከለ'ከለ]

impediment

ኢም'ፔደመንት -ስ- እንቅፋት

speech

-ስ- ያ'ነጋገር ጉድለት (ም'ባሌ ፡ መ'ን ፋነፍ)

impending
ኢም'ፔንዲንግ -ቅ- በቅርብ ጊዜ ይሆናል ተብሎ የ'ሚያ'ሠ'ጋ

impenetrable
ኢም'ፔነትረበል -ቅ- ሲገቡበት የ'ማይ'ቻል (ደ'ን ወዘተ)

impenitent
ኢም'ፔኒተንት -ቅ- ን'ስሐ የ'ማይገባ ፣ የ'ማ ያርመው

imperative
ኢም'ፔረቲቭ -ቅ- አ'ዛዥ ፣ ትእዛዝ ሰጪ

imperceptible
ኢምፐ'ሴፕተበል -ቅ- ባይን የ'ማይ'ታይ

imperfect
ኢም'ፐ፡ፊክት -ቅ- ፍ'ጹም ያልሆነ ፣ ጉድለት ያ'ለ'በት

imperial
ኢም'ፒሪየል -ቅ- ንጉሠ ነገሥታዊ

imperil
ኢም'ፔረል -ግ- አደጋ ላይ መጣል [ጣለ]

imperishable
ኢም'ፔሪሸበል -ቅ- የ'ማይሞት ፣ የ'ማይጠፋ

impermeable
ኢም'ፐ፡ሚየበል -ቅ- ዝናብ የ'ማያስገ'ባ (የዝናብ ልብስ ዓይነት)

impersonal
ኢም'ፐ፡ሰነል -ቅ- የ'ማያ'ዳ'ላ ፣ የተ'ለየ ሰውን የ'ማይነካ

impersonate
ኢም'ፐ፡ሰኔይት -ግ- ሌላ ሰው መ'መሰል [ተመ'ሰለ] (ለማ'ታለል ወይን'ም ለቧልት)

impertinence
ኢም'ፐ፡ቲነንስ -ስ- አስቸ'ጋሪ'ነት ፣ አ'ዋኪ'ነት (በንግ'ግር) ፣ ብልግ'ና

imperturbable
ኢምፐ'ተ፡በበል -ቅ- ለማ'ን'ኛው'ም ነገር ደ ንታ የሌ'ለው ፣ የ'ማይ'ጨ'ነቅ

impervious
ኢም'ፐ፡ቪየስ -ቅ- ውሃ የ'ማይገባው

impetuous
ኢም'ፔትዩወስ -ቅ- ሳያ'ስብ በኀይል የ'ሚ ሠራ ፣ ች'ኩል ፣ በፍጥነት የታ'ሰበ ፣ የተሠ'ራ ፣ በኀይል የ'ሚንቀሳ'ቀስ

impiety
ኢም'ፓየቲ -ስ- ሃይማኖት ተቃዋሚ'ነት ፣ ምግባረ ቢስ'ነት ፣ እግዚአብሔርን አለመፍ ራት

implacable
ኢመፐ'ላከበል -ቅ- ሐ'ሳቡን የ'ማይለ'ውጥ፣ ች'ኮ ፣ መንቻ'ካ ፣ በጥላ'ቻ የተሞ'ላ

implement
'ኢምፐ'ለመንት -ስ- መ'ሣሪያ

implicate
'ኢምፕለኬይት -ግ- አንድ ሰው የጥፋት ተካ ፋይ መሆኑን ማሳ'የት [አሳ'የ]

implication
ኢምፐለ'ኬይሽን -ስ- እውነተ'ኛ ፍርድ ፣ ሌላ ውን ጥፋተ'ኛ ማድረግ

implicit
ኢምፐ'ሊሲት -ቅ- ሳይ'ነገር የታ'ወቀ ፣ መጠ 'የቅ የ'ማያስፈ'ልገው

implore
ኢምፐ'ሎ፡ -ግ- መለ'መን [ለ'መነ] ፣ መ'ለማ መጥ [ተለማ'መጠ]

imply
ኢምፐ'ላይ -ግ- ሐ'ሳብ ማቅረብ [አቀ'ረበ]

impolite
ኢምፐ'ላይት -ቅ- ያልተቀ'ጣ ፣ ያልታ'ረመ

import
ኢም'ፖ፡ት -ግ- ማስመ'ጣት [አስመ'ጣ] (ሸቀጣ ሸቀጥ ከው'ጭ አገር)
'ኢምፖት -ስ- ጠቅላ'ላ ሐ'ሳብ ፣ ትርጉም

importance
ኢም'ፖ፡ተንስ -ስ- ዋጋ (ላንድ ነገር) ፣ አስፈ 'ላጊ'ነት

impose
ኢም'ፐውዝ -ግ- መጫን [ጫነ] (ቀረጥ ወዘተ)፣ ማስቀ'መጥ [አስቀ'መጠ] ፣ እንዲ'ቀ'በሉ ማስ ገ'ደድ [አስገ'ደደ] (ሕ'ግን ወዘተ)

imposing
ኢም'ፐውዚንግ -ቅ- አስደ'ናቂ (በመጠኑ ፣ በጠባዩ ፣ በመልኩ፣ ምክንያት)

imposition
ኢምፐ'ዚሽን -ስ- ጭነት (የቀረጥ) ፣ በቅጣት መልክ ለተማሪ የ'ሚ'ሰጥ የቤት ሥራ ፣ የ'ማይ 'ገ'ባ ማስቸ'ገር

impossible
ኢም'ፖሰበል -ቅ- የ'ማይ'ቻል

impostor

ኢም'ፖስተ -ስ- ሌላውን መስሎ መ'ታየት (ለማ'ታለል) ፣ ያልሆነውን ነ'ኝ እ'ያለ የ'ሚ ያ'ታልል

impotence

'ኢምፖተንስ -ስ- ድካም ፣ አለመቻል

impoverish

ኢም'ፖቨሪሽ -ግ- ማደኽየት [አደኸ'የ]

impregnable

ኢምፕ'ሬግነበል -ቅ- መከራ የ'ማይበ'ግረው፣ መከራ የ'ማይፈታው

impregnate

ኢምፕ'ሬግኔይት -ግ- ማስረ'ገዝ [አስረ'ገዘ]

soak

-ግ- ማጥለቅለቅ [አጠለቀ'ለቀ] (እፈ ሳሽ ውስጥ)

impress

ኢምፕ'ሬስ -ግ- ማስደ'ነቅ [አስደ'ነቀ]፣ ስ'ሜ ት መማረክ [ማ'ረከ]

impression

ኢምፕ'ሬሽን -ስ- ስ'ሜት ፣ ምል'ክት (የማ ኅተም ወዘተ)

impressionable

ኢምፕ'ሬሽነበል -ቅ- በቀ'ላሉ የ'ሚያምን

impressive

ኢምፕ'ሬሲቭ -ቅ- አስገ'ራሚ ፣ ስ'ሜት የ ሚቀሰ'ቅስ ፣ ስ'ሜት ማራኪ

imprint

'ኢምፕሪንት -ስ- ምል'ክት ፣ (የማኅተም ወ ዘተ)

imprison

ኢምፕ'ሪዘን -ግ- እሥር ቤት ማስገ'ባት [አስ ገ'ባ]

imprisonment

ኢምፕ'ሪዘንመንት -ስ- መ'ታሠር ፣ እሥር ቤት መግባት ፣ እሥር ቤት ውስጥ ያሳ'ለፉት ጊዜ

improbable

ኢምፕ'ሮበበል -ቅ- የ'ሚያ'ጠራ'ጥር ፣ እው ነት ሊሆን የ'ማይችል፣ እውነት ሊ'ደ'ረግ የ'ማ ይችል

impromptu

ኢምፕ'ሮምትዩ -ቅ- ያልተዘጋ'ጀ'በት ፣ በድ ንገት ያደ'ረጉት ፣ ያሉት

improper

ኢምፕ'ሮፐ -ቅ- ሕ'ገ ወ'ጥ ፣ ባለጌ ፣ ሊ'ና'ገ ሩት የ'ማይ'ገ'ባ

impropriety

ኢምፕረፕ'ራየቲ -ስ- ብልግ'ና ፣ ሊሠሩት የ'ማይ'ገ'ባ ሥራ

improve

ኢምፕ'ሩ:ቭ -ግ- ማ'ሻሻል [አ'ሻሻለ]

improvise

'ኢምፕረቫይዝ -ግ- ድንገተ'ኛ አ'ጋጣሚን እንደም'ንም መ'ወጣት [ተወ'ጣ]

imprudent

ኢምፕ'ሩ:ደንት -ቅ- ች'ኩል ፣ የ'ማያ'ስብ

impudence

'ኢምፕዩደንስ -ስ- ድፍረት (ሰውን ባለማ' በር)

impulse

'ኢምፐልስ -ስ- ም'ኞት ፣ ፍ'ላጎት ፣ በል ቢ የ'ሚል ስ'ሜት ፣ የ'ሚገፋ'ፋ ስ'ሜት

impulsive

ኢም'ፐልሲቭ -ቅ- በስ'ሜት ብ'ቻ የ'ሚሠ

impunity

ኢም'ፕዩ:ነቲ -ስ- ከቅጣት ነጻ መሆን

impure

ኢምፕ'ዩወ -ቅ- ንጹሕ ያልሆነ ፣ ቆሻሻ ፣ የ ደባ'ለቀ ፣ ውጥንቅጥ

impurity

ኢምፕ'ዩረቲ -ስ- አለመጥራት ፣ ያ'ደፈ መሆን

in

'ኢን -መዋ- በ . . . ውስጥ ፣ እ . . . ውስጥ

inability

ኢነ'ቢለቲ -ቅ- አለመቻል

inaccessible

ኢነክ'ሴሰበል -ቅ- የ'ማይ'ደ'ረስ'በት ፡ የራቀ

innaccuracy

ኢ'ናክዩረሲ -ስ- ስሕተት ፣ የተ'ን'ቀቄ ጉድ ለት

inaction

ኢ'ናክሽን -ስ- ሥራ አለመሥራት ፡ ሥራ መፍታት

nadequate

ኢ'ናዲክወት -ቅ- በቂ ያልሆነ ፡ ብቁ'ነት የለ 'ለው

inadmissible
ኢነድ'ሚሰበል -ቅ- የ'ማይ'ቀ'በሉት
inadvertent
ኢነድ'ቨ፡ተንት -ቅ- ዝንጉ ፣ የ'ማይ'ጠነ'ቀቅ ፣ ድንገተ'ኛ
inane
ኢ'ኔይን -ቅ- ጅል ፣ ሞ'ኝ
inanimate
ኢ'ናነመት -ቅ- ግዑዝ ፣ ሕይወት የሌ'ለው
inapplicable
ኢነፐ'ሊከበል -ቅ- እሥራ ላይ ሊውል የ'ማይችል
inappropriate
ኢነፐ'ረውፐሪየት -ቅ- የ'ማይስማ'ማ ፣ የ'ማይ'ገ'ባ
inarticulate
ኢና'ቲክዩለት -ቅ- በቀ'ላሉ መ'ናገር የ'ማይችል ፣ ግልጽ ሆኖ ያልተነ'ገረ ፣ ያ'ነጋገር እ'ስከክ የጎ'ደለው
inattentive
ኢነ'ቴንቲቭ -ቅ- ሐ'ሳቡ የባ'ከነ ፣ ሐ'ሳበ ብኩን
inaudible
ኢ'ኖ፡ ደበል -ቅ- ሊ'ሰማ የ'ማይ'ቻል
inaugurate
ኢ'ኖ፡ግየሬይት -ቅ- መ'ርቆ መክፈት [ከ'ፈተ] ማስተዋወቅ [አስተዋ'ወቀ] (አ'ዲስ መምህር ሹ'ም ወዘተ በስብሰባ ላይ)
inborn
ኢን'ቦ፡ን -ቅ- የተፈጥሮ ፣ ሲ'ወ'ለዱ አብሮ የተገ'ኘ (ጠባይ ወዘተ)
incalculable
ኢን'ካልክዩለበል -ቅ- ሊቆ'ጠር የ'ማይ'ቻል ፣ በጣም ብዙ
incandescent
ኢንካን'ዴሰንት -ቅ- ቦ'ግ ያለ ፣ የደ'መቀ ብርሃን
incapable
ኢን'ኬይፐበል -ቅ- የ'ማይ'ችል ፣ ችሎታ የሌ'ለው ፣ ደካማ
incense
'ኢንሴንስ -ስ- እጣ'ን
incentive
ኢን'ሴንቲቭ -ቅ- አ'ነሣሽ (ሥራ እንዲሠሩ የ'ሚያደርግ)

inception
ኢን'ሴፐሽን -ስ- መጀ'መር ፣ መወ'ጠን
incessant
ኢን'ሴሰንት -ቅ- የ'ማያ'ቋርጥ ፣ ያልተ'ቋ'ረጠ ፣ ቀ'ጣይ
inch
'ኢንች -ስ- ሁለ'ት ሳንቲሜትር ተ'ኩል (ለመለ'ኪያ)
incident
'ኢንሲደንት -ስ- ሁኔቴ ፣ ድርጊ'ት
incidental
ኢንሲ'ዴንተል -ቅ- አብሮ ያ'ለ ግን ከፍሬ ነገሩ ው'ጭ የሆነ ፣ ትንሽ'ና ዋጋ ቢስ የሆነ
incinerator
ኢን'ሲነሬይተ -ስ- ቆሻሻ ማ'ቃጠያ በርሜል (ከቆርቆ'ሮ የተሠ'ራ)
incite
ኢን'ሳይት -ግ- ማ'ደፋፈር [አ'ደፋ'ፈረ] ፣ መገፋፋት [ገፋ'ፋ] (አንድ ነገር እንዲያደርጉ)
inclement
ኢንክ'ሌመንት -ቅ- መጥፎ ፣ አስቸ'ጋሪ (አ'የር) ፣ ምሕረት የሌ'ለው
inclination
ኢንክሊ'ኔይሽን -ስ- ዝን'ባሌ
incline
ኢንክ'ላይን -ግ- ማዘንበል [አዘነ'በለ]
incline
'ኢንክላይን -ስ- ዘቅዛ'ቃ ቦታ
include
ኢንክ'ሉ፡ድ -ግ- መጨ'መር [ጨ'መረ]
inclusive
ኢንክ'ሉ፡ሲቭ -ቅ- አ'ጠቃላይ ፣ የ'ሚጨ'ም (ሁ'ሉን ነገር)
incoherent
ኢንኮ'ሂረንት -ቅ- ያልተያያዘ (ለንግ'ግር)
income
'ኢንከም -ስ- ገቢ (ለገንዘብ)
incomparable
ኢን'ኮምፐረበል -ቅ- ተወዳዳሪ የሌ'ለው ተመሳሳይ የሌ'ለው
incompatibility
ኢንክምፓተ'ቢሊቲ -ስ- አለመስማማት
incompatible
ኢንክም'ፓተበል -ቅ- የ'ማይስማ'ማ

incompetence
ኢን'ኮምፒተንስ -ስ- የችሎታ ጉድለት ፣ የዕውቀት ማነስ
incomplete
ኢንኮምፕ'ሊይት -ቅ- ሙሉ ያልሆነ ፣ ጉድለት ያ'ለው
incomprehensible
ኢንኮምፕሪ'ሄንሰበል -ቅ- ሊ'ረ'ዱት የ'ማይ'ቻል ፣ የ'ማይገባ
inconceivable
ኢንከን'ሲይቨበል -ቅ- የ'ማይ'ታ'ሰብ
inconsiderate
ኢንከን'ሲደረት -ቅ- ለሌሎ'ች የ'ማያ'ስብ ፣ ይሉኝታ ቢስ
inconsistent
ኢንከንሲስ'ተንት -ቅ- የ'ሚ'ለዋ'ወጥ (በሐ'ሳብ ወዘተ) ፣ አንድ መሥመር ወዘተ ተከ'ትሎ የ'ማይሄድ ፣ ራሱን በራሱ የ'ሚ'ቃ'ወም
inconspicuous
ኢንከንስ'ፒክዩወስ -ቅ- በቀ'ላሉ ጎልቶ የ'ማይ'ለ'ይ ፣ ኢምንት
inconvenience
ኢንከን'ቪይኒየንስ -ስ- ሁከት ፡ ችግር ፡ አለመ'መቸት
incorporate
ኢን'ኮ፡ፐሬይት -ግ- ማ'ዋሐድ [አ'ዋሐደ] ፣ በአንድ አካል ውስጥ ሌላ ነገር መጨ'መር [ጨ'መረ]
incorrigible
ኢን'ኮሪጀበል -ቅ- የ'ማይ'ታ'ረም
increase
ኢንክ'ሪይስ -ግ- መጨ'መር [ጨ'መረ] ፣ ማብ'ዛት [አበ'ዛ] ፡ ማ'ተ'ለቅ [አ'ተ'ለቀ]
incredible
ኢንክ'ሬደበል -ቅ- የ'ማይ'ታ'መን
incredulity
ኢንክሬድ'ዩ፡ለቲ -ስ- አለማመን ፣ ማመን አለመቻል
incriminate
ኢንክ'ሪመኔይት -ግ- ጥፋተ'ኛ ማድረግ [አደ'ረገ] ፡ መወንጀል [ወነ'ጀለ]
incubate
'ኢንክዩቤይት -ግ- ዕንቁላል እንዲ'ፈለ'ፈል እመፈልፈያ መኪና ውስጥ ማስቀ'መጥ [አስቀ'መጠ] ፡ መፈልፈል [ፈለ'ፈለ] (ለዕ'ንቁላል)
incur
ኢን'ከ፡ -ግ- ማምጣ'ት [አመ'ጣ] (በራስ ላይ ዕዳ ፣ መከራ ጥላ'ቻ ወዘተ)
incurable
ኢንክ'ዩረበል -ቅ- የ'ማይድን ፣ ፈውስ የሌ'ለው (ለበ'ሽታ)
incursion
ኢን'ከ፡ሽን -ስ- ድንገተ'ኛ ወረራ ፣ ግጥሚያ (ለጦር'ነት)
indebted
ኢን'ዴተድ -ቅ- ባለውለታ ፣ ባለዕዳ (የገንዘብ)
indecent
ኢን'ዲይሰንት -ቅ- ባለጌ ፣ ነውረ'ኛ
indecision
ኢንደ'ሲዠን -ስ- ው'ሳኔ መስጠት አለመቻል፣ ለመወ'ሰን ማመንታት
indecisive
ኢንደ'ሳይሲቭ -ቅ- ው'ሳኔ መስጠት የ'ማይ'ችል ፣ ተጠራጣሪ
indeed
ኢን'ዲይድ -ተግ- በርግጥ
indefinite
ኢን'ዴፈኒት -ቅ- ያልተወ'ሰነ ፣ ጉልህ ያልሆነ ፣ እርግጠ'ኛ'ነቱ ያል'ታ'ወቀ
indelible
ኢን'ዴለበል -ቅ- ሊጠፋ የ'ማይችል ፣ ሊ'ፋቅ የ'ማይ'ቻል
indemnity
ኢን'ዴምኒቲ -ስ- ካሣ ፣ ዋስት'ና
indent
ኢን'ዴንት -ግ- አ'ዲስ አንቀጽ መጀ'መር [ጀ'መረ]
independence
ኢንደ'ፔንደንስ -ስ- ነጻ'ነት ፡ ራስን መቻል ከማ'ንም በታ'ች አለመሆን
indestructible
ኢንደስት'ረክተበል -ቅ- የማይ'ደ'መ'ሰስ
indeterminate
ኢንደ'ተ፡መነት -ቅ- ያልተወ'ሰነ ፣ ግልጽ ያልሆነ ፣ እርግጠ'ኛ ያልሆነ
index
'ኢንዴክስ -ስ- ያርእስት ማውጫ ፣ አመልካች
index-finger
'ኢንዴክስ'ፊንገ -ስ- ሌባ ጣት

indicate
'ኢ.ንዲኬይት -ግ- ማመልከት [አመለ'ከተ]
indication
ኢ.ንዲ'ኬይሽን -ስ- ምል'ክት ፣ ማመልከት
indicator
'ኢ.ንዲኬይተ -ስ- አመልካች ፣ አሳ'ይ
indict
ኢ.ን'ዳይት -ግ- መ'ክሰስ [ተከ'ሰሰ]
indictment
ኢ.ን'ዳይትመንት -ስ- ክ'ስ ፣ የክ'ስ ደብዳ'ቤ
indifference
ኢ.ን'ዲፈረንስ -ስ- ግ'ዴ'ለሽ'ነት (ከማ'ን'ኛ ው'ም ወገን አለመሆን)
indigenous
ኢ.ን'ዲጂነስ -ቅ- ያንድ አገር ተወ'ላጅ ፣ አገሬ (ሕዝብ)
indigestion
ኢ.ንዲ'ጂስችን -ስ- የምግብ አለመንሸራሸር
indignant
ኢ.ን'ዲግነንት -ቅ- ቁ'ጡ
indirect
ኢ.ንዲ'ሬክት -ቅ- ቀ'ጥተ'ኛ ያልሆነ
indiscreet
ኢ.ንዲስክ'ሪይት -ቅ- ምስጢር የ'ማይይ'ዝቅ
indiscretion
ኢ.ንዲስክ'ሬሽን -ስ- ምስጢር ማውጣት ፣ ምስጢር መያ'ዝቅ አለመቻል
indiscriminate
ኢ.ንዲስክ'ሪመነት -ቅ- አለመለ'የት (ክፉ'ና ደ'ጉን)
indispensible
ኢ.ንዲስ'ፔንስበል -ቅ- በጣም አስፈ ላጊ. ሊ'ተው የ'ማይ ቻል
indisposition
ኢ.ንዲስፖ'ዚሽን -ስ- ሕመም (ቀ'ላል) ፣ ጥላ ቻ አለመሻት
indistinct
ኢ.ንዲስ'ቲንክት -ቅ- ግልጽ ያልሆነ (ለይ ቶ ሊ'ለይ የ'ማይ'ቻል
individual
ኢ.ንዲ'ቪጁወል -ስ- ሰው
-ቅ- የ'ያንዳንዱ
indolence
'ኢ.ንዶለንስ -ስ- ስንፍ'ና

indomitable
ኢ.ን'ዶሚተበል -ቅ- የ'ማይ'ሸ'ነፍ ፣ የ'ማይ 'በ'ገር
indoor
'ኢ.ን'ዶ፡ -ስ- የቤት ውስጥ ፣ አቤት ውስጥ ያ'ለ
induce
ኢ.ንድ'ዩ፡ስ -ግ- ማሳ'መን [አሳ'መነ] (አንድ ነገር እንዲያደርግ)
inducement
ኢ.ንድ'ዩ፡ስመንት -ስ- አንድ ነገር ለመሥ ራት መገፋፋት
indulge
ኢ.ን'ደልጅ -ግ- አንድ ነገር ከመጠን በላይ ማድረግ [አደ'ረገ]
indulgence
ኢ.ን'ደልጀንስ -ስ- የፈ'ለጉትን ማድረግ የ'ማይ'ወ'ደድ ተግባር በብዛት መፈ'ጸም
permission
-ስ- ፈቃድ
industrial
ኢ.ን'ደስትሪየል -ቅ- የኢንዱስትሪ
industrious
ኢ.ን'ደስትሪየስ -ቅ- ትጉህ ሠ'ራተ'ኛ
industry
'ኢ.ንደስትሪ -ስ- ሥራ ፣ ኢንዱስትሪ
inedible
ኢ.'ኔደበል -ቅ- የ ማይበ'ላ
ineffective
ኢ.ኒ'ፌክቲቭ -ቅ- የ'ማይሠራ ፣ የ'ማይረባ
inefficient
ኢ.ኒ'ፊሸንት -ቅ- አጥጋቢ ያልሆነ (በሥራ)
ineligible
ኢ.'ኔለጀበል -ቅ- በቂ ችሎታ የሌ'ለው (ለመ 'መረጥ)
inept
ኢ.'ኔፕት -ቅ- እ'ጁ የተሳ'ሰረ ፣ ጉልድፍ (እሥራ ላይ) ፣ ሥራ የ'ማያልክፈ'ክፉ
inert
ኢ.'ነ፡ት -ቅ- ለመሥራት ፣ ለመንቀሳቀስ ኀይል የሌ'ለው
inestimable
ኢ.'ኔስቲመበል -ቅ- የ'ማይ'ገ'መት ፣ ዋጋው እ'ጅግ ከ'ፍ ያለ

inevitable
ኢ'ኔቪተበል -ቅ- የ'ማያመልጡት ፣ ግ'ዴታ ያ'ለ'በት ፣ የ'ማይሸሹት

inexhaustible
ኢኔ'ዞ:ስተበል -ቅ- የ'ማያልቅ፣የ'ማያ'ጽ'ርጥ

inexplicable
ኢኔክስፐ'ሊከበል -ቅ- ሊ'ገ'ለጽ የ'ማይ'ቻል

infallible
ኢን'ፋለበል -ቅ- እንከን የ'ሌለው ፣ ኀጢአት የ'ማይሠራ

infamous
'ኢንፈመስ -ቅ- በኃጢአት የተበ'ከለ ፣ በጣም ተንኰለ'ኛ ፣ ሐፍረት ቢስ

infant
'ኢንፈንት -ስ- ሕፃን

infantile
'ኢንፈንታይል -ቅ- የሕፃን

infantry
'ኢንፈንትሪ -ስ- እግረ'ኛ ወታ'ደር

infatuated
ኢን'ፋትዩዌይተድ -ቅ- በ'ማይረባ ፍቅር አእ ምሮውን ያ'ጣ

infatuation
ኢንፋትዩ'ዌይሸን -ስ- አእምሮ የ'ሚያሳ'ጣ ፍቅር

infect
ኢን'ፌክት -ግ- በ'ሽታ ማስያዝ [አስያዘ] ፣ በ'ሽታ ማስተላለፍ [አስተላ'ለፈ]

infection
ኢን'ፌክሸን -ስ- በ'ሽታ መያዝ (የተላ'ለፈ)

infectious
ኢንፌክሸስ -ቅ- የ'ሚ'ተላ'ለፍ ፣ ተላላፊ (በ'ሽታ)

infer
ኢን'ፈ: -ግ- ከመረ'መሩ በኋላ አስተያየት መስጠት [ሰ'ጠ]

inferiority
ኢፊሪ'ዮሪቲ -ስ- ዝ'ቅተ'ኛ'ነት

infernal
ኢን'ፈ:ናል -ቅ- ገሀ'ነማዊ ፣ ሰይጣናዊ

inferno
ኢን'ፈ:ነው -ስ- ገሀ'ነም ፣ እቶን

infest
ኢን'ፌስት -ግ- መውረር [ወ'ረረ] (ሆድም ፣ ትል ፣ ወዘተ)

infidel
'ኢንፊደል -ቅ- አረመኔ ፣ አላማኒ ፣ ጣኦት አምላኪ

infiltrate
'ኢንፊልትሬየት -ግ- ቀስ በቀ'ስ እ'የገ'ቡ መውረር [ወ'ረረ]

infinite
'ኢንፊኒት -ቅ- መጨ'ረሻ የሌ'ለው

infinitive
ኢን'ፊኒቲቭ -ስ- ንኡስ አንቀጽ (ሰዋሰው)

infinitesimal
...ፊኒ'ቴሲመል -ቅ- በጣም ት'ንሽ ፣ ደ...

infinity
ኢን'ፊኒቲ -ስ- መጨ'ረሻ የሌ'ለው ጊዜ ፣ ቦ... ወይን'ም ቁጥር

infirm
ኢን'ፈ:ም -ቅ- ደካማ (በእርጅ'ና ምክንያት)፣ አእምሮ ደካማ

infirmity
ኢን'ፈ:ሚቲ -ስ- ድካም ፣ አለመጽ'ናት

inflammable
ኢንፍ'ላመበል -ቅ- የ'ሚ'ቃ'ጠል (... ወዘተ)

inflammation
ኢንፍለ'ሜይሽን -ስ- እብጠት ፣ እበጥ (የ' ያ'ቃ'ጥል)

inflate
ኢንፍ'ሌይት -ግ- መንፋት [ነ'ፋ] ፣ በአ' መሙላት [ሞ'ላ]

inflict
ኢንፍ'ሊክት -ግ- ክፉ ነገር እንዲደርስ ማ... ረግ [አደ'ረገ] ፣ ማ'ሠቃየት [አ'ሠቃ'የ] (በ... ምታት ፣ በመቅጣት ወዘተ)

influence
'ኢንፍሉወንስ -ግ- ማግባባት [አግባ'ባ]
-ስ- አግባብ ፣ ተጽእኖ

influential
ኢንፍሉ'ዌንሸል -ቅ- አግባብ ያ'ለው ፣ ሥል ጣን ያ'ለው

influenza
ኢንፍሉ'ዌንዛ -ስ- ኢንፍሉዌንዛ ፣ ጉንፋን

influx
ኢንፍለክስ -ግ- በብዛት መግባት [ገ'ባ] (አገር ውስጥ)
inform
ኢን'ፎ:ም -ግ- ማስታወቅ [አስታ'ወቀ]፣ መንገር [ነ'ገረ]
informal
ኢን'ፎ:መል -ቅ- በይፋ ያልሆነ ፣ ሥርዓት ፡ ደምብ ያልተከ'ተለ ፣ መዝናናት ያ'ለ'በት
informant
ኢን'ፎ:መንት -ስ- ተጠ'ያቂ ፣ አስረ'ጂ
information
ኢንፈ'ሜይሽን -ስ- ማስታወቂያ ፣ ወሬ ፣ ከሌላ ሰው ያገ'ኙት ዕውቀት
informative
ኢን'ፎ:መቲቭ -ቅ- አስታዋቂ ፣ አስረ'ጂ
informer
ኢን'ፎ:መ -ስ- ሰ'ላይ (ለፖሊስ የ'ሚነግር) ፣ ጠ'ቋሚ
infrequent
ኢንፍ'ሪይክወንት -ቅ- የ'ማያዘወ'ትር ፣ አልፎ አልፎ የ'ሚ'ደ'ረግ
infringe
ኢንፍ'ሪንጅ -ግ- መጣስ [ጣሰ] (ሕ'ግ ፣ ውል፡ ደምብ)
infuriate
ኢንፍ'ዩሪዬይት -ግ- ማ'ናደድ [አ'ና'ደደ] ፡ ማስቆ'ጣት [አስ'ቆጣ]
ingenious
ኢን'ጂኒየስ -ቅ- ብልኅ ፡ ሠዋቂ (መ'ቀኣጠራ ያ በመሥራት)
ngenuity
ኢንጅን'ዩወቲ -ስ- ብልኅነት ፡ ዕውቀት
ingot
'ኢንገት -ስ- መፍሬም ወርቅ ወይን'ም ብረት (የጡብ ቅርፅ ያ'ለው)
ingratitude
ኢንግ'ራቲትዩድ -ስ- ምስጋና ቢስ'ነት ውለታ ቢስ'ነት
ingredient
ኢንግ'ሪይዲየንት -ስ- ምግብ ሲ'ሠ'ራ የ'ሚ'ጨ'መር'በት ነገር ሁ'ሉ
inhabitant
ኢን'ሀቢተንት -ስ- ያገር ነዋሪ
inhabit
ኢን'ሀቢት -ግ- መኖር [ኖረ] (ባንድ ቦታ ፡ ባንድ አገር)
inhale
ኢን'ሄይል -ግ- አ'የር ወደ ውስጥ መሳብ [ሳበ]
inherent
ኢን'ሂረንት -ቅ- አብሮ የተፈ'ጠረ
inherit
ኢን'ሄሪት -ግ- መውረስ [ወ'ረሰ]
inhuman
ኢንሀ'ዩ:መን -ቅ- ጨ'ካኝ ፣ ከሰብአዊ ስ'ሜት የተራ'ቆተ
inimitable
ኢ'ኒመተበል -ቅ- አምሳ'ያ የሌ'ለው ፡ ል'ዩ
iniquity
ኢ'ኒክወቲ -ስ- ኀጢአት ፡ በደል
initial
ኢ'ኒሸል -ቅ- የመጀ'መሪያ
-ስ- የስም መጀ'መሪያ ፊደሎ'ች
initiate
ኢ'ኒሺዬይት -ግ- ሐ'ሳብ ማፍለቅ [አፈ'ለቀ]
initiation
ኢኒሺ'ዬይሽን -ስ- በማኅበራዊ ኑሮ ውስጥ ተካፋይ እንዲሆን ማግባት ፣ ሐሳ'ብ ማፍለቅ
initiative
ኢ'ኒሺየቲቭ -ስ- ሐሳ'ብ አፍላቂ'ነት
inject
ኢን'ጀክት -ግ- መውጋት [ወ'ጋ] (መርፌ)
injection
ኢንጀክሽን -ስ- ትእዛዝ ፣ የሰው መብት እንዳይ'ነ'ካ የ'ሚያ'ዝ የፍርድቤት ትእዛዝ
injunction
ኢን'ጀንክሽን -ስ- መርፌ (መድኀኒት)
injure
'ኢንጀ -ግ- መጉዳት [ጎ'ዳ]
injury
'ኢንጀሪ -ስ- ጉዳት ፡ ቁስል
injustice
ኢን'ጀስቲስ -ስ- አድልዎ (ለፍርድ)
ink
'ኢንክ -ስ- ቀለም (መጻፊያ)
inkstand
'ኢንክስታንድ -ስ- የቀለም ቢልቃጥ ፡ ለም ቀንድ

inland
'ኢን'ላንድ -ቅ- የአገር ውስጥ
inlet
'ኢንሌት -ስ- መፍሰሻ ፣ መሄጃ ፣ መግቢያ (የውሃ ፣ የአ'የር)
inmate
'ኢንሜይት -ስ- ሆስፒታል ውስጥ የተ'ኛ ሕመምተ'ኛ (የእእምሮ)
inmost
'ኢንመውስት -ቅ- በጣም እውስጥ ያ'ለ ጥልቅ
inn
'ኢን -ስ- ት'ንሽ ሆቴል ቤት
innate
ኢ'ኔይት -ቅ- አብሮ የተፈ'ጠረ ፣ በተፈጥሮ ያ'ለ
inner
'ኢነ -ቅ- የውስጥ ፣ ማእከላይ
innermost
'ኢነመውስት -ቅ- ጥልቅ ፣ የውስጥ
innkeeper
'ኢንኪፐ -ስ- ባለት'ንሽ ሆቴል
innocence
'ኢነሰንስ -ስ- ንጽሕ'ና (ከጥፋት) ፣ ከደሙ ንጹሕ ፣ የማይጎዳ
innumerable
ኢን'ዩ፡መረበል -ቅ- የ'ማይ'ቈ'ጠር
innovate
'ኢነቬየት -ግ- አ'ዲስ ነገር መፍጠር [ፈ'ጠረ]፡ ለውጥ ማድረግ [አደ'ረገ]
inoculate
ኢ'ኖክዩሌይት -ግ- መርፌ መውጋት [ወ'ጋ] (በ'ሽታ ለመ'ከላከል)
inoffensive
ኢነ'ፌንሲቭ -ቅ- ክፋት የሌ'ለው ፡ የማይጎዳ
inopportune
ኢኖፐት'ዩን -ቅ- የ'ማይስማ'ማ (ጊዜ)
inordinate
ኢ'ኖዶነት -ቅ- የ'ሚያበዛ ፡ መጠን የ'ማያውቅ ፡ መጠን የ'ለሽ
inquest
'ኢንክዌስት -ግ- ፍርድ ማ'ጣራት [አ'ጣ'ራ] (በተለ'ይ የነፍስ ግ'ዳይ)
inquire
ኢንክ'ዋየ -ግ- መጠ'የቅ [ጠ'የቀ]
inquiry
ኢንክ'ዋሪ -ስ- ጥ'ያቄ ፣ ምርመራ
inquisitive
ኢንክ'ዊዘቲቭ -ቅ- ሁ'ሉን ለማወቅ የ'ሚሻ ፣ ወሬ አ'ሳዳጅ
insane
ኢን'ሴይን -ቅ- እብድ
insanity
• ኢን'ሳነቲ -ስ- እብደት
insatiable
ኢን'ሴይሸበል -ቅ- የ'ማይጠግብ ፡ በ'ቃ'ኝ የ'ማይል
inscribe
ኢንስክ'ራይብ -ግ- መጻፍ [ጻፈ] ፡ መቅረፅ [ቀ'ረፀ] (ለጽሑፍ)
inscription
ኢንስክ'ሪፕሽን -ስ- ጽሕፈት ፣ ጽሑፍ
insect
'ኢንሴክት -ስ- ተባይ
insecure
ኢንሰክ'ዩወ -ቅ- ያል'ረጋ ፡ አደጋ ያ'ለ'በት ለሕይወት የ'ሚያ'ሠ'ጋ
insert
ኢን'ሰ፡ት -ግ- ማግባት [አገ'ባ] (አንድ ነገ እሌላው ውስጥ)
inset
'ኢንሴት -ግ- በተጨ'ማሪ ማግባት [አገ'ባ]
-ስ- በተጨ'ማሪ'ነት የገ'ባ ነገር
inside
ኢን'ሳይድ -ተግ- በ . . . ውስጥ
insidious
ኢን'ሲዲየስ -ቅ- እየተጎ'ተተ የ'ሚገባ (ለክፉ ነገር) ፡ ለማጥፋት በድ'ብቅ የ'ሚሠራ
insight
'ኢንሳይት -ስ- ማስተዋል ፡ አስተዋይ'ነት ፡ ጠልቆ የመ'ረዳት ችሎታ
insignificant
ኢንሲግ'ኒፊከንት -ቅ- ዋጋ የሌ'ለው (ለነገር)
insinuate
ኢን'ሲኑዩዌይት -ግ- ቀ'ጥተ'ኛ ባልሆነ መንገድ ሐሳ'ብ መግለጽ [ገ'ለጸ]

insinuation
ኢንሲንዩ'ዌይሽን -ስ- ሳይ'ና'ገሩ ሐ'ሳብ መግለጽ

insist
ኢን'ሲስት -ግ- ሐ'ሳብ አለመለ'ወጥ [-ለ'ወጠ] ፤ አጥብቆ ማዘዝ [አ'ዘዘ] ፤ መጠ'የቅ [ጠ'የቀ]

insolent
'ኢንሰለንት -ቅ- ተሳዳቢ ፤ ደ'ፋር ፤ ባለጌ

insolence
'ኢንሰለንስ -ስ- ብልግ'ና ፤ ድፍረት

insoluble
ኢን'ሶልዩበል -ቅ- ፍ'ች የ'ማይ'ገ'ኝ'ለት

insolvent
ኢን'ሶልቨንት -ቅ- የከ'ሰረ ፤ እዳውን መክፈል የ'ማይችል

insomnia
ኢን'ሶምኒየ -ስ- እንቅልፍ ማጣት

inspect
ኢንስ'ፔክት -ግ- ማየት [አ'የ] ፤ መመርመር [መረ'መረ]

inspection
ኢንስ'ፔክሽን -ስ- ምርመራ ፤ ጥን'ቃቄ ያ'ለ'በት ቁጥ'ጥር

inspector
ኢንስ'ፔክተ -ስ- መርማሪ ፤ ተቆጣጣሪ

inspiration
ኢንስፐ'ሬይሽን -ስ- መ'ነሣሻ ሐ'ሳብ ፤ ድንገት የፈ'ለቀ ጥሩ ሐ'ሳብ

inspire
ኢንስ'ፓየ -ግ- ሐ'ሳብ መስጠት [ሰ'ጠ] ፤ ማ'ነሣሣት [አ'ነሣ'ሣ]

instability
ኢንስተ'ቢሊቲ -ስ- አለመ'ረጋጋት

install
ኢንስ'ቶል -ግ- መሾም [ሾ'መ] (መ'ሣሪያ)

instalment
ኢንስ'ቶልመንት -ስ- ለተ'ወሰነ ዕዳ ዋጋውን በ'የጊዜው መክፈል

instance
'ኢንስተንስ -ስ- ሁኔታ ፤ ም'ሳሌ (ለአንድ ነገር ማስረ'ጃ የ'ሚሆን)

instant
'ኢንስተንት -ስ- አ'ጭር ጊዜ
-ቅ- ወድያው የተደ'ረገ ፤ የሆነ

instantaneous
ኢንስተን'ቴይኒየስ -ቅ- ወዲያውኑ የ'ሚሆን

instantly
'ኢንስተንትሊ -ተግ- አሁኑኑ ፤ በፍጥነት

instead
ኢንስ'ቴድ -ተግ- በ . . . ፋንታ ፤ በ . . . ምት'ክ

instep
'ኢንስቴፕ -ስ- የእግር ጉ'ብታ ፤ የላይ'ኛው የግር ክፍል (በጣቶ'ች'ና በተረከዝ መሀል ያ'ለ)

instigate
'ኢንስቲጌይት -ግ- ማ'ነሣሣት [አ'ነሣ'ሣ]

instil
ኢንስ'ቲል -ግ- ቀስ በቀ'ስ ማስተማር [አስተማረ] ፤ ማንጠባጠብ [አንጠባ'ጠበ]

instinct
'ኢንስቲንክት -ስ- በተፈጥሮ ስ'ሜት የ'ሚ'ሠ'ራ ሥራ ፤ ደመ ነፍስ

institute
'ኢንስቲትዩት -ስ- የትምህርት ድር'ጅት

instruct
ኢንስት'ረክት -ግ- ማስተማር [አስተማረ] ፤ ማሠልጠን [አሠለ'ጠነ]
order
-ግ- ማዘዝ [አ'ዘዘ]

instruction
ኢንስት'ረክሽን -ስ- ትምህርት
order
-ስ- ትእዛዝ

instructor
ኢንስት'ረክተ -ስ- አስተማሪ ፤ አሠልጣኝ

instrument
'ኢንስትሩመንት -ስ- መ'ሣሪያ

insubordination
ኢንሰቦ:ዲ'ኔይሽን -ስ- አለመ'ታዘዝ ፤ እምቢ ተ'ኛ'ነት

insufficient
ኢንሰ'ፊሸንት -ቅ- የ'ማይበቃ ፤ ያልተ'ሟላ

insular
'ኢንስዩለ -ቅ- የደሴት ፤ ደሴት መ'ሰል ፤ የራሱን ጎሳ ብ'ቻ የ'ሚደግ'ፍ ፤ አስተያየቱ ጠባብ

insulate

'ኢንሹሌይት -ግ- ማ'ገድ [አ'ገደ] (ሙቀት ፣ ኤሌክትሪክ ወዘተ)

insulation

ኢንሹ'ሌይሽ -ስ- ማ'ገጃ (ሙቀት ፣ ኤሌክትሪክ ወዘተ)

insulator

'ኢንሹሌይተ -ስ- ማ'ገጃ ፣ መ'ከላከያ መ'ግሪያ (የሙቀት ፣ የድምፅ ወዘተ) ፣ የኤሌክትሪክ ሽቦ የ'ሚያልፍ'በት ሲኒ የመ'ሰለ መ'ግሪያ

insult

'ኢን'ሰልት -ግ- መስደብ [ሰ'ደበ] ፣ ማ'ዋረድ [አ'ዋ'ረደ]

insurance

ኢን'ሾ:ረንስ -ስ- ዋስት'ና ፣ ኢንሹራንስ

insure

ኢን'ሾ: -ግ- ማ'ረጋገጥ [አ'ረጋ'ገጠ] ፤ ኢንሹራንስ መግባት [ገ'ባ]

insurgent

ኢን'ሰ:ጀንት -ቅ- ሽ'ፍታ ፣ ዐመፀ'ኛ (በመንግሥት ላይ ወዘተ)

insurmountable

ኢንሰ'ማውንተበል -ቅ- ሊ'ሸ'ነፍ የ'ማይ'ቻል ፣ የ'ማይ'ዘ'ለቅ

insurrection

ኢንሰ'ሬክሽን -ስ- ማ'መፅ ፣ የሕዝብ በመንግሥት ላይ ብጥ'ብጥ ማንሣት

intact

ኢን'ታክት -ቅ- አደጋ ያልደ'ረሰ'በት ፣ ያልተጎ'ዳ ፣ ያልተነ'ካ

intake

'ኢንቴይክ -ስ- በተወ'ሰነ ጊዜ የ'ሚገባ የሰው ፣ የተማሪ ወዘተ ብዛት

intangible

ኢን'ታንጀበል -ቅ- የ'ማይ'ዳ'ሰስ ፣ ግዙፍ ያልሆነ ፤ በግልጽ የ'ማይ'ረ'ዱት ፣ ደብዛ'ዛ

integral

'ኢንተግረል -ቅ- ዋ'ና ፣ እ'ጅግ አስፈ'ላጊ ፣ የ'ማይ'ነ'ጠል

integrity

ኢን'ቴግረቲ -ስ- ቀ'ጥተ'ኛ'ነት ፣ ታ'ማኝ'ነት ፣ ፍ'ጹም'ነት ፣ ሙሉ'ነት

intellect

'ኢንተሌክት -ስ- የአእምሮ ማስተዋል ችሎታ ፣ የማወቅ ችሎታ ፣ ብልኀ'ነት

intellectual

ኢንተ'ሌክቹወል -ቅ- ዐዋቂ ፣ ግእምር ፣ ምሁር

intelligence

ኢን'ቴሊጀንስ -ስ- ዕውቀት ፣ ል'ቡና

intelligible

ኢን'ቴለጀበል -ቅ- ሊ'ረ'ዱት የ'ሚ'ቻል

intemperance

ኢን'ቴምፐረንስ -ስ- ከመጠን በላይ የሆነ ነገር ፣ ከመጠን በላይ ማድረግ ፤ ስ'ካራም'ነት

intend

ኢን'ቴንድ -ግ- ማ'ሰብ [አ'ሰበ] ፣ ማ'ቀድ [ዐ'ቀደ]

intense

ኢን'ቴንስ -ቅ- ኀይለ'ኛ ፣ ከ'ባድ ፣ ጥልቅ (ስስ'ሜት)

intent

ኢን'ቴንት -ስ- ዐቅድ

intention

ኢን'ቴንሽን -ስ- ሐ'ሳብ

intercede

ኢንተ'ሲይድ -ግ- ማ'ማለድ [አ'ማ'ለደ]

intercept

ኢንተ'ሴፐት -ግ- እፈ'ለጉት ቦታ እንዳይደርሱ ማ'ሰናከል [አ'ሰና'ከለ] ፣ ማ ፣ ገድ [አ'ገደ] (ሰው ፣ ደብዳ'ቤ ፣ ጠላት ወዘተ)

intercession

ኢንተ'ሴሽን -ስ- ማ'ማለድ ፣ ምልጃ

interchange

ኢንተ'ቼይንጅ -ግ- መለ'ዋወጥ [ተለ'ዋወጠ]

intercommunication

ኢንተከምዩኒ'ኬይሽን -ስ- የእርስ በርስ ግን'ኙ'ነት

intercourse

'ኢንተኮ:ስ -ስ- እርስ በርስ መ'ገናኘት ፤ በፈቃደ ሥጋ ማወቅ

interdependent

ኢንተደ'ፔንደንት -ቅ- መ'ረዳዳት የ'ሚፈ'ልግ

interdict

ኢንተ'ዲክት -ስ- የማ'ገጃ ሕ'ግ

interest

'ኢንተሬስት -ስ- ዝን'ባሌ

money

-ስ- ትርፍ ፣ አራጣ (በንግድ)

interesting
'ኢንትሬስቲንግ -ቅ- አስተያየት የ'ሚስብ ፣ ቸ'ል የ'ማይሉት

interested
'ኢንትሬስተድ -ቅ- አስተያየቱን ወዳንድ ነገ ር ያዘነ'በለ ፣ ዝን'ባሌ ያ'ለው

interfere
ኢንተ'ፊየ -ግ- ጣልቃ መግባት [ገ'ባ]

interference
ኢንተ'ፊረንስ -ስ- ጣልቃ ገ'ብ'ነት

interim
'ኢንተሪም -ቅ- ጊዜያዊ

interior
ኢን'ቲሪየ -ቅ- ውስጣዊ ፣ የውስጥ

interjection
ኢንተ'ጀክሽን -ስ- ቃለ አ'ጋ'ኖ (ሰዋሰው)

interlude
'ኢንተልዩ:ድ -ስ- በሁለ'ት ድርጊ'ቶ'ች መሀ' ከል አ'ጭር ጊዜ (የዕረፍት)

interlock
ኢንተ'ሎክ -ግ- ማ'ያያዝ [አ'ያያዘ]

intermarriage
ኢንተ'ማሪጅ -ስ- በል'ዩ ል'ዩ ጎሳዎ'ች መካ 'ከል የ'ሚ'ደ'ረግ ጋብቻ ፤ በቅርብ ዘመድ መካ 'ከል የ'ሚ'ደ'ረግ ጋብቻ

intermediate
ኢንተ'ሚይዲየት -ቅ- መካ'ከለ'ኛ ፣ ማዕከ ላዊ፣በሁለ'ት ሁናቴዎ'ች መካ'ከል ያ'ለ ፣ የ'ሚ 'ፈ'ጸም ድር'ጊት

interment
ኢን'ተ:መንት -ስ- ሥርዓተ ቀብር

intermission
ኢንተ'ሚሽን -ስ- ት'ንሽ ዕረፍት

intermittent
ኢንተ'ሚተንት -ቅ- በ'የጊዜው የ'ሚያ'ቋ'ር ጥ ወይን'ም እያ'ነሰ የ'ሚሄድ

intern
ኢን'ተ:ን -ግ- እሥር ቤት ማስገ'ባት [አስገ'ባ]

internal
ኢን'ተ:ነል -ቅ- ውስጣዊ

international
ኢንተ'ናሽነል -ቅ- ኢንተርናሲዮናል (ብዙ መ ንግሥታትን የ'ሚ'መለ'ከት

internee
ኢንተ:'ኒ -ስ- ግዞተ'ኛ ፣ እሥረ'ኛ (ለጊዜው)

internment
ኢን'ተ:ንመንት -ስ- መ'ታሠር (ለጊዜው)

interpolate
ኢን'ተ:ፐሌይት -ግ- ምል'ክት ማድረግ [አደ 'ረገ] (በድርሰት ላይ አስተያየትን በመጻፍ)

interpret
ኢን'ተ:ፐረት -ግ- መተርጐም [ተረ'ጐመ] ፡ 'ፍች መስጠት [ሰ'ጠ]

interpretation
ኢንተፐረ'ቴይሽን -ስ- ትርጉም ፣ ፍ'ች

interpreter
ኢን'ተ:ፐረተ -ስ- አስተርጓሚ ፣ ትርጉማን

interrogate
ኢን'ቴረጌይት -ግ- መመርመር [መረ'መረ] (ለፖሊስ ፣ ለዳ'ኛ ወዘተ)

interrogation
ኢንቴረ'ጌይሽን -ስ- ጥ'ያቄ

interrogative
ኢንተ'ሮገቲቭ -ቅ- መጠ'ይቅ

interrupt
ኢንተ'ረፕት -ግ- ማ'ቋረጥ [አ'ቋ'ረጠ]

interruption
ኢንተ'ረፕሽን -ስ- ማ'ቋረጥ

intersect
ኢንተ'ሴክት -ግ- ለሁለ'ት መክፈል [ከ'ፈለ]፡ መገመስ [ገ'መሰ]

intersperse
ኢንተስ'ፐ:ስ -ግ- አልፎ አልፎ ማስቀ'መጥ [አስቀ'መጠ]

interval
'ኢንተቨል -ስ- የዕረፍት ጊዜ (በሁለ'ት ድር ጊ'ቶ'ች መካ'ከል) ፤ በሁለ'ት ነገሮ'ች መካ'ከል ያ'ለ ክፍት ቦታ

intervene
ኢንተ'ቪይን -ግ- በመካ'ከል መግባት [ገ'ባ] ጥ'ልቅ ማለት [አለ]

intervention
ኢንተ'ቬንሽን -ስ- ጣልቃ ገ'ብ'ነት

interview
'ኢንተቭዩ: -ስ- ጥ'ያቄ'ና መልስ

intestate
ኢን'ቴስቴይት -ቅ- ሳይ'ና'ዘዝ የሞተ

intestinal
ኢንቴስ'ታይነል -ቅ- የአንጀት ፣ የሆድቃ
intestine
ኢን'ቴስቲን -ስ- አንጀት
intimacy
'ኢንቲመሲ -ስ- የቅርብ ወዳጅ'ነት ፣ የግ'ል የሆነ ጉ'ዳይ
intimate
'ኢንቲመት -ቅ- የቅርብ ወዳጅ
intimation
ኢንቲ'ሚይሽን -ስ- ት'ንሽ ሐ'ሳብ መስጠት ፡ ማስታወቅ
intimidate
ኢን'ቲሚዴይት -ግ- ማስፈራራት [አስፈራ'ራ]፡ መዛት [ዛተ]
intimidation
ኢንቲመ'ዴይሽን -ስ- ማስፈራራት ፣ ዛ'ቻ
into
'ኢንቱ -ተግ- ወደ ፣ ወደ . . . ውስጥ
intolerable
ኢን'ቶለረበል -ቅ- የማይ'ታ'ገሡት
intolerance
ኢን'ቶለረንስ -ስ- አለመ'ታገሥ
intonation
ኢንተ'ኔይሽን -ስ- የድምፅ መውደቅ'ና መ'ነ ሣት (የንግ'ግር)
intoxicate
ኢን'ቶክሲኬይት -ግ- ማስከ'ር [አስ'ከረ]
intoxication
ኢንቶክሲ'ኬይሽን -ስ- ስካር
intoxicated
ኢን'ቶክሲኬይተድ -ቅ- የሰ'ከረ ፡ ስ'ካራም ፡ የጠ'ጣ
intransitive
ኢንት'ራንሲቲቭ -ቅ- የ'ማይ'ሻ'ገር (ግ'ሥ ፡ ነዋሰው)
intrepid
ኢንት'ሬፒድ -ቅ- ደ'ፋር ፡ የ'ማይፈራ
intricate
'ኢንትሪከት -ቅ- የተጠላ ሰበ ፡ ግልጽ ያልሆነ
intrigue
'ኢንትሪይግ -ግ- መዶ'ለት [ዶ'ለተ] ፡ ነገር መሥራት [ሠ'ራ]
-ስ- ዱ'ለታ
intrinsic
ኢንት'ሪንሲክ -ቅ- እውነተ'ኛ (ዋጋ ወዘተ)
introduction
ኢንትረ'ደክሽን -ስ- መቅድም ፣ ማስተዋወቅ
introductory
ኢንትረ'ደክተሪ -ቅ- የመጀ'መሪያ ፣ አስተዋ ዋቂ
introspection
ኢንትረስ'ፔክሽን -ስ- ማ'ሰላሰል ፣ ስ'ሜትን፡ ሐ'ሳብን መመርመር
intrude
ኢንት'ሩ፡ድ -ግ- ጥ'ልቅ ማለት [አለ]
intrusion
ኢንት'ሩ፡ዠን -ስ- ጥ'ልቅ ማለት ፣ ጣልቃ ገ'ብ 'ነት
intuition
ኢንትዩ'ዊሽን -ስ- ብዙ ባለማ'ሰብ የተገ'ኘ ዕውቀት ፡ የተፈጥሮ ዕውቀት
inundate
'ኢነንዴይት -ግ- ማጥለቅለቅ [አጥለቀ'ለቀ]
inure
ኢን'ዩወ -ግ- ከአንግዳ ነገር ጋር መ'ለማመድ [ተለማ'መደ]
invade
ኢን'ቬይድ -ግ- መውረር [ወ'ረረ]
invalid
ኢን'ቫሊድ -ቅ- ዋጋ ቢስ
invalid
'ኢንቨሊድ -ስ- ደ'ውይ ፡ አካለ ጉደሎ ፡ አካለ ስንኩል
invaluable
ኢን'ቫልዩወበል -ቅ- ባለ ብዙ ዋጋ ፡ ዋጋው ሊ'ገ'መት የ'ማይ'ቻል
invariable
ኢን'ቬሪየበል -ቅ- የ'ማይ'ለ'ወጥ
invasion
ኢን'ቬይዠን -ስ- ወረራ (ለጦር'ነት)
invent
ኢን'ቬንት -ግ- አ'ዲስ ነገር ማውጣት [አወ 'ጣ] ፡ መፈልሰፍ [ፈለ'ሰፈ]
invention
ኢን'ቬንሽን -ስ- አ'ዲስ ነገር ወይን'ም ሐ'ሳብ፣ አ'ዲስ የተሠ'ራ ፡ የተፈለ'ሰፈ ነገር

inventor
ኢን'ቬንተ -ስ- አ'ዲስ ነገር ወይን'ም ሐሳ'ብ ፈጣሪ

inventory
'ኢንቨንትሪ -ስ- የዕቃ ዝርዝር (የቤት ወዘተ)

inverse
'ኢንቨ፡ስ -ቅ- ተቃራኒ ፣ የተገለ'በጠ (የውስጡ ወደ ው'ጭ)

invert
ኢን'ቨ፡ት -ግ- መገልበጥ [ገለ'በጠ] (የውስጡን ወደ ው'ጭ)

invest
ኢን'ቬስት -ግ- ገንዘብ ማውጣት [አወ'ጣ] (ጥቅም ፡ ትርፍ ለ'ሚያመጣ ተግባር)

investigate
ኢን'ቬስትጌይት -ግ- መመርመር [መረ'መረ]

investigation
ኢንቬስተ'ጌይሽን -ስ- ምር'ምር

investigator
ኢን'ቬስቲጌይተ -ስ- መርማሪ

investment
ኢን'ቬስትመንት -ስ- እንግድ ላይ የዋለ ገንዘብ

investor
ኢን'ቬስተ -ስ- ገንዘብ የሚያወጣ (ጥቅም ፡ ትርፍ ለሚያመጣ ተግባር)

inveterate
ኢን'ቬተረት -ቅ- መሠረቱ የቆ'የ ፣ ሥር የተ'ከለ (ልምድ ፡ አደልዎ ወዘተ) ፣ ች'ኮ ፣ ደረቅ

invidious
ኢን'ቪዲየስ -ቅ- መጥፎ ስ'ሜት ፡ ም'ቀ'ኝ'ነት የ'ሚቀሰ'ቅስ

invigilate
ኢን'ቪጂሌይት -ግ- ተፈ'ታ'ኞ'ች መጠ'በቅ [ጠ'በቀ] (ለመ'ቆጣጠር)

invigorating
ኢን'ቪገሬይቲንግ -ቅ- የ'ሚያ'ነቃ'ቃ ፡ የ'ሚያ'ነቃ'ቃ

invincible
ኢን'ቪንሲበል -ቅ- የ'ማይ'ሸ'ነፍ

invisible
ኢን'ቪዚበል -ቅ- የ'ማይ'ታ'ይ

invitation
ኢንቪ'ቴይሽን -ስ- ግብዣ

invite
ኢን'ቫይት -ግ- መጋበዝ [ጋ'በዘ]

invoice
'ኢንቮይስ -ስ- የዋጋ ዝርዝር

invoke
ኢን'ቮውክ -ግ- እርዳታ መጠ'የቅ [ጠ'የቀ] ፣ ምስ'ክር'ነት መጥራት [ጠ'ራ]

involuntary
ኢን'ቮለንተሪ -ቅ- ያለፈቃድ የሆነ ፣ ሳይ'ታ'ሰብ የሆነ

involve
ኢን'ቮልቭ -ግ- ማስገ'ባት [አስገ'ባ] (ጣንድ ጉ'ዳይ ውስጥ)

invulnerable
ኢን'ቨልነረበል -ቅ- ጉዳት የ'ማይደርስ'በት

inward
'ኢንወድ -ቅ- ውስጣዊ

iodine
'አየዲይን -ስ- አዮዲን ፣ በት'ኩስ ቁስል ላይ የ'ሚፈ'ስ የ'ሚቆጠ'ቁጥ መድኃኒት

irate
አይ'ሬይት -ቅ- የተቆ'ጣ ፣ የተና'ደደ

iris
'አይሪስ -ስ- ያይን ብረት ፣ የአበባ ዓይነት (ቅጠሉ የሠይፍ ቅርፅ ያ'ለው)

irksome
'ኧ፡ክሰም -ቅ- የ'ሚሰለ'ች ፣ ች'ክ የ'ሚል ፣ አ'ዋኪ

iron
'አየን -ስ- ብረት
clothes-
-ስ- ካው'ያ

ironical
አ'ሮኒክል -ቅ- ውስጠ ፌዝ ያ'ለ'በት ፡ ፌዝ'ኛ ፣ ም'ፀት ያ'ለ'በት (ንግ'ግር)

irony
'አረኒ -ስ- ውስጠ ፌዝ ንግ'ግር ፡ ፌዝ ፡ ም'ፀት

irrational
ኢ'ራሽነል -ቅ- ሳይ'ታ'ሰብ የተሠ'ራ ፣ አስተ'ካካይ የማ'ሰብ ችሎታ የሌ'ለው ፣ በጣም ሞ'ኝ

irreconcilable
ኢሬከን'ሳይለበል -ቅ- የ'ማይ'ታ'ረቅ ፡ የ'ማይስማ'ማ

irredeemable
ኢረ'ዲይመበል -ቅ- ሊያስተካ'ክሉት የ'ማይ'ቻል ፣ ሊጠ'ግኑት የ'ማይ'ቻል

irregular
ኢ'ሬግዩለ -ቅ- ሕ'ገ ወ'ጥ ፣ ያልተስተካ'ከለ ፤ ከተለ'መደው ሥርዓት ው'ጭ የሆነ

irrelevant
ኢ'ሬለቨንት -ቅ- ከጉ'ዳዩ የራቀ ፣ አግባብ የሌ'ለው

irreparable
ኢ'ሬፐረበል -ቅ- ሊ'ጠ'ገን የ'ማይ'ቻል

irrepressible
ኢሪፐ'ሬሰበል -ቅ- ሊ'ቆጣ'ጠሩት የ'ማይ'ቻል ፣ ሊገቱት የ'ማይ'ቻል

irreproachable
ኢረፐ'ረውቸበል -ቅ- እንከን የሌ'ለው ፣ ጥፋት የሌ'ለው

irresistible
ኢረ'ዚስተበል -ቅ- የ'ማይመ'ከቱት ፣ ስ'ሜትን የ'ማያስገ'ታ ፣ ማራኪ

irresolute
ኢ'ሬዘሉዩት -ቅ- አ'ወላዋይ ፣ ተጠራጣሪ

irresponsible
ኢረስ'ፖንሰበል -ቅ- ኀላፊ'ነት የ'ማይ'ሰ'ማው ፤ አእምሮው ያልበ'ሰለ

irretrievable
ኢረት'ሪይቨበል -ቅ- ሊ'መ'ለስ የ'ማይ'ቻል፣ ሊ'ጠ'ገን የ'ማይ'ቻል

irreverent
ኢ'ሬቨረንት -ቅ- በሃይማኖት የ'ሚያሾፍ ፤ አንቋሻሽ

irrevocable
ኢ'ሬቨከበል -ቅ- የ'ማይ'ለ'ወጥ

irrigate
'ኢሪጌይት -ግ- በመስኖ ውሃ ማጠ'ጣት [አጠ'ጣ] (አትክልት)

irrigation
ኢረ'ጌይሽን -ስ- የመስኖ ውሃ

irritable
'ኢረተበል -ቅ- በቀ'ላሉ የ'ሚ'ና'ደድ

irritate
'ኢረቴይት -ግ- ማስቆ'ጣት [አስቆ'ጣ] ፤ መተነኳኰስ [ተነኳ'ኰሰ] (ሰው'ነት)

irritation
ኢረ'ቴይሽን -ግ- ቁ'ጣ ፤ መብላት (ሰው'ነት ለ'ሚያሳ'ክክ)

island
'አይለንድ -ስ- ደሴት

isle
'አይል -ስ- ደሴት

islet
'አይለት -ግ- ት'ንሽ ደሴት

isolate
'አይሰሌይት -ግ- ለ'ይቶ ማኖር [አኖረ]

isolation
አይሰ'ሌይሽን -ስ- ተለ'ይቶ መኖር ፣ ብ'ቸ'ኛ'ነት

issue
'ኢሹ -ግ- መውጣት [ወ'ጣ] (ለፈሳሽ ወዘተ)፣ እ'ትሞ ማውጣት [አወ'ጣ] (መጻሕፍት ወዘተ) -ስ- ልጅ ፣ ዘር ፤ እ'ትም

isthmus
'ኢስመስ -ስ- ል'ሳነ ምድር

it
'ኢት -ተስ- እርሱ ፣ እርሷ (ሰው ላልሆነ ፣ ለግዑዝ ጾታ)

itch
'ኢች -ስ- መብላት (ሲያሳ'ክክ) ፣ እከክ

item
'አይተም -ስ- ከዝርዝር ጽሑፍ ውስጥ አንድ ዕቃ

itinerary
ኢ'ቲነሪ -ስ- በጉዞ የጉብ'ኝት ዝግ'ጅት

its
'ኢትስ -ተስ- የርሱ ፣ የርሷ (ሰው ላልሆነ ፣ ለግዑዝ ጾታ)

itself
ኢት'ሴልፍ -ተስ- እራሱ ፣ እራሷ (ሰው ላልሆነ ፣ ለግዑዝ ጾታ)

ivory
'አይቨሪ -ስ- የዝሆን ጥርስ

J

jab
'ጃብ -ግ- መውጋት [ወ'ጋ] ፣ መነ'ስም [ነ'ሰመ]
jack
'ጃክ -ስ- ክሪክ ፣ የመኪና ጎ'ማ ማንሻ
jackal
'ጃኮ:ል -ስ- ቀበሮ
jackass
'ጃካስ -ስ- አህ'ያ (ወንድ) ፤ ቂል
jacket
'ጃከት -ስ- ጉርድ ኮት
jack-knife
'ጃክናይፍ -ስ- ት'ልቅ ሰንጢ
jade
'ጄይድ -ስ- አረንጓዴ ደንጊያ ፤ ጊ'ኛ
jaded
'ጄይደድ -ቅ- የደ'ከመው ፣ የዛለ
jag
'ጃግ -ስ- የሾለ ነገር ፤ ቡ'ጭቅ (የልብስ ወዘተ)
jail
'ጄይል -ስ- እሥር ቤት
jailer
'ጄይለ -ስ- እሥር ቤት ጠ'ባቂ
jam
'ጃም -ግ- መ'ታፈግ [ታ'ፈገ]
-ስ- ማርማላታ
janitor
'ጃኒተ -ስ- ቤት ጠራጊ ፣ ቤት ጠ'ባቂ ፣ በ'ረ'ኛ ፣ ቤት ተከባካቢ
January
'ጃንዩወሪ -ስ- ጥ'ር (የወር ስም)
Japan
ጀ'ፓን -ስ- ጃ'ፓን
jar
'ጃ: -ግ- መ'ጋጨት [ተጋ'ጨ]
-ስ- የዕቃ መያዣ (ከሸክላ ወይን'ም ከብርጭ'ቆ የተሠ'ራ)
jaundice
'ጆ:ንዲስ -ስ- የወፍ በ'ሽታ (ዓይን ብጫ የ'ሚያደርግ በ'ሽታ)
jaunt
'ጆ:ንት -ስ- ሽ'ርሽ'ር
jaw
'ጆ: -ስ- መንጋጋ ፣ መንጋጨ'ላ
jealous
'ጄለስ -ቅ- ቀ'ናተ'ኛ
jealousy
'ጄለሲ -ስ- ቅናት
jeer
'ጂየ -ግ- ማፌዝ [አፌዘ]
jelly
'ጄሊ -ስ- የረ'ጋ (ፈሳሽ) ፣ ዝልግልግ ነገር
jellyfish
'ጄሊፊሽ -ስ- ዝልግልግ ዐሣ
jemmy
'ጄሚ -ስ- የሣጥን መክፈቻ ብረት (በተለ'ይ የሌቦ'ች)
jeopardize
'ጄፐዳይዝ -ግ- አደጋ ላይ መጣል [ጣለ]
jeopardy
'ጄፐዲ -ስ- አደጋ
jerk
'ጀ:ክ -ስ- ድንገተ'ኛ እንቅስ'ቃሴ ፣ ብርገ፡ ወዘተ
jerky
'ጀ:ኪ -ቅ- የሚያንገጫ'ግጭ ፣ ድንገተ'ኛ (ብርገጋ)
jersey
'ጀ:ዚ -ስ- ሹ'ራብ (የገላ)
jest
'ጄስት -ግ- መቀ'ለድ [ቀ'ለደ]
jet
'ጄት -ስ- ት'ንሽ ቀዳዳ ውሃ'ና አ'የር በኀይል የ'ሚወ'ጣ'በት ፤ ጄት አውሮ'ፕላን
-ቅ- በጣም ጥቁር
jettison
'ጄቲሰን -ግ- መጣል [ጣለ] (ዕቃ ከመርከብ ላይ ማዕበል ሲ'ነ'ሣ ለማቅለል)
jetty
'ጄቲ -ስ- የመርከብ መቆሚያ (በወደብ)
Jew
ጆ'ዩ: -ቅ- ይሁዲ

jewel
ጁ'ወል -ስ- ዕንቁ
jeweller
ጁ'ውለ -ስ- ጌጣጌጥ ነ'ጋዴ ፣ ጌጣጌጥ ሠ'ራ ተ'ኛ
jewelry
ጁ'ወልሪ -ስ- ጌጣጌጥ
Jewish
ጁ'ዊሽ -ቅ- የይሁዲ
jig
'ጂግ -ግ- መጨ'ፈር [ጨ'ፈረ]
jilt
'ጂልት -ግ- የጋብ'ቻ ውል አለመፈ'ጸም [-ፈ'ጸመ] (ቃል ካ'ሠሩ በኋላ)
jingle
'ጂንገል -ግ- መንቃጨል [ተን.ቃ'ጨለ]
-ስ- መንቃጨል
job
'ጆብ -ስ- ሥራ ፣ ተግባር
jocular
'ጆክዩለ -ቅ- ተጫዋች ፣ ቀ'ላጅ
jog
'ጆግ -ግ- መሥገር [ሠ'ገረ] ፣ መነ'ሸም [ነ'ሸመ]
join
'ጆይን -ግ- ማ'ጋጠም [አ'ጋ'ጠመ] (ሁለ'ት ነገር'ች) ፣ ማኅበርተ'ኛ መሆን [ሆነ]
joiner
'ጆይነ -ስ- አናጢ
joinery
'ጆይነሪ -ስ- ያናጢ'ነት ሥራ
joint
'ጆይንት -ስ- መ'ጋጠሚያ ፣ አንጓ (የጣት ፣ የእ'ጅ ወዘተ) ፣ ብ'ልት (የሥጋ)
-ቅ- የጋራ
jointly
'ጆይንትሊ -ተግ- ባንድ'ነት ፣ የጋር'ዮሽ
joist
'ጆይስት -ስ- ወጋግራ
joke
'ጆውክ -ስ- ቀልድ
joker
'ጆውከ -ቅ- ተጫዋች ፣ ቀ'ላጅ
cards
-ስ- የተለ'የ የመ'ጫወቻ ካርታ ስም ፣ ጆከር
jolly
'ጆሊ -ቅ- ደ'ስተ'ኛ
jolt
'ጆልት -ግ- መንዘፍዘፍ [ተንዘፈ'ዘፈ]
-ስ- ድንገተ'ኛ እንቅስ'ቃሴ
jostle
'ጆሰል -ግ- መ'ጋፋት [ተጋ'ፋ]
jot
'ጆት -ቅ- በጣም ት'ንሽ
-ግ- ማስታወሻ በጽሑፍ መያዝ [ያዘ]
journal
'ጀ፡ነል -ስ- በ'የቀኑ የተፈ'ጸመ ሥራ ማስ ረ'ጃ ጽሑፍ
newspaper
-ስ- ጋዜጣ
journalism
'ጀ፡ነሊዝም -ስ- ጋዜጣ የማ'ዘጋጀት ሞያ
journalist
'ጀ፡ነሊስት -ስ- ጋዜጠ'ኛ
journey
'ጀ፡ኒ -ስ- ጉዞ (ረ'ጅም)
jovial
'ጆውቪየል -ቅ- የተደ'ሰተ
jowl
'ጃውል -ስ- ወፍራም ጉንጭ (የተንጠለ'ጠለ)
joy
'ጆይ -ስ- ደ'ስታ
joyful
'ጆይፉል -ቅ- ደ'ስተ'ኛ
jubilant
'ጁቢለንት -ቅ- በጣም የተደ'ሰተ ፣ በደ'ስታ የፈነ'ደቀ
jubilation
ጁቢ'ሌይሽን -ስ- ታ'ላቅ ደ'ስታ
jubilee
ጁ'ቢሊ -ስ- ኢ'ዮቤልዩ
judge
'ጀጅ -ግ- መዳኘት [ዳ'ኘ]
-ስ- ዳ'ኛ ፣ ፈራጅ

judgement
'ጀጅመንት -ስ- ፍርድ
judicial
ጁ'ዲሽል -ት- ሕ'ጋዊ
judicious
ጁ'ዲሽስ -ት- አ'መዛዛኝ ፣ ብልኀተ'ኛ ፣ ፍርድ ዐዋቂ
jug
'ጀግ -ስ- ማንቆርቆሪያ ፣ ማብረጃ
juggle
'ጀግል -ግ- እ'የወረ'ወሩ'ና እ'የተ'ለቡ መ'ጫወት [ተጫ'ወተ]
juggler
'ጀግለር -ስ- እ'የወረ'ወረ'ና እ'የተ'ለበ የ'ሚ'ጫ'ወት ሰው
juice
ጁ'ስ -ስ- ጭ'ማቂ (የፍሬ ወዘተ)
juicy
ጁ'ሲ -ት- ውኃ የሞ'ላ'በት (ፍሬ ወዘተ)
July
ጁላ'ላይ -ስ- ሐምሌ
jumble
'ጀምበል -ግ- ያለ ሥርዓት መደበላለቅ [ደበ ላ'ለቀ]
-ስ- የተደበላ'ለቀ ነገር ፣ ዥርቻር ፣ ቅጣ የተጨ'መረ'በት እድብ
jump
'ጀምፕ -ግ- መዝለል [ዘ'ለለ]
-ስ- ዝ'ላይ
jumper
'ጀምፐ -ስ- ዘላይ
sweater
-ስ- ሹ'ራብ (የገላ)
junction
'ጀንክሽን -ስ- መ'ጋጠሚያ (የመንገድ ፣ የባቡር ሐዲድ)
juncture
'ጀንክቸ -ስ- መ'ጋጠሚያ ቦታ
June
ጁ፡ን -ስ- ሰኔ (የወር ስም)
jungle
'ጀንገል -ስ- ደ'ን
junior
ጁ'ንየ -ት- አነስተ'ኛ
junk
'ጀንክ -ስ- ው'ዳቂ ነገር ፣ ቆሻሻ ፣ የቢና'ች መርከብ
junket
'ጀንከት -ግ- በዐል ማድረግ [አደ'ረገ]
juror
'ጁረ -ስ- ዳ'ኛ
jury
'ጁሪ -ስ- ዳ'ኞ'ች
just
'ጀስት -ት- ል'ክ
justice
'ጀስቲስ -ስ- ትክ'ክለ'ኛ ፍርድ ፣ ቅን ፍርድ
jut
'ጀት -ግ- ወጣ ብሎ መ'ታየት [ታ'የ]
juvenile
ጁ፡ቨናይል -ት- ወ'ጣት ፣ የወ'ጣት ፣ የወ'ጣ ት'ነት ጠባይ ያ'ለው
juxtaposition
ጀክስተፐ'ዚሽን -ስ- ጎ'ን ለጎ'ን መ'ቀመጥ ወይን'ም ማስቀ'መጥ

keel
'ኪይል -ስ- መርከብ ሲ'ሠ'ራ እርስበርሱ የ'ሚያ'ያይዘው እንጨት ፣ ብረት
keen
'ኪይን -ት- በንቁ ያ'ሰበ'በት ፣ ጎይለ'ኛ (ነፋስ ወዘተ)
keenness
'ኪይንስ -ስ- በንቁ ማ'ሰብ
keep
'ኪይፕ -ግ- መጠ'በቅ [ጠ'በቀ]
keeper
'ኪይፐ -ስ- ጠ'ባቂ

keeping
'ኪይፒንግ -ስ- ጥ'በቃ

keepsake
'ኪይፕሴይክ -ስ- ማስታወሻ (የስጦታ ዕቃ)

keg
'ኬግ -ስ- ት'ንሽ የንጨት በርሜል

kennel
'ኬ፡ነል -ስ- የው'ሻ ቤት

kerb
'ከ፡ብ -ስ- የመንገድ ጠርፍ ፣ በመንገድ ዳር'ና ዳር ያ'ለ አግድም ጥርብ ድንጊያ

kerchief
'ከ፡ቺይፍ -ስ- የጠጉር ሻሽ

kernel
'ከነል -ስ- በፍራፍሬ ውስጥ የ'ሚ'ገ'ኝ ጠን ካ'ራ ፍሬ (ም'ሳሌ ፣ የኮክ)

kettle
'ኬተል -ስ- ጀበና

key
'ኪይ -ስ- ቁልፍ

keyhole
'ኪሆውል -ስ- የቁልፍ ቀዳዳ

keystone
'ኪስተውን -ስ- የማዕዘን ድንጊያ

kick
'ኪክ -ስ- መርገጥ [ረ'ገጠ] (በግር መምታት)

kid
'ኪድ -ስ- የፍ'የል ግልገል
child
-ስ- ት'ንሽ ልጅ

kidnap
'ኪድናፕ -ስ- ማፈን [አ'ፈነ] (ሰው ለመስረቅ)

kidnapper
'ኪድናፕ -ስ- አ'ፋኝ

kidney
'ኪድኒ -ስ- ኩላሊት

kill
'ኪል -ግ- መግደል [ገ'ደለ]

kiln
'ኪልን -ስ- የሸክላ መተ'ኮሻ ምድ'ጃ

kilo
'ኪይለው -ስ- ኪሎ (መለ'ኪያ)

kin
'ኪን -ስ- ተወ'ላጅ (ዘመድ)

kind
'ካይንድ -ቅ- ርኅሩኅ
-ስ- ዓይነት

kindle
'ኪንደል -ግ- መለ'ኰስ ፣ [ለ'ኰሰ]፣ማ'ቀጣጠል [አ'ቀጣ'ጠለ]

kindling
'ኪንድሊንግ -ስ- እሳት መለ'ኰሻ እንጨት

kindness
'ካይንድነስ -ስ- ርኅራኄ

kindred
'ኪንድረድ -ስ- ተ'ወላጅ ፣ ዘመድ

king
'ኪንግ -ስ- ንጉሥ

kingdom
'ኪንግደም -ስ- መንግሥት ፣ የንጉሥ ግዛት

kink
'ኪንክ -ስ- መ'ጣመም (የሽቦ ፣ የገመድ የጠጉር) ፣ መ'ቆጣጠር

kiosk
'ኪዮስክ -ስ- የጥቃ'ቅን ዕቃዎ'ች መሸጫ ት'ንሽ ሱቅ ፣ ኪዮስክ

kiss
'ኪስ -ግ- መሳም [ሳመ]
-ስ- መሳም

kit
'ኪት -ስ- መ'ሣሪያ (የአንድ የእ'ጅ ሠ'ራተ'ኛ፣ የጉዞ ዕቃ (የወ'ታ'ደር ወዘተ)

kitbag
'ኪትባግ -ስ- ማሲኖዳ

kitchen
'ኪችን -ስ- ወጥ ቤት ፣ ማድቤት

kite
'ካይት -ስ- ጭልፊ'ት ፣ ውልብልቢት (መ'ጫወቻ)

kitten
'ኪተን -ስ- ት'ንሽ ድ'መት

knack
'ናክ -ስ- ል'ዩ ችሎታ ፣ ሞያ

knapsack
'ናፕሳክ -ስ- ስ'ል'ቻ (በጀርባ የ'ሚ'ሸ'ከሙት)

knave
'ኔይቭ -ስ- የ'ማይ'ታ'መን ሰው ፣ ወ'ራ'ዳ ሰው
cards
-ስ- ወለድ (በካርታ ጨዋታ)
knead
'ኒይድ -ግ- ማቡካት [አቦ'ካ]
kneading trough
'ኒይዲንግ ት'ሮፍ -ስ- ገበታ ፣ ማቡኪያ
knee
'ኒይ -ስ- ጉልበት
kneecap
'ኒይካፕ -ስ- ሎሚ (የጉልበት)
kneel
'ኒይል -ግ- መንበርከክ [ተንበረ'ከከ]
knell
'ኔል -ስ- በቀብር ጊዜ የ'ሚ'ሰ'ማ የመረ'ዋ ድምፅ
knick-knack
'ኒክናክ -ስ- ተራ ጌጣ ጌጥ
knife
'ናይፍ -ስ- ቢ'ላዋ ፣ ካ'ራ
knight
'ናይት -ስ- ማዕረግ ያ'ለው ሰው
knit
'ኒት -ግ- ሹ'ራብ መሥራት [ሠ'ራ]
knitting
'ኒቲንግ -ስ- የሹ'ራብ ሥራ
knob
'ኖብ -ስ- ት'ንሽ ክ'ብ ነገር ፣ የመዝጊያ መክፈቻ መያዣ
knock
'ኖክ -ግ- ማንኳኳት [አንኳ'ኳ]
knocker
'ኖክ -ስ- በ'ር የ'ሚያንኳ'ኳ
knockout
'ኖካውት -ስ- ተጋጣሚን ከጨዋታ የ'ሚያስ ወ'ጣው በ'ትር (በቦክስ ጨዋታ) ፣ የጥሎ ማለፍ ጨዋታ (በስፖርት)
knot
'ኖት -ስ- ቋ'ጥር (የገመድ ወዘተ)
know
'ነው -ግ- ማወቅ [ዐ'ወቀ]
knowledge
'ኖለጅ -ስ- ዕውቀት ፣ ማወቅ
knowledgeable
'ኖለጀበል -ቅ- ዐዋቂ
knuckle
'ነክል -ስ- የጣቶ'ች መ'ጋጠሚያ (ለእ'ጅ)

label
'ሌይበል -ስ- ምል'ክት (በጠርሙስ ወዘተ)
laboratory
ለ'ቦረትሪ -ስ- ላቦራተሪ
laborious
ለ'ቦ፡ሪየስ -ቅ- ለመሥራት የ'ሚያስቸ'ግር
labour
'ሌይበ -ስ- ሥራ
childbirth
-ስ- ምጥ
labourer
'ሌይበረ -ስ- ሠ'ራተ'ኛ ፣ የቀን ሞያተ'ኛ
lace
'ሌይስ -ስ- ጥልፍ ሥራ፤ሲር፤የጫ'ማ ማሠሪያ
lacerated
'ላሰሬይተድ -ቅ- የተበጣ'ጠሰ (ለሰው'ነት)
lack
'ላክ -ስ- እጦት
lacquer
'ላከ -ስ- ቀለም (ወፍራም)
lactic
'ላክቲክ -ቅ- የወተት
lad
'ላድ -ስ- ወንድ ልጅ ፣ ጉብል
ladder
'ላደ -ስ- መሰላል
ladle
ሌይደል -ስ- ጭልፋ

lady
'ሌይዲ -ስ- ወይዘር
lag
'ላግ -ግ- ወደኋላ መቅረት [ቀ'ረ]
-ስ- መዘግየት
lair
'ሌየ -ስ- ጎሬ (የአውሬ)
laity
'ሌይቲ -ስ- ተራ ሕዝብ ፣ መ'ይምናን
lake
'ሌይክ -ስ- ሐይቅ
lamb
'ላም -ስ- ጠ'ቦት ፣ ተ'ቦት
lame
'ሌይም -ቅ- የሰ'ለለ (ለእግር) ፣ ሽባ
lament
ለ'ሜንት -ግ- ወ'ዮ ማለት [አለ]
lamentable
'ላመንተበል -ቅ- የ'ሚያሳ'ዝን
lamentation
ላመን'ቴይሽን -ስ- ሰቆቃው ፣ ወ'ዮታ
lamp
'ላምፕ -ስ- ፋኖስ ፣ እም'ፑል
lampblack
'ላምፕብላክ -ስ- ጥቀርሻ
lamp-post
'ላምፕፖስት -ስ- የመብራት እንጨት (ኤሌ ክትሪክ)
lamp-shade
'ላምፕሼይድ -ስ- የእም'ፑል ሽፋን
lance
'ላ፡ንስ -ስ- ጦር
land
'ላንድ -ስ- መሬት ፣ አገር
-ግ- ማረፍ [ዐ'ረፈ] (ለአውሮ'ፕላን ወ ዘተ)
anding
'ላንዲንግ -ስ- ማረፍ ፣ ማሳ'ረፍ ፣ የአውሮ'ፕ ላን ማረፊያ'ና መ'ነሻ ቦታ ፣ በቤት ደረጃ መካ' ከል የ'ሚ'ገ'ኝ ጠፍጣ'ፋ ቦታ ፣ ደረጃ ካለ'ቀ በኋላ እበ'ሩ አጠገብ የ'ሚ'ገ'ኘው ጠፍጣ'ፋ ቦታ

landlady
'ላንድሌይዲ -ስ- የቤት ባለቤት ፣ ቤት አ'ከ ራይ (ሴት)
landlord
'ላንድሎ፡ድ -ስ- የቤት ባለቤት ፣ ቤት አ'ከራይ (ወንድ)
landmark
'ላንድማ፡ክ -ስ- ያገር ምል'ክት ፣ የመሬት ወሰን መለ'ያ ምል'ክት
landowner
'ላንደውነ -ስ- ባለመሬት ፣ ባለርስት
landscape
'ላንድስኬይፕ -ስ- ያገር አ'ካባቢ
landslide
'ላንድስላይድ -ስ- ናዳ
lane
'ሌይን -ስ- ጠ'ባብ መንገድ ፣ ስርጥ መንገድ
language
'ላንግዊጅ -ስ- ቋንቋ
languid
'ላንግዊድ -ቅ- የዛለ ፣ ደካማ ፣ ፈዛዛ
languish
'ላንግዊሽ -ግ- መፍዘዝ [ፈ'ዘዘ] ፣ መድከም [ደ'ከመ] ፣ መዛል [ዛለ]
languor
'ላንገ -ስ- ድካም ፣ መዛል ፣ መፍዘዝ
lanky
'ላንኪ -ቅ- ተ'ጭን'ና ረ'ጅም ፣ ሰላላ መላላ ፣ መንግ'ና
lantern
'ላንተን -ስ- ፋኖስ
lap
'ላፕ -ስ- ጭን
-ግ- መልከስከስ [ለከ'ለከ] (ለመጠ ጥ)
lapel
ለ'ፔል -ስ- የኮት የደረት ታ'ጣፊ (ከአንገትጌው ጋር የ'ሚ'ያያዝ)
lapse
'ላፕስ -ግ- ቀስ በቀ'ስ እየተረ'ሳ መሄድ [ሄደ] (ለሕ'ግ ፣ ለባህል)
-ስ- ቀስ በቀ'ስ እ'የቀ'ረ መሄድ ፣ (ለሕ 'ግ ለባህል) ፣ በንግ'ግር ት'ንሽ ስንተት
larceny
'ላ፡ሰኒ -ስ- ስርቆት (ለጥ'ቃቅን ነገር)

lard
'ላ:ድ -ስ- ያሣማ ስብ

larder
'ላ:ደ -ስ- ጓዳ (የምግብ ማስቀ'መጫ)

large
'ላ:ጅ -ቅ- ሰ'ፊ ፣ ት'ልቅ

largely
'ላ:ጅሊ -ተግ- በብዛት ፣ ይበልጡን

lark
'ላ:ክ -ግ- መ'ቃለድ [ተቃ'ለደ]

larva
'ላ:ቨ -ስ- ትል (ወጺያው እንደተፈለ'ፈለ) ፣ እጭ

larynx
'ላሪንክስ -ስ- ማንቁርት

lash
'ላሽ -ግ- መግረፍ [ገ'ረፈ]

lass
'ላስ -ስ- ልጃገረድ ፣ የከንፈር ወዳጅ

lassitude
'ላሲትዩ:ድ -ስ- ድካም ፣ መታከት

last
'ላ:ስት -ግ- መቆ'የት [ቆ'የ]
final
-ቅ- መጨ'ረሻ

lasting
'ላ:ስቲንግ -ቅ- የ'ሚቆ'ይ ፣ ነዋሪ ፣ ዕድሜ ያ'ለው

lastly
'ላ:ስትሊ -ተግ- በመጨ'ረሻ

latch
'ላች -ስ- መወርወሪያ ፣ መቀርቀሪያ (የበ'ር ፣ የመስኮት)

late
'ሌይት -ቅ- የዘገ'የ ፣ ከጥቂት ጊዜ በፊት የነ'በረ ፣ ያ'ረፈ (የሞተ)

lately
'ሌይትሊ -ተግ፡ ከጥቂት ጊዜ በፊት ፣ በቅርብ ጊዜ

latent
'ሌይተንት -ቅ- የተደ'በቀ ፣ የ'ማይሠራ ፣ የ'ማይንቀሳ'ቀስ

lateral
'ላተረል -ቅ- የጐ'ን ፣ በስተጎ'ን ያ'ለ ፣ ከጎ'ን ያ'ለ

latest
'ሌይተስት -ቅ- አ'ዲስ ፣ ዘመናዊ

lath
'ላስ -ስ- ሳንቃ

lather
'ላ:ዘ -ስ- አረፋ ፣ ኮረፋ

latitude
'ላቲትዩ:ድ -ስ- ነጻ'ነት (የሐሳ'ብ ወዘተ) ፣ ኬንትሮስ (መልከዐ ምድር)

latrine
ለት'ሪይን -ስ- (የተቆ'ፈረ የሰገራ ጉድጓድ)

latter
'ላተ -ቅ- የኋለ'ኛ ፣ የአሁን (ጊዜ) ፣ በመጨ'ረሻ የተጠ'ቀሰ ወዘተ

latterly
'ላተሊ -ተግ- በቅርብ ጊዜ ፣ በአሁኑ ዘመን

lattice
'ላቲስ -ስ- እንደ ወንፊት የተሠ'ራ የሽቦ ፡ የእንጨት አጥር

laud
'ሎ:ድ -ግ- ማመስገን [አመሰ'ገነ]

laudible
'ሎ:ደበል -ቅ- የሚ'መሰ'ገን ፣ ምስጋና የ'ሚ'ገ'ባው

laugh
'ላ:ፍ -ግ- መሣቅ [ሣቀ]

laughable
'ላ:ፈበል -ቅ- የ'ሚያ'ሥቅ

laughter
'ላ:ፍተ -ስ- ሣቅ

launch
'ሎ:ንች -ስ- ት'ንሽ በሞተር የ'ሚ'ነ'ዳ ጀልባ
-ግ- እንዲንቀሳ'ቀስ ማድረግ [አደ'ረገ] ፣ መጀ'መር [ጀ'መረ]

laundress
'ሎ:ንድረስ -ስ- ልብስ አጣቢ ሴት

laundry
'ሎ:ንድሪ -ስ- የልብስ ማጠቢያ ቦታ ፡ የልብስ ንጽሕ'ና መስጫ

lavatory
'ላቨትሪ -ስ- የንጽሕ'ና ቦታ ፣ ሰገራ ቤት

lavish
’ላቪሽ -ግ- በብዙ መስጠት [ሰ'ጠ] ፣ ማባከን [አባ'ከነ]

law
’ሎ: -ስ- ሕ'ግ

law-court
’ሎ:’ኮ:ት -ስ- ፍርድ ቤት

lawful
’ሎ:ፉል -ቅ- ሕ'ጋዊ

lawn
’ሎ:ን -ስ- መስክ ፣ ጨ'ፌ

lawsuit
’ሎ:ሱት -ስ- ክ'ስ

lawyer
’ሎ:የ -ስ- ጠበቃ (ሕ'ግ የተማረ)

lax
’ላክስ -ቅ- ልል (ለሕ'ግ)

laxative
’ላክሰቲቭ -ስ- የ'ሚያስቀ'ምጥ መድኃኒት ፣ ሆድ የ'ሚያላ'ላ መድኃኒት ፣ የሆድ ድርቀት የ'ሚያስ'ወ'ግድ መድኃኒት

lay
’ሌይ -ግ- ማ'ጋደም [አ'ጋ'ደመ] ፣ መጣል [ጣለ] (ለዕንቁላል)

layer
’ሌየ -ስ- ውፍረት (የዝርግ ነገር) ፣ መሥመር (በጽጥ'ኝ ወዘተ) ፣ እሻል (ለመሬት)

layman
’ሌይመን -ስ- ተራ ሰው (ክህነት የሌ'ለው) ፣ መሃ'ይምን

laze
’ሌይዝ -ግ- ጊዜን በከንቱ ማሳ'ለፍ [አሳ'ለፈ]፣ ማውደልደል [አውደለ'ደለ]

laziness
’ሌይዚነስ -ስ- ስንፍ'ና

lazy
’ሌይዚ -ቅ- ሰነፍ

lead
’ሌድ -ስ- እርሳስ (ማዕ'ድን)

lead
’ሊይድ -ግ- መምራት [መ'ራ]

leader
’ሊይደ -ስ- መሪ

leading
’ሊይዲንግ -ስ- መሪ ፣ ዋ'ና

leaf
’ሊይፍ -ስ- ቅጠል

leaflet
’ሊይፍለት -ስ- ት'ንሽ ጽሑፍ

league
’ሊይግ -ስ- ማኅበር

leak
’ሊይክ -ግ- ማንጠብጠብ [አንጠበ'ጠበ] (ውሃ) ፣ መስረቅ [ሰ'ረቀ] (ለውሃ)

leakage
’ሊይኪጅ -ስ- ቀዳዳ ፣ ሽንቁር (ውሃ የ'ሚያፈ'ስ ፣ የ'ሚሰርቅ)

leaky
’ሊይኪ -ቅ- የ'ሚያንጠበ'ጥብ ፣ የ'ሚያፈ'ስ የ'ሚሰርቅ (ውሃ)

lean
’ሊይን -ግ- መ'ደገፍ [ተደ'ገፈ]
not fat
-ቅ- ቀ'ጭን ፣ ያልሰ'ባ

leap
’ሊይፕ -ግ- መዝለል [ዘ'ለለ]

learn
’ለ:ን -ግ- መ'ማር [ተማረ] ፣ ማወቅ [ዐ'ወ

learned
’ለ:ነድ -ቅ- የተማረ ፣ ዐዋቂ

learner
’ለ:ነ -ስ- ተማሪ

learning
’ለ:ኒንግ -ስ- ትምህርት

lease
’ሊይስ -ግ- ቤት ወይን'ም መሬት ለረ'ጅ ጊዜ ማ'ከራየት [አ'ከራ'የ]

leaseholder
’ሊይስሆውልደ -ስ- ቤት ወይን'ም መሬ ለተወ'ሰነ ጊዜ የተከራ'የ

leash
’ሊይሽ -ስ- ማሠሪያ (ጠፍር ፣ ሰንሰለት ፣ ው'ሻ)

least
’ሊይስት -ቅ- የመጨ'ረሻ ፣ ያ'ነሰ

leather
’ሌዘ -ስ- ቆዳ

leave
’ሊይቭ -ግ- መተው [ተወ] ፤ መሄድ [ሄደ]

leaven
’ሌቨን -ስ- እርሾ

leavings
’ሊይቪንግዝ -ስ- ፍር'ፋሪ ፣ ትርፍራፊ

lecherous
’ሌቸረስ -ቅ- ቅንዝረ'ኛ ፣ ሴሰ'ኛ

lecture
’ሌክቸ -ስ- ንግ'ግር ፣ ትምህርት (ለብዙ ሰው፣ ተማሪ የ'ሚ'ደ'ረግ ፣ የሚነገር)

lecturer
’ሌክቸረ -ስ- ተናጋሪ ፣ አስተማሪ

ledger
’ሌጀ -ስ- የሒሳብ መያዣ መዝገብ

leech
’ሊይች -ስ- አልቅ'ት

leer
’ሊየ -ግ- በፈቃደ ሥጋ አስተያየት መ'መል ከት [ተመለ'ከተ] ፤ በክፉ አስተያየት ማየት [አ'የ]

left
’ሌፍት -ቅ- ግራ (አቅጣ'ጫ) ፤ የተተወ

left-handed
ሌፍት’ሀንደድ -ቅ- ግራ'ኝ (በግራ እ'ጁ መሥ ራት የ'ሚቀናው)

leg
’ሌግ -ስ- ባት ፣ ቅልጥም

legacy
’ሌገሲ -ስ- ቅርስ ፣ ውርስ (በኑዛዜ የተገ'ኘ)

legal
’ሊይገል -ቅ- ሕ'ጋዊ

legality
ሊ’ጋሊቲ -ስ- ሕ'ጋዊ'ነት

legalize
’ሊይገላይዝ -ግ- ሕ'ጋዊ ማድረግ [አደ'ረገ]

legate
’ሌገት -ስ- መልእክተ'ኛ (የሮማው ፓ'ፓ)

legation
ለ’ጌይሽን -ስ- ሌጋሲዮን

legend
’ሌጀንድ -ስ- አፈ ታሪክ

leggings
’ሌጊንግዝ -ስ- ገምባ'ሌ

legibility
ሌጀ’ቢሊቲ -ስ- ለመ'ነበብ መ'ቻል

legible
’ሌጀበል -ቅ- የ'ሚ'ነ'በብ

legion
’ሊይጀን -ስ- የጦር ሠራዊት ክፍል ፣ ማኅበር፤ እልቆ መሣፍርት የሌ'ለው ሰው

legislate
’ሌጂስሌይት -ግ- ሕ'ግ ማውጣት [አወ'ጣ]

legislation
ሌጂስ’ሌይሽን -ስ- ሕ'ግ

legitimate
ለ’ጂተመት -ሕ- ሕ'ጋዊ ፣ ተገቢ

leisure
’ሌዠ -ስ- የዕረፍት ጊዜ ፣ የመዝናኛ ጊዜ

leisurely
’ሌዠሊ -ቅ- ዝ'ግተ'ኛ ፣ ተዝናኝ

lemon
’ሌመን -ስ- የባሕር ሎሚ

lemonade
ሌመ’ኔይድ -ስ- ሎሚናት

lend
’ሌንድ -ግ- ማበ'ደር [አበ'ደረ]፣ ማዋስ [አዋሰ]

lender
’ሌንደ -ስ- አበ'ዳሪ ፣ አዋሽ

length
’ሌንግU -ስ- እርዝመት ፣ እርዝማኔ

lengthen
ሌንገ'ሀን -ግ- ማርዘም [አረ'ዘመ]

lengthy
’ሌንግU -ቅ- በጣም ረ'ጂም

lenient
’ሊይኒየንት -ቅ- ትዕግሥተ'ኛ ፣ ልል (አ'ሳብ ግ'ትር ያልሆነ)

lens
’ሌንዝ -ስ- የካሜራ ፣ የመነ'ጽር መስተዋት

Lent
’ሌንት -ስ- ጾመ አርባ ፣ ሑዳዴ

lentil
’ሌንተል -ስ- ም'ስር (የእህል ዓይነት)

leopard
’ሌፐድ -ስ- ነብር ፡ ነምር

leper
'ሌፐ -ስ- ቆማጣ ፤ ሥጋ ደዌ ያ'ደረ'በት ሰው
leprosy
'ሌፕረሲ -ስ- ቁምጥ'ና ፤ ሥጋ ደዌ በ'ሽታ
less
'ሌስ -ቅ- ያ'ነሰ
lessen
'ሌሰን -ግ- ማሳ'ነስ [አሳ'ነሰ]
lesson
'ሌሰን -ስ- ትምህርት ፤ የ'ሚ'ማሩት ነገር ፤ ማስጠንቀቂያ
let
'ሌት -ግ- መልቀቅ [ለ'ቀቀ] ፤ መተው [ተወ]
letter
'ሌተ -ስ- ደብዳ'ቤ
lettuce
'ሌተስ -ስ- ሰላጣ
level
'ሌቨል -ቅ- ደልዳ'ላ ፤ ዝርግ ፤ ለ'ጥ ያለ
lever
'ሊይቨ -ስ- ሰቅስቆ ማንሻ (ብረት ፤ እንጨት)
levity
'ሌቨቲ -ስ- ያለቦታው የ'ሚ'ደ'ረግ ቧልት ፤ ቁም ነገር አ'ቃ'ሎ ማየት
levy
'ሌቪ -ግ- ቀረጥ መጣል [ጣለ]
-ስ- በሕግ የተጣለ ቀረጥ
lewd
ል'ዩ፡ውድ -ቅ- ባለጌ ፡ ሐፍረተ ቢስ (በፈቃደ ሥጋ ነገር)
liability
ላየ'ቢሊቲ -ስ- ኀላፊ'ነት የመኖር ስ'ሜት ፤ የ'ሚያ'ገድ ነገር (ለሥራ ወዘተ) ፤ የመክፈል ኀላፊ'ነት
liable
'ላየበል -ቅ- በኀ'ጸዩ'የ'ሚያገባው (ሊ'ወ'ቀስ የ'ሚ'ገ'ባው) ፤ ሊሆን የ'ሚችል
liaison
ሊ'ዬይዘን -ስ- ግን'ኙ'ነት ፡ ኅብረት
liar
'ላየ -ቅ- ውሸ፡ታም ፡ ቀጣፊ
libel
'ላይበል -ስ- የሰው ክብር ነ'ክ የሆነ ጽሑፍ

liberal
'ሊበረል -ቅ- ነጻ አ'ሳቢ ፤ አስተሳሰበ ሰ'ፊ
generous
-ቅ- ቸር
liberate
'ሊበሬይት -ግ- ነጻ ማውጣት [አወ'ጣ]
liberty
'ሊበቲ -ስ- ነጻ'ነት
librarian
ላይብ'ሬሪየን -ስ- ሀ'ቃቢ መጻሕፍት
library
'ላይብረሪ -ስ- ቤተ መጻሕፍት
licence
'ላይሰንስ -ስ- ፈቃድ (የመኪና መንጃ ፤ የመ'ሣሪያ ወዘተ)
license
'ላይሰንስ -ግ- የሥራ ፈቃድ መስጠት [ሰ'ጠ]
licensed
'ላይሰንስት -ቅ- ፈቃድ ያ'ለው
licentious
ላይ'ሴንሸስ -ቅ- ሐፍረተ ቢስ (በፈቃደ ሥጋ ነገር)
lick
'ሊክ -ግ- መላስ [ላሰ]
lid
'ሊድ -ስ- ሽፋን ፤ እ'ፊያ ፤ ክዳን
lie
'ላይ -ግ- መዋሸት [ዋ'ሸ]
-down
-ግ- መ'ጋደም [ተ'ጋ'ደመ] ፤ ማ'ጋደም [አ'ጋ'ደመ]
life
'ላይፍ -ስ- ሕይወት ፤ ኑሮ
lifebelt
'ላይፍቤልት -ስ- ከመስጠም የ'ሚያድን መ'ሣሪያ (ከቡሽ የተሠ'ራ)
lifeless
'ላይፍለስ -ቅ- ሕይወት የሌ'ለው ፡ የሞተ ፡ ም'ውት
lift
'ሊፍት -ግ- ማንሣት [አነ'ሣ]
-ስ- አሳንሰር
ligament
'ሊገመንት -ስ- ጅ'ማቶ'ች ፤ ማ'ያያዣ ገመድ

light
'ላይት -ስ- ብርሃን ፣ መብራት
not heavy
-ቅ- ተ'ላል

lighting
'ላይቲንግ -ስ- መብራት (የቤት)

lighter
'ላይተ -ስ- ሲጋራ ማ'ቃጠያ ፣ ማ'ቀጣጠያ (መ'ግሪያ)

lighthouse
'ላይትሀውስ -ስ- መርከቦ'ች ከጽ'ተ'ኝ ጋር እን ዳይ'ጋ'ጩ የ'ሚያመለ'ክት ብርሃን ያ'ለ'በት ሕንፃ

lightning
'ላይትኒንግ -ስ- መብረቅ

lights
'ላይትስ -ስ- የከብት ሆድቃ

like
'ላይክ -ግ- መውደድ [ወ'ደደ]
-ቅ- የ'ሚመስል

likely
'ላይክሊ -ቅ- ሊሆን የ'ሚችል ፣ ምናልባት'ነት ያ'ለው

likeness
'ላይክነስ -ስ- አምሳ'ያ

lilt
'ሊልት -ስ- የዜማ አ'መታት

limb
'ሊም -ስ- እግር'ና እ'ጅ

lime
'ላይም -ስ- ሎሚ ፣ ኖራ

limestone
'ላይምስተውን -ስ- በሀ ወይም ተፎርፎች ድን ጋይ

limit
'ሊሚት -ግ- መወ'ሰን [ወ'ሰነ]
-ስ- ወሰን

limitation
ሊሚቴይሽን -ስ- ወሰን ፣ ድ'ካ

limp
'ሊምፕ -ግ- ማንከስ [አነ'ከሰ]

limpid
'ሊምፒድ -ቅ- የጠ'ራ ፣ ኩል'ል ያለ ፣ በው ስጡ የ'ሚያሳ'ይ (ውሃ ፣ አ'የር ፣ ዓይን)

line
'ላይን -ስ- መሥመር

linen
'ሊነን -ስ- ከተልባ እግር የተሠ'ራ ጨርቅ

liner
'ላይነ -ስ- ታ'ላቅ መርከብ (ለመንገደ'ኞ'ች)

linger
'ሊንገ -ግ- ወደኋላ ማለት [አለ] ፣ መቆ'የት [ቆ'የ]

linguist
'ሊንግዊስት -ስ- የቋንቋዎ'ች ጥናት ሊቅ

liniment
'ሊኒመንት -ስ- መ'ታሻ ቅባት (ለአ'በጠ'ና ለ'ጓ'ጓለ ሰው'ነት)

lining
'ላይኒንግ -ስ- ገበር

link
'ሊንክ -ስ- ማ'ያያዣ

lint
'ሊንት -ስ- ጥጥ (የቁስል)

lion
'ላየን -ስ- አንበ'ሳ

lip
'ሊፕ -ስ- ከንፈር

liquid
'ሊክዊድ -ስ- ፈሳሽ ነገር

liquidate
'ሊክዊዴይት -ግ- መደምሰስ [ደመ'ሰሰ] ፣ መ ክፈል [ከ'ፈለ] (እዳ) ፣ የንግድ ድር'ጅት ገንዘቡን ለዕዳ በመክፈል መዝጋት [ዘ'ጋ]

liquor
'ሊከ -ስ- አልኮል'ነት ያ'ለው መጠ'ጥ

lisp
'ሊስፕ -ስ- መንተባተብ [ተንተባ'ተበ] ("ሰ" ንና "ዘ" ን ደኅና አድርጎ ባለመ'ናገር)

list
'ሊስት -ስ- ዝርዝር

listen
'ሊስን -ግ- ማ'ዳመጥ [አ'ዳ'መጠ]

listener
'ሊስነ -ስ- አድማጭ ፣ ሰሚ

listless
'ሊስትለስ -ቅ- ደካማ ፣ ስልቹ

literacy

'ሊተረሲ -ስ- የማንበብ'ና የመጻፍ ችሎታ

literal

'ሊተረል -ቅ- ያለ ትርጓሜ ፣ እንደ ጽሑፉ ፣ ል'ክ ፣ ፍ'ጹም ስሕተት የሌ'ለ'በት

literary

'ሊተረሪ -ቅ- የሥነ ጽሑፍ ፣ ሥነ ጽሑፋዊ

literate

'ሊተረት -ቅ- የማንበብ'ና የመጻፍ ችሎታ ያ 'ለው

literature

'ሊትረቸ -ስ- ሥነ ጽሑፍ

litre

'ሊይተ -ስ- ሊትር (የፈሳሽ መለ'ኪያ)

litter

'ሊተ -ስ- ው'ዳቂ ፣ ል'ቃሚ ፣ ቆሻሻ

little

'ሊተል -ቅ- ት'ንሽ ፣ አ'ጭር ፣ ጥቂት

live

'ላይቭ -ቅ- ንቁ ፣ ሕይወት ያ'ለው

live

'ሊቭ -ግ- መኖር [ኖረ]

livelihood

'ላይቭሊሁድ -ስ- ወረት የ'ሚ'ገ'ኝ'በት ሥራ፣ መ'ተዳደሪያ ሥራ

lively

'ላይቭሊ -ቅ- ንቁ ፣ የተደ'ሰተ በፍጥነት የ' ሚንቀሳ'ቀስ

liver

'ሊቨ -ስ- ጉ'በት

liverish

'ሊቨሪሽ -ቅ- ጉ'በቱ በመ'ታመም የ'ሚ'ሠ ቃ'ይ

livery

'ሊቨሪ -ስ- የቤት አገልጋይ መ'ለ'ዮ ልብስ

livestock

'ላይቭስቶክ -ስ- ከብት (የከብት ሀብት)

livid

'ሊቪድ -ቅ- መልኩ የገረ'ጣ (በቁ'ጣ ፣ በሕ መም)

living

'ሊቪንግ -ቅ- የ'ሚኖር ፣ ሕያው
-ስ- ወረት የ'ሚ'ገ'ኝ'በት ሥራ

living-room

'ሊቪንግ ሩም -ስ- የእንግዳ መ'ቀበያ ክፍል ፡ እልፍ'ኝ (ሳሎን)

lizard

'ሊዘድ -ስ- እንሽላሊት

load

'ለውድ -ስ- ሸክም

loaf

'ለውፍ -ስ- ዳ'ቦ

loan

'ለውን -ስ- ብ'ድር ፣ ውሰት

loath

'ለውዝ -ቅ- ወደኋላ የ'ሚል ፣ ፈቃድ የሌ'ለው (አንድ ነገር ለማድረግ)

loathe

'ለውዝ -ግ- በጣም መጥላት [ጠ'ላ] ፣ መ'ጸየፍ [ተጸ'የፈ]

lobby

'ሎቢ -ስ- ት'ንሽ አ'ዳራሽ ፣ በቤት ውስጥ መ'ተላለፊያ ቦታ

lobe

'ለውብ -ስ- ለምለም ጆር ፣ ጆር ልም

local

'ለውከል -ቅ- ያንድ ቦታ ፣ ያገሬው

locality

ለው'ካለቲ -ስ- አንድ ነገር ያ'ለ'በት ቦታ ፡ አንድ ድርጊ'ት የተፈ'ጸመ'በት ቦታ

locate

ለው'ኬይት -ግ- አንድ ነገር ያ'ለ'በትን ቦታ ማግኘት [አገ'ኘ]

location

ለው'ከይሽን -ስ- ቦታ ፣ ሥፍራ

lock

'ሎክ -ግ- መቆ'ለፍ [ቆ'ለፈ]
-ስ- የበ'ር ቁልፍ ፣ የጠጉር ቁ'ጥራት

locker

'ሎከ -ስ- ቁልፍ ያ'ለው ት'ንሽ ቁም ሣጥን ፣ ሣጥን

locket

'ሎኪት -ስ- እንደ አሸንክታብ በአንገት ላይ የ'ሚንጠለ'ጠል የማስታወሻ ስጦታ

locksmith

'ሎክስሚስ -ስ- ቁልፍ ሠ'ሪተ'ኛ (የቤት)

locomotion
ለውከ'መውሽን -ስ- ወደፊት መሄድ ፣ መንቀሳቀስ ፣ ካንድ ቦታ ወደ ሌላው መሄድ መቻል

locomotive
ለውከ'መውቲቭ -ስ- የ'ሚያንቀሳ'ቅስ ፣ ባቡር ጎ'ታች ሞተር

locust
'ለውከስት -ስ- አንበጣ ፣ አምበጣ

lodge
'ሎጅ -ግ- መኖር [ኖረ] ፣ (በሰው ዘንድ ለጊዜው'ና ገንዘብ እ'የከ'ፈሉ)

lodger
'ሎጀ -ስ- ገንዘብ እ'የ'ከ'ፈለ በሌላ ሰው ቤት ደ'ባል ሆኖ የ'ሚኖር ሰው

lodging
'ሎጂንግ -ስ- ካንድ መኖሪያ ቤት ውስጥ የተከ ራ'ዩት ክፍል

lodging-house
'ሎጂንግ 'ሀውስ -ስ- ፓንሲዮን፣ ለቀን ወይ'ንም ለሳ'ምንት የ'ሚ'ከራዩት የቤት ክፍል

loft
'ሎፍት -ስ- በጣራ'ና በኮርኒስ መካ'ከል ያ'ለው ክፍት ቦታ

lofty
'ሎፍቲ -ቅ- ረ'ጅም (ለቤት ፣ ለተራራ)

log
'ሎግ -ስ- የግንድ ቱ'ማጅ

logic
'ሎጂክ -ስ- የማስተዋል ጥበብ ፣ ትምህርት ፣ የመ'ከራከር'ና የማሳ'መን ችሎታ

logical
ሎጂክል -ቅ- ጉልህ ፣ ትክ'ክል (ለሐሳ'ብ) አስተዋይ አእምሮ የ'ሚ'ቀ'በለው አስተያየት፣

loin
'ሎይን -ስ- ሽንጥ ፣ የሽንጥ ሥጋ

loiter
'ሎይተ -ግ- ያለሥራ ባ'የቦታው መ'ገተር [ተ ገ'ተረ]

loneliness
'ለውንሊነስ -ስ- ብ'ቸ'ኝ'ነት

lonely
'ለውንሊ -ቅ- ብ'ቸ'ኛ

long
'ሎንግ -ቅ- ረ'ጅም
-ግ- መናፈቅ [ና'ፈቀ

longevity
ሎን'ጀቨቲ -ስ- ረ'ጅም ዕድሜ

longing
'ሎንጊንግ -ስ- ናፍቆት

longitude
'ሎንጊትዩ:ድ -ስ- ቀ'ጥ ያለ መሥመር ፣ ኬንትሮስ (መልክአ ምድር)

longsighted
ሎንግ'ሳይተድ -ቅ- የወደፊቱን የ'ሚያ'ስብ ፣ አርቆ አ'ሳቢ ፣ ዓይኑ ቅርብ ማየት የ'ማይችል

longstanding
ሎንግስ'ታንዲንግ -ቅ- የኖረ ፣ የቆ'የ

look
'ሉክ -ግ- መ'መልከት [ተመለ'ከተ] ፣ አተኩ'ሮ ማየት [አ'የ]

looking-glass
'ሉኪንግ ግ'ላ:ስ -ስ- መስታወት (የመልክ ማያ)

lookout
'ሉካውት -ስ- ዘበ'ኛ (አገር የ'ሚጠ'ብቅ) ፣ መጠ'በቂያ ቦታ

loom
'ሉ:ም -ስ- የሸ'ማኔ ዕቃ
-ግ- ብ'ቅ ማለት [አለ] (በ'ሚያስፈራ ሁናቴ)

loop
'ሉ:ፐ -ስ- ቋጥር (የገመድ ፣ የሺቦ) ፣ ቋ'ጥራት

loophole
'ሉፐሆውል -ስ- ከሕ'ግ ማምለጫ ምክንያት፣ ከም'ሽግ ውስጥ ለመተ'ኰሻ የተበ'ጀ ቀዳዳ

loose
'ሉ:ስ -ቅ- የተፈ'ታ ፣ የላ'ላ ፣ ልል

loosen
'ሉ:ሰን -ግ- መፍታት [ፈ'ታ] ፣ ማላላት [አላ'ላ]

loot
'ሉ:ት -ግ- መዝረፍ [ዘ'ረፈ)
-ስ- የተዘ'ረፈ ዕቃ

lop
'ሎፕ -ግ- መቆርጠፍ [ቆረ'ጠፈ] ፣ ማስተካከል [አስተካ'ከለ] (የዛፍ ቅርንጫፍ ወዘተ) ፣ መጣል [ጣለ] (ለእንስሳት ጆሮ)

lop-sided
ሎፕ'ሳይደድ -ቅ- የተዛ'ባ ፣ ያልተስተካ'ከለ

loquacious
ለውክ'ዌይሸስ -ቅ- ለፍላፊ ፣ ቀባጣሪ

lord
'ሎ:ድ -ስ- ገ'ዥ ፣ ጌታ

lordly
'ሎ:ድሊ -ቅ- የተከ'በረ ፣ ግርማ ያ'ለው ፣ ቀብ ራ'ራ

lore
'ሎ: -ስ- አፈ ታሪክ

lorry
'ሎሪ -ስ- የጭነት መኪና

lose
'ሉ:ዝ -ግ- ማጥፋት [አጠ'ፋ] ፣ መጣል [ጣለ]
game
-ግ- ውር'ርድ መ'ሸነፍ [ተሸ'ነፈ]

loser
'ሉ:ዘ -ስ- ተሸ'ናፊ (በውር'ርድ)

loss
'ሎስ -ስ- ኪሳራ ፣ ማጣት ፣ የጠ'ፋ ነገር ፣ ጉዳት ፣ ሐዘን

lot
'ሎት -ስ- ብዛት ያ'ለው ነገር ፤ በሀ'ራጅ የ'ሚ'ሸጥ ዕቃ ፤ ቁ'ራጭ መሬት
fate
-ስ- እጣ ፣ ዕ'ድል

lotion
'ለውሸ'ን -ስ- ቅባት (ለጠጉር ፣ ለፊት)

lottery
'ሎተሪ -ስ- ሎተሪ

loud
'ላውድ -ቅ- ከ'ፍተ'ኛ (ለጩኸት)

lounge
'ላውንጅ -ስ- ማረፊያ ክፍል
-ግ- ተዝናንቶ መ'ቀመጥ [ተቀ'መጠ]

louse
'ላውስ -ስ- ቅማል

lousy
'ላውዚ -ቅ- ቅማላም ፣ በጣም መጥፎ ፣ ወ'ራዳ

love
'ለቭ -ግ- ማፍቀር [አፈ'ቀረ] ፣ መውደድ [ወ'ደደ]

loveliness
'ለቭሊነስ -ስ- ቁንጅ'ና ፣ ውብ'ነት ፣ ተወ'ዳጅ'ነት

lovely
'ለቭሊ -ቅ- ያማረ ፣ ቆንጆ ፣ ውብ ፣ ተወ'ዳጅ

lover
'ለቨ -ስ- አፍቃሪ ፣ ወዳጅ ውሽ'ማ

loving
'ለቪንግ -ቅ- ወ'ዳድ ፣ የ'ሚወ'ድ ፣ የ'ሚያፈ ቅር

low
'ለው -ቅ- ዝ'ቅ ያለ ፣ ወ'ራ'ዳ

lower
'ለወ -ግ- ዝ'ቅ ማድረግ [አደ'ረገ]

loyal
'ሎየል -ቅ- ታ'ማኝ

loyalty
'ሎየልቲ -ስ- ታ'ማኝ'ነት

lubricant
'ሉብሪከንት -ስ- ቅባት (ለመኪና ፣ ለዕቃ)

lubricate
'ሉብሪኬይት -ግ- ቅባት መቀ'ባት [ቀ'ባ] (ብ ረታ ብረት ፣ መኪና)

lubrication
ሉብሪ'ኬይሸን -ስ- የመኪና ቅባት

lucid
'ሉሲድ -ቅ- ግልጽ (ለንግ'ግር)

luck
'ለክ -ስ- ዕ'ድል

lucky
'ለኪ -ቅ- ዕ'ድለ'ኛ

lucrative
'ሉ:ክረቲቭ -ቅ- ብዙ ገንዘብ የ'ሚያስገ'ኝ

ludicrous
'ሉ:ዲክረስ -ቅ- አ'ሥቂ'ኝ ፣ የ'ቀሀ

luggage
'ለጊጅ -ስ- የመንገድ ጓዝ (ሻንጣ'ና የመሳ 'ሰለው)

luke-warm
ሉ:ክ'ዎ:ም -ቅ- ለ'ብ ያለ (ለውሃ ወዘተ)

lull
'ለል -ግ- ጸ'ጥ ማድረግ [አደ'ረገ] ፣ እ'ሹሩሩ ማለት [አለ]
-ስ- ጸ'ጥታ (ለጥቂት ጊዜ)

lullaby
'ለለባይ -ስ- እ'ሹሩሩ (ልጅ ለማስተ'ኛት የ'ሚ'ዘ'ፈን ዘፈን)

lumbago
ለም'ቤይጎው -ስ- የጀርባ ቁርጥማት

lumber
'ለምበ -ስ- ጠርብ
luminous
'ሉ:ሚነስ -ቅ- የ'ሚያበራ
lump
'ለምፕ -ስ- ቁራጭ (ት'ልቅ) ፣ እብጥ
lumpy
'ለምፒ -ቅ- የጎ'ጉስ (ለሰበት ፣ ለገንፎ)
lunacy
'ሉ:ነሲ -ስ- እብደት
lunar
'ሉ:ነ -ቅ- የጨረቃ
lunatic
'ሉ:ነቲክ -ቅ- እብድ
lunch
'ለንች -ስ- ምሳ
luncheon
'ለንቸን -ስ- ግብር (የምሳ)
lung
'ለንግ -ስ- ሳምባ
lunge
'ለንጅ -ግ- መሻጥ [ሻጠ] (በጦር ወዘተ)
lure
'ሉ:ዐ -ግ- አባብሎ አደጋ ላይ መጣል [ጣለ]፣ ማ'ታለል [አ'ታ'ለለ]
lurid
'ሉ:ሪድ -ቅ- አስፈ'ሪ ፣ አ'ሠቃቂ ፣ ቀለመ ደ'ማት
lurk
'ለ:ክ -ግ- ማድፈጥ [አደ'ፈጠ] ፣ ማድባት [አደ'ባ]
luscious
'ለሽስ -ቅ- እስንምጂ ፣ በጣም የጸለለ'ና የ'ሚ ጣ'ፍጥ ጣዕም ያ'ለው (ለፍራፍሬ)
lust
'ለስት -ስ- ፍትወተ ሥጋ ፣ ጠንካ'ራ ፍ'ላጎት
lustre
'ለስተ -ስ- አንጸባራቂ ፣ ጽርየት
luxuriant
'ለክዥ:ሪየንት -ቅ- ጥቅጥ'ቅ ብሎ የበ'ቀለ (ሣር ፣ ጠጉር) ፣ የተትረፈ'ረፈ
luxurious
ለክ'ዥ:ሪየስ -ቅ- ድሎታም ፣ ም'ቾት ያ'ለው
luxury
'ለክሸሪ -ስ- ድሎት ፣ ም'ቾት
lynch
'ሊንች -ግ- መ'ግደል [ተገ'ደለ] (ታ'ፍኖ በመ ወ'ሰድ ፣ በሕዝብ ያለ ፍርድ)
lyric
'ሊሪክ -ስ- የዘፈን ቃላት ፣ ለዘፈን የተመ'ቹ አጫ'ጭር ግጥሞ'ች

mace
'ሜይስ -ስ- በትረ አርን
machine
መ'ሺይን -ስ- መኪና
machinery
መ'ሺይነሪ -ስ- የመኪና ዕቃ ፣ የመኪና ሥራ
mackintosh
'ማኪንቶሽ -ስ- የዝናም ልብስ
mad
'ማድ -ቅ- እብድ
Madam
'ማደም -ስ- እ'ሜቴ ፣ እ'መቤቴ
madman
'ማድመን -ስ- ያ'በደ ሰው
madness
'ማድነስ -ስ- እብደት
magazine
ማገ'ዚይን -ስ- መጽሔት
of firearms
-ስ- የጥ'ይት ካርታ ፣ የጦር መ'ጋሪያ ፣ የጥ'ይት ወዘተ ዕቃ ቤት
maggot
'ማገት -ስ- የፍራፍሬ ፣ የሥጋ ትል
magic
'ማጂክ -ስ- ጥንቆላ

magician
መ'ጂሽን -ስ- ጠንቋይ
magistrate
'ማጂስትሬይት -ስ- ዳ'ኛ (በዝ'ቅተ'ኛ ፍርድ ቤት)
magnanimity
ማግነ'ኒመቲ -ስ- ቸር'ነት ፣ ባለ ጥሩ ባሕር ይ'ነት
magnet
'ማግነት -ስ- መግነጢስ
magnetic
ማግ'ኔቲክ -ቅ- መግነጢሳዊ
magnificent
ማግ'ኒፊሰንት -ቅ- ት'ልቅ ፣ ድንቅ
magnify
'ማግኒፋይ -ግ- ማጉላት [አጎ'ላ] ፣ ት'ልቅ ማድረግ [አደ'ረገ]
magnifying-glass
'ማግኒፋይንግ ግላ፡ስ -ስ- ማጉያ መነ'ጥር
magnitude
'ማግኒትዩ፡ድ -ስ- መጠን ፣ ት'ልቅ'ነት
mahogany
መ'ሆገኒ -ስ- ጥቁር እንጨት
maid
'ሜይድ -ስ- ገረድ
maiden
'ሜይደን -ስ- ልጃገረድ ፣ ሳዱ'ላ
mail
'ሜይል -ስ- ደብዳ'ቤ ፣ ፖስታ
maim
'ሜይም -ግ- የሰው ገላ መቆራረጥ [ቆራ'ረጠ] ፣ አካለ ስንኩል ማድረግ [አደ'ረገ]
main
'ሜይን -ቅ- ዋ'ና
mainland
'ሜይንለንድ -ስ- አገር ፣ አህጉር (ደሴት ያል ሆነ)
mainly
'ሜይንሊ -ተግ- ይበልጡን
maintain
ሜይን'ቴይን -ግ- መ'ከባከብ [ተከባ'ከበ] ፣ መጠ'በቅ [ጠ'በቀ]
say
-ግ- መ'ናገር [ተና'ገረ]
maintenance
'ሜይተነንስ -ስ- አ'ያያዝ ፣ አ'ጠባበቅ (በተለ'ይ ለሕይወት መጠ'በቂያ)
maize
'ሜይዝ -ስ- በ'ቆ'ሎ ፣ ባርማሽ'ላ
majestic
መ'ጀስቲክ -ቅ- ግርማዊ
majesty
'ማጀስቲ -ስ- ግርማ
major
'ሜይጀ -ቅ- ዋ'ና
military
-ስ- ሻለቃ
majority
መ'ጆረቲ -ስ- የ'ሚበልጠው ፣ አብዛ'ኛው ፣ ሕዝብ ወዘተ
make
'ሜይክ -ግ- መሥራት [ሠ'ራ] ፣ ማድረግ [አደ'ረገ]
make-believe
'ሜይክ ፣ በሊይቭ -ስ- ማስመ'ሰል
maker
'ሜይከ -ግ- አድራጊ
makeshift
'ሜይክሺፍት -ስ- ጊዜያዊ 'ምት'ክ (የተሻለ እስኪ'ገ'ኝ)
make-up
'ሜይከፕ -ስ- የመልክ ማሣ'መሪያ ቅባት ወዘተ
malady
'ማለዲ -ስ- ሕመም ፣ በ'ሽታ
malaria
ማ'ሌሪየ -ስ- ወባ ፣ ንዳድ
male
'ሜይል -ቅ- ተባዕት
malevolent
መ'ሌቨለንት -ቅ- ክፉ አ'ሳቢ ፣ ተንኰለ'ኛ
malice
'ማሊስ -ስ- ክፉ ሐሳ'ብ ፣ ሰውን የመጉዳ ፍ'ላጎት ፣ ተንኰል
malicious
መ'ሊሽስ -ቅ- ክፉ ፣ ክፉ አድራጊ ፣ ተንኰለ'ኛ
malignant
መ'ሊግነንት -ቅ- በሰው ላይ ክፋት የ'ሚያ'ስብ ፣ በጥላ'ቻ የተሞ'ላ

malleable
'ማሊየበል -ቅ- በቀ'ላሉ ቅርፅ ሊ'ሰ'ጠው የ'ሚ'ቻል

mallet
'ማለት -ስ- የንጨት መዶሻ

malnutrition
ማልንዩት'ሪሽን -ስ- በደምብ ባለመ'መገብ የ'ሚ'ፈ'ጠር ሁናቴ

malt
'ሞልት -ስ- ብቅል (የጠ'ላ ፣ የቢራ)

maltreat
ማልት'ሪይት -ግ- መበ'ደል [በ'ደለ]

mammal
'ማመል -ስ- የ'ሚያጠቡ እንስሳት፣ ጡት ያ'ላ'ቸው እንስሳት

mammoth
'ማመስ -ቅ- በጣም ት'ልቅ

man
'ማን -ስ- ሰው

manage
'ማነጅ -ግ- ማስተዳደር [አስተዳ'ደረ] ፣ መምራት [መ'ራ] (ለሥራ) ፤ በ'ሚ'ገ'ባ መያዝ [ያዘ]

management
'ማነጅመንት' -ስ- አስተዳደር ፣ አ'መራር

manager
'ማነጀ -ስ- አስተዳዳሪ ፣ ሥራ መሪ

mane
'ሜይን -ግ- ጋ'ማ (የፈረስ ፣ የአንበሳ)

manger
'ሜይንጀ -ስ- የከብት መ'መገቢያ ፣ ግርግም

mangle
'ማንገል -ስ- የልብስ መጭመቂያ ፣ መጠምዘዢያ መኪና
-ግ- መቆራረጥ [ቆራ'ረጠ] ፣ መበጣጠስ [በጣ'ጠሰ]

ፉ **manhood**
'ማንሁድ -ስ- ጉልምስ'ና ፣ አካለ መጠን ፣ ጉብዝ'ና

· **mania**
'ሜይኒየ -ስ- እብደት ፤ ላንድ ነገር ከ'ሚ'ገ'ባ በላይ ማ'ሰብ

maniac
'ሜይኒያክ -ስ- አእምሮውን የሳተ ሰው ፣ በጣም ያ'በደ ሰው

manicure
'ማኒክዩወ -ስ- እ'ጅን ፣ ጥፍሮ'ችን መ'ከባከብ

manifest
'ማኒፌስት -ግ- መግለጽ [ገ'ለጸ] ፣ ማሳ'የት [አሳ'የ]
-ቅ- ግልጽ

manifold
'ማኒፎውልድ -ቅ- ብዙ ቅርፅ ያ'ለው ፣ ል'ዩ ል'ዩ አገልግሎት የ'ሚሰጥ

manipulate
መ'ኒፐዩሌይት -ግ- በ'ጅ መሥራት [ሠ'ራ] ፤ መ'ቆጣጠር [ተቆጣ'ጠረ] ፤ አሳ'ምሮ መሥራት [ሠ'ራ]

mankind
ማን'ካይንድ -ስ- የሰው ዘር

manly
'ማንሊ -ቅ- ጀግና ፣ ጎበዝ

manner
'ማነ -ስ- ሁናቴ ፣ ጠባይ

manoeuvre
መ'ኑቨ -ስ- የጦር'ነት እንቅስ'ቃሴ ዕ'ቅድ

manor
'ማነ -ስ- የባለመሬቱ ቤት የ'ሚ'ገ'ኝ'በት ርስት

mansion
'ማንሽን -ስ- ታ'ላቅ ቤት ፣ አ'ዳራሽ

manslaughter
'ማንስሎ፡ተ -ስ- በስሕተት ነፍስ መግደል

mantle
'ማንተል -ስ- ካ'ባ ፤ የማሾ ክ'ር

manual
'ማንዩውል -ቅ- የእ'ጅ
book
-ስ- መምሪያ መጽሐፍ

manufacture
ማንዩ'ፋክቸ -ግ- በብዛት ሠርቶ ማውጣት

manufacturer
ማንዩ'ፋክቸረ -ስ- ባለፋብሪካ

manure
መን'ዩወ -ስ- የመሬት ማዳበሪያ መድኃኒት ፤ ፍግ

manuscript
'ማንዩስክሪፕት -ስ- የእ'ጅ ጽሑፍ

many
'ሜኒ -ቅ- ብዙ ፣ አ'ያሌ
map
'ማፕ -ስ- ካርታ (የመሬት)
mar
ማ፡ -ግ- ማ'ጸላሸት [አ'በላ'ሸ] ፣ ማጥፋት [አጠ'ፋ] ፣ ማፈራረስ [አፈራ'ረሰ]
marble
'ማ፡ቦል -ስ- እብነ በረድ
march
'ማ፡ች -ግ- በሰልፍ መ'ጓዝ [ተጓዘ]
March
'ማ፡ች -ስ- መ'ጋቢት (የወር ስም)
mare
'ሜየ -ስ- ሴት ፈረስ ፣ ባዝራ
margin
'ማ፡ጂን -ስ- ሕ'ዳግ (የመጽሐፍ ወዘተ) ፣ ዳር (የሒደት ወዘተ)
marine
መ'ሪይን -ስ- የጦር መርከበ'ኛ
-ቅ- የባሕር
marital
'ማሪተል -ቅ- የጋብ'ቻ
maritime
'ማሪታይም -ስ- የባሕር ንግድ
mark
'ማ፡ክ -ግ- ምል'ክት ማድረግ [አደ'ረገ]
-ስ- ምል'ክት
market
'ማ፡ክት -ስ- ገበያ
market-place
'ማ፡ክትፕሌይስ -ስ- ገበያ
marksman
'ማ፡ክስመን -ስ- ጥሩ አ'ነጣጣሪ ፣ ተ'ኩሶ የ'ማ ይስት
maroon
መ'ሩ:ን -ቅ- ወደ ተ'ደ'ነት የ'ሚያደላ ዐ'ና'ማ ተለም
leave stranded
-ግ- ሰውን ብቻ'ውን ላይ ጥሎ መሄድ [ሄደ] (ም'ላሌ ፣ ሰው በሌ'ለ'በት ደሴት ወዘተ)
marquee
ማ፡'ኪይ -ስ- ዳ'ስ ፣ ት'ልቅ ድንኳን

marriage
'ማሪጅ -ስ- ጋብ'ቻ
married
'ማሪድ -ቅ- ያገ'ባ ፣ ባለትዳር
marrow
'ማሬው -ስ- ዱ'ባ ፣ መቅኒ፣መቅን (የቅልጥም ቅልጥም
marry
'ማሪ -ግ- ማግባት [አገ'ባ]
marsh
'ማ፡ሽ -ስ- ረግረግ
marshal
'ማ፡ሸል -ስ- ስልፍ ጠ'ባቂ ፣ ስልፍ ተቆጣጣሪ
mart
'ማ፡ት -ስ- ገበያ ፣ ሐ'ራጅ የ'ሚ'ባል'በት ቤት
martial
'ማ፡ሸል -ቅ- የወ'ታ'ደር ፣ ወ'ታ'ደራዊ
martyr
'ማ፡ተ -ስ- ሰማዕት
marvel
'ማ፡ቨል -ግ- መ'ደነቅ [ተደ'ነቀ] ፣ መ'ደናገር [ተደና'ገረ] (በመ'ደሰት)
marvellous
'ማ፡ቨለስ -ቅ- አስደ'ናቂ ፣ ግሩም (በመ'ደሰት)
masculine
'ማስኪዩሊን -ስ- ተባዕት ፣ ወንድ
mash
'ማሽ -ግ- ማድቀቅ [አደ'ቀቀ] ፣ መደፍጠጥ [ደፈ'ጠጠ] (ለመጥ ምግብ'ቹ)
mask
'ማ፡ስክ -ስ- ሽፋን (የፊት መሸ'ሸጊያ'ና ልላ ቅርጽ የ'ሚለጥ)
mason
'ሜይሰን -ስ- ድንጊያ ጠራቢ
masquerade
'ማስከሬይድ -ቅ- ማ'ታለል ፣ እውነት ያልሆነ
mass
'ማስ -ስ- ክብደት
religious service
-ስ- ቅ'ዳሴ
majority
-ስ- ያብላጫ ሕዝብ ፣ ብዙ ቦታ የተከ'ማ'ቸ ሕዝብ

massacre
'ማሰከ -ግ- መግደል [ገ'ደለ] ፣ መፍጀት [ፈ'ጀ] (ለሰው)

massage
'ማሳ:ጅ -ግ- ማሸት [አ'ሸ] (ሰው'ነት)

massive
'ማሲቭ -ቅ- በጣም ተ'ልቅ'ና ከ'ባድ

mast
'ማ:ስት -ስ- የመርከብ ተራዳ

master
'ማ:ስተ -ስ- ጌታ ፣ መሪ ፣ አ'ዛዥ

masterful
'ማ:ስተፉል -ቅ- ኀይለ'ኛ (ገዢ) ፣ ሥልጣኑን በሌሎ'ች ላይ መጠርጋት የ'ሚወ'ድ ፣ የ'ሚችል ፣ ታ'ላቅ ችሎታ ያ'ለው

masticate
'ማስቲኬይት -ግ- ማ'ኘክ [አ'ኘከ] ፣ ማ'ላመጥ [አ'ላመጠ]

mat
'ማት -ስ- ሰሌን (የወለል ምንጣፍ)

match
'ማች -ስ- ክብሪት
resemble
-ግ- መ'መሳሰል [ተመሳ'ሰለ]
sport
-ስ- ግጥሚያ (ስፖርት)

match-maker
'ማችሜይከ -ስ- አ'ባባይ ፣ አ'ማች (ለጋብ'ቻ)

mate
'ሜይት -ስ- የሥራ ጓ'ደ'ኛ ፣ ጓ'ደ'ኛ ፣ ሚስት ፣ ባል

material
መ'ቲሪየል -ስ- ጨርቃ ጨርቅ ፣ አንድ ዕቃ የ'ሚ'ሠራ'በት ነገር

materialize
መ'ቲሪየላይዝ -ግ- እው'ነት ማድረስ [አደ'ረሰ] ፣ እሥራ ላይ ማዋል [አ'ዋለ]

maternal
መ'ተ:ነል -ቅ- የእ'ናት ፣ እ'ናታዊ

maternity
መ'ተ:ነቲ -ስ- እ'ናት'ነት

mathematics
ማስ'ማቲክስ -ስ- የሒሳብ ትምህርት ፣ የሒሳብ ዕውቀት

matriculation
መትሪክዩ'ሌይሽን -ስ- የሁለ'ተ'ኛ ደረጃ ትምህርት ቤት መልቀቂያ ፈተና

matrimony
'ማትሪመኒ -ስ- ጋብ'ቻ

matron
'ሜይትረን -ስ- ዕትዓር ብዙ ጊዜ የኖረ'ች ሴት ፣ ያገቡ ድር'ጅት ኀላፊ የሆን'ች ሴት (በሆስፒታል ወዘተ)

matter
'ማተ -ስ- ነገር ፣ ጉ'ዳይ

matter-of-fact
ማተረ'ቭፋክት -ቅ- ተራ (ሁኔታ) ፣ ደንታ የለ'ለው ፣ እውነቱ ብ'ቻ የ'ሚገ'ደው

matting
'ማቲንግ -ስ- ሳጣራ ፣ ሰሌን ወዘተ

mattress
'ማትረስ -ስ- ፍራሽ

mature
መ'ቹዋ -ቅ- የበ'ሰለ (ለሰው)

maturity
መ'ቹረቲ -ስ- እድገት ፣ መብሰል (ስዕድሜ)

maul
'ሞ:ል -ግ- መቦጫጨቅ [ቦጫ'ጨቀ] ፣ የጭ'ካኔ ተግባር መፈ'ጸም [ፈ'ጸመ]

mauve
'መውቭ -ቅ- ጠቆ'ር ያለ ሰማያዊ

May
'ሜይ -ስ- ግንቦት

may
'ሜይ -ግ- መቻል [ቻለ] ፣ ፈቃድ መ'ቀበል [ተቀ'በለ] (እንደ ሪ'ፓት ግ'ም ፐር'ሚሬን ፣ ም'ኞትን'ና ፈቃድን ይገልጣል)

maybe
'ሜይቢ -ተግ- ሊሆን ይችላል ፣ ምናልባት

mayor
'ሜየ -ስ- ከን'ቲባ ፣ የከተማ ገ'ዥ

maze
'ሜይዝ -ስ- መግቢያ'ና መውጫው የ'ማይ'ታ'ወ'ቅ መንገድ ፣ የተወሳ'ሰበ ጉ'ዳይ ፣ ሐ'ሳብ

me
'ሚይ -ተስ- እኔን ፣ ለኔ

meadow
'ሜደው -ስ- መስክ

meagre
'ሚገ -ቅ- ት'ንሽ ፥ የ'ማይበቃ (ምግብ ወዘተ)
meal
'ሚይል -ስ- ምግብ (የተዘጋ'ጀ)
mean
'ሚይን -ቅ- ንብጋ'ባ ፥ ቆጥቋ'ጣ (ለገንዘብ ወዘተ) ፥ እስቀ'ያሚ ፥ የ'ማይ'ገ'ባ (ለጠባይ)
meaning
'ሚይኒንግ -ስ- ትርጉም ፥ ፍ'ች
means
'ሚይንዝ -ስ- መንገድ ፥ ብልኀት
meantime
'ሚይን:ታይም -ተግ- ወዲያው'ም፥በ'ዚያው'ም ጊዜ፥በ'ዚሁ'ም መካ'ከል
meanwhile
ሚይን'ዋይል -ተግ- ወዲያ'ው'ም ፥ በ'ዚያው'ም ፥ በ'ዚሁ'ም መካ'ከል
measles
'ሚይዘልዝ -ስ- ኩ'ፍ'ኝ
measure
'ሜዠ -ግ- መለ'ካት [ለ'ካ]
meat
'ሚይት -ስ- ሥጋ
mechanic
ሚ'ካኒክ -ስ- ሜካኒክ
medal
'ሜዶል -ስ- ኒሻን ፥ ሊሻን
meddle
'ሜዶል -ግ- ጥ'ል'ቅ ማለት [አለ] (በሰው ን'ዳይ)
mediate
'ሚ፤ዲዩይት -ግ- መሸምገል [ሸመ'ገለ] (ለግ(ታረቅ)
medical
'ሜዲክል -ቅ- የመድኃኒት
medication
ሜዲ'ኬይሽን -ስ- መድኃኒት ፥ ሕ'ክም'ና
medicinal
መ'ዲሰነል -ቅ- መድኃኒት'ነት ያ'ለው
medicine
'ሜደሰን -ስ- መድኃኒት

medieval
ሜ'ዲይቨል -ስ- ማእከላዊ ዘመን (ከ፩ሺ፩፻ እስከ ፩ሺ፭፻ ዓ ም ገደማ ያ'ለው የአውሮ'ፓ ታሪክ)
meditate
'ሜደቴይት -ግ- አጥልቆ ማ'ሰብ [አ'ሰበ] ፥ ከል'ብ ማ'ሰላሰል [አ'ሰላ'ሰለ]
medium
'ሚይዲየም -ቅ- መካ'ከለ'ኛ ፥ ደልዳ'ላ (ለቁመት)
meek
'ሚይክ -ቅ- ትሑት ፥ ታ'ዛዥ ፥ መከራን ታ'ጋሽ
meet
'ሚይት -ግ- መ'ገናኘት [ተገና'ኘ]
meeting
'ሚይቲንግ -ስ- ስብሰባ ፥ መ'ገናኘት
melancholy
'ሜለንኮሊ -ስ- ጥልቅ ሐዘን ፥ ጭንቀ
mellow
'ሜለው -ቅ- የበ'ሰለ ፥ ለስላ'ሳ'ና ጣፋጭ ፥ ዕድሜ ያስተማረው ፥ የተዝና'ና
melodious
መ'ለውዲየስ -ቅ- ጣዕመ ዜማ ያ'ለው
melody
'ሜለዲ -ስ- ጣዕመ ዜማ
melon
'ሜለን -ስ- ከርቡሽ ፥ በ'ጢኽ
melt
'ሜልት -ግ- መቅለጥ [ቀ'ለጠ] ፥ ማቅለጥ [አቀ'ለጠ]
member
'ሜምበ -ስ- አባል
membrane
'ሜምብሬይን -ስ- ሥሥ ሽፋን (የሰውን ፥ የእንስሳን ሥጋ የ'ሚያ'ገና'ኝ ፥ የ'ሚሸ'ፍን)
memento
መ'ሜንተው -ስ- የማስታወሻ ዕቃ (ያንዱን ሰው የተለ'የ ሁናቴ የ'ሚያስታ'ውሱ'በት)
memoir
'ሜምዋ -ስ- የራስ ታሪክ ፥ የሰው ታሪክ (ያ'ቴት በመጽሐፍ መልክ)
memorable
'ሜመረበል -ቅ- የ'ሚታ'ወስ ፥ የ'ማይረ'ሳ

memorial
መ'ሞ:ሪየል -ስ- መ'ታሰቢያ (የጦር'ነት ፣ የታላ'ላቅ ሰዎ'ች)

memorize
'ሜመራይዝ -ግ- ማስታወስ [አስታ'ወሰ] ፡ በቃል ማጥናት [አጠ'ና]

memory
'ሜመሪ -ስ- ት'ዝታ

menace
'ሜነስ -ግ- መዛት [ዛተ] ፣ ማስፈራራት [አስ ፈራ'ራ]

menacing
'ሜነሲንግ -ስ- አስፈ'ሪ ፣ የ'ሚዝት

menagerie
ሞ'ናጀሪ -ስ- የዱር እንስሳት ማኖሪያ ቦታ (በተለ'ይ ካገር አገር እ'የተዘዋ'ወሩ ለሰው የ'ሚ 'ታ'ዩ)

mend
'ሜንድ -ግ- መጠ'ገን [ጠ'ገነ]

menial
'ሚይኒየል -ቅ- ወ'ራ'ዳ (ሥራ)
-ስ- የቤት አገልጋይ

menstruation
ሜንስትሩ'ዌይሸን -ስ- አደፍ ፣ እንግዳ (የሴት ደም)

mental
'ሜንተል -ቅ- የአእምሮ

mentality
ሜን'ታለቲ -ስ- አእምሮ ፣ አስተሳሰብ

mention
'ሜንሸን -ግ- መጥቀስ [ጠ'ቀሰ]

mercantile
'መ:ከንታይል -ቅ- የንግድ ፣ የነ'ጋዴ

mercenary
'መ:ሰንሪ -ስ- በገንዘብ የተገ'ዛ ወ'ታ'ደር
greedy
-ቅ- ስለገንዘብ ብ'ቻ የ'ሚያ'ስብ ፣ ቆጥ ቋ'ጣ

merchandise
'መ:ቸንዳይዝ -ስ- የንግድ ዕቃ

merchant
'መ:ቸንት -ስ- ነ'ጋዴ

merciful
'መ:ሲፉል -ቅ- መሐሪ ፣ ርኅሩኅ

mercury
'መ:ክዩሪ -ስ- ባዜቃ

mercy
'መ:ሲ -ስ- ምሕረት

mere
'ሚየ -ቅ- ተጨ'ማሪ'ም ፣ ተቀ'ናሽ'ም የሌ'ለ 'በት ፣ ቀ'ላል (ብ'ቻ)

merely
'ሚየሊ -ተግ- እን ዲያው ፣ ብ'ቻ ፣ በቀ'ላሉ

merge
'መ:ጅ -ግ- መ'ደባለቅ [ተደባ'ለቀ]

merger
'መ:ጀ -ስ- የሁለ'ት ድር'ጅቶ'ች መ'ዋሐድ (የን ግድ)

merit
'ሜሪት -ስ- ሽ'ልማት የሚያስገኝ ተገቢ'ነት ፣ የመ'መስገን ተገቢ'ነት

mermaid
'መ:ሜይድ -ስ- ጂራቱ የሀሣ የተቀ'ረው ሰው 'ነቱ ግን የሰው ቅርፅ ያ'ለው ፍጡር

merriment
'ሜሪሜንት -ስ- ደ'ስታ

merry
'ሜሪ -ቅ- ደ'ስተ'ኛ

mesh
'ሜሽ -ስ- መረብ ፣ መርበብ (ዐሣ ማጥመጃ)

mess
'ሜስ -ስ- ዝረክራ'ካ'ነት ፣ የንጽሕ'ና ጉድለት አለመ'ሰተር

message
'ሜሰጅ -ስ- መልእክት

messenger
'ሜሰንጀ -ስ- መልእክተ'ኛ ፣ ተላላኪ

metal
'ሜተል -ስ- ብረታ ብረት

metallic
ሜ'ታሊክ -ቅ- ብረት መ'ሰል ፣ የብረት ፣ ብ ረት ያ'ለ'በት

meter
'ሚይተ -ስ- መቁጠሪያ (የኤሌትሪክ ፡ የውሃ ወዘተ)

method
ሜሰድ -ስ- መንገድ (የአ'ሠራር)

methodical

ሜ'ሶዲካል -ት- ሥርዓት ጠ'ባቂ ፣ በደምብ'ና በሥርዓት የተሠ'ራ

meticulous

ሚ'ቲክዩለስ -ት- ለጥቃ'ቅን ነገር ሁ'ሉ የ'ሚ 'ጠነ'ቀ'ቅ ፣ በጣም ጥንቁቅ

metre

'ሚይተ -ስ- ሜትር (መለ'ኪያ)

metropolis

ሜት'ሮፖሊስ -ስ- ዋ'ና ከተማ ፣ መዲና

metropolitan

ሜትሮ'ፖሊተን -ት- የዋ'ና ከተማ ፣ የሊቀ ጳ'ጳሳት ወይን'ም የስብከተ ሀገሩ

mettle

'ሜተል -ስ- ጉብዝ'ና፣መከራን መቻል (ለሰው ፣ ለፈረስ)

microbe

'ማይክረውብ -ስ- ሚክሮብ ፣ ረቂቃን ነፍሳት

microscope

'ማይክረስኮፕ -ስ- ሚክሮስኮ'ፕ ፣ ጥቃ'ቅን ነገሮ'ች አጉልቶ የ'ሚያሳ'ይ መነ'ጽር

midday

ሚድ'ዴይ -ስ- ቀትር ፣ ተሲዓት

middle

'ሚደል -ት- መካ'ከለ'ኛ

middleman

'ሚደልማን -ስ- ጅምላ ነ'ጋዴ ፣ አማካኝ ሰው (እንደ ደ'ላላ ያ'ለ)

middling

'ሚድሊንግ -ት- መካ'ከለ'ኛ (ለዓይነት ፣ ለመ ጠን)

midge

'ሚጅ -ስ- ት'ንኝ

midget

'ሚጂት -ስ- ድንክ

midnight

'ሚድናይት -ስ- እ'ኩለ ሌሊት

midst

'ሚድስት -ስ- መካ'ከል

midsummer

ሚድ'ሰመ -ስ- የበጋ እ'ጋማሽ

midwife

'ሚድዋይፍ -ስ- አ'ዋላጅ

might

'ማይት -ስ- ኀይል

mighty

'ማይቲ -ት- ኀይለ'ኛ ፣ ት'ልቅ

migrant

'ማይግረንት -ስ- ስ'ደተ'ኛ (ወደ ሌላ አገር የ'ሚሄድ)

migrate

ማይግ'ሬይት -ግ- አገሩን ለ'ቆ ወደሌላ አገር መሄድ [ሄደ] (ለመኖር)

mild

'ማይልድ -ት- ለስላ'ሳ ፣ ጥን'ካሬ የሌ'ለው ፣ ቀ'ላል (ቅጣት ወዘተ)

mildew

'ሚልድዩው -ስ- አረቄ

mile

'ማይል -ስ- ማይል (የርቀት መለ'ኪያ)

milestone

'ማይልስተውን -ስ- የመንገድ ርቀት መንገሪያ ድንጊያ (አልፎ አልፎ በመንገድ ዳር የተ ተ'ከለ)

militant

'ሚሊተንት -ት- ተጣይ ፣ ተዋጊ (ለእምነት ወዘተ)

military

'ሚሊተሪ -ት- ወ'ታ'ደራዊ

milk

'ሚልክ -ስ- ወተት

milkmaid

'ሚልክሜይድ -ስ- ወተት አላቢ ሴት

milky

'ሚልኪ -ስ- ወተት የ'ሚመስል (ፈሳሽ)

mill

'ሚል -ስ- ወፍጮ

millennium

ሚ'ሌኒየም -ስ- አንድ ሺህ ዓመት ፣ ከምፅአት በኋላ ክርስቶስ በመሬት ላይ የ'ሚነግሥ'በት ዘመን ፣ የሰላም'ና የደ'ስታ'ንት ዘመን

miller

'ሚለ -ስ- ባለወፍጮ ፣ በወፍጮ ቤት የ'ሚ ሠራ

millet

'ሚሊት -ስ- የዳጉ'ሳ'ና የጠጁ ዓይነት እህል

milliner
'ሚሊነ -ስ- የሴት ባርኔጣ ሠሪ'ና ሻጭ
million
'ሚልየን -ስ- ሚሊዮን ፥ እልፍ አእላፋት
millstone
'ሚልስተውን -ስ- የወፍጮ ድንጊያ
mimic
'ሚሚክ -ግ- ሰው መቀ'ጸል [ቀ'ጸለ]፥ ሰው መቀ'ንጠጥ [ቀን'ጠጠ] ፥ የሰው አ'ነጋገር እስ መ'ስሎ መ'ናገር [ተና'ገረ]
mimicry
'ሚሚክሪ -ስ- ሰውን ቅ'ጸላ (ለአ'ነጋገር) ፥ ቅ'ንጠጣ
mince
'ሚንስ -ግ- መክተፍ [ከ'ተፈ]
mincing machine
'ሚንሲንግ ፥ መ'ሺይን -ስ- የሥጋ መፍጫ መኪና
mind
'ማይንድ -ስ- አእምሮ ፥ አንጐል ፥ አስተሳሰብ
-ግ- መ'ቃወም [ተቃ'ወመ] ፥ መ'ጠን ቀቅ [ተጠን'ቀቀ]
mine
'ማይን -ተስ- የኔ
mineral
'ሚነረል -ስ- የማዕድ'ን ቦታ (የተቆ'ፈረ) ማዕ'ድን
mingle
'ሚንግል -ግ- መ'ደባለቅ [ተደባ'ለቀ] ፥ ማ'ደ ባለቅ [አ'ደባ'ለቀ]
miniature
'ሚኒቸ -ስ- በጣም ት'ን'ሽ ሥዕል ፥ ያንድ ቅር ፅ ት'ን'ሽ ምስል
minimize
'ሚኒማይዝ -ግ- ማሳ'ነስ [አሳ'ነሰ]
minimum
'ሚኒመም -ቅ- በተቻለ መጠን ያ'ነሰ
mining
'ማይኒንግ -ስ- የማዕ'ድን ሥራ
minister
'ሚኒስተ -ግ- ማገልገል [አገለ'ገለ] ፥ መርዳት [ረ'ዳ]
-ስ- ሚኒስትር ፥ ካህን
ministerial
ሚኒስ'ቲሪየል -ቅ- የሚኒስትር ፥ የሚኒስቴር

ministry
'ሚኒስትሪ -ስ- ሚኒስቴር (መሥሪያ ቤት)
minor
'ማይነ -ቅ- ዝ'ቅተ'ኛ ፥ ያ'ነሰ ፥ ዋጋ የሌ'ለው
-ስ- ከሃያ ዓመት በታ'ች ያ'ለ ሰው
minority
ማይ'ኖሪቲ -ስ- ጥቂቶ'ች ፥ በቁጥር ያ'ነሱ
minstrel
'ሚንስትረል -ስ- እ'የዞረ የ'ሚዘፍን አዝማሪ
mint
'ሚንት -ስ- ገንዘብ የ'ሚ'ሠ'ራ'በት ቦታ
herb
-ስ- ሚንታ
minus
'ማይነስ -ቅ- ያ'ነሰ ፥ የተቀ'ነሰ'ለት
minute
'ሚኒት -ስ- ደቂቃ ፥ ቃለ ጉባኤ
minute
ማይን'ዩ፡ት -ቅ- በጣም ት'ን'ሽ ፥ ደ'ቃቅ
miracle
'ሚረክል -ስ- ተአ'ምር ፥ የ'ሚያስደ'ንቅ ነገር ያልተለ'መደ ነገር
miraculous
ሚ'ራክዩለስ -ቅ- አስገ'ራሚ ፥ ተአ'ምራዊ
mire
'ማየ -ስ- ጭቃ ፥ እርንታ ፥ ቆሻሻ
mirror
'ሚረ -ስ- መስታዎት (ማያ)
mirth
'መ፡ስ -ስ- መ'ደሰት ፥ ሣቅ
misapprehension
ሚሳፕረ'ሄንሽን -ስ- በትክ'ክል አለመ'ረዳት
misbehave
ሚስቢ'ሄይቭ -ግ- አመለቢስ መሆን [ሆነ] ፥ መጥፎ አመል ማሳየት [አሳ'የ] ፥ መባለግ [ባ 'ለገ]
miscalculate
ሚስ'ካልኩሌይት -ግ- ስሕተት ማድረግ [አ ደ'ረገ] (ባ'ሰቡት ፥ በገ'መቱት ነገር)
miscarriage
'ሚስካሪጅ -ስ- ማስወ'ረድ (ልጅ)
miscarry
ሚስ'ካሪ -ግ- እፍ'ጻሚ አለመድረስ [-ደ'ረሰ]፥ ማስወ'ረድ [አስወ'ረደ] (ለእርግዝ'ና)

miscellaneous

ሚስ'ሌይኒየስ -ቅ- ል'ዩ ል'ዩ ፣ ድብልቅልቅ

mischief

'ሚስቺፍ -ስ- እ'ዋኪ'ነት ፣ ክልፍልፍ'ነት ክፋት ፣ በጥባጭ'ነት

mischievous

'ሚስቺቨስ -ቅ- ቅልብልብ ፣ እ'ዋኪ ፣ በጥ ባጭ

misdemeanour

ሚስደ'ሚይነ -ስ- መጥፎ ሥራ ፣ ተሳሳፊ'ነት (ሕ'ግን)

miserly

'ማይዘሊ -ቅ- ሥ'ሥታም ፣ ገብጋ'ባ ፣ ቆጥ ቋ'ጣ

miserable

'ሚዝረበል -ቅ- በጣም ያልተደ'ሰተ ፣ መከራ ያጠ'ቃው ፣ መከረ'ኛ

misery

'ሚዘሪ -ስ- መከራ ፣ ች'ግር

misfortune

ሚስ'ፎ፡ቹን -ስ- መጥፎ ዕ'ድል

misgiving

ሚስ'ጊቪንግ -ስ- ጥር'ጣሬ ፣ ፍርሀት

mishap

'ሚስሀፕ -ስ- ድንገተ'ኛ አደጋ (ቀለ'ል ያለ)

mislay

ሚስ'ሌይ -ግ- ዕቃ ያኖሩ'በትን ቦታ ማጣት [አ'ጣ] ፣ ለጊዜው ማጣት [አ'ጣ]

mislead

ሚስ'ሊይድ -ግ- ማ'ታለል [አ'ታለለ] ፣ ማ'ሳ ሳት [አ'ሳሳተ]

misplace

ሚስፕ'ሌይስ -ግ- ያለቦታው ማስቀ'መጥ [አ ስቀ'መጠ]

misrepresentation

ሚስሬፕሪዘን'ቴይሽን -ስ- እ'ያ'ወቁ የ'ሚያቀር ቡት ማ'ሳሳቻ ፣ ትክ'ክል ያልሆነ ወሬ

miss

'ሚስ -ግ- ለመድረስ ፣ ለመምታት ፣ ለማግ ኘት ወዘተ አለመቻል [-ቻለ]

Miss

'ሚስ -ስ- ወይዘሪት

missile

'ሚሳይል -ስ- ተወርዋሪ የጦር መ'ሣሪያ ፡ ተስፈንጣሪ መ'ሣሪያ

missing

'ሚሲንግ -ቅ- የጠ'ፋ

mission

'ሚሽን -ስ- ተግባር ፣ መልእክት ፣ መልእክ 'ኞ'ች ፤ በሕይወት ሙሉ የ'ሚፈ'ጸም ተግባ

religious

-ስ- ሚስዮን (የሃይማኖት ስብከት ድ 'ጅት)

missionary

'ሚሽነሪ -ስ- የወንጌል መልእክተ'ኛ ፡ ሚ ዮናዊ ሰው

mist

'ሚስት -ስ- ጭጋግ

mistake

ሚስ'ቴይክ -ግ- መ'ሳሳት [ተሳሳተ]

mistaken

ሚስ'ቴይክን -ቅ- የተሳሳተ

Mister

'ሚስተ -ስ- አቶ

mistress

'ሚስትረስ -ስ- ው'ሽማ (ሴት) ወዳጅ

employer

-ስ- እ'መቤት

mistrust

ሚስት'ረስት -ግ- አለማመን [-አ'መነ]፡ መ'ጠ ራጠር [ተጠራ'ጠረ]

misunderstanding

ሚስንደስ'ታንዲንግ -ስ- አለመግባባት

misuse

ሚስ'ዩ፡ዝ -ግ- ማ'በላሸት [አ'በላ'ሸ] ፡ ያለ ቦታው ማዋል [አዋለ]

misuse

ሚስ'ዩ፡ስ -ስ- ማ'በላሸት ፣ አንድ ነገር በ'ሚ 'ገ'ባው ቦታ አለማዋል

mite

'ማይት -ስ- በጣም ት'ንሽ ነገር ፡ ት'ንሽ ሕፃን

mitigate

'ሚቲጌይት -ግ- ማ ባባል [አ'ሻሻለ] ፡ ማለ 'ዘብ [አለ'ዘበ]

mitten

'ሚተን -ስ- የሱፍ እ'ጅ ሹ'ራብ (አራ'ቱን ጣት ለብ'ቻ አውራ ጣት ለብ'ቻ የ'ሚሸ'ፍን)

ሊክስ -ግ- መደባለቅ [ደባ'ለቀ] ፣ መ'ደባለቅ [ተደባ'ለቀ]

ıture

ሚክስቸ -ስ- የተደባ'ለቀ ነገር ፣ ማ'ደባለቅ

ix-up

'ሚክሰፐ -ስ- አለመግባባት ፣ መ'ሳሳት

noan

'መውን -ግ- ማቃሰት [አቃ'ሰተ] (ከሥቃይ የተነ'ሣ)

moat

'መውት -ስ- በቤት ዙሪያ ያ'ለ የውሃ አጥር (ለመ'ከላከያ)

mob

'ሞብ -ስ- ሕ'ገ ወ'ጥ ሰዎ'ች ፣ የተሰበ'ሰቡ ሰዎ'ች (ብጥ'ብጥ ለማንሣት ፣ አንድ ሁናቴ ለመ'መልከት)

mobile

'መውባይል -ቅ- የ'ሚንቀሳ'ቀስ

mock

'ሞክ -ግ- ማፌዝ [አፌዘ]

mockery

'ሞከሪ -ስ- ፌዝ

mode

'መውድ -ስ- ያ'ደራረግ ወይ'ን'ም ያ'ሠራር መ'ን ገድ ፣ ዘዴ ፣ ሞድ (የልብስ)

model

'ሞደል -ስ- ያንድ ነገር ት'ን'ሽ ቅርፅ ፣ እንደ ም'ሳሌ የ'ሚ'ገለ'በጥ ነገር ፣ ሞድ የ'ምታሳ'ይ ሴት ልጅ ፣ ጥሩ ም'ሳሌ (ሊ'ገለ'በጥ የ'ሚ'ገ 'ባው)

moderate

'ሞደረት -ቅ- መካ'ከለ'ኛ

modern

'ሞደን -ቅ- ዘመናዊ ፣ አ'ዲስ ሐ'ሳብ ያ'ለው

modest

'ሞደስት -ቅ- ትሑት ፣ ጭ'ምት

modification

ሞዲፊ'ኬይሽን -ስ- ማ'ሻሻል ፣ ት'ን'ሽ ለውጥ

modify

'ሞዲፋይ -ግ- ማ'ሻሻል [አ'ሻሻለ] ፣ ት'ን'ሽ ለውጥ ማድረግ [አደ'ረገ]

moist

'ሞይስት -ቅ- እርጥብ ፣ ዝናማም

moisten

'ሞይሰን -ግ- ማርጠብ [አረ'ጠበ]

moisture

'ሞይስቸ -ስ- እርጥበት

mole

'መውል -ስ- ፍልፈል ፣ ማርያም የሳመ'ችው ምል'ክት (በሰው'ነት ላይ)

molest

'መሌስት -ግ- ጥ'ልቅ ማለት [አለ] (በሰው ሥራ) ፣ ማ'ወክ [አ'ወከ] (አ'ያ'ወቂ)

molten

'ሞልተን -ቅ- የቀ'ለጠ (ለብረታ ብረት)

moment

'መውመንት -ስ- ቅጽበት ፣ አፍታ

momentary

'መውመንትሪ -ቅ- አንድ አፍታ የቆ'የ

momentous

መ'ሜንተስ -ቅ- በጣም አስፈ'ላጊ

monarch

'ሞነክ -ስ- የበላይ ገዥ ፣ ንጉሥ

monarchy

'ሞነኪ -ስ- ንጉሣዊ አ'ገዛዝ ፣ ግዛቱ በአንድ ከ'ፍተ'ኛ ሥልጣን ሥር ያ'ለ መንግሥት

monastery

'ሞነስትሪ -ስ- ገዳም

Monday

'መንዴይ -ስ- ሰ'ኞ

monetary

'መነትሪ -ቅ- የገንዘብ

money

'መኒ -ስ- ገንዘብ

mongrel

'ሞንግረል -ስ- መጢቃ ፣ ዘሩ የተደባ'ለቀ እንስሳ (ው'ሻ ፣ ወዘተ)

monitor

'ሞኒተ -ስ- መካሪ ፣ አስጠንቃቂ ሰው ፣ የትም ህርት ክፍል አለቃ (ተማሪ)

monk

'መንክ -ስ- መነኩሴ

monkey

'መንኪ -ስ- ዝንጀሮ

monopoly

መ'ኖፖሊ -ስ- አንድ ዓይነት ንግድ ያለ ተወ ዳዳሪ መያዝ

monotonous
መ'ኖተነስ -ቅ- አሰልቺ

monster
'ሞንስተ -ስ- ታ'ላቅ አስፈ'ሪ ፍጡር ወይን'ም ት'ልቅ ተክል

monstrous
'ሞንስትረስ -ቅ- በጣም ት'ልቅ ፣ አስደንጋጭ ፣ አስፈ'ሪ

month
'መን<u>ሰ</u> -ስ- ወር

monument
'ሞንዩመንት -ስ- ሐውልት

mood
'ሙ:ድ -ስ- አ'ኳኋን ፣ ስ'ሜት

moody
'ሙ:ዲ -ቅ- አመለ'ኛ ፣ ነጭና'ጫ ፣ አመለቢስ

moon
'ሙ:ን -ስ- ጨረቃ

moonlight
'ሙ:ንላይት -ስ- የጨረቃ ብርሃን

moor
'ሞ: -ስ- ሰ'ፊ ጠፍ ሜዳ ፤ ቱርክ ፣ (የቱርክ አገር ሰው)
-ግ- ጀልባ እወንዝ ዳር ማሠር [አ'ሠረ]

moot
'ሙ:ት -ቅ- አ'ጠራጣሪ ፣ አ'ከራካሪ
-ግ- ለመ'ነጋገር ማቅረብ [አቀ'ረበ] (አንድ ጉዳ'ይ)

mop
'ሞፐ -ስ- ወለል መጥረጊያ ፣ ብት'ቶ (በን ጨት ላይ የታ'ሠረ)

mope
'መውፐ -ግ- ስላንድ እ'ክል ማ'ሰላሰል [አ'ሰ ላ'ሰለ]

moral
'ሞረል -ቅ- ጥሩ ፣ የተቀ'ጣ ፣ ግብረ ገ'ባዊ ፣ ባለ ምግባር

morale
መ'ራ:ል -ስ- ውስጣዊ ስ'ሜት (ስለ ድፍረት ፣ መ'ተማመን)

morals
'ሞረልዝ -ስ- ግብረ ገ'ብ'ነት

morality
መ'ራሊቲ -ስ- ግብረ ገ'ብ'ነት

morbid
'ሞ:ቢድ -ቅ- አእምሮው ያልተተካ'ከለ ፣ 'መመ ፤ በሰው ሥቃይ የ'ሚ'ደ'ሰት

more
'ሞ: -ቅ- ተጨ'ማሪ ፣ ይበልጥ

moreover
ሞ'ረውቨ -ተግ- ከ'ዚህ በላይ

morning
'ሞ:ኒንግ -ስ- ጧት ፡ ንጋት

morose
መ'ረውስ -ቅ- ጭፍግ'ግ ያለው ፣ ሊ'ነ የ'ማይሻ ፣ የማይጠዳው ፣ አይጠዴ

morsel
'ሞ:ሰል -ስ- ቁ'ራሽ (ምግብ)

mortal
'ሞ:ተል -ቅ- መዋቲ

mortar
'ሞ:ተ -ስ- የተደባ'ለቀ ሲሚንቶ
military
-ስ- አ'ዳፍኔ (የጦር መ'ሣሪያ ዓነ
utensil .
-ስ- ሙቀ'ጫ

mortgage
'ሞ:ጊጅ -ስ- ንብረትን ዋስ በማድረግ ገን መ'በደር

mortify
'ሞ:ቲፋይ -ግ- በሰው ፊት ማሳ'ፈር [አሳ'ፈ ሰው ማሳ'ዘን [አሳ'ዘነ] ፤ ሰው'ነት በ በጾሎት ማድከም [አደ'ከመ]

mortuary
'ሞ:ትዩወሪ -ስ- ሬሳ እስኪ'ቀ'በር የ'ሚ'ቀ ጥ'በት ቦታ (በሐኪም ቤት ግ'ቢ) ፣ የሬሳ (

mosque
'ሞስክ -ስ- መስጊድ (የእስላሞ'ች ቤተ መ ደስ)

mosquito
ሞስ'ኪተው -ስ- ቢምቢ ፣ የወባ ትን'ኝ

moss
'ሞስ -ስ- የደንጊያ ፣ የእንጨት ሽበት (በደ ጊያ ፣ በእንጨት ወይን'ም በርጥብ ቦታ ላ የ'ሚበቅል አረንጓዴ ወይን'ም ብጫ ተክል

most
'መውስት -ቅ- የ'ሚበልጥ

stly
መውስት፣ሊ -ተግ- ይበልጡን

th
ሞፀ -ስ- ብል ፣ ቁንቁን

ther
መዘ -ስ- እ'ናት

ther-in-law
መዘሪንሎ፡ -ስ- አማት (የባል ወይን'ም የሚ ስት እ'ናት)

tion
መውሽን -ስ- እንቅስ'ቃሴ

tive
ሞውቲቭ -ስ- የ'ሚያ'ነሣ'ሣ ምክንያት (አን ድ ነገር ለማድረግ)

tor
ሞውተ -ስ- ሞቶር

tor-car
ሞውተ'ካ፡ -ስ- መኪና ፣ አውቶሚቢል

ttled
ሞተልድ -ቅ- ል'ዩ ል'ዩ ቀለም በገላው ላይ የጣለ'በት

otto
'ሞተው -ስ- አ'ጭር ም'ሳሌያዊ አ'ነጋገር (የ ጠባይን ሕ'ግጋት የ'ሚ'ና'ገር) ፣ ሕይወት የ'ሚ 'መ'ራ'በት ም'ሳሌ

ould
'ሞልድ -ግ- ቅርፅ መስጠት [ሰ'ጠ] ፣ መልክ መስጠት [ሰ'ጠ]

oult
ሞልት -ግ- የላባ መርገፍ [ረ'ገፈ] (አዲስ ለማ ብቀል)

ound
'ማውንድ -ስ- ት'ንሽ የደንጊያ ፣ የአፈር ቁ'ልል

ount
'ማውንት -ግ- መውጣት [ወ'ጣ] (አንድ፡ነገር ላይ)

ountain
'ማውንቴን -ስ- ተራራ

ountainous
'ማውንተነስ -ቅ- ተራራ'ማ

ourn
'ሞ፡ን -ግ- ማልቀስ [አለ'ቀሰ] (ለሞተ ሰው)

mourner
'ሞ፡ነ -ስ- አልቃሽ

mournful
'ሞ፡ንፉል -ቅ- ያ'ዘነ

mourning
'ሞ፡ኒንግ -ስ- ልቅሶ ፣ ለቅሶ

mouse
'ማውስ -ስ- አይጥ

mousetrap
'ማውስትራፕ -ስ- ያይጥ ወጥመድ

moustache
መስ'ታ፡ሽ -ስ- ሪዝ

mouth
'ማውፀ -ስ- አፍ

mouthful
'ማውፀፉል -ስ- አፍ ሙሉ

mouthpiece
'ማውፀፒይስ -ስ- ዋቢ ፣ ጠበቃ ፣ የሌላውን ሐሳ'ብ የ'ሚገልጽ ሰው ፣ ጋዜጣ ወዘተ፤ወደአፍ የ'ሚ'ደ'ረገው የሙዚቃ መሣሪያ (ዋሽንት) ወዘተ ክፍል

movable
'ሙ፡ቨበል -ቅ- የ'ሚንቀሳ'ቀስ

move
'ሙ፡ቭ -ግ- ማንቀሳቀስ [አንቀሳ'ቀሰ]፣ መንቀ ሳቀስ [ተንቀሳ'ቀሰ]

movement
'ሙ፡ቭመንት -ስ- እንቅስ'ቃሴ

moving
'ሙ፡ቪንግ -ቅ- ተንቀሳቃሽ

mow
'መው -ግ- ማጨድ [አ'ጨደ]

much
'መች -ቅ- ብዙ ፣ እ'ያሌ

muck
'መክ -ስ- ቆሻሻ ፣ ጉድፍ

mucus
'ምዩከስ -ስ- ንፍጥ

mud
'መድ -ስ- ጭቃ

muddle
'መደል -ስ- ሥርዓት የሌ'ለው ፣ ዝብርቅርቅ ነገር

muddy
'መዲ -ቅ- ጭቃ'ማ

muffin
'መፈን -ስ- ቂ'ጣ (ጠቃጠቆ ያ'ለ'በት)

muffle
'መፈል -ግ- ማ'ፈን [አ'ፈነ] ፣ ማድከም [አደ'ከመ] (ድምፅ) ፣ መ'ሸፋፈን [ተሸፋ'ፈነ]

muffler
'መፍለ -ስ- ሻል (ወፍራም)

mug
'መግ -ስ- ኩ'ባ'ያ

mule
'ምዩ:ል -ስ- በቅሎ

multiple
'መልቲፕል -ቅ- ል'ዩ ል'ዩ ክፍል ያ'ለው ፡ ብዙ

multiplication
መልቲፕሊ'ኬይሽን -ስ- ማብዛት ፣ ማ'ባዛት

multiply
'መልቲፕላይ -ግ- ማብዛት [አበ'ዛ] ፡ ማ'ባዛት [አ'ባ'ዛ]

mumble
'መምበል -ግ- ማነብነብ [አነበ'ነበ] ፣ ንግ'ግርን ግልጽ አድርጎ አለመ'ናገር [-ተና'ገረ]

mummy
'መሚ -ስ- በመድኃኒት እንዳይፈርስ'ና እንዳይበሰ'ብስ የተደ'ረገ አስከሬን

mumps
'መምፕስ -ስ- ጆሮ ደ'ግፍ

munch
'መንች -ግ- አጥብቆ ማ'ላመጥ [አ'ላ'መጠ] ፡ ማ''ኘክ [አ''ኘከ]

municipal
ምዩ'ኒሲፐል -ቅ- ከከተማ አስተዳደር ጋር ግን''ኙ'ነት ያ'ለው

municipality
ምዩኒሲ'ፓሊቲ -ስ- ማ'ዘጋጃ ቤት

munitions
ምዩ'ኒሽንዝ -ስ- የጦር መ'ሣሪያ መደ'ብር (የጥ'ይት ወዘተ)

mural
ም'ዩረል -ስ- እግድግ'ዳ ላይ የተሣለ ሥ'ዕል
-ቅ- የግድግ'ዳ

murder
'መ:ደ -ግ- መግደል [ገ'ደለ] (ሰው)
-ስ- ነፍስ ግ'ዳይ

murderer
'መ:ደረ -ስ- ነፍሰ ገዳይ

murky
'መ:ኪ -ቅ- ጥቁር ፣ ያልጠ'ራ ፡ የደበ'ዘዘ

murmur
'መ:መ -ግ- ማጉረምረም [አጉረመ'ረመ]

muscle
'መሰል -ስ- ጡንቻ

muscular
'መስክዩለ -ቅ- ጡንቻ'ማ ፣ የጡንቻ

museum
መዩ'ዚየም -ስ- ቤተ መዘ'ክር (ታሪካውያ[ን] ቅርሶ'ች የ'ሚ'ቀ'መጡ'በት'ና ለሕዝብ የ'ሚ'ታ'ዩ'በት ቤት)

mushroom
'መሽሩም -ስ- እንጉዳይ

music
ም'ዩዚክ -ስ- ሙዚቃ

musket
'መስኪት -ስ- መስኪ'ቶ (ጠመንጃ)

muslim
'መዝሊም -ቅ- እስላም

muslin
'መዝሊን -ስ- ቀ'ጭን የጥጥ ጨርቅ

must
'መስት -ግ- መ'ገባት [ተገ'ባ]

mustard
'መስተድ -ስ- ሰናፍ'ጭ

muster
'መስተ -ግ- መሰብሰብ [ሰበ'ሰበ] (ወ'ታ'ደ[ር] ወዘተ ለቁጥ'ጥር)

musty
'መስቲ -ቅ- የሻ'ገተ ፡ የሻጋታ ሽ'ታ ያ'ለ[ው]

mutation
ምዩ'ቴይሽን -ስ- ለውጥ ፡ ል'ዩ'ነት

mute
ም'ዩ:ት -ቅ- ድዳ

mutilate
ም'ዩ:ቲሌይት -ግ- የሰው አካል መቆራረ[ጥ] [ቆረ'ረጠ] ፡ አካለ ስንኩል ማድረግ [አደ'ረ[ገ]]

mutiny
ምዩቲኒ -ስ- ብጥ'ብጥ ፡ አድማ (የመርከበ'ኞ'ች ፡ የጦር ሠራዊት)

mutter
'መተ -ግ- ማንብነብ [አነበ'ነበ] ፡ ማጉረምረም [አጉረመ'ረመ]

mutton
'መተን -ስ- የበግ ሥጋ

mutual
ምዩቹዩወል -ቅ- የወል ፡ የጋራ ፡ የርስበርስ

muzzle
'መዘል -ስ- አፍ'ና አፍንጫ (የው'ሻ ፡ የቀበሮ ወዘተ) ፡ አፈ ሙዝ (የጠመንጃ)

my
'ማይ -ተስ- የኔ

myself
ማይ'ሴልፍ -ተስ- (እኔ) ራሴ

mysterious
ሚስ'ቲሪየስ -ቅ- ምስጢራዊ ፡ የተሸ'ሸገ ፡ መፍትሔ የሌ'ለው ሊ'ረ'ዱት የ'ማይ'ቻል

mystery
'ሚስተሪ -ስ- ምስጢር ፡ ድብቅ ፡ ሊ'ረ'ዱት የማ'ይቻል ነገር

myth
'ሚስ -ስ- የጥንት ታሪክ ፡ አፈ ታሪክ

mythical
'ሚሲከል -ቅ- ል'ብ ወ'ለድ'ነት ያ'ለው (የጥ'ንት ታሪክ) ፡ አፈታሪካዊ

nag
'ናግ -ግ- መጨቅጨቅ [ጨቀ'ጨቀ] ፡ መነዝነዝ [ነዘ'ነዘ]

nail
'ኔይል -ስ- ምስማር ፡ ሚስማር ፡ ችንካር
finger-
-ስ- ጥፍር (የእ'ጅ)

naive
ና'ይቭ -ቅ- ቂላቂል ፡ ጅል ፡ ሞ'ኝ ፡ የ'ዋህ

naked
'ኔይክድ -ቅ- ራቁት ፡ የተራ'ቆተ ፡ ልብሱን ያለ ፡ ያልተሸ'ፈነ

name
'ኔይም -ስ- ስም

namely
'ኔይምሊ -ተግ- ማለት ፡ ይኸው'ም

namesake
'ኔይምሴይክ -ስ- ሞክሼ

nanny
'ናኒ -ስ- ልጅ አሳ'ዳጊ ፡ ሞግዚት (ሴት)

nanny-goat
'ናኒጎውት -ስ- ሴት ፍ'የል

nap
'ናፕ -ስ- ትንሽ እንቅልፍ ፡ ሸለብታ

nape
'ኔይፕ -ስ- ማጅራት

napkin
'ናፕኪን -ስ- የገበታ ፎጣ ፡ አፍ መጥረጊያ ፎጣ

narcotic
ና፡ኮቲክ -ቅ- የ'ሚያደነ'ዝዝ ፡ የ'ሚያስተ'ኛ መድኃኒት

narrate
ነ'ሬይት -ግ- ታሪክ ማውራት [አወ'ራ] ፡ መተ'ረክ [ተ'ረከ]

narration
ነ'ሬይሽን -ስ- ታሪክ ፡ መተ'ረክ (ያንድ አገር ወይ'ንም መንግሥት)

narrative
'ናረቲቭ -ስ- ታሪክ

narrator
ነ'ሬይተ -ስ- አውሪ ተረት ተ'ራች

narrow
'ናረው -ቅ- ጠ'ባብ

nasal
'ኔይዘል -ቅ- የአፍንጫ

nasty
'ና:ስቲ -ቅ- አስቀ'ያሚ ፣ ሽ'ታው ወይን'ም ጣዕሙ የ'ሚያስጠ'ላ ፣ የ'ማይስማ'ማ

natal
'ኔይተል -ቅ- የልደት ፣ የመ'ወለድ

nation
'ኔይሽን -ስ- አገር'ና ሕዝብ

national
'ናሽነል -ቅ- ብሔራዊ

nationality
ናሽ'ናለቲ -ስ- ዜግ'ነት

native
'ኔይቲቭ -ቅ- ያገር ተ'ወላጅ

natural
'ናቸረል -ቅ- ጠባያዊ ፣ የተለ'መደ

naturalization
ናቸረላይ'ዜይሽን -ግ- የሌላ አገር ዜግ'ነት መያዝ [ያዘ]

naturally
'ናቸረሊ -ተግ- በርግጥ ፣ በተለምዶ

nature
'ኔይቸ -ስ- ሥነ ፍጥረት

naught
'ኖ:ት -ስ- ምን'ም ነገር
zero
-ስ- ዜሮ

naughty
'ኖ:ቲ -ቅ- ቅልብልብ ፣ የ'ማይታ'ዘዝ (ሕፃን)፣ በጥባጭ

nausea
'ኖ:ሲየ -ስ- የትውኪያ ፣ የማስታወክ ስ'ሜት ፣ ቅልሽል'ሽታ

nautical
'ኖ:ቲክል -ቅ- ከባሕር ጉዞ ጋር ግን'ኙ'ነት ያ'ለው

naval
'ኔይቨል -ቅ- የባሕር ኃይል

nave
'ኔይቭ -ስ- , በቤተ ክርስቲያን መካ'ከለ'ኛው ቦታ (ሕዝቡ የ'ሚቆም'በት) ፣ ቅኔ ማሕሌት

navel
'ኔይቨል -ስ- እም'ብርት

navigable
'ናቪገበል -ቅ- መርከብ ሊሄድ'በት የ'ሚችል (ወንዝ)

navigate
'ናቪጌይት -ግ- መርከብ መንዳት [ነ'ዳ]

navvy
'ናቪ -ስ- የ'ጅ ሠ'ራተ'ኛ (ከባ'ድ ሥራ የ'ሚ ሠራ) ፣ የጉልበት ሥራ የ'ሚሠራ

navy
'ኔይቪ -ስ- የባሕር ኀይል

navy-blue
ኔይቪ ብ'ሉ: -ቅ- ጥቁር ሰማያዊ

near
'ኒየ -ተግ- ቅርብ

nearly
'ኒየሊ -ተግ- ያህል

nearsighted
ኒየ'ሳይቲድ -ቅ- እሩቅ ማየት የ'ማይችል

neat
'ኒይት -ቅ- ንጹሕ ፣ ሥርዓት ያ'ለው ፣ የተሰ 'ተረ

nebulous
'ኔብዩለስ -ቅ- ደብዛ'ዛ ፣ ጉልህ ያልሆነ

necessary
'ኔሰሰሪ -ቅ- አስፈ'ላጊ

necessity
ነ'ሴሲቲ -ስ- አስፈ'ላጊ ነገር

neck
'ኔክ -ስ- አንገት

necklace
'ኔክለስ -ስ- ድሪ ፣ ያንገት ጌጥ

necklet
'ኔክለት -ስ- ድሪ ፣ ያንገት ጌጥ

necktie
'ኔክታይ -ስ- ክራቫት

need
'ኒይድ -ስ- ፍ'ላጎት ፣ እጦት ፣ ች'ግር
-ግ- መፈ'ለግ [ፈ'ለገ]

needle
'ኒይደል -ስ- መርፌ

needy
'ኒይዲ -ቅ- ድሃ ፣ የተቸ'ገረ ፣ ምስኪን ፣ ች'ግ ረ'ኛ

negative
’ኔገቲቭ -ቅ- አፍራሽ ፣ አሉታ
neglect
ነግ’ሌክት -ግ- ቸ'ል ማለት [አለ] ፣ ች' ላ ማለ ት [አለ]
negligence
’ኔግሊጀንስ -ስ- ቸ'ልተ'ኛ'ነት
negligent
’ኔግሊጀንት -ቅ- ቸ'ልተ'ኛ ፣ ጥንቁቅ ያልሆነ
negligible
’ኔግሊጀበል -ቅ- ቸ'ል የ'ሚሉት፣ዋጋ የሌ'ለው
negotiate
ኒ’ገውሺዬይት -ግ- ወደ ስምም'ነት ለመድ ረስ መ'ወያየት [ተወያ'የ] ፣ የስምም'ነት ድር' ድር ማድረግ [አደ'ረገ]
negro
’ኒይግረው -ቅ- ሻንቅ'ላ
neigh
’ኔይ -ግ- እንደ ፈረስ መሬጥ [ሬጠ]
-ስ- የፈረስ ጩኸት
neighbour
’ኔበ -ስ- ጎረቤት ፣ መንደርተ'ኛ
neighbourhood
’ኔበሁድ -ስ- አቅራ'ቢያ (በቤት)
neighbouring
’ኔበሪንግ -ቅ- ቅርብ ፣ አ'ካባቢ
neither
’ናይዘ -ተግ- ሆነ . . . ወይም (በአፍራሽ'ነት)
nephew
’ኔፍዩ -ስ- የወንድ'ም ፣ የእኅት ልጅ
nerve
’ነ:ቭ -ስ- የስ'ሜት ሥር'ች
nervous
’ነ:ቨስ -ቅ- በቀ'ላሉ የ'ሚደነ'ግጥ
nest
’ኔስት -ስ- የወፍ ጎ'ጆ
nestle
’ኔስል -ግ- መ'ፈጋፈግ [ተፈጋ'ፈገ] (ሙቀ ትና ምቾት ለማግኘት)
nestling
’ኔስሊንግ -ስ- ገና መብረር የ'ማይችል ወፍ
net
’ኔት -ስ- መርበብ ፣ መረብ

nettle
’ኔተል -ስ- ሳ'ማ ፣ አለብላቢት
network
’ኔትወ:ክ -ስ- የአንድ መሥሪያ ቤት ቅርንጫ ፎ'ች ፣ ግን'ኙ'ነት ያ'ላ'ቸው የራዲዮ ጣቢያዎ' ች ፣ የተጠላ'ለፈ ነገር (እንደ መርበብ)
neuter
ን’ዩተ -ቅ- ግዑዝ (ጾታ)
neutral
ን’ዩትረል -ቅ- አማካኝ የሆነ ፣ ከሁለ'ቱ'ም ወገን ያልሆነ ፣ ገለልተ'ኛ
never
’ኔቨ -ተግ- በፍ'ጹም ፣ በምን'ም ጊዜ
nevertheless
ኔቨዘ’ሌስ -ተግ- ቢሆን'ም ፣ ይሁን'ና ፣ ሆ ኖ'ም
new
ን’ዩው -ቅ- አ'ዲስ
newcomer
ን’ዩከመ -ስ- አ'ዲስ ገ'ብ ፣ አ'ዲስ መጪ
news
ን’ዩዝ -ስ- ወሬ ፣ ዜና
newspaper
ን’ዩዝፔይፐ -ስ- ጋዜጣ
next
’ኔክስት -ቅ- የ'ሚቀ'ጥል ፣ ቀ'ጣይ
nearest
’ኒረስት -ቅ- የቀ'ረበ ፣ በጣም ቅርብ የሆነ
nib
’ኒብ -ስ- የብዕር ሜኖ
nibble
’ኒበል -ግ- ጥ'ቂም ጥ'ቂም እ'ያደ'ረጉ መብ ላት [በ'ላ] (ለትና'ንሽ እንስሳት) ፤ (ሁ'ለት ል'ብ መሆን [ሆነ] (ለማድረግ ለመ'ቀበል እየ'ፈ'ለጉ)
nice
’ናይስ -ቅ- ጥሩ ፣ ያማረ
nick
’ኒክ -ስ- ጭረት (ለቁስል)
nickname
’ኒክኔይም -ስ- በስም ላይ ተጨ'ማሪ የቁል ምጫ ፣ የመቀ'ለጃ ፣ የማፌዣ ስም (ም'ሳሌ ፣ አ'ጭሩን ሰው 'ዛፉ' ማለት)
niece
’ኒይስ -ስ- የወን'ድም ፣ የእኅት ልጅ (ሴት)

niggard
'ኒገድ -ቅ- ሥ'ሥታም ፣ ገብጋ'ባ
nigger
'ኒገ -ስ- ጥቁር ቡና'ማ (ቀለም) ፣ ጠጻራ (የጥ ላ'ቻ መ'ጠሪያ)
night
'ናይት -ስ- ሌሊት ፣ ጨ'ለማ
nightcap
'ናይትካፕ -ስ- የመ'ኝታ ቆብ ፣ ከመ'ኝታ በፊት የ'ሚ'ጠ'ጣ መጠ'ጥ
nightfall
ናይትፎ፡ል -ስ- ም'ሽት
nightmare
'ናይትሜየ -ስ- ቅዠት
nil
'ኒል -ቅ- ምን'ም ፣ ዜሮ
nimble
'ኒምበል -ቅ- ፈ'ጣን ፣ ንቁ (በቶሎ የ'ሚገ ባው)
nine
'ናይን -ቅ- ዘጠ'ኝ
nineteen
ናይን'ቲይን -ቅ- ዐሥራ ዘጠ'ኝ
nineteenth
'ናይን'ቲንስ -ቅ- ዐሥራ ዘጠን'ኛ
ninetieth
'ናይንቲየስ -ቅ- ዘጠና'ኛ
ninth
'ናይንስ -ቅ- ዘጠን'ኛ
ninety
'ናይንቲ -ቅ- ዘጠና
nip
'ኒፕ -ግ- መቆንጠጥ [ቆን'ጠጠ] ፣ መንከስ [ነ'ከሰ]
nipple
'ኒፕል -ስ- የጡት አፍንጫ ፣ የጡት ጫፍ
no
'ነው -ተግ- አይደ'ለም ፣ የ'ለም
nobility
ነ'ቢሊቲ -ስ- ባለክብር'ነት ፣ መሳፍንት
noble
'ነውበል -ቅ- የተከ'በረ ፣ ገበዝ ፣ የ'ሚ'ደ'ነቅ ከ'ፍ ያለ ማዕረግ ያ'ለው

nobody
'ነውበዲ -ቅ- ማን'ም
nod
'ኖድ -ቅ- ራስ መነቅነቅ [ነቀ'ነቀ] (ለመስ ማማት ፣ ሰላምታ ለመስጠት)
noise
'ኖይዝ -ስ- ዋካታ
nominal
'ኖሚነል -ቅ- ለስሙ ያህል ፣ በጣም ትን'ሽ
nominate
'ኖሚኔይት -ቅ- መሰ'የም [ሰ'የመ]
nominative
'ኖሚነቲቭ -ቅ- ባለቤ (በሰዋሰው)
nominee
ኖሚ'ኒይ -ስ- በምርጫ ላይ የ'ሚያ'ገፋት ፣ ለመ'መረጥ የቃ'ጨ
nonchalant
'ኖንሸለንት -ቅ- የ'ማይገ'ደው ፣ ግ'ዴ'ለሽ ፣ ስ'ሜቱ የቀዘ'ቀዘ
non-commital
ኖንክ'ሚተለ -ቅ- እ'ሺ'ም እም'ቢ'ም የ'ማ ይል ፣ አስተያየቱን የ'ሚሸ'ሽግ ፣ ከማ'ን'ኛው ም ወገን ያልሆነ (በጥል)
none
'ነን -ተስ- ማን'ም
nonsense
'ኖንሰንስ -ስ- ትርኪ ምርኪ ፣ የ'ማይረባ
nook
'ኑክ -ስ- ራ'ቅ ያለ ቦታ (ገለ'ል ብለው የ'ሚ'ቀ 'መጡ'በት)
noon
'ኑ፡ን -ስ- ቀትር
noose
'ኑ፡ስ -ስ- ሸምቀ'ቆ (የሰው መስቀያ)
nor
'ኖ፡ -መሃ- ወይ'ም ፣ ወይን'ም
normal
'ኖ፡መል -ቅ- የተለመ'ደ ፣ ያ'ተመ'መጡ ፣ ያል ተበላ'ሸ (ለአእምሮ)
north
'ኖ፡ስ -ስ- ሰሜን
northern
'ኖ፡ዘን -ቅ- ሰሜናዊ

nose
'ነውዝ -ስ- አፍንጫ

nosegay
'ነውዝጌይ -ስ- ያበባ እ'ቅፍ

nostalgia
ኖስ'ታልጅየ -ስ- ያገር ናፍቆት ፤ ያ'ለፈ ሁናቴ ት'ዝታ

nostril
'ኖስትረል -ስ- ያፍንጫ ቀዳዳ

not
'ኖት -ተግ- አይደ'ለም

notable
'ነውተበል -ቅ- የታ'ወቀ

notch
'ኖች -ስ- የተፋረ ነገር (በሰንጢ) ፤ ስርጉዳት

note
'ነውት -ስ- ማስታወሻ (አ'ጭር ጽሑፍ)
-ግ- ጠንቅቆ ማስተዋል [አስተዋለ]

note-book
'ነውትቡክ -ስ- ማስታወሻ መጻፊያ ደብተር

noted
'ነውተድ -ቅ- የታ'ወቀ ፤ ዝ'ነ'ኛ

notepaper
'ነውትፔይፐ -ስ- ረቂት ማውጫ ወረቀት ፤ ደብዳ'ቤ መጻፊያ ወረቀት

nothing
'ነሲንግ -ተግ- ምን'ም

notice
'ነውቲስ -ግ- ማስተዋል [አስተዋለ]
-ስ- ማስታወቂያ

noticeable
'ነውቲሰበል -ቅ- በቀ'ላሉ የ'ሚ'ታ'ይ ፤ ጉልህ

notify
'ነውቲፋይ -ግ- ማመልከት [አመለ'ከተ] ፤ ማስታወቅ [አስታ'ወቀ]

notion
'ነውሽን -ስ- ሐ'ሳብ ፤ አስተያየት

notoriety
ነውተ'ራየቲ -ስ- መጥፎ ዝ'ና

notorious
ነ'ቶሪየስ -ቅ- በመጥፎ ተግባር የታ'ወቀ

notwithstanding
ኖትዊዝስ'ታንዲንግ -ተግ- ቢሆን'ም ፤ ሆኖ'ም

nought
'ኖ፡ት -ስ- ምን'ም ነገር ፤ ዜሮ

noun
'ናውን -ስ- ስም ፤ ነ'ባር ፤ ዘር

nourish
'ነሪሽ -ግ- መመ'ገብ [መ'ገበ]

novel
'ኖቨል -ስ- ረ'ጅም ል'ብ ወለ'ድ ታሪክ (በስ'ድ ጽሑፍ የተጻፈ)
-ቅ- አ'ዲስ'ና አስገ'ራሚ

novelty
'ኖቨልቲ -ስ- አ'ዲስ'ነት

November
ነ'ቬምበ -ስ- ኅዳር

novice
'ኖቪስ -ቅ- ልምድ የሌ'ለው ፤ ጀ'ማሪ
-ስ- በተባሕትዎ ብዙ ጊዜ ያልቆ'የ(ች)

now
'ናው -ተግ- አሁን

nowadays
'ናወደይዝ -ተግ- ባሁኑ ጊዜ ፤ ባሁኑ ዘመን

nowhere
'ነዌየ -ተግ- የት'ም

noxious
'ኖክሽስ -ቅ- መርዛም ፤ የ'ሚጎዳ ፤ ጎጂ

nozzle
'ኖዘል -ስ- የቧን'ቧ መፈሻ'ረሻ (ውሃ የ'ሚፈ'ስ'በት) ፤ የቧን'ቧ አፈ ሙዝ

nucleus
'ን'ዩክሊየስ -ስ- የአቶም እምብርት ፤ ያንድ ነገር መሀል (እምብርት)

nude
'ን'ዩ፡ድ -ቅ- ራቁት

nudge
'ነጅ -ግ- መጐንተል [ጐን'ተለ] ፤ በክርን ጎ'ሰም ማድረግ [አደ'ረገ]

nudity
'ን'ዩ፡ዲቲ -ስ- ራቁት'ነት

nuisance
'ን'ዩስንስ -ስ- አ'ዋኪ ፤ በጥባጭ ሰው

null
'ነል -ቅ- ዋጋ ቢስ

numb
'ነም -ቅ- የደነ'ዘዘ
-ግ- ማደንዘዝ [አደነ'ዘዘ]
number
'ነምበ -ስ- ቁጥር
numeral
ን'ዩመረል -ስ- አኀዝ
numerical
ንዩ'ሜሪከል -ቅ- የቁጥር
numerous
ን'ዩመረስ -ቅ- ብዙ ፣ እ'ያሌ
nun
'ነን -ስ- መነኩሲት
nunnery
'ነነሪ -ስ- የመነኩሳዪያት ገዳም
nuptial
'ነፕሸል -ቅ- የሠርግ ፣ የጋብ'ቻ
nurse
'ነ:ስ -ግ- ማስታመም [አስታ'መመ]
nursemaid
'ነ:ስሜይድ -ስ- ልጅ አሳ'ዳጊ (ሴት)
nurture
'ነ:ቸ -ግ- ማሳ'ደግ [አሳ'ደገ] (ለሕፃን)
nut
'ነት -ስ- ለውዝ
nutriment
ን'ዩትሪመንት -ስ- ምግብ (ለጤና ተስማሚ)
nutrition
ንዩት'ሪሽን -ስ- ምግብ
nutshell
'ነትሼል -ስ- የለውዝ ቅር'ፊት
nutty
'ነቲ -ቅ- የለውዝ ጣዕም ያ'ለው
nuzzle
'ነዘል -ግ- ባፍንጫ መ'ታከክ [ታ'ከከ] (በተለ'ይ ለእንስሳት)

oaf
'ኦውፍ: -ቅ- ባለጌ ፣ ያልሠለ'ጠነ ፣ ጅላጅል ፣ ሞ'ኛ ሞ'ኝ
oak
ኦውክ -ስ- ባ'ሉጥ (የዛፍ ዓይነት)
oar
'ኦ: -ስ- መቅዘፊያ
oasis
ኦ'ዌይሲስ -ስ- የምድረ በዳ ኩሬ ውሃ
oath
'ኦውስ -ስ- መሐላ ፣ ስድብ ፣ እርግማን
oatmeal
'ኦውትሚይል -ስ- የአ'ጃ ዱቄት
oats
'ኦውትስ -ስ- አ'ጃ
obdurate
'ኦብጅዩረት -ቅ- ች'ኮ ፣ መንቻ'ካ
obedient
ኦ'ቢይዲየንት -ቅ- ታ'ዛዥ
obeisance
ኦ'ቢይሰንስ -ስ- በአክብሮት እ'ጅ መንሣት ፣ መ'ታዘዝ
obelisk
'ኦበሊስክ -ስ- ከደንጊያ ተጠርቦ የተሠ'ራ አራ'ት ማዕዘን ያ'ለው ሐውልት
obese
ኦ'ቢይስ -ቅ- በጣም ወፍራም (ለሰው)
obesity
ኦ'ቢይሲቲ -ስ- ያለመጠን ውፍረት
obey
ኦ'ቤይ -ግ- መ'ታዘዝ [ታ'ዘዘ]
obituary
ኦ'ቢቹሪ -ስ- የሙት ታሪክ (በጋዜጣ ወዘተ)
object
ኦብ'ጀክት -ግ- መ'ቃወም [ተቃ'ወመ]
object
'ኦብጀክት -ስ- ነገር ፣ ዐላማ

objection
ኧብ'ጀክሽን -ስ- መ'ቃወም
objectionable
ኧብ'ጀክሽነበል -ቅ- የ'ማያስደ'ስት ፣ የ'ሚ'ቃ'ወሙት
objective
ኧብ'ጀክቲቭ -ስ- ግብ ፣ ዐላማ
obligation
ኦብሊ'ጌይሽን -ስ- ግ'ዴታ
obligatory
ኧብ'ሊገትሪ -ቅ- አስገ'ዳጅ ፣ ግ'ዴታዊ
oblige
ኧብ'ላይጅ -ግ- ውለታ መዋል [ዋለ] ፣ ማስገ'ደድ [አስገ'ደደ]
oblique
ኧብ'ሊይክ -ቅ- ሠ'ያፍ (መሥመር) ፣ ቀ'ጥተ'ኛ ያልሆነ ፣ ዘንበ'ል ያለ ፣ ያዘ'መመ
obliterate
ኧብ'ሊተሬይት -ግ- መደምሰስ [ደመ'ሰሰ] ፣ መፋቅ [ፋቀ]
obliteration
ኧብሊተ'ሬይሽን -ስ- መደምሰስ ፣ ድምሰሳ ፣ መፋቅ
oblivion
ኧብ'ሊቪየን -ስ- መ'ረሳት ፣ መ'ዘንጋት
oblivious
ኧብ'ሊቪየስ -ቅ- የረ'ሳ ፣ የዘነ'ጋ ፣ ዝንጉ
oblong
'ኦብሎንግ -ቅ- አራት ማዕዘን (ሁለ'ት ጎ'ኑ በርዝመት የ'ሚ'መሳ'ሰል) ፣ ሞላላ
obnoxious
ኧብ'ኖክሸስ -ቅ- የ'ሚያስጠ'ላ ፣ ደ'ስ የ'ማያ'ሰ'ኝ (ለጠባይ)
obscene
ኧብ'ሲይን -ቅ- ባለጌ ፣ አስቀ'ያሚ ፣ ስለፈቃደ ሥጋ በይፋ የ'ሚ'ና'ገር ፣ ነውር የ'ማያውቅ
obscenity
ኧብ'ሴነቲ -ስ- ብልግ'ና ፣ አስቀ'ያሚ'ነት ፣ ነውር አለማወቅ
obscure
ኧብስክ'ዩወ -ቅ- ግልጽ ያልሆነ ፣ የተሠ'ወረ
obsequious
ኧብ'ሲይክዊየስ -ቅ- ተለማማጭ

observant
ኧብ'ዘ፡ቨንት -ስ- ተመልካች ፣ አስተዋይ ፣ ታ'ዛቢ
observation
ኦብዘ'ቬይሽን -ስ- መ'መልከት ፣ ማስተዋል
observe
ኧብ'ዘ፡ቭ -ግ- መ'መልከት [ተመለ'ከተ] ፣ ማስተዋል [አስተዋለ]
observer
ኧብ'ዘ፡ቨ -ስ- ተመልካች ፣ ታ'ዛቢ
obsession
ኧብ'ሴሽን -ስ- ሐሳብን መ'ማረክ (ከፍርሃት ፣ ትክክል ካልሆነ ሐሳብ የተነ'ሣ)
obsolete
'ኦብሰሊይት -ቅ- ዘመናዊ ያልሆነ ፣ ያረጀ ፣ እሥራ ላይ የ'ማይውል
obstacle
'ኦብስተክል -ስ- መሰናክል ፣ ዕንቅፋት
obstinate
'ኦብስቲነት -ቅ- ችʼኮ ፣ በአንድ ሐሳብ ችʼክ የ'ሚል
obstruct
ኧብስት'ረክት -ግ- ማ'ደናቀፍ [አ'ደና'ቀፈ] ፣ እንቅፋት መሆን [ሆነ]
obtain
ኧብ'ቴይን -ግ- ማግኘት [አገ'ኘ]
obtrusive
ኧብት'ሩዚቭ -ቅ- ል'ታይ ባይ ፣ ሥ'ሉጥ
obtuse
ኧብ'ትዩስ -ቅ- ፈዛዛ ፣ ደ'ደብ ፣ ቶሎ የ'ማይ ገባው
obverse
'ኦብቨስ -ስ- የንጉሥ መልክ ፣ ዘውድ ያ'ለ'በት የመሐ'ለቅ መልክ ፣ ዘውድ (የመሐ'ለቅ)
obvious
'ኦብቪየስ -ቅ- ግልጽ
occasion
ኧ'ኬይዥን -ስ- ጊዜ (ት'ልቅ) ፣ በዐል
occasionally
ኧ'ኬይዠነሊ -ተግ- አልፎ አልፎ
occult
ኦ'ከልት -ቅ- የአስማት
occupant
'ኦክዩፐንት -ስ- ነዋሪ ፣ ያዥ (ሥፍራ)

occupation
ኦክዩ'ፔይሽን -ስ- ተግባር ፣ ሥራ

occupy
'ኦክዩፓይ -ግ- መያዝ [ያዘ] ፣ መውረር [ወ'ረ ረ] (ሳገር)

occur
ኦ'ከ: -ግ- መሆን [ሆነ] ፣ መድረስ [ደ'ረሰ] (ለነገር) ፣ ት'ዝ ማለት [አለ]

ocean
'ኦውሽን -ስ- ውቅያኖስ

octagon
'ኦክተጎን -ስ- ስ'ምንት ጎ'ን ያ'ለው ቅርፅ

October
ኦክ'ተውበ -ስ- ጥቅምት

oculist
'ኦክዩሊስት -ስ- ያይን ሐኪም

odd
'ኦድ -ቅ- ለሁለ'ት የ'ማይ'ከ'ፈል (ለሒሳብ) ፣ ጥንድ ያልሆነ ፣ ያልተለ'መደ ፣ እንግዳ (ለሁ ኔቴ)

oddment
ኦድመንት -ስ- ርዝ'ራሽር ፣ ቁርጥራጭ

odds
'ኦድዝ -ስ- ል'ዩ'ነት ፡ አለመ'መጣጠን ፣ ዕድል (የጥሩ ወይ'ንም የመጥፎ)

ode
'ኦውድ -ስ- ረዘ'ም ያለ ግጥም (ረጃጅም'ና አጫ'ጭር ስን'ኞች ያ'ሉት)

odious
'ኦውዲየስ -ቅ- የ'ሚ'ጠ'ላ

odour
'ኦውደ -ስ- 'ሽ'ታ ፡ መዓዛ

of
'ኦቭ -መዋ- የ . . .

off
'ኦፍ -ተግ- ወዲያ ፡ ወደው'ጭ

offal
'ኦፈል -ስ- ሆድቃ (የእንስሳት)፣ ቆሻሻ ፣ ው 'ዳቂ

offence
ኦ'ፌንስ -ስ- ሕ'ግ መጣስ

offend
ኦ'ፌንድ -ስ- ማስቀ'የም [አስቀ'የመ] ፣ መስ ደብ [ሰ'ደበ]

offensive
ኦ'ፌንሲቭ -ቅ- አ'ናዳጅ ፣ አሳ'ዛኝ ፣ አስቀ 'ያ'ሚ

offer
'ኦፈ -ግ- ለስጦታ ማቅረብ [አቀ'ረበ] ፣ ለመ ሸጥ ማስማማት [አስማ'ማ] ፣ መሥዋዕት ማቅ ረብ [አቀ'ረበ]

offering
'ኦፈሪንግ -ስ- መሥዋዕት

alms

-ስ- ለምጽዋት የወ'ጣ ገንዘብ

offhand
ኦፍ'ሀንድ -ቅ- ያለመ'ዘጋጀት ፣ ሳያ'ስብ የድ ፍረት ንግግር የ'ሚያደርግ

careless

-ቅ- ግ'ዴ'ለሽ ፣ የ'ማይ'ጠን'ቀቅ

office
'ኦፊስ -ስ- ሥራ ፣ ተግባር

building

-ስ- ቢሮ ፣ መሥሪያ ቤት

officer
'ኦፊሰ -ስ- ባለ ሥልጣን

military

-ስ- የጦር መኰ'ንን

official
ኦ'ፊሸል -ስ- ሹም ፣ ባለሥልጣን
-ቅ- ይፋ ፣ የመንግሥት

offshoot
'ኦፍሹት -ስ- ቅርንጫፍ

offspring
'ኦፍስፕሪንግ -ስ- ልጆ'ች

often
'ኦፈን -ተግ- ሁልጊዜ ፣ ዘወትር

Oh
'ኦው -ቃአ- እንዴ! ወይጉድ!

oil
'ኦይል -ስ- ዘይት

oilcan
'ኦይልካን -ስ- የዘይት ማንቆርቆርያ ቆርቆ'ሮ (ባለጡት)

oilcloth
'ኦይልክሎስ -ስ- ውሃ የማይዘልቀው ጨርቅ

oily
'ኦይሊ -ቅ- በቅባት የተበ'ከለ

ointment
'አይንትመንት -ስ- ቅባት
old
'ኦልድ -ቅ- አሮጌ ፣ ሽማግ'ሌ
old-fashioned
ኦልድ'ፋሽንድ -ቅ- ዘመናዊ ያልሆነ ፣ ጊዜ ያ'ለፈ'በት ፣ ባህልን ተከ'ታይ
olive
'ኦሊቭ -ስ- ወይራ ፣ ወደ ብጫ'ነት ያዘነ'በለ አረንጓዴ ቀለም
omen
'ኦውሜን -ስ- ገ'ድ ፣ ምል'ክት (መጪውን ሁናቴ የ'ሚያሳ'ይ)
ominous
'ኦሚነስ -ቅ- አደጋ ሊያመጣ የ'ሚችል
omission
ኦ'ሚሽን -ስ- መግደፍ ፣ ግድፈት
omit
ኦ'ሚት -ግ- መተው [ተወ] ፣ መግደፍ [ገ'ደፈ]
omnibus
'ኦምኒበስ -ስ- አውቶቡስ
omnipotent
ኦም'ኒፐተንት -ቅ- ሁ'ሉን የ'ሚችል ፣ ከሃሌ ኩሉ (ለእግዚአብሔር)
omniscient
ኦም'ኒሲየንት -ቅ- ሁ'ሉን የ'ሚያውቅ (ለእግ ዚአብሔር)
on
'ኦን -መዋ- በ . . . ላይ ፣ በ
once
'ወንስ -ተግ- አንድ ጊዜ ፣ አንዲት ጊዜ
one
'ወን -ቅ- አንድ ፣ አንዲት
onerous
'ኦነረስ -ቅ- አስቸ'ጋሪ ፣ አ'ዋኪ (ለሥራ)
oneself
ወን'ሴልፍ -ተስ- ራስ
onion
'አንየን -ስ- ሽንኩርት
onlooker
'ኦንሉከ -ስ- ተመልካች
only
'ኦውንሊ -ቅ- ብ'ቻ ፣ የተለ'የ ፣ መ'ሰል የሌ ለው
onslaught
'ኦንስሎ፡ት -ስ- ከ'ባድ ግጥሚያ (ለጠላት)
onus
'ኦውነስ -ስ- ኀላፊ'ነት ፣ ሸክም
onward
'ኦንወድ -ተግ- ወደፊት
onyx
'ኦኒክስ -ስ- መረግድ
ooze
'ኡ፡ዝ -ግ- ማገርት [አ'ኘር]
opaque
ኦ'ፔይክ -ቅ- በውስጡ የ'ማያሳ'ይ ፣ ብርሃን የ'ማያስገ'ባ ፣ ጥቅጥ'ቅ ያለ
open
'ኦውፕን -ግ- መክፈት [ከ'ፈተ]
opening
'ኦውፕኒንግ -ስ- ቀዳዳ
operate
'ኦፐሬይት -ግ- መሥራት [ሠ'ራ] ፣ ማ'ሠ'ራት [አ'ሠ'ራ]
-on
-ግ- መቅደድ [ቀ'ደደ] (ሕ'ክም'ና)
operation
ኦፐ'ሬይሽን -ስ- ሥራ
medical
-ስ- ኦፔራሲዮን ፣ ሰው'ነትን ለህ'ክም'ና መቅደድ
operative
'ኦፐረቲቭ -ቅ- ሠሪ
-ስ- ሠ'ራተ'ኛ (ይበልጡን የፋብሪካ ፡ ሜካኒክ)
opinion
ኦ'ፒንየን -ስ- አስተያየት ፣ ፍርድ ፣ እምነት ፡ ግ'ምት
opponent
ኦ'ፐውነንት -ስ- ጠላት ፣ ተቃዋሚ ፣ ባላንጣ
opportune
'ኦፐቹ፡ን -ቅ- ተስማሚ
opportunity
ኦፐ'ቹ፡ኒቲ -ስ- ም'ቹ ጊዜ (ሥራ ለመሥራት)
oppose
ኦ'ፐውዝ -ግ- መ'ቃወም [ተቃ'ወመ]

opposite

'ኦፐሲት -ቅ- ፊት ለፊት የሆነ ፣ ተቃራኒ ፣ የ'ማይስማ'ማ ፣ እቅጣ'ጫው የተለያ'የ

opposition

ኦፐ'ዚሽን -ስ- መ'ቃወም ፣ ተቃዋሚ ክፍል

oppress

ኧፐ'ሬስ -ግ- መጨ'ቆን [ጨ'ቆነ]

oppressive

ኧፐ'ሬሲቭ -ቅ- ጨ'ቋኝ

oppressor

ኧፐ'ሬሰ -ስ- ጨ'ቋኝ (ሰው)

optical

'ኦፐቲከል -ቅ- የዓይን

optician

ኦፐ'ቲሽን -ስ- መነ'ጥር ሠ'ሪተ'ኛ (መነ'ጽር ሠ'ሪተ'ኛ)

optimist

'ኦፕቲሚስት -ስ- በጥሩ ተምኔት የ'ሚያምን ሰው ፣ ሁናቴዎ'ችን ሁሉ በቅን የ'ሚያይ ሰው

option

'ኦፐሽን -ስ- የፈ'ለጉትን የመምረጥ መብት

or

'ኦ: -መየ- ወይን'ም ፣ ወይ'ም

oral

'ኦረል -ቅ- የቃል ፣ የአፍ

orange

'ኦረንጅ -ስ- ብርቱካን

oration

ኦ'ሬይሽን -ስ- ንግ'ግር (በሕዝብ ፊት)

orator

'ኦረተ -ስ- ንግ'ግር ሀዋቂ ፣ እንደበተ ርቱእ ፣ ጥሩ ተናጋሪ

oratory

'ኦረተሪ -ስ- ንግ'ግር የማድረግ ሀብት

orb

'ኦ:ብ -ስ- ሉል (ንጉሥ በ'ጁ የ'ሚይዘው ፣ መስቀል ያ'ለ'በት) ፣ ክ'ብ ነገር (ም'ሳሌ ፣ ፀሐይ ፣ ጨረቃ ፣ ከዋክብ ፣ ምድር)

orbit

'ኦ:ቢት -ግ- አንድን ነገር መዞር [ዞረ] (በፈለክ)
-ስ- አንድ ፈለክ በሌላው ዙሪያ የ'ሚያደርገው መዞር ፣ ዑደት

orchard

'ኦ:ቸድ -ስ- የፍራፍሬ ተክል ቦታ

orchestra

'ኦ:ከስትረ -ስ- የሙዚቃ ጓ'ድ

ordain

ኦ:'ዴይን -ግ- ክህነት መስጠት [ሰ'ጠ] ፣ መካን [ካነ] ፤ ማዘዝ [አ'ዘዘ]

ordeal

ኦ:'ዲይል -ስ- አ'ዋኪ የገ-ብዝ'ና መለ'ኪያ ፈተና

order

'ኦ:ደ -ግ- ማዘዝ [አ'ዘዘ]

instruction

-ስ- ሥርዓት

sequence

-ስ- ቅደም ተከ'ተል

orderly

'ኦ:ደሊ -ቅ- ጥሩ ሥርዓት ያ'ለው ፣ የተሸ'ከፈ፣ የተሰ'ተረ

servant

-ስ- የሆስፒታል ተላላኪ ፣ ያንድ መኰን'ን ተላላኪ

ordinance

'ኦ:ዲነንስ -ስ- ትእዛዝ ፣ ሕ'ግ ፣ ዐዋጅ ፣ ሃይማኖታዊ ክብረ በዓል

ordinary

'ኦ:ደንሪ -ቅ- ተራ ፣ የተለ'መደ ፣ መና'ኛ

ordination

ኦ:ዲ'ኔይሽን -ስ- መ'ሾም ፡ መሾም (መንፈሳዊ)

ordnance

'ኦ:ድነንስ -ስ- መድፈ'ኛ ክፍል ፣ የጦር መ'ሣሪያ'ና የምግብ መደ'ብር (የወ'ታ'ደር)

ore

'ኦ: -ስ- የብረታ ብረት አፈር (ገና ያልነ'ጠረ)

organ

'ኦ:ገን -ስ- የሰው'ነት ክፍል

musical

-ስ- ኦርጋኖን (እንደ ፒያኖ ያ'ለ የሙዚቃ መ'ሣርያ)

organic

ኦ:'ጋኒክ -ቅ- የሰው'ነት ፡ የአካል ፣ ሕይወት ያ'ለው

organization

ኦ:ገናይ'ዜይሽን -ስ- ድር'ጅት

organize
'ኦ:ገናይዝ -ግ- ማ'ደራጀት [አ'ደራ'ጀ] ፣ መልክ መስጠት [ሰ'ጠ]
orgy
'ኦ:ጂ -ስ- መ'ሳከር ፣ ቅጥ ማጣት (በታ'ላቅ ግብዣ ላይ) ፣ መፈንጠዝ
Orient
'ኦ:ሪዬንት -ስ- ምሥራቃዊ የዓለም ክፍል
orientate
'ኦ:ሪዬንቴይት -ግ- ማልመድ [አለ'መደ] ፣ አንድ ነገር ማሳ'ወቅ [አሳ'ወቀ]
orifice
'ኦሪፊስ -ስ- ት'ን'ሽ ቀዳዳ ፣ የዋ'ሻ አፍ ወዘተ
origin
'ኦሪጂን -ስ- መጀ'መሪያ ፣ ምንጭ ፣ ትውል'ድ
original
ኦ'ሪጂነል -ቅ- የመጀ'መሪያ ፣ ለመጀ'መሪያ ጊዜ የተሠ'ራ ፣ አዲ'ስ ፣ እንቁ
originate
ኦ'ሪጂኔይት -ግ- ማስገ'ኘት [አስገ'ኘ] ፣ መፍጠር [ፈ'ጠረ]
ornament
'ኦ:ነመንት -ስ- ጌጣጌጥ
ornate
ኦ':ኔይት -ቅ- ያጌጠ
orphan
'ኦ:ፈን -ስ- እ'ናለ ማውታ ፣ የሙት ልጅ
orphanage
'ኦ:ፈኒጅ -ስ- የሙት ልጀ'ች የ'ሚ'ረ'ዱ'በት ድር'ጅት
orthodox
ኦ:ሰዶክስ -ቅ- በአስተያየቱ ትክ'ክለ'ኛ ፣ እምነቱ ያልተቃ'ወሰ
church
-ስ- ኦርቶዶክሳዊት ቤተ ክርስቲያን
orthography
ኦ:'ሶግረፊ -ስ- ትክ'ክለ'ኛ አ'ጻጻፍ (ፊደሉ ያልተሳሳተ)
oscillate
'ኦሲሌይት -ግ- መ'ወዛወዝ [ተወዛ'ወዘ] ፣ ማ'ወዛወዝ [አ'ወዛ'ወዘ]
ostensible
ኦስ'ቴንሲበል -ቅ- እውነተ'ኛውን ምክንያት ለመሸ'ፈን የቀ'ረበ (ምክንያት)

ostentation
ኦስቴን'ቴይሽን -ስ- ል'ታይ ል'ታይ ማለት ፣ ል'ታወቅ ል'ታወቅ ማለት
ostracize
'ኦስትረሳይዝ -ግ- ለ'ይቶ ማስቀ'ረት [አስቀ'ረ] ፣ ማጋዝ [አጋዘ] (ግዞት)
ostrich
'ኦስትሪች -ስ- ሰጎን
other
'አ<u>ሀ</u> -ቅ- ሌላ ፣ ል'ዩ ፣ ተጨ'ማሪ
otherwise
'አ<u>ሀ</u>ዋይዝ -ተግ- አለበለ'ዚያ
our
'አወ -ቅ- የ'ኛ
ours
'አወዝ -ተስ- የ'ኛ
ourselves
አወ'ሴልቭዝ -ተስ- (እ'ኛ) ራሳ'ችን
oust
'አውስት -ግ- ማስወ'ገድ [አስወ'ገደ] ፣ ወደ ውጪ ማ'ባረር [አ'ባ'ረረ]
out
'አውት -ተግ- እው'ጭ ፣ ወደ ው'ጭ
outburst
'አውት'በ:ስት -ስ- ስ'ሜት ለመግለጽ መገንፈል
outcast
'አውት'ካ:ስት -ስ- የተጠ'ላ ፣ የተባረ'ረ ከማኅበራዊ ኑሮ ው'ጭ የሆነ
outcome
'አውትከም -ስ- ው'ጤት
outcry
'አውትክራይ -ስ- እቤቱታ ፣ ጩኸት (የብዙ ሰዎ'ች)
outdoor
አውት'ዶ: -ቅ- የው'ጭ (ከቤት)
outer
'አውተ -ቅ- የው'ጭ
outfit
'አውትፊት -ስ- ለተለ'የ ነገር የ'ሚውል ሙሉ ልብስ ፣ መ'ሣሪያ
organization
-ስ- ድር'ጅት ፣ ጓ'ድ ፣ ወ'ሮበ'ላ

outhouse
'አውትሀውስ -ስ- ከዋ'ናው ቤት የተለ'የ ፡ የዕቃ ፡ የእንስሳት ቤት

outing
'አውቲንግ -ስ- ሽ'ር'ሽር

outlandish
አውት'ላዲሽ -ቅ- እንግዳ የ'ሚመስል ፡ ያል ተለ'መደ

outlaw
'አውትሎ፡ -ስ- ሽፍታ ፡ ወንበዴ ፡ ደመ ከልብ

outlay
'አውትሌይ -ስ- ወጪ (ገንዘብ)

outlet
'አውትሌት -ስ- መውጫ ፡ መፍሰሻ (ለፈሳሽ ነገር)

outline
'አውትላይን -ስ- ዋ'ና ዋ'ናውን ሐ'ሳብ መግለጫ አ'ጭር ጽሑፍ

outlook
'አውትሉክ -ስ- ካንድ ቦታ የ'ሚ'ታ'ይ ትእ'ይንት ፡ ወደፊት የ'ሚ'ፈ'ጸም ፡ የ'ሚሆን ነገር፣ ያስተሳስብ መንገድ

outnumber
አውት'ነምበ -ግ- በቁጥር መብለጥ [በ'ለጠ] ፡ ባብዛት ማ'ጣፋት [አ'ጣ'ፋ]

outpost
'አውትፖውስት -ስ- ፈን'ጠር ያለ መንደር ፡ ከሠ'ል'ጣኔ ራ'ቅ ያለ መንደር ፣ ራቅ ያ'ለ ት'ን'ሽ የጦር ሠፈር

output
'አውትፑት -ስ- ው'ጤት (ከፋብሪካ ወዘተ የ'ሚ'ገ'ኝ)

outrage
'አውትሬይጅ -ስ- ታ'ላቅ ወንጀል ፡ ታ'ላቅ የጭ'ካኔ ተግባር

outrageo.s
አውት'ሬይጀስ -ቅ- አ'ሠ'ቃቂ ፡ አስደንጋጭ

outset
'አውትሴት -ስ- መጀ'መሪያ

outside
አውት'ሳይድ -ስ- ው'ጭ
-ቅ- የው'ጭ

outsider
አውት'ሳይደ -ስ- ያንድ ማኅበር አባል ያል ሆነ ፡ ብዙ ተስፋ የሌ'ለው ሰው (በውድ'ድር)

outskirts
'አውትስከትስ -ስ- የከተማ ዳር'ቻ

outspoken
አውትስ'ፖውከን -ቅ- ግልጽ ፡ እውነት ተና'ጋሪ ፡ የ'ማይደ'ብቅ

outstanding
አውትስ'ታንዲንግ -ቅ- በጣም ጥሩ ፡ መ'ሰል የሌ'ለው ፣ ገና ያልተፈ'ጸመ ፡ ያላ'ለቀ
unpaid
-ቅ- ያልተከ'ፈለ (ዱቤ ወዘተ) ፡ ው'ዝፍ (ሒሳብ)

outstretched
አውትስት'ሬችድ -ቅ- የተዘረ'ጋ

outward
'አውትወድ -ተግ- ወደ ው'ጭ

outwit
አውት'ዊት -ግ- ከ'ፍ ባለ ብልኅት ማ'ሸ'ነፍ [አ'ሸ'ነፈ]

oval
'ኦውቨል -ቅ- የእንቁላል ቅርፅ ያ'ለው ፡ ሽሞ ልሙል

oven
'አቨን -ስ- ምድ'ጃ

over
'ኦውቨ -ተግ- በ . . . ላይ
-ቅ- ያ'ለቀ ፡ የተፈ'ጸመ

overall
ኦውቨ'ሮ፡ል -ቅ- ጠቅላ'ላ ፡ አ'ጠቃላይ
garment
-ስ- የሥራ ልብስ ፡ ቱ'ታ

overcast
ኦቨ'ካ፡ስት -ቅ- በደ'መና የተሸ'ፈነ ፡ የጨፈ'ገገ

overcoat
'ኦውቨኮውት -ስ- ካ'ፖርት

overcome
ኦውቨ'ከም -ግ- ማ'ሸ'ነፍ [አ'ሸ'ነፈ]

overcrowded
ኦውቨክ'ራውደድ -ቅ- የተጣ'በበ (በሰዎች ፣ መ'ፈናፈኛ የሌ'ለው

overdraft
'ኦውቨድራ፡ፍት -ስ- የባንክ አ'ላፊ እዳ ፡ ከበ'ተ'መጠው በላይ የወ'ጣ ገንዘብ (ከባንክ)

overdue
ኦውቨድ'ዩ፡ -ቅ- የዘገ'የ ፣ በጊዜው ያልተከ'ፈለ (ው'ዝፍ እዳ)

overflow
ኦቨፍ'ለው -ግ- ሞልቶ መፍሰስ [ፈ'ሰሰ]

overgrown
ኦውቨግ'ረውን -ቅ- አለመጠን ያ'ደገ ፣ ያረ'ጀ (ለአትክልት ወዘተ) ፣ በልምላሜ የተሸ'ፈነ ፣ ያለ ዕድሜው በጣም የረ'ዘመ (ለልጅ)

overhang
ኦውቨ'ሀንግ -ግ- ማንጠልጠል [አንጠለ'ጠለ]

overhaul
ኦውቨ'ሆ፡ል -ግ- ማ'ደስ [አ'ደሰ] ፣ መቅደም [ቀ'ደመ] (በሩ'ጫ)

overload
ኦውቨ'ለውድ -ግ- ያለመጠን መጫን [ጫነ]

overlook
ኦወቨ'ሉክ -ግ- ቸ'ል ማለት [አለ] ፣ ትይ'ዩ መሆን [ሆነ]

overpower
ኦውቨ'ፓወ -ግ- ማ'ሸ'ነፍ [አ'ሸ'ነፈ] ፣ ከሥልጣን ሥር ማድረግ [አደ'ረገ]

overrun
ኦውቨ'ረን -ግ- መውረር [ወ'ረረ] (በፍጥነት)

overseas
ኦውቨ'ሲይዝ -ስ- ባሕር ማዶ

overseer
'ኦውቨሲየ -ስ- ተቆጣጣሪ (የሠ'ራተ'ኞ'ች)

oversight
'ኦውቨሳይት -ስ- ግድፈት ፣ ስሕተት

oversleep
ኦውቨስ'ሊይፕ -ስ- ከተወ'ሰነው ጊዜ ይበልጥ መተ'ኛት ፣ ጋድሚያ'ነት

overtake
ኦውቨ'ቴይክ -ግ- መቅደም [ቀ'ደመ]

overthrow
ኦውቨስ'ረው -ግ- መገልበጥ [ገለ'በጠ] (መንግሥትን) ፣ ማ'ሸ'ነፍ [አ'ሸ'ነፈ]

overtime
'ኦውቨታይም -ስ- ከተመ'ደበው የሥራ ጊዜ በላይ ያ'ለፈ የሥራ ጊዜ ፣ ለ'ዚህ ጊዜ የ'ሚ'ከ'ፈል ገንዘብ

overture
'ኦውቨቸ -ስ- ለኦፔራ ወይን'ም ለትያትር መቅድም የ'ሚሆን ሙዚቃ

overturn
ኦውቨ'ተ፡ን -ግ- መገልበጥ [ገለ'በጠ]

overweight
ኦውቨ'ዌይት -ቅ- ብዙ ክብደት ያ'ለው
-ስ- ከመጠን በላይ የሆነ ውፍረት

overwhelm
ኦውቨ'ዌልም -ግ- ማ'ሸ'ነፍ [አ'ሸ'ነፈ] (ተወዳዳሪ በሌ'ለው ኀይል) ፣ ማጥለቅለቅ [አጥለቀ'ለቀ]

owe
'ኦው -ግ- ባለዳ መሆን [ሆነ]

owl
'አውል -ግ- ጉ'ጉት (የወፍ ዓይነት)

own
'ኦውን -ግ- መ'ገናዘብ [ተገና'ዘበ] ፣ ባለቤት መሆን [ሆነ]

owner
'ኦውነ -ስ- ባለቤት ፣ ባለመብት

ownership
'ኦውነሺፕ -ስ- ባለቤት'ነት

ox
'ኦክስ -ስ- በሬ

oyster
'ኦይስተ -ስ- ኦይስተር (የ'ሚ'በ'ላ ዶንጊያ ለ'በስ ዐሣ)

pace
'ፔይስ -ስ- ፍጥነት (የርም'ጃ፣የሩ'ጫ)፣እርም'ጃ

pacific
ፐ'ሲፊክ -ቅ- ጸ'ጥ ያለ ፣ ሰላማዊ

Pacific
ፐ'ሲፊክ -ቅ- ፓ'ሲፊክ (የውቅያኖስ ስም)

pacify
'ፓሲፋይ -ግ- ጸ'ጥ ማድረግ [አደ'ረገ]

pack
'ፓክ -ስ- እሥር ፣ ረብጣ
-ግ- ዕቃ ለጉዞ ማሣሠር [አሣ'ሠረ]
package
'ፓከጅ -ስ- ት'ንሽ እሥር ፣ ረብጣ
packet
'ፓክት -ስ- ት'ንሽ እሥር ፣ ፓ'ኮ
packing
'ፓኪንግ -ስ- ማሠሪያ ጉዝጓዝ ፣ ማ'ሸጊያ ጉዝጓዝ
packed
'ፓክድ -ቅ- የታ'ሠረ ፣ የታ'ሸገ (ዕቃ)
pad
'ፓድ -ስ- ዕቃ እንዳይ'ጎ'ዳ ለጉዝጓዝ የ'ሚሆን ለስላ'ሳ ጨርቅ ፤ ገበር
padding
'ፓዲንግ -ስ- የማ'ሸጊያ ጉዝጓዝ (ዕቃ እንዳ ይ'በላ'ሽ)
paddle
'ፓደል -ግ- ጥልቀት በሌ'ለው ወንዝ በግር መሄድ [ሄደ] ፤ መቅዘፍ [ቀ'ዘፈ]
-ስ- መቅዘፊያ
paddock
'ፓዶክ -ስ- የፈረሶ'ች ማሠልጠኛ ወይን'ም መኖሪያ መስክ
padlock
'ፓድሎክ -ስ- ጓጉንቸር ቁልፍ
paediatrics
ፒዲ'ያትሪክስ -ስ- የሕፃናት በ'ሽታ'ና የሕ 'ክም'ናው ጥናት
pagan
'ፔይገን -ስ- አረመኔ ፣ በብዙ አማልክት የ'ሚ ያምን ሰው
page
'ፔይጅ -ስ- ገ'ጽ (የመጽሐፍ.
servant
-ስ- ተላላኪ ፣ አሽከር (በሆቴል ፣ በክ በብ ወዘተ)
pageant
'ፓጀንት -ስ- የበዓል ሰልፍ (የጥንት ባህል የ'ሚያሳ'ይ)
pail
'ፔይል -ስ- ባልዲ ፣ ሸንክ'ሎ
pain
'ፔይን -ስ- ሕማም ፣ ሥቃይ (የሰው'ነት)
painful
'ፔይንፉል -ቅ- የ'ሚያ'ም ፣ የ'ሚየ'ሠቃ'
painstaking
'ፔይንዝቴይኪንግ -ቅ- ጥንቁቅ (በሥራ) ባተሌ
paint
'ፔይንት -ግ- መቀ'ባት [ቀ'ባ] (ለቀለም) መሣል [ሣለ] (ለሥዕል)
-ስ- ቀለም (የቤት ወዘተ)
painter
'ፔይንተ -ስ- ቀለም ቀ'ቢ ፤ ሥዕል ሠዓሊ
painting
'ፔይንቲንግ -ስ- ሥዕል
pair
'ፔየ -ስ- ሁለ'ት ፣ ጥንድ
pal
'ፓል -ስ- የቅርብ ጓ'ደ'ኛ
palace
'ፓለስ -ስ- ቤተ መንግሥት
palatable
'ፓለተበል -ቅ- የ'ሚጥም ፣ የ'ሚጣ'ፍጥ ጣዕም ፣ ለአእምሮ)
palate
'ፓለት -ስ- ት'ናጋ
pale
'ፔይል -ቅ- የገረ'ጣ
-ስ- የሾለ ረ'ጅም የአጥር እንጨት
paling
'ፔይሊንግ -ስ- የንጨት አጥር
palisade
ፓሊ'ሴይድ -ስ- በሾለ እንጨት ወይን'ም ረት ዘንግ የታጠ'ረ አጥር
pall
'ፖ:ል -ግ- መሰልቸት [ሰለ'ቸ]
-ስ- ግምጃ (የሬሳ መሸ'ፈኛ)
pallid
'ፓሊድ -ቅ- የገረ'ጣ
palm
'ፓ:ም -ስ- መዳፍ ፤ ዘምባባ
palmist
'ፓ:ሚስት -ስ- ጠንቋይ (መዳፍ ተመል የ'ሚናገር)

palpable
'ፓልፐበል -ቅ- በቀ'ላሉ ሊ'ዳ'ሰስ የ'ሚችል፣ ለአእምሮ ጉልህ የሆነ

palpitation
ፓልፒ'ቴይሽን -ስ- የል'ብ በፍጥነት መም ታት

palsy
'ፖ:ልዚ -ስ- የእ'ጅ እንቅጥ'ቃጤ (በ'ሽታ)

paltry
'ፖ:ልትሪ -ቅ- ዋጋ ቢስ

pamper
'ፓምፐ -ግ- ማንቀባረር [አንቀባ'ረረ]

pamphlet
'ፓምፍለት -ስ- ት'ንሽ መጽሐፍ

pan
'ፓን -ስ- መጥበሻ ፣ ድስት (ወዘተ)

pancake
'ፓንኬይክ -ስ- ከዱቄት ከዘይት'ና ከወተት የ'ሚ'ሠ'ራ ኬክ (ት'ኩሱን የ'ሚ'በላ)

pancreas
'ፓንክሪያስ -ስ- ጣ'ፊያ

pander
'ፓንደ -ግ- ማ'ቃጠር [አ'ቃ'ጠረ] (ለሴት) ፤ ማ'በረታታት [አ'በረታ'ታ] (ከፉን ሰው)

pane
'ፔይን -ስ- መስተዋት (የመስኮት ፣ አንድ ክፍል)

panel
'ፓነል -ስ- የግድግ'ዳ አንዱ ክፍል ፤ አራ'ት ማእዘን የሆነ እንጨት ፤ ለመፍረድ የተጠ'ሩ (በእንግሊዝ አገር) ሰዎ'ች የስም ዝርዝር ፤ በው ይ'ይት የ'ሚ'ካ'ፈሉ ሰዎ'ች

pang
'ፓንግ -ስ- ውጋት ፣ ድንገተ'ኛ ሕማም

panic
'ፓኒክ -ስ- መ'ሸበር ፣ ሽ'ብር (ከፍርሃት የተ ነ'ሣ)

panorama
'ፓነራ:መ -ስ- ጠቅላ'ላ የመሬት አ'ቀማመጥ ፣ ትእ'ይንት

pant
'ፓንት -ግ- ማለከለክ [አለከ'ለከ]

panther
'ፓንሰ -ስ- ግ'ሥ'ላ

pantry
'ፓንትሪ -ስ- ግ'ጀት ፣ የምግብ ቤት መ'ሣሪያ የ'ሚ'ቀ'መጥ'በት ክፍል

pants
'ፓንትስ -ስ- የውስጥ ሱ'ሪ

paper
'ፔይፐ -ስ- ወረቀት
news
-ስ- ጋዜጣ

par
'ፓ: -ስ- የዋጋ መ'ተካከል

parable
'ፓረበል -ስ- ም'ሳሌ

parachute
'ፓረሹት -ስ- ጃንጥላ (ከአውሮ'ፕላን የ'ሚ 'ወ'ረድ'በት)

parade
ፐ'ሬይድ -ግ- በሰልፍ መ'ጓዝ [ተጓዘ]
-ስ- ሰልፍ

paradise
'ፓረዳይስ -ስ- ገ'ነት

paradox
'ፓረዶክስ -ስ- ለመጀ'መሪያ ሲሰሙት እው ነት የ'ማይመስል ነገር ግን እውነት ሊሆን የ'ሚ ችል

paraffin
'ፓረፊን -ስ- ነዳጅ

paragraph
'ፓረግራ:ፍ -ስ- አንቀጽ (በጽሑፍ)

parallel
'ፓረሌል -ቅ- ጎ'ን ለጎ'ን የተ'ኰለ'ኰለ ትይ'ዩ (መሥመር)

paralyse
'ፓረላይዝ -ግ- ማስለል [አስ'ለለ] ፣ ሽባ ማድ ረግ [አደ'ረገ] ፤ አቅም ማሳ'ጣት [አሳ'ጣ]

paralysis
ፐ'ራለሲስ -ስ- ሽባ'ነት ፣ መስለል

paramount
'ፓረማውንት -ቅ- በጣም አስፈ'ላጊ ፣ ላ'ቅ ያለ

parapet
'ፓረፔት -ስ- በጣራ ፣ በመንገድ ፣ በድልድይ ዳር'ና ዳር ያ'ለ ግንብ

paraphrase
'ፓረፍሬይዝ -ግ- እንድ ጽሑፍ በቀ'ላል እ'ነጋገር ፈ'ቶ መ'ናገር [ተና'ገረ]

parasite
'ፓረሳይት -ስ- ሰው'ነት የሚበሉ ተባዮ'ች ፤ ለሰው ሸክም ሆኖ የ'ሚኖር ሰው

parasol
'ፓርሶል -ስ- ጃንጥላ (ለፀሐይ መ'ከላከያ)

parcel
'ፓ:ሰል -ስ- እሥር ፤ ረብጣ

parched
'ፓ:ችድ -ቅ- በና ፤ ደረቅ

parchment
'ፓ:ችመንት -ስ- ብራ'ና

pardon
'ፓ:ደን -ግ- ይቅር ማለት [አለ]
-ስ- ይቅር'ታ

pare
'ፔየ -ግ- መፋቅ [ፋ'ቀ] (እንጨት) ፤ መከር ከም [ከረ'ከመ] ፤ መላጥ [ላጠ]

parent
'ፔረንት -ስ- ወላጆ'ች (አ'ባት ወይን'ም እ'ናት)

parenthesis
ፔ'ሬንሰሲስ -ስ- ቅ'ንፍ (በጽሑፍ)

parenthood
'ፔረንትሁድ -ስ- ወላጅ'ነት

paring
'ፔሪንግ -ስ- ቁ'ራጭ ፤ ፍቅ'ፋቂ

parish
'ፓሪሽ -ስ- ሰበካ (ያንድ ቄስ)

parity
'ፓሪቲ -ስ- እ'ኩል'ነት (የማዕረግ)

park
'ፓ:ክ -ግ- መኪና ቦታ አስይዞ ማቆም [አ ቆመ]
place
-ስ- መ'ናፈሻ ቦታ

parley
'ፓ:ሊ -ስ- የእርቅ ድር'ድር (በሁለ'ት መሪዎ'ች መካ'ከል)

parliament
'ፓ:ለመንት -ስ- የምክር ቤት (ያንድ መንግ ሥት)

parlour
'ፓለ -ስ- ል'ዩ የእንግዳ መ'ቀበያ ክፍል

arochial
ፐ'ረውኪየል -ቅ- ሐ'ሳበ ው'ሱን ፤ ጠ'ባብ አስተያየት ያ'ለው

parole
ፐ'ሮል -ግ- ቃል በመ'ቀበል እሥረ'ኛ መፍ ታት [ፈ'ታ]
-ስ- ቃል መስጠት

parrot
'ፓረት -ስ- በቀበ'ቃ (የወፍ ዓይነት)

parry
'ፓሪ -ስ- መመ'ከት [መ'ከተ] (ለበ'ትር)

parsimonious
ፓ:ሲ'መውኒየስ -ቅ- ሥ'ሥታም ፤ ነብ'ጋ (ገንዘብ) ፤ ንፉግ

parson
'ፓ:ሰን -ስ- ካህን

part
'ፓ:ት -ስ- ክፍል

partake
ፓ:'ቴይክ -ግ- መ'ሳተፍ [ተሳ'ተፈ]

partial
'ፓ:ሸል -ቅ- በከፊል የሆነ ፤ ያልተፈ'ጸመ እ'ዳዩ ፤ አድልዎ የ'ሚያደርግ

participate
ፓ'ቲሲፔይት -ግ- መ'ካፈል [ተካ'ፈለ] (ለ ሥራ)

particle
'ፓ:ቲክል -ስ- ት'ን'ሽ ቁ'ራጭ ፤ ሰብርባሪ እ'ገባብ (ሰዋስው)

particular
ፐ'ቲኩዩለ -ቅ- ል'ዩ ፤ የተለ'የ
fussy
-ቅ- በጣም ጥንቁቅ

parting
'ፓ:ቲንግ -ስ- መለያየት

partisan
'ፓ:ቲዛን -ስ- ነጭ ለባሽ ፤ ተዋጊ ፤ አርበ'ኛ

partition
ፓ:'ቲሽን -ስ- መከፈያ ፤ መከፈል ፤ ሁለ'ት ክፍሎ'ች የ'ሚለ'ይ ግድግ'ዳ ፤ ግንቦ ወዘተ

partly
'ፓ:ትሊ -ተግ- በከፊል

partner
'ፓ:ትነ -ስ- የሥራ ጓ'ደ'ኛ ፣ ሽርካ

party
'ፓ:ቲ -ስ- ግብዣ
political
-ስ- የፖ'ሊቲካ ማኅበር

pass
'ፓ:ስ -ግ- ማለፍ [አ'ለፈ]
a law
-ግ- ሕ'ግ ማውጣት [አወ'ጣ]
give
-ግ- ማቀ'በል [አቀ'በለ]
ticket
-ስ- በነጻ የመግቢያ መ'ታወቂያ ወረ ቀት

passage
'ፓሰጅ -ስ- መ'ተላለፊያ
fare
-ስ- የጉዞ ዋጋ (የመርከብ)

passenger
'ፓሰንጀ -ስ- መንገደ'ኛ

passer-by
'ፓ:ሰ'ባይ -ስ- ተላላፊ ፣ መንገደ'ኛ

passion
'ፓሽን -ስ- ታ'ላቅ ስ'ሜት ፣ ጥልቅ ስ'ሜት ፣ ፍ'ላጎት

passive
'ፓሲቭ -ቅ- የ'ማይሠራ ፣ ተገብሮ (ሰዋሰው)

passport
'ፓ:ስፖ:ት -ስ- የይለፍ ወረቀት

past
'ፓ:ስት -ቅ- ያ'ለፈ
-ስ- ያ'ለፈ ጊዜ

paste
'ፔይስት -ስ- መጣብቅ ፣ ማ'ሸጊያ

pasteboard
'ፔይስትቦ:ድ -ስ- ነ'ጭ ወፍራም ወረቀት ፣ ክርታስ

pastime
'ፓ:ስታይም -ስ- የጊዜ ማ'ሳ'ለፊያ ሥራ (ለመ 'ደሰት ፣ ለመዝናኛ)

pastoral
'ፓስተረል -ቅ- ከከብት እ'ረ'ኛ'ና ከሕይወቱ ጋር ግን'ኙ'ነት ያ'ለው ፣ የጳ'ጳስ

pastry
'ፔይስትሪ -ስ- ኬክ

pasture
'ፓ:ስቸ -ስ- የከብት ማዋያ መስክ ፣ የግጦሽ ቦታ

pat
'ፓት -ግ- መጠብጠብ [ጠበ'ጠበ] (ሕፃናትን)

patch
'ፓች -ስ- መ'ጣፊያ (ጨርቅ)

patchy
'ፓቺ -ቅ- ጥሩ'ነቱ ሙሉ ያልሆነ ፣ በመጠኑ ሆነ በዓይነት ያልተስተካ'ከለ

patent
'ፔተንት -ስ- አንድ ነገር ባንድ ሰው ፣ ባንድ ኩ'ባንያ የተሠ'ራ የተፈለ'ሰፈ መሆኑን ማ'ረጋገጫ ሰነድ

paternal
ፐ'ተ:ነል -ቅ- አ'ባታዊ

path
'ፓ:ስ -ስ- የግር መንገድ ፣ የግረ'ኛ መንገድ ፣ ስርጥ መንገድ

pathetic
ፐ'ሴቲክ -ቅ- አሳ'ዛኝ

pathos
'ፔይሶስ -ስ- የሐዘን ስ'ሜት የ'ሚቀሰ'ቅስ ነገር ፣ ሁናቴ

pathway
'ፓ:ስዌይ -ስ- መ'ተላለፊያ ፣ ጠ'ባብ መንገድ

patient
'ፔይሽንት -ስ- ሕመምተ'ኛ
-ቅ- ቻይ ፣ ትዕግሥተ'ኛ

patriotic
ፓትሪ'ዮቲክ -ቅ- ያገር ፍቅር ያ'ለው ፣ ለሀገሩ ተቆርቋሪ

patrol
ፐት'ረውል -ግ- መፈ'ተሽ [ፈ'ተሸ] (አንድ ቦታ በወ'ታ'ደር) ፣ ዘብ መቆም [ቆመ]

patron
'ፔይትረን -ስ- ጠ'ባቂ ፣ ተከባካቢ ፣ ረ'ዳት
customer
-ስ- ደምበ'ኛ (የንግድ)

patronize
'ፓትረናይዝ -ግ- በዝ'ቅተ'ኛ መንፈስ እ'የተ መለ'ከቱ መርዳት [ረ'ዳ] ፤ የበላይ ተጠባባቂ መሆን [ሆነ] (የድር'ጅት ወዘተ)
a shop
-ግ- ደምበ'ኛ መሆን [ሆነ] (የሱቅ)
patter
'ፓተ -ስ- የመንጠብጠብ ድምፅ ፤ የፈ'ጣን እርምጃ ድምፅ ፤ ፈ'ጣን እ'ንጋገር (ያ'ሥቂ'ኝ ሰው)
pattern
'ፓተን -ስ- ሐረግ ፤ አንድ ነገር ለመሣል የ'ሚ'ገለ'በጥ ቅርፅ ፤ ማንገድ ፤ ዓይነት ፤ ም'ሳሌ ወዘተ
paunch
'ፖ:ንች -ስ- ቦርጭ
pauper
'ፖ:ፐ -ስ- ድሃ ፤ በተራድኦ ገንዘብ የ'ሚኖር ድሃ ሰው
pause
'ፖ:ዝ -ግ- ለጥቂት ጊዜ ማረፍ [ዐ'ረፈ]
pave
'ፔይቭ -ግ- መደልደል [ደለ'ደለ] (መንገድ)
pavement
'ፔይቭመንት -ስ- በመኪና መንገድ ዳር'ና ዳር ያ'ለ የእግረ'ኛ መሄጃ ፤ የግረ'ኛ መንገድ
pavilion
ፐ'ቪልየን -ስ- ዳስ
paving
'ፔይቪንግ -ስ- ንጣፍ ደንጊያ (የመንገድ)
paw
'ፖ: -ስ- መዳፍ (የእንስሳት)
pawn
'ፖ:ን -ስ- መያዣ ዕቃ (ለገንዘብ ብ'ድር)
chess
-ስ- ወ'ታ'ደር (በሰንጠረጅ ጨዋታ)
agent
-ስ- መ'ሣሪያ (ለክፉ ሥራ ፤ ለሰው)
pawnbroker
'ፖ:ንብረውክ -ስ- ገንዘብ አበ'ዳሪ (መያዣ ተቀ'ብሎ)
pay
'ፔይ -ግ- መክፈል ፤ [ከ'ፈለ]
salary
-ስ- ደመወዝ

payment
'ፔይመንት -ስ- ክፍ'ያ ፤ መክፈል
pea
'ፒ:ይ -ስ- አተር
peace
'ፒ:ይስ -ስ- ሰላም ፤ እርጋታ ፤ ፀ'ጥታ
peaceful
'ፒ:ይስፉል -ቅ- ሰላማዊ ፤ ፀ'ጥ ያለ
peach
'ፒ:ይች -ስ- ኮክ
peak
'ፒ:ይክ -ስ- የተራራ ጫፍ
peal
'ፒ:ይል -ግ- በጣም መደ'ወል [ደ'ወለ]
-ስ- ከፍተ'ኛ የደወል ድምፅ
peanut
'ፒ:ነት -ስ- ለውዝ ·
pearl
'ፐ:ል -ስ- ሉል
peasant
'ፔዘንት -ስ- ገበሬ ፤ ባላገር
pebble
'ፔበል -ስ- ጠጠር
peck
'ፔክ -ግ- መጠቅጠቅ [ጠቀ'ጠቀ] (ለዶሮ ፤ ለወፍ)
peculiar
ፐክ'ዩሊየ -ቅ- ያልተለ'መደ ፤ እንግዳ (ለሁኔታ) ፤ የተለ'የ (ጠባይ)
peculiarity
ፐክዩሊ'ያሪቲ -ስ- ል'ዩ ጠባይ
pecuniary
ፔክ'ዩኒየሪ -ቅ- የገንዘብ
pedal
'ፔዶል -ስ- በእግር እንዲሠራ የ'ሚ'ደ'ረግ (መወስወሻ ፤ ፍሬሲዮን ወዘተ)
pedantic
ፐ'ዳንቲክ -ቅ- ዐዋቂ ነ'ኝ ባይ ፤ ለጥ.ቃ'ቅን ነገር ል'ጠንቀቅ ባይ ፤ ለ'ዛ የሌ'ለው (ዐዋቂ) ፤ ጥራዝ ነ'ጠቅ
pedestal
'ፔደስተል -ስ- በምድ ፤ ሐውልት ወዘተ የ'ሚ.ቆም'በት መሠረት

edestrian
ፐ'ዴስትሪየን -ስ- እግረ'ኛ
-ቅ- እስልቺ

edigree
'ፔዲግሪይ -ስ- ትውል'ድ ፣ የትውል'ድ ሐረግ

edlar
'ፔድለ -ስ- ሱቅ በደረቴ ፣ ከቦታ ወደ ቦታ የ'ሚ'ዘዋ'ወር'ና ዕቃ የ'ሚሸጥ ነ'ጋዴ

eel
'ፒይል -ስ- ል'ጣጭ (የፍራፍሬ)

eep
'ፒይፐ -ግ- በቀዳዳ ውስጥ መ'መልከት [ተመ ለ'ከተ] ፣ ማሾ'ለቅ [አሾ'ለቀ]

eer
'ፒየ -ግ- ቀረብ ብሎ ማየት [አ'የ]
noble
-ስ- ከ'ፍ ያለ ማዕረግ ያ'ለው ሰው

eevish
'ፒይቪሽ -ቅ- በቀ'ላሉ የ'ሚ'ቆ'ጣ ፣ በት'ንሹ የ'ሚ'ና'ደድ

eg
'ፔግ -ስ- ማንጠልጠያ (በግድግ'ዳ ላይ የተ ሰ'ካ)

elican
'ፔሊከን -ስ- ይብራ

ellet
'ፔለት -ስ- ት'ንሽ ፣ ክ'ብ ቁ'ራጭ
shotgun
-ስ- የረሽ ፍን'ጣቂ

elt
'ፔልት -ስ- አንጋ'ሬ ፣ ቆዳ

en
'ፔን -ስ- ብዕር
enclosure
-ስ- ጋጥ ፣ ጉረ'ኖ

enal
'ፒይነል -ቅ- የወንጀል

enalize
'ፒይነላይዝ -ግ- መቅጣት [ቀ'ጣ] (መ'ቀጮ በመጣል)

enalty
'ፔነልቲ -ስ- መ'ቀጫ ፣ መ'ቀጮ

enance
'ፔነንስ -ስ- የን'ሥሐ ቅጣት

pencil
'ፔንሰል -ስ- እርሳስ (መጻፊያ)

pendant
'ፔንደንት -ስ- ያንገት ጌጥ (በድሪ ላይ የተን ጠለ'ጠለ)

pending
'ፔንዲንግ -ቅ- የተንጠለ'ጠለ (ው'ሳኔ ያላገ'ኘ)

pendulum
'ፔንድዩለም -ስ- ወዲያ'ና ወዲህ የ'ሚ'ወዛ 'ወዝ መ'ሣሪያ (የሰዓት)

penetrate
'ፔነትሬይት -ግ- መግባት [ገ'ባ] ፣ መ'ነስነስ [ተነሰ'ነሰ]

peninsuler
ፐ'ኒንስዩለ -ስ- ል'ሳን ምድር (ከብዙ ወገን በውሃ የተከ'በበ የብስ)

penis
ፒይ'ነስ -ስ- የወንድ አባል ፣ የወንድ ሐፍረተ ሥጋ (ቁላ)

penitence
'ፔኒተንስ -ስ- ን'ሥሐ

penitent
'ፔኒተንት -ቅ- ተነ'ሣሒ

penitentiary
ፔኒ'ቴንሸሪ -ስ- እሥር ቤት (በተለ'ይ እሥረ 'ኛው ወደ በ'ጎ ተግባር እንዲ'መ'ለስ የ'ሚ'ደ 'ከም'በት)

pen-knife
'ፔንናይፍ -ስ- ሰንጢ

pennant
'ፔነንት -ስ- ጠ'ባብ'ና ረ'ጅም ሦስት ማዕዘን ያ'ለው ሰን'ደቅ ዐላማ

penniless
'ፔኒለስ -ቅ- በጣም ደሀ ፣ መንጻ'ካ ደሀ

pension
'ፔንሽን -ስ- የጡረታ አበ'ል ፣ ኪራይ ተከ ፍሎ የ'ሚ'ታ'ደር'በት ቤት

pensive
'ፔንሲቭ -ቅ- ያ'ዘነ ፣ ሐ'ሳብ የገ'ባው

pentagon
'ፔንተጎን -ስ- አ'ምስት ማዕዘን ያ'ለው ቅርፅ

pentecost
'ፔንተኮስት -ስ- በዓለ ኀምሳ ፣ ጴንጠቆስጤ

penultimate
ፔ'ንል·ቲመት -ቅ- ከመጨ'ረሻ በፊት ያ'ለ (ነገር)

penury
'ፔንዩሪ -ስ- ከል'ክ ያ'ለፈ ችግረ'ኛ'ነት

people
'ፒይፐል -ስ- ሕዝብ

pepper
'ፔፐ -ስ- በርበ'ሬ ፡ ቁንዶ በርበ'ሬ

peppermint
'ፔፐሚንት -ስ- ፔፔርሚንት

perambulator
ፐ'ራምብዩሌይተ -ስ- የሕፃናት ጋሪ (ሕፃናት ማንሸራሸሪያ)

perceive
ፐ'ሲይቭ -ግ- ማስተዋል [አስተዋለ] ፡ ማየት [አ'የ] ፡ መ'ረዳት [ተረ'ዳ]

perch
'ፐ:ች -ስ- የወፎ'ች መሥፈሪያ አግድም ብረት፣ እንጨት

roost

-ግ- ማረፍ [ዐ'ረፈ] (ለወፍ)

percent
ፐ'ሰንት -ተግ- ከመቶ ፡ በመቶ

perdition
ፐ'ዲሽን -ስ- ጥፋት (በሰው ላይ የ'ሚመጣ) ፡ ዘለዓለማዊ ኩነኔ

peremptory
'ፔረምትሪ -ቅ- እም'ቢታ የ'ማይ'ቀ'በል ፡ በመፀ'ኛ

perennial
ፐ'ሬኒየል -ቅ- ከመት ዓመት የ'ሚቆ'ይ ፡ ብዙ ዓመታት የ'ሚቆ'ይ (አትክልት)

perfect
'ፐ:ፊክት -ቅ- ፍ'ጹም ፡ እንከን የሌ'ለው

perfection
ፐ'ፌክሽን -ስ- ፍ'ጹም'ነት ፡ እንከን የ'ለሽ'ነት

perfidious
ፐ'ፊዲየስ -ቅ- እምነተቢስ ፡ ከሓዲ (እምነት አጉዳይ)

perfidy
'ፐ:ፊዲ -ስ- ክሕደት

perforate
'ፐ:ፈሬይት -ግ- መሸንቆር [ሸነ'ቆረ] (በተ
ብዙ ሸንቁሮ'ች

perform
ፐ'ፎ:ም -ግ- መሥራት [ሠ'ራ] ፡ ማድረግ [አ
'ረገ]

perfume
'ፐ:ፍዩም -ስ- ጥሩ ሽ'ታ

liquid

-ስ- ሽ'ቶ

perfunctory
ፐ'ፈንክተሪ -ቅ- ጥን'ቃቄ ያ'ነሰው ፡ ለግ
ይውጣ የተሠ'ራ

perhaps
ፐ'ሀፐስ -ተግ- ምናልባት

peril
'ፔረል -ስ- ከ'ባድ አደጋ ፡ ከ'ባድ መከራ

period
'ፒሪየድ -ስ- ጊዜ ፤ ነጥብ (በረፍተ ነገር ማ
ሚያ)

menstruation

-ስ- የአደፍ ጊዜ

periodical
ፒሪ'ዮዲክል -ስ- መጽሔት
-ቅ- በተወ'ሰነ ጊዜ የ'ሚሆን

periodically
ፒሪ'ዮዲክሊ -ተግ- በ'የጊዜው

periphery
ፐ'ሪፈሪ -ስ- ዳር ፡ ዳር'ቻ

perish
'ፔሪሽ -ግ- መጥፋት [ጠ'ፋ] ፡ መሞት [ሞ

perjury
'ፐ:ጀሪ -ስ- የሐ'ሰት ፡ የመዋሸት ወንጀል
ምስ'ክር'ነት)

perky
'ፐ:ኪ -ቅ- ንቁ ፡ እምነቱን'ና በጉዳ'ዩ አ'ሳ
መሆኑን የ'ሚያሳ'ይ ፡ በራሱ የ'ሚ'ተማ'መ

permanent
'ፐ:መነንት -ቅ- ቀዋሚ ፡ ነዋሪ ፡ የ'ማይ'
'ወጥ

permeate
'ፐ:ሚዬይት -ግ- መስፋፋት [ተስፋ'ፋ] ፡ መ
ባት [ገ'ባ] (ለውሃ)

permission
ፐ'ሚሽን -ስ- ፈቃድ
permit
ፐ'ሚት -ግ- ፈቃድ መስጠት [ሰ'ጠ]
permit
'ፐ:ሚት -ቅ- ፈቃድ
pernicious
ፐ'ኒሽስ -ቅ- በጣም የ'ሚጎዳ ፣ አደገ'ኛ ፣ ክፉ
perpendicular
ፐ:ፐን'ዲክዩለ -ቅ- ቀ'ጥ ያለ (መሥመር ወዘተ)
perpetual
ፐ'ፔቹውል -ቅ- ዘለዓለማዊ ፣ ነዋሪ ፣ መጨ'ረሻ የሌ'ለው ፣ ተደጋጋሚ
perplex
ፐ'ፕ'ሌክስ -ግ- ማ'ደናገር [አ'ደና'ገረ] ፣ የ'ሚያደርገውን ማሳ'ጣት [አሳ'ጣ]
persecute
'ፐ:ሲክዩ:ት -ግ- ማ'ሳደድ [አ'ሳ'ደደ] (ለሃይማኖት ወዘተ)
persevere
ፐሲ'ቪየ -ግ- መቀ'ጠል [ቀ'ጠለ] (ተስፋ ባለመቁረጥ)
Persian
'ፐ:ሽን -ቅ- የፋርስ ፣ የኢራን ፣ ኢራናዊ
persist
ፐ'ሲስት -ግ- በሐ'ሳብ መጽናት [ጸ'ና]
person
'ፐ:ሰን -ስ- ሰው
personal
'ፐ:ሰነል -ቅ- የግል
personnel
ፐሰ'ኔል -ስ- ሠ'ራተ'ኞ'ች (የመሥሪያ ቤት)
perspiration
ፐስፐ'ሬይሽን -ስ- ማላብ ፣ ላብ
persuade
ፐስ'ዌይድ -ግ- ማሳ'መን [አሳ'መነ] ፣ በመ'ወያየት ወይን'ም በክር'ክር ሐ'ሳብ እንዲ'ቀ'በሉ ማድረግ [አደ'ረገ]
pert
'ፐ:ት -ቅ- ደ'ፋር ፣ አክብሮት የ'ማያሳ'ይ
pertinent
'ፐ:ቲነንት -ቅ- ከጉ'ዳዩ ጋር የተያያዘ ፣ ጉ'ዳዩን የ'ሚነካ

perturbed
ፐ'ተ:ብድ -ቅ- የታ'ወከ ፣ የተጨ'ነቀ
peruse
ፐ'ሩ:ዝ -ግ- በጥን'ቃቄ ማንበብ [አነ'በበ]
pervade
ፐ'ቬይድ -ግ- መስፋፋት [ተስፋ'ፋ] (አዲስ ፡ ሥል'ጣኔ ወዘተ)
pervert
ፐ'ቨ:ት -ግ- ማ'ጣመም [አ'ጣመመ] (ያ'ጉን ነገር) ፤ የሰው አእምሮ ከትክ'ክለ'ኛ መንገዱ ማውጣት [አወ'ጣ] ፣ ማዛባት [አ'ዛ'ባ] ፣ ለክፉ ማዋል (አዋለ)
pervert
'ፐ:ቨ:ት -ስ- ከሰው የተለ'የ ጠባይ ያ'ለው ፣ ሴሰ'ኛ ፣ ከተፈጥሮ ው'ጭ የሆነ ሥራ የ'ሚሠራ (ለግብረ ሥጋ)
pessimist
'ፔሰሚስት -ቅ- ሁልጊዜ ክፉ ነገር ይመጣል ብሎ የ'ሚያምን
pest
'ፔስት -ስ- አ'ዋኪ ነገር
animals
-ስ- የ'ሚጎዱ ነፍሳት ፣ ትን'ንሽ እንስሳት ፤ መቅሠፍት ፤ ብጥብጭ ፣ ሁከተ'ኛ ሰው ወይ'ም ነገር
pet
'ፔት -ስ- ለ'ማዳ ት'ንሽ እንስሳ
person
-ስ- በተለ'ይ የ'ሚ'ወ'ደድ (ተማሪ ወዘተ)
caress
-ግ- ማሻሸት [አሻ'ሸ] (ሴት)
petal
'ፔተል -ስ- ያበባ ቅጠል (ከአበባው ዙሪያ ቅጠል)
petition
ፐ'ቲሽን -ስ- ይግባ'ኝ ፣ አቤቱታ
petrol
'ፔትረል -ስ- ቤንዚን
petticoat
'ፔቲኮውት -ስ- ቡ'ፍ ያለ የሴት የውስጥ ልብስ ፣ ቡ'ፋንት
petty
'ፔቲ -ቅ- ጥቃ'ቅን (ዋጋ የሌ'ለው)

antasy

'ፋንተሲ -ስ- እውነት'ነት የሌ'ለው ታሪክ ፣ ሕልም የ'ሚመስል ሐ'ሳብ ፣እንደሕልም ያ'ለ ነገር

hantom

'ፋንተም -ስ- ረቂቅ ፍጡር ፣ የማይ'ዳ'ሰስ ቅርፅ ፣ እውነት'ነት የሌ'ለው

pharmaceutical

ፋ:መስ'ዩቲከል -ቅ- የመድኃኒት ቅ'መማ

pharmacy

'ፋ:መሲ -ስ- መድኃኒት ቅ'መማ

phase

'ፌይዝ -ስ- ባንድ ተመላልሶ በ'ሚ'ደ'ረግ ሁናቴ ውስጥ የእድገት ወይን'ም የለውጥ ጊዜ

philanthropist

ፊ'ላንስረፒስት ቅ- የሰውን ልጅ ወ'ዳድ ፣ በጎ አድራጊ ፣ ሰብአዊ ፍቅር ያ'ደረ'በት

philology

ፊ'ሎለጂ -ስ- የቋንቋዎ'ች ትምህርት

philosophy

ፊ'ሎሰፊ -ስ- ፍልስፍ'ና

phlegmatic

ፊሌግ'ማቲክ -ቅ- በቀ'ላሉ የ'ማይ'ሸ'በር

phonetic

ፊ'ኔቲክ -ቅ- እንዳ'ነባበቡ የተጻፈ ፣ የድምፅ

photograph

'ፊውተግራ:ፍ -ስ- ፎቶግራፍ

phrase

ፍ'ሬይዝ -ስ- ሐረግ (ሰዋሰው)

physician

ፊ'ዚሽን -ስ- ሐኪም

physics

'ፊዚክስ -ስ- ፊዚክስ (የኀይል'ና የጥንተ ነገ ር'ች ጠባይ ጥናት)

physiognomy

ፊዚ'ዮነሚ -ስ- መልክ ፣ የመልክ ቅርፅ'ና ጠቅላ'ላ ሁኔታው

physique

ፊ'ዚይክ -ስ- የሰው'ነት ቅርፅ

piano

ፒ'ያነው -ስ- ፒያኖ

pick

'ፒክ -ግ- መልቀም [ለ'ቀመ]

choose

-ግ- መምረጥ [መ'ረጠ]

tool

-ስ- መቆ'ፈሪያ ፣ ዶማ

pickaxe

'ፒካክስ -ስ- ዶማ

picnic

'ፒክኒክ -ስ- የሽር'ሽር ቦታ (ምግብ ተይዞ የ'ሚ'ኬድ'በት)

picture

'ፒክቸ -ስ- ሥዕል

picturesque

ፒክቸ'ሬስክ -ቅ- ያማረ (ትእ'ይንት ፣ ለመሣል የ'ሚስማ'ማ)

pie

'ፓይ -ስ- ከሥጋ ወይን'ም ከፍራፍሬ'ና ከሊጥ የተሰና'ዳ ምግብ (የተጋ'ገረ)

piece

'ፒይስ -ስ- ቁራ'ጭ ነገር

piecemeal

'ፒይስሚይል -ተግ- ት'ንሽ በት'ንሽ ፣ በተበ ታ'ተነ ሁናቴ

pierce

'ፒየስ -ግ- መውጋት [ወ'ጋ] (በመ'ሣሪያ)

piety

'ፓየቲ -ስ- ሃይማኖተ'ኛ'ነት

pig

'ፒግ -ስ- ዐሣማ

pigeon

'ፒጀን -ስ- እርግብ

pigtail

'ፒግቴይል -ስ- በስተኋላ የወ'ረደ የጠጉር ጉን ጉን

pike

'ፓይክ -ስ- ዶማ

pile

'ፓይል -ስ- ዐሣ የ'ሚበላ ዐሣ

-ግ- መከ'መር [ከ'መረ] ፣ መቆ'ለል [ቆ'ለለ]

pilfer

'ፒልፈ -ግ- መስረቅ [ሰ'ረቀ] (ለጥቃ'ቅን ነገር)

pilgrim
’ፒልግሪም -ስ- የተቀ'ደሱ ቦታዎ'ች ለመ
'ሳለም የ'ሚ'ጓዝ ሰው ፣ ተሳላሚ (ም'ሳሌ ፣
ኢ'የሩሳሌም ፣ መ'ካ)

pilgrimage
’ፒልግሪሚጅ -ስ- ወደተቀ'ደሱ ቦታዎ'ች የ
'ሚ'ደ'ረግ ጉዞ

pill
’ፒል -ስ- ክኒን ፣ እንክብ'ል (መድኃኒት)

pillage
’ፒለጅ -ግ- መዝረፍ [ዘ'ረፈ]

pillar
’ፒለ -ስ- ዐምድ

pillar-box
’ፒለቦክስ -ስ- ዐምድ መ'ሰል የፖስታ ማስገ
'ቢያ ሣጥን (በመንገድ ዳ'ር የቆመ)

pillion
’ፒለየን -ስ- መ'ፈናጠጫ ወምበር (በሞቶር
ቢስክሌት ኋላ)

pillow
’ፒለው -ስ- ትራስ

pillow-case
’ፒለውኬይስ -ስ- የትራስ ልብስ

pilot
’ፓይለት -ስ- መርከብ ነጂ ፣ አውሮ'ፕላን
ነጂ

pimp
’ፒምፕ -ግ- ማ'ቃጠር [አ'ቃ'ጠረ] (ሴት
ለወንድ)

pimple
’ፒምፑል -ስ- ብጉር

pin
’ፒን -ግ- በስፒል ማ'ያያዝ [አ'ያያዘ] (ወረ
ቀት)

straight

-ስ- ስፒል

safety-

-ስ- መርፌ ቁልፍ

pinafore
’ፒነፎ፡ -ስ- ሽ'ርጥ (የሕፃናት ፣ ልብሳ'ቸው
እንዳይቆ'ሽሽ)

pincers
’ፒንሰዝ -ስ- ጉጠት

pinch
’ፒንች -ግ- መቆንጠጥ [ቆነ'ጠጠ]

pine
’ፓይን -ግ- መድከም [ደ'ከመ] (ከበ'ሽታ፣ከሐ
ዘን የተነ'ሣ) ፤ የጋለ ፍ'ላጎት መኖር [ኖረ]
(አንድ ነገር ለማድረግ)

pineapple
’ፓይናፑል -ስ- አናናስ

pinion
’ፒንየን -ግ- እ'ጅ ማሰር [አ'ሰረ] (ከሰው
'ውነት ጋር)

-ስ- የወፍ ክንፍ

pink
’ፒንክ -ቅ- ክፍት ቀ'ይ

pinnacle
’ፒንክል -ስ- ጫፍ (የቤት፣የተራራ ወዘተ) ፣
ቁንጮ

pioneer
ፓየ’ኒየ -ስ- አንዱን ያ'ለ'ማ አገር ለማልማት
ከሄዱ ሰዎ'ች አንዱ ፤ ያንድ ዕ'ቅድ መሪ ፣ ያን
ድ ሥራ ጀ'ማሪ

pious
’ፓየስ -ቅ- ሃይማኖታዊ ፣ ጊዜውን ለሃይማ
ኖት ተግባር የሰ'ጠ

pip
’ፒፕ -ስ- ፍሬ (የፍራፍሬ)

pipe
’ፓይፕ -ስ- ቧንቧ

smoking

-ስ- ፒ'ፓ (የትምባሆ ማጨሻ)

flute

-ስ- ዋሽ'ንት

pirate
’ፓይረት -ስ- የባሕር ወንበዴዎ'ች ፣ መርከብ
ዘራፊዎ'ች

pistol
’ፒስተል -ስ- ሽ'ጉጥ

piston
’ፒስተን -ስ- ፒስቶን

pit
’ፒት -ስ- ጉድጓድ

pitch
’ፒች -ስ- የድምፅ ከ'ፍተ'ኛ'ነት'ና ዝ'ቅተ'ኛ'ነት
tar
-ስ- ሬንጅ
throw
-ግ- መወርወር [ወረ'ወረ]
sport
-ስ- የስፖርት ሜዳ
a tent
-ግ- ድንኳን መትከል [ተ'ከለ]

pitcher
’ፒቸ -ስ- እንሥራ

piteous
’ፒትየስ -ቅ- አሳ'ዛኝ

pitfall
’ፒትፎ:ል -ስ- የአውሬ ማጥመጃ ጉድጓድ ፥ የተደ'በቀ አደጋ

pith
’ፒስ -ስ- ከል'ጣጭ በታች ያ'ለው ሥሥ ሽፋን (የፍራፍሬ ወዘተ)
importance
-ስ- ቁም ነገር (የንግ'ግር)
vigour
-ስ- ጥን'ካሬ ፥ ኀይል

pity
’ፒቲ -ስ- ሐዘን ፥ ርኅራኄ

pivot
’ፒቨት -ስ- መሽከርከሪያ ሹል መ'ሣሪያ

placard
ፕ’ላካ:ድ -ስ- ሕዝብን ለማስታወቅ የተጻፈ ጽሑፍ

placate
ፕለ’ኬይት -ግ- ማ'ረጋጋት [አ'ረጋጋ] ፥ ቁ'ጣ ማብረድ [አበ'ረደ]

place
ፕ’ሌይስ -ስ- ቦታ

placenta
ፕለ’ሴንተ -ስ- የእንግዴ ልጅ

placid
ፕ’ላሲድ -ቅ- ጸ'ጥ ያለ

plague
ፕ’ሌይግ -ስ- ኀይለ'ኛ ተላላፊ በ'ሽታ ፥ ቸፈር
disturb
-ግ- ማ'ወክ [አ'ወከ] ፥ መበጥበጥ [በጠ'በጠ]

plain
ፕ’ሌይን -ስ- ለ'ጥ ያለ ቦታ ፥ ሜዳ
undecorated
-ቅ- ጌጣጌጥ የሌ'ለ'በት
understandable
-ቅ- ግልጽ

plaintiff
ፕ’ሌይንቲፍ -ስ- ከሳሽ

plaintive
ፕ’ሌይንቲቭ -ቅ- የ'ሚያሳ'ዝን (ድምፅ)

plan
ፕ’ላን -ግ- ማ'ቀድ [ዐ'ቀደ]
-ስ- ዕ'ቅድ

plane
ፕ’ሌይን -ቅ- ጠፍጣ'ፋ
aero-
-ስ- አውሮ'ፕላን
tool
-ስ- መላጊያ

planet
ፕ’ላኔት -ስ- ፈለክ (ከፀሐይ ጭፍሮ'ች አንዱ)

plank
ፕ’ላንክ -ስ- ጣውላ

plant
ፕ’ላ:ንት -ስ- ተክል

plantation
ፕላን’ቴይሽን -ስ- አትክልት

plaque
ፕ’ላክ -ስ- የድንጊያ ፥ የሸክላ ጽ'ላት (በግድ'ግ'ዳ ላይ እንዲጌጥ የ'ሚንጠለ'ጠል)

plaster
ፕ’ላ:ስተ -ስ- ፕላስተር ፥ እቁስል ላይ የ'ሚ'ለ'ጠፍ መድ'ኃኒት'ነት ያ'ለው መለ'ጠፊያ
of Paris
-ስ- ጀሶ
a wall etc
-ግ- መምረግ [መ'ረገ] (በጭቃ)

plastic
ፕ'ላስቲክ -ስ- ፕላስቲክ
-ቅ- በቀ'ላሉ የ'ሚ'ለ'መጥ ፣ ቅርፁ የ'ሚ'ለ'ወጥ

plate
ፕ'ሌይት -ስ- ዝርግ ሳሕን ፣ ሥሥ'ና ዝርግ የብረት ፣ የብ'ር ወዘተ ዕቃ

plateau
ፕ'ላቶው -ስ- በደጋ አገር ላይ ሜዳ'ማ ቦታ

platform
ፕ'ላትፎ፡ም -ስ- ከ'ፍ ያለ የተናጋሪ መቆሚያ ቦታ

plausible
ፕ'ሎ፡ዘበል -ቅ- እውነት የ'ሚመስል ፣ የ'ሚ ያሳ'ምን ፣ ሊ'ታ'መን የ'ሚችል

play
ፕ'ሌይ -ግ- መ'ጫወት [ተጫ'ወተ]
theatrical
-ስ- ቴያትር (ጽሑፍ)

plea
ፕ'ሊይ -ስ- ል'መና ፡ ማመልከቻ

plead
ፕ'ሊይድ -ግ- ምክንያት ለዳ'ኛ ማቅረብ [አቀ'ረበ] (ክ'ስ ሲያቀርቡ)
beseech
-ግ- መ'ለማመን [ተለማ'መነ]

pleasant
ፕ'ሌዘንት -ቅ- አስደ'ሳች

pleasantry
ፕ'ሌዘንትሪ -ስ- አስደ'ሳች ጭውው'ውት

please
ፕ'ሊይዝ -ግ- መ'ደሰት [ተ'ደ'ሰተ]
-ተግ ፡ ቃአ- እባ'ክዎን ፡ እባ'ክህን

pleasure
ፕ'ሌገር -ስ- ደ'ስታ

pleat
ፕ'ሊይት -ስ- ሽን'ሽን (የልብስ)

pledge
ፕ'ሌጅ -ግ- ቃል መግባት [ገ'ባ]
-ስ- ውለታ መግባት (አንድ ዕቃ እሰው ዘንድ በማስቀ'መጥ የገ'ባውን ውለታ ሲፈ'ጽም ዕቃውን ለመውሰድ)

plenty
ፕ'ሌንቲ -ስ- ብዛት ፡ መትረፍረፍ

pliable
ፕ'ላየበል -ቅ- በቀ'ላሉ የ'ሚ'ታ'ጠፍ
mind
-ቅ- በቀ'ላሉ የሰውን ሐ'ሳብ የ'ሚ'ቀ'በል

pliers
ፕ'ላየዝ -ስ- የጉጠት ዓይነት መ'ገሬያ

plight
ፕ'ላይት -ስ- አ'ዋኪ ፣ አሳ'ዛኝ ሁኔታ
promise
-ግ- ተስፋ መስጠት [ሰ'ጠ] (ለጋብ'ቻ)

plimsolls
ፕ'ሊምሶልዝ -ስ- የላስቲክ ሶል ያ'ለው የሸራ ጫ'ማ (የስፖርት)

plinth
ፕ'ሊንስ -ስ- ያንድ ሐውልት መቆሚያ ድን'ጋይ

plod
ፕ'ሎድ -ግ- እየተጎ'ተቱ መ'ራመድ [ተራ'መደ] ፡ መሥራት [ሠ'ራ] (ለዕረፍት)

plot
ፕ'ሎት -ግ- መሸ'መቅ [ሸ'መቀ]
-ስ- ሽ'መቃ
story
-ስ- ያንድ መጽሐፍ ታሪክ ፍሬ ነገር
land
-ስ- ትን'ሽ ቁ'ራጭ መሬት

plough
ፕ'ላው -ግ- ማረስ [አ'ረሰ]
-ስ- ማረሻ

pluck
ፕ'ለክ -ግ- መልቀም [ለ'ቀመ] (ፍራፍሬ ከዛፍ) ፡ መ'ቅጠፍ [ቀጠ'ፈ] (አበባ) ፡ መንቀል [ን'ቀለ] [ላባ]

plug
ፕ'ለግ -ስ- ውታፍ ፣ የኤሌክትሪክ መሰ'ኪያ

plumage
ፕ'ሉሚጅ -ስ- የወፍ ላባ

plumber
ፕ'ለመ -ስ- ቧምቧ ሠ'ራተ'ኛ

plumbing
ፕ'ለሚንግ -ስ- በቤት ውስጥ ያ'ለ 'ውሃ ቧምቧ'ና የውሃ ጋን

plume
ፕ'ሉ:ም -ስ- ላባ ፣ ከላባ የተሠ'ራ ጌጥ
plump
ፕ'ለምፕ -ስ- ወፍራም ፣ ወደል (ለሰው ፣ ለእንስሳ) ፣ ድምቡ'ጭ ያለ
plunder
ፕ'ለንደ -ግ- መዝረፍ [ዘ'ረፈ] ፣ መበዝበዝ [በዘ'በዘ]
-ስ- የተዘ'ረፈ ዕቃ
plunge
ፕ'ለንጅ -ግ- መጥለቅ [ጠ'ለቀ] ፣ ማጥለቅ [አጠ'ለቀ] (እውሃ ውስጥ)
plural
ፕ'ሉረል -ስ- የብዙ ቁጥር (ሰዋሰው)
plus
ፕ'ለስ -ስ- የድ'ምር ምል'ክት
-ቅ- ተጨ'ማሪ
plush
ፕ'ለሽ -ስ- ከፈይ
-ቅ- የተቀማ'ጠለ
ply
ፕ'ላይ -ግ- የንግድ ሥራ ማ'ካሄድ [አ'ካሄደ]
-ስ- ቃ'ጫ (አንዱ ክ'ር)
pneumatic
ንዩ'ማቲክ -ቅ- በአ'የር የ'ሚ'ሠ'ራ ፣ በአ'የር የተሞ'ላ
pneumonia
ንዩ'መውኒየ -ስ- የሳም'ባ እብጠት በ'ሽታ
poach
'ፐውች -ግ- መስረቅ [ሰ'ረቀ] (ለከብት ፣ ለአደን ወዘተ)
pocket
'ፓኪት -ስ- ኪስ
pod
'ፖድ -ስ- የእሸት ል'ጣጭ (የአተር የባቄላ ወዘተ)
podgy
'ፖጂ -ቅ- አጭር'ና ወፍራም ፣ ዶፍዷ'ፋ
poem
'ፐውም -ስ- ግጥም ፣ ቅኔ
poet
'ፐውት -ስ- ግጥም ገጣሚ ፣ ባለቅኔ ፣ ባለግጥም
poetry
'ፐውትሪ -ስ- ቅኔ ፣ ግጥም ፣ ሥነ ግጥም
point
'ፖይንት -ስ- ነጥብ ፣ ነቁጥ
place, spot
-ስ- ቦታ
indicate
-ግ- ማመልከት [አመለ'ከተ]
pointed
'ፖይንተድ -ቅ- ሹል
of remarks
-ቅ- የተለ'የ ሰውን የ'ሚነካ (አ'ነጋገ
pointer
'ፖይንተ -ስ- ማመልከቻ (ዘንግ)
poise
'ፖይዝ -ስ- በራስ መ'ተማመን ፣ ኩሩ'ነት
የተመ'ዛነ አ'ቋቋም
poison
'ፖይዘን -ስ- መርዝ
-ግ- በመርዝ መግደል [ገ'ደለ]
poisonous
'ፖይዝነስ -ቅ- መርዛም ፣ መርዘ'ኛ
poke
'ፐውክ -ግ- መቆስቆስ [ቆሰ'ቆሰ] (በጣት በበ'ትር ወዘተ)
poker
'ፐውከ -ስ- የእሳት መቆስቆሻ (ብረት)
pole
'ፖውል -ስ- አጣና ፣ ዘንግ ፣ ምሰ'ሶ
geographical
-ስ- ዋልታ (የሰሜን ፣ የደቡብ)
police
ፐ'ሊስ -ስ- ፖሊስ (ድር'ጅት)
policeman
ፐ'ሊስመን -ስ- ፖሊስ (ሰው)
policy
'ፖሊሲ -ስ- አቅዋም ፣ ዐቅድ (የመንግሥ
insurance
-ስ- ስምም'ነት (የኢንሹራንስ)
polish
'ፖሊሽ -ግ- መጥረግ [ጠ'ረገ] (እንዲያበ
አድርጎ) ፣ መኰላት [ኰ'ላ]
-ስ- የጫ'ማ ቀለም
refinement
-ስ- መልካም አስተዳደግ

polite
ፐ'ላይት -ቅ- የታ'ረመ ፣ የተቀ'ጣ

politics
'ፖሊቲክስ -ስ- ፖለቲካ

poll
'ፖውል -ስ- የምርጫ መዝገብ ፣ ቦታ ፣ ድምፅ መስጠት ወዘተ (ለሕዝብ እንደራሴዎ'ች)

pollen
'ፖለን -ስ- በአበባ ውስጥ ያለ ብ'ጫ ዱቄት (ሌሎ'ች አበቦ'ች እንዲ'ራ'ቡ የ'ሚያደርግ)

pollute
ፐ'ሉ፡ት -ግ- ማሳ'ደፍ [አሳ'ደፈ] ፣ ማጉደፍ [አጉ'ደፈ]

pollution
ፐ'ሉሽን -ስ- እድፍ'ነት ፣ ጉድፍ'ነት

polygamy
ፐ'ሊገሚ -ስ- ከአንድ የበ'ለጠ ሚስት ማግባት

polyglot
'ፖሊግሎት -ስ- አ'ያሌ ቋንቋዎ'ች የ'ሚያውቅ ሰው
-ቅ- በብዙ ቋንቋዎ'ች የተጻፈ

polytheism
ፖሊ'ቢይዝም -ስ- በብዙ አማልክት አምልኮ

pomegranate
'ፖሚግራኔት -ስ- ሮማን (የፍሬ ዓይነት)

pomp
'ፖምፕ -ስ- ግሩም የሆነ ሰልፍ

pompous
'ፖምፐስ -ቅ- ል'ታይ ል'ታይ ባይ ፣ ባለግርማ

pond
'ፖንድ -ስ- ኩሬ

ponder
'ፖንደ -ግ- አጥልቆ ማ'ሰብ [አ'ሰበ] ፣ አተኩ'ሮ ማ'ሰብ [አ'ሰበ]

ponderous
'ፖንደረስ -ቅ- በጣም ከ'ባድ ፣ በቀ'ላሉ የ'ማይንቀሳ'ቀስ

pontoon
ፖን'ቱ፡ን -ስ- በውሃ ላይ የ'ሚንሳ'ፈፍ የድልድይ ድጋፍ (በጀልባ ላይ የቆመ)

pony
'ፐውኒ -ስ- ድንክ ፈረስ

pool
'ፑ፡ል -ስ- ኩሬ
resources
-ግ- መደባለቅ [ደባ'ለቀ] (ሀብትን ፣ ትርፍን ለመ'ካፈል)

poor
'ፖ፡ -ቅ- ድሀ ፣ ች'ግረ'ኛ
weak
-ቅ- ደካማ (በትምህርት ወዘተ)
pitiful
-ቅ- አሳ'ዛኝ

popular
'ፖፒዩለ -ቅ- የታ'ወቀ ፣ ዝ'ነ'ኛ

population
ፖፒዩ'ሌይሽን -ስ- ሕዝብ

porch
'ፖ፡ች -ስ- መግቢያ (ጣራ መሳይ ያ'ለው በ'ር)

porcupine
ፖ፡ክዩፓይን -ስ- ጃርት

pore
'ፖ፡ -ስ- ት'ንሽ ቀዳዳ (በሰው'ነት ቆዳ)
concentrate on
-ግ- አተ'ኩሮ ማ'ሰብ [አ'ሰበ]

pork
'ፖ፡ክ -ስ- ያሣማ ሥጋ

porous
'ፖ፡ረስ -ቅ- ውሃ የ'ሚያፈ'ስ ፣ ቀዳዳ ያ'ለው ፣ ውሃ የ'ማይቋ'ጥር

porridge
'ፖሪጅ -ስ- አጥሚት ፣ ሙቅ (ከአ'ጃ፣ከውሃ'ና ከወተት የተሠ'ራ)

port
'ፖ፡ት -ስ- መስኮት (በመርከብ ውስጥ)
harbour
-ስ- የመርከብ ወደብ

portable
'ፖ፡ተበል -ቅ- በእ'ጅ ሊ'ያዝ የ'ሚችል (ለማ'ጓጓዝ)

portal
'ፖ፡ተል -ስ- ት'ልቅ በ'ር

portent
'ፖ፡ቴንት -ስ- ምል'ክት (ወደፊት የ'ሚሆነውን የ'ሚያመለ'ክት)

porter
'ፖ:ተ -ስ- ተሸ'ካሚ ፤ ኩሊ ፤ በ'ረ'ኛ (በሆቴል እንግዳ ከው'ጭ የ'ሚ'ቀ'በል)

portion
'ፖ:ሽን -ስ- ድርሻ ፤ ክፍ'ያ ፤ ቁ'ራ'ሽ

portly
'ፖ:ትሊ -ቅ- ወፍራም ፤ ግዙፍ (በተለ'ይ ለሽማግ'ሌ'ች)

portrait
'ፖ:ትሬይት -ስ- የሰው ፤ የእንስሳ ሥዕል

pose
'ፖውዝ -ግ- ሰ'ው'ነት ማስተካከል [አስተ ካ'ከለ] (ለፎቶግራፍ አንሺ)

pretend

-ግ- መምሰል [መ'ሰለ] (ሌላ ሰው)

set (question)

-ግ- ጥ'ያቄ ማቅረብ [አቀ'ረበ]

position
ፐ'ዚሽን -ስ- ቦታ ፤ ሁኔታ

positive
'ፖዘቲቭ -ቅ- እርግጠ'ኛ ፤ የ'ማያ'ጠራ'ጥር

possess
ፐ'ዜስ -ግ- መ'ገናዘብ [ተገና'ዘበ]

possessive
ፐ'ዜሲቭ -ቅ- ሰውን ፤ ማ'ና'ቸውን'ም ነገር የራሱ ለማድረግ የ'ሚጥር ፤ አ'ገናዛቢ (ሰዋ ሰው)

possible
'ፖሲበል -ቅ- የ'ሚ'ቻል ፤ ሊሆን የ'ሚችል

post
'ፖውስት -ስ- እመሬት ላይ የተተ'ከለ እን ጨት

mail

-ስ- ፖስታ ፤ ደብዳ'ቤ

appointment

-ስ- ሹመት (የሥራ)

despatch

-ግ- ደብዳ'ቤ በፖስታ መላክ [ላከ]

postcard
'ፖውስትካ:ድ -ስ- ፖስትካርድ

poster
'ፖውስተ -ስ- የተለ'ጠፈ ማስታወቂያ

posterior
ፖስ'ቲሪየ -ስ- ኋላ ፤ ጳ'ሌ ፤ ቂጥ

-ቅ- በተራ ፤ በጊዜ የኋለ'ኛ የሆነ

after in time

-ቅ- በኋላ ያ'ለ ፤ ያ'ለፈ

posterity
ፖስ'ቴረቲ -ስ- መጪ ትውል'ድ ፤ የልጅ ልጅ

posthumous
'ፖስትዩመስ -ቅ- ከሞት በኋላ ፤ ከደራሲው ሞት በኋላ የታ'ተመ

postman
'ፖውስትመን -ስ- ፖስታ አ'ዳይ

postmaster
'ፖውስትማ:ስተ -ስ- የፖስታ ቤት ሹም

postmortem
ፖውስት'ሞ:ተም -ስ- በበድን ላይ የ'ሚ'ደ'ረግ የሕ'ክም'ና ምርመራ (ያ'ሟሟቱን ሁኔታ ለማ 'ረጋገጥ)

post-office
'ፖውስትኦፊስ -ስ- የፖስታ ቤት

postpone
ፖስ'ፖውን -ግ- ማስተላለፍ [አስተላለ ፈ ገር ፤ ተ'ዳይ)

postscript
'ፖውስክሪፕት -ስ- ደብዳ'ቤ ከተጻፈ'ና ከተ ፈ'ረመ በኋላ የ'ሚ'ጻፍ ተጨ'ማሪ ጽሑፍ ፤ ጥ'ያቄ

postulate
'ፖስትዩሌይት -ግ- ሐ'ሳብ ማቅረብ [አቀ'ረበ] (ለክር'ክር ፤ ለውይ'ይት)

posture
'ፖስቸ -ስ- የሰው'ነት አ'ቋቋም (ቀ'ጥ ያለ ፤ ያዘነ'በለ ወዘተ)

posy
'ፖውዚ -ስ- ያበባ እ'ቅፍ

pot
'ፖት -ስ- ማሰሮ

potato
ፐ'ቴይቶው -ስ- ድ'ን'ች

potent
'ፖውተንት -ቅ- ችሎታ ያ'ለው ፤ ኀይለ'ኛ

potential
ፐ'ቴንሽል -ስ- ወደፊት ሊሆን ፤ ሊ'ደ ረ የ'ሚችል ነገር ወይን'ም ሁኔታ

potion
'ፖውሽን -ስ- መድኃኒት'ነት ያ'ለው ፣ መር ዝ'ነት ያ'ለው ወይን'ም አስካሪ መጠ'ጥ

potter
'ፖተ -ስ- ሸክላ ሠሪ

pottery
'ፖተሪ -ስ- የሸክላ ዕቃ

pouch
'ፓውች -ስ- የቆዳ ከረጢት ፣ ቦርሳ

poultice
'ፖልቲስ -ስ- በቆ'ሰለ ወይን'ም ባ'በጠ ሰው'ነት ላይ የ'ሚ'ደ'ረግ በሙቅ ወሃ ፣ በተቀ'ቀለ ተልባ ፣ በሰናፍ'ጭ የተዘፈ'ዘፈ ጨርቅ

poultry
'ፖልትሪ -ስ- ክንፍ ያ'ላቸው የቤት እንስሳት (ዶሮ ፣ ዳ'ክዬ ወዘተ)

pounce
'ፓውንስ -ግ- ዘ'ሎ መ'ከመር [ተከ'መረ] (አደን ላይ)

pound
'ፓውንድ -ግ- መውቀጥ [ወ'ቀጠ] ፣ ማድቀቅ [አደ'ቀቀ]
-ስ- የእንግሊዝ ገንዘብ (ፓውንድ)

pour
'ፖ: -ግ- መፍሰስ [ፈ'ሰሰ] ፣ ማፍሰስ [አፈ'ሰሰ]

pout
'ፓውት -ግ- ከንፈር በማውጣት አለመ'ደሰትን መግለጽ [ገ'ለጸ]

poverty
'ፖቨቲ -ስ- ድህ'ነት

powder
'ፓውደ -ስ- ዱቄት
cosmetic
-ስ- ፓውደር (መልክ ማሳ'መሪያ ዱቄት)

power
'ፓወ -ስ- ችሎታ ፣ ኀይል
authority
-ስ- ሥልጣን

practical
ፕ'ራክቲክል -ቅ- ብልኀተ'ኛ (ለእ'ጅ ሥራ)፣ ብቁ ፣ ጠቃሚ

practically
ፕ'ራክቲክሊ -ተግ- ገደማ ፣ አቅራ'ቢያ ፣ በውነቱ ፣ በግብር

practice
ፕ'ራክቲስ -ስ- ልም'ምድ (ለመ'ማር)
habitual action
-ስ- ልምድ

practise
ፕ'ራክቲስ -ግ- መ'ለማመድ [ተለማ'መደ] ፣ መሠልጠን [ሠለ'ጠነ]
carry out profession
-ግ- ሞያን እሥራ ላይ ማዋል [አዋለ]

pragmatic
ፕራግ'ማቲክ -ቅ- ሁናቴን እንዳ'ለ አይቶ የ'ሚፈርድ ፣ የ'ሚሠራ (በተወ'ሰነ እምነት ሳይሆን)

praise
ፕ'ሬይዝ -ግ- ማመስገን [አመሰ'ገነ]
-ስ- ምስጋና

prance
ፕ'ራ:ንስ -ግ- መዝለል [ዘ'ለለ] (ለፈረስ)

prank
ፕ'ራንክ -ስ- ቢልት ፣ ቀልድ (ጉዳት የ'ሚያስከ'ትል)

prate
ፕ'ሬይት -ግ- መቀባጠር [ቀባ'ጠረ]

prattle
ፕ'ራተል -ግ- መንተባተብ [ተንተባ'ተበ] (እንደ ሕፃን)

pray
ፕ'ሬይ -ግ- መጸ'ለይ [ጸ'ለየ]

prayer
ፕ'ሬየ -ስ- ጸሎት

preach
ፕ'ሪይች -ግ- መስበክ [ሰ'በከ] (ሃይማኖት)

preacher
ፕ'ሪቸ -ስ- ሰባኪ

precarious
ፕሪ'ኬሪየስ -ቅ- እርግጠ'ኛ ያልሆነ ፣ ድንገት ሊሆን በ'ሚችል ሁኔታ ላይ የተመሠ'ረተ ፣ አ'ጠራጣሪ

precaution
ፕሪ'ኮ:ሽን -ስ- ጥን'ቃቄ

precede
ፕሪ'ሲይድ -ግ- መቅደም [ቀ'ደመ] (በጊዜ ፤ በቦታ ፤ በቅደም ተከ'ተል)

precedent
ፕ'ሬሲደንት -ስ- ያ'ለፈ ነገር (ለወደፊት እን ደ ም'ሳሌ የ'ሚ'ወ'ሰድ ፤ በፍርድ ወዘተ)

precept
ፕ'ሪሴፕት -ስ- የግብረ ገ'ብ'ነት ሕ'ግ

precinct
ፕ'ሪሲንክት -ስ- ቅጥር ግ'ቢ (በቤተ ክርስቲ ያን ፤ በገዳም ዙሪያ)

precious
ፕ'ሬሸስ -ቅ- ዋጋው የላቀ ፤ ው'ድ

precipice
ፕ'ሬሲፒስ -ስ- ዥ'ው ያለ ገደል ፤ ታ'ላቅ አደጋ

precis
ፕ'ሬይሲ -ስ- አሕጽሮተ ጽሑፍ

precise
ፕሪ'ሳይስ -ቅ- በትክ'ክል የተነ'ገረ ፤ ግልጥ ፤ ል'ክ

preclude
ፕሪክ'ሉ፡ድ -ግ- መከልከል [ከለ'ከለ] ፤ ማ'ገድ [አ'ገደ]

precocious
ፕሪ'ከውሸስ -ቅ- ብልጥ (ያለ ዕድሜው)

predatory
ፕ'ሬደትሪ -ቅ- በዘረፋ የ'ሚኖር ፤ እየነ'ጠቀ የ'ሚኖር

predecessor
ፕ'ሪይዲሴስ -ስ- በሥራ ቀዳሚ'ነት ያ'ለው ፤ በሥራው ላይ የቆ'የ'ና በቦታው ሌላ ሰው የተተ 'ካ'በት

predicament
ፕሪ'ዲከመንት -ስ- አሥጊ ሁናቴ ፤ የ'ማያስ ደ'ስት ሁናቴ (ማምለጥ የ'ማይ'ቻል)

predominate
ፕሪ'ዶሚኔይት -ግ- መብለጥ [በ'ለጠ] ፤ በቁ ጥር መላቅ [ላቀ]

preface
ፕ'ሬፈስ -ስ- መቅድም

prefer
ፕሪ'ፈ፡ -ግ- መምረጥ [መ'ረጠ]

prefix
ፕ'ሪይፊክስ -ስ- ባዕድ መነ'ሻ (ሰዋስው)

pregnant
ፕ'ሬግነንት -ቅ- ያረ'ገዘ ፤ የፀ'ነሰ

prejudice
ፕ'ሬጁዲስ -ስ- ማስረ'ጃ የሌ'ለው መጥፎ አስ ተያየት ፤ ያለ ማስረጃ ፍርድ መስጠት

preliminary
ፕረ'ሊሚነሪ -ቅ- መቅድማዊ ፤ የመጀ'መሪያ

prelude
ፕ'ሬልዩድ -ስ- መቅድም

premature
ፕ'ሬመቸ -ቅ- ያለዕድሜው ፤ ጊዜው የደ'ረሰ

premier
ፕ'ሬሚየ -ቅ- በአስፈ'ላጊ'ነቱ የመ'ጀ'መሪያ 'ነትን የያዘ
-ስ- ጠቅላይ ሚኒስትር

premonition
ፕሬመ'ኒሽን -ስ- ክፉ ነገር እንደ'ሚመጣ ማ መን

preoccupation
ፕሪዮክዩ'ፔይሽን -ስ- ስለአንድ ነገር ጥልቅ ሐሳብ መ'ያዝ

preparation
ፕሬፐ'ሬይሽን -ስ- ዝግ'ጅት

prepare
ፕሪ'ፔየ -ግ- ማ'ዘጋጀት [አ'ዘጋ'ጀ]

preponderance
ፕሪ'ፖንደረንስ -ስ- የቁጥር ፤ የክብደት ፤ የኀ ይል ወዘተ ብልጫ

preposition
ፕሬፐ'ዚሽን -ስ- መስተዋድድ (ሰዋስው)

prerogative
ፕሪ'ሮገቲቭ -ስ- የተለ'የ መብት

presage
ፕሪ'ሴይጅ -ግ- መ'ነበይ [ተነ'በየ] (ክፉ ነገር መምጣቱን)

prescribe
ፕረስክ'ራይብ -ግ- ማዘዝ [አ'ዘዘ] (ለመድኃ ኒት) ፤ ሕ'ግ ማውጣት [አወ'ጣ]

prescription
ፕሪስክ'ሪፕሽን -ስ- ትእዛዝ (የሐኪም)

presence
ፕ'ሬዘንስ -ስ- መ'ገኘት (ባንድ ቦታ)

present
ፕ'ሬዘንት -ቅ- ያ'ለ ፣ በሥራ ላይ ያ'ለ ፣ ያሁ ን ጊዜ

present
ፕ'ሬዘንት -ስ- ስጦታ ፣ ሽ'ልማት

present
ፕሪ'ዜንት -ግ- ማቅረብ [አቀ'ረበ]
offer gift
-ግ- ስጦታ መስጠት [ሰ'ጠ]
exhibit, show
-ግ- ማሳ'የት [አሳ'የ]

presently
ፕ'ሬዘንትሊ -ተግ- ከጥቂት ጊዜ በኋላ ፣ በቅርቡ
american
-ተግ- በአሁኑ ጊዜ

preserve
ፕሪ'ዘ፡ቭ -ግ- መጠ'በቅ [ጠ'በቀ] ፣ ማኖር [አ'ኖረ] ፣ ማቆ'የት [አቆ'የ]

preside
ፕሪ'ዛይድ -ግ- ሊቀ መንበር መሆን [ሆነ] ፣ ስብሰባ በሊቀ መንበር'ነት መምራት [መ'ራ]

president
ፕ'ሬዚደንት -ስ- ፕሬዚዶንት ፣ አፈ ጉባኤ ፣ ሊቀ መንበር

press
ፕ'ሬስ -ግ- መጫ'መቅ [ጨ'መቀ] ፣ መ'ጫን [ተጫነ]
printing
-ስ- ማ'ተሚያ መኪና
journalism
-ስ- ጋዜጠ'ኞች
urge
-ግ- መወትወት [ወተ'ወተ]

pressure
ፕ'ሬሽ -ስ- መ'ጫን ፣ ክብደት

prestige
ፕሬስ'ቲይጅ -ስ- ክብር

presume
ፕሪዥዩም -ግ- መገ'መት [ገ'መተ]
impudently
-ግ- ከመጠን በላይ ማለፍ [አ'ለፈ]

pretend
ፕሪ'ቴንድ -ግ- ማስመ'ሰል [አስመ'ሰለ]

protext
ፕ'ሪይቴክስት -ስ- ትክ'ክለ'ኛ ያልሆነ ምክን ያት

pretty
ፕ'ሪቲ -ቅ- ያማረ ፣ ቆንጆ ፣ ውብ

prevail
ፕሪ'ቬይል -ግ- ድል መንሣት [ነ'ሣ] ፣ መሰ ናክል ማስወ'ገድ [አስወ'ገደ] ፣ መስፋፋት [ተስፋ'ፋ]
persuade
-ግ- ማሳ'መን [አሳ'መነ]

prevalent
ፕ'ሬቨለንት -ቅ- የተስፋ'ፋ

prevaricate
ፕሪ'ቫሪኬይት -ግ- መዋሸት [ዋ'ሸ] ፣ ጠማማ መልስ መስጠት [ሰ'ጠ]

prevent
ፕሪ'ቬንት -ግ- መከልከል [ከለ'ከለ]

previous
ፕ'ሪይቪየስ -ቅ- የቀድሞ ፣ ያ'ለፈ

prey
ፕ'ሬይ -ስ- ታ'ድኖ የ'ሚ'በ'ላ እንስሳ ፣ አደን

price
ፕ'ራይስ -ስ- ዋጋ

priceless
ፕ'ራይስለስ -ቅ- ባለ ብዙ ዋጋ ፣ ዋጋው ሊ'ገ 'መት የ'ማይ'ቻል

prick
ፕ'ሪክ -ግ- መውጋት [ወ'ጋ] (በሹል ነገር)

prickle
ፕ'ሪክል -ስ- እሾህ (ት'ንሽ)

pride
ፕ'ራይድ -ስ- ኩራት ፣ ክብር

priest
ፕ'ሪይስት -ስ- ቄስ ፣ ካህን

prig
ፕ'ሪግ -ስ- ግ'ብዝ ፣ ተመጻዳቂ

prim
ፕ'ሪም -ቅ- በቀ'ላሉ የ'ሚደነ'ግጥ

primary
ፕ'ራይመሪ -ቅ- መጀ'መሪያ ፣ ዋ'ና ፣ የበ'ለጠ አስተያየት የ'ሚ'ሰ'ጠው

prime

ፕ'ራይም -ቅ- እካለ መጠን ፣ ጤና'ማ

most important

-ቅ- በጣም አስፈ'ላጊ

primer

ፕ'ራይመ -ስ- ያንደ'ኛ ደረጃ ት/ቤት መ'ማሪያ መጽሐፍ

primitive

ፕ'ሪመቲቭ -ቅ- በሥል'ጣኔ ወደኋላ የቀ'ረ

prince

ፕ'ሪንስ -ስ- ልዑል

princess

ፕ'ሪን'ሴስ -ስ- ልዕልት

principal

ፕ'ሪንሲፐል -ቅ- ዋ'ና ፣ የበ'ለጠ ዋጋ ያ'ለው ፣ ባለት'ልቅ ማዕረግ

capital sum

-ስ- ወ'ለድ የ'ሚ'ገ'ኝ'በት ዋ'ና ገንዘብ

principle

ፕ'ሪንሲፐል -ስ- ጠቅላ'ላ እምነት ፣ መሠረታውያን የግብረ ገ'ብ'ነት ሕ'ጎ'ች

print

ፕ'ሪንት -ግ- ማ'ተም [አ'ተመ]

type

-ስ- እ'ትም

printer

ፕ'ሪንተ -ስ- አ'ታሚ

printing-press

'ሪንቲንግፕሬስ -ስ- ማ'ተሚያ ቤት

prior

ፕ'ራየ -ስ- አበምኔት ፣ አለቃ

-ቅ- ያ'ለፈ ፣ የቀ'ደመ

priority

ፕ'ራዮሪቲ -ስ- ቅድሚያ

priory

ፕ'ራየሬ -ስ- ያበምኔት መኖሪያ ቤት

prison

ፕ'ሪዘን -ስ- እሥር ቤት ፣ ወህኒ ቤት

prisoner

ፕ'ሪዘነ -ስ- እሥረ'ኛ

privacy

ፕ'ሪቨሲ -ስ- ግ'ለ'ኛ'ነት

private

ፕ'ራይቨት -ቅ- የግ'ል

privation

ፕራይ'ቬይሸን -ስ- የምግብ እጦት ፣ ድህ'ነ ለሕይወት የ'ሚያስፈ'ልጉትን ነገሮ'ች ማጣ

privilege

ፕ'ሪቪሊጅ -ስ- ል'ዩ መብት

privy

ፕ'ሪቪ -ቅ- ምስጢር ዐዋቂ

-ስ- የሽንት ቤት

prize

ፕ'ራይዝ -ስ- ሽ'ልማት

pro

ፕ'ረው -ስ- አንድ ሰው ለመደ'ገፍ የ'ሚ'ረግ ክር'ክር ፣ የ'ሚደ'ግፍ

probable

ፕ'ሮበበል -ቅ- ሊሆን የ'ሚችል

probe

ፕ'ረውብ -ግ- መመርመር [መረ'መረ]

-ስ- መመርመሪያ መ'ሣሪያ (ሐኪ ቁስል የ'ሚመረ'ምር'በት)

probity

ፕ'ረውቢቲ -ስ- ታ'ማ'ኝ'ነት (በተለ'ይ ግድ)

problem

ፕ'ሮብለም -ስ- እ'ክል ፣ አስቸ'ጋሪ ጉ'ዳይ የ'ሚ'ታ'ሰብ'በት ጉ'ዳይ

procedure

ፕረ'ሲይጀ -ስ- መንገድ (ሥራ የመሥራት

proceed

ፕረ'ሲይድ -ግ- ወደፊት ማምራት [አመ' መቀ'ጠል [ቀ'ጠለ]

proceeds

ፕ'ረውሲይድዝ -ስ- ትርፍ ገንዘብ (የሽ'ያጭ

process

ፕ'ረውሴስ -ስ- ተከታትሎ የተደ'ረገ ድር'ጊ'

procession

ፕረ'ሴሽን -ስ- ሥርዓተ ጉዞ ፣ ሰላማዊ ሰልፍ ሰልፍ

proclaim

ፕረክ'ሌይም -ግ- ማ'ወጅ [ሀ'ወጀ]

proclamation

ፕሮክለ'ሜይሽን -ስ- ዐዋጅ

procrastinate

ፕረክ'ራስቲኔይት -ግ- ሥራን ለሌላ ጊዜ ያ ግሞ ማስተላለፍ [አስተላ'ለፈ] ፡ በ'የጊዜ ማዘግየት [አዘገ'የ]

procure

ፐረኪ'ዩወ -ግ- ማግኘት [አገ'ኘ] (በድካም ወዘተ) ፤ ማ'ቃጠር [አ.ቃ'ጠረ] [ሴት ለወንድ]

prod

ፕ'ሮድ -ግ- እንዲሠሩ መጐትጐት [ጐተ 'ጐተ] ፤ መጎንተል [ጎነ'ተለ]

prodigal

ፕ'ሮዲገል -ቅ- ገንዘብ አባካኝ ፤ ሀብቱን ነኻሪ

prodigious

ፕረ'ዲጀስ -ቅ- የ'ሚያስገ'ርም ፤ ታ'ላቅ ፤ አስደ'ናቂ

prodigy

ፕ'ሮዲጂ -ስ- ል'ዩ ስጦታ ያ'ለው ሕፃን ፤ በጣም አስደ'ናቂ (ከሥነ ፍጥረት ሥርዓት ው'ጭ በመሆኑ)

produce

ፕረድ'ዩ:ስ -ግ- ማስገ'ኘት [አስገ'ኘ] ፤ መውለድ [ወ'ለ ደ]

produce

ፕ'ሮድዩስ -ስ- ምርት ፤ ው'ጤት (የሥራ)

producer

ፕረ'ድዮስ -ስ- ባለፋብሪካ

theatrical

-ስ- የቲያትር ዝግ'ጅት መሪ

product

ፕ'ሮዶክት -ስ- ውጤት (የፋብሪካ)

profane

ፕረ'ፌይን -ቅ- የተቀ'ደሰ ነገር የ'ሚጠላ ፤ የሃይማኖት ያልሆነ (ጽሑፍ)

profess

ፕረ'ፌስ -ግ- ማ'ረጋገጥ [አ'ረጋ'ገጠ] (እምነት) ፤ ማ'ታለል [አ'ታ'ለለ] ፤ በውሸት ሆነ ማለት [አለ]

profession

ፕረ'ፌሽን -ስ- ሞያ

professor

ፕረ'ፌሰ -ስ- የዩኒቨርስቲ መምህር

profile

ፕ'ረውፋይል -ስ- መልክ (በአንድ በ'ኩል) ፤ ያንድ ሰው አ'ጭር የሕይወት ታሪክ (በመጽሐፍ ፡ በጋዜጣ)

profit

ፕ'ሮፊት -ግ- ማትረፍ [አተ'ረፈ]

-ስ- ትርፍ

profitable

ፕ'ሮፊተበል -ቅ- ጠቃሚ ፤ ትርፍ ያ'ለው

profiteer

ፕሮፊ'ቲየ -ስ- ከ'ሚ'ገ'ባው በላይ ትርፍ የ'ሚያገ'ኝ (የንግድ ዕቃ በገበያ በጠ'ፋ ጊዜ)

profligate

ፕ'ሮፍሊገት -ቅ- ገንዘብ አባካኝ ፤ ግብረ ገ'ብ'ነት የሌ'ለው ፤ ል'ቅ

profound

ፕረ'ፋውንድ -ቅ- በጣም ጥልቅ (ሐ'ሳብ)

profuse

ፕረፍ'ዩስ -ቅ- ገንዘብ አባካኝ ፤ ቀምጣ'ላ ፤ የተትረፈ'ረፈ ፤ በጣም ቸር

profusion

ፕረፍ'ዩዠን -ስ- መትረፍረፍ ፤ ቀምጣ'ላ'ነት

progeny

ፕ'ሮጀኒ -ስ- ልጆ'ች ፤ ዘር ፤ የልጅ ልጅ

prognostication

ፕሮግኖስቲ'ኬይሽን -ስ- ትንቢት ፤ ምል'ክት (ወደፊት ለ'ሚሆነው)

programme

ፕ'ረውግራም -ስ- የሥራ ዕ'ቅድ ቅደም ተከ'ተል

progress

ፕ'ረውግረስ -ስ- እርም'ጃ ፤ መ'ሻሻል

progress

ፕረግ'ረስ -ግ- መ'ራመድ [ተራ'መደ] (በሥራ ወዘተ)

prohibit

ፕረ'ሂቢት -ግ- መከልከል [ከለ'ከለ]

project

ፕረ'ጀክት -ግ- ዕ'ቅድ ማውጣት [አወ'ጣ] ፤ ብርሃን ፤ ፊልም ፤ ጥላ በአንድ ነገር ላይ አርፎ እንዲ'ታ'ይ ማድረግ [አደ'ረገ] ፤ የአንድን ነገር ሁናቴ ፤ ጠባይ ደኅና አድርጎ ማሳ'የት [አሳ'የ] ፤ ተርፎ መውጣት [ወ'ጣ]

project

ፕ'ረጀክት -ስ- የሥራ ዕ'ቅድ

projector

ፕሮ'ጀክተ -ስ- የሲኒማ ማሳ'ያ መኪና

proletariat

ፕሮለ'ቴሪየት -ስ- በጉልበታ'ቸው ትርፍ የ'ሚኖሩ'ና የግ'ል ንብረት የሌ'ላ'ቸው ሞያተ'ኞ'ች

prolong
ፕረ'ሎንግ -ግ- ማስረ'ዘም [አስረ'ዘመ] (ለጊ ዜ)
prominent
ፕ'ሮሚነንት -ቅ- የተመ'ረጠ ፡ የተከ'በረ ፡ ከ'ፍ ያለ
promiscuous
ፕረ'ሚስክዩወስ -ቅ- ሴሰ'ኛ ፡ ከብዙ ሰው ጋር ፈቃደ ሥጋ የ'ሚፈ'ጽም
promise
ፕ'ሮሚስ -ግ- ተስፋ መስጠት [ሰ'ጠ]
-ስ- ተስፋ
promote
ፕረ'መውት -ግ- ከ'ፍ ማድረግ [አደ'ረገ] (በደረጃ)
initiate
-ግ- መጀ'መር [ጀ'መረ] (ለዕ'ቅድ)
promotion
ፕረ'መውሽን -ስ- የማዕረግ እድገት
prompt
ፕ'ሮምት -ግ- ማ'ነሣሣት [አ'ነሣ'ሣ] (አንድ ሰው አንድ ሥራ እንዲሠራ)
quick
-ቅ- ቀልጣ'ፋ
theatrical
-ግ- የተረ'ሳ ቃል ፡ ሐረግ ማስታወስ [አስታ'ወሰ] (ለተናጋሪ ፡ ለቴአትር ሠ'ራተ'ኛ)
promulgate
ፕ'ሮሙልጌይት -ግ- ማ'ወጅ [ዐ'ወጀ] (አ'ዲስ ሕ'ግ ፡ ደንብ)
prone
ፕ'ረውን -ቅ- የተጋ'ደመ (ራስ ደፍቶ ፡ በግምባር)
disposed
-ቅ- ዝን ባሌ ያ'ለው
prong
ፕ'ሮንግ -ስ- ጣት (የሹ'ካ ወዘተ)
pronoun
ፕ'ረውናውን -ስ- ተውላጠ ስም
pronounce
ፕረ'ናውንስ -ግ- መ'ናገር [ተና'ገረ] ፡ አንድ ቃል መጥራት [ጠ'ራ]
pronunciation
ፕረነንሲ'ዩይሽን -ስ- አ'ጠራር ፡ አ'ባባል ፡ አ'ነጋገር

proof
ፕ'ሩፍ -ስ- ማስረ'ጃ
printing
-ስ- የ'ሚ'ታ'ረም የማኅተም ጽሑፍ
impervious to
-ቅ- የተፈ'ተነ ፡ ፍቱን (ውሃ ባለማስገ'ባት)
prop
ፕ'ሮፕ -ስ- ድጋፍ (የእንጨት)
propagate
ፕ'ሮፐጌይት -ግ- እንዲስፋ'ፋ ማድረግ [አደ'ረገ] (ዕውቀት ፡ ወሬ ወዘተ)
'multiply
-ግ- እንዲ'ባ'ዛ ማድረግ [አደ'ረገ] (ተክል ፡ እንስሳት)
propel
ፕረ'ፔል -ግ- መግፋት [ገ'ፋ] (ወደፊት)
propeller
ፕረ'ፔለ -ስ- መዘ'ውር (የአውሮ'ፕላን ፡ የመርከብ) ፡ ቢልቢ'ላ
propensity
ፕረ'ፔንሲቲ -ስ- የተፈጥሮ ዝን'ባሌ
proper
ፕ'ሮፐ -ቅ- ተገቢ ፡ ደምበ'ኛ
properly
ፕ'ሮፐሊ -ተግ- በ'ሚ'ገ'ባ ፡ በደምብ
property
ፕ'ሮፐቲ -ስ- ንብረት ፡ ሀብት
land
-ስ- መሬት ፡ ርስት
prophecy
ፕ'ሮፈሲ -ስ- ትንቢት
prophesy
ፕ'ሮፈሳይ -ግ- መ'ንበይ [ተነ'በየ]
prophet
ፕ'ሮፊት -ስ- ነቢ'ይ
propitiate
ፕረ'ፒሺዬይት -ግ- መ'ለማመን [ተለማ'መነ] (ቁ'ጣ ለማብረድ ፡ ድጋፍ ለማግ'ኘት)
propitious
ፕረ'ፒሽስ -ቅ- ተስማሚ ፡ የሥራ መ'ቃናት ሊያመጣ የ'ሚችል

proportion
ፕረ'ፖ፡ሽን -ስ- መጠን ፤ አንድ ነገር ከሌላው ጋር በመጠን ፣ በብዛት ወዘተ ያ'ለው ግን'ኙ'ነት

proposal
ፕረ'ፐውዘል -ስ- ሐ'ሳብ (የ'ሚቀርብ)
marriage
-ስ- የጋብ'ቻ ጥ'ያቄ ፣ ማጨት

propose
ፕረ'ፐውዝ -ግ- ሐ'ሳብ ማቅረብ [አቀ'ረበ]
marriage
-ግ- ለጋብ'ቻ መጠ'የቅ [ጠ'የቀ] ፣ ማጨት [አ'ጨ]

proposition
ፕሮፐ'ዚሽን -ስ- ለስምም'ነት ሐ'ሳብ ማቅረብ

propound
ፕረ'ፐውንድ -ግ- ሐ'ሳብ ማቅረብ [አቀ'ረበ] (ለው'ሳኔ ለስምም'ነት)

proprietor
ፕረፕ'ራየተ -ስ- ባለንብረት ፣ ባለቤት

propriety
ፕረፕ'ራየቲ -ስ- የተመሰ'ገነ አመል ፣ ተስማሚ'ነት

prosaic
ፕረው'ዜይክ -ቅ- ተራ ፡ አስልቺ ፣ ብዙ የ'ማያሳ'ስብ

prose
ፕ'ረውዝ -ስ- ስ'ድ ንባብ

prosecute
ፕ'ሮሲክዩ፡ት -ግ- መክሰስ [ከ'ሰሰ]

prospect
ፕ'ሮስፔክት -ግ- መቆ'ፈርን መፈ'ለግ [ፈ'ለገ]
-ስ- ወደፊት የ'ሚሆነው ው'ጤት
view
-ስ- ትዕ'ይንት

prosper
ፕ'ሮስፐ -ግ- መበልጸግ [በለ'ጸገ]

prosperity
ፕሮስ'ፔረቲ -ስ- ብልጽግ'ና

prosperous
ፕ'ሮስፐረስ -ቅ- ባለጸ'ጋ

prostitute
ፕ'ሮስቲትዩ፡ት -ስ- ሴተ'ኛ አዳሪ

prostitution
ፕሮስቲት'ዩ፡ሽን -ስ- ሴተ'ኛ አዳሪ'ነት

prostrate
ፕ'ሮስትሬይት -ቅ- የተዘ'ረረ ፡ የተዘረ'ጋ (ፊቱን ደፍቶ)

protect
ፕረ'ቴክት -ግ- መ'ከላከል [ተከላ'ከለ] ፣ መከታ መሆን [ሆነ]

protest
ፕረ'ቴስት -ግ- በነገሩ አለመስማማትን መግለጽ [ገ'ለጸ] ፤ አቤቱታ ማ'ሰ'ማት [አ'ሰ'ማ]

Protestant
ፕ'ሮቴስተንት -ስ- ፕሮቴስታንት ፡ የሉተር ተከ'ታይ

protestation
ፕሮቴስ'ቴይሽን -ስ- አቤቱታ

protracted
ፕረት'ራክቲድ -ቅ- ጊዜ የፈ'ጀ ፣ የቆ'የ

protrude
ፕረት'ሩ፡ድ -ግ- ወደ ው'ጭ መውጣት [ወ'ጣ] (ማፈንገጥ)

protruberance
ፕረት'ሩ፡በረንስ -ስ- አፈንግጦ የወ'ጣ ነገር ፡ አፈንግጦ መውጣት

proud
ፕ'ራውድ -ቅ- ኩሩ

prove
ፕ'ሩ፡ቭ -ግ- ማስረ'ጃ መስጠት [ሰ'ጠ]

proverb
ፕ'ሮቨ፡ብ -ስ- ም'ሳሌ

provide
ፕረ'ቫይድ -ስ- ማቅረብ [አቀ'ረበ] ፣ ማ'ዘጋጀት [አ'ዘጋ'ጀ]

providence
ፕ'ሮቪደንስ -ስ- የእግዚአብሔር ፈቃድ ፡ የእግዚአብሔር ጥ'በቃ

province
ፕ'ሮቪንስ -ስ- አውራ'ጃ

provision
ፕረ'ቪዠን -ስ- መ'ሰናዶ ፣ መ'ሰናዳት

provisions
ፕረ'ቪዠንዝ -ስ- ሥንቅ

provisional
ፕረ'ቪዠነል -ቅ- ጊዜያዊ ፣ የ'ማይቆ'ይ

provoke
ፕረ'ቨውክ -ግ- ማ'ነሣሣት [አ'ነሣ'ሣ] ፤ ማስ ቆ'ጣት [አስቆ'ጣ] ፤ ጠብ ማጫር [አጫረ]

prowess
ፕ'ራዌስ -ስ- ብልኀት ፤ ችሎታ (የመ'ዋጋት)፣ ጉብዝ'ና

prowl
ፕ'ራውል -ግ- ለማ'ደን በዝ'ግታ ወዲያ'ና ወዲ ህ ማለት [አለ] (ለአውሬ) ፤ ማድባት [አደ'ባ]

proximity
ፕሮክ'ሲሚቲ -ስ- ቅርብ'ነት

proxy
ፕ'ሮክሲ -ቅ- ወ'ኪል'ነት ፤ ወ'ኪል

prudence
ፕ'ሩ፡ደንስ -ስ- ጥን'ቃቄ

prudish
ፕ'ሩ፡ዲሽ -ቅ- እስመ'ሳይ ፤ የ'ማይፈ'ልግ መ ሳይ (ግብረ ሥጋ)

prune
ፕ'ሩ፡ን -ግ- በመቁረጥ ማስተካከል [አስተካ ከለ] (ዛፍ ቁጥቋጦ ወዘተ) ፤ ማ'ረም [አ'ረመ] (ጽሑፍ ወዘተ)

pry
ፕ'ራይ -ግ- የሰው ምስጢር ለማወቅ መሻት [ሻ] ፤ መሰ'ለል [ሰ'ለለ]

psalm
'ሳ፡ም -ስ- መዝሙረ ዳዊት

pseudonym
ስ'ዩደኒም -ስ- የውሸት ስም (እንድ ደራሲ የ'ሚሠራ'በት)

psychology
ሳይ'ኮለጂ -ስ- የሰውን አእምሮ ፤ አስተሳሰብ የ'ሚያጠና ትምህርት ፤ ሥነ ልቡና

puberty
ፕ'ዩ፡በቲ -ስ- የጉርምስ'ና ወቅት ፤ አንድ ሰው ለመውለድ የ'ሚችል'በት ዕድሜ ፤ መባለቅ

public
'ፐብሊክ -ስ- ሕዝብ
-ቅ- ሕዝባዊ

publish
'ፐብሊሽ -ግ- ማሳ'ተም [አሳ'ተመ] (መጽ ሐፍ)

pucker
'ፐከ -ግ- ማ'ኰሳተር [አ'ኰሳ'ተረ] (ለግምባር)

puddle
'ፐደል -ስ- ኩሬ (የዝናም ውሃ የተጠራ'ቀመ 'በት)

puerile
ፕ'ዩ፡ራይል -ቅ- የሕፃን ሥራ ፤ ቂላቂል ፤ እንቶ ፈንቶ

puff
'ፐፍ -ግ- እ'ፍ ማለት [አለ] ፤ ቡ'ል'ቅ ቡ'ል 'ቅ ማድረግ [አደ'ረገ] ፤ ማለክለክ [አለከ'ለከ]

puffy
'ፐፊ -ቅ- ያ'በጠ ፤ የተነ'ፋ

pugnacious
ፐግ'ኔሸስ -ቅ- አምባጓሮ ወ'ዳድ ፤ ጠብ አጫሪ (ለማደ'ኛ)

pull
'ፑል -ግ- መጐ'ተት [ጐ'ተተ]

pullet
'ፑሌት -ስ- ጫጩ'ት

pulley
'ፑሊ -ስ- መዘ'ውር (የወሃ መቅጃ ወዘተ)

pullover
'ፑለውቨ -ስ- ሹ'ራብ (ከሸሚዝ በላይ የ'ሚ'ለ 'በስ) ፤ የገላ ሹ'ራብ

pulp
'ፐልፕ -ስ- የደ'ቀቀ የተፈ'ጨ እርጥብ ነገር (ፍራፍሬ ወዘተ)

pulpit
'ፑልፒት -ስ- ሰባኪ የ'ሚቆም'በት ከ'ፍ ያለ ቦታ ፤ ምስባክ

pulsate
ፐል'ሴይት -ግ- ትʼር ትʼር ማለት [አለ]

pulse
'ፐልስ -ስ- ት'ርታ (የደም ሥር)

pummel
'ፐመል -ግ- መደብደብ [ደበ'ደበ] (ሠምታት፣ በእ'ጅ)

pump
'ፐምፕ -ግ- መንፋት [ነ'ፋ] (አ'የር ወዘተ)
-ስ- መ'ንፊያ

pumpkin
'ፐምኪን -ስ- ዱ'ባ

pun
'ፐን -ስ- ኅብር እ'ነጋገር ፤ ሁለ'ት ትርጉም ያ'ለው እ'ነጋገር

punch
'ፐንች -ግ- በቡ'ጢ መምታት [መ'ታ]
punctilious
ፐንክ'ቲሊየስ -ቅ- ለጥቃ'ቅን ነገር የ'ሚ'ጠ
ን'ቀቅ (ሥራን በመፈ'ጸም)
punctual
'ፐንክቹውል -ቅ- ጊዜ ጠ'ባቂ ፡ በቀጠሮ
ሰዓት የ'ሚ'ገ'ኝ ፡ ቀጠሮ አክባሪ
punctuation
ፐንክቹ'ዌይሽን -ስ- ሥርዐተ ነጥብ (በጽሑፍ)
puncture
'ፐንክቸ -ስ- ቀዳዳ (የጐ'ማ ወዘተ)
pungent
'ፐንጀንት -ስ- ኀይለ'ኛ ሽ'ታ ፡ ጣዕም
punish
'ፐኒሽ -ግ- መቅጣት [ቀ'ጣ]
punishment
'ፐኒሽመንት -ስ- ቅጣት ፡ መ'ቀጫ
puny
ፕ'ዩ:ኒ -ቅ- ት'ንሽ'ና ደካማ
pup
'ፐፕ -ስ- ቡ'ች'ላ
pupil
ፕ'ዩ:ፐል -ስ- ተማሪ
of eye
-ስ- የዓይን ብሌን
puppet
'ፐፐት -ስ- የንጨት አሻንጉ'ሊት (በክ'ር የ
'ሚንቀሳ'ቀስ)
purchase
'ፐ:ቸስ -ግ- መግዛት [ገ'ዛ] (ዕቃ)
thing bought
-ስ- የተገ'ዛ ዕቃ
pure
ፕ'ዩወ -ቅ- ንጹሕ ፡ ምን'ም ነገር ያልተደባ
'ለቀ'በት
purgative
'ፐ:ገቲቭ -ስ- የ'ሚያስቀ'ምጥ መድኃኒት
purgatory
'ፐ:ገትሪ -ስ- ኀጢያት የ'ሚያነጹ'በት ቦታ
(ከሞት በኋላ) ፡ መካነ ን'ስሐ
purge
'ፐ:ጅ -ግ- ማ'ጣራት [አ'ጣ'ራ] ፡ ማጽዳት
[አጸ'ዳ] ፡ ከሶ መጠ'ጣት [ጠ'ጣ]

political
-ግ- ከፖ'ለቲካ ማኅበር የ'ማያ'ስፈ'ልጉ
አባሉ'ች ማስወ'ጣት [አስወ'ጣ]
purify
ፕ'ዩ:ሪፋይ -ግ- ማ'ጣራት [አ'ጣ'ራ] ፡ ንጹሕ
ማድረግ [አደ'ረገ]
purity
ፕ'ዩ:ሪቲ -ስ- ንጽሕ'ና ፡ ጥራት
purple
'ፐ:ፐል -ቅ- ሐምራዊ
purport
ፐ'ፖ:ት -ግ- ማስመ'ሰል [አስመ'ሰለ] (ያልሆ
ነውን)
-ስ- ፍ'ች ፡ ዋ'ና ሐ'ሳብ
purpose
'ፐ:ፐስ -ስ- ምክንያት ፡ ዓላማ ፡ ዕ'ቅድ ፡ ግብ
on-
-ተግ- በማወቅ ፡ በውቆ
purposely
'ፐ:ፐስሊ -ተግ- በማወቅ ፡ በውቆ
purr
'ፐ: -ግ- ማንኳረፍ [አንኳ'ረፈ] (ለድ'መት
በተደ'ሰተ ጊዜ)
purse
'ፐ:ስ -ስ- የገንዘብ ቦርሳ (የሴት)
pursue
ፐስ'ዩ: -ግ- መ'ከተል [ተከ'ተለ]
purulent
ፕ'ዩሩለንት -ቅ- መግላም ፡ የ'ሚመግል
purvey
ፐ'ቬይ -ግ- የምግብ ሸቀጥ ለሺ'ያጭ ማቅ
ረብ [አቀ'ረበ]
pus
'ፐስ -ስ- መግል
push
'ፑሽ -ግ- መግፋት [ገ'ፋ]
put
'ፑት -ግ- ማስቀ'መጥ [አስቀ'መጠ]
-aside
አ'ሳይድ -ግ- ወደጐ'ን ማስቀ'መጥ [አስቀ
'መጠ]
-on
'ኦን -ግ- መልበስ [ለ'በሰ] ፡ ማድረግ [አደ
'ረገ] (ሜ'ማ ፡ መነ'ጽር)

-up
'አፕ -ግ- ማ'ዘጋጀት [አ'ዘጋ'ጀ] (ለእንግዳ)
-up with
'አፕ 'ዊዝ -ግ- መ'ታገሥ [ታ'ገሠ]

putrid
ፕ'ዩትሪድ -ቅ- የተ'ላ ፡ የሸ'ተተ (ለሥጋ)

putty
'ፑቲ -ስ- በዘይት የተደባ'ለቀ ስሚንቶ (ለመስተዋት ማጣበቂያ) ፡ ስቱ'ኮ

puzzle
'ፓዘል -ስ- በቀ'ላሉ ሊ'ረ'ዱት የ'ማይ'ቻል ነገር ፡ ሁናቴ ፡ እንቆቅ'ልሽ
-ግ- መ'ጨነቅ [ተጨ'ነቀ]

pyjamas
ፐ'ጃ፡ማዝ -ስ- የመኝ'ታ ልብስ ፡ ፒጃማ

pyramid
'ፒረሚድ -ስ- ሀረም

pyre
'ፓየ -ስ- አስከሬን የ'ሚ'ቃ'ጠል'በት የእንጨት ክ'ምር

pyx
'ፒክስ -ስ- ሥጋ ወደሙ የ'ሚ'ቀመጥ'በት ማኅን

quack
ክ'ዋክ -ስ- የዳ'ክ'የ ጩኸት
doctor
-ስ- ውሸተ'ኛ ሐኪም ፡ አጭበርባሪ ሐኪም (ሐኪም ሳይሆን ነ'ኝ ባይ)

quadrangle
ክ'ዎድራንገል -ስ- አራ'ት ማዕዘን የሆነ ለም ለም አጥር ግ'ቢ ፡ አራት ማዕዘን ያ'ለው ቅርፅ

quagmire
ክ'ዋግማየ -ስ- ረግረግ

quadruped
ክ'ዋድሩፒድ -ስ- አራ'ት እግር ያ'ለውእንስሳ

quail
ክ'ዌይል -ግ- በፍርሀት መንቀጥቀጥ [ተንቀጠ'ቀጠ]

quaint
ክ'ዌይንት -ቅ- እንግዳ ፡ ያልተለ'መደ (ነገር ግን አስተያየትን ማራኪ)

quake
ክ'ዌይክ -ግ- መንቀጥቀጥ [ተንቀጠ'ቀጠ] ፡ መንዘፍዘፍ [ተንዘፈ'ዘፈ] (ከፍርሀት የተነ'ሣ)

qualify
ክ'ዋሊፋይ -ግ- ለአንድ ተግባር ተስማሚ መ መሆን [ሆነ]
become trained
ለአንድ ተግባር ማሠልጠን [አሠለ'ጠነ]

quality
ክ'ዎሊቲ -ስ- ዓይነት

qualm
ክ'ዋ፡ም -ስ- ትን'ሽ ጥር'ጣሬ (አንድ ሰው ስለ ሠ'ራው ወይን'ም ስለ'ሚሠራው ሥራ) ፡ ቅልሽልሽ'ታ

quandary
ክ'ዎንደሪ -ስ- ግራ የ'ሚያ'ጋ'ባ ች'ግር ፡ እ'ክል

quantity
ክ'ዎንቲቲ -ስ- ብዛት

quarrel
ክ'ዎረል -ግ- መ'ጣላት [ተጣ'ላ]
-ስ- ጥል

quarrelsome
ክ'ዎረልሰም -ቅ- አምባጓር'ኛ ፡ ተጣይ

quarry
ክ'ዎሪ -ስ- ድንጋይ ፡ አሸዋ የ'ሚ'ገ'ኝ'በት ጎድጓ'ዳ ቦታ
prey
-ስ- የ'ሚ'ታ'ደን እንስሳ ፡ አደን

quarter
ክ'ዎ፡ተ -ስ- ሩብ ፡ አንድ አ'ራ'ተ'ኛ
area
-ስ- መኖሪያ ሠፈር

quash
ክ'ዎሽ -ግ- ውድቅ ማድረግ [አደ'ረገ] (በፍርድ ቤት)

quavering
ክ'ዌይቨሪንግ -ቅ- ቀጥ.ቀ'ጣ (ለድምፅ)

quay
'ኪይ -ስ- የመርከብ መቆሚያ ቦታ

queen
ክ'ዊይን -ስ- ንግሥት ፣ እቴጌ ፣ የንጉሥ ባለቤት (ሚስት)

queer
ክ'ዊየ -ቅ- እንግዳ (ለጠባይ)

quell
ክ'ዌል -ግ- ጸ'ጥ ማድረግ [አደ'ረገ] (ብጥ'ብጥ)

quench
ክ'ዌንች -ግ- ማጥፋት [አጠ'ፋ] (ለእሳት)
thirst
-ግ- መቁረጥ [ቆ'ረጠ] (ለጥም)

querulous
ክ'ዌሩለስ -ቅ- አጉረምራሚ ፣ ደ'ስ ያላለው ፣ የከ'ፋው

query
ክ'ዊየሪ -ግ- መጠ'የቅ [ጠ'የቀ] ፣ መ'ጠራጠር [ተጠራ'ጠረ]

quest
ክ'ዌስት -ስ- ፍ'ለጋ

question
ክ'ዌስችን -ስ- ጥ'ያቄ

queue
ክ'ዩ: -ስ- የወረፋ መሥመር

quibble
ክ'ዊበል -ግ- መሸሽ መፈ'ለግ [ፈ'ለገ] (በክርክር)
play on words
-ግ- ሁለ'ት ትርጉም በያዘ አ'ነጋገር መ'ናገር [ተና'ገረ] ፣ በጎብር መ'ናገር [ተና'ገረ]

quick
ክ'ዊክ -ቅ- ፈ'ጣን

quickly
ክ'ዊክሊ -ተግ- በፍጥነት

quiet
ክ'ዋየት -ቅ- ፀ'ጥ ያለ ፣ ሰላማዊ

quill
ክ'ዊል -ስ- ላባ (ረ'ጅም)

quilt
ክ'ዊልት -ስ- ለሐፍ (ወፍራም የብርድ ልብስ)

quit
ክ'ዊት -ግ- እርግ'ፍ አድርጎ መተው [ተወ]

quite
ክ'ዋይት -ተግ- በፍ'ጹም ፣ በጣም
-ተግ- በመጠኑ
almost
-ቃአ- በውነት ፣ በርግጥ

quiver
ክ'ዊቨ -ግ- መንቀጥቀጥ [ተንቀጠ'ቀጠ]
-ስ- የፍላ'ፃ ማሕደር

quixotic
ክዊክ'ሶቲክ -ቅ- ለጥ.ቀ'ቅን ነገር ታ'ላቅ ዋጋ የ'ሚሰጥ ፣ ሌሎ'ችን ለመርዳት እራሱን የ'ሚጎዳ

quiz
ክ'ዊዝ -ስ- የጥ'ያቄ'ና የመልስ ውድ'ድር ፣ የዕውቀት መፈተ'ኛ ጥ'ያቄ

quota
ክ'ወውተ -ስ- ድርሻ ፣ ላንዱ የተወ'ሰነ'ለት ድርሻ (በተለ'ይ ወደ አንድ አገር ለመግባት የተፈ'ቀደ የሰው ብዛት ፣ የንግድ ዕቃ መጠን)

quotation
ክወው'ቴይሽን -ስ- ጥቅስ

quotation-mark
ክወው'ቴይሽን'ማ:ክ -ስ- የጥቅስ ምል'ክት ፣ ትእምርተ ጥቅስ ("   ")

quote
ክ'ወውት -ግ- መጥቀስ [ጠ'ቀሰ] (የሰው ንግ'ግር ፣ ጽሑፍ)

quotient
ክ'ወውሽንት -ስ- አንድ ቁጥር ከተከ'ፈለ በኋላ የ'ሚ'ገ'ኘው ው'ጤት

R

rabbit
'ራቢት -ስ- ጥንቸል

rabble
'ራበል -ስ- ል'ቃሚ ሕዝብ ፡ ሥርዐት የሌ'ለ ለው የተሰበ'ሰበ ሕዝብ ፤ ጀሌ

rabid
'ራቢድ -ቅ- ያ'በደ ው'ሻ ፤ ኀይለ'ኛ ፡ ቁ'ጡ

rabies
'ሬይቢይዝ -ስ- የው'ሻ እብደት በ'ሽታ

race
'ሬይስ -ስ- እሽቅድ'ድም
human
-ስ- ዘር (የሰው)
compete
-ግ- መሽቀዳደም [ተሽቀዳ'ደመ]

rack
'ራክ -ስ- የዕቃ መደርደሪያ (የሳሕን ወዘተ)

racket
'ራኬት -ስ- የቴኒስ መምቻ

racy
'ሬይሲ -ቅ- የ'ማይ'ሰለ'ች ፡ አስደ'ሳች ፡ ሕያው (መጽሐፍ ፡ ቴያትር ፡ ፊልም ወዘተ)

radiant
'ሬይዲየንት -ቅ- ደ'ስተ'ኛ ፡ ያማ'ረ'በት ፤ ጨረር የ'ሚያ'ስራ'ጭ ፡ የ'ሚያበራ

radiate
'ሬይዲዬይት -ግ- ማ'ስራጨት [አ'ሰራ'ጨ] (ለጨረር ፡ ለሙቀት)

radiator
'ሬይዲዬይተ -ስ- የቤት ማሞቂያ ፤ የመኪና ሰሊንደር ማቀዝቀዣ መ'ሣሪያ ፡ ራዲያተር

radical
'ራዲከል -ቅ- መሠረታዊ ፡ ፍ'ጹም
political
-ቅ- ተቃዋሚ ፡ ፍ'ጹም ለውጥ ፈ'ላጊ (በፖ'ለቲካ)

radio
'ሬይዲየው -ስ- ራዲዮ

radish
'ራዲሽ -ስ- ፍጅል ፤ ሥሩ ነ'ጭ የሆነ እንደ ሰላ'ጣ የ'ሚ'በ'ላ የካሮት ቅርፅ ያለው ተክል

radius
'ሬይዲየስ -ስ- ሬዲየስ ፤ በአንድ ክበብ ከመሀ'ከሉ እስከ ዳሩ ያ'ለው ርቀት

raffle
'ራፉል -ስ- ሎተሪ (የዕቃ)

raft
'ራፍት -ስ- ታንኳ (ከአንድ ግንድ ወይን'ም ከአንድ እሥር የተሠ'ራ)

rafter
'ራፍተ -ስ- ከንች (የቤት)

rag
'ራግ -ስ- ብት'ቶ

ragamuffin
'ራገመፊን -ስ- ልብሱ ያ'ለ'ቀ'በት ፡ ሰው (በተለ'ይ ልጅ)

rage
'ሬይጅ -ስ- ቁ'ጣ
-ግ- መ'ቆጣት [ተቆ'ጣ]

ragged
'ራጊድ -ቅ- የተበጣ'ጠሰ ፡ ብት'ቶ የሆነ የተተለ'ተለ (ልብስ) ፤ ኰስኳ'ሳ

raid
'ሬይድ -ግ- መግጠም [ገ'ጠመ] (ጦር'ነት) አደጋ መጣል [ጣለ] ፤ መውረር [ወ'ረረ]
-ስ- ግጥሚያ ፤ አደጋ ፡ ወረራ

rail
'ሬይል -ስ- ሐዲድ (የባቡር) ፤ የቤት ደረጃ መ'ደገፊያ ብረት
abuse
-ግ- መ'ሳደብ [ተሳ'ደበ]

railway
'ሬይልዌይ -ስ- የባቡር ሐዲድ

rain
'ሬይን -ስ- ዝናም ፡ ዝናብ

rainbow
'ሬይንበው -ስ- ቀስተ ደ'መና

raincoat
'ሬይንኰውት -ስ- የዝናም ልብስ

rainy season
'ሬይኒ 'ሲይዘን -ስ- የዝናም ወራት ፡ ወር'ን ዝናማት ፡ ክረምት

raise
'ሬይዝ -ግ- ማንሣት [አነ'ሣ]
-ስ- እድገት (የደመወዝ)

raisin
'ሬይዘን -ስ- ዘቢብ

rake
'ሬይክ -ስ- ባለጣት አፈር ማስተካከያ
waster
-ስ- ገንዘብ አባካኝ

rally
'ራሊ -ስ- የስፖርተ'ኞ'ች ፣ የፖሊቲካ ደ'ጋፊ ዎ'ች ስብሰባ
support
-ግ- ማ'ጃገን [አ'ጃ'ገነ]

ram
'ራም -ግ- መግጨት [ገ'ጨ] (ባንድ ነገር)
male sheep
-ስ- ወጠጤ (በግ)

ramble
'ራምበል -ግ- ወዲያ'ና ወዲህ መሄድ [ሄደ] (ሽ'ር'ሽ'ር)

ramp
'ራምፕ -ስ- መንሸራተቻ'፡ ሸተት'ያ

rampart
'ራምፓ፡ት -ስ- የም'ሽግ ግድግ'ዳ

ramshackle
'ራምሻክል -ቅ- ያረ'ጀ'ና የተሰባ'በረ

ranch
'ራ፡ንች -ስ- ት'ልቅ የርሻ'ና የከብት ማርቢያ ቦታ

rancid
'ራንሲድ -ስ- የቆ'የ ፡ የ'ሚሸ'ት (ቅቤ ፡ ዘይት)

rancour
'ራንከ -ስ- መጥፎ ስ'ሜት ፡ መ'መረር ፡ ጥላ'ቻ (የቆ'የ'ና ት'ልቅ)

random
'ራንደም -ቅ- ያለብልሃት ፡ ያለማ'ሰብ የተ ሠ'ራ
at
-ተግ- እ'ዚህ'ና እ'ዚያ ፡ መላ በማጣት

range
'ሬይንጅ -ስ- ሰ'ፊ ግልጥ መሬት
distance
-ስ- ርቀት (የጦር መ'ሣርያ የ'ሚመ ታው)
of mountains
-ስ- የተራሮ'ች ሰንሰለት
array
-ስ- የዕቃ ዓይነት'ና ብዛት
wander
-ግ- ረ'ጅም ጉዞ መሄድ [ሄደ]
put in order
-ግ- መደርደር [ደረ'ደረ]

rank
'ራንክ -ስ- ማዕረግ
rotting
-ቅ- የበሰ'በሰ አትክልት

rankle
'ራንክል -ግ- በአእምሮ መ'መላለስ [ተመላ 'ለሰ] (መጥፎ ስ'ሜት)

ransack
'ራንሳክ -ግ- መዝረፍ [ዘ'ረፈ] ፣ አንድ ነገር አጥብቆ መፈ'ለግ [ፈ'ለገ]

ransom
'ራንሰም -ግ- መዋገርት [ዋ'ገረ] ፡ ገንዘብ በመ ክፈል ከግዞት ማስለ'ቀቅ [አስለ'ቀቀ]-
-ስ- ለተያዘ ሰው ማስለ'ቀቂያ የ'ሚ'ከ 'ፈል ገንዘብ ፡ ቤዛ

rant
'ራንት -ግ- መጮኽ [ጮ'ኸ] (በን'ዴት) ፡ እ'የ ጮ'ኹ መዘላበድ [ዘላ'በደ]

rap
'ራፕ -ግ- መቆርቆር [ቆረ'ቆረ] (መምታት)

rapacious
ረ'ፔይሸስ -ቅ- ዘራፊ ፡ አሙዳሚ ፣ ቀንቋ'ና ፡ ሥ'ሥታም (በተ'ለ'ይ ለገንዘብ)

rape
'ሬይፕ -ግ- አስገ'ድዶ መ'ገናኘት [ተገና'ኘ] ፡ መድፋት [ደ'ፋ] (ሴት)

rapid
'ራፒድ -ቅ- ፈ'ጣን

rapt
'ራፕት -ስ- በሐ'ሳብ የተመ'ሠጠ

rapture
'ራፕቸ -ስ- ታ'ላቅ ደ'ስታ ፣ ሐ'ሴት

rare
'ሬየ -ቅ- በብዛት የ'ማይ'ገ'ኝ ፣ ያልተለ'መደ፣ ሁልጊዜ የ'ማይ'ደ'ረግ ፣ ከል'ክ ያ'ለፈ ጥሩ

rascal
'ራ፡ስክል -ስ- የ'ማይረባ ፣ ተንኮለ'ኛ ፣ አ'ታላይ

rash
'ራሽ -ስ- የሰው'ነት መንደብደብ
hasty
-ቅ- በጣም ች'ኩል

rasher
'ራሸ -ስ- ቀ'ጭን ያሣማ ሥጋ ቁ'ራጭ

rasp
'ራ፡ስፕ -ስ- የንጨት መሞ'ረጃ ሞረድ

rat
'ራት -ስ- አይጥ (ት'ልቅ)

rate
'ሬይት -ስ- የተወ'ሰነ ዋጋ ፣ ፍጥነት

rather
'ራ፡ዘ -ተግ- ይልቅ
to a great extent
-ተግ- . . . መሳይ

ratify
'ራቲፋይ -ግ- ማጽደቅ [አጸ'ደቀ] (ሕ'ግ)

ration
'ራሽን -ስ- መቁነን

rational
'ራሽነል -ቅ- ማስተዋል ያ'ለ'በት ፣ አስተዋይ ፣ ብልኅነተ'ኛ

rattle
'ራተል -ግ- መንኳኳት (ተንኳ'ኳ)

raucous
'ሮ፡ከስ -ቅ- ሻካራ (ለድምፅ)

ravage
'ራቪጅ -ስ- ማፈራረስ ፣ መደምሰስ ፣ በጣም መጉዳት

rave
'ሬይቭ -ግ- በቁ'ጣ መጮ'ኽ [ጮ'ኽ] ፣ በቁ'ጣ መ'ናገር [ተና'ገረ]

raven
'ሬይቨን -ስ- ቁራ

ravenous
'ራቨነስ -ቅ- በጣም የራበው

ravine
ረ'ቪይን -ስ- በሁለ'ት ገደል መካ'ከል ያ'ለ ክፍት ቦታ ፣ ጥልቀት ያ'ለው ሸለቆ

ravish
'ራቪሽ -ግ- በኀይል መቀ'ማት [ቀ'ማ] ፣ መንጠቅ [ነ'ጠቀ] ፣ መድፋት [ደ'ፋ] (ለሴት) ፣ በደ'ስታ መሙላት [ሞ'ላ]

ravishing
'ራቪሺንግ -ቅ- በጣም ቆ'ንጆ ፣ ውብ ፣ ያማረ

raw
'ሮ፡ -ቅ- ጥሬ (ያልበ'ሰለ)
inexperienced
-ቅ- ልምድ የሌ'ለው ፣ ጀ'ማሪ

ray
'ሬይ -ስ- ጮ'ራ

raze
'ሬይዝ -ግ- ሕ'ንፃ ፣ ከተማ ማፈራረስ [አፈራ'ረሰ] ፣ መደምሰስ [ደመ'ሰሰ]

razor
'ሬይዘ -ስ- ምላ'ጭ

reach
'ሪይች -ግ- መድረስ [ደ'ረሰ]

react
ሪ'ያክት -ግ- አጸፋ መመ'ለስ [መ'ለሰ] (ከአንድ ሁናቴ ፣ ድር'ጊት ስ'ሜት በኋላ)

reaction
ሪ'ያክሽን -ስ- ከአንድ ሁናቴ ፣ ድር'ጊት ፣ ስ'ሜት በኋላ የ'ሚ'ታ'ይ የሰው ጠባይ ፣ አጸፋ

read
'ሪይድ -ግ- ማንበብ [አነ'በበ]

ready
'ሬዲ -ቅ- የተዘጋ'ጀ ፣ ዝግ'ጁ

ready-made
ሬዲ'ሜይድ -ቅ- የተዘጋ'ጀ ፣ ወዲያው እንደ'ራ ሊያውሉት የ'ሚ'ቻል (ለልብስ ወዘተ)

real
'ሪየል -ቅ- እውነት

realistic
ሪየ'ሊስቲክ -ቅ- አስተዋይ ፣ ከእውነት ያ'ራቀ

realize
’ሪየላይዝ -ግ- መ'ገንዘብ [ተገነ'ዘበ]
accomplish
-ግ- እሥራ ላይ ማዋል [አዋለ] ፣ መፈ'ጸም [ፈ'ጸመ]

realm
’ሬልም -ስ- መንግሥት ፣ አገር ግዛት

reap
’ሪይፐ -ግ- ማጨድ [አ'ጨደ] (ለሰብል)

rear
’ሪየ -ግ- ማርባት [አረ'ባ] (ለከብት)
behind part
-ስ- ጀርባ ፣ ኋላ
raise
-ግ- ማሳ'ደግ [አሳ'ደገ]

reason
’ሪይዘን -ግ- ማስተዋል [አስተዋለ]
cause
-ስ- ምክንያት
intellect
-ስ- አእምሮ

reasonable
’ሪይዘነበል -ቅ- ምክንያት ያ'ለው ፣ ተገቢ ፣ ል'ክ ፤ ተመጣጣኝ ፣ ከል'ክ ያላ'ለፈ ፣ ተገቢ (ዋጋ)

reassure
ሪየ’ሾ: -ግ- ማጽናናት [አጽና'ና] ፣ እንደገና ማ'ረጋገጥ [አ'ረጋ'ገጠ] ፣ ፍርሀትና ጥር'ጣሬ ማራቅ [አራቀ]

rebate
’ሪይቤይት -ስ- እንደገና የተከ'ፈለ ገንዘብ (የተስተካ'ከለ) ፤ የዋጋ ቅ'ናሽ
-ግ- መቀ'ነስ [ቀ'ነሰ] (ዋጋ)

rebel
ሪ’ቤል -ግ- መሸ'ፈት [ሸ'ፈተ]

rebel
’ሬበል -ስ- ሽፍታ

rebellion
ሪ’ቤልየን -ስ- ሽ'ፈታ ፣ መሸ'ፈት

rebound
ሪ’ባውንድ -ግ- ነጥሮ መ'መለስ [ተመ'ለሰ] (ለኳስ)
-ስ- መንጠር (ለኳስ)

rebuff
ሪ’በፍ -ግ- ማሳ'ፈር [አሳ'ፈረ] (በደ'ግ የመ'ጣን ሰው)

rebuke
ሪብ’ዩ:ክ -ግ- መገ'ሠፅ [ገ'ሠፀ]

recalcitrant
ሪ’ካልሲትረንት -ቅ- እምቢተ'ኛ ፣ ች'ኮ

recall
ሪ’ኮ:ል -ግ- ማስታወስ [አስታ'ወሰ]
memory
-ስ- ት'ዝታ
call back
-ግ- መመ'ለስ [መ'ለሰ] (እው'ጭ አገር የተሾመን ሰው)

recant
ሪ’ካንት -ግ- ቀደ'ም ብሎ የተና'ገሩት ትክ'ክል አለመሆኑን መግለጽ [ገ'ለጸ]

recede
ሪ’ሲይድ -ግ- ወደኋላ ማለት [አለ] ፣ ወደኋላ ማፈግፈግ [አፈገ'ፈገ]

receipt
ሪ’ሲይት -ስ- ደ'ረሰ'ኝ ፣ ፋክቱር

receive
ሪ’ሲይቭ -ግ- መ'ቀበል [ተቀ'በለ] ፤ ማስተናገድ [አስተና'ገደ]

receiver
ሪ’ሲይቨ -ስ- ተቀ'ባይ
telephone
-ስ- የቴሌፎን መስሚያ'ና መ'ናገሪያ መ'ሣሪያ
dealer in stolen property
-ስ- የተሰ'ረቀ ዕቃ የ'ሚሸጥ ነ'ጋዴ

recent
’ሪይሰንት -ቅ- ከጥቂት ጊዜ በፊት የሆነ

receptacle
ሪ’ሰፕተ:ከል -ስ- ዕቃ ፣ መያዣ

reception
ሪ’ሴፕሽን -ስ- አ'ቀባበል
party
-ስ- የመስተንግዶ ግብዣ

receptive
ሪ’ሴፕቲቭ -ቅ- ተቀ'ባይ (ለትምህርት ፣ ለሐ'ሳብ)

recess
ሪ'ሴስ -ስ- ሰር'ጓዳ ቦታ (በቤት ውስጥ ወዘተ)
break for rest
-ስ- ትንሽ ዕረፍት

recession
ሪ'ሴሽን -ስ- የኢኮኖሚ ድቀት (ጊዜ)

recipe
'ሬሰፒ -ስ- የምግብ አ'ሠራር ዘዴ ፣ የምግብ አ'ቀማመም ፤ በአንድ ዓይነት ምግብ አ'ሠራር የ'ሚገቡ ል'ዩ ል'ዩ ነገሮ'ች

recipient
ሪ'ሲፒየንት -ስ- ተቀ'ባይ

reciprocal
ሪ'ሲፕረክል -ቅ- ከሁለ'ት ወገን የሆነ (ስም ም'ነት ፣ ስ'ሜት ፣ መስጠት'ና መ'ቀበል)

reciprocate
ሪ'ሲፕረኬይት -ግ- አጸፋውን መመ'ለስ [መ'ለሰ]

recital
ሪ'ሳይተል -ስ- ለሕዝብ የ'ሚቀርብ (የሙዚቃ ፣ የቅኔ በዐል)

recite
ሪ'ሳይት -ግ- ግጥም ማንበብ [አነ'በበ] (በቃል)

reckless
'ሬክሌስ -ቅ- የ'ማይ'ጠነ'ቀቅ ፣ ንዝህላል

reckon
'ሬከን -ግ- ማወቅ [ዐ'ወቀ]
guess
-ግ- ግ'ሰብ [አ'ሰበ] (ለሒሳብ)
add up
-ግ- መደ'መር [ደ'መረ]

reclaim
ሪክ'ሌይም -ግ- መብትን መጠ'የቅ [ጠ'የቀ] (የተሰ'ረቀን ፣ የተዘ'ረፈን)
recultivate
-ግ- ጠፍ መሬት እንደገና ማረስ [አ'ረሰ]

recline
ሪክ'ላይን -ግ- ጋደ'ም ብሎ መ'ቀመጥ [ተቀ'መጠ] ፣ ደ'ገ'ፍ ብሎ መ'ቀመጥ [ተቀ'መጠ]

recluse
ሪክ'ሉ:ስ -ስ- ባሕታዊ ፣ በተባሕትዎ የ'ሚኖር ፣ መ'ናኒ

recognize
'ሬከግናይዝ -ግ- ማወቅ [ዐ'ወቀ] ፣ መለ'የ [ለ'የ]

recoil
ሪ'ኮይል -ግ- መርገጥ [ረ'ገጠ] (ጠመንጃ ሲ'ተኮስ)

recollect
ሬከ'ሌክት -ግ- ማስታወስ [አስታ'ወሰ]

recommend
ሬከ'ሜንድ -ግ- አደራ ማለት [አለ] ፣ አን ነገር ጠቃ'ሚ'ነቱን'ና ጥሩ'ነቱን መ'ናገር [ተ'ገረ]

recompense
'ሬከምፔንስ -ግ- መካሥ [ካሠ]

reconcile
'ሬከንሳይል -ግ- ማስታረቅ [አስታ'ረቀ]

recondition
ሪከን'ዲሽን -ግ- መጠ'ገን [ጠ'ገነ] ፣ ማ'ደ [አ'ደሰ] (የተበ'ላ'ሸ ነገር)

reconnaissance
ሪ'ኮነሰንስ -ስ- ስ'ለላ (አንድን አገር ከመ'ንት በፊት) ፤ ቀድሞ ሁናቴን ማጥናት

reconnoitre
ሬከ'ኖይተ -ግ- አገር መሰ'ለል [ሰ'ለለ] (ከ ውረር በፊት)

reconstruct
ሪከንስት'ረክት -ግ- እንደገና ማቆም [አቆመ መሥራት [ሠ'ራ] (ለቤት ፣ ለሕንፃ)

record
'ሪኮ:ድ -ግ- መመዝገብ [መዘ'ገበ] (ጉ'ዳይ ድምፅ)

record
'ሬኮ:ድ -ስ- ሸክላ (የሙዚቃ)
account
-ስ- መዝገብ

recount
ሪ'ካውንት -ግ- ወሬ ማውራት [አወ'ራ]

recoup
ሪ'ኩፕ -ግ- የከ'ሰሩትን ፣ የተሸ'ነፉትን ገ ዘብ መመ'ለስ [መ'ለሰ]

recourse
ሪ'ኮ:ስ -ስ- እርዳታ መጠ'የቅ

recover

ሪ'ከቨ -ግ- እንደገና ማግኘት [አገ'ኘ] (የጠ'ፋ ነገር)

from illness

-ግ- መዳን [ዳነ]

recreation

ሬክሪ'ዬይሽን -ስ- መዝናናት ፣ መ'ደሰት (ከሥራ በኋላ)

recrimination

ሪክሪሚ'ኔይሽን -ስ- እርስበርስ መ'ካሰስ ፣ መ'ዛለፍ ፣ መ'ወቃቀስ

-ግ- እርስበርስ መ'ካሰስ [ተካ'ሰሰ] ፣ መ'ዛለፍ [ተዛ'ለፈ] ፣ መወ'ቃቀስ [ተወቃ'ቀሰ]

recruit

ሪክ'ሩ፡ት -ግ- መመልመል [መለ'መለ] (ወ'ታ'ደር ወዘተ)

-ስ- በመሠልጠን ላይ ያ'ለ ወ'ታ'ደር

rectangular

ሬክ'ታንጉለ -ቅ- ባለ አራ'ት ማዕዘን (ባንጻር ያ'ሉ ሁለ'ት ጎ'ኖ'ቹ የ'ሚ'መሳ'ሰሉ)

rectify

'ሬክቲፋይ -ግ- ማስተካከል [አስተካ'ከለ] (ስሕተትን)

recumbent

ሪ'ከምበንት -ቅ- የተጋ'ደመ

recuperate

ሪ'ኩፐሬይት -ግ- ማገ'ገም [አገ'ገመ] (ከሕመም)

recur

ሪ'ከ፡ -ግ- እንደገና መሆን [ሆነ] ፣ ብዙ ጊዜ ተመላልሶ መሆን [ሆነ] ፣ ማገርሸት [አገረ'ሸ] (ሕመም)

red

'ሬድ -ቅ- ቀ'ይ

redden

'ሬደን -ግ- መቅላት [ቀ'ላ]

redeem

ሪ'ዲይም -ግ- ማዳን [አዳነ] (እዳ ከፍሎ)

religious

-ግ- መዋጀት [ዋ'ጀ]

redhanded

ሬድ'ሃንዲድ -ቅ- ወንጀል በ'ሚፈ'ጽም'በት ጊዜ የተያዘ ፣ እ'ጅ ከፍንጅ የተያዘ (ወንጀለ'ኛ)

redistribute

ሪዲስት'ሪብዩት -ግ- መደልደል [ደለ'ደለ] ፣ ማ'ከፋፈል [አ'ከፋ'ፈለ] (እንደገና)

redolent

'ሬደለንት -ቅ- ጥሩ መዓዛ ያ'ለው ፣ ጥሩ ጥሩ የ'ሚሸ'ት

-of

-ቅ- የ'ሚያስታ'ውስ

redress

ሪድ'ሬስ -ግ- መካሥ [ካሠ]

-ስ- ካሣ

reduce

ሪድ'ዩስ -ግ- ማሳ'ነስ [አሳ'ነሰ] ፣ መቀ'ነስ [ቀ'ነሰ]

reduction

ሪ'ደክሽን -ስ- መቀ'ነስ

of price

-ስ- ቅ'ናሽ (የዋጋ)

redundant

ሪ'ደንደንት -ቅ- ከስፈ'ላጊ በላይ ፣ ትርፍ(ለሠ'ራተ'ኞ'ች ወዘተ) ፣ ከ'ሚያስፈ'ልገው በላይ ቃላት የ'ሚያስገ'ባ ፣ ሳያስፈ'ልግ የተደጋ'ገመ (ቃላት)

reed

'ሪይድ -ስ- ሸምበ'ቆ ፣ መቃ

reedy

'ሪይዲ -ቅ- ቀ'ጭን'ና ከ'ፍ ያለ (ለድምፅ)

reef

'ሪይፍ -ስ- በባሕር መካ'ከል የ'ሚ'ገ'ኙ ቋጥ'ኞ'ች ።

-ግ- ጠቅልሎ ማሠር [አ'ሠረ] (ለመርከብ ሸራ)

reek

'ሪይክ -ግ- መከርፋት [ከረ'ፋ]

reel

'ሪይል -ግ- መንገዳገድ [ተንገዳ'ገደ] (በስካር ወዘተ)

dance

-ስ- ጭ'ፈራ (ስም'ንት ሰዎ'ች ያ'ሉ'በት)

bobbin

-ስ- መጠቅለያ ፣ ማጠንጠኛ ፣ ማቅለሚያ

reimburse

ሪይም'በ፡ስ -ግ- ያወ'ጡትን ገንዘብ መ'ከፈል [ተከ'ፈለ]

refer
ሪ'ፈ: -ግ- ማ'መላከት [አ'መላ ከረ] (ለጽሑፍ)
to
-ግ- መጥቀስ [ጠ'ቀሰ] (ለንግ'ግር)
referee
ሬፈ'ሪይ -ስ- ዳ'ኛ (ለጨዋታ) ፣ ያደራ ወረ ቀት የላከ ሰው
reference
'ሬፍረንስ -ስ- የተጠ'ቀሰ መጻሕፍት (በድር ሰት ወዘተ)
recommendation
-ስ- ያደራ ወረቀት
refill
ሪ'ፊል -ግ- እንደገና መሙላት [ሞ ላ]
refine
ሪ'ፋይን -ግ- ማ'ጣራት [አ'ጣ'ራ] (ስኳይት ወዘተ)
refined
ሪ'ፋይንድ -ቅ- የተጣ'ራ
refinement
ሪ'ፋይንመንት -ስ- የማ'ጣራት ተግባር (ን ጹሕ ለማድረግ) ፣ ጥሩ አስተዳደግ
refinery
ሪ'ፋይነሪ -ስ- ማ'ጣሪያ መኪና ወይን'ም ቦታ
reflect
ሪፍ'ሌክት -ግ- ማስተጋባት [አስተጋ'ባ] (ለብ ርሃን)
meditate
-ግ- በነገሩ ማ'ሰብ [አ'ሰበ]
reflection
ሪፍ'ሌክሽን -ስ- ማስተጋባት
thought
-ስ- ሐ'ሳብ
reform
ሪ'ፎ:ም -ግ- ማ'ሻሻል [አ'ሻሻለ] ፣ መ'ሻሻል [ተሻሻለ]
reformatory
ሪ'ፎ:መትሪ -ስ- ማ'ሻሻል (አ'ዲስ ሕ'ግ) ፣ አመል ማ'ረሚያ (ለሕፃናት'ና ለወ'ጣቶ'ች)
refractory
ሪፍ'ራክተሪ -ቅ- የ'ማይ'ታ'ዘዝ ፣ እምቢተ'ኛ
refrain
ሪፍ'ሬይን -ግ- ወደኋላ ማለት [አለ] (ከመ'ና ገር) ፣ ማቆም [አቆመ] (አንድ ነገር ከመሥራት)

refreshing
ሪፍ'ሬሺንግ -ቅ- የ'ሚያ'በረታ'ታ ፣ የ'ሚያ[illegible] ና'ና (ሰው'ነት)
refreshment
ሪፍ'ሬሽመንት -ስ- ቀለ'ል ያለ ምግብ'ና መ[illegible] ጠ'ጥ ፣ ቁርስ ፣ መቅሰስ
refrigerator
ሪፍ'ሪጀሬይተ -ስ- ማቀዝቀዣ መኪና ፣ የ[illegible] ረዣ ቤት
refuge
'ሬፍዩ:ጅ -ስ- መ'ሸሸጊያ ቦታ ፣ ከአደጋ የ'ሚ[illegible] መልጡ'በት ቦታ ፣ ተገን
refugee
ሬፍዩ'ጂይ -ስ- ስ'ደተ'ኛ
refund
'ሪፈንድ -ስ- ተመ'ላሽ ገንዘብ (ከተከ'ፈለ [illegible] ኋላ)
refuse
ሪፍ'ዩ:ዝ -ግ- እምቢ ማለት [አለ] ፣ አለመ'ቀ[illegible] በል [ተቀ'በለ]
refuse
'ሬፍዩስ -ስ- አድፍ ፣ ጉድፍ
refute
ሪፍ'ዩ:ት -ግ- ትክ'ክል አለመሆኑን ማስረ'ዳት [አስረ'ዳ]
regain
ሪ'ጌይን -ግ- እንደገና ማግኘት [አገ'ኘ] ማስመ'ለስ [አስመ'ለሰ]
regal
'ሪይገል -ቅ- ንጉሣዊ ፣ ለንጉሥ የ'ሚስማ'ማ[illegible]
regale
ሪ'ጌይል -ግ- በምግብ'ና በመጠ'ጥ ሰውን ራስን ማስደ'ሰት [አስደ'ሰተ]
regard
ሪ'ጋ:ድ -ግ- መ'መልከት [ተመለ'ከተ] (አ[illegible] ብቶ)
esteem
-ስ- ክብር
regardless
ሪ'ጋ:ድሌስ -ተግ- ዋጋ ሳይሰጡ ፣ ሳይ'መ[illegible] ነቱ ፣ ችላ በማለት
regent
'ሪይጀንት -ስ- ባለሙሉ ሥልጣን እን'ደራሴ (የንጉሥ ሥራ የ'ሚሠራ)

regime
ሬ'ዥይም -ስ- የመንግሥት ዓይነት (ለመጥፎ)፤ የኑሮ ዓይነት

regiment
'ሬጂመንት -ስ- ክፍለ ጦር (በኰሎኔል የ'ሚ'ታ'ዘዝ)

region
'ሪይጀን -ስ- ክፍለ ሀገር ፥ ወረዳ ፥ አ'ካባቢ

register
'ሬጂስተ -ግ- መመዝገብ [መዘ'ገበ]
official list
-ስ- መዝገብ
give one's name
-ግ- ስምን ማስመዝገብ [አስመዘ'ገበ]

registration
ሬጂስት'ሬይሽን -ስ- ምዝገባ

regret
ሪግ'ሬት -ስ- መ'ፀፀት [ተፀ'ፀተ]

regrettable
ሪግ'ሬተበል -ቅ- አሳ'ዛኝ ፥ የ'ሚያሳ'ዝን

regular
'ሬግዩለ -ቅ- የተለ'መደ ፥ ተመሳሳይ የሆነ ፥ እ'የተደጋ'ገመ የ'ሚሆን

regulate
'ሬግዩሌይት -ግ- ማስተካከል [አስተካ'ከለ]

regulation
ሬግዩ'ሌይሽን -ስ- ደንብ ፥ ሕ'ግ ፥ ሥርዓት

rehabilitate
ሪሃ'ቢሊቴይት -ግ- ድኩማንን ማሠልጠን [አሠለ'ጠነ] ፥ ራሳ'ቸውን እንዲችሉ ወንጀለ'ኞ'ችን በትምህርት ማ'ሻሻል [አ'ሻሻለ]

rehearse
ሪ'ኸ፡ስ -ግ- መ'ለማመድ [ተለማ'መደ] (ቴያትር ወዘተ)

reign
'ሬይን -ግ- መንገሥ [ነ'ገሠ]
-ስ- ዘመነ መንግሥት

rein
'ሬይን -ስ- ገብ ፥ መግቻ

reinforce
ሪዪን'ፎ፡ስ -ግ- ማጠንከር [አጠነ'ከረ]

reinstate
ሪዪንስ'ቴይት -ግ- እሹመት ላይ መመ'ለስ [መ'ለሰ]፥ወደቀድሞው ቦታ መመ'ለስ [መ'ለሰ]

reiterate
ሪ'ይተሬይት -ግ- ደጋግሞ መና'ገር [ተና'ገረ]፥ መሥራት [ሠ'ራ]

reject
ሪ'ጀክት -ግ- አለመ'ቀበል [-ተቀ'በለ]

reject
'ሪጀክት -ስ- የ'ሚ'ጣል ዕቃ (ስብርባሪ ወዘተ)

rejoice
ሪ'ጆይስ -ግ- መ'ደሰት [ተደ'ሰተ]

rejoin
ሪ'ጆይን -ግ- እንደገና መ'ገናኘት [ተገና'ኘ]

rejoinder
ሪ'ጆይንደ -ስ- መልስ ፥ ም'ላሽ (የጥ'ያቄ ፥ የክር'ክር)

rejuvenate
ሪ'ጁቨኔይት -ግ- እንደገና ወ'ጣት ማድረግ [አደ'ረገ]

relapse
ሪ'ላፕስ -ግ- ወደ ቀድሞው መጥፎ ሁናቴ መ'መለስ [ተመ'ለሰ] ፥ ማገርሸት [አገረ'ሸ]

relate
ሪ'ሌይት -ግ- ማውራት [አወ'ራ] ፥ መተ'ረት [ተ'ረተ]

relation
ሪ'ሌይሽን -ስ- ግን'ኙ'ነት
kinsman
-ስ- ዘመድ

relative
'ሬለቲቭ -ቅ- አ'ንፃሪ (እንዳ'ነጋገሩ ሊ'ተረ'ጐም የ'ሚችል ቃል)
kinsman
-ስ- ዘመድ

relax
ሪ'ላክስ -ግ- መዝናናት [ተዝና'ና]

relaxation
ሪላክ'ሴይሽን -ስ- መዝናናት

relay
'ሪሌይ -ግ- እምነትን መጣል [ጣለ]

release
ሪ'ሊይስ -ግ- መፍታት [ፈ'ታ] ፥ መልቀቅ [ለ'ቀቀ]

relegate
'ሬለጌይት -ግ- ከሹመት ዝ'ቅ ማድረግ [አደ'ረገ] ፤ አንድ ጉ'ዳይ ለው'ሳኔ ማስተላለፍ [አስተላ'ለፈ] (ለሌላ ሰው)
relent
ሪ'ሌንት -ግ- መሐሪ መሆን [ሆነ]
relentless
ሪ'ሌንትለስ -ቅ- ምሕረት የሌ'ለው ፣ ጨ'ካኝ
relevant
'ሬለቨንት -ቅ- ተገቢ'ነት ያ'ለው ፣ ከጉ'ዳዩ ጋር የተያያዘ
reliable
ሪ'ላየበል -ቅ- ታ'ማኝ ፣ እምነት የ'ሚ'ጣል'በት
relic
'ሬሊክ -ስ- ታሪካዊ ዕቃ ፤ ያንድ የሞተ ቅ'ዱስ ሰው የማስታወሻ ዕቃ (ዐፅሙ ወዘተ)
relief
ሪ'ሊይፍ -ስ- ዕረፍት (ከሐ'ሳብ ፣ ከበ'ሽታ)
replacement
-ስ- ተተኪ 'ሰው (በሥራ ላይ)
sculpture
-ስ- ከደንጊያ የተፈለ'ፈለ የምስል'ነት ቅርፅ ያ'ለው
relieve
ሪ'ሊይቭ -ግ-መ'ገላገል [ተገላ'ገለ] (ከሐ'ሳብ ፣ ከበ'ሽታ)
replace
-ግ- መ'ተካት [ተተ'ካ] (በሥራ)
religion
ሪ'ሊጅን -ስ- ሃይማኖት
religious
ሪ'ሊጀስ -ቅ- ሃይማኖተ'ኛ
relinquish
ሪ'ሊንክዊሽ -ግ- መተው [ተወ] ፤ መ'ሰናበት [ተሰና'በተ] (ከሥራ) ፣ መልቀቅ ፣ [ለ'ቀቀ] (የያዘውን ነገር)
relish
'ሬሊሽ -ስ- ቅመማቅመም ፣ የ'ሚጣ'ፍጥ ፣ እ'ጅ የ'ሚያስቆረ'ጥም
enthusiasm
-ስ- ኀይለ'ኛ ፍ'ላጎት
reluctant
ሪ'ለክተንት -ቅ- ለማድረግ የ'ማይወ'ድ ፣ ወደ ኋላ የ'ሚል ፣ እንገራጋሪ

rely
ሪ'ላይ -ግ- መ'መካት [ተመ'ካ] ፣ እምነት መጣል [ጣለ] (በሰው ላይ)
remain
ሪ'ሜይን -ግ- መቅረት [ቀ'ረ]
remainder
ሪ'ሜይንደ -ስ- ቀሪ
remains
ሪ'ሜይንዝ -ስ- ቀሪ ፣ ትርፍ ፤ የቤት ፍ'ራሽ ፤ አስከሬን
remark
ሪ'ማ:ክ -ግ- መ'ናገር [ተና'ገረ] ፣ አስተያየት መስጠት [ሰ'ጠ]
-ስ- ንግ'ግር ፣ አስተያየት (የተነ'ገረ ወይን'ም የተጻፈ)
remarkable
ሪ'ማ:ከበል -ቅ- በጣም ጥሩ ፣ ግሩም ፤ ያልተ ለ'መደ
remedy
'ሬመዲ -ግ- ማዳን [አዳነ] ፤ ማ'ቃናት [አ'ቃ'ና] ፣ መፍትሔ ማግኘት [አገ'ኘ]
-ስ- መድኃኒት (ለበ'ሽታ ፣ ለመከራ)
remember
ሪ'ሜምበ -ስ- ማስታወስ [አስታ'ወሰ] ፣ ት'ዝ ማለት [አለ]
remembrance
ሪ'ሜምብረንስ -ስ- ማስታወስ
remind
ሪ'ማይንድ -ግ- ማስታወስ [አስታ'ወሰ]
remission
ሪ'ሚሽን -ስ- የእስር ጊዜ ቅ'ነሳ
remnant
'ሬምነንት -ስ- ቀሪ ፣ ትርፍ
remonstrate
'ሬመንስትሬይት -ግ- ስሕተት መንገር [ነ'ገረ] ፤ አለመስማማትን መግለጽ [ገ'ለጸ]
remorse
ሪ'ሞ:ስ -ስ- ፀፀት ፣ ሐዘን (ላ'ለፈ ነገር)
remorseless
ሪ'ሞ:ስሌስ -ቅ- ምሕረት የሌ'ለው ፣ ርኅራኄ የለ'ለው
remote
ሪ'መውት -ቅ- ሩቅ ፣ ዳር (ለአገር)

move

ሪ'ሙ:ቭ -ግ- መውሰድ [ወ'ሰደ] ፤ ወደሌላ ቦታ ማ'ዛወር [አ'ዛ'ወረ] ፤ ማስወ'ገድ [አስወ'ገደ]

munerate

ሪም'ዩ:ነሬይት -ግ- መክፈል [ከ'ፈለ] ፤ ገንዘብ መስጠት [ሰ'ጠ] (ለአንድ አገልግሎት)

muneration

ሪምዩነ'ሬይሽን -ስ- ለአገልግሎት የ'ሚ'ከ'ፈል ገንዘብ

nd

'ሬንድ -ግ- መሸርከት [ሸረ'ከተ] ፤ መሠን ጠቅ [ሠነ'ጠቀ]

nder

'ሬንደ -ግ- መልስ መስጠት [ሰ'ጠ] ፤ መ'ልሶ መክፈል [ከ'ፈለ] ፤ መተርጐም [ተረ'ጐመ] (ቋንቋን)

endezvous

'ሮንደ.ቩ: -ስ- ቀጠሮ (የጓ'ደ'ኞ'ች ፤ የወዳ ጆ'ች)

enegade

'ሬነጌይድ -ስ- ከሓዲ ፤ መናፍቅ

enew

ሪን'ዩ: -ግ- ማ'ደስ [አ'ደሰ]

enounce

ሪ'ናውንስ -ግ- መካድ [ካደ]

enovate

'ሬነቬይት -ግ- እንደገና ማ'ደስ [አ'ደሰ] ፤ ወደ ቀድሞው ሁናቴ አ'ድሶ መመ'ለስ [መ'ለሰ]

enown

ሪ'ናውን -ስ- ዝ'ና ፤ ስመ ጥር'ነት

ent

'ሬንት -ስ- ኪራይ (የቤት)

tear in cloth

-ስ- ቀዳዳ (የልብስ)

occupy house etc.

-ግ- መ'ከራየት [ተከራ'የ] (ለቤት ወዘተ)

eorganize

ሪ'ዮገናይዝ -ግ- እንደገና ማ'ደራጀት [አ'ደ ራ'ጀ] ፤ መልክ መስጠት [ሰ'ጠ]

epair

ሪ'ፔየ -ግ- መጠ'ገን [ጠ'ገነ]

epartee

ሬፓ'ቲይ -ስ- ፈ'ጣን ፤ ቧልት ያ'ለ'በት አ'ሥ ቂ'ኝ መልስ (በንግ'ግር)

repay

ሪ'ፔይ -ግ- መክፈል [ከ'ፈለ] (ብ'ድር)

repeal

ሪ'ፒይል -ግ- የወ'ጣ ሕ'ግ መሻር [ሻረ]

repeat

ሪ'ፒይት -ግ- መደጋገም [ደጋ'ገመ] ፤ መድ ገም [ደ'ገመ]

repel

ሪ'ፔል -ግ- ማ'ባረር [አ'ባ'ረረ] ፤ አለመ'ቀ በል [-ተቀ'በለ]

repent

ሪ'ፔንት -ግ- ን'ሥሐ መግባት [ገ'ባ]

repercussion

ሪፐ'ከሽን -ስ- ካንድ ሁናቴ በኋላ የ'ሚ'ከ'ተ ለው ው'ጤት ፤ የ'ሚያስተጋ'ባ ድምፅ

repetition

ሬፒ'ቲሽን -ስ- መድገም ፤ መ'ልሶ ማድረግ

replace

ሪፕ'ሌይስ -ግ- መተ'ካት [ተ'ካ]

replenish

ሪፕ'ሌኒሽ -ግ- እንደገና መሙላት [ሞ'ላ]

replica

'ሬፕሊካ -ስ- አምሳ'ያ ፤ እስመ'ስሎ የተሠ'ራ ሥዕል

reply

ሪፕ'ላይ -ግ- መልስ መስጠት [ሰ'ጠ]

report

ሪ'ፖ:ት -ግ- ስላ'ዩት ፤ ስለሰ'ሙት ፤ ስለሠ'ሩት ጉ'ዳይ መ'ናገር [ተና'ገረ]

rumour

-ስ- ወሬ ፤ ጭምጭምታ

sound of explosion

-ስ- ተኩስ

reporter

ሪ'ፖ:ተ -ስ- ጋዜጠ'ኛ

repose

ሪ'ፖውዝ -ግ- ማረፍ [ዐ'ረፈ]

-ስ- ዕረፍት

represent

ሬፕረ'ዜንት -ግ- መ'ወ'ከል [ተወ'ከለ]

representative

ሬፕረ'ዜንተቲቭ -ስ- ወ'ኪል

-ቅ- የ'ሚመ'ስል ፤ የተወ'ከለ

repress

ሪፕ'ሬስ -ግ- መጨ'ቆን [ጨ'ቆነ] ፡ መግታት [ገ'ታ]

reprieve

ሪፕ'ሪይቭ -ግ- ምሕረት መስጠት [ሰ'ጠ] (ከ ስ'ቅላት ፡ ከሞት ቅጣት) ፡ ለጊዜው ፍርድ እንዳ ይ'ፈ'ጸም ማ'ገድ [አ'ገደ]

reprimand

'ሬፕሪማ፡ንድ -ግ- መገ'ሠፅ [ገ'ሠፀ]

-ስ- ተግሣፅ

reprint

ሪፕ'ሪንት -ግ- ደግሞ ማ'ተም [አ'ተመ]

reprisal

ሪፕ'ራይዘል -ስ- ለመ'በቀል ማጥቃት (በጦ ር'ነት) ፡ ክፋትን በክፋት መመ'ለስ

reproach

ሪፕ'ረውች -ግ- መዝለፍ [ዘ'ለፈ] ፡ መውቀስ [ወ'ቀሰ]

reproduce

ሪፕሪድ'ዩ፡ስ -ግ- መ'ባዛት [ተባ'ዛ] ፡ መ'ዋ ለድ [ተዋ'ለደ]

reproduction

ሪፕረ'ዶክሽን -ስ- መ'ባዛት ፡ መ'ዋለድ

facsimile

-ስ- ትክ'ክለ'ኛ ግል'ባጭ

reproof

ሪፕ'ሩ፡ፍ -ስ- ዘለፋ

reptile

'ሬፕ፡ታይል -ስ- በደረቱ የ'ሚ'ሳብ ፍጡር (እ ባብ ወዘተ)

republic

ሪ'ፐብሊክ -ስ- ሬፑብሊክ ፡ የመንግሥቱ ሥ ልጣን በሕዝብ እንደራሴዎ'ች እ'ጅ ያ'ለ የመንግሥት አስተዳደር

repudiate

ሪፕ'ዩዲዩይት -ግ- አለመ'ቀበል [-ተቀ'በለ]፡ መካድ [ካደ] (መጥፎን ልጅ ወዘተ)

repugnant

ሪ'ፐግነንት -ቅ- ማስጠ'ሎ ፡ አ'ጸ'ያፊ

repulse

ሪ'ፐልስ -ግ- ወደኋላ መመ'ለስ [መ'ለሰ] (ጠ ላት) ፡ መመ'ከት [መ'ከተ]

repulsive

ሪ'ፐልሲቭ -ቅ- አስቀ'ያሚ ፡ የ'ሚያስጠ'ላ

reputation

ሬፑዩ'ቴይሽን -ስ- ዝ'ና ፡ ስም

requost

ሪክ'ዌስት -ግ- መጠ'የቅ [ጠ'የቀ] (ፈቃደ

require

ሪክ'ዋየ -ግ- ማስፈ'ለግ [አስፈ'ለገ] ፡ ማዘ [አ'ዘዘ] ፡ መጠ'የቅ [ጠ'የቀ] (እንደ መብት በሥልጣን)

requisite

'ሬክዊዚት -ቅ- አስፈ'ላጊ ፡ ሊተውት የ' ይ'ቻል

requisition

ሬክዊ'ዚሽን -ግ- በጦር'ነት ጊዜ ከሕዝብ ን ንት ወዘተ መውሰድ [ወ'ሰደ]

-ስ- ለግዥ በጽሑፍ ዕቃ መጠ'የ

rescind

ሪ'ሲንድ -ግ- መፋት [ፋተ] (ሕ'ግን ፡ ደንብን

rescue

'ሬስክዩ፡ -ግ- ማዳን [አዳነ] (ከአደጋ) ፡ ከ ላት ፡ ከእሥር ቤት ነጻ ማድረግ [አደ'ረገ]

research

ሪ'ስ፡ች -ግ- ምር'ምር ማድረግ [አደ'ረገ]

-ስ- ምር'ምር ፡ ጥናት (ለትምህርት ዘተ)

resemble

ሪ'ዜምበል -ግ- መምሰል [መ'ሰለ]

resent

ሪ'ዜንት -ግ- መ'ቃወም [ተቃ'ወመ] ፡ አለ ስማማት [-ተስማ'ማ] ፡ እንደ ውርደት መቁ [ቆ'ጠረ]

roservation

ሬዘ'ቬይሽን -ስ- ጥር'ጣሬ (ድንገተ'ኛ) ፡ ከ 'ናዝር ከመሥራት መ'ቆጠብ

special area

-ስ- የተከ'ለለ ቦታ

pre-booking

-ስ- ቦታ መያዝ (በባቡር ፡ አውሮ'ፕ ወዘተ)

reserve

ሪ'ዘ፡ቭ -ስ- ክ'ልል ቦታ

reticence

-ስ- መ'ቆጠብ (ከንግ'ግር)

store

-ስ- የተቀ'መጠ ገንዘብ ፡ በቂ (ለስ

book seat etc.

-ግ- አስቀ'ድሞ ቦታ መያዝ [ያዘ] (በ ቡር ፡ በአውሮ'ፕላን ወዘተ)

reservoir
'ሬዘቮዋ: -ስ- የውሃ ማ'ከማቻ ጋን
reside
ሪ'ዛይድ -ግ- መኖር [ኖረ] (ባንድ ቦታ)
residence
'ሬዚደንስ -ስ- መኖርያ ቤት ፤ መኖርያ ጊዜ
resident
'ሬዚደንት -ስ- ነዋሪ (ባንድ ቦታ)
-ቅ- ነዋሪ
residue
'ሬዚድዩ -ስ- ጭ'ላጭ ፤ ዝ'ቃጭ
resign
ሪ'ዛይን -ግ- ሥራ መልቀቅ [ለ'ቀቀ] (በራስ ፈቃድ)
resignation
ሬዚግ'ኔይሽን -ስ- ሥራ መልቀቅ (በራስ ፈቃድ)
resigned
ሪ'ዛይንድ -ቅ- ታ'ጋሽ ፤ ያ'ጋጠመውን በት ዕግሥት የ'ሚ'ቀ'በል ፤ የ'ማያጉረመ'ርም
resilient
ሪ'ዚሊየንት -ቅ- ወደቀድሞው ሁኔቴ መ'መ ለስ የ'ሚችል (ከደ'ቀቀ ፤ ከተጨ'መቀ ወዘተ በኋላ)
resin
'ሬዚን -ስ- ሙ'ጫ
resist
ሪ'ዚስት -ግ- መመከት [መ'ከተ] ፤ እለመ'በ ገር [-ተበ'ገረ] ፤ መ'ቃወም [ተቃ'ወመ]
resolute
'ሬዘሉት -ቅ- የጸ'ና ፤ የ'ማያ'ወላ'ውል ፤ ደ'ፋር
resolution
ሬዘ ሉ:ሽን -ስ- ጽናት ፤ አለማ'ወላወል
motion
-ስ- ው'ሳኔ
resolve
ሪ'ዞልቭ -ግ- መወ'ሰን [ወ'ሰነ] ፤ መበተን [በ'ተነ] (ጉባኤ ፤ ስብሰባ)
resonant
'ሬዘነንት -ቅ- የ'ሚያስተጋ'ባ ፤ የ'ሚነ'ብ (ለድምፅ)

resort
ሪ'ዞ:ት -ስ- የመ'ደሰቻ ቦታ ፤ ለዕረፍት የ'ሚ'ኬድ'በት ሥፍራ ፤ አገር
means of help
-ስ- መ'ረጃ
go for help to
-ግ- እርዳታ መጠ'የቅ [ጠ'የቀ]
resource
ሪ'ሶ:ስ -ስ- ምንጭ (የገንዘብ ፤ የሀብት ወዘተ)
expedient
-ስ- ዘዴ ፤ ብልኀት
resources
ሪ'ሶ:ሲዝ -ስ- የተፈጥሮ ሀብት (ማዕ'ድን ወዘተ) ፤ የገንዘብ ምንጭ
respect
ሪስ'ፔክት -ግ- ማክበር [አከ'በረ]
-ስ- ክብር
respectable
ሪስ'ፔክተበል -ቅ- ጨዋ ፤ ታ'ማኝ ፤ የ'ሚ'ከ'በር
respiration
ሬስፐ'ሬይሽን -ስ- ትንፋሽ ፤ መተንፈስ
respite
'ሬስፓት -ስ- ት'ንሽ ዕረፍት (ከሥራ ፤ ከድካም ፤ ከ'ማያስደ'ስት ነገር)
resplendent
ሪስፕ'ሌንደንት -ቅ- ያሸበ'ረቀ ፤ ያጌጠ ፤ ያማ ረ'በት (በአ'ለባበስ)
respond
ሪስ'ፖንድ -ግ- መመ'ለስ [መ'ለሰ] (ንግ'ግር ፤ ሐሳብ)
react favourably
-ግ- ሐ'ሳብ ተቀብሎ አንድ ነገር ማድረግ [አደ'ረገ]
response
ሪስ'ፖንስ -ስ- መልስ
responsibility
ሪስፖንስ'ቢሊቲ -ስ- ኀላፊ'ነት ፤ የኀላፊ'ነት ስ'ሜት
level-headedness
-ስ- ታ'ማኝ'ነት
responsible
ሪስ'ፖንሰበል -ቅ- ኀላፊ ፤ ታ'ማኝ ፤ እምነት የ'ሚ'ጣል'በት

rest

’ሬስት -ግ- ማረፍ [ዐ'ረፈ]

instrument

-ስ- ድጋፍ ፣ መደ'ገፊያ

remainder

-ስ- ቀሪ

restaurant

’ሬስትሮንት -ስ- ሆቴል ፣ ሬስቶራንት

restitution

ሬስቲት’ዩ:ሽን -ስ- ካሣ

restore

ሪስ’ቶ: -ግ- መመ'ለስ [መ'ለሰ] (የወ'ሰዱትን ነገር) ፣ መጠ'ገን [ጠ'ገነ]

restrain

ሪስት’ሬይን -ግ- ወደኋላ መግፋት [ገ'ፋ] ፣ ወደኋላ መያዝ [ያ'ዘ] ፣ ማ'ገድ [አ'ገደ] ፣ መግታት [ገ'ታ]

restrict

ሪስት’ሪክት -ግ- መወ'ሰን [ወ'ሰነ] (እንቅስ'ቃሴን)

result

ሪ’ዘልት -ስ- ው'ጤት

resume

ሪዝ’ዩ:ም -ግ- መቀ'ጠል [ቀ'ጠለ] (ሥራ)

resurrection

ሬዘ’ሬክሽን -ስ- ትንሣኤ

retail

’ሪይቴይል -ግ- መቸርቸር [ቸረ'ቸረ]

by-

-ተግ- በችርቻሮ (የተሸጠ)

retailer

’ሪይቴይለ -ስ- ቸርቻሪ

retain

ሪ’ቴይን -ግ- ማቆየት [አቆ'የ] ፣ ማስቀ'ረት [አስቀ'ረ]

retaliate

ሪ’ታሊዩይት -ግ- ክፋትን በክፋት መመ'ለስ [መ'ለሰ] ፣ መ'በቀል [ተበ'ቀለ]

retard

ሪ’ታ:ድ -ግ- ማዘግየት [አዘገ'የ]

retire

ሪ’ታየ -ግ- በእርጅ'ና ምክንያት ሥራን ማቆም [አቆመ]

withdraw

-ግ- ገለ'ል ማለት [አለ] ፣ ለመ'ኝታ መሄድ [ሄደ]

retort

ሪ’ቶ:ት -ግ- በቁ'ጣ መልስ መስጠት [ሰ'ጠ]

container

-ስ- የውሃ ማፍያ ብርጭ'ቆ በላቦራቶሪ ውስጥ

retract

ሪት’ራክት -ግ- ቃል ማንሣት [አነ'ሣ] (የተና'ገሩትን)

retreat

ሪት’ሪይት -ግ- ወደኋላ ማለት [አለ] ፣ ማፈግፈግ [አፈገ'ፈገ]

retribution

ሬትሪብ’ዩ:ሽን -ስ- ቅጣት (የኃጢአት ፣ የጥፋት)

retrieve

ሪት’ሪይቭ -ግ- ማስመ'ለስ [አስመ'ለሰ] (የጠ'ፋ የተሰ'ረቀ ዕቃ) ፣ የሰው ሀብት መመ'ለስ [መ'ለሰ]

retrospect

’ሬትረስፔክት -ስ- ያ'ለፈውን ጊዜ ፣ ያ'ለፉትን ሁኔታዎ'ች ማስታወስ

return

ሪ’ተ:ን -ግ- መመለስ [መ'ለሰ] ፣ መ'መለስ [ተመ'ለሰ]

profit

-ስ- ትርፍ

reunion

ሪ’ዩኒየን -ግ- እንደገና መ'ገናኘት [ተገና'ኘ] (የጓ'ደ'ኞ'ች ፣ የባልንጀሮ'ች)

reveal

ሪ’ቪየል -ግ- መግለጽ [ገ'ለጸ]

revel

’ሬቨል -ግ- መ'ደሰት [ተደ'ሰተ] ፣ መጨ'ፈር [ጨ'ፈረ] ፣ በዐል ማድረግ [አደ'ረገ]

revelation

ሬቨ’ሌይሽን -ስ- ራእይ ፣ የተገ'ለጸ ነገር

revenge

ሪ’ቬንጅ -ግ- መ'በቀል [ተበ'ቀለ]

-ስ- በቀል

revenue
'ሬቨንዩ፡ -ስ- የመንግሥት ያመት ገቢ (ከቀረጥ) ፣ ያገር ውስጥ ገቢ መሥሪያ ቤት

reverberate
ሪ'ቨ፡በሬይት -ግ- ማስተጋባት [አስተጋ'ባ] (ለድምፅ)

revere
ሪ'ቪየ -ግ- ማክበር [አከ'በረ] (በተለ'ይ ለተቀ'ደሱ ነገሮ'ች)

reverence
'ሬቨረንስ -ስ- ክብር (ለተቀ'ደሱ ነገሮ'ች)

reverse
ሪ'ቨ፡ስ -ግ- መገልበጥ [ገለ'በጠ]
a car
-ግ- ወደኋላ መሄድ [ሄደ] (ለመኪና)

revert
ሪ'ቨ፡ት -ግ- ወደ ቀድሞ ሁናቴ መ'መለስ [ተመ'ለሰ]

review
ሪቭ'ዩ፡ -ግ- እንደገና መ'መልከት [ተመለ'ከተ] መከ'ለስ [ከ'ለሰ] (ለትምህርት)
theatrical
-ስ- ል'ዩ ል'ዩ የመ'ደሰቻ ትርኢቶ'ች

revile
ሪ'ቫይል -ግ- አጥብቆ መንቀፍ [ነ'ቀፈ] እም'ሮ መውቀስ [ወ'ቀሰ]

revise
ሪ'ቫይዝ -ግ- እንደገና መ'መልከት [ተመለ'ከተ] ፣ ማጥናት [አጠ'ና]

revive
ሪ'ቫይቭ -ግ- ሕይወት መስጠት [ሰ'ጠ] ፣ ሕይወት ማግ'ኘት [አገ'ኘ] ፣ እንደገና እሥራ ላይ ማዋል [አዋለ]

revoke
ሪ'ቮውክ -ግ- ሕ'ግ መሻር [ሻረ] ፣ የተና'ገሩትን ማንሣት [አነ'ሣ] ፣ የፈ'ቀዱትን እንደገና መከልከል [ከለ'ከለ]

revolt
ሪ'ቮልት -ግ- መሸ'ፈት [ሸ'ፈተ] ፣ ማ'መፅ [ሀ'መፀ]
-ስ- ሽ'ፍታ ፣ ሀመፅ

revolting
ሪ'ቮልቲንግ -ቅ- የ'ሚያስጠ'ላ ፡ የ'ሚያ'ሠ'ቅቅ

revolution
ሬቨ'ሉ፡ሽን -ስ- መዞር ፣ መሽከርከር (እን'ጽ ገ.ዜ)
political
-ስ- ብጥ'ብጥ ፣ ሁከት (የፖለቲካ)

revolutionary
ሬቨ'ሉ፡ሽንሪ -ቅ- መሠረታዊ ለውጥ እንዲሆን የ'ሚደ'ግፍ ፣ የ'ሚያደርግ ፣ ሁከተ'ኛ (የፖለቲካ) ፣ የሰውን የኑሮ ሁናቴ የ'ሚለ'ውጥ

revolve
ሪ'ቮልቭ -ግ- መዞር [ዞረ]

revolver
ሪ'ቮልቨ -ስ- ሽ'ጉጥ (ፍ'ሻሌ)

revulsion
ሪ'ቨልሽን -ስ- መ'ጸየፍ (የመጥላት መንፈስ)

reward
ሪ'ዎ፡ድ -ግ- መሸ'ለም [ሸ'ለመ]
-ስ- ሽ'ልማት

rhapsody
'ራፕሰዲ -ስ- የፍ'ጹም ደ'ስታን ስ'ሜት መግለጽ (በንግ'ግር ፣ በግጥም ፣ በሙዚቃ)

rhetoric
'ሬተሪክ -ስ- በቃላት ያሸበ'ረቀ አ'ነጋገር (ውስጡ ፍሬ ቢስ የሆነ)

rheumatism
'ሩ፡መቲዝም -ስ- ቁርጥማት

rhinoceros
ራይ'ኖሰረስ -ስ- አውራሪስ

rhyme
'ራይም -ስ- ቤት (በግጥም)

rhythm
'ሪዘም -ስ- የዜማ አ'ጣጣል ፣ ስን'ኝ

rib
'ሪብ -ስ- የጎድን አጥንት

ribald
'ሪቦልድ -ቅ- ንግ'ግሩ ብልግ'ና የተም'ላ(ሰው)፣ ፌዘ'ኛ ፣ ያ'ለ'ዘበ (አ'ነጋገር ፣ ሣቅ)

ribbon
'ሪበን -ስ- ቀ'ጭን መቀ'ነት ፣ ጥብጣብ

rice
'ራይስ -ስ- ሩዝ

rich
'ሪች -ቅ- ሀብታም
sweet
-ቅ- ጣፋጭ ፣ ቅባት የበ'ዛ'በት (ምግብ)

rickety
'ሪከቲ -ቅ- የተንቃ'ነቀ ፣ የወላ'ለቀ ፣ የ'ሚ'ሰ'በር (በተለ'ይ ለመ'ጋጠሚያ)

riddle
'ሪደል -ስ- እንቆቅ'ልሽ

ride
'ራይድ -ግ- መጋለብ [ጋ'ለበ]

ridge
'ሪጅ -ስ- ጉ'ብታ (የተራራ ወዘተ)

ridicule
'ሪዲክዩ:ል -ግ- ማ'ቂያቂል [አ'ቂያቂለ]

ridiculous
ሪ'ዲክዩለስ -ቅ- የ'ሚያ'ሥቅ ፣ የሚ'ፌገ'በት

rife
'ራይፍ -ቅ- የተስፋ'ፋ (በ'ሽታ ወዘተ)

riff-raff
'ሪፍ 'ራፍ -ስ- ል'ቃሚ ፣ ዱር'ዬ

rifle
'ራይፉል -ስ- ጠመንጃ (ጠበንጃ)

rift
'ሪፍት -ስ- ሥን'ጥቅ

rig
'ሪግ -ግ- ማጭበርበር [አጭበረ'በረ] (ለምርጫ)
clothes
-ስ- ልብስ

right
'ራይት -ቅ- ል'ክ
direction
-ስ- ቀ'ኝ (አቅጣ'ጫ)
justice
-ስ- መብት
-ግ- ማስተካከል [አስተካ'ከለ]

righteous
'ራይቸስ -ቅ- ጻድቅ

rigid
'ሪጂድ -ቅ- ቀ'ጥ ያለ ፣ በቀ'ላሉ የ'ማይ'ታ'ጠፍ ፣ ደረቅ (ለጠባይ)

rigorous
'ሪገረስ -ቅ- ድካም ያ'ለ'በት ፣ አድካሚ (ለሥራ) ፣ ደረቅ (ለጠባይ)

rim
'ሪም -ስ- ወፈ'ር ያለ ጠርዝ (በተለ'ይ የክ'ብ ነገር)

rind
'ራንድ -ስ- ቅርፊ'ት ፣ ቆዳ ፣ ል'ጣጭ (የፍራፍሬ ወዘተ)

ring
'ሪንግ -ስ- ቀለበት
sound
-ግ- መደ'ወል [ደ'ወለ]
encircle
-ግ- መክበብ [ከ'በበ]

ringleader
'ሪንግሊ:ደ -ስ- የወ'ሮበ'ሎ'ች አለቃ ፣ የሽፍ'ቶ'ች ሹም

ringlet
'ሪንግሌት -ስ- የጠ'ጉር ቋ'ጥራት ፣ ትን'ሽ ቀለበት ወይን'ም ክ'ብ ነገር

rinse
'ሪንስ -ግ- ማለቅለቅ [አለቀ'ለቀ]

riot
'ራየት -ስ- ኃ'ላቅ ብጥ'ብጥ (ሰዎ'ች የ'ሚያ'ነሡት) ፣ ሁካታ ፣ ሁከት

rip
'ሪፕ -ግ- መሸርከት [ሸረ'ከተ]

ripe
'ራይፕ -ቅ- የበ'ሰለ (ለፍራፍሬ) ፣ የደ'ረሰ (ለፍርድ ወዘተ)

ripple
'ሪፐል -ስ- ቀለበት (በውሃ ውስጥ ድንጋይ ሲ'ጣል የ'ሚ'ታ'ይ)

rise
'ራይዝ -ግ- መነሣት [ተነ'ሣ]
growth
-ስ- እድገት
sun-
-ስ- መውጣት (የፀሐይ)
of sun
-ግ- መውጣት [ወ'ጣ] (ለፀሐይ)

risk
'ሪስክ -ግ- ራስን አደጋ ላይ መጣል [ጣለ] (አንድ ነገር ለማዳን)
-ስ- አደጋ ሊያመጣ የ'ሚችል ነገር

rite
'ራይት -ስ- ሥርዓተ ቅ'ዳሴ ፣ ሥርዓተ ማሕሌት

ritual
'ሪቸውል -ስ- ሥርዓተ ቅ'ዳሴ ፣ ሥርዓተ ማሕሌት

rival
'ራይቨል -ስ- ባላንጣ ፣ ተፎካካሪ ፣ ተቀናቃኝ
-ቅ- ባላንጣ ፣ ተፎካካሪ ፣ ተቀናቃኝ

rivalry
'ራይቨልሪ -ስ- ባላንጣ'ነት ፣ ተፎካካሪ'ነት ፣ ተቀናቃኝ'ነት

river
'ሪቨ -ስ- ወንዝ

rivet
'ሪቨት -ስ- ብረት'ና ብረት ማ'ያያዣ ሚስማር (ሊ'ነ'ቀል የ'ማይ'ቻል)

rivulet
'ሪቭዩሌት -ስ- ቀ'ጭን ጅረት

road
'ረውድ -ስ- መንገድ

roam
'ረውም -ግ- መንከራተት [ተንከራ'ተተ]

roar
'ሮ: -ግ- ማግሳት [አገ'ሳ] (ለአንበሳ)

roast
'ረውስት -ግ- መጥበስ [ጠ'በሰ]

rob
'ሮብ -ግ- መዝረፍ [ዘ'ረፈ]

robber
'ሮበ -ስ- ዘራፊ ፣ ወንበዴ (ወምበዴ)

robe
'ረውበ -ስ- መ'ጐናጸፊያ

robust
ረው'በስት -ቅ- ጠንካ'ራ ፣ ወፍራም ፣ ደንዳ'ና፣ ጤና'ማ

rock
'ሮክ -ስ- ቋጥ'ኝ
oscillate
-ግ- መ'ወዛወዝ [ተወዛ'ወዘ] (ወደኋላ'ና ወደፊት)
-a baby
-ግ- እ'ሹሩሩ ማለት [አለ]

rocket
'ሮኬት -ስ- ሮኬት ፣ ተስፈንጣሪ መ'ሣሪያ (በራሱ ኃይል)

rod
'ሮድ -ስ- ረ'ጅም በ'ትር ፣ ሽመል

rogue
'ረውግ -ስ- በጥባጭ ፣ ሁከተ'ኛ ፣ ወ'ሮበ'ላ ፣ ዱር'ዬ ፣ የ'ማይ'ታ'መን ፣ ወንጀለ'ኛ

role
'ሮውል -ስ- በቴአትር አንድ ተዋናይ የ'ሚሠራው ክፍል ፣ በአንድ ሥራ የአንድ ሰው ል'ዩ ተግባር

roll
'ሮውል -ግ- መንከባለል [ተንከባ'ለለ]
-up
-ግ- መጠቅለል [ጠቀ'ለለ]
of bread
-ስ- ት'ንሽ ዳ'ቦ
of paper etc.
-ስ- ጥቅ'ል (የወረቀት ወዘተ)

romance
ረው'ማንስ -ስ- ፍቅር
book
-ስ- ል'ብ ወ'ለድ የፍቅር ታሪክ መጽሐፍ

romantic
ረው'ማንቲክ -ቅ- የፍቅር ስ'ሜት የ'ሚሰጥ

romp
'ሮምፕ -ግ- መ'ሯሯጥ [ተሯሯጠ] (ለጨዋታ)

roof
'ሩ:ፍ -ስ- ጣራ

rook
'ሩክ -ስ- አነ'ስ ያለ የቁራ ዓይነት ወፍ

room
'ሩ:ም -ስ- ክፍል (የቤት)
space
-ስ- ቦታ

roomy
’ሩ:ሚ -ቅ- ሰ'ፊ (ለቦታ)

rooster
’ሩ:ስተ -ስ- አውራ ዶሮ

root
’ሩ:ት -ስ-. ሥር
source
-ስ- ምንጭ ፣ መሠረት

rope
’ረውፕ -ስ- ገመድ

rose
’ረውዝ -ስ- ጽ'ጌረዳ

roster
’ሮስተ -ስ- የስም ዝርዝር (የሥራ ተረ'ኞ'ች)

rostrum
’ሮስትረም -ስ- ተናጋሪ የ'ሚቆም'በት ከ'ፍ ያለ ቦታ

rot
’ሮት -ግ- መበስበስ [በሰ'በሰ] ፡ መሽተት [ሸ'ተተ] (ለሥጋ ወዘተ)

rota
’ረውተ -ስ- የተረ'ኞ'ች መዝገብ ፣ ዝርዝር (የሥራ ፣ በተራ የ'ሚ'ሠ'ራ)

rotation
ረው'ቴይሽን -ስ- መዞር

rotten
’ሮተን -ቅ- የበሰ'በሰ

rotund
ረው'ተንድ -ቅ- የተድበለ'በለ (ለሰው) ፣ ጉል ህ'ና ጥልቅ (ለድምፅ)

rouge
’ሩ:ዥ -ስ- የከንፈር ፣ የጉንጭ ቀ'ይ ቀለም (የሴቶ'ች)

rough
’ረፍ -ቅ- ሻካራ
crude, harsh
-ቅ- ጨ'ካኝ ፣ ርኅራኄ የሌ'ለው
stormy, of weather
-ቅ- መጥፎ አ'የር (ነፋስ)
in unfinished state
-ቅ- ሥራው ንጹሕ ያልሆነ (ዕቃ) ፣ እን ደነገሩ የተሠ'ራ ፣ የተጀራ'ረገ

round
’ራውንድ -ቅ- ክ'ብ

rouse
’ራውዝ -ግ- መቀስቀስ [ቀሰ'ቀሰ] ፡ ማስነ'ሣት [አስነ'ሣ]

rout
’ራውት -ግ- መደምሰስ [ደመ'ሰሰ] ፡ ፈ'ጽሞ ማ'ሸ'ነፍ [አ'ሸነፈ] (ጠላትን)

route
’ሩ:ት -ስ- መንገድ (የመ'ጓገር)

routine
ሩ'ቲይን -ስ- የተለ'መደ ሥራ (ተመላልሶ የ'ሚ'ሠ'ራ)

rove
’ረውቭ -ግ- መዞር [ዞረ] (አገር ላገር)

row
’ረው -ግ- መቅዘፍ [ቀ'ዘፈ]

row
’ራው -ስ- ጥል ፡ ዋካታ ፣ ጫጫታ (በክር'ክር)

rowdy
’ራውዲ -ቅ- የ'ሚያ'ውክ ፣የ'ሚበጠ'ብጥ፡የ'ሚ ጮኽ (ሰው)

royal
’ሮየል -ቅ- ንጉሣዊ

rub
’ረብ -ግ- መፈ'ተግ [ፈ'ተገ] ፡ መፈግፈግ [ፈገ'ፈገ]
-out
-ግ- መፋቅ [ፋቀ] (ጽሑፍ)
-off
-ግ- ማጥፋት [አጠ'ፋ] (ከጥቁር ሰሌዳ)

rubber
’ረበ -ስ- ላስቲክ
eraser
-ስ- ላ'ጲስ

rubbish
’ረቢሽ -ስ- ጉድፍ ፣ ቆሻሻ
nonsense
-ስ- ትርኪ ምርኪ ፣ እንቶ ፈንቶ

rubble
’ረበል -ስ- የተከሰ'ከሰ ድንጋይ ፡ ሽክላ

rubicund
’ሩ:ቢከንድ -ቅ- ደም የመ'ሰለ ቀ'ይ መልክ ያ'ለው

ruby
'ሩ:ቢ -ስ- ሩቢ
in watch
-ስ- ደንጊያ (የሰዓት)

rude
'ሩ:ድ -ቅ- በደምብ ያልተሠ'ራ
impolite
-ቅ- ባለጌ ፤ ነውረ'ኛ

rudimentary
ሩ:ዲ'ሜንትሪ -ቅ- ጥልቅ ያልሆነ ፤ (ሓ'ሳብ፣ ለጥናት ወዘተ)፣ ለጥናት ቀ'ላል ፤ ፍ'ጻሜ ያላገ'ኘ

rue
'ሩ: -ግ- መ'ፀፀት [ተፀ'ፀተ] ፤ ማዘን [አ'ዘነ]

ruffian
'ረፊየን -ስ- ወንበዴ ፤ ወንጀል የመፈ'ጸም ዝን'ባሌ ያ'ለው ሰው

ruffle
'ረፈል -ግ- ማ'ጨማተር [አ'ጨማ'ተረ] (ለል ብስ) ፤ ማ'በላሸት [አ'በላ'ሸ] (ለፀጉር ወዘተ)
annoy
-ግ- ማስቆ'ጣት [አስቆ'ጣ] ፤ ፀ'ጥታ መንሣት [ነ'ሣ]

rug
'ረግ -ስ- ትን'ሽ ምንጣፍ (የወለል) ፤ ትን'ሽ ወፍራም የብርድ ልብስ ለእግር ማሞቂያ የ'ሚ ሆን

rugged
'ረጊድ -ቅ- ኃይለ'ኛ ፤ ብርቱ ፤ ወ'ጣ ገ'ባ ፣ ያልተስተካ'ከለ (ለመሬት) ፤ የተኰማ'ተረ (ለፊት)

ruin
'ሩዊን -ስ- ፍርስራሽ ፣ ፍ'ራሽ

rule
'ሩ:ል -ግ- መግዛት [ገ'ዛ] (አስተዳደር)
law
-ስ- ሕ'ግ ፣ ደምብ
measure
-ስ- ማሥመሪያ
draw lines
-ግ- ማሥመር [አሠ'መረ]

ruler
'ሩ:ለ -ስ- አገረ ገዥ ፣ ንጉሥ
for drawing lines
-ስ- ማሥመሪያ

rum
'ረም -ስ- ሩም (መጠ'ጥ)
strange
-ቅ- እንግዳ ፤ ያልተለ'መደ (ሁኔታ ፤ ነገር)

rumble
'ረምበል -ግ- መንጓጓት [ተንጓ'ጓ] ፣ መንጻ ጻት [ተንጻ'ጻ]

ruminate
'ሩ:ሚኔይት -ግ- ማ'ሰላሰል [አ'ሰላ'ሰለ] ፤ ማመ ስኳት [አመሰ'ኳ]

rumour
'ሩ:መ -ስ- ጭምጭምታ ፤ ወሬ

rump
'ረምፕ -ስ- ቂጥ (የእንስሳ) ፤ የወፍ የጅራት ጫፍ

rumple
'ረምፐል -ግ- ማ'ጨማተር [አ'ጨማ'ተረ] ፤ ማቆ'ሸሸ [አቆ'ሸሸ]

run
'ረን -ግ- መሮጥ [ሮጠ]
operate a machine, business etc.
-ግ- እንዲሠራ ማድረግ [አደ'ረገ] (መኪና ወዘተ) ፤ ማ'ካሄድ [አ'ካሄደ] (የንግድ ሥራ)

rung
'ረንግ -ስ- መ'ወጣጫ (የመሰላል)

runner
'ረነ -ስ- ሯጭ
messenger
-ስ- ተላላኪ

rupture
'ረፕቸ -ግ- መስበር [ሰ'በረ]
strain
-ግ- ሥጋ መ'ቆረጥ [ተቆ'ረጠ] (ሸክም በማንሣት)
breach
-ስ- መ'ቀያየም [ተቀያ'የመ]

rural
'ሩ:ረል -ቅ- ያገር ቤት ፣ የባላገር

ruse
'ሩ:ዝ -ስ- ማ'ታለል ፣ ማጭበርበር

rush

'ረሽ -ግ- መፍጠን [ፈ'ጠነ] ፣ በፍ'ጥነት መሄድ [ሄደ] ፣ መምጣት [መ'ጣ]

rust

'ረስት -ግ- መዛግ [ዛገ]
-ስ- ዝገት

rustic

'ረስቲክ -ቅ- የባላገር ፣ ያገር ቤት

rustle

'ረስል -ግ- መንኰሻኰሽ [ተንኰሻ'ኰሸ]

rut

'ረት -ስ- የመኪና ጎ'ማ የሄደ'በት ምል'ክት ወዘተ)

ruthless

'ሩስለስ -ቅ- ምሕረት የሌ'ለው ፣ ጨ'ካኝ

sabbath

ሳበስ -ስ- ሰንበት ፣ ቅዳሜ (ለአይሁድ) ፣ እሑድ (ለክርስቲያን)

sable

ሴይበል -ቅ- ጥቁር

sabotage

ሳበታ:ዥ -ስ- ዐውቆ ማጥፋት ፣ በእ'ሥራ ላይ እድማ ማድረግ ፣ ያንድ አገር የመ'ከላከያ ድር'ጅት ለማ'ሰናከል ማ'ደም

sabre

'ሰይበ -ስ- ጎራዴ

sack

'ሳክ -ስ- ኬሻ ፣ ጆን'ያ

dismissal

-ስ- ከሥራ ማስወ'ገድ ፣ ማስወ'ጣት

plunder

-ግ- መዝረፍ [ዘ'ረፈ]

sackcloth

'ሳክ ክሎስ -ስ- የማቅ ልብስ

sacrament

'ሳክረመንት -ስ- ምስጢር (የቤተ ክርስቲያን፣ ም'ሳሌ ፣ ቊርባን ፣ ተክሊል ወዘተ)

sacred

'ሴይክረድ -ቅ- የተቀ'ደሰ ፣ ቅ'ዱስ

sacrifice

'ሳክሪፋይስ -ግ- መሠ'ዋት [ሠ'ዋ]
-ስ- መሥዋዕት

sacrilege

'ሳክሪሊጅ -ስ- ማርከስ (ለሃይማኖት)

sad

'ሳድ -ግ- ማዘን [አ'ዘነ]
-ቅ- ያ'ዘነ

saddle

'ሳደል -ስ- ኮር'ቻ

sadism

'ሳዲዝም -ስ- ሰውን በማ'ሠቃየት መ'ደሰ[ት]

safe

'ሴይፍ -ቅ- ምን'ም የ'ማያስፈ'ራ (ለቦታ) አማን የሆነ

money

-ስ- የብረት ሣጥን (ለገንዘብ)

safeguard

'ሴይፍጋ:ድ -ግ- መ'ጠንቀቅ [ተጠነ'ቀቀ] ([ለ]ሰው ፣ ለአንድ ነገር) ፣ ደኅና አድርጎ መጠ'በ[ቅ] [ጠ'በቀ]

safety

'ሴይፍቲ -ስ- ጸ'ጥታ ፣ ደኅን'ነት

safety-pin

'ሴይፍቲፒን -ስ- መርፌ ቁልፍ

sag

'ሳግ -ግ- መንከርፈፍ [ተንከረ'ፈፈ] ፣ መ[...] ገብ [ረ'ገበ] (ለገመድ)

sagacious

ሰ'ጌይሸስ -ቅ- ጥበበ'ኛ ፣ ብልኀተ'ኛ ፣ ብል[...] (ለእንስሳ)

sage

'ሴይጅ -ቅ- ነጣ ያለ አረንጓዴ ፣ ብልኀተ'ኛ ጥበበ'ኛ ፣ ዘዴ'ኛ
-ስ- ብልኀተ'ኛ ሰው

sail
’ሴይል -ስ- ሸራ (የመርከብ)
-ግ- በባሕር መ'ጓዝ [ተጓዘ]

sailor
’ሴይለ -ስ- መርከበ'ኛ

saint
’ሴይንት -ቅ- ጻድቅ ፣ ቅ'ዱስ

sake (for the-of)
’ሴይክ -መዋ- ስለ . . . ፣ ለ . . . ሲል

salad
’ሳለድ -ስ- ሰላጣ

salary
’ሳለሪ -ስ- ደመወዝ

sale
’ሴይል -ግ- መሸጥ [ሸጠ]
-ስ- በቅ'ናሽ የመሸጫ ጊዜ

salesman
’ሴይልዝመን -ስ- የን'ግድ ወ'ኪል ፣ እ'የዞረ እንዲሸጥ የተቀ'ጠረ ሰው

saliva
ሰ’ላይቨ -ስ- ምራቅ

sallow
’ሳለው -ቅ- የደፈ'ረሰ (መልክ)

sally
’ሳሊ -ስ- ድንገተ'ኛ ግጥሚያ (በጠላት የተከ'በቡ ወ'ታ'ደሮ'ች የ'ሚያደርጉት) ፣ ድንገተ'ኛ ፈዝ ያ'ለ'በት መልስ

salmon
’ሳመን -ስ- ሳልሞን (ት'ልቅ ዐሣ ፣ ሥጋው የ'ሚ'በላ)

salon
’ሳሎን -ስ- እ'ዳራሽ ፣ የቁንጅ'ና ቤት

salt
’ሶልት -ስ- ጨው

salutation
ሳልዩ’ቴይሽን -ስ- ሰላምታ

salute
ሰ’ሉ:ት -ግ- ሰላምታ መስጠት [ሰ'ጠ]
-ስ- ሰላምታ

salvage
’ሳልቪጅ -ግ- ማዳን [አዳነ] (ከአደጋ)

salvation
ሳል’ቬይሽን -ስ- ድኅነት

salve
’ሳልቭ -ስ- የቁስል ፣ የተቃ'ጠለ ሰው'ነት ፣ የእበጥ ቅባት

salver
’ሳልቨ -ስ- የብ'ር ትሪ (ደብዳ'ቤ ፣ ካርድ የ'ሚ ቀርብ'በት)

salvo
’ሳልቨው -ስ- የመድፍ ሰላምታ (ለበዐል፣ለታ'ላቅ የመንግሥት እንግዳ ወዘተ የ'ሚ'ተ'ኮስ)

same
’ሴይም -ቅ- ያው ፣ የታ'ወቀው

sample
’ሳ:ምፐል -ስ- ለዓይነት የ'ሚቀርብ ዕቃ ወዘተ

sanctify
’ሳንክቲፋይ -ግ- መቀ'ደስ [ቀ'ደሰ] ፣ መ'ባ ረክ [ባ'ረከ]

sanctimonious
ሳንክቲ’መውኒየስ -ቅ- ጻድቅ መሳይ

sanction
’ሳንክሽን -ግ- ሥልጣን መስጠት [ሰ'ጠ] ፣ ማጽደቅ [አጸ'ደቀ]
political
-ስ- ንግድ ማ'ገድ ፣ ሕ'ግ በመጣስ የ'ሚወድቅ ቅጣት

sanctity
’ሳንክቲቲ -ስ- ቅ'ድስ'ና

sanctuary
’ሳንክቹሪ -ስ- መቅደስ

sand
’ሳንድ -ስ- አሸዋ

sandal
’ሳንደል -ስ- ነጠላ ጫ'ማ

sandwich
’ሳንድዊጅ -ስ- በመካ'ከሉ ሥጋ ፣ እንቁላል ወዘተ ያ'ለበት ሁለ'ት የዳቦ ቁራ'ጭ

sane
’ሴይን -ቅ- አእምሮው ያልተና'ወጠ ፣ የተደ ላ'ደለ አእምሮ ያ'ለው

sanguine
’ሳንግዊን -ቅ- ባለተስፋ ፣ የተማ'መነ ፣ እንደ ደም የቀ'ላ

sanitary
’ሳኒትሪ -ቅ- ጽዳት ያ'ለው

sanity
'ሳኒቲ -ስ- የአእምሮ ጤን'ነት

sap
'ሳፕ -ስ- በእትክልት ግንድ ውስጥ የ'ሚ'ተላ'ለፍ ፈሳሽ (እትክልት የ'ሚ'መ'ገቡትን ምግብ የ'ሚያስተላ'ልፍ)
drain
-ግ- ማድከም [አደ'ከመ]

sapling
'ሳፕሊንግ -ስ- ሊጋ ዛፍ

sarcasm
'ሳ፡ካዝም -ስ- ፌዝ ፤ ልግጫ

sardonic
ሳ፡'ዶኒክ -ቅ- ፌዘ'ኛ ፤ አ'ላጋጭ ፤ አሿፊ

sash
'ሳሽ -ስ- መቀ'ነት

Satan
'ሴይተን -ስ- ሰይጣን

satchel
'ሳቸል -ስ- ት'ን'ሽ የመጸሕፍት መያዣ ፤ የ'ጅ ቦርሳ

satiate
'ሴሺዬይት -ግ- ማጥገብ [አጠ'ገበ] (ለምግብ)

satire
'ሳታየ -ስ- ፌዝ ፤ ቧልት (የማኅበራዊ ኑሮን ሁናቴ የ'ሚ'መለ'ከት)

satisfy
'ሳቲስፋይ -ግ- መጥገብ [ጠ'ገበ] ፤ መስማማት [ተስማ'ማ]

saturate
'ሳቹሬይት -ግ- መርጠብ [ረ'ጠበ] ፤ መበስበስ [በሰ'በሰ] (በውሃ)

Saturday
'ሳተዴይ -ስ- ቅዳሜ

sauce
'ሶ፡ስ -ስ- መረቅ

saucepan
'ሶ፡ስፐን -ስ- እ'ጀታ ያ'ለው ብረት ድስት (ብረ'ድስት)

saucer
'ሶ፡ሰ -ስ- የስኒ ማስቀ'መጫ

saunter
'ሶ፡ንተ -ግ- መንሸራሸር [ተንሸራ'ሸረ] (ለሽ'ርሽ'ር)

sausage
'ሶሲጅ -ስ- ቋሊማ

savage
'ሳቪጅ -ስ- አውሬ
-ቅ- ያልሠለ'ጠነ ፤ ጨ'ካኝ

save
'ሴይቭ -ግ- መቆ'ጠብ [ቆ'ጠበ]
rescue
-ግ- ማዳን [አዳነ]

saviour
'ሴይቭየ -ግ- አዳኝ ፤ መድኃኒት

savour
'ሴይቨ -ግ- ማ'ጣጣም [አ'ጣጣመ] ፤ እ'ያ'ጣጠሙ መብላት [በ'ላ]
-ስ- ጣዕም (በጣም ጥሩ)

saw
'ሶ፡ -ስ- መጋዝ

sawdust
'ሶ፡ደስት -ስ- ሴጋቱራ

say
'ሴይ -ግ- ማለት [አለ]

saying
'ሴይንግ -ስ- ም'ሳሌ

scab
ስ'ካብ -ስ- የቁስል ቅርፊ'ት ፤ ሽንኮፍ

scabbard
ስ'ካበድ -ስ- አፎት ፤ ሰገባ

scaffold
ስ'ካፈውልድ -ስ- የሰው መስቀያ እንጨት ፤ ቤት ሲ'ሠ'ራ መ'ወጣጫ የ'ሚሆን እንጨት

scaffolding
ስ'ካፈውልዲንግ -ስ- ቤት ሲ'ሠ'ራ የ'ሚቆም እንጨት (መ'ወጣጫ'ና መቆሚያ)

scald
ስ'ኮ፡ልድ -ግ- በሞ'ቃት ውሃ መ'ቃጠል [ተቃ'ጠለ] ፤ በውሃ መንፈር [ነ'ፈረ]

scale
ስ'ኬይል -ግ- መውጣት [ወ'ጣ] (ተራራ ወዘተ)
balance
-ስ- ሚዛን
of fish
-ስ- ቅር'ፊት (የዐሣ)

scalp
ስ'ካልፐ -ስ- የራስ ቆዳ

scamper
ስ'ካምፐ -ግ- መ'ፈትለክ [ተፈተ'ለከ]

scan
ስ'ካን -ግ- መ'መልከት [ተመለ'ከተ] ፣ በጥን'ቃቄ መመርመር [መረ'መረ]

scandal
ስ'ካንደል -ስ- የሐሜት ወሬ ፣ አሳ'ፋሪ ድር'ጊ'ት ፣ ስምን የ'ሚያጠፋ ወሬ

scant
ስ'ካንት -ቅ- በጣም ጥቂት ፣ የ'ማይበቃ

scanty
ስ'ካንቲ -ቅ- ሥሥ (ለልብስ) ፣ በቂ ያልሆነ ፣ በጣም ጥቂት ወይን'ም ት'ንሽ

scapegoat
ስ'ኬይፐገውት -ስ- ሌሎ'ች ባጠ'ፉት ጥፋት የ'ሚ'ወ'ቀስ ፣ የ'ሚ'ቀ'ጣ

scar
ስ'ካ: -ስ- ጠባሳ ፣ ኅጻኗ'ሳ

scarce
ስ'ኬየስ -ቅ- በብዛት የ'ማይ'ገ'ኝ

scarcely
ስ'ኬስሊ -ተግ- ምን'ም ያህል

scare
ስ'ኬየ -ግ- ማስፈ'ራት [አስፈ'ራ]

scarecrow
ስ'ኬክረው -ስ- በርሻ ላይ ወፍ ለመ'ከላከል የ'ሚቆም ምስል

scarf
ስ'ካ:ፍ -ስ- ሻል ፣ ያንገት ጥምጥም

scarlet
ስ'ካ:ለት -ቅ- ደማቅ ቀ'ይ ፣ ቅርምዝ

scathing
ስ'ኬይዚንገ -ቅ- መራር (ለንግ'ግር)

scatter
ስ'ካተ -ግ- መበተን [በ'ተነ]

scavenger
ስ'ካቨንጀ -ስ- መንገድ ጠራጊ ፣ ጥምብ አንሣ (አሞራ ፣ ጅብ)

scene
'ሲይን -ስ- የ'ሚ'ታ'ይ ነገር ፣ አንድ ድር'ጊ'ት የተፈ'ጸመ 'በት ቦታ ፣ ትዕይንት ,
embarrassing incident
-ስ- አሳ'ፋሪ ድር'ጊ'ት

scenery
'ሲይነሪ -ስ- የአገር ቤት ትዕ'ይንት
theatrical
-ስ- የቴያትር መድረክ ግድግ'ዳዎ'ች ሥዕል

scent
'ሴንት -ስ- ሽ'ታ

sceptical
ስ'ኬፕቲከል -ቅ- አላማኚ ፣ ተጠራጣሪ (ይበልጡን ለሃይማኖት)

schedule
'ሼጅዩል -ስ- የ'ሚ'ፈ'ጸሙ ጉዳዮ'ች ዝርዝር'ና የሚ'ፈ'ጸም'በት ጊዜ መግለጫ ፣ የሥራ ፕሮግራም

scheme
ስ'ኪይም -ስ- የሥራ ዕቅድ፣ ሥርዓት የያዘ የሥራ ዕ'ቅድ

schism
'ሲዝም -ስ- መ'ከፋፈል ፣ መ'ለያየት (በሐ'ሳብ)

scholar
ስ'ኮለ -ስ- ተማሪ
learned person
-ስ- የተማረ ሰው ፣ ምሁር

scholarship
ስ'ኮለሺፕ -ስ- የመ'ማርያ ገንዘብ (ከድር'ጅት ፣ ከመንግሥት ወዘተ የ'ሚ'ሰ'ጥ)
learning
-ስ- ትምህርት

school
ስ'ኩ:ል -ስ- ትምህርት ቤት ፣ ተማሪ ቤት

schoolmaster
ስ'ኩ:ልማ:ስተ -ስ- አስተማሪ (ተባዕት)

science
'ሳየንስ -ስ- ሥነ ጥበብ ፣ ሳይንስ

scientific
ሳይን'ቲፊክ -ቅ- ሥነ ጥበባዊ ፣ ሳይንሳዊ

scissors
'ሲዘዝ -ስ- መቀስ ፣ መቁረጫት

scoff
ስ'ኮፍ -ግ- ማፌዝ [አፌዘ]
scold
ስ'ከውልድ -ግ- መ'ሳደብ [ተሳ'ደበ] ፣ መዝለፍ [ዘ'ለፈ]
scope
ስ'ከውፕ -ስ- ዐላማ ፣ ሐ'ሳብ (የሥራ)፤ መጠን (የሥራ ፣ ያስተያየት)
scorch
ስ'ኮ:ች -ግ- መለብለብ [ለበ'ለበ] (ለእሳት)
score
ስ'ኮ: -ግ- ግብ ማስገ'ባት [አስገ'ባ] (ለስፖርት)
-ስ- ግብ
twenty
-ቅ- ሃያ
musical
-ስ- የሙዚቃ ድርሰት የተጻፈ'በት መጽሐፍ ፣ የሙዚቃ ድርሰት
scorn
ስ'ኮ:ን -ግ- ማፌዝ [አፌዘ]
scorpion
ስ'ኮ:ፒየን -ስ- ጊንጥ
scoundrel
ስ'ካውንድረል -ስ- ጠማማ ሰው ፣ የ'ማይ'ታ'መን ሰው ፣ ወንጀለ'ኛ
scour
ስ'ካወ -ግ- እያ'ሹ እ'የፈ'ተጉ ማጠብ [አ'ጠበ]
scourge
ስ'ከ:ጅ -ስ- ጉማ'ሬ ፣ አለንጋ
scout
ስ'ካውት -ስ- ቃፊር (የወ'ታ'ደር)
scowl
ስ'ካውል -ግ- ፊት ማጨፍገግ [አ'ጨፈ'ገገ]
scramble
ስክ'ራምበል -ግ- መፍጨርጨር [ተፍጨረ'ጨረ] (ተራራ ለመውጣት) ፤ እንቁላል በቀ'ለጠ ቅባት መ'ቶ መጥበስ [ጠ'በሰ]
scrap
ስክ'ራፕ -ስ- ፍር'ፋሪ ፣ ልቅምቃሚ ነገር ፣ ትርፍራፊ (ለማ'ን'ኛውም ነገር)
scrape
ስክ'ሬይፕ -ግ- መ'ፏጠጥ [ፏ'ጠጠ] ፣ መፋቅ [ፋቀ]

scratch
ስክ'ራች -ግ- ማከክ [አ'ከከ] ፣ መጫር [ጫረ] (በ'ጅ)
-ስ- ጭረት
scrawl
ስክ'ሮ:ል -ግ- መቦጫጨር [ቦጫ'ጨረ] (ለጽሕፈት)
scream
ስክ'ሪይም -ግ- መጮኸ [ጮኸ]
-ስ- ጩኸት
screen
ስክ'ሪይን -ግ- መጋረድ [ጋ'ረደ] ፣ መከ'ለል [ከ'ለለ]
protection
-ስ- መ'ጋረጃ ፣ መከ'ለያ
cinema
-ስ- የሲኒማ መ'ጋረጃ ፣ የሲኒማ ማሳ'ያ የጨርቅ ቅ'ስት
screw
ስክ'ሩ: -ግ- መቦርቦር [ቦረ'ቦረ]
-ስ- ጥርስ ያ'ለው ሚስማር
screwdriver
ስክ'ሩ:ድራይቨ -ስ- ጠመንጃ መፍቻ
scribble
ስክ'ሪበል -ግ- መቦጫጨር [ቦጫ'ጨረ] (ለጽሕፈት)
scripture
ስክ'ሪፕቸ -ስ- መጽሐፍ ቅ'ዱስ ፣ የመጽሐፍ ቅ'ዱስ ጥናት
scroll
ስክ'ሮል -ስ- ጥቅ'ል ጽሑፍ
scrub
ስክ'ረብ -ግ- መፈግፈግ [ፈገ'ፈገ] (ለማጽዳት)
scruple
ስክ'ሩ:ፐል -ስ- ትክ'ክለ'ኛውን ፍርድ ለመስጠት ያለመቻል ጥር'ጣሬ
scrupulous
ስክ'ሩ:ፐዩለስ -ቅ- አንድ ነገር በትክ'ክል ለመሥራት የ'ሚ'ጠን'ቀቅ ፣ ጥንቁቅ
scrutinize
ስክ'ሩ:ቲናይዝ -ግ- አጥብቆ መመርመር [መረ'መረ]
scuffle
ስ'ከፉል -ስ- ት'ን'ሽ እምባጓሮ (ፉ'ላ ያ'ለ'በት)

sculpture
ስ ከልፕቸ -ስ- ምስል (ከደንጊያ ፣ ከእንጨት፣ ከብረት ተፈልፍሎ የተሠ'ራ)

scum
ስ'ከም -ስ- ውሃ ወይ'ም ሌላ ፈሳሽ ሲፈላ ባናቱ ላይ የ'ሚ'ታይ አሰር ፣ አረፋ
worthless people
-ስ- ወ'ራ'ዳ ሰዎ'ች

scurry
ስ'ከሪ -ግ- በፍጥነት መሮጥ [ሮጠ] ፣ ብ'ር ብሎ መሄድ [ሄደ] (በተለ'ይ በአጫ'ጭር እር ም'ጃ)

scuttle
ስ'ከተል -ግ- መርከብ ማስጠም [አሰ'ጠመ] (ዐውቆ ፣ ቀዳዳ በመብሳት)
run away
-ግ- መሸሽ [ሸ'ሸ]

scythe
'ሳይ‍ዟ -ስ- ማጭድ (ት'ልቅ)

sea
'ሲይ -ስ- ባሕር

seal
'ሲይል -ግ- ማ'ተም [አ'ተመ]
-ስ- ማኅተም
stick down
-ግ- ማ'ሸግ [አ'ሸገ]
-ስ- ማ'ሸጊያ ሰም

seam
'ሲይም -ስ- ስፌት (የልብስ)

search
'ሰ፡ች -ግ- መፈ'ለግ [ፈ'ለገ]
by police
መበርበር [በረ'በረ]

seashore
'ሲሾ፡ -ስ- የባሕር ዳር

seaside
'ሲሳይድ -ስ- የባሕር ዳር (ቦታ ፣ ከተማ)

season
'ሲዘን -ስ- ጊዜ ፣ ወቅት ፣ ያመት ክፍል (ለም 'ሳሌ ፣ ክረምት በጋ ወዘተ)

seasonable
'ሲዘነበል -ቅ- ከጊዜው ጋር የተስማ'ማ (አ 'የር) ፤ በፈ'ለጉት ጊዜ የተገ'ኘ (እርዳታ ፣ ምክር ፣ ስጦታ ወዘተ)

seasoning
'ሲዘኒንግ -ስ- ቅመማቅመም

seat
'ሲይት -ስ- ወምበር ፣ መ'ቀመጫ ፤ ቂጥ

secede
ሰ'ሲይድ -ግ- መ'ነጠል [ተነ'ጠለ] (ካገር ፣ ለማኅበር ወዘተ)

secluded
ሴክ'ሉ፡ዲድ -ቅ- የተለ'የ ፣ ል'ዩ (ለቦታ)

second
'ሴከንድ -ስ- ረ'ዳት ፣ መከታ ፣ አ'ጋ'ዥ
in number
-ቅ- ሁለተ'ኛ
of rulers
-ቅ- ዳግማዊ
time unit
-ስ- ሴኮንድ

secondary
'ሴከንደሪ -ቅ- ሁለ'ተ'ኛ ፤ ዋጋ የሌ'ለው (በአስፈ'ላጊ'ነት)

secondhand
ሴከንድ'ሐንድ -ቅ- የተሠ'ራ'በት ፣ አ'ዲስ ያልሆነ

secret
'ሲክረት -ስ- ምስጢር
-ቅ- ምስጢራዊ

secretary
'ሴክረቴሪ -ስ- ጸሓፊ

sect
'ሴክት -ስ- ሀራጥቃ ፣ ያንድ ሃይማኖት ል'ዩ ክፍል

section
'ሴክሽን -ስ- ክፍል

sector
'ሴክተ -ስ- የከተማ ፣ የቦታ ፣ የኤኮኖሚ ወዘተ ክፍል

secular
'ሴክዩለ -ቅ- ዓለማዊ (መንግሥት) ፣ ሥጋዊ (መንፈሳዊ ያልሆነ)

secularism
'ሴክዩለሪዝም -ስ- ሃይማኖትን'ና መንግሥትን የ'ሚለ'ይ የመንግሥት አ'ገዛዝ

secure
ሰክ'ዩወ -ግ- እንዲ'ጠ'በቅ ማድረግ [አደ'ረገ] (ከአደጋ) ፤ ሥራ ማግኘት [አገ'ኘ]
-ቅ- ጸ'ጥ ያለ ፣ የ'ማያ'ሠ'ጋ

security
ሰክ'ዩሪቲ -ስ- ጸ'ጥታ ፣ ሰላም ፣ መ'ረጋጋት
person
-ስ- ዋስ
guarantee
-ስ- መያዣ

sedate
ሰ'ዴይት -ቅ- ረጋ ያለ ፣ ጭ'ምት ፣ ኩስታ'ራ (ለሰው ጠባይ)

sedative
'ሴዶቲቭ -ቅ- የ'ሚያ'ረጋ'ጋ ፣ የ'ሚያደነ'ዝዝ (መድኃኒት)

sediment
'ሴዲመንት -ስ- ዝ'ቃጭ ፣ አተላ

sedition
ሰ'ዲሽን -ስ- ብጥ'ብጥ ም'ነሣሣ ንግ'ግር ፣ ተግባር (በመንግሥት ላይ)

seduce
ሰድ'ዩ፡ስ -ግ- መ'ጻራት [ተጻ'ራ] ፣ ከቶ ሥራ ለመፈ'ጸም ማባበል [አባ'በለ]

see
'ሲይ -ግ- ማየት [አ'የ] ፤ መ'ረዳት [ተረ'ዳ]

seed
'ሲይድ -ስ- ዘር (የተክል)

seedling
'ሲይድሊንግ -ስ- ችግ'ኝ

seedy
'ሲይዲ -ቅ- ጎስቋ'ላ ፤ ፍሬያ'ማ

seek
'ሲይክ -ግ- መፈለግ [ፈ'ለገ] ፣ መሻት [ሻ]

seem
'ሲይም -ግ- መምሰል [መ'ሰለ]

seemly
'ሲይምሊ -ቅ- \ጥሩ አመል ፣ የተስማ'ማ (ለጊዜው)

seer
'ሲየ፡ -ስ- ወደፊት የ'ሚሆነውን በውቃ'ለሁ የ'ሚል ነቢ'ይ

seethe
'ሲይዝ -ግ- መ'ናደድ [ተና'ደደ] ፤ በጣም መፍላት [ፈ'ላ] ,

segment
'ሴግመንት -ስ- ቁ'ራጭ ፣ ብ'ጣሽ ፣ ክፍል (ካንድ ነገር የተከ'ፈለ)

segregate
'ሴግሪጌይት -ግ- መለ'የት [ለ'የ] ፣ ከሌላው ለ'ይቶ ማስቀ'መጥ [አስቀ'መጠ]

seize
'ሲይዝ -ግ- መያዝ [ያዘ] ፤ ለቀ'ም ማድረግ [አደ'ረገ]

seldom
'ሴልደም -ተግ- አንዳንድ ጊዜ ፣ አልፎ አልፎ

select
ሲ'ሌክት -ግ- መምረጥ [መ'ረጠ]

self
'ሴልፍ -ጸተስ- ራስ
my-
-ጸተስ- ራሴ

self-centred
ሴልፍ'ሴንተድ -ቅ- ራሱን ብ'ቻ ወ'ዳድ

self-conscious
ሴልፍ'ኮንሸስ -ቅ- ይሉኝተ'ኛ ፣ ዓይነ አ'ፋር

selfish
'ሴልፊሽ -ቅ- ራስን ወ'ዳድ

sell
'ሴል -ግ- መሸጥ [ሸጠ]

semester
ሲ'ሜስተ -ስ- የትምህርት ክፍለ ዓመት (ለሁለ'ት የተከ'ፈለ)

semicolon
ሴሚ'ከውለን -ስ- ድር'ብ ሠረዝ (;)

semitic
ሲ'ሚቲክ -ቅ- ሴማዊ

senate
'ሴነት -ስ- የሕ'ግ መወ'ሰኛ ምክር ቤት

send
'ሴንድ -ግ- መላክ [ላከ]

senile
'ሲይናይል -ቅ- የጃ'ጀ ፣ የገረ'ጀፈ

senior
'ሲይንየ -ቅ- የ'ሚበልጥ ፣ ሹም ፣ በዕድሜ የ'ሚበልጥ

sensation
ሴን'ሲይሽን -ስ- ግሩም ፡ ድንቅ ነገር
feeling
-ስ- የስ'ሜት ችሎታ (ለስላሳ'ነት ፡ መደብዘዝ ወዘተ)

sense
'ሴንስ -ግ- መ'ሰማት [ተሰ'ማ] (መስማት ፡ ማሽተት ፡ ጣዕም ፡ ስ'ሜት ፡ ማየት)
common-
-ስ- ዕውቀት (ልማዳዊ)
physical, touch e.g.
-ስ- ስ'ሜት ፡ ሕዋስ

sensible
'ሴንሲበል -ቅ- ዐዋቂ ፡ የ'ሚ'ቀ'በሉት ፡ የ'ሚ'ረ'ዱት ፡ እስተዋይ

sensitive
'ሴንሰቲቭ -ቅ- ስ'ሜት ያ'ለው
irritable
-ቅ- በቀ'ላሉ ተናዳጅ ፡ የ'ሚ'ቆ'ጣ
painful
-ቅ- የ'ሚያ'ም

sensual
'ሴንስዩወል -ቅ- ዓለማዊ ፡ ለምግብ ፡ ለመጠ'ጥ'ና ለፈቃደ ሥጋው የ'ሚኖር ፡ ፍትወተ'ኛ

sentence
'ሴንተንስ ·ስ- ዐረፍተ ነገር
legal
-ግ- መፍረድ [ፈ'ረደ] (ለመቅጣት)
judgement
-ስ- ፍርድ

sentiment
'ሴንቲመንት -ስ- ስ'ሜት

sentimental
ሴንቲ'ሜንተል -ቅ- አዛኝ ፡ ርኅሩኅ ፡ ስ'ሜቱ የ'ሚማ'ርከው

sentinel
'ሴንቲነል -ስ- ዘብ ፡ ተረ'ኛ ወ'ታ'ደር (የ'ሚጠ'ብቅ)

sentry
'ሴንትሪ -ስ- ዘብ ፡ ተረ'ኛ ወ'ታ'ደር (የ'ሚጠ'ብቅ)

separate
'ሴፐሬይት -ግ- , መለ'የት [ለ'የ]

separate
'ሴፐረት -ቅ- የተለ'የ ፡ ል'ዩ ፡ ሌላ

September
ሴፐ'ቴምበ -ስ- መስከረም

septic
'ሴፕቲክ -ቅ- የተመ'ረዘ ፡ መግል የ'ቋ'ጠረ (ለቁስል)

sepulchre
'ሴፑልከ -ስ- መቃብር

sequel
'ሲይክወል -ቅ- የ'ሚ'ከ'ተል ፡ ተከ'ታይ (ታሪክ ፡ ወሬ)

sequence
'ሲይክወንስ -ስ- ተከታታይ'ነት

serenade
ሴረ'ኔይድ -ስ- በም'ሽት በገላጣ ቦታ የ'ሚ'ዘ'ፈን ዘፈን ወይን'ም የ'ሚ'ጫ'ወቱት ሙዚቃ (በተለ'ይ የፍቅር)

serene
ሰ'ሪይን -ቅ- ሰላማዊ ፡ ፍ'ጹም ፀ'ጥታ ያ'ለ'በት ፡ የረ'ጋ (ሀውከት የሌ'ለ'በት)

sergeant
'ሳ:ጀንት -ስ- ያምሳ አለቃ

serial
'ሲሪየል -ስ- ተከታታይ (ታሪክ ፡ ቁጥር ወዘተ)

series
'ሲሪዝ -ስ- ተመሳሳይ'ና ተከታታይ ነገር

serious
'ሲሪየስ -ቅ- ቁም ነገረ'ኛ ፡ ቁም ነገራም ፡ ኮስታ'ራ
grave
-ቅ- ከ'ባድ

sermon
'ሰ:መን -ስ- ስብከት

serpent
'ሰ:ፐንት -ስ- እባብ

servant
'ሰ:ቨንት -ስ- አገልጋይ ፡ ሎሌ ፡ አሽከር

serve
'ሰ:ቭ -ግ- ማገልገል [አገለ'ገለ]

service
'ሰ:ቪስ -ስ- አገልግሎት

servile
'ሰ:ቫይል -ቅ- ተለማማጭ

ervitude
'ሰ:ቪትዩ:ድ -ስ- ባር'ነት
session
'ሴሽን -ስ- ጉባኤ ፣ ስብሰባ ፣ ችሎት
set
'ሴት -ግ- ሥራ መደልደል [ደለ'ደለ]
solidify
-down
-ግ- ማስቀ'መጥ [አስቀ'መጠ]
-ግ- መርጋት [ረ'ጋ] (ዕቃ)
-aside
-ግ- ማቆ'የት [አቆ'የ]
-on fire
-ግ- ማ'ቃጠል [አ'ቃ'ጠለ] ፣ መለ'ኮስ [ለ'ኮሰ] ፣ ማ'ያያዝ [አ'ያያዘ] (ለእሳት)
-free
-ግ- ነጻ ማውጣት [አወ'ጣ]
-ስ- ዓይነታቸው አንድ የሆኑ ዕቃዎ'ች፣አንዱ የሌላው ክፍል የሆኑ ዕቃዎ'ች
setback
'ሴትባክ -ስ- እንቅፋት
setting
'ሴቲንግ -ስ- አ'ካባቢ (ለቦታ) ፤ አንድ ነገር የ'ሚ'ገ'ጠም'በት ቦታ (ጌጣጌጥ)
settle
'ሴተል -ግ- መ'ቀመጥ [ተቀ'መጠ] ፣ ማረፍ [ዐ'ረፈ] ፣ ዕዳ መክፈል [ከ'ፈለ]
colonize
-ግ- መ'ሠራት [ተሠ'ራ] (ባገር ላይ)
settlement
'ሴተልመንት -ስ- ሠፈር ፣ መሥፈሪያ (ቦታ)
seven
'ሴቨን -ቅ- ሰባ'ት
seventeen
ሴቨን'ቲይን -ቅ- ዐሥራ ሰባ'ት
seventh
'ሴቨንስ -ቅ- ሰባ'ተ'ኛ
seventieth
'ሴቨንቲየስ -ስ- ሰባ'ኛ
seventy
'ሴቨንቲ -ቅ- ሰባ
sever
'ሴቨ -ግ- መቁረጥ [ቈ'ረጠ] (ገመድ ለሁለ'ት)፤ ማ'ቋረጥ [አ'ቋ'ረጠ] (ወዳጅ'ነት)

several
'ሴቨረል -ቅ- ብዙ ፣ አ'ያሌ
severe
ሰ'ቪየ -ቅ- ከ'ባድ (ለነገር)
sew
'ሰው -ግ- መስፋት [ሰ'ፋ] (ልብስ)
sewage
'ሱዊጅ -ስ- ሠገራ ፣ እበር ፣ ዓይነ ምድር (በ'ቧምቧ ውስጥ የ'ሚ'ፈ'ስ)
sewer
'ሱወ -ስ- የሠገራ ቧምቧ (ከምድር በታ'ች)
sex
'ሴክስ -ስ- ግብረ ሥጋ
gender
-ስ- ጾታ
sexual
'ሴክስዩወል -ቅ- ፈቃደ ሥጋዊ ፣ ከፈቃደ ሥጋ ጋር ግን'ኙ'ነት ያ'ለው
shabby
'ሻቢ -ቅ- አሮጌ (ልብስ) ፣ ብት'ቶ
shackle
'ሻክል -ስ- እግር ብረት
shade
'ሼይድ -ስ- ጥላ
-ግ- ማጥላት [አጠ'ላ] ፣ መከ'ለል [ከ'ለለ] ፣ መጋረድ [ጋ'ረደ]
shadow
'ሻደው -ስ- ጥላ (የሰው ፣ ያንድ ነገር)
shady
'ሼይዲ -ቅ- ጥላ'ማ
of reputation
-ቅ- የ'ማይ'ታመን ፣ መጥፎ ስም ያ'ለው
shaft
'ሻ:ፍት -ስ- ቀ'ጭን ረ'ጅም ብረት ፤ እንዳ ፤ የመጥረቢያ ረ'ጅም እ'ጀታ ፤ የጋሪ መጎ'ተቻ ጋድሚያ እንጨት (ከሁለ'ት አንዱ)
shaggy
'ሻጊ -ቅ- ጠጉረ ከርዳ'ዳ ፤ ረ'ጅም'ና ያልተ በ'ጠረ ጠጉር ያ'ለው
shake
'ሼይክ -ግ- መወዝወዝ [ወዘ'ወዘ]
tremble
-ግ- መንቀጥቀጥ [ተንቀጠ'ቀጠ]

shall
'ሻል -ግ- (ትንቢት መግለጫ ረ'ዳት ግሥ)
shallow
'ሻለው -ቅ- ጥልቀት የሌ'ለው (ለውሃ) ፤ ጥራ ዝ ነ'ጠቅ
sham
'ሻም -ቅ- አ'ታላይ ፣ እውነት'ነት የሌ'ለው
shamble
'ሻምበል -ግ- መ'ወዛወዝ [ተወዛ'ወዘ] ፣ እየተ ጉ'ተቱ መሄድ [ሄደ] (ለሰው)
shambles
'ሻምበልዝ -ስ- ሥርዓት'ና ወግ የሌ'ለው ቦታ ወይን'ም ሁናቴ ፤ የደም መፍሰሻ ቦታ ፣ ብዙ ሰዎ'ች የ'ሚ'ገ'ደሉ'በት ቦታ ፤ ቄራ
shame
'ሼይም -ስ- ሐፍረት
shape
'ሼይፕ -ግ- ቅርፅ መስጠት [ሰ'ጠ] ፣ መቅረፅ [ቀ'ረፀ]
-ስ- ቅርፅ
share
'ሼየ -ግ- ማ'ካፈል [አ'ካ'ፈለ]
portion
-ስ- ድርሻ ፣ ክፍ'ያ ፣ እጣ
of plough
-ስ- ስለት (የማረሻ)
shareholder
'ሼሆልደ -ስ- ባለእጣ (ባለአክሲዮን)
sharp
'ሻ፡ፕ -ቅ- ስለታም
sharpen
'ሻፐን -ግ- መቅረፅ [ቀረፀ] ፣ መሳል [ሳለ] (ስለት)
shatter
'ሻተ -ግ- መሰባበር [ሰባ'በረ]
shave
'ሼይቭ -ግ- መላጨት [ላ'ጨ] (ጢምን)
shawl
'ሾ፡ል -ስ- ሸ'ማ
she
'ሺይ -ተስ- እርሷ ፣ እ'ሷ
sheaf
'ሺይፍ -ስ- ነዶ
shear
'ሺየ -ግ- መሸ'ለት [ሸ'ለተ]
sheath
'ሺይስ -ስ- አፎት ፣ ሰገባ
shed
'ሼድ -ግ- መጣል [ጣለ] ፣ ማፍሰስ [አፈ'ሰሰ] (ውሃ ፣ ደም ወዘተ)
sheen
'ሺይን -ስ- ብሩህ'ነት
sheep
'ሺይፕ -ስ- በግ
sheer
'ሺየ -ቅ- ፍ'ጹም ፤ ገደላ'ማ ፣ ዥ'ው ያለ (ገደል)
-ግ- አቅጣ'ጫን መለ'ወጥ [ለ'ወጠ] (ለመርከብ)
sheet
'ሺይት -ስ- ያልጋ ምንጣፍ (አንሶላ) ፤ ሉህ (ወረቀት)
shelf
'ሼልፍ -ስ- ዕቃ መደርደሪያ ፣ ጨንጎት
shell
'ሼል -ግ- መፈልፈል [ፈለ'ፈለ] (እተር ወዘተ)
casing
-ስ- ቀለህ
hard cover
-ስ- ቅርፌ'ት (የዕንቁላል ፣ የለውዝ ወዘተ) ፤ ዛጎል
of cannon
-ስ- የመድፍ ጥ'ይት
shelter
'ሼልተ -ግ- መ'ጠጋት [ተጠ'ጋ] (ራስን ከአ ደጋ ለማዳን) ፣ መ'ጠለል [ተጠ'ለለ]
protection
-ስ- መ'ጠጊያ (ከአደጋ) ፣ መ'ጠለያ (ከዝናም)
cover
-ስ- የዘበ'ኛ ቤት
shelve
'ሼልቭ -ግ- ማዘግየት [አዘገ'የ] (ለጉ'ዳይ) ፤ እመደርደሪያ ውስጥ ማስቀ'መጥ [አስቀ'መጠ]
shepherd
'ሼፐድ -ስ- እ'ረ'ኛ ፣ በግ ጠ'ባቂ

shield
ʼሺይልድ -ግ- መከታ መሆን [ሆነ]
-ስ- ጋ'ሻ (መ'ከላከያ)

shift
ʼሺፍት -ግ- ወደ ጐ'ን ማድረግ [አደ'ረገ] ፣ ካንድ ቦታ ወደ ሌላው መውሰድ [ወ'ሰደ]

shin
ʼሺን -ስ- መሀል አገዳ

shine
ʼሻይን -ግ- ማብራት [አበ'ራ]

ship
ʼሺፐ -ስ- መርከብ

ship
ʼሺፐ -ግ- መጫን (ካንድ አገር ወደ ሌላው ለመውሰድ)

shirk
ʼሸ፡ክ -ግ- ሥራ በ'ሚ'ገ'ባ አለመሥራት [-ሠ'ራ] ፣ ማልኰስኰስ [አልኰሰ'ኰሰ] ፣ ተግባር አለመፈ'ጸም [-ፈ'ጸመ] ፣ መስነፍ ፣ [ሰ'ነፈ]

shirt
ʼሸ፡ት -ስ- ሸሚዝ

shiver
ʼሺቨ -ግ- መንቀጥቀጥ [ተንቀጠ'ቀጠ]

shock
ʼሾክ -ስ- ድን'ጋጤ ፣ ንዝረት

shoe
ʼሹ፡ -ስ- ጫ'ማ

shoemaker
ʼሹ፡ሜይከ -ስ- ጫ'ማ ሰፊ

shoot
ʼሹ፡ት -ግ- መተ'ኰስ [ተ'ኰሰ] (ጦር መ'ሣሪያ)፣ ኳስ ወደ ግብ አስተካክሎ መምታት [መ'ታ]

shop
ʼሾፐ -ስ- ሱቅ

shopkeeper
ʼሾፐኪይፐ -ስ- ባለሱቅ

shore
ʼሾ፡ -ስ- የባሕር ዳር

short
ʼሾ፡ት -ቅ- አ'ጭር

shorten
ʼሾ፡ተን -ግ- ማሳ'ጠር [አሳ'ጠረ]

shortly
ʼሾ፡ትሊ -ተግ- ከጥቂት ጊዜ በኋላ

shot
ʼሾት -ስ- ተኩስ ፣ አ'ተኳኰስ

shoulder
ʼሸውልደ -ስ- ትከ'ሻ

shout
ʼሻውት -ግ- መጮኸ [ጮኸ]
-ስ- ጩኸት

shovel
ʼሸቨል -ስ- አካፋ
-ግ- በአካፋ መዛቅ [ዛቀ]

show
ʼሸው -ግ- ማሳ'የት [አሳ'የ]
appearance
-ስ- ለይምሰል
theatrical
-ስ- ትርኢት (የቴያትር)

shower
ʼሻወ -ስ- መ'ጠመቂያ (ለመ'ታጠብ)
of rain
-ስ- ካ'ፍያ

shred
ሽ'ሬድ -ግ- መተልተል [ተለ'ተለ]
-ስ- የተተለ'ተለ ነገር

shrew
ሽ'ሩ፡ -ስ- ፍልፈል አፈር ፣ ጨቅጫ'ቃ ሴ

shrewd
ሽ'ሩ፡ውድ -ቅ- ሙ'ሌ ፣ ብልጥ ፣ ተንኰለ'

shriek
ሽ'ሪይክ -ግ- መጮኸ [ጮኸ] ፣ መንጐር ጐረ]

shrill
ሽ'ሪል -ስ- ቀ'ጭን ከ'ፍ ያለ ድምፅ ፣ መ ረር

shrine
ሽ'ራይን -ስ- የተቀ'ደሰ ቦታ ፣ መ'ሳለ ቦታ

shrink
ሽ'ሪንክ -ግ- መ'ኰማተር [ተኰማ'ተረ]

shrivel
ሽ'ሪቨል -ግ- መ'ጨማደድ [ተጨማ'ደደ]

shroud
ሽ'ራውድ -ስ- ከፈን ፣ መከ'ፈኛ ጨርቅ

shrub
ሽ'ረብ -ግ- ቁጥቋጦ (ት'ንሽ)

shrug
ሽ'ረግ -ግ- ትከ'ሻ መነቀነቅ [ነቀ'ነቀ] (ግ'ድ የ'ለ'ኝም ለማለት)

shudder
'ሸደ -ግ- በድንገት መንዘፍዘፍ [ተንዘፈ'ዘፈ] ፣ መንቀጥቀጥ [ተንቀጠ'ቀጠ]

shuffle
'ሸፈል -ግ- መ'ጐተት [ተጐ'ተተ] (ሲሄዱ) ፣ ካርታ መበ'ወዝ [በ'ወዘ]

shun
'ሸን -ግ- መራቅ [ራቀ] (ከነገር)

shut
'ሸት -ግ- መዝጋት [ዘ'ጋ]
-up
-ግ- ዝምበል ፣ አፍክን ዝጋ

shutter
'ሸተ -ስ- ተጠቅላይ'ና ተዘርጊ የመስኮት መዝጊያ (ከእንጨት ፣ ከብረት የተሠ'ራ)

shy
'ሻይ -ቅ- ዓይነ አ'ፋር

sick
'ሲክ -ቅ- ሕሙም ፣ ሕመምተ'ኛ

sickle
'ሲክል -ስ- ማጭድ

sickness
'ሲክነስ -ስ- ሕመም

side
'ሳይድ -ስ- ጎ'ን (የሰው'ነት ክፍል)
direction
-ስ- ጎ'ን (አቅጣ'ጫ)

sideways
'ሳይድዌይዝ -ተግ- እግድም ፣ ወደ ጎ'ን

seige
'ሲይጅ -ስ- የመውረሪያ ጊዜ (በጦር'ነት ከተማ ፣ ም'ሽግ)

seive
'ሲቭ -ስ- ወንፊት

sift
'ሲፍት -ግ- መንፋት [ነ'ፋ] (በወንፊት)

sigh
'ሳይ -ግ- እህ ማለት [አለ] (ከድካም ፣ ከሐዘን ፣ ከመንሰፍሰፍ የተነ'ሣ)

sight
'ሳይት -ግ- ማየት [አ'የ] (ተ'ረብ በማለት)
-ስ- ማየት ፣ የማየት ችሎታ
spectacle
-ስ- ትርኢት

sign
'ሳይን -ግ- መፈ'ረም [ፈ'ረመ]
-ስ- ምል'ክት

signal
'ሲግነል -ስ- ምል'ክት (የትራፊክ ወዘተ)

signify
'ሲግኒፋይ -ግ- ማለት [አለ] (ለቃል) ፣ ማመልከት [አመለ'ከተ] (ለቃል)

signature
'ሲግነቸ -ስ- ፊርማ

signboard
'ሳይንቦ:ድ -ስ- የሱቅ ፣ የሆቴል ፣ ወዘተ ስም ተጽፎ የ'ሚ'ታ'ይ'በት ሰሌዳ

significant
ሲግ'ኒፊከንት -ቅ- አስፈ'ላጊ ፣ ዐቢ'ይ ፣ በጣም አስፈ'ላጊ'ነትን የ'ሚያመለ'ክት

silence
'ሳይለንስ -ስ- ጸ'ጥታ ፣ ዝ'ምታ

silent
'ሳይለንት -ቅ- ጸ'ጥ ያለ

silk
'ሲልክ -ስ- ሐ'ር

silly
'ሲሊ -ቅ- ቂል ፣ ሞ'ኝ ፣ ጅል

silver
'ሲልቨ -ስ- ብ'ር (ማዕ'ድን)

similar
'ሲሚለ -ቅ- ተመሳሳይ ፣ የ'ሚመስል

simmer
'ሲመ -ግ- መንተክተክ [ተንተከ'ተከ] (ወጥ ወዘተ) ፣ በን'ዴት መትከን [ተ'ከነ]

simple
'ሲምፐል -ቅ- ቀ'ላል ፣ የ'ማያስቸ'ግር

simplicity
ሲምፐ'ሊሲቲ -ስ- ቀ'ላል'ነት (አለማስቸ'ገር)

simulate
'ሲምዩሌይት -ግ- መቅዳት [ቀ'ዳ] (ሌላው የ'ሚያደርገውን) ፣ ማስመ'ሰል [አስመ'ሰለ] (ያልሆነውን)

simultaneously
ሲሙል'ቴይኒየስሊ -ተግ- ባንድ ጊዜ (የሆነ ፣ የተደ'ረገ)

sin
'ሲን -ግ- ኃጢአት መሥራት [ሠ'ራ]

since
'ሲንስ -ተግ- ከ . . . ጀምሮ

sincere
ሲን'ሲየ -ቅ- ታ'ማኝ ፣ እውነተ'ኛ ፣ ል'ባዊ

sinew
'ሲንዩ -ስ- ጅ'ማት (የሰው'ነት)

sing
'ሲንግ -ግ- መዝፈን [ዘ'ፈነ] ፣ መዘ'መር [ዘ'መረ]

singe
'ሲንጅ -ግ- መ'ለብለብ [ተለበ'ለበ] (የጠጉር ጫፍ ወዘተ)

single
'ሲንገል -ቅ- ነጠላ ፣ ብ'ቻ
unmarried
-ቅ- ያላገ'ባ

singular
'ሲንግዩለ -ቅ- ነጠላ (እጥፍ ያልሆነ)
unusual
-ቅ- እንግዳ ፣ ያልተለ'መደ

sinister
'ሲኒስተ -ቅ- አደገ'ኛ ፣ እኩይ ፣ በ'ጎ ፈቃድ የ'ማያሳ'ይ

sink
'ሲንክ -ግ- መስጠም [ሰ'ጠመ]
-ስ- ሰሐን (መ'ታጠቢያ)

sip
'ሲፕ -ግ- ፉ'ት ማለት [አለ]

sir
'ሰ: -ስ- ጌታዬ

sirloin
'ሰ:ሎይን -ስ- ጭ'ቅ'ና

sister
'ሲስተ -ስ- እኅት

sister-in-law
'ሲስተሪንሎ: -ስ- የወንድ'ም ሚስት

sistrum
'ሲስትረም -ስ- ጸናጽል

sit
'ሲት -ግ- መ'ቀመጥ [ተቀ'መጠ]

site
'ሳይት -ስ- ቦታ (አንድ ነገር የተፈ'ጸመ'በት ፣ የ'ሚ'ፈ'ጸም'በት)

situated
'ሲትዩዌይተድ -ቅ- የ'ሚ'ገ'ኘው ፣ ያ'ለ'በት (ቦታ)

situation
ሲትዩ'ዌይሽን -ስ- ሁናቴ ፣ ሁኔታ

six
'ሲክስ -ቅ- ስ'ድስት

sixteen
ሲክስ'ቲይን -ቅ- ዐሥራ ስ'ድስት

sixteenth
ሲክስ'ቲይንስ -ቅ- ዐሥራ ስ'ድስተ'ኛ

sixth
'ሲክስ -ቅ- ስ'ድስተ'ኛ

sixty
'ሲክስቲ -ቅ- ስድሳ (ስልሳ)

size
'ሳይዝ -ስ- መጠን ፣ ል'ክ

sizzle
'ሲዘል -ግ- ችስ ማለት [አለ] (ውሃ በእሳት ላይ ሲፈ'ስ)

skate
ስ'ኬይት -ግ- በበረዶ ላይ መንሸራተት [ተንሸራ'ተተ] (ለመ'ጫወት)

skein
ስ'ኬይን -ስ- ል'ቃቂት (የጥጥ ፣ የሱፍ ወዘተ)

skeleton
ስ'ኬሌተን -ስ- ዐፅም (ሳይ'ለያ'ይ)

sketch
ስ'ኬች -ግ- መንደፍ [ነ'ደፈ] (ሥዕል)
-ስ- ንድፍ ፣ ሥዕል

skewer
ስክ'ዩወ -ስ- ሥጋ እየተሰ'ካ የ'ሚ'ጠ'በስ'በት ቀ'ጭን ረ'ጅም ሹል ብረት

skid
ስ'ኪድ -ግ- መንሸራተት [ተንሸራ'ተተ] ፣ ማዳለጥ [አዳ'ለጠ]

skill
ስ'ኪል -ስ- ከ'ፍተ'ኛ ችሎታ ፣ ብልኀት ፣ ጥበብ (አንድ ነገር የመሥራት)

skilful
ስ'ኪልፉል -ቅ- ብልኀተ'ኛ ፣ ጥበበ'ኛ

skim
'ስኪም -ግ- መግፈፍ [ገ'ፈፈ] (ለስልባቦት)

skimp
ስ'ኪምፕ -ግ- የ'ማይበቃውን እሥራ ላይ ማዋል [እዋለ] ፣ የ'ሚበቃ አለመስጠት [-ሰ'ጠ]

skin
ስ'ኪን -ስ- ቆዳ

skinny
ስ'ኪኒ -ቅ- በጣም ከ'ሲ'ታ ፣ ቆዳው ከአጥንቱ ጋር የተጣ'በቀ

skip
ስ'ኪፕ -ግ- እንጣ'ጥ እንጣ'ጥ ማለት [አለ] ፤ ች'ላ ማለት [አለ] ፤ ማለፍ [አ'ለፈ]

skirmish
ስ'ከ፡ሚሽ -ስ- ግ'ጭት (ቀ'ላል ፣ በወ'ታ'ደር መካ'ከል)

skirt
ስ'ከ፡ት -ስ- ሽ'ርጥ

skulk
ስ'ከልክ -ግ- ማድባት [አደ'ባ] ፤ ቀ'ስ ብሎ ማምለጥ [አመ'ለጠ] (ከሥራ ላይ)

skull
'ስከል -ስ- ጭንቅ'ላት ፣ የራስ ቅል

sky
ስ'ካይ -ስ- ሰማይ

slack
ስ'ላክ -ቅ- ልል ፣ ቸ'ልተ'ኛ ፣ ሰነፍ

slam
ስ'ላም -ግ- በ'ር በኀይል መዝጋት [ዘ'ጋ] ፣ መደርገም [ደረ'ገመ]

slander
ስ'ላ፡ንደ -ግ- ማማት [አ'ማ] ፣ ስም ማጥፋት [አጠ'ፋ]
-ስ- ሐሜት ፣ ስም ማጥፋት

slang
ስ'ላንግ -ስ- ተራ ቋንቋ (ለጽሑፍ የ'ማይበ'ጅ)

slant
ስ'ላ፡ንት -ግ- መ'ዘቅዘቅ [ተዘቀ'ዘቀ] (ለመንገድ ፣ ወዘተ)

slap
ስ'ላፕ -ግ- በጥ'ፊ መምታት [መ'ታ]

slash
ስ'ላሽ -ግ- መቦ'ደስ [ቦ'ደሰ] ፣ መብጣት [በ'ጣ] (በተለይ በምላ'ጭ) ፤ መግረፍ [ገ'ረፈ] (በአለንጋ)

slat
ስ'ላት -ስ- ቀ'ጭን እንጨት ፣ ብረት

slate
ስ'ሌይት -ስ- ጽ'ላት (ለመጻፊያ)

slaughter
ስ'ሎ፡ተ -ግ- ማረድ [አ'ረደ]፣ መባረክ [ባ'ረከ]

slaughterhouse
ስ'ሎ፡ተሀውስ -ስ- ቄራ

slave
ስ'ሌይቭ -ስ- ባሪያ

slavery
ስ'ሌይቨሪ -ስ- ባር'ነት

slay
ስ'ሌይ -ግ- ማረድ [አ'ረደ] ፣ መግደል [ገ'ደለ]

sleek
ስ'ሊይክ -ቅ- ለስላ'ሳ'ና ያማረ (ም'ሳሌ ፣ ለጠጉር)

sleep
ስ'ሊይፕ -ግ- ተ'ኛ [መተ'ኛት] ፤ ማሳለፍ [አሳ'ለፈ] ጊዜን ፣ ሕመም ወዘተ

sleepy
ስ'ሊይፒ -ቅ- የደ'ከመው ፤ እንቅልፋም ፤ የፈ'ዘዘ

sleet
ስ'ሊይት -ስ- በረዶ (ከዝናም ጋር የተደባ'ለቀ)

sleeve
ስ'ሊይቭ -ስ- እ'ጅጌ

sleight
ስ'ላይት -ስ- የማ'ታለል ጨዋታ (በእ'ጅ ቅልጥፍ'ና የ'ሚ'ሠ'ራ ወዘተ)

slender
ስ'ሌንደ -ቅ- ቀ'ጭን

slice
ስ'ላይስ -ግ- መቁረጥ [ቆ'ረጠ] (ሥሥ አድርጎ)

slide
ስ'ላይድ -ግ- መንሸራተት [ተንሸራ'ተተ]

slight
ስ'ላይት -ቅ- ት'ንሽ ፣ ጥቂት
insult
-ስ- ጽርፈት ፣ ማንጓጠጥ

slim
ስ'ሊም -ቅ- ቀ'ጭን (ለሰው)

slime
ስ'ላይም -ስ- ጭቃ (ቀ'ጭን)

sling
ስ'ሊንግ -ግ- መወርወር (ወረ'ወረ) ፣ መወን ጨፍ [ወነ'ጨፈ]
-ስ- ወንጭፍ

slink
ስ'ሊንክ -ግ- ሹክ'ክ ብሎ መሄድ [ሄደ]

slip
ስ'ሊፕ -ግ- ማዳለጥ [አዳ'ለጠ]
mistake
-ስ- ስሕተት
underclothes
-ስ- የውስጥ ልብስ (የሴት)
pillow-
-ስ- የትራስ ልብስ

slippers
ስ'ሊፐዝ -ስ- የቤት ጫ'ማ

slippery
ስ'ሊፐሪ -ቅ- አዳላጭ

slipshod
ስ'ሊፕሾድ -ቅ- ደንታ ቢስ (ለሥራ ፣ ለአ'ለባ በስ)

slit
ስ'ሊት -ግ- መብጣት [በ'ጣ]
ስ- ብጥ ፣ ብጣት

slogan
ስ'ለውገን -ስ- ዐረፍተ ነገር ፣ በቀ'ላሉ የ'ሚ ጠና ሐረግ (የፖለቲካ ፣ ሕዝብ ለማ'ነሣሣት ፣ አንድ ነገር ለማሳ'ወቅ ፣ ያንድን ማኅበር ዓላማ ለመግለጽ)

slop
ስ'ሎፕ -ግ- መ'ፈንጠቅ [ተፈነ'ጠቀ] ፣ ተርፎ መፍሰስ [ፈ'ሰሰ]
-s
-ስ- ቆሻሻ ውሃ (የወጥ ቤት እ'ጣቢ)

slope
ስ'ለውፕ -ስ- ዳገት ፣ ዐቀበት ፣ ቁልቁለት

slot
ስ'ሎት -ስ- ቀዳዳ (የፖስታ ሣጥን ፣ ወዘተ)

slothful
ስ'ለውስፉል -ቅ- ሰነፍ ፣ ሀኬተ'ኛ

slouch
ስ'ላውች -ግ- መ'ጐተት [ተጐ'ተተ] ፣ ተዝለ ፍልፎ መ'ቀመጥ [ተቀ'መጠ]

slovenly
ስ'ለቨንሊይ -ቅ- ጠ'ፍ ያላለ ፣ ስለ ሥራው የ'ማይ'ጠነ'ቀቅ ፣ ያ'ደፈ ልብስ የለ'በሰ

slow
ስ'ለው -ቅ- ዝ'ግ ያለ ፣ ቀርፋ'ፋ

sludge
ስ'ለጅ -ስ- እተላ ፣ ዝ'ቃጭ ፣ ወፍራም ጭቃ ፣ ቆሻሻ ፣ ዘይት ፣ ቅባት

slug
ስ'ለግ -ስ- የቅጠል ትል

sluggish
ስ'ለጊሽ -ቅ- ሰነፍ ፣ በፍጥነት የ'ማይሠራ ፣ ቀርፋ'ፋ

sluice
ስ'ሉ:ስ -ስ- የ'ሚ'ከ'ፈት'ና የ'ሚ'ዘ'ጋ የውሃ ማ'ገጃ (ለቦይ ውሃ ወዘተ)

slum
ስ'ለም -ስ- ቆሸ'ሸ ያለ ሠፈር ፣ ንጽሕ'ና የሌ 'ለው ሠፈር ፣ መንደር

slumber
ስ'ለምበ -ግ- ማንቀላፋት [አንቀላ'ፋ]

slump
ስ'ለምፕ -ግ- መ'ደገፍ [ተደ'ገፈ] (ከድካም የተነ'ሣ) ፣ ተዝለፍልፎ መ'ቀመጥ [ተቀ'መጠ]
-ስ- የንግድ ዕቃ የ'ማይ'ነ'ሣ'በት ጊዜ

slur
ስ'ለ: -ግ- መንተባተብ [ተንተባ'ተበ]
-ስ- ግ'ዋረድ ፣ ነቀፌታ

slush
ስ'ለሽ -ስ- ማጥ (ለጭቃ) ፣ በከፊል የቀ'ለጠ በረዶ

slut
ስ'ለት -ስ- አመንዝራ ፣ መጥፎ ስም ያ'ላት ሴት

sly
ስ'ላይ -ቅ- አ'ታላይ ፣ ብልጣብልጥ ፣ በሥ 'ውር የ'ሚሠራ

ňack
ስ'ማክ -ግ- በጥ'ፊ መምታት [መ'ታ]
blow
-ስ- ጥ'ፊ
taste
-ስ- ጣዕም

nall
ስ'ሞ፡ል -ቅ- ት'ንሽ

nallpox
ስ'ሞ፡ልፖክስ -ስ- ፈንጣጣ

nart
ስ'ማ፡ት -ግ- ማ'ቃጠል [አ'ቃ'ጠለ] ፣ መለብ ለብ [ለበ'ለበ] (ለቁስል)
well-dressed
-ቅ- ጥሩ አድርጎ የለ'በሰ
clever
-ቅ- ጮ'ሌ

nash
ስ'ማሽ -ግ- በኀይል መስበር [ሰ'በረ] ፣ መሰ ባበር [ሰባ'በረ]

nattering
ስ'ማተሪንግ -ስ- ት'ንሽ ፣ ጥቂት ዕውቀት

near
ስ'ሚየ -ግ- መቀ'ባት [ቀ'ባ] (በቅባት ነገር) ፣ መበ'ከል [በ'ከለ] (በቆሻሻ) ፣ ማ'በስ [አ'በሰ] (ያ'ደፈ እጅ)

nell
ስ'ሜል -ግ- ማሽተት [አሸ'ተተ]
-ስ- ሽ'ታ ፣ ክርፋት ፣ ግማት

nelt
ስ'ሜልት -ግ- ማቅለጥ [አቀ'ለጠ] (ብረት ወዘተ)

mile
ስ'ማይል -ግ- ፈገ'ግ ማለት [አለ]

mite
ስ'ማይት -ግ- በኀይል መምታት [መ'ታ]

mith
ስ'ሚስ -ስ- ብረት ቀጥቃጭ ፣ ባለ'ጅ

moke
ስ'መውክ -ግ- ማጤስ [አጤሰ] (ሲጃራ) ፣ መ ጤስ [ጤሰ]
of fire etc.
-ስ- ጢስ

smoker
ስ'መውክ -ስ- ሲጃራ ጠ'ጪ ፣ ሲጃራ አጢያሽ

smoky
ስ'መውኪ -ቅ- ጭጋጋም (ለአ'የር) ፣ ጢሳም

smooth
ስ'ሙ፡ዝ -ቅ- ለስላ'ሳ ፤ ያለ እንቅፋት የ'ሚንቀ ሳ'ቀስ

smother
ስ'መዘ -ግ- በጨርቅ አ'ፍኖ መግደል [ገ'ደለ]፣ አንቆ መግደል [፡'ደለ]

smoulder
ስ'መውልደ -ግ- ነበልባል ሳይኖረው ቀስ በ ቀ'ስ መ'ቃጠል [ተ'ቃጠለ]

smudge
ስ'መጅ -ግ- መበ'ከል [በ'ከለ] (በቆሻሻ)

smug
ስ'መግ -ቅ- ግ'ብዝ ፣ በራሱ ታ'ላቅ'ነት ወይ ን'ም ደኅን'ነት የ'ሚ'ደ'ሰት

smuggle
ስ'መገል -ግ- ቀረጥ ያልተከ'ፈለ'በት ዕቃ አገር ውስጥ ማስገ'ባት [አስገ'ባ] ፣ ወይን'ም ካገር ማውጣት [አወ'ጣ] ፣ የኮንትሮባንድ ሥራ መሥራት [ሠ'ራ]

smut
ስ'መት -ስ- ጉድፍ
obscenity
-ስ- ብልግ'ና

snack
ስ'ናክ -ስ- ቀ'ላል ምግብ ፣ ቁርስ ፣ መቅሰስ

snag
ስ'ናግ -ስ- እንቅፋት ፣ ች'ግር (ድንገተ'ኛ)

snail
ስ'ኔይል -ስ- ቀንድ አውጣ

snake
ስ'ኔይክ -ስ- እባብ

snap
ስ'ናፕ -ስ- ቀ'ጭ ማለት
of dog
-ግ- መንከስ [ነ'ከሰ] ፣ ለቀ'ም ማድረግ [አደ'ረገ] (ለው'ሻ በጥርስ)
answer rudely
-ግ- በቁ'ጣ መመ'ለስ [መ'ለሰ]

snare
ስ'ኔየ -ስ- ወጥመድ

snarl
ስ'ና:ል -ግ- ጥርስ አውጥቶ መጮኽ [ጮኸ] (ለውሻ በተቆ'ጣ ጊዜ) ፣ እም'ር መ'ናገር [ተና'ገረ]

snatch
ስ'ናች -ግ- መቀ'ማት [ቀ'ማ] ፣ መንጠቅ [ነ'ጠቀ] ፣ መመንጩቅ [መነ'ጩቀ]

sneak
ስ'ኒይክ -ግ- ማድባት [አደ'ባ]
-ስ- ስብቅያ ፣ ስብቀት

sneer
ስ'ኒየ -ግ- በፈገግታ በሰው ላይ ማፌዝ [አፌዘ] ፣ መዘ'በት [ዘ'በተ]

sneeze
ስ'ኒይዝ -ግ- ማንጠስ [አነ'ጠሰ]

sniff
ስ'ኒፍ -ግ- ባፍንጫ መሳብ [ሳበ]

snip
ስ'ኒፐ -ግ- መቁረጥ [ቆ'ረጠ] (በመቀስ)

sniper
ስ'ናይፐ -ስ- የመ'ሸገ ነፍጠ'ኛ ፣ ያደ'ፈጠ ነፍጠ'ኛ

snivel
ስ'ኒቨል -ግ- መ'ነባረር [ተነባ'ረረ] ፣ ማልቀስ [አለ'ቀሰ] (ለሕፃን)

snob
ስ'ኖብ -ስ- ኩራተ'ኛ ፣ ሰው የ'ሚንቅ ፣ ያላቅሙ የ'ሚንጠራ'ራ ፣ ው'ጥር

snore
ስ'ኖ: -ግ- ማንኮራፋት [አንኮራ'ፋ] ፣ ማኩረፍ [አኩ'ረፈ] (በእንቅልፍ)

snort
ስ'ኖ:ት -ግ- ፉ'ር ማለት [አለ] (ለፈረስ)

snout
ስ'ናውት -ስ- የእንስሳት አፍንጫ (እንደ ዐሣማ አፍንጫ ያለ)

snow
ስ'ነው -ግ- ጥጥ የ'ሚመስል በረዶ (እመዳይ)

snub
ስ'ነብ -ግ- ማሳ'ፈር [አሳ'ፈረ]
-nosed
-ቅ- ት'ንሽ ደፍጣ'ጣ ከወደጫፉ ቀና ያለ አፍንጫ ያ'ለው

snuff
ስ'ነፍ -ስ- ሱ'ረት ፣ ስንቆ

snug
ስ'ነግ -ቅ- ሙቀት ያ'ለው'ና ም'ቹ (ለቤ

snuggle
ስ'ነገል -ግ- መ'ታከክ [ታ'ከከ] (ለም'ቾት ለሙቀት)

so
'ሰው -ተግ- እንደ'ዚህ
very
-ተግ- በጣም
that
-ተግ- እንዲህ (ነው)

soak
'ሰውክ -ግ- በውሃ መዘፍዘፍ [ዘፈ'ዘፈ] ፣ መ
ከር [ነ'ከረ]

soap
'ሰውፐ -ስ- ሳሙና

soapsuds
'ሰውፐሰድዝ -ስ- የሳሙና አረፋ

soar
'ሶ: -ግ- መምጠቅ [መ'ጠቀ] ፣ ርቆ ወደላ
መብረር [በ'ረረ]

sob
'ሶብ -ግ- እየተንሰቀ'ሰቁ ማልቀስ [አለ'ቀ

sober
'ሰውበ -ቅ- ያልሰ'ከረ ፣ እራሱን የ'ሚ'ቆ'
'ጠር

sociable
'ሰውሸበል -ቅ- ተግባቢ ፣ ትብ'ብር ፣ ወ
ጅ'ነት የ'ሚያሳ'ይ

social
'ሰውሸል -ቅ- ማኅበራዊ ፣ ከሌሎ'ች ጋር አ
ር የ'ሚኖር

society
ሶ'ሳየቲ -ስ- ማኅበር

sock
'ሶክ -ስ- የግር ሹ'ራብ (አ'ጭር)

socket
'ሶክት -ስ- መሰ'ኪያ (የኤሌክትሪክ ወዘተ) ያይን ጉድጓድ

sofa
'ሰውፈ -ስ- ሶፋ ፣ ረ'ጅም ም'ቾት ያ'ለው ባ
መ'ደገፊያ ወንበር (ል'ብም ወንበር)

soft
’ሶፍት -ቅ- ለስላ'ሳ

soil
’ሶይል -ግ- ማቆ'ሸሽ [አቆ'ሸሸ]
earth
-ስ- ዐፈር

solace
’ሰውለስ -ግ- ማጽናናት [አጽና'ና]
-ስ- የ'ሚያጽና'ና ፣ ጭንቅ የ'ሚቀ'ንስ

solar
’ሰውለ -ቅ- የፀሐይ

solder
’ሶልደ -ግ- መበ'የድ [በ'የደ]

soldier
’ሶልጀ -ስ- ወ'ታ'ደር

sole
’ሰውል -ቅ- ብ'ቻ
exclusive
-ቅ- የተለ'የ

solemn
’ሶለም -ቅ- የተከ'በረ'ና ጸ'ጥ ያለ ፣ ተከ'ባሪ ፣ ክብረ በዓላዊ

solicitous
ሰ’ሊሲተስ -ቅ- ደ'ግ አ'ሳቢ (ለሌሎች) ፣ አንድ ነገር ለመሥራት የ'ሚጓ'ጓ ፣ በጣም ጥንቁቅ (ለጥቃ'ቅን ነገሮ'ች)

solid
’ሶሊድ -ቅ- ጠንካ'ራ ፣ ብርቱ ፣ ጥኑ

solidarity
ሶሊ’ዳሪቲ -ስ- ኅብረት ፣ አንድ'ነት (ለጋራ ጥቅም)

solitary
’ሶለትሪ -ቅ- ብ'ቸ'ኛ

solitude
’ሶሊትዩ:ድ -ስ- ብ'ቸ'ኝ'ነት

solution
ሰ’ሉሽን -ስ- መፍትሔ
answer
-ስ- መልስ (ለሒሳብ)
chemical
-ስ- የተቀ'መመ

solve
’ሶልቭ -ግ- መፍትሔ ማግኘት [አገ'ኘ] ፣ ማው ጣት [አወ'ጣ] (ለሒሳብ)

sombre
’ሶምበ -ስ- ጭፍግ'ግ ያለው ፣ የጠ'ቆረ

some
’ሰም -ቅ ፣ ተስ- ጥቂት ፣ አንዳንድ

somewhat
’ሰምዎት -ተግ- በመጠኑ

somebody
’ሰምበዲ -ስ- አንድ ሰው

somehow
’ሰምሀው -ተግ- እንደ ምን'ም

someone
’ሰምወን -ስ- አንድ ሰው

something
’ሰምቢንግ -ስ- አንድ ነገር ፣ ነገር

sometime
’ሰምታይም -ተግ- አንድ ጊዜ

somewhere
’ሰምዌየ -ተግ- አንድ ቦታ ፣ የት'ም

son
’ሰን -ስ- ልጅ (ተባዕት)

song
’ሶንግ -ስ- ዘፈን ፣ መዝሙር

son-in-law
’ሰኒንሎ: -ስ- አማች ፣ የልጅ ባል

soon
’ሱ:ን -ተግ- በፍጥነት ፣ አሁኑን

soot
’ሱት -ስ- ጥቀርሻ ፣ ጥላሸት

soothe
’ሱ:ዝ -ግ- ን'ዴት ፣ ቁ'ጣ ማ'ባረድ [አ'ባ'ረደ] ፣ ሕመም ፣ ውጋት ማብረድ [አበ'ረደ]

sop
’ሶፕ -ስ- ማባበያ ፣ ገ'ም ማ'ሰ'ኛ ፣ ፍትፍት

sophisticated
ሰፊስቲ’ኬይተድ -ቅ- የሠለ'ጠነ ፣ ከተሜ ፣ ዘበናይ

sordid
’ሶ:ዲድ -ቅ- ቆሻሻ ፣ ወ'ራ'ዳ (አመል) ፣ ም'ቹ ያልሆነ ፣ አሳ'ዛኝ (ለሁናቴ)

sorcerer
’ሶ:ሰረ -ስ- አስማተ'ኛ ፣ ጠንቋይ

sore
’ሶ፡ -ስ- ቁስል
-ቅ- የቆ'ሰለ

sorghum
'ሶ፡ገም -ስ- ማሽ'ላ
sorrow
'ሶረው -ስ- ሐዘን
sorry (to be)
'ሶሪ -ግ- ማዘን [አ'ዘነ] ፣ መፀ'ፀት [ተፀ'ፀተ]
sort
'ሶ፡ት -ግ- መለ'የት [ለ'የ] (በወገን በወገኑ)
soul
'ሰውል -ስ- ነፍስ
sound
'ሳውንድ -ስ- ድምፅ
in health
-ቅ- ጤና'ማ
structurally firm
-ቅ- ጠንካ'ራ
soup
'ሱፕ -ስ- ሾርባ
sour
'ሳወ -ቅ- የኮመ'ጠጠ ፣ ኮምጣ'ጣ
source
'ሶ፡ስ -ስ- ምንጭ ፣ አንድ ነገር የ'ሚ'ገ'ኝ'በት ሥር
south
'ሳውስ -ስ- ደቡብ
southern
'ሰ<u>ዘ</u>ን -ቅ- ደቡባዊ
southward
'ሳውስወደ -ተግ- ወደ ደቡብ
sovereign
'ሶቭረን -ስ- ንጉሥ ፣ ነጻ መንግሥት ፣ ጠቅላይ መሪ (አ'መራር)
-ቅ- ራሱን የቻለ የመንግሥት ግዛት፣ ነጻ (ንጉሥ ፣ መንግሥት)
sow
'ሰው -ግ- መዝራት [ዘ'ራ]
sow
'ሳው -ስ- እንስት ዐሣማ
space
ስ'ፔይስ -ስ- ቦታ
outer-
-ስ- ጠፈር
seating
-ስ- መ'ቀመጫ ፣ ማረፊያ (ለቦታ)

spacious
ስ'ፔይሽስ -ቅ- ሰ'ፊ ቦታ
spade
ስ'ፔይድ -ስ- አካፋ
span
ስ'ፓን -ቅ- ስፋት (የቦታ ወይን'ም የጊዜ)
-ስ- ስንዝር
spank
ስ'ፓንክ -ግ- መምታት [መ'ታ] (ለሕፃናት በተለ'ይ እመ'ቀመጫ ላይ)
spanner
ስ'ፓነ -ስ- መፍቻ (ኪያቬ)
spare
ስ'ፔየ -ግ- መተው [ተወ] ፣ ማዳን [አዳነ]
extra
-ስ- መለወ'ጫ (ዕቃ)
not wanted
-ቅ- ሌላ ፣ ትርፍ
spark
ስ'ፓ፡ክ -ስ- የሳት ፍን'ጣቂ
sparkle
ስ'ፓ፡ክል -ግ- ማብለጭለጭ [አብለጨ'ለጨ]
sparse
ስ'ፓ፡ስ -ቅ- ች'ፍግ ያላለ ፣ የሣ'ሣ (ለጠጉር ፣ ለሣር ወዘተ)
spasm
ስ'ፓዝም -ስ- ድንገተ'ኛ እንቅስ'ቃሴ (የሰው'ነት)
spasmodic
ስፓዘ'ሞዲክ -ቅ- አልፎ አልፎ የ'ሚሆን ፣ ጊዜ እ'ያሳ'ለፈ ደጋግሞ የ'ሚሆን
spatter
ስ'ፓተ -ግ- መ'ረጨት [ተረ'ጨ] ፣ መርጨት [ረ'ጨ]
spawn
ስ'ፖ፡ን -ስ- የንቁራሪት ፣ የዐሣ ወዘተ እንቁላል
-ግ- እንቁላል መጣል [ጣለ] (ለእንቁራሪት ፣ ለዐሣ)
speak
ስ'ፒየክ -ግ- መ'ናገር [ተና'ገረ]
spear
ስ'ፒየ -ግ- መውጋት [ወ'ጋ] (በጦር)
-ስ- ጦር

special
ስ'ፔሸል -ቅ- ል'ዩ ፥ የተለ'የ
specific
ስፐ'ሲፊክ -ቅ- የተወ'ሰነ ፥ የተለ'የ
specimen
ስ'ፔሲመን -ስ- ለዓይነት ያህል የ'ሚቀርብ ነገር
specious
ስ'ፒይሸስ -ቅ- ጥሩ መሳይ ፥ እውነት መሳይ
speck
ስ'ፔክ -ስ- ነቁጥ ፥ ጉድፍ
speckled
ስ'ፔክልድ -ቅ- ነቁጣም ፥ ባለነቁጥ ፥ ዝንጉር ጉር
spectacle
ስ'ፔክተክል -ስ- ትርኢይት
spectacles
ስ'ፔክተክልዝ -ስ- መነ'ጥር ፥ መነ'ጽር
spectator
ስፔክ'ቴይተ -ስ- ተመልካች (አንድ ትርኢት)
spectre
ስ'ፔክተ -ስ- መንፈስ (የ'ሚ'ታይ) ፤ ወደፊት ስለ'ሚመጣው ች'ግር ወዘተ የ'ሚያስጨ'ንቅ ፍርሃት
speculate
ስ'ፔክዩሌይት -ግ- ማ'መዛዘን [አ'መዛ'ዘነ] ፥ በአእምሮ ወደፊት የ'ሚሆነውን ማወቅ [ዐ'ወቀ]
in business
-ግ- ወደፊት ያተርፈ'ኛል ብሎ መግዛት [ገ'ዛ] ፥ መሸጥ [ሸጠ]
speech
ስ'ፒይች -ስ- ንግ'ግር
speed
ስ'ፒይድ -ስ- ፍጥነት
spell
ስ'ፔል -ግ- እ'ጻጻፍ
of time
-ስ- ጊዜ (አ'ጭር)
magic
-ስ- ድግምት (የጥንቆላ)
spend
ስ'ፔንድ -ግ- ማጥፋት [አጠ'ፋ] (ለገንዘብ)
time
-ግ- ማሳ'ለፍ [አሳ'ለፈ] (ለጊዜ)

sperm
ስ'ፐ፡ም -ስ- ዘር (ኀጢአት)
sphere
ስ'ፊየ -ስ- ክበብ
spherical
ስ'ፌሪክል -ቅ- ክ'ብ
spice
ስ'ፓይስ -ግ- መቀ'መም [ቀ'መመ]
-ስ- ቅመም
spicy
ስ'ፓይሲ -ቅ- የተቀ'መመ ፥ የተመ'ጠነ ፥ ቅመም ያ'ለ'በት
spider
ስ'ፓይደ -ስ- ሸረሪት
spike
ስ'ፓይክ -ስ- የሾለ ብረት ወይን'ም እንጨት ፤ የእህል እሸት
spill
ስ'ፒል -ግ- ማፍሰስ [አፈ'ሰሰ]
-ስ- ማ'ቀጣጠያ (ለእሳት)
spin
ስ'ፒን -ግ- መፍተል [ፈ'ተለ] ፥ ማሾር [አሾረ] (በማዞር)
spinach
ስ'ፒነች -ስ- ጎ'መን (ስፒናች)
spindle
ስ'ፒንደል -ስ- ቀለም ፥ ማቅለሚያ ፥ ማጠን ጠ'ኛ
spine
ስ'ፓይን -ስ- አ'ከርካሪ ፤ የሾለ ነገር (ም'ሳሌ ፥ የጃርት ወስፈንጠር ፥ እሾህ)
spinster
ስ'ፒንስተ -ስ- ሳዱ'ላ ፥ ያላገ'ባች ሴት
spiny
ስ'ፓይኒ -ቅ- እሾኻ'ማ ፥ ሹል ነገር የበ'ዛ'በት ፥ ያ'ለ'በት
spiral
ስ'ፓይረል -ቅ- ጠምዛ'ዛ ፥ ካንድ ነጥብ እ'የ ዞረ'ና እ'የሰ'ፋ የ'ሚሄድ
spire
ስ'ፓየ -ስ- ረ'ጅም'ና ሾጣጣ የሆነ (የቤተ ክርስቲያን ወዘተ) ጫፍ

spirit
ስ'ፒሪት -ስ- መንፈስ
zeal
-ስ- ወ'ኔ
alcohol
-ስ- አልኮል (መጠ'ጥ)
mood
-ስ- ሁናቴ

spirit-lamp
ስ'ፒሪት'ላምፕ -ስ- ላምባ ፣ ኩ'ራዝ

spiritual
ስ'ፒሪችዩወል -ቅ- መንፈሳዊ

spit
ስ'ፒ፡ት -ግ- እንት'ፍ ማለት [አለ] ፣ መትፋት [ተፋ]
for roasting
-ስ- ረ'ጅም ብረት (ለሥጋ መጥበሻ)

spite
ስ'ፓይት -ስ- ጥላ'ቻ
in-of
-ተግ- ምን'ም እንኳ(ን)

spiteful
ስ'ፓይትፉል -ቅ- ተንኳሽ (ለጥል)

splash
ስፕ'ላሽ -ግ- መርጨት [ረ'ጨ]

splendid
ስፕ'ሌንደድ -ቅ- ድንቅ
-ተግ- በገፍ ፣ በብዛት

splice
ስፕ'ላይስ -ግ- መቀ'ጠል [ቀ'ጠለ] (ገመድ በመፍተል ፣ እንጨት እንዱን ካንዱ ውስጥ በመሰ'ካት)

splint
ስፕ'ሊንት -ስ- መጠ'ገኛ (እንጨት ፣ ለተሰ'በረ ዐጥንት)

splinter
ስፕ'ሊንተ -ስ- ሹል ስን'ጣሪ ፣ ስ'ባሪ (የን ጨት ፣ የደንጊያ ፣ የመስተዋት ወዘተ)

split
ስፕ'ሊት -ግ- መሠንጠቅ [ሠነ'ጠቀ]

splutter
ስፕ'ለተ -ግ- መንተባተብ [ተንተባ'ተበ] (ከድ ን'ጋጤ የተነ'ሣ) ፣ መርጨት [ረ'ጨ] (ቀለም ከብእር)

spoil
ስ'ፖይል -ግ- ማጥፋት [አጠ'ፋ] ፣ ማ'በላሸት [አ'በላ'ሸ]

spokesman
ስ'ፖውክስመን -ስ- ቃል አቀ'ባይ ፣ በአንድ ማኅበር ስም ተናጋሪ

sponge
ስ'ፖንጅ -ስ- ስፍንግ

sponsor
ስ'ፖንሰ -ስ- ኀላፊ ፣ የክርስት'ና አ'ባት ፣ ተጠ 'ያቂ

spontaneous
ስፖን'ቴይኒየስ -ቅ- ያለመ'ዘጋጀት ፣ ድንገ ተ'ኛ ፣ በስ'ሜት የተሠ'ራ

spool
ስ'ፑ፡ል -ስ- ማጠንጠኛ ፣ በከራ

spoon
ስ'ፑ፡ን -ስ- ማንካ ፣ ማንኪያ

sporadic
ስፐ'ራዲክ -ቅ- አልፎ አልፎ የ'ሚሆን ፣ የ'ሚ 'ደ'ረግ ፣ የ'ሚ'ታ'ይ

sport
ስ'ፖ፡ት -ስ- ስፖርት

spout
ስ'ፓውት -ስ- አፍ ፣ ጡት (የጀበና ፣ የማንቆ ርቆሪያ ወዘተ)

sprain
ስፕ'ሬይን -ግ- ወለ'ም ማለት [አለ]
-ስ- ወለምታ

sprawl
ስፕ'ሮ፡ል -ግ- መ'ጋደም [ተጋ'ደመ] ፣ መ'ዘ ረር [ተዘ'ረረ]

spray
ስፕ'ሬይ -ግ- መርጨት [ረ'ጨ] (መድኃኒት ፣ ፈሳሽ)
-ስ- የ'ሚ'ረ'ጭ ነገር

spread
ስፕ'ሬድ -ግ- መስፋፋት [ተስፋ'ፋ] ፣ መ'ዘ ርጋት [ተዘረ'ጋ] ፣ መቀ'ባት [ቀ'ባ] (ቅቤ)

spree
ስፕ'ሪይ -ስ- የደ'መቀ ት'ንሽ በዐል ፣ ድንገ ተ'ኛ የጠባይ መ'ለወጥ (በመጠ'ጥ'ና በዝ'ሙት ወዘተ)

sprightly
ስፕ'ራይትሊ -ቅ- ቀልጣ'ፋ ፣ ንቁ

spring
ስፕ'ሪንግ -ስ- ሞ'ላ ፣ የተወ'ጠረ'ና የ'ሚያረ ገ'ርግ ሽቦ
season
-ስ- ጸደይ
jump
-ግ- መዝለል [ዘ'ለለ]
a jump
-ስ- ዝ'ላይ
water
-ስ- ምንጭ
springy
ስፕ'ሪንጊ -ቅ- አረግራጊ ፣ የ'ሚያንጥር
sprinkle
ስፕ'ሪንክል -ግ- መርጨት [ረ'ጨ] ፣ ማርከፍ ከፍ [አርከፈ'ከፈ]
sprint
ስፕ'ሪንት -ግ- መሮጥ [ሮጠ] ፣ መሽቀዳደም [ተሽቀዳ'ደመ] (አ'ጭር ርቀት)
sprout
ስፕ'ራውት -ግ- ማቆንጐል [አቆን'ጐለ]
spruce
ስፕ'ሩ:ስ -ቅ- ልብስ ያማረ'በት ፣ የተሽቀረ 'ቀረ
spry
ስፕ'ራይ -ቅ- ቀልጣ'ፋ ፣ ንቁ
spur
ስ'ፐ: -ግ- ማ'ጃገን [አ'ጃ'ገነ] ፣ መኰልኰል [ኰለ'ኰለ] (ለፈረስ ፣ ለበቅሎ)
-ስ- በፈረሰ'ኛ ጫ'ማ ላይ ያ'ለ የፈረስ መኰልኰያ ብረት
spurn
ስ'ፐ:ን -ግ- ማ'ባረር [አ'ባ'ረረ] (በጥላ'ቻ)
spurt
ስ'ፐ:ት -ግ- ፍትል'ክ ማለት [አለ] (ለሰው) ፣ ፈ'ን ማለት [አለ] (ለፈሳሽ)
spy
ስ'ፓይ -ግ- መሰ'ለል [ሰ'ለለ]
-ስ- ሰ'ላይ
squabble
ስክ'ዎበል -ግ- እ'የጮኹ መ'ከራከር [ተከራ 'ከረ] (በ'ማይረባ ነገር)
squalid
ስክ'ዎሊድ -ቅ- ቆሻሻ ፣ እድፋም ፣ አ'ፀ'ያፊ ፣ ድህ'ነት ያጠ'ቃው

squall
ስክ'ዎ:ል -ስ- ድንገተ'ኛ ነፋስ (ይበልጡን ከበ ረዶ'ና ከዝናም ጋር የተደባ'ለቀ)
squander
ስክ'ዎንደ -ግ- ማባከን [አባ'ከነ] ፣ መንዛት [ነ'ዛ] (ለገንዘብ ወዘተ)
square
ስክ'ዌየ -ቅ- አራት ማዕዘን
piazza
-ስ- አ'ደባባይ
squash
ስክ'ዎሽ -ግ- መጭመቅ [ጨ'መቀ]
-ስ- ጭ'ማቂ (የሎሚ ፣ የብርቱካን ወዘተ) ፣ ት'ንሽ ዱ'ባ ፣ ዙ'ኪኒ
squat
ስክ'ዎት -ግ- ያለፈቃድ በሰው ቦታ ፣ ሕንፃ ውስጥ መ'ቀመጥ [ተቀ'መጠ]
squeak
ስክ'ዊይክ -ግ- ሲ'ጥ ማለት [አለ]
squeal
ስክ'ዊይል -ግ- መጮኽ [ጮኸ] (ለትን'ንሽ እንስሳት ፣ ከፍርሃት'ና ከሥቃይ የተነ'ሣ)
squeeze
ስኪ'ዊይዝ -ግ- መጭመቅ [ጨ'መቀ] ፣ ማፍ ረጥረጥ [አፍረጠ'ረጠ]
squint
ስክ'ዊንት -ግ- መንሸዋረር [ተንሸዋ'ረረ]
-ስ- መንሸዋረር
squirt
ስክ'ወ:ት -ግ- ፈ'ን ማለት [አለ] ፣ ፍጭ'ጭ ማለት [አለ]
stab
ስ'ታብ -ግ- መውጋት [ወ'ጋ] (በስለት)
stable
ስ'ቴይበል -ስ- ጋጣ (የፈረስ)
firm
-ቅ ጽኑ ፣ የተደላ'ደለ
stack
ስ'ታክ -ስ- ክ'ምር (የድርቆሽ ፣ የሣር) ፣ በደ ምብ የተደረ'ደሩ መጻሕፍት ፣ እንጨት ወዘተ)
stadium
ስ'ቴይዲየም -ስ- የስፖርት ክ'ብ ሜዳ ፣ ስታ ዲየም

staff

ስ'ታ:ፍ -ስ- ሠ'ራተ'ኞ'ች (ከአንድ አለቃ ሥር ያ'ሉ)

stick

-ስ- ምርኩዝ ፣ ዘንግ

stage

ስ'ቴይጅ -ስ- ከ'ፍተ'ኛ ቦታ (በቴአትር) ፣ መድረክ

of journey

-ስ- መናኸሪያ

stagger

ስ'ታግ -ግ- መንገዳገድ [ተንገዳ'ገደ]

stagnant

ስ'ታግነንት -ቅ- የ'ማይንቀሳ'ቀስ ፣ የታ'ገደ (ውሃ)

inactive

-ቅ- እርምጃ የ'ማያሳ'ይ ፣ መ'ሻሻል የ'ማያሳ'ይ

staid

ስ'ቴይድ -ቅ- እርምጃ የ'ማይወ'ድ

stain

ስ'ቴይን -ግ- መበ'ከል [በ'ከለ]

-ስ- እድፍ

stair

ስ'ቴየ -ስ- ደረጃ (የቤት) ፣ ዕርከን

staircase

ስ'ቴየኬይስ -ስ- ደረጃዎ'ች (የቤት)

stake

ስ'ቴይክ -ስ- ችካል ፤ ለውር'ርድ የተቀ'መጠ ገንዘብ

stale

ስ'ቴይል -ቅ- ደረቅ ፣ ያረ'ጀ (ዳ'ቦ ፣ ወዘተ)

stalk

ስ'ቶ:ክ -ግ- ማድባት [አደ'ባ] (ወደ አደን ለመድረስ)

of plant

-ስ- አገዳ

stall

ስ'ቶ:ል -ስ- ጋጣ ፣ የከብት ማ'ጕሪያ (ለአንድ ከብት)

-ግ- ወደ ኋላ ማለት [አለ]

stallion

ስ'ታሊየን -ስ- ያልተኰላ'ሸ ፈረስ (ተባዕት)

stamina

ስ'ታመነ -ስ- አለመድከም ፣ ንቃት

stammer

ስ'ታመ -ግ- መንተፍተፍ [ተንተጠ'ተጠ] (ለን ግ'ግር ቃል በመደጋገም)

stamp

ስ'ታምፕ -ግ- ማ'ተም [አ'ተመ]

with foot

-ግ- መርገጥ [ረ'ገጠ]

official mark

-ስ- ማኅተም

postage

-ስ- ቴምብር

stand

ስ'ታንድ -ግ- መቆም [ቆመ] ፣ አለመ'ለወጥ [-ተለ'ወጠ] ፤ መ'ታገሥ [ታ'ገሠ]

standard

ስ'ታንደድ -ስ- መለ'ኪያ (ለሌሎ'ች ነገ ሮ'ች)

flag

-ስ- የቤተ መንግሥት ሰንደቅ ዓላማ

normal

-ቅ- የተለ'መደ

star

ስ'ታ: -ስ- ኮከብ

starch

ስ'ታ:ች -ስ- የልብስ ማድረቂያ ዱቄት ፤ በዱ ቄት ውስጥ የ'ሚ'ገ'ኝ የምግብ ዓይነት

stare

ስ'ቴየ -ግ- አፍ'ጦ ማየት [አ'የ] ፣ ት'ኩረ ብሎ ማየት [አ'የ]

stark

ስ'ታ:ክ -ቅ- የተራ'ቆተ ፣ ባዶ (ለመሬት) ፤ ደረቅ ፣ ራቁት (ለሰውነ'ት)

start

ስ'ታ:ት -ግ- መጀ'መር [ጀ'መረ] ፣ መወ'ጠን [ወ'ጠነ]

startling

ስ'ታ:ትሊንግ -ቅ- አስገ'ራሚ ፣ አስፈ'ሪ

starve

ስ'ታ:ቭ -ግ- መ'ራብ [ተራበ]፣ በረብ መ'ሠ ቃየት [ተሠቃ'የ]

state

ስ'ቴይት -ስ- አገር'ና ሕዝብ (በመንግሥት የ'ሚ'ተዳ'ደር)

condition
-ስ- ሁናቴ
say
-ግ- መ'ናገር [ተና'ገረ] (አንድ ነገር)
governmental
-ቅ- መንግሥታዊ

stately
ስ'ቴይትሊ -ቅ- የተከ'በረ ፣ ባላገርግ

statement
ስ'ቴይትመንት -ስ- ንግ'ግር ፣ መግለጫ

statesman
ስ'ቴይትስመን -ስ- ታ'ላቅ የመንግሥት ባለ ሥልጣን

station
ስ'ቴይሽን -ስ- ጣቢያ ፣ ማቆሚያ
position
-ስ- ደረጃ (ማዕረግ)
railway
-ስ- ለገሀር ፣ ባቡር ጣቢያ
place
-ግ- ዘብ ማቆም [አቆመ]

stationery
ስ'ቴይሽነሪ -ስ- የጽሕፈት መ'ሣሪያ

statistics
ስታ'ቲስቲክስ -ስ- የል'ዩ ል'ዩ ነገሮ'ች ዝር ዝር ሒሳብ

statue
ስ'ታቹ -ስ- ሐውልት

stature
ስ'ታቸ -ስ- ቁመት ፣ እርዝማኔ
standing
-ስ- ማዕረግ

status
ስ'ቴይተስ -ስ- ሁናቴ ፣ ማዕረግ

statute
ስ'ታቹት -ስ- ሕ'ግ (ሕ'ግ አውጭዎ'ች ያወ 'ጡት)

staunch
ስ'ቶ:ንች -ቅ- ታ'ማኝ ፣ እምነት የ'ሚ'ጣል 'በት ፣ ቀ'ጥተ'ኛ (ለጓ'ደ'ኛ'ና ፣ በሐ'ሳብ ለ'ሚ ደ'ገፍ)
-ግ- ከቁስል ደም እንዳይፈ'ስ ማቆም [አቆመ]

stave
ስ'ቴይቭ -ስ- ዱ'ላ ፣ በ'ትር
off-
-ግ- ለጊዜው መከልከል [ከለ'ከለ] ፣ ለጊዜው ማራቅ [አራቀ] (አደጋ ፣ መዐት ወዘተ)

stay
ስ'ቴይ -ግ- መቆ'የት [ቆ'የ] ፣ መኖር [ኖረ]

stead
ስ'ቴድ -ስ- ቦታ ፣ ፋንታ (በሌላ)

steadfast
ስ'ቴድፋስት -ቅ- ታ'ማ'ኝ ፣ የ'ማይ'ለ'ወጥ

steady
ስ'ቴዲ -ቅ- ታ'ማኝ ፣ የ'ማያ'ወላ'ውል የ'ማይ'ና'ወጥ ፣ የጸ'ና

steal
ስ'ቲይል -ግ- መስረቅ [ሰ'ረቀ]

stealthy
ስ'ቴልሲ -ቅ- በጥን'ቃቄ'ና በስ'ውር የተደ 'ረገ

steam
ስ'ቲይም -ስ- እንፋሎት

steamer
ስ'ቲይመ -ስ- መርከብ (በሞቶር የ'ሚ'ነ'ዳ)

steel
ስ'ቲይል -ስ- ብረት

steep
ስ'ቲይፕ -ቅ- ኸፍ'ው ያለ ፣ ቀ'ጥ ያለ (ገደል)

steeple
ስ'ቲይፐል -ስ- ቁንጮ ፣ ጫፍ (የቤተ ክርስ ቲያን)

steer
ስ'ቲየ -ግ- መንዳት [ነ'ዳ] (ለመኪና ወዘተ)

stem
ስ'ቴም -ስ- ግንድ

stench
ስ'ቴንች -ስ- መጥፎ ሽ'ታ ፣ ክርፋት ፣ ግማት

step
ስ'ቴፕ -ግ- መ'ራመድ [ተራ'መደ]

grade, stair

-ስ- ደረጃ (የቤት)

pace

-ስ- እርም'ጃ

measure

-ስ- ው'ሳኔ

stepbrother

ስ'ቴፕብረዘ -ስ- የሚስት ወይን'ም የባል ወን ድ'ም

stepchild

ስ'ቴፕቻይድ -ስ- የንጀራ ልጅ

stepdaughter

ስ'ቴፕዶ፡ተ -ስ- የንጀራ ልጅ (እንስት)

stepfather

ስ'ቴፕፋ፡ዘ -ስ- የንጀራ እ'ባት

stepmother

ስ'ቴፕመዘ -ስ- የንጀራ እ'ናት

stepsister

ስ'ቴፕሲስተ -ስ- የንጀራ እ'ናት ወይን'ም የእ ንጀራ እ'ባት ሴት ልጅ

stepson

ስ'ቴፕሰን -ስ- የንጀራ ልጅ (ወንድ)

stereotyped

ስ'ቲሪየታይፕት -ቅ- ገልባጭ ፣ እራሱ ሐ'ሳብ ማፍለቅ የ'ማይችል

sterile

ስ'ቴራይል -ቅ- መ'ካን ፣ የተኰላ'ሸ ፣ የተቀ ጠ'ቀጠ (እንስሳ)

clean

-ቅ- ንጹሕ ፣ ከተውሳክ የነጻ

stew

ስት'ዩ፡ -ግ- ወጥ መሥራት [ሠ'ራ]

-ስ- ወጥ

steward

ስት'ዩወድ -ስ- የመሬት ወ'ኪል ፡ የመሬት ሹም ፣ እ'ዛዥ ፣ እ'ጋፋሪ (የቤት)

cabin attendant

-ስ- በመርከብ ፣ በአውሮ'ፕላን ላይ አስተናጋጅ

stick

ስ'ቲክ -ግ- ማ'ጣበቅ [እ'ጣ'በቀ]

jam

-ግ- ማስገ'ባት [እስገ'ባ] ፣ መዶል [ዶለ] ፣ መሳግ [ሳገ]

-to

-ግ- እለመ'ለ'የት [-ተለ'የ]፣ አለመተው [-ተወ] ፣ የሙ'ጥ'ኝ ማለት [አለ]

staff

-ስ- ምርኩዝ ፣ ዱ'ላ ፣ በ'ትር

stiff

ስ'ቲፍ -ቅ- ደረቅ ፣ ግ'ትር

stifle

ስ'ታይፋል -ግ- ማ'ፈን [አ'ፈነ] (እንዳይተነፍስ)

stifling

ስ'ታይፍሊንግ -ቅ- አፋ'ኝ ፣ የ'ሚያንቅ

still

ስ'ቲል -ተግ- ገና

quiet

-ቅ- ጸ'ጥተ'ኛ ፣ የ'ማይንቀሳ'ቀስ

quieten

-ግ- ዝ'ም ማ'ሰ'ኘት [አ'ሰ'ኘ]

still-born

ስ'ቲልቦ፡ን -ስ- ሞቶ የተወ'ለደ

stimulate

ስ'ቲምዩሌይት -ግ- ማ'ነሣሣት [እ'ነሣ'ሣ]

sting

ስ'ቲንግ -ግ- መንደፍ [ነ'ደፈ] (ለንብ ወዘተ)

stingy

ስ'ቲንጂ -ቅ- ሥ'ሥታም ፣ ገብጋ'ባ

stink

ስ'ቲንክ -ግ- መሽተት [ሸ'ተተ] ፣ መከርፋት [ከረ'ፋ]

-ስ- ግማት ፣ መጥፎ ሽ'ታ ፣ ክርፋት

stipend

ስ'ታይፔንድ -ስ- ደመወዝ (የትምህርት ወዘተ)

stipulate

ስ'ቲፕዩሌይት -ግ- እጥብቆ መጠ'የቅ [ጠ'የቀ] (ለአንድ ስምም'ነት እስፈ'ላጊ የሆነውን)

stir

ስ'ተ፡ -ግ- ማ'ማሰል [እ'ማ'ሰለ] ፣ ማ'ወክ ፣ [እ'ወከ] ፣ መበጥበጥ [በጠ'በጠ]

-up

-ግ- ብጥ'ብጥ ማንሣት [እነ'ሣ]

stirrup

ስ'ቲረፕ -ስ- እርካብ

stitch
ስ'ቲች -ግ- መጣፍ [ጣፈ] ፣ መጥቀም [ጠ'ቀመ] (ለልብስ)
-ስ- ስፌት (የጨርቅ)

stock
ስ'ቶክ -ግ- የሸቀጥ ዕቃ ገዝቶ መደርደር [ደረ'ደረ]
goods
-ስ- ሸቀጥ
of rifle
-ስ- ሰደፍ

stocking
ስ'ቶኪንግ -ስ- ረ'ጅም የእግር ሹ'ራብ

stocky
ስ'ቶኪ. -ቅ- አ'ጭር ፣ ወፍራም'ና ጠንካ'ራ

stoke
ስ'ተውክ -ግ- መማገድ [ማ'ገደ]

stolid
ስ'ቶሊድ -ቅ- ግ'ድ የሌ'ለው ፣ ስለአንድ ሁናቴ ስ'ሚቱን የ'ማይገልጽ

stomach
ስ'ተመክ -ስ- ሆድ (ለሰው)

stone
ስ'ተውን -ግ- መውገር [ወ'ገረ]
-ስ- ድንጊያ

stony
ስ'ተውኒ -ቅ- ድንጊያ'ማ

stool
ስ'ቱ:ል -ስ- ወምበር ፣ በርጩ'ማ
faeces
-ስ- ዓይነ ምድር

stoop
ስ'ቱ:ፕ -ግ- ማጐንበስ [አጐን'በሰ]

stop
ስ'ቶፕ -ግ- መቆም [ቆመ] ፣ ቀ'ጥ ማለት [አለ]
-ስ- መቆሚያ

stopper
ስ'ቶፐ -ስ- ቆርኬ ፣ ውታፍ

store
ስ'ቶ: -ስ- ሱቅ ፣ መደ'ብር ፣ ዕቃ ቤት
-ግ- ማስቀ'መጥ [አስቀ'መጠ] (ማካበት)

storey
ስ'ቶ:ሪ -ስ- ፎቅ ቤት ፣ ደርብ

storm
ስ'ቶ:ም -ስ- አውሎ ነፋስ ፣ ማዕበል ፣ መውጅ

story
ስ'ቶ:ሪ -ስ- ተረት ፣ ታሪክ

story-teller
ስ'ቶ:ሪቴለ -ስ- ተ'ራች

stout
ስ'ታውት -ቅ- ወፍራም ፣ ዘርጣ'ጣ

stove
ስ'ተውቭ -ስ- ምድ'ጃ

stow
ስ'ተው -ግ- መደርደር [ደረ'ደረ] ፣ ማስቀ'መጥ [አስቀ'መጠ] (በዕቃ ቤት) ፣ ማ'ሸግ [አ'ሸገ] (በማሠር)

straddle
ስት'ራደል -ግ- እንፈራ'ጦ መቆም [ቆመ] ወይ'ም መ'ቀመጥ [ተቀ'መጠ]

straggle
ስት'ራገል -ግ- መ'በታተን [ተበታ'ተነ]

straight
ስት'ሬይት -ቅ- ቀ'ጥ ያለ ፣ ቀጥተ'ኛ
honest
-ቅ- ታ'ማኝ ፣ ቅን

straighten
ስት'ሬይተን -ግ- ማ'ቃናት [አ'ቃ'ና] ፣ ቀ'ጥ ማድረግ [አደ'ረገ]

straightforward
ስትሬይት'ፎ:ወድ -ቅ- የ'ማያ'ውክ (ሥራ)
honest
-ቅ- ታ'ማኝ ፣ ግልጽ (ለጠባይ)

strain
ስት'ሬይን -ግ- ማጥለል [አጠ'ለለ]
tire out
-ግ- በሥራ ማድከም [አደ'ከመ]
fatigue
-ስ- ድካም

strait
ስት'ሬይት -ስ- የባሕር ወሽመጥ

stranded
ስት'ራንዲድ -ቅ- ያለርዳታ የቀ'ረ (መ'ጓጓዣ 'በማጣት)

strange
ስት'ሬይንጅ -ቅ- እንግዳ (ነገር)
unusual
-ቅ- ያልተለ'መደ
unexplained
-ቅ- ግሩም ፣ ድንቅ

stranger
ስት'ሬይንጀ -ስ- እንግዳ (ለሰው)

strangle
ስት'ራንገል -ግ- አንቆ መግደል [ገ'ደለ]

strap
ስት'ራፕ -ስ- ጠፍር

strategem
ስት'ራተጀም -ስ- ብልኀት (ጠላትን በጦር 'ነት የ'ሚያ'ሸ'ንፉ'በት)

strategy
ስት'ራተጂ -ስ- የጦር ዐቅድ

straw
ስት'ሮ፡ -ስ- ገለባ
for drinking
-ስ- መጠ'ጥ መምጠጫ ብር

stray
ስት'ሬይ -ግ- መጥፋት [ጠ'ፋ] (መንገድ በመ ሳት)

stream
ስት'ሪይም -ስ- ጅረት ፣ ባለማ'ቋረጥ የ'ሚጐ ርፍ ፣ ፈሳሽ ፣ ጋዝ ፣ ሰው ፣ ዕቃ ወዘተ

street
ስት'ሪይት -ስ- ጎዳና ፣ መንገድ

strenuous
ስት'ሬንዩወስ -ቅ- ኀይለ'ኛ ፣ ከ'ባድ (ለሥራ)

stress
ስት'ሬስ -ግ- ማጥበቅ [አጠ'በቀ] (ለቃላት)
-ስ- ድካም

stretch
ስት'ሬች -ግ- መዘርጋት [ዘ'ረጋ]

stretcher
ስት'ሬቸ -ስ- ታ'ጣፊ አልጋ ፣ የበ'ሽተ'ኛ ማ 'መላለሻ አልጋ

strew
ስት'ሩ. -ግ- መበ'ተን [በ'ተነ] ፣ መርጨት [ረ'ጨ] ፣ መነስነስ [ነስ'ነሰ]

stricken
ስት'ሪከን -ቅ- የተጐ'ዳ ፣ መከራ ያጠ'ቃው
-in years
-ቅ- በጣም ያረ'ጀ ፣ የሸመ'ገለ

strict
ስት'ሪክት -ቅ- ጥብቅ ፣ የ'ማያ'ወላ'ውል

stride
ስት'ራይድ -ግ- በረ'ጅሙ መ'ራመድ [ተራ 'መደ] ፣ እንጣ'ጥ ብሎ መ'ሻገር [ተሻ'ገረ]

strife
ስት'ራይፍ -ስ- ጥል ፣ ሁከት

strike
ስት'ራይክ -ግ- መምታት [መ'ታ] ፣ ለደመ ወዝ ጭ'ማሪ ማ'ደም [አ'ደመ]
-ስ- አድማ

string
ስት'ሪንግ -ስ- ክ'ር ፣ ሲባጎ

strip
ስት'ሪፕ -ግ- መላጥ [ላጠ] (ዛፍ ወዘተ) ፣ ማው ለቅ [አወ'ለቀ] (ልብስ)
-ስ- ረ'ጅም ቁ'ራጭ (ጨርቅ ፣ መሬት ወዘተ)

stripe
ስት'ራይፕ -ስ- ሰንበር (በሰው'ነት ላይ የ'ሚ 'ታ'ይ)
coloured line
-ስ- ዝንጉርጉር መሥመር
military
-ስ- ምል'ክት (የወ'ታ'ደር ሹመት ፣ የ'V' ቅርፅ ያ'ለው)

stripling
ስት'ሪፕሊንግ -ስ- ጎልማ'ሳ

strive
ስት'ራይቭ -ግ- ት'ልቅ ጥረት ማድረግ [አደ'ረገ]

stroke
ስት'ረውክ -ግ- ማሻሸት [አሻ'ሸ] ፣ መደባበስ [ደባ'በሰ]
blow
-ስ- በ'ትር (የተመ'ቱት)

stroll
ስት'ሮ:ል -ግ- መንሸርሸር [ተንሸረ'ሸረ] (ለሽ 'ርሽ'ር)

strong
ስት'ሮንግ -ቅ- ኀይለ'ኛ

stronghold
ስት'ሮንግሆልድ -ስ- ም'ሽግ
strop
ስት'ሮፕ -ስ- መሳያ ጠፍር
structure
ስት'ረክቸ -ስ- አቋም ፣ አንድ ነገር የተሠ'ራ'በት ፣ የተገጣ'ጠመ'በት ፣ የተደራጀ'በት መንገድ
building
-ስ- ታ'ላቅ ሕንፃ
struggle
ስት'ረገል -ግ- መታገል [ታ'ገለ]
-ስ- ትግል
strut
ስት'ረት -ግ- በኩራት መ'ራመድ [ተራ'መደ]፣ መ'ወጠር [ተወ'ጠረ] (ለኩራት)
-ስ- ወጋግራ ፣ የድጋፍ እንጨት
stub
ስ'ተብ -ስ- ቁ'ራጭ ፣ ብ'ጣሽ (የሲጃራ የእርሳስ ወዘተ)
-out
-ግ- መተርኮስ [ተረ'ኮሰ] (ለሲጃራ)
stubble
ስ'ተበል -ስ- ቀምቀ'ሞ (የጢም ጠጉር)
grain
-ስ- ቆረን (የእህል)
stubborn
ስ'ተበን -ቅ- ች'ኮ ፣ ገ'ታ'ራ ፣ መንቻ'ካ
stud
ስ'ተድ -ስ- ከልብስ ጋር ያልተሰ'ፋ ያንገትጌ ቁልፍ
student
ስት'ዩ:ደንት -ስ- ተማሪ ፣ ደ'ቀ መዝሙር
study
ስ'ተዲ -ግ- ማጥናት [አጠ'ና]
room
-ስ- ቢሮ (እመኖሪያ ቤት ውስጥ)
stuff
ስ'ተፍ -ስ- ጨርቃጨርቅ
nonsense
-ስ- ፍሬ ቢስ
push in
-ግ- ማ'ጨቅ [አ'ጨቀ]

stuffy
ስ'ተፊ -ቅ- አ'የር ያ'ነሰው ቦታ
stumble
ስ'ተምበል -ግ- መ'ደናቀፍ [ተደና'ቀ .]
stump
ስ'ተምፕ -ስ- ሥር (ግንዱ የተቆ'ረጠ ት)
of limb etc.
-ስ- ጉምድ (ተቆርጦ የቀ'ረ) ፣ ዱ'ሽ
stun
ስ'ተን -ግ- በመምታት ነፍስ ን.' ዲስት ማድረግ [አደ'ረገ]
stupid
ስት'ዩ:ፒድ -ቅ- ደንቆሮ ፣ የ'ማይገባው ፣ ሞ'ኝ
stupor
ስት'ዩ:ፐ -ስ- አእምሮን የመሳት ሁናተ (ከመድኃኒት ፣ ከመጠ'ጥ ወዘተ የተነ'ሣ)
sturdy
ስ'ተ:ዲ -ቅ- ጠንካ'ራ
stutter
ስ'ተተ -ግ- መንተባተብ [ተንተባ'ተበ ፣ መንገዝገዝ [ተንገዘ'ገዘ]
sty
ስ'ታይ -ስ- ያሣማ ጋጣ
style
ስ'ታይል -ስ- መንገድ ፣ ዘዴ (የ'ጸጸፍ ወዘተ)
suave
ስ'ዋ:ቭ -ቅ- የታ'ረመ ፣ ጠ'ፍ ያለ፣ ጥሩ ጠባይ ያ'ለው
subdue
ሰብድ'ዩ: -ግ- ማ'ሸ'ነፍ [አ'ሸ'ነፈ] ፡ ጸ'ጥተ'ኛ'ና ለስላ'ሳ ማድረግ [አደ'ረገ]
subhuman
ሰብ'ህ'ዩ:መን -ቅ- ከሰው ተፈጥሮ በታ'ች የሆነ
subject
'ሰብጀክት -ስ- ተገዥ
grammar
-ስ- ባለቤት (ለዋለው)
academic
-ስ- ትምህርት (የተለ'የ)
subject
ሰብ'ጀክት -ግ- መ'ገደድ [ተገ'ደደ] ፡ መ'ገዛት [ተገ'ዛ] ፣ መገ'በር [ገ'በረ]

sublime
ሱብ'ላይም -ቅ- ፍ'ጹም የተከ'በረ ፣ ባለግርማ፣ እ'ጅግ የላቀ
holy
-ቅ- ቅ'ዱስ

submarine
ሰብመ'ሪይን -ስ- በባሕር ውስጥ የ'ሚሄድ መርከብ

submerge
ሰብ'መ:ጅ -ግ- መጥለቅ [ጠ'ለቀ]፣ መስጠም [ሰ'ጠመ] ፣ መ'ዘፈቅ [ተዘ'ፈቀ]

submission
ሰብ'ሚሽን -ስ- መ'ማረክ ፣ መ'ሸነፍ
legal
-ስ- ማስረ'ጃ ማቅረብ (ለዳ'ኛ)

submit
ሰብ'ሚት -ግ- ማቅረብ [አቀ'ረበ]
surrender
-ግ- መ'ሸነፍ [ተሸ'ነፈ]

subordinate
ሰ'ቦ:ዲነት -ቅ- የበታ'ች (ለማዕረግ)

subscribe
ሰብስክ'ራይብ -ግ- አስተዋፅኦ ማድረግ [አደ'ረገ] (የገንዘብ ወዘተ)

subsequent
'ሰብሰክዌንት -ቅ- ተከ'ታይ

subservient
ሰብ'ሰ:ቪየንት -ቅ- ትሕት'ና አብዛር ፣ ተቅለ ስላሽ ፣ ሽቁጥቁጥ

subside
ሰብ'ሰይድ -ግ- ጸ'ጥ ማለት [አለ] ፣ (ለነፋስ) ፣ እ'ያ'ነሰ መሄድ [ሄደ] (ለጎርፍ)

subsidiary
ሰብ'ሲዲየሪ -ስ- ቅርንጫፍ (የድር'ጅት)

subsidy
'ሰብሲዲ -ስ- መንግሥት የ'ሚሰጠው የርዳታ ገንዘብ (ላንድ ድር'ጅት)

substance
'ሰብስተንስ -ስ- ነገር (ለዕቃ)

substantial
ሰብስ'ታንሽል -ቅ- ት'ልቅ ፡ ብዙ ፡ ጠንካ'ራ

substitute
'ሰብስቲትዩ:ት -ግ- መተ'ካት [ተ'ካ]
-ስ- ምት'ክ ፡ ተለ'ዋጭ

subterfuge
'ሰብተፍዩ:ጅ -ስ- ማ'ታለል ፣ ተንኰል ፣ የ' ፈ'ልጉትን ነገር በተንኮል ማግኘት

subterranean
ሰብተ'ሬይኒየን -ስ- ከመሬት በታ'ች

subtle
'ሰተል -ቅ- ጮ'ሌ ፣ ብልጥ

subtract
ሰብት'ራክት -ግ- መቀ'ነስ [ቀነ'ሰ]

suburb
'ሰበ:ብ -ስ- በከተማ ዳር ያ'ለ መንደር

subversive
ሰብ'ቨ:ሲቭ -ቅ- መንግሥት ፣ ሃይማኖት ወ ተቃዋሚ

subway
'ሰብዌይ -ስ- ከመሬት በታ'ች የ'ሚሄድ መ ላለሻ ባቡር

succeed
ሰክ'ሲይድ -ግ- መተ'ካት [ተ'ካ] ፡ እፈ'ለ ግብ መድረስ [ደ'ረሰ]
prosper
-ግ- መ'ከናወን [ተከና'ወነ] ፡
ው'ጤት ማግኘት [አገ'ኘ]

success
ሰክ'ሴስ -ስ- ተብዝ'ና ፣ ከን'ውን

successor
ሰክ'ሴሰ -ስ- ወራ'ሽ ፡ ምት'ክ

succour
'ሰከ -ስ- እርዳታ (በች'ግር ፣ በሐዘን ጊዜ)
-ግ- ማጽናናት [አጽና'ና] ፣ መር [ረ'ዳ]

succulent
'ሰክዩለንት -ቅ- ጣፋጭ ፡ እ'ጅ የ'ሚያስ 'ጥም ያ ውሃ የሞ'ላው (ለፍራፍሬ)

succumb
ሰ'ከም -ግ- መ'ሸነፍ [ተሸ'ነፈ] ፣ መ [ሞተ]

such
'ሰች -ቅ- እንደ'ዚህ

suck
'ሰክ -ግ- መምጠጥ [መ'ጠጠ] ፡ መ [ጠ'ባ]

sudden
'ሰደን -ቅ- ድንገተ'ኛ

suds
'ሰድዝ -ስ- አረፋ (የሳሙና)

sue
'ሱ: -ግ- መክሰስ [ከ'ሰሰ] (በሕ'ግ ፡ ቀጣሪን ስላልከ'ፈለው ደመወዝ) ፤ መ'ለማመጥ [ተለማ'መጠ] (ለዕርቅ ፡ ለምሕረት)

suet
'ሱዊት -ስ- ሞራ

suffer
'ሰፈ -ግ- መ'ታመም [ታ'መመ] ፡ መ'ጨነቅ [ተጨ'ነቀ] ፡ መ'ሠቃየት [ተሠቃ'የ]

suffice
ሰ'ፋይስ -ግ- መብቃት [በ'ቃ].

sufficient
ሰ'ፊሸንት -ቅ- በቂ

suffix
'ሰፊክስ -ስ- ባዕድ መ'ነሻ [ሰዋስው)

suffocate
'ሰፈኬይት -ግ- መ'ታነቅ [ታ'ነቀ] ፡ መ'ታፈን [ታ'ፈነ] (ከአ'የር እጦት የተነ'ሣ)

suffrage
'ሰፍሪጅ -ስ- የምርጫ መብት (የሕዝብ እንደ ራሴን)

sugar
'ሹገ -ስ- ሱ'ካር

sugar-cane
'ሹገ ኬይን -ስ- ሸንኮር አገዳ

suggest
ሰ'ጀስት -ግ- ሐ'ሳብ ማቅረብ [አቀ'ረበ]

suggestion
ሰ'ጀስትየን -ስ- የ'ሚቀርብ ሐ'ሳብ

suicide
'ሱዊሳይድ -ስ- ራስን መግደል ፡ የራስን ሕይወት ማጥፋት

suit
ስ'ዩ:ት -ስ- ሙሉ ልብስ (ከአንድ ዓይነት ጨርቅ)
petition
-ስ- አቤቱታ ፡ ክ'ስ (ለፍርድ ቤት)
fit
-ግ- መስማማት [ተስማ'ማ] ፡ መ'መቸት [ተመ'ቸ]

suitable
ስ'ዩ:ተበል -ቅ- ተስማሚ ፡ ም'ቹ

suitcase
ስ'ዩ:ትኬይስ -ስ- የልብስ ሻንጣ

suitor
'ስዩ:ተ -ስ- ሊያጭ የ'ሚመጣ ፡ ጋብቻ ጠ'ያቂ ወንድ

sulk
'ሰልክ -ግ- የፈ'ለጉትን ባለማግኘት ማኩረፍ [አኩ'ረፈ] (ለሕፃን)

sulky
'ሰልኪ -ቅ- አኩራፊ

sullen
'ሰለን -ቅ- አኩራፊ ፡ የ'ማይጠዳው ፡ የጨፈ'ገገ (ሰማይ)

sulphur
'ሰልፈ -ስ- ድ'ኝ

sultry
'ሰልትሪ -ስ- ከ'ባድ ፡ ሞ'ቃት አ'የር

sum
'ሰም -ስ- ድ'ምር
mathematical
-ስ- ጠቅላላ ድ'ምር

summary
'ሰመሪ -ስ- ማ'ጠቃለያ (ለጽሑፍ) ፡ አ'ጭር መግለጫ

summer
'ሰመ -ስ- በጋ

summit
'ሰሚት -ስ- ጫፍ (የተራራ) ፤ ከ'ፍተ'ኛ (ጉባኤ ስብሰባ)

summon
'ሰመን -ግ- መሰብሰብ [ሰበ'ሰበ] ፡ መጥራት [ጠ'ራ] (ለጥ'ሪ)

summons
'ሰመንዝ -ስ- መጥሪያ (የክ'ስ)

sumptuous
'ሰምችዩወስ -ቅ- በጣም ም'ቹ ፡ ድሎት ያ'ለው ፡ ዋጋው ከ'ፍ ያለ

sun
'ሰን -ስ- ፀሐይ

sunbeam
'ሰንቢይም -ስ- የፀሐይ ጮ'ራ ፡ ጨረር

sunburn
'ሰንበ:ን -ስ- ፀሐይ ያ'ቃ'ጠለው ሰው'ነት

Sunday
’ሰንዴይ -ስ- እሑድ

sunflower
’ሰንፍላወ -ስ- የሱፍ አበባ

sunken
’ሰንከን -ቅ- ዝ'ቅተ'ኛ ፣ ረ'ባ'ዳ (ቦታ) ፣ የጐ ደ'ጐደ (ለመልክ)

sunlight
’ሰንላይት -ስ- የፀሐይ ብርሃን

sunny
’ሰኒ -ቅ- ፀሐያ'ማ

sunrise
’ሰንራይዝ -ስ- የፀሐይ መውጣት ፣ የጀምበር መውጣት

sunset
’ሰንሴት -ስ- የፀሐይ መጥለቅ ፣ የጀምበር መጥለቅ

sunshade
’ሰንሼይድ -ስ- ጥላ (በ'ጅ የ'ሚ'ያዝ)

sunshine
’ሰንሻይን -ስ- የፀሐይ ብርሃን (ፈገ'ግ ያለ)

sunstroke
’ሰንስትረውክ -ስ- የፀሐይ ም'ች

superannuation
ሱፐራንዩ’ዌይሽን -ስ- የጡረታ አበ'ል ፣ ከሥ ራ በጡረታ መውጣት

superb
ሱ’ፐ፡ብ -ቅ- ግሩም ፣ ድንቅ ፣ እን ከን የሌ'ለው

supercilious
ሱፐ’ሲሊየስ -ቅ- ፌዘ'ኛ ፣ አልግጭ ፣ እ'ቡይ

superficial
ሱፐ’ፊሸል -ቅ- ጥራዝ ነ'ጠቅ ፣ ጥልቅ'ነት የሌ'ለው ፣ ዐዋቂ መሳይ

superfluous
ሱ’ፐ፡ፍሉወስ -ቅ- ከ'ሚ'ፈ'ለገው በላይ ፣ ከመ ጠን በላይ

superhuman
ሱፐህ’ዩ፡መን -ቅ- ከሰው ዐቅም በላይ ፣ ከሰው ተፈጥሮ በላይ የሆነ

superimpose
ሱፐሪም’ፐውዝ -ግ- መደ'ረብ [ደ'ረበ] ፣ በ ላይ ማስቀ'መጥ [አስቀ'መጠ]

superintendent
ሱፐሪን’ቴንደንት -ስ- ተቆጣጣሪ ፣ ያንድ ድር 'ጅት ሹም

superior
ሱ’ፒሪየ -ቅ- የበላይ

superiority
ሱፒሪ’ዮረቲ -ስ- የበላይ'ነት

superlative
ሱ’ፐ፡ለቲቭ -ቅ- እ'ጅግ በጣም ጥሩ
-ስ- እ'በላላጭ ደረጃ (ሰዋስው)

supermarket
’ሱፐማ፡ከት -ስ- በ'ያይነቱ ሸቀጣሸቀጥ የ'ሚ 'ሸጥ'በት የተሟ'ላ ት'ልቅ መደ'ብር

supernatural
ሱፐ’ናቸረል -ቅ- መለኮታዊ ፣ ከሰው ዐቅም በላይ

supersede
ሱፐ’ሲይድ -ግ- መ'ተካት [ተተ'ካ]

superstition
ሱፐስ’ቲሽን -ስ- በጥንቆላ ፣ በአስማት'ና በል'ዩ ል'ዩ ምል'ክቶ'ች ማመን

superstitious
ሱፐስ’ቲሽስ -ቅ- በጣኦት አምልኮ አማኝ

superstructure
’ሱፐስትረክቸ -ስ- የቤት ዋ'ና አካል (ከመሠ ረት በላይ ያ'ለው)

supervise
’ሱፐቫይዝ -ግ- መ'ቆጣጠር [ተቆጣ'ጠረ]

supervision
ሱፐ’ቪዝን -ስ- ቁጥ'ጥር

supervisor
’ሱፐቫይዘ -ስ- ተቆጣጣሪ

supine
’ሱፓይን -ቅ- የተንጋ'ለለ ፣ ኀይል የጐ'ደ ለው ፣ የ'ማይንቀሳ'ቀስ

supper
’ሰፐ -ስ- ራት

supple
’ሰፐል -ቅ- ልል ፣ በቀ'ላሉ የ'ሚ'ታ'ጠፍ

supplement
’ሰፐሊመንት -ስ- ተጨ'ማሪ ነገር ፣ ች'ግርን ለማ'ሟላት የተጨ'መረ ነገር

supplication
ሰፐሊ’ኬሽን -ስ- የል'ብ ጸሎት ፣ አቤቱታ

supply
ሰፐ'ላይ -ግ- ማቅረብ [አቀ'ረበ] ፣ መስጠት [ሰ'ጠ]
-ስ- ሥንቅ ፣ ምግብ

support
ሰ'ፖ:ት -ግ- መርዳት [ረ'ዳ]
-ስ- እርዳታ

supporter
ሰ'ፖ:ተ -ስ- ረ'ዳት

suppose
ሰ'ፐውዝ -ግ- ማ'ሰብ [አ'ሰበ] ፡ ሊሆን ይች ላ'ል ብሎ ማ'ሰብ [አ'ሰበ]

suppress
ሰፐ'ሬስ -ግ- መጨ'ቆን [ጨ'ቆነ]

supremacy
ሱፐ'ሬመሲ -ስ- ታ'ላቅ'ነት ፣ መላቅ ፡ የበላ ይ'ነት

supreme
ሱፐሪይም -ቅ- የላቀ ፡ ታ'ላቅ፣ብልጫ ያ'ለው፡ ከ'ፍተ'ኛ

sure
'ሾ: -ቅ- እርግጥ

surely
'ሾ:ሊ -ተግ- በርግጥ ፣ በውነት

surf
'ሰ:ፍ -ስ- የማዕበል አረፋ

surface
'ሰ:ፈስ -ስ- ፊት (ያንድ ነገር የላይ'ኛው መል ኩ)

surfeit
'ሰ:ፊት -ግ- ከመጠን በላይ መመ'ገብ [መ'ገበ]
-ስ- ከመጠን በላይ መብላት ፣ መጠ'ጣት ወዘተ

surge
'ሰ:ጅ -ግ- መስገግ [ሰ'ገገ] (ለብዙ ሰዎ'ች ወዘተ)

surgeon
'ሰ:ጀን -ስ- ቀዳጅ ሐኪም

surly
'ሰ:ሊ -ቅ- በጥቂቱ የ'ሚ'ቀ'የም ፣ እኩራፊ

surmise
ሰ'ማይዝ -ግ- ማ'ሰብ [አ'ሰበ] (ሊሆን የ'ሚ ችለውን)

surmount
ሰ'ማውንት -ግ- ማ'ሸ'ነፍ [አ'ሸ'ነፈ] ፣ መ'ወ ጣት [ተወ'ጣ] (ች'ግርን)

surname
'ሰ:ኔይም -ስ- ያ'ባት ስም (ባ'ባት በ'ኩል የመ'ጣ የቤተሰብ ስም)

surpass
ሰ'ፓ:ስ -ግ- መላቅ [ላቀ] ፡ መብለጥ [በ'ለጠ]

surplus
'ሰ:ፐለስ -ስ- ትርፍ ፡ ከስፈ'ላጊ በላይ ያ'ለ ነገር

surprise
ሰፕ'ራይዝ -ግ- ማስደንገጥ [አስደነ'ገጠ]
-ስ- አስገ'ራሚ ፣ ያልጠ'በቁት ነገር

surrender
ሰ'ሬንደ -ግ- እ'ጅን መስጠት [ሰ'ጠ]
-ስ- እ'ጅን መስጠት

surreptitious
ሰሬፕ'ቲሸስ -ቅ- በድ'ብቅ ፡ በምስጢር የተ ሠ'ራ ፣ የተገ'ኘ (እምነትን በማጉደል)

surroundings
ሰ'ራውንዲንግዝ -ስ- አ'ካባቢ

survey
ሳ'ቨይ -ግ- መሬትን መለ'ካት [ለ'ካ] ፣ መቀ 'የስ [ቀ'የሰ] ፡ ጠቅላ'ላ ጥናት ማድረግ [አደ 'ረገ]

survey
'ሰ:ቬይ -ስ- ጠቅላ'ላ ምር'ምር ፣ ጥናት

surveyor
ሰ'ቬየ -ስ- መሬት ቀ'ያሽ (ጅኦሜትራ)

survive
ሰ'ቫይቭ -ግ- መዳን [ዳነ] ፣ ማለፍ [አ'ለፈ] (መከራን) ፣ መትረፍ [ተ'ረፈ] (ከመከራ)

susceptible
ሰ'ሴፕቲበል -ቅ- ደካማ ፣ በስ'ሜት በቀ'ላሉ የ'ሚ'ማ'ረክ ፣ በቀ'ላሉ ሊ'ለ'ወጥ የ'ሚችል

suspect
ሰስ'ፔክት -ግ- መ'ጠራጠር [ተጠራ'ጠረ]

suspend
ሰስ'ፔንድ -ግ- ማንጠልጠል [አንጠለ'ጠለ] ፣ መስቀል [ሰ'ቀለ] ፣ መ'ሰቀል [ተሰ'ቀለ]
dismiss temporarily
-ግ- መ'ታገድ [ታ'ገደ] (ከሥራ)

suspenders
ሰስ'ፔንደዝ -ስ- የግር ሹ'ራብ መያዣ (ላስ ቲክ'ነት ያ'ለው)
American
-ስ- የሱ'ሪ መያዣ (ላስቲክ'ነት ያ'ለው)

suspense
ሰስ'ፔንስ -ስ- እርግጠ'ኛ ያልሆነ ጉ'ጉት (ስለ ወሬ ፣ ው'ሳኔ ወዘተ)

suspension
ሰስ'ፔንሽን -ስ- የመኪና ሞ'ላ
dismissal
-ስ- ማ'ገድ (ከሥራ)

suspicion
ሰስ'ፒሽን -ስ- ጥር'ጣሬ

sustained
ሰስ'ቴይንድ -ቅ- ቀ'ጣይ ፣ የ'ማያ'ቋ'ርጥ (ለ ሥራ) ፤ የተደ'ገፈ (ለኑሮ)

swagger
ስ'ዋገ -ግ- መንጐራደድ [ተንጐራ'ደደ] ፤ እየ ደነ'ፋ መ'ናገር [ተና'ገረ]

swallow
ስ'ዎለው -ግ- መዋጥ [ዋጠ] (ለምብል)

swamp
ስ'ዎምፕ -ስ- አሮንቃ ፣ ጨቀጨቅ

swan
ስ'ዎን -ስ- ዝ'ይ ፣ የውሃ ዶሮ

swarm
ስ'ዎ:ም -ስ- የንብ መንጋ

swathe
ስ'ዌይዝ -ግ- በጨርቅ መጠቅለል [ጠቀ'ለለ]

sway
ስ'ዌይ -ግ- መ'ወዝወዝ [ተወዘ'ወዘ]

swear
ስ'ዌየ -ግ- መማል [ማለ]
use bad language
-ግ- መስደብ [ሰ'ደበ]

sweat
ስ'ዌት -ግ- ማላብ [አላበ]
-ስ- ላብ

sweep
ስ'ዊይፕ -ግ- መጥረግ [ጠ'ረገ] (ቤት)

sweet
ስ'ዊይት -ቅ- ጣፋጭ
-ስ- ከረሜ'ላ

sweetheart
ስ'ዊይትሃ:ት -ስ- ወዳጅ ፣ ፍቅር

swell
ስ'ዌል -ግ- ማበጥ [አ'በጠ]

swelling
ስ'ዌሊንግ -ስ- እበጥ ፣ እብጠት

sweltering
ስ'ዌልተሪንግ -ቅ- ከሙቀት የተነ'ሣ የተዝ ለፈ'ለፈ ፣ ሐሩር ያ'ደ'ከመው

swerve
ስ'ወ:ቭ -ግ- ማግለል [አገ'ለለ] ፣ መንገድ መለ'ወጥ [ለ'ወጠ]

swift
ስ'ዊፍት -ቅ- ፈ'ጣን

swill
ስ'ዊል -ስ- ፍር'ፋሪ ፣ ት'ራፊ (ለምግብ) ያሣማ ምግብ (የተበጠ'በጠ)
gulp down
-ግ- መገ'ጠም [ገ'ጠመ] (ወሃ)

swim
ስ'ዊም -ግ- መዋኘት [ዋ''ኘ]

swindle
ስ'ዊንደል -ግ- ማ'ታለል [አ'ታ'ለለ] ፣ ማጭ በርበር [አጭበረ'በረ]
-ስ- ማ'ታለል ፣ ማጭበርበር

swindler
ስ'ዊንደለ -ቅ- አ'ታላይ ፣ አጭበርባሪ

swine
ስ'ዋይን -ስ- ዐሣማ

swing
ስ'ዊንግ -ግ- መ'ወዛወዝ [ተወዛ'ወዘ] ፤ ሲ'ሶ ሽ መ'ጫወት [ተጫ'ወተ]፣ዥ'ውዥ'ው መ'ጫ ወት [ተ'ጫ'ወተ]
-ስ- ሲ'ሶሽ ፣ ዥ'ውዥ'ው
play apparatus
-ስ- የሲ'ሶሽ ወንበር ፣ የዥ'ውዥ'ው ወንበር

swipe
ስ'ዋይፕ -ግ- መለ'ተም [ለ'ተመ] (መምታት)

swirl
ስ'ወ:ል -ግ- መዞር [ዞረ] (አዝዋሪት)

switch
ስ'ዊች -ስ- ማብሪያ (ለኤሌክትሪክ)
-on
-ግ- ማብራት [አበ'ራ] (ለመብራት)
-off
-ግ- ማጥፋት [አጠ'ፋ] (ለመብራት)
transfer
-ግ- መለዋወጥ [ለዋ'ወጠ] (ሐ'ሳብን በንግ'ግር)

swivel
ስ'ዊቨል -ግ- በአንድ ነገር ላይ መዞር [ዞረ]

swoon
ስ'ውːን -ግ- መዝለፍለፍ [ተዝለፈ'ለፈ]፤ እእምሮ መሳት [ሳተ]

swoop
ስ'ውːፕ -ግ- ሽ'ው ብሎ መውረድ [ወ'ረደ]፤ ድንገት አደጋ መጣል [ጣለ]

sword
'ሶːድ -ስ- ጎራዴ ፣ ሠይፍ

sycamore
'ሲከሞː -ስ- ዋርካ (ወርካ)

syce
'ሳይስ -ስ- ለ'ጓሚ (የፈረስ ፣ የበቅሎ)

syllable
'ሲለበል -ስ- ክፍለ ቃል

syllabus
'ሲለበስ -ስ- መርሐ ትምሀርት

symbol
'ሲምበል -ስ- ምል'ክት

symmetrical
ሲ'ሜትሪከል -ቅ- ተመሳሳይ (ቅርፅ ፣ መጠን)፣ ሁለ'ቱም ጎ'ን የ'ሚ'መሳ'ሰል

sympathy
'ሲምፐቢ -ስ- ርኅራኄ ፣ እርስበርስ መስማማት ፣ እንዱ ለሌላው ማ'ሰብ

symptom
'ሲምተም -ስ- የበ'ሽታ ምል'ክት ፣ አንድ ነገር መኖሩን የ'ሚያመለ'ክት ምል'ክት

synagogue
'ሲነጎግ -ስ- የአይሁድ ቤተ መቅደስ ፣ ምኩራብ አይሁድ

synchronize
'ሲንክረናይዝ -ግ- ማስተካከል [አስተካ'ከለ] (ሰዓት አንድ ዓይነት ጊዜ እንዲነግር) ፣ ባንድ ጊዜ እንዲሄድ ማድረግ [አደ'ረገ]

syndicate
'ሲንዲከት -ስ- ማኅበር (የል'ዩ ል'ዩ ሞያ)

synonym
'ሲነኒም -ስ- ተመሳሳይ ትርጉም ያ'ለው ቃል

synopsis
ሲ'ኖፕሲስ -ስ- አሕጽሮተ ጽሑፍ ፤ ዋ'ና ሐ'ሳብ ፣ ፍሬ ነገር (የመጽሐፍ ፣ የቴአትር ፣ የፊልም ወዘተ)

syntax
'ሲንታክስ -ስ- አ'ገባብ (የዐረፍተ ነገር)

synthetic
ሲን'ቤቲክ -ቅ- ሰው ሠ'ራሽ

syphilis
'ሲፊሊስ -ስ- ቂ'ጥ'ኝ

syringe
ስ'ሪንጅ -ስ- መርፌ (የሐኪም) ፤ ፈሳሽ መምጠጫ'ና ማፍሰሻ መ'ሣሪያ

syrup
'ሲረፕ -ስ- ጣፋጭ መጠ'ጥ (ከሱ'ካር'ና ከውሃ ወይን'ም ከሱ'ካር'ና ከፍራፍሬ ጭ'ማቂ የተ'ሠ'ራ)

system
'ሲስተም -ስ- ሕ'ግ ፣ ደምብ

systematic
ሲስ'ተማቲክ -ቅ- ደምበ'ኛ ፣ በደምብ የ'ሚሠራ

systematically
ሲስተ'ማቲክሊ -ተግ- በሕ'ግ ፣ በደምብ ፣ በተራ

T

tab
'ታብ -ስ- የጨርቅ ምል'ክት (ለማዕረግ)
tabernacle
'ታበናክል -ስ- ደብተራ እሪት
table
'ቴይበል -ስ- ጠረ'ጴዛ
tablecloth
'ቴይቡልክሎ፡ስ -ስ- የጠረ'ጴዛ ልብስ
tablespoon
'ቴይቡልስፑ፡ን -ስ- የሾርባ ማንካ
tablet
'ታብሌት -ስ- ክኒን (መድኃኒት)
taboo
ታ'ቡ፡ -ስ- ሃይማኖት ወይን'ም ሥነ ምግባር እንዳይ'ነ'ካ ፣ እንዳይ'ደ'ረግ ፣ በይፋ እንዳ'ይ'ነ'ገር የ'ሚከለ'ክለው ነገር
tabulate
'ታብዩሌይት -ግ- በወግ መመ'ደብ [መ'ደበ]
tacit
'ታሲት -ቅ- ሳይ'ና'ገር (ራስ በመነቅነቅ መስማማት'ና አለመስማማትን) የ'ሚገልጽ
tack
'ታክ -ስ- ት'ንሽ ሚስማር (ራሱ ሰፋ ያለ)
-ስ- ስፌት (እንዱ)
stitch
-ግ- መወስወስ [ወሰ'ወሰ]
tackle
'ታክል -ስ- መ'ሣሪያ
approach
-ግ- መፍትሔ መፈ'ለግ [ፈ'ለገ]
football
-ግ- መያዝ [ያዘ] (ተጫዋቾ'ችን)
tacky
'ታኪ -ቅ- መጣብቅ'ነት ያ'ለው ፣ የ'ሚያ'ጣ'ብቅ
tact
'ታክት -ስ- ብልኀት (ሰውን ሳይጎዱ የ'ሚ'ወ'ጡ'በት)
tactics
'ታክቲክስ -ስ- ዕቅድ ፣ ብልኀት (የወ'ታ'ደር)
tag
'ታግ -ስ- ምል'ክት ፣ የዋጋ መግለጫ ወረቀት
stock phrase
-ስ- በ'የጊዜው የ'ሚ'ነ'ገር ፣ የተለ'መደ የ'ሚ'ጠ'ቀስ ሐረግ ፣ ዐረፍተ ነገር
tail
'ቴይል -ስ- ጂራት
tailor
'ቴይለ -ስ- ልብስ ሰፊ ፣ መኪና ሰፊ
tainted
'ቴይንቲድ -ቅ- እ'ጅ እ'ጅ የ'ሚል (ምግብ)
take
'ቴይክ -ግ- መውሰድ [ወ'ሰደ]
tale
'ቴይል -ግ- ታሪክ ፣ ስለአንድ ሁናቴ የ'ሚ'ነ'ገር ወሬ
talent
'ታለንት -ግ ስጦታ ፣ ችሎታ ፣ ተውህቦ
talisman
'ታሊዝመን -ስ- አሽንክታብ ፣ ጠልሰም
talk
'ቶ፡ክ -ግ- መ'ናገር [ተና'ገረ]
-ስ- ንግ'ግር
lecture
-ስ- ንግ'ግር
talkative
'ቶ፡ክቲቭ -ቅ- ለፍላፊ ፣ ቀባጣሪ ፣ ምላስ'ኛ
tall
'ቶ፡ል -ቅ- ረ'ጅም
tame
'ቴይም -ቅ- ለ'ማዳ (ለእውሬ)
-ግ- ማልመድ [አለ'መደ]
tamper
'ታምፐ -ግ- ጥ'ልቅ ማለት [አለ]
tan
'ታን -ግ- ቆዳ ማልፋት [አለ'ፋ]
sun-
-ስ- በፀሐይ የጠቆ'ረ ሰው'ነት
become sunburned
-ግ- በፀሐይ መ'ቃጠል [ተቃ'ጠለ] (ለ'መልክ)

tandem
'ታንደም -ስ- ሁለ'ት ሰዎ'ች የ'ሚጋ'ልቡት ቢሲክሌት (ባለሁ'ለት መወስወሻ)

tang
'ታንግ -ስ- መጣጣ ጣዕም ፣ የተለ'የ ጣዕም ፣ ሽ'ታ ያ'ለው ነገር

tangible
'ታንጀበል -ቅ- ግዑዝ ፣ በእጅ የ'ሚ'ዳ'ሰስ ፣ ግልጽ ፣ ደብዛ'ዛ ያልሆነ

tangle
'ታንገል -ግ- መ'ወታተብ [ተወታ'ተበ] (ለ ክ'ር ፣ ለጠጉር ወዘተ)
-ስ- ውትብትብ ክ'ር ፣ ጠጉር (ወዘተ)

tank
'ታንክ -ስ- የወሃ ማ'ጠራቀሚያ ፣ የመኪና ቤንዚን መያዣ
military
-ስ- ታንክ (ብረት ለ'በስ መኪና)

tantalize
'ታንተላይዝ -ግ- ማጓጓት [አጓ'ጓ] ፣ ተስፋ እ'የሰ'ጡ አለመፈ'ጸም [-ፈ'ጸመ]

tap
'ታፕ -ስ- የቧምቧዋ ውሃ መክፈቻ
-ግ- ማንኳኳት [አንኳ'ኳ] (በ'ር ወዘተ)

tape
'ቴይፕ -ስ- ቀ'ጭን ፣ ረ'ጅም ከጨርቅ ፣ ከወ ረቀት የተሠ'ራ የዕቃ ማሠሪያ
-ስ- የቴ'ፕ ክ'ር

taper
'ቴይፐ -ግ- እ'የቀ'ጠነ መሄድ [ሄደ] (ከአ ንድ ወገን)
-ስ- ጧፍ

tapestry
'ታፔስትሪ -ስ- ገብረ ምንጣፍ (የግድግ'ዳ ፣ የወለል)

tapeworm
'ቴፕወ:ም -ስ- የኮሶ ትል

tar
'ታ: -ስ- ሬንጅ

target
'ታ:ገት -ስ- ዓላማ (የተኩስ) ፣ በቦምብ የ'ሚ 'ደበ'ደብ ቦታ ፣ ግብ (የሥራ)

tariff
'ታ:ሪፍ -ስ- ቁርጥ ዋጋ (በሆቴ'ሉ ፣ ለሆቴል ምግብ ፣ ለመ'ኝታ ወዘተ) ፣ አገር ውስጥ በ'ሚ ገቡ ዕቃዎ'ች ላይ የ'ሚ'ጣል የቀረጥ ዝርዝር

tarnish
'ታ:ኒሽ -ግ- መደብዘዝ [ደበ'ዘዘ] ፣ ማደብዘዝ [አደበ'ዘዘ] (ከመቆ'የት የተነ'ሣ)

tarpaulin
ታ'ፖ:ሊን -ስ- ውሃ የ'ማያስገ'ባ ልብስ በሬንጅ የተነ'ከረ ሸራ

tart
'ታ:ት -ስ- ኬክ (መርመላታ'ና ፍሬ ያ'ለ'በት)
taste
-ቅ- ኮምጣ'ጣ ጣዕም ያ'ለው

task
'ታ:ስክ -ስ- ሥራ ፣ ተግባር

tassel
'ታሰል -ስ- ባለጌጥ ዘርፍ ፣ መርገፍ

taste
'ቴይስት -ግ- መቅመስ [ቀ'መሰ]
-ስ- ቅምሻ ፣ ጣዕም ፣ አ'መራረጥ

tasty
'ቴይስቲ -ቅ- የ'ሚጥም ፣ የ'ሚጣ'ፍጥ

tattered
'ታተድ -ቅ- የተበጫ'ጨቀ ፣ የተተለ'ተለ (ለ ልብስ)

tattoo
ታ'ቱ: -ስ- ው'ቅራት ፣ ንቅሳት

taunt
'ቶ:ንት -ግ- መ'ተናኮል [ተተና'ኮለ] ፣ ነገር መቆስቆስ [ቆሰ'ቆሰ] (በንግ'ግር)

taut
'ቶ:ት -ቅ- የተወ'ጠረ (ገመድ ፣ የደም ሥር ወዘተ)

tavern
'ታቨን -ስ- መጠ'ጥ ቤት ፣ መሸታ ቤት

tawny
'ቶ:ኒ -ቅ- ጠየ'ም ያለ ብጫ

tax
'ታክስ -ስ- ቀረጥ
-ግ- መቅረጥ [ቀ'ረጠ]

taxi
'ታክሲ -ስ- ታክሲ

tea
'ቲይ -ስ- ሻይ

teach
'ቲይች -ግ- ማስተማር [አስተማረ]

teacher

'ቲይቸ -ስ- አስተማሪ

team

'ቲይም -ስ- ቡድን ፤ ጋሪ የ'ሚጎ'ትቱ ሁለ'ት ወይን'ም የበ'ለጡ ፈረሶ'ች ፣ በሬዎ'ች ወዘተ

tear

'ቲየ -ስ- ቅ'ድ (የጨርቅ) ፣ መቅደድ [ቀ'ደደ]

tear

'ቲየ -ስ- ዕንባ

tease

'ቲይዝ -ግ- ማ'ናደድ [አ'ና'ደደ] ፣ መ'ቃለድ [ተቃ'ለደ] (ለጨዋታ ወይ'ም ለመጉዳት)

teaspoon

'ቲይስፑ፡ን -ስ- የሻይ ፣ የቡ'ና ማንካ

teat

'ቲይት -ስ- የጡት ጫፍ (የእንስት) ፤ የጡ'ጦ አፍ

technique

ቴክ'ኒይክ -ስ- አንድ ነገር የመሥራት ብልኀት (በተለ'ይ ሜካኒካዊ)

tedious

'ቲይድየስ -ቅ- ረ'ጅም'ና አሰልቺ ፣ አድካሚ፤ ዝ'ግ ያለ'ና አስተያየትን የ'ማይማ'ርክ

teem

'ቲይም -ግ- መ'ሞላት [ተሞ'ላ] ፣ በብዛት መ'ገኘት [ተገ'ኘ]

teenager

'ቲይኔይጀ -ስ- ዕድሜው በዐሥራ ሦስት'ና በሃያ ዓመት መካ'ከል ያ'ለ ወ'ጣት

teetotal

ቲ'ቶተል -ቅ- የ'ሚያሰክር መጠ'ጥ የ'ማይጠ'ጣ ፣ የ'ሚያሰክር መጠ'ጥ እንዳይ'ጠ'ጣ የ'ሚደ'ግፍ

telegram

'ቴለግራም -ስ- ቴሌግራም

telephone

'ቴለፈውን -ስ- ቴሌፎን

telescope

'ቴለስከውፕ -ስ- ቴሌስኮ'ፕ (የሩቁን አቅርቦ የ'ሚያሳ'ይ መነ'ፅር)

television

'ቴለቪዠን -ስ- ቴሌቪዥን

tell

'ቴል -ግ- መንገር [ነ'ገረ]

temerity

ቲ'ሜሪቲ -ስ- የማይ'ገ'ባ ድፍረት ፤ ችኩ'ል'ነት ፣ አለመ'ጠንቀቅ

temper

'ቴምፐ -ስ- አመል (ቁ'ጡ'ነት ፣ ገ'ራም'ነት)
-ስ- ጠንካ'ራ'ነት (ለብረት)

steel

-ግ- ማጠንከር [አጠነ'ከረ] (ለብረት ለመስተዋት ፣ በሙቀት)

temperament

ቴምፐረመንት -ስ- አመል (ቁ'ጡ'ነት ፣ ን'ዴተ'ኛ'ነት ፣ ፀ'ጥተ'ኛ'ነት ወዘተ)

temperance

'ቴምፐረንስ -ስ- አለማብዛት ፣ መጠነ'ኛ'ነት ራስን ከአስካሪ መጠ'ጥ መከልከል

temperate

'ቴምፐረት -ቅ- መካ'ከለ'ኛ (ለአ'የር ሙቀት)

temperature

'ቴምፐረቸ -ስ- ያ'የር ሁናቴ (ሙቀት ወይን'ም ቅዝ'ቃዜ) ፤ ሙቀት (የሰው'ነት ከት'ኩሳት የተነ'ሣ)

tempest

'ቴምፔስት -ስ- ኀይለ'ኛ ነፋስ ፣ ዝናም ወዘተ

temple

'ቴምፐል -ስ- ቤተ መቅደስ

temporal

'ቴምፐረል -ቅ- ኀላፊ ፣ የ'ማይቆ'ይ ፣ ጊዜያዊ ፤ ምድራዊ ፣ ዓለማዊ

temporary

'ቴምፐረሪ -ቅ- ጊዜያዊ ፣ ጥቂት ጊዜ ብ'ቻ የ'ሚቆ'ይ

tempt

'ቴምት -ግ- መ'ፈታተን [ተፈታ'ተነ] ፣ ክፉ ሥራ እንዲሠሩ ማባበል [አባ'በለ]

temptation

ቴም'ቴይሸን -ስ- ፈተና (የሠይጣን)

ten

'ቴን -ቅ- ዐ'ሥር

tenable

'ቴነበል -ቅ- የ'ሚ'ደ'ገፍ ፣ የ'ሚ'ቀ'በሉት (ሐ'ሳብ)

tenacious

ተ'ኔይሸስ -ቅ- ተስፋ የ'ማይቆርጥ ፣ የያዘውን የ'ማይለ'ቅ ፤ አ'ሳበ ጥብቅ

tenacity

ተ’ናሲቲ -ስ- ተስፋ አለመቁረጥ ፣ በሐ'ሳብ መጥበቅ

tenant

’ቴነንት -ስ- ኪራየተ'ኛ (የመሬት ፣ የቤት ወዘተ) ፣ ጢሰ'ኛ

tend

’ቴንድ -ግ- ማዘንበል [አዘነ'በለ] ፣ መጠበቅ [ጠ'በቀ] (ለእንስሳ)

tendency

’ቴንደንሲ -ስ- ዝን'ባሌ

tender

’ቴንደ -ቅ- ርኅሩኅ ፣ ገር ፣ ለስላ'ሳ

offer

-ግ- ማ'ቅረብ [አ'ቀ'ረበ]

tendon

’ቴንደን -ስ- ጅ'ማት

tendril

’ቴንድሪል -ስ- ቀምበጥ (የ'ሚ'ሳቡ እትክልት)

tense

’ቴንስ -ስ- ድርጊ'ቱ የ'ሚ'ፈ'ጸም'በትን ፣ የተፈ'ጸመ'በትን ጊ፣ የ'ሚያሳ'ይ የግ'ሥ ዓይነት ፣ ጊዜ (ሰዋስው)

unrelaxed

-ቅ- ግ'ትር ፣ ያልተዝናና (ለሰው'ነት ወዘተ)

tension

’ቴንሽን -ስ- አለመግባባት ፣ ግ'ጭት (የሐ'ሳብ)

tent

’ቴንት -ስ- ድንኳን

tentative

’ቴንተቲቭ -ቅ- ለሙ'ከራ ያህል የተደ'ረገ ፣ ጊዜያዊ

tenth

’ቴንስ -ቅ- ዐ'ሥረ'ኛ

tent-peg

’ቴንት’ፔግ -ስ- ካስማ

tenure

’ቴንየ -ስ- ይዞታ (የመሬት ፣ የፖሊቲካ ሥራ)

tepid

’ቴፒድ -ቅ- ለ'ብ ያለ (ለውሃ)

term

’ተ:ም -ስ- የትምህርት ክፍለ ዓመት (ለሁለ'ት ወዘተ የተከ'ፈለ)፤ፍርድ ቤቶ'ች ችሎት የ'ሚያስችሉ'በት ወራት

expression

-ስ- ቃል

of bargain

-ስ- ስምም'ነት (ለገበያ)

terminal

’ተ:ሚነል -ቅ- መጨ'ረሻ (የባቡር መጨ'ረሻ ጣቢያ)

terminate

’ተ:ሚኔይት -ግ- መጨ'ረስ [ጨ'ረሰ] ፣ መፈ'ጸም [ፈ'ጸመ]

terminus

’ተ:ሚነስ -ስ- የአውቶቡስ መጨ'ረሻ ጣቢያ

termite

’ተ:ማይት -ስ- ምስጥ

terrace

’ቴረስ -ስ- ደልዳ'ላ ቦታ

terrain

ቴ’ሬይን -ስ- የመሬት አ'ቀማመጥ

terrible

’ቴሪበል -ቅ- በጣም አስደንጋጭ ፣ አስፈ'ሪ ፣ አሳ'ዛኝ

terrify

’ቴሪፋይ -ግ- ማስፈራራት [አስፈራ'ራ] ፣ ማስደንገጥ [አስደነ'ገጠ]

territory

’ቴሪትሪ -ስ- ግዛት ፣ በግዛት ውስጥ ያ'ለ አገር

terror

’ቴረ -ስ- ፍርሃት ፣ ድን'ጋጤ

terse

’ተ:ስ -ቅ- አ'ጭር'ና መሥመሩን ያ'ለ'ቀቀ (ለንግ'ግር)

test

’ቴስት -ግ- መፈ'ተን [ፈ'ተነ] ፣ መሞ'ከ፤ (ሞ'ከረ]

testament

’ቴስተመንት -ስ- ኑዛዜ

biblical

-ስ- ኪዳን

testicle
'ቴስቲክል -ስ- ቆለጥ
testify
'ቴስቲፋይ -ግ- መመስከር [መሰ'ከረ]
testimonial
ቴስት'መውኒየል -ስ- የምስ'ክር ወረቀት (የሠ'ራተ'ኛ ጠባይ)
testimony
'ቴስተመኒ -ስ- ምስ'ክር
text
'ቴክስት -ስ- ጽሑፍ (መጽሐፍ) ፤ የመጽሐፍ ቅ'ዱስ ጥቅስ
textbook
'ቴክስትቡክ -ስ- የመ'ማሪያ መጽሐፍ
textiles
'ቴክስታየልዝ -ስ- ጨርቃጨርቅ
texture
'ቴክስቸ -ስ- ያንድ ነገር የለስላ'ሳ'ነቱ ፤ የሻካራ'ነቱ ወዘተ ሁናቴ ፤ የድር'ና የማግ አ'ቀማመጥ (በጨርቃጨርቅ ፋብሪካ)
than
'ሻን -መሃ- ከ . . . ይልቅ
thank
'ሷንክ -ስ- ማመስገን [አመሰ'ገነ]
thank you
'ሷንክዩ አመሰ'ግና'ለሁ ፤ እግዚአብሔር ይስጥ'ል'ኝ
that
'ዛት -አተስ ያ ፤ ያ'ች
-አቅ- ያ ፤ ያ'ች
-መዋ- እንደ
thatch
'ሷች -ስ- የሣር ክዳን ፤ ክፈክፋ
-ግ- በሣር መክደን [ከ'ደነ] ፡ መክፋክፋ [ከፈ'ከፈ]
thaw
'ሶ፡ -ግ- መሟሟት [ሟ'ሟ] (ለበረዶ)
the
'ዘ, 'ዘ -ተመሥ- -ው ፡ -ዋ
-ዎቹ ፡ -ዎቹ
theatre
'ሲየትር -ስ- ቴአትር ፤ በሀ ስፒታል በ'ሽተ'ኞ'ች የ'ሚ'ቀ'ደዱ'በት ክፍል
theft
ሴፍት -ስ- ስርቆት

their
'ዜየ -ገተስ- የ'ነሱ ፤ የ'ነርሱ
theme
'ሲይም -ስ- ዋ'ና ሐ'ሳብ ፤ ዋ'ና ቁም ነገር (የመጽሐፍ ፤ የንግ'ግር)
then
'ዜን -ተግ- እንግዲህ ፤ ያን ጊዜ ፤ ታዲያ
after that
-ተግ- ከ'ዚያ በኋላ
thence
'ዜንስ -ተግ- ከ'ዚያ
theology
ሲ'ዮለጂ -ስ- ቃለ እግዚአብሔር ፤ ነገረ መለኮት
theory
'ሲየሪ -ስ- አስተያየት ፤ በሳይንሳዊ መንገድ ያልተረ'ጋ'ገጠ እምነት ወይን'ም ልምድ
therapy
'ሴረፒ -ስ- ሕ'ክም'ና
there
'ዜየ -አተስ- እ'ዚያ
therefore
'ዜፎ፡ -መዋ- ስለ'ዚህ
-ቃአ- እ'ነሆ
thermometer
ሰ'ሞመተ -ስ- የሙቀት መለ'ኪያ መ'ሣሪያ (ቴርሞሜትር)
these
'ዚይዝ -አተስ- እ'ነ'ዚህ
they
'ዜይ -ተስ- እ'ነሱ
thick
'ሲክ -ቅ- ወፍራም ፡ ጥቅ'ጥቅ ያለ
thicken
'ሲክን -ግ- ማወ'ፈር [አወ'ፈረ]
thicket
'ሲከት -ስ- ቁጥቋጦ
thickness
'ሲክነስ -ስ- ውፍረት
thief
'ሲይፍ -ስ- ሌባ
thigh
'ሳይ -ስ- ጭን

in
’ሲ̲ን -ቅ- ቀ'ጭን
ing
’ሲ̲ንግ -ስ- ነገር ፣ ዕቃ
ink
’ሲ̲ንክ -ግ- ማ'ሰብ [አ'ሰበ]
ird
’ሰ̲፡ድ -ቅ- ሢሶ ፣ አን'ድ ሦስተ'ኛ ፣ ሦስት'ያ
irst
’ሰ̲፡ስት -ስ- ጥም
irsty
’ሰ̲፡ስቲ -ቅ- የጠ'ማው ፣ የተጠ'ማ
irteen
ሰ̲’ቲይን -ቅ- ዐሥራ ሦስት
irteenth
ሰ̲’ቲይንሰ̲ -ቅ- ዐሥራ ሦስተ'ኛ
irtieth
’ሰ̲፡ቲየሰ̲ -ቅ- ሠላሳ'ኛ
irty
’ሰ̲፡ቲ -ቅ- ሠላሳ
is
’ዚ̲ስ -አ.ተ.ስ- ይህ ፣ ይህ'ች
ong
’ሶ̲ንግ -ስ- ጠፍር (መ'ጫ'ኛ ፣ ጅራፍ ወዘተ)
orn
’ሶ̲፡ን -ስ- እሾህ
orough
’ሰ̲ረ -ቅ- ጥንቁቅ ፣ ለጥ.ቃ'ቅን ነገር የ'ሚ'ጠ
ን'ቀቅ
oroughfare
’ሰ̲ረፌየ -ስ- ዥ'ው ያለ ጎዳና
ough
’ዞ̲ው -መዋ- ቢሆን'ም ፣ ሆኖ'ም
ought
’ሶ̲፡ት -ስ- ሐ'ሳብ
oughtful
’ሶ̲፡ትፉል -ቅ- ል'ባም ፣ አ'ሳቢ
oughtless
’ሶ̲፡ትሌስ -ቅ- ሐ'ሳበ ቢስ ፣ ል'በ ቢስ
ousand
’ሳ̲ውዘንድ -ቅ- ሽህ ፣ ሺ

thrash
ሰ̲’ራሽ -ግ- መደብደብ [ደበ'ደበ] ፣ ደኅና እድርጎ መግረፍ [ገ'ረፈ] ፣ መውቃት [ወ'ቃ] (እህል)
thread
ሰ̲’ሬድ -ስ- ክ'ር
of screw
ጥርስ (የሚሰማር)
threadbare
ሰ̲’ሬድቤየ -ቅ- እ'ላቂ (ጨርቅ)
threat
ሰ̲’ሬት -ስ- ዛ'ቻ
threaten
ሰ̲’ሬተን -ግ- መዛት [ዛተ]
three
’ሰ̲ሪይ -ቅ ሦስት
thresh
ሰ̲’ሬሽ -ግ- መውቃት [ወ'ቃ]
threshold
ሰ̲’ሬሽሆልድ -ስ- ምድራክ ፣ መድረክ
thrifty
ሰ̲’ሪፍቲ -ቅ- ገንዘብ ቆ'ጣቢ
thrill
ሰ̲’ሪል -ስ- ጥልቅ ስ'ሜት ፣ ጥልቅ የደ'ስታ ስ'ሜት
thrive
ሰ̲’ራይቭ -ግ- መፋፋት [ፋ'ፋ] ፣ ማደግ [አ'ደገ] ፣ መበልጸግ [በለ'ጸገ]
throat
ሰ̲’ረውት -ስ- ጉሮ'ሮ
throb
ሰ̲’ሮብ -ግ- መጠዝጠዝ [ጠዘ'ጠዘ] (ለቁስል) ፣ በፍጥነት መምታት [መ'ታ] (ለል'ብ ፣ ለት'ርታ)
throne.
ሰ̲’ረውን -ስ- ዙፋን
throng
ሰ̲’ሮንግ -ግ- መ'ታፈግ [ታ'ፈገ] ፣ መ'ጋፋት [ተጋ'ፋ]
-ስ- የተሰበ'ሰበ ሕዝብ
throttle
ሰ̲’ሮተል -ግ- ማነቅ [አ'ነቀ]

through

ሰ'ሩ፡ -መዋ- በ . . . ውስጥ

by means of

-መዋ- በ . . . አማካኝ'ነት

throw

ሰ'ረው -ግ- መወርወር [ወረ'ወረ]

thrust

ሰ'ረስት -ግ- መውጋት [ወ'ጋ] ፣ መሻጥ [ሻጠ]

push

-ግ- መጠቅጠቅ [ጠቀ'ጠቀ]

thud

'ሰድ -ግ- እንዘ'ፍ ማለት [አለ]

thumb

ሰም -ስ- አውራ ጣት

thump

'ሰምፕ -ስ- ኀይለ'ኛ በ'ትር (በጡ'ጫ)

-ግ- መምታት [መ'ታ] (በጡ'ጫ)

thunder

'ሰንደ -ስ- ነጐድጓድ

Thursday

'ሰ፡ዝዴይ -ስ- ሐሙስ

thus

'ዘስ -ተግ- እንዲህ ፣ ስለ'ዚህ ፣ በ'ዚህ ሁኔ'ቴ

thwart

'ሰዎ፡ት -ግ- ማ'ገድ [አ'ገደ] ፣ ማ'ሰናከል [አ'ሰና'ከለ] (ሐ'ሳብ ፣ ምኞ'ት)

tick

'ቲክ -ስ- ጭረት (ል'ክ'ነትን የ'ሚያመለ'ክት '✓')

insect

-ስ- ደም መጣጭ ተባይ (መ'ዥገር፡ ወዘተ)

ticket

'ቲኬት -ስ- የመግቢያ ወረቀት (ቲኬት)

tickle

'ቲክል -ግ- መኰርኰር [ኰረ'ኰረ] (እንዲ ሥቁ ለማድረግ)

ticklish

'ቲክሊሽ -ቅ- ሲኰረ'ኰሩት የ'ሚሽኰረ'መም

difficult

-ቅ- ለመሥራት አ'ዋኪ

tide

'ታይድ -ስ- ማዕበል ፣ ሞገድ (የባሕር)

tidings

'ታይዲንግዝ -ስ- ወሬ

tidy

'ታይዲ -ቅ- ንጹሕ ፣ የተስ'ተረ ፣ ጠ'ፍ

tie

'ታይ -ግ- ማሠር [አ'ሠረ]

-ስ- ክራቫት

tier

'ቲየ -ስ- ደረጃ'ነት ያ'ለው በመሥመር የተ ረ'ደረ መ'ቀመጫ ፣ መደርደሪያ ወዘተ

tiff

'ቲፍ -ስ- ጭቅ'ጭቅ ፣ አለመግባባት (ቀ'ላ

tiger

'ታይገ -ስ- ነብር ፣ ነምር

tight

'ታይት -ቅ- ጥብቅ ፣ ጠ'ባብ

tighten

'ታይተን -ግ- ማጥበቅ [አጠ'በቀ] ፣ ማጥበ [አጠ'በበ] ፣ በውል ማሠር [አ'ሠረ]

till (until)

'ቲል -ተግ- እስከ . . . ድረስ

till

'ቲል -ግ- ማረስ [አ'ረሰ]

cash

-ስ- መሳቢያ (የገንዘብ ማስቀ'መጫ)

tilt

'ቲልት -ግ- ማዘንበል [አዘን'በለ]

timber

'ቲምበ -ስ- ሳንቃ

time

'ታይም -ስ- ሰዓት ፣ ጊዜ ፣ ዘመን

timely

'ታይምሊ -ተግ- በደኅና ጊዜ ፣ በሰዓቱ ፣ በ ስማሚ ጊዜ

timetable

'ታይም'ቴይበል -ስ- የጊዜ ሠሌዳ

timid

'ቲሚድ -ቅ- ዓይን አ'ፋር ፣ ፈሪ

timorous

'ቲመረስ -ቅ- ዓይን አ'ፋር ፣ ፈሪ

tin

'ቲን -ስ- ቆርቆ'ሮ

container

-ስ- ታኒካ

tincture
'ቲንክቸ -ስ- ቀለም (መንከሪያ) ፥ በአልኮል ውስጥ የ'ሚሟ'ሟ መድኃኒት

tinder
'ቲንደ -ስ- እሳት ማ'ቀጣጠያ ፥ መለ'ኮሻ

tinged
'ቲንጅድ -ቅ- በቀ'ላሉ የቀ'ለመ

tingle
'ቲንገል -ግ- መውረር [ወ'ረረ] (ስ'ሜት)

tinker
'ቲንከ -ስ- እ'የዞረ የብረት ድስት'ና መጥበሻ ወዘተ የ'ሚያበ'ጅ ሰው
-ግ- መጐራጐር [ጐራ'ጐረ] (ሳያውቁ ለማበ'ጀት መሞ'ከር)

tinkle
'ቲንክል -ግ- መክለል [ከ'ለለ]

tinted
'ቲንቲድ -ቅ- የቀ'ለመ

tiny
'ታይኒ -ቅ- በጣም ት'ንሽ

tip
'ቲፕ -ስ- ጫፍ
gratuity
-ስ- ጉርሻ (የገንዘብ)
advice
-ስ- ጠቃሚ ምክር
-ግ- መገልበጥ [ገለ'በጠ] ፥ ማፍሰስ [አፈ'ሰሰ]

tipsy
'ቲፕሲ -ቅ- ሞ'ቅ ያለው (በመጠ'ጥ)

tiptoe
'ቲፕተው -ግ- በእግር ጣት መሄድ [ሄደ] (ከ'ቴ እንዳይ'ሰ'ማ)

tiptop
'ቲፕ'ቶፕ -ቅ- ዋ'ና ፥ ላ'ቂያ ወይን'ም ብልጫ ያ'ለው

tirade
ተ'ሬይድ -ስ- ቁ'ጣ የተመ'ላ ረ'ጅም ንግ'ግር

tire
'ታየ -ግ- መድከም [ደ'ከመ]

tiresome
'ታየሰም -ቅ- አስቆ'ጪ ፥ አሰልቺ ፥ አድካሚ

tissue
'ቲሹ: -ስ- ቀ'ጭን'ና በውስጡ የ'ሚያሳ'ይ ሠርቅ ፥ ወረቀት ፥ የሥጋ ልባስ ወዘተ ፥ ሥጋ (የሰው'ነት)

titbit
'ቲትቢት -ስ- የ'ሚጣ'ፍጥ ምግብ ት'ንሽ ጉርሻ ፥ የ'ሚያጓ'ጓ ወሬ ፥ ጭምጭምታ

tithe
'ታይዝ -ስ- ዐሥራት
-ግ- ዐሥራት ማውጣት [አወ'ጣ]

title
'ታይተል -ስ- አርእስት
rank
-ስ- ማዕርግ

titter
'ቲተ -ግ- እየተሽኮረ'መመ መሣቅ [ሣቀ] ፥ በዝ'ቅተ'ኛ ድምፅ መሣቅ [ሣቀ]

to
'ቱ: -መዋ- ወደ ፥ ለ ፥ እስከ

toad
'ተውድ -ስ- ጉርጥ (የእንቁራሪት ዓይነት ፍጡር)

toast
'ተውስት -ስ- የተጠ'በሰ ዳ'ቦ (ቶስት)

tobacco
ተ'ባከው -ስ- ትምባሆ

today
ቱ'ዴይ -ተግ- ዛሬ ፥ ባሁኑ ጊዜ

toddle
'ቶደል -ግ- መውተርተር [ተውተረ'ተረ] (እንደ ሕፃን እርም'ጃ)

toe
'ተው -ስ- የእግር ጣት

toenail
'ተውኔይል -ስ- የግር ጣት ጥፍር

toffee
'ቶፊ -ስ- ከወተት የተሠ'ራ ከረሜ'ላ

together
ቱ'ጌዘ -ተግ- አንድ'ነት ፥ አንድላይ ፥ አብሮ

toil
'ቶይል -ግ- መሥራት [ሠ'ራ] ፥ መጣር [ጣረ]
-ስ- ከ'ባድ ሥራ

toilet
'ቶይለት -ስ- ሠገራ ቤት ፣ ሽንት ቤት ፣ ልብስ መለባበስ'ና ጠጉር ማበጣጠር
token
'ተውከን -ስ- መ'ታወቂያ ፣ ምል'ክት ፣ ለወዳ'ጅ'ነት ምል'ክት እንዲሆን የተሰ'ጠ ስጦታ
tolerance
'ቶለረንስ -ስ- ትዕግሥት ፣ ቻይ'ነት
toll
'ቶል -ግ- መረ'ዋ መምታት [መ'ታ].
-ስ- የይለፍ ቀረጥ (በአንድ መንገድ ወይን'ም ድልድይ ላይ ለማለፍ)
tomato
ተ'ማ:ተው -ስ- ቲማቲም
tomb
'ቱ:ም -ስ- መቃብር
tomboy
'ቶምቦይ -ቅ- ወንዳወንድ (ለሴት)
tomorrow
ተ'ሞረው -ተግ- ነገ
tone
'ተውን -ስ- የሙዚቃ ድምፅ
tongs
'ቶንግዝ -ስ- ወረንጦ
tongue
'ተንግ -ስ- መላስ ፣ ምላስ
tonic
'ቶኒክ -ስ- ማ'ነቃቂያ መድኃኒት
tonight
ቱ'ናይት -ተግ- ዛሬ ማታ
too
'ቱ: -ተግ- ደግሞ ፣ እ'ጅግ ፣ -ም
tool
'ቱ:ል -ስ- መ'ሣሪያ (የሠ'ራተ'ኞ'ች)
tooth
'ቱ:ስ -ስ- ጥርስ
toothache
'ቱ:ቴይክ -ስ- የጥርስ በ'ሽታ ፣ የጥርስ ሕመም
toothpick
'ቱ:ስፒክ -ስ- የጥርስ መጎርጎሪያ (እንጨት)
top
'ቶፕ -ስ- ራስ ፣ ጫፍ ፣ አናት
cover
-ስ- መክደኛ

topaz
'ተውፓዝ -ስ- ዕንቈ'ጳዝዮን
topic
'ቶፒክ -ስ- አርእስት
topple
'ቶፐል -ግ- ተንገዳግዶ መውደቅ [ወ'ደቀ]
torch
'ቶ:ች -ስ- ፋና ፣ ችቦ
torment
'ቶ:ሜንት -ግ- ማስጨ'ነቅ [አስጨ'ነቀ] ፣ ማ'ሠቃየት [አ'ሠቃ'የ]
-ስ- ጭንቀት ፣ ሥቃይ
tornado
ቶ:'ኔደው -ስ- ኀይለ'ኛ ዐውሎ ነፋስ
torpid
'ቶ:ፒድ -ቅ- ደካማ ፣ የደነ'ዘዘ ፣ ኅታታ
torrent
'ቶረንት -ስ- ጎርፍ ፣ በቁ'ጣ መገንፈል
torso
'ቶ:ሰው -ስ- እ'ጅ ፣ እግር'ና ራስ የሌ'ለው ምስል
tortoise
'ቶ:ተስ -ስ- ኤሊ.
torture
'ቶ:ቸ -ግ- ማ'ሠቃየት [አ'ሠቃ'የ]
-ስ- ሥቃይ ፣ ሕማም
toss
'ቶስ -ግ- ማኀን [አ:ነነ] ፣ ወደ ላይ ማስፈን'ጠር [አስፈን'ጠረ] (ም'ሳሌ መሐ'ለቅ ወዘተ) ፣ መ'ገላበጥ [ተገላ'በጠ] (በመ'ኝታ)
total
'ተውተል -ስ- ሙሉ ፣ ፍ'ጹም
-ቅ- ድምር
totter
'ቶተ -ግ- መንገዳገድ [ተንገዳ'ገደ] (ሲሄዱ)
touch
'ተች -ግ- መንካት [ነ'ካ]
touchy
'ተቺ -ቅ- ፈጥኖ ተቆጪ ፣ ቁ'ጡ ፣ አኩራፊ
tough
'ተፍ -ቅ- ጠንካ'ራ ፣ ኀይለ'ኛ ፣ የ'ማይ'በ'ገር
tour
'ቶ: -ግ- መዞር [ዞረ] (አገር)

tourist
'ቱ:ሪስት -ስ- አገር ጐብኚ
tournament
'ቱ:ነመንት -ስ- ግጥሚያ (የስፖርት)
tow
'ተው -ግ- መጐ'ተት [ጐ'ተተ] ፡ መሳብ[ሳበ] (መርከብ ፡ መኪና ወዘተ በገመድ)
towards
ተ'ዎ:ድዝ -መዋ- ወደ ፡ በ . . . አቅጣ'ጫ
towel
'ታወል -ስ- ፎጣ
tower
'ታወ -ስ- ጥቅም ፡ ከ'ፍተ'ኛ ግምብ
town
'ታውን -ስ- ከተማ
-hall
-ስ- የማ'ዘጋጃ ቤት አ'ዳራሽ ፡ ማ'ዘጋጃ ቤት
toxic
'ቶክሲክ -ቅ- የመርዝ ፡ መርዛም
toy
'ቶይ -ስ- መ'ጫወቻ ፡ አሻንጉ'ሊት
trace
ት'ሬይስ -ግ- ፈ'ልጎ ማግኘት [አገ'ኘ]
-ስ- ምል'ክት ፡ ፋና
trachoma
ትረ'ኮውመ -ስ- ዓይነ መያዝ (ተላላፊ የዓ ይን በ'ሽታ)
track
ት'ራክ -ግ- መ'ከታተል [ተከታ'ተለ] (ለእ ንስሳ)
-ስ- ስርጥ መንገድ ፡ የባቡር ሐዲዶ'ች
tractor
ት'ራክተ -ስ- ማረሻ መኪና
trade
ት'ሬይድ -ግ- መነ'ገድ [ነገደ] ፡ መሸ'ቀጥ [ሸ'ቀጠ]
-ስ- መግዛት ፡ መሸጥ ፡ መነ'ገድ ፡ ሞያ (ሥራ)
trader
ት'ሬይደ -ስ- ነ'ጋዴ ፡ ሸ'ቃጭ
tradeunion
ትሬይደ'ዩ:ኒየን -ስ- የሞያተ'ኞ'ች ማኅበር
tradition
ትረ'ዲሽን -ስ- ልምድ ፡ ባህል ፡ ወግ

traffic
ት'ራፊክ -ስ- ተሽከርካሪ መኪናዎ'ች (በመን ገድ ላይ)
tragedy
ት'ራጀዲ -ስ- የሰውን ድቀት ፡ ሐዘን የ'ሚያ ሳ'ይ ታሪክ ወይ'ም ቴአትር ፡ አሳ'ዛኝ ሁናቴ (በሰው ሕይወት)
tragic
ት'ራጂክ -ቅ- በጣም አሳ'ዛኝ
trail
ት'ሬይል -ግ- በመሬት ላይ መጎ'ተት [ጎ'ተተ] ፡ እኋላ መቅረት [ቀ'ረ] (በጉዞ)
-ስ- ኰረኰንች መንገድ ፡ ዱካ
train
ት'ሬይን -ግ- ማሠልጠን [አሠለ'ጠነ] (ለእን ስሳት)
learn
-ግ- መ'ማር [ተማረ] ፡ መ'ለማመድ (ተለማ'መደ]
sport
-ግ- መ'ለማመድ [ተለማ'መደ] (ለስ ፖርት)
railway
-ስ- የምድር ባቡር
trainer
ት'ሬይነ -ስ- አሠልጣኝ ፡ ገሪ
trait
ት'ሬት -ስ- የጠባይ ዓይነት ፡ መ'ለዩ ጠባይ
traitor
ት'ሬተ -ስ- ከ'ዳተ'ኛ
tram
ት'ራም -ስ- ትራም (በከተማ ውስጥ የ'ሚሄድ የምድር ባቡር)
tramp
ት'ራምፕ -ግ- መርገጥ [ረ'ገጠ] (ለመ'ታ'ደር]
-ስ ዘዋሪ ፡ ቤት የሌ'ለው ፡ ከዘ:ታ':ጋ
trample
ት'ራምፕል -ግ- መረጋ'ረግ [ረመ'ረመ] ፡ ማ በረየት [አበረ'የ]
trance
ት'ራ:ንስ -ስ- ራስን አለማወቅ ፡ ነፍስን መሳት
tranquil
ት'ራንክዊል -ቅ- ጸ'ጥተ'ኛ ለማዊ
transact
ትራን'ሳክት -ግ- መ'ገበያየት [ተገበያ'የ]

transaction
ትራን'ሳክሽን -ስ- መ'ገበያየት
transcribe
ትራንስክ'ራይብ -ግ- በሌላ ፊደል መጻፍ [ጻፈ]፣ በሙሉ መጻፍ [ጻፈ] ፣ መገልበጥ [ገለ'በጠ] (ጽሑፍ)
transfer
ት'ራንስፈ፡ -ግ- ማ'ዛወር [አ'ዛ'ወረ]
-ስ- ዝው'ውር
transferable
ትራንስ'ፈ፡ረበል -ቅ- የ'ሚ'ዛ'ወር ፣ ሊ'ዛ'ወር የ'ሚችል
transform
ትራንስ'ፎ፡ም -ግ- መለ'ወጥ [ለ'ወጠ] (ካንድ ሁናቴ ወደ ሌላ)
transgress
ትራንዝግ'ሬስ -ግ- መጣስ [ጣሰ]፣ መ'ተላለፍ [ተላ'ለፈ] (ሕ'ግን)
transit
ት'ራንሲት -ስ- አላፊ (መንገደ'ኛ ፣ ሳያርፍ)
transition
ትራን'ዚሽን -ስ- መ'ሸጋገሪያ (ጊዜ)
transitive
ት'ራንዚቲቭ -ቅ- ተሻጋሪ (ለሰዋሰው ፣ ግ'ሥ)
translate
ትራንስ'ሌይት -ግ- መተርጐም [ተረ'ጐመ] (ካንድ ቋንቋ ወደ ሌላው)
transparent
ትራንስ'ፓረንት -ቅ- በውስጡ የ'ሚያሳ'ይ
transport
ት'ራንስፖ፡ት -ግ- ማ'መላለስ [አ'መላ'ለሰ] ፣ ማጓዝ [አጓዘ]
-ስ- ማ'መላለሻ (መኪና፣በቅሎ ወዘተ)
trap
ት'ራፕ -ግ- ማጥመድ [አጠ'መደ]
-ሴ- ወጥመድ
trash
ት'ራሽ -ስ- ቆሻሻ ፣ ወ'ራ'ዳ ነገር ፣ ምናምን
travel
ት'ራቨል -ግ- መ'ጓዝ [ተ'ጓዘ]
-ስ- ጉዞ ፣ መንገድ
traverse
ትራ'ቨ፡ስ -ግ- መ'ሻገር [ተሻ'ገረ]፣ ማ'ቋረጥ [አ'ቋ'ረጠ] (ለነገር)
tray
ት'ሬይ -ስ- ትሪ
treacherous
ት'ሬቸረስ -ቅ- ከ'ዳተ'ኛ
tread
ት'ሬድ -ግ- መርገጥ [ረ'ገጠ] ፣ መ'ራመድ [ተራ'መደ]
treadle
ት'ሬደል -ስ- መወስወሻ (የስፌት መኪና ወዘተ)
treason
ት'ሪይዘን -ስ- ዐመጽ ፣ በሀገር ላይ ማ'መጽ ፣ እምነት ማጉደል
treasure
ት'ሬዠ -ስ- መዝገብ (ዋጋ ያ'ለው ዕቃ)
-ግ- በጥን'ቃቄ ማስቀ'መጥ [አስቀ'መጠ]
treat
ት'ሪይት -ግ- ማ'ከም [አ'ከመ]
handle
-ግ- በተለ'የ ሁናቴ መያዝ [ያዘ] (ለክፉ፣ ለደ'ግ)
invite
-ግ- መጋበዝ [ጋ'በዘ]
invitation
-ስ- ግብዞ ማብላት ፣ ማጠ'ጣት ማስተናገድ
treaty
ት'ሪይቲ -ስ- ውል ፣ ስምም'ነት (በመንግሥታት መካ'ከል)
treble
ት'ሬበል -ቅ- ሦስት እጥፍ ፣ ሦስት እ'ጅ
-ግ- ሦስት ማድረግ [አደ'ረገ]
musical
-ስ- ከ'ፍተ'ኛ ድምፅ (በሙዚቃ)
tree
ት'ሪይ -ስ- ዛፍ
trellis
ት'ሬሊስ -ስ- የእንጨት አጥር (እንደመረብ የተሠ'ራ) ፣ ፍርግርግ የንጨት አጥር
tremble
ት'ሬምበል -ግ- መንቀጥቀጥ [ተንቀጠ'ቀጠ
with fear
-ግ- መብረክረክ [ተብረከ'ረከ]

tremendous
ትረ'ሜንደስ -ቅ- አስገ'ራሚ ፣ አስደ'ናቂ ፣ ታ'ላቅ ፣ ጎ'ያል

tremor
ት'ሬመ -ስ- ቀ'ላል የመሬት መንቀጥቀጥ ፣ የፍርሀት ስ'ሜት

trench
ት'ሬንች -ስ- ቦይ ፣ በረ'ጅሙ የተቆ'ፈረ ቦይ (ለወ'ታ'ደር ም'ሽግ)

trend
ት'ሬንድ -ስ- ዝን'ባሌ

trespass
ት'ሬስፐስ -ግ- ኀጢአት መሥራት [ሠ'ራ] ፣ መ'ተላለፍ [ተላ'ለፈ]
on land
-ግ- የሰውን ድንበር መጣስ [ጣሰ]፣ መግፋት [ገ'ፋ]

tress
ት'ሬስ -ስ- ኩልኩ'ሉ (የጠጉር)

trestle
ት'ሬሰል -ስ- የጠረ'ጴዛ መቆሚያ

trial
ት'ራይል -ስ- ምርመራ (ለጻ'ኝ'ነት) ፣ ሙ'ከራ

triangle
ት'ራያንገል -ስ- ሦስት ማዕዘን

triangular
ትራ'ያንግዩለ -ቅ- ባበለሦስት ማዕዘን

tribe
ት'ራይብ -ስ- ነገድ ፣ ጎሳ

tribunal
ትራይብ'ዩ:ነል -ስ- ል'ዩ ፍርድ ቤት (ለአንድ ለተለ'የ ጉ'ዳይ)

tribute
ት'ሪበዩ:ት -ስ- ምስጋና (የውለታ) ፣ ግብር (አንድ መ'ንግሥት ከሌላው የ'ሚ'ቀ'በለው) ፣ ግብር (የገንዘብ ወዘተ)

trick
ት'ሪክ -ግ- ማ'ታለል [አ'ታ'ለለ] ፣ ማሞ'ኘት [አሞ'ኘ]

trickle
ት'ሪክለ -ግ- በትንሹ መፍሰስ [ፈ'ሰሰ] በት'ንሹ ማፍሰስ [አፈ'ሰሰ] (ለውሃ)

tricky
ት'ሪኪ -ቅ- አስቸ'ጋሪ (ለመ'ረዳት ፣ ለመግ ባባት)

trifle
ት'ራይፉል -ስ- ተራ ነገር ፣ ት'ንሽ ጣፋጭ ኬክ ፣ መርመላታ ወዘተ
-ግ- ማሞ'ኘት [አሞ'ኘ] ፣ የቂል ሥራ መሥራት [ሠ'ራ]

trigger
ት'ሪገ -ስ- ምላ'ጭ (የጠመንጃ)

trim
ት'ሪም -ቅ- የተስተካ'ከለ
-ግ- ማስተካከል [አስተካ'ከለ]

trinity
ት'ሪኒቲ -ስ- ሥ'ላሴ

trinket
ት'ሪንከት -ስ- መና'ኛ ጌጥ

trio
ት'ሪየው -ስ- አንድ ሥራ የ'ሚሠሩ ሦስት ሰዎ'ች (ሙዚቀ'ኞ'ች ፣ ዘፋኞ'ች ወዘተ)

trip
ት'ሪፕ -ስ- አ'ጭር ጉዞ
stumble
-ግ- መ'ደናቀፍ [ተደና'ቀፈ]

tripe
ት'ራይፕ -ስ- ጨ'ጓ'ራ (የከብት)
nonsense
-ስ- ዋጋ የሌ'ለው ንግ'ግር

triple
ት'ሪፐል -ቅ- ሦስት እጥፍ

tripod
ት'ራይፖድ -ስ- ባለሦስት እግር ማስቀ'መጫ (ጠረ'ጴዛ ፣ ወንበር ወዘተ)

trite
ት'ራይት -ቅ- ተራ (ለንግ'ግር ፣ ብዙ ጊዜ የተ መላ'ለሰ)

triumph
ት'ራየምፍ -ግ- ድል በመንሣት መደ'ሰት [ተደ'ሰተ]

trivial
ት'ሪቪየል -ቅ- ተራ ፣ ዋጋ ቢስ

troop
ት'ሩ:ፕ -ስ- ሠራዊት ፣ የጦር ሠራዊት

trophy
ት'ረውፊ -ስ- ዋንጫ (ለስፖርት)

trot
ት'ሮት -ግ- መስገር [ሰ'ገረ] ፣ ኰ'ስ ኰ'ስ ማለት [አለ] (ለሰው)

trouble
ት'ረበል -ግ- ማስቸ'ገር [አስቸ'ገረ] ፥ ማ'ወክ [አ'ወከ]
-ስ- ች'ግር

troublesome
ት'ረበልሰም -ቅ- አውከተ'ኛ ፥ አስቸ'ጋሪ

trough
ት'ሮፍ -ስ- ገርግም (የእንስሳት መ'መገቢያ ዕቃ)

trousers
ት'ራውዘዝ -ስ- ሱ'ሪ

trowel
ት'ራወል -ስ- የሲሚንቶ መለ'ጠፊያ ማንኪ

truant
ት'ሩወንት -ስ- ከትምህርት ቤት የ'ሚቀር ሕፃን (ለጨዋታ ሲል)

truce
ት'ሩ:ስ -ስ- ጦር'ነት ለጥቂት ጊዜ ለማቆም መስማማት

truck
ት'ረክ -ስ- ጋሪ ፥ መንኰራኲር (ለዕቃ መጫኛ)

trudge
ት'ረጅ -ስ- መ'ጐተት [ተጐ'ተተ] (ሲሄዱ)

true
ት'ሩ: -ስ- እውነት

trumpet
ት'ረምፐት -ስ- ጡሩምባ ፥ መለከት

truncheon
ት'ረንቸን -ስ- ቆመጥ ፥ አ'ጭር ዱ'ላ ፥ (የፖ'ሊስ)

trunk
ት'ረንክ -ስ- ግንድ
of elephant
-ስ- ኩምቢ
of body
-ስ- ዛላ ፥ አካል
container
-ስ- ት'ልቅ ሣጥን (የብረት)

truss
ት'ረስ -ግ- ማሰር [አ'ሰረ]

trust
ት'ረስት -ግ- መ'ተማመን [ተማ'መነ] ፥ ማመን [አ'መነ] ፥ አደራ መስጠት [ሰ'ጠ]
-ስ- እምነት

trustee
ትረስ'ቲይ -ስ- ባላደራ (ዎ'ች)

trustworthy
ት'ረስትወርዚ -ቅ- ታ'ማኝ ፥ እሙን ፥ እምነት የ'ሚ'ጣል'በት

truth
ት'ሩ:ስ -ስ- እውነት

try
ት'ራይ -ግ- መሞ'ከር [ሞ'ከረ] ፥ መፈ'ተን [ፈ'ተነ]

trying
ት'ራይንግ -ስ- አ'ዋኪ ፥ አስቸ'ጋሪ ፥ አ'ናዳጅ

tub
'ተብ -ስ- የገላ መታጠቢያ በርሚል

tube
ት'ዩ:ብ -ስ- ቧምቧ (ቱ'ቦ)

tuberculosis
ቱበክዩ'ለውሲስ -ስ- የሳምባ ነቀርሳ

tuck
'ተክ -ግ- አጥፎ ማስገ'ባት [አስገ'ባ] (ያልጋ ልብስ ሲያነ'ጥፉ እፍራሽ ውስጥ)

Tuesday
ት'ዩዝዴይ -ስ- ማክሰ'ኞ

tuft
'ተፍት -ስ- ቁንጮ ፥ ተ'ሬ (የጠጕር) ፥ አንድ'ነት ች'ፍ'ግ ያለ (ግር ፥ ጠጕር ወዘተ)

tug
'ተግ -ግ- በኀይል መጎተት [ጎ'ተተ]

tuition
ትዩ'ዊሽን -ስ- ማስተማር

tumble
'ተምበል -ግ- መውደቅ [ወ'ደቀ] (በተለ'ይ በኀይል'ና በፍጥነት)

tumour
ቱ'ዩመ -ስ- የጠ'ጠረ እበጥ ፥ ያህ'ያ ከንታሮት

tumult
ት'ዩ:መልት -ስ- ጩኸት ፥ ዋካታ ፥ ረብሻ ፥ የአእምሮ መ'ታወክ

tune
ት'ዩ:ን -ስ- ጣዕመ ዜማ

tunic
ት'ዩ:ኒክ -ስ- እ'ጀጠ'ባብ

tunnel
'ተነል -ስ- በመሬት ፣ በተራራ ውስጥ የተፈ ለ'ፈለ የዋ'ሻ መንገድ

turbulent
'ተ:ብዩለነት -ቅ- የተጨ'ነቀ ፣ የተቸ'ገረ ፣ የተቆ'ጣ (ሕዝብ)

turf
'ተ:ፍ -ስ- ለምለም ሣር ፣ ስርዶ

turkey
'ተ:ኪ -ስ- የፈረንጅ ዶሮ

turmoil
'ተ:ሞይል -ስ- ብጥ'ብጥ ፣ ሁከት

turn
'ተ:ን -ግ- መዞር [ዞረ]
-round
-ግ- ወደኋላ መዞር [ዞረ]

turquoise
'ተ:ክዎይዝ -ስ- አረንጓዴ ፈርጥ ፣ አረንጓዴ'ና ሰማያዊ ቀለም

turret
'ተሬት -ስ- ት'ንሽ ጥቅም ፣ በጦር መርከብ ፣ በታንክ ፣ በአውሮ'ፕላን ላይ የ'ሚዞር የጦ: መ'ሣሪያ ቤት

turtle
'ተ:ተል -ስ- የባሕር ኤሊ

turtle-dove
'ተ:ተል'ደቭ -ስ- ዋኔ

tusk
'ተስክ -ስ- የዝሆን ፣ የከርከሮ ረ'ጅም ጥርስ

tussle
'ተሰል -ስ- ኀይለ'ኛ ትግል

tutor
ት'ዩተ -ስ- አስተማሪ ፣ አሠልጣኝ

twang
ት'ዋንግ -ስ- የተወ'ጠረ ክ'ር ፣ ሽቦ ተስቦ ሲ'ለ'ቀቅ የ'ሚያ'ሰ'ማው ድምፅ

tweezers
ት'ዊይዘዝ -ስ- ወረንጦ

twelfth
ት'ዌልፍ፟ስ -ቅ- ሀሥራ ሁለ'ተ'ኛ

twelve
ት'ዌልቭ -ቅ- ዐሥራ ሁለ'ት

twentieth
ት'ዌንቲየ፟ስ -ቅ- ሃያ'ኛ

twenty
ት'ዌንቲ -ቅ- ሃያ (ሀያ)

twice
ት'ዋይስ -ተግ- ሁለ'ት ጊዜ

twig
ት'ዊግ -ስ- ቀም'በጥ (የዛፍ ፣ የተክል)

twilight
ት'ዋይላይት -ስ- የፀሐይ ጥልቀት ብርሃን

twin
ት'ዊን -ስ- መንት'ያ ፣ መንታ (ልጆ'ች)

twine
ት'ዋይን -ስ- ሲባጎ
-ግ- መ'ጠምጠም [ተጠመ'ጠመ]

twinge
ት'ዊንጅ -ስ- ውጋት (ድንገተ'ኛ)

twinkle
ት'ዊንክል -ግ- ማብለጭለጭ [አብለጨ'ለጨ]

twirl
ት'ወ:ል -ግ- መ'ዟዟር [ተዟዟረ] (ብዙ ጊዜ) ፣ መ'ጠማዘዝ [ተጠማ'ዘዘ]

twist
ት'ዊስት -ግ- መጠምዘዝ [ጠመ'ዘዘ]
-ስ- ጥም'ዝ ፣ ጥምዛዛ

twitch
ት'ዊች -ግ- መንቀጥቀጥ [ተንቀጠ'ቀጠ] (ድን ገተ'ኛ የጡንቻ)

twitter
ት'ዊተ -ስ- የወፍ ጫጫታ

two
ቱ: -ቅ- ሁለ'ት

type
'ታይፕ -ስ- ዓይነት
-ግ- በጽሕፈት መኪና መጻፍ [ጻፈ]

typewriter
'ታይፕራይተ -ስ- የጽሕፈት መኪና

typhoon
ታይ'ፉ:ን -ስ- ከ'ባድ አውሎ ነፋስ

typhus
'ታይፈስ -ስ- ተስቦ በ'ሽታ

typical
'ቲፒከል -ቅ- የተለ'መደ ፣ ደምበ'ኛ

tyrant
'ታረንት -ስ- ጨ'ካኝ'ና ፍትሕ የ'ማያውቅ ገ'ዥ ፣ የበታ'ቹን የ'ሚያጠቃ

udder
’እደ -ስ- ጡት (የእንስሳት)
ugly
’አግሊ -ቅ- ፉንጋ ፣ መልከ ጥፉ
ulcer
’አልሰ -ስ- የ'ሚመግል ቁስል
ulterior
አል’ቲሪየ -ቅ- የተደ'በቀ (ለሰው ሐ'ሳብ)
ultimate
’አልተመት -ቅ- የመጨ'ረሻ
ultimatum
አልተ’ሜይተም -ስ- ማስጠንቀቂያ ፣ ዛ'ቻ
umbilical cord
አም’ቢልከል’ኮ፡ድ -ስ- እትብት
umbrage
’አምብረጅ -ስ- መ'ከፋት ፣ መ'ቀየም (ከመ'በደል ስ'ሜት የተነ'ሣ)
umbrella
አምብ’ሬለ -ስ- ጥላ ፣ ጃንጥላ
umpire
’አምፓየ -ስ- ዳ'ኛ (ለስፖርት
unable
አ’ኔይበል -ቅ- የ'ማይችል
unaccustomed
አነ’ከስተምድ -ቅ- ልምድ የሌ'ለው
unanimous
ዩ’ናነመስ -ቅ- ሁ'ሉም አንድ ሐ'ሳብ ያ'ላ'ቸው (በስምም'ነት) ፣ አንድ ል'ብ አንድ ቃል የሆኑ (በስምም'ነት)
unarmed
አ’ና፡ምድ -ቅ- የጦር መ'ሣርያ ያልያዘ ፣ መ'ከላከያ የሌ'ለው
unassuming
አነስ’ዩ፡ሚንግ -ቅ- ትሑት ፣ አ'ለሁ አ'ለሁ የ'ማይል
unavoidable
አነ’ቮይደበል -ቅ- ቸ'ል የ'ማይሉት ፣ ሊ፡ቁት የ'ማይ'ቻል ፣ የ'ማይቀር
unaware
አነ’ዌየ -ቅ- ያላ'ወቀ ፣ ያላስተዋለ

unbecoming
አንበ’ከሚንግ -ቅ- የ'ማይስማ'ማ ፣ የ'ማይ'ገ'ባ
of dress
-ቅ- የ'ማያምር
unbearable
አን’ቤረበል -ቅ- የ'ማይ'ቻል ፣ የ'ማይ'ታ'ገሡት
unbiased
አን’ባየስት -ቅ- የ'ማያ'ዳ'ላ ፣ አድልዎ የ'ሌ'ለ'በት
uncertain
አን’ሰ፡ተን -ቅ- እርግጠ'ኛ ያልሆነ ፣ ያልተረጋ'ገጠ
uncle
’አንከል -ስ- አ'ጎት ፣ ያክስት ባል
uncomfortable
አን’ከምፈተበል -ስ- ም'ቹ'ነት የሌ'ለው ፣ ም'ቹ ያልሆነ ፣ የ'ማይ'መ'ች
unconscious
አን’ኮንሸስ -ቅ- እእምሮውን የሳተ ፣ የ'ማያውቅ ፣ ሳያ'ስቡት የተደ'ረገ
uncouth
አን’ኩ፴ -ቅ- ያልታ'ረመ ፣ ባለጌ ፣ ስ'ድ ፣ እስከ'ፊ ጠባይ ያ'ለው
under
’አንደ -መዋ- ታ'ች ፣ በ . . . ታ'ች ፣ ከ . . . ታ'ች
underclothes
’አንደክለውዝዝ -ስ- የውስጥ ልብስ ፣ ገላ ነ'ክ
underdog
’አንደዶግ -ስ- የሰው ዝ'ቅተ'ኛ ፣ የሰው መቀ'ለጃ'ና መ'ሣለቂያ ፣ የ'ማይ'ቃ'ና'ለት (አሳዛኝ ሰው)
underestimate
አንደ’ሬስቲሜይት -ስ- ዝ'ቅ አርጎ መገ'መት [ገ'መተ]
undergo
አንደ’ገው -ግ- መከራን ታ'ግሶ ማሳ'ለፍ [አሳ'ለፈ] ፣ አንድ ነገር ማለፍ [አ'ለፈ]

underhand
እንደ'ሃንድ -ቅ- የ'ማይ'ታ'መን ፣ ድብቅብቅ፣ (ነገር)

underline
እንደ'ላይን -ግ- ከበታ'ች ማሥመር [አሠ'መረ] (ለጽሑፍ) ፤ አንድ ነገር ማጥበቅ [አጠ'በቀ] የበ'ለጠ አስተያየት መስጠት [ሰ'ጠ]

underneath
እንደ'ኒይ፱ -መዋ- በ . . . ታ'ች ፣ ከ . . . ታ'ች

understand
አንደስ'ታንድ -ግ- መግባት [ገ'ባ] ፣ መ'ረዳት [ተረ'ዳ]

undertake
እንደ'ቴይክ -ግ- አንድ ሥራ ለመሥራት መስማማት [ተስማ'ማ]

undertaker
'እንደቴይከ -ስ- ገ'ናዥ ፤ ሥራ ተቋራጭ

underwear
'እንደዌየ -ስ- የውስጥ ልብስ ፣ ገላ ነ'ክ

underworld
'እንደወ:ልድ -ስ- የወንበዴዎ'ች ማኅበር ወ'ሮበ'ሎች
hell
-ስ- ገሀ'ነመ እሳት

undesirable
እንደ'ዛረበል -ቅ- ዋየ'ማይ'ፈ'ለግ ፣ የተጠ'ላ ፣ ያልተወ'ደደ

undo
እን'ዱ: -ግ- መፍታት [ፈ'ታ] (እሥር ፣ ቁልፍ ወዘተ)

undress
እንድ'ሬስ -ግ- ማውለቅ [አወ'ለቀ] (ለልብስ)

undulating
'እንድዩሌይቲንግ -ቅ- ወ'ጣ ገ'ባ (የመሬት ወዘተ)

uneasy
እ'ኒይዚ -ቅ- የተጨ'ነቀ ፣ የ'ማይ'መ'ች

uneven
እ'ኒይቨን -ቅ- ያልተስተካ'ከለ ፣ ወ'ጣ ገ'ባ

unexpected
እንኢክስ'ፔክተድ -ቅ- ያልጠ'በቁት ፣ ያልተጠ'በቀ ፣ ድንገተ'ኛ

unfair
እን'ፌየ -ቅ- ግፍ ፣ በደል ፣ ትክ'ክል ያልሆነ (አድራጎት)

unfit
እን'ፊት -ቅ- የማይስማ'ማ ፣ ጤናው በመጥፎ ሁናቴ ላይ ያ'ለ

unfortunate
እን'ፎ:ቸነት -ቅ- ዕ'ድለ ቢስ ፣ የሚያሳ'ዝን

unhappy
እን'ሀፒ -ቅ- ያ'ዘነ ፣ የከ'ፋው

unhealthy
እን'ሄልሲ -ቅ- የታ'መመ ፣ ጤና የሌ'ለው ፣ አእምሮ ወይን'ም ሰው'ነት የ'ሚጎዳ

unification
ዩኒፊ'ኬይሽን -ስ- መ'ዋሐድ ፣ አንድ'ነት

uniform
'ዩኒፎ:ም -ስ- መ'ለ'ዮ ልብስ (ዩኒፎርም)
same
-ስ- አንድ ዓይነት

unify
'ዩኒፋይ -ግ- ማ'ዋሐድ [አ'ዋሐደ] ፣ አንድ ማድረግ [አደ'ረገ]

unilateral
ዩኒ'ላተረል -ቅ- ያንድ ወገን (በስምም'ነት ፣ በጥል)

union
'ዩኒየን -ስ- አንድ'ነት ፣ ኅብረት

unique
ዩ'ኒይክ -ቅ- የተለ'የ ፣ ል'ዩ ጠባይ ያ'ለው

unit
'ዩኒት -ስ- ራሱን የቻለ አንድ ክፍል

unite
ዩ'ናይት -ግ- ማ'ዋሐድ [አ'ዋሐደ] ፣ አንድ ማድረግ [አደ'ረገ]

unity
'ዩነቲ -ስ- አንድ'ነት ፣ ኅብረት

universal
ዩነ'ቨ:ሰል -ስ- ጠቅላ'ላ ፣ የወል ፣ የሁ'ሉ ፣ ለሁ'ሉ የ'ሚሆን

universe
'ዩነቨስ -ስ- ዓለም'ና በሥነ ፍጥረት ውስጥ ያ'ለው ነገር ሁ'ሉ

university
ዩነ'ቨ:ሰቲ -ስ- ከ'ፍተ'ኛ ትምህርት ቤት ፣ ዩኒቨርሲቲ

unkempt
እን'ኬምት -ቅ- ጠ'ፍ ያላለ ፣ ጠጉሩ ያልተበ'ጠረ

unless
እን'ሌስ -ተግ- ከ . . . በስተቀ'ር
unload
እን'ለውድ -ግ- ጭነት ማ'ራገፍ [አ'ራ'ገፈ]
unlucky
እን'ለኪ -ቅ- ዕ'ድለ ቢስ
unmoved
እን'ሙቭድ -ቅ- ስ'ሜት የሌ'ለው ፣ የ'ማያ
ዝን
unnatural
አ'ንናቸረል -ቅ- ያልተለ'መደ ፣ ጉድ ፤ ግሩም
unnecessary
አ'ኔሰሰሪ -ቅ- የ'ማያስፈ'ልግ ፣ ሊቀር የ'ሚ
ችል
unpleasant
እንፕ'ሌዘንት -ቅ- የ'ማያስደ'ስት ፣ አሳ'ዛኝ
unqualified
እንክ'ዎለፋይድ -ቅ- ያልተማረ ፣ ያልሠለ'ጠነ
የተለ'የ ሞያ የሌ'ለው
unravel
እን'ራቨል -ግ- መተርተር [ተረ'ተረ] ፣ መለ
ያየት [ለያ'የ] (ለክ'ር)
unreasonable
እን'ሪይዘነበል -ቅ- ምክንያት የሌ'ለው ፣ የ'ማ
ይመስል
excessive
-ቅ- ከ'ሚ'ገ'ባ በላይ
unreliable
እንሪ'ላየበል -ቅ- እምነት የ'ማይ'ጣል'በት
unruly
እን'ሩ፡ሊ -ቅ- የ'ማይ'ታ'ዘዝ ፣ ስ'ድ
unsatisfactory
እንሳተስ'ፋክትሪ -ቅ- የ'ማያጠግብ (ምክንያ
ት) ፣ በቂ ያልሆነ
unscrew
እንስክ'ሩ፡ -ግ- መንቀል [ነ'ቀለ] (ለሚስማር ፣
ለቡሽ)
unscrupious
እንስ'ክሩ፡ፕዩለስ -ቅ- ጨ'ካኝ ፣ ራሱን ወ'ዳድ ፣
ይሉኝታ ቢስ
unseemly
እን'ሲይምሊ -ቅ- የ'ማይ'ገ'ባ ፣ ነውር ፤ ከጊ
ዜው ጋር የ'ማይስማ'ማ

unselfish
እን'ሴልፊሽ -ቅ- ራሱን የ'ማይወ'ድ ፣ ስስ
ብ'ቻ የ'ማይል
unsettled
እን'ሴተልድ -ቅ- የተጨነ'ቀ ፣ የሐ'ሳብ ዕረ
ፍት የሌ'ለው ፤ ያልተከ'ፈለ ዕዳ ፤ የመጨ'ረሻ
ው'ሳኔ ያላገ'ኘ
unsightly
እን'ሳይትሊ -ቅ- የ'ማያምር ፣ የ'ሚያስጠ'ላ ፣
አስቀ'ያሚ ፣ ማስጠ'ሎ
unskilled
እንስ'ኪልድ -ቅ- ያልሠለ'ጠነ ፣ ሞያ ቢስ
unsteady
እንስ'ቴዲ -ቅ- ቀ'ጥ ያላለ ፣ የተንገደገ'ደ
(በመ'ራመድ) ፤ እምነት የ'ማይ'ጣል'በት
untie
እን'ታይ -ግ- መፍታት [ፈ'ታ] (እስርን)
until
እን'ቲል -መዋ- እስከ . . . ድረስ
untimely
እን'ታይምሊ -ቅ- ያለ ጊዜው ፣ በ'ማይ'መ'ች
ጊዜ የመ'ጣ
untrue
እንት'ሩ፡ -ቅ- ውሸት ፣ ከውነት የራቀ
unusual
እን'ዩዡወል -ቅ- ያልተለ'መደ ፣ እንግዳ (ለነ
ገር)
unwell
እን'ዌል -ቅ- የታ'መመ ፣ ጤና ያ'ጣ
unwilling
እን'ዊሊንግ -ቅ- ፈቃደ'ኛ'ነት የሌ'ለው ፣ የ
'ማይፈ'ልግ (አንድ ነገር ለማድረግ ስምም'ነት
የሌለ'ው)
unwise
እን'ዋይዝ -ቅ- ብልኀ ያልሆነ ፣ ሞ'ኝ ፣ ቂል
unworthy
እን'ወ፡ዚ -ቅ- የ'ማይረባ ፣ መ'ናኛ ፣ ክብር
የ'ማይ'ገ'ባው
up
'አፕ -ተግ- ላይ ፣ . . . ላይ ፣ ወደ . . . ላይ ፣
እስከ . . .
-to
እስከ . . . ድረስ

upbraid
አፕብ'ሬይድ መዝለፍ [ዘ'ለፈ]

upheaval
አፕ'ሂይቨል -ስ- ብጥ'ብጥ (ት'ልቅ) ፤ ድንገተ'ኛ'ና በ'የቦታው የተሰራ'ጨ ለውጥ

uphill
'አፕ'ሂል -ተግ- ወደ ላይ

uphold
'አፕ'ሆልድ -ግ- መደ'ገፍ [ደ'ገፈ]

upholstery
አፕ'ሆልስትሪ -ስ- ሥጋ'ጃ ፣ መ'ጋረጃ ፣ የሶፋ ወንበር ፣ ፍራሽ'ና የመ'ሰሉት ዕቃዎ'ች

upkeep
'አፕኪይፕ -ስ- የመ'ከባከቢያ ዋጋ

financial

-ስ- የገንዘብ እርዳታ (ላንድ ሰው ኑሮ)

upon
አ'ፖን -መዋ- በ . . . ላይ

upper
'አፐ -ቅ- የላይ

upright
'አፕራይት -ቅ- ቀ'ጥ ያለ ፣ የ'ሚ'ከ'በር ፣ ቅን

uprising
'አፕራይዚንግ -ቅ- ብጥ'ብጥ

uproar
'አፕሮ: -ስ- ጩኸት ፣ ሁከት

uproot
አፕ'ሩ:ት -ግ- መንቀል [ነ'ቀለ] ፣ መመንገል [መነ'ገለ]

upset
አፕ'ሴት -ቅ- ያ'ዘነ ፣ የተጨ'ነቀ

overturn

-ግ- መገላበጥ [ገለ'በጠ]

perturb

-ግ- ማ'ናደድ [አ'ና'ደደ] ፣ ማስቀ'የም [አስቀ'የመ]

upside-down
አፕሳይድ'ዳውን -ቅ- የተገለ'በጠ ፣ ሥርዓት ያ'ጣ ፣ የተመሰቃ'ቀለ

upstart
'አፕስታ:ት -ስ- እምባ ገ'ነን

up-to-date
አፕቱ'ዴይት -ቅ- ዘመናዊ ፣ ስለመጨ'ረሻው የመ'ሻሻል እርምጃ የ'ሚያውቅ

upward
'አፕወድ -ተግ- ወደላይ

urban
'ኧበን -ቅ- የከተማ

urchin
'ኧቺን -ስ- ዘዋሪ ት'ንሽ ልጅ

urge
'ኧጅ -ግ- ማ'ጻፈር [አ'ጻ'ፈረ] ፣ ከል'ብ መለ'መን [ለ'መነ] (አንድ ነገር እንዲያደርጉ)

urgent
'ኧጀንት -ቅ- አስቸ'ኳይ

urine
'ዩሪን -ስ- ሽንት

us
'አስ -ተስ- ለእ'ኛ ፣ እ'ኛን

usage
'ዩዚጅ -ስ- በልምድ የተወ'ሰነ ሕ'ግ (ለቋንቋ ወዘተ) ፣ የተለ'መደ ሥርዓት

use
'ዩዝ -ግ- እሥራ ላይ ማዋል [አዋለ] ፣ ባንድ ነገር መሥራት [ሠ'ራ]

use
'ዩስ -ስ- ጥቅም ፣ አገልግሎት ፣ እርባን

useful
'ዩስፉል -ቅ- ጠቃሚ ፣ ለተግባር የ'ሚውል

useless
'ዩስለስ -ቅ- ጥቅም የሌ'ለው ፣ የ'ማይረባ

usher
'አሸ -ስ- አስተናባሪ ፣ አስተናጋጅ

usual
'ዩዡወል -ቅ- የተለ'መደ

usurer
'ዩዠረ -ስ- ገንዘብ በከ'ፍተ'ኛ አራጣ የ'ሚያበ'ድር ሰው

usurp
ዩ'ዘ:ፕ -ግ- ያለአግባብ መንጠቅ [ነ'ጠቀ] (የመንግሥት ሥልጣን ወዘተ)

utensil
ዩ'ቴንሰል -ስ- የወጥ ቤት ቁሳቁስ

utilize
'ዩቲላይዝ -ግ- እጥቅም ላይ ማዋል [አዋለ]

utmost
'እትመውስት -ቅ- የ'ሚበልጠው ፣ ብልጫ ያ'ለው ፣ የመጨ'ረሻ (በርቀት)

utter
'አተ -ግ- መ'ናገር [ተና'ገረ]
complete
-ቅ- ፍ'ጹም

utterance
'አተረንስ -ስ- ንግ'ግር ፣ ያ'ነጋገር ሁናቴ

uvula
'ኡቩዩላ -ስ- እንጥል

vacancy
'ቬይከንሲ -ስ- ባዶ ቦታ (ለሥራ) ፣ ክፍት ቦታ (ለሥራ)

vacant
'ቬይከንት -ቅ- ባዶ
absent-minded
-ቅ- ተሳሳ ፣ ዝንጉ

vacate
ቨ'ኬይት -ግ- መልቀቅ [ለ'ቀቀ] (ቦታን)

vacation
'ቨኬይሸን -ስ- የዕረፍት ጊዜ

vaccination
ቫክሲ'ኔይሸን -ስ- ክ'ትባት

vacillate
'ቫሲሌይት -ግ- ሐ'ሳብ አለመቁረጥ [-ቆ'ረጠ] ፣ ማ'ወላወል [አ'ወላ'ወለ]

vacuum
'ቫክዩም -ስ- ባዶ ቦታ ፣ ምን'ም ነገር የሌ'ለ'በት ቦታ
vacuumcleaner
-ስ- የኤሌክትሪክ ቤት መጥረጊያ

vagabond
'ቫገቦንድ -ስ- ወ'ሮበ'ላ ፣ ኣውደልዳይ ፣ ወ'መኔ ፣ እባጊ'ዮ ፣ ወመኔ

vagina
ቨ'ጃይነ -ስ- የሴት አባለ ዘር ፣ ብልት (እምስ)

vagrant
'ቬይግረንት -ስ- በ'የቦታው እየተዘዋ'ወረ የ'ሚለምን ሰው የተወ'ሰነ መኖሪያ የሌ'ለው

vague
'ቬይግ -ቅ- ግልጽ ያልሆነ ፣ ደብዛ'ዛ

vain
'ቬይን -ቅ- ከንቱ ፣ ዋጋ ቢስ ፣ በከንቱ የ'ሚ'ኩራ
-in
-ተግ- በከንቱ

vale
'ቬይል -ስ- ሸለቆ

valet
'ቫሌ -ስ- አልባሽ (ወንድ)

valiant
'ቫሊየንት -ቅ- ደ'ፋር ፣ ጎበዝ

valid
'ቫሊድ -ቅ- ሕ'ጋዊ
of argument
-ቅ- ትክ'ክለ'ኛ (ለክር'ክር)

valise
ቫ'ሊይስ -ስ- ት'ንሽ ሻንጣ (የመንገድ)

valley
'ቫሊ -ስ- ሸለቆ

valour
'ቫለ -ስ- ድፍረት ፣ ጉብዝ'ና (በጦር ሜዳ)

value
'ቫልዩ -ስ- ዋጋ

valve
'ቫልቭ -ስ- ቫልቮላ ፣ የ'ሚፈ'ስ ነገር ማ'ገ ወይን'ም መልቀቂያ መ'ሣሪያ

van
'ቫን -ስ- የጭነት መኪና (የተሸ'ፈነ) ፣ የተ 'ፈነ ፉርጎ
military
-ስ- ግምባር ቀ'ደም ፣ የፊታውራሪ ጦ

vanguard
'ቫንጋ:ድ -ስ- ግምባር ቀ'ደም፣ የፊታውራሪ ጦር

vanish
'ቫኒሽ -ግ- መጥፋት [ጠ'ፋ]፣ እ'ልም ማለት [አለ]

vanity
'ቫኒቲ -ስ- ከንቱ'ነት

vanquish
'ቫንክዊሽ -ግ- ድል መንሣት [ነ'ሣ]፣ ማስገ'በር [አስገ'በረ] (በጦር'ነት)

vapour
'ቬይፐ -ስ- እንፋሎት

variable
'ቬሪየበል -ቅ- ተለ'ዋ/ጭ፣ የ'ሚ'ለ'ወጥ እምነት የ'ማይ'ጣል'በት

varnish
'ቫ:ኒሽ -ግ- ቀለም መቀ'ባት [ቀ'ባ]

variety
ቨ'ራየቲ -ስ- ል'ዩ ል'ዩ ዓይነት

vary
'ቬሪ -ግ- መ'ለየት [ተለ'የ]፣ ል'ዩ'ነት ማሳ'የት [አሳ'የ]፣ መ'ለዋወጥ [ተለዋ'ወጠ]

vase
'ቫ:ዝ -ስ- ያበባ ማስቀ'መጫ

vassal
'ቫሰል -ስ- ተወ'ራጅ፣ አገልጋይ፣ ሎሌ

vast
'ቫ:ስት -ቅ- ሰ'ፊ

vat
'ቫት -ስ- ት'ልቅ ጋን

vault
'ቮ:ልት -ስ- ምድር ቤት
-ግ- እ'መር ማለት [አለ] (አንድ ነገር ተደ'ግፎ)
-ስ- ቅ'ሥት'ነት ያ'ለው ጣራ

veal
'ቪይል -ስ- የጥ'ጃ ሥጋ

veer
'ቪየ -ግ- አቅጣ'ጫ መለ'ወጥ [ለ'ወጠ] (በተለ'ይ ለነፋስ፣ ለሐ'ሳብ)

vegetable
'ቬጅተበል -ስ- አትክልት (የምግብ)

vegetation
ቬጀ'ቴይሸን -ስ- ተክላተክል፣ ልምላሜ

vehemence
'ቪየመንስ -ስ- ኀይለ ቃል፣ መራራ ውስጣዊ ስ'ሜት

vehicle
'ቪይክል -ስ- ተሽከርካሪ

veil
'ቬይል -ስ- ዓይነ ርግብ

vein
'ቬይን -ስ- የደም ሥር፣ በቅጠል ላይ የ'ሚ'ታዩ መሥመሮ'ች

velocity
ቨ'ሎሰቲ -ስ- ፍጥነት

velvet
'ቬልቨት -ስ- ከፈይ

vendor
'ቬንደ -ቅ- ሻጭ

veneer
ቨ'ኒየ -ስ- ቀ'ጭን ሽፋን፣ ልባጥ (በጠረ'ጴዛ በወምበር ወዘተ)

venerable
'ቬነረበል -ቅ- ሊ'ከ'በር የ'ሚ'ገ'ባው (በዕድሜው በጠባዩ ምክንያት)

vengeance
'ቬንጀንስ -ስ- በቀል

venison
'ቬነዘን -ስ- የሚዳ'ቋ ሥጋ፣ የአጋዘን ሥጋ

venom
'ቬነም -ስ- የእባብ መርዝ፣ ጥላ'ቻ

vent
'ቬንት -ስ- ያ'የር፣ የውሃ ማስገ'ቢያ ቀዳዳ

ventilation
ቬንቲ'ሌይሸን -ስ- ነፋስ መስጫ

venture
'ቬንቸ -ግ- መሞ'ከር [ሞ'ከረ]
-ስ- ወደፊት ሊሆን የ'ሚችለውን መ'ሞት (ለንግድ)

veracity
ቨ'ራሲቲ -ስ- እውነት፣ ል'ክ'ነት

verb
'ቨ:ብ -ስ- ግ'ሥ፣ አንቀጽ (ሰዋስው)

verbal
'ቨ:በል -ቅ- የቃል፣ የንግ'ግር፣ የግሥ

verbose
ቨ'በውስ -ቅ- ለፍላፊ፣ ብዙ ተናጋሪ

verdant
'ቨ:ደንት -ቅ- ለምለም
verdict
'ቨ:ዲክት -ስ- ፍርድ ፣ ው'ሳኔ (የዳ'ኞች)
verge
'ቨ:ጅ -ስ- ዳር ፣ ጫፍ
verify
'ቬሪፋይ -ግ- መመርመር [መረ'መረ] ፣ ማስረ'ጃ መፈ'ለግ [ፈ'ለገ] (ለተናገሩት ነገር እውነት'ነት)
veritable
'ቬሪተበል -ቅ- እውነተ'ኛ ፣ በትክ'ክል የተሰ'የመ
vermicide
'ቨ:ሚሳይድ -ስ- በሆድ ውስጥ ያ'ሉ ትሎ'ችን መግደያ መድኃኒት
vermilion
ቨ'ሚልየን -ቅ- ብሩህ ቀ'ይ (ቀለም)
vermin
'ቨ:ሚን -ስ- ትል ፣ አይጥ ወዘተ
vernacular
ቨ'ናክዩለ -ስ- ተራ ቋን'ቋ (የጽሑፍ ያልሆነ)
versatile
'ቨ:ሰታይል -ቅ- ባለ ብዙ ሞያ ፣ ብዙ ሥራ ሊሠራ የ'ሚችል ፣ ለብዙ አገልግሎት የ'ሚውል
verse
'ቨ:ስ -ስ- ቁጥር (የመጽሐፍ ቅ'ዱስ)
poetry
-ስ- የግጥም ክፍል
version
'ቨ:ሸን -ስ- አ'ትም ፣ በሌላ ቋንቋ ትርጉም (ያንድ መጽሐፍ)
story
-ስ- ታሪክ (አንድ ሰው ስለ አንድ ሁኔታ የ'ሚያወራው የራሱ አስተያየት)
vertical
'ቨ:ቲክል -ቅ- ቀ'ጥ ያለ
very
'ቬሪ -ተግ- በጣም
vessel
'ቬሰል -ስ- ዕቃ (መያዣ)
ship
-ስ- መርከብ

vest
'ቬስት -ስ- የውስጥ ልብስ
vestige
'ቬስቲጅ -ስ- ያ'ለፈ ነገር ምል'ክት
vestments
'ቬስትመንትስ -ስ- ልብሰ ተክህኖ ፣ አልባሳት ፣ የክብረ በዓል ልብስ
veteran
'ቬተረን -ስ- የጥንት ወ'ታ'ደር ፣ የተረ'ፈተ ወ'ታ'ደር
veterinary surgeon
'ቬትሪነሪ'ሰ:ጀን -ስ- የከብት ሐኪም
vex
'ቬክስ -ግ- ማ'ናደድ [አ'ና'ደደ] ፣ ማስቆ'ጣት [አስቆ'ጣ]
viaduct
'ቫየደክት -ስ- በጣም ረ'ጅም ድልድይ (ባቡር፣ መኪና ወዘተ የ'ሚያልፍ'በት)
vibrate
ቫይብ'ሬይት -ግ- መንዘር [ነ'ዘረ]
vice
'ቫይስ -ስ- መጥፎ ልምድ (ከግብረ ገብ'ነት የወ'ጣ) ፣ ድክማ ሥጋዊ ጠባይ
assistant
-ስ- ምክ'ትል
wickedness
-ስ- ክፋት
vicinity
ቪ'ሲኒቲ -ስ- አቅራ'ቢያ ፣ አ'ካባቢ
vicious
'ቪሸስ -ቅ- ጨ'ካኝ ፣ አረመኔ (ለጠባይ) ፡ ክፉ ፣ አመለ'ኛ (ለፈረስ)
vicissitude
ቪ'ሲሲትዩ:ድ -ስ- መ'ለዋወጥ (በተለ'ይ ለዕድል)
victim
'ቪክቲም -ስ- ያለጥፋቱ የ'ሚ'ሠቃ'ይ ሰው ወይን'ም እንስሳ
victor
'ቪክተ -ቅ- አ'ሸ'ናፊ ፣ ድል ነ'ሺ ፣ ባለ ድል ፣ ድል አድራጊ
victory
'ቪክተሪ -ስ- ድል ፣ ማ'ሸ'ነፍ
victuals
'ቪተልዝ -ስ- ምግብ ፣ ቀ'ለብ

vie
'ቫይ -ግ- መ'ፎካከር [ተፎካ'ከረ] ፣ መ'ወዳደር [ተወዳ'ደረ]

view .
ቭ'ዩ: -ግ- ማየት [አ'የ]
-ስ- ትዕ'ይንት

viewpoint
ቭ'ዩ:ፖይንት -ስ- አስተያየት ፣ ግ'ምት (አስተያየት)

vigil
'ቪጂል -ስ- ነቅቶ ማደር (ለጸሎት ፣ ለጥ'በቃ)

vigilance
'ቪጂለንስ -ስ- ጥንቁቅ ጥ'በቃ፣ንቃት (ለጥበቃ)

vigour
'ቪገ -ስ- ኀይል ፣ ጥን'ካሬ ፣ ብርታት

vile
'ቫይል -ቅ- አ'ሥቃቂ ፣ እ'ጅግ መጥፎ ፣ አሳ'ፋሪ

villa
'ቪለ -ስ- ቪ'ላ ፣ በአንድ አጥር ግ'ቢ ውስጥ ያ'ለ ቤት

village
'ቪለጅ -ስ- ያገር ቤት መንደር

villain
'ቪለን -ስ- መጥፎ ሰው ፣ ክፉ ሰውን የ'ሚጎዳ ሰው

vindicate
'ቪንዲኬይት -ግ- እውነተ'ኛ'ነትን ማስረ'ዳት [አስረ'ዳ]

vindictive
ቪን'ዲክቲቭ -ቅ- በቀለ'ኛ ፡ ጡ'ካኝ

vine
'ቫይን -ስ- የወይን ተክል

vinegar
'ቪኒገ -ስ- ኮምጣ'ጤ ፡ መጣጥ

violate
'ቫየሌይት -ግ- መጣስ [ጣሰ] \
law
-ግ- መድፈር [ደ'ፈ] (ሴት ያለፈቃዷ)

violent
'ቫየለንት -ቅ- ብርቱ ፡ ኀይለ'ኛ ፡ ቁ'ጡ

violet
'ቫየለት -ቅ- ወይሰማያዊ'ነት የ'ሚያይላ ሐምራዊ

violin
ቫየ'ሊን -ስ- ቫየሊን ፣ (መሰንቆ ባለአራት ጭራ)

viper
'ቫየፐ -ስ- እ'ፉኝት (መርዛም እባብ)

virgin
'ቨ:ጂን -ስ- ድንግል
soil
-ቅ- ድንግል (ለመሬት)

virile
'ቪራይል -ቅ- ወንድ (ጠንካ'ራ)

virtue
'ቨ:ቹ -ስ- ምግባር (ጥሩ)

virtuous
'ቨ:ቹወስ -ቅ- ባለ ጥሩ ምግባር ፣ ደ'ግ

visa
'ቪያዘ -ስ- ቢዛ (የይለፍ ወረቀት ፣ ይብዳ'ር)

visage
'ቪዚጅ -ስ- የሰው ፊት ፣ መልክ

viscous
'ቪስከስ -ቅ- መጣብቅ'ነት ያ'ለው

visible
'ቪዘበል -ቅ- የ'ሚ'ታ'ይ ፡ ያልተሸ'ሸገ

vision
'ቪዥን -ስ- ራእይ
power of sight
-ስ- የማየት ኀይል

visit
'ቪዚት -ግ- መጎብኘት [ጎበ'ኘ]
-ስ- ጉብ'ኝት

visitor
'ቪዚተ -ስ- ጎብኚ ፣ ጠያቂ (የታመመ ወዘተ)

visual
'ቪዥዩወል -ቅ- ለማየት የ'ሚ ቻል
-aids
-ስ- ለትምህርት መግለጫ የ ሥዕል ሥዕሎች

vital
'ቫይትል -ቅ- ዋ'ና (ነገር) ፡ በጣም አስ (ለኑሮ ወዘተ)

vitality
ቪ'ታሊቲ -ስ- ሕያው'ነት ፡ ንቁ'ነት

vivacity
ቪ'ቫሲቲ -ስ- ንቁ'ነት
vivid
'ቪቪድ -ቅ- ጠንካ'ራ ፣ ኀይለ'ኛ ፣ ሕያው (የአ'ገላለጽ)
vocabulary
ቮ'ካብዩለሪ -ስ- አንድ ሰው የ'ሚያውቃ'ቸው'ና በንግ'ግሩ የ'ሚያስገ'ባቸው የቃላት ብዛት ፣ የቃላት ዝርዝር መጽሐፍ
vocal
'ቮውከል -ቅ- የድምፅ ፣ ድምፃዊ
vocation
ቮ'ኬይሽን -ስ- የተለ'የ ሞያ
vociferous
ቮ'ሲፈረስ -ቅ- በጣም የ'ሚጮ'ኽ
vogue
'ቮውግ -ስ- የጊዜው ሞድ
voice
'ቮይስ -ስ- ድምፅ
void
'ቮይድ -ስ- ባዶ'ነት
not valid
-ቅ- ዋጋ ቢስ
volatile
'ቮለታይል -ቅ- በቀ'ላሉ የ'ሚተ'ን ፣ ጠባዩ በ'የጊዜው የ'ሚ'ለዋ'ወጥ፣ደ'ስተ'ኛ፣ፈገግተ'ኛ
volcano
ቮል'ኬይነው -ስ- እሳተ ገሞራ
volley
'ቮሊ -ስ- እ'ሩምታ (ለተኩስ)
volley-ball
'ቮሊቦ:ል -ስ- የመረብ ኳስ ፣ ቮሊ ቦል
volt
'ቮልት -ስ- የኤሌክትሪክ ኀይል መጠን
voluble
'ቮልዩበል -ቅ- የ'ሚ'ና'ገር ፣ በፍጥነት'ና በ'ቀ'ላሉ መ'ናገር የ'ሚችል
volume
'ቮልዩም -ስ- ጥራዝ
measure
-ስ- ይዘት
radio
-ስ- ድምፅ (ለራዲዮ ፣ ከ'ፍተ'ኛ'ነቱ'ና ዝ'ቅተ'ኛ'ነቱ)
voluminous
ቨል'ዩሚነስ -ቅ- ት'ልቅ ፣ ሰ'ፊ
voluntary
'ቮለንትሪ -ቅ- ፈቃደ'ኛ
volunteer
ቮለን'ቲየ -ስ- በፈቃዱ የ'ሚሠራ ሰው ፣ ሳ
'ገ'ደድ የ'ሚሠራ ሰው
-ግ- በፈቃድ መሥራት [ሠ'ራ]
voluptuous
ቨ'ለፕቸወስ -ቅ- በግብረ ሥጋ መ'ደሰት የ'
ያበዛ'ና በተትረፈ'ረፈ ኑሮ የ'ሚኖር
vomit
'ቮሚት -ግ- ማስታወክ [አስታ'ወከ] ፣ ማ
መ'ለስ [አስመ'ለሰ]
voracious
ቨ'ሬይሽስ -ቅ- ሆዳም
vote
'ቮውት -ግ- መምረጥ [መ'ረጠ] ፣ (ያገር መ
ዎ'ችን ፣ የሕዝብ እንደራሴዎ'ችን)
voter
'ቮውተ -ስ- መራጭ
vouch (for)
'ቫውች -ግ- መ'ዋስ [ተዋሰ] ፣ ለእውነቱ መ
ስከር [መሰ'ከረ]
voucher
'ቫውቸ -ስ- ቫውቸር ፣ ባለሥልጣን የፈ'ረ
'በት የገንዘብ ማዘዣ ወረቀት
vow
'ቫው -ግ- ስለት መ'ሳል [ተሳለ]
vowel
'ቫወል -ስ- አ'ናባቢ ፊደል ፣ ድምፅ ሰ
ፊደል
voyage
'ቮየጅ -ስ- ጉዞ
vulgar
'ቨልገ -ቅ- ስ'ድ ፣ ባለጌ
vulgarity
ቨል'ጋረቲ -ስ- ስ'ድ'ነት ፣ ባለጌ'ነት
vulnerable
'ቨልነረበል -ቅ- በቀ'ላሉ የ'ሚ'ጎ'ዳ ፣ በ
'ላሉ የ'ሚቆስል
vulture
'ቨልቸ -ስ- ጥምብ አንሣ (የሞራ ዓይነት)
vulva
'ቨልቨ -ስ- የሴት ብ'ልት ቀዳዳ

wad
'ዎድ -ስ- ወፍራም ለስላ'ሳ ቁ'ራጭ ጨርቅ (ዕቃ ወይን'ም ቁስል ለማሠር የ'ሚያገለ 'ግል)

wadding
'ዎዲንግ -ስ- ዕቃ ማ'ሸጊያ (ጥጥ ወዘተ)

wade
'ዌይድ -ግ- ጥልቀት የሌ'ለውን ወንዝ በእ ግር መ'ሻገር [ተሻ'ገረ]

wafer
'ዌይፈ -ስ- ቀ'ጭን ጠፍጣ'ፋ ብስኩት (ም'ሳ ሌ ፣ ከጀላ'ቲ ጋር የ'ሚ'በ'ላ)
communion
-ስ- አ'ኮቴት (ቁርባን)

waft
'ዎፍት -ግ- ማርበብ [አረ'በበ] ፣ በቀ'ስታ እንዲስ'ፍ ማድረግ [አደ'ረገ]

wag
'ዋግ -ግ- መነቅነቅ [ነቀ'ነቀ]
joker
-ስ- ቀልደ'ኛ ሰው

wage
'ዌይጅ -ግ- ጦር ማንሣት [አነ'ሣ]
-ስ- ዋጋ (የቀን ሞያተ'ኛ)

wager
'ዌይጀ -ግ- መ'ወራረድ [ተወራ'ረደ]
-ስ- ውር'ርድ

waggon
'ዋገን -ስ- የጭነት ፉርጎ ፣ ባለአ'ራት እግር የጭ'ነት ተሽከርካሪ

waif
'ዌይፍ -ስ- የጠ'ፋ ሰው ወይን'ም እንስሳ ፣ አሳ'ዳጊ የሌ'ለው ልጅ

wail
'ዌይል -ግ- መጮኽ [ጮ'ኸ] ፣ ወ'ዮ፡ታ ማ'ሰ 'ማት [አ'ሰ'ማ]

waist
'ዌይስት -ስ- ወገብ

waistcoat
'ዌይስትኮውት -ስ- ሰደ'ርያ

wait
'ዌይት -ግ- መጠ'በቅ [ጠ'በቀ]
at table
-ግ- ማሳ'ለፍ [አሳ'ለፈ] (በግብዣ)

waiter
'ዌይተ -ስ- አሳ'ላፊ (ቦይ)

wake
'ዌይክ -ግ- መንቃት [ነ'ቃ]
-up
-ግ- መቀስቀስ [ቀሰ'ቀሰ] ፣ መ'ቀስቀስ [ተቀሰ'ቀሰ]

walk
'ዎ፡ክ -ግ- መሄድ [ሄደ]፣መ'ራመድ [ተራ'መደ]

walking-stick
'ዎ፡ኪንግስ'ቲክ -ስ- ከዘራ

wall
'ዎ፡ል -ስ- ግድግ'ዳ

wallet
'ዋለት -ስ- የገንዘብ ቦርሳ

wallpaper
'ዎ፡ልፔይፐ -ስ- የግድግ'ዳ ወረቀት

waltz
'ዎ፡ልስ -ስ- ወልስ (የዳንስ ዓይነት)

wan
'ዎን -ቅ- የገረ'ጣ (በሕመም) ፣ የዛለ (ከድ ካም የተነ'ሣ)

wand
'ዎንድ -ስ- ቀ'ጭን በ'ትር (በተለ'ይ ምትሃተ 'ኞ'ች የ'ሚይዙት)

wander
'ዎንደ -ግ- መንገድን መሳት [ሳተ] ፣ መንከ ራተት [ተንከራ'ተተ]

wane
'ዌይን -ግ- ማነስ [አ'ነሰ] (ለጨረቃ ወዘተ)

want
'ዎንት -ግ- መፈ'ለግ [ፈ'ለገ] ፣ መከ'ጀል [ከ'ጀለ]
-ስ- ፍ'ላጎት ፣ ከ'ጀላ ፣ እምሮት

wanton
'ዎንተን -ቅ- ግብረ ገ'ብ'ነት የሌ'ለው
-ስ- መረን የወ'ጣች ሴት

war
'ዎ፡ -ስ- ጦር'ነት
warble
'ዎ፡በል -ስ- የወፍ ቶጪት ፤ የወፍ ጫጫታ
ward
'ዎ፡ድ -ስ- የ'ሚያሳ'ድጉት ልጅ ፤ ልጅ ማሳ'ደግ
city district
-ስ- የከተማ ክፍል (ለአስተዳደር የተከ'ፈለ) ፤ በእስር ቤት ፤ በሆስፒታል ያንድ ሕንፃ ል'ዩ ል'ዩ ክፍሎ'ች
wardrobe
'ዎ፡ድረውብ -ስ- የልብስ መስቀያ
warehouse
'ዌየሃውስ -ስ- የሸቀጣሸቀጥ ፤ የዕቃ መጋዘን
wares
'ዌየዝ -ስ- የ'ሚ'ሸጥ ዕቃ (በሱቅ)
warfare
'ዎ፡ፌየ -ስ- ጦር'ነት
warm
'ዎ፡ም -ቅ- ሙቅ
warmth
'ዎ፡ምስ -ስ- ሙቀት ፤ ግለት
warn
'ዎ፡ን -ግ- ማስጠንቀቅ [አስጠን'ቀቀ]
warning
'ዎ፡ኒንግ -ስ- ማስጠንቀቂያ
warp
'ዎ፡ፕ -ግ- መ'ጣመም [ተጣ'መመ] (ለእንጨት)
warrant
'ዎረንት -ስ- መጥሪያ (ለክ'ስ) ፤ በቂ ምክንያት
-ግ- ሕ'ጋዊ ፈቃድ ማግኘት [አገ'ኘ]
warren
'ዎረን -ስ- ጉድጓድ (የጥንቸል ወዘተ)
warrior
'ዎሪየ -ስ- ተዋጊ ፡ ጦረ'ኛ
warship
'ዎ፡ሺፕ -ስ- የጦር መርከብ
wart
'ዎ፡ት -ስ- ኪንታሮት
wary
'ዌሪ -ቅ- ጥንቁቅ ፤ አደጋ ሊደርስ ይችላል ብሎ የ'ሚ'ጠን'ቀቅ

wash
'ዎሽ -ግ- ማጠብ [አ'ጠበ]
-one's self
-ግ- መ'ታጠብ [ታ'ጠበ]
washer
'ዎሸ -ስ- አጣቢ
washing
'ዎሺንግ -ስ- የ'ሚ'ታ'ጠብ ልብስ
wasp
'ዎስፕ -ስ- የው'ሻ ንብ
waste
'ዌይስት -ግ- ማባከን [አባ'ከነ] ፤ ማጥፋት [አጠ'ፋ]
wastrel
'ዌይስትረል -ስ- ገንዘብ አባካኝ
watch
'ዎች -ግ- መ'መልከት [ተመለ'ከተ]
guard
-ግ- መጠ'በቅ [ጠ'በቀ]
wrist-
-ስ- የእ'ጅ ሰዓት
watchman
'ዎችመን -ስ- ዘበ'ኛ ፤ ጠ'ባቂ
water
'ዎ፡ተ -ስ- ውሃ
water-closet
'ዎ፡ተክሎዚት -ስ- ሰገራ ቤት ፡ ሽንት ቤት
watercress
'ዎ፡ተክሬስ -ስ- ጉ'ጉብሌ
waterfall
'ዎ፡ተፎ፡ል -ስ- ፏፏቴ
watering-can
'ዎ፡ተሪንግካን -ስ- የአትክልት ማጠ'ጫ ዕቃ (ባለጡት) ፡ ማሰራጫ
waterlogged
'ዎ፡ተሎግድ -ቅ- በውሃ የራሰ (ጀልባ ፡ እንጨት ወዘተ) ፤ ውሃ ያጥለቀ'ለቀው
water-melon
'ዎ፡ተሜለን -ስ- ክርብሽ ፤ በ'ጢ'ኸ
waterproof
'ዎ፡ተፕሩ፡ፍ -ቅ- ውሃ የ'ማይገባው
waterworks
'ዎ፡ተወክስ -ስ- ውሃ ማ'ጣሪያ ሕንፃ ፡ የውሃ ማ'ደያ መምሪያ ቤት

watery
'ዎ:ተሪ -ቅ- ውሃ ውሃ የ'ሚል ፣ ወሃ'ማ ፣ ጣዕም የሌ'ለው

wave
'ዌይቭ -ግ- እ'ጅ ማ'ወዛወዝ [አ'ወዛ'ወዘ]
-ስ- ማዕበል

waver
'ዌይቨ -ግ- ማመንታት [አመነ'ታ] ፣ ማ'ወላወል [አ'ወላ'ወለ]

wavy
'ዌይቪ -ቅ- የማዕበል ቅርፅ ያ'ለው ፣ በማዕበል የተመ'ላ

wax
'ዋክስ -ስ- ሰም

way
'ዌይ -ስ- መንገድ ፣ አ'ኳኋን ፣ አቅጣ'ጫ

wayfarer
'ዌይፌረ -ስ- የእግር መንገደ'ኛ

waylay
ዌ'ይሌይ -ግ- ማድፈጥ [አደ'ፈጠ] (አደጋ ለመጣል ፣ ለመዝረፍ ወዘተ)

wayward
'ዌይወድ -ቅ- ፀመፀ'ኛ ፣ የ'ማይ'ታ'ዘዝ (ይበልጡን ለሕፃናት)

we
'ዊይ -ተስ- እ'ኛ

weak
'ዊይክ -ቅ- ደካማ

weaken
'ዊይክን -ግ- ማድከም [አደ'ከመ]

weakling
'ዊይክሊንግ -ስ- ደካማ ሰው ፣ እንስሳ

weakness
'ዊይክነስ -ስ- ድካም ፣ ደካማ'ነት

weal
'ዊይል -ስ- ሰንበር (ከተመ'ቱ በኋላ በሰው'ነት ላይ የ'ሚ'ታ'ይ) ፣ ጥሩ ዕ'ድል ፣ ደ'ስታ (የመ'ላው ሕዝብ)

wealth
'ዌልስ -ስ- ሀብት

wealthy
'ዌልሲ -ቅ- ሀብታም

wean
'ዊይን -ግ- ጡት ማስጣል [አስጣለ] ፣ ከመጥፎ ጓ'ደ'ኛ ጋር መ'ገናኘት ፣ መጥፎ ልምድ ማስተው [አስተወ]

weapon
'ዌፐን -ስ- የጦር መ'ሣሪያ

wear
'ዌየ -ግ- መልበስ [ለ'በሰ]
-out
-ግ- ማለቅ [አ'ለቀ] (ለልብስ)

weariness
'ዊሪነስ -ስ- ድካም ፣ መታከት

weary
'ዊይሪ -ግ- ማድከም [አደ'ከመ] ፣ ማታከት [አታ'ከተ]
-ቅ- ታካች ፣ የደ'ከመ

weather
'ዌዘ -ስ- አ'የር ፣ ነፋስ

weave
'ዊይቭ -ግ- ሸ'ማ መሥራት [ሠ'ራ]

weaver
'ዊይቨ -ስ- ሸ'ማኔ

web
'ዌብ -ስ- የሸረሪት ድር

wed
'ዌድ -ግ- ማግባት [አገ'ባ] (ለሚስት ፣ ለባል)

wedding
'ዌዲንግ -ስ- ሠርግ

wedge
'ዌጅ -ስ- ሽብ'ልቅ (እንጨት መፍለ'ጫ) ፣ ቅርቃር ፣ ውሻል (ሦስት ማዕዘን ያ'ለው መደ'ገፊያ እንጨት)

Wednesday
'ዌንዝዴይ -ስ- ረቡዕ

weed
'ዊይድ -ግ- ማ'ረም [አ'ረመ] (ለአ'ረሙ'ም)
-ስ- አ'ረሙ'ም

week
'ዊይክ -ስ- ሳ'ምንት

weekend
ዊ'ከኢንድ -ስ- የሳ'ምንት መጨ'ረሻ (ቅዳሜ ና እሑድ)

weekly
'ዊይክሊ -ተግ- በ'የሳ'ምንቱ

weep
'ዊይፐ -ግ- ማልቀስ [አለ'ቀሰ]

weigh
'ዌይ -ግ- መመ'ዘን [መ'ዘነ]

weight
'ዌይት -ስ- ክብደት
balance
-ስ- ሚዛን ፣ መመ'ዘኛ

weird
'ዊየድ -ቅ- ያልተለ'መደ ፣ እንግዳ ፣ በዓለም ውስጥ የሌ'ለ

welcome
'ዌልከም -ግ- በደኅና መ'ቀበል [ተቀ'በለ] ፣ እንኳን ደኅና ገ'ቡ ማለት [አለ]

weld
'ዌልድ -ግ- መበ'የድ [በ'የደ] ፣ ብረት ከብ ረት ጋር ማ'ጣበቅ [አ'ጣ'በቀ]

welfare
'ዌልፌየ -ስ- ደኅን'ነት

well
'ዌል -ቅ- ጥሩ ፣ ደኅና
fit
-ቅ- ጤና'ማ
water
-ስ- የውሃ ጉድጓድ

well-behaved
ዌልበ'ሄይቭድ -ቅ- ባለ ጥሩ ጠባይ ፣ የታ'ረመ

well-baing
ዌል'ቢይንግ -ስ- ደኅን'ነት

well-off
ዌል'እፍ -ቅ- የተደላ'ደለ ሀብት ያ'ለው

well-to-do
ዌል ቱ'ዱ: -ቅ- ሀብታም ፣ የተመቻ'ቸ ፣ የተደ ላ'ደለ (በሀብት)

welter
'ዌልተ -ስ- መዓት (የዱ'ላ) ፣ ሥርዓት የሌ 'ለው የሕዝብ ብዛት

west
'ዌስት -ስ- ምዕራብ

westward
'ዌስትወድ -ተግ- ወደ ምዕራብ

wet
'ዌት -ግ- መንከር [ነ'ከረ] ፣ ማርጠብ [አረ 'ጠበ]
-ቅ- እርጥብ

whale
'ዌይል -ስ- ዐሣ አንበሪ ፣ ዐሣነባሪ

what
'ዎት -መተስ- ምንድ'ን ፣ ምን

wheat
'ዊይት -ስ- ስንዴ

wheedle
'ዊይደል -ግ- መ'ለማመጥ [ተለማ'መጠ]

wheel
'ዊይል -ስ- የተሽከርካሪ እግር
steering-
-ስ- መዘ'ውር ፣ መሪ (የመኪና)

wheelbarrow
'ዊይል ባረው -ስ- የ'ጅ ጋሪ (በ'ጅ የ'ሚ'ገ'ፋ)

wheeze
'ዊይዝ -ግ- በችግር መተንፈስ [ተነ'ፈሰ] (ተ 'ጭን ድምፅ እ'ያ'ሰ'ሙ)

whelp
'ዌልፐ -ስ- የው'ሻ ቡ'ች'ላ ፣ ስ'ድ አ'ደግ ልጅ ፣ ሰው

when
'ዌን -መተግ- መ'ቼ
-ተግ- በ . . . ጊዜ
-መዩ- ስ . . .

whence
'ዌንስ -ተግ- ከየት ፣ ከወዴት

whenever
ዌ'ኔቨ -ተግ- በ . . . ጊዜ

where
'ዌየ -መተግ- ወዴት ፣ የት
-ዘተስ- የም . . . . .
-መዩ- . . . በት . . .

wherever
'ዌሬቨ -ተግ- በ. . . ቦታ

whet
'ዌት -ግ- መሳል [ሳለ] (ለስለት) ፣ ማጎምጀት [አጎመ'ጀ]

whether
'ዌዘ -መዩ- የ . . . እንደሆነ

whetstone

'ዊትስተውን -ስ- መሳያ ድንጊያ ፣ መሳል ፣ ለሆቴ

whey

'ዌይ -ስ- አሬራ

which

'ዊች -መቅ- የት'ኛው
-ዘተስ- የም . . .

whiff

'ዊፍ -ስ- ሽ'ታ ፣ ትንፋሽ ፣ ት'ንሽ የአ'የር እ'ፍታ

while

'ዋይል -ተግ- በ . . . ጊዜ
short time
-ስ- አንድ አፍታ

whim

'ዊም -ስ- አምሮት (ም'ኞት ፣ የእርጉዝ ሴት)

whimper

'ዊምፐ -ግ- መጮኽ [ጮኸ] (ለትና'ንሽ እን ስሳት ፣ ለሕፃን ከሥቃይ ፣ ከፍርሀት የተነ'ሣ)

whimsical

'ዊምዚክል -ቅ- አምሮት ያ'ለው ፣ አምሮት የያዘው

whine

'ዋይን -ግ- ማልቀስ [አለ'ቀሰ] (ለው'ሻ)

whip

'ዊፕ -ግ- መገረፍ [ገ'ረፈ]
-ስ- ጅራፍ ፣ መገረፊያ ፣ አለንጋ

whirl

'ወ:ል -ግ- እንደአዘዋሪት ፣ እንደዐውሎ ነፋስ መዞር [ዞረ]

whirlpool

'ወ:ልፑ:ል -ስ- ::ዘዋሪት

whirlwind

ወ:ልዊንድ -ስ- አውሎ ነፋስ

whisk

'ዊስክ -ግ- መምታት [መ'ታ] (ላእንቁላል ፣ ለሊጥ ወዘተ)
-ስ- ᵒምታት
fly-
-ስ- የዝንብ ጭራ (የዝምብ መ'ከላከያ)

whiskers

'ዊስከዝ -ስ- ሪዝ (ያንበ'ሳ ፣ የድ'መት ወዘተ)

whisper

'ዊስፐ -ግ- ማሾክሾክ [አሾክ'ሾከ] (በለሆስታ መ'ናገር)
-ስ- ሹክሹክታ ፣ የለሆስታ ንግ'ግር

whistle

'ዊሰል -ግ- ማፏጨት [አፏ'ጨ]
-ስ- ፉጨት
instrument
-ስ- ፊሽኪያ (ፊሽካ)

white

'ዋይት -ቅ- ነ'ጭ

whiten

'ዋይተን -ግ- ማንጣት [አነ'ጣ] ፣ ነ'ጭ ማድ ረግ [አደ'ረገ]

whiteness

'ዋይትኔስ -ስ- ንጣት

white-wash

'ዋይትዎሽ -ስ- ኖራ (የቤት መለቅለቂያ)

whittle

'ዊተል -ግ- መተፍተፍ [ተፈ'ተፈ] ፣ መቅ ረፍ [ቀ'ረፈ] (ለእንጨት ወዘተ)

who

'ሁ: -መተስ- ማ'ን
-ዘተ(· የም . . . ፣ የ . . .

whoever

ሁ'ዌቨ -ተስ- ማ'ንም

whole

'ሆውል -ቅ- ሙሉ ፣ ጠቅላ'ላ

wholesale

'ሆውልሴይል -ስ- ጅምላ

wholesome

'ሆውልሰም -ቅ- ደኅና ፣ ጤና'ማ

wholly

'ሆውሊ -ተግ- በሙሉ

whom

'ሁ:ም -መተስ- ማ'ንን

whooping-cough

'ሁፒንግኮፍ -ስ- ት ክታ ፣ ት'ክት'ክ (ሳል

whose

'ሁ:ዝ -መተስ- የማ'ን

why

'ዋይ -መተግ- ለምን

wick

'ዊክ -ስ- ፈትል (የኩ'ራዝ · 'ማ)

wicked
'ዊክድ -ቅ- ክፉ ፣ ጠማማ (ለጠባይ)
wicker
'ዊክ -ስ- የሸምበ'ቆ እንጨት (ቅርጫት ወዘተ የ'ሚ'ሠ'ራ'በት)
wicket
'ዊክት -ስ- ት'ንሽ በ'ር (በት'ልቅ በ'ር መካ'ከል ያ'ለ)
wide
'ዋይድ -ቅ- ሰ'ፊ
widen
'ዋይደን -ቅ- ማስፋት [አሰ'ፋ]
widespread
'ዋይድስፕሬድ -ቅ- የተሰራ'ጨ
widow
'ዊደው -ስ- ጋለሞታ (ባሏ የሞተ'ባት)
widower
'ዊደወ -ስ- ሚስቱ የሞተ'ች'በት ወንድ
width
'ዊድስ -ስ- ስፋት
wife
'ዋይፍ -ስ- ሚስት
wig
'ዊግ -ስ- የተፈጥሮ ያልሆነ ሰው ሠ'ራ'ሽ ጠጉር (እራስ ላይ የ'ሚ'ደ'ፋ)
wild
'ዋይልድ -ቅ- አውሬ
wilderness
'ዊልደኔስ -ስ- ምድረ በዳ
wildness
'ዋይልደኔስ -ስ- አውሬ'ነት
wile
'ዋይል -ስ- ማ'ታለል ፡ ተንኮል (የሠይጣን ወዘተ)
wilful
'ዊልፉል -ቅ- የ'ማይ'ታ'ዘዝ ፡ የራሱን መንገድ ብ'ቻ የ'ሚ'ከ'ተ'ተል
will
'ዊል -ስ- ፍ'ላጎት
legal
-ስ- የኑዛዜ ቃል (ለሀብት)
willing
'ዊሊንግ -ቅ- ፈቃደ'ኛ

wilt
'ዊልት -ግ- ማጠውለግ [አጠወ'ለገ] (ለእትክልት)
wily
'ዋይሊ -ቅ- አ'ታላይ ፣ ተንኮለ'ኛ
win
'ዊን -ግ- ማ'ሸ'ነፍ [አ'ሸ'ነፈ] ፣ መርታት [ረ'ታ]
wince
'ዊንስ -ግ- ወደ ኋላ ማለት [አለ] (ሰው ሊ'መ'ታ ሲ'ቃ'ጣ)
winch
'ዊንች -ስ- ማጠንጠኛ ፣ መጠቅለያ
wind
'ዊንድ -ስ- ነፋስ
wind
'ዋይንድ -ግ- መጠምዘዝ [ጠመ'ዘዘ] ፣ ማዞር [አዞረ] ፣ መሙላት [ሞ'ላ] (ሰዓት)
windfall
'ዊንድፎ፡ል -ስ- ነፋስ የጣለው ፍሬ
luck
-ስ- ድንገተ'ኛ ዕ'ድል
windlass
'ዊንድለስ -ስ- ማጠንጠኛ ፣ መጠቅለያ
windmill
'ዊንድሚል -ስ- የነፋስ ወፍጮ
window
'ዊንደው -ስ- መስኮት
windy
'ዊንዲ -ቅ- ነፋሳም
wine
'ዋይን -ስ- የወይን ጠ'ጅ
wing
'ዊንግ -ስ- ክንፍ
wink
'ዊንክ -ግ- ዓይን መጥቀስ [ጠቀ'ሰ] ፡ ዓይን በግቶ መክፈት [ከ'ፈ'ተ]
winnow
'ዊነው -ግ- ማንገዋለል [አዘ'ራ] (ፍሬውን ከእ'ብት ለመለ'የት)
winter
'ዊንተ -ስ- ክረምት

wipe
'ዋይፐ -ግ- መጥረግ [ጠ'ረገ] ፣ መወልወል [ወለ'ወለ]

wire
'ዋየ -ስ- ሽቦ
telegram
-ስ- ቴሌግራም

wireless
'ዋየሌስ -ስ- ራዲዮ
telegraphy
-ስ- የነፋስ ስልክ

wiry
'ዋሪ -ቅ- ቀ'ጭን'ና ጠንካ'ራ ፣ ጠምዛ'ዛ (ለሰው)

wisdom
'ዊዝደም -ስ- ጥበብ ፣ ብልኀት

wise
'ዋይዝ -ቅ- ብልኅ

wish
'ዊሽ -ግ- መ'መኘት [ተመ'ኘ]
-ስ- ም'ኞት

wishful
'ዊሽፉል -ቅ- የ'ሚ'መ'ኝ (እንደፍ'ላጎቱ እን ዲሆን'ለት)

wistful
'ዊስትፉል -ቅ- አዘ'ን ያለ ፣ ያልጠ'ጻው

wit
'ዊት -ስ- ቀልድ
person
ቀልደ'ኛ ሰው

witch
'ዊች -ስ- ሟርተ'ኛ ፣ ጠንቋይ (ለሴት)

with
'ዊ<u>ዝ</u> -መዋ- ከ . . . ጋር

withdraw
ዊ<u>ዝ</u>ድ'ሮ፡ -ግ- ወደ ኋላ ማለት [አለ]
accusation
ክ'ስ ማንሣት [አነ'ሣ]

wither
'ዊ<u>ዘ</u> -ግ- መድረቅ [ደ'ረቀ] (ለእትክልት)

withhold
ዊ<u>ዝ</u>'ሆልድ -ግ- ይዞ አለመስጠት [-ሰ'ጠ] ፣ ወደኋላ ማስቀ'ረት [አስቀ'ረ]

within
ዊ'<u>ዚ</u>ን -ተግ- በ . . . ውስጥ

without
ዊ'<u>ዟ</u>ውት -ተግ- ያለ

withstand
ዊ<u>ዝ</u>ስ'ታንድ -ግ- መቋቋም [ተ'ቋቋመ] ፣ መ ቃወም [ተቃ'ወመ]

witness
'ዊትነስ -ግ- መ'መልከት [ተመ'ለ'ከተ] ፣ መ መስከር [መሰ'ከረ]
-ስ- ምስ'ክር

witty
'ዊቲ -ቅ- ቀልደ'ኛ ፣ ጨዋተ'ኛ ፣ ሚወራ ዕዋቂ (በንግ'ግር)

wizard
'ዊዘድ -ስ- አስማተ'ኛ ፣ ጠንቋይ (ለወንድ)

wobble
'ዎበል -ግ- መ'ንቃነቅ [ተነቃ'ነቀ] ፣ መ'ወ ዛወዝ [ተወዛ'ወዘ] ፣ ማ'ወላወል [አ'ወላ'ወለ]

woe
'ወው -ስ- ወ'ዮታ ፣ ሐዘን ፣ ች'ግር

wolf
'ውልፍ -ስ- ተኩላ

woman
'ውመን -ስ- ሴት

womb
'ውም -ስ- ማሕፀን

wonder
'ወንደ -ግ- መ'ደነቅ [ተደ'ነቀ] ፣ መ'ገረም [ተገ'ረመ]

wonderful
'ወንደፉል -ቅ- አስደ'ናቂ ፣ ገሩም

woo
'ው፡ -ግ- ሴት ማባበል [አባ'በለ] ፣ ማግባባት [አግባ'ባ] (ለማፍቀር ፣ ለማግባት)

wood
'ውድ -ስ- እንጨት
forest
-ስ- ደ'ን

wooden
'ውደን -ቅ- ከንጨት የተሠ'ራ ፣ የንጨት

woodpecker
'ውድፔከ -ስ- ግንደ ቆርቆር

woodwork
'ውድወ:ክ -ስ- እናጢ'ነት
wooden part
-ስ- ከንጨት በሙሉ ወይን'ም በከፊል የተሠ'ራ

wool
'ውል -ስ- ሱፍ

woollen
'ውለን -ቅ- የሱፍ ፣ ከሱፍ የተሠ'ራ

woolly
'ውሊ -ቅ- በሱፍ የተሸ'ፈነ ፣ ከሱፍ የተሠ'ራ ፣ ሱፍ የ'ሚመስል
vague
-ቅ- ግልጽ ያልሆነ (ለሰው)

word
'ወ:ድ -ስ- ቃል

work
'ወ:ክ -ግ- መሥራት [ሠ'ራ]
-ስ- ሥራ

worker
'ወ:ከ -ስ- ሠ'ራተ'ኛ

workman
'ወክ:መን -ስ- የእ'ጅ ሠ'ራተ'ኛ

works
'ወ:ክስ -ስ- ጽሑፍ ፣ ድርሰት
musical
የሙዚቃ ድርሰት
factory
ፋብሪካ

workshop
'ወ:ክሾፕ -ስ- ቀለ'ል ያሉ የእ'ጅ ሙያዎ'ች የ'ሚ'ሠ'ሩ'በት ቤት
garage
-ስ- ጋራጅ

world
'ወ:ልድ -ስ- ዓለም

worm
'ወ:ም -ስ- ትል

worn-out
ዎ:ን'አውት -ቅ- ያረ'ጀ ፣ ያ'ለቀ (ለልብስ ወዘተ)

worry
'ወሪ -ግ መ'ጨነቅ [ተጨ'ነቀ] ፣ ማስጨ'ነቅ [አስጨ'ነቀ]

worse
'ወ:ስ -ቅ- የከ'ፋ

worsen
'ወ:ሰን -ግ- ማከፋት [አከ'ፋ]

worship
'ወ:ሺፕ -ግ- ማምለክ [አመ'ለከ]
-ስ- አምልኮ

worshipper
'ወ:ሺፐ -ስ- አምላኪ

worst
'ወ:ስት -ቅ- እ'ጅግ የከ'ፋ

worth
'ወ:ሷ -ስ- ዋጋ
-ቅ- የ'ሚያወጣ ፣ የ'ሚ'ገ'መት

worthy
'ወ:ዢ -ቅ- የ'ሚ'ገ'ባው ፣ ተገቢ ፣ ጥሩ ግ'ምት ያ'ለው

wound
'ውንድ -ግ- ማቁሰል [አቆ'ሰለ]
-ስ- ቁስል

wrangle
'ራንገል -ግ- መ'ጨቃጨቅ [ተጨቃ'ጨቀ]፣ መ'ነታረክ [ተነታ'ረከ]

wrap
'ራፕ -ግ- መጠቅለል [ጠቀ'ለለ]

wrapper
'ራፐ -ስ- መጠቅለያ (ወረቀት ፣ ዕቃ ለመላክ)

wrath
'ሮ:ሷ -ስ- ቁ'ጣ ፣ መዐት

wreath
'ሪይሷ -ስ- የአበባ ዕ'ቅፍ (በቃሬዛ ላይ የ'ሚ'ቀ'መጥ)

wreck
'ሬክ -ግ- መስጠም [ሰ'ጠመ] ፣ ማስጠም [አሰ'ጠመ] (ለመርከብ)፣መ'ሰባበር [ተሰባ'በረ]

wreckage
'ሬኪጅ -ስ- ስብርባሪ (በተለ'ይ የመርከብ)

wrench
'ሬንች -ግ- መገንጠል [ገነ'ጠለ] ፣ በኀይል መጠምዘዝ [ጠመ'ዘዘ]
spanner
-ስ- የእንግሊዝ መፍቻ

wrest
'ሬስት -ግ- መንጠቅ [ነ'ጠቀ]

wrestle
'ሬስል -ግ- መ'ታገል [ታ'ገለ]

wretch
'ሬች -ስ- መንጿ'ካ ፣ ዕ'ድለ ቢስ ፣ ች'ግረ'ኛ

wriggle
'ሪገል -ግ- መስለክለክ [ተስለከ'ለከ] (እባብ ወዘተ)

wring
'ሪንግ -ግ- መጠምዘዝ [ጠመ'ዘዘ] (ለልብስ)

wrinkle
'ሪንክል -ስ- የግንባር እ'ጥፋት

wrist
'ሪስት -ስ- የእ'ጅ አንጓ ፣ አምባር መ‐ያ

wrist-watch
'ሪስት ዎች -ስ- የእ'ጅ ሰዓት

writ
'ሪት -ስ- አንድ ነገር ለማድረግ ወይን'ም ላለማድረግ የ'ሚያ'ዝ የንጉሥ ደብዳ'ቤ
written accusation
-ስ- የክ'ስ ማመልከቻ

write
'ራይት -ግ- መጻፍ [ጻፈ]

writer
'ራይተ -ስ- ጸሐፊ ፣ ደራሲ

writhe
'ራይዝ -ግ- መንፈራገጥ [ተንፈራ'ገጠ] (ከሕመም የተነ'ሣ)

writing
'ራይቲንግ -ስ- ጽሑፍ ፣ ድርሰት

wrong
'ሮንግ -ስ- ስሕተት
-ቅ- ስሕተት
-ግ- መጉዳት [ጎ'ዳ] ፣ መበደል [በ'ደለ]

wry
'ራይ -ቅ- መራራ (ለንግ'ግር) ፣ የተኰሳ'ተረ (ለመልክ)

X-rays
'ኤክስሬይዝ -ስ- ራ'ጂ ፣ ኤክስሬይ

X-rayed
'ኤክስሬይድ -ግ- ራ'ጂ መ'ነሣት [ተነ'ሣ]

yacht
'ዮት -ስ- አነስተ'ኛ መርከብ (መንሸራሸሪያ)

yap
'ያፕ -ስ- የቡ'ች'ላ ጩኸት

yard
'ያ:ድ -ስ- ያጥር ግ'ቢ አትክልት ቦታ
measure
-ስ- ያርድ (መለ'ኪያ ፣ የርዝመት)

yarn
'ያ:ን -ስ- ማግ (የጥጥ ፣ የሱፍ ወዘተ)
story
-ስ- ወሬ (አንድ ሰው ስላ'የው ሁናቴ የ'ሚያወራው)

yawn
'ዮ:ውን -ግ- ማፋሸግ [አፋ'ሸገ] ፣ ማ'ዛጋት [አ'ዛ'ጋ]

year
'ዪእ -ስ- ዓመት

yearly
'ዪ-እሊ -ቅ- ዓመታዊ
-ተግ- በ'ያመቱ

yearn
'ዪ፡ን -ግ- መናፈቅ [ና'ፈቀ]

yeast
'ይስት -ስ- እርሾ

yell
'ዬል -ግ- መጮኽ [ጮኸ] ፣ መ'ቆጣት [ተ'ቆጣ]

yellow
'ዬለው -ቅ- ብጫ ፣ ወይባ

yelp
'ዬልፕ -ስ- የው'ሻ ጩኸት (ከተመ'ታ በኋላ)

yes
'ዬስ -ተግ- አዎን ፣ አዎ

yesterday
'ዬስተዴይ -ስ- ትናንት ፣ ትናንት'ና

yet
'ዬት -ተግ- እስካሁን ድረስ ፣ ገና

yield
'ዪልድ -ግ- መ'ማረክ [ተማ'ረከ] ፣ መ'ሸነፍ [ተሸ'ነፈ]
· *agriculture*
-ግ- መ'መረት [ተመ'ረተ]

yoke
'የውክ -ስ- ቀንበር

yolk
'የውክ -ስ- አስኳል

yonder
'ዮንደ -ቅ- ማዶ
-ተግ- በማዶ

you
'ዩ፡ -ተስ- አንተ ፣ አንቺ ፣ እርስዎ ፣ እ'ናንተ

young
'የንግ -ቅ- ወ'ጣት ፣ ለጋ

your
'ዮ፡ -ገቅ- ያንተ ፣ ያንቺ ፣ የርስዎ ፣ የ'ናንተ

yours
'ዮ፡ዝ -ገተስ፣ቅ- ያንተ ፣ ያንቺ ፣ የርስዎ ፣ የ'ናን·

yourself
ዮ፡'ሴልፍ -ጸተስ- እራስህ ፣ እራስሽ ፣ እራስ፡

youth
'ዩሰ -ስ- ወ'ጣት ፣ ወ'ጣት'ነት

yuletide
'ዩወልታይድ -ስ- የገ'ና በዐል ሰሞን

Z

zeal
'ዚይል -ስ- የጋለ ፍ'ላጎት

zealot
'ዜለት -ስ- ለሃይማኖቱ የ'ሚቀና ፣ ለእምነቱ የ'ሚ'ቆረ'ቆር

zealous
'ዜለስ -ቅ- የጋለ ፍ'ላጎት ያ'ለው

zebra
'ዜብረ -ስ- የሜዳ አህ'ያ

zenith
'ዜኒሰ -ስ- ጫፍ ፣ ቁንጮ ፣ ፀሐይ በተሲያት የ'ም'ት'ታ'ይ'በት ቦታ

zephyr
'ዜፈ -ስ- አስደ'ሳች ነፋስ

zero
'ዚይረው -ስ- ዜሮ ፣ ምን'ም ፣ ባዶ

zest
'ዜስት -ስ- ታ'ላቅ ፍ'ላጎት ፣ በታ'ላቅ ደ'ስታ ያንድ ነገር ተካፋይ መሆን

zigzag
'ዚግዛግ -ግ- መ'ጠማዘዝ [ተጠማ'ዘዘ]
-ቅ- ጠምዛ'ዛ (መንገድ ወዘተ)

zinc
'ዚንክ -ስ- ዚንክ ፣ ቆርቆ'ሮ

zip

'ዚፕ -ስ- ተተርጋታሪ'ና ተገ'ጣሚ የብረት ቁልፍ ፣ ዚ'ፕ

zone

'ዞውን -ስ- ክ'ልል

zoo

'ዙ፡ -ስ- ል'ዩ ል'ዩ አራዊት'ና እንስሳት ለሕዝብ እንዲ'ታ'ዩ የ'ሚ'ጠ'በቁ'በት ቦታ

zoology

ዙ'ዎለጂ -ስ- ዙኦሎጂ ፣ የእንስሳት ሥነ ፍጥረት ጥናት

Printed in the United States
220114BV00001B/19/A

9 781843 560159